C

S

DICTIONARY

HarperCollins Publishers
Westerhill Road
Bishopbriggs
Glasgow
G64 2QT

Third Edition 2012
Reissued 2013

Reprint 10 9 8 7 6 5 4 3 2 1 0

© HarperCollins Publishers 2013

ISBN 978-0-00-753812-6

Collins® is a registered trademark of
HarperCollins Publishers Limited

Scrabble® is a registered trademark of
J.W Spear & Sons Ltd, a subsidiary of
Mattel, Inc. © 2012 Mattel

www.collinsdictionary.com

A catalogue record for this book is
available from the British Library

Typeset by Davidson Publishing
Solutions, Glasgow

Printed in Italy by Lego SpA, Lavis
(Trento)

EDITORS
Gerry Breslin
Ian Brookes
Lorna Gilmour
Robert Groves
Robbie Guillory
Andrew Holmes
Persephone Lock

COMPUTING SUPPORT
Thomas Callan

FOR THE PUBLISHER
Lucy Cooper
Kerry Ferguson
Elaine Higgleton
Sharon McTeir

Introduction

The *Collins Gem Scrabble Dictionary* is the ideal reference book for people who play Scrabble for enjoyment, in a social or family setting. This dictionary doesn't include every word eligible for Scrabble, but does contain the most commonly used of the 270,000 words in *Collins Official Scrabble Words* 2011, the definitive Scrabble wordlist. The concise definitions in the *Gem Scrabble Dictionary* allow players to check the meaning of words, as well as to use the book for settling arguments during games.

The *Collins Gem Scrabble Dictionary* contains words of up to 7 letters in length. However, references to longer words playable in Scrabble are included. These longer words output in bold, and are introduced by a chevron symbol (>). Because this dictionary is designed for family play, it does not include offensive terms. Such words are, on the other hand, included in the *Collins Official Scrabble Words* 2011, the complete wordlist for tournaments and club competitions, along with words of 8–15 letters.

Words are listed in alphabetical order, although some inflected forms are grouped together or run on from the base form entry to save space. Inflected forms which are run on from the base form entry appear in bold, after the definition. Definitions are given for base forms of words where the meaning is not self-explanatory. A black triangle symbol (▶) is used to refer readers to another related entry in the dictionary. Inflections which are separate from their base form are referred back to the main entry in this way.

Two-letter words

A sound knowledge of the 124 two-letter words is crucial to success in Scrabble. Where many inexperienced Scrabble players go wrong is that they think the longer a word is, the better it is to know, as it's likely to score more. In fact, the key to a good Scrabble vocabulary is a good knowledge of short words.

The reason for that is you can use the short words to 'hook' the word you want to play on to the board, allowing you to play parallel to another word, rather than always going through it crosswise. That way you will usually make more than one word each shot, gaining you a higher score.

Notice how by using the same letters from your rack, you have scored seventeen more points. But notice also that little word **FA** which enabled you to fit the play in. And there we have the first, essential thing you have to know to improve your game: **all the allowable two letter words**. Yes, all of them.

There are 124 of these to learn, but to make the list more manageable, you can divide them into three groups:

1. The ones you already know.
2. The ones you already know, but may not have realized were words.
3. The ones you probably don't know.

There are thirty-seven two-letter words which most people would know and which would appear in most dictionaries:

AH	AM	AN	AS	AT	AX	AY	BE	BY	DO	EH
GO	HA	HE	HI	HO	IF	IN	IS	IT	LA	LO
MA	ME	MY	NO	OF	OH	ON	OR	OX	PA	SO
TO	UP	US	WE							

So straight away you only have eighty-seven new ones to learn. But it's not even as bad as that, because now we move on to the second group: the ones you know, but don't know you know.

These include:

Contractions

AD (advertisement)   **PO** (chamberpot)

BI (bisexual)   **RE** (regarding)

MO (moment)   **TA** (thank you)

OP (operation)

Interjections and exclamations

AW	ER	HM	MM	OI	OW	OY
SH	ST	UH	UM	UR	YA	YO

Letters of the alphabet

AR	EF	EL	EM	EN	ES	EX

Then add in **ID** (the psychiatric term), **PI** (the Greek letter and mathematical term), and **YE** (the old form of **YOU**), and that's another thirty-one taken care of with no trouble at all.

Fifty-six to go. These are the ones you probably don't know, so let's set them out where you can get the measure of them:

AA	AB	AE	AG	AI	AL	BA	BO	CH	DA	DE
DI	EA	ED	EE	ET	FA	FE	FY	GI	GU	IO
JA	JO	KA	KI	KO	KY	LI	MI	MU	NA	NE
NU	NY	OB	OD	OE	OM	OO	OS	OU	PE	QI
SI	TE	TI	UG	UN	UT	WO	XI	XU	YU	ZA
ZO										

Once you're happy with the common two-letter words, have a go at mastering the unusual ones. These really are the essential first step to improving your game.

Special Scrabble Words

To help family players learn and use some of the most useful words in the game, the *Collins Gem Scrabble Dictionary* includes a number of special panel entries, drawing attention to more than 200 words of particular interest or utility. For the most part these are words which are less likely to form part of a novice player's natural vocabulary, and the emphasis is on particularly useful three-letter words, on high probability seven-letter bonus words, on words that are especially useful when you have either too many vowels on your rack or too many consonants, and on selected shorter words that use the high value consonants **J**, **K**, **Q**, **X** and **Z**. But just for fun we have also featured a few of the unusual and exciting words of the kind that Scrabble players dream about. Realistically, you may well never get the chance to play words like **ZOOTAXY**, **TZADDIQ** and **QUETZAL**. But imagine the thrill (and the score!) if you did...

The *Collins Gem Scrabble Dictionary* is designed to be useful to new players and Scrabble veterans alike – we hope you enjoy using it!

Abbreviations

adj	adjective
adv	adverb
conj	conjunction
det	determiner
interj	interjection
n	noun
pl	plural
prep	preposition
pron	pronoun
vb	verb

Aa

A forms a two-letter word when followed by any one of **A, B, D, E, G, H, I, L, M, N, R, S, T, W, X** and **Y** – 16 letters out of 26 – so it's a really useful tile. There are also a number of short high-scoring words beginning with **A**. **Axe** (10 points) and **adze** (14 points) are good examples, but don't forget their US variants, **ax** (9 points) and **adz** (13 points). Also remember their plurals and the verb form **axed** (12 points). **Aye** (6) and **ay** (5) are handy for tight corners.

AA n volcanic rock

AAH vb exclaim in pleasure **aahed, aahing, aahs**

AAL n Asian shrub or tree

> An **aal** is an East Indian shrub, useful for getting rid of annoying multiples of A.

AALII n bushy shrub **aaliis**

> An **aalii** is a tropical tree, great for getting rid of surplus As and Is.

AALS ▶ aal

AARGH ▶ argh

AARRGH ▶ argh

AARRGHH ▶ argh

AARTI n Hindu ceremony **aartis**

AAS ▶ aa

AB n abdominal muscle

ABA n type of Syrian cloth

ABAC n mathematical diagram

ABACA n species of banana **abacas**

ABACI ▶ abacus

ABACK adv

ABACS ▶ abac

ABACTOR n cattle thief

ABACUS n

ABAFT adv by the rear of (a ship) ▷ adj closer to the stern

ABAKA n abaca abakas

ABALONE n

ABAMP = abampere

ABAMPS ▶ abamp

ABAND vb abandon abanded

ABANDON vb, n

ABANDS ▶ aband

ABAS ▶ aba

ABASE vb abased, abaser, abasers, abases

ABASH vb cause to feel ill at ease, **abashed**

ABASHED adj

ABASHES ▶ abash

ABASIA n disorder affecting ability to walk **abasias**

ABASING ▶ abase

ABASK adv in pleasant warmth

ABATE vb abated, abater, abaters, abates, abating

ABATIS n rampart of felled trees

ABATOR n person who effects an abatement **abators**

ABATTIS = abatis

ABATTU adj dejected

ABATURE n trail left by hunted stag

ABAXIAL adj facing away from the axis

ABAXILE adj away from the axis

ABAYA n Arab outer garment **abayas**
ABB n yarn used in weaving
ABBA n Coptic bishop
ABBACY n office of abbot or abbess
ABBAS ▸ abba
ABBE n French abbot
ABBED adj displaying strong abdominal muscles
ABBES ▸ abbe
ABBESS n in charge of a convent
ABBEY n abbeys
ABBOT n abbotcy, abbots
ABBS ▸ abb
ABCEE n alphabet abcees
ABDABS n highly nervous state
ABDOMEN n
ABDUCE vb abduct abduced, abduces
ABDUCT vb abducts
ABEAM adj at right angles to a ship
ABEAR vb bear or behave **abears**
ABED adv in bed
ABEIGH adv aloof
ABELE n white poplar tree **abeles**
ABELIA n garden plant with pink or white flowers **abelian, abelias**
ABET vb abets, abettal, abetted, abetter, abettor
ABEYANT > abeyance
ABFARAD n unit of

capacitance
ABHENRY n unit of inductance
ABHOR vb abhors
ABID ▸ abide
ABIDDEN ▸ abide
ABIDE vb abided, abider, abiders, abides
ABIDING adj, n
ABIES n fir tree
ABIETIC adj as in abietic acid yellowish powder
ABIGAIL n maid for a lady
ABILITY n
ABIOSES ▸ abiosis
ABIOSIS n absence of life abiotic
ABITUR n German examination abiturs
ABJECT adj, vb abjects
ABJOINT vb cut off
ABJURE vb deny or renounce on oath abjured, abjurer, abjures
ABLATE vb remove by ablation ablated, ablates
ABLATOR n heat shield of a space craft
ABLAUT n vowel gradation ablauts
ABLAZE adj, adv
ABLE adj, vb
ABLED adj having physical powers
ABLEISM n discrimination against disabled people ableist
ABLER ▸ able
ABLES ▸ able
ABLEST ▸ able

ABLET n freshwater fish ablets
ABLING ▸ able
ABLINGS adv possibly
ABLINS adv Scots word meaning perhaps
ABLOOM adj in flower
ABLOW adj blooming
ABLUENT n substance used for cleansing
ABLUSH adj blushing
ABLUTED adj washed thoroughly
ABLY adv
ABMHO n unit of electrical conductance abmhos
ABOARD adv, adj
ABODE n, vb aboded, abodes, aboding
ABOHM n unit of resistance abohms
ABOIL adj boiling
ABOLISH vb
ABOLLA n Roman cloak abollae, abollas
ABOMA n South American snake abomas
ABOMASA > abomasum
ABOMASI > abomasus
ABOON Scots word for ▸ above
ABORAL adj away from the mouth
ABORD vb accost aborded, abords
ABORE ▸ abear
ABORNE adj Shakespearean form of auburn
ABORT vb, n aborted
ABORTEE n woman having an abortion

ABORTER ▸ abort
ABORTS ▸ abort
ABORTUS n aborted fetus
ABOUGHT ▸ aby
ABOULIA = abulia
ABOULIC ▸ aboulia
ABOUND vb abounds
ABOUT adv
ABOUTS prep about
ABOVE adv, n aboves
ABRADE vb wear down by friction abraded, abrader, abrades
ABRAID vb awake abraids
ABRAM adj auburn
ABRASAX = abraxas
ABRAXAS n ancient charm composed of Greek letters
ABRAY vb awake abrayed, abrays
ABRAZO n embrace abrazos
ABREACT vb alleviate through abreaction
ABREAST adj
ABREGE n abridgment abreges
ABRI n shelter or place of refuge, esp in wartime
ABRIDGE vb
ABRIM adj full to the brim
ABRIN n poisonous compound abrins
ABRIS ▸ abri
ABROACH adj (of a cask, barrel, etc) tapped
ABROAD adv, adj, n abroads

ABROOKE vb bear or tolerate
ABROSIA n condition involving refusal to eat
ABRUPT adj, n abrupts
ABS ▸ ab
ABSCESS n, vb
ABSCIND vb cut off
ABSCISE vb separate or be separated by abscission
ABSCISS n cutting off
ABSCOND vb
ABSEIL vb, n abseils
ABSENCE n being away
ABSENT adj, vb absents
ABSEY n alphabet abseys
ABSINTH = absinthe
ABSIT n leave from college absits
ABSOLVE vb
ABSORB vb absorbs
ABSTAIN vb
ABSURD adj, n absurds
ABTHANE n ancient Scottish church territory
ABUBBLE adj bubbling
ABULIA n pathological inability to take decisions abulias, abulic
ABUNA n male head of Ethiopian family abunas
ABUNE Scots word for ▸ above
ABURST adj bursting
ABUSAGE n wrong use
ABUSE vb, n abused, abuser, abusers, abuses, abusing

ABUSION n wrong use or deception
ABUSIVE adj
ABUT vb abuts
ABUTTAL = abutment
ABUTTED ▸ abut
ABUTTER n owner of adjoining property
ABUZZ adj noisy, busy with activity etc
ABVOLT n unit of potential difference in the electromagnetic system abvolts
ABWATT n unit of power abwatts
ABY vb pay the penalty for

> Remember this word can be expanded to **baby** and **gaby** and also to **abye** and **abys**.

ABYE = aby
ABYEING ▸ abye
ABYES ▸ abye
ABYING ▸ aby
ABYS ▸ aby
ABYSM archaic word for ▸ abyss
ABYSMAL adj
ABYSMS ▸ abysm
ABYSS n
ABYSSAL adj of the ocean depths
ABYSSES ▸ abyss
ACACIA n acacias
ACADEME n place of learning
ACADEMY n
ACAI n berry acais
ACAJOU n type of mahogany acajous
ACALEPH n invertebrate

ACANTH n acanthus

ACANTHA n thorn or prickle

ACANTHI ▷ acanthus

ACANTHS ▷ acanth

ACAPNIA n lack of carbon dioxide

ACARI ▷ acarus

ACARIAN ▷ acarus

ACARID n small arachnids ▷ adj of these arachnids acarids

ACARINE n acarid

ACAROID adj resembling a mite

ACARUS n type of mite

ACATER n buyer of provisions acaters

ACATES n provisions

ACATOUR n buyer of provisions

ACAUDAL adj having no tail

ACCA n academic

ACCABLE adj dejected or beaten

ACCAS ▷ acca

ACCEDE vb acceded, acceder, accedes

ACCEND vb set alight accends

ACCENT n, vb accents

ACCEPT vb accepts

ACCESS n, vb

ACCIDIA = accidie

ACCIDIE n spiritual sloth

ACCINGE vb put a belt around

ACCITE vb summon accited, accites

ACCLAIM vb, n

ACCLOY vb choke or clog **accloys**

ACCOAST vb accost

ACCOIED ▷ accoy

ACCOIL n welcome ▷ vb gather together accoils

ACCOMPT vb account

ACCORD n, vb accords

ACCOST vb, n accosts

ACCOUNT n, vb

ACCOURT vb entertain

ACCOY vb soothe accoyed

ACCOYLD ▷ accoil

ACCOYS ▷ accoy

ACCRETE vb grow together

ACCREW vb accrue accrews

ACCRUAL n act of accruing

ACCRUE vb accrued, accrues

ACCURSE vb curse

ACCURST = accursed

ACCUSAL n accusation

ACCUSE vb

ACCUSED n person accused of a crime

ACCUSER ▷ accuse

ACCUSES ▷ accuse

ACE n, adj, vb aced

ACEDIA = accidie

ACEDIAS ▷ acedia

ACEQUIA n irrigation ditch

ACER n type of tree

ACERATE = acerated

ACERB adj bitter acerber

ACERBIC adj

ACEROLA n cherry-like fruit

ACEROSE adj shaped

like a needle **acerous**

ACERS ▷ acer

ACES ▷ ace

ACETA ▷ acetum

ACETAL n colourless liquid acetals

ACETATE n salt or ester of acetic acid

ACETIC adj of or involving vinegar

ACETIFY vb become vinegar

ACETIN n type of acetate acetins

ACETONE n colourless liquid used as a solvent

ACETOSE = acetous

ACETOUS adj containing acetic acid

ACETUM n solution that has dilute acetic acid as solvent

ACETYL n containing the monovalent group CH_3CO- **acetyls**

ACH interj Scots expression of surprise

ACHAGE n pain achages

ACHAR n spicy pickle made from mango

ACHARNE adj furiously violent

ACHARS ▷ achar

ACHARYA n religious teacher and spiritual guide

ACHATES ▷ acates

ACHE n, vb ached

ACHENE n type of fruit achenes

ACHENIA ▷ achenium

ACHES ▷ ache

ACHIER ▷ achy

ACHIEST ▸ achy

ACHIEVE vb

ACHING ▸ ache

ACHINGS ▸ ache

ACHIOTE n annatto

ACHIRAL adj of a tuber producing arrowroot

ACHKAN n man's coat in India achkans

ACHOLIA n bile condition

ACHOO interj sound of a sneeze

ACHY adj affected by a continuous dull pain

ACICULA n needle-shaped part

ACID n, adj acider, acidest

ACIDIC adj containing acid

ACIDIER ▸ acid

ACIDIFY vb convert into acid

ACIDITY n quality of being acid

ACIDLY ▸ acid

ACIDS ▸ acid

ACIDY ▸ acid

ACIFORM adj shaped like a needle

ACINAR adj of small sacs

ACING ▸ ace

ACINI ▸ acinus

ACINIC ▸ acinus

ACINOSE ▸ acinus

ACINOUS ▸ acinus

ACINUS n parts of a gland

ACKEE n tropical tree ackees

ACKER = acca

ACKERS ▸ acker

ACKNEW ▸ acknow

ACKNOW vb recognize acknown, acknows

ACLINIC adj unbending

ACMATIC adj highest or ultimate

ACME n acmes

ACMIC = acmatic

ACMITE n chemical with pyramid-shaped crystals acmites

ACNE n

ACNED adj marked by acne

ACNES ▸ acne

ACNODAL ▸ acnode

ACNODE n mathematical term acnodes

ACOCK adv cocked

ACOLD adj feeling cold

ACOLYTE n

ACOLYTH n acolyte

ACONITE n poisonous plant with hoodlike flowers

ACORN n

ACORNED adj covered with acorns

ACORNS ▸ acorn

ACOUCHI n South American rodent with a white-tipped tail acouchy

ACQUEST n something acquired

ACQUIRE vb

ACQUIS n as in acquis communautaire European Union laws

ACQUIST n acquisition

ACQUIT vb

ACQUITE vb acquit

ACQUITS ▸ acquit

ACRASIA n lack of willpower

ACRASIN n chemical

ACRATIC ▸ acrasia

ACRAWL adv crawling

ACRE n

ACREAGE n, adj

ACRED adj having acres of land

ACRES ▸ acre

ACRID adj acrider

ACRIDIN n acridine

ACRIDLY ▸ acrid

ACROBAT n

ACROGEN n flowerless plant

ACROMIA > acromion

ACRONIC adj acronical

ACRONYM n

ACROSS adv

ACROTER n plinth

ACROTIC adj of a surface

ACRYLIC adj, n

ACRYLYL n type of monovalent group

ACT n, vb

ACTA n minutes of meeting

ACTABLE ▸ act

ACTANT n grammatical term actants

ACTED ▸ act

ACTIN n protein

ACTINAL adj part of a jellyfish

ACTING n, adj actings

ACTINIA n type of sea anemone

ACTINIC adj (of radiation) producing a photochemical effect

ACTINON = actinide

ACTINS ▸ actin

ACTION n, vb actions
ACTIVE adj, n actives
ACTON n jacket actons
ACTOR n
ACTORLY adj of or
relating to an actor
ACTORS ▶ actor
ACTRESS n
ACTS ▶ act
ACTUAL adj
ACTUALS pl n
commercial
commodities that
can be bought and
used
ACTUARY n statistician
who calculates
insurance risks
ACTUATE vb
ACTURE n action
actures
ACUATE adj sharply
pointed
ACUITY n keenness of
vision or thought
ACULEI ▶ aculeus
ACULEUS n prickle or
spine, such as the
thorn of a rose
ACUMEN n acumens
ACUSHLA n Irish
endearment
ACUTE adj, n acutely,
acuter, acutes,
acutest
ACYCLIC adj not cyclic
ACYL n member of the
monovalent group of
atoms RCO-
ACYLATE vb chemical
ACYLOIN n organic
chemical compound
ACYLS ▶ acyl
AD n

ADAGE n adages,
adagial
ADAGIO adv, n adagios
ADAMANT adj, n
ADAPT vb adapted
ADAPTER = adaptor
ADAPTOR n
ADAPTS ▶ adapt
ADAW vb subdue
adawed, adawing,
adaws
ADAXIAL adj facing the
axis
ADAYS adv daily
ADD vb addable
ADDAX n antelope
addaxes
ADDED ▶ add
ADDEDLY ▶ add
ADDEEM vb adjudge
addeems
ADDEND n any of a set
of numbers that is to
be added
ADDENDA > addendum
ADDENDS ▶ addend
ADDER n adders
ADDIBLE adj addable
ADDICT n, vb addicts
ADDIES ▶ addy
ADDING n act or
instance of addition
▶ adj of, for, or relating
to addition addings
ADDIO interj farewell
▶ n cry of addio
ADDLE vb become
muddled ▶ adj
indicating a muddled
state addled, addles,
addling
ADDOOM vb adjudge
addooms
ADDRESS n, vb addrest

ADDS ▶ add
ADDUCE vb mention
something as evidence
or proof adduced,
adducer, adduces
ADDUCT vb movement
of a muscle ▶ n
compound adducts
ADDY n e-mail address
ADEEM vb cancel
adeemed, adeems
ADENINE n chemical
ADENOID adj of or
resembling a gland
ADENOMA n tumour
occurring in glandular
tissue
ADENYL n enzyme
adenyls
ADEPT n, adj adepter,
adeptly, adepts
ADERMIN n vitamin
ADHAN n call to prayer
adhans
ADHARMA n wickedness
ADHERE vb adhered,
adherer, adheres
ADHIBIT vb administer
or apply
ADIEU n adieus, adieux

Very useful when
you want to say
goodbye to a surplus
of vowels. And
remember its plural
can be either **adieus**
or **adieux**.

ADIOS sentence
substitute Spanish for
goodbye
ADIPIC adj as in adipic
acid crystalline solid
used in the
preparation of nylon

ADIPOSE *adj* of or containing fat ▷ *n* animal fat

ADIPOUS *adj* made of fat

ADIPSIA *n* complete lack of thirst

ADIT *n* shaft into a mine, for access or drainage **adits**

ADJIGO *n* SW Australian yam plant with edible tubers **adjigos**

ADJOIN *vb* adjoins

ADJOINT *n* type of mathematical matrix

ADJOURN *vb*

ADJUDGE *vb*

ADJUNCT *n*

ADJURE *vb* command (to do) **adjured, adjurer, adjures, adjuror**

ADJUST *vb* adjusts

ADLAND *n* advertising industry and the people who work in it **adlands**

ADMAN *n* man who works in advertising

ADMASS *n* mass advertising

ADMEN ▸ adman

ADMIN *n* administration **admins**

ADMIRAL *n*

ADMIRE *vb* admired, admirer, admires

ADMIT *vb* admits

ADMIX *vb* mix or blend admixed, admixes, admixt

ADNATE *adj* growing closely attached

to an adjacent part or organ

ADNEXA *pl n* organs adjoining the uterus **adnexal**

ADNOUN *n* adjective used as a noun **adnouns**

ADO *n*

ADOBE *n* sun-dried brick **adobes**

ADOBO *n* Philippine dish **adobos**

ADONIS *n* beautiful young man

ADONISE *vb* adorn

ADONIZE *vb* adorn

ADOORS *adv* at the door

ADOPT *vb*

ADOPTED *adj* having been adopted

ADOPTEE *n* one who has been adopted

ADOPTER *n* person who adopts

ADOPTS ▸ adopt

ADORE *vb* adored, adorer, adorers, adores, adoring

ADORN *vb* adorned, adorner, adorns

ADOS ▸ ado

ADOWN *adv* down

ADOZE *adv* asleep

ADPRESS *vb* press together

ADRAD *adj* afraid

ADREAD *vb* dread **adreads**

ADRED *adj* filled with dread

ADRENAL *adj* near the kidneys ▷ *n* adrenal gland

ADRIFT *adv*

ADROIT *adj*

ADRY *adj* dry

ADS ▸ ad

ADSORB *vb* condense to form a thin film **adsorbs**

ADSUKI = adzuki

ADSUKIS = adsuki

ADSUM *sentence substitute* I am present

ADUKI = adzuki

ADUKIS ▸ aduki

ADULATE *vb* flatter or praise obsequiously

ADULT *adj, n* adultly, adults

ADUNC *adj* hooked

ADUST *vb* dry up or darken by heat **adusted, adusts**

ADVANCE *vb, n, adj*

ADVECT *vb* move horizontally in air **advects**

ADVENE *vb* add as extra **advened, advenes**

ADVENT *n* advents

ADVERB *n* adverbs

ADVERSE *adj*

ADVERT *n* advertisement ▷ *vb* draw attention (to) **adverts**

ADVEW *vb* look at **advewed, advews**

ADVICE *n* advices

ADVISE *vb*

ADVISED *adj* considered, thought-out

ADVISEE *n* person receiving advice

ADVISER *n*

ADVISES ▸ advise

ADVISOR = adviser

ADWARD vb award **adwards**

ADWARE n computer software **adwares**

ADWOMAN n woman working in advertising **adwomen**

ADYTA ▶ adytum

ADYTUM n sacred place in ancient temples

ADZ = adze

This is the American spelling of **adze**, and is one of the essential short words to know for using the Z.

ADZE n woodworking tool ▷ vb use an adze **adzed, adzes, adzing**

ADZUKI n type of plant **adzukis**

AE determiner one

AECIA ▶ aecium

AECIAL ▶ aecium

AECIDIA ▶ aecidium

AECIUM n area of some fungi

AEDES n type of mosquito which transmits yellow fever and dengue

AEDILE n magistrate of ancient Rome **aediles**

AEDINE adj of a species of mosquito

AEGIS n aegises

AEMULE vb emulate **aemuled, aemules**

AENEOUS adj brass-coloured or greenish-gold

AENEUS n aquarium fish

AEOLIAN adj of or relating to the wind

AEON n immeasurably long period of time

This little word gets played when you have too many vowels. And it has a partner **eoan**, meaning of the dawn: but beware, unlike **aeon**, it does not take a plural S.

AEONIAN adj everlasting

AEONIC ▶ aeon

AEONS ▶ aeon

AERATE vb **aerated, aerates, aerator**

AERIAL adj, n **aerials**

AERIE a variant spelling (esp US) of ▶ eyrie

This word for an eagle's nest is a great one for dealing with a surplus of vowels. And it has several variants: **aery, aiery, ayrie, eyrie** and **eyry**.

AERIED adj in a very high place

AERIER ▶ aery

AERIES ▶ aerie

AERIEST ▶ aery

AERIFY vb change or cause to change into a gas

AERILY ▶ aery

AERO n of or relating to aircraft or aeronautics

AEROBAT n person who does stunt flying

AEROBE n organism that requires oxygen to survive **aerobes**

AEROBIA ▶ aerobium

AEROBIC adj designed for or relating to aerobics

AEROBOT n unmanned aircraft used esp in space exploration

AEROGEL n colloid

AEROS ▶ aero

AEROSAT n communications satellite

AEROSOL n

AERUGO (esp of of bronze) another name for ▶ verdigris

AERUGOS ▶ aerugo

AERY adj lofty, insubstantial, or visionary

AESC n rune **aesces**

AESIR n chief of the Norse gods

AETHER = ether

AETHERS ▶ aether

AFALD adj single

AFAR adv, n

AFARA n African tree **afaras**

AFARS ▶ afar

AFAWLD adj single

AFEAR vb frighten

AFEARD an archaic or dialect word for ▶ afraid

AFEARED = afeard

AFEARS ▶ afear

AFF adv off

AFFABLE adj affably

AFFAIR n

AFFAIRE n love affair

AFFAIRS pl n personal or business interests

AFFEAR vb frighten **affeard**

AFFEARE vb frighten **affeares**

AFFEARS ▸ affear

AFFECT vb, n **affects**

AFFEER vb assess **affeers**

AFFIANT n person who makes an affidavit

AFFICHE n poster

AFFIED ▸ affy

AFFIES ▸ affy

AFFINAL ▸ affine

AFFINE adj involving transformations which preserve collinearity ▷ n relation by marriage

AFFINED adj closely related

AFFINES ▸ affine

AFFIRM vb **affirms**

AFFIX vb, n **affixal, affixed, affixer, affixes**

AFFLICT vb

AFFLUX n flowing towards a point

AFFOORD vb consent

AFFORCE vb strengthen

AFFORD vb **affords**

AFFRAP vb strike **affraps**

AFFRAY n, vb **affrays**

AFFRET n furious attack **affrets**

AFFRONT n, vb

AFFY vb trust **affyde, affying**

AFGHAN n type of biscuit

AFGHANI n monetary unit of Afghanistan

AFGHANS ▸ afghan

AFIELD adj

AFIRE adj on fire

AFLAJ ▸ falaj

AFLAME adj burning

AFLOAT adj, adv

AFOOT adj, adv

AFORE adv before

AFOUL adj in or into a state of difficulty, confusion, or conflict (with)

AFRAID adj

AFREET n powerful evil demon or giant monster **afreets**

AFRESH adv

AFRIT = afreet

AFRITS ▸ afrit

AFRO n

AFRONT adv in front

AFROS ▸ afro

AFT adv, adj

AFTER adv

AFTERS n sweet course of a meal

AFTMOST adj furthest towards rear

AFTOSA n foot-and-mouth disease **aftosas**

AG n agriculture

AGA n title of respect

AGACANT adj irritating

AGAIN adv

AGAMA n small lizard **agamas**

AGAMETE n reproductive cell

AGAMI n South American bird

AGAMIC adj asexual

AGAMID = agama

AGAMIDS ▸ agamid

AGAMIS ▸ agami

AGAMOID n lizard of the agamid type

AGAMONT another name for ▸ schizont

AGAMOUS adj without sex

AGAPAE ▸ agape

AGAPAI ▸ agape

AGAPE adj (of the mouth) wide open ▷ n love feast among the early Christians **agapeic, agapes**

AGAR n

AGARIC n type of fungus **agarics**

AGAROSE n gel used in chemistry

AGARS ▸ agar

AGAS ▸ aga

AGAST adj aghast

AGATE n, adv **agates**

AGATISE = agatize

AGATIZE vb turn into agate

AGATOID adj like agate

AGAVE n tropical plant **agaves**

AGAZE adj gazing at something

AGAZED adj amazed

AGE n, vb

AGED adj **agedly**

AGEE adj awry, crooked, or ajar ▷ adv awry

AGEING n fact or process of growing old ▷ adj becoming or growing older **ageings**

AGEISM n discrimination against people on the grounds of age **ageisms, ageist, ageists**

AGELAST n someone who never laughs

AGELESS adj apparently never growing old

AGELONG adj lasting for a very long time

AGEMATE n person the same age as another person

AGEN archaic form of ▶ **again**

AGENCY n

AGENDA n **agendas, agendum**

AGENE n chemical used to whiten flour **agenes**

AGENISE = **agenize**

AGENIZE vb whiten using agene

AGENT n, vb **agented**

AGENTRY n acting as agent

AGENTS ▶ **agent**

AGER n something that ages **agers**

AGES ▶ **age**

AGEUSIA n lack of the sense of taste

AGGADA n explanation in Jewish literature **aggadah, aggadas**

AGGADIC adj of aggada

AGGADOT ▶ **aggada**

AGGER n rampart

AGGERS adj aggressive

AGGIE n American agricultural student **aggies**

AGGRACE vb add grace to

AGGRADE vb build up by the deposition of sediment

AGGRATE vb gratify

AGGRESS vb attack first or begin a quarrel

AGGRI adj of African beads

AGGRO n aggressive behaviour **aggros**

AGGRY adj of African beads

AGHA = **aga**

AGHAS ▶ **agha**

AGHAST adj

AGILA n eaglewood **agilas**

AGILE adj **agilely, agiler, agilest, agility**

AGIN prep against, opposed to

AGING = **ageing**

AGINGS ▶ **aging**

AGINNER n someone who is against something

AGIO n difference between the nominal and actual values of a currency **agios**

AGISM = **ageism**

AGISMS ▶ **agism**

AGIST vb care for and feed (cattle or horses) for payment **agisted**

AGISTER n person who grazes cattle for money

AGISTOR n person who grazes cattle for money

AGISTS ▶ **agist**

AGITA n acid indigestion

AGITANS adj as in **paralysis agitans** Parkinson's disease

AGITAS ▶ **agita**

AGITATE vb

AGITATO adv (to be performed) in an agitated manner

AGITPOP n use of pop music to promote political propaganda

AGLARE adj glaring

AGLEAM adj glowing

AGLEE = **agley**

AGLET n metal tag **aglets**

AGLEY adj awry

AGLOO = **aglu**

AGLOOS ▶ **agloo**

AGLOW adj

AGLU n breathing hole made in ice by a seal **aglus**

AGLY Scots word for ▶ **wrong**

AGLYCON n chemical compound

AGMA n symbol used to represent a velar nasal consonant **agmas**

AGNAIL another name for > **hangnail**

AGNAILS ▶ **agnail**

AGNAME n name additional to first name and surname

AGNAMED adj having an agname

AGNAMES ▶ **agname**

AGNATE adj related through a common male ancestor ▷ n descendant by male

links from a common
male ancestor
agnates, agnatic
AGNISE *vb* acknowledge
agnised, agnises
AGNIZE *vb* acknowledge
agnized, agnizes
AGNOMEN *n* name used
by ancient Romans
AGNOSIA *n* loss of
power to recognize
familiar objects
agnosic
AGO *adv*
AGOG *adj*
AGOGE *n* ancient Greek
tempo **agoges**
AGOGIC *n* musical
accent **agogics**
AGOING *adj* moving
AGON *n* ancient Greek
festival
AGONAL *adj* of agony
AGONE *an archaic word
for* ▸ **ago**
AGONES ▸ **agon**
AGONIC *adj* forming no
angle
AGONIES ▸ **agony**
AGONISE = **agonize**
AGONIST *n* any muscle
that is opposed in
action by another
muscle
AGONIZE *vb*
AGONS ▸ **agon**
AGONY *n*
AGOOD *adv* seriously or
earnestly
AGORA *n* place of
assembly in ancient
Greece **agorae**,
agoras, agorot
AGOROTH ▸ **agorot**

AGOUTA *n* Haitian
rodent **agoutas**
AGOUTI *n* rodent
agoutis
AGOUTY *n* agouti
AGRAFE = **agraffe**
AGRAFES ▸ **agrafe**
AGRAFFE *n* loop and
hook fastening
AGRAPHA > **agraphon**
AGRASTE ▸ **aggrace**
AGRAVIC *adj* of zero
gravity
AGREE *vb*
AGREED *adj* determined
by common consent
AGREES ▸ **agree**
AGREGE *n* winner in
examination for
university teaching
post **agreges**
AGRIA *n* appearance of
pustules **agrias**
AGRIN *adv* grinning
AGRISE *vb* fill with fear
agrised, agrises
AGRIZE *vb* fill with fear
agrized, agrizes
AGROUND *adv, adj*
AGRYZE *vb* fill with fear
agryzed, agryzes
AGS ▸ **ag**
AGUE *n* periodic fever
with shivering
AGUED *adj* suffering
from fever
AGUES ▸ **ague**
AGUISE *vb* dress
aguised, aguises
AGUISH ▸ **ague**
AGUIZE *vb* dress
aguized, aguizes
AGUNA *n* (in Jewish law)
woman whose

husband will not grant
her a divorce **agunah,
agunot**
AGUTI *n* aġouti **agutis**
AH *interj* exclamation
expressing surprise,
joy, etc ▷ *vb* say ah
AHA *interj* exclamation
AHCHOO *interj* sound
made by someone
sneezing
AHEAD *adv*
AHEAP *adv* in a heap
AHED ▸ **ah**
AHEIGHT *adv* at height
AHEM *interj* clearing
of the throat in
order to attract
attention
AHENT *adv* behind
AHI *n* yellowfin tuna

┃ A very useful one to
┃ catch!

AHIGH *adv* at height
AHIMSA *n* the law of
reverence for every
form of life **ahimsas**
AHIND *adv* behind
AHING ▸ **ah**
AHINT *adv* behind
AHIS ▸ **ahi**
AHOLD *n* holding
aholds
AHORSE *adv* on
horseback
AHOY *interj*
AHS ▸ **ah**
AHULL *adv* with sails
furled
AHUNGRY *adj* very
hungry
AHURU *n* type of small
pink cod of SW Pacific
waters **ahurus**

AI n shaggy-coated slow-moving animal of South America

AIA n female servant in East **aias**

AIBLINS Scots word for ▸ **perhaps**

AID n, vb

AIDA n cotton fabric with a natural mesh

AIDANCE n help

AIDANT adj helping

AIDAS ▸ **aida**

AIDE n

AIDED ▸ **aid**

AIDER ▸ **aid**

AIDERS ▸ **aider**

AIDFUL adj helpful

AIDING ▸ **aid**

AIDLESS adj without help

AIDMAN n military medical assistant **aidmen**

AIDOI adj of the genitals

AIDOS Greek word for ▸ **shame**

AIDS ▸ **aid**

AIERIES ▸ **aiery**

AIERY n eyrie

AIGA n Māori word for family **aigas**

AIGHT adv

AIGLET = **aglet**

AIGLETS ▸ **aiglet**

AIGRET = **aigrette**

AIGRETS ▸ **aigret**

AIKIDO n Japanese self-defence **aikidos**

AIKONA interj South African expression meaning no

AIL vb trouble, afflict

AILANTO n Asian tree

AILED ▸ **ail**

AILERON n

AILETTE n shoulder armour

AILING adj

AILMENT n

AILS ▸ **ail**

AIM vb, n aimed, aimer, aimers

AIMFUL adj with purpose or intention

AIMING ▸ **aim**

AIMLESS adj

AIMS ▸ **aim**

AIN variant of ▸ **ayin**

AINE adj French word for elder (male)

> Though it doesn't score much it is useful to remember that you have too many vowels. And it can be extended to **ainee**, the feminine form.

AINEE adj French word for elder (female)

AINGA n Māori word for village **aingas**

AINS ▸ **ain**

AINSELL n Scots word meaning own self

AIOLI n garlic mayonnaise **aiolis**

AIR n, vb

AIRBAG n safety device in a car **airbags**

AIRBASE n centre from which military aircraft operate

AIRBOAT n boat

AIRBUS n commercial passenger aircraft

AIRCON n air conditioner **aircons**

AIRCREW n

AIRDATE n date of a programme broadcast

AIRDROP n delivery of supplies by parachute ▸ vb deliver (supplies, etc) by an airdrop

AIRED ▸ **air**

AIRER n device on which clothes are hung to dry **airers**

AIREST ▸ **air**

AIRFARE n money for an aircraft ticket

AIRFLOW n flow of air past a moving object

AIRFOIL = **aerofoil**

AIRGAP n gap between parts in an electrical machine **airgaps**

AIRGLOW n faint light in the night sky

AIRGUN n gun fired by compressed air **airguns**

AIRHEAD n stupid person

AIRHOLE n hole that allows the passage of air

AIRIER ▸ **airy**

AIRIEST ▸ **airy**

AIRILY adv in a light-hearted and casual manner

AIRING n exposure to air for drying or ventilation **airings**

AIRLESS adj

AIRLIFT n, vb

AIRLIKE ▸ **air**

AIRLINE n

AIRLOCK n

AIRMAIL n, adj, vb

AIRMAN n **airmen**

AIRN Scots word for
► iron

AIRNED ► airn

AIRNING ► airn

AIRNS ► airn

AIRPARK n car park at airport

AIRPLAY n broadcast performances of a record on radio

AIRPORT n

AIRPOST n system of delivering mail by air

AIRPROX n near collision involving aircraft

AIRS pl n manners put on to impress people

AIRSHED n air over a particular geographical area

AIRSHIP n

AIRSHOT n shot that misses the ball completely

AIRSHOW n occasion when an air base is open to the public

AIRSICK adj nauseated from travelling in an aircraft

AIRSIDE n part of an airport nearest the aircraft

AIRSTOP n helicopter landing-place

AIRT n point of the compass ▷ vb direct
airted, airth

AIRTHED ► airth

AIRTHS ► airth

AIRTIME n time divisions on radio and TV

AIRTING ► airt

AIRTS ► airt

AIRWARD adj into air

AIRWAVE n radio wave used in radio and television broadcasting

AIRWAY n air route used regularly by aircraft airways

AIRWISE adv towards the air

AIRY adj

AIS ► ai

AISLE n aisled, aisles

AISLING Irish word for
► dream

AIT n islet, esp in a river

AITCH n letter h or the sound represented by it aitches

AITS ► ait

AITU n half-human half-divine being aitus
| This demigod is often played to dispose of an excess of vowels.

AIVER n working horse aivers

AIZLE n Scots word for hot ashes aizles

AJAR adv, adj

AJEE = agee
| This is a Scots word meaning ajar often useful for disposing of the J. It has an alternative spelling agee.

AJIVA n Jainist term for non-living thing ajivas

AJOWAN n plant related to caraway ajowans

AJUGA n garden plant ajugas

AJUTAGE n nozzle

AJWAN n plant related to caraway ajwans

AKA n type of New Zealand vine akas
| One of the key short words when it comes to using the K.

AKATEA n New Zealand vine with white flowers akateas

AKE vb old spelling of ache

AKEAKE n New Zealand tree akeakes

AKED ► ake

AKEDAH n binding of Isaac in Bible akedahs

AKEE = ackee

AKEES ► akee

AKELA n adult leader of a pack of Cub Scouts akelas

AKENE = achene

AKENES ► akene

AKENIAL ► achene

AKES ► ake

AKHARA n (in India) gymnasium akharas

AKIMBO adj as in with arms akimbo

AKIN adj

AKING ► ake

AKIRAHO n small New Zealand shrub with white flowers

AKITA n large dog akitas

AKKAS slang word for
► money

AKRASIA n weakness of will akratic

AKVAVIT = aquavit
AL = aal
ALA n winglike structure
ALAAP n part of raga in Indian music **alaaps**
ALACK archaic or poetic word for ▶ alas
ALAE ▶ ala
ALALIA n complete inability to speak **alalias**
ALAMEDA n public walk lined with trees
ALAMO n poplar tree
ALAMODE n soft light silk used for shawls and dresses, esp in the 19th century
ALAMORT adj exhausted and downcast
ALAMOS ▶ alamo
ALAN n member of ancient European nomadic people
ALAND vb come onto land **alands**
ALANE Scots word for ▶ alone
ALANG n type of grass in Malaysia **alangs**
ALANIN n alanine
ALANINE n chemical
ALANINS ▶ alanin
ALANNAH interj term of endearment ▶ n cry of alannah
ALANS ▶ alan
ALANT n flowering plant used in herbal medicine **alants**
ALANYL n chemical found in proteins **alanyls**

ALAP n Indian vocal music without words
ALAPA n part of raga in Indian music **alapas**
ALAPS ▶ alap
ALAR adj relating to, resembling, or having wings or alae
ALARM n, vb alarmed, alarms
ALARUM n alarm, esp a call to arms ▶ vb raise the alarm **alarums**
ALARY adj of, relating to, or shaped like wings
ALAS adv
ALASKA n dessert made of cake and ice cream **alaskas**
ALASTOR n avenging demon
ALATE adj having wings or winglike extensions ▶ n winged insect
ALATED adj having wings
ALATES ▶ alate
ALATION n state of having wings
ALAY vb allay **alayed, alaying, alays**
ALB n long white robe worn by a Christian priest
ALBA n song of lament **albas**
ALBATA n variety of German silver consisting of nickel, copper, and zinc **albatas**
ALBE old word for ▶ albeit

ALBEDO n ratio of the intensity of light **albedos**
ALBEE archaic form of ▶ albeit
ALBEIT conj
ALBERGO n Italian word for inn
ALBERT n watch chain **alberts**
ALBINAL ▶ albino
ALBINIC ▶ albino
ALBINO n albinos
ALBITE n type of mineral **albites, albitic**
ALBIZIA n mimosa
ALBS ▶ alb
ALBUGO n opacity of the cornea **albugos**
ALBUM n
ALBUMEN ▶ albumin
ALBUMIN n
ALBUMS ▶ album
ALCADE = alcalde
ALCADES ▶ alcade
ALCAIC n verse consisting of strophes with four tetrametric lines **alcaics**
ALCAIDE n commander of a fortress or castle
ALCALDE n (in Spain and Spanish America) the mayor or chief magistrate in a town
ALCAYDE n alcaide
ALCAZAR n Moorish palaces or fortresses
ALCHEMY n
ALCHERA n mythical Golden Age
ALCHYMY old spelling of ▶ alchemy

ALCID n bird of the auk family **alcids**

ALCO = **alko**

ALCOHOL n

ALCOOL n form of pure grain spirit distilled in Quebec **alcools**

ALCOPOP n

ALCORZA n Spanish sweet

ALCOS ▸ alco

ALCOVE n

ALCOVED adj with or in an alcove

ALCOVES ▸ alcove

ALDEA n Spanish village **aldeas**

ALDER n

ALDERN adj made of alder wood

ALDERS ▸ alder

ALDOL n colourless or yellowish oily liquid **aldols**

ALDOSE n type of sugar **aldoses**

ALDRIN n brown to white poisonous crystalline solid **aldrins**

ALE n

ALEC = **aleck**

ALECK n irritatingly oversmart person **alecks**

ALECOST another name for > **costmary**

ALECS ▸ alec

ALEE adj on or towards the lee

ALEF n first letter of Hebrew alphabet **alefs**

ALEFT adv at or to left

ALEGAR n malt vinegar **alegars**

ALEGGE vb alleviate **alegged, alegges**

ALEMBIC n anything that distils

ALENCON n elaborate lace worked on a hexagonal mesh

ALENGTH adv at length

ALEPH n first letter in the Hebrew alphabet **alephs**

ALEPINE n type of cloth

ALERCE n wood of the sandarac tree **alerces**

ALERION n eagle in heraldry

ALERT adj, n, vb **alerted, alerter, alertly, alerts**

ALES ▸ ale

ALETHIC adj of philosophical concepts

ALEURON n outer layer of seeds

ALEVIN n young fish, esp a young salmon or trout **alevins**

ALEW n cry to call hunting hounds

ALEWIFE n North American fish

ALEWS ▸ alew

ALEXIA n disorder of the central nervous system **alexias, alexic**

ALEXIN n complement **alexine, alexins**

ALEYE vb allay **aleyed, aleyes, aleying**

ALF n uncultivated Australian

ALFA n type of grass

ALFAKI n expert in Muslim law **alfakis**

ALFALFA n

ALFAQUI n expert in Muslim law

ALFAS ▸ alfa

ALFEREZ n Spanish standard-bearer

ALFORJA n saddlebag made of leather or canvas

ALFREDO adj cooked with a cheese and egg sauce

ALFS ▸ alf

ALGA n multicellular organism **algae, algal, algas**

ALGATE adv anyway

ALGATES adv anyway

ALGEBRA n

ALGESES ▸ algesis

ALGESIA n capacity to feel pain **algesic**

ALGESIS n feeling of pain

ALGETIC ▸ algesia

ALGID adj chilly or cold

ALGIN n seaweed solution

ALGINIC adj as in **alginic acid** powdery substance extracted from kelp

ALGINS ▸ algin

ALGOID adj resembling or relating to algae

ALGOR n chill **algors**

ALGUM n type of wood mentioned in Bible **algums**

ALIAS adv, n **aliases**

ALIBI n, vb **alibied, alibies, alibis**

ALIBLE adj nourishing

ALICANT n wine from Alicante in Spain

ALIDAD = alidade

ALIDADE *n* surveying instrument

ALIDADS ▸ alidad

ALIEN *adj, n, vb* aliened

ALIENEE *n* person to whom a transfer of property is made

ALIENER ▸ alien

ALIENLY ▸ alien

ALIENOR *n* person who transfers property to another

ALIENS ▸ alien

ALIF *n* first letter of Arabic alphabet

ALIFORM *adj* wing-shaped

ALIFS ▸ alif

ALIGHT *vb, adj, adv* alights

ALIGN *vb* aligned, aligner, aligns

ALIKE *adj, adv*

ALIMENT *n* something that nourishes the body ▷ *vb* support or sustain

ALIMONY *n*

ALINE *a rare spelling of* ▸ align; alined, aliner, aliners, alining

ALIPED *n* bat-like creatures ▷ *adj* having digits connected by a membrane alipeds

ALIQUOT *adj* of or denoting an exact divisor of a number ▷ *n* exact divisor

ALISMA *n* marsh plant alismas

ALISON = alyssum

ALISONS ▸ alison

ALIST *adj* leaning over

ALIT *rare past tense and past participle of* ▸ alight

ALIUNDE *adj* from a source under consideration

ALIVE *adj*

ALIYA *n* immigration to Holy Land

ALIYAH *n* immigration to the Holy Land aliyahs

ALIYAS ▸ aliya

ALIYOS *n* remission of sin in Jewish faith

ALIYOT ▸ aliyah

ALIYOTH ▸ aliyah

ALIZARI *n* madder from Middle East

ALKALI *n*

ALKALIC *adj* geographical term

ALKALIN *adj* leaning over

ALKALIS ▸ alkali

ALKANE *n* saturated hydrocarbon alkanes

ALKANET *n* European plant whose roots yield a red dye

ALKENE *n* unsaturated hydrocarbon alkenes

ALKIE = alky

ALKIES ▸ alky

ALKINE *n* alkyne alkines

ALKO *n* heavy drinker or alcoholic alkos

ALKOXY *adj* of type of chemical compound containing oxygen

ALKY *n* heavy drinker or alcoholic

ALKYD *n* synthetic resin alkyds

ALKYL *n* of or containing the monovalent group CnH_2n+1 alkylic, alkyls

ALKYNE *n* any unsaturated aliphatic hydrocarbon alkynes

ALL *adj, adv, n*

ALLAY *vb* allayed, allayer, allays

ALLEDGE *vb* allege

ALLEE *n* avenue allees

ALLEGE *vb*

ALLEGED *adj* stated but not proved

ALLEGER ▸ allege

ALLEGES ▸ allege

ALLEGGE *vb* alleviate

ALLEGRO *adv, n*

ALLEL *n* form of gene

ALLELE *n* genes with alternative characteristics alleles, allelic

ALLELS ▸ allel

ALLERGY *n*

ALLEY *n*

ALLEYED *adj* having alleys

ALLEYS ▸ alley

ALLHEAL *n* plants with reputed healing powers

ALLICE *n* species of fish allices

ALLICIN *n* chemical found in garlic

ALLIED *adj*

ALLIES ▸ ally

ALLIS *n* species of fish allises

ALLIUM *n* type of plant **alliums**

ALLNESS *n* being all

ALLOBAR *n* form of element

ALLOD = allodium

ALLODIA > allodium

ALLODS ▶ allod

ALLONGE *n* paper extension to bill of exchange

ALLONS *interj* French word meaning let's go

ALLONYM *n* name assumed by a person

ALLOT *vb* allots

ALLOVER *n* fabric completely covered with a pattern

ALLOW *vb* allowed, allows

ALLOXAN *n* chemical found in uric acid

ALLOY *n, vb* alloyed, alloys

ALLS ▶ all

ALLSEED *n* type of plant

ALLUDE *vb* alluded, alludes

ALLURE *n, vb* allured, allurer, allures

ALLUVIA ▶ alluvium

ALLY *vb, n* allying

ALLYL *n* containing the monovalent group CH₂:CHCH₂⁻ **allylic**, **allyls**

ALLYOU *pron* all of you

ALMA *n* Egyptian dancing girl

ALMAH *n* Egyptian dancing girl **almahs**

ALMAIN *n* German dance **almains**

ALMANAC *n*

ALMAS ▶ alma

ALME *n* Egyptian dancing girl

ALMEH *n* Egyptian dancing girl **almehs**

ALMEMAR *n* area in a synagogue

ALMERY *n* cupboard for church vessels

ALMES ▶ alme

ALMIRAH *n* cupboard

ALMNER *n* almoner

ALMNERS ▶ almoner

ALMOND *n* almonds, almondy

ALMONER *n* formerly, a hospital social worker

ALMONRY *n* house of an almoner, usually the place where alms were given

ALMOST *adv*

ALMOUS *Scots word for* ▶ alms

ALMS *pl n*

ALMSMAN *n* person who gives or receives alms **almsmen**

ALMUCE *n* fur-lined hood or cape **almuces**

ALMUD *n* Spanish unit of measure

ALMUDE *n* Spanish unit of measure **almudes**

ALMUDS ▶ almud

ALMUG *n* type of wood mentioned in Bible **almugs**

ALNAGE *n* measurement in ells

ALNAGER *n* inspector of cloth

ALNAGES ▶ alnage

ALNICO *n* alloy including iron, nickel, and cobalt **alnicos**

ALOD *n* feudal estate with no superior

ALODIA ▶ alodium

ALODIAL ▶ alodium

ALODIUM = allodium

ALODS ▶ alod

ALOE *n*

ALOED *adj* containing aloes

ALOES *another name for* > eaglewood

ALOETIC ▶ aloe

ALOFT *adv, adj*

ALOGIA *n* inability to speak **alogias**

ALOHA *a Hawaiian word for* ▶ hello

ALOHAS ▶ aloha

ALOIN *n* crystalline compound **aloins**

ALONE *adv* alonely

ALONG *adv*

ALONGST *adv* along

ALOO *n* (in Indian cookery) potato

ALOOF *adj* aloofly

ALOOS ▶ aloo

ALOUD *adv, adj*

ALOW *adj* in or into the lower rigging of a vessel, near the deck

ALOWE *Scots word for* ▶ ablaze

ALP *n* high mountain

ALPACA *n* alpacas, alpacca

ALPEEN *n* Irish cudgel **alpeens**

ALPHA *n* first letter in the Greek alphabet **alphas**

ALPHORN n wind instrument

ALPHYL n univalent radical **alphyls**

ALPINE adj, n **alpines**

ALPS ► **alp**

ALREADY adv

ALRIGHT adj

ALS ► **al**

ALSIKE n clover native to Europe and Asia **alsikes**

ALSO adv

ALSOON = **alsoone**

ALSOONE adv as soon

ALT n octave directly above the treble staff

ALTAR n **altars**

ALTER vb **altered, alterer**

ALTERN adj alternate

ALTERNE n neighbouring but different plant group

ALTERS ► **alter**

ALTESSE n French word for highness

ALTEZA n Spanish word for highness **altezas**

ALTEZZA n Italian word for highness

ALTHAEA n type of plant **althea**

ALTHEAS ► **althea**

ALTHO conj short form of although

ALTHORN n valved brass musical instrument

ALTO n, adj

ALTOIST n person who plays the alto saxophone

ALTOS ► **alto**

ALTS ► **alt**

ALU ► **aloo**

ALUDEL n pear-shaped vessel **aludels**

ALULA n tuft of feathers **alulae, alular, alulas**

ALUM n double sulphate of aluminium and potassium

ALUMIN n aluminium oxide

ALUMINA n aluminium oxide

ALUMINE n French word for alumina

ALUMINS ► **alumin**

ALUMISH adj like alum

ALUMIUM old name for ► aluminium

ALUMNA n female graduate of a school, college, etc **alumnae**

ALUMNI ► **alumnus**

ALUMNUS n graduate of a college

ALUMS ► **alum**

ALUNITE n white, grey, or reddish mineral

ALURE n area behind battlements **alures**

ALUS ► **alu**

ALVEARY n beehive

ALVEOLE n alveolus

ALVEOLI ► **alveolus**

ALVINE adj of or relating to the intestines or belly

ALWAY = **always**

ALWAYS adv

ALYSSUM n

AM see ► **be**

AMA n vessel for water

AMABILE adj sweet

AMADODA pl n grown men

AMADOU n spongy substance made from fungi **amadous**

AMAH n (in the East, formerly) a nurse or maidservant **amahs**

AMAIN adv with great strength, speed, or haste

AMAKOSI ► **inkhosi**

AMALGAM n

AMANDLA n

AMANITA n type of fungus

AMARANT n amaranth

AMARNA adj pertaining to the reign of the Pharaoh Akhenaton

AMARONE n strong dry red Italian wine

AMAS ► **ama**

AMASS vb **amassed, amasser, amasses**

AMATE vb match **amated, amates**

AMATEUR n, adj

AMATING ► **amate**

AMATION n lovemaking

AMATIVE a rare word for ► **amorous**

AMATOL n explosive mixture **amatols**

AMATORY adj relating to romantic or sexual love

AMAUT n hood on an Inuit woman's parka for carrying a child **amauts**

AMAZE vb **amazed, amazes**

AMAZING adj

AMAZON n any tall, strong, or aggressive

woman **amazons**

AMBACH = ambatch

AMBAGE n ambiguity ambages

AMBAN n Chinese official **ambans**

AMBARI = ambary

AMBARIS ▸ ambari

AMBARY n tropical Asian plant that yields a fibre similar to jute

AMBASSY n embassy

AMBATCH n tree or shrub

AMBEER n saliva coloured by tobacco juice **ambeers**

AMBER n, adj

AMBERED adj fixed in amber

AMBERS ▸ amber

AMBERY adj like amber

AMBIENT adj, n

AMBIT n limits or boundary **ambits**

AMBITTY adj crystalline and brittle

AMBLE vb, n ambled, ambler, amblers, ambles

AMBLING n walking at a leisurely pace

AMBO n early Christian pulpit

AMBOINA = amboyna ambones, ambos

AMBOYNA n mottled curly-grained wood

AMBRIES ▸ ambry

AMBROID = amberoid

AMBRY n cupboard in the wall of a church

AMBSACE n double ace, the lowest throw at dice

AMBUSH n, vb

AME n soul

AMEARST old form of ▸ amerce

AMEBA = amoeba

AMEBAE ▸ ameba

AMEBAN ▸ ameba

AMEBAS ▸ ameba

AMEBEAN = amoebean

AMEBIC ▸ ameba

AMEBOID = amoeboid

AMEER n (formerly) the ruler of Afghanistan ameers

AMELIA n congenital absence of arms or legs **amelias**

AMEN n, vb

AMENAGE vb tame

AMEND vb

AMENDE n public apology

AMENDED ▸ amend

AMENDER ▸ amend

AMENDES ▸ amende

AMENDS n recompense for injury, insult, etc

AMENE adj pleasant

AMENED ▸ amen

AMENING ▸ amen

AMENITY n

AMENS ▸ amen

AMENT n mentally deficient person

AMENTA ▸ amentum

AMENTAL ▸ amentum

AMENTIA n severe mental deficiency, usually congenital

AMENTS ▸ ament

AMENTUM = ament

AMERCE vb punish by a fine **amerced, amercer, amerces**

AMES ▸ ame

AMESACE = ambsace

AMI n male friend

AMIA n species of fish

AMIABLE adj amiably

AMIAS ▸ amia

AMICE n item of clothing **amices**

AMICI ▸ amicus

AMICUS n Latin for friend

AMID prep, n

AMIDASE n enzyme

AMIDE n any organic compound containing the group $-CONH_2$ **amides, amidic**

AMIDIN n form of starch

AMIDINE n crystalline compound

AMIDINS ▸ amidin

AMIDO adj containing amide

AMIDOL n chemical used in developing photographs **amidols**

AMIDONE n pain-killing drug

AMIDS = amid

AMIDST = amid

AMIE n female friend amies

AMIGA n Spanish female friend **amigas**

AMIGO n friend **amigos**

AMILDAR n manager in India

AMIN = amine

AMINE n chemical amines, aminic

AMINITY n amenity

AMINO n of, consisting of, or containing the group of atoms $-NH_2$

AMINS ▶ amin

AMIR n (formerly) the ruler of Afghanistan **amirate, amirs**

AMIS ▶ ami

AMISES ▶ ami

AMISS adv, adj, n **amisses**

AMITIES ▶ amity

AMITY n

AMLA n species of Indian tree **amlas**

AMMAN = amtman

AMMANS ▶ amman

AMMETER n

AMMINE n chemical compound **ammines**

AMMINO adj containing ammonia molecules

AMMIRAL old word for ▶ **admiral**

AMMO n ammunition

AMMON n Asian wild sheep

AMMONAL n explosive

AMMONIA n

AMMONIC adj of ammonia

AMMONO adj using ammonia

AMMONS ▶ ammon

AMMOS ▶ ammo

AMNESIA n amnesic

AMNESTY n, vb

AMNIA ▶ amnion

AMNIC adj relating to amnion

AMNIO n amniocentesis

AMNION n innermost of two membranes enclosing an embryo **amnions**

AMNIOS ▶ amnio

AMNIOTE n group of animals

AMOEBA n amoebae, amoeban, amoebas, amoebic

AMOK n amoks

AMOKURA n type of sea bird

AMOLE n American plant **amoles**

AMOMUM n plant of ginger family **amomums**

AMONG prep amongst

AMOOVE vb stir someone's emotions **amooved, amooves**

AMORAL adj

AMORANT > amorance

AMORCE n small percussion cap **amorces**

AMORET n sweetheart **amorets**

AMORINI ▶ amorino

AMORINO = amoretto

AMORISM ▶ amorist

AMORIST n lover or a writer about love

AMOROSA n lover

AMOROSO adv (to be played) lovingly ▷ n sherry

AMOROUS adj

AMORT adj in low spirits

AMOSITE n form of asbestos

AMOTION n act of removing

AMOUNT n, vb **amounts**

AMOUR n (secret) love affair **amours**

AMOVE vb stir someone's emotions **amoved, amoves, amoving**

AMOWT = amaut

AMOWTS ▶ amowt

AMP n ampere ▷ vb excite or become excited

AMPASSY n ampersand

AMPED ▶ amp

AMPERE n amperes

AMPHORA n two-handled ancient Greek or Roman jar

AMPING ▶ amp

AMPLE adj ampler, amplest

AMPLIFY vb

AMPLY adv fully or generously

AMPOULE n small sealed glass vessel

AMPS ▶ amp

AMPUL n ampoule

AMPULE = ampoule

AMPULES ▶ ampule

AMPULLA n dilated end part of certain tubes in the body

AMPULS ▶ ampul

AMPUTEE n person who has had a limb amputated

AMREETA = amrita

AMRIT n liquid used in the Amrit Ceremony

AMRITA n ambrosia of the gods that bestows immortality **amritas**

AMRITS ▶ amrit

AMTMAN n magistrate in parts of Europe **amtmans**

AMTRAC n amphibious tracked vehicle

AMTRACK n amphibious tracked vehicle

AMTRACS ▸ amtrac

AMU n unit of mass

AMUCK = amok

AMUCKS ▸ amuck

AMULET n amulets

AMUS ▸ amu

AMUSE vb amused, amuser, amusers, amuses

AMUSIA n inability to recognize musical tones amusias, amusic

AMUSING adj mildly entertaining

AMUSIVE adj deceptive

AMYGDAL n almond

AMYL n chemical compound

AMYLASE n enzyme

AMYLENE another name (no longer in technical usage) for ▸ pentene

AMYLIC adj of or derived from amyl

AMYLOID n complex protein ▷ adj starchlike

AMYLOSE n type of chemical

AMYLS ▸ amyl

AMYLUM another name for ▸ starch

AMYLUMS ▸ amylum

AN adj form of **a** used before vowels ▷ n additional condition

ANA adv in equal quantities ▷ n collection of reminiscences

ANABAS n type of fish

ANADEM n garland for the head anadems

ANAEMIA n

ANAEMIC adj having anaemia

ANAGOGE n allegorical interpretation anagogy

ANAGRAM n

ANAL adj

ANALGIA = analgesia

ANALITY n quality of being psychologically anal

ANALLY ▸ anal

ANALOG = analogue

ANALOGA ▸ analogon

ANALOGS ▸ analog

ANALOGY n

ANALYSE vb

ANALYST n

ANALYTE n substance that is being analyzed

ANALYZE = analyse

ANAN interj expression of failure to understand

ANANA n pineapple

> More than two As on your rack is bad news, but there are a number of short words that use three As, of which this word is one.

ANANAS n plant related to the pineapple

ANANKE n unalterable necessity anankes

ANAPEST = anapaest

ANAPHOR n word referring back to a previous word

ANARCH n instigator or personification of anarchy anarchs

ANARCHY n

ANAS ▸ ana

ANATA n Buddhist belief anatas

ANATASE n rare blue or black mineral

ANATMAN = anata

ANATOMY n

ANATTA n annatto anattas

ANATTO = annatto

ANATTOS ▸ anatto

ANAXIAL adj asymmetrical

ANBURY n soft spongy tumour occurring in horses and oxen

ANCE dialect form of ▸ once

ANCHO n chili pepper

ANCHOR n, vb

ANCHORS pl n brakes of a motor vehicle

ANCHOS ▸ ancho

ANCHOVY n

ANCHUSA n Eurasian plant

ANCIENT adj, n

ANCILE n mythical Roman shield ancilia

ANCILLA n Latin word for servant

ANCLE old spelling of ▸ ankle

ANCLES ▸ ancle

ANCOME n inflammation ancomes

ANCON n projecting bracket anconal, ancone

ANCONES ▸ ancone

ANCORA adv Italian for encore

ANCRESS n female anchorite

AND n

ANDANTE adv, n

ANDIRON n iron stand for supporting logs in a fireplace

ANDRO n type of sex hormone

ANDROID n, adj

ANDROS ▶ andro

ANDS ▶ and

ANDVILE old form of ▶ anvil

ANE Scots word for ▶ one

ANEAR adv nearly ▷ vb approach **aneared, anears**

ANEATH Scots word for ▶ beneath

ANELACE = anlace

ANELE vb anoint, esp to give extreme unction to **aneled, aneles, aneling**

ANELLI pl n pasta shaped like small rings

ANEMIA n anaemia **anemias**

ANEMIC = anaemic

ANEMONE n

ANENST dialect word for ▶ against

ANENT prep lying against

ANERGIA n anergy

ANERGIC ▶ anergy

ANERGY n lack of energy

ANERLY Scots word for ▶ only

ANEROID adj not containing a liquid ▷ n

barometer that does not contain liquid

ANES ▶ ane

ANESTRA ▶ anestrus

ANESTRI ▶ anestrus

ANETHOL n substance derived from oil of anise

ANETIC adj medically soothing

ANEURIN a less common name for ▶ thiamine

ANEW adv

ANGA n part in Indian music

ANGAKOK n Inuit shaman

ANGARIA n species of shellfish

ANGARY n right to use the property of a neutral state during a war

ANGAS ▶ anga

ANGEKOK n Inuit shaman

ANGEL n, vb angeled

ANGELIC adj very kind, pure, or beautiful

ANGELS ▶ angel

ANGELUS n series of prayers

ANGER n, vb angered

ANGERLY adv old form of angrily

ANGERS ▶ anger

ANGICO n South American tree angicos

ANGINA n anginal, anginas

ANGIOMA n tumour consisting of a mass of blood vessels or lymphatic vessels

ANGLE n, vb angled

ANGLER n anglers

ANGLES ▶ angle

ANGLICE adv in English

ANGLIFY = anglicize

ANGLING n art or sport of fishing with a hook and line

ANGLIST = anglicist

ANGLO n White inhabitant of the US not of Latin extraction **anglos**

ANGOLA = angora

ANGORA n angoras

ANGRIER ▶ angry

ANGRIES ▶ angry

ANGRILY ▶ angry

ANGRY adj, n

ANGST n angsts

ANGSTY adj displaying angst

ANGUINE adj of, relating to, or similar to a snake

ANGUISH n, vb

ANGULAR adj

ANHINGA n type of bird

ANI n tropical bird

ANICCA n Buddhism belief aniccas

ANICUT n dam in India anicuts

ANIGH adv near

ANIGHT adv at night

ANIL n West Indian shrub

ANILE adj of or like a feeble old woman

ANILIN n aniline

ANILINE n colourless oily liquid

ANILINS ▶ anilin

ANILITY ▶ anile

ANILS ▶ anil

ANIMA n feminine principle as present in the male unconscious

ANIMACY n state of being animate

ANIMAL n, adj animals

ANIMAS ▶ anima

ANIMATE vb, adj

ANIMATO adv (to be performed) in a lively manner

ANIME n type of Japanese animation animes

ANIMI ▶ animus

ANIMIS ▶ animus

ANIMISM n belief that natural objects possess souls animist

ANIMUS n hatred, animosity

ANION n ion with negative charge anionic, anions

ANIS ▶ ani

ANISE n plant with liquorice-flavoured seeds

ANISEED n

ANISES ▶ anise

ANISIC ▶ anise

ANISOLE n colourless pleasant-smelling liquid used as a solvent

ANKER n old liquid measure for wine ankers

ANKH n ancient Egyptian symbol ankhs

ANKLE n, vb ankled, ankles

ANKLET n ornamental chain worn round the

ankle anklets

ANKLING ▶ ankle

ANKLONG n Asian musical instrument

ANKLUNG n Asian musical instrument

ANKUS n stick used, esp in India, for goading elephants ankuses

ANKUSH n Indian weapon

ANLACE n medieval short dagger with a broad tapering blade anlaces

ANLAGE n organ or part in the earliest stage of development anlagen, anlages

ANLAS = anlace

ANLASES ▶ anlas

ANN n old Scots word for a widow's pension

ANNA n former Indian coin worth one sixteenth of a rupee

ANNAL n recorded events of one year annals

ANNAS ▶ anna

ANNAT n singular of annates

ANNATES pl n money paid to the Pope

ANNATS ▶ annat

ANNATTA n annatto

ANNATTO n tropical tree

ANNEAL vb toughen by heating and slow cooling ▷ n act of annealing anneals

ANNELID n type of worm with a segmented body

ANNEX vb seize (territory)

ANNEXE n extension to a building

ANNEXED ▶ annex

ANNEXES ▶ annexe

ANNICUT n dam in India

ANNO adv Latin for in the year

ANNONA n American tree or shrub annonas

ANNOY vb annoyed, annoyer, annoys

ANNS ▶ ann

ANNUAL adj, n annuals

ANNUITY n

ANNUL vb

ANNULAR adj ring-shaped ▷ n ring finger

ANNULET n moulding in the form of a ring

ANNULI ▶ annulus

ANNULS ▶ annul

ANNULUS n area between two concentric circles

ANOA n type of small cattle anoas

ANOBIID n any type of beetle

ANODAL ▶ anode

ANODE n anodes, anodic

ANODISE = anodize

ANODIZE vb coat (metal) with a protective oxide film by electrolysis

ANODYNE n, adj

ANOESES ▶ anoesis

ANOESIS n feeling without understanding anoetic

ANOINT vb **anoints**

ANOLE n type of lizard **anoles**

ANOLYTE n part of electrolyte around anode

ANOMALY n

ANOMIC ▶ anomie

ANOMIE n lack of social or moral standards **anomies, anomy**

ANON adv

ANONYM n anonymous person or publication

ANONYMA n promiscuous woman

ANONYMS ▶ anonym

ANOPIA n inability to see **anopias**

ANOPSIA n squint in which the eye turns upwards

ANORAK n **anoraks**

ANOREXY old name for ▶ anorexia

ANOSMIA n loss of the sense of smell **anosmic**

ANOTHER adj

ANOUGH adj enough

ANOW adj old form of enough

ANOXIA n lack or absence of oxygen **anoxias, anoxic**

ANS pl n as in **ifs and ans** things that might have happened, but which did not

ANSA n either end of Saturn's rings **ansae**

ANSATE adj having a handle or handle-like part

ANSATED adj ansate

ANSWER n, vb **answers**

ANT n

ANTA n pilaster

ANTACID n substance that counteracts acidity ▷ adj having the properties of this substance

ANTAE ▶ anta

ANTAR old word for ▶ cave

ANTARA n South American panpipes **antaras**

ANTARS ▶ antar

ANTAS ▶ anta

ANTBEAR n aardvark

ANTBIRD n South American bird

ANTE n player's stake in poker ▷ vb place (one's stake) in poker **anted, anteed**

ANTEFIX n carved ornament

ANTEING ▶ ante

ANTENNA n insect's feeler

ANTES ▶ ante

ANTHEM n, vb **anthems**

ANTHER n **anthers**

ANTHILL n mound near an ants' nest

ANTHOID adj resembling a flower

ANTHRAX n

ANTI adj opposed (to) ▷ n opponent of a party, policy, or attitude

ANTIAIR adj countering attack by aircraft or missile

ANTIAR another name for ▶ upas

ANTIARS ▶ antiar

ANTIBUG adj acting against computer bugs

ANTIC n actor in a ludicrous or grotesque part ▷ adj fantastic

ANTICAL adj position of plant parts

ANTICAR adj opposed to cars

ANTICK vb perform antics

ANTICKE adj old form of antique

ANTICKS ▶ antick

ANTICLY adv grotesquely

ANTICS pl n

ANTIENT old spelling of ▶ ancient

ANTIFAT adj acting to remove or prevent fat

ANTIFLU adj acting against influenza

ANTIFOG adj preventing the buildup of moisture on a surface

ANTIFUR adj opposed to the wearing of fur garments

ANTIGAY adj hostile to homosexuals

ANTIGEN n

ANTIGUN adj opposed to the possession of guns

ANTIJAM adj preventing jamming

ANTILOG n number whose logarithm to a given base is a

ANTIMAN *adj* opposed to men

ANTING *n* rubbing of ants by birds on their feathers **antings**

ANTIPOT *adj* opposed to illegal use of marijuana

ANTIQUE *n, adj, vb*

ANTIRED *adj* of a particular colour of antiquark

ANTIS ▸ anti

ANTISAG *adj* preventing sagging

ANTISEX *adj* opposed to sexual activity

ANTITAX *adj* opposed to taxation

ANTIWAR *adj* opposed to war

ANTLER *n* antlers

ANTLIA *n* butterfly proboscis **antliae**

ANTLIKE *adj* of or like an ant or ants

ANTLION *n* type of insect resembling a dragonfly

ANTONYM *n*

ANTRA ▸ antrum

ANTRAL ▸ antrum

ANTRE *n* cavern or cave **antres**

ANTRUM *n* natural cavity, esp in a bone **antrums**

ANTS ▸ ant

ANTSIER ▸ antsy

ANTSY *adj* restless, nervous, and impatient

ANURAL *adj* without a tail

ANURAN *n* type of amphibian **anurans**

ANURIA *n* result of a kidney disorder **anurias, anuric**

ANUROUS *adj* lacking a tail

ANUS *n* anuses

ANVIL *n, vb* anviled, anvils

ANXIETY *n*

ANXIOUS *adj*

ANY *adj, adv*

ANYBODY *n*

ANYHOW *adv*

ANYMORE *adv* at present

ANYON *n* (in mathematics) projective representation of a Lie group

ANYONE *pron, n* anyones

ANYONS ▸ anyon

ANYROAD *a* northern English dialect word for **▸ anyway**

ANYTIME *adv* at any time

ANYWAY *adv* anyways

ANYWHEN *adv* at any time

ANYWISE *adv* in any way or manner

ANZIANI *n* Italian word for councillors

AORIST *n* tense of the verb in classical Greek **aorists**

AORTA *n* aortae, aortal, aortas, aortic

AOUDAD *n* wild mountain sheep

aoudads

APACE *adv* swiftly

APACHE *n* Parisian gangster or ruffian **apaches**

APADANA *n* ancient Persian palace hall

APAGE *interj* Greek word meaning go away

APAGOGE *n* reduction to absurdity

APAID ▸ apay

APANAGE = appanage

APAREJO *n* kind of packsaddle made of stuffed leather cushions

APART *adv*

APATHY *n*

APATITE *n* pale green to purple mineral, found in igneous rocks

APAY *vb* old word meaning satisfy **apayd, apaying, apays**

APE *n, vb*

APEAK *adj* in a vertical or almost vertical position

APED ▸ ape

APEDOM *n* state of being an ape **apedoms**

APEEK *adv* nautical word meaning vertically

APEHOOD *n* state of being an ape

APELIKE ▸ ape

APEMAN *n* primate thought to have been the forerunner of humans **apemen**

APEPSIA n digestive disorder

APEPSY n apepsia

APER n person who apes

APERCU n outline **apercus**

APERIES ▶ apery

APERS ▶ aper

APERT adj open

APERY n imitative behaviour

APES ▶ ape

APETALY ▶ apetalous

APEX n apexes

APGAR n as in **apgar score** system for determining the condition of an infant at birth

APHAGIA n refusal or inability to swallow

APHAKIA n absence of the lens of an eye

APHASIA n disorder of the central nervous system **aphasic**

APHELIA ▶ aphelion

APHESES ▶ aphesis

APHESIS n gradual disappearance of an unstressed vowel at the beginning of a word **aphetic**

APHID n

APHIDES ▶ aphis

APHIDS ▶ aphid

APHIS n type of aphid such as the blackfly

APHONIA n loss of the voice caused by damage to the vocal tract

APHONIC adj affected with aphonia ▷ n

person affected with aphonia

APHONY = aphonia

APHOTIC adj characterized by or growing in the absence of light

APHTHA n small ulceration **aphthae**

APHYLLY ▶ aphyllous

APIAN adj of, relating to, or resembling bees

APIARY n

APICAL adj of, at, or being an apex ▷ n sound made with the tip of the tongue **apicals**

APICES plural of ▶ apex

APICIAN adj of fine or dainty food

APICULI ▶ apiculus

APIECE adv

APIEZON adj as in **apiezon oil** oil left by distillation

APING ▶ ape

APIOL n substance formerly used to assist menstruation **apiols**

APISH adj stupid or foolish **apishly**

APISM n behaviour like an ape **apisms**

APLANAT n aplanatic lens

APLASIA n congenital absence of an organ

APLENTY adv in plenty

APLITE n type of igneous rock **aplites, aplitic**

APLOMB n aplombs

APNEA = apnoea

APNEAL ▶ apnea

APNEAS ▶ apnea

APNEIC ▶ apnea

APNOEA n temporary inability to breathe **apnoeal, apnoeas, apnoeic**

APO n type of protein

APOCARP n apocarpous gynoecium or fruit

APOCOPE n omission of the final sound or sounds of a word

APOD n animal without feet

APODAL adj (of snakes, eels, etc) without feet

APODE n animal without feet **apodes**

APODOUS = apodal

APODS ▶ apod

APOGAMY n type of reproduction in some ferns

APOGEAL ▶ apogee

APOGEAN ▶ apogee

APOGEE n point of moon's orbit **apogees, apogeic**

APOLLO n strikingly handsome youth **apollos**

APOLOG = apologue

APOLOGS ▶ apolog

APOLOGY n

APOLUNE n point in a lunar orbit

APOMICT n organism, esp a plant, produced by apomixis

APOOP adv on the poop deck

APOPLEX vb afflict with apoplexy

APORIA n doubt, real or professed, about what to do or say **aporias**

APORT adj on or towards the port side

APOS ▸ apo

APOSTIL n marginal note

APOSTLE n

APOTHEM n geometrical term

APOZEM n medicine dissolved in water **apozems**

APP n application program

APPAID ▸ appay

APPAIR vb old form of impair **appairs**

APPAL vb **appall**

APPALLS ▸ appall

APPALS ▸ appall

APPALTI ▸ appalto

APPALTO n Italian word for contact

APPARAT n Communist Party organization

APPAREL n, vb

APPAY old word for ▸ **satisfy**

APPAYD ▸ appay

APPAYS ▸ appay

APPEACH old word for ▸ **accuse**

APPEAL vb, n **appeals**

APPEAR vb **appears**

APPEASE vb

APPEL n stamp of the foot, used to warn of one's intent to attack **appels**

APPEND vb **appends**

APPERIL old word for ▸ **peril**

APPLAUD vb

APPLE n apples

APPLET n computing program **applets**

APPLEY adj resembling or tasting like an apple

APPLIED adj

APPLIER ▸ apply

APPLIES ▸ apply

APPLY vb

APPOINT vb

APPORT n production of objects at a seance **apports**

APPOSE vb place by side or near to each other **apposed, apposes**

APPRESS vb press together

APPRISE vb make aware (of) **apprize**

APPRO n approval

APPROOF old word for ▸ **trial appros**

APPROVE vb

APPS ▸ app

APPUI n support

APPUIED ▸ appuy

APPUIS ▸ appui

APPULSE n close approach of two celestial bodies

APPUY vb support **appuyed, appuys**

APRAXIA n disorder of the central nervous system **apraxic**

APRES prep French word for after

APRICOT n, adj

APRON n, vb **aproned, aprons**

APROPOS adv

APROTIC adj (of solvents) neither accepting nor donating hydrogen ions

APSARAS n Hindu water sprite

APSE n arched or domed recess, esp in a church **apses**

APSIDAL ▸ apsis

APSIDES ▸ apsis

APSIS n points in the elliptical orbit of a planet or satellite

APSO n Tibetan terrier **apsos**

APT adj, vb

APTAMER n artificially-created DNA or RNA molecule

APTED ▸ apt

APTER ▸ apt

APTERAL adj (esp of a classical temple) not having columns at the sides

APTERIA ▸ apterium

APTERYX n kiwi (the bird)

APTEST ▸ apt

APTING ▸ apt

APTLY ▸ apt

APTNESS ▸ apt

APTOTE n noun without inflections **aptotes, aptotic**

APTS ▸ apt

APYRASE n enzyme

AQUA n water **aquae** | This Latin word for water, together with its plural **aquae** or **aquas**, comes up over and over again.

AQUAFER n aquifer

AQUAFIT n type of aerobic exercise done in water

AQUARIA ▷ aquarium

AQUAS ▷ aqua

AQUATIC adj, n

AQUAVIT n grain- or potato-based spirit

AQUEOUS adj of, like, or containing water

AQUIFER n deposit of rock containing water used to supply wells

AQUILON n name for the north wind

AQUIVER adj quivering

AR n letter R

ARAARA another name for ▷ trevally

ARAARAS ▷ araara

ARABA n Asian carriage **arabas**

This is one of the short words that can help you deal with a surplus of As.

ARABESK = arabesque

ARABIC adj as in **gum arabic** gum exuded by certain acacia trees

ARABICA n high-quality coffee bean

ARABIN n essence of gum arabic **arabins**

ARABIS n type of plant

ARABISE vb make or become Arab

ARABIZE vb make or become Arab

ARABLE adj, n **arables**

ARACHIS n Brazilian plant

ARAISE vb old form of raise **araised, araises**

ARAK = arrack

ARAKS ▷ arak

ARALIA n type of plant **aralias**

ARAME n Japanese edible seaweed **arames**

ARAMID n synthetic fibre **aramids**

ARANEID n member of the spider family

ARAR n African tree

ARAROBA n Brazilian leguminous tree

ARARS ▷ arar

ARAYSE vb old form of raise **araysed, arayses**

ARB short for ▷ arbitrage

ARBA n Asian carriage **arbas**

ARBITER n

ARBLAST n arbalest

ARBOR n revolving shaft or axle in a machine

ARBORED adj having arbors

ARBORES ▷ arbor

ARBORET n old name for an area planted with shrubs

ARBORIO n as in **arborio rice** variety of round-grain rice used for making risotto

ARBORS ▷ arbor

ARBOUR n **arbours**

ARBS ▷ arb

ARBUTE old name for ▷ arbutus

ARBUTES ▷ arbute

ARBUTUS n evergreen shrub with strawberry-like berries

ARC n, vb

ARCADE n, vb **arcaded, arcades**

ARCADIA n traditional idealized rural setting

ARCANA n either of the two divisions of a pack of tarot cards **arcanas**

ARCANE adj

ARCANUM n profound secret or mystery known only to initiates

ARCED ▷ arc

ARCH n, vb, adj

ARCHAEA n order of prokaryotic microorganisms

ARCHAEI ▷ archaeus

ARCHAIC adj

ARCHEAN ▷ archaean

ARCHED adj provided with or spanned by an arch or arches

ARCHEI ▷ archeus

ARCHER n **archers**

ARCHERY n

ARCHES ▷ arch

ARCHEST ▷ arch

ARCHEUS n spirit believed to inhabit a living thing

ARCHFOE n chief enemy

ARCHIL a variant spelling of ▷ orchil

ARCHILS ▷ archil

ARCHINE n Russian unit of length equal to about 71 cm

ARCHING ▷ arch

ARCHIVE n, vb

ARCHLET n small arch

ARCHLY ▶ arch
ARCHON n (in ancient Athens) one of the nine chief magistrates **archons**
ARCHWAY n passageway under an arch
ARCING ▶ arc
ARCINGS ▶ arc
ARCKED ▶ arc
ARCKING ▶ arc
ARCMIN n 1/60 of a degree of an angle **arcmins**
ARCO adv musical direction meaning with bow ▷ n bow of a stringed instrument **arcos**
ARCS ▶ arc
ARCSEC n 1/3600 of a degree of an angle **arcsecs**
ARCSINE n trigonometrical function
ARCTIC adj, n **arctics**
ARCTIID n type of moth
ARCTOID adj like a bear
ARCUATE adj shaped or bent like an arc or bow
ARCUS n circle around the cornea of the eye **arcuses**
ARD n primitive plough
ARDEB n unit of dry measure **ardebs**
ARDENCY ▶ ardent
ARDENT adj
ARDOR = ardour
ARDORS ▶ ardor
ARDOUR n **ardours**
ARDRI n Irish high king

ARDRIGH n Irish high king
ARDRIS ▶ ardri
ARDS ▶ ard
ARDUOUS adj
ARE n, vb
AREA n
AREACH vb old form of reach
AREAD vb old word meaning declare **areads**
AREAE ▶ area
AREAL ▶ area
AREALLY ▶ area
AREAR n old form of arrear
AREAS ▶ area
AREAWAY n passageway
ARECA n type of palm tree **arecas**
ARED ▶ aread
AREDD ▶ aread
AREDE vb old word meaning declare **aredes, areding**
AREFIED ▶ arefy
AREFIES ▶ arefy
AREFY vb dry up
AREG a plural of ▶ erg
AREIC adj relating to area
ARENA n **arenas**
ARENE n aromatic hydrocarbon **arenes**
ARENITE n any arenaceous rock
ARENOSE adj sandy
ARENOUS adj sandy
AREOLA n **areolae, areolar, areolas**
AREOLE n space outlined on a surface **areoles**

AREPA n Colombian cornmeal cake **arepas**
ARERE adv old word meaning backwards
ARES ▶ are
ARET vb old word meaning entrust
ARETE n sharp ridge separating two glacial valleys **aretes**
ARETS ▶ aret
ARETT vb old word meaning entrust **aretted, aretts**
AREW adv old word meaning in a row
ARF n barking sound **arfs**
ARGAL = argali
ARGALA n Indian stork **argalas**
ARGALI n wild sheep **argalis**
ARGALS ▶ argal
ARGAN n Moroccan tree
ARGAND n lamp with a hollow circular wick **argands**
ARGANS ▶ argan
ARGENT n silver **argents**
ARGH interj cry of pain
ARGHAN n agave plant **arghans**
ARGIL n clay, esp potters' clay **argils**
ARGLE vb quarrel **argled, argles, argling**
ARGOL n chemical compound **argols**
ARGON n
ARGONON n inert gas
ARGONS ▶ argon

ARGOSY n large merchant ship

ARGOT n argotic, argots

ARGUE vb argued, arguer, arguers, argues

ARGUFY vb argue or quarrel, esp over something trivial

ARGUING ▶ argue

ARGULI ▶ argulus

ARGULUS n parasite on fish

ARGUS n any of various brown butterflies arguses

ARGUTE adj shrill or keen

ARGYLE adj a diamond-shaped pattern ▷ n sock made of this argyles

ARGYLL n sock with diamond pattern argylls

ARGYRIA n staining of skin by exposure to silver

ARHAT n Buddhist who has achieved enlightenment arhats

ARIA n

ARIARY n currency of Madagascar

ARIAS ▶ aria

ARID adj arider, aridest, aridity, aridly

ARIEL n type of Arabian gazelle ariels

ARIETTA n short aria ariette

ARIGHT adv rightly

ARIKI n first-born male

or female in a notable family **arikis**

ARIL n appendage on certain seeds

ARILED adj having an aril

ARILLI ▶ arillus

ARILLUS n aril

ARILS ▶ aril

ARIOSE adj songlike

ARIOSI ▶ arioso

ARIOSO n recitative with the lyrical quality of an aria **ariosos**

ARIOT adv riotously

ARIPPLE adv in ripples

ARISE vb arisen, arises

ARISH n field that has been mown **arishes**

ARISING ▶ arise

ARISTA n stiff bristle aristae, aristas

ARISTO n aristocrat aristos

ARK n, vb arked, arking

ARKITE n passenger in ark arkites

ARKOSE n type of sandstone arkoses, arkosic

ARKS ▶ ark

ARLE vb make downpayment arled, arles, arling

ARM n limbs from the shoulder to the wrist ▷ vb supply with weapons

ARMADA n armadas

ARMBAND n band worn on the arm

ARMED adj

ARMER ▶ arm

ARMERS ▶ arm

ARMET n close-fitting medieval visored helmet with a neck guard **armets**

ARMFUL n as much as can be held in the arms armfuls

ARMHOLE n opening in a garment through which the arm passes

ARMIES ▶ army

ARMIGER n person entitled to bear heraldic arms

ARMIL n bracelet

ARMILLA n bracelet

ARMILS ▶ armil

ARMING n act of taking arms or providing with arms armings

ARMLESS ▶ arm

ARMLET n band worn round the arm armlets

ARMLIKE ▶ arm

ARMLOAD n amount carried in the arms

ARMLOCK vb grip someone's arms

ARMOIRE n large cabinet

ARMOR = armour

ARMORED = armoured

ARMORER = armourer

ARMORS ▶ armor

ARMORY = armoury

ARMOUR n, vb armours

ARMOURY n

ARMPIT n armpits

ARMREST n part of a chair or sofa that supports the arm

ARMS ▶ arm

ARMSFUL ▶ armful

ARMURE n silk or wool

fabric with a small
cobbled pattern
armures
ARMY n
ARNA n Indian water
buffalo **arnas**
ARNATTO n annatto
ARNICA n temperate or
arctic plant **arnicas**
ARNOTTO n annatto
ARNUT n plant with
edible tubers **arnuts**
AROBA n Asian carriage
arobas
AROHA n love,
compassion, or
affection **arohas**
AROID n type of plant
aroids
AROINT vb drive away
aroints
AROLLA n European
pine tree **arollas**
AROMA n aromas
AROSE past tense of
▸ **arise**
AROUND adv
AROUSAL ▸ **arouse**
AROUSE vb aroused,
arouser, arouses
AROW adv in a row
AROYNT vb old word
meaning to drive away
aroynts
ARPA n website
concerned with
structure of the
internet **arpas**
ARPEN n old French
measure of land
arpens
ARPENT n former
French unit of length
arpents

ARRACK n alcoholic
drink distilled from
grain or rice **arracks**
ARRAH interj Irish
exclamation
ARRAIGN vb
ARRANGE vb
ARRANT adj
ARRAS n tapestry
wall-hanging
ARRASED adj having an
arras
ARRASES ▸ **arras**
ARRAY n, vb arrayal,
arrayed, arrayer,
arrays
ARREAR n singular of
arrears
ARREARS pl n
ARRECT adj pricked up
ARREEDE vb old word
meaning declare
ARREST vb, n arrests
ARRET n judicial
decision **arrets**
ARRIAGE n Scottish
feudal service
ARRIBA interj
exclamation of
pleasure or approval
ARRIDE vb old word
meaning gratify
arrided, arrides
ARRIERE adj French
word meaning
old-fashioned
ARRIERO n Spanish
word for mule driver
ARRIS n sharp edge at
the meeting of two
surfaces **arrises**
ARRISH n corn stubble
ARRIVAL n
ARRIVE vb arrived,

arriver, arrives
ARROBA n unit of
weight in
Spanish-speaking
countries **arrobas**
ARROW n
ARROWED adj having
an arrow pattern
ARROWS ▸ **arrow**
ARROWY adj like an
arrow
ARROYO n usually dry
stream bed **arroyos**
ARS ▸ **ar**
ARSENAL n
ARSENIC n, adj
ARSENO adj containing
arsenic
ARSHEEN n old measure
of length in Russia
ARSHIN n old measure
of length in Russia
ARSHINE n old measure
of length in Russia
ARSHINS ▸ **arshin**
ARSINE n colourless
poisonous gas **arsines**
ARSINO adj containing
arsine
ARSIS n long or stressed
syllable in a metrical
foot
ARSON n arsons
ART n
ARTAL a plural of ▸ **rotl**
ARTEL n cooperative
union **artels**
ARTERY n
ARTFUL adj
ARTI n ritual performed
in homes and temples
ARTIC n articulated
vehicle
ARTICLE n, vb

ARTICS ▸ artic

ARTIER, arties, artiest, artily ▸ **arty**

ARTIS ▸ arti

ARTISAN n

ARTIST n

ARTISTE n

ARTISTS ▸ artist

ARTLESS adj

ARTS ▸ art

ARTSIER ▸ artsy

ARTSIES ▸ artsy

ARTSMAN old word for ▸ craftsman

ARTSMEN ▸ artsman

ARTSY adj interested in the arts ▸ n person interested in the arts

ARTWORK n all the photographs and illustrations in a publication

ARTY adj, n

ARUGOLA n salad plant

ARUGULA another name for ▸ rocket

ARUHE n edible root of a fern **aruhes**

ARUM n type of plant **arums**

ARUSPEX variant spelling of ▸ haruspex

ARVAL adj of ploughed land

ARVO n afternoon **arvos**

ARY dialect form of ▸ any

ARYL n of, consisting of, or containing an aromatic group **aryls**

AS adv, n

ASANA n any of various postures in yoga **asanas**

ASAR ▸ as

ASARUM n dried strong-scented root **asarums**

ASCARED adj afraid

ASCARID n type of parasitic nematode

ASCARIS n ascarid

ASCAUNT adv old word meaning slantwise

ASCEND vb ascends

ASCENT n ascents

ASCESES ▸ ascesis

ASCESIS n exercise of self-discipline

ASCETIC adj, n

ASCI ▸ ascus

ASCIAN n person living in the tropics **ascians**

ASCIDIA ▸ ascidium

ASCITES n accumulation of serous fluid in the peritoneal cavity **ascitic**

ASCONCE adv old form of askance

ASCOT n type of cravat **ascots**

ASCRIBE vb

ASCUS n saclike structure in fungi

ASDIC an early form of ▸ sonar

ASDICS ▸ asdic

ASEA adv towards the sea

ASEITY n existence derived from itself, having no other source

ASEPSES ▸ asepsis

ASEPSIS n aseptic condition

ASEPTIC adj, n

ASEXUAL adj

ASH n, vb

ASHAKE adv shaking

ASHAME vb make ashamed

ASHAMED adj

ASHAMES ▸ ashame

ASHCAKE n cornmeal bread

ASHCAN n large metal dustbin **ashcans**

ASHED ▸ ash

ASHEN adj

ASHERY n place where ashes are made

ASHES ▸ ash

ASHET n shallow oval dish or large plate **ashets**

ASHFALL n dropping of ash from a volcano

ASHIER ▸ ashy

ASHIEST ▸ ashy

ASHINE adv old word meaning shining

ASHING ▸ ash

ASHIVER adv shivering

ASHKEY n winged fruit of the ash **ashkeys**

ASHLAR n block of hewn stone ▸ vb build with ashlars **ashlars, ashler**

ASHLERS ▸ ashler

ASHLESS ▸ ash

ASHMAN n man who shovels ashes **ashmen**

ASHORE adv, adj

ASHRAF ▸ sherif

ASHRAM n religious retreat where a Hindu holy man lives

ASHRAMA n stage in

Hindu spiritual life

ASHRAMS ▶ ashram

ASHTRAY n

ASHY adj pale greyish

ASIAGO n type of cheese asiagos

ASIDE adv, n asides

ASINICO n old Spanish word for fool

ASININE adj

ASK vb say (something) in a form that requires an answer

ASKANCE adv, vb askant

ASKANTS ▶ askant

ASKARI n (in East Africa) a soldier or policeman askaris

ASKED ▶ ask

ASKER ▶ ask

ASKERS ▶ ask

ASKESES ▶ askesis

ASKESIS n practice of self-discipline

ASKEW adj

ASKING ▶ ask

ASKINGS ▶ ask

ASKLENT Scots word for ▶ aslant

ASKOI ▶ askos

ASKOS n ancient Greek vase

ASKS ▶ ask

ASLAKE vb slake aslaked, aslakes

ASLANT adv at a slant (to), slanting (across)

ASLEEP adj

ASLOPE adj sloping

ASLOSH adj awash

ASMEAR adj smeared

ASOCIAL n person who avoids social contact

ASP n small poisonous snake

ASPECT n, vb aspects

ASPEN n, adj aspens

ASPER n former Turkish monetary unit

ASPERGE vb sprinkle

ASPERS ▶ asper

ASPERSE vb spread false rumours about

ASPHALT n, vb

ASPHYXY n ▶ asphyxia

ASPIC n

ASPICK old word for ▶ asp

ASPICKS ▶ aspick

ASPICS ▶ aspic

ASPIDIA ▶ aspidium

ASPINE old word for ▶ aspen

ASPINES ▶ aspine

ASPIRE vb aspired, aspirer, aspires

ASPIRIN n

ASPIS n horned viper aspises

ASPISH adj like an asp

ASPORT vb old word meaning take away asports

ASPOUT adv spouting

ASPRAWL adv sprawling

ASPREAD adv spreading

ASPRO n associate professor at an academic institution aspros

ASPROUT adv sprouting

ASPS ▶ asp

ASQUAT adv squatting

ASQUINT adj with a glance from the corner of the eye

ASRAMA n stage in Hindu spiritual life asramas

ASS n donkey

ASSAGAI = assegai

ASSAI adv (usually preceded by a musical direction) very ▶ n Brazilian palm tree

ASSAIL vb assails

ASSAIS ▶ assai

ASSAM n (in Malaysia) tamarind as used in cooking assams

ASSART vb clear ground for cultivation assarts

ASSAULT n, vb

ASSAY n analysis of a substance ▶ vb make such an analysis assayed, assayer, assays

ASSEGAI n, vb

ASSENT n, vb assents

ASSERT vb asserts

ASSES ▶ ass

ASSESS vb

ASSET n assets

ASSEVER vb old form of asseverate

ASSEZ adv (as part of a musical direction) fairly

ASSIEGE vb old form of besiege

ASSIGN vb, n assigns

ASSIST vb, n assists

ASSIZE n sitting of a legislative assembly assized

ASSIZER n weights and measures official

ASSIZES ▶ assize

ASSLIKE ▶ ass

ASSOIL vb absolve assoils

ASSORT vb arrange or distribute equally assorts

ASSOT vb old word meaning make infatuated assots

ASSOTT vb besot

ASSUAGE vb

ASSUME vb

ASSUMED adj false

ASSUMER ▶ assume

ASSUMES ▶ assume

ASSURE vb

ASSURED adj, n

ASSURER ▶ assure

ASSURES ▶ assure

ASSUROR ▶ assure

ASSWAGE old spelling of ▶ assuage

ASTABLE adj not stable

ASTARE adv staring

ASTART old word for ▶ start

ASTARTS ▶ astart

ASTASIA n inability to stand

ASTATIC adj not static

ASTATKI n fuel derived from petroleum

ASTEISM n use of irony

ASTELIC ▶ astely

ASTELY n lack of central cylinder in plants

ASTER n plant with daisy-like flowers

ASTERIA n gemstone with starlike light effect

ASTERID n variety of flowering plant

ASTERN adv, adj

ASTERS ▶ aster

ASTERT vb start asterts

ASTHENY = asthenia

ASTHMA n asthmas

ASTHORE n Irish endearment

ASTILBE n type of plant

ASTIR adj

ASTONE vb old form of ▶ astonish

ASTONED ▶ astone

ASTONES ▶ astone

ASTONY vb old form of ▶ astonish

ASTOOP adv stooping

ASTOUND vb

ASTRAL adj of stars ▷ n oil lamp astrals

ASTRAND adv on shore

ASTRAY adv

ASTRICT vb bind, confine, or constrict

ASTRIDE adv, adj

ASTROID n hypocycloid having four cusps

ASTRUT adv old word meaning in a protruding way

ASTUN vb old form of astonish astuns

ASTUTE adj astuter

ASTYLAR adj without columns or pilasters

ASUDDEN adv old form of suddenly

ASUNDER adv, adj

ASWARM adj filled, esp with moving things

ASWAY adv swaying

ASWIM adv floating

ASWING adv swinging

ASWIRL adv swirling

ASWOON adv swooning

ASYLA ▶ asylum

ASYLEE n person who is granted asylum asylees

ASYLUM n asylums

AT n

ATAATA n grazing marine gastropod ataatas

ATABAL n N African drum atabals

ATABEG n Turkish ruler atabegs

ATABEK n Turkish ruler atabeks

ATABRIN n drug formerly used for treating malaria

ATACTIC adj attribute of a polymer

ATAGHAN a variant of ▶ yataghan

ATALAYA n watchtower in Spain

ATAMAN n elected leader of the Cossacks atamans

ATAP n palm tree of S Asia ataps

ATARAXY = ataraxia

ATAVIC ▶ atavism

ATAVISM n atavist

ATAXIA n lack of muscular coordination ataxias, ataxic, ataxics

ATAXIES ▶ ataxy

ATE past tense of ▶ eat

ATEBRIN n drug formerly used to treat malaria

ATELIC adj of action without end

ATELIER n workshop, artist's studio

ATEMOYA *n* tropical fruit tree

ATES *n* shop selling confectionery

ATHAME *n* witch's ceremonial knife **athames**

ATHANOR *n* alchemist's furnace

ATHEISE *vb* speak atheistically

ATHEISM *n* belief that there is no God **atheist**

ATHEIZE *vb* speak atheistically

ATHEOUS *adj* without a belief in god

ATHIRST *adj* having an eager desire

ATHLETA *n* old form of ▶ **athlete**

ATHLETE *n*

ATHODYD *another name* for ▶ **ramjet**

ATHRILL *adv* feeling thrills

ATHROB *adv* throbbing

ATHWART *adv* transversely

ATIGI *n* type of parka worn by the Inuit in Canada **atigis**

ATILT *adj* in a tilted or inclined position

ATIMIES ▶ **atimy**

ATIMY *n* loss of honour

ATINGLE *adv* tingling

ATISHOO *n* sound of a sneeze

ATLAS *n* **atlases**

ATLATL *n* Native American throwing

stick **atlatls**

ATMA = **atman**

ATMAN *n* personal soul or self **atmans**

ATMAS ▶ **atma**

ATOC *n* skunk

ATOCIA *n* inability to have children **atocias**

ATOCS ▶ **atoc**

ATOK *n* skunk

ATOKAL *adj* having no children

ATOKE *n* part of a worm **atokes**

ATOKOUS *adj* having no children

ATOKS ▶ **atok**

ATOLL *n* **atolls**

ATOM *n*

ATOMIC *adj*

ATOMICS *n* science of atoms

ATOMIES ▶ **atomy**

ATOMISE = **atomize**

ATOMISM *n* ancient philosophical theory **atomist**

ATOMIZE *vb*

ATOMS ▶ **atom**

ATOMY *n* atom or minute particle

ATONAL *adj* (of music) not written in an established key

ATONE *vb* atoned, atoner, atoners, atones

ATONIA *n* lack of normal muscle tone **atonias**

ATONIC *adj* carrying no stress ▷ *n* unaccented or unstressed syllable **atonics**

ATONIES ▶ **atony**

> The plural of **atony**, this is another of the most frequently played 7-letter bonus words that it is essential to know.

ATONING ▶ **atone**

ATONY *n* lack of normal tone or tension, as in muscles

ATOP *adv* on top

ATOPIC *adj* of or relating to hypersensitivity to certain allergens

ATOPIES ▶ **atopy**

ATOPY *n* tendency to be hypersensitive to certain allergens

ATRESIA *n* absence of or unnatural narrowing of a body channel **atresic**, **atretic**

ATRIA ▶ **atrium**

ATRIAL ▶ **atrium**

ATRIP *adj* (of an anchor) no longer caught on the bottom

ATRIUM *n* upper chamber of either half of the heart **atriums**

ATROPHY *n*, *vb*

ATROPIA *n* atropine

ATROPIN = **atropine**

ATS ▶ **at**

ATT *n* old Siamese coin

ATTABOY *sentence substitute* expression of approval or exhortation

ATTACH *vb*

ATTACHE *n* specialist attached to a diplomatic mission

ATTACK vb, n **attacks**

ATTAIN vb **attains**

ATTAINT vb pass judgment of death ▷ n dishonour

ATTAP n palm tree of South Asia **attaps**

ATTAR n fragrant oil made from roses **attars**

ATTASK old word for > **criticize**

ATTASKS ▶ **attask**

ATTASKT ▶ **attask**

ATTEMPT vb, n

ATTEND vb **attends**

ATTENT old word for > **attention**

ATTENTS ▶ **attent**

ATTEST vb **attests**

ATTIC n **attics**

ATTIRE n, vb **attired, attires**

ATTONCE adv old word for at once

ATTONE vb old word meaning appease **attoned, attones**

ATTORN vb acknowledge a new owner of land as one's landlord **attorns**

ATTRACT vb

ATTRAP vb adorn **attraps**

ATTRIST vb old word meaning to sadden

ATTRIT vb wear down or dispose of gradually

ATTRITE vb wear down

ATTRITS ▶ **attrit**

ATTUENT adj carrying out attrition

ATTUITE vb perceive by attuition

ATTUNE vb adjust or accustom (a person or thing) **attuned, attunes**

ATUA n spirit or demon **atuas**

ATWAIN adv old word meaning into two parts

ATWEEL Scots word for ▶ **well**

ATWEEN an archaic or Scots word for ▶ **between**

ATWIXT old word for ▶ **between**

ATYPIC adj not typical

AUA n yellow-eye mullet **auas**

> This Maori word for a kind of mullet is very often played to balance a rack by getting rid of a surplus of vowels.

AUBADE n song or poem greeting the dawn **aubades**

AUBERGE n inn or tavern

AUBURN adj, n **auburns**

AUCEPS n old word meaning person who catches hawks

AUCTION vb, n

AUCUBA n Japanese laurel **aucubas**

AUDAD n wild African sheep **audads**

AUDIAL adj of sound

AUDIBLE adj, n, vb **audibly**

AUDIENT n person who hears

AUDILE n person with a faculty for auditory imagery ▷ adj of or relating to such a person **audiles**

AUDING n practice of listening to try to understand **audings**

AUDIO adj, n

AUDIT n, vb **audited**

AUDITEE n one who is audited

AUDITOR n person qualified to audit accounts

AUDITS ▶ **audit**

AUE interj Maori exclamation

> Another Maori exclamation, so useful for getting rid of surplus vowels. But unlike **aua** it does not take an S.

AUF old word for ▶ **oaf**

AUFGABE n word used in psychology to mean task

AUFS ▶ **auf**

AUGEND n number to which a number is added **augends**

AUGER n tool for boring holes **augers**

AUGHT adv in any least part ▷ n less common word for nought **aughts**

AUGITE n black or greenish-black mineral **augites, augitic**

AUGMENT vb, n

AUGUR vb, n **augural, augured, augurer,**

augurs

AUGURY n foretelling of the future

AUGUST adj dignified and imposing ▷ n auguste

AUGUSTE n type of circus clown

AUGUSTS ▶ august

AUK n sea bird with short wings

AUKLET n type of small auk **auklets**

AUKS ▶ auk

AULA n hall **aulas**

AULD a Scots word for ▶ old

AULDER ▶ auld

AULDEST ▶ auld

AULIC adj relating to a royal court

AULNAGE n measurement in ells

AULOI ▶ aulos

AULOS n ancient Greek pipes

AUMAIL old word for ▶ enamel

AUMAILS ▶ aumail

AUMBRY = ambry

AUMIL n manager in India **aumils**

AUNE n old French measure of length **aunes**

AUNT n

AUNTER old word for > adventure

AUNTERS ▶ aunter

AUNTIE n aunt

AUNTIES ▶ aunty

AUNTLY adj of or like an aunt

AUNTS ▶ aunt

AUNTY = auntie

AURA n **aurae**

AURAL adj **aurally**

AURAR plural of ▶ eyrir

AURAS ▶ aura

AURATE n salt of auric acid

AURATED adj combined with auric acid

AURATES ▶ aurate

AUREATE adj covered with gold, gilded

AUREI ▶ aureus

AUREITY n attributes of gold

AURELIA n large jellyfish

AUREOLA = aureole

AUREOLE n halo

AURES ▶ auris

AUREUS n gold coin of the Roman Empire

AURIC adj of or containing gold in the trivalent state

AURICLE n upper chamber of the heart

AURIFY vb turn into gold

AURIS n medical word for ear

AURIST a former name for > audiology

AURISTS ▶ aurist

AUROCHS n recently extinct European wild ox

AURORA n bands of light seen in the sky **aurorae, auroral, auroras**

AUROUS adj of or containing gold, esp in the monovalent state

AURUM n gold **aurums**

AUSFORM vb temper steel

AUSPEX = augur

AUSPICE n patronage or guidance

AUSTERE adj

AUSTRAL adj southern ▷ n former monetary unit of Argentina

AUSUBO n tropical tree **ausubos**

AUTARCH n absolute ruler

AUTARKY n policy of economic self-sufficiency

AUTEUR n director **auteurs**

AUTHOR n, vb **authors**

AUTISM n **autisms**

AUTIST n autistic person **autists**

AUTO n automobile ▷ vb travel in an automobile

AUTOBUS n motor bus

AUTOCAR n motor car

AUTOCUE n

AUTOED ▶ auto

AUTOING ▶ auto

AUTOMAN n car manufacturer

AUTOMAT n vending machine

AUTOMEN ▶ automan

AUTONYM n writing published under the real name of an author

AUTOPEN n mechanical device used to produce imitation signatures

AUTOPSY n

AUTOPUT n motorway in the former Yugoslavia

AUTOS ▸ auto

AUTOVAC n vacuum pump in a car petrol tank

AUTUMN n autumns

AUTUMNY adj like autumn

AUXESES ▸ auxesis

AUXESIS n increase in cell size without division

AUXETIC n something that promotes growth

AUXIN n plant hormone that promotes growth auxinic, auxins

AVA adv at all ▷ n Polynesian shrub

AVAIL vb, n

AVAILE old word for ▸ lower availed

AVAILES ▸ availe

AVAILS ▸ avail

AVAL adj of a grandparent

AVALE old word for ▸ lower

AVALED ▸ avale

AVALES ▸ avale

AVALING ▸ avale

AVANT prep before

AVANTI interj forward!

AVARICE n

AVAS ▸ ava

AVAST sentence substitute stop! cease!

AVATAR n appearance of a god in animal or human form avatars

AVAUNT sentence substitute go away! depart! ▷ vb go away; depart avaunts

AVE n expression of welcome or farewell

AVEL a variant of ▸ ovel

AVELLAN adj of hazelnuts

AVELS ▸ avel

AVENGE vb avenged, avenger, avenges

AVENIR n future avenirs

AVENS n any of several temperate or arctic rosaceous plants avenses

AVENTRE old word for ▸ thrust

AVENUE n avenues

AVER vb state to be true

AVERAGE n, adj, vb

AVERRED ▸ aver

AVERS ▸ aver

AVERSE adj

AVERT vb averted, averter, averts

AVES ▸ ave

AVGAS n aviation fuel avgases

AVIAN adj of or like a bird ▷ n bird avians

AVIARY n

AVIATE vb pilot or fly in an aircraft aviated, aviates

AVIATIC adj pertaining to aviation

AVIATOR n

AVID adj avider, avidest

AVIDIN n protein found in egg-white avidins

AVIDITY n quality or state of being avid

AVIDLY ▸ avid

AVIETTE n aeroplane driven by human strength

AVIFORM adj like a bird

AVINE adj of birds

AVION n aeroplane

AVIONIC ▸ avionics

AVIONS ▸ avion

AVISE old word for ▸ advise

AVISED ▸ avise

AVISES ▸ avise

AVISING ▸ avise

AVISO n boat carrying messages avisos

AVITAL adj of a grandfather

AVIZE old word for ▸ advise

AVIZED ▸ avize

AVIZES ▸ avize

AVIZING ▸ avize

AVO n Macao currency unit

AVOCADO n

AVOCET n long-legged wading bird avocets

AVODIRE n African tree

AVOID vb avoided, avoider, avoids

AVOS ▸ avo

AVOSET n avocet avosets

AVOUCH vb vouch for

AVOURE old word for ▸ avowal

AVOURES ▸ avoure

AVOUTRY old word for > adultery

AVOW vb avowal, avowals, avowed, avower, avowers, avowing

AVOWRY old word for ▸ avowal

AVOWS ▸ avow

AVOYER n former Swiss magistrate avoyers

AVRUGA n herring roe **avrugas**

AVULSE vb take away by force **avulsed, avulses**

AVYZE old word for ▶ **advise**

AVYZED ▶ **avyze**

AVYZES ▶ **avyze**

AVYZING ▶ **avyze**

AW variant of ▶ **all**

AWA adv away

AWAIT vb **awaited, awaiter, awaits**

AWAKE vb, adj **awaked**

AWAKEN vb awake **awakens**

AWAKES ▶ **awake**

AWAKING ▶ **awake**

AWARD vb, n **awarded, awardee, awarder, awards**

AWARE adj **awarer, awarest**

AWARN vb old form of warn **awarned, awarns**

AWASH adv, adj

AWATCH adv watching

AWATO n New Zealand caterpillar **awatos**

AWAVE adv in waves

AWAY adv, adj, n

AWAYDAY n day trip taken for pleasure

AWAYES old word for ▶ **away**

AWAYS ▶ **away**

AWDL n traditional Welsh poem **awdls**

AWE n, vb

AWEARY old form of ▶ **weary**

AWED ▶ **awe**

AWEE adv for a short time

AWEEL interj Scots word meaning well

AWEIGH adj (of an anchor) no longer hooked onto the bottom

AWEING ▶ **awe**

AWELESS ▶ **awe**

AWES ▶ **awe**

AWESOME adj

AWETO n New Zealand caterpillar **awetos**

AWFUL adj, adv

AWFULLY adv in an unpleasant way

AWFY adv

AWHAPE old word for ▶ **amaze**

AWHAPED ▶ **awhape**

AWHAPES ▶ **awhape**

AWHATO n New Zealand caterpillar **awhatos**

AWHEEL adv on wheels **awheels**

AWHETO n New Zealand caterpillar **awhetos**

AWHILE adv

AWHIRL adv whirling

AWING ▶ **awe**

AWK n type of programming language **awks**

This provides a useful high-scoring outlet for what can be the awkward letters W and K.

AWKWARD adj

AWL n pointed tool for piercing wood, leather, etc

AWLBIRD n woodpecker

AWLESS ▶ **awe**

AWLS ▶ **awl**

AWLWORT n type of aquatic plant

AWMOUS Scots word for ▶ **alms**

AWMRIE n cupboard for church vessels **awmries**

AWMRY n cupboard for church vessels

AWN n bristles on grasses **awned**

AWNER n machine for removing awns **awners**

AWNIER ▶ **awny**

AWNIEST ▶ **awny**

AWNING n **awnings**

AWNLESS ▶ **awn**

AWNS ▶ **awn**

AWNY adj having awns

AWOKE past tense of ▶ **awake**

AWOKEN ▶ **awake**

AWOL n person who is absent without leave **awols**

AWORK adv old word meaning at work

AWRACK adv in wrecked condition

AWRONG adv old word meaning wrongly

AWRY adj

AWSOME adj old form of awesome

AX = **axe**

AXAL adj of an axis

AXE n, vb

AXEBIRD n nightjar

AXED ▶ **axe**

AXEL n ice-skating movement **axels**

AXEMAN n man who wields an axe, esp to cut down trees **axemen**

AXENIC adj (of a biological culture) free from other microorganisms

AXES ▸ axis

AXIAL adj forming or of an axis **axially**

AXIL n angle where the stalk of a leaf joins a stem

AXILE adj of, relating to, or attached to the axis

AXILLA n area under a bird's wing **axillae**

AXILLAR = axillary

AXILLAS ▸ axilla

AXILS ▸ axil

AXING ▸ axe

AXINITE n crystalline substance

AXIOM n axioms

AXION n type of hypothetical elementary particle **axions** n

AXIS n

AXISED adj having an axis

AXISES ▸ axis

AXITE n type of gunpowder **axites**

AXLE n

AXLED adj having an axle

AXLES ▸ axle

AXLIKE ▸ ax

AXMAN = axeman

AXMEN ▸ axman

AXOID n type of curve **axoids**

AXOLOTL n aquatic salamander of central America

AXON n threadlike extension of a nerve cell **axonal, axone**

AXONEME n part of cell consisting of proteins

AXONES ▸ axone

AXONIC ▸ axon

AXONS ▸ axon

AXSEED n crown vetch **axseeds**

AY adv ever ▸ n expression of agreement

AYAH n native maidservant or nursemaid **ayahs**

AYE n, adv

AYELP adv yelping

AYES ▸ aye

AYGRE old word for ▸ **eager**

AYIN n 16th letter in the Hebrew alphabet **ayins**

AYONT adv beyond

AYRE old word for ▸ **air**

AYRES ▸ ayre

AYRIE old word for ▸ **eyrie**

AYRIES ▸ ayrie

AYS ▸ ay

AYU n small Japanese fish **ayus**

This comes up quite often, being an extension of both **ay** and **yu**, showing how important it is to know those little 'hook' words.

AYWORD n old word meaning byword **aywords**

AZALEA n azaleas

AZAN n call to prayer **azans**

AZERTY n European version of keyboard

AZIDE n type of chemical compound **azides**

AZIDO adj containing an azide

AZIMUTH n arc of the sky between the zenith and the horizon

AZINE n organic compound **azines**

AZIONE n musical drama **aziones**

AZLON n fibre made from protein **azlons**

AZO adj of the divalent group -N:N-

Azo is a chemical term you will want to play often, but it does not take an S. It takes an N to form **azon**.

AZOIC adj without life

AZOLE n organic compound **azoles**

AZOLLA n tropical water fern **azollas**

AZON n type of drawing paper

AZONAL adj not divided into zones

AZONIC adj not confined to a zone

AZONS ▸ azon

AZOTE an obsolete name for ▸ **nitrogen**

AZOTED ▶ azote

AZOTES ▶ azote

AZOTH n panacea postulated by Paracelsus **azoths**

AZOTIC adj of, containing, or concerned with nitrogen

AZOTISE = azotize

AZOTIZE vb combine or treat with nitrogen or a nitrogen compound

AZOTOUS adj containing nitrogen

AZUKI = adzuki

AZUKIS ▶ azuki

AZULEJO n Spanish porcelain tile

An **azulejo** is a kind of brightly coloured tile, beautiful in its combination of the J and Z.

AZURE n, adj

AZUREAN adj azure

AZURES ▶ azure

AZURINE n blue dye

AZURITE n azure-blue mineral associated with copper deposits

AZURN old word for ▶ azure

AZURY adj bluish

AZYGIES ▶ azygy

AZYGOS n biological structure not in a pair

AZYGOUS adj developing or occurring singly

AZYGY n state of not being joined in a pair

AZYM n unleavened bread

AZYME n unleavened bread **azymes**

AZYMITE n member of a church using unleavened bread in the Eucharist

AZYMOUS adj unleavened

AZYMS ▶ azym

Bb

B forms a two-letter word before every vowel except **U** – and with **Y** as well. With a **B** in your rack, you can play lots of short words that will give you relatively high scores. The best of these are **box** (12 points), **bez** (14 points), and **biz** (14 points), but don't forget **bay** (8), **by** (7), **bow** (8), **boy** (8), **buy** (8), and **bye** (8).

BA *n* symbol for the soul in Ancient Egyptian religion

BAA *vb* the characteristic bleating sound of a sheep ▷ *n* cry made by a sheep **baaed, baaing, baaings**

BAAL *n* any false god or idol **baalim, baalism, baals**

BAAS *South African word for* ▷ **boss**

BAASES ▷ **baas**

BAASKAP *n* (in South Africa) control by Whites of non-Whites

BABA *n* small cake of leavened dough

BABACO *n* greenish-yellow egg-shaped fruit **babacos**

BABALAS *adj* drunk

BABAS ▷ **baba**

BABASSU *n* Brazilian palm tree with hard edible nuts

BABBITT *vb* line (a bearing) or face (a surface) with a similar soft alloy

BABBLE *vb, n* **babbled**

BABBLER *n* person who babbles

BABBLES ▷ **babble**

BABBLY ▷ **babble**

BABE *n*

BABEL *n* **babels**

BABES ▷ **babe**

BABESIA *n* parasite causing infection in cattle

BABICHE *n* thongs or lacings of rawhide

BABIED, babier, babies, babiest ▷ **baby**

BABKA *n* cake **babkas**

BABLAH *n* type of acacia **bablahs**

BABOO = **babu**

BABOOL *n* type of acacia **babools**

BABOON *n* **baboons**

BABOOS ▷ **baboo**

BABOOSH = **babouche**

BABU *n* title or form of address used in India

BABUCHE = **babouche babudom, babuism**

BABUL *n* N African and Indian tree with small yellow flowers **babuls**

BABUS ▷ **babu**

BABY *n, adj, vb* **babying, babyish**

BABYSAT ▷ **babysit**

BABYSIT *vb* look after a child in its parents' absence

BAC *n* baccalaureate

BACALAO *n* dried salt cod

BACCA *n* berry **baccae**

BACCARA = **baccarat**

BACCARE = **backare**

BACCAS ▷ **bacca**

BACCATE *adj* like a berry in form, texture, etc

BACCHIC *adj* riotously drunk

BACCHII > bacchius

BACCIES ▶ baccy

BACCO n tobacco baccoes, baccos

BACCY n tobacco

BACH = batch

BACHA n Indian English word for young child bachas

BACHCHA n Indian English word for young child

BACHED, baches, baching, bachs ▶ bach

BACILLI > bacillus

BACK n, vb, adj, adv

BACKARE interj instruction to keep one's distance; back off

BACKBIT > backbite

BACKED adj having a back or backing

BACKER n backers

BACKET n shallow box backets

BACKFIT vb overhaul nuclear power plant

BACKHOE n digger ▷ vb dig with a backhoe

BACKIE n ride on the back of someone's bicycle backies

BACKING n

BACKLIT adj illuminated from behind

BACKLOG n

BACKLOT n area outside a film and television studio used for outdoor filming

BACKOUT n instance of withdrawing (from an agreement, etc)

BACKRA n white person backras

BACKS ▶ back

BACKSAW n small handsaw

BACKSET n reversal

BACKSEY n sirloin

BACKUP n support or reinforcement backups

BACLAVA = baklava

BACON n

BACONER n pig that weighs between 83 and 101 kg, from which bacon is cut

BACONS ▶ bacon

BACS ▶ bac

BACULA ▶ baculum

BACULUM n bony support in the penis of certain mammals

BAD adj not good ▷ n unfortunate or unpleasant events collectively ▷ adv badly badder, baddest

BADDIE n bad character in a story, film, etc, esp an opponent of the hero

BADDIES ▶ baddy

BADDISH ▶ bad

BADDY = baddie

BADE ▶ bid

BADGE n, vb badged

BADGER n, vb badgers

BADGES ▶ badge

BADGING ▶ badge

BADIOUS adj chestnut; brownish-red

BADLAND > badlands

BADLY adv poorly

BADMAN n hired gunman, outlaw, or criminal

BADMASH n evil-doer ▷ adj naughty or bad

BADMEN ▶ badman

BADNESS ▶ bad

BADS ▶ bad

BADWARE n software designed to harm a computer system

BAEL n type of spiny Indian tree baels

BAETYL n magical meteoric stone baetyls

BAFF vb strike ground with golf club baffed

BAFFIES pl n slippers

BAFFING ▶ baff

BAFFLE vb, n baffled, baffler, baffles

BAFFS ▶ baff

BAFFY n golf club

BAFT n coarse fabric bafts

BAG n, vb

BAGARRE n brawl

BAGASS = bagasse

BAGASSE n pulp of sugar cane or similar plants

BAGEL n hard ring-shaped bread roll bagels

BAGFUL n amount (of something) that can be held in a bag bagfuls

BAGGAGE n

BAGGED ▶ bag

BAGGER n person who packs groceries baggers

BAGGIE n plastic bag

BAGGIER ▶ baggy

BAGGIES ▶ baggy

BAGGILY ▶ baggy

BAGGING ▶ bag

BAGGIT *n* unspawned salmon **baggits**

BAGGY = bagie

BAGH *n* (in India and Pakistan) a garden **baghs**

BAGIE *n* turnip **bagies**

BAGLESS *adj* (esp of a vacuum cleaner) not containing a bag

BAGLIKE ▶ bag

BAGMAN *n* travelling salesman **bagmen**

BAGNIO *n* brothel **bagnios**

BAGPIPE *vb* play the bagpipes

BAGS ▶ bag

BAGSFUL ▶ bagful

BAGUET = baguette

BAGUETS ▶ baguet

BAGUIO *n* hurricane **baguios**

BAGWASH *n* laundry that washes clothes without drying or pressing them

BAGWIG *n* 18th-century wig with hair pushed back into a bag **bagwigs**

BAGWORM *n* type of moth

BAH *interj* expression of contempt or disgust

BAHADA = bajada

BAHADAS ▶ bahada

BAHADUR *n* title formerly conferred by the British on distinguished Indians

BAHT *n* standard monetary unit of Thailand, divided into 100 satang **bahts**

BAHU *n* **bahus**

BAHUT *n* decorative cabinet **bahuts**

BAIL *n, vb* **bailed**

BAILEE *n* person to whom the possession of goods is transferred under a bailment **bailees**

BAILER ▶ bail

BAILERS ▶ bail

BAILEY *n* outermost wall or court of a castle **baileys**

BAILIE *n* (in Scotland) a municipal magistrate **bailies**

BAILIFF *n*

BAILING ▶ bail

BAILLI *n* magistrate

BAILLIE *variant of ▶ bailie*

BAILLIS ▶ bailli

BAILOR *n* person who retains ownership of goods but entrusts possession of them to another under a bailment **bailors**

BAILOUT *n* instance of helping (a person, organization, etc) out of a predicament

BAILS ▶ bail

BAININ *n* Irish collarless jacket made of white wool **bainins**

BAINITE *n* mixture of iron and iron carbide found in incompletely hardened steels

BAIRN *n* **bairnly, bairns**

BAIT *n, vb* **baited, baiter, baiters**

BAITH *adj* both

BAITING ▶ bait

BAITS ▶ bait

BAIZA *n* Omani unit of currency **baizas**

BAIZE *n, vb* **baized, baizes, baizing**

BAJADA *n* sloping surface formed from rock deposits **bajadas**

BAJAN *n* freshman at Aberdeen University **bajans**

BAJRA *n* Indian millet **bajras, bajree**

BAJREES ▶ bajree

BAJRI = bajra

BAJRIS ▶ bajri

BAJU *n* Malay jacket **bajus**

BAKE *vb, n* **baked, baken**

BAKEOFF *n* baking competition

BAKER *n* **bakers**

BAKERY *n*

BAKES ▶ bake

BAKGAT *adj* fine, excellent, marvellous

BAKING *n* process of cooking bread, cakes, etc ▶ *adj* (esp of weather) very hot and dry **bakings**

BAKKIE *n* **bakkies**

BAKLAVA *n* rich pastry of Middle Eastern origin **baklawa**

BAKRA *n* White person, esp one from Britain ▶ *adj* (of people) White, esp British **bakras**

BAL *n* balmoral

BALADIN n dancer

BALANCE n, vb

BALAS n red variety of spinel, used as a gemstone **balases**

BALATA n tropical American tree yielding a latex-like sap **balatas**

BALBOA n standard currency unit of Panama **balboas**

BALCONY n

BALD adj, vb **balded**, **balder**, **baldest**

BALDIE ▶ **baldy**

BALDIER ▶ **baldy**

BALDIES ▶ **baldy**

BALDING adj becoming bald

BALDISH ▶ **bald**

BALDLY ▶ **bald**

BALDRIC n wide silk sash or leather belt worn across the body

BALDS ▶ **bald**

BALDY adj bald ▶ n bald person

BALE = bail

BALED ▶ **bale**

BALEEN n whalebone **baleens**

BALEFUL adj

BALER ▶ **bail**

BALERS ▶ **bail**

BALES ▶ **bale**

BALING ▶ **bale**

BALISE n electronic beacon used on a railway **balises**

BALISTA = ballista

BALK vb, n **balked**, **balker**, **balkers**

BALKIER ▶ **balky**

BALKILY ▶ **balky** **balking**, **balks**

BALKY adj inclined to a stop abruptly and unexpectedly

BALL n, vb

BALLAD n, vb

BALLADE n verse form

BALLADS ▶ **ballad**

BALLAN n species of fish **ballans**

BALLANT vb write a ballad

BALLAST n, vb

BALLAT vb write a ballad **ballats**

BALLED ▶ **ball**

BALLER n ball-game player **ballers**

BALLET n **ballets**

BALLIES ▶ **bally**

BALLING ▶ **ball**

BALLIUM = bailey

BALLON n light, graceful quality **ballons**

BALLOON n, vb

BALLOT n, vb **ballots**

BALLOW n heavy club **ballows**

BALLUTE n inflatable balloon parachute

BALLY another word for ▶ **ballyhoo**

BALM n, vb **balmed**

BALMIER ▶ **balmy**

BALMILY ▶ **balmy**

BALMING ▶ **balm**

BALMS ▶ **balm**

BALMY adj (of weather) mild and pleasant

BALNEAL adj of or relating to baths or bathing

BALONEY n foolish talk; nonsense

BALOO n bear **baloos**

BALS ▶ **bal**

BALSA n

BALSAM n, vb **balsams**, **balsamy**

BALSAS ▶ **balsa**

BALTI n spicy Indian dish served in a metal dish

BALTIC adj very cold

BALTIS ▶ **balti**

BALU = baloo

BALUN n electrical device **baluns**

BALUS ▶ **balu**

BAM vb cheat

BAMBI n born-again middle-aged biker

BAMBINI ▶ **bambino**

BAMBINO n young child, esp an Italian one

BAMBIS ▶ **bambi**

BAMBOO n **bamboos**

BAMMED, **bammer**, **bammers**, **bamming** ▶ **bam**

BAMPOT n fool **bampots**

BAMS ▶ **bam**

BAN vb, n

BANAK n type of Central American tree **banaks**

BANAL adj **banaler**, **banally**

BANANA n

BANANAS adj crazy

BANC n as in in banc sitting as a full court

BANCO n call made in gambling games **bancos**

BANCS ▶ **banc**

BAND n, vb

BANDA n African thatched hut

BANDAGE n, vb

BANDAID adj (of a solution or remedy) temporary

BANDANA = bandanna

BANDAR n species of monkey

BANDARI n Indian English word for female monkey

BANDARS ▸ bandar

BANDAS ▸ banda

BANDBOX n lightweight usually cylindrical box for hats

BANDEAU n narrow ribbon worn round the head

BANDED ▸ band

BANDER ▸ band

BANDERS ▸ band

BANDH n (in India) a general strike **bandhs**

BANDIED ▸ bandy

BANDIER ▸ bandy

BANDIES ▸ bandy

BANDING n practice of grouping schoolchildren according to ability

BANDIT n

BANDITO n Mexican bandit

BANDITS ▸ bandit

BANDOG n ferocious dog **bandogs**

BANDOOK = bundook

BANDORA = bandore

BANDORE n 16th-century musical instrument

BANDROL = banderole

BANDS ▸ band

BANDSAW n power saw with continuous blade

BANDURA n type of lute

BANDY adj, vb

BANE n, vb baned

BANEFUL adj destructive, poisonous, or fatal

BANES ▸ bane

BANG vb banged

BANGER n bangers

BANGING ▸ bang

BANGKOK n type of straw hat

BANGLE n bangled, bangles

BANGS ▸ bang

BANI ▸ ban

BANIA = banyan

BANIAN = banyan

BANIANS ▸ banian

BANIAS ▸ bania

BANING ▸ bane

BANISH vb

BANJAX vb ruin; destroy
Meaning to ruin or confound, this is a great word to remember, with its high-scoring combination of J and X.

BANJO n banjoes, banjos

BANK n, vb banked

BANKER n manager or owner of a bank bankers

BANKET n gold-bearing conglomerate found in South Africa bankets

BANKING = bank

BANKIT = banquette

BANKITS ▸ bankit

BANKS ▸ bank

BANKSIA n

BANNED ▸ ban

BANNER n, vb, adj banners

BANNET n bonnet bannets

BANNING ▸ ban

BANNOCK n round flat cake made from oatmeal or barley

BANNS pl n

BANOFFI = banoffee

BANQUET n, vb

BANS = banns

BANSELA = bonsela

BANSHEE = banshie

BANT n string ▸ vb tie with string

BANTAM n bantams

BANTED ▸ bant

BANTENG n wild ox

BANTER vb, n banters

BANTIES ▸ banty

BANTING ▸ bant

BANTS ▸ bant

BANTY n bantam

BANYA n traditional Russian steam bath

BANYAN n banyans

BANYAS ▸ banya

BANZAI interj patriotic cheer, battle cry, or salutation banzais

BAOBAB n baobabs

BAP n baps

BAPTISE = baptize

BAPTISM n

BAPTIST n one who baptizes

BAPTIZE vb

BAPU n spiritual father **bapus**

BAR n, vb

BARACAN = barracan

BARAZA n place where public meetings are held **barazas**

BARB n, vb

BARBAL adj of a beard

BARBATE adj having tufts of long hairs

BARBE n Waldensian missionary

BARBED ▶ barb

BARBEL n long thin growth that hangs from the jaws of certain fishes, such as the carp

BARBELL n

BARBELS ▶ barbel

BARBER n, vb barbers

BARBES ▶ barbe

BARBET n type of small tropical bird **barbets**

BARBIE short for > barbecue

BARBIES ▶ barbie

BARBING ▶ barb

BARBOLA n small models of flowers, etc made from plastic paste

BARBS ▶ barb

BARBULE n very small barb

BARBUT n open-faced helmet **barbuts**

BARBY n barbecue

BARCA n boat barcas

BARCHAN n crescent-shaped shifting sand dune

BARCODE n

BARD n, vb

BARDASH n kept boy in a homosexual relationship

BARDE = bard

BARDED ▶ barde

BARDES ▶ barde

BARDIC ▶ bard

BARDIE n type of Australian grub

BARDIER ▶ bard

BARDIES ▶ bardie

BARDING ▶ bard

BARDISM ▶ bard

BARDO n (in Tibetan Buddhism) the state of the soul between its death and its rebirth **bardos**

BARDS ▶ bard

BARDY ▶ bard

BARE adj, vb bared

BAREFIT > barefoot

BAREGE n light silky gauze fabric made of wool ▷ adj made of such a fabric **bareges**

BARELY adv

BARER ▶ bare

BARES ▶ bare

BAREST ▶ bare

BARF vb vomit ▷ n act of vomiting **barfed, barfing**

BARFLY n person who frequents bars

BARFS ▶ barf

BARFUL adj presenting difficulties

BARGAIN n, vb

BARGE n, vb barged

BARGEE n person in charge of a barge **bargees**

BARGES ▶ barge

BARGEST = barghest

BARGING ▶ barge

BARGOON Canadian word for ▶ bargain

BARHOP vb visit several bars in succession **barhops**

BARIC adj of or containing barium

BARILLA n impure mixture of sodium carbonate and sodium sulphate

BARING ▶ bare

BARISH adj quite thinly covered

BARISTA n person who makes and sells coffee in a coffee bar

BARITE n colourless or white mineral **barites**

BARIUM n bariums

BARK vb

BARKAN = barchan

BARKANS ▶ barkan

BARKED ▶ bark

BARKEEP n barkeeper

BARKEN vb become dry with a bark-like outer layer **barkens**

BARKER n person at a fairground who calls loudly to passers-by in order to attract customers **barkers**

BARKHAN = barchan

BARKIER ▶ barky

BARKING adj mad ▷ adv extremely

BARKS ▶ bark

BARKY adj having the texture or appearance of bark

BARLESS ▶ bar

BARLEY n, sentence

substitute **barleys**

BARLOW n type of strong knife **barlows**

BARM n yeasty froth on fermenting malt liquors

BARMAID n

BARMAN = **bartender**

BARMEN ▸ **barman**

BARMIE = **barmy**

BARMIER ▸ **barmy**

BARMKIN n protective wall around castle

BARMPOT n foolish or deranged person

BARMS ▸ **barm**

BARMY adj

BARN n, vb **barned**

BARNET n hair **barnets**

BARNEY n noisy fight or argument ▸ vb argue or quarrel **barneys**

BARNIER ▸ **barny**

BARNING ▸ **barn**

BARNS ▸ **barn**

BARNY adj reminiscent of a barn

BAROCCO = **baroque**

BAROCK = **baroque**

BAROCKS ▸ **barock**

BAROLO n red Italian wine **barolos**

BARON n

BARONET n

BARONG n broad-bladed cleaver-like knife used in the Philippines **barongs**

BARONNE n baroness

BARONS ▸ **baron**

BARONY n domain or rank of a baron

BAROQUE n, adj

BARP n hillock or bank of stones **barps**

BARQUE n sailing ship, esp one with three masts **barques**

BARRA n barramundi

BARRACE n record of teams entering a sports contest

BARRACK vb

BARRAGE n, vb

BARRAS ▸ **barra**

BARRAT n fraudulent dealings **barrats**

BARRE n rail at hip height used for ballet practice ▸ vb execute guitar chords by laying the index finger over some or all of the strings ▸ adv by using the barre

BARRED ▸ **bar**

BARREED ▸ **barre**

BARREL n, vb **barrels**

BARREN adj

BARRENS pl n (in North America) a stretch of land that is sparsely vegetated

BARRES ▸ **barre**

BARRET n small flat cap resembling a biretta **barrets**

BARRICO n small container for liquids

BARRIE adj very good

BARRIER n, vb

BARRIES ▸ **barry**

BARRING ▸ **bar**

BARRIO n Spanish-speaking quarter in a town or city, esp in the US **barrios**

BARRO adj embarrassing

BARROOM n room or building where alcoholic drinks are served over a counter

BARROW n **barrows**

BARRY n mistake or blunder

BARS ▸ **bar**

BARTEND vb serve drinks from a bar

BARTER vb, n **barters**

BARTON n farmyard **bartons**

BARTSIA n type of semiparasitic plant

BARWARE n glasses, etc used in a bar

BARWOOD n red wood from small African tree

BARYE n unit of pressure **baryes**

BARYON n elementary particle that has a mass greater than or equal to that of the proton **baryons**

BARYTA = **barite**

BARYTAS ▸ **baryta**

BARYTE = **baryta**

BARYTES ▸ **baryte**

BARYTIC ▸ **baryta**

BARYTON n bass viol with sympathetic strings as well as its six main strings

BAS ▸ **ba**

BASAL adj of, at, or constituting a base **basally**

BASALT n **basalts**

BASAN n sheepskin tanned in bark **basans**

BASANT n Pakistani spring festival **basants**

BASCULE *n* drawbridge that operates by a counterbalanced weight

BASE *n, vb, adj* based

BASEEJ *pl n* Iranian volunteer militia

BASELY ▶ base

BASEMAN *n* fielder positioned near a base basemen

BASEN Spencerian spelling of ▶ basin

BASENJI *n* small breed of dog

BASER ▶ base

BASES ▶ basis

BASEST ▶ base

BASH *vb, n*

BASHAW *n* important or pompous person bashaws

BASHED, basher, bashers, bashes ▶ bash

BASHFUL *adj*

BASHING ▶ bash

BASHLIK *n* Caucasian hood bashlyk

BASHO *n* grand tournament in sumo wrestling

BASIC *adj, n* basics

BASIDIA ▶ basidium

BASIFY *vb* make basic

BASIJ ▶ baseej

BASIL *n*

BASILAR *adj* of or situated at a base

BASILIC > basilica

BASILS ▶ basil

BASIN *n* basinal, basined

BASINET *n* close-fitting medieval helmet of light steel usually with a visor

BASING ▶ base

BASINS ▶ basin

BASION *n* (in anatomy) midpoint on the forward border of the foramen magnum basions

BASIS *n*

BASK *vb* basked

BASKET *n* baskets

BASKING ▶ bask

BASKS ▶ bask

BASMATI *n* variety of long-grain rice with slender aromatic grains

BASNET = basinet

BASNETS ▶ basnet

BASOCHE *n* society of medieval French lawyers who performed comic plays

BASON = basin

BASONS ▶ bason

BASQUE *n* tight-fitting bodice for women basqued, basques

BASS *vb* basse, bassed, basser, basses, bassest

BASSET *n* breed of hound ▷ *vb* (of rock) protrude through earth's surface bassets, bassett

BASSI ▶ basso

BASSIER ▶ bassy

BASSING ▶ bass

BASSIST *n* player of a double bass, esp in a jazz band

BASSLY ▶ bass

BASSO *n* singer with a bass voice

BASSOON *n*

BASSOS ▶ basso

BASSY *adj* manifesting strong bass tones

BAST *n* fibrous material used for making rope, matting, etc

BASTA *interj* enough; stop

BASTE *vb* basted, baster, basters, bastes

BASTI *n* (in India) a slum inhabited by poor people

BASTIDE *n* small isolated house in France

BASTILE = bastille

BASTING *n* loose temporary stitches

BASTION *n*

BASTIS ▶ basti

BASTLE *n* fortified house bastles

BASTO *n* ace of clubs in certain card games bastos

BASTS ▶ bast

BASUCO *n* cocaine-based drug basucos

BAT *n, vb* batable

BATATA *n* sweet potato batatas

BATAVIA *n* variety of lettuce with smooth pale green leaves

BATBOY *n* boy who works at baseball games batboys

BATCH *n, vb* batched,

batcher, batches

BATE *vb* (of hawks) to jump violently from a perch or the falconer's fist

BATEAU *n* light flat-bottomed boat used on rivers in Canada and the northern US **bateaux**

BATED ▶ bate

BATES ▶ bate

BATFISH *n* type of angler fish with a flattened scaleless body

BATFOWL *vb* catch birds by temporarily blinding them with light

BATGIRL *n* girl who works at baseball games

BATH *n, vb*

BATHE *vb* bathed, bather

BATHERS *pl n* swimming costume

BATHES ▶ bathe

BATHING ▶ bathe

BATHMAT *n* mat to stand on after a bath

BATHMIC > bathmism

BATHOS *n*

BATHS ▶ bath

BATHTUB *n* bath, esp one not permanently fixed

BATHYAL *adj* relating to an ocean depth of between 200 and 2000 metres

BATIK *n, vb* batiked, batiks

BATING ▶ bate

BATISTE *n* fine plain-weave cotton fabric: used esp for shirts and dresses

BATLER *n* flat piece of wood for beating clothes, etc before washing **batlers, batlet**

BATLETS ▶ batlet

BATLIKE ▶ bat

BATMAN *n* batmen

BATON *n, vb* batoned, batons, batoon

BATOONS ▶ batoon

BATS ▶ bat

BATSMAN *n* batsmen

BATT ▶ bat

BATTA *n* soldier's allowance **battas**

BATTEAU = bateau

BATTED ▶ bat

BATTEL *vb* make fertile **battels**

BATTEN *n, vb* battens

BATTER *vb, n*

BATTERO *n* heavy club

BATTERS ▶ batter

BATTERY *n, adj*

BATTIER ▶ batty

BATTIES ▶ batty

BATTIK = batik

BATTIKS ▶ battik

BATTILL *old spelling of* ▶ battle

BATTING ▶ bat

BATTLE *n, vb* battled, battler, battles

BATTS ▶ batt

BATTU *adj* (in ballet) involving a beating movement

BATTUE *n* beating of woodland or cover to force game to flee in the direction of hunters **battues**

BATTUTA *n* (in music) a beat

BATTUTO *n*

BATTY *adj, n*

BATWING *adj* shaped like the wings of a bat, as a black tie, collar, etc

BAUBEE = bawbee

BAUBEES ▶ baubee

BAUBLE *n* baubles

BAUCHLE *vb* shuffle along

BAUD *n* unit used to measure the speed of transmission of electronic data

BAUDRIC = baldric

BAUDS ▶ baud

BAUERA *n* small evergreen Australian shrub **baueras**

BAUK = balk

BAUKED ▶ bauk

BAUKING ▶ bauk

BAUKS ▶ bauk

BAULK ▶ balk

BAULKED ▶ balk

BAULKER ▶ balk

BAULKS ▶ balk

BAULKY = balky

BAUR *n* humorous anecdote; joke **baurs**

BAUSOND *adj* (of animal) dappled with white spots

BAUXITE *n*

BAVIN *n* impure limestone **bavins**

BAWBEE *n* former

Scottish silver coin **bawbees**

BAWBLE = bauble

BAWBLES ▶ bawble

BAWCOCK n fine fellow

BAWD n person who runs a brothel, esp a woman

BAWDIER ▶ bawdy

BAWDIES ▶ bawdy

BAWDILY ▶ bawdy

BAWDKIN = baldachin

BAWDRIC n heavy belt to support sword

BAWDRY n obscene talk or language

BAWDS ▶ bawd

BAWDY adj, n

BAWL vb, n bawled, bawler, bawlers

BAWLEY n small fishing boat bawleys

BAWLING ▶ bawl

BAWLS ▶ bawl

BAWN n fortified enclosure

BAWNEEN = bainin

BAWNS ▶ bawn

BAWR = bawr

BAWRS ▶ bawr

BAWSUNT adj black and white in colour

BAWTIE n name for a dog bawties, bawty

BAXTER old variant of ▶ baker

BAXTERS ▶ baxter

BAY n, vb

BAYAMO n Cuban strong wind bayamos

BAYARD n bay horse bayards

BAYE vb bathe

BAYED ▶ bay

BAYES ▶ baye

BAYING ▶ bay

BAYLE n barrier bayles

BAYMAN n fisherman baymen

BAYONET n, vb

BAYOU n (in the southern US) a sluggish marshy tributary of a lake or river bayous

BAYS ▶ bay

BAYT = bate

BAYTED ▶ bayt

BAYTING ▶ bayt

BAYTS ▶ bayt

BAYWOOD n light soft wood of a tropical American mahogany tree

BAYYAN n Islamic declaration bayyans

BAZAAR n bazaars, bazar

BAZARS ▶ bazar

BAZAZZ = pizzazz

BAZOO a US slang word for ▶ mouth

BAZOOKA n portable rocket launcher that fires an armour-piercing projectile

BAZOOS ▶ bazoo

BAZOUKI = bouzouki

BAZZAZZ ▶ pizzazz

BE vb exist or live

BEACH n, vb beached, beaches

BEACHY adj with gentle sandy slopes

BEACON n, vb beacons

BEAD n, vb beaded

BEADER n person making things with beads beaders

BEADIER ▶ beady

BEADILY ▶ beady

BEADING n strip of moulding used for edging furniture

BEADLE n (formerly) a minor parish official who acted as an usher beadles

BEADMAN = beadsman

BEADMEN ▶ beadman

BEADS ▶ bead

BEADY adj

BEAGLE n, vb beagled

BEAGLER n person who hunts with beagles

BEAGLES ▶ beagle

BEAK n, vb beaked

BEAKER n beakers

BEAKIER ▶ beak

BEAKS ▶ beak

BEAKY ▶ beak

BEAM n, vb beamed

BEAMER n full-pitched ball bowled at the batsman's head beamers

BEAMIER ▶ beam

BEAMILY ▶ beam

BEAMING ▶ beam

BEAMISH adj smiling

BEAMLET n small beam

BEAMS ▶ beam

BEAMY ▶ beam

BEAN n, vb

BEANBAG n small cloth bag filled with dried beans and thrown in games

BEANED ▶ bean

BEANERY n cheap restaurant

BEANIE n close-fitting woollen hat

BEANIES ▸ beany

BEANING ▸ bean

BEANO n celebration or party beanos

BEANS ▸ bean

BEANY = beanie

BEAR vb, n

BEARCAT n lesser panda

BEARD n, vb bearded

BEARDIE n another name for bearded loach

BEARDS ▸ beard

BEARDY adj having a beard

BEARE = bear

BEARED ▸ bear

BEARER n bearers

BEARES ▸ beare

BEARHUG n wrestling hold in which the arms are locked tightly round an opponent's chest and arms

BEARING ▸ bear

BEARISH adj like a bear

BEARS ▸ bear

BEAST n, vb beasted

BEASTIE n small animal

BEASTLY adj, adv

BEASTS ▸ beast

BEAT vb, n, adj

BEATBOX n drum machine simulated by a human voice

BEATEN ▸ beat

BEATER n device used for beating beaters

BEATH vb dry; heat beathed, beaths

BEATIER ▸ beaty

BEATIFY vb take first step towards making (a dead person) a saint

BEATING ▸ beat

BEATS ▸ beat

BEATNIK n young person in the late 1950s who rebelled against conventional attitudes, etc

BEATS ▸ beat

BEATY adj (of music) having a strong rhythm

BEAU n boyfriend or admirer

BEAUFET = buffet

BEAUFIN = biffin

BEAUISH adj vain and showy

BEAUS ▸ beau

BEAUT n, adj, interj beauts

BEAUTY n, interj, vb

BEAUX ▸ beau

BEAVER n, vb beavers

BEAVERY n place for keeping beavers

BEBEERU n tropical American tree

BEBLOOD vb stain with blood

BEBOP = bop

BEBOPS ▸ bebop

BEBUNG n vibrato effect on clavichord bebungs

BECALL vb use insulting words about someone becalls

BECALM vb becalms

BECAME ▸ become

BECAP vb put cap on becaps

BECASSE n woodcock

BECAUSE conj

BECHALK vb mark with chalk

BECHARM vb delight

BECK n, vb

BECKE = beak

BECKED ▸ becke

BECKES ▸ becke

BECKET n clevis forming part of one end of a sheave beckets

BECKING ▸ beck

BECKS ▸ beck

BECLASP vb embrace

BECLOAK vb dress in cloak

BECLOG vb put clogs on beclogs

BECLOUD vb cover or obscure with a cloud

BECLOWN vb clown around

BECOME vb becomes

BECRAWL vb crawl all over

BECRIME vb make someone guilty of a crime

BECROWD vb crowd with something

BECRUST vb cover with crust

BECURL vb curl becurls

BECURSE vb curse becurst

BED n, vb

BEDAD interj by God (oath)

BEDAMN vb damn bedamns

BEDASH vb sprinkle with liquid

BEDAUB vb smear with something sticky or dirty bedaubs

BEDAWIN = bedouin

BEDAZE vb daze bedazed, bedazes

BEDBATH n washing of a sick person in bed

BEDBUG n small blood-sucking wingless insect that infests dirty houses **bedbugs**

BEDDED ▸ bed

BEDDER n (at some universities) a college servant employed to keep students' rooms in order **bedders**

BEDDING ▸ bed

BEDE n prayer

BEDECK vb cover with decorations **bedecks**

BEDEL archaic spelling of ▸ **beadle**

BEDELL ▸ **beadle**

BEDELLS ▸ **bedell**

BEDELS ▸ **bedel**

BEDEMAN = beadsman

BEDEMEN ▸ **bedeman**

BEDERAL = bedral

BEDES ▸ **bede**

BEDEVIL vb harass, confuse, or torment

BEDEW vb wet or cover with or as if with drops of dew **bedewed, bedews**

BEDFAST an archaic word for ▸ **bedridden**

BEDGOWN n nightdress

BEDHEAD n untidy state of hair, esp caused by sleeping

BEDIDE ▸ **bedye**

BEDIGHT vb array or adorn ▷ adj adorned or bedecked

BEDIM vb make dim or obscure **bedims**

BEDIRTY vb make dirty

BEDIZEN vb dress or decorate gaudily or tastelessly

BEDLAM n

BEDLAMP n bedside light

BEDLAMS ▸ **bedlam**

BEDLESS ▸ **bed**

BEDLIKE adj like a bed

BEDMATE n person who shares a bed

BEDOUIN n member of any of the nomadic tribes of Arabs

BEDPAN n **bedpans**

BEDPOST n vertical support on a bedstead

BEDRAIL n rail along the side of a bed connecting the headboard with the footboard

BEDRAL n minor church official **bedrals**

BEDRAPE vb adorn

BEDRID = bedridden

BEDRITE > **bedright**

BEDROCK n

BEDROLL n portable roll of bedding

BEDROOM n, adj

BEDROP vb drop on **bedrops, bedropt**

BEDRUG vb drug excessively **bedrugs**

BEDS ▸ **bed**

BEDSIDE n area beside a bed ▷ adj placed at or near the side of the bed

BEDSIT n furnished sitting room with a bed **bedsits**

BEDSORE n

BEDTICK n case containing stuffing in mattress

BEDTIME n time when one usually goes to bed

BEDU adj relating to beduins

BEDUCK vb duck under water **beducks**

BEDUIN variant of ▸ **bedouin**

BEDUINS ▸ **beduin**

BEDUMB vb make dumb **bedumbs**

BEDUNCE vb cause to look or feel foolish

BEDUNG vb spread with dung **bedungs**

BEDUST vb cover with dust **bedusts**

BEDWARD adj towards bed

BEDWARF vb hamper growth of

BEDYDE ▸ **bedye**

BEDYE vb dye **bedyed, bedyes**

BEE n

BEEBEE n air rifle **beebees**

BEECH n beechen, beeches, beechy

BEEDI n Indian cigarette beedie, beedies

BEEF n, vb

BEEFALO n cross between cow and buffalo

BEEFED ▸ **beef**

BEEFIER ▸ **beefy**

BEEFILY ▸ **beefy**

BEEFING ▸ **beef**

BEEFS ▸ **beef**

BEEFY adj

BEEGAH = bigha

BEEGAHS ▸ **beegah**

BEEHIVE n
BEELIKE ▶ bee
BEELINE n, adj
BEEN ▶ be
BEENAH n
understanding; insight beenahs
BEENTO n person who has resided in Britain ▷ adj of, relating to, or characteristic of such a person beentos
BEEP n high-pitched sound, such as that of a car horn ▷ vb (cause to) make this noise beeped, beeper, beepers, beeping, beeps
BEER n
BEERAGE n brewing industry
BEERIER ▶ beery
BEERILY ▶ beery
BEERS ▶ beer
BEERY adj smelling or tasting of beer
BEES ▶ bee
BEESOME = bisson
BEESWAX n wax secreted by bees, used in polishes etc ▷ vb polish with such wax
BEET n, vb beet
BEETFLY n type of fly which is a common pest of beets and mangel-wurzels
BEETING ▶ beet
BEETLE n, adj, vb beetled
BEETLER n one who operates a beetling machine
BEETLES ▶ beetle

BEETS ▶ beet
BEEVES ▶ beef
BEEYARD n place where bees are kept
BEEZER n person or chap ▷ adj excellent beezers
BEFALL vb befalls
BEFANA n Italian gift-bearing good fairy befanas
BEFELD ▶ befall
BEFELL ▶ befall
BEFFANA = befana
BEFIT vb befits
BEFLAG vb decorate with flags beflags
BEFLEA vb infect with fleas befleas
BEFLECK vb fleck
BEFLUM vb fool; deceive beflums
BEFOAM vb cover with foam befoams
BEFOG vb surround with fog befogs
BEFOOL vb make a fool of befools
BEFORE adv, prep
BEFOUL vb make dirty or foul befouls
BEFRET vb fret about something befrets
BEG vb
BEGAD interj emphatic exclamation
BEGALL vb make sore by rubbing begalls
BEGAN ▶ begin
BEGAR n compulsory labour begars
BEGAT ▶ beget
BEGAZE vb gaze about or around begazed, begazes

BEGEM vb decorate with gems begems
BEGET vb begets
BEGGAR n, vb beggars
BEGGARY n extreme poverty or need
BEGGED ▶ beg
BEGGING ▶ beg
BEGHARD n member of a 13th century Christian brotherhood
BEGIFT vb give gift or gifts to begifts
BEGILD vb gild begilds, begilt
BEGIN vb start
BEGINNE = beginning begins
BEGIRD vb surround begirds, begirt
BEGLAD vb make glad beglads
BEGLOOM vb make gloomy
BEGNAW vb gnaw at begnaws
BEGO vb harrass; beset begoes, begoing, begone
BEGONIA n
BEGORAH = begorra
BEGORED adj smear with gore
BEGORRA interj emphatic exclamation, regarded as a characteristic utterance of Irishmen
BEGOT past participle of ▶ beget
BEGRIM = begrime
BEGRIME vb make dirty
BEGRIMS ▶ begrim
BEGROAN vb groan at
BEGS ▶ beg

BEGUILE vb

BEGUIN another name for ► **beghard**

BEGUINE n S American dance

BEGUINS ► **beguin**

BEGULF vb overwhelm **begulfs**

BEGUM n Muslim woman of high rank **begums**

BEGUN past participle of ► **begin**

BEGUNK vb delude; trick **begunks**

BEHALF n

BEHAVE vb behaved, **behaver, behaves**

BEHEAD vb beheads

BEHELD ► **behold**

BEHEST n behests

BEHIGHT vb entrust

BEHIND adv, n, prep, adj **behinds**

BEHOLD vb beholds

BEHOOF n advantage or profit **behoofs**

BEHOOVE = behove

BEHOTE = behight

BEHOTES ► **behote**

BEHOVE vb be necessary or fitting for **behoved, behoves**

BEHOWL vb howl at **behowls**

BEIGE adj, n

BEIGEL = bagel

BEIGELS ► **beigel**

BEIGES ► **beige**

BEIGIER ► **beige**

BEIGNE variant of ► **beignet**

BEIGNES ► **beigne**

BEIGNET n square deep-fried pastry served hot and sprinkled with icing sugar

BEIGY ► **beige**

BEIN adj financially comfortable

BEING ► **be**

BEINGS ► **be**

BEINKED adj daubed with ink

BEJADE vb jade; tire **bejaded, bejades**

BEJANT = bajan

BEJANTS ► **bejant**

BEJESUS interj exclamation of surprise ▷ n as in the **bejesus** mild expletive

BEJEWEL vb decorate with or as if with jewels

BEKAH n half shekel **bekahs**

BEKISS vb smother with kisses

BEKNAVE vb treat as a knave

BEKNOT vb tie a knot or knots in **beknots**

BEKNOWN adj known about

BEL n unit for comparing two power levels or measuring the intensity of a sound

BELABOR = belabour

BELACE vb decorate with lace **belaced, belaces**

BELADY vb call a lady

BELAH n Australian tree which yields a useful timber **belahs**

BELAMY n close friend

BELAR = belah

BELARS ► **belar**

BELATE vb cause to be late

BELATED adj

BELATES ► **belate**

BELAUD vb praise highly **belauds**

BELAY vb secure a line to a pin or cleat ▷ n attachment (of a climber) to a mountain **belayed, belayer, belays**

BELCH vb, n belched, **belcher, belches**

BELDAM n old woman, esp an ugly or malicious one **beldame, beldams**

BELEAP vb leap over **beleaps, beleapt**

BELEE vb put on sheltered side **beleed, beleees**

BELFRY n

BELGA n former Belgian monetary unit worth five francs

BELGARD n kind gaze

BELGAS ► **belga**

BELIE vb belied

BELIEF n beliefs

BELIER ► **belie**

BELIERS ► **belie**

BELIES ► **belie**

BELIEVE vb

BELIKE adv perhaps

BELIVE adv speedily

BELL n, vb

BELLBOY n man or boy employed in a hotel, club, etc, to carry luggage and answer calls for service

BELLE n beautiful woman, esp the most attractive woman at a function

BELLED ▶ bell

BELLEEK n kind of thin fragile porcelain with a lustrous glaze

BELLES ▶ belle

BELLHOP = bellboy

BELLIED ▶ belly

BELLIES ▶ belly

BELLING ▶ bell

BELLMAN n man who rings a bell, esp (formerly) a town crier **bellmen**

BELLOCK vb shout

BELLOW vb, n

BELLOWS pl n instrument for pumping a stream of air into something

BELLS ▶ bell

BELLY n, vb

BELON n type of oyster

BELONG vb belongs

BELONS ▶ belon

BELOVE vb love

BELOVED adj, n

BELOVES ▶ belove

BELOW adv, prep

BELOWS ▶ bellows

BELS ▶ bel

BELT n, vb belted

BELTER n outstanding person or event **belters**

BELTING n material used to make a belt or belts ▷ adj excellent

BELTMAN n (formerly) a member of a beach lifesaving team **beltmen**

BELTS ▶ belt

BELTWAY n people and institutions located in the area bounded by the Washington Beltway

BELUGA n large white sturgeon belugas

BELYING ▶ belie

BEMA n speaker's platform in the assembly in ancient Athens

BEMAD vb cause to become mad

BEMADAM vb call a person madam

BEMADS ▶ bemad

BEMAS ▶ bema

BEMATA ▶ bema

BEMAUL vb maul bemauls

BEMAZED adj amazed

BEMBEX n type of wasp bembix

BEMEAN a less common word for ▶ demean

BEMEANS ▶ bemean

BEMEANT ▶ bemean

BEMEDAL vb decorate with medals

BEMETE vb measure bemeted, bemetes

BEMIRE vb soil with or as if with mire bemired, bemires

BEMIST vb cloud with mist bemists

BEMIX vb mix thoroughly bemixed, bemixes, bemixt

BEMOAN vb bemoans

BEMOCK vb mock bemocks

BEMOIL vb soil with mud bemoils

BEMOUTH vb endow with a mouth

BEMUD vb cover with mud bemuds

BEMUSE vb confuse

BEMUSED adj

BEMUSES ▶ bemuse

BEN n mountain peak ▷ adv in ▷ adj inner

BENAME an archaic word for ▶ name

BENAMED ▶ bename

BENAMES ▶ bename

BENCH n, vb benched

BENCHER n member of the governing body of one of the Inns of Court

BENCHES ▶ bench

BENCHY adj (of a hillside) hollowed out in benches

BEND vb, n

BENDAY vb (printing) reproduce using Benday technique bendays

BENDED ▶ bend

BENDEE = bendy

BENDEES ▶ bendee

BENDER n drinking bout benders

BENDIER ▶ bendy

BENDING ▶ bend

BENDLET n narrow diagonal stripe on heraldic shield

BENDS ▶ bend

BENDY adj, n bendys

BENE n blessing

BENEATH prep, adv

BENEFIC adj a rare word for beneficent

BENEFIT n, vb

BENEMPT a past participle of ▸ **name**

BENES ▸ **bene**

BENET vb trap (something) in a net **benets**

BENGA n type of Kenyan popular music featuring guitars **bengas**

BENI n sesame plant

BENIGHT vb shroud in darkness

BENIGN adj

BENIS ▸ **beni**

BENISON n blessing, esp a spoken one

BENJ another word for ▸ **bhang**

BENJES ▸ **benj**

BENNE another name for ▸ **sesame**

BENNES ▸ **benne**

BENNET n Eurasian and N African plant with yellow flowers **bennets**

BENNI n sesame

BENNIES ▸ **benny**

BENNIS ▸ **benni**

BENNY n amphetamine tablet, esp benzedrine: a stimulant

BENOMYL n fungicide

BENS ▸ **ben**

BENT adj, n

BENTHAL ▸ **benthos**

BENTHIC ▸ **benthos**

BENTHON ▸ **benthos**

BENTHOS n animals and plants living at the bottom of a sea or lake

BENTIER ▸ **benty**

BENTO n thin lightweight box used in Japanese cuisine **bentos**

BENTS ▸ **bent**

BENTY adj covered with bentgrass

BENUMB vb make numb or powerless **benumbs**

BENZAL n transparent crystalline substance **benzals**

BENZENE n flammable poisonous liquid used as a solvent, insecticide, etc

BENZIL n yellow compound radical **benzils**

BENZIN = **benzine**

BENZINE n volatile liquid used as a solvent **benzins** ▸ **benzin**

BENZOIC adj of, containing, or derived from benzoic acid or benzoin

BENZOIN n gum resin used in ointments, perfume, etc

BENZOL n crude form of benzene **benzole**, **benzols**

BENZOYL n of, consisting of, or containing the monovalent group C_6H_5CO-

BENZYL n of, consisting of, or containing the monovalent group $C_6H_5CH_2-$ **benzyls**

BEPAINT vb dye; paint

BEPAT vb pat **bepats**

BEPEARL vb decorate with pearls

BEPELT vb pelt energetically **bepelts**

BEPITY vb feel great pity for

BEPROSE vb (of poetry) reduce to prose

BEPUFF vb puff up **bepuffs**

BEQUEST n

BERAKE vb rake thoroughly **beraked**, **berakes**

BERATE vb **berated**, **berates**

BERAY vb soil; defile **berayed**, **berays**

BERBERE n hot-tasting Ethiopian paste

BERBICE n as in berbice chair large armchair with long arms that can be folded inwards to act as leg rests

BERCEAU n arched trellis for climbing plants

BERDASH = **berdache**

BERE n barley

BEREAVE vb deprive (of) something or someone valued, esp through death

BEREFT adj

BERES ▸ **bere**

BERET n berets

BERETTA n type of pistol

BERG n iceberg

BERGAMA n type of Turkish rug

BERGEN n large rucksack with a capacity of over 50 litres **bergens**

BERGERE *n* type of French armchair

BERGS ▶ berg

BERGYLT *n* large northern marine food fish

BERHYME *vb* mention in poetry **berime**

BERIMED ▶ berime

BERIMES ▶ berime

BERK *n* stupid person

BERKO *adj* berserk

BERKS ▶ berk

BERLEY *n* bait scattered on water to attract fish ▷ *vb* scatter (bait) on water **berleys**

BERLIN *n* fine wool yarn used for tapestry work, etc **berline, berlins**

BERM *n, vb* **berme, bermed**

BERMES ▶ berme berming, berms

BEROB *vb* rob

BEROBED *adj* wearing a robe

BEROBS ▶ berob

BERRET = beret

BERRETS ▶ berret

BERRIED ▶ berry

BERRIES ▶ berry

BERRY *n, vb*

BERSEEM *n* Mediterranean clover grown as a forage crop and to improve the soil

BERSERK *adj, n*

BERTH *n, vb*

BERTHA *n* wide deep capelike collar, often of lace, usually to cover up a low neckline

berthas

BERTHE *n* type of lace collar

BERTHED ▶ berth

BERTHES ▶ berthe

BERTHS ▶ berth

BERYL *n* beryls

BES *variant of* ▶ **beth**

BESAINT *vb* give saint status to

BESANG ▶ besing

BESAT ▶ besit

BESAW ▶ besee

BESCOUR *vb* scour thoroughly

BESEE *vb* provide for; mind

BESEECH *vb* beseeke

BESEEM *vb* be suitable for **beseems**

BESEEN ▶ besee

BESEES ▶ besee

BESES ▶ bes

BESET *vb* besets

BESHAME *vb* cause to feel shame

BESHINE *vb* illuminate **beshone**

BESHOUT *vb* shout about

BESHREW *vb* wish evil on

BESIDE *prep*

BESIDES *prep, adv*

BESIEGE *vb*

BESIGH *vb* sigh for **besighs**

BESING *vb* sing about joyfully **besings**

BESIT *vb* suit; fit **besits**

BESLAVE *vb* treat as slave

BESLIME *vb* cover with slime

BESMEAR *vb* smear over

BESMILE *vb* smile on

BESMOKE *vb* blacken with smoke

BESMUT *vb* blacken with smut **besmuts**

BESNOW *vb* cover with snow **besnows**

BESOIN *n* need **besoins**

BESOM *n* broom made of twigs ▷ *vb* sweep with a besom **besomed, besoms**

BESORT *vb* fit **besorts**

BESOT *vb* make stupid or muddled **besots**

BESPAKE ▶ bespoke

BESPAT ▶ bespit

BESPATE ▶ bespit

BESPEAK *vb* indicate or suggest

BESPED ▶ bespeed

BESPEED *vb* get on with (doing something)

BESPICE *vb* flavour with spices

BESPIT *vb* cover with spittle **bespits**

BESPOKE *adj* (esp of a suit) made to the customer's specifications

BESPORT *vb* amuse oneself

BESPOT *vb* mark with spots **bespots**

BESPOUT *vb* speak pretentiously

BEST *adj* most excellent of a particular group etc ▷ *adv* in a manner surpassing all others ▷ *n* utmost effort ▷ *vb* defeat

BESTAD = bestead

BESTAIN vb stain

BESTAR vb decorate with stars **bestars**

BESTEAD vb serve; assist

BESTED ▶ best

BESTI Indian English word for ▶ shame

BESTIAL adj

BESTICK vb cover with sharp points

BESTILL vb cause to be still

BESTING ▶ best

BESTIR vb cause (oneself) to become active **bestirs**

BESTIS ▶ besti

BESTORM vb assault

BESTOW vb bestows

BESTREW vb scatter or lie scattered over (a surface)

BESTRID ▶ bestride

BESTROW = bestrew

BESTS ▶ best

BESTUCK ▶ bestick

BESTUD vb set with, or as with studs **bestuds**

BESUNG ▶ besing

BESWARM vb swarm over

BET n, vb

BETA n second letter in the Greek alphabet, a consonant, transliterated as b

BETAINE n sweet-tasting alkaloid that occurs in the sugar beet

BETAKE vb as in betake oneself go **betaken, betakes**

BETAS ▶ beta

BETAXED adj burdened with taxes

BETCHA interj bet you

BETE = beet

BETED ▶ bete

BETEEM vb accord **beteeme, beteems**

BETEL n betels

BETES ▶ bete

BETH n second letter of the Hebrew alphabet transliterated as b

BETHANK vb thank

BETHEL n seaman's chapel **bethels**

BETHINK vb cause (oneself) to consider or meditate

BETHORN vb cover with thorns

BETHS ▶ beth

BETHUMB vb (of books) wear by handling

BETHUMP vb thump hard

BETID ▶ betide

BETIDE vb happen (to) **betided, betides, betight**

BETIME vb befall **betimed, betimes**

BETING ▶ bete

BETISE n folly or lack of perception **betises**

BETITLE vb give title to

BETOIL vb tire through hard work **betoils**

BETOKEN vb indicate or signify

BETON n concrete **betons**

BETONY n North American plant

BETOOK the past tense of ▶ betake

BETOSS vb toss about

BETRAY vb betrays

BETREAD vb tread over

BETRIM vb decorate **betrims**

BETROD ▶ betread

BETROTH vb promise to marry or to give in marriage

BETS ▶ bet

BETTA n fighting fish **bettas**

BETTED ▶ bet

BETTER adj more excellent than others ▷ adv in a more excellent manner ▷ pl n one's superiors ▷ vb improve upon **betters**

BETTIES ▶ betty

BETTING ▶ bet

BETTONG n short-nosed rat kangaroo

BETTOR n person who bets **bettors**

BETTY n type of short crowbar

BETWEEN adv, prep

BETWIXT adv between

BEURRE n butter **beurres**

BEVEL n slanting edge ▷ vb slope **beveled, beveler, bevels**

BEVER n snack **bevers**

BEVIES ▶ bevy

BEVOMIT vb vomit over

BEVOR n armour protecting lower part

of face **bevors**

BEVUE n careless error **bevues**

BEVVIED ▶ bevvy

BEVVIES ▶ bevvy

BEVVY n alcoholic drink ▷ vb drink alcohol

BEVY n

BEWAIL vb bewails

BEWARE vb bewared, bewares

BEWEARY vb cause to be weary

BEWEEP vb express grief through weeping **beweeps**

BEWENT ▶ bego

BEWEPT ▶ beweep

BEWET vb make wet **bewets**

BEWHORE vb treat as a whore

BEWIG vb adorn with a wig **bewigs**

BEWITCH vb

BEWORM vb fill with worms **beworms**

BEWORRY vb beset with worry

BEWRAP vb wrap up **bewraps, bewrapt**

BEWRAY an obsolete word for ▶ betray

BEWRAYS ▶ bewray

BEY n (in the Ottoman empire) a title given to senior officers, provincial governors, and certain other officials

A **bey** was an official in the Ottoman empire. If someone plays this remember

that you can of course put an O in front of it to make obey.

BEYLIC n province ruled over by a bey **beylics, beylik**

BEYLIKS ▶ beylik

BEYOND prep, adv, n **beyonds**

BEYS ▶ bey

BEZ n part of deer's horn

This word for the tine of a deer's horn is one of the essential short words for using the Z.

BEZANT n medieval Byzantine gold coin **bezants**

BEZAZZ another word for ▶ pizzazz

BEZEL n sloping edge of a cutting tool **bezels**

BEZES ▶ bez

BEZIL archaic word for ▶ alcoholic

BEZILS ▶ bezil

BEZIQUE n card game for two or more players

This card game played with two decks of cards combines the Q and Z and would make a wonderful bonus word.

BEZOAR n hard mass, such as a stone or hairball, in the stomach and intestines of animals **bezoars**

BEZZANT = bezant

BEZZAZZ ▶ bezazz

BEZZLE vb drink to excess **bezzled, bezzles**

BHAGEE = bhaji

BHAGEES ▶ bhagee

BHAI n Indian form of address for a man **bhais**

BHAJAN n singing of devotional songs and hymns **bhajans**

BHAJEE = bhaji

BHAJEES ▶ bhajee

BHAJI n Indian deep-fried savoury of chopped vegetables in spiced batter **bhajia, bhajis**

BHAKTA n Hindu term for devotee of God **bhaktas**

BHAKTI n loving devotion to God leading to nirvana **bhaktis**

BHANG n preparation of Indian hemp used as a narcotic and intoxicant

BHANGRA n Punjabi folk music combined with elements of Western pop music

BHANGS ▶ bhang

BHARAL n wild Himalayan sheep **bharals**

BHAT n currency of Thailand

BHAVAN n (in India) a large house or building **bhavans, bhawan**

BHAWANS ▶ bhawan

BHEESTY ▶ bhishti

BHEL = bael

BHELS ▶ bhel

BHIKHU n fully ordained Buddhist monk **bhikhus**

BHINDI n bindhi

BHINDIS ▶ bhindi

BHISHTI n (formerly in India) a water-carrier **bhistee, bhisti, bhistie**

BHISTIS ▶ bhisti

BHOONA ▶ bhuna

BHOONAS ▶ bhoona

BHOOT = bhut

BHOOTS ▶ bhoot

BHUNA n Indian sauce **bhunas**

BHUT n Hindu term for type of ghost **bhuts**

BI short for > bisexual

BIALI = bialy

BIALIES ▶ bialy

BIALIS ▶ biali

BIALY n type of bagel **bialys**

BIAS n, vb, adj, adv biased, biases, biasing, biassed, biasses

BIAXAL = biaxial

BIAXIAL adj (esp of a crystal) having two axes

BIB = bibcock

BIBASIC adj with two bases

BIBB n wooden support on a mast for the trestletrees

BIBBED ▶ bib

BIBBER n drinker **bibbers**

BIBBERY n drinking to excess

BIBBING ▶ bib

BIBBLE n pebble **bibbles**

BIBBS ▶ bibb

BIBCOCK n tap with a nozzle bent downwards

BIBELOT n attractive or curious trinket

BIBFUL n as in spill a bibful to divulge secrets **bibfuls**

BIBLE n any book containing the sacred writings of a religion **bibles**

BIBLESS ▶ bib

BIBLIKE ▶ bib

BIBLIST = biblicist

BIBS ▶ bib

BICARB n bicarbonate of soda **bicarbs**

BICCIES ▶ biccy

BICCY n biscuit

BICE n medium blue colour

BICEP = biceps

BICEPS n

BICES ▶ bice

BICHIR n African freshwater fish with an elongated body **bichirs**

BICHORD adj having two strings for each note

BICKER vb, n bickers

BICKIE short for ▶ biscuit

BICKIES ▶ bickie

BICOLOR = bicolour

BICORN adj having two horns or hornlike parts **bicorne, bicorns**

BICRON n billionth part of a metre **bicrons**

BICYCLE n, vb

BID vb, n

BIDARKA n canoe covered in animal skins, esp sealskin, used by the Inuit of Alaska

BIDDEN ▶ bid

BIDDER ▶ bid

BIDDERS ▶ bid

BIDDIES ▶ biddy

BIDDING ▶ bid

BIDDY n woman, esp an old gossipy one

BIDE vb bided

BIDENT n instrument with two prongs **bidents**

BIDER ▶ bide

BIDERS ▶ bide

BIDES ▶ bide

BIDET n bidets

BIDI = beedi

BIDING ▶ bide

BIDINGS ▶ bide

BIDIS ▶ bidi

BIDON n oil drum **bidons**

BIDS ▶ bid

BIELD n shelter ▷ vb shelter or take shelter **bielded, bields**

BIELDY adj sheltered

BIEN adv well

BIENNIA ▶ biennium

BIER n biers

BIFACE n prehistoric stone tool **bifaces**

BIFF n blow with the fist ▷ vb give (someone) such a blow **biffed**

BIFFER n someone, such

as a sportsperson, who has a reputation for hitting hard **biffers**

BIFFIES ▶ biffy

BIFFIN n variety of red cooking apple

BIFFING ▶ biff

BIFFINS ▶ biffin

BIFFO n fighting or aggressive behaviour ▷ adj aggressive **biffos**

BIFFS ▶ biff

BIFFY n outdoor toilet

BIFID adj divided into two by a cleft in the middle **bifidly**

BIFILAR adj having two parallel threads, as in the suspension of certain measuring instruments

BIFLEX adj bent or flexed in two places

BIFOCAL adj having two different focuses

BIFOLD adj that can be folded in two places

BIFORM adj having or combining the characteristics of two forms, as in a centaur

BIG adj of considerable size, height, number, or capacity ▷ adv on a grand scale ▷ vb build

BIGA n chariot drawn by two horses **bigae**

BIGAMY n

BIGENER n hybrid between individuals of

different genera

BIGEYE n type of red marine fish **bigeyes**

BIGFEET ▶ bigfoot

BIGFOOT n yeti ▷ vb throw one's weight around

BIGG n type of barley

BIGGED ▶ big

BIGGER ▶ big

BIGGEST ▶ big

BIGGETY ▶ biggity

BIGGIE n something big or important **biggies**

BIGGIN n plain close-fitting cap

BIGGING ▶ big

BIGGINS ▶ biggin

BIGGISH ▶ big

BIGGITY adj conceited

BIGGON = biggin

BIGGONS ▶ biggon

BIGGS ▶ big

BIGGY = biggie

BIGHA n in India, unit for measuring land **bighas**

BIGHEAD n conceited person

BIGHORN n large wild mountain sheep

BIGHT n long curved shoreline ▷ vb fasten or bind with a bight **bighted, bights**

BIGLY ▶ big

BIGNESS ▶ big

BIGOS n Polish stew **bigoses**

BIGOT n bigoted

BIGOTRY n attitudes, behaviour, or way of thinking of a bigot

BIGOTS ▶ bigot

BIGS ▶ big

BIGTIME adj important

BIGWIG n important person **bigwigs**

BIJOU adj (of a house) small but elegant ▷ n something small and delicately worked **bijous, bijoux**

A **bijou** is a French word for a jewel, and it is indeed a jewel to play, getting rid of awkward letters for a good score. And remember that the plural can be **bijous** or **bijoux**.

BIKE = bicycle

BIKED ▶ bike

BIKER n person who rides a motorcycle **bikers**

BIKES ▶ bike

BIKEWAY n cycle lane

BIKIE n member of a motorcycle gang **bikies**

BIKING ▶ bike

BIKINGS ▶ bike

BIKINI n bikinis

BIKKIE slang word for ▶ biscuit

BIKKIES ▶ bikkie

BILAYER n part of cell membrane

BILBIES ▶ bilby

BILBO n (formerly) a sword with a marked temper and elasticity **bilboa**

BILBOAS ▶ bilboa bilboes, bilbos

BILBY n Australian marsupial with long

pointed ears and grey fur

BILE n, vb **biled, biles**

BILEVEL n hairstyle with two different lengths

BILGE n, vb **bilged, bilges, bilgier, bilging, bilgy**

BILIAN n type of tree used for its wood **bilians**

BILIARY adj of bile, the ducts that convey bile, or the gall bladder ▷ n disease found in dogs

BILIMBI n type of fruit-bearing tree

BILING ▶ **bile**

BILIOUS adj

BILK vb cheat, esp by not paying ▷ n swindle or cheat **bilked, bilker, bilkers, bilking, bilks**

BILL n, vb

BILLBUG n type of weevil

BILLED ▶ **bill**

BILLER n stem of a plant **billers**

BILLET vb, n **billets**

BILLIE = **billy**

BILLIES ▶ **billy**

BILLING n prominence given in programmes, advertisements, etc. to performers or acts

BILLION n, determiner

BILLMAN n person who uses a billhook **billmen**

BILLON n alloy consisting of gold or silver and a base metal **billons**

BILLOW n, vb **billows**

BILLOWY adj full of or forming billows

BILLS ▶ **bill**

BILLY n

BILLYO n as in **like billyo** phrase used to emphasize or intensify something **billyoh, billyos**

BILOBAR = **bilobate**

BILOBED = **bilobate**

BILSTED n American gum tree

BILTONG n strips of dried meat

BIMA = **bema**

BIMAH = **bema**

BIMAHS ▶ **bimah**

BIMANAL = **bimanous**

BIMAS ▶ **bima**

BIMBLE n as in **bimble box** type of dense Australian tree

BIMETAL n material made from two sheets of metal

BIMODAL adj having two modes

BIMORPH n assembly of piezoelectric crystals

BIN n, vb

BINAL adj twofold

BINARY adj, n

BINATE adj occurring in two parts or in pairs

BIND vb, n

BINDER n **binders**

BINDERY n bookbindery

BINDHI = **bindi**

BINDHIS ▶ **bindhi**

BINDI n decorative dot worn in the middle of the forehead, esp by Hindu women

BINDING ▶ **bind**

BINDIS ▶ **bindi**

BINDLE n small packet **bindles**

BINDS ▶ **bind**

BINE n climbing or twining stem of various plants

BINER n clip used by climbers **biners**

BINES ▶ **bine**

BING n heap or pile, esp of spoil from a mine

BINGE n, vb **binged**

BINGER n person who is addicted to crack cocaine **bingers**

BINGES ▶ **binge**

BINGIES ▶ **bingy**

BINGING ▶ **binge**

BINGLE n minor crash or upset, as in a car or on a surfboard ▷ vb layer (hair) **bingled, bingles**

BINGO n, sentence substitute **bingoes, bingos**

BINGS ▶ **bing**

BINGY Australian slang for ▶ **stomach**

BINIOU n small high-pitched Breton bagpipe **binious**

BINIT n (computing) early form of bit **binits**

BINK n ledge **binks**

BINMAN another name for ▶ **dustman**

BINMEN ▶ **binman**

BINNED ▶ **bin**

BINNING ▶ **bin**

BINOCLE n binocular-style telescope

BINOCS > binocular

BINS ▶ **bin**

BIO short for
> **biography**
BIOBANK n small glass or
BIOCHIP n small glass or
silicon plate
containing an array of
biochemical molecules
or structures
BIOCIDE n substance
used to destroy living
things
BIODATA n information
regarding an
individual's education
and work history
BIODOT n temperature-
sensitive device stuck
to the skin in order to
monitor stress
biodots
BIOFACT n item of
biological information
BIOFILM n thin layer of
living organisms
BIOFUEL n gaseous,
liquid, or solid
substance of biological
origin used as a fuel
▷ vb fuel (a vehicle, etc)
using biofuel
BIOG short form of
> **biography**
BIOGAS n gaseous fuel
produced by the
fermentation of
organic waste
BIOGEN n hypothetical
protein **biogens**
BIOGENY n principle
that a living organism
must originate from
a parent form similar
to itself
BIOGS ▶ **biog**

BIOHERM n mound of
material laid down by
sedentary marine
organisms
BIOLOGY n
BIOMASS n total number
of living organisms in a
given area
BIOME n major
ecological community
biomes
BIONIC adj
BIONICS n study of
biological functions to
create electronic
versions
BIONOMY n laws of life
BIONT n living thing
biontic, bionts
BIOPHOR n hypothetical
material particle
BIOPIC n film based on
the life of a famous
person **biopics**
BIOPSIC ▶ **biopsy**
BIOPSY n, vb **bioptic**
BIOS ▶ **bio**
BIOTA n plant and
animal life of a
particular region or
period **biotas**
BIOTECH n
biotechnology
BIOTIC adj of or relating
to living organisms ▷ n
living organism **biotics**
BIOTIN n vitamin of the
B complex, abundant
in egg yolk and liver
biotins
BIOTITE n black or dark
green mineral of the
mica group
BIOTOPE n small area

that supports its own
distinctive community
BIOTRON n
climate-control
chamber
BIOTYPE n group of
genetically identical
plants within a
species, produced by
apomixis
BIPACK n obsolete
filming process
bipacks
BIPARTY adj involving
two parties
BIPED n, adj
BIPEDAL adj having two
feet
BIPEDS ▶ **biped**
BIPLANE n two-legged
BIPOD n two-legged
support or stand
bipods
BIPOLAR adj having
two poles
BIPRISM n prism having
a highly obtuse angle
to facilitate beam
splitting
BIRCH n, vb **birched,**
birchen, birches
BIRCHIR ▶ **bichir**
BIRD n, vb
BIRDDOG n dog used or
trained to retrieve
game birds
BIRDED ▶ **bird**
BIRDER n birdwatcher
birders
BIRDIE n score of one
stroke under par for a
hole ▷ vb play (a hole)
in one stroke under par
birdied, birdies

BIRDING ▷ **bird**

BIRDMAN n man concerned with birds, such as a fowler or ornithologist **birdmen**

BIRDS ▷ **bird**

BIREME n ancient galley having two banks of oars **biremes**

BIRETTA n stiff square cap worn by the Catholic clergy

BIRIANI = **biryani**

BIRK n birch tree ▷ adj consisting of or made of birch

BIRKEN adj relating to the birch tree

BIRKIE n spirited or lively person ▷ adj lively **birkier, birkies**

BIRKS ▷ **birk**

BIRL = **burl**

BIRLE = **burl**

BIRLED ▷ **birl**

BIRLER ▷ **birl**

BIRLERS ▷ **birl**

BIRLES ▷ **birle**

BIRLING ▷ **birl**

BIRLINN n small Scottish boat

BIRLS ▷ **birl**

BIRO n tradename of a kind of ballpoint pen **biros**

BIRR vb make or cause to make a whirring sound ▷ n whirring sound **birred, birring, birrs**

BIRSE n bristle **birses**

BIRSIER ▷ **birsy**

BIRSLE vb roast **birsled, birsles**

BIRSY adj bristly

BIRTH n, vb **birthed, births**

BIRYANI n Indian rice-based dish

BIS adv twice ▷ **sentence substitute** encore! again!

BISCUIT n, adj

BISE n cold dry northerly wind

BISECT vb **bisects**

BISES ▷ **bise**

BISH n mistake **bishes**

BISHOP n, vb **bishops**

BISK a less common spelling of ▷ **bisque**

BISKS ▷ **bisk**

BISMAR n type of weighing scale **bismars**

BISMUTH n pinkish-white metallic element

BISNAGA n type of cactus

BISOM ▷ **besom**

BISOMS ▷ **bisom**

BISON n buffalo

BISONS ▷ **bison**

BISQUE n thick rich soup made from shellfish **bisques**

BISSON adj blind

BIST a form of the second person singular of ▷ **be**

BISTATE adj involving two states

BISTER = **bestir**

BISTERS ▷ **bister**

BISTORT n Eurasian plant with a spike of small pink flowers

BISTRE n water-soluble pigment **bistred, bistres**

BISTRO n **bistros**

BIT n small piece, portion, or quantity

BITABLE ▷ **bite**

BITCH n, vb **bitched**

BITCHING = **bitching**

BITCHES ▷ **bitch**

BITCHY adj spiteful or malicious

BITE vb, n **biter, biters, bites, biting, bitings**

BITLESS adj without a bit

BITMAP n picture created by colour or shading on a visual display unit ▷ vb create a bitmap of **bitmaps**

BITO n African and Asian tree

BITONAL adj consisting of black and white tones

BITOS ▷ **bito**

BITOU n as in **bitou bush** type of sprawling woody shrub

BITS ▷ **bit**

BITSER n mongrel dog **bitsers**

BITSIER ▷ **bitsy**

BITSY adj very small

BITT n strong post on the deck of a ship for securing lines ▷ vb secure (a line) by means of a bitt

BITTE interj you're welcome

BITTED ▷ **bitt**

BITTEN ▷ **bite**

BITTER adj, n, adv, vb

BITTERN n

BITTERS pl n

bitter-tasting spirits flavoured with plant extracts

BITTIE n small piece

BITTIER ▶ bitty

BITTIES ▶ bittie

BITTING ▶ bitt

BITTOCK n small amount

BITTOR n bittern **bittors, bittour**

BITTS ▶ bitt

BITTUR n bittor

BITTURS ▶ bittur

BITTY adj lacking unity, disjointed

BITUMED adj covered with bitumen

BITUMEN n

BIVALVE adj (marine mollusc) with two hinged segments to its shell ▷ n sea creature that has a shell consisting of two hinged valves and breathes through gills

BIVIA ▶ bivium

BIVINYL another word for > butadiene

BIVIOUS adj offering a choice of two different ways

BIVIUM n parting of ways

BIVOUAC n, vb

BIVVIED ▶ bivvy

BIVVIES ▶ bivvy

BIVVY n small tent or shelter ▷ vb camp in a bivouac

BIZ n business

BIZARRE adj, n

BIZARRO n bizarre person

BIZAZZ = pizazz

BIZE n dry, cold wind in France **bizes**

BIZNAGA = bisnaga

BIZONAL ▶ bizone

BIZONE n place comprising two zones **bizones**

BIZZES ▶ biz

BIZZIES ▶ bizzy

BIZZO n empty and irrelevant talk or ideas **bizzos**

BIZZY n policeman

BLAB vb **blabbed**

BLABBER vb talk without thinking ▷ n person who blabs

BLABBY adj talking too much; indiscreet

BLABS ▶ blab

BLACK adj, n, vb **blacked**

BLACKEN vb

BLACKER ▶ black

BLACKLY ▶ black

BLACKS ▶ black

BLAD = blaud

BLADDED ▶ blad

BLADDER n

BLADE n **bladed**

BLADER n person skating with in-line skates **bladers**

BLADES ▶ blade

BLADIER ▶ blady

BLADING n act or instance of skating with in-line skates

BLADS ▶ blad

BLADY adj as in **blady grass** coarse leafy Australasian grass

BLAE adj bluish-grey **blaer**

BLAES n hardened clay or shale

BLAEST ▶ blae

BLAFF n West Indian stew **blaffs**

BLAG vb obtain by wheedling or cadging ▷ n robbery, esp with violence **blagged, blagger, blags**

BLAGUE n pretentious but empty talk **blaguer, blagues**

BLAH n worthless or silly talk ▷ adj uninteresting ▷ vb talk nonsense or boringly **blahed, blahing, blahs**

BLAIN n blister, blotch, or sore on the skin **blains**

BLAISE = blaes

BLAIZE = blaes

BLAM n representation of the sound of a bullet being fired

BLAME vb, n

BLAMED euphemistic word for ▶ damned **blamer, blamers, blames, blaming**

BLAMS ▶ blam

BLANCH vb

BLANCO n whitening substance ▷ vb whiten (something) with blanco **blancos**

BLAND adj, n, vb **bland out blanded, blander, blandly, blands**

BLANK adj, n, vb **blanked, blanker**

BLANKET *n, adj, vb*

BLANKLY ▶ blank

BLANKS ▶ blank

BLARE *vb, n* blared, blares, blaring

BLARNEY *n* flattering talk ▷ *vb* cajole with flattery

BLART *vb* sound loudly and harshly blarted, blarts

BLASE *adj* indifferent or bored through familiarity

BLASH *n* splash blashes

BLASHY *adj* windy and rainy

BLAST *n, vb, interj*

BLASTED *adv* extreme or extremely ▷ *adj* blighted or withered

BLASTER ▶ blast

BLASTIE *n* ugly creature

BLASTS ▶ blast

BLASTY *adj* gusty

BLAT *vb* cry out or bleat like a sheep

BLATANT *adj*

BLATE *adj* shy; ill at ease blater, blatest

BLATHER *vb* speak foolishly ▷ *n* foolish talk

BLATS ▶ blat

BLATT *n* newspaper

BLATTED ▶ blat

BLATTER *n, vb* prattle

BLATTS ▶ blatt

BLAUBOK *n* South African antelope

BLAUD *vb* slap blauded, blauds

BLAW *vb* blow blawed, blawing, blawn

BLAWORT *n* harebell .

BLAWS ▶ blaw

BLAY *n* small river fish blays

BLAZAR *n* type of active galaxy blazars

BLAZE *vb, n* blazed

BLAZER *n* blazers

BLAZES *pl n* hell

BLAZING ▶ blaze

BLAZON *vb* proclaim publicly ▷ *n* coat of arms blazons

BLEACH *vb, n*

BLEAK *adj, n* bleaker, bleakly, bleaks, bleaky

BLEAR *vb* make (eyes or sight) dim with or as if with tears ▷ *adj* bleary bleared, blearer, blears

BLEARY *adj*

BLEAT *vb, n* bleated, bleater, bleats

BLEB *n* fluid-filled blister on the skin blebby, blebs

BLED ▶ bleed

BLEE *n* complexion; hue

BLEED *vb*

BLEEDER *n* despicable person

BLEEDS ▶ bleed

BLEEP *n, vb* bleeped

BLEEPER *n* small portable radio receiver that makes a bleeping signal

BLEEPS ▶ bleep

BLEES ▶ blee

BLELLUM *n* babbler; blusterer

BLEMISH *n, vb*

BLENCH *vb*

BLEND *vb, n*

BLENDE *n* mineral consisting mainly of zinc sulphide

BLENDED ▶ blend

BLENDER *n*

BLENDES ▶ blende

BLENDS ▶ blend

BLENNY *n* small fish with a tapering scaleless body

BLENT *a past participle of* ▶ blend

BLERT *n* foolish person blerts

BLESBOK *n* S African antelope

BLESS *vb* blessed, blesser, blesses, blest

BLET *n* state of decay in certain fruits, due to overripening ▷ *vb* go soft

BLETHER ▶ blather blets, bletted

BLEW ▶ blow

BLEWART = blawort

BLEWITS *n* type of edible fungus with a pale brown cap and a bluish stalk

BLEY = blay

BLEYS ▶ bley

BLIGHT *n, vb* blights

BLIGHTY *n* home country; home leave

BLIKSEM *interj* South African expression of surprise

BLIMEY *interj* exclamation of surprise or annoyance

BLIMP *n* small airship blimps

BLIMY = blimey

BLIN Scots word for ▶ blind

BLIND adj, vb, n blinded, blinder, blindly, blinds

BLING adj, n blinger, blings, blingy

BLINI pl n Russian pancakes made of buckwheat flour and yeast blinis

BLINK vb, n blinked

BLINKER n provide (a horse) with blinkers ▷ n flashing light for sending messages

BLINKS ▶ blink

BLINNED ▶ blin

BLINS ▶ blin

BLINTZ n thin pancake folded over a filling usually of apple, cream cheese, or meat blintze

BLINY = blini

BLIP n a sound such as that produced by an electronic device ▷ vb produce such a noise blipped, blips

BLISS n, vb blissed, blisses

BLIST archaic form of ▶ blessed

BLISTER n, vb

BLIT vb move (a block of data) in a computer's memory

BLITE n type of herb blites

BLITHE adj

BLITHER = blether

BLITS ▶ blit

BLITTED ▶ blit

BLITTER n circuit that transfers large amounts of data within a computer's memory

BLITZ n, vb blitzed, blitzer, blitzes

BLIVE = belive

BLOAT vb cause to swell, as with liquid or air ▷ n abnormal distention of the abdomen in cattle, sheep, etc

BLOATED adj

BLOATER n

BLOATS ▶ bloat

BLOB n, vb blobbed, blobby, blobs

BLOC n

BLOCK n, vb

BLOCKED adj functionally impeded by amphetamine

BLOCKER n person or thing that blocks

BLOCKIE n owner of a small property, esp a farm

BLOCKS ▶ block

BLOCKY adj like a block, esp in shape and solidity

BLOCS ▶ bloc

BLOG n, vb blogged, blogger, blogs

BLOKART n single-seat three-wheeled vehicle propelled by the wind

BLOKE n blokes

BLOKEY = blokeish

BLOKIER = blokey

BLOKISH = blokeish

BLOND adj (of men's

hair) of a light colour ▷ n person, esp a man, having light-coloured hair and skin

BLONDE n, adj blonder, blondes

BLONDS ▶ blond

BLOOD n, vb

BLOODED adj (of horses, cattle, etc) of good breeding

BLOODS ▶ blood

BLOODY adj, adv, vb

BLOOEY adj out of order; faulty blooie

BLOOK n blooks

BLOOM n, vb

BLOOMED adj (of a lens) coated to reduce light lost by reflection

BLOOMER n stupid mistake

BLOOMS ▶ bloom

BLOOMY adj having a fine whitish coating on the surface

BLOOP vb (baseball) hit a ball into air beyond infield blooped

BLOOPER n stupid mistake

BLOOPS ▶ bloop

BLOOSME = blossom

BLORE n strong blast of wind blores

BLOSSOM n, vb

BLOT n, vb

BLOTCH n, vb

BLOTCHY adj covered in or marked by blotches

BLOTS ▶ blot

BLOTTED ▶ blot

BLOTTER n sheet of blotting paper

BLOTTO adj extremely drunk

BLOTTY adj covered in blots

BLOUBOK = blaubok

BLOUSE n, vb bloused, blouses

BLOUSON n short loose jacket with a tight waist

BLOUSY adj loose; blouse-like

BLOW vb, n

BLOWBY n leakage of gas past the piston of an engine at maximum pressure **blowbys**

BLOWED ▸ blow

BLOWER n mechanical device, such as a fan, that blows **blowers**

BLOWFLY n fly that lays its eggs in meat

BLOWGUN = blowpipe

BLOWIE n bluebottle

BLOWIER ▸ blowy

BLOWIES ▸ blowie

BLOWING n

BLOWN ▸ blow

BLOWOFF n discharge of a surplus fluid

BLOWOUT n

BLOWS ▸ blow

BLOWSE n large, red-faced woman

BLOWSED = blowsy

BLOWSES ▸ blowse

BLOWSY adj fat, untidy, and red-faced

BLOWUP n fit of temper **blowups**

BLOWY adj windy

BLOWZE variant of ▸ blowse

BLOWZED = blowsy

BLOWZES ▸ blowze

BLOWZY = blowsy

BLUB a slang word for ▸ blubber

BLUBBED ▸ blub

BLUBBER n, vb, adj, n

BLUBS ▸ blub

BLUCHER n high shoe with laces over the tongue

BLUDE Scots form of ▸ blood

BLUDES ▸ blude

BLUDGE vb, n bludged

BLUDGER n person who scrounges

BLUDGES ▸ bludge

BLUDIE Scots form of ▸ bloody

BLUDIER ▸ bludie

BLUDY = bludie

BLUE n, adj, vb

BLUECAP another name for ▸ bluetit

BLUED ▸ blue

BLUEFIN another name for ▸ tunny

BLUEGUM n widely cultivated Australian tree

BLUEING ▸ blue

BLUEISH = bluish

BLUEJAY n N American jay

BLUELY ▸ blue

BLUER ▸ blue

BLUES pl n type of music

BLUEST ▸ blue

BLUESY ▸ blues

BLUET n N American plant with small four-petalled blue flowers

BLUETIT n

BLUETS ▸ bluet

BLUETTE n short, brilliant piece of music

BLUEY adj bluish ▸ n informal Australian word meaning blanket **blueys**

BLUFF vb, n, adj bluffed, bluffer, bluffly, bluffs

BLUGGY = bloody

BLUID Scots word for ▸ blood

BLUIDS ▸ bluid

BLUIDY ▸ bluid

BLUIER ▸ bluey

BLUIEST ▸ bluey

BLUING ▸ blue

BLUINGS ▸ blue

BLUISH adj slightly blue

BLUME Scots word for ▸ bloom

BLUMED ▸ blume

BLUMES ▸ blume

BLUMING ▸ blume

BLUNDER n, vb

BLUNGE vb mix clay with water blunged

BLUNGER n large vat in which the contents are mixed by rotating arms

BLUNGES ▸ blunge

BLUNK vb ruin; botch blunked, blunker, blunks

BLUNT adj, vb, n blunted, blunter, bluntly, blunts

BLUR vb, n

BLURB n, vb blurbed, blurbs

BLURRED ▸ blur

BLURRY ▸ blur

BLURS ▸ blur

BLURT vb utter suddenly and involuntarily **blurted, blurter, blurts**

BLUSH vb, n **blushed**

BLUSHER n cosmetic for giving the cheeks a rosy colour

BLUSHES ▸ blush

BLUSHET n modest young woman

BLUSTER vb, n

BLYPE n piece of skin peeled off after sunburn **blypes**

BO interj exclamation uttered to startle or surprise someone ▸ n fellow, buddy

BOA n

BOAB short for ▸ baobab

BOABS ▸ boab

BOAK = boke

BOAKED ▸ boak

BOAKING ▸ boak

BOAKS ▸ boak

BOAR n

BOARD n, vb **boarded**

BOARDER n

BOARDS ▸ board

BOARISH adj coarse, cruel, or sensual

BOARS ▸ boar

BOART = bort

BOARTS ▸ boart

BOAS ▸ boa

BOAST vb, n **boasted, boaster, boasts**

BOAT n, vb **boated**

BOATEL n waterside hotel catering for boating people **boatels**

BOATER n **boaters**

BOATFUL ▸ boat

BOATIE n boating enthusiast **boaties**

BOATING n rowing, sailing, or cruising in boats as a form of recreation

BOATMAN n man who works on, hires out, or repairs boats **boatmen**

BOATS ▸ boat

BOB vb, n

BOBA n type of Chinese tea

BOBAC = bobak

BOBACS ▸ bobac

BOBAK n type of marmot **bobaks**

BOBAS ▸ boba

BOBBED ▸ bob

BOBBER n type of float for fishing **bobbers**

BOBBERY n mixed pack of hunting dogs ▸ adj noisy or excitable

BOBBIES ▸ bobby

BOBBIN n

BOBBING ▸ bob

BOBBINS ▸ bobbin

BOBBISH adj cheery

BOBBITT vb sever the penis of

BOBBLE n, vb **bobbled, bobbles**

BOBBLY adj (of fabric) covered in small balls; worn

BOBBY n

BOBCAT n N American feline **bobcats**

BOBECHE n candle drip-catcher

BOBLET n two-man bobsleigh **boblets**

BOBOL n type of fraud ▸ vb commit a bobol **bobols**

BOBOTIE n dish of curried mince

BOBS ▸ bob

BOBSLED = bobsleigh

BOBSTAY n stay between a bowsprit and the stem of a vessel

BOBTAIL n docked tail ▸ adj having the tail cut short ▸ vb dock the tail of

BOBWIG n type of short wig **bobwigs**

BOCAGE n wooded countryside characteristic of northern France **bocages**

BOCCA n mouth **boccas**

BOCCE = boccie

BOCCES ▸ bocce

BOCCI = boccie

BOCCIA = boccie

BOCCIAS ▸ boccia

BOCCIE n Italian version of bowls **boccies**

BOCCIS ▸ bocci

BOCK a variant spelling of ▸ boke

BOCKED ▸ bock

BOCKEDY adj (of a structure, piece of furniture, etc) unsteady

BOCKING ▸ bock

BOCKS ▸ bock

BOD n person

BODACH n old man **bodachs**

BODDLE = bodle

BODDLES ▸ boddle

BODE vb portend or presage **boded**

BODEFUL adj portentous

BODEGA n shop in a Spanish-speaking country that sells wine **bodegas**

BODES ▶ bode

BODGE vb make a mess of **bodged**

BODGER adj worthless or second-rate **bodgers**

BODGES ▶ bodge

BODGIE n unruly or uncouth young man, esp in the 1950s ▷ adj inferior **bodgier, bodgies**

BODGING ▶ bodge

BODHI n as in **bodhi tree** holy tree of Buddhists

BODHRAN n shallow one-sided drum popular in Irish and Scottish folk music

BODICE n **bodices**

BODIED ▶ body

BODIES ▶ body

BODIKIN n little body

BODILY adj, adv

BODING ▶ bode

BODINGS ▶ bode

BODKIN n blunt large-eyed needle **bodkins**

BODLE n small obsolete Scottish coin **bodles**

BODRAG n enemy attack **bodrags**

BODS ▶ bod

BODY n **bodying**

BOEP n South African word for a big belly **boeps**

BOERBUL n crossbred mastiff used esp as a watchdog

BOET n brother **boets**

BOEUF n as in **boeuf bourguignon** casserole of beef, vegetables, herbs, etc, cooked in red wine

BOFF n boffin ▷ vb hit **boffed**

BOFFIN n scientist or expert

BOFFING ▶ boff

BOFFINS ▶ boffin

BOFFO adj very good

BOFFOLA n great success

BOFFOS ▶ boffo

BOFFS ▶ boff

BOG n, vb

BOGAN n youth who dresses and behaves rebelliously **bogans**

BOGART vb monopolize or keep to oneself selfishly **bogarts**

BOGBEAN = buckbean

BOGEY n evil or mischievous spirit ▷ vb play (a hole) in one stroke over par **bogeyed, bogeys**

BOGGARD = boggart

BOGGART n ghost or poltergeist

BOGGED ▶ bog

BOGGER n lavatory **boggers**

BOGGIER ▶ bog

BOGGING ▶ bog

BOGGISH ▶ bog

BOGGLE vb **boggled, boggler, boggles**

BOGGY ▶ bog

BOGIE = bogey

BOGIED ▶ bogie

BOGIES ▶ bogy

BOGLAND n area of wetland

BOGLE n rhythmic dance performed to ragga music ▷ vb perform such a dance **bogled, bogles, bogling**

BOGMAN n body of a person found preserved in a peat bog **bogmen**

BOGOAK n oak or other wood found preserved in peat bogs; bogwood **bogoaks**

BOGONG n large nocturnal Australian moth **bogongs**

BOGS ▶ bog

BOGUS adj **bogusly**

BOGWOOD = bogoak

BOGY = bogey

BOGYISM = bogeyism

BOGYMAN = bogeyman

BOGYMEN ▶ bogyman

BOH = bo

BOHEA n black Chinese tea **boheas**

BOHEMIA n area frequented by unconventional (esp creative) people

BOHO short for **> bohemian**

BOHOS ▶ boho

BOHRIUM n element artificially produced in minute quantities

BOHS ▶ boh

BOI n lesbian who dresses like a boy

BOIL vb, n boiled

BOILER n boilers

BOILERY n place where water is boiled to extract salt

BOILING adj, n

BOILOFF n quantity of liquified gases lost in evaporation

BOILS ▶ boil

BOING vb rebound making a noise boinged, boings, boink

BOINKED ▶ boink

BOINKS ▶ boink

BOIS ▶ boi

BOITE n artist's portfolio boites

BOK n S African antelope This useful K word, meaning an antelope, that can take quite a number of front extensions, forming words like blesbok, reitbok, rhebok, and, even, if you are lucky, jambok or sjambok

BOKE vb retch or vomit ▷ n retch boked, bokes, boking

BOKO slang word for ▶ nose

BOKOS ▶ boko

BOKS ▶ bok

BOLA n missile used by

gauchos and Indians of South America

BOLAR adj relating to clay

BOLAS = bola

BOLASES ▶ bolas

BOLD adj, n

BOLDEN vb make bold boldens

BOLDER, boldest, boldly, bolds ▶ bold

BOLE n tree trunk

BOLERO n boleros

BOLES ▶ bole

BOLETE n type of fungus boletes

BOLETI ▶ boletus

BOLETUS n type of fungus

BOLIDE n large exceptionally bright meteor that often explodes bolides

BOLINE n (in Wicca) a knife bolines

BOLIVAR n standard monetary unit of Venezuela, equal to 100 céntimos

BOLIVIA n type of woollen fabric

BOLL n rounded seed capsule of cotton, flax, etc ▷ vb form into a boll

BOLLARD n

BOLLED, bollen, bolling, bolls ▶ boll

BOLO n large single-edged knife, originating in the Philippines

BOLOGNA n type of sausage

BOLONEY a variant spelling of ▶ baloney

BOLOS ▶ bolo

BOLSHIE adj difficult or rebellious ▷ n any political radical bolshy

BOLSON n desert valley surrounded by mountains, with a shallow lake at the centre bolsons

BOLSTER vb, n

BOLT n, vb bolted, bolter, bolters, bolting, bolts

BOLUS = bole

BOLUSES ▶ bolus

BOMA n enclosure set up to protect a camp, herd of animals, etc bomas

BOMB n, vb

BOMBARD vb, n

BOMBAST n pompous language ▷ vb speak pompous language

BOMBAX n type of S American tree

BOMBE n dessert of ice cream lined or filled with custard, cake crumbs, etc ▷ adj (of furniture) having a projecting swollen shape

BOMBED ▶ bomb

BOMBER n bombers

BOMBES ▶ bombe

BOMBING ▶ bomb

BOMBLET n small bomb

BOMBO n inferior wine

BOMBORA n submerged reef

BOMBOS ▸ bombo

BOMBS ▸ bomb

BOMBYX n type of moth

BOMMIE n outcrop of coral reef **bommies**

BON adj good

BONA n goods

BONACI n type of fish **bonacis**

BONANZA n

BONASUS n European bison

BONBON n sweet **bonbons**

BONCE n head **bonces**

BOND n, vb

BONDAGE n

BONDED adj consisting of, secured by, or operating under a bond or bonds

BONDER = bondstone

BONDERS ▸ bonder

BONDING n process by which individuals become emotionally attached to one another = bondsman

BONDMAN = bondsman

BONDMEN ▸ bondman

BONDS ▸ bond

BONDUC n type of North American tree **bonducs**

BONE n, vb **boned**

BONER n blunder **boners**

BONES ▸ bone

BONESET n N American plant with flat clusters of small white flowers

BONEY = bony

BONEYER ▸ boney

BONFIRE n

BONG n deep reverberating sound, as of a large bell ▸ vb make a deep reverberating sound **bonged, bonging**

BONGO n small drum played with the fingers **bongoes, bongos**

BONGS ▸ bong

BONHAM n piglet **bonhams**

BONIATO n sweet potato

BONIE = bonny

BONIER ▸ bony

BONIEST ▸ bony

BONING ▸ bone

BONINGS ▸ bone

BONISM n doctrine that the world is good, although not the best of all possible worlds **bonisms, bonist, bonists**

BONITA slang term for ▸ heroin

BONITAS ▸ bonita

BONITO n small tunny-like marine food fish **bonitos**

BONJOUR interj hello

BONK vb have sex with **bonked**

BONKERS adj crazy

BONKING ▸ bonk

BONKS ▸ bonk

BONNE n housemaid or female servant **bonnes**

BONNET n, vb **bonnets**

BONNIE = bonny

BONNIER ▸ bonny

BONNIES ▸ bonny

BONNILY ▸ bonny

BONNOCK n thick oatmeal cake

BONNY adj, adv

BONOBO n type of anthropoid ape of central W Africa **bonobos**

BONSAI n

BONSELA n small gift of money

BONSOIR interj good evening

BONUS n **bonuses**

BONXIE n great skua **bonxies**

BONY adj

BONZA = bonzer

BONZE n Chinese or Japanese Buddhist priest or monk

BONZER adj excellent

BONZES ▸ bonze

BOO interj, vb

BOOAI ▸ boohai

BOOAIS ▸ booai

BOOAY ▸ boohai

BOOAYS ▸ booay

BOOB n foolish mistake ▸ vb make a foolish mistake ▸ adj of poor quality, similar to that provided in prison **boobed**

BOOBIE = booby

BOOBIES ▸ booby **boobing**

BOOBIRD n person who boos

BOOBISH ▸ booby

BOOBOO n blunder

BOOBOOK n

BOOBOOS ▷ booboo
BOOBS ▷ boob
BOOBY n foolish person
BOOCOO = beaucoup
BOOCOOS ▷ boocoo
BOODIE n type of kangaroo
BOODIED ▷ boody
BOODIES ▷ boody
BOODLE n money or valuables, counterfeit, or used as a bribe ▷ vb give or receive money corruptly or illegally **boodled, boodler, boodles**
BOODY vb sulk
BOOED ▷ boo
BOOFIER ▷ boofy
BOOFY adj muscular and strong but stupid
BOOGER n dried mucus from the nose **boogers**
BOOGEY = boogie
BOOGEYS ▷ boogey
BOOGIE vb dance to fast pop music ▷ n session of dancing to pop music **boogied, boogies, boogy**
BOOH = boo
BOOHAI n as in up the boohai thoroughly lost **boohais**
BOOHED ▷ booh
BOOHING ▷ booh
BOOHOO vb sob or pretend to sob noisily ▷ n distressed or pretended sobbing **boohoos**
BOOHS ▷ booh
BOOING ▷ boo

BOOJUM n American tree **boojums**
BOOK n, vb booked
BOOKEND n one of a pair of supports for holding books upright
BOOKER ▷ book
BOOKERS ▷ book
BOOKFUL ▷ book
BOOKIE short for > bookmaker
BOOKIER ▷ booky
BOOKIES ▷ bookie
BOOKING n
BOOKISH adj fond of reading
BOOKLET n
BOOKMAN n learned person **bookmen**
BOOKOO = boocoo
BOOKOOS ▷ bookoo
BOOKS ▷ book
BOOKSIE ▷ booksy
BOOKSY adj inclined to be bookish or literary
BOOKY adj bookish
BOOL n bowling bowl ▷ vb play bowls **booled, booling, bools**
BOOM vb, n
BOOMBOX n portable stereo system
BOOMED ▷ boom
BOOMER n large male kangaroo **boomers**
BOOMIER ▷ boomy
BOOMING ▷ boom
BOOMKIN n short boom projecting from the deck of a ship
BOOMLET n small boom in business, birth rate, etc
BOOMS ▷ boom

BOOMY adj characterized by heav[y] bass sound
BOON n
BOONER n young working-class person from Canberra **booners**
BOONIES short form of > boondocks
BOONS ▷ boon
BOOR n
BOORD obsolete spellin[g] of ▷ board
BOORDE obsolete spelling of ▷ board
BOORDES ▷ boorde
BOORDS ▷ boord
BOORISH adj ill-mannered, clumsy or insensitive
BOORKA = burka
BOORKAS ▷ boorka
BOORS ▷ boor
BOOS ▷ boo
BOOSE = booze
BOOSED ▷ boose
BOOSES ▷ boose
BOOSHIT adj very goo[d]
BOOSING ▷ boose
BOOST n, vb boosted
BOOSTER n small additional injection o[f] a vaccine
BOOSTS ▷ boost
BOOT n, vb
BOOTCUT adj (of trousers) slightly flar[e] at the bottom of the legs
BOOTED adj wearing boots
BOOTEE n baby's soft shoe **bootees**

BOOTERY n shop where boots and shoes are sold

BOOTH n booths

BOOTIE n Royal Marine

BOOTIES ▶ booty

BOOTING ▶ boot

BOOTLEG adj produced, distributed, or sold illicitly ▷ vb make, carry, or sell (illicit goods) ▷ n something made or sold illicitly

BOOTS ▶ boot

BOOTY n

BOOZE n, vb boozed

BOOZER n person who is fond of drinking boozers

BOOZES ▶ booze

BOOZEY = boozy

BOOZIER ▶ boozy

BOOZILY ▶ boozy

BOOZING ▶ booze

BOOZY adj inclined to or involving excessive drinking of alcohol

BOP vb dance to pop music ▷ n form of jazz with complex rhythms and harmonies

BOPEEP n quick look; peek bopeeps

BOPPED adj, bopper, boppers, bopping, bops ▶ bop

BOPS ▶ bop

BOR n neighbour

BORA n Aboriginal ceremony

BORACES ▶ borax

BORACIC = boric

BORAGE n Mediterranean plant

with star-shaped blue flowers borages

BORAK n rubbish boraks

BORAL n type of fine powder borals

BORANE n any compound of boron and hydrogen boranes

BORAS ▶ bora

BORATE n salt or ester of boric acid ▷ vb treat with borax, boric acid, or borate borated, borates

BORAX n soluble white mineral occurring in alkaline soils and salt deposits boraxes

BORAZON n extremely hard form of boron nitride

BORD obsolete spelling of ▶ board

BORDAR n smallholder who held cottage in return for menial work bordars

BORDE obsolete spelling of ▶ board

BORDEL = bordello

BORDELS ▶ bordel

BORDER n, vb borders

BORDES ▶ borde

BORDS ▶ bord

BORDURE n outer edge of a shield, esp when decorated distinctively

BORE vb make (someone) weary by being dull

BOREAL adj of or relating to the north or

the north wind

BOREAS n name for the north wind

BORED ▶ bore

BOREDOM n

BOREE = myall

BOREEN n country lane or narrow road boreens

BOREES ▶ boree

BOREL adj unlearned

BORER n machine or hand tool for boring holes borers

BORES ▶ bear

BORGO n small attractive medieval village borgos

BORIC adj of or containing boron

BORIDE n compound in which boron is the most electronegative element borides

BORING n, adj borings

BORK vb dismiss from job unfairly borked, borking, borks

BORM vb smear with paint, oil, etc bormed, borming, borms

BORN adj

BORNA n as in borna disease viral disease found in mammals, esp horses

BORNE ▶ bear

BORNEOL n white solid terpene alcohol

BORNITE n type of mineral

BORNYL n as in bornyl alcohol white solid alcohol from a

Malaysian tree **bornyls**
BORON n
BORONIA n Australian aromatic flowering shrub
BORONIC ▸ boron
BORONS ▸ boron
BOROUGH n
BORREL adj ignorant **borrell**
BORROW vb **borrows**
BORS ▸ bor
BORSCH = borscht
BORSCHT n Russian soup based on beetroot **borshch, borsht**
BORSHTS ▸ borsht
BORSIC n composite material used in aviation **borsics**
BORSTAL n
BORT n inferior grade of diamond used for cutting and drilling or, in powdered form, as an industrial abrasive **bortier, borts**
BORTSCH = borscht **borty, bortz**
BORTZES ▸ bortz
BORZOI n borzois
BOS ▸ bo
BOSBOK = bushbuck
BOSBOKS ▸ bosbok
BOSCAGE n mass of trees and shrubs
BOSH n empty talk, nonsense
BOSHBOK = bushbuck **boshes**
BOSHTA = boshter
BOSHTER adj excellent
BOSIE n (in cricket)

another term for googly **bosies**
BOSK n small wood of bushes and small trees
BOSKAGE = boscage
BOSKER adj excellent
BOSKET n clump of small trees or bushes **boskets**
BOSKIER ▸ bosky
BOSKS ▸ bosk
BOSKY adj containing or consisting of bushes or thickets
BOSOM n, adj, vb **bosomed, bosoms**
BOSOMY adj (of a woman) having large breasts
BOSON n type of elementary particle **bosonic, bosons**
BOSQUE = bosk
BOSQUES ▸ bosque
BOSQUET = bosket
BOSS n, vb, adj
BOSSBOY n Black African foreman of a gang of workers
BOSSDOM n bosses collectively
BOSSED, bosser, bosses, bossest ▸ boss
BOSSET n either of the rudimentary antlers found in young deer **bossets**
BOSSIER ▸ bossy
BOSSIES ▸ bossy
BOSSILY ▸ bossy
BOSSING n act of shaping malleable metal
BOSSISM n domination

of political organizations by bosses
BOSSY = boss
BOSTON n card game for four, played with two packs **bostons**
BOSTRYX n phenomenon in which flowers develop on one side only
BOSUN = boatswain
BOSUNS ▸ bosun
BOT n larva of a botfly
BOTA n leather container
BOTANIC = botanical
BOTANY n
BOTARGO n relish consisting of the roe of mullet or tunny, salted and pressed into rolls
BOTAS ▸ bota
BOTCH vb, n **botched, botcher, botches**
BOTCHY adj clumsily done or made
BOTE n compensation given for injury or damage to property
BOTEL = boatel
BOTELS ▸ botel
BOTES ▸ bote
BOTFLY n type of stout-bodied hairy fly
BOTH pron, adj, determiner
BOTHAN n unlicensed drinking house **bothans**
BOTHER vb, n, interj **bothers**
BOTHIE = bothy
BOTHIES ▸ bothy

BOTHOLE n hole made by the larva of the botfly

BOTHRIA > **bothrium**

BOTHY n hut used for temporary shelter

BOTNET n network of infected computers **botnets**

BOTONE adj having lobes at the ends **botonee**

BOTS n digestive disease of horses and some other animals

BOTT = **bot**

BOTTE n thrust or hit

BOTTED > **bot**

BOTTEGA n workshop; studio

BOTTES > **botte**

BOTTIES > **botty**

BOTTINE n light boot for women or children

BOTTING > **bot**

BOTTLE n, vb **bottled**

BOTTLER n exceptional person or thing

BOTTLES > **bottle**

BOTTOM n, adj, vb **bottoms**

BOTTS > **bott**

BOTTY n diminutive for bottom

BOTULIN n potent toxin which causes botulism

BOUBOU n long flowing garment **boubous**

BOUCHE n notch cut in top corner of shield

BOUCHEE n small pastry case filled with a savoury mixture

BOUCHES > **bouche**

BOUCLE n looped yarn giving a knobbly effect ⊳ adj of or designating such a yarn or fabric

BOUCLEE n support for a cue in billiards using the hand

BOUCLES > **boucle**

BOUDIN n French version of a black pudding **boudins**

BOUDOIR n woman's bedroom or private sitting room

BOUFFE n type of light or satirical opera common in France during the 19th century **bouffes**

BOUGE vb move **bouged, bouges**

BOUGET n budget **bougets**

BOUGH n **boughed, boughs**

BOUGHT > **buy**

BOUGHTS > **buy**

BOUGIE n medical instrument **bougies**

BOUGING > **bouge**

BOUILLI n stew

BOUK n bulk; volume **bouks**

BOULDER n, vb

BOULE = **boulle**

BOULES n game popular in France

BOULLE adj relating to a type of marquetry much used on French furniture from the 17th century ⊳ n something ornamented with such

marquetry **boulles**

BOULT = **bolt**

BOULTED > **boult**

BOULTER > **boult**

BOULTS > **boult**

BOUN vb prepare to go out

BOUNCE vb, n **bounced**

BOUNCER n person employed at a disco etc to remove unwanted people

BOUNCES > **bounce**

BOUNCY adj

BOUND > **bind**

BOUNDED adj (of a set) having a bound

BOUNDEN adj morally obligatory

BOUNDER n morally reprehensible person

BOUNDS pl n limit

BOUNED > **boun**

BOUNING > **boun**

BOUNS > **boun**

BOUNTY n

BOUQUET n

BOURBON n whiskey made from maize

BOURD n prank

BOURDER n prankster

BOURDON n 16-foot organ stop of the stopped diapason type

BOURDS > **bourd**

BOURG n French market town, esp one bèside a castle **bourgs**

BOURKHA = **burka**

BOURLAW n byrlaw

BOURN n (in S Britain) stream **bourne**

BOURNES > **bourne**

BOURNS > **bourn**

BOURREE n traditional French dance in fast duple time

BOURSE n stock exchange of continental Europe, esp Paris **bourses**

BOURSIN n tradename of a smooth white creamy cheese, often flavoured with garlic

BOUSE vb raise or haul with a tackle **boused, bouses**

BOUSIER ▸ bousy

BOUSING ▸ bouse

BOUSY adj drunken; boozy

BOUT n

BOUTADE n outburst

BOUTON n knob-shaped contact between nerve fibres **boutons**

BOUTS ▸ bout

BOUVIER n large powerful dog

BOVATE n obsolete measure of land **bovates**

BOVID n type of ruminant **bovids**

BOVINE n **bovines**

BOVVER n rowdiness, esp caused by gangs of teenage youths **bovvers**

BOW vb, n

BOWAT n lamp **bowats**

BOWBENT adj bent; bow-like

BOWED adj lowered, bent forward, or curved

BOWEL n, vb **boweled,** bowels

BOWER n, vb **bowered, bowers, bowery**

BOWES ▸ bough

BOWET n = bowat

BOWETS ▸ bowet

BOWFIN n N American freshwater fish **bowfins**

BOWGET obsolete variant of ▸ budget

BOWGETS ▸ bowget

BOWHEAD n type of large-mouthed arctic whale

BOWIE n as in bowie knife type of hunting knife

BOWING n musical technique **bowings**

BOWKNOT n decorative knot usually having two loops and two loose ends

BOWL n, vb

BOWLDER n = boulder

BOWLED ▸ bowl

BOWLEG n leg curving outwards like a bow between the ankle and the thigh **bowlegs**

BOWLER n player who sends (a ball) towards the batsman **bowlers**

BOWLESS ▸ bow

BOWLFUL n = bowl

BOWLIKE ▸ bow

BOWLINE n line used to keep the sail taut against the wind

BOWLING n

BOWLS n

BOWMAN n archer **bowmen**

BOWNE = boun

BOWNED ▸ bowne

BOWNES ▸ bowne

BOWNING ▸ bowne

BOWPOT = boughpot

BOWPOTS ▸ bowpot

BOWR n muscle **bowrs**

BOWS ▸ bow

BOWSAW n saw with a thin blade in a bow-shaped frame **bowsaws**

BOWSE = bouse

BOWSED ▸ bowse

BOWSER n tanker containing fuel for aircraft, military vehicles, etc **bowsers**

BOWSES ▸ bowse

BOWSEY = bowsie

BOWSEYS ▸ bowsey

BOWSHOT n distance an arrow travels from the bow

BOWSIE n low-class, mean or obstreperous person **bowsies**

BOWSING ▸ bowse

BOWWOW n imitation of the bark of a dog ▸ vb make a noise like a dog **bowwows**

BOWYANG n band worn round trouser leg below knee

BOWYER n person who makes or sells archery bows **bowyers**

BOX n, vb

BOXBALL n street ball game

BOXCAR n closed railway freight van **boxcars**

BOXED ▶ box

BOXEN ▶ box

BOXER n boxers

BOXES ▶ box

BOXFISH another name for ▶ trunkfish

BOXFUL = box

BOXFULS ▶ box

BOXHAUL vb bring (a square-rigger) onto a new tack by backwinding the foresails and steering hard round

BOXIER ▶ boxy

BOXIEST ▶ boxy

BOXILY ▶ boxy

BOXING n boxings

BOXLIKE ▶ box

BOXPLOT n (in statistics) type of graph

BOXROOM n small room in which boxes, cases, etc may be stored

BOXTIES n

BOXTY n type of Irish potato pancake

BOXWOOD n hard yellow wood of the box tree, used to make tool handles, etc

BOXY adj squarish or chunky

BOY n, vb

BOYAR n member of an old order of Russian nobility **boyard**

BOYARDS ▶ boyard

BOYARS ▶ boyar

BOYAU n connecting trench **boyaux**

BOYCHIK n young boy

BOYCOTT vb, n

BOYED ▶ boy

BOYF n boyfriend **boyfs**

BOYG n troll-like mythical creature **boygs**

BOYHOOD n state or time of being a boy

BOYING ▶ boy

BOYISH adj of or like a boy in looks, behaviour, or character

BOYKIE n **boykies**

BOYLA n Australian Aboriginal word for magician **boylas**

BOYO n boy or young man: often used in direct address **boyos**

BOYS ▶ boy

BOYSIER ▶ boysy

BOYSY adj suited to or typical of boys or young men

BOZO n man, esp a stupid one **bozos**

BRA = brassiere

BRAAI vb grill or roast (meat) over open coals **braaied, braais**

BRAATA n small portion added to a purchase to encourage the customer to return **braatas**

BRABBLE rare word for ▶ squabble

BRACCIA ▶ braccio

BRACCIO n former unit of measurement; length of man's arm

BRACE n, vb **braced**

BRACER n person or thing that braces

BRACERO n Mexican World War II labourer

BRACERS ▶ bracer

BRACES pl n pair of straps worn over the shoulders for holding up the trousers

BRACH n bitch hound

BRACHAH n blessing

BRACHES ▶ brach

BRACHET ▶ brach

BRACHIA ▶ brachium

BRACHOT ▶ brachah

BRACHS ▶ brach

BRACING adj, n

BRACK = barmbrack

BRACKEN n, vb

BRACKET n, vb

BRACKS ▶ brack

BRACT n bracted, bracts

BRAD n small tapered nail with a small head

BRADAWL n small boring tool

BRADDED ▶ brad

BRADOON = bridoon

BRADS ▶ brad

BRAE n hill or slope **braes**

BRAG vb, n **bragged, bragger**

BRAGGY adj boastful

BRAGLY ▶ brag

BRAGS ▶ brag

BRAHMA n breed of domestic fowl

BRAHMAN n member of highest Hindu caste

BRAHMAS ▶ brahma

BRAHMIN = brahman

BRAID vb, n, adj, adv

BRAIDE adj given to deceit

BRAIDED adj (of a river or stream) flowing in several shallow interconnected channels

BRAIDER ▶ braid

BRAIDS ▶ braid

BRAIL n one of several lines fastened to a fore-and-aft sail to aid in furling it ▷ vb furl (a fore-and-aft sail) using brails **brailed**

BRAILLE n system of writing for the blind ▷ vb print or write using this method

BRAILS ▶ brail

BRAIN n, vb **brained, brains**

BRAINY adj

BAIRD vb appear as shoots **brairds**

BRAISE vb **braised, braises, braize**

BRAIZES ▶ braize

BRAK n crossbred dog ▷ adj (of water) slightly salty

BRAKE = bracken

BRAKED ▶ brake

BRAKES ▶ brake

BRAKIER ▶ braky

BRAKING ▶ brake

BRAKS ▶ brak

BRAKY adj **brambly**

BRALESS ▶ bra

BRAMBLE n Scots word for blackberry **brambly**

BRAME n powerful feeling of emotion **brames**

BRAN n

BRANCH n, vb **branchy**

BRAND n, vb

BRANDED adj identifiable as being the product of a particular company

BRANDER ▶ brand

BRANDS ▶ brand

BRANDY n, vb

BRANE n hypothetical component of string theory **branes**

BRANGLE vb quarrel noisily

BRANK vb walk with swaggering gait **branked**

BRANKS pl n (formerly) iron bridle used to restrain scolding women

BRANKY adj ostentatious

BRANLE n old French country dance performed in a linked circle **branles**

BRANNED ▶ bran

BRANNER n person or machine that treats metal with bran

BRANNY adj having the appearance or texture of bran

BRANS ▶ bran

BRANSLE another word for ▶ brantle

BRANT n type of small goose

BRANTLE n French country dance

BRANTS ▶ brant

BRAS ▶ bra

BRASCO n lavatory

brascos

BRASERO n metal grid for burning coals

BRASES ▶ bra

BRASH adj, n, vb **brashed, brasher, brashes, brashly**

BRASHY adj loosely fragmented

BRASIER = brazier

BRASIL = brazil

BRASILS = brasil

BRASS n, vb **brassed, brasses**

BRASSET = brassart

BRASSIE n former name for a golf club **brassy**

BRAST = burst

BRASTS ▶ brast

BRAT n **brats**

BRATTLE vb make a rattling sound

BRATTY ▶ brat

BRAUNCH old variant of ▶ branch

BRAVA n professional assassin

BRAVADO n, vb

BRAVAS ▶ brava

BRAVE adj, n, vb **braved bravely, braver, bravers, bravery, braves, bravest**

BRAVI ▶ bravo

BRAVING ▶ brave

BRAVO interj, n, vb **bravoed, bravoes, bravos**

BRAVURA n display of boldness or daring **bravure**

BRAW adj fine or excellent, esp in appearance or dress

▷ *pl n* best clothes
brawer, brawest

BRAWL *n, vb* brawled,
brawler

BRAWLIE *adj* in good
health

BRAWLS ▶ brawl

BRAWLY ▶ braw

BRAWN *n* brawned,
brawns

BRAWNY *adj* muscular
and strong

BRAWS *n* fine apparel

BRAXIES ▶ braxy

BRAXY *n* acute and
usually fatal bacterial
disease of sheep

BRAY *vb, n* brayed,
brayer, brayers,
braying, brays

BRAZA *n* Spanish unit
of measurement
brazas

BRAZE *vb* join (two
metal surfaces) with
brass ▷ *n* high-melting
solder or alloy used in
brazing **brazed**

BRAZEN *adj, vb* brazens

BRAZER ▶ braze

BRAZES ▶ braze

BRAZIER *n*

BRAZIL *n* red wood used
for cabinetwork **brazils**

BRAZING ▶ braze

BREACH *n, vb*

BREAD *n, vb* breaded,
breads

BREADTH *n*

BREADY *adj* having the
appearance or texture
of bread

BREAK ▶ bracken

BREAKER *n*

BREAKS ▶ bracken

BREAKUP *n* separation
or disintegration

BREAM *n, vb* breamed,
breams

BREARE = brier

BREARES ▶ breare

BREAST *n, vb* breasts

BREATH *n*

BREATHE *vb*

BREATHS ▶ breath

BREATHY *adj* (of the
speaking voice)
accompanied by an
audible emission of
breath

BRECCIA *n* type of rock

BRECHAM *n* straw
horse-collar **brechan**

BRED *n*

BREDE *archaic spelling of*
▶ braid

BREDED ▶ brede

BREDES ▶ brede

BREDIE *n* meat and
vegetable stew
bredies

BREDING ▶ brede

BREDREN > brethren

BREDRIN > brethren

BREDS ▶ bred

BREE *n* broth, stock, or
juice

BREED *vb, n*

BREEDER *n* person who
breeds plants or
animals

BREEDS ▶ breed

BREEKS *pl n* trousers

BREEM = breme

BREENGE *vb* lunge
forward ▷ *n* violent
movement

BREER *another word for*
▶ braird

BREERED ▶ breer

BREERS ▶ breer

BREES ▶ bree

BREESE = breeze

BREESES ▶ breese

BREEST ▶ breast

BREESTS ▶ breast

BREEZE *n, vb* breezed,
breezes

BREEZY *adj* windy

BREGMA *n* point on the
top of the skull

BREHON *n* (formerly)
judge in Ireland
brehons

BREI *vb* speak with a
uvular r, esp in
Afrikaans

BREID *n* bread **breids**

BREIING ▶ brei

BREINGE = breenge

BREIS ▶ brei

BREIST *Scot word for*
▶ breast

BREISTS ▶ breist

BREKKY *slang word for*
> breakfast

BREME *adj* well-known

BREN *n* type of machine
gun

BRENNE *vb* burn
brennes

BRENS ▶ bren

BRENT *n* type of goose
▷ *adj* steep **brenter,
brents**

BRER *n* brother: usually
prefixed to a name

BRERE = brier

BRERES ▸ brere

BRERS ▸ brer

BRETON n hat with an upturned brim and a rounded crown **bretons**

BREVE n accent placed over a vowel to indicate shortness **breves**

BREVET n document entitling a commissioned officer to hold temporarily a higher military rank ▷ vb promote by brevet

BREVETE adj patented

BREVETS ▸ brevet

BREVIER n (formerly) size of printer's type approximately equal to 8 point

BREVIS ▸ brewis

BREVITY n

BREW vb, n

BREWAGE n product of brewing

BREWED ▸ brew

BREWER ▸ brew

BREWERS ▸ brew

BREWERY n

BREWING n quantity of a beverage brewed at one time

BREWIS n bread soaked in broth, gravy, etc

BREWPUB n pub that incorporates a brewery on its premises

BREWS ▸ brew

BREWSKI n beer

BREY = brei

BREYED ▸ brey

BREYING ▸ brey

BREYS ▸ brey

BRIAR n

BRIARD n medium-sized dog **briards**

BRIARED ▸ briar

BRIARS ▸ briar

BRIARY ▸ briar

BRIBE vb, n **bribed**

BRIBEE n one who is bribed **bribees**

BRIBER ▸ bribe

BRIBERS ▸ bribe

BRIBERY n process of giving or taking bribes

BRIBES ▸ bribe

BRIBING ▸ bribe

BRICHT Scot word for ▸ **bright**

BRICK n, vb **bricked**

BRICKEN adj made of brick

BRICKIE n bricklayer

BRICKLE variant of ▸ **brittle**

BRICKS ▸ brick

BRICKY ▸ brickie

BRICOLE n billiards shot

BRIDAL adj of a bride or a wedding ▷ n wedding or wedding feast **bridals**

BRIDE n **brided, brides**

BRIDGE n, vb **bridged, bridges**

BRIDIE n semicircular pie containing meat and onions **bridies**

BRIDING ▸ bride

BRIDLE n, vb **bridled, bridler, bridles**

BRIDOON n horse's bit: small snaffle used in double bridles

BRIE = bree

BRIEF adj, n, vb **briefed, briefer, briefly**

BRIEFS pl n men's or women's underpants without legs

BRIER = brier

BRIERED ▸ brier

BRIERS ▸ brier

BRIERY ▸ brier

BRIES ▸ brie

BRIG n two-masted square-rigged ship

BRIGADE n, vb

BRIGAND n

BRIGHT adj, adv

BRIGHTS pl n high beam of the headlights of a motor vehicle

BRIGS ▸ brig

BRIGUE vb solicit **briqued, brigues**

BRIK n Tunisian pastry

BRIKI = cezve

BRIKIS ▸ briki

BRIKS ▸ brik

BRILL n type of European flatfish popular as a food fish **briller**

BRILLO n tradename for a type of scouring pad impregnated with a detergent **brillos**

BRILLS ▸ brill

BRIM n, vb

BRIMFUL adj completely filled with

BRIMING n phosphorescence of sea

BRIMMED ▸ brim

BRIMMER n vessel, such as a glass or bowl, filled to the brim

BRIMS ▸ brim

BRIN n thread of silk

from silkworm

BRINDED *adj* streaky or patchy

BRINDLE *n* brindled animal

BRINE *n, vb* brined, briner, briners, brines

BRING *vb* bringer, brings

BRINIER ▸ briny

BRINIES ▸ briny

BRINING ▸ brine

BRINISH ▸ brine

BRINJAL *n*

BRINK *n* brinks

BRINNY *n* stone, esp when thrown

BRINS ▸ brin

BRINY *adj* very salty

BRIO *n* liveliness

BRIOCHE *n* soft roll or loaf made from a very light yeast dough, sometimes mixed with currants

BRIONY = bryony

BRIOS ▸ brio

BRIQUET = briquette

BRIS *n* ritual circumcision of male babies

BRISANT ▸ brisance

BRISE *n* type of jump

BRISES ▸ bris

BRISK *adj, vb* brisked

BRISKEN *vb* make or become more lively or brisk

BRISKER ▸ brisk

BRISKET *n* beef from the breast of a cow

BRISKLY ▸ brisk

BRISKS ▸ brisk

BRISKY another word for

▸ **brisk**

BRISSES ▸ bris

BRISTLE *n, vb* bristly

BRISTOL *n as in* bristol **board** type of heavy cardboard

BRISURE *n* mark of cadency in heraldry

BRIT *n* young of a herring, sprat, or similar fish

BRITH = bris

BRITHS ▸ brith

BRITS ▸ brit

BRITSKA = britzka

BRITT *n* young herring or sprat

BRITTLE *adj, n* brittly

BRITTS ▸ britt

BRITZKA *n* long horse-drawn carriage

BRIZE = breeze

BRIZES ▸ brize

BRO *n* family member

BROACH *vb, n*

BROAD *adj, n*

BROADAX = broadaxe

BROADEN *vb*

BROADER ▸ broad

BROADLY ▸ broad

BROADS ▸ broad

BROCADE *n, vb*

BROCAGE another word for ▸ **brokerage**

BROCARD *n* basic principle of civil law

BROCH *n* (in Scotland) a circular dry-stone tower large enough to serve as a fortified home

BROCHAN *n* type of thin porridge

BROCHE *adj* woven

with a raised design, as brocade **broched, broches**

BROCHO = brachah

BROCHOS ▸ brocho

BROCHS ▸ broch

BROCK *n* badger

BROCKED *adj* having different colours

BROCKET *n* small tropical American deer with small unbranched antlers

BROCKIT = brocked

BROCKS ▸ brock

BROCOLI = broccoli

BROD *vb* prod brodded

BRODDLE *vb* poke or pierce (something)

BRODKIN = brodekin

BRODS ▸ brod

BROG *n* bradawl

BROGAN *n* heavy laced, usually ankle-high, work boot **brogans**

BROGGED ▸ brog

BROGH ▸ broch

BROGHS ▸ brogh

BROGS ▸ brog

BROGUE *n* brogues

BROIDER *archaic word for* ▸ **embroider**

BROIL *vb* cook by direct heat under a grill ▸ *n* process of broiling **broiled**

BROILER *n* young tender chicken for roasting

BROILS ▸ broil

BROKAGE another word for ▸ **brokerage**

BROKE *vb* broked

BROKEN ▸ bracken

BROKER n, vb **brokers**

BROKERY n work done by a broker

BROKES ▸ broke

BROKING ▸ broke

BROLGA n **brolgas**

BROLLY n

BROMAL n synthetic liquid formerly used medicinally **bromals**

BROMATE = **brominate**

BROME n type of grass **bromes**

BROMIC adj of or containing bromine in the trivalent or pentavalent state

BROMID = **bromide**

BROMIDE n chemical compound used in medicine and photography

BROMIDS ▸ bromid

BROMIN ▸ bromine

BROMINE n

BROMINS ▸ bromin

BROMISE = **bromize**

BROMISM n bromine poisoning

BROMIZE vb treat with bromine

BROMMER n S African word for bluebottle

BROMO n something that contains bromide **bromos**

BRONCS ▸ bronc

BROND n old form of

brand bronds

BRONZE n, adj, vb **bronzed**

BRONZEN adj made of or the colour of bronze

BRONZER n cosmetic applied to the skin to simulate a sun tan

BRONZES ▸ bronze

BRONZY ▸ bronze

BROO n brow of hill

BROOCH n, vb

BROOD n, vb **brooded**

BROODER n structure used for rearing young chickens or other fowl

BROODS ▸ brood

BROODY adj moody and sullen

BROOK n, vb **brooked**

BROOKIE n brook trout

BROOKS ▸ brook

BROOL n low roar **brools**

BROOM n, vb **broomed, brooms**

BROOMY adj covered with growth of broom

BROOS ▸ broo

BROOSE n race at country wedding **brooses**

BROS ▸ bro

BROSE n oatmeal or pease porridge, sometimes with butter or fat added **broses**

BROSIER ▸ brosy

BROSY adj smeared with porridge

BROTH n

BROTHEL n

BROTHER n, interj, vb

BROTHS ▸ broth

BROTHY adj having appearance or texture of broth

BROUGH = **broch**

BROUGHS ▸ brough

BROUGHT ▸ bring

BROUZE = **broose**

BROUZES ▸ brouze

BROW n

BROWED adj having a brow

BROWN n, adj, vb **browned, browner**

BROWNIE n

BROWNS ▸ brown

BROWNY ▸ brown

BROWS ▸ brow

BROWSE vb, n **browsed**

BROWSER n

BROWSES ▸ browse

BROWST n brewing (of ale, tea) **browsts**

BROWSY ▸ browse

BRR = brrr

| This is useful if your consonant-heavy rack is giving you the shivers. And if you are even colder, **brrr** is available.

BRRR interj used to suggest shivering

BRU South African word for ▸ **friend**

BRUCHID n type of beetle

BRUCIN = brucine

BRUCINE n bitter poisonous alkaloid resembling strychnine

BRUCINS ▸ brucin

BRUCITE n white

translucent mineral

BRUCKLE adj brittle

BRUGH n large house **brughs**

BRUHAHA = brouhaha

BRUIN n name for a bear, used in children's tales, fables, etc **bruins**

BRUISE n, vb **bruised**

BRUISER n strong tough person

BRUISES ▸ bruise

BRUIT vb report ▷ n abnormal sound heard within the body **bruited, bruiter, bruits**

BRULE n a mixed-race person of Canadian Indian and White (usually French-Canadian) ancestry **brules**

BRULOT n coffee-based alcoholic drink, served flaming **brulots**

BRULYIE = brulyie

BRULZIE n noisy dispute

BRUMAL adj of, characteristic of, or relating to winter

BRUMBY n

BRUME n heavy mist or fog **brumes**

BRUMMER = brommer **brumous**

BRUNCH n breakfast and lunch combined ▷ vb eat brunch

BRUNET adj dark brown **brunets**

BRUNG ▸ bring

BRUNT n, vb **brunted,**

brunts

BRUS ▸ bru

BRUSH n, vb

BRUSHED adj treated with a brushing process

BRUSHER ▸ brush

BRUSHES ▸ brush

BRUSHUP n the act or an instance of tidying one's appearance

BRUSHY adj like a brush

BRUSK = brusque

BRUSKER ▸ brusk

BRUSQUE adj

BRUSSEN adj bold

BRUST = burst

BRUSTS ▸ brust

BRUT adj (of champagne or sparkling wine) very dry ▷ n very dry champagne

BRUTAL adj

BRUTE n, adj **bruted, brutely**

BRUTER n diamond cutter **bruters**

BRUTES ▸ brute

BRUTIFY less common word for > brutalize

BRUTING n diamond cutting

BRUTISH adj of or like an animal

BRUTISM n stupidity; vulgarity

BRUTS ▸ brut

BRUX vb grind one's teeth **bruxed, bruxes, bruxing**

BRUXISM n habit of grinding the teeth,

esp unconsciously

BRYONY n wild climbing hedge plant

BUAT = bowat

BUATS ▸ buat

BUAZE n fibrous African plant **buazes**

BUB n youngster

BUBA another name for ▸ yaws

BUBAL n any of various antelopes

BUBALE n large antelope **bubales**

BUBALIS ▸ bubal

BUBALS ▸ bubal

BUBAS ▸ buba

BUBBA n ordinary American person **bubbas**

BUBBLE n, vb **bubbled**

BUBBLER n drinking fountain

BUBBLES ▸ bubble

BUBBLY adj excited and lively ▷ n champagne

BUBINGA n reddish-brown wood from African tree

BUBKES n very small amount

BUBKIS n

BUBO n inflammation and swelling of a lymph node, esp in the armpit or groin **buboed, buboes, bubonic**

BUBS ▸ bub

BUBU = boubou

BUBUKLE n red spot on skin

BUBUS ▸ bubu

BUCARDO n type of

Spanish mountain goat, recently extinct

BUCCAL adj of or relating to the cheek

BUCCINA n curved Roman horn

BUCHU n S African shrub whose leaves are used as an antiseptic and diuretic **buchus**

BUCK n, vb **bucked**

BUCKEEN n (in Ireland) poor young man who aspires to the habits and dress of the wealthy

BUCKER ▶ buck

BUCKERS ▶ buck

BUCKET vb **buckets**

BUCKEYE n N American tree with erect clusters of white or red flowers and prickly fruits

BUCKIE n whelk or its shell **buckies**

BUCKING ▶ buck

BUCKISH ▶ buck

BUCKLE n, vb **buckled**

BUCKLER n small round shield worn on the forearm ▷ vb defend

BUCKLES ▶ buckle

BUCKO n lively young fellow: often a term of address **buckoes, buckos**

BUCKRAM n cotton or linen cloth stiffened with size, etc ▷ vb stiffen with buckram

BUCKS ▶ buck

BUCKSAW n

woodcutting saw

BUCKSOM = buxom

BUCKU = buchu

BUCKUS ▶ bucku

BUCOLIC adj, n

BUD n swelling on a plant that develops into a leaf or flower ▷ vb produce buds **budded, budder, budders**

BUDDHA n person who has achieved a state of perfect enlightenment **buddhas**

BUDDIED, buddier, buddies, buddiest ▶ buddy

BUDDLE n sloping trough in which ore is washed ▷ vb wash (ore) in a buddle **buddled, buddles**

BUDDY n friend ▷ vb act as a friend to ▷ adj friendly

BUDGE vb, n **budged, budger**

BUDGERO = budgerow

BUDGERS ▶ budge

BUDGES ▶ budge

BUDGET n, vb, adj **budgets**

BUDGIE n short form of budgerigar **budgies**

BUDGING ▶ budge

BUDLESS ▶ bud

BUDLIKE ▶ bud

BUDMASH ▶ badmash

BUDO n combat and spirit in martial arts **budos**

BUDS ▶ bud

BUDWORM n pest that

eats tree leaves and buds

BUFF n, adj, vb

BUFFA ▶ buffo

BUFFALO n, vb

BUFFE ▶ buffo

BUFFED ▶ buff

BUFFEL adj as in **buffel grass** grass used for pasture in Africa, India, and Australia

BUFFER = buff

BUFFERS ▶ buffer

BUFFEST ▶ buff

BUFFET n, vb **buffets**

BUFFI ▶ buffo

BUFFIER ▶ buffy

BUFFING ▶ buff

BUFFO n (in Italian opera of the 18th century) comic part, esp one for a bass

BUFFOON n

BUFFOS ▶ buffo

BUFFS ▶ buff

BUFFY adj having appearance or texture of buff

BUFO n type of toad **bufos**

BUG n, vb

BUGABOO n imaginary source of fear

BUGBANE n European plant whose flowers are reputed to repel insects

BUGBEAR n thing that causes obsessive anxiety

BUGEYE n oyster-dredging boat **bugeyes**

BUGGAN n evil spirit

buggane, buggans

RUGGED ▸ bug

BUGGERY n anal intercourse

BUGGIER ▸ buggy

BUGGIES ▸ buggy

BUGGIN = buggan

BUGGING ▸ bug

BUGGINS ▸ buggin

BUGGY n light horse-drawn carriage ▷ adj infested with bugs

BUGLE n, vb bugled, bugler, buglers, bugles

BUGLET n small bugle buglets

BUGLING ▸ bugle

BUGLOSS n hairy Eurasian plant with clusters of blue flowers

BUGONG = bogong

BUGONGS ▸ bugong

BUGOUT n act of running away bugouts

BUGS ▸ bug

BUGSEED n form of tumbleweed

BUGSHA = buqsha

BUGSHAS ▸ bugsha

BUGWORT another name for ▸ bugbane

BUHL = boulle

BUHLS ▸ buhl

BUHR ▸ burr

BUHRS ▸ burr

BUHUND n type of Norwegian dog buhunds

BUIBUI n black cloth worn as a shawl by

Muslim women buibuis

BUIK = book

BUIKS ▸ buik

BUILD vb, n builded

BUILDER n person who constructs houses and other buildings

BUILDS ▸ build

BUILDUP n gradual approach to a climax or critical point

BUILT ▸ build

BUIRDLY adj well-built

BUIST vb brand sheep with identification mark buisted, buists

BUKE = book

BUKES ▸ buke

BUKSHEE n person in charge of paying wages bukshi

BUKSHIS ▸ bukshi

BULB n, vb

BULBAR adj of or relating to a bulb, esp the medulla oblongata

BULBED ▸ bulb

BULBEL = bulbil

BULBELS ▸ bulbel

BULBIL n small bulblike organ growing on plants such as the onion and tiger lily bulbils

BULBING ▸ bulb

BULBLET n small bulb at base of main bulb

BULBOUS adj

BULBS ▸ bulb

BULBUL n songbird of tropical Africa and Asia bulbuls

BULGE n, vb bulged,

bulger, bulgers, bulges

BULGHUR = bulgur

BULGIER ▸ bulge

BULGINE = bullgine

BULGING ▸ bulge

BULGUR n kind of dried cracked wheat bulgurs

BULGY ▸ bulge

BULIMIA n eating disorder bulimic, bulimus, bulimy

BULK n, vb bulkage, bulked

BULKER n ship that carries unpackaged cargo bulkers

BULKIER ▸ bulky

BULKILY ▸ bulky

BULKING n expansion of excavated material to a volume greater than that of the excavation from which it came

BULKS ▸ bulk

BULKY adj

BULL adj

BULLA n leaden seal affixed to a papal bull

BULLACE n small Eurasian tree of which the damson is the cultivated form

BULLAE ▸ bulla

BULLARY n boilery for preparing salt

BULLATE adj puckered or blistered in appearance

BULLBAT another name for ▸ nighthawk

BULLDOG n

BULLED ▸ bull

BULLER vb make

bubbling sound **bullers**

BULLET n, vb **bullets**

BULLIED ▶ **bully**

BULLIER ▶ **bully**

BULLIES ▶ **bully**

BULLING ▶ **bull**

BULLION n

BULLISH adj like a bull

BULLOCK n, vb

BULLOSA adj as in **epidermolysis bullosa** type of genetic skin disorder

BULLOUS adj blistered

BULLPEN n large cell where prisoners are confined together temporarily

BULLS ▶ **bull**

BULLY n, vb, adj

BULRUSH n

BULSE n purse or bag for diamonds **bulses**

BULWARK n, vb

BUM n buttocks or anus ▷ vb get by begging ▷ adj of poor quality

BUMALO = **bummalo**

BUMBAG n small bag attached to a belt and worn round the waist **bumbags**

BUMBAZE vb confuse; bewilder

BUMBLE vb speak, do, or move in a clumsy way ▷ n blunder or botch **bumbled, bumbler, bumbles**

BUMBO n drink with gin or rum, nutmeg, lemon juice, etc

BUMBOAT n any small boat used for ferrying

goods to a ship at anchor or at a mooring

BUMBOS ▶ **bumbo**

BUMELIA n thorny shrub

BUMF n official documents or forms **bumfs**

BUMKIN = **bumpkin**

BUMKINS ▶ **bumkin**

BUMMALO n Bombay duck

BUMMED ▶ **bum**

BUMMEL n stroll

BUMMELS ▶ **stroll**

BUMMER n unpleasant or disappointing experience **bummers**

BUMMEST ▶ **bum**

BUMMING ▶ **bum**

BUMMLE Scots variant of ▶ **bumble**

BUMMLED ▶ **bummle**

BUMMLES ▶ **bummle**

BUMMOCK n submerged mass of ice projecting downwards

BUMP vb, n **bumped**

BUMPER n, adj, vb **bumpers**

BUMPH = **bumf**

BUMPHS ▶ **bumph**

BUMPIER ▶ **bumpy**

BUMPILY ▶ **bumpy**

BUMPING ▶ **bump**

BUMPKIN n

BUMPS ▶ **bump**

BUMPY adj having an uneven surface

BUMS ▶ **bum**

BUMSTER adj (of trousers) cut low so as to reveal the top part of the buttocks

BUN n

BUNA n synthetic rubber **bunas**

BUNCE n windfall; boom ▷ vb charge someone too much money **bunced, bunces**

BUNCH n, vb **bunched**

BUNCHES pl n hair tied into two sections

BUNCHY adj composed of or resembling bunches

BUNCING ▶ **bunce**

BUNCO n swindle, esp one by confidence tricksters ▷ vb swindle **buncoed, buncos**

BUND n embankment or German federation ▷ vb form into an embankment **bunde, bunded**

BUNDH = **bandh**

BUNDHS ▶ **bundh**

BUNDIED ▶ **bundy**

BUNDIES ▶ **bundy** **bunding, bundist**

BUNDLE n, vb **bundled, bundler, bundles**

BUNDOOK n rifle

BUNDS ▶ **bund**

BUNDT n type of sweet cake **bundts**

BUNDU n largely uninhabited wild region far from towns **bundus**

BUNDY n time clock at work ▷ vb register arrival or departure from work on a time clock

BUNG n, vb **bunged**

BUNGEE n strong elastic

cable **bungees**

BUNGEY n firework **bungers**

BUNGEY = bungee

BUNGEYS ▶ bungey

BUNGIE = bungee

BUNGIES ▶ bungy

BUNGING ▶ bung

BUNGLE vb, n bungled, bungler, bungles

BUNGS ▶ bung

BUNGY ▶ bungee

BUNIA = bunnia

BUNIAS ▶ bunia

BUNION n bunions

BUNJE = bungee

BUNJEE = bungee

BUNJEES ▶ bunjee

BUNJIE = bungee

BUNJIES ▶ bunjie

BUNJY = bungee

BUNK n, vb bunked

BUNKER n, vb bunkers

BUNKING ▶ bunk

BUNKO = bunco

BUNKOED ▶ bunko

BUNKOS ▶ bunko

BUNKS ▶ bunk

BUNKUM n nonsense bunkums

BUNN = bun

BUNNET = bonnet

BUNNETS ▶ bunnet

BUNNIA n Hindu shopkeeper **bunnias**

BUNNIES ▶ bunny

BUNNS ▶ bunn

BUNNY n child's word for a rabbit

BUNRAKU n Japanese puppet theatre

BUNS pl n buttocks

BUNSEN n as in bunsen

burner gas burner used in scientific labs **bunsens**

BUNT vb (of an animal) butt (something) with the head or horns ▷ n act or an instance of bunting

BUNTAL n straw obtained from leaves of the talipot palm **buntals**

BUNTED ▶ bunt

BUNTER n batter who deliberately taps ball lightly **bunters**

BUNTIER ▶ bunt

BUNTING n

BUNTS ▶ bunt

BUNTY ▶ bunt

BUNYA n tall dome-shaped Australian coniferous tree **bunyas**

BUNYIP n bunyips

BUOY n, vb

BUOYAGE n system of buoys

BUOYANT adj

BUOYED ▶ buoy

BUOYING ▶ buoy

BUOYS ▶ buoy

BUPKES = bubkes

BUPKIS = bubkis

BUPKUS = bubkes

BUPPIE n affluent young Black person

BUPPIES ▶ buppy

BUPPY ▶ buppie

BUQSHA n former Yemeni coin **buqshas**

BUR ▶ burr

BURA = buran

BURAN n blizzard, with

the wind blowing from the north and reaching gale force **burans**

BURAS ▶ bura

BURB n suburb

BURBLE vb, n burbled, burbler, burbles

BURBLY adj burbling

BURBOT n freshwater fish of the cod family that has barbels around its mouth **burbots**

BURBS ▶ burb

BURD Scots form of ▶ bird

BURDASH n fringed sash worn over coat

BURDEN n, vb burdens

BURDIE Scots form of ▶ birdie

BURDIES ▶ burdie

BURDOCK n weed with prickly burrs

BURDS ▶ burd

BUREAU n bureaus, bureaux

BURET = burette

BURETS ▶ buret

BURETTE n glass tube for dispensing known volumes of fluids

BURG n fortified town

BURGAGE n (in England) tenure of land or tenement in a town or city, which originally involved a fixed money rent

BURGEE n triangular or swallow-tailed flag flown from the mast of a merchant ship **burgees**

BURGEON vb, n

BURGER n hamburger **burgers**

BURGESS n (in England) citizen or freeman of a borough

BURGH n Scottish borough **burghal**

BURGHER n citizen

BURGHS ▸ burgh

BURGHUL = bulgur

BURGLAR n, vb

BURGLE vb burgled, **burgles**

BURGOO n porridge **burgoos, burgout**

BURGS ▸ burg

BURHEL = bharal

BURHELS ▸ burhel

BURIAL n burials

BURIED ▸ bury

BURIER n person or thing that buries **buriers**

BURIES ▸ bury

BURIN n steel chisel used for engraving metal, wood, or marble **burins**

BURITI n type of palm tree **buritis**

BURK = berk

BURKA = burqa

BURKAS ▸ burka

BURKE vb murder in such a way as to leave no marks on the body, usually by suffocation **burked, burker, burkers, burkes**

BURKHA n all-enveloping garment worn by Muslim women

burkhas

BURKING ▸ burke

BURKITE ▸ burke

BURKS ▸ burk

BURL n small knot or lump in wool ▷ vb remove the burls from (cloth)

BURLAP n coarse fabric woven from jute, hemp, or the like **burlaps**

BURLED ▸ burl

BURLER ▸ burl

BURLERS ▸ burl

BURLESK = burlesque

BURLEY = berley

BURLEYS ▸ burley

BURLIER ▸ burly

BURLILY ▸ burly

BURLING ▸ burl

BURLS ▸ burl

BURLY adj

BURN vb, n burned

BURNER n part of a stove or lamp that produces the flame **burners**

BURNET n type of rose **burnets**

BURNIE n sideburn **burnies**

BURNING ▸ burn

BURNISH vb, n

BURNOUS n long circular cloak with a hood, worn esp by Arabs

BURNOUT n failure of a mechanical device from excessive heating

BURNS ▸ burn

BURNT ▸ burn

BUROO n government office from which

unemployment benefit is distributed **buroos**

BURP n, vb burped

BURPEE n type of physical exercise movement **burpees**

BURPING ▸ burp

BURPS ▸ burp

BURQA n garment worn by Muslim women in public **burqas**

> This Arab garment illustrates the fact that Q doesn't always have to be followed by U. It has several variants including **burka** and **burkha**.

BURR n small rotary file ▷ vb form a rough edge on (a workpiece) **burred**

BURREL = bharal

BURRELL variant of ▸ bharal

BURRELS ▸ burrel

BURRER n person who removes burrs **burrers**

BURRHEL = burrel

BURRIER ▸ burry

BURRING ▸ burr

BURRITO n tortilla folded over a filling of minced beef, chicken, cheese, or beans

BURRO n donkey, esp one used as a pack animal **burros**

BURROW n, vb burrows

BURRS ▸ burr

BURRY adj full of or covered in burs

BURS ▸ burr

BURSA n small fluid-filled sac that reduces friction between movable parts of the body **bursae, bursal**

BURSAR n **bursars**

BURSARY n

BURSAS ▸ bursa

BURSATE ▸ bursa

BURSE n flat case used at Mass as a container for the corporal

BURSEED n type of plant

BURSERA adj of a type of gum tree

BURSES ▸ burse

BURST vb, n, adj **bursted, bursten, burster, bursts**

BURTHEN archaic word for ▸ burden

BURTON n type of hoisting tackle **burtons**

BURWEED n any of various plants that bear burs, such as the burdock

BURY vb **burying**

BUS n, vb

BUSBAR n electrical conductor **busbars**

BUSBIES ▸ busby

BUSBOY n waiter's assistant **busboys**

BUSBY n tall fur hat worn by some soldiers

BUSED ▸ bus

BUSERA n Ugandan alcoholic drink made from millet:

sometimes mixed with honey **buseras**

BUSES ▸ bus

BUSGIRL n waiter's assistant

BUSH n, vb

BUSHED adj extremely tired

BUSHEL n obsolete unit of measure equal to 8 gallons ▸ vb alter or mend (a garment) **bushels**

BUSHER ▸ bush

BUSHERS ▸ bush

BUSHES ▸ bush

BUSHFLY n small black Australian fly that breeds in faeces and dung

BUSHIDO n feudal code of the Japanese samurai

BUSHIE = bushy

BUSHIER ▸ bushy

BUSHIES ▸ bushy

BUSHILY ▸ bushy

BUSHING = bush

BUSHMAN n **bushmen**

BUSHPIG n wild brown or black forest pig of tropical Africa and Madagascar

BUSHTIT n small grey active North American songbird

BUSHWA n nonsense **bushwah, bushwas**

BUSHY adj, n

BUSIED, busier, busies, busiest ▸ busy

BUSILY adv in a busy manner

BUSING ▸ bus

BUSINGS ▸ bus

BUSK vb act as a busker ▸ n strip of whalebone, wood, steel, etc, inserted into the front of a corset **busked, busker, buskers**

BUSKET n bouquet **buskets**

BUSKIN n (formerly) sandal-like covering

BUSKING ▸ busk

BUSKINS ▸ buskin

BUSKS ▸ busk

BUSKY = bosky

BUSLOAD n number of people bus carries

BUSMAN n person who drives a bus **busmen**

BUSS archaic or dialect word for ▸ kiss

BUSSED ▸ bus

BUSSES ▸ bus

BUSSING ▸ bus

BUSSU n type of palm tree **bussus**

BUST n, adj, vb

BUSTARD n type of bird

BUSTED = bust

BUSTEE = basti

BUSTEES ▸ bustee

BUSTER n person or thing destroying something as specified **busters**

BUSTI = basti

BUSTIC n type of small American tree **bustics**

BUSTIER n close-fitting strapless women's top

BUSTING ▸ bust

BUSTIS ▸ busti

BUSTLE vb, n **bustled, bustler, bustles**

BUSTS ▶ bust
BUSTY adj (of a woman) having a prominent bust
BUSUUTI n garment worn by Ugandan women
BUSY adj, vb busying
BUT prep, adj, n
BUTANE n gas used for fuel butanes
BUTANOL n colourless substance
BUTCH adj markedly or aggressively masculine ▶ n lesbian who is noticeably masculine
BUTCHER n, vb
BUTCHES ▶ butch
BUTE n drug used illegally to dope horses
BUTENE n pungent colourless gas butenes
BUTEO n type of American hawk buteos
BUTES ▶ bute
BUTLE vb act as butler butled
BUTLER n, vb butlers
BUTLERY n butler's room
BUTLES ▶ butle
BUTLING ▶ butle
BUTMENT = abutment
BUTS ▶ but
BUTT n, vb
BUTTALS n abuttal
BUTTE n isolated steep flat-topped hill
BUTTED ▶ butt
BUTTER n, vb butters

BUTTERY n (in some universities) room in which food and drink are sold to students ▶ adj containing, like, or coated with butter
BUTTES ▶ butte
BUTTIES ▶ butty
BUTTING ▶ butt
BUTTLE vb act as butler buttled, buttles
BUTTOCK n either of the two fleshy masses that form the human rump ▶ vb perform a kind of wrestling manoeuvre on a person
BUTTON n, vb
BUTTONS n page boy
BUTTONY ▶ button
BUTTS ▶ butt
BUTTY n sandwich
BUTUT n Gambian monetary unit worth one hundredth of a dalasi bututs
BUTYL adj of or containing any of four isomeric forms of the group C_4H_9– ▶ n of, consisting of, or containing any of four isomeric forms of the group C_4H_9– butyls
BUTYRAL n type of resin
BUTYRIC adj as in butyric acid type of acid
BUTYRIN n colourless liquid found in butter
BUTYRYL n radical of butyric acid
BUVETTE n roadside café

BUXOM adj buxomer, buxomly
BUY vb, n buyable
BUYBACK n repurchase by a company of some or all of its shares from an early investor
BUYER n customer buyers
BUYING n as in panic buying
BUYINGS ▶ buying
BUYOFF n purchase buyoffs
BUYOUT n purchase of a company buyouts
BUYS ▶ buy
BUZUKI = bouzouki
BUZUKIA ▶ buzuki
BUZUKIS ▶ buzuki
BUZZ n, vb
BUZZARD n
BUZZCUT n very short haircut
BUZZED ▶ buzz
BUZZER n buzzers
BUZZES ▶ buzz
BUZZIER ▶ buzzy
BUZZING ▶ buzz
BUZZWIG n bushy wig
BUZZY adj making a buzzing sound
BWANA n (in E Africa) master, often used as a respectful form of address bwanas
BWAZI = buaze
BWAZIS ▶ bwazi
BY prep, adv, n
BYCATCH n unwanted fish and sea animals caught along with the desired kind

BYCOKET n former italian high-crowned hat

BYDE = bide

BYDED ▶ byde

BYDES ▶ byde

BYDING ▶ byde

BYE n situation where a player or team wins a round by having no opponent ▷ interj goodbye ▷ sentence substitute goodbye

BYELAW n rule made by a local authority **byelaws**

BYES ▶ bye

BYGONE adj **bygones**

BYKE n bicycle; byked; bykes, byking

BYLANE n side lane or alley off a road **bylanes**

BYLAW n rule made by a local authority **bylaws**

BYLINE n line under the title of a newspaper or magazine article giving the author's name ▷ vb give a byline to **bylined, byliner,**

bylines

BYLIVE = bellve

BYNAME n nickname **bynames**

BYNEMPT ▶ bename

BYPASS n, vb bypast

BYPATH n little-used path or track, esp in the country **bypaths**

BYPLACE n private place

BYPLAY n secondary action or talking carried on apart while the main action proceeds **byplays**

BYRE n shelter for cows

BYREMAN n man who works in byre **byremen**

BYRES ▶ byre

BYRL = birl

BYRLADY interj short for By Our Lady

BYRLAW = bylaw

BYRLAWS ▶ byrlaw

BYRLED ▶ byrl

BYRLING ▶ byrl

BYRLS ▶ byrl

BYRNIE n archaic word for coat of mail **byrnies**

BYROAD n secondary or slde road **byroads**

BYROOM n private room **byrooms**

BYS ▶ by

BYSSAL adj of mollusc's byssus

BYSSI ▶ byssus

BYSSINE adj made from flax

BYSSOID adj consisting of fine fibres

BYSSUS n mass of threads that attaches an animal to a hard surface

BYTALK n trivial conversation **bytalks**

BYTE n bytes

BYWAY n minor road **byways**

BYWONER n poor tenant-farmer

BYWORD n **bywords**

BYWORK n work done outside usual working hours **byworks**

BYZANT = bezant

BYZANTS ▶ byzant

Cc

C can be a tricky letter to use, especially as it only forms a single two-letter word **ch**. But if you remember this, you won't waste time racking your brains for two-letter words. There are, however, plenty of good three-letter words beginning with **C**. **Cox** scores 12 points, while **caw**, **cow**, and **coy** are each worth 8 and **caz**, **coz**, and **cuz** are worth 14. It's also a good idea to remember the short words starting with **C** that don't contain any vowels: **cly** and **cwm** as well as **ch**.

CAA *a Scot word for*
▶ **call**

CAAED ▶ **caa**

CAAING ▶ **caa**

CAAS ▶ **caa**

CAB *n, vb*

CABA = **cabas**

CABAL *n, vb*

CABALA *a variant spelling of* ▶ **kabbalah**

CABALAS ▶ **cabala**

CABALS ▶ **cabal**

CABANA *n* tent used as a dressing room by the sea **cabanas**

CABARET *n*

CABAS *n* reticule

CABBAGE *n, vb* **cabbagy**

CABBALA *a variant spelling of* ▶ **kabbalah**

CABBED ▶ **cab**

CABBIE *n* taxi driver **cabbies**

CABBING ▶ **cab** **cabby**

CABER *n* tree trunk

tossed in competition at Highland games **cabers**

CABEZON *n* large fish

CABILDO *n* Spanish municipal council

CABIN *n, vb* **cabined**

CABINET *n*

CABINS ▶ **cabin**

CABLE *n, vb* **cabled**

CABLER *n* cable broadcasting company **cablers**

CABLES ▶ **cable**

CABLET *n* small cable **cablets**

CABLING ▶ **cable**

CABMAN *n* driver of a cab **cabmen**

CABOB *vb* roast on a skewer **cabobs**

CABOC *n* type of Scottish cheese **cabocs**

CABOMBA *n* type of aquatic plant

CABOOSE *n* guard's van on a train

CABOVER *adj* of a truck or lorry in which the cab is over the engine

CABRE *adj* heraldic term designating an animal rearing

CABRIE *n* pronghorn antelope **cabries**

CABRIO *short for* ▶ **cabriolet**

CABRIOS ▶ **cabrio**

CABRIT *n* pronghorn antelope **cabrits**

CABS ▶ **cab**

CACA *n* heroin

CACAO = **cocoa**

CACAOS = **cocoa**

CACAS ▶ **caca**

CACHACA *n* white Brazilian rum made from sugar cane

CACHE *n, vb* **cached, caches**

CACHET n, vb **cachets**

CACHEXY = **cachexia**

CACHING ▶ **cache**

CACHOU = **catechu**

CACHOUS ▶ **catechu**

CACIQUE n American Indian chief in a Spanish-speaking region

CACKIER ▶ **cacky**

CACKLE vb, n **cackled, cackler, cackles**

CACKY adj of or like excrement

CACODYL n oily poisonous liquid with a strong garlic smell

CACOEPY n bad or mistaken pronunciation

CACOLET n seat fitted to the back of a mule

CACONYM n erroneous name

CACOON n large seed of the sword-bean **cacoons**

CACTI ▶ **cactus**

CACTOID adj resembling a cactus

CACTUS n

CACUMEN n apex

CAD n

CADAGA n eucalyptus tree **cadagas, cadagi**

CADAGIS ▶ **cadagi**

CADAVER n corpse

CADDICE = **caddis**

CADDIE n, vb **caddied, caddies**

CADDIS n type of coarse woollen yarn, braid, or fabric

CADDISH ▶ **cad**

CADDY = **caddie**

CADDYSS = **caddis**

CADE n juniper tree ▷ adj (of a young animal) left by its mother and reared by humans

CADEAU n present **cadeaux**

CADEE old form of ▶ **cadet**

CADEES ▶ **cadee**

CADELLE n type of beetle that feeds on flour, grain, and other stored foods

CADENCE n, vb **cadency**

CADENT adj having cadence

CADENZA n

CADES ▶ **cade**

CADET n **cadets**

CADGE vb **cadged**

CADGER n person who cadges **cadgers**

CADGES ▶ **cadge**

CADGIER ▶ **cadgy**

CADGING ▶ **cadge**

CADGY adj cheerful

CADI n judge in a Muslim community

CADIE n messenger **cadies**

CADIS ▶ **cadi**

CADMIC ▶ **cadmium**

CADMIUM n

CADRANS n instrument used in gemcutting

CADRE n group of people trained to form the core of a political or military unit **cadres**

CADS ▶ **cad**

CADUAC n windfall **caduacs**

CADUCEI ▶ **caduceus**

CAECA ▶ **caecum**

CAECAL ▶ **caecum**

CAECUM n pouch at the beginning of the large intestine

CAEOMA n aecium in some rust fungi that has no surrounding membrane **caeomas**

CAERULE = **cerule**

CAESAR n any emperor, autocrat, dictator, or other powerful ruler **caesars**

CAESE interj Shakespearean interjection

CAESIUM n

CAESTUS = **cestus**

CAESURA n

CAFARD n feeling of severe depression **cafards**

CAFE n small or inexpensive restaurant serving light refreshments **cafes**

CAFF n café

CAFFEIN = **caffeine**

CAFFILA n caravan train

CAFFS ▶ **caff**

CAFILA = **caffila**

CAFILAS ▶ **cafila**

CAFTAN = **kaftan**

CAFTANS ▶ **kaftan**

CAG = **cagoule**

CAGANER n figure of a squatting defecating person

CAGE n, vb **caged**

CAGEFUL n amount which fills a cage to capacity

CAGER n basketball player **cagers**

CAGES ▸ cage

CAGEY adj cagier, cagiest, cagily

CAGING ▸ cage

CAGMAG adj done shoddily ▸ vb chat idly **cagmags**

CAGOT n member of a class of French outcasts **cagots**

CAGOUL = cagoule

CAGOULE n

CAGOULS ▸ cagoul

CAGS ▸ cag

CAGY = cagey

CAHIER n notebook **cahiers**

CAHOOT n partnership **cahoots**

CAHOW n Bermuda petrel **cahows**

CAID n Moroccan district administrator **caids**

CAILLE n quail **cailles**

CAIMAC = caimacam

CAIMACS ▸ caimac

CAIMAN = cayman

CAIMANS ▸ caiman

CAIN n (in Scotland and Ireland) payment in kind **cains**

CAIQUE n long narrow light rowing skiff used on the Bosporus **caiques**

CAIRD n travelling tinker **cairds**

CAIRN n

CAIRNED adj marked by a cairn

CAIRNS ▸ cairn

CAIRNY adj covered with cairns

CAISSON ▸ cofferdam

CAITIFF n cowardly or base person ▸ adj cowardly

CAITIVE n captive

CAJAPUT = cajuput

CAJEPUT = cajuput

CAJOLE vb cajoled, cajoler, cajoles

CAJON n Peruvian wooden box used as a drum **cajones**

CAJUN n music of the Cajun people

CAJUPUT n small tree or shrub

CAKE n, vb caked, cakes, cakey, cakier, cakiest, caking, caky

CALALOO = calalu

CALALU n edible leaves of various plants **calalus**

CALAMAR n any member of the squid family

CALAMI ▸ calamus

CALAMUS n tropical Asian palm

CALANDO adv (to be performed) with gradually decreasing tone and speed

CALASH n horse-drawn carriage with low wheels and a folding top

CALATHI ▸ calathus

CALCAR n spur or spurlike process **calcars**

CALCED adj wearing shoes

CALCES ▸ calx

CALCIC adj of, containing, or concerned with lime or calcium

CALCIFY vb harden by the depositing of calcium salts

CALCINE vb oxidize (a substance) by heating

CALCITE n colourless or white form of calcium carbonate

CALCIUM n

CALCULI ▸ calculus

CALDERA n large basin-shaped crater at the top of a volcano

CALDRON = cauldron

CALECHE a variant of ▸ calash

CALEFY vb make warm

CALENDS pl n first day of each month in the ancient Roman calendar

CALESA n horse-drawn buggy **calesas**

CALF n calfs

CALIBER = calibre

CALIBRE n

CALICES ▸ calix

CALICHE n bed of sand or clay in arid regions

CALICLE = calycle

CALICO n calicos

CALID adj warm

CALIF = caliph

CALIFS ▸ calif

CALIGO n speck on the cornea causing poor vision **caligos**

CALIMA n Saharan dust-storm **calimas**
CALIPEE n edible part of the turtle found next to the lower shell
CALIPER = **calliper**
CALIPH n Muslim ruler **caliphs**
CALIVER n type of musket
CALIX n cup
CALK = **caulk**
CALKED, calker, calkers, calkin, calking, calkins, calks ► **calk**
CALL vb name ▷ n cry, shout
CALLA n S African plant with a white funnel-shaped spathe enclosing a yellow spadix
CALLAIS n type of green stone
CALLAN = **callant**
CALLANS ► **callan**
CALLANT n youth
CALLAS ► **calla**
CALLBOY n person who notifies actors when it is time to go on stage
CALLED ► **call**
CALLEE n computer function being used **callees**
CALLER n person or thing that calls, esp a person who makes a brief visit ▷ adj (of food, esp fish) fresh **callers**
CALLET n scold **callets**
CALLID adj cunning
CALLING n

CALLOP n edible Australian freshwater fish **callops**
CALLOSE n carbohydrate found in plants
CALLOUS adj, vb
CALLOW adj, n **callows**
CALLS ► **call**
CALLUNA n type of heather
CALLUS n, vb
CALM adj, n, vb
CALMANT n sedative
CALMED ► **calm**
CALMER ► **calm**
CALMEST ► **calm**
CALMIER ► **calmy**
CALMING ► **calm**
CALMLY ► **calm**
CALMS ► **calm**
CALMY adj tranquil
CALO n military servant
CALOMEL n colourless tasteless powder
CALORIC adj of heat or calories ▷ n hypothetical fluid formerly postulated as the embodiment of heat
CALORIE n **calory**
CALOS ► **calo**
CALOTTE n skullcap worn by Roman Catholic clergy
CALOYER n monk of the Greek Orthodox Church, esp of the Basilian Order
CALP n type of limestone
CALPA n Hindu unit of time
CALPAC n large black

brimless hat **calpack, calpacs**
CALPAIN n type of enzyme
CALPAS ► **calpa**
CALPS ► **calp**
CALQUE ► **caulk**
CALQUED ► **calque**
CALQUES ► **calque**
CALTHA n marsh marigold **calthas**
CALTRAP = **caltrop**
CALTROP n floating Asian plant
CALUMBA n Mozambiquan root used for medicinal purposes
CALUMET n peace pipe
CALUMNY n
CALVARY n representation of Christ's crucifixion
CALVE vb **calved**
CALVER vb prepare fish for cooking **calvers**
CALVES ► **calf**
CALVING ► **calve**
CALX n powdery metallic oxide formed when an ore or mineral is roasted **calxes**
CALYCES ► **calyx**
CALYCLE n cup-shaped structure, as in the coral skeleton
CALYPSO n
CALYX n **calyxes**
CALZONE n folded pizza filled with cheese, tomatoes, etc **calzoni**
CAM n, vb
CAMA n hybrid offspring

of a camel and a llama

CAMAIEU n cameo

CAMAIL n covering of chain mail **camails**

CAMAN n wooden stick used to hit the ball in shinty **camans**

CAMARON n shrimp

CAMAS = camass

CAMASES ▸ camas

CAMASH = camass

CAMASS n type of North American plant

CAMBER n, vb cambers

CAMBIA ▸ cambium

CAMBIAL ▸ cambium

CAMBISM ▸ cambist

CAMBIST n dealer or expert in foreign exchange

CAMBIUM n meristem that increases the girth of stems and roots

CAMBOGE n type of gum resin

CAMBREL a variant of ▸ gambrel

CAMBRIC n fine white linen fabric

CAME ▸ come

CAMEL n

CAMELIA = camellia

CAMELID adj of or relating to camels ▸ n any animal of the camel family

CAMELOT n supposedly idyllic period or age

CAMELRY n troops mounted on camels

CAMELS ▸ camel

CAMEO n, vb cameoed, cameos

CAMERA n camerae

CAMERAL adj of or relating to a judicial or legislative chamber

CAMERAS ▸ camera

CAMES ▸ canvas

CAMESE = camise

CAMESES ▸ camese

CAMION n lorry, or, esp formerly, a large dray camions

CAMIS n light robe

CAMISA n smock camisas

CAMISE n loose light shirt, smock, or tunic originally worn in the Middle Ages camises

CAMISIA n surplice

CAMLET n tough waterproof cloth camlets

CAMMED ▸ cam

CAMMIE n webcam award **cammies**

CAMMING ▸ cam

CAMO n short for camouflage

CAMOGIE n form of hurling played by women

CAMOODI a Caribbean name for ▸ anaconda

CAMORRA n secret criminal group

CAMOS ▸ camo

CAMOTE n type of sweet potato camotes

CAMP vb, adj

CAMPANA n bell or bell shape

CAMPED ▸ camp

CAMPER n person who lives or temporarily

stays in a tent, cabin, etc **campers**

CAMPERY n campness

CAMPEST ▸ camp

CAMPHOL another word for ▸ borneol

CAMPHOR n

CAMPI ▸ campo

CAMPIER ▸ campy

CAMPILY ▸ campy

CAMPING ▸ camp

CAMPION n red, pink, or white wild flower

CAMPLE vb argue campled, **camples**

CAMPLY ▸ camp

CAMPO n level or undulating savanna country

CAMPONG n in Malaysia, a village

CAMPOS ▸ campo

CAMPOUT n camping trip

CAMPS ▸ camp

CAMPUS n, vb

CAMPY adj effeminate

CAMS ▸ cam

CAMSHO adj crooked

CAMUS n type of loose robe camuses

CAMWOOD n W African leguminous tree

CAN vb, n

CANADA n canada goose **canadas**

CANAKIN = cannikin

CANAL n, vb canaled, canals

CANAPE n small piece of bread or toast with a savoury topping canapes

CANARD n false report

canards

CANARY n, vb

CANASTA n card game like rummy, played with two packs

CANBANK n container for receiving cans for recycling

CANCAN n lively high-kicking dance performed by a female group **cancans**

CANCEL vb, n **cancels**

CANCER n **cancers**

CANCHA n toasted maize **canchas**

CANDELA n

CANDENT adj emitting light as a result of being heated to a high temperature

CANDID adj, n

CANDIDA n yeastlike parasitic fungus which causes thrush

CANDIDS ▶ candid

CANDIE n South Indian unit of weight

CANDIED adj

CANDIES ▶ candy

CANDIRU n parasitic freshwater catfish of the Amazon region

CANDLE n, vb **candled, candler, candles**

CANDOCK n type of water lily, or horsetail

CANDOR = candour

CANDORS ▶ candor

CANDOUR n honesty and straightforwardness

CANDY n, vb

CANE n, vb **caned**

CANEH n Hebrew unit of length **canehs**

CANELLA n fragrant cinnamon-like inner bark of a W Indian tree, used as a spice and in medicine

CANER ▶ cane

CANERS ▶ cane

CANES ▶ cane

CANFUL n amount a can will hold **canfuls**

CANG = cangue

CANGLE vb wrangle **cangled, cangles**

CANGS ▶ cang

CANGUE n (formerly in China) a wooden collar worn as a punishment **cangues**

CANID n animal of the dog family **canids**

CANIER ▶ cany

CANIEST ▶ cany

CANIKIN = cannikin

CANINE adj, n **canines**

CANING n beating with a cane as a punishment **canings**

CANKER n, vb **cankers**

CANKERY adj like a canker

CANKLE n thickened calfs on an overweight person **cankles**

CANN vb direct a ship's steering

CANNA n type of tropical plant

CANNACH n cotton grass

CANNAE vb can not

CANNAS ▶ canna

CANNED ▶ can

CANNEL n type of dull coal **cannels**

CANNER n person or organization whose job is to can foods **canners**

CANNERY n factory where food is canned

CANNIE = canny

CANNIER ▶ canny

CANNILY ▶ canny

CANNING ▶ can

CANNOLI n Sicilian pudding of pasta shells filled with sweetened ricotta

CANNON n, vb **cannons**

CANNOT vb

CANNS ▶ cann

CANNULA n narrow tube for insertion into a bodily cavity

CANNY adj, adv

CANOE n, vb **canoed, canoer, canoers, canoes**

CANOLA n cooking oil extracted from a variety of rapeseed **canolas**

CANON n

CANONIC = canonical

CANONRY n office, benefice, or status of a canon

CANONS ▶ canon

CANOPIC adj of ancient Egyptian vase

CANOPY n, vb

CANS ▶ can

CANSFUL ▶ canful

CANSO n love song **cansos**

CANST vb form of 'can' used with the pronoun *thou* or its relative form

CANT n, vb, adj

CANTAL n French cheese

CANTALA n tropical American plant, the agave

CANTALS ▸ cantal

CANTAR variant form of ▸ kantar

CANTARS ▸ cantar

CANTATA n musical work consisting of arias, duets, and choruses

CANTATE n 98th psalm sung as a nonmetrical hymn

CANTDOG = canthook

CANTED ▸ cant

CANTEEN n

CANTER vb move at gait between trot and gallop **canters**

CANTEST ▸ cant

CANTHAL ▸ canthus

CANTHI ▸ canthus

CANTHUS n inner or outer corner or angle of the eye

CANTIC ▸ cant

CANTICO vb dance as part of an act of worship

CANTIER ▸ canty

CANTILY ▸ canty

CANTINA n bar or wine shop, esp in a Spanish-speaking country

CANTING ▸ cant

CANTION n song

CANTLE n back part of a saddle that slopes upwards ▸ vb set up, or stand, on high **cantled, cantles**

CANTLET n piece

CANTO = cantus

CANTON n, vb **cantons**

CANTOR n man employed to lead services in a synagogue **cantors**

CANTOS ▸ canto

CANTRAP = cantraip

CANTRED n district comprising a hundred villages **cantref**

CANTRIP n magic spell ▸ adj (of an effect) produced by black magic

CANTS ▸ cant

CANTUS n medieval form of church singing

CANTY adj lively

CANULA = cannula

CANULAE ▸ canula

CANULAR adj shaped like a cannula

CANULAS ▸ canula

CANVAS n, vb

CANVASS vb, n

CANY adj cane-like

CANYON n **canyons**

CANZONA n type of 16th- or 17th-century contrapuntal music

CANZONE n Provençal or Italian lyric, often in praise of love or beauty **canzoni**

CAP n, vb

CAPA n type of Spanish cloak

CAPABLE adj **capably**

CAPAS ▸ capa

CAPE n, vb **caped**

CAPELAN another word for ▸ capelin

CAPELET n small cape

CAPELIN n type of small marine food fish

CAPER n, vb **capered, caperer**

CAPERS pl n pickled flower buds of a Mediterranean shrub used in sauces

CAPES ▸ cape

CAPEX n capital expenditure **capexes**

CAPFUL n quantity held by a (usually bottle) cap **capfuls**

CAPH n letter of the Hebrew alphabet **caphs**

CAPI ▸ capo

CAPIAS n (formerly) a writ directing the arrest of a named person

CAPING ▸ cape

CAPITA ▸ caput

CAPITAL n, adj

CAPITAN another name for ▸ hogfish

CAPITOL n (in America) building housing the state legislature

CAPIZ n bivalve shell of a mollusc **capizes**

CAPLE n horse **caples**

CAPLESS ▸ cap

CAPLET n medicinal tablet, usually oval in shape, coated in a soluble substance

caplets

CAPLIN = capelin

CAPLINS ▶ caplin

CAPO n device used to raise the pitch of a stringed instrument

CAPON n castrated cock fowl fattened for eating **capons**

CAPORAL n strong coarse dark tobacco

CAPOS ▶ capo

CAPOT n winning of all the tricks by one player ▷ vb score a capot (against)

CAPOTE n long cloak or soldier's coat, usually with a hood **capotes**

CAPOTS ▶ capot

CAPOUCH = capuche

CAPPED, capper, cappers, capping ▶ cap

CAPRATE n any salt of capric acid

CAPRIC adj (of a type of acid) smelling of goats

CAPRICE = capriccio

CAPRID n any member of the goat family **caprids**

CAPRIFY vb induce figs to ripen

CAPRINE adj of or resembling a goat

CAPRIS pl n women's tight-fitting trousers

CAPROCK n layer of rock that overlies a salt dome

CAPROIC adj as in caproic acid oily acid

found in milk

CAPS ▶ cap

CAPSID n outer protein coat of a mature virus **capsids**

CAPSIZE vb

CAPSTAN n rotating cylinder round which a ship's rope is wound

CAPSULE n, adj, vb

CAPTAIN n, vb

CAPTAN n type of fungicide **captans**

CAPTION n, vb

CAPTIVE n, adj, vb

CAPTOR n **captors**

CAPTURE vb, n

CAPUCHE n large hood or cowl, esp that worn by Capuchin friars

CAPUERA variant of > capoeira

CAPUL = caple

CAPULS ▶ capul

CAPUT n main or most prominent part of an organ or structure

CAR n

CARABAO n water buffalo

CARABID n type of beetle

CARABIN = carbine

CARACAL n lynx with reddish fur, which inhabits deserts of N Africa and S Asia

CARACK = carrack

CARACKS ▶ carrack

CARACOL = caracole

CARACT n sign or symbol **caracts**

CARACUL n fur from the

skins of newly born lambs of the karakul sheep

CARAFE n **carafes**

CARAMBA n Spanish interjection similar to 'wow!'

CARAMEL n, vb

CARANNA n gumlike substance

CARAP n crabwood

CARAPAX n carapace

CARAPS ▶ carap

CARAT n

CARATE n tropical disease **carates**

CARATS ▶ carat

CARAUNA = caranna

CARAVAN n, vb

CARAVEL n two- or three-masted sailing ship

CARAWAY n

CARB n carbohydrate

CARBARN n streetcar depot

CARBEEN n Australian eucalyptus tree

CARBENE n neutral divalent free radical, such as methylene: CH_2

CARBIDE n

CARBIES ▶ carby

CARBINE n

CARBO n carbohydrate

CARBON n **carbons**

CARBORA n former name for the koala

CARBOS ▶ carbo

CARBOY n large bottle with a protective casing **carboys**

CARBS ▶ carb

CARBY n short for carburettor

CARCAKE n (formerly, in Scotland) a cake traditionally made for Shrove Tuesday

CARCASE ▶ carcass

CARCASS n, vb

CARCEL n French unit of light **carcels**

CARD n, vb

CARDAN n as in **cardan joint** type of universal joint

CARDECU n old French coin (a quarter of a crown)

CARDED ▶ card

CARDER ▶ card

CARDERS ▶ card

CARDI n cardigan

CARDIA n lower oesophageal sphincter

CARDIAC adj, n

CARDIAE ▶ cardia

CARDIAS ▶ cardia

CARDIE short for ▶ cardigan

CARDIES ▶ cardie

CARDING ▶ card

CARDIO adj exercising heart ▷ n cardiovascular exercise **cardios**

CARDIS ▶ cardi

CARDON n variety of cactus **cardons**

CARDOON n thistle-like S European plant

CARDS ▶ card

CARDUUS n thistle

CARDY = **cardie**

CARE vb, n **cared**

CAREEN vb tilt over to one side **careens**

CAREER n, vb, adj **careers**

CAREFUL adj

CAREME n period of Lent **caremes**

CARER n person who looks after someone who is ill or old, often a relative **carers**

CARES ▶ care

CARESS n, vb

CARET n proofreading symbol **carets**

CAREX n any member of the sedge family

CARFARE n fare that a passenger is charged for a ride on a bus, etc

CARFAX n place where principal roads or streets intersect **carfox**

CARFUL n maximum number of people a car will hold **carfuls**

CARGO n, vb **cargoed, cargoes, cargos**

CARHOP n waiter or waitress at a drive-in restaurant ▷ vb work as a carhop **carhops**

CARIAMA another word for ▶ **seriema**

CARIBE n piranha **caribes**

CARIBOU n

CARICES ▶ carex

CARIED adj (of teeth) decayed

CARIERE obsolete word for ▶ **career**

CARIES n

CARINA n keel-like part or ridge **carinae**

CARINAL adj keel-like

CARINAS ▶ carina

CARING adj feeling or showing care and compassion for other people ▷ n practice or profession of providing social or medical care **carings**

CARIOCA n Brazilian dance similar to the samba

CARIOLE n small open two-wheeled horse-drawn vehicle

CARIOSE n carious

CARIOUS adj (of teeth or bone) affected with caries

CARITAS n divine love; charity

CARJACK vb

CARK vb break down **carked, carking, carks**

CARL another word for ▶ churl

CARLE n carl

CARLES ▶ carle

CARLESS ▶ car

CARLIN ▶ carling

CARLINE ▶ carling

CARLING n fore-and-aft beam in a vessel **carlins**

CARLISH adj churlish

CARLOAD n amount that can be carried by a car

CARLOCK n type of Russian isinglass

CARLOT n boor **carlots**

CARLS ▸ carl

CARMAN n man who drives a car or cart **carmen**

CARMINE adj, n

CARN n cairn

CARNAGE n

CARNAL adj, vb **carnals**

CARNET n type of customs licence **carnets**

CARNEY = carny

CARNEYS ▸ carney

CARNIE = carny

CARNIED ▸ carny

CARNIER ▸ carny

CARNIES ▸ carny

CARNIFY vb be altered so as to resemble skeletal muscle

CARNOSE adj fleshy

CARNS ▸ carn

CARNY vb coax or cajole or act in a wheedling manner ▸ n person who works in a carnival ▸ adj sly

CARNYX n bronze Celtic war trumpet

CAROACH = caroche

CAROB n pod of a Mediterranean tree, used as a chocolate substitute **carobs**

CAROCH = caroche

CAROCHE n stately ceremonial carriage used in the 16th and 17th centuries

CAROL n, vb caroled, caroler

CAROLI ▸ carolus

CAROLS ▸ carol

CAROLUS n any of several coins struck in the reign of a king called Charles

CAROM n shot in which the cue ball is caused to contact one object ball after another ▸ vb carambole **caromed**

CAROMEL vb turn into caramel

CAROMS ▸ carom

CARON n inverted circumflex **carons**

CAROTID n either of the two arteries supplying blood to the head ▸ adj of either of these arteries

CAROTIN = carotene

CAROUSE vb

CARP n, vb

CARPAL n wrist bone **carpale, carpals**

CARPED ▸ carp

CARPEL n carpels

CARPER ▸ carp

CARPERS ▸ carp

CARPET n, vb carpets

CARPI ▸ carpus

CARPING adj tending to make petty complaints ▸ n petty complaint

CARPOOL vb share the use of a single car to travel to work or school

CARPORT n shelter for a car, consisting of a roof supported by posts

CARPS ▸ carp

CARPUS n set of eight bones of the wrist

CARR n area of bog or fen in which scrub has become established

CARRACK n galleon used as a merchantman **carract**

CARRAT = carat

CARRATS ▸ carrat

CARRECT = carrack

CARREL n small individual study room or private desk **carrell, carrels**

CARRICK n as in carrick bend type of knot

CARRIED ▸ carry

CARRIER n

CARRIES ▸ carry

CARRION n

CARROCH variant of ▸ caroche

CARROM ▸ carom

CARROMS ▸ carrom

CARRON n as in carron oil ointment of limewater and linseed oil

CARROT n carrots

CARROTY adj (of hair) reddish-orange

CARRS ▸ carr

CARRY vb

CARRYON n fuss or commotion

CARS ▸ car

CARSE n riverside area of flat fertile alluvium **carses**

CARSEY slang word for ▸ toilet

CARSEYS ▸ carsey

CARSICK adj nauseated from riding in a car

CART n, vb

CARTA n charter
CARTAGE n process or cost of carting
CARTAS ▶ carta
CARTE n fencing position
CARTEL n association of competing firms formed to fix prices **cartels**
CARTER ▶ cart
CARTERS ▶ cart
CARTES ▶ carte
CARTFUL n amount a cart can hold
CARTING ▶ cart
CARTON n, vb **cartons**
CARTOON n, vb
CARTOP adj designed to be transported on top of a vehicle
CARTS ▶ cart
CARTWAY n way by which carts travel
CARVE vb carved
CARVEL = caravel
CARVELS ▶ carvel
CARVEN ▶ carve
CARVER n carving knife **carvers**
CARVERY n restaurant where customers pay a set price for unrestricted helpings
CARVES ▶ carve
CARVIES ▶ carvy
CARVING n
CARVY n caraway seed
CARWASH n drive-through structure containing automated equipment for washing cars

CASA n house
CASABA n kind of winter muskmelon **casabas**
CASAS = casa
CASAVA = cassava
CASAVAS ▶ casava
CASBAH n citadel of a N African city **casbahs**
CASCADE n, vb
CASCARA n bark of a N American shrub, used as a laxative
CASCO n Argentinian homestead **cascos**
CASE n, vb
CASEASE n proteolytic enzyme
CASEATE vb undergo caseation
CASED ▶ case
CASEFY vb make or become similar to cheese
CASEIC adj relating to cheese
CASEIN n phosphoprotein forming the basis of cheese **caseins**
CASEMAN n in printing, a person who sets and corrects type **casemen**
CASEMIX n mix or type of patients treated by a hospital or medical unit
CASEOSE n peptide produced by the peptic digestion of casein
CASEOUS adj of or like cheese
CASERN n (formerly) a billet or accommodation for

soldiers in a town **caserne, caserns**
CASES ▶ case
CASETTE variant of **> cassette**
CASEVAC vb evacuate (a casualty) from a combat zone, usu by air
CASES ▶ case
CASHAW n winter squash **cashaws**
CASHBOX n box for holding cash
CASHED ▶ cash
CASHES ▶ cash
CASHEW n cashews
CASHIER n, vb
CASHING ▶ cash
CASHOO n catechu **cashoos**
CASING n **casings**
CASINI ▶ casino
CASINO n **casinos**
CASITA n small house **casitas**
CASK n, vb **casked**
CASKET n, vb **caskets**
CASKIER ▶ casky
CASKING ▶ cask
CASKS ▶ cask
CASKY adj (of wine) having a musty smell due to resting too long in the cask
CASPASE n type of enzyme
CASQUE n helmet or a helmet-like process or structure **casqued, casques**
CASSABA = casaba
CASSATA n ice cream usually containing nuts and candied fruit

CASSAVA n

CASSENA = cassina

CASSENE = cassina

CASSIA n tropical plant whose pods yield a mild laxative **cassias**

CASSINA n American tree **cassine**

CASSINO n card game for two to four players

CASSIS n blackcurrant cordial

CASSOCK n

CASSONE n highly-decorated Italian dowry chest

CASSPIR n armoured military vehicle

CAST n, vb

CASTE n

CASTED adj having a caste

CASTER n person or thing that casts **casters**

CASTES ▸ caste

CASTING ▸ cast

CASTLE n, vb

CASTLED adj like a castle in construction

CASTLES ▸ castle

CASTOCK n kale stalk

CASTOFF n person or thing that has been discarded or abandoned

CASTOR = caster

CASTORS ▸ castor

CASTORY n dye derived from beaver pelts

CASTRAL adj relating to camps

CASTS ▸ cast

CASUAL adj, n **casuals**

CASUIST n person who attempts to resolve moral dilemmas

CASUS n event

CAT n, vb

CATALO = cattalo

CATALOG = catalogue

CATALOS ▸ catalo

CATALPA n tree of N America and Asia with bell-shaped whitish flowers

CATAPAN n governor in the Byzantine Empire

CATARRH n

CATASTA n platform on which slaves were presented for sale

CATAWBA n type of red North American grape

CATBIRD n North American songbird

CATBOAT n sailing vessel

CATCALL n, vb

CATCH vb seize, capture ▸ n device for fastening a door, window, etc **catched, catchen**

CATCHER n person or thing that catches, esp in a game or sport

CATCHES ▸ catch

CATCHT = catched

CATCHUP a variant spelling (esp US) of ▸ ketchup

CATCHY adj

CATCLAW n type of shrub; black bead

CATCON n catcons

CATE n delicacy

CATECHU n astringent resinous substance

CATELOG obsolete word for ▸ catalogue

CATENA n connected series, esp of patristic comments on the Bible **catenae, catenas**

CATER vb

CATERAN n (formerly) a member of a band of brigands in the Scottish highlands

CATERED ▸ cater

CATERER n

CATERS ▸ cater

CATES pl n choice dainty food

CATFACE n deformity of the surface of a tree trunk, caused by fire or disease

CATFALL n line used as a tackle for hoisting an anchor to the cathead

CATFISH n fish with whisker-like barbels round the mouth

CATFLAP n small flap in a door to let a cat go through

CATGUT n strong cord used to string musical instruments and sports rackets **catguts**

CATHEAD n fitting at the bow of a vessel for securing the anchor when raised

CATHECT vb invest mental or emotional energy in

CATHODE n

CATHOLE n hole in a ship through which ropes are passed

CATHOOD n state of being a cat
CATION n positively charged ion **cations**
CATJANG n tropical shrub
CATKIN n catkins
CATLIKE ▶ cat
CATLIN = catling
CATLING n long double-edged surgical knife for amputations
CATLINS ▶ catlin
CATMINT n Eurasian plant with scented leaves that attract cats
CATNAP vb doze ▶ n short sleep or doze **catnaps**
CATNEP = catmint
CATNEPS ▶ catnep
CATNIP = catmint
CATNIPS ▶ catmint
CATS ▶ cat
CATSKIN n skin and/or fur of a cat
CATSPAW n person used by another as a tool
CATSUIT n one-piece usually close-fitting trouser suit
CATSUP a variant (esp US) of ▶ ketchup
CATSUPS ▶ catsup
CATTABU n cross between common cattle and zebu
CATTAIL n reed mace
CATTALO n hardy breed of cattle
CATTED ▶ cat
CATTERY n place where cats are bred or looked after

CATTIE = catty
CATTIER ▶ catty
CATTIES ▶ catty
CATTILY ▶ catty
CATTING ▶ cat
CATTISH ▶ cat
CATTLE pl n
CATTY adj, n
CATWALK n
CATWORM n type of carnivorous worm
CAUCUS n, vb
CAUDA n area behind the anus of an animal
CAUDAD adv towards the tail or posterior part
CAUDAE ▶ cauda
CAUDAL adj at or near an animal's tail
CAUDATE adj having a tail or a tail-like appendage ▶ n lizard-like amphibian
CAUDEX n thickened persistent stem base of some herbaceous perennial plants
CAUDLE n hot spiced wine drink made with gruel, formerly used medicinally ▶ vb make such a drink **caudled, caudles**
CAUDRON Spenserian spelling of ▶ **cauldron**
CAUF n cage for holding live fish in the water
CAUGHT ▶ catch
CAUK n type of barite
CAUKER n one who caulks **caukers**
CAUKS ▶ cauk

CAUL n membrane sometimes covering a child's head at birth
CAULD a Scot word for ▶ cold
CAULDER ▶ cauld
CAULDS ▶ cauld
CAULES ▶ caulis
CAULINE adj relating to or growing from a plant stem
CAULIS n main stem of a plant
CAULK vb fill in (cracks) with paste etc **caulked, caulker, caulks**
CAULOME n plant's stem structure, considered as a whole
CAULS ▶ caul
CAUM = cam
CAUMED ▶ caum
CAUMING ▶ caum
CAUMS ▶ caum
CAUP n type of quaich **caups**
CAUSA n reason or cause **causae**
CAUSAL adj of or being a cause ▶ n something that suggests a cause **causals**
CAUSE n something that produces a particular effect ▶ vb be the cause of **caused, causen, causer, causers, causes**
CAUSEY n cobbled street ▶ vb cobble **causeys**
CAUSING ▶ cause

CAUSTIC adj, n
CAUTEL n craftiness **cautels**
CAUTER n cauterising instrument **cauters**
CAUTERY n coagulation of blood or destruction of body tissue by cauterizing
CAUTION n, vb
CAUVES ▶ **cauf**
CAVA n Spanish sparkling wine
CAVALLA n type of tropical fish **cavally**
CAVALRY n
CAVAS ▶ **cava**
CAVASS n Turkish armed police officer
CAVE n, vb
CAVEAT n warning ▷ vb introduce a caveat **caveats**
CAVED ▶ **cave**
CAVEL n drawing of lots among miners for an easy and profitable place at the coalface **cavels**
CAVEMAN n **cavemen**
CAVER ▶ **caving**
CAVERN n, vb **caverns**
CAVERS ▶ **caving**
CAVES ▶ **cave**
CAVETTI ▶ **cavetto**
CAVETTO n concave moulding, shaped to a quarter circle in cross section
CAVIAR n **caviare, caviars**
CAVIE n hen coop
CAVIER = **caviar**
CAVIERS ▶ **cavier**

CAVIES ▶ **cavy**
CAVIL vb, n **caviled, caviler, cavils**
CAVING n sport of exploring caves **cavings**
CAVITY n
CAVORT vb **cavorts**
CAVY n type of small rodent
CAW n, vb **cawed, cawing, cawings**
CAWK = **cauk**
CAWKER n metal projection on a horse's shoe to prevent slipping **cawkers**
CAWKS ▶ **cawk**
CAWS ▶ **caw**
CAXON n type of wig **caxons**
CAY n low island or bank composed of sand and coral fragments
CAYENNE n very hot condiment
CAYMAN n S American reptile similar to an alligator **caymans**
CAYS ▶ **cay**
CAYUSE n small American Indian pony used by cowboys **cayuses**
CAZ short for ▶ **casual**

Caz is slang for casual, and is one of the essential short words for using the Z.
CAZIQUE = **cacique**
This word means an American Indian chief, and its plural

caziques was once played as a 9-timer (that is, a word spanning two triple-word squares) earning the highest score for a single word ever officially recorded in a game of Scrabble, 392 points.

CEAS = **caese**
CEASE vb **ceased, ceases, ceasing**
CEAZE obsolete spelling of ▶ **seize**
CEAZED ▶ **ceaze**
CEAZES ▶ **ceaze**
CEAZING ▶ **ceaze**
CEBID n any member of the Cebidae family of New World monkeys **cebids, ceboid**
CEBOIDS ▶ **ceboid**
CECA ▶ **cecum**
CECAL ▶ **cecum**
CECALLY ▶ **cecum**
CECILS pl n fried meatballs
CECITIS n inflammation of the c(a)ecum
CECITY n rare word for blindness
CECUM = **caecum**
CEDAR n, adj
CEDARED adj covered with cedars
CEDARN adj relating to cedar
CEDARS ▶ **cedar**
CEDARY adj like cedar
CEDE vb **ceded, ceder, ceders, cedes**
CEDI n standard monetary unit of

Ghana, divided into 100 pesewas

CEDILLA n

CEDING ▶ cede

CEDIS ▶ cedi

CEDRATE n citron

CEDRINE adj relating to cedar

CEDULA n form of identification in Spanish-speaking countries **cedulas**

CEE n third letter of the alphabet **cees**

CEIBA n type of tropical tree **ceibas**

CEIL vb line (a ceiling) with plaster, boarding, etc **ceiled, ceiler, ceilers**

CEILI variant spelling of ▶ ceilidh

CEILIDH n

CEILING n, vb

CEILIS ▶ ceili

CEILS ▶ ceil

CEL short for ▶ celluloid

CELADON n type of porcelain having a greyish-green glaze: mainly Chinese

CELEB n celebrity **celebs**

CELERY n

CELESTA n instrument like a small piano **celeste**

CELIAC = coeliac

CELIACS ▶ celiac

CELL n

CELLA n inner room of a classical temple **cellae**

CELLAR n, vb **cellars**

CELLED adj cellular

CELLI ▶ cello

CELLING n formation of cells

CELLIST ▶ cello

CELLO n **cellos**

CELLOSE n disaccharide obtained by the hydrolysis of cellulose by cellulase

CELLS ▶ cell

CELLULE n very small cell

CELOM = coelom

CELOMIC ▶ celom

CELOMS ▶ celom

CELOSIA = cockscomb

CELOTEX n tradename for a type of insulation board

CELS ▶ cel

CELT n stone or metal axelike instrument with a bevelled edge **celts**

CEMBALI ▶ cembalo

CEMBALO n, vb

CEMBRA n Swiss pine **cembras**

CEMENT n, vb

CEMENTA ▶ cementum

CEMENTS ▶ cement

CENACLE n supper room, esp one on an upper floor

CENDRE adj ash-blond

CENOTE n natural well formed by the collapse of an overlying limestone crust **cenotes**

CENS n type of annual property rent

CENSE vb burn incense near or before (an altar, shrine, etc) **censed**

CENSER n container for burning incense **censers**

CENSES ▶ cense

CENSING ▶ cense

CENSOR n, vb **censors**

CENSUAL ▶ census

CENSURE n, vb

CENSUS n, vb

CENT n

CENTAGE n rate per hundred

CENTAI ▶ centas

CENTAL n unit of weight equal to 100 pounds (45.3 kilograms) **centals**

CENTARE = centiare

CENTAS n monetary unit of Lithuania

CENTAUR n

CENTAVO n monetary unit in Portugal and many Latin American countries

CENTER = centre

CENTERS ▶ center

CENTILE n (in statistics) another word for percentile

CENTIME n

CENTIMO n monetary unit of Costa Rica, Paraguay, Peru, and Venezuela

CENTNER n unit of weight equivalent to 100 pounds (45.3 kilograms)

CENTO n piece of writing composed of quotations from other authors **centos**

CENTRA ▶ centrum

CENTRAL adj, n

CENTRE n, vb

CENTRED adj mentally and emotionally confident, focused, and well-balanced

CENTRES ▶ centre

CENTRIC adj being central or having a centre

CENTRUM n main part or body of a vertebra

CENTRY obsolete variant of ▶ sentry

CENTS ▶ cent

CENTU n Lithuanian money unit

CENTUM adj denoting or belonging to the Indo-European languages in which original velar stops (k) were not palatalized ▷ n hundred **centums**

CENTURY n

CEORL n freeman of the lowest class in Anglo-Saxon England **ceorls**

CEP another name for ▶ porcino

CEPAGE n grape variety or type of wine **cepages**

CEPE another spelling of ▶ cep

CEPES ▶ cepe

CEPHEID n type of variable star with a regular cycle of variations in luminosity

CEPS ▶ cep

CERAMAL = cermet

CERAMIC n, adj

CERASIN n meta-arabinic acid

CERATE n hard ointment or medicated paste

CERATED adj (of certain birds, such as the falcon) having a cere

CERATES ▶ cerate

CERATIN = keratin

CERCAL adj of or relating to a tail

CERCI ▶ cercus

CERCIS n type of tree or shrub

CERCUS n one of a pair of sensory appendages on some insects and other arthropods

CERE n soft waxy swelling at the base of the upper beak of a parrot ▷ vb wrap (a corpse) in a cerecloth

CEREAL n cereals

CEREBRA ▶ cerebrum

CERED ▶ cere

CEREOUS adj waxlike

CERES ▶ cere

CERESIN n white wax extracted from ozocerite

CEREUS n type of tropical American cactus

CERGE n large altar candle **cerges**

CERIA n ceric oxide **cerias**

CERIC adj of or containing cerium in the tetravalent state

CERING ▶ cere

CERIPH = serif

CERIPHS ▶ ceriph

CERISE adj cherry-red ▷ n moderate to dark red colour **cerises**

CERITE n hydrous silicate of cerium **cerites**

CERIUM n steel-grey metallic element **ceriums**

CERMET n materials consisting of a metal matrix with ceramic particles disseminated through it **cermets**

CERNE obsolete variant of > encircle

CERNED ▶ cerne

CERNES ▶ cerne

CERNING ▶ cerne

CERO n type of large food fish

CEROON n hide-covered bale **ceroons**

CEROS ▶ cero

CEROTIC adj as in cerotic acid white insoluble odourless wax

CEROUS adj of or containing cerium in the trivalent state

CERRADO n vast area of tropical savanna in Brazil

CERRIAL adj relating to the cerris

CERRIS n Turkey oak

CERT n certainty

CERTAIN adj

CERTES adv with certainty

CERTIE n as in by my certie assuredly

CERTIFY vb
CERTS ▸ cert
CERTY n as in **by my certy** assuredly
CERULE adj sky-blue
CERUMEN n wax secreted by glands in the external ear
CERUSE n white lead **ceruses**
CERVEZA n Spanish word for beer
CERVID n type of ruminant mammal characterized by the presence of antlers **cervids**
CERVINE adj resembling or relating to a deer
CERVIX n
CESIOUS = caesious
CESIUM = caesium
CESIUMS ▸ cesium
CESS n any of several special taxes, such as a land tax in Scotland ▸ vb tax or assess for taxation
CESSE obsolete variant of ▸ **cease**
CESSED ▸ cess
CESSER n coming to an end of a term interest or annuity **cessers**
CESSES ▸ cess
CESSING ▸ cess
CESSION n ceding
CESSPIT = cesspool
CESTA n in jai alai, the basket used to throw and catch the pelota **cestas**
CESTI ▸ cestus
CESTODE n type of

parasitic flatworm such as the tapeworms
CESTOI ▸ cestos
CESTOID adj (esp of tapeworms and similar animals) ribbon-like in form ▸ n ribbon-like worm
CESTOS = cestus
CESTUI n legal term to designate a person **cestuis**
CESTUS n girdle of Aphrodite (Venus) decorated to cause amorousness
CESURA a variant spelling of ▸ **caesura**
CESURAE ▸ cesura
CESURAL ▸ cesura
CESURAS ▸ cesura
CESURE = caesura
CESURES ▸ cesure
CETANE n colourless liquid hydrocarbon, used as a solvent **cetanes**
CETE n group of badgers **cetes**
CETYL n univalent alcohol radical **cetyls**
CEVICHE n Peruvian seafood dish
CEZVE ▸ cezves
CH pron obsolete from of I
CHA n tea
CHABLIS n dry white French wine
CHABOUK n type of whip **chabuk**
CHABUKS ▸ chabuk
CHACE obsolete variant of ▸ **chase**

CHACED ▸ chace
CHACES ▸ chace
CHACHKA n cheap trinket
CHACING ▸ chace
CHACK vb bite **chacked, chacks**
CHACMA n type of baboon with coarse greyish hair, occurring in S and E Africa **chacmas**
CHACO = shako
CHACOES ▸ chaco
CHACOS ▸ chaco
CHAD n small pieces removed during the punching of holes in punch cards, printer paper, etc
CHADAR = chuddar
CHADARS ▸ chadar
CHADDAR = chuddar
CHADDOR = chuddar
CHADO n Japanese tea ceremony
CHADOR = chuddar
CHADORS ▸ chador
CHADOS ▸ chador
CHADRI n shroud which covers the body from head to foot
CHADS ▸ chad
CHAEBOL n large, usually family-owned, business group in South Korea
CHAETA n the chitinous bristles on the body of annelids **chaetae, chaetal**
CHAFE vb chafed
CHAFER n large beetle **chafers**

CHAFES ▶ chafe

CHAFF n, vb **chaffed**

CHAFFER vb haggle

CHAFFS ▶ chaff

CHAFFY ▶ chaff

CHAFING ▶ chafe

CHAFT n jaw **chafts**

CHAGAN n Mongolian royal or imperial title **chagans**

CHAGRIN n, vb

CHAI n tea, esp as made in India with added spices

CHAIN n, vb

CHAINE adj (of a dance turn) producing a full rotation for every two steps taken ▶ vb produce a full rotation for every two steps taken

CHAINED ▶ chain

CHAINES ▶ chaine

CHAINS ▶ chain

CHAIR n, vb **chaired, chairs**

CHAIS ▶ chai

CHAISE n light horse-drawn carriage **chaises**

CHAKRA n (in yoga) any of the seven major energy centres in the body **chakras**

CHAL n in Romany, person or fellow

CHALAH = challah

CHALAHS ▶ chalah

CHALAN vb (in India) to cause an accused person to appear before a magistrate **chalans**

CHALAZA n one of a pair of spiral threads holding the yolk of a bird's egg in position

CHALCID n type of tiny insect

CHALDER n former Scottish dry measure

CHALEH = challah

CHALEHS ▶ chaleh

CHALET n **chalets**

CHALICE n

CHALK n, vb **chalked, chalks, chalky**

CHALLA = challah

CHALLAH n type of bread

CHALLAN = chalan

CHALLAS ▶ challa

CHALLIE = challis

CHALLIS n lightweight plain-weave fabric

CHALLOT ▶ challah

CHALLY = challis

CHALONE n any internal secretion that inhibits a physiological process or function

CHALOT ▶ chalah

CHALOTH ▶ chalah

CHALS ▶ chal

CHALUPA n Mexican dish

CHALUTZ n member of an organization of immigrants to Israeli agricultural settlements

CHAM an archaic word for ▶ khan

CHAMADE n (formerly) a signal by drum or trumpet inviting an enemy to a parley

CHAMBER n, vb

CHAMBRE adj (of wine) at room temperature

CHAMETZ n leavened food which may not be eaten during Passover

CHAMFER n ▶ chase

CHAMISA n American shrub

CHAMISE = chamiso

CHAMISO n fourwing saltbush

CHAMLET = camlet

CHAMMY = chamois

CHAMOIS n small mountain antelope or a pice of leather from its skin, used for polishing ▶ vb polish with a chamois **chamoix**

CHAMP vb

CHAMPAC n type of tree **champak**

CHAMPED ▶ champ

CHAMPER ▶ champ

CHAMPS ▶ champ

CHAMPY adj (of earth) churned up (by cattle, for example)

CHAMS ▶ cham

CHANA n (in Indian cookery) chickpeas **chanas**

CHANCE n, vb **chanced**

CHANCEL n

CHANCER n unscrupulous or dishonest opportunist

CHANCES ▶ chance

CHANCEY = chancy

CHANCRE n small hard growth which is the first sign of syphilis

CHANCY adj

CHANG n loud discordant noise

CHANGA interj in Indian English, an expression of approval or agreement

CHANGE n, vb changed, changer, changes

CHANGS ▶ chang

CHANK n shell of several types of sea conch, used to make bracelets chanks

CHANNEL n, vb

CHANNER n gravel

CHANOYO a variant of ▶ chado

CHANOYU = chado

CHANSON n song

CHANT vb, n chanted

CHANTER n (on bagpipes) pipe on which the melody is played

CHANTEY the usual US spelling of ▶ shanty

CHANTIE n chamber pot

CHANTOR = chanter

CHANTRY n endowment for the singing of Masses for the soul of the founder or others designated by him

CHANTS ▶ chant

CHANTY = shanty

CHAO n Vietnamese rice porridge

CHAOS n chaoses, chaotic

CHAP n, vb

CHAPATI n (in Indian cookery) flat thin

unleavened bread

CHAPE n metal tip or trimming for a scabbard

CHAPEAU n hat

CHAPEL n chapels

CHAPES ▶ chape

CHAPESS n woman

CHAPKA = czapka

CHAPKAS ▶ chapka

CHAPLET n garland for the head ▷ vb create a garland

CHAPMAN n travelling pedlar **chapmen**

CHAPPAL n one of a pair of sandals, usually of leather, worn in India

CHAPPED ▶ chap

CHAPPIE n man or boy

CHAPPY adj (of skin) chapped

CHAPS ▶ chap

CHAPT adj chapped

CHAPTER n, vb

CHAR vb, n

CHARA n type of green freshwater algae

CHARACT n distinctive mark

CHARADE n

CHARAS another name for ▶ hashish

CHARD n variety of beet **chards**

CHARE = char

CHARED ▶ char

CHARES ▶ char

CHARET obsolete variant of ▶ chariot

CHARETS ▶ charet

CHARGE vb, n charged

CHARGER n

CHARGES ▶ charge

CHARIER ▶ chary

CHARILY adv cautiously

CHARING ▶ char

CHARIOT n, vb

CHARISM = charisma

CHARITY n

CHARK vb char

CHARKA = charkha

CHARKAS ▶ charkha

CHARKED ▶ chark

CHARKHA n (in India) a spinning wheel, esp for cotton

CHARKS ▶ chark

CHARLEY n as in **charley horse** muscle stiffness after strenuous exercise

CHARLIE n fool

CHARM n, vb

CHARMED adj delighted or fascinated

CHARMER n

CHARMS ▶ charm

CHARNEL adj ghastly ▷ n ghastly thing

CHARPAI = charpoy

CHARPIE n lint pieces used to make surgical dressings

CHARPOY n type of bedstead

CHARQUI n meat, esp beef, cut into strips and dried

CHARR = char

CHARRED ▶ char

CHARRO n Mexican cowboy **charros**

CHARRS ▶ charr

CHARRY adj of or relating to charcoal

CHARS ▶ char

CHART n, vb

CHARTA n charter **chartas**

CHARTED ▶ chart

CHARTER n, vb

CHARTS ▶ chart

CHARY adj

CHAS ▶ cha

CHASE vb, n **chased**

CHASER n milder drink drunk after another stronger one **chasers**

CHASES ▶ chase

CHASING ▶ chase

CHASM n, vb **chasmal, chasmed, chasmic, chasms**

CHASMY adj full of chasms

CHASSE n one of a series of gliding steps in ballet ▷ vb perform either of these steps **chassed, chasses**

CHASSIS n

CHASTE adj

CHASTEN vb

CHASTER ▶ chaste

CHAT n, vb

CHATBOT n computer program

CHATEAU n

CHATON n in jewellery, a stone with a reflective metal foil backing **chatons**

CHATS ▶ chat

CHATTA n umbrella **chattas**

CHATTED ▶ chat

CHATTEL n

CHATTER vb, n

CHATTI n (in India) an earthenware pot **chattis**

CHATTY adj

CHAUFE obsolete variant of ▶ chafe

CHAUFED ▶ chaufe

CHAUFER = chauffer

CHAUFES ▶ chaufe

CHAUFF obsolete variant of ▶ chafe

CHAUFFS ▶ chauff

CHAUMER n chamber

CHAUNCE archaic variant of ▶ chance

CHAUNGE archaic variant of ▶ change

CHAUNT a less common variant of ▶ chant

CHAUNTS ▶ chaunt

CHAUVIN n chauvinist

CHAVE n old dialect term for "I have"

CHAVVY adj relating to or like a chav

CHAW vb chew (tobacco), esp without swallowing it ▷ n something chewed, esp a plug of tobacco **chawed, chawer, chawers, chawing**

CHAWK n jackdaw **chawks**

CHAWS ▶ chaw

CHAY n plant of the madder family **chaya**

CHAYAS ▶ chaya

CHAYOTE n tropical climbing plant

CHAYS ▶ chay

CHAZAN n cantor **chazans** ▶ chazan

CHAZZAN variant of ▶ chazan

CHAZZEN = chazzan

CHE pron dialectal form meaning "I"

CHEAP adj, adv, n, vb **cheaped**

CHEAPEN vb lower the reputation of

CHEAPER ▶ cheap

CHEAPIE n something inexpensive

CHEAPLY ▶ cheap

CHEAPO n very cheap and possibly shoddy thing **cheapos**

CHEAPS ▶ cheap

CHEAPY = cheapie

CHEAT vb, n **cheated, cheater, cheats**

CHEBEC n type of boat **chebecs**

CHECHIA n Berber skullcap

CHECK vb, n **checked**

CHECKER = chequer

CHECKS ▶ check

CHECKUP n

CHECKY adj having squares of alternating tinctures or furs

CHEDDAR n type of smooth hard yellow or whitish cheese

CHEDER n Jewish religious education **cheders**

CHEDITE = cheddite

CHEEK n, vb **cheeked, cheeks**

CHEEKY adj

CHEEP n young bird's high-pitched cry ▷ vb utter a cheep **cheeped, cheeper, cheeps**

CHEER vb, n **cheered, cheerer**

CHEERIO interj, n, sentence substitute

CHEERLY adv cheerful or cheerfully

CHEERO = cheerio

CHEEROS ▷ cheero

CHEERS interj drinking toast ▷ sentence substitute drinking toast

CHEERY adj

CHEESE n, vb cheesed, cheeses

CHEESY adj like cheese

CHEETAH n

CHEF n, vb

CHEFDOM n state or condition of being a chef

CHEFED, cheffed, chefing, chefs ▷ chef

CHEGOE = chigger

CHEGOES ▷ chigger

CHEKA n secret police set up in Russia in 1917 chekas

CHEKIST n member of the cheka

CHELA n disciple of a religious teacher chelae, chelas

CHELATE n coordination compound ▷ adj of or possessing chelae ▷ vb form a chelate

CHELLUP n noise

CHELOID a variant spelling of ▷ keloid

CHELONE n hardy N American plant

CHELP vb (esp of women or children) to chatter or speak out of turn chelped, chelps

CHEMIC vb bleach ▷ n chemist chemics

CHEMISE n woman's loose-fitting slip

CHEMISM n chemical action

CHEMIST n

CHEMMY n gambling card game

CHEMO n short form of chemotherapy chemos

CHENAR n oriental plane tree chenars

CHENET another word for ▷ genip

CHENETS ▷ chenet

CHENIX n ancient measure, slightly more than a quart

CHEQUE n

CHEQUER n piece used in Chinese chequers ▷ vb make irregular in colour or character

CHEQUES ▷ cheque

CHEQUY n ▷ checky

CHER adj dear or expensive chere

CHERISH vb

CHEROOT n cigar with both ends cut flat

CHERRY n, adj, vb

CHERT n microcrystalline form of silica cherts, cherty

CHERUB n cherubs

CHERUP n chirrup

CHERUPS ▷ cherup

CHERVIL n aniseed-flavoured herb

CHESIL n gravel or shingle chesils

CHESNUT rare variant of ▷ chestnut

CHESS n

CHESSEL n mould used in cheese-making

CHESSES ▷ chess

CHEST n, vb chested, chests

CHESTY adj symptomatic of chest disease

CHETAH = cheetah

CHETAHS ▷ cheetah

CHETH = heth

CHETHS ▷ cheth

CHETNIK n member of a Serbian nationalist paramilitary group

CHETRUM n monetary unit in Bhutan

CHEVAL n as in cheval glass full-length mirror that can swivel

CHEVEN n chub chevens

CHEVET n semicircular or polygonal east end of a church chevets

CHEVIED ▷ chevy

CHEVIES ▷ chevy

CHEVIN n cheven

CHEVINS ▷ chevin

CHEVIOT n type of British sheep reared for its wool

CHEVRE n any cheese made from goats' milk chevres

CHEVRET n type of goats' cheese

CHEVRON n, vb

CHEVY = chivy

CHEW vb, n chewed, chewer, chewers

CHEWET n type of meat pie **chewets**

CHEWIE n chewing gum

CHEWIER ▶ chewy

CHEWIES ▶ chewy

CHEWING ▶ chew

CHEWINK n towhee

CHEWS ▶ chew

CHEWY adj requiring a lot of chewing ▷ n dog's chewable toy

CHEZ prep at the home of

CHI n 22nd letter of the Greek alphabet

> Chi is a letter of the Greek alphabet, and can also be spelt khi.

CHIA n plant of the mint family

CHIACK vb tease or banter ▷ n good-humoured banter **chiacks**

CHIANTI n dry red Italian wine

CHIAO n Chinese coin equal to one tenth of one yuan

CHIAS ▶ chia

CHIASM = chiasma

CHIASMA n biological term

CHIASMI > chiasmus

CHIASMS ▶ chiasma

CHIAUS = chouse

CHIB vb in Scots English, stab or slash with a sharp weapon ▷ n sharp weapon **chibbed**

CHIBOL n spring onion **chibols**

CHIBOUK n Turkish tobacco pipe with an extremely long stem

CHIBS ▶ chib

CHIC adj, n

CHICA n Spanish young girl

CHICANA n female chicano

CHICANE n obstacle in a motor-racing circuit ▷ vb deceive or trick by chicanery

CHICANO n American citizen of Mexican origin

CHICAS ▶ chica

CHICER ▶ chic

CHICEST ▶ chic

CHICH another word for > chickpea

CHICHA n Andean drink made from fermented maize **chichas**

CHICHES > chickpea

CHICHI adj affectedly pretty or stylish ▷ n quality of being affectedly pretty or stylish **chichis**

CHICK n

CHICKEE n opensided, thatched building on stilts

CHICKEN n, adj, vb

CHICKS ▶ chick

CHICLE n gumlike substance obtained from the sapodilla **chicles**

CHICLY ▶ chic

CHICO n spiny chenopodiaceous shrub

CHICON = chicory

CHICONS ▶ chicon

CHICORY n

CHICOS ▶ chico

CHICS ▶ chic

CHID ▶ chide

CHIDDEN ▶ chide

CHIDE vb chided, chider, chiders, chides, chiding

CHIEF n, adj chiefer

CHIEFLY adv especially ▷ adj of or relating to a chief or chieftain

CHIEFRY = chiefery

CHIEFS ▶ chief

CHIEL n young man **chield, chields, chiels**

CHIFFON n, adj

CHIGGER n parasitic larva of various mites

CHIGNON n knot of hair pinned up at the back of the head ▷ vb make a chignon

CHIGOE = chigger

CHIGOES ▶ chigoe

CHIGRE = chigger

CHIGRES ▶ chigre

CHIK n slatted blind

CHIKARA n Indian seven-stringed musical instrument

CHIKHOR = chukar

CHIKOR = chukar

CHIKORS ▶ chikor

CHIKS ▶ chik

CHILD n, vb

CHILDE n young man of noble birth

CHILDED ▶ child

CHILDER dialect variant of > children

CHILDES ▶ childe

CHILDLY ▸ child

CHILDS ▸ child

CHILE *a variant spelling of* ▸ **chilli**

CHILES ▸ chile

CHILI = chilli

CHILIAD *n* group of one thousand

CHILIES ▸ chili

CHILIS ▸ chili

CHILL *n, vb, adj* chilled

CHILLER *n* cooling or refrigerating device

CHILLI *n* chillis

CHILLS ▸ chill

CHILLUM *n* short pipe, usually of clay, used esp for smoking cannabis

CHILLY *adj*

CHIMAR = chimere

CHIMARS ▸ chimar

CHIMB = chime

CHIMBLY = chimney

CHIMBS ▸ chime

CHIME *n, vb* chimed, chimer

CHIMER = chimere

CHIMERA *n* unrealistic hope or idea

CHIMERE *n* gown worn by bishops

CHIMERS ▸ chime

CHIMES ▸ chime

CHIMING ▸ chime

CHIMLA = chimney

CHIMLAS ▸ chimla

CHIMLEY = chimney

CHIMNEY *n, vb*

CHIMO *interj* Inuit greeting and toast

CHIMP *n* chimpanzee chimps

CHIN *n, vb*

CHINA *n*

CHINAR = chenar

CHINARS ▸ chinar

CHINAS ▸ china

CHINCH *another name for a* ▸ **bedbug**

CHINCHY *adj* tightfisted

CHINDIT *n* Allied soldier fighting behind the Japanese lines in Burma during World War II

CHINE = chime

CHINED ▸ chine

CHINES ▸ chine

CHINING ▸ chine

CHINK *n, vb* chinked, chinks, chinky

CHINNED ▸ chin

CHINO *n* durable cotton twill cloth

CHINONE *n* benzoquinone

CHINOOK *n* wind found in the Rocky Mountains

CHINOS *pl n* trousers made of a kind of hard-wearing cotton

CHINS ▸ chin

CHINTS *obsolete variant of* ▸ **chintz**

CHINTZ *n*

CHINTZY *adj* of or covered with chintz

CHINWAG *n* chat

CHIP *n, vb* chipped

CHIPPER *vb* chirp or chatter

CHIPPIE = chippy

CHIPPY *n* fish-and-chip shop ▸ *adj* resentful or

oversensitive about being perceived as inferior

CHIPS ▸ chip

CHIPSET *n* highly integrated circuit on the motherboard of a computer

CHIRAL ▸ chirality

CHIRK *vb* creak, like a door ▸ *adj* spritely; high-spirited chirked, chirker, chirks

CHIRL *vb* warble chirled, chirls

CHIRM *n* chirping of birds ▸ *vb* (esp of a bird) to chirp chirmed, chirms

CHIRO *n* informal name for chiropractor chiros

CHIRP *vb, n* chirped, chirper, chirps

CHIRPY *adj*

CHIRR *vb* (esp of certain insects, such as crickets) to make a shrill trilled sound ▸ *n* sound of chirring chirre, chirred

CHIRREN *n* dialect form of children

CHIRRES ▸ chirre

CHIRRS ▸ chirr

CHIRRUP *vb, n*

CHIRT *vb* squirt chirted, chirts

CHIRU *n* Tibetan antelope chirus

CHIS ▸ chi

CHISEL *n, vb* chisels

CHIT *n, vb*

CHITAL *n* type of deer chitals**

CHITIN n outer layer of the bodies of arthropods **chitins**

CHITLIN n pig intestine cooked and served as a dish

CHITON n (in ancient Greece and Rome) a loose woollen tunic **chitons**

CHITS ▸ chit

CHITTED ▸ chit

CHITTER vb twitter or chirp

CHITTY adj, vb

CHIV n knife ▸ vb stab (someone)

CHIVARI = charivari

CHIVE n, vb **chived, chives**

CHIVIED ▸ chivy

CHIVIES ▸ chivy

CHIVING ▸ chive

CHIVS ▸ chiv

CHIVVED ▸ chiv

CHIVVY = chivy

CHIVVY vb harass or nag ▸ n hunt

CHIZ n cheat ▸ vb cheat **chizz, chizzed, chizzes**

CHLAMYS n woollen cloak worn by ancient Greek soldiers

CHLORAL n colourless oily liquid with a pungent odour

CHLORIC adj of or containing chlorine in the pentavalent state

CHLORID n type of chlorine compound

CHLORIN = chlorine

CHOANA n posterior nasal aperture **choanae**

CHOBDAR n in India and Nepal, king's macebearer or attendant

CHOC short form of > chocolate

CHOCCY n chocolate ▸ adj made of, tasting of, smelling of, or resembling chocolate

CHOCHO = chayote

CHOCHOS ▸ chocho

CHOCK n, vb, adv **chocked**

CHOCKER adj full up

CHOCKO = choco

CHOCKOS ▸ chocko

CHOCKS ▸ chock

CHOCO n member of the Australian army **chocos**

CHOCS ▸ choc

CHOCTAW n movement in ice-skating

CHODE ▸ chide

CHOENIX = chenix

CHOG n core of a piece of fruit **chogs**

CHOICE n, adj **choicer, choices**

CHOIR n, vb **choired, choirs**

CHOKE vb, n

CHOKED adj disappointed or angry

CHOKER n tight-fitting necklace **chokers**

CHOKES ▸ choke

CHOKEY n slang word for prison ▸ adj involving, caused by, or causing choking **chokeys, chokier, chokies**

CHOKING ▸ choke

CHOKO n chokos

CHOKRA n in India, a boy or young man **chokras**

CHOKRI n in India, a girl or young woman **chokris**

CHOKY = chokey

CHOLA n Hispanic girl **cholas**

CHOLATE n salt of cholic acid

CHOLENT n meal prepared on Friday and left to cook until eaten for Sabbath lunch

CHOLER n bad temper

CHOLERA n

CHOLERS ▸ choler

CHOLI n short-sleeved bodice, as worn by Indian women

CHOLIC adj as in cholic acid crystalline acid found in bile

CHOLINE n colourless viscous soluble alkaline substance present in animal tissues

CHOLIS ▸ choli

CHOLLA n type of spiny cactus **chollas**

CHOLO n chicano gangster **cholos**

CHOLTRY n caravanserai

CHOMETZ = chametz

CHOMMIE n (in informal South African English) friend

CHOMP vb chew noisily ▷ n act or sound of chewing in this manner **chomped, chomper, chomps**

CHON n North and South Korean monetary unit

CHONDRE another word for ▷ chondrule

CHONDRI > chondrus

CHOOF vb go away **choofed, choofs**

CHOOK n, vb **chooked, chookie, chooks**

CHOOM n Englishman **chooms**

CHOON n choons

CHOOSE vb **chooser, chooses**

CHOOSEY = choosy

CHOOSY adj

CHOP vb, n

CHOPIN ▷ chopine

CHOPINE n sandal-like shoe popular in the 18th century

CHOPINS ▷ chopin

CHOPPED ▷ chop

CHOPPER n, vb

CHOPPY adj

CHOPS ▷ chop

CHORAGI > choragus

CHORAL adj

CHORALE n slow stately hymn tune

CHORALS ▷ choral

CHORD n straight line joining two points on a curve ▷ vb provide (a melodic line) with chords

CHORDA n in anatomy, a cord **chordae**

CHORDAL ▷ chord

CHORDED ▷ chord

CHORDEE n painful penile erection, a symptom of gonorrhoea

CHORDS ▷ chord

CHOREA n disorder of the nervous system **choreal, choreas**

CHORED ▷ chore

CHOREE n trochee **chorees**

CHOREGI > choregus

CHOREIC ▷ chorea

CHORES ▷ chore

CHOREUS = choree

CHORIA ▷ chorion

CHORIAL ▷ chorion

CHORIC adj in the manner of a chorus

CHORINE n chorus girl

CHORING ▷ chore

CHORION n outer membrane forming a sac around an embryo

CHORISM ▷ chorisis

CHORIST n choir member

CHORIZO n kind of highly seasoned pork sausage of Spain or Mexico

CHOROID adj resembling the chorion, esp in being vascular ▷ n vascular membrane of the eyeball

CHORRIE n dilapidated old car

CHORTEN n Buddhist shrine

CHORTLE vb, n

CHORUS n large choir ▷ vb sing or say together

CHOSE ▷ choose

CHOSEN ▷ choose

CHOSES ▷ choose

CHOTA adj (in British Empire Indian usage) small

CHOTT a variant spelling of ▷ shott

CHOTTS ▷ chott

CHOU n type of cabbage

CHOUGH n large black Eurasian and N African bird of the crow family **choughs**

CHOUSE vb to cheat **choused, chouser, chouses**

CHOUSH n Turkish messenger

CHOUT n blackmail **chouts**

CHOUX ▷ chou

CHOW n, vb

CHOWDER n thick soup containing clams or fish ▷ vb to make a chowder of

CHOWED ▷ chow

CHOWING ▷ chow

CHOWK n marketplace or market area **chowks**

CHOWRI n fly-whisk **chowris, chowry**

CHOWS ▷ chow

CHOWSE = chouse

CHOWSED ▷ chowse

CHOWSES ▷ chowse

CHRISM n consecrated oil used for anointing in some churches

CHRISMA > chrismon

CHRISMS ▸ chrism

CHRISOM = chrism

CHRISTY n skiing turn for stopping or changing direction quickly

CHROMA n attribute of a colour **chromas**

CHROME n, vb, adj **chromed**

CHROMEL n nickel-based alloy

CHROMES ▸ chrome

CHROMIC adj of or containing chromium in the trivalent state

CHROMO n picture produced by lithography **chromos**

CHROMY ▸ chrome

CHROMYL n of, consisting of, or containing the divalent radical CrO_2

CHRONIC adj, n

CHRONON n unit of time

CHUB n European freshwater fish of the carp family

CHUBBY adj

CHUBS ▸ chub

CHUCK vb, n **chucked**

CHUCKER n person who throws something

CHUCKIE n small stone

CHUCKLE vb, n

CHUCKS ▸ chuck

CHUCKY = chuckie

CHUDDAH = chuddar

CHUDDAR n large shawl or veil **chudder**

CHUDDY n chewing gum

CHUFA n type of sedge

chufas

CHUFF vb (of a steam engine) move while making a puffing sound ▷ n puffing sound of or as if of a steam engine ▷ adj boorish

CHUFFED adj very pleased

CHUFFER ▸ chuff

CHUFFS ▸ chuff

CHUFFY adj boorish and surly

CHUG n, vb **chugged, chugger, chugs**

CHUKAR n common Indian partridge **chukars**

CHUKKA n period of play in polo **chukkar, chukkas, chukker**

CHUKOR = chukar

CHUKORS ▸ chukor

CHUM n, vb

CHUMASH n printed book containing one of the Five Books of Moses

CHUMLEY = chimney

CHUMMED ▸ chum

CHUMMY adj friendly ▷ n chum

CHUMP n, vb **chumped, chumps**

CHUMS ▸ chum

CHUNDER vb vomit ▷ n vomit

CHUNK n, vb **chunked, chunks**

CHUNKY adj

CHUNNEL n rail tunnel linking England and France

CHUNNER = chunter

CHUNTER vb mutter or grumble incessantly in a meaningless fashion

CHUPATI = chupatti

CHUPPA variant of ▸ **chuppah**

CHUPPAH n canopy under which a marriage is performed

CHUPPAS ▸ chuppa

CHUPPOT ▸ chuppah

CHUR interj expression of agreement

CHURCH n, vb

CHURCHY adj like a church, church service, etc

CHURL n surly ill-bred person **churls**

CHURN n, vb **churned, churner, churns**

CHURR = chirr

CHURRED ▸ churr

CHURRO n Spanish dough stick snack **churros**

CHURRS ▸ churr

CHURRUS n hemp resin

CHUSE obsolete variant of ▸ **choose**

CHUSES ▸ chuse

CHUSING ▸ chuse

CHUT interj expression of surprise or annoyance ▷ vb make such an expression

CHUTE n, vb **chuted, chutes, chuting, chutist**

CHUTNEE = chutney

CHUTNEY n

CHUTZPA = chutzpah

CHYACK = chiack

CHYACKS ▶ chyack
CHYLDE archaic word for
▶ **child**
CHYLE n milky fluid
formed in the small
intestine during
digestion **chyles**
CHYLIFY vb to be turned
into chyle
CHYLOUS ▶ chyle
CHYME n partially
digested food that
leaves the stomach
chymes
CHYMIC = chemic
CHYMICS ▶ chymic
CHYMIFY vb to form
into chyme
CHYMIST = chemist
CHYMOUS ▶ chyme
CHYND adj chined
CHYPRE n perfume
made from
sandalwood **chypres**
CHYTRID n variety of
fungus
CIAO an informal word
for ▶ hello
CIBOL = chibol
CIBOLS ▶ cibol
CIBORIA ▶ ciborium
CIBOULE = chibol
CICADA n cicadae,
cicadas, cicala
CICALAS ▶ cicala
CICALE ▶ cicala
CICELY n type of plant
CICERO n measure for
type that is somewhat
larger than the pica
ciceros
CICHLID n type of
tropical freshwater
fish popular in

aquariums
CICOREE = chicory
CICUTA n spotted
hemlock **cicutas**
CID n leader
CIDARIS n sea urchin
CIDE Shakespearean
variant of ▶ **decide**
CIDED ▶ cide
CIDER n ciders, cidery
CIDES ▶ cide
CIDING ▶ cide
CIDS ▶ cid
CIEL = ceil
CIELED ▶ ciel
CIELING ▶ ciel
CIELS ▶ ciel
CIERGE = cerge
CIERGES ▶ cierge
CIG = cigarette
CIGAR n
CIGARET = cigarette
CIGARS ▶ cigar
CIGGIE = cigarette
CIGGIES ▶ ciggie
CIGGY > cigarette
CIGS ▶ cig
CILIA ▶ cilium
CILIARY adj of or
relating to cilia
CILIATE n type of
protozoan
CILICE n haircloth fabric
or garment **cilices**
CILIUM n short thread
projecting from a cell
that causes movement
CILL a variant spelling
(used in the building
industry) for ▶ **sill**
CILLS ▶ cill
CIMAR = cymar
CIMARS ▶ cimar
CIMELIA n (especially,

ecclesiastical)
treasures
CIMEX n type of
heteropterous insect,
esp the bedbug
cimices
CIMIER n crest of a
helmet **cimiers**
CINCH n easy task ▷ vb
fasten a girth around
(a horse) **cinched,
cinches**
CINCT adj encircled
CINDER n, vb cinders,
cindery
CINE n as in cine
camera camera able
to film moving pictures
CINEAST = cineaste
CINEMA n cinemas
CINEOL n colourless oily
liquid with a
camphor-like odour
and a spicy taste
cineole, cineols
CINEREA n grey matter
of the brain and
nervous system
CINERIN n either of two
organic compounds
used as insecticides
CINES ▶ cine
CINGULA ▶ cingulum
CINQUE n number five
in cards, dice, etc
cinques
CION = scion
CIONS ▶ cion
CIPHER n, vb ciphers
CIPHONY n ciphered
telephony
CIPOLIN n Italian
marble with
alternating white and

CIPPI ▶ cippus
CIPPUS n pillar bearing an inscription
CIRCA prep
CIRCAR n in India, part of a province circars
CIRCLE n, vb circled, circler, circles
CIRCLET n circular ornament worn on the head
CIRCLIP n type of fastener
CIRCS pl n circumstances
CIRCUIT n, vb
CIRCUS n circusy
CIRE adj (of fabric) treated with a heat or wax process to make it smooth ▷ n such a surface on a fabric cires
CIRL n bird belonging to the bunting family cirls
CIRQUE n steep-sided semicircular hollow found in mountainous areas cirques
CIRRATE adj bearing or resembling cirri
CIRRI ▶ cirrus
CIRROSE = cirrate
CIRROUS = cirrate
CIRRUS n
CIRSOID adj resembling a varix
CIS adj having two groups of atoms on the same side of a double bond
CISCO n whitefish, esp the lake herring of cold

deep lakes of North America ciscoes, ciscos
CISSIER ▶ cissy
CISSIES ▶ cissy
CISSING n appearance of pinholes, craters, etc, in paintwork
CISSOID n geometric curve whose two branches meet in a cusp at the origin and are asymptotic to a line parallel to the y-axis
CISSUS n type of climbing plant
CISSY = sissy
CIST n wooden box for holding ritual objects used in ancient Rome and Greece ▷ vb make a cist cisted
CISTERN n
CISTIC adj cist-like
CISTRON n section of a chromosome that encodes a single polypeptide chain
CISTS ▶ cist
CISTUS n type of plant
CIT n pejorative term for a town dweller
CITABLE ▶ cite
CITADEL n
CITAL n court summons citals
CITATOR n legal publication
CITE vb cited, citer, citers, cites
CITESS n female cit
CITHARA n ancient stringed musical

instrument
CITHER = cittern
CITHERN ▶ cittern
CITHERS ▶ cither
CITHREN = cithara
CITIED adj having cities
CITIES ▶ city
CITIFY vb cause to conform to or adopt the customs, habits, or dress of city people
CITING ▶ cite
CITIZEN n
CITO adv swiftly
CITOLA n type of medieval stringed instrument citolas
CITOLE a rare word for ▶ cittern
CITOLES ▶ citole
CITRAL n volatile liquid with a lemon-like odour citrals
CITRATE n any salt or ester of citric acid
CITRIC adj of or derived from citrus fruits or citric acid
CITRIN n vitamin P
CITRINE n brownish-yellow variety of quartz: a gemstone
CITRINS ▶ citrin
CITRON n lemon-like fruit of a small Asian tree citrons
CITROUS = citrus
CITRUS n type of tropical or subtropical tree or shrub
CITRUSY = citrussy
CITS ▶ cit
CITTERN n medieval

stringed instrument

CITY n

CITYFY = citify

CIVE = chive

CIVES ▶ cive

CIVET n spotted catlike African mammal **civets**

CIVIC adj

CIVICS n study of the rights and responsibilities of citizenship

CIVIE = civvy

CIVIES ▶ civie

CIVIL adj civilly, civils

CIVISM n good citizenship **civisms**

CIVVIES ▶ civvy

CIVVY n civilian

CIZERS archaic spelling of ▶ scissors

CLABBER vb to cover with mud

CLACH n stone

CLACHAN n small village

CLACHS ▶ clach

CLACK n sound made by two hard objects striking each other ▷ vb make this sound **clacked**

CLACKER n object that makes a clacking sound

CLACKS ▶ clack

CLAD vb

CLADDED adj covered with cladding

CLADDER ▶ clad

CLADDIE another name for ▶ korari

CLADE n group of organisms sharing a

common ancestor **clades**

CLADISM ▶ cladist

CLADIST n proponent of cladistics

CLADODE n stem resembling and functioning as a leaf

CLADS ▶ clad

CLAES Scots word for ▶ clothes

CLAG n sticky mud ▷ vb stick, as mud **clagged**

CLAGGY adj stickily clinging, as mud

CLAGS ▶ clag

CLAIM vb, n claimed, claimer, claims

CLAM n, vb

CLAMANT adj noisy

CLAMBE old variant of ▶ climb

CLAMBER vb, n

CLAME archaic variant of ▶ claim

CLAMES ▶ claim

CLAMMED ▶ clam

CLAMMER n person who gathers clams

CLAMMY adj

CLAMOR = clamour

CLAMORS ▶ clamor

CLAMOUR n, vb

CLAMP n, vb clamped

CLAMPER n spiked metal frame fastened to the sole of a shoe ▷ vb to tread heavily

CLAMPS ▶ clamp

CLAMS ▶ clam

CLAN n

CLANG vb, n clanged

CLANGER n

CLANGOR = clangour

CLANGS ▶ clang

CLANK n, vb clanked, clanks

CLANKY adj making clanking sounds

CLANS ▶ clan

CLAP vb, n

CLAPNET n net that can be closed instantly by pulling a string

CLAPPED ▶ clap

CLAPPER n, vb

CLAPS ▶ clap

CLAPT ▶ clap

CLAQUE n group of people hired to applaud

CLAQUER = claqueur

CLAQUES ▶ claque

CLARAIN n one of the four major lithotypes of banded coal

CLARET n, adj, vb clarets

CLARIES ▶ clary

CLARIFY vb

CLARINI ▶ clarino

CLARINO adj relating to a high passage for the trumpet in 18th-century music ▷ n high register of the trumpet

CLARION n obsolete high-pitched trumpet ▷ adj clear and ringing ▷ vb proclaim loudly

CLARITY n

CLARKIA n N American plant cultivated for its red, purple, or pink flowers

CLARO n mild light-coloured cigar

claroes, claros

CLART vb to dirty **clarted**

CLARTS pl n lumps of mud, esp on shoes

CLARTY adj dirty, esp covered in mud

CLARY n European plant with aromatic leaves and blue flowers

CLASH vb, n **clashed, clasher, clashes**

CLASP n, vb **clasped, clasper, clasps, claspt**

CLASS n, vb **classed, classer**

CLASSES ▸ classis

CLASSIC adj, n

CLASSIS n governing body of elders or pastors

CLASSON n elementary atomic particle

CLASSY adj

CLAST n fragment of a clastic rock

CLASTIC adj composed of fragments ▸ n **clast**

CLASTS ▸ clast

CLAT n irksome or troublesome task ▸ vb to scrape

CLATCH vb to move making a squelching sound

CLATS ▸ clat

CLATTED ▸ clat

CLATTER n, vb

CLAUCHT vb to seize by force **claught**

CLAUSAL ▸ clause

CLAUSE n **clauses**

CLAUT = clat

CLAUTED ▸ claut

CLAUTS ▸ claut

CLAVATE adj shaped like a club with the thicker end uppermost

CLAVE n one of a pair of hardwood sticks struck together to make a hollow sound

CLAVER vb talk idly ▸ n idle talk **clavers**

CLAVES ▸ clave

CLAVI ▸ clavus

CLAVIE n tar-barrel traditionally set alight in Moray in Scotland on Hogmanay

CLAVIER n any keyboard instrument

CLAVIES ▸ clavie

CLAVIS n key

CLAVUS n corn on the toe

CLAW n, vb **clawed, clawer, clawers, clawing, claws**

CLAXON = klaxon

CLAXONS ▸ claxon

CLAY n, vb **clayed, clayey, clayier, claying, clayish**

CLAYPAN n layer of stiff impervious clay situated just below the surface of the ground

CLAYS ▸ clay

CLEAN adj, vb, adv **cleaned**

CLEANER n person or thing that removes dirt

CLEANLY adv easily or smoothly ▸ adj habitually clean or neat

CLEANS ▸ clean

CLEANSE vb

CLEANUP n process of cleaning up or eliminating something

CLEAR adj, adv, vb **cleared, clearer**

CLEARLY adv in a clear, distinct, or obvious manner

CLEARS ▸ clear

CLEAT n wedge ▸ vb supply or support with a cleat or cleats **cleated, cleats**

CLEAVE vb split apart ▸ n split **cleaved**

CLEAVER n

CLEAVES ▸ cleave

CLECHE adj (in heraldry) voided so that only a narrow border is visible

CLECK vb (of birds) to hatch ▸ n piece of gossip **clecked, clecks, clecky**

CLEEK n large hook, such as one used to land fish ▸ vb to seize **cleeked, cleekit, cleeks**

CLEEP = clepe

CLEEPED ▸ cleep

CLEEPS ▸ cleep

CLEEVE n cliff **cleeves**

CLEF n **clefs**

CLEFT ▸ cleave

CLEFTED ▸ cleave

CLEFTS ▸ cleave

CLEG another name for a > **horsefly**

CLEGS ▸ cleg

CLEIK = cleek

CLEIKS ▶ cleek

CLEM vb be hungry or cause to be hungry

CLEMENT adj (of weather) mild

CLEMMED ▶ clem

CLEMS ▶ clem

CLENCH vb, n

CLEOME n type of herbaceous or shrubby plant **cleomes**

CLEPE vb call by the name of **cleped, clepes, cleping, clept**

CLERGY n

CLERIC n **clerics**

CLERID n beetle that preys on other insects **clerids**

CLERISY n learned or educated people

CLERK n, vb **clerked**

CLERKLY adj of or like a clerk ▷ adv in the manner of a clerk

CLERKS ▶ clerk

CLERUCH n settler in a cleruchy

CLEUCH = clough

CLEUCHS ▶ cleuch

CLEUGH = clough

CLEUGHS ▶ cleugh

CLEVE = cleeve

CLEVER adj

CLEVES ▶ cleeve

CLEVIS n type of fastening used in agriculture

CLEW n ball of thread, yarn, or twine ▷ vb coil or roll into a ball **clewed, clewing, clews**

CLICHE n expression or idea that is no longer effective because of overuse ▷ vb use a cliché (in speech or writing) **cliched, cliches**

CLICK n, vb **clicked, clicker**

CLICKET vb make a click

CLICKS ▶ click

CLIED ▶ cly

CLIENT n **clients**

CLIES ▶ cly

CLIFF n, vb **cliffed, cliffs, cliffy, clift, clifted, clifts, clifty**

CLIMATE n, vb

CLIMAX n, vb

CLIMB vb, n **climbed**

CLIMBER n person or thing that climbs

CLIMBS ▶ climb

CLIME n place or its climate **climes**

CLINAL ▶ cline

CLINCH vb, n

CLINE n variation within a species **clines**

CLING vb, n **clinged, clinger, clings, clingy**

CLINIC n **clinics**

CLINK n, vb **clinked**

CLINKER n fused coal left over in a fire or furnace ▷ vb form clinker during burning

CLINKS ▶ clink

CLINT n section of a limestone pavement separated from others by fissures **clints**

CLIP vb, n

CLIPART n large collection of simple drawings stored in a computer

CLIPE = clype

CLIPED ▶ clipe

CLIPES ▶ clipe

CLIPING ▶ clipe

CLIPPED ▶ clip

CLIPPER n

CLIPPIE n bus conductress

CLIPS ▶ clip

CLIPT old inflection of ▶ clip

CLIQUE n, vb **cliqued, cliques**

CLIQUEY adj exclusive, confined to a small group **cliquy**

CLIT > clitoris

CLITIC adj (of a word) incapable of being stressed ▷ n clitic word **clitics**

CLITS ▶ clit

CLITTER vb to stridulate

CLIVERS = cleavers

CLIVIA n plant belonging to the Amaryllid family **clivias**

CLOACA n cavity in most animals into which the alimentary canal and the genital and urinary ducts open **cloacae, cloacal, cloacas**

CLOAK n, vb **cloaked, cloaks**

CLOAM adj made of clay or earthenware ▷ n clay or earthenware pots, dishes, etc, collectively **cloams**

CLOBBER vb, n

CLOCHE n **cloches**

CLOCK n, vb **clocked, clocker, clocks**

CLOD n, vb **clodded, cloddy, clodly, clods**

CLOFF n cleft of a tree **cloffs**

CLOG vb, n **clogged**

CLOGGER n clogmaker

CLOGGY ▶ **clog**

CLOGS ▶ **clog**

CLOISON n partition

CLOKE = **cloak**

CLOKED ▶ **cloke**

CLOKES ▶ **cloke**

CLOKING ▶ **cloke**

CLOMB a past tense and past participle of ▶ **climb**

CLOMP = **clump**

CLOMPED ▶ **clomp**

CLOMPS ▶ **clomp**

CLON = **clone**

CLONAL ▶ **clone**

CLONE n, vb **cloned, cloner, cloners, clones**

CLONIC ▶ **clonus**

CLONING ▶ **clone**

CLONISM n series of clonic spasms

CLONK vb made a loud dull thud ▶ n loud thud **clonked, clonks**

CLONS ▶ **clon**

CLONUS n type of convulsion

CLOOP n sound made when a cork is drawn from a bottle **cloops**

CLOOT n hoof

CLOOTIE adj as in

clootie dumpling kind of dumpling

CLOOTS ▶ **cloot**

CLOP vb, n **clopped, clops**

CLOQUE n fabric with an embossed surface **cloques**

CLOSE vb shut ▶ n end, conclusion ▶ adj near ▶ adv closely, tightly **closed, closely, closer, closers, closes, closest**

CLOSET n, adj, vb **closets**

CLOSEUP n photo taken close to subject

CLOSING ▶ **close**

CLOSURE n, vb

CLOT n, vb

CLOTBUR n burdock

CLOTE n burdock **clotes**

CLOTH n

CLOTHE vb **clothed**

CLOTHES n garments

CLOTHS ▶ **cloth**

CLOTS ▶ **clot**

CLOTTED ▶ **clot**

CLOTTER vb to clot

CLOTTY adj full of clots

CLOTURE n closure in the US Senate ▶ vb end (debate) in the US Senate by cloture

CLOU n crux; focus

CLOUD n, vb **clouded, clouds**

CLOUDY adj

CLOUGH n gorge or narrow ravine **cloughs**

CLOUR vb to thump or dent **cloured, clours**

CLOUS ▶ **clou**

CLOUT n, vb **clouted, clouter, clouts**

CLOVE n tropical evergreen myrtaceous tree

CLOVEN ▶ **cleave**

CLOVER n **clovers, clovery**

CLOVES ▶ **clove**

CLOVIS n as in **clovis point** flint projectile dating from the 10th millennium b.c.

CLOW n clove

CLOWDER n collective term for a group of cats

CLOWN n, vb **clowned, clowns**

CLOWS ▶ **clow**

CLOY vb cause weariness through an excess of something initially pleasurable

CLOYE vb to claw

CLOYED ▶ **cloy**

CLOYES ▶ **cloye**

CLOYING adj

CLOYS ▶ **cloy**

CLOZE adj as in **cloze test** test of the ability to understand text **clozes**

CLUB n, vb **clubbed**

CLUBBER n person who regularly frequents nightclubs

CLUBBY adj sociable, esp effusively so

CLUBMAN n man who is an enthusiastic member of a club or clubs **clubmen**

CLUBS ▸ club

CLUCK *n, vb* clucked, clucks

CLUCKY *adj* wishing to have a baby

CLUDGIE *n* toilet

CLUE *n, vb* clued, clueing, clues, cluing

CLUMBER *n* type of thickset spaniel

CLUMP *n, vb* clumped, clumper, clumps, clumpy

CLUMSY *adj*

CLUNCH *n* hardened clay

CLUNG ▸ cling

CLUNK *n* dull metallic sound ▸ *vb* make such a sound clunked

CLUNKER *n* dilapidated old car or other machine

CLUNKS ▸ clunk

CLUNKY *adj* making a clunking noise

CLUPEID *n* type of fish

CLUSIA *n* tree of the tropical American genus Clusia clusias

CLUSTER *n, vb*

CLUTCH *vb, n*

CLUTCHY *adj* (of a person) tending to cling

CLUTTER *vb, n*

CLY *vb* to steal or seize clying

> A little word meaning to seize or steal, this can be useful when you are short of vowels.

CLYPE *vb* tell tales ▸ *n*

person who tells tales

CLYPEAL ▸ clypeus

CLYPED ▸ clype

CLYPEI ▸ clypeus

CLYPES ▸ clype

CLYPEUS *n* cuticular plate on the head of some insects

CLYPING ▸ clype

CLYSTER *a former name for an* ▸ **enema**

CNEMIAL ▸ cnemis

CNEMIS *n* shin or tibia

CNIDA *n* nematocyst **cnidae**

COACH *n, vb* coached

COACHEE *n* person who receives training from a coach

COACHER ▸ coach

COACHES ▸ coach

COACHY *n* coachman ▸ *adj* resembling or pertaining to a coach

COACT *vb* to act together coacted, coactor, coacts

COADMIT *vb* to admit together

COAEVAL *n* contemporary

COAGENT ▸ coagency

COAGULA ▸ coagulum

COAITA *n* spider monkey coaitas

COAL *n, vb*

COALA = koala

COALAS ▸ coala

COALBIN *n* bin for holding coal

COALBOX *n* box for holding coal

COALED ▸ coal

COALER *n* ship, train,

etc, used to carry or supply coal **coalers**

COALIER ▸ coal

COALIFY *vb* to turn into coal

COALING ▸ coal

COALISE *vb* to form a coalition **coalize**

COALMAN *n* man who delivers coal **coalmen**

COALPIT *n* pit from which coal is extracted

COALS ▸ coal

COALY ▸ coal

COAMING *n* raised frame round a ship's hatchway for keeping out water

COANNEX *vb* to annex with something else

COAPT *vb* to secure coapted, coapts

COARB *n* spiritual successor **coarbs**

COARSE *adj*

COARSEN *vb*

COARSER ▸ coarse

COAST *n, vb* coastal, coasted

COASTER *n* small mat placed under a glass

COASTS ▸ coast

COAT *n, vb*

COATE = quote

COATED *adj* covered with an outer layer, film, etc

COATEE *n* short coat, esp for a baby **coatees**

COATER *n* machine that applies a coating to something **coaters**

COATES ▸ coate

COATI n type of omnivorous mammal
COATING n
COATIS ▸ coati
COATS ▸ coat
COAX vb
COAXAL = coaxial
COAXED, coaxer, coaxers, coaxes ▸ coax
COAXIAL adj (of a cable) transmitting by means of two concentric conductors separated by an insulator
COAXING ▸ coax
COB n stalk of an ear of maize ▷ vb beat, esp on the buttocks
COBAEA n tropical climbing shrub cobaeas
COBALT n cobalts
COBB = cob
COBBED ▸ cob
COBBER n friend cobbers
COBBIER ▸ cobby
COBBING ▸ cob
COBBLE n, vb cobbled
COBBLER n
COBBLES pl n coal in small rounded lumps
COBBS ▸ cobb
COBBY adj short and stocky
COBIA n large dark-striped game fish cobias
COBLE n small single-masted flat-bottomed fishing boat cobles
COBLOAF n round loaf

of bread
COBNUT another name for ▸ hazelnut
COBNUTS ▸ cobnut
COBRA n cobras, cobric
COBS ▸ cob
COBURG n rounded loaf with a cross cut on the top coburgs
COBWEB n cobwebs
COBZA n Romanian lute cobzas
COCA n dried leaves of a S American shrub which contain cocaine
COCAIN = cocaine
COCAINE n
COCAINS ▸ cocain
COCAS ▸ coca
COCCAL ▸ coccus
COCCI ▸ coccus
COCCIC ▸ coccus
COCCID n type of homopterous insect coccids
COCCO n taro
COCCOID ▸ coccus
COCCOS ▸ cocco
COCCOUS ▸ coccus
COCCUS n any spherical or nearly spherical bacterium
COCCYX n
COCH obsolete variant of ▸ coach
COCHAIR vb to chair jointly
COCHES ▸ coch
COCHIN n large breed of domestic fowl cochins
COCHLEA n spiral tube in the internal ear
COCK n, vb

COCKADE n feather or rosette worn on a hat as a badge
COCKED ▸ cock
COCKER n devotee of cockfighting ▷ vb pamper or spoil by indulgence cockers
COCKET n document issued by a customs officer cockets
COCKEYE n eye affected with strabismus or one that squints
COCKIER ▸ cocky
COCKIES ▸ cocky
COCKILY ▸ cocky
COCKING ▸ cock
COCKISH adj wanton
COCKLE n, vb cockled
COCKLER n person employed to gather cockles
COCKLES ▸ cockle
COCKNEY n native of London, esp of its East End ▷ adj characteristic of cockneys or their dialect
COCKPIT n
COCKS ▸ cock
COCKSHY n target aimed at in throwing games
COCKSY adj cocky
COCKUP n something done badly ▷ vb ruin or spoil cockups
COCKY adj, n
COCO n coconut palm
COCOA n cocoas
COCOMAT n mat made from coconut fibre
COCONUT n

COCOON n, vb cocoons

COCOPAN n (in South Africa) a small wagon running on narrow-gauge railway lines used in mines

COCOS ▶ coco

COCOTTE n small fireproof dish in which individual portions of food are cooked

COCOYAM n food plant of West Africa with edible underground stem

COCTILE adj made by exposing to heat

COCTION n boiling

COD n, adj, vb

CODA n final part of a musical composition

CODABLE adj capable of being coded

CODAS ▶ coda

CODDED ▶ cod

CODDER n cod fisherman or his boat codders

CODDING ▶ cod

CODDLE vb, n coddled, coddler, coddles

CODE n, vb

CODEC n set of electrical equipment codecs

CODED ▶ code

CODEIA n codeine codeias

CODEIN = codeine

CODEINA obsolete variant of ▶ codeine

CODEINE n drug used as a painkiller

CODEINS ▶ codein

CODEN n identification code assigned to a publication codens

CODER n person or thing that codes coders

CODES ▶ code

CODETTA n short coda

CODEX n volume of manuscripts of an ancient text

CODFISH n fish

CODGER n old man codgers

CODICES ▶ codex

CODICIL n addition to a will

CODIFY vb

CODILLA n coarse tow of hemp and flax

CODILLE n in the cardgame ombre, term indicating that the game is won

CODING ▶ code

CODINGS ▶ code

CODIST n codifier codists

CODLIN = codling

CODLING n young cod

CODLINS ▶ codlin

CODON n part of a DNA molecule codons

CODRIVE vb take alternate turns driving a car with another person codrove

CODS ▶ cod

COED adj educating both sexes together ▷ n school or college that educates both sexes together

COEDIT vb edit (a book, newspaper, etc) jointly coedits

COEDS ▶ coed

COEHORN n type of small artillery mortar

COELIAC adj of or relating to the abdomen ▷ n person who has coeliac disease

COELOM n body cavity of many multicellular animals coelome, coeloms

COEMPT vb buy up something in its entirety coempts

COENACT vb to enact jointly

COENURE variant form of ▶ coenurus

COENURI ▶ coenurus

COEQUAL n equal ▷ adj of the same size, rank, etc

COERCE vb coerced, coercer, coerces

COERECT vb to erect together

COESITE n polymorph of silicon dioxide

COEVAL n contemporary ▷ adj contemporary coevals

COEXERT vb to exert together

COEXIST vb

COFF vb buy coffed

COFFEE n, adj coffees

COFFER n chest, esp for storing valuables ▷ vb store

COFFERS > cofferdam

COFFIN n, vb

COFFING ▶ coff

COFFINS ▶ coffin

COFFLE n (esp formerly) a line of slaves, beasts, etc, fastened together ▷ vb to fasten together in a coffle **coffled, coffles**

COFFRET n small coffer

COFFS ▶ coff

COFOUND vb to found jointly

COFT ▶ coff

COG n, vb

COGENCE ▶ cogent

COGENCY ▶ cogent

COGENER n congener

COGENT adj

COGGED ▶ cog

COGGER n deceiver **coggers**

COGGIE n quaich or drinking cup **coggies**

COGGING ▶ cog

COGGLE vb wobble or rock **coggled, coggles, coggly**

COGIE = coggie

COGIES ▶ cogie

COGITO n philosophical theory **cogitos**

COGNAC n cognacs

COGNATE adj derived from a common original form ▷ n cognate word or language

COGNISE = cognize

COGNIZE vb perceive, become aware of, or know

COGON n type of coarse tropical grass used for thatching **cogons**

COGS ▶ cog

COGUE n wooden pail

or drinking vessel **cogues**

COGWAY n rack railway **cogways**

COHAB n cohabitor

COHABIT vb

COHABS ▶ cohab

COHEAD vb to head jointly **coheads**

COHEIR n person who inherits jointly with others **coheirs**

COHEN ▶ kohen

COHENS ▶ cohen

COHERE vb hold or stick together **cohered**

COHERER n electrical component

COHERES ▶ cohere

COHIBIT vb to restrain

COHO n type of Pacific salmon **cohoe, cohoes**

COHOG n quahog, an edible clam **cohogs**

COHORN = coehorn

COHORNS ▶ coehorn

COHORT n band of associates **cohorts**

COHOS ▶ coho

COHOSH n type of North American plant

COHOST vb to host jointly **cohosts**

COHUNE n tropical feather palm **cohunes**

COIF vb arrange the hair of ▷ n close-fitting cap worn in the Middle Ages

COIFED adj wearing a coif

COIFFE vb to coiffure

COIFFED ▶ coif

COIFFES ▶ coiffe

COIFING ▶ coif

COIFS ▶ coif

COIGN vb wedge ▷ n quoin **coigne, coigned**

COIGNES ▶ coigne

COIGNS ▶ coign

COIL vb, n, coiled, coiler, coilers, coiling, coils

COIN n, vb

COINAGE n

COINED ▶ coin

COINER ▶ coin

COINERS ▶ coin

COINFER vb infer jointly

COINING ▶ coin

COINOP adj (of a machine) operated by putting a coin in a slot

COINS ▶ coin

COINTER vb to inter together

COIR n coconut fibre, used for matting **coirs**

COIT n buttocks

COITAL ▶ coitus

COITION = coitus

COITS ▶ coit

COITUS n

COJOIN vb to conjoin **cojoins**

COJONES pl n testicles

COKE n, vb **coked**

COKES n fool **cokeses**

COKIER ▶ coky

COKIEST ▶ coky

COKING ▶ coke

COKY adj like coke

COL n high mountain pass

COLA n dark brown fizzy soft drink **colas**

COLBIES ▶ colby

COLBY *n* type of mild-tasting hard cheese **colbys**

COLD *adj*, *n* **colder**, **coldest**

COLDIE *n* cold can or bottle of beer **coldies**

COLDISH ▸ **cold**

COLDLY ▸ **cold**

COLDS ▸ **cold**

COLE = **cabbage**

COLEAD *vb* to lead together **coleads**, **coled**

COLES ▸ **cole**

COLETIT *n* coal tit

COLEUS *n* Old World plant

COLEY = **coalfish**

COLEYS ▸ **coley**

COLIBRI *n* hummingbird

COLIC *n*

COLICIN *n* bacteriocidal protein

COLICKY *adj* relating to or suffering from colic

COLICS ▸ **colic**

COLIES ▸ **coly**

COLIN *n* quail **colins**

COLITIC ▸ **colitis**

COLITIS *n* inflammation of the colon

COLL *vb* to embrace

COLLAGE *n*, *vb*

COLLAR *n*, *vb*

COLLARD *n* variety of the cabbage with a crown of edible leaves

COLLARS ▸ **collar**

COLLATE *vb*

COLLECT *vb*, *n*

COLLED ▸ **coll**

COLLEEN *n* girl

COLLEGE *n*

COLLET *n* (in a jewellery setting) a band or coronet-shaped claw that holds an individual stone ▸ *vb* mount in a collet **collets**

COLLIDE *vb*

COLLIE *n*

COLLIED ▸ **colly**

COLLIER *n* coal miner

COLLIES ▸ **colly**

COLLING *n* embrace

COLLINS *n* type of cocktail

COLLOID *n* suspension of particles in a solution ▸ *adj* of or relating to the gluelike translucent material found in certain degenerating tissues

COLLOP *n* small slice of meat **collops**

COLLS ▸ **coll**

COLLUDE *vb*

COLLY *n* soot or grime, such as coal dust ▸ *vb* begrime

COLOBI ▸ **colobus**

COLOBID ▸ **colobus**

COLOBUS *n* type of Old World monkey

COLOG *n* logarithm of the reciprocal of a number

COLOGNE *n*

COLOGS ▸ **colog**

COLON *n* **colone**

COLONEL *n*

COLONES ▸ **colone**

COLONI ▸ **colonus**

COLONIC *adj* of or relating to the colon ▸ *n* irrigation of the colon

COLONS ▸ **colon**

COLONUS *n* ancient Roman farmer

COLONY *n*

COLOR = **colour**

COLORED US spelling of ▸ **coloured**

COLORER ▸ **color**

COLORS ▸ **color**

COLORY = **coloury**

COLOSSI > **colossus**

COLOUR *n* appearance of things as a result of reflecting light ▸ *vb* apply colour to **colours**

COLOURY *adj* possessing colour

COLS ▸ **col**

COLT *n*, *vb*

COLTAN *n* metallic ore **coltans**

COLTED ▸ **colt**

COLTER = **coulter**

COLTERS ▸ **coulter**

COLTING ▸ **colt**

COLTISH *adj* inexperienced

COLTS ▸ **colt**

COLUGO *n* flying lemur **colugos**

COLUMEL *n* in botany, the central column in a capsule

COLUMN *n*, *vb* **columns**

COLURE *n* either of two great circles on the celestial sphere **colures**

COLY *n* S African arboreal bird

COLZA n oilseed rape, a Eurasian plant with bright yellow flowers **colzas**

COMA n

COMADE ▶ comake

COMAE ▶ coma

COMAKE vb to make together **comaker, comakes**

COMAL ▶ coma

COMARB ▶ coarb

COMARBS ▶ comarb

COMART n covenant **comarts**

COMAS ▶ coma

COMATE adj having tufts of hair ▶ n companion **comates**

COMATIC ▶ coma

COMATIK variant of ▶ komatik

COMB n, vb

COMBAT vb, n **combats**

COMBE = comb

COMBED ▶ comb

COMBER n long curling wave **combers**

COMBES ▶ combe

COMBI n combination boiler

COMBIER ▶ comby

COMBIES ▶ comby

COMBINE vb, n

COMBING ▶ comb

COMBIS ▶ combi

COMBLE n apex; zenith **combles**

COMBO n small group of jazz musicians **combos**

COMBS ▶ comb

COMBUST adj invisible due to proximity to the sun ▶ vb burn

COMBY adj comb-like ▶ n combination boiler

COME vb

COMEDIC adj of or relating to comedy

COMEDO the technical name for ▶ blackhead

COMEDOS ▶ comedo

COMEDY n

COMELY adj

COMER n person who comes **comers**

COMES ▶ come

COMET n

COMETH ▶ come

COMETIC ▶ comet

COMETS ▶ comet

COMFIER ▶ comfy

COMFIT n sugar-coated sweet **comfits**

COMFORT n, vb

COMFREY n tall plant with bell-shaped flowers

COMFY adj comfortable

COMIC adj, n

COMICAL adj

COMICE n kind of pear **comices**

COMICS ▶ comic

COMING ▶ come

COMINGS ▶ come

COMIQUE n comic actor

COMITAL adj relating to a count or earl

COMITIA n ancient Roman assembly

COMITY n friendly politeness, esp between different countries

COMIX n comic books in general

COMM n as in comm

badge small wearable badge-shaped radio transmitter and receiver

COMMA n

COMMAND vb, n

COMMAS ▶ comma

COMMATA ▶ comma

COMMEND vb

COMMENT n, vb

COMMER ▶ comer

COMMERE n female compere

COMMERS ▶ commer

COMMIE adj communist **commies**

COMMIS n apprentice waiter or chef ▶ adj (of a waiter or chef) apprentice

COMMIT vb commits

COMMIX a rare word for ▶ mix

COMMIXT ▶ commix

COMMO short for ▶ communist

COMMODE n seat with a hinged flap concealing a chamber pot

COMMODO = comodo

COMMON adj, n, vb

COMMONS n people not of noble birth viewed as forming a political order

COMMOS ▶ commo

COMMOT n in medieval Wales, a division of land **commote, commots**

COMMOVE vb disturb

COMMS pl n communications

COMMUNE n, vb

COMMUTE vb, n

COMMY = commie

COMODO adv (to be performed) at a convenient relaxed speed

COMOSE another word for ▷ **comate**

COMOUS adj hairy

COMP n person who sets and corrects type ▷ vb set or correct type

COMPACT adj, n, vb

COMPAGE obsolete form of > **compages**

COMPAND vb (of a transmitter signal) to compress before, and expand after, transmission

COMPANY n, vb

COMPARE vb

COMPART vb to divide into parts

COMPAS n rhythm in flamenco

COMPASS n, vb

COMPAST adj rounded

COMPEAR vb in Scots law, to appear in court

COMPED > compositor

COMPEER n person of equal rank, status, or ability ▷ vb to equal

COMPEL vb compels

COMPEND n compendium

COMPER n person who regularly enters competitions

COMPERE n, vb

COMPERS ▷ comper

COMPETE vb

COMPILE vb

COMPING ▷ comp

COMPLEX adj, n, vb

COMPLIN = compline

COMPLOT n plot or conspiracy ▷ vb plot together

COMPLY vb

COMPO n mixture of materials, such as mortar, plaster, etc ▷ adj intended to last for several days

COMPONE = compony

COMPONY adj made up of alternating metal and colour, colour and fur, or fur and metal

COMPORT vb behave (oneself) in a specified way

COMPOS ▷ compo

COMPOSE vb

COMPOST n, vb

COMPOT = compote

COMPOTE n fruit stewed with sugar

COMPOTS ▷ compot

COMPS ▷ comp

COMPT obsolete variant of ▷ **count**

COMPTED ▷ compt

COMPTER n formerly, a prison

COMPTS ▷ count

COMPUTE vb, n

COMRADE n

COMS pl n one-piece woollen undergarment with long sleeves and legs

COMTE n European nobleman **comtes**

COMUS n wild party **comuses**

CON vb, n, prep

CONACRE n farming land let for a season or for eleven months ▷ vb to let conacre

CONARIA > conarium

CONATUS n effort or striving of natural impulse

CONCAVE adj, vb

CONCEAL vb

CONCEDE vb

CONCEDO interj I allow; I concede (a point)

CONCEIT n, vb

CONCENT n concord, as of sounds, voices, etc

CONCEPT n

CONCERN n, vb

CONCERT n

CONCH = concha

CONCHA n any bodily organ or part resembling a shell in shape **conchae, conchal, conchas**

CONCHE vb (in chocolate-making) to use a conche **conched, conches**

CONCHIE n conscientious objector

CONCHO n American metal ornament **conchos**

CONCHS ▷ conch

CONCHY = conchie

CONCISE adj, vb

CONCOCT vb

CONCORD n state of peaceful agreement, harmony ▷ vb to agree

CONCREW vb to grow together

CONCUPY n concupiscence

CONCUR vb **concurs**

CONCUSS vb injure (the brain) by a fall or blow

COND old inflection of ▶ **con**

CONDEMN vb

CONDER n person who directs the steering of a vessel **conders**

CONDIE n culvert; tunnel **condies**

CONDIGN adj (esp of a punishment) fitting

CONDO n condominium **condoes**

CONDOLE vb express sympathy with someone in grief, pain, etc

CONDOM n **condoms**

CONDONE vb

CONDOR n large vulture of S America **condors**

CONDUCE vb lead or contribute (to a result)

CONDUCT n, vb

CONDUIT n

CONDYLE n rounded projection on the articulating end of a bone

CONE n, vb **coned, cones**

CONEY = **cony**

CONEYS ▶ **coney**

CONF n online forum

CONFAB n conversation ▷ vb converse **confabs**

CONFECT vb prepare

by combining ingredients

CONFER vb **confers**

CONFESS vb

CONFEST adj admitted

CONFIDE vb

CONFINE vb, n

CONFIRM vb

CONFIT n preserve **confits**

CONFIX vb to fasten

CONFLUX n merging or following togther, especially of rivers

CONFORM vb

CONFS ▶ **conf**

CONFUSE vb

CONFUTE vb prove wrong

CONGA n dance performed by a number of people in single file ▷ vb dance the conga **congaed, congas**

CONGE n permission to depart or dismissal, esp when formal ▷ vb to take one's leave

CONGEAL vb

CONGED ▶ **conge**

CONGEE ▶ **conge**

CONGEED ▶ **congee**

CONGEES ▶ **congee**

CONGER n **congers**

CONGES ▶ **conge**

CONGEST vb crowd or become crowded to excess

CONGII ▶ **congius**

CONGIUS n unit of liquid measure equal to 1 Imperial gallon

CONGO = **congou**

CONGOES ▶ **congou**

CONGOS ▶ **congo**

CONGOU n kind of black tea from China **congous**

CONGREE vb to agree

CONGRUE vb to agree

CONI ▶ **conus**

CONIA = **coniine**

CONIAS ▶ **coniine**

CONIC adj having the shape of a cone

CONICAL adj

CONICS n branch of geometry

CONIDIA > **conidium**

CONIES ▶ **cony**

CONIFER n

CONIINE n colourless poisonous soluble liquid alkaloid found in hemlock

CONIMA n gum resin from the conium hemlock tree **conimas**

CONIN = **coniine**

CONINE = **coniine**

CONINES ▶ **conine**

CONING ▶ **cone**

CONINS ▶ **conin**

CONIUM n N temperate umbelliferous plant, esp hemlock **coniums**

CONJECT vb to conjecture

CONJEE vb prepare as, or in, a conjee (a gruel of boiled rice and water) **conjeed, conjees**

CONJOIN vb join or become joined

CONJURE vb perform tricks that appear to

be magic
CONJURY n magic
CONK n nose ▷ vb strike (someone) on the head or nose **conked**
CONKER n
CONKERS n game played with conkers tied on strings
CONKIER ▷ conky
CONKING ▷ conk
CONKS ▷ conk
CONKY adj affected by the timber disease, conk
CONN = con
CONNATE adj existing in a person or thing from birth
CONNE = con
CONNECT vb
CONNED ▷ con
CONNER = conder
CONNERS ▷ conner
CONNES ▷ conne
CONNIE n connies
CONNING ▷ con
CONNIVE vb
CONNOTE vb imply or suggest
CONNS ▷ conn
CONOID n geometric surface ▷ adj conical, cone-shaped **conoids**
CONQUER vb
CONS ▷ con
CONSEIL n advice
CONSENT n, vb
CONSIGN vb
CONSIST vb
CONSOL n consolidated annuity, a British government bond
CONSOLE vb, n

CONSOLS pl n irredeemable British government securities
CONSORT vb, n
CONSPUE vb spit on with contempt
CONSTER obsolete variant of > **construe**
CONSUL n consuls
CONSULT vb
CONSUME vb
CONTACT n, vb, interj
CONTAIN vb
CONTE n tale or short story, esp of adventure
CONTECK n contention
CONTEMN vb regard with contempt
CONTEND vb
CONTENT n meaning or substance of a piece of writing ▷ adj satisfied with things as they are ▷ vb make (someone) content
CONTES ▷ conte
CONTEST n, vb
CONTEXT n
CONTO n former Portuguese monetary unit worth 1000 escudos
CONTORT vb twist out of shape
CONTOS ▷ conto
CONTOUR n, vb
CONTRA n counter-argument **contras**
CONTRAT old form of > **contract**
CONTROL n, vb
CONTUND vb to pummel
CONTUSE vb injure

(the body) without breaking the skin
CONURE n small American parrot **conures**
CONUS n any of several cone-shaped structures
CONVECT vb to circulate hot air by convection
CONVENE vb
CONVENT n, vb
CONVERT vb, n
CONVEX adj, vb
CONVEY vb **conveys**
CONVICT vb, n, adj
CONVIVE vb to feast together
CONVO n conversation
CONVOKE vb call together
CONVOS ▷ convo
CONVOY n, vb, **convoys**
CONY n rabbit
COO vb, n, interj
COOCOO old spelling of ▷ **cuckoo**
COOED ▷ coo
COOEE interj call to attract attention ▷ vb utter this call ▷ n calling distance **cooeed, cooees**
COOER ▷ coo
COOERS ▷ coo
COOEY = cooee
COOEYED ▷ cooey
COOEYS ▷ cooey
COOF n simpleton **coofs**
COOING ▷ coo
COOINGS ▷ coo

COOK *vb, n* cooked
COOKER *n* cookers
COOKERY *n*
COOKEY = cookie
COOKEYS ▶ cookey
COOKIE *n* cookies
COOKING ▶ cook
COOKOFF *n* cookery competition
COOKOUT *n* party where a meal is cooked and eaten out of doors
COOKS ▶ cook
COOKTOP *n* flat unit for cooking in saucepans or the top part of a stove
COOKY = cookie
COOL *adj, vb, n*
COOLANT *n*
COOLED ▶ cool
COOLER *n* container for making or keeping things cool coolers
COOLEST ▶ cool
COOLIE *n* unskilled Oriental labourer coolies
COOLING *n as in* regenerative cooling
COOLISH ▶ cool
COOLLY ▶ cool
COOLS ▶ cool
COOLTH *n* coolness coolths
COOLY = coolie
COOM *n* waste material ▷ *vb* to blacken
COOMB ▶ comb
COOMBE ▶ comb
COOMBES ▶ coombe
COOMBS ▶ comb
COOMED ▶ coom

COOMIER ▶ coomy
COOMING ▶ coom
COOMS ▶ coom
COOMY *adj* grimy
COON *n* raccoon
COONCAN *n* card game for two players, similar to rummy
COONDOG *n* dog trained to hunt raccoons
COONS ▶ coon
COONTIE *n* evergreen plant of S Florida coonty
COOP *n, vb* cooped
COOPER *n* person who makes or repairs barrels ▷ *vb* make or mend (barrels, casks, etc) coopers
COOPERY = cooperage
COOPING ▶ coop
COOPS ▶ coop
COOPT *vb* coopted, coopts
COORIE = courie
COORIED ▶ coorie
COORIES ▶ coorie
COOS ▶ coo
COOSEN = cozen
COOSENS ▶ coosen
COOSER *n* stallion coosers
COOSIN = cozen
COOSINS ▶ coosin
COOST *Scots form of* ▶ cast
COOT *n*
COOTCH *n* hiding place ▷ *vb* hide
COOTER *n* type of freshwater turtle

cooters
COOTIE ▶ louse
COOTIES ▶ cootie
COOTS ▶ coot
COP = copper
COPAIBA *n* resin obtained from certain tropical trees copaiva
COPAL *n* resin used in varnishes
COPALM *n* aromatic resin copalms
COPALS ▶ copal
COPAY *n* amount payable for treatment by person with medical insurance copays
COPE *vb, n*
COPECK = kopeck
COPECKS ▶ copeck
COPED ▶ cope
COPEN *n* shade of blue copens
COPEPOD *n* type of minute crustacean
COPER *n* horse-dealer ▷ *vb* smuggle liquor to deep-sea fishermen copered, copers
COPES ▶ cope
COPIED ▶ copy
COPIER *n* machine that copies copiers
COPIES ▶ copy
COPIHUE *n* Chilean bellflower
COPILOT *n* second pilot of an aircraft
COPING *n* sloping top row of a wall copings
COPIOUS *adj*
COPITA *n* tulip-shaped sherry glass copitas

COPLOT vb plot together **coplots**

COPOUT n act of avoiding responsibility **copouts**

COPPED ▶ copper

COPPER n, adj, vb **coppers, coppery**

COPPICE n, vb

COPPIES ▶ coppy

COPPIN n ball of thread

COPPING ▶ copper

COPPINS ▶ coppin

COPPLE n hill rising to a point **copples**

COPPRA = copra

COPPRAS ▶ coppra

COPPY n small wooden stool

COPRA n dried oil-yielding kernel of the coconut **coprah**

COPRAHS ▶ coprah

COPRAS ▶ copra

COPS ▶ copper

COPSE = coppice

COPSED ▶ copse

COPSES ▶ copse

COPSHOP n police station

COPSIER ▶ copsy

COPSING ▶ copse

COPSY adj having copses

COPTER n helicopter **copters**

COPULA n verb used to link the subject and complement of a sentence **copulae, copular, copulas**

COPY n, vb

COPYBOY n formerly, in journalism, boy who carried copy and ran errands

COPYCAT n person who imitates or copies someone ▶ vb to imitate with great attention to detail

COPYING ▶ copy

COPYISM n slavish copying

COPYIST n person who makes written copies

COQUET vb behave flirtatiously **coquets**

COQUINA n soft limestone

COQUITO n Chilean palm tree yielding edible nuts and a syrup

COR interj exclamation of surprise, amazement, or admiration

CORACLE n

CORAL n, adj

CORALLA > corallum

CORALS ▶ coral

CORAM prep before, in the presence of

CORANTO = courante

CORBAN n gift to God **corbans**

CORBE obsolete variant of ▶ corbel

CORBEAU n blackish green colour

CORBEIL n carved ornament in the form of a basket of fruit, flowers, etc

CORBEL n stone or timber support sticking out of a wall ▶ vb lay (a stone or brick) so that it forms a corbel **corbels**

CORBES ▶ corbe

CORBIE n raven or crow **corbies**

CORBINA n type of North American whiting

CORBY = corbie

CORCASS n in Ireland, marshland

CORD n, adj, vb

CORDAGE n lines and rigging of a vessel

CORDATE adj heart-shaped

CORDED adj tied or fastened with cord

CORDER ▶ cord

CORDERS ▶ cord

CORDIAL adj, n

CORDING ▶ cord

CORDITE n

CORDOBA n standard monetary unit of Nicaragua

CORDON n, vb **cordons**

CORDS pl n trousers made of corduroy

CORE n, vb **cored**

COREIGN vb to reign jointly

CORELLA n white Australian cockatoo

COREMIA > coremium

CORER ▶ core

CORERS ▶ core

CORES ▶ core

CORF n wagon or basket used formerly in mines

CORGI n short-legged sturdy dog **corgis**

CORIA ▶ corium

CORIES ▸ cory
CORING ▸ core
CORIOUS adj leathery
CORIUM n deep inner layer of the skin **coriums**
CORIVAL = corrival
CORIXID n type of water bug
CORK n, vb, adj
CORKAGE n restaurant's charge for serving wine bought elsewhere
CORKED adj (of wine) spoiled through having a decayed cork
CORKER n splendid or outstanding person or thing **corkers**
CORKIER ▸ corky
CORKING adj excellent
CORKIR n lichen from which red or purple dye is made **corkirs**
CORKS = corky
CORKY = corked
CORM n
CORMEL n new small corm arising from the base of a fully developed one **cormels**
CORMOID adj like a corm
CORMOUS ▸ corm
CORMS ▸ corm
CORMUS n corm
CORN n, vb
CORNAGE n rent fixed according to the number of horned cattle pastured
CORNCOB n core of an

ear of maize, to which the kernels are attached
CORNEA n corneae, corneal, corneas
CORNED adj preserved in salt or brine
CORNEL n type of plant such as the dogwood and dwarf cornel **cornels**
CORNER n, vb corners
CORNET = cornett
CORNETS ▸ cornet
CORNETT n musical instrument
CORNFED adj fed on corn
CORNFLY n small fly
CORNI ▸ corno
CORNICE n, vb
CORNIER ▸ corny
CORNIFY vb turn soft tissue hard
CORNILY ▸ corny
CORNING ▸ corn
CORNIST n horn-player
CORNO n French horn
CORNROW n hairstyle in which the hair is plaited in close parallel rows ▸ vb style the hair in a cornrow
CORNS ▸ corn
CORNU n part or structure resembling a horn or having a hornlike pattern **cornua, cornual**
CORNUS n any member of the genus Cornus, such as dogwood
CORNUTE adj having or resembling cornua

▸ vb to make a cuckold of
CORNUTO n cuckold
CORNY adj
CORODY n feudal law
COROLLA n petals of a flower collectively
CORONA n ring of light round the moon or sun **coronae**
CORONAL n circlet for the head ▸ adj of or relating to a corona or coronal
CORONAS ▸ corona
CORONEL n iron head of a tilting spear
CORONER n
CORONET n
CORONIS n symbol used in Greek writing
COROZO n tropical American palm whose seeds yield a useful oil **corozos**
CORPORA ▸ corpus
CORPS n
CORPSE n, vb corpsed, corpses
CORPUS n collection of writings, esp by a single author
CORRADE vb to erode by the abrasive action of rock particles
CORRAL n enclosure for cattle or horses ▸ vb put in a corral **corrals**
CORREA n correas
CORRECT adj, vb
CORRIDA the Spanish word for ▸ bullfight
CORRIE = cirque

CORRIES ▶ corrie
CORRODE vb
CORRODY = corody
CORRUPT adj, vb
CORS ▶ cor
CORSAC n type of fox of central Asia **corsacs**
CORSAGE n small bouquet worn on the bodice of a dress
CORSAIR n pirate
CORSE n corpse **corses**
CORSET n, vb **corsets**
CORSEY n pavement or pathway **corseys**
CORSIVE n corrodent
CORSLET = corselet
CORSNED n ordeal to discover innocence or guilt
CORSO n promenade **corsos**
CORTEGE n
CORTEX n
CORTILE n open, internal courtyard **cortili**
CORTIN n adrenal cortex extract
CORTINA n weblike part of certain mushrooms
CORTINS ▶ cortin
CORULER n joint ruler
CORVEE n day's unpaid labour owed by a feudal vassal to his lord **corvees**
CORVES ▶ corf
CORVET = curvet
CORVETS ▶ corvet
CORVID n any member of the crow family **corvids**
CORVINA = corbina

CORVINE adj of, relating to, or resembling a crow
CORVUS n type of ancient hook
CORY n catfish belonging to the South American Corydoras genus
CORYLUS n hazel genus
CORYMB n flat-topped flower cluster ▶ vb be corymb-like **corymbs**
CORYPHE n coryphaeus
CORYZA n acute inflammation in the nose **coryzal, coryzas**
COS = cosine
COSE vb get cosy
COSEC = cosecant
COSECH n hyperbolic cosecant **cosechs**
COSECS ▶ cosec
COSED ▶ cose
COSES ▶ cose
COSET n mathematical set **cosets**
COSEY n tea cosy **coseys**
COSH n heavy blunt weapon ▶ vb hit with a cosh **coshed**
COSHER vb pamper or coddle **coshers**
COSHERY n Irish chief's right to lodge at his tenants' houses
COSHES ▶ cosh
COSHING ▶ cosh
COSIE = cosy
COSIED ▶ cosy
COSIER n cobbler **cosiers**

COSIES ▶ cosy
COSIEST ▶ cosy
COSIGN vb to sign jointly **cosigns**
COSILY ▶ cosy
COSINE n **cosines**
COSING ▶ cose
COSMEA n plant of the genus Cosmos **cosmeas**
COSMIC adj
COSMID n segment of DNA **cosmids**
COSMIN = cosmine
COSMINE n substance resembling dentine
COSMINS ▶ cosmin
COSMISM n Russian cultural and philosophical movement **cosmist**
COSMOID adj (of the scales of coelacanths and lungfish) consisting of two inner bony layers and an outer layer of cosmine
COSMOS n
COSS another name for ▶ kos
COSSACK n Slavonic warrior-peasant
COSSES ▶ coss
COSSET vb, n **cossets**
COSSIE n informal name for a swimming costume **cossies**
COST n, vb
COSTA n riblike part, such as the midrib of a plant leaf **costae**
COSTAL n strengthening rib of an insect's wing **costals**

COSTAR *n* actor who shares the billing with another ▷ *vb* share the billing with another actor

COSTARD *n* English variety of apple tree

COSTARS ▷ costar

COSTATE *adj* having ribs

COSTE *vb* to draw near

COSTEAN *vb* to mine for lodes

COSTED ▷ cost

COSTER *n* person who sells fruit, vegetables etc from a barrow costers

COSTES ▷ coste

COSTING *n* as in marginal costing

COSTIVE *adj* having or causing constipation

COSTLY *adj*

COSTREL *n* flask, usually of earthenware or leather

COSTS ▷ cost

COSTUME *n, vb*

COSTUS *n* Himalayan herb with an aromatic root

COSY *adj, n, vb* cosying

COT *n, vb*

COTAN = cotangent

COTANS > cotangent

COTE ▷ cot

COTEAU *n* hillside coteaux

COTED ▷ cot

COTERIE *n* exclusive group, clique

COTES ▷ cote

COTH *n* hyperbolic cotangent coths

COTHURN = cothurnus

COTIDAL *adj* (of a line on a tidal chart) joining points at which high tide occurs simultaneously

COTING ▷ cot

COTINGA *n* tropical bird

COTISE = cottise

COTISED ▷ cotise

COTISES ▷ cotise

COTLAND *n* grounds that belong to a cotter

COTS ▷ cot

COTT ▷ cot

COTTA *n* short form of surplice cottae

COTTAGE *n, vb*

COTTAR = cotter

COTTARS ▷ cottar

COTTAS ▷ cotta

COTTED ▷ cot

COTTER *n* pin or wedge used to secure machine parts ▷ *vb* secure (two parts) with a cotter

COTTERS ▷ cottier

COTTID *n* type of fish typically with a large head, tapering body, and spiny fins cottids

COTTIER = cotter

COTTING ▷ cot

COTTISE *n* type of heraldic decoration ▷ *vb* (in heraldry) decorate with a cottise

COTTOID *adj* resembling a fish of the genus Cottus

COTTON *n, vb* cottons, cottony, cottown

COTTS ▷ cott

COTTUS *n* type of fish with four yellowish knobs on its head

COTWAL *n* Indian police officer cotwals

COTYLAE ▷ cotyle

COTYLE *n* cuplike cavity cotyles

COTYPE *n* type specimen in biological study cotypes

COUCAL *n* type of ground-living bird of Africa, S Asia, and Australia, with long strong legs coucals

COUCH *n, vb*

COUCHE *adj* in heraldry (of a shield), tilted

COUCHED ▷ couch

COUCHEE *n* reception held late at night

COUCHER ▷ couch

COUCHES ▷ couch

COUDE *adj* relating to the construction of a reflecting telescope

COUGAN *n* drunk and rowdy person cougans

COUGAR *n* cougars

COUGH *vb, n* coughed, cougher, coughs

COUGUAR = cougar

COULD ▷ can

COULDST *vb* form of 'could' used with the pronoun thou or its relative form

COULEE *n* flow of molten lava coulees

COULIS *n* thin purée of vegetables or fruit

COULOIR n deep gully on a mountain side, esp in the French Alps

COULOMB n

COULTER n blade at the front of a ploughshare

COUNCIL n, adj

COUNSEL n, vb

COUNT vb, n counted

COUNTER n, vb, adv

COUNTRY n

COUNTS ▶ count

COUNTY n, adj

COUP n, vb

COUPE n sports car with two doors and a sloping fixed roof

COUPED ▶ coup

COUPEE n dance movement coupees

COUPER n dealer coupers

COUPES ▶ coupe

COUPING ▶ coup

COUPLE n, vb coupled

COUPLER n mechanical device

COUPLES ▶ couple

COUPLET n

COUPON n coupons

COUPS ▶ coup

COUPURE n entrenchment made by beseiged forces behind a breach

COUR obsolete variant of ▶ cover

COURAGE n

COURANT n courante ▷ adj (of an animal) running

COURB vb to bend courbed, courbs

COURD obsolete variant

of ▶ covered

COURE obsolete variant of ▶ cover

COURED ▶ coure

COURES ▶ coure

COURIE vb nestle or snuggle couried

COURIER n, vb

COURIES ▶ courie

COURING ▶ cour

COURLAN another name for ▶ limpkin

COURS ▶ cour

COURSE n, vb coursed

COURSER n swift horse

COURSES another word for ▶ menses

COURT n, vb courted

COURTER n suitor

COURTLY adj ceremoniously polite

COURTS ▶ court

COUSIN n cousins

COUTA n coutas

COUTEAU n large two-edged knife used formerly as a weapon

COUTER n armour designed to protect the elbow couters

COUTH adj refined ▷ n refinement couther

COUTHIE adj sociable

COUTHS ▶ couth

COUTHY adj couthier ▶ couthie

COUTIL n type of tightly-woven twill cloth coutils

COUTURE n, adj

COUVADE n custom in certain cultures relating to childbirth

COUVERT another word for ▶ cover

COUZIN n South African word for a friend couzins

COVARY vb vary together maintaining a certain mathematical relationship

COVE n, vb coved

COVELET n small cove

COVEN n meeting of witches covens

COVENT ▶ convent

COVENTS ▶ convent

COVER vb, n covered, coverer, covers

COVERT adj, n coverts

COVERUP n concealment of a mistake, crime, etc

COVES ▶ cove

COVET vb coveted, coveter, covets

COVEY n small flock of grouse or partridge coveys

COVIN n conspiracy between two or more persons

COVING = cove

COVINGS ▶ coving

COVINS ▶ covin

COVYNE = covin

COVYNES ▶ covyne

COW n, vb

COWAGE n tropical climbing plant cowages

COWAL n shallow lake or swampy depression supporting vegetation cowals

COWAN n drystone waller cowans

COWARD n, vb cowards

COWBANE n poisonous marsh plant

COWBELL n bell hung around a cow's neck

COWBIND n any of various bryony plants, esp the white bryony

COWBIRD n American oriole with a dark plumage and short bill

COWBOY n, vb cowboys

COWED ► cow

COWEDLY ► cow

COWER vb cowered, cowers

COWFISH n type of trunkfish with hornlike spines over the eyes

COWFLAP n cow dung

COWFLOP n foxglove

COWGIRL n female cowboy

COWHAGE = cowage

COWHAND = cowboy

COWHEEL n heel of a cow, used as cooking ingredient

COWHERB n European plant with clusters of pink flowers

COWHERD n person employed to tend cattle

COWHIDE n hide of a cow ▷ vb to lash with a cowhide whip

COWIER ► cowy

COWIEST ► cowy

COWING ► cow

COWISH adj cowardly

COWITCH another name for ► cowage

COWK vb retch or feel

nauseated cowked, cowking, cowks

COWL = cowling

COWLED adj wearing a cowl

COWLICK n tuft of hair over the forehead

COWLING n cover on an engine

COWLS ► cowl

COWMAN n man who owns cattle cowmen

COWP = coup

COWPAT n pool of cow dung cowpats

COWPEA n type of tropical climbing plant cowpeas

COWPED ► cowp

COWPIE n cowpat cowpies

COWPING ► cowp

COWPLOP n cow dung

COWPOKE n cowboy

COWPOX n disease of cows

COWPS ► cowp

COWRIE n brightly-marked sea shell cowries

COWRITE vb to write jointly cowrote

COWRY = cowrie

COWS ► cow

COWSHED n byre

COWSKIN = cowhide

COWSLIP n

COWTREE n South American tree that produces latex

COWY adj cowlike

COX n, vb

COXA n technical name for the hipbone

or hip joint coxae, coxal

COXALGY = coxalgia

COXCOMB = cockscomb

COXED ► cox

COXES ► cox

COXIB n anti-inflammatory drug coxibs

COXIER ► coxy

COXIEST ► coxy

COXING ► cox

COXITIS n inflammation of the hip joint

COXLESS ► cox

COXY adj cocky

COY adj, vb

COYDOG n cross between a coyote and a dog coydogs

COYED, coyer, coyest, coying, coyish, coyly, coyness ► coy

COYOTE n coyotes

COYPOU = coypu

COYPOUS ► coypou

COYPU ► coypus

COYS ► coy

COZ archaic word for ► cousin

> Coz is an old word for **cousin** and a good one to know for using the Z.

COZE vb to chat cozed

COZEN vb cheat, trick cozened, cozener, cozens

COZES ► coze

COZEY n tea cosy cozeys, cozie

COZIED ► cosy

COZIER n cobbler coziers

COZIES ▸ cozey
COZIEST ▸ cozy
COZILY ▸ cozy
COZING ▸ coze
COZY ▸ cosy
COZYING ▸ cozy
COZZES ▸ coz
CRAAL vb to enclose in a craal (or kraal) **craaled, craals**
CRAB n crabbed
CRABBER n crab fisherman
CRABBIT adj bad-tempered
CRABBY adj bad-tempered
CRABS ▸ crab
CRACK vb, n, adj
CRACKED adj damaged by cracking ▷ n sharp noise
CRACKER n
CRACKET n low stool, often one with three legs
CRACKLE vb, n
CRACKLY adj making a cracking sound
CRACKS ▸ crack
CRACKUP n physical or mental breakdown
CRACKY adj full of cracks
CRACOWE n medieval shoe with a sharply pointed toe
CRADLE n, vb **cradled, cradler, cradles**
CRAFT n, vb crafted
CRAFTER n person doing craftwork
CRAFTS ▸ craft
CRAFTY adj

CRAG n
CRAGGED = craggy
CRAGGY adj
CRAGS ▸ crag
CRAIC n Irish word meaning fun **craics**
CRAIG a Scot word for ▸ crag
CRAIGS ▸ craig
CRAKE n bird of the rail family, such as the corncrake ▷ vb to boast **craked, crakes, craking**
CRAM vb, n
CRAMBE n any plant of the genus Crambe **crambes**
CRAMBO n word game **crambos**
CRAME n merchant's booth or stall **crames**
CRAMESY = cramoisy
CRAMMED ▸ cram
CRAMMER n person or school that prepares pupils for an examination
CRAMP n, vb
CRAMPED adj
CRAMPER n spiked metal plate used as a brace for the feet in throwing the stone
CRAMPET n cramp iron **crampit**
CRAMPON n spiked plate strapped to a boot for climbing on ice ▷ vb climb using crampons
CRAMPS ▸ cramp
CRAMPY adj affected

with cramp
CRAMS ▸ cram
CRAN n unit of capacity used for measuring fresh herring, equal to 37.5 gallons
CRANAGE n use of a crane
CRANCH vb to crunch
CRANE n, vb **craned, cranes**
CRANIA ▸ cranium
CRANIAL adj of or relating to the skull
CRANING ▸ crane
CRANIUM n
CRANK n, vb, adj **cranked, cranker**
CRANKLE vb to bend or wind
CRANKLY adj vigorously
CRANKS ▸ crank
CRANKY ▸ crank
CRANNOG n ancient Celtic lake or bog dwelling
CRANNY n, vb
CRANS ▸ cran
CRANTS n garland carried in front of a maiden's bier
CRAP n rubbish, nonsense ▷ vb defecate
CRAPAUD n frog or toad
CRAPE = crepe; **craped, crapes, crapier, craping**
CRAPLE = grapple
CRAPLES ▸ craple
CRAPOLA n rubbish
CRAPPED ▸ crap
CRAPPIE n N American freshwater fish)

CRAPPY adj worthless, lousy

CRAPS ▶ crap

CRAPY ▶ crape

CRARE n type of trading vessel **crares**

CRASES ▶ crasis

CRASH n, vb, adj crashed, crasher, crashes

CRASIS n fusion or contraction of two adjacent vowels into one

CRASS adj crasser, crassly

CRATCH n rack for holding fodder for cattle, etc

CRATE n, vb crated

CRATER n bowl-shaped opening at the top of a volcano ▷ vb make or form craters **craters**

CRATES ▶ crate

CRATHUR n ▶ cratur

CRATING ▶ crate

CRATON n stable part of the earth's continental crust **cratons**

CRATUR n whisky or whiskey **craturs**

CRAUNCH = crunch

CRAVAT n, vb **cravats**

CRAVE vb craved

CRAVEN adj, n, vb **cravens**

CRAVER ▶ crave

CRAVERS ▶ crave

CRAVES ▶ crave

CRAVING n intense desire or longing

CRAW n pouchlike part of a bird's oesophagus

CRAWDAD n crayfish

CRAWL vb, n crawled

CRAWLER n servile flatterer

CRAWLS ▶ crawl

CRAWLY adj feeling like creatures are crawling on one's skin

CRAWS ▶ craw

CRAY n crayfish

CRAYER = crare

CRAYERS ▶ crayer

CRAYON n, vb crayons

CRAYS ▶ cray

CRAZE n, vb

CRAZED adj wild and uncontrolled

CRAZES ▶ craze

CRAZIER ▶ crazy

CRAZIES ▶ crazy

CRAZILY ▶ crazy

CRAZING ▶ craze

CRAZY adj, n

CREACH = creagh

CREACHS ▶ creach

CREAGH n foray **creaghs**

CREAK n, vb creaked, creaks, creaky

CREAM n, adj, vb creamed

CREAMER n powdered milk substitute for use in coffee

CREAMS ▶ cream

CREAMY adj resembling cream in colour, taste, or consistency

CREANCE n long light cord used in falconry

CREANT adj formative

CREASE n, vb creased, creaser, creases, creasy

CREATE vb created, creates

CREATIC adj relating to flesh or meat

CREATIN = creatine

CREATOR n person who creates

CRECHE n place where small children are looked after **creches**

CRED n short for credibility

CREDAL ▶ creed

CREDENT adj believing or believable

CREDIT n, vb

CREDITS pl n list of people responsible for the production of a film, programme, or record

CREDO n creed **credos**

CREDS ▶ cred

CREE vb to soften grain by boiling or soaking

CREED n creedal, creeds

CREEING ▶ cree

CREEK n creeks

CREEKY adj abounding in creeks

CREEL n wicker basket used by anglers ▷ vb to fish using creels creeled, creels

CREEP vb, n creeped

CREEPER n, vb

CREEPIE n low stool

CREEPS ▶ creep

CREEPY adj

CREES ▶ cree

CREESE ▶ kris

CREESED ▶ creese

CREESES ▶ creese

CREESH vb to lubricate

CREESHY adj greasy

CREM n crematorium

CREMANT adj (of wine) moderately sparkling

CREMATE vb

CREME n cream ▷ adj (of a liqueur) rich and sweet **cremes**

CREMINI n variety of mushroom

CREMONA = **cromorna**

CREMOR n cream **cremors**

CREMS ▷ **crem**

CREMSIN = **cremosin**

CRENA n cleft or notch **crenas**

CRENATE adj having a scalloped margin, as certain leaves

CRENEL n opening formed in the top of a wall having slanting sides ▷ vb crenellate **crenels**

CREOLE n, adj **creoles**

CREOSOL n insoluble oily liquid

CREPE n, vb creped, **crepes**

CREPEY = **crepy**

CREPIER ▷ **crepy**

CREPING ▷ **crepe**

CREPON n thin material made of fine wool and/or silk **crepons**

CREPS pl n

CREPT ▷ **creep**

CREPY adj (esp of the skin) having a dry wrinkled appearance like crepe

CRESOL n aromatic compound **cresols**

CRESS n **cresses**

CRESSET n metal basket mounted on a pole

CRESSY ▷ **cress**

CREST n, vb

CRESTA adj as in **cresta run** high-speed tobogganing down a steep narrow passage

CRESTAL ▷ **crest**

CRESTED ▷ **crest**

CRESTON n hogback

CRESTS ▷ **crest**

CRESYL n tolyl **cresyls**

CRETIC n metrical foot **cretics**

CRETIN n stupid person **cretins**

CRETISM n lying

CRETONS pl n

CREVICE n

CREW n, vb

CREWCUT n very short haircut

CREWE n type of pot

CREWED ▷ **crew**

CREWEL n fine worsted yarn used in embroidery ▷ vb to embroider in crewel **crewels**

CREWES ▷ **crewe**

CREWING ▷ **crew**

CREWMAN n member of a ship's crew **crewmen**

CREWS ▷ **crew**

CRIA n baby llama, alpaca, or vicu

CRIANT adj garish

CRIAS ▷ **cria**

CRIB n, vb cribbed, cribber

CRIBBLE vb to sift

CRIBLE adj dotted

CRIBS ▷ **crib**

CRICK n, vb cricked

CRICKET n, vb

CRICKEY = **crikey**

CRICKS ▷ **crick**

CRICKY = **crikey**

CRICOID adj of or relating to part of the larynx ▷ n this cartilage

CRIED ▷ **cry**

CRIER n (formerly) official who made public announcements **criers**

CRIES ▷ **cry**

CRIKEY interj expression of surprise

CRIM short for
> **criminal**

CRIME n, vb crimed

CRIMEN n crime

CRIMES ▷ **crime**

CRIMINA ▷ **crimen**

CRIMINE interj expression of surprise

CRIMING ▷ **crime**

CRIMINI ▷ **crime**

CRIMINY interj cry of surprise

CRIMMER a variant spelling of ▷ **krimmer**

CRIMP vb fold or press into ridges ▷ n act or result of crimping crimped, crimper

CRIMPLE vb crumple, wrinkle, or curl

CRIMPS ▷ **crimp**

CRIMPY ▷ **crimp**

CRIMS ▷ **crim**

CRIMSON adj, n, vb
CRINAL adj relating to the hair
CRINATE adj having hair
CRINE vb to shrivel **crined, crines**
CRINGE vb, n **cringed, cringer, cringes**
CRINGLE n eye at the edge of a sail
CRINING ▷ **crine**
CRINITE adj covered with soft hairs or tufts ▷ n sedimentary rock
CRINKLE n, vb
CRINKLY adj wrinkled ▷ n old person
CRINOID n type of primitive echinoderm
CRINOSE adj hairy
CRINUM n type of mostly tropical plant **crinums**
CRIOLLO n native or inhabitant of Latin America of European descent ▷ adj of, relating to, or characteristic of a criollo or criollos
CRIOS n multicoloured woven woollen belt **crioses**
CRIPE variant of ▷ **cripes**
CRIPES interj expression of surprise
CRIPPLE n, vb
CRIS variant of ▷ **kris**
CRISE n crisis
CRISES ▷ **crisis**
CRISIC adj relating to a crisis
CRISIS n
CRISP adj, n, vb

CRISPED = crispate
CRISPEN vb to make crisp
CRISPER n compartment in a refrigerator
CRISPIN n cobbler
CRISPLY ▷ **crisp**
CRISPS ▷ **crisp**
CRISPY adj
CRISSA ▷ **crissum**
CRISSAL ▷ **crissum**
CRISSUM n area or feathers surrounding the cloaca of a bird
CRISTA n structure resembling a ridge or crest **cristae**
CRIT abbreviation of ▷ **criticism**
CRITH n unit of weight for gases **criths**
CRITIC n critics
CRITS ▷ **crit**
CRITTER a dialect word for ▷ **creature**
CRITTUR = critter
CRIVENS interj expression of surprise
CROAK vb, n **croaked**
CROAKER n animal, bird, etc, that croaks
CROAKS ▷ **croak**
CROAKY ▷ **croak**
CROC short for ▷ **crocodile**
CROCEIN n any one of a group of red or orange acid azo dyes
CROCHE n knob at the top of a deer's horn **croches**
CROCHET vb, n
CROCI ▷ **crocus**

CROCINE adj relating to the crocus
CROCK n earthenware pot or jar ▷ vb become or cause to become weak or disabled
CROCKED adj injured
CROCKET n carved ornament in the form of a curled leaf or cusp
CROCKS ▷ **crock**
CROCS ▷ **croc**
CROCUS n flowering plant
CROFT n, vb **crofted**
CROFTER n owner or tenant of a small farm, esp in Scotland or northern England
CROFTS ▷ **croft**
CROG vb ride on a bicycle as a passenger **crogged**
CROGGY n ride on a bicycle as a passenger
CROGS ▷ **crog**
CROJIK n triangular sail **crojiks**
CROMACK = crummock
CROMB = crome
CROMBEC n African Old World warbler with colourful plumage
CROMBED ▷ **cromb**
CROMBS ▷ **cromb**
CROME n hook ▷ vb use a crome **cromed, cromes, croming**
CRONE n crones
CRONET n hair which grows over the top of a horse's hoof **cronets**
CRONIES ▷ **crony**

CRONISH ▸ crone

CRONK adj unfit **cronker**

CRONY n

CROODLE vb to nestle close

CROOK n, vb

CROOKED adj

CROOKER ▸ crook

CROOKS ▸ crook

CROOL vb spoil **crooled, crools**

CROON vb, n **crooned, crooner, croons**

CROOVE n animal enclosure **crooves**

CROP n, vb

CROPFUL n quantity that can be held in the craw

CROPPED ▸ crop

CROPPER n person who cultivates or harvests a crop

CROPPIE = croppy

CROPPY n rebel in the Irish rising of 1798

CROPS ▸ crop

CROQUET n, vb

CROQUIS n rough sketch

CRORE n (in Indian English) ten million **crores**

CROSIER n staff carried by bishops as a symbol of pastoral office ▸ vb bear or carry such a cross

CROSS vb, n, adj

CROSSE n light staff used in playing lacrosse

CROSSED, crosser, crosses, crossly, crost ▸ cross

CROTAL n any of various lichens used in dyeing wool

CROTALA > crotalum **crotals**

CROTCH n

CROTON n type of shrub or tree, the seeds of which yield croton oil **crotons**

CROTTLE = crotal

CROUCH vb, n

CROUP n, vb **croupe, crouped**

CROUPER obsolete variant of ▸ crupper

CROUPES ▸ croupe

CROUPON n type of highly-polished flexible leather

CROUPS ▸ croup

CROUPY ▸ croup

CROUSE adj lively, confident, or saucy

CROUT n sauerkraut

CROUTE n small round of toasted bread on which a savoury mixture is served **croutes**

CROUTON n

CROUTS ▸ crout

CROW n, vb

CROWBAR n, vb

CROWD n, vb **crowded, crowder**

CROWDIE n porridge of meal and water

CROWDS ▸ crowd **crowdy**

CROWEA n Australian shrub with pink flowers **croweas**

CROWED, crower, crowers, crowing ▸ crow

CROWN n, vb **crowned**

CROWNER n promotional label

CROWNET n coronet

CROWNS ▸ crown

CROWS ▸ crow

CROZE n recess cut at the end of a barrel or cask to receive the head

CROZER n machine which cuts grooves in cask staves **crozers**

CROZES ▸ croze

CROZIER = crosier

CRU n (in France) a vineyard, group of vineyards, or wine-producing region

CRUBEEN n pig's trotter

CRUCES ▸ crux

CRUCIAL adj

CRUCIAN n European fish

CRUCIFY vb

CRUCK n wooden timber supporting the end of certain roofs **crucks**

CRUD n sticky or encrusted substance ▸ interj expression of disgust, disappointment, etc ▸ vb cover with a sticky or encrusted substance **crudded**

CRUDDLE vb to curdle

CRUDDY adj dirty or unpleasant

CRUDE adj, n crudely, cruder, crudes, crudest, crudity

CRUDS ▶ crud

CRUDY adj raw

CRUE obsolete variant of ▶ crew

CRUEL adj crueler

CRUELLS = cruels

CRUELLY ▶ cruel

CRUELS n disease of cattle and sheep

CRUELTY n

CRUES ▶ crew

CRUET n cruets

CRUISE n, vb cruised

CRUISER n

CRUISES = cruizie

CRUISIE = cruizie

CRUIVE n animal enclosure cruives

CRUIZIE n oil lamp

CRULLER n light sweet ring-shaped cake, fried in deep fat

CRUMB n, vb, adj crumbed, crumber

CRUMBLE vb, n

CRUMBLY adj

CRUMBS interj expression of dismay or surprise

CRUMBUM n rogue

CRUMBY adj full of crumbs

CRUMEN n deer's larmier or tear-pit crumens

CRUMMIE n cow with a crumpled horn

CRUMMY adj of poor quality ▷ n lorry that carries loggers to work from their camp

CRUMP vb thud or explode with a loud dull sound ▷ n crunching, thudding, or exploding noise ▷ adj crooked crumped, crumper

CRUMPET n

CRUMPLE vb, n crumply

CRUMPS ▶ crump

CRUMPY adj crisp

CRUNCH vb, n crunchy

CRUNK n form of hip-hop music originating in the Southern US

CRUNKED adj excited or intoxicated

CRUNKLE Scots variant of ▶ crinkle

CRUNKS ▶ crunk

CRUNODE n mathematical term

CRUOR n blood clot cruores, cruors

CRUPPER n strap that passes from the back of a saddle under a horse's tail

CRURA ▶ crus

CRURAL adj of or relating to the leg or thigh

CRUS n leg, esp from the knee to the foot

CRUSADE n, vb

CRUSADO n former gold or silver coin of Portugal

CRUSE n small earthenware jug or pot cruses

CRUSET n goldsmith's crucible crusets

CRUSH vb, n crushed, crusher, crushes

CRUSIAN variant of ▶ crucian

CRUSIE = cruizie

CRUSIES ▶ crusie

CRUSILY adj (in heraldry) strewn with crosses

CRUST n, vb

CRUSTA n hard outer layer crustae

CRUSTAL adj of or relating to the earth's crust

CRUSTED ▶ crust

CRUSTS ▶ crust

CRUSTY adj, n

CRUSY = cruizie

CRUTCH n, vb

CRUVE = cruive

CRUVES ▶ cruve

CRUX n cruxes

CRUZADO = crusado

CRUZIE = cruizie

CRUZIES ▶ cruzie

CRWTH n ancient stringed instrument of Celtic origin crwths

> This old Celtic musical instrument makes a fine tune when your rack is all consonants.

CRY vb shed tears ▷ n fit of weeping

CRYBABY n person, esp a child, who cries too readily

CRYING ▶ cry

CRYINGS ▶ cry

CRYOGEN n substance used to produce low temperatures

CRYONIC ► cryonics
CRYPT n cryptal
CRYPTIC adj
CRYPTO n person who is a secret member of an organization or sect
CRYPTON n krypton
CRYPTOS ► crypto
CRYPTS ► crypt
CRYSTAL n, adj
CSARDAS n type of Hungarian folk dance
CTENE n locomotor organ found in ctenophores (or comb jellies) **ctenes**
CTENOID adj toothed like a comb, as the scales of perches
CUATRO n four-stringed guitar **cuatros**
CUB n, adj, vb
CUBAGE = cubature
CUBAGES > cubature
CUBANE n rare octahedral hydrocarbon **cubanes**
CUBBED ► cub
CUBBIER ► cubby
CUBBIES ► cubby
CUBBING ► cub
CUBBISH ► cub
CUBBY n, adj
CUBE n, vb
CUBEB n SE Asian woody climbing plant with brownish berries **cubebs**
CUBED ► cube
CUBER ► cube
CUBERS ► cube
CUBES ► cube
CUBHOOD n state of being a cub
CUBIC adj, n
CUBICA n fine shalloon-like fabric
CUBICAL adj of or related to volume
CUBICAS ► cubica
CUBICLE n
CUBICLY ► cubic
CUBICS ► cubic
CUBING ► cube
CUBISM n style of art in which objects are represented by geometrical shapes **cubisms, cubist, cubists**
CUBIT n old measure of length based on the length of the forearm
CUBITAL adj of or relating to the forearm
CUBITI ► cubitus
CUBITS ► cubit
CUBITUS n elbow
CUBLESS adj having no cubs
CUBOID adj shaped like a cube ▷ n geometric solid whose six faces are rectangles **cuboids**
CUBS ► cub
CUCKING adj as in **cucking stool** stool in which suspected witches were tested
CUCKOLD n man whose wife has been unfaithful ▷ vb be unfaithful to (one's husband)
CUCKOO n, adj, interj, vb **cuckoos**
CUD n

CUDBEAR another name for ► orchil
CUDDEN n young coalfish **cuddens**
CUDDIE = cuddy
CUDDIES ► cuddy
CUDDIN = cudden
CUDDINS ► cuddin
CUDDLE n, vb cuddled, cuddler, cuddles, cuddly
CUDDY n small cabin in a boat
CUDGEL n, vb cudgels
CUDS ► cud
CUDWEED n type of temperate plant
CUE n, vb cued, cueing
CUEINGS ► cueing
CUEIST n snooker or billiards player **cueists**
CUES ► cue
CUESTA n long low ridge with a steep scarp slope and a gentle back slope **cuestas**
CUFF n, vb cuffed
CUFFIN n man
CUFFING ► cuff
CUFFINS ► cuffin
CUFFLE vb scuffle cuffled, cuffles
CUFFO adv free of charge
CUFFS ► cuff
CUIF = coof
CUIFS ► cuif
CUING ► cue
CUIRASS n piece of armour, of leather or metal covering the chest and back ▷ vb equip with a cuirass

CUISH = cuisse

CUISHES ▸ cuish

CUISINE n

CUISSE n piece of armour for the thigh

CUISSER = cooser cuisses

CUIT n ankle

CUITER vb to pamper cuiters

CUITS ▸ cuit

CUITTLE vb to wheedle

CUKE n cucumber cukes

CULCH n the basis of an oyster bed culches

CULCHIE n rough or unsophisticated country-dweller from outside Dublin

CULET n flat face at the bottom of a gem culets

CULEX n type of mosquito culexes, culices

CULICID n type of dipterous insect

CULL vb, n

CULLAY n soapbark tree cullays

CULLED ▸ cull

CULLER n person employed to cull animals cullers

CULLET n waste glass for melting down to be reused cullets

CULLIED ▸ cully

CULLIES ▸ cully

CULLING ▸ cull

CULLION n rascal

CULLIS = coulisse

CULLS ▸ cull

CULLY n pal ▷ vb to trick

CULM n coal-mine waste ▷ vb to form a culm or grass stem culmed

CULMEN n summit culmina

CULMING ▸ culm

CULMS ▸ culm

CULOTTE > culottes

CULPA n act of neglect culpae

CULPRIT n

CULT n, adj

CULTCH = culch

CULTER = coulter

CULTERS ▸ culter

CULTI ▸ cultus

CULTIC adj of or relating to a religious cult

CULTIER ▸ culty

CULTISH adj intended to appeal to a small group of fashionable people

CULTISM ▸ cult

CULTIST ▸ cult

CULTS ▸ cult

CULTURE n, vb

CULTUS another word for ▸ cult

CULTY ▸ cultish

CULVER an archaic or poetic name for ▸ pigeon

CULVERS ▸ culver

CULVERT n

CUMARIC ▸ cumarin

CUMARIN = coumarin

CUMBENT adj lying down

CUMBER vb obstruct or hinder ▷ n hindrance or

burden **cumbers**

CUMBIA n Colombian style of music cumbias

CUMEC n unit of volumetric rate of flow cumecs

CUMIN n cumins

CUMMER n gossip cummers

CUMMIN = cumin

CUMMINS ▸ cummin

CUMQUAT = kumquat

CUMSHAW n (used, esp formerly, by beggars in Chinese ports) a present or tip

CUMULET n variety of domestic fancy pigeon

CUMULI ▸ cumulus

CUMULUS n

CUNDIES ▸ cundy

CUNDUM n early form of condom cundums

CUNDY n sewer

CUNEAL = cuneiform

CUNEATE adj wedge-shaped: cuneate leaves are attached at the narrow end

CUNEI ▸ cuneus

CUNETTE n small trench dug in the main ditch of a fortification

CUNEUS n small wedge-shaped area of the cerebral cortex

CUNNER n fish of the wrasse family cunners

CUNNING adj, n

CUP n, vb

CUPCAKE n small cake baked in a cup-shaped

foil or paper case

CUPEL n refractory pot in which gold or silver is refined ▷ vb refine (gold or silver) by means of cupellation **cupeled, cupeler, cupels**

CUPFUL n amount a cup will hold **cupfuls**

CUPGALL n gall found on oakleaves

CUPHEAD n type of bolt or rivet with a cup-shaped head

CUPID n figure representing the Roman god of love **cupids**

CUPLIKE adj

CUPMAN n drinking companion **cupmen**

CUPOLA n, vb **cupolar, cupolas**

CUPPA n cup of tea **cuppas**

CUPPED ▷ cup

CUPPER = cuppa

CUPPERS ▷ cupper

CUPPIER ▷ cuppy

CUPPING ▷ cup

CUPPY adj cup-shaped

CUPRIC adj of or containing copper in the divalent state

CUPRITE n red secondary mineral

CUPROUS adj of or containing copper in the monovalent state

CUPRUM an obsolete name for ▷ **copper**

CUPRUMS ▷ cuprum

CUPS ▷ cup

CUPSFUL ▷ cupful

CUPULA n dome-shaped structure **cupulae**

CUPULAR = cupulate

CUPULE n cup-shaped part or structure **cupules**

CUR n mongrel dog

CURABLE adj **curably**

CURACAO n orange-flavoured liqueur **curacao**

CURACY n work or position of a curate

CURAGH = currach

CURAGHS ▷ curagh

CURARA = curare

CURARAS ▷ curara

CURARE n poisonous resin of a S American tree **curares, curari**

CURARIS ▷ curari

CURAT n cuirass

CURATE n, vb **curated, curates**

CURATOR n

CURATS ▷ curat

CURB n, vb **curbed, curber, curbers**

CURBING the US spelling of ▷ **kerbing**

CURBS ▷ curb

CURCH n woman's plain cap or kerchief **curchef, curches**

CURCUMA n type of tropical Asian tuberous plant

CURD n coagulated milk, used to make cheese ▷ vb turn into or become curd **curded, curdier, curding**

CURDLE vb **curdled, curdler, curdles**

CURDS ▷ curd

CURDY ▷ curd

CURE vb, n **cured, curer, curers, cures**

CURET = curette

CURETS ▷ curet

CURETTE n surgical instrument for scraping tissue from body cavities ▷ vb scrape with a curette

CURF n type of limestone

CURFEW n **curfews**

CURFS ▷ curf

CURIA n papal court and government of the Roman Catholic Church **curiae, curial, curias**

CURIE n standard unit of radioactivity **curies**

CURIET n cuirass **curiets**

CURING ▷ cure

CURIO n curios

CURIOSA n curiosities

CURIOUS adj

CURITE n oxide of uranium and lead **curites**

CURIUM n radioactive element artificially produced from plutonium **curiums**

CURL n, vb **curled**

CURLER n **curlers**

CURLEW n **curlews**

CURLI pl n curled hairlike processes on the surface of the E. coli bacterium

CURLIER ▶ curly
CURLIES pl n as in have by the short and curlies have completely in one's power
CURLILY ▶ curly
CURLING n game like bowls, played with heavy stones on ice
CURLS ▶ curl
CURLY adj tending to curl
CURN n grain (of corn etc)
CURNEY ▶ curny
CURNIER ▶ curny
CURNS ▶ curn
CURNY adj granular
CURPEL = crupper
CURPELS ▶ curpel
CURR vb to purr
CURRACH a Scot or Irish name for ▶ coracle
CURRAGH ▶ currach
CURRAN n black bun currans
CURRANT n
CURRED ▶ curr
CURRENT adj, n
CURRIE = curry
CURRIED ▶ curry
CURRIER n person who curries leather
CURRIES ▶ curry
CURRING ▶ curr
CURRISH adj of or like a cur
CURRS ▶ curr
CURRY n, vb
CURS ▶ cur
CURSAL ▶ cursus
CURSE vb, n cursed, curser, cursers, curses

CURSI ▶ cursus
CURSING ▶ curse
CURSIVE n, adj
CURSOR n cursors
CURSORY adj
CURST ▶ curse
CURSUS n Neolithic parallel earthworks
CURT adj
CURTAIL vb
CURTAIN n, vb
CURTAL adj cut short ▷ n animal whose tail has been docked curtals
CURTANA n unpointed sword displayed at a coronation as an emblem of mercy
CURTATE adj shortened
CURTAXE = curtalaxe
CURTER ▶ curt
CURTEST ▶ curt
CURTESY n widower's life interest in his wife's estate
CURTLY ▶ curt
CURTSEY = curtsy
CURTSY n, vb
CURULE adj (in ancient Rome) of the highest rank, esp one entitled to use a curule chair
CURVATE adj curved
CURVE n, vb curved, curves
CURVET n horse's low leap with all four feet off the ground ▷ vb make such a leap curvets
CURVEY = curvy
CURVIER ▶ curve
CURVING ▶ curve

CURVITY n curvedness
CURVY ▶ curve
CUSCUS n large Australian nocturnal possum
CUSEC n unit of flow equal to 1 cubic foot per second cusecs
CUSH n cushion
CUSHAT n wood pigeon cushats
CUSHAW = cashaw
CUSHAWS ▶ cushaw
CUSHES ▶ cush
CUSHIE = cushat
CUSHIER ▶ cushy
CUSHIES ▶ cushie
CUSHILY ▶ cushy
CUSHION n, vb
CUSHTY interj exclamation of pleasure, agreement, approval, etc
CUSHY adj
CUSK n type of food fish of northern coastal waters, with a single long dorsal fin cusks
CUSP n pointed end, esp on a tooth cuspal
CUSPATE adj having a cusp or cusps cusped
CUSPID n tooth having one point cuspids
CUSPIER ▶ cuspy
CUSPIS n (in anatomy), tapering structure
CUSPS ▶ cusp
CUSPY adj (of a computer program) well-designed and user-friendly
CUSS n curse, oath ▷ vb swear (at)

CUSSED adj obstinate

CUSSER = cooser

CUSSERS ▶ cusser

CUSSES ▶ cuss

CUSSING ▶ cuss

CUSSO n tree of the rose family **cussos**

CUSTARD n

CUSTOCK = castock

CUSTODE n custodian

CUSTODY n

CUSTOM n, adj

CUSTOMS n duty charged on imports or exports

CUSTOS n superior in the Franciscan religious order

CUSTREL n knave

CUSUM n analysis technique used in statistics **cusums**

CUT vb

CUTAWAY adj (of a drawing or model) having part of the outside omitted to reveal the inside ▷ n man's coat cut diagonally from the front waist to the back of the knees

CUTBACK n decrease or reduction ▷ vb shorten by cutting

CUTBANK n steep banking at a bend in a river

CUTCH = catechu

CUTCHA adj crude

CUTCHES ▶ cutch

CUTDOWN n decrease

CUTE adj cutely, cuter

CUTES ▶ cutis

CUTESIE = cutesy

CUTEST ▶ cute

CUTESY adj affectedly cute or coy

CUTEY = cutie

CUTEYS ▶ cutey

CUTICLE n

CUTIE n person regarded as appealing or attractive, esp a girl or woman **cuties**

CUTIKIN = cutikin

CUTIN n waxy waterproof substance **cutins**

CUTIS a technical name for the ▶ skin

CUTISES ▶ cutis

CUTLAS = cutlass

CUTLASS n

CUTLER n maker of cutlery **cutlers**

CUTLERY n

CUTLET n cutlets

CUTLINE n caption

CUTOFF n limit or termination **cutoffs**

CUTOUT n cutouts

CUTOVER n transitional period in IT system changeover

CUTS ▶ cut

CUTTAGE n propagation by using parts taken from growing plants

CUTTER n person or tool that cuts **cutters**

CUTTIER ▶ cutty

CUTTIES ▶ cutty

CUTTING ▶ cut

CUTTLE vb to whisper **cuttled, cuttles**

CUTTO n large knife **cuttoe, cuttoes**

CUTTY adj short or cut short ▷ n something cut short

CUTUP n joker or prankster **cutups**

CUTWORK n type of openwork embroidery

CUTWORM n caterpillar of various types of moth

CUVEE n individual batch or blend of wine **cuvees**

CUVETTE n shallow dish or vessel for holding liquid

CUZ n cousin **cuzzes**

> **Cuz** is another word for **cousin**, great for using the Z.

CUZZIE n close friend or family member **cuzzies**

CWM = cirque

> **Cwm** is a Welsh word meaning a valley, a useful one to remember because it doesn't contain any vowels.

CWMS ▶ cwm

CWTCH vb be snuggled up **cwtched, cwtches**

> This delightful Welsh word meaning to cuddle is not likely to come up, but might just help you out of a tight spot one day when your rack is all consonants.

CYAN n highly saturated green-blue ▷ adj of this colour

CYANATE n any salt or ester of cyanic acid

CYANIC adj as in cyanic acid colourless volatile liquid acid

CYANID n cyanide

CYANIDE n, vb

CYANIDS ▷ cyanid

CYANIN ▷ cyanine

CYANINE n blue dye used in photography

CYANINS ▷ cyanin

CYANISE vb turn into cyanide

CYANITE a variant spelling of ▷ kyanite

CYANIZE = cyanise

CYANO adj containing cyanogen

CYANS ▷ cyan

CYATHI ▷ cyathus

CYATHIA > cyathium

CYATHUS n ancient measure of wine

CYBER adj involving computers

CYBORG n (in science fiction) a living being enhanced by computer implants **cyborgs**

CYBRID n cytoplasmic hybrid **cybrids**

CYCAD n type of tropical or subtropical plant **cycads**

CYCAS n palm tree of the genus Cycas **cycases**

CYCASIN n glucoside, toxic to mammals, occurring in plants

CYCLASE n enzyme which acts as a catalyst

in the formation of a cyclic compound

CYCLE vb, n cycled

CYCLER = cyclist

CYCLERS ▷ cyclist

CYCLERY n business dealing in bicycles and bicycle accessories

CYCLES ▷ cycle

CYCLIC adj recurring or revolving in cycles

CYCLIN n type of protein

CYCLING n ▷ cycle

CYCLINS ▷ cyclin

CYCLISE = cyclize

CYCLIST n

CYCLIZE vb be cyclical

CYCLO n type of rickshaw

CYCLOID adj resembling a circle ▷ n mathematical curve

CYCLONE n

CYCLOPS n type of copepod characterized by having one eye

CYCLOS ▷ cyclo

CYCLUS n cycle

CYDER = cider

CYDERS ▷ cyder

CYESES ▷ cyesis

CYESIS the technical name for ▷ pregnancy

CYGNET n cygnets

CYLICES ▷ cylix

CYLIX a variant of ▷ kylix

CYMA n moulding with a double curve, part concave and part convex **cymae**

CYMAR n woman's short fur-trimmed jacket, popular in the 17th and 18th centuries

cymars

CYMAS ▷ cyma

CYMATIA > cymatium

CYMBAL n

CYMBALO another name for ▷ dulcimer **cymbals**

CYME n type of flower cluster

CYMENE n colourless insoluble liquid **cymenes**

CYMES ▷ cyme

CYMLIN = cymling

CYMLING n pattypan squash

CYMLINS ▷ cymling

CYMOID adj resembling a cyme or cyma

CYMOL = cymene

CYMOLS ▷ cymol

CYMOSE adj having the characteristics of a cyme

CYMOUS adj relating to a cyme

CYNIC n, adj

CYNICAL adj

CYNICS ▷ cynic

CYPHER = cipher

CYPHERS ▷ cypher

CYPRES n legal doctrine

CYPRESS n

CYPRIAN n prostitute or dancer

CYPRID n cypris **cyprids**

CYPRINE adj relating to carp

CYPRIS n member of the genus Cypris (small bivalve freshwater crustaceans)

CYPRUS = cypress

CYPSELA n dry

one-seeded fruit of the daisy and related plants

CYST n

CYSTEIN = cysteine

CYSTIC adj of, relating to, or resembling a cyst

CYSTID n cystidean **cystids**

CYSTINE n sulphur-containing amino acid

CYSTOID adj resembling a cyst or bladder ▷ n tissue mass that resembles a cyst but lacks an outer membrane

CYSTS ▶ cyst

CYTASE n cellulose-dissolving enzyme **cytases**

CYTE n biological cell **cytes**

CYTISI ▶ cytisus

CYTISUS n any plant of the broom genus, Cytisus

CYTODE n mass of protoplasm without a nucleus **cytodes**

CYTOID adj resembling a cell

CYTON n main part of a neuron **cytons**

CYTOSOL n solution in a biological cell

CZAPKA n leather and felt peaked military helmet of Polish origin **czapkas**

CZAR = tsar

CZARDAS n Hungarian national dance of alternating slow and fast sections

CZARDOM ▶ czar

CZARINA variant spellings (esp US) of ▶ tsarina

CZARISM a variant spelling (esp US) of ▶ tsarism

CZARIST ▶ czarism

CZARS ▶ czar

Dd

D forms a two-letter word before every vowel except **U**. There are plenty of good three-letter words beginning with **D**, particularly those with a **Y** or **W**: **day**, **dye** and **dew** are worth 7 points each, for example. And don't forget **dex** and **dux** for 11 points each and the invaluable **dzo** for 13 points.

DA n Burmese knife

DAAL n (in Indian cookery) split pulses **daals**

DAB vb, n

DABBA n in Indian cookery, round metal box used to transport hot food **dabbas**

DABBED ▶ dab

DABBER n pad used by printers for applying ink by hand **dabbers**

DABBING ▶ dab

DABBITY n temporary tattoo

DABBLE vb **dabbled, dabbler, dabbles**

DABS ▶ dab

DABSTER n incompetent or amateurish worker

DACE n **daces**

DACHA n country cottage in Russia **dachas**

DACITE n volcanic rock **dacites**

DACK vb remove the trousers from (someone) by force **dacked**

DACKER vb walk slowly **dackers**

DACKING ▶ dack

DACKS ▶ dack

DACOIT n (in India and Myanmar) a member of a gang of armed robbers **dacoits**

DACOITY n (in India and Myanmar) robbery by an armed gang

DACRON n US tradename for a synthetic polyester fibre or fabric **dacrons**

DACTYL n metrical foot of three syllables, one long followed by two short

DACTYLI > dactylus

DACTYLS ▶ dactyl

DAD n, vb

DADA n nihilistic artistic movement of the early 20th century

DADAH n illegal drugs **dadahs**

DADAISM = dada

DADAIST ▶ dada

DADAS ▶ dada

DADDED ▶ dad

DADDIES ▶ daddy

DADDING ▶ dad

DADDLE vb walk unsteadily **daddled, daddles**

DADDOCK n core of a dead tree

DADDY n father

DADGUM mild form of ▶ damned

DADO n, vb **dadoed, dadoes, dadoing, dados**

DADS ▶ dad

DAE a Scot word for ▶ do

DAEDAL adj skilful or intricate

DAEING ▶ dae
DAEMON = demon
DAEMONS ▶ daemon
DAES ▶ dae
DAFF vb frolic daffed
DAFFIER ▶ daffy
DAFFIES ▶ daffy
DAFFILY ▶ daffy
DAFFING ▶ daff
DAFFS ▶ daff
DAFFY another word for
▶ daft
DAFT adj
DAFTAR Indian word for
▶ office
DAFTARS ▶ daftar
DAFTER ▶ daft
DAFTEST ▶ daft
DAFTIE n foolish person
dafties
DAFTLY ▶ daft
DAG n character ▷ vb
cut daglocks from
sheep
DAGABA n shrine for
Buddhist relics
dagabas
DAGGA n daggas
DAGGED ▶ dag
DAGGER ▶ dag
DAGGERS ▶ dag
DAGGIER ▶ daggy
DAGGING ▶ dag
DAGGLE vb trail through
water daggled,
daggles
DAGGY adj amusing
DAGLOCK n dung-caked
lock of wool around
the hindquarters of a
sheep
DAGOBA n
dome-shaped
Buddhist shrine

dagobas
DAGS ▶ dag
DAGWOOD n European
shrub
DAH n long sound used
in combination with
the short sound in the
spoken representation
of Morse and other
telegraphic codes
DAHL = dhal
DAHLIA n dahlias
DAHLS ▶ dahl
DAHOON n evergreen
shrub dahoons
DAHS ▶ dah
DAIDLE vb waddle
about daidled,
daidles
DAIKER vb walk slowly
daikers
DAIKO n Japanese drum
DAIKON another name
for ▶ mooli
DAIKONS ▶ daikon
DAIKOS ▶ daiko
DAILIES ▶ daily
DAILY adj, adv, n
DAIMEN adj occasional
DAIMIO = daimyo
DAIMIOS ▶ daimio
DAIMOKU n Nichiren
Buddhist chant
DAIMON = demon
DAIMONS ▶ daimon
DAIMYO n magnate in
Japan from the 11th to
the 19th century
daimyos
DAINE vb condescend
dained, daines,
daining
DAINT adj dainty
DAINTY adj, n

DAIRIES ▶ dairy
DAIRY n, adj
DAIS n daises
DAISIED ▶ daisy
DAISIES ▶ daisy
DAISY n
DAK n system of mail
delivery or passenger
transport

A **dak** is an old mail
or transport system,
often useful for
disposing of the K.

DAKER vb walk slowly
dakered, dakers
DAKOIT = dacoit
DAKOITI = dakoit
DAKOITS ▶ dakoit
DAKOITY n armed
robbery
DAKS an informal name
for ▶ trousers
DAL = decalitre
DALAPON n herbicide
DALASI n standard
monetary unit of The
Gambia, divided into
100 bututs dalasis
DALE n
DALED = daleth
DALEDH n letter of
Hebrew alphabet
daledhs
DALEDS ▶ daled
DALES ▶ dale
DALETH n fourth letter
of the Hebrew
alphabet,
transliterated as d or,
when final, dh daleths
DALGYTE another name
for ▶ bilby
DALI n type of tree dalis
DALLE ▶ dalles

DALLES pl n stretch of a river between high rock walls, with rapids and dangerous currents
DALLIED ▶ dally
DALLIER ▶ dally
DALLIES ▶ dally
DALLOP n semisolid lump **dallops**
DALLY vb
DALS ▶ dal
DALT n foster child
DALTON n atomic mass unit **daltons**
DALTS ▶ dalt
DAM n, vb
DAMAGE vb, n damaged, damager
DAMAGES pl n money awarded as compensation for injury or loss
DAMAN n the Syrian rock hyrax **damans**
DAMAR = dammar
DAMARS ▶ dammar
DAMASK n, vb damasks
DAMBROD n draughtboard
DAME n dames
DAMFOOL adj foolish
DAMIANA n herbal medicine
DAMMAR n any of various resins obtained from SE Asian trees dammars
DAMME interj exclamation of surprise
DAMMED ▶ dam
DAMMER = dammar

DAMMERS ▶ dammer
DAMMING ▶ dam
DAMMIT interj exclamation of surprise
DAMN interj, adj, vb
DAMNED adj condemned to hell ▷ adv extreme or extremely
DAMNER n person who damns damners
DAMNIFY vb cause loss or damage to (a person)
DAMNING ▶ damn
DAMNS ▶ damn
DAMOSEL = damsel
DAMOZEL = damoiselle
DAMP adj, n, vb damped
DAMPEN vb dampens
DAMPER n dampers
DAMPEST ▶ damp
DAMPIER ▶ dampy
DAMPING n moistening or wetting
DAMPISH ▶ damp
DAMPLY ▶ damp
DAMPS ▶ damp
DAMPY adj damp
DAMS ▶ dam
DAMSEL n damsels
DAMSON n damsons
DAN n
DANAZOL n type of drug
DANCE vb, n danced, dancer, dancers, dances
DANCEY adj of, relating to, or resembling dance music dancier
DANCING ▶ dance
DANCY adj (of music)

appropriate for dancing
DANDER n stroll ▷ vb stroll danders
DANDIER ▶ dandy
DANDIES ▶ dandy
DANDIFY vb dress like or cause to resemble a dandy
DANDILY ▶ dandy
DANDLE vb move (a child) up and down on one's knee dandled, dandler, dandles
DANDY n, adj
DANELAW n Danish law in parts of Anglo-Saxon England
DANG a euphemistic word for ▶ damn
DANGED ▶ dang
DANGER n, vb dangers
DANGING ▶ dang
DANGLE vb, n dangled, dangler, dangles, dangly
DANGS ▶ dang
DANIO n type of tropical freshwater fish danios
DANISH n sweet pastry
DANK adj, n danker, dankest, dankish, dankly, danks
DANNIES ▶ danny
DANNY n hand (used esp when addressing children)
DANS ▶ dan
DANSEUR n male ballet dancer
DANT vb intimidate danted, danting
DANTON = daunton

DANTONS ▸ danton

DANTS ▸ dant

DAP vb engage in type of fly fishing

DAPHNE n ornamental Eurasian shrub **daphnes**

DAPHNIA n

DAPHNID n water flea

DAPPED ▸ dap

DAPPER adj, n **dappers**

DAPPING ▸ dap

DAPPLE vb mark or become marked with spots or patches of a different colour ▸ n mottled or spotted markings ▸ adj marked with dapples or spots **dappled, dapples**

DAPS ▸ dap

DAPSONE n antimicrobial drug

DAQUIRI n rum cocktail

DARAF n unit of elastance equal to a reciprocal farad **darafs**

DARB n something excellent

DARBAR n hall in Sikh temple **darbars**

DARBIES ▸ handcuffs

DARBS ▸ darb

DARCIES ▸ darcy

DARCY n unit expressing the permeability coefficient of rock **darcys**

DARE vb, n **dared**

DAREFUL adj daring

DARER ▸ dare

DARERS ▸ dare

DARES ▸ dare

DARESAY vb venture to say

DARG n day's work

DARGA n Muslim shrine

DARGAH n tomb of a Muslim saint **dargahs**

DARGAS ▸ darga

DARGLE n wooded hollow **dargles**

DARGS ▸ darg

DARI n variety of sorghum

DARIC n gold coin of ancient Persia **darics**

DARING adj, n **darings**

DARIOLE n small cup-shaped mould

DARIS ▸ dari

DARK adj, n, vb **darked**

DARKEN vb **darkens**

DARKER, darkest, darking, darkish ▸ dark

DARKLE vb grow dark **darkled, darkles**

DARKLY ▸ dark

DARKNET n covert communication network on the Internet

DARKS ▸ dark

DARLING n, adj

DARN vb, n

DARNED adj damned

DARNEL n weed that grows in grain fields **darnels**

DARNER, darners, darning, darns ▸ darn

DAROGHA n in India, manager

DARRAIN vb clear of guilt

DARRAYN vb clear of guilt

DARRE vb dare **darred, darres, darring**

DARSHAN n Hindu blessing

DART n, vb **darted**

DARTER n type of aquatic bird **darters**

DARTING ▸ dart

DARTLE vb move swiftly **dartled, dartles**

DARTRE n skin disease **dartres**

DARTS n game in which darts are thrown at a dartboard

DARZI n tailor in India **darzis**

DAS ▸ da

DASH vb, n **dashed**

DASHEEN another name for ▸ taro

DASHEKI n upper garment

DASHER n one of the boards surrounding an ice-hockey rink **dashers**

DASHES ▸ dash

DASHI n clear stock made from dried fish and kelp

DASHIER ▸ dashy

DASHIKI n large loose-fitting buttonless upper garment

DASHING adj

DASHIS ▸ dashi

DASHPOT n device for damping vibrations

DASHY adj showy

DASSIE n type of hoofed rodent-like animal **dassies**

DASTARD n contemptible sneaking coward

DASYPOD n armadillo

DASYURE n

DATA n

DATABLE ▸ date

DATABUS n computing term

DATAL adj slow-witted ▸ n day labour **datals**

DATARIA n Roman Catholic office

DATARY n head of the dataria

DATCHA = dacha

DATCHAS ▸ datcha

DATE n, vb

DATED adj **datedly**

DATER n person who dates **daters**

DATES ▸ date

DATING n any of several techniques for establishing the age of objects **datings**

DATIVAL ▸ dative

DATIVE adj, n **datives**

DATO n chief of any of certain Muslim tribes in the Philippine Islands **datos**

DATTO n Datsun car **dattos**

DATUM n **datums**

DATURA n type of plant **daturas**, **daturic**

DAUB vb, n

DAUBE n braised meat stew

DAUBED ▸ daub

DAUBER ▸ daub

DAUBERS ▸ daub

DAUBERY n act or an instance of daubing

DAUBES ▸ daube

DAUBIER ▸ daub

DAUBING ▸ daub

DAUBRY n unskilful painting

DAUBS ▸ daub

DAUBY ▸ daub

DAUD n lump or chunk of something ▸ vb (in dialect) whack **dauded**, **dauding**, **dauds**

DAULT n foster child **daults**

DAUNDER vb stroll **daunders**

DAUNER vb stroll **dauners**

DAUNT vb **daunted**, **daunter**

DAUNTON vb dishearten

DAUNTS ▸ daunt

DAUPHIN n

DAUR a Scot word for ▸ dare

DAURED ▸ daur

DAURING ▸ daur

DAURS ▸ daur

DAUT vb fondle **dauted**

DAUTIE n darling **dauties**

DAUTING ▸ daut

DAUTS ▸ daut

DAVEN vb pray **davened**, **davens**

DAVIDIA n Chinese shrub

DAVIES ▸ davy

DAVIT n crane, usu one of a pair, at a ship's side, for lowering and hoisting a lifeboat **davits**

DAVY n miner's safety lamp

DAW n archaic, dialect, or poetic name for a jackdaw ▸ vb old word for dawn

This is another name for a **jackdaw**. It is worth remembering that not only does this little word take D, K, N, S and T at the back, to make **dawd**, **dawk**, **dawn**, **daws** and **dawt**, but you can put an A on the front of it to make **adaw**.

DAWAH n practice of educating non-Muslims about the message of Islam **dawahs**

DAWBAKE n foolish or slow-witted person

DAWBRY n unskilful painting

DAWCOCK n male jackdaw

DAWD vb thump **dawded**, **dawding**

DAWDLE vb **dawdled**, **dawdler**, **dawdles**

DAWDS ▸ dawd

DAWED, **dawen**, **dawing**, **dawish** ▸ daw

DAWK = dak

DAWKS ▸ dawk

DAWN n, vb **dawned**

DAWNER vb stroll
dawners
DAWNEY adj (of a person) dull or slow
DAWNING ▸ dawn
DAWNS ▸ dawn
DAWS ▸ daw
DAWT vb fondle
dawted
DAWTIE n darling
dawties
DAWTING ▸ dawt
DAWTS ▸ dawt
DAY n
DAYAN n senior rabbi, esp one who sits in a religious court
dayanim, dayans
DAYBED n narrow bed for day use **daybeds**
DAYBOAT n small sailing boat with no sleeping accommodation
DAYBOOK n book in which transactions are recorded as they occur
DAYBOY n boy who attends a boarding school but returns home each evening **dayboys**
DAYCARE n
DAYCH vb thatch **dayched, dayches**
DAYFLY another name for ▸ **mayfly**
DAYGIRL n girl who attends a boarding school but returns home each evening
DAYGLO n fluorescent colours

DAYGLOW n fluorescent colours
DAYLILY n any of various plants having lily-like flowers
DAYLIT ▸ daylight
DAYLONG adv lasting the entire day
DAYMARE n bad dream during the day
DAYMARK n navigation aid
DAYNT adj dainty
DAYPACK n small rucksack
DAYROOM n communal living room in a residential institution
DAYS adv during the day, esp regularly
DAYSACK n rucksack
DAYSIDE n side of a planet nearest the sun
DAYSMAN n umpire **daysmen**
DAYSTAR a poetic word for ▸ **sun**
DAYTALE n day labour
DAYTIME n time from sunrise to sunset
DAYWEAR n clothes for everyday or informal wear
DAYWORK n daytime work
DAZE vb, n **dazed, dazedly, dazer, dazers, dazes, dazing**
DAZZLE vb, n **dazzled, dazzler, dazzles**
DE prep of or from
DEACON n, vb **deacons**
DEAD adj, n, adv, vb

DEADBOY ▸ deadman
DEADED ▸ dead
DEADEN vb **deadens**
DEADER ▸ dead
DEADERS ▸ dead
DEADEST ▸ dead
DEADEYE n either of two disclike blocks used to tighten a shroud on a boat
DEADING ▸ dead
DEADLY adj, adv
DEADMAN n item used in construction **deadmen**
DEADPAN adv, adj, n
DEADS ▸ dead
DEAF adj
DEAFEN vb **deafens**
DEAFER, deafest, deafish, deafly ▸ deaf
DEAIR vb remove air from **deaired, deairs**
DEAL n, vb, adj
DEALATE adj (of insects) having lost their wings after mating ▸ n insect that has shed its wings
DEALER n **dealers**
DEALING ▸ deal
DEALS ▸ deal
DEALT ▸ deal
DEAN n, vb **deaned**
DEANER n shilling **deaners**
DEANERY n office or residence of a dean
DEANING ▸ dean
DEANS ▸ dean
DEAR n, adj
DEARE vb harm **deared**
DEARER ▸ dear
DEARES ▸ deare
DEAREST ▸ dear

DEARIE = **deary**
DEARIES ▸ **deary**
DEARING ▸ **deare**
DEARLY *adv* very much
DEARN *vb* hide **dearnly, dearns**
DEARS ▸ **dear**
DEARTH *n* **dearths**
DEARY *n* term of affection: now often sarcastic or facetious
DEASH *vb* remove ash from **deashed, deashes**
DEASIL *adv* in the direction of the apparent course of the sun ▸ *n* motion in this direction **deasils**
DEASIUL *n* motion towards the sun
DEASOIL *n* motion towards the sun
DEATH *n*
DEATHLY *adv, adj*
DEATHS ▸ **death**
DEATHY ▸ **death**
DEAVE *vb* deafen **deaved, deaves, deaving**
DEAW *n* dew **deawie, deaws, deawy**
DEB *n* debutante
DEBACLE *n*
DEBAG *vb* remove the trousers from (someone) by force **debags**
DEBAR *vb*
DEBARK *vb* remove the bark from (a tree) **debarks**
DEBARS ▸ **debar**
DEBASE *vb* debased,

debaser, debases
DEBATE *n, vb* debated, debater, debates
DEBAUCH *vb* make (someone) bad or corrupt, esp sexually ▸ *n* instance or period of extreme dissipation
DEBBIER ▸ **debby**
DEBBIES ▸ **debby**
DEBBY *n* debutante ▸ *adj* of, or resembling a debutante
DEBE *n* tin
DEBEAK *vb* remove part of the beak of poultry to reduce the risk of such habits as feather-picking or cannibalism **debeaks**
DEBEARD *vb* remove beard from mussel
DEBEL *vb* beat in war **debels**
DEBES ▸ **debe**
DEBILE *adj* lacking strength
DEBIT *n, vb* debited
DEBITOR *n* person in debt
DEBITS ▸ **debit**
DEBONE *vb* remove bones from **deboned, deboner, debones**
DEBOSH *vb* debauch
DEBOSS *vb* carve a design into
DEBOUCH *vb* move out from a narrow place to a wider one ▸ *n* outlet or passage, as for the exit of troops
DEBRIDE *vb* remove dead tissue from

DEBRIEF *vb*
DEBRIS *n*
DEBS ▸ **deb**
DEBT *n*
DEBTED *adj* in debt
DEBTEE *n* person owed a debt **debtees**
DEBTOR *n* **debtors**
DEBTS ▸ **debt**
DEBUD = **disbud**
DEBUDS ▸ **debud**
DEBUG *vb, n* **debugs**
DEBUNK *vb* expose the falseness of **debunks**
DEBUR *vb* remove burs from (a piece of machined metal)
DEBURR *vb* remove burrs from (a workpiece) **deburrs**
DEBURS ▸ **debur**
DEBUS *vb* unload (goods) or (esp of troops) to alight from a motor vehicle **debused, debuses**
DEBUT *n, vb* debuted, debuts
DEBYE *n* unit of electric dipole moment **debyes**
DECAD *n* ten years
DECADAL ▸ **decade**
DECADE *n* **decades**
DECADS ▸ **decad**
DECAF *n* decaffeinated coffee ▸ *adj* decaffeinated
DECAFF *n* decaffeinated coffee **decaffs**
DECAFS ▸ **decaf**
DECAGON *n* geometric figure with ten faces
DECAL *vb* transfer

(a design) by decalcomania **decaled**

DECALOG = decalogue **decals**

DECAMP vb decamps

DECANAL adj of or relating to a dean or deanery

DECANE n liquid alkane hydrocarbon **decanes**

DECANI adv be sung by the decanal side of a choir

DECANT vb decants

DECAPOD n creature, such as a crab, with five pairs of walking limbs ▷ adj of, relating to, or belonging to these creatures

DECARB vb decoke **decarbs**

DECARE n ten ares or 1000 square metres **decares**

DECAY vb, n **decayed, decayer, decays**

DECCIE n decoration **deccies**

DECEASE n

DECEIT n **deceits**

DECEIVE vb

DECENCY n

DECENT adj

DECERN vb decree or adjudge **decerns**

DECIARE n one tenth of an are or 10 square metres

DECIBEL n

DECIDE vb

DECIDED adj

DECIDER n thing that determines who wins a match or championship

DECIDES ▷ decide

DECIDUA n membrane lining the uterus of some mammals during pregnancy

DECILE n one of nine actual or notional values of a variable dividing its distribution into ten groups with equal frequencies **deciles**

DECIMAL n, adj

DECIME n former French coin **decimes**

DECK n, vb

DECKED adj having a wooden deck or platform

DECKEL = deckle

DECKELS ▷ deckel

DECKER ▷ deck

DECKERS ▷ deck

DECKING n wooden platform in a garden

DECKLE n frame used to contain pulp on the mould in the making of handmade paper **deckled, deckles**

DECKO n look ▷ vb have a look **deckoed, deckos**

DECKS ▷ deck

DECLAIM vb

DECLARE vb

DECLASS vb lower in social status or position

DECLAW vb remove claws from **declaws**

DECLINE vb, n

DECO adj as in art deco style of art, jewellery, design, etc

DECOCT vb extract the essence from (a substance) by boiling **decocts**

DECODE vb **decoded, decoder, decodes**

DECOKE vb decarbonize **decoked, decokes**

DECOLOR vb bleach

DECOR n decors

DECORUM n

DECOS ▷ deco

DECOY n, vb **decoyed, decoyer, decoys**

DECREE n, vb **decreed, decreer, decrees**

DECREET n final judgment or sentence of a court

DECREW vb decrease **decrews**

DECRIAL, decried, decrier, decries ▷ decry

DECROWN vb depose

DECRY vb

DECRYPT vb decode (a message)

DECTET n ten musicians **dectets**

DECUMAN n large wave

DECUPLE vb increase by ten times ▷ n amount ten times as large as a given reference ▷ adj increasing tenfold

DECURIA n group of ten

DECURVE vb curve downwards

DECURY n (in ancient

Rome) a body of ten men

DEDAL = daedal

DEDANS n open gallery at the server's end of the court

DEDIMUS n legal term

DEDUCE vb deduced, deduces

DEDUCT vb deducts

DEE a Scot word for ▶ die

DEED n, vb, adj deeded, deeder, deedest

DEEDFUL adj full of exploits

DEEDIER ▶ deedy

DEEDILY ▶ deedy

DEEDING ▶ deed

DEEDS ▶ deed

DEEDY adj hard-working

DEEING ▶ dee

DEEJAY n disc jockey ▷ vb work or act as a disc jockey **deejays**

DEEK vb look at

DEELY adj as in **deely boppers** hairband with two bobbing antennae-like attachments

DEEM vb deemed, deeming, deems

DEEN n din **deens**

DEEP adj, n

DEEPEN vb deepens

DEEPER ▶ deep

DEEPEST ▶ deep

DEEPIE n 3D film **deepies**

DEEPLY ▶ deep

DEEPS ▶ deep

DEER n

DEERE adj serious

DEERFLY n insect related to the horsefly

DEERLET n ruminant mammal

DEERS ▶ deer

DEES ▶ dee

DEET n insect-repellent **deets**

DEEV n mythical monster

DEEVE vb deafen deeved, deeves, deeving

DEEVS ▶ deev

DEEWAN n chief of a village in India **deewans**

DEF adj very good

DEFACE vb defaced, defacer, defaces

DEFAME vb attack the good reputation of defamed, defamer, defames

DEFANG vb remove the fangs of **defangs**

DEFAST adj defaced

DEFASTE adj defaced

DEFAT vb remove fat from **defats**

DEFAULT n, vb

DEFEAT n, vb defeats

DEFECT n, vb defects

DEFENCE n

DEFEND vb defends

DEFENSE = defence

DEFER vb defers

DEFFER ▶ def

DEFFEST ▶ def

DEFFLY archaic word = deftly

DEFFO interj definitely: an expression of agreement or consent

DEFI n challenge

DEFIANT adj marked by resistance or bold opposition, as to authority

DEFICIT n

DEFIED, defier, defiers, defies ▶ defy

DEFILE vb, n defiled, defiler, defiles

DEFINE vb defined, definer, defines

DEFIS ▶ defi

DEFLATE vb

DEFLEA vb remove fleas from **defleas**

DEFLECT vb turn

DEFLEX vb turn downwards

DEFO interj

DEFOAM vb remove foam from **defoams**

DEFOCUS vb put out of focus

DEFOG vb clear of vapour **defogs**

DEFORCE vb withhold (property, esp land) wrongfully or by force from the rightful owner

DEFORM vb deforms

DEFOUL vb defile defouls

DEFRAG vb defragment defrags

DEFRAUD vb

DEFRAY vb defrays

DEFROCK vb deprive (a priest) of priestly status

DEFROST vb

DEFROZE > defreeze

DEFT adj **defter,**

deftest, deftly

DEFUEL *vb* remove fuel from **defuels**

DEFUNCT *adj, n*

DEFUND *vb* stop funds to **defunds**

DEFUSE *vb* **defused, defuser, defuses, defuze**

DEFUZED ▶ **defuze**

DEFUZES ▶ **defuze**

DEFY *vb* **defying**

DEG *vb* water (a plant, etc)

DEGAGE *adj* unconstrained in manner

DEGAME *n* tree of South and Central America **degames, degami**

DEGAMIS ▶ **degami**

DEGAS *vb* remove gas from (a container, vacuum tube, liquid, adsorbent, etc) **degases**

DEGAUSS *n* demagnetize

DEGERM *vb* remove germs from **degerms**

DEGGED ▶ **deg**

DEGGING ▶ **deg**

DEGLAZE *vb* dilute meat sediments (in a pan) in order to make a sauce or gravy

DEGOUT *n* disgust **degouts**

DEGRADE *vb*

DEGRAS *n* emulsion used for dressing hides

DEGREE *n*

DEGREED *adj* having a degree

DEGREES ▶ **degree**

DEGS ▶ **deg**

DEGU *n* small S American rodent

DEGUM *vb* remove gum from **degums**

DEGUS ▶ **degu**

DEGUST *vb* taste, esp with care or relish **degusts**

DEHISCE *vb* (of the seed capsules of some plants) to burst open spontaneously

DEHORN *vb* remove or prevent the growth of the horns of (cattle, sheep, or goats) **dehorns**

DEHORT *vb* dissuade **dehorts**

DEI ▶ **deus**

DEICE *vb* free or be freed of ice **deiced, deicer, deicers, deices**

DEICIDE *n* act of killing a god

DEICING ▶ **deice**

DEICTIC *adj* proving by direct argument

DEID *a Scot word for* ▶ **dead**

DEIDER ▶ **deid**

DEIDEST ▶ **deid**

DEIDS ▶ **deid**

DEIF *a Scot word for* ▶ **deaf**

DEIFER ▶ **deif**

DEIFEST ▶ **deif**

DEIFIC *adj* making divine or exalting to the position of a god

DEIFIED ▶ **deify**

DEIFIER ▶ **deify**

DEIFIES ▶ **deify**

DEIFORM *adj* having the form or appearance of a god

DEIFY *vb*

DEIGN *vb* **deigned, deigns**

DEIL *a Scot word for* ▶ **devil**

DEILS ▶ **deil**

DEINDEX *vb* cause to become no longer index-linked

DEISEAL *n* clockwise motion

DEISM *n* belief in God but not in divine revelation **deisms, deist, deistic, deists**

DEITIES ▶ **deity**

DEITY *n*

DEIXES ▶ **deixis**

DEIXIS *n* use or reference of a deictic word

DEJECT *vb* have a depressing effect on ▷ *adj* downcast

DEJECTA *pl n* waste products excreted through the anus

DEJECTS ▶ **deject**

DEJEUNE *n* lunch

DEKARE *n* unit of measurement equal to ten ares **dekares**

DEKE *vb* movement used in ice hockey or box lacrosse ▷ *n* such a shot or movement **deked, dekeing, dekes, deking**

DEKKO *n* look ▷ *vb* have a look **dekkoed, dekkos**

DEL n differential operator

DELAINE n sheer wool or wool and cotton fabric

DELAPSE vb be inherited

DELATE vb (formerly) to bring a charge against **delated, delates, delator**

DELAY vb, n **delayed, delayer, delays**

DELE n sign indicating that typeset matter is to be deleted ▷ vb mark (matter to be deleted) with a dele

DELEAD vb remove lead from **deleads**

DELEAVE vb separate copies

DELEBLE adj able to be deleted

DELED ▷ dele

DELEING ▷ dele

DELENDA pl n items for deleting

DELES ▷ dele

DELETE vb **deleted, deletes**

DELF n kind of earthenware **delfs**

DELFT n tin-glazed earthenware, typically having blue designs on white **delfts**

DELI n delicatessen

DELIBLE adj able to be deleted

DELICE n delicacy **delices**

DELICT n wrongful act for which the person

injured has the right to a civil remedy **delicts**

DELIGHT n, vb

DELIME vb remove lime from **delimed, delimes**

DELIMIT vb

DELIRIA ▷ delirium

DELIS ▷ deli

DELISH adj delicious

DELIST vb remove from a list **delists**

DELIVER vb

DELL n

DELLIES ▷ delly

DELLS ▷ dell

DELLY n delicatessen

DELO an informal word for ▷ delegate

DELOPE vb shoot into the air **deloped, delopes**

DELOS ▷ delo

DELOUSE vb rid (a person or animal) of lice

DELPH n kind of earthenware

DELPHIC adj obscure or ambiguous

DELPHIN n fatty substance from dolphin oil

DELPHS ▷ delph

DELS ▷ del

DELT n deltoid muscle

DELTA n **deltaic, deltas, deltic**

DELTOID n muscle acting to raise the arm ▷ adj shaped like a Greek capital delta

DELTS ▷ delt

DELUDE vb **deluded,**

deluder, deludes

DELUGE n, vb **deluged, deluges**

DELUXE adj rich, elegant, superior, or sumptuous

DELVE vb **delved, delver, delvers, delves, delving**

DEMAGOG = demagogue

DEMAIN n demesne

DEMAINE n demesne

DEMAINS ▷ demain

DEMAN vb reduce the workforce of (a plant, industry, etc)

DEMAND vb, n **demands**

DEMANS ▷ deman

DEMARK vb demarcate **demarks**

DEMAST vb remove the mast from **demasts**

DEMAYNE n demesne

DEME n (in preclassical Greece) the territory inhabited by a tribe

DEMEAN vb

DEMEANE n demesne

DEMEANS ▷ demean

DEMENT vb deteriorate mentally, esp because of old age

DEMENTI n denial

DEMENTS ▷ dement

DEMERGE vb separate a company from another

DEMERIT n fault, disadvantage ▷ vb deserve

DEMERSE vb immerse

DEMES ▷ deme

DEMESNE n land surrounding a house

DEMETON n insecticide

DEMIC adj of population

DEMIES ▶ demy

DEMIGOD n being who is part mortal, part god

DEMIREP n woman of bad repute, esp a prostitute

DEMISE n, vb demised, demises

DEMISS adj humble

DEMIST vb remove condensation from (a windscreen) demists

DEMIT vb resign (an office, position, etc) demits

DEMIVEG n person who eats poultry and fish, but no red meat ▷ adj denoting a person who eats poultry and fish, but no red meat

DEMO n, vb

DEMOB vb demobilize demobs

DEMODE adj out of fashion

DEMODED adj out of fashion

DEMOED ▶ demo

DEMOING ▶ demo

DEMON n

DEMONIC adj evil

DEMONRY ▶ demon

DEMONS ▶ demon

DEMOS n people of a nation regarded as a political unit demoses

DEMOTE vb demoted, demotes

DEMOTIC adj of the common people ▷ n demotic script of ancient Egypt

DEMOUNT vb remove (a motor, gun, etc) from its mounting or setting

DEMPT ▶ deem

DEMUR vb, n

DEMURE adj, vb, n demured, demurer, demures

DEMURS ▶ demur

DEMY n size of printing paper, 17 ½ by 22 ½ inches (444.5 × 571.5 mm)

DEN n, vb

DENAR n standard monetary unit of Macedonia, divided into 100 deni denari

DENARII ▶ denarius

DENARS ▶ denar

DENARY adj calculated by tens

DENAY vb deny denayed, denays

DENDRON = dendrite

DENE n narrow wooded valley denes

DENET vb remove from the Net Book Agreement denets

DENGUE n viral disease transmitted by mosquitoes dengues

DENI n monetary unit of the Former Yugoslav Republic of Macedonia, worth

one hundredth of a denar

DENIAL n denials

DENIED ▶ deny

DENIER n deniers

DENIES ▶ deny

DENIM n

DENIMED adj wearing denim

DENIMS pl n jeans or overalls made of denim

DENIS ▶ deni

DENIZEN n inhabitant ▷ vb make a denizen

DENNED ▶ den

DENNET n carriage for one horse dennets

DENNING ▶ den

DENOTE vb denoted, denotes

DENS ▶ den

DENSE adj densely, denser, densest

DENSIFY vb make or become dense

DENSITY n

DENT n, vb

DENTAL adj, n dentals

DENTARY n lower jawbone with teeth

DENTATE adj having teeth or teethlike notches

DENTED ▶ dent

DENTEL n architectural term dentels

DENTEX n large predatory fish

DENTIL n architectural ornament dentils

DENTIN = dentine

DENTINE n

DENTING ▶ dent

DENTINS ▶ dentin
DENTIST n
DENTOID adj
resembling a tooth
DENTS ▶ dent
DENTURE n false tooth
DENUDE vb denuded,
denuder, denudes
DENY vb denying
DEODAND n (formerly)
a thing that had
caused a death and
was forfeited to the
crown for a charitable
purpose
DEODAR n Himalayan
cedar with drooping
branches deodara,
deodars
DEODATE n offering to
God
DEONTIC adj of or
relating to such ethical
concepts as obligation
and permissibility
DEORBIT vb go out of
orbit
DEOXY adj having less
oxygen than a specified
related compound
DEPAINT vb depict
DEPART vb departs
DEPECHE n message
DEPEND vb depends
DEPERM vb
demagnetize deperms
DEPICT vb depicts
DEPLANE vb disembark
from an aeroplane
DEPLETE vb
DEPLORE vb
DEPLOY vb deploys
DEPLUME vb deprive of
feathers

DEPONE vb declare
(something) under
oath deponed,
depones
DEPORT vb deports
DEPOSAL n deposition;
giving of testimony
under oath
DEPOSE vb deposed,
deposer, deposes
DEPOSIT vb, n
DEPOT n, adj depots
DEPRAVE vb
DEPRESS vb
DEPRIVE vb
DEPSIDE n organic
chemical compound
DEPTH n depths
DEPUTE vb, n deputed,
deputes
DEPUTY n
DEQUEUE vb remove
(an item) from a queue
of computing tasks
DERAIGN vb contest
(a claim, suit, etc)
DERAIL vb, n derails
DERANGE vb disturb the
order or arrangement of
DERAT vb remove rats
from
DERATE vb assess the
value of some types of
property at a lower
rate than others for
local taxation
derated, derates
DERATS ▶ derat
DERAY vb go mad
derayed, derays
DERBIES ▶ derby
DERBY n
DERE vb injure dered,
deres

DERHAM = dirham
DERHAMS ▶ derham
DERIDE vb derided,
derider, derides
DERIG vb remove
equipment, e.g. from
stage set derigs
DERING ▶ dere
DERIVE vb derived,
deriver, derives
DERM = derma
DERMA n beef or fowl
intestine used as a
casing for certain
dishes, esp kishke
DERMAL adj of or
relating to the skin
DERMAS ▶ derma
DERMIC ▶ dermis
DERMIS another name
for ▶ corium
DERMOID adj of or
resembling skin ▶ n
congenital cystic
tumour whose walls
are lined with
epithelium
DERMS ▶ derm
DERN n concealment
DERNFUL adj sorrowful
DERNIER adj last
DERNLY adv sorrowfully
DERNS ▶ dern
DERO n tramp or
derelict deros
DERRICK n, vb
DERRIES ▶ derry
DERRIS n E Indian
woody climbing plant
DERRO n vagrant
derros
DERRY n derelict house,
esp one used by tramps,
drug addicts, etc

DERTH = dearth
DERTHS ▸ derth
DERV n
DERVISH n member of a Muslim religious order noted for a frenzied whirling dance
DERVS ▸ derv
DESALT vb desalts
DESAND vb remove sand from **desands**
DESCALE vb remove a hard coating from inside (a kettle or pipe)
DESCANT n, adj, vb
DESCEND vb
DESCENT n
DESCRY vb catch sight of
DESEED vb remove the seeds from (eg a fruit) **deseeds**
DESERT n, vb deserts
DESERVE vb
DESEX n desexualize **desexed**, **desexes**
DESHI = desi
DESI adj in Indian English, indigenous or local
DESIGN vb, n designs, desine
DESINED ▸ desine
DESINES ▸ desine
DESIRE vb, n desired, desirer, desires
DESIST vb desists
DESK n
DESKILL vb mechanize or computerize (a job) thereby reducing the skill required to do it
DESKING n desks and related furnishings in

a given space, eg an office
DESKMAN n police officer in charge in police station
deskmen
DESKS ▸ desk
DESKTOP adj, n
DESMAN n either of two molelike amphibious mammals
desmans
DESMID n type of mainly unicellular freshwater green alga
desmids
DESMINE n type of mineral
DESMOID adj resembling a tendon or ligament ▷ n very firm tumour of connective tissue
DESNOOD vb remove the snood of a turkey poult to reduce the risk of cannibalism
DESORB vb change from an adsorbed state to a gaseous or liquid state **desorbs**
DESOXY = deoxy
DESPAIR n, vb
DESPISE vb
DESPITE prep, n, vb
DESPOIL vb
DESPOND vb lose heart or hope
DESPOT n despots
DESSE n desk
DESSERT n
DESSES ▸ desse
DESTAIN vb remove stain from

DESTINE vb set apart or appoint
DESTINY n
DESTOCK vb reduce the amount of stock
DESTROY vb
DESUGAR vb remove sugar from
DESYNE = design
DESYNED ▸ desyne
DESYNES ▸ desyne
DETACH vb
DETAIL n, vb details
DETAIN vb detains
DETECT vb detects
DETENT n locking piece of a mechanism, often spring-loaded to check the movement of a wheel in one direction only
DETENTE n
DETENTS ▸ detent
DETENU n prisoner
DETENUE n female prisoner
DETENUS ▸ detenu
DETER vb
DETERGE vb wash or wipe away
DETERS ▸ deter
DETEST vb detests
DETICK vb remove ticks from **deticks**
DETINUE n action brought by a plaintiff to recover goods wrongfully detained
DETORT vb pervert **detorts**
DETOUR n, vb detours
DETOX n treatment to rid the body of poisonous substances

▷ **vb** undergo treatment to rid the body of poisonous substances **detoxed, detoxes**

DETRACT *vb*

DETRAIN *vb* leave or cause to leave a railway train, as passengers, etc

DETRUDE *vb* force down or thrust away or out

DETUNE *vb* change pitch of (stringed instrument) **detuned, detunes**

DEUCE *vb, n*

DEUCED *adj* damned

DEUCES ▶ **deuce**

DEUCING ▶ **deuce**

DEUS *n* god

DEUTON old form of ▶ **deuteron**

DEUTONS ▶ **deuton**

DEUTZIA *n* shrub with clusters of pink or white flowers

DEV = deva
Dev is a Sanskrit word for a good spirit; related words are **deev** and **deva**

DEVA *n* (in Hinduism and Buddhism) divine being or god

DEVALL *vb* stop **devalls**

DEVALUE *vb*

DEVAS ▶ **deva**

DEVEIN *vb* remove vein from **deveins**

DEVEL = **devvel**

DEVELED ▶ **devel**

DEVELOP *vb*

DEVELS ▶ **devel**

DEVEST variant spelling of ▶ **divest**

DEVESTS ▶ **devest**

DEVIANT *adj, n*

DEVIATE *vb*

DEVICE *n* **devices**

DEVIL *n, vb* **deviled**

DEVILET *n* young devil

DEVILRY *n*

DEVILS ▶ **devil**

DEVIOUS *adj*

DEVISAL *n* act of inventing, contriving, or devising

DEVISE *vb, n* **devised**

DEVISEE *n* person to whom property, esp realty, is devised by will

DEVISER ▶ **devise**

DEVISES ▶ **devise**

DEVISOR *n* person who devises property, esp realty, by will

DEVLING *n* young devil

DEVOICE *vb* make (a voiced speech sound) voiceless

DEVOID *adj*

DEVOIR *n* duty **devoirs**

DEVOLVE *vb*

DEVON *n* bland processed meat in sausage form, eaten cold in slices **devons**

DEVORE *n* velvet fabric with a raised pattern **devores**

DEVOT *n* devotee

DEVOTE *vb*

DEVOTED *adj*

DEVOTEE *n*

DEVOTES ▶ **devote**

DEVOTS ▶ **devot**

DEVOUR *vb* **devours**

DEVOUT *adj*

DEVS ▶ **dev**

DEVVEL *vb* strike with blow **devvels**

DEW *n, vb*

DEWAN *n* (formerly in India) the chief or finance minister of a state ruled by an Indian prince

DEWANI *n* post of dewan **dewanis, dewanny**

DEWANS ▶ **dewan**

DEWAR *n* as in **dewar flask** type of vacuum flask **dewars**

DEWATER *vb* remove water from

DEWAX *vb* remove wax from **dewaxed, dewaxes**

DEWCLAW *n* nonfunctional claw on a dog's leg

DEWDROP *n* drop of dew

DEWED ▶ **dew**

DEWFALL *n* formation of dew

DEWFULL obsolete form of ▶ **due**

DEWIER ▶ **dewy**

DEWIEST ▶ **dewy**

DEWILY ▶ **dewy**

DEWING ▶ **dew**

DEWITT *vb* kill, esp hang unlawfully **dewitts**

DEWLAP *n* **dewlaps, dewlapt**

DEWLESS ▶ **dew**

DEWOOL *vb* remove wool from **dewools**

DEWORM vb rid of worms **deworms**

DEWS ▸ dew

DEWY adj

DEX n dextroamphetamine **dexes**

> Short for Dexedrine®, a stimulant drug, this is another of the key words to know for using the X. It can be extended to **dexy** or **dexie**.

DEXIE n pill containing dextroamphetamine **dexies**

DEXTER adj of or on the right side of a shield, etc, from the bearer's point of view ▸ n small breed of beef cattle **dexters**

DEXTRAL adj of, relating to, or located on the right side, esp of the body

DEXTRAN n polysaccharide compound

DEXTRIN n sticky substance obtained from starch

DEXTRO adj dextrorotatory or rotating to the right

DEXY = dexie

DEY n title given to commanders or governors of the Janissaries of Algiers **deys**

DEZINC vb remove zinc from **dezincs**

DHAK n tropical Asian tree **dhaks**

DHAL n dhals

DHAMMA variant of ▸ **dharma**

DHAMMAS ▸ dhamma

DHANSAK n any of a variety of Indian dishes

DHARMA n dharmas, dharmic

DHARNA n (in India) a method of obtaining justice **dharnas**

DHIMMI n non-Muslim living in a state governed by sharia law **dhimmis**

DHOBI n (in India, Malaya, East Africa, etc, esp formerly) a washerman **dhobis**

DHOL n type of Indian drum

DHOLE n fierce canine mammal **dholes**

DHOLL = dhal

DHOLLS ▸ dholl

DHOLS ▸ dhol

DHOOLY = doolie

DHOORA = durra

DHOORAS ▸ dhoora

DHOOTI = dhoti

DHOOTIE = dhoti

DHOOTIS ▸ dhootis

DHOTI n dhotis

DHOURRA = durra

DHOW n Arab sailing ship **dhows**

DHURNA = dharna

DHURNAS ▸ dhurna

DHURRA = durra

DHURRAS ▸ dhurra

DHURRIE = durrie

DHUTI = dhoti

DHUTIS ▸ dhuti

DI ▸ deus

DIABASE n altered dolerite

DIABLE n type of sauce **diables**

DIABOLO n game using a spinning top and a cord fastened to two sticks

DIACID n lead plaster **diacids**

DIACT n two-rayed

DIADEM n, vb diadems

DIADROM n complete course of pendulum

DIAGRAM n, vb

DIAGRID n diagonal structure network

DIAL n, vb

DIALECT n

DIALED, dialer, dialers, dialing ▸ dial

DIALIST n dial-maker

DIALLED ▸ dial

DIALLEL n interbreeding among a group of parents

DIALLER ▸ dial

DIALOG = dialogue

DIALOGS ▸ dialog

DIALS ▸ dial

DIALYSE vb separate by dialysis **dialyze**

DIAMIDE n compound containing two amido groups

DIAMIN = diamine

DIAMINE n any chemical compound containing two amino groups in its molecules

DIAMINS ▸ diamin

DIAMOND n, adj, vb

DIAMYL *adj* with two amyl groups

DIANDRY *n* practice of having two husbands

DIANE *adj as in* steak diane kind of steak

DIANOIA *n* perception and experience regarded as lower modes of knowledge

DIAPASE = diapason

DIAPER *n* nappy ▷ *vb* decorate with a geometric pattern **diapers**

DIAPIR *n* anticlinal fold in which the brittle overlying rock has been pierced by material, such as salt, from beneath **diapirs**

DIAPSID *n* reptile with two holes in rear of skull

DIARCH *adj* (of a vascular bundle) having two strands of xylem

DIARCHY *n* government by two states, individuals, etc

DIARIAL ▷ diary

DIARIAN ▷ diary

DIARIES ▷ diary

DIARISE *vb* diarize

DIARIST *n* person who writes a diary

DIARIZE *vb* record in diary

DIARY *n*

DIASCIA *n* S African plant, usu with pink flowers

DIASTEM = diastema

DIASTER *n* stage in cell division

DIATOM *n* microscopic unicellular alga **diatoms**

DIATRON *n* circuit that uses diodes

DIAXON *n* bipolar cell **diaxons**

DIAZIN = diazine

DIAZINE *n* organic compound

DIAZINS ▷ diazin

DIAZO *adj* relating to a method for reproducing documents ▷ *n* document produced by this method **diazoes**

DIAZOLE *n* type of organic compound

DIAZOS ▷ diazo

DIB *vb* fish by allowing the bait to bob and dip on the surface

DIBASIC *adj* (of an acid) containing two acidic hydrogen atoms

DIBBED ▷ dib

DIBBER = dibble

DIBBERS ▷ dibber

DIBBING ▷ dib

DIBBLE *n* small gardening tool ▷ *vb* make a hole in (the ground) with a dibble **dibbled, dibbler, dibbles**

DIBBS *n* money

DIBBUK *variant spelling of* ▷ dybbuk

DIBBUKS ▷ dibbuk

DIBS ▷ dib

DIBUTYL *adj* with two butyl groups

DICAMBA *n* type of weedkiller

DICAST *n* juror in ancient Athens **dicasts**

DICE *n, vb* diced, dicer, dicers, dices

DICEY *adj*

DICH *interj* archaic expression meaning "may it do"

DICHORD *n* two-stringed musical instrument

DICHT *vb* wipe dichted, dichts

DICIER ▷ dicey

DICIEST ▷ dicey

DICING ▷ dice

DICINGS ▷ dice

DICKENS *n* euphemism for devil

DICKER *vb* trade (goods) by bargaining ▷ *n* petty bargain or barter **dickers**

DICKEY = dicky

DICKEYS ▷ dickey

DICKIE = dicky

DICKIER ▷ dicky

DICKIES ▷ dicky

DICKTY = dicty

DICKY *n, adj*

DICLINY > diclinous

DICOT *n* type of flowering plant **dicots**

DICOTYL *n* type of flowering plant

DICT *vb* dictate

DICTA ▷ dictum

DICTATE *vb, n*

DICTED ▷ dict

DICTIER ▷ dicty

DICTING ▶ dict

DICTION n

DICTS ▶ dict

DICTUM n dictums

DICTY adj conceited; snobbish

DICYCLY ▶ dicyclic

DID ▶ do

DIDACT n instructive person didacts

DIDAKAI = didicoy

DIDAKEI = didicoy

DIDDER vb shake with fear didders

DIDDIER ▶ diddy

DIDDIES ▶ diddy

DIDDLE vb diddled, diddler, diddles

DIDDLEY n worthless amount

DIDDLY n worthless amount

DIDDY n female breast or nipple ▷ adj of or relating to a diddy

DIDICOI = didicoy

DIDICOY n (in Britain) a person who lives like a Gypsy but is not a true Romany

DIDIE = didy

DIDIES ▶ didy

DIDO n antic didoes, didos

DIDST form of the past tense of ▶ do

DIDY n woman's breast

DIE vb, n

DIEB n N African jackal

DIEBACK n disease of trees and shrubs ▷ vb (of plants) to suffer from dieback

DIEBS ▶ dieb

DIED ▶ die

DIEDRAL = dihedral

DIEDRE n large shallow groove or corner in a rock face diedres

DIEHARD n

DIEING ▶ die

DIEL n 24-hour period

DIENE n type of hydrocarbon dienes

DIEOFF n process of dying in large numbers dieoffs

DIES ▶ die

DIESEL vb, n diesels

DIESES ▶ diesis

DIESIS n (in ancient Greek theory) any interval smaller than a whole tone

DIESTER n synthetic lubricant

DIET n, vb, adj

DIETARY adj of or relating to a diet ▷ n regulated diet

DIETED ▶ diet

DIETER ▶ diet

DIETERS ▶ diet

DIETHER n chemical compound

DIETHYL adj as in diethyl ether

DIETINE n low-ranking diet

DIETING ▶ diet

DIETIST another word for > dietitian

DIETS ▶ diet

DIF = diff

DIFF n (slang) difference

DIFFER vb differs

DIFFORM adj irregular in form

DIFFS ▶ diff

DIFFUSE vb, adj

DIFS ▶ dif

DIG vb, n

DIGAMMA n letter of the Greek alphabet

DIGAMY n second marriage

DIGEST vb, n digests

DIGGED a past tense of ▶ dig

DIGGER n diggers

DIGGING ▶ dig

DIGHT vb adorn or equip, as for battle dighted, dights

DIGICAM n digital camera

DIGIT n

DIGITAL adj, n

DIGITS ▶ digit

DIGLOT n bilingual book diglots

DIGLYPH n ornament in Doric frieze with two grooves

DIGNIFY vb

DIGNITY n

DIGONAL adj of or relating to a symmetry operation

DIGOXIN n glycoside extracted from the leaves of the woolly foxglove

DIGRAPH n two letters used to represent a single sound

DIGRESS vb

DIGS ▶ dig

DIHEDRA ▶ dihedron

DIKA n wild mango dikas

DIKAST = dicast

DIKASTS ▶ dikast

DIKDIK n small African antelope **dikdiks**

DIKE = dyke

DIKED ▶ dike

DIKER n builder of dikes **dikers**

DIKES ▶ dike

DIKING ▶ dike

DIKKOP n type of brownish shore bird with a large head and eyes **dikkops**

DIKTAT n dictatorial decree **diktats**

DILATE vb **dilated**

DILATER = dilator

DILATES ▶ dilate

DILATOR n something that dilates an object

DILDO n object used as a substitute for an erect penis **dildoe**

DILDOES ▶ dildo

DILDOS ▶ dildo

DILEMMA n

DILL vb, n **dilled**

DILLI n dilly bag; small bag, esp one made of plaited grass and used for carrying food

DILLIER ▶ dilly

DILLIES ▶ dilly

DILLING ▶ dill

DILLIS ▶ dilli

DILLS ▶ dill

DILLY adj foolish ▷ n person or thing that is remarkable

DILUENT adj causing dilution or serving to dilute ▷ n substance used for or causing dilution

DILUTE vb, adj **diluted, dilutee, diluter, dilutes**

DILUTOR n thing intended to have a diluting effect

DILUVIA > diluvium

DIM adj, vb

DIMBLE n wooded hollow; dingle **dimbles**

DIME n

DIMER n type of molecule

DIMERIC adj of a dimer

DIMERS ▶ dimer

DIMES ▶ dime

DIMETER n type of verse

DIMITY n light strong cotton fabric with woven stripes or squares

DIMLY, dimmed, dimmer, dimmers, dimmest ▶ dim

DIMMING n as in global dimming decrease in the amount of sunlight reaching the earth

DIMMISH ▶ dim

DIMNESS ▶ dim

DIMORPH n either of two forms of a substance that exhibits dimorphism

DIMOUT n reduction of lighting **dimouts**

DIMP n in Northern English dialect, a cigarette butt

DIMPLE n, vb **dimpled, dimples, dimply**

DIMPS ▶ dimp

DIMPSY n twilight

DIMS ▶ dim

DIMWIT n stupid person **dimwits**

DIN n, vb

DINAR n **dinars**

DINDLE another word for ▶ **dinnle**

DINDLED ▶ dindle

DINDLES ▶ dindle

DINE vb **dined**

DINER n

DINERIC adj of or concerned with the interface between immiscible liquids

DINERO n money **dineros**

DINERS ▶ diner

DINES ▶ dine

DINETTE n alcove or small area for use as a dining room

DINFUL adj noisy

DING n small dent in a vehicle ▷ vb ring or cause to ring, esp with tedious repetition

DINGBAT n any unnamed object

DINGE n dent ▷ vb make a dent in (something) **dinged**

DINGER n (in baseball) home run **dingers**

DINGES n jocular word for something whose name is unknown or forgotten

DINGEY = dinghy

DINGEYS ▶ dingey

DINGHY n, vb

DINGIED ▶ dingey

DINGIER ▶ dingy

DINGIES ▶ dingy

DINGILY ▶ dingy

DINGING ▶ dinge

DINGLE n small wooded hollow or valley **dingles**

DINGO n, vb dingoed, **dingoes**

DINGS ▶ ding

DINGUS = dinges

DINGY adj, vb

DINIC n remedy for vertigo **dinics**

DINING ▶ dine

DINITRO adj containing two nitro groups

DINK adj neat or neatly dressed ▶ vb carry (a second person) on a horse, bicycle, etc ▶ n ball struck delicately **dinked, dinker, dinkest**

DINKEY n small locomotive **dinkeys**

DINKIE n affluent married childless person ▶ adj designed for or appealing to dinkies

DINKIER ▶ dinky

DINKIES ▶ dinkie

DINKING ▶ dink

DINKLY adj neat

DINKS ▶ dink

DINKUM n dinkums

DINKY adj small and neat

DINMONT n neutered sheep

DINNA vb a Scots word for do not

DINNAE vb (Scots) do not

DINNED ▶ din

DINNER vb, n dinners

DINNING ▶ din

DINNLE vb shake dinnled, dinnles

DINO n dinosaur **dinos**

DINS ▶ din

DINT variant of ▶ dent

DINTED ▶ dint

DINTING ▶ dint

DINTS ▶ dint

DIOBOL n ancient Greek coin **diobols**

DIOCESE n

DIODE n diodes

DIOECY n state of being dioecious

DIOL n any of a class of alcohols that have two hydroxyl groups in each molecule **diols**

DIOPTER = dioptre

DIOPTRE n unit for measuring the refractive power of a lens

DIORAMA n miniature three-dimensional scene

DIORISM n definition; clarity

DIORITE n dark coarse-grained igneous plutonic rock

DIOTA n type of ancient vase **diotas**

DIOXAN n colourless insoluble toxic liquid **dioxane, dioxans**

DIOXID = dioxide

DIOXIDE n

DIOXIDS ▶ dioxid

DIOXIN n poisonous chemical by-products

of certain weedkillers **dioxins**

DIP vb, n

DIPHASE adj of, having, or concerned with two phases

DIPHONE n combination of two speech sounds

DIPLEX adj (in telecommunications) permitting the transmission of simultaneous signals in both directions

DIPLOE n spongy bone separating the two layers of compact bone of the skull **diploes**

DIPLOIC adj relating to diploe

DIPLOID adj denoting a cell or organism with pairs of homologous chromosomes ▶ n diploid cell or organism

DIPLOMA vb, n

DIPLON another name for ▶ deuteron

DIPLONS ▶ diplon

DIPLONT n animal or plant that has the diploid number of chromosomes in its somatic cells

DIPNET vb fish using fishing net on pole **dipnets**

DIPNOAN n lungfish

DIPODIC ▶ dipody

DIPODY n metrical unit consisting of two feet

DIPOLAR ▶ dipole

DIPOLE n two equal but opposite electric charges or magnetic poles separated by a small distance **dipoles**

DIPPED ▸ dip

DIPPER n ladle used for dipping **dippers**

DIPPIER ▸ dippy

DIPPING ▸ dip

DIPPY adj odd, eccentric, or crazy

DIPS ▸ dip

DIPSAS n type of snake

DIPSHIT n stupid person

DIPSO n (slang) dipsomaniac or alcoholic **dipsos**

DIPT ▸ dip

DIPTERA n order of insects with two wings

DIPTYCA = diptych

DIPTYCH n painting on two hinged panels

DIQUARK n particle in physics

DIQUAT n type of herbicide **diquats**

DIRAM n money unit of Tajikistan **dirams**

DIRDAM = dirdum

DIRDAMS ▸ dirdam

DIRDUM n tumult **dirdums**

DIRE adj

DIRECT adj, adv, vb directs

DIREFUL = dire

DIRELY ▸ dire

DIREMPT vb separate with force

DIRER ▸ dire

DIREST ▸ dire

DIRGE n dirges

DIRHAM n standard monetary unit of Morocco **dirhams, dirhem**

DIRHEMS ▸ dirhem

DIRIGE n dirge **diriges**

DIRK n dagger, formerly worn by Scottish Highlanders ▸ vb stab with a dirk **dirke, dirked**

DIRKES ▸ dirke

DIRKING ▸ dirk

DIRKS ▸ dirk

DIRL vb tingle; vibrate **dirled, dirling, dirls**

DIRNDL n full gathered skirt **dirndls**

DIRT vb, n

DIRTBAG n filthy person

DIRTED ▸ dirt

DIRTIED, dirtier, dirties, dirtily ▸ dirty

DIRTING ▸ dirt

DIRTS ▸ dirt

DIRTY adj, vb

DIS = diss

DISA n type of orchid

DISABLE vb

DISALLY vb separate

DISARM vb disarms

DISAS ▸ disa

DISAVOW vb

DISBAND vb

DISBAR vb deprive (a barrister) of the right to practise

DISBARK = disembark

DISBARS ▸ disbar

DISBUD vb remove superfluous buds from (a plant, esp a fruit tree) **disbuds**

DISC n, vb

DISCAGE vb release from cage

DISCAL adj relating to or resembling a disc

DISCANT = descant

DISCARD vb, n

DISCASE vb remove case from

DISCED ▸ disc

DISCEPT vb discuss

DISCERN vb

DISCERP vb divide

DISCI ▸ discus

DISCIDE vb split

DISCING ▸ disc

DISCO vb, n **discoed, discoer**

DISCOID adj like a disc ▸ n dislike object

DISCORD n, vb

DISCOS ▸ disco

DISCS ▸ disc

DISCURE old form of > discover

DISCUS n

DISCUSS vb

DISDAIN n, vb

DISEASE vb, n

DISEDGE vb render blunt

DISEUR = diseuse

DISEURS ▸ diseur

DISEUSE n (esp formerly) an actress who presents dramatic recitals

DISFAME n discredit

DISFORM vb change form of

DISGEST vb digest

DISGOWN vb remove gown from

DISGUST n, vb

DISH n, vb

DISHED adj shaped like a dish

DISHELM vb remove helmet from

DISHES ▶ dish

DISHFUL n the amount that a dish is able to hold

DISHIER ▶ dishy

DISHING ▶ dish

DISHOME vb deprive of home

DISHORN vb remove horns from

DISHPAN n large pan for washing dishes, pots, etc

DISHRAG n dishcloth

DISHY adj good-looking

DISJECT vb break apart

DISJOIN vb disconnect or become disconnected

DISJUNE n breakfast

DISK = disc

DISKED ▶ disk

DISKING ▶ disk

DISKS ▶ disk

DISLEAF vb remove leaf or leaves from

DISLEAL archaic form of ▶ disloyal

DISLIKE vb, n

DISLIMB vb remove limbs from

DISLIMN vb efface

DISLINK vb disunite

DISLOAD vb unload

DISMAL adj

DISMALS pl n gloomy state of mind

DISMAN vb remove men from **dismans**

DISMASK vb remove mask from

DISMAST vb break off the mast or masts of (a sailing vessel)

DISMAY vb, n dismayed

DISMAYL vb remove a coat of mail from

DISMAYS ▶ dismay

DISME old form of ▶ dime

DISMES ▶ disme

DISMISS vb, sentence substitute

DISNEST vb remove from nest

DISOBEY vb

DISOMIC adj having an extra chromosome in the haploid state **disomy**

DISOWN vb **disowns**

DISPACE vb move or travel about

DISPARK vb release

DISPART vb separate

DISPEL vb **dispels**

DISPEND vb spend

DISPLAY vb, n

DISPLE vb punish **displed, disples**

DISPONE vb transfer ownership

DISPORT vb indulge (oneself) in pleasure ▶ n amusement

DISPOSE vb

DISPOST vb remove from post

DISPRAD old form of ▶ dispread

DISPRED old spelling of ▶ dispread

DISPUTE n, vb

DISRANK vb demote

DISRANK vb punish (an officer) by lowering in rank

DISROBE vb undress

DISROOT vb uproot

DISRUPT vb

DISS vb treat (a person) with contempt

DISSAVE vb spend savings

DISSEAT vb unseat

DISSECT vb

DISSED ▶ diss

DISSENT vb, n

DISSERT n give or make a dissertation; dissertate

DISSES ▶ diss

DISSING ▶ diss

DISTAFF n rod on which wool etc is wound for spinning

DISTAIN vb stain; tarnish

DISTAL adj (of a bone, limb, etc) situated farthest from the point of attachment

DISTANT adj

DISTEND vb

DISTENT adj bloated; swollen

DISTICH n unit of two verse lines

DISTIL vb **distill, distils**

DISTOME n parasitic flatworm

DISTORT vb

DISTRIX n splitting of the ends of hairs

DISTUNE vb cause to be out of tune

DISTURB vb
DISTYLE n temple with two columns
DISUSE vb, n
DISUSED adj no longer used
DISUSES ▶ disuse
DISYOKE vb unyoke
DIT vb stop something happening ▷ n short sound used in the spoken representation of telegraphic codes
DITA n tropical shrub
DITAL n key for raising pitch of lute string **ditals**
DITAS ▶ dita
DITCH n, vb ditched, ditcher, ditches
DITE vb set down in writing dited, dites
DITHER vb, n dithers, dithery
DITHIOL n chemical compound
DITING ▶ dite
DITONE n interval of two tones **ditones**
DITS ▶ dit
DITSIER ▶ ditsy
DITSY = ditzy
DITT = dit
DITTANY n aromatic plant
DITTAY n accusation; charge **dittays**
DITTED ▶ dit
DITTIER ▶ ditty
DITTIES ▶ ditty
DITTING ▶ dit
DITTIT ▶ dit
DITTO n, adv, sentence substitute, vb dittoed,

dittos
DITTS ▶ ditt
DITTY vb, n
DITZ n silly scatterbrained person ditzes
DITZIER ▶ ditzy
DITZY adj silly and scatterbrained
DIURNAL adj happening during the day or daily ▷ n service book containing all the canonical hours except matins
DIURON n type of herbicide **diurons**
DIV n stupid or foolish person
DIVA n
DIVAN n divans
DIVAS ▶ diva
DIVE vb, n dived
DIVER n person who works or explores underwater
DIVERGE vb
DIVERS adj various ▷ determiner various
DIVERSE vb, adj
DIVERT vb diverts
DIVES ▶ dive
DIVEST vb divests
DIVI alternative spelling of ▶ divvy
DIVIDE vb, n
DIVIDED adj split
DIVIDER n
DIVIDES ▶ divide
DIVIED ▶ divvied
DIVINE adj, vb, n divined, diviner, divines
DIVING ▶ dive

DIVINGS ▶ dive
DIVIS ▶ divi
DIVISIM adv separately
DIVISOR n
DIVNA vb do not
DIVO n male diva
DIVORCE n, vb
DIVOS ▶ divo
DIVOT n small piece of turf divots
DIVS ▶ div
DIVULGE vb
DIVULSE vb tear apart
DIVVIED ▶ divvy
DIVVIER ▶ divvy
DIVVIES ▶ divvy
DIVVY vb divide and share ▷ adj stupid ▷ n stupid person
DIVVYING > divvying
DIWAN = dewan
DIWANS ▶ diwan
DIXI interj I have spoken
DIXIE n large metal pot for cooking, brewing tea, etc **dixies**
DIXIT n statement dixits
DIXY = dixie
DIYA n small oil lamp, usu made from clay diyas
DIZAIN n ten-line poem dizains
DIZEN archaic word for ▶ bedizen
DIZENED ▶ dizen
DIZENS ▶ dizen
DIZZARD n dunce
DIZZIED, dizzier, dizzies, dizzily ▶ dizzy
DIZZY adj, vb
DJEBEL a variant spelling of ▶ jebel

DJEBELS ▸ djebel
DJEMBE n W African drum **djembes**
DJIBBAH = jubbah
DJIN = jinn
DJINN ▸ djinni
DJINNI = jinni
DJINNS ▸ djinn
DJINNY = jinni
DJINS ▸ djin
DO vb perform or complete (a deed or action) ▸ n party, celebration
DOAB n alluvial land between two converging rivers
DOABLE adj capable of being done
DOABS ▸ doab
DOAT = dote; doated, doater, doaters, doating, doats
DOB vb as in dob in inform against or report **dobbed**
DOBBER n informant or traitor **dobbers**
DOBBIE = dobby
DOBBIES ▸ dobby
DOBBIN n name for a horse
DOBBING ▸ dob
DOBBINS ▸ dobbin
DOBBY n attachment to a loom, used in weaving small figures
DOBHASH n interpreter
DOBIE n cannabis **dobies**
DOBLA n medieval Spanish gold coin, probably worth 20 maravedis **doblas**
DOBLON a variant

spelling of **>** doubloon
DOBLONS ▸ doblon
DOBRA n standard monetary unit of São Tomé e Principe **dobras**
DOBRO n type of acoustic guitar **dobros**
DOBS ▸ dob
DOBSON n larva of dobsonfly **dobsons**
DOBY = dobie
DOC = doctor
DOCENT n voluntary worker who acts as a guide **docents**
DOCETIC adj believing in docetism
DOCHMII › dochmius
DOCHT ▸ dow
DOCIBLE adj easily tamed
DOCILE adj dociler
DOCK n, vb
DOCKAGE n charge levied upon a vessel for using a dock
DOCKED ▸ dock
DOCKEN n something of no value or importance **dockens**
DOCKER n person employed to load and unload ships **dockers**
DOCKET n, vb **dockets**
DOCKING ▸ dock
DOCKISE = dockize
DOCKIZE vb convert into docks
DOCKS ▸ dock
DOCO n (slang) documentary **docos**
DOCQUET = docket
DOCS ▸ doc

DOCTOR n, vb **doctors**
DOD vb clip
DODDARD adj archaic word for missing branches; rotten
DODDED ▸ dod
DODDER vb, n **dodders, doddery**
DODDIER ▸ doddy
DODDIES ▸ doddy
DODDING ▸ dod
DODDLE n something easily accomplished **doddles**
DODDY n bad mood ▸ adj sulky
DODGE vb, n **dodged**
DODGEM n bumper car **dodgems**
DODGER n person who evades a responsibility or duty **dodgers**
DODGERY n deception
DODGES ▸ dodge
DODGIER ▸ dodgy
DODGING ▸ dodge
DODGY adj
DODKIN n coin of little value **dodkins**
DODMAN n snail **dodmans**
DODO n **dodoes, dodoism, dodos**
DODS ▸ dod
DOE n
DOEK n square of cloth worn on the head by women **doeks**
DOEN ▸ do
DOER n active or energetic person **doers**
DOES ▸ do
DOESKIN n skin of a

deer, lamb, or sheep

DOEST ▶ do

DOETH ▶ do

DOF informal South African word for ▶ stupid

DOFF vb doffed, doffer, doffers, doffing, doffs

DOG n, vb

DOGATE n office of doge dogates

DOGBANE n N American plant

DOGBOLT n bolt on cannon

DOGCART n light horse-drawn two-wheeled cart

DOGDOM n world of dogs dogdoms

DOGE n (formerly) chief magistrate of Venice or Genoa

DOGEAR vb fold down the corner of (a page) ▶ n folded-down corner of a page dogears

DOGEATE n office of doge

DOGEDOM n domain of doge

DOGES ▶ doge

DOGEY = dogie

DOGEYS ▶ dogey

DOGFACE n WW2 US soldier

DOGFISH n small shark

DOGFOX n male fox

DOGGED ▶ dog

DOGGER n Dutch fishing vessel with two masts **doggers**

DOGGERY n surly behaviour

DOGGESS n female dog

DOGGIE = doggy

DOGGIER ▶ doggy

DOGGIES ▶ doggy

DOGGING ▶ dog

DOGGISH adj of or like a dog

DOGGO adv

DOGGONE interj exclamation of annoyance, disappointment, etc ▶ vb damn ▶ adj damnedest

DOGGREL = doggerel

DOGGY n child's word for a dog ▶ adj of or like a dog

DOGHOLE n squalid dwelling place

DOGIE n motherless calf

DOGIES ▶ dogie

DOGLEG n sharp bend ▶ vb go off at an angle ▶ adj of or with the shape of a dogleg doglegs

DOGLIKE ▶ dog

DOGMA n

DOGMAN n person who directs a crane whilst riding on an object being lifted by it

DOGMAS ▶ dogma

DOGMATA ▶ dogma

DOGMEN ▶ dogman

DOGNAP vb carry off and hold (a dog), usually for ransom dognaps

DOGS ▶ dog

DOGSHIP n condition of

being a dog

DOGSKIN n leather from dog's skin

DOGSLED n sleigh drawn by dogs

DOGTOWN n community of prairie dogs

DOGTROT n gently paced trot

DOGVANE n light windvane mounted on the side of a vessel

DOGWOOD n type of tree or shrub

DOGY = dogie

DOH n in tonic sol-fa, first degree of any major scale ▶ interj exclamation of annoyance when something goes wrong

dohs

> This is one of the very useful short words denoting a note of the musical scale.

DOHYO n sumo wrestling ring **dohyos**

DOILED = doilt

DOILIES ▶ doily

DOILT adj foolish **doilter**

DOILY n

DOING ▶ do

DOINGS pl n deeds or actions

DOIT n former small copper coin of the Netherlands

DOITED adj foolish or childish, as from senility **doitit**

DOITKIN = doit

DOITS ▶ doit

DOJO n room or hall for the practice of martial arts **dojos**

DOL n unit of pain intensity, as measured by dolorimetry

DOLCE n dessert ▷ adv (to be performed) gently and sweetly **dolces, dolci**

DOLE n, vb **doled**

DOLEFUL adj

DOLENT adj sad

DOLENTE adv (to be performed) in a sorrowful manner

DOLES ▶ dole

DOLIA ▶ dolium

DOLINA = doline

DOLINAS ▶ dolina

DOLINE n depression of the ground surface formed in limestone regions **dolines**

DOLING ▶ dole

DOLIUM n genus of molluscs

DOLL n, vb as in **doll up**

DOLLAR n **dollars**

DOLLDOM ▶ doll

DOLLED ▶ doll

DOLLIED ▶ dolly

DOLLIER n person who operates a dolly

DOLLIES ▶ dolly

DOLLING ▶ doll

DOLLISH ▶ doll

DOLLOP n, vb **dollops**

DOLLS ▶ doll

DOLLY adj, n, vb

DOLMA n vine leaf stuffed with a filling of meat and rice

DOLMAN n long Turkish outer robe **dolmans**

DOLMAS ▶ dolma

DOLMEN n prehistoric monument **dolmens**

DOLOR = dolour

DOLORS ▶ dolor

DOLOS n knucklebone of a sheep, buck, etc, used esp by diviners **dolosse**

DOLOUR n grief or sorrow **dolours**

DOLPHIN n

DOLS ▶ dol

DOLT n doltish, **dolts**

DOM n title given to various monks and to certain of the canons regular

DOMAIN n

DOMAINE n French estate where wine is made

DOMAINS ▶ domain

DOMAL adj of a house

DOMATIA ▶ domatium

DOME n, vb **domed, domes**

DOMETT n wool and cotton cloth **dometts**

DOMIC adj dome-shaped

DOMICAL ▶ dome

DOMICIL ▶ domicile

DOMIER ▶ domy

DOMIEST ▶ domy

DOMINE n clergyman

DOMINEE n minister of the Dutch Reformed Church

DOMINES ▶ domine

DOMING ▶ dome

DOMINIE n minister or clergyman: also used as a term of address

DOMINO n dominos

DOMOIC adj as in **domoic acid** kind of amino acid

DOMS ▶ dom

DOMY adj having a dome or domes

DON vb, n

DONA n Spanish lady

DONAH n woman **donahs**

DONARY n thing given for holy use

DONAS ▶ dona

DONATE vb donated, **donates, donator**

DONDER vb beat (someone) up ▷ n wretch **donders**

DONE ▶ do

DONEE n person who receives a gift **donees**

DONER n as in **doner kebab** grilled meat and salad served in pitta bread with chilli sauce

DONG n deep reverberating sound of a large bell ▷ vb (of a bell) to make a deep reverberating sound

DONGA n steep-sided gully created by soil erosion **dongas**

DONGED ▶ dong

DONGING ▶ dong

DONGLE n electronic device **dongles**

DONGOLA n leather tanned using a particular method

DONGS ▶ dong

DONING n act of giving blood **donings**

DONJON n heavily fortified central tower of a castle **donjons**

DONKEY n donkeys

DONKO n tearoom or cafeteria in a factory, wharf area, etc **donkos**

DONNA n Italian lady

DONNARD = donnert

DONNART = donnert

DONNAS ▶ donna

DONNAT n lazy person **donnats**

DONNE = donnee

DONNED ▶ don

DONNEE n subject or theme **donnees**

DONNERD adj stupid

DONNERT adj stunned

DONNES ▶ donne

DONNIES ▶ donny

DONNING ▶ don

DONNISH adj serious and academic

DONNISM n loftiness

DONNOT n lazy person **donnots**

DONNY = danny

DONOR n donors

DONS ▶ don

DONSHIP n state or condition of being a don

DONSIE adj rather unwell **donsier, donsy**

DONUT n doughnut

DONUTS ▶ donut

DONZEL n man of high birth **donzels**

DOO a Scot word for

▶ dove

DOOB n cannabis cigarette **doobie**

DOOBIES ▶ doobie

DOOBREY n thingumabob **doobrie**

DOOBS ▶ doob

DOOCE vb dismiss (an employee) because of comments they have posted on the Internet **dooced, dooces, doocing**

DOOCOT n dovecote **doocots**

DOODAD = doodah

DOODADS ▶ doodad

DOODAH n unnamed thing **doodahs**

DOODIES ▶ doody

DOODLE vb, n doodled, doodler, doodles

DOODOO n excrement **doodoos, doody**

DOOFER n thingamajig **doofers**

DOOFUS n slow-witted or stupid person

DOOK n wooden plug driven into a wall to hold a nail, screw, etc ▷ vb dip or plunge **dooked**

DOOKET n dovecote **dookets**

DOOKING ▶ dook

DOOKS ▶ dook

DOOL n boundary marker

DOOLAN n Roman Catholic **doolans**

DOOLE ▶ dool

DOOLEE ▶ doolie

DOOLEES ▶ doolee

DOOLES ▶ doole

DOOLIE n enclosed couch on poles for carrying passengers **doolies**

DOOLS ▶ dool

DOOLY = doolie

DOOM n, vb doomed, doomful

DOOMIER ▶ doomy

DOOMILY ▶ doomy

DOOMING ▶ doom

DOOMS ▶ doom

DOOMY adj despondent or pessimistic

DOON = down

DOONA n large quilt used as a bed cover **doonas**

DOOR n

DOORMAN n man employed to be on duty at the entrance to a large public building

DOORMAT n mat for wiping dirt from shoes before going indoors

DOORMEN ▶ doorman

DOORN n thorn **doorns**

DOORS ▶ door

DOORWAY n

DOOS ▶ doo

DOOSRA n delivery in cricket **doosras**

DOOWOP n style of singing in harmony **doowops**

DOOZER = doozy

DOOZERS ▶ doozer

DOOZIE = doozy

DOOZIES ▶ doozie

DOOZY n something excellent

DOP vb curtsy ▷ n tot or small drink, usually alcoholic ▷ vb fail to reach the required standard in (an examination, course, etc)

DOPA n precursor to dopamine

DOPANT n element or compound used to dope a semiconductor **dopants**

DOPAS ▶ dopa

DOPATTA n headscarf

DOPE n, vb, adj **doped**

DOPER n person who administers dope **dopers**

DOPES ▶ dope

DOPEY adj

DOPIAZA n Indian meat or fish dish cooked in onion sauce

DOPIER ▶ dopy

DOPIEST ▶ dopy

DOPILY ▶ dopey

DOPING ▶ dope

DOPINGS ▶ dope

DOPPED ▶ dop

DOPPER n member of an Afrikaner church that practises a stict Calvinism **doppers**

DOPPIE n cartridge case **doppies**

DOPPING ▶ dop

DOPPIO n double measure, esp of espresso coffee **doppios**

DOPS ▶ dop

DOPY = dopey

DOR n European dung beetle

DORAD n South American river fish

DORADO n large marine percoid fish **dorados**

DORADS ▶ dorad

DORB = dorba

DORBA n stupid, inept, or clumsy person **dorbas**

DORBS ▶ dorb

DORBUG n type of beetle **dorbugs**

DORE n walleye fish

DOREE n type of fish **dorees**

DORES ▶ dore

DORHAWK n nightjar

DORIC adj rustic

DORIES ▶ dory

DORIS n woman

DORISE ▶ dorize

DORISED ▶ dorise

DORISES ▶ dorise

DORIZE vb become Doric **dorized, dorizes**

DORK n stupid person **dorkier**

DORKISH adj stupid or contemptible

DORKS ▶ dork

DORKY ▶ dork

DORLACH n quiver of arrows

DORM = dormitory

DORMANT n, adj

DORMER n **dormers**

DORMICE > dormouse

DORMIE adj (in golf) leading by as many holes as there are left

DORMIN n hormone found in plants **dormins**

DORMS ▶ dorm

DORMY = dormie

DORNECK = dornick

DORNICK n heavy damask cloth

DORNOCK n type of coarse fabric

DORP n small town

DORPER n breed of sheep **dorpers**

DORPS ▶ dorp

DORR = dor

DORRED ▶ dor

DORRING ▶ dor

DORRS ▶ dor

DORS ▶ dor

DORSA ▶ dorsum

DORSAD adj towards the back or dorsal aspect

DORSAL adj, n **dorsals**

DORSE n type of small fish

DORSEL another word for ▶ dossal

DORSELS ▶ dorsel

DORSER n hanging tapestry **dorsers**

DORSES ▶ dorse

DORSUM n the back

DORT vb sulk **dorted**

DORTER n dormitory **dorters**

DORTIER ▶ dorty

DORTING ▶ dort

DORTOUR = dorter

DORTS ▶ dort

DORTY adj haughty, or sullen

DORY n spiny-finned edible sea fish

DOS ▶ do

DOSAGE = dose

DOSAGES ▶ dosage

DOSE n, vb dosed

DOSEH n former Egyptian religious ceremony **dosehs**

DOSER ▶ dose

DOSERS ▶ dose

DOSES ▶ dose

DOSH n money **doshes**

DOSING ▶ dose

DOSS vb, n

DOSSAL n ornamental hanging used in churches **dossals**

DOSSED ▶ doss

DOSSEL = dossal

DOSSELS ▶ dossel

DOSSER n bag or basket for carrying objects on the back **dossers**

DOSSES ▶ doss

DOSSIER n

DOSSIL n lint for dressing wound **dossils**

DOSSING ▶ doss

DOST a singular form of the present tense (indicative mood) of ▶ do

DOT n, vb

DOTAGE n dotages

DOTAL ▶ dot

DOTANT another word for ▶ dotard

DOTANTS ▶ dotant

DOTARD n person who is feeble-minded through old age **dotards**

DOTCOM n dotcoms

DOTE vb doted, doter, doters, dotes

DOTH a singular form of the present tense of ▶ do

DOTIER ▶ doty

DOTIEST ▶ doty

DOTING ▶ dote

DOTINGS ▶ dote

DOTISH adj foolish

DOTS ▶ dot

DOTTED ▶ dot

DOTTEL = dottle

DOTTELS ▶ dottel

DOTTER ▶ dot

DOTTERS ▶ dot

DOTTIER ▶ dotty

DOTTILY ▶ dotty

DOTTING ▶ dot

DOTTLE n tobacco left in a pipe after smoking ▷ adj relating to dottle

DOTTLED adj foolish

DOTTLER ▶ dottle

DOTTLES ▶ dottle

DOTTREL = dotterel

DOTTY adj

DOTY adj (of wood) rotten

DOUANE n customs house **douanes**

DOUAR = duar

DOUARS ▶ douar

DOUBLE adj, adv, n, vb doubled, doubler

DOUBLES n game between two pairs of players

DOUBLET n man's close-fitting jacket, with or without sleeves

DOUBLY adv in a greater degree, quantity, or measure

DOUBT n, vb doubted, doubter, doubts

DOUC n Old World monkey

DOUCE adj quiet doucely, doucer, doucest

DOUCET n former flute-like instrument doucets

DOUCEUR n gratuity, tip, or bribe

DOUCHE n stream of water onto or into the body ▷ vb cleanse or treat by means of a douche **douched, douches**

DOUCINE n type of moulding for cornice

DOUCS ▶ douc

DOUGH n doughs

DOUGHT ▶ dow

DOUGHTY adj brave and determined

DOUGHY adj resembling dough in consistency, colour, etc

DOUK = douk

DOUKED ▶ douk

DOUKING ▶ douk

DOUKS ▶ douk

DOULA n woman trained to provide support to families during pregnancy, childbirth, and time following the birth doulas

DOULEIA = dulia

This word refers to the inferior veneration accorded to saints and angels, as distinct from **latria**, the veneration accorded to God alone, and is another of the few seven-letter words that use all five vowels. It's surprising how often you want to do this!

DOUM *n as in* **doum palm** variety of palm tree

DOUMA = **duma**

DOUMAS ▷ **douma**

DOUMS ▷ **doum**

DOUN = **down**

DOUP *n* bottom **doups**

DOUR *adj*

DOURA = **durra**

DOURAH = **durra**

DOURAHS ▷ **dourah**

DOURAS ▷ **doura**

DOURER ▷ **dour**

DOUREST ▷ **dour**

DOURINE *n* infectious venereal disease of horses

DOURLY ▷ **dour**

DOUSE *vb, n* doused, douser, dousers, douses, dousing

DOUT *vb* extinguish douted, douter, douters, douting, douts

DOUX *adj* sweet

DOVE *vb, n*

DOVECOT = **dovecote**
doved

DOVEISH *adj* dovelike

DOVEKEY = **dovekie**

DOVEKIE *n* small short-billed auk

DOVELET *n* small dove

DOVEN *vb* pray dovened, dovens

DOVER *vb* doze ▷ *n* doze dovered, dovers

DOVES ▷ **dove**

DOVIE *Scots word for* ▷ **stupid**

DOVIER ▷ **dovie**

DOVIEST ▷ **dovie**

DOVING ▷ **dove**

DOVISH ▷ **dove**

DOW *vb* archaic word meaning be of worth

DOWABLE *adj* capable of being endowed

DOWAGER *n*

DOWAR = **duar**

DOWARS ▷ **dowar**

DOWD *n* woman who wears unfashionable clothes

DOWDIER ▷ **dowdy**

DOWDIES ▷ **dowdy**

DOWDILY ▷ **dowdy**

DOWDS ▷ **dowd**

DOWDY *adj, n*

DOWED ▷ **dow**

DOWEL *n, vb* doweled, dowels

DOWER *n* life interest in a part of her husband's estate allotted to a widow by law ▷ *vb* endow dowered, dowers

DOWERY = **dowry**

DOWF *adj* dull; listless

DOWIE *adj* dull and dreary dowier, dowiest

DOWING ▷ **dow**

DOWL *n* fluff

DOWLAS *n* coarse fabric

DOWLE = **dowl**

DOWLES ▷ **dowle**

DOWLIER ▷ **dowly**

DOWLNE *obsolete form of* ▷ **down**

DOWLNES ▷ **dowlne**

DOWLNEY ▷ **dowlne**

DOWLS ▷ **dowl**

DOWLY *adj* dull

DOWN *adv, adj, vb, n*

DOWNA *obsolete Scots form of* ▷ **cannot**

DOWNBOW *n* (in music) a downward stroke of the bow across the strings

DOWNED ▷ **down**

DOWNER *n* barbiturate, tranquillizer, or narcotic **downers**

DOWNIER ▷ **downy**

DOWNING ▷ **down**

DOWNS *pl n*

DOWNY *adj*

DOWP = **doup**

DOWPS ▷ **dowp**

DOWRIES ▷ **dowry**

DOWRY *n*

DOWS ▷ **dow**

DOWSE = **douse**; dowsed, dowser, dowsers, dowses

DOWSET = **doucet**

DOWSETS ▷ **dowset**

DOWSING ▷ **dowse**

DOWT *n* cigarette butt dowts

DOXIE = **doxy**

DOXIES ▷ **doxy**

DOXY *n* opinion or doctrine, esp concerning religious matters

DOY *n* beloved person:

used esp as an endearment

DOYEN n doyenne, doyens

DOYLEY = doily

DOYLEYS ▶ doyley

DOYLIES ▶ doyly

DOYLY = doily

DOYS ▶ doy

DOZE vb, n

DOZED adj (of timber or rubber) rotten or decayed

DOZEN vb dozened, dozens, dozenth

DOZER ▶ doze

DOZERS ▶ doze

DOZES ▶ doze

DOZIER ▶ dozy

DOZIEST ▶ dozy

DOZILY ▶ dozy

DOZING ▶ doze

DOZINGS ▶ doze

DOZY adj

DRAB adj, n, vb drabbed

DRABBER n one who frequents low women

DRABBET n yellowish-brown fabric of coarse linen

DRABBLE vb make or become wet or dirty

DRABBY adj promiscuous

DRABLER = drabble

DRABLY ▶ drab

DRABS ▶ drab

DRAC = drack

DRACENA = dracaena

DRACHM = dram

DRACHMA n former monetary unit of Greece

DRACHMS ▶ drachm

DRACK adj (esp of a woman) unattractive

DRACO n as in draco lizard flying lizard

DRACONE n large container towed by a ship

DRAD ▶ dread

DRAFF n residue of husks used as a food for cattle draffs, draffy

DRAFT = draught

DRAFTED ▶ draft

DRAFTEE a conscript

DRAFTER ▶ draft

DRAFTS ▶ draft

DRAFTY = draughty

DRAG vb, n

DRAGEE n sweet made of a nut, fruit, etc, coated with a hard sugar icing dragees

DRAGGED ▶ drag

DRAGGER ▶ drag

DRAGGLE vb make or become wet or dirty by trailing on the ground

DRAGGY adj slow or boring

DRAGNET n net used to scour the bottom of a pond or river

DRAGON n dragons

DRAGOON n, vb

DRAGS ▶ drag

DRAIL n weighted hook used in trolling ▷ vb fish with a drail drailed, drails

DRAIN n, vb drained

DRAINER n person or thing that drains

DRAINS ▶ drain

DRAKE n drakes

DRAM n small amount of a strong alcoholic drink, esp whisky ▷ vb drink a dram

DRAMA n

DRAMADY = dramedy

DRAMAS ▶ drama

DRAMEDY n television or film drama in which there are important elements of comedy

DRAMMED ▶ dram

DRAMS ▶ dram

DRANK ▶ drink

DRANT vb drone dranted, drants

DRAP a Scot word for ▶ drop

DRAPE vb, n draped

DRAPER n drapers

DRAPERY n

DRAPES pl n material hung at an opening or window to shut out light or to provide privacy

DRAPET n cloth drapets

DRAPEY adj hanging in loose folds

DRAPIER n draper

DRAPING ▶ drape

DRAPPED ▶ drap

DRAPPIE n little drop, esp a small amount of spirits

DRAPPY n drop (of liquid)

DRAPS ▶ drap

DRASTIC n, adj

DRAT interj exclamation of annoyance ▷ vb curse drats

DRATTED adj wretched

DRAUGHT vb, n, adj

DRAUNT = drant

DRAUNTS ▶ draunt

DRAVE archaic past of ▶ drive

DRAW vb, n

DRAWBAR n strong metal bar on a tractor, locomotive, etc

DRAWEE n person or organization on which payment is drawn **drawees**

DRAWER n

DRAWERS pl n undergarment worn on the lower part of the body

DRAWING ▶ draw

DRAWL vb, n **drawled, drawler, drawls, drawly**

DRAWN ▶ draw

DRAWS ▶ draw

DRAY vb pull using cart ▷ n low cart used for carrying heavy loads

DRAYAGE n act of transporting something a short distance

DRAYED ▶ dray

DRAYING ▶ dray

DRAYMAN n driver of a dray **draymen**

DRAYS ▶ dray

DRAZEL n low woman **drazels**

DREAD vb, n, adj **dreaded, dreader, dreadly, dreads**

DREAM n, vb, adj **dreamed**

DREAMER n person who dreams habitually

DREAMS ▶ dream

DREAMT ▶ dream

DREAMY adj

DREAR = dreary

DREARE obsolete form of ▶ drear

DREARER ▶ drear

DREARES ▶ dreare

DREARS ▶ drear

DREARY adj, n

DRECK n rubbish **drecks, drecky**

DREDGE vb, n **dredged, dredger, dredges**

DREE vb endure **dreed, dreeing, drees**

DREG n small quantity

DREGGY adj like or full of dregs

DREGS pl n

DREICH adj dreary

DREIDEL n spinning top **dreidl**

DREIDLS ▶ dreidl

DREIGH = dreich

DREK = dreck

DREKS ▶ drek

DRENCH vb, n **drent**

DRERE obsolete form of ▶ drear

DRERES ▶ drere

DRESS n, vb, adj **dressed**

DRESSER n

DRESSES ▶ dress

DRESSY adj (of clothes) elegant

DREST ▶ dress

DREVILL n offensive person

DREW ▶ draw

DREY n squirrel's nest **dreys**

DRIB vb flow in drops **dribbed, dribber**

DRIBBLE vb, n **dribbly**

DRIBLET n small amount

DRIBS ▶ drib

DRICE n pellets of frozen carbon dioxide **drices**

DRIED ▶ dry

DRIEGH adj tedious

DRIER, driers, dries, driest ▶ dry

DRIFT vb, n **drifted**

DRIFTER n person who moves aimlessly from place to place or job to job

DRIFTS ▶ drift

DRIFTY ▶ drift

DRILL n, vb **drilled, driller, drills**

DRILY adv in a dry manner

DRINK vb, n

DRINKER n person who drinks

DRINKS ▶ drink

DRIP vb, n **dripped, dripper**

DRIPPY adj mawkish, insipid, or inane

DRIPS ▶ drip

DRIPT ▶ drip

DRIVE vb guide the movement of (a vehicle) ▷ n journey by car, van, etc

DRIVEL n, vb **drivels**

DRIVEN ▶ drive

DRIVER n person who drives a vehicle **drivers**

DRIVES ▶ drive

DRIVING ▶ drive

DRIZZLE n, vb **drizzly**

DROGER n W Indian boat **drogers, drogher**

DROGUE n any funnel-like device used as a sea anchor **drogues**

DROGUET n woollen fabric

DROICH n dwarf **droichs**

DROICHY adj dwarfish

DROID = **android**

DROIDS ▶ droid

DROIL vb carry out boring menial work **droiled, droils**

DROIT n legal or moral right or claim **droits**

DROLE adj amusing ▷ n scoundrel **droler, droles, drolest**

DROLL vb, adj **drolled, droller, drolls, drolly**

DROME ▶ aerodrome

DROMES ▶ drome

DROMIC adj relating to running track

DROMOI ▶ dromos

DROMON = **dromond**

DROMOND n sailing vessel of the 12th to 15th centuries

DROMONS ▶ dromon

DROMOS n Greek passageway

DRONE n, vb **droned, droner, droners, drones**

DRONGO n tropical songbird **drongos**

DRONIER ▶ drony

DRONING ▶ drone

DRONISH ▶ drone

DRONY adj monotonous

DROOB n pathetic person **droobs**

DROOG n ruffian **droogs**

DROOK = **drouk**

DROOKED ▶ drook

DROOKIT = **droukit**

DROOKS ▶ drook

DROOL vb **drooled, drools**

DROOLY adj tending to drool

DROOME obsolete form of ▶ **drum**

DROOMES ▶ drum

DROOP vb, n **drooped, droops**

DROOPY adj hanging or sagging downwards

DROP vb, n

DROPFLY n (angling) artificial fly

DROPLET n

DROPOUT n person who rejects conventional society ▷ vb abandon or withdraw (from an institution or group)

DROPPED ▶ drop

DROPPER n small tube with a rubber part at one end

DROPPLE n trickle

DROPS ▶ drop

DROPSY n illness in which watery fluid collects in the body

DROPT ▶ drop

DROSERA n insectivorous plant

DROSHKY n four-wheeled carriage, formerly used in Russia **drosky**

DROSS n **drosses, drossy**

DROSTDY n office of landdrost

DROUGHT n

DROUK vb drench **drouked**

DROUKIT adj drenched

DROUKS ▶ drouk

DROUTH = **drought**

DROUTHS ▶ drouth

DROUTHY adj thirsty or dry

DROVE ▶ drive

DROVED ▶ drive

DROVER n person who drives sheep or cattle **drovers**

DROVES ▶ drive

DROVING ▶ drive

DROW n sea fog

DROWN vb **drownd**

DROWNDS ▶ drown

DROWNED ▶ drown

DROWNER ▶ drown

DROWNS ▶ drown

DROWS ▶ drow

DROWSE vb, n **drowsed, drowses**

DROWSY adj

DRUB vb beat as with a stick ▷ n blow, as from a stick **drubbed, drubber, drubs**

DRUCKEN adj drunken

DRUDGE n, vb **drudged, drudger, drudges**

DRUG n, vb **drugged**

DRUGGER n druggist

DRUGGET n coarse

fabric used as a protective floor-covering, etc

DRUGGIE n drug addict

DRUGGY ▸ drug

DRUGS ▸ drug

DRUID n druidic, druidry, druids

DRUM n, vb

DRUMBLE vb be inactive

DRUMLIN n streamlined mound of glacial drift

DRUMLY adj dismal; dreary

DRUMMED ▸ drum

DRUMMER n person who plays a drum or drums

DRUMMY n (in South Africa) drum majorette

DRUMS ▸ drum

DRUNK ▸ drink

DRUNKEN adj drunk or frequently drunk

DRUNKER ▸ drink

DRUNKS ▸ drink

DRUPE n fleshy fruit with a stone, such as the peach or cherry

DRUPEL = drupelet

DRUPELS ▸ drupel

DRUPES ▸ drupe

DRUSE n aggregate of small crystals within a cavity

DRUSEN pl n small deposits of material on the retina

DRUSES ▸ druse

DRUSIER ▸ drusy

DRUSY adj made of tiny crystals

DRUXIER ▸ druxy

DRUXY adj (of wood) having decayed white spots

DRY adj, vb dryable

DRYAD n wood nymph dryades, dryadic, dryads

DRYBEAT vb beat severely

DRYER, dryers, dryest, drying, dryings ▸ dry

DRYISH adj fairly dry

DRYLAND adj of an arid area

DRYLOT n livestock enclosure drylots

DRYLY = drily

DRYNESS ▸ dry

DRYS ▸ dry

DRYSUIT n waterproof rubber suit for wearing in esp cold water

DRYWALL n wall built without mortar ▸ vb build a wall without mortar

DRYWELL n type of sewage disposal system

DSO = zho

> A **dso** is a kind of Himalayan ox; the other forms are **dzo**, **zho**, **dzho** and **zo** and it's worth remembering all of them.

DSOBO = zobo

DSOBOS ▸ dsobo

DSOMO = zhomo

DSOMOS ▸ dsomo

DSOS ▸ dso

DUAD a rare word for ▸ pair

DUADS ▸ duad

DUAL adj, n, vb

DUALIN n explosive substance dualins

DUALISE = dualize

DUALISM n state of having two distinct parts dualist

DUALITY n state or quality of being two or in two parts

DUALIZE vb cause to have two parts

DUALLED ▸ dual

DUALLY ▸ dual

DUALS ▸ dual

DUAN n poem duans

DUAR n Arab camp

DUARCHY n diarchy

DUARS ▸ duar

DUB vb, n, dubbed, dubber, dubbers

DUBBIN n thick grease applied to leather to soften and waterproof it

DUBBING ▸ dub

DUBBINS ▸ dubbin

DUBBO adj stupid ▸ n stupid person dubbos

DUBIETY n

DUBIOUS adj

DUBNIUM n chemical element

DUBS ▸ dub

DUBSTEP n

DUCAL adj of a duke ducally

DUCAT n former European gold or silver coin ducats

DUCDAME interj

Shakespearean
nonsense word
DUCE n leader **duces**
DUCHESS n, vb
DUCHIES ▸ duchy
DUCHY n
DUCI ▸ duce
DUCK n, vb ducked,
ducker, duckers
DUCKIE = ducky
DUCKIER ▸ ducky
DUCKIES ▸ ducky
DUCKING ▸ duck
DUCKPIN n short
bowling pin
DUCKS ▸ duck
DUCKY n darling or dear
▸ adj delightful
DUCT vb, n ductal,
ducted
DUCTILE adj
DUCTING ▸ duct
DUCTS ▸ duct
DUCTULE n small duct
DUD n, adj
DUDDER n
door-to-door
salesman **dudders**
DUDDERY n place
where old clothes are
sold
DUDDIE adj ragged
duddier, duddy
DUDE vb dress
fashionably ▸ n man
duded
DUDEEN n clay pipe
with a short stem
dudeens
DUDES ▸ dude
DUDGEON n anger or
resentment
DUDHEEN n type of pipe
DUDING ▸ dude

DUDISH ▸ dude
DUDISM n being a dude
dudisms
DUDS ▸ dud
DUE vb, adj, n, adv dued
DUEFUL adj proper
DUEL n, vb dueled,
dueler, duelers,
dueling, duelist,
duelled, dueller
DUELLI ▸ duello
DUELLO n art of
duelling **duellos**
DUELS ▸ duel
DUENDE n Spanish
goblin **duendes**
DUENESS ▸ due
DUENNA n (esp in
Spain) elderly woman
acting as chaperone to
a young woman
duennas
DUES pl n membership
fees
DUET n, vb dueted,
dueting, duets,
duett, duetted
DUETTI ▸ duetto
DUETTO = duet
DUETTOS ▸ duetto
DUETTS ▸ duett
DUFF adj broken or
useless ▸ vb change
the appearance of or
give a false appearance
to (old or stolen goods)
▸ n rump or buttocks
duffed
DUFFEL n duffels
DUFFER n duffers
DUFFEST ▸ duff
DUFFING ▸ duff
DUFFLE = duffel
DUFFLES ▸ duffle

DUFFS ▸ duff
DUFUS = doofus
DUFUSES ▸ dufus
DUG ▸ dig
DUGITE n medium-sized
Australian venomous
snake **dugites**
DUGONG n dugongs
DUGOUT n dugouts
DUGS ▸ dig
DUH interj ironic
response to a question
or statement

> This word provides
> a useful front hook
> to **uh**.

DUHKHA = dukkha
DUHKHAS ▸ duhkha
DUI ▸ duo
DUIKER n small African
antelope **duikers**
DUING ▸ due
DUIT n former Dutch
coin **duits**
DUKA n shop dukas
DUKE vb, n duked
DUKEDOM n
DUKERY n duke's
domain
DUKES pl n fists
DUKING ▸ duke
DUKKA n mix of ground
roast nuts and spices
dukkah
DUKKAHS ▸ dukkah
DUKKAS ▸ dukka
DUKKHA n Buddhist
belief that all things
are suffering
dukkhas
DULCET adj, n dulcets
DULCIAN n precursor to
the bassoon
DULCIFY vb make

pleasant or agreeable

DULCITE n sweet substance **dulcose**

DULE n suffering; misery **dules**

DULIA n veneration accorded to saints **dulias**

DULL adj, vb

DULLARD n dull or stupid person

DULLED, duller, dullest, dullier, dulling, dullish, dulls, dully, dulness ▸ dull

DULOSES ▸ dulosis

DULOSIS n behaviour where one species of ant forces members of another to work for them **dulotic**

DULSE n seaweed with large red edible fronds **dulses**

DULY adv

DUMA n elective legislative assembly established by Tsar Nicholas II

DUMAIST n member of duma

DUMAS ▸ duma

DUMB vb, adj **dumbed, dumber, dumbest, dumbing, dumbly**

DUMBO n slow-witted unintelligent person **dumbos**

DUMBS ▸ dumb

DUMDUM n soft-nosed bullet **dumdums**

DUMELA sentence substitute hello

DUMKA n Slavonic

lyrical song **dumky**

DUMMIED ▸ dummy

DUMMIER ▸ dummy

DUMMIES ▸ dummy

DUMMY adj, n, vb

DUMOSE adj bushlike **dumous**

DUMP vb, n

DUMPBIN n unit in a bookshop displaying a particular publisher's books

DUMPED ▸ dump

DUMPEE n person dumped from a relationship **dumpees**

DUMPER ▸ dump

DUMPERS ▸ dump

DUMPIER ▸ dumpy

DUMPIES ▸ dumpy

DUMPILY ▸ dumpy

DUMPING ▸ dump

DUMPISH = dumpy

DUMPLE vb form into dumpling shape **dumpled, dumples**

DUMPS pl n state of melancholy or depression

DUMPY n, adj

DUN adj, vb, n

DUNAM n unit of area measurement **dunams**

DUNCE n

DUNCERY n duncelike behaviour

DUNCES ▸ dunce

DUNCH vb push against gently **dunched, dunches**

DUNCISH adj duncelike

DUNDER n cane juice lees **dunders**

DUNE n dunes

DUNG n, vb **dunged**

DUNGEON vb, n

DUNGER n old decrepit car **dungers**

DUNGIER, dunging, dungs, dungy ▸ dung

DUNITE n ultrabasic igneous rock **dunites, dunitic**

DUNK vb **dunked, dunker, dunkers, dunking, dunks**

DUNLIN n small sandpiper **dunlins**

DUNNAGE n loose material used for packing cargo

DUNNART n type of insectivorous marsupial

DUNNED, dunner, dunness, dunnest ▸ dun

DUNNIER ▸ dunny

DUNNIES ▸ dunny

DUNNING ▸ dun

DUNNISH ▸ dun

DUNNITE n explosive containing ammonium picrate

DUNNO vb slang for don't know

DUNNOCK n hedge sparrow

DUNNY n in Australia, toilet ▷ adj relating to dunny

DUNS ▸ dun

DUNSH = dunch

DUNSHED ▸ dunsh

DUNSHES ▸ dunsh

DUNT n blow ▷ vb strike

or hit **dunted,
dunting, dunts**
DUO = duet
DUODENA
> **duodenum**
DUOLOG = duologue
DUOLOGS ▶ duolog
DUOMI ▶ duomo
DUOMO n cathedral in
Italy **duomos**
DUOPOLY n siuation
when control of a
commodity is vested
in two producers or
suppliers
DUOS ▶ duo
DUOTONE n process for
producing halftone
illustrations
DUP vb open
DUPABLE ▶ dupe
DUPATTA n scarf worn
in India
DUPE vb, n **duped,
duper, dupers,
dupery, dupes,
duping**
DUPION n silk fabric
made from the threads
of double cocoons
dupions
DUPLE adj having two
beats in a bar
DUPLET n pair of
electrons shared
between two atoms in
a covalent bond
duplets
DUPLEX vb duplicate
▷ n apartment on two
floors ▷ adj having two
parts
DUPLIED ▶ duply
DUPLIES ▶ duply

DUPLY vb give a second
reply
DUPPED ▶ dup
DUPPIES ▶ duppy
DUPPING ▶ dup
DUPPY n spirit or ghost
DUPS ▶ dup
DURA = durra
DURABLE adj **durably**
DURAL n alloy of
aluminium and copper
durals
DURAMEN another name
for > **heartwood**
DURANCE n
imprisonment
DURANT n tough,
leathery cloth
durants
DURAS ▶ dura
DURBAR n (formerly)
the court of a native
ruler or a governor in
India **durbars**
DURDUM = dirdum
DURDUMS ▶ durdum
DURE vb endure **dured**
DUREFUL adj lasting
DURES ▶ dure
DURESS n duresse
DURGAH = dargah
DURGAHS ▶ durgah
DURGAN n dwarf
durgans
DURGIER ▶ durgy
DURGY adj dwarflike
DURIAN n SE Asian tree
whose very large oval
fruits have a hard spiny
rind and an evil smell
durians
DURING prep
DURION = durian
DURIONS ▶ durion

DURMAST n large
Eurasian oak tree with
lobed leaves
DURN ▶ darn
DURNED ▶ durn
DURNING ▶ durn
DURNS ▶ durn
DURO n silver peso of
Spain or Spanish
America
DUROC n breed of pig
durocs
DUROS ▶ duro
DUROY n coarse
woollen fabric
duroys
DURR = durra
DURRA n Old World
variety of sorghum
with hairy flower
spikes and round
seeds, cultivated for
grain and fodder
durras
DURRIE n cotton carpet
made in India, often in
rectangular pieces
fringed at the ends
DURRIES ▶ durry
DURRS ▶ durr
DURRY n cigarette
DURST past tense of
▶ **dare**
DURUM n variety of
wheat cultivated
mainly in the
Mediterranean region,
used chiefly to make
pastas **durums**
DURZI n Indian tailor
durzis
DUSH vb strike hard
**dushed, dushes,
dushing**

DUSK n, adj, vb **dusked**

DUSKEN vb grow dark **duskens**

DUSKER ▸ **dusk**

DUSKEST ▸ **dusk**

DUSKIER ▸ **dusky**

DUSKILY ▸ **dusky**

DUSKING, duskish, duskly, dusks ▸ **dusk**

DUSKY adj

DUST n, vb

DUSTBIN n

DUSTED ▸ **dust**

DUSTER n **dusters**

DUSTIER ▸ **dusty**

DUSTILY ▸ **dusty**

DUSTING ▸ **dust**

DUSTMAN n **dustmen**

DUSTOFF n casualty evacuation helicopter

DUSTPAN n short-handled shovel

DUSTRAG n cloth for dusting

DUSTS ▸ **dust**

DUSTUP n quarrel, fight, or argument **dustups**

DUSTY adj

DUTCH n wife **dutches**

DUTEOUS adj dutiful or obedient

DUTIED adj liable for duty

DUTIES ▸ **duty**

DUTIFUL adj

DUTY n

DUUMVIR n one of two coequal magistrates or officers

DUVET n **doona**

DUVETS ▸ **duvet**

DUVETYN n soft napped velvety fabric of cotton, silk, wool, or rayon

DUX n (in Scottish and certain other schools) the top pupil in a class or school **duxes**

> A **dux** is a leader, and is often useful for disposing of the X.

DUYKER n = **duiker**

DUYKERS ▸ **duyker**

DVANDVA n class of compound words

DVORNIK n Russian doorkeeper

DWAAL n state of absent-mindedness **dwaals**

DWALE n deadly nightshade **dwales**

DWALM vb faint **dwalmed**, dwalms

DWAM n stupor or daydream ▸ vb faint or fall ill **dwammed**, dwams

DWANG n short piece of wood inserted in a timber-framed wall **dwangs**

DWAUM = **dwam**

DWAUMED ▸ **dwaum**

DWAUMS ▸ **dwaum**

DWEEB n stupid or uninteresting person **dweebs**

DWEEBY adj like or typical of a dweeb

DWELL vb, n **dwelled**, dweller, dwells, dwelt

DWILE n floor cloth

dwiles

DWINDLE vb

DWINE vb languish **dwined**, dwines, dwining

DYABLE ▸ **dye**

DYAD n operator that is the unspecified product of two vectors

DYADIC adj of or relating to a dyad ▸ n sum of a particular number of dyads **dyadics**

DYADS ▸ **dyad**

DYARCHY = **diarchy**

DYBBUK n (in Jewish folklore) the body of a person possessed by the soul of a dead sinner **dybbuks**

DYE n, vb **dyeable**, dyed, dyeing, dyeings

DYELINE = **diazo**

DYER ▸ **dye**

DYERS ▸ **dye**

DYES ▸ **dye**

DYESTER n dyer

DYEWEED n plant that produces dye

DYEWOOD n any wood from which dyes and pigments can be obtained

DYING ▸ **die**

DYINGLY ▸ **die**

DYINGS ▸ **die**

DYKE n, vb **dyked**, dykes, dyking

DYKON n **dykons**

DYNAMIC adj, n

DYNAMO n **dynamos**

DYNAST n hereditary ruler **dynasts**

DYNASTY n
DYNE n cgs unit of force
DYNEIN n class of proteins **dyneins**
DYNEL n trade name for synthetic fibre **dynels**
DYNES ▶ dyne
DYNODE n electrical component **dynodes**

DYSLOGY n uncomplimentary remarks
DYSODIL n yellow or green mineral
DYSPNEA = dyspnoea
DYSURIA n difficult or painful urination
dysuric, dysury
DYVOUR n debtor

dyvours
DYVOURY n bankruptcy
DZEREN n Chinese yellow antelope
dzerens
DZHO = zho
DZHOS ▶ dzho
DZO a variant spelling of
▶ zo
DZOS ▶ zo

Ee

E is the most common tile in the game and, while it is only worth one point, as the most frequent letter in English it is extremely useful, especially when it comes to forming bonus words scoring an extra 50 points. Many words contain two or more **E**s, so, unlike many tiles, it does no harm to have two **E**s on your rack and even three can be manageable. Keep in mind three-letter words formed by an **E** on either side of a consonant, like **eye**, **ewe** and **eve** (6 points each), and **eke** (7). **E** can also be handy for getting rid of double consonants: think of words like **egg** or **ebb** (each 5 points). **E** also combines well with **K**: as well as **eke**, we have **elk** and **eek** (both 7), and **ewk** (10). If you have an **X** on your rack, **E** offers you all kinds of options: just think of all the words that begin with **ex-**, like **exhaust** (17), which will give you a 50-point bonus if you use all of your tiles to form it. And don't forget **ex** itself, a nice little word that earns you 9 points, and also the very useful **exo** for 10 points. Just as important are **jee** for 10 points, **zee** for 12 points and **zed** for 13 points.

EA *n* river

EACH *pron, determiner, adv*

EADISH *n* aftermath

EAGER *adj, n* eagerer, eagerly, eagers

EAGLE *n, vb* eagled, eagles

EAGLET *n* young eagle eaglets

EAGLING ▸ eagle

EAGRE *n* tidal bore, esp of the Humber or Severn estuaries

eagres

EALE *n* beast in Roman legend **eales**

EAN *vb* give birth **eaned, eaning**

EANLING *n* newborn lamb

EANS ▸ ean

EAR *n, vb*

EARACHE *n* pain in the ear

EARBALL *n* device used in acupressure

EARBASH *vb* talk incessantly

EARBOB *n* earring earbobs

EARBUD *n* small earphone **earbuds**

EARCON *n* sound representing object or event **earcons**

EARD *vb* bury **earded, earding**

EARDROP *n* pendant earring

EARDRUM *n*

EARDS ▸ eard

EARED adj having an ear or ears

EARFLAP n either of two pieces of fabric or fur attached to a cap

EARFUL n scolding or telling-off **earfuls**

EARING n line fastened to a corner of a sail for reefing **earings**

EARL n

EARLAP = earflap

EARLAPS ▶ earlap

EARLDOM n rank, title, or dignity of an earl or countess

EARLESS ▶ ear

EARLIER ▶ early

EARLIES ▶ early

EARLIKE ▶ ear

EARLOBE n fleshy lower part of the outer ear

EARLOCK n curl of hair close to ear

EARLS ▶ earl

EARLY adv before the expected or usual time ▷ adj occurring or arriving before the correct or expected time ▷ n something which is early

EARMARK vb, n

EARMUFF n item of clothing for keeping the ears warm

EARN vb earned, earner, earners

EARNEST adj, n

EARNING ▶ earn

EARNS ▶ earn

EARPICK n instrument for removing ear wax

EARPLUG n piece of soft

material placed in the ear to keep out water or noise

EARRING n

EARS ▶ ear

EARSHOT n

EARST adv first; previously

EARTH n, vb earthed

EARTHEN adj made of baked clay or earth

EARTHLY adj, n

EARTHS ▶ earth

EARTHY adj

EARWAX nontechnical name for ▶ cerumen

EARWIG n, vb earwigs

EARWORM n irritatingly catchy tune

EAS ▶ ea

EASE n, vb eased

EASEFUL adj characterized by or bringing ease

EASEL n

EASELED adj mounted on easel

EASELS ▶ easel

EASER ▶ ease

EASERS ▶ ease

EASES ▶ ease

EASIED, easier, easies, easiest ▶ easy

EASILY adv

EASING n as in **quantitative easing easings**

EASLE n hot ash **easles**

EASSEL adv easterly

EASSIL adv easterly

EAST n, adj, adv, vb **easted**

EASTER n most important festival of

the Christian Church

EASTERN adj

EASTERS ▶ easter

EASTING n net distance eastwards made by a vessel moving towards the east

EASTLIN adj easterly

EASTS ▶ east

EASY adj, vb **easying**

EAT vb

EATABLE adj fit or suitable for eating

EATAGE n grazing rights **eatages**

EATCHE n adze **eatches**

EATEN ▶ eat

EATER ▶ eat

EATERIE = eatery

EATERS ▶ eat

EATERY n restaurant or eating house

EATH adj easy **eathe, eathly**

EATING ▶ eat

EATINGS ▶ eat

EATS ▶ eat

EAU = ea

EAUS ▶ eau

EAUX ▶ eau

EAVE n overhanging edge of a roof

EAVED adj having eaves

EAVES ▶ eave

EBAUCHE n rough sketch

EBAYER n any person who uses eBay **ebayers**

EBAYING n buying or selling using eBay

EBB vb, n ebbed

EBBET n type of newt **ebbets**

EBBING ▶ ebb

EBBLESS ▸ ebb
EBBS ▸ ebb
EBON poetic word for
▸ **ebony**
EBONICS n dialect used
by African-Americans
EBONIES = ebony
EBONISE = ebonize
EBONIST n carver of
ebony
EBONITE another name
for ▸ **vulcanite**
EBONIZE vb stain or
otherwise finish in
imitation of ebony
EBONS ▸ ebon
EBONY n, adj
EBOOK n book in
electronic form
ebooks
EBRIATE adj drunk
EBRIETY n drunkenness
EBRIOSE adj drunk
ECAD n organism
whose form has been
affected by its
environment **ecads**
ECARTE n card game
for two, played with
32 cards and king high
ecartes
ECBOLE n digression
ecboles
ECBOLIC adj hastening
labour or abortion ▸ n
drug or agent that
hastens labour or
abortion
ECCE interj behold
ECCO interj look there
ECCRINE adj of or
denoting glands that
secrete externally
ECDEMIC adj not

indigenous or endemic
ECDYSES ▸ ecdysis
ECDYSIS n shedding of
the cuticle in
arthropods or the
outer epidermal layer
in reptiles
ECDYSON > ecdysone
ECESIC ▸ ecesis
ECESIS n establishment
of a plant in a new
environment
ECH = eche
ECHAPPE n leap in
ballet
ECHARD n water that is
present in the soil but
cannot be utilized by
plants **echards**
ECHE vb eke out **eched**
ECHELLE n ladder; scale
ECHELON n, vb
ECHES ▸ eche
ECHIDNA n
ECHING ▸ eche
ECHINI ▸ echinus
ECHINUS n ovolo
moulding between the
shaft and the abacus
of a Doric column
ECHIUM n type of
Eurasian and African
plant **echiums**
ECHO n, vb **echoed,**
echoer, echoers,
echoes
ECHOEY adj
ECHOIC adj
characteristic of or
resembling an echo
ECHOIER ▸ echoey
ECHOING ▸ echo
ECHOISE = echoize
ECHOISM n

onomatopoeia as a
source of word
formation **echoist**
ECHOIZE vb repeat like
echo
ECHOS ▸ echo
ECHT adj real
ECLAIR n finger-shaped
pastry filled with
cream and covered
with chocolate **eclairs**
ECLAT n brilliant
success **eclats**
ECLIPSE n, vb
ECLOGUE n pastoral or
idyllic poem, usually in
the form of a
conversation or
soliloquy
ECLOSE vb emerge
eclosed, ecloses
ECO n ecology activist
ECOCIDE n total
destruction of an area
of the natural
environment
ECOD = egad
ECOLOGY n
ECOMAP n diagram
showing the links
between an individual
and their community
ecomaps
ECONOMY n, adj
ECONUT n
environmentalist
econuts
ECORCHE n anatomical
figure without the skin
ECOS ▸ eco
ECOTAGE n sabotage for
ecological motives
ECOTONE n zone
between two major

ecological communities

ECOTOUR n holiday taking care not to damage environment

ECOTYPE n organisms within a species that have adapted to a particular environment

ECRU adj pale creamy-brown ▷ n greyish-yellow to a light greyish colour **ecrus**

ECSTASY n

ECTASES ▶ ectasis

ECTASIA n distension or dilation of a duct, vessel, or hollow viscus **ectasis, ectatic**

ECTHYMA n local inflammation of the skin

ECTOPIA n congenital displacement of an organ or part **ectopic, ectopy**

ECTOZOA ▶ ectozoon

ECTYPAL ▶ ectype

ECTYPE n copy as distinguished from a prototype **ectypes**

ECU n any of various former French gold or silver coins

ECUELLE n covered soup bowl with handles

ECURIE n team of motor-racing cars **ecuries**

ECUS ▶ ecu

ECZEMA n **eczemas**

ED n education

EDACITY > edacious

EDAMAME n immature soybeans boiled in the pod

EDAPHIC adj of or relating to the physical and chemical conditions of the soil

EDDIED ▶ eddy

EDDIES ▶ eddy

EDDISH n pasture grass

EDDO = taro

EDDOES ▶ eddo

EDDY n, vb **eddying**

EDEMA = oedema

EDEMAS ▶ edema

EDEMATA ▶ edema

EDENIC adj delightful, like the Garden of Eden

EDENTAL adj having few or no teeth

EDGE n, vb **edged, edger, edgers, edges**

EDGIER ▶ edgy

EDGIEST ▶ edgy

EDGILY ▶ edgy

EDGING n anything placed along an edge to finish it ▷ adj relating to or used for making an edge **edgings**

EDGY adj

EDH n character of the runic alphabet **edhs**

EDIBLE adj

EDIBLES pl n articles fit to eat

EDICT n **edictal, edicts**

EDIFICE n

EDIFIED ▶ edify

EDIFIER ▶ edify

EDIFIES ▶ edify

EDIFY vb

EDILE variant spelling of ▶ aedile

EDILES ▶ edile

EDIT n, vb **edited, editing**

EDITION n, vb

EDITOR n **editors**

EDITRIX n female editor

EDITS ▶ edit

EDS ▶ ed

EDUCATE vb

EDUCE vb evolve or develop **educed, educes, educing**

EDUCT n substance separated from a mixture without chemical change

EDUCTOR ▶ educe

EDUCTS ▶ educt

EE Scots word for ▶ eye

EECH = eche

EECHED ▶ eech

EECHES ▶ eech

EECHING ▶ eech

EEJIT Scots and Irish word for ▶ idiot

EEJITS ▶ eejit

EEK interj indicating shock or fright

EEL n

EELFARE n young eel

EELIER ▶ eel

EELIEST ▶ eel

EELLIKE adj resembling an eel

EELPOUT n marine eel-like blennioid fish

EELS ▶ eel

EELWORM n any of various nematode worms

EELY ▶ eel

EEN ▶ ee

EERIE adj **eerier, eeriest, eerily, eery**

EEVEN n evening

eevens

EEVN n evening

EEVNING n evening

EEVNS ▸ eevn

EF n the letter F

EFF vb say the word 'fuck'

EFFABLE adj capable of being expressed in words

EFFACE vb effaced, effacer, effaces

EFFECT n, vb

EFFECTS pl n personal belongings

EFFED ▸ eff

EFFEIR vb suit effeirs

EFFENDI n (in the Ottoman Empire) a title of respect

EFFERE = effeir

EFFERED ▸ effere

EFFERES ▸ effere

EFFETE adj

EFFIGY n

EFFING ▸ eff

EFFINGS ▸ eff

EFFLUX n effluence

EFFORCE vb force

EFFORT n efforts

EFFRAY = affray

EFFRAYS ▸ effray

EFFS ▸ ef

EFFULGE vb radiate

EFFUSE vb pour or flow out ▷ adj (esp of an inflorescence) spreading out loosely effused, effuses

EFS ▸ ef

EFT n dialect or archaic name for a newt ▷ adv again

EFTEST adj nearest at hand

EFTS ▸ eft

EFTSOON > eftsoons

EGAD n mild oath or expression of surprise egads

EGAL adj equal

EGALITE n equality

EGALITY n equality

EGALLY ▸ egal

EGENCE n need egences, egency

EGER = eagre

EGERS ▸ eger

EGEST vb excrete (waste material)

EGESTA pl n anything egested, as waste material from the body

EGESTED ▸ egest

EGESTS ▸ egest

EGG n, vb

EGGAR = egger

EGGARS ▸ eggar

EGGCUP n cup for holding a boiled egg eggcups

EGGED ▸ egg

EGGER n moth with brown body and wings eggers

EGGERY n place where eggs are laid

EGGHEAD n intellectual person

EGGIER ▸ eggy

EGGIEST ▸ eggy

EGGING ▸ egg

EGGLER n egg dealer: sometimes itinerant egglers

EGGLESS ▸ egg

EGGMASS n

intelligentsia

EGGNOG n drink made of raw eggs, milk, sugar, spice, and brandy or rum eggnogs

EGGS ▸ egg

EGGWASH n beaten egg for brushing on pastry

EGGY adj soaked in or tasting of egg

EGIS rare spelling of ▸ aegis

EGISES ▸ egis

EGMA mispronunciation of ▸ enigma

EGMAS ▸ egma

EGO n

EGOISM n egoisms

EGOIST n person who is preoccupied with his own interests egoists

EGOITY n essence of the ego

EGOLESS adj without an ego

EGOS ▸ ego

EGOTISE = egotize

EGOTISM n concern only for one's own interests and feelings

EGOTIST n conceited boastful person

EGOTIZE vb talk or write in self-important way

EGRESS = emersion

EGRET n lesser white heron egrets

EH interj exclamation of surprise or inquiry ▷ vb say 'eh' ehed, ehing, ehs

EIDE ▸ eidos

EIDENT adj diligent

EIDER n Arctic duck
eiders
EIDETIC adj (of images) exceptionally vivid, allowing recall of something ▷ n person with eidetic ability
EIDOLA ▶ eidolon
EIDOLIC ▶ eidolon
EIDOLON n unsubstantial image
EIDOS n intellectual character of a culture or a social group
EIGHT n, adj
EIGHTH n number eight in a series ▷ adj coming after the seventh and before the ninth ▷ adv after the seventh person, position, event, etc **eighths**
EIGHTS ▶ eight
EIGHTVO another word for ▶ octavo
EIGHTY n, adj, determiner
EIGNE adj firstborn
EIK variant form of ▶ eke
EIKED ▶ eik
EIKING ▶ eik
EIKON variant spelling of ▶ icon
EIKONES ▶ eikon
EIKONS ▶ eikon
EIKS ▶ eik
EILD n old age
EILDING n fuel
EILDS ▶ eild
EINA interj exclamation of pain
EINE pl n eyes
EINKORN n variety of wheat of Greece and

SW Asia
EIRACK n young hen **eiracks**
EIRENIC variant spelling of ▶ irenic
EISEL n vinegar **eisell**
EISELLS ▶ eisell
EISELS ▶ eisel
EISH interj South African exclamation
EISWEIN n wine made from grapes frozen on the vine
EITHER pron, adv, determiner
EJECT vb
EJECTA pl n matter thrown out by a volcano or during a meteorite impact
EJECTED ▶ eject
EJECTOR n person or thing that ejects
EJECTS ▶ eject
EKE vb increase, enlarge, or lengthen **eked, ekes, eking**
EKISTIC ▶ ekistics
EKKA n type of one-horse carriage **ekkas**
EKPWELE n former monetary unit of Equatorial Guinea **ekuele**
EL n American elevated railway
ELAIN = triolein
ELAINS ▶ elain
ELAN n style and vigour
ELANCE vb throw a lance **elanced, elances**
ELAND n **elands**

ELANET n bird of prey **elanets**
ELANS ▶ elan
ELAPID n mostly tropical type of venomous snake **elapids**
ELAPINE adj of or like an elapid
ELAPSE vb elapsed, **elapses**
ELASTIC adj, n
ELASTIN n fibrous scleroprotein
ELATE vb fill with high spirits, exhilaration, pride or optimism
ELATED adj extremely happy and excited
ELATER n elaterid beetle **elaters**
ELATES ▶ elate
ELATING ▶ elate
ELATION n
ELATIVE adj denoting a grammatical case in Finnish and other languages ▷ n elative case
ELBOW n, vb elbowed, **elbows**
ELCHEE n ambassador **elchees, elchi**
ELCHIS ▶ elchi
ELD n old age
ELDER adj, n
ELDERLY adj
ELDERS ▶ elder
ELDEST adj oldest
ELDIN n fuel **elding**
ELDINGS ▶ elding
ELDINS ▶ eldin
ELDRESS n woman elder

ELDRICH = eldritch

ELDS ▸ eld

ELECT vb, adj **elected**

ELECTEE n someone who is elected

ELECTOR n someone who has the right to vote in an election

ELECTRO vb (in printing) make a metallic copy of a page

ELECTS ▸ elect

ELEGANT adj

ELEGIAC adj, n

ELEGIES ▸ elegy

ELEGISE = elegize

ELEGIST ▸ elegize

ELEGIT n writ delivering debtor's property to plaintiff **elegits**

ELEGIZE vb compose an elegy or elegies (in memory of)

ELEGY n

ELEMENT n

ELEMI n fragrant resin obtained from various tropical trees **elemis**

ELENCH n refutation in logic

ELENCHI > elenchus

ELENCHS ▸ elench

ELEVATE vb

ELEVEN n, adj, determiner **elevens**

ELEVON n aircraft control surface usually fitted to tailless or delta-wing aircraft **elevons**

ELF n, vb **elfed, elfhood**

ELFIN adj, n

ELFING ▸ elf

ELFINS ▸ elfin

ELFISH adj of, relating to, or like an elf or elves ▷ n supposed language of elves

ELFLAND another name for ▸ **fairyland**

ELFLIKE ▸ elf

ELFLOCK n lock of hair

ELFS ▸ elf

ELHI adj informal word for or relating to elementary high school

ELIAD n glance **eliads**

ELICHE n pasta in the form of spirals **eliches**

ELICIT vb **elicits**

ELIDE vb **elided, elides, eliding**

ELINT n electronic intelligence **elints**

ELISION n

ELITE n, adj **elites**

ELITISM n **elitist**

ELIXIR n **elixirs**

ELK n

ELKHORN n as in **elkhorn fern** fern with a large leaf like an elk's horn

ELKS ▸ elk

ELL n obsolete unit of length

ELLAGIC adj of an acid derived from gallnuts

ELLIPSE n

ELLOPS = elops

ELLS ▸ ell

ELLWAND n stick for measuring lengths

ELM n

ELMEN adj of or relating to elm trees

ELMIER ▸ elmy

ELMIEST ▸ elmy

ELMS ▸ elm

ELMWOOD n wood from an elm tree

ELMY adj of or relating to elm trees

ELOCUTE vb speak as if practising elocution

ELODEA n type of American plant **elodeas**

ELOGE = eulogy

ELOGES ▸ eloge

ELOGIES ▸ elogy

ELOGIST ▸ elogy

ELOGIUM = eulogy

ELOGY = eulogy

ELOIGN vb remove (oneself, one's property, etc) to a distant place **eloigns, eloin**

ELOINED ▸ eloin

ELOINER ▸ eloign

ELOINS ▸ eloin

ELOPE vb **eloped, eloper, elopers, elopes, eloping**

ELOPS n type of fish **elopses**

ELPEE n LP, long-playing record **elpees**

ELS ▸ el

ELSE adv

ELSHIN n cobbler's awl **elshins, elsin**

ELSINS ▸ elsin

ELT n young female pig

ELTCHI variant of ▸ **elchee**

ELTCHIS ▸ eltchi

ELTS ▸ elt

ELUANT = eluent

ELUANTS ▸ eluant

ELUATE n solution of adsorbed material obtained during the process of elution **eluates**

ELUDE vb **eluded, eluder, eluders, eludes, eluding**

ELUENT n solvent used for eluting **eluents**

ELUSION ▶ **elude**

ELUSIVE adj

ELUSORY adj avoiding the issue

ELUTE vb wash out (a substance) by the action of a solvent **eluted, elutes, eluting, elution, elutor, elutors**

ELUVIA ▶ **eluvium**

ELUVIAL ▶ **eluvium**

ELUVIUM n mass of sand, silt, etc

ELVAN n type of rock **elvans**

ELVER n young eel **elvers**

ELVES ▶ **elf**

ELVISH = **elfish**

ELYSIAN adj delightful, blissful

ELYTRA ▶ **elytrum**

ELYTRAL ▶ **elytron**

ELYTRON n either of the horny front wings of beetles and some other insects **elytrum**

EM n square of a body of any size of type, used as a unit of measurement

EMACS n powerful computer program

emacsen

EMAIL n electronic mail ▷ vb send a message by electronic mail **emailed, emailer, emails**

EMANANT ▶ **emanate**

EMANATE vb

EMBACE variant of ▶ **embase**

EMBACES ▶ **embace**

EMBAIL vb enclose in a circle **embails**

EMBALE vb bind **embaled, embales**

EMBALL vb enclose in a circle **emballs**

EMBALM vb **embalms**

EMBANK vb protect, enclose, or confine with an embankment **embanks**

EMBAR vb close in with bars

EMBARGO n, vb

EMBARK vb **embarks**

EMBARS ▶ **embar**

EMBASE vb degrade or debase **embased, embases**

EMBASSY n

EMBASTE ▶ **embase**

EMBATHE vb bathe with water

EMBAY vb form into a bay **embayed**

EMBAYLD ▶ **embail**

EMBAYS ▶ **embay**

EMBED vb, n **embeds**

EMBER n **embers**

EMBLAZE vb cause to light up

EMBLEM n, vb

EMBLEMA n mosaic

decoration

EMBLEMS ▶ **emblem**

EMBLIC n type of Indian tree **emblics**

EMBLOOM vb adorn with blooms

EMBODY vb

EMBOG vb sink down into a bog **embogs**

EMBOGUE vb go out through a narrow channel or passage

EMBOIL vb enrage or be enraged **emboils**

EMBOLI ▶ **embolus**

EMBOLIC adj of or relating to an embolus or embolism

EMBOLUS n material that blocks a blood vessel

EMBOLY n infolding of an outer layer of cells so as to form a pocket in the surface

EMBOSK vb hide or cover **embosks**

EMBOSOM vb enclose or envelop, esp protectively

EMBOSS vb create a decoration that stands out on (a surface) **embost**

EMBOUND vb surround or encircle

EMBOW vb design or create (a structure) in the form of an arch or vault **embowed**

EMBOWEL vb bury or embed deeply

EMBOWER vb enclose in or as in a bower

EMBOWS ▸ embow

EMBOX vb put in a box emboxed, emboxes

EMBRACE vb, n

EMBRAID vb braid or interweave

EMBRAVE vb adorn or decorate

EMBREAD vb braid

EMBROIL vb

EMBROWN vb make or become brown

EMBRUE variant spelling of ▸ imbrue

EMBRUED ▸ embrue

EMBRUES ▸ embrue

EMBRUTE variant of ▸ imbrute

EMBRYO n embryon, embryos

EMBUS vb cause (troops) to board a transport vehicle embused, embuses

EMBUSY vb keep occupied

EMCEE n master of ceremonies ▸ vb act as master of ceremonies (for or at) emceed, emcees

EMDASH n long dash in punctuation

EME n uncle

EMEER variant of ▸ emir

EMEERS ▸ emeer

EMEND vb emended, emender, emends

EMERALD n, adj

EMERGE vb emerged, emerges

EMERIED ▸ emery

EMERIES ▸ emery

EMERITA adj retired, but

retaining an honorary title ▸ n woman who is retired, but retains an honorary title

EMERITI ▸ emeritus

EMEROD n haemorrhoid emerods, emeroid

EMERSE ▸ emersed

EMERSED adj protruding above the surface of the water

EMERY n hard mineral used for smoothing and polishing ▸ vb apply emery to

EMES ▸ eme

EMESES ▸ emesis

EMESIS technical name for ▸ vomiting

EMETIC n, adj emetics

EMETIN = emetine

EMETINE n white bitter poisonous alkaloid

EMETINS ▸ emetin

EMEU variant of ▸ emu

EMEUS ▸ emeu

EMEUTE n uprising or rebellion emeutes

EMIC adj of or relating to a significant linguistic unit

EMICANT ▸ emicate

EMICATE vb twinkle

EMIGRE n someone who has left his native country for political reasons emigres

EMINENT adj

EMIR n

EMIRATE n emir's country

EMIRS ▸ emir

EMIT vb emits, emitted

EMITTER n person or thing that emits

EMLETS pl n as in blood-drop emlets Chilean plant

EMMA n former communications code for the letter A emmas

EMMER n variety of wheat emmers

EMMESH variant of ▸ enmesh

EMMET n tourist or holiday-maker emmets

EMMEW vb restrict emmewed, emmews

EMMOVE vb cause emotion in emmoved, emmoves

EMMY n award for outstanding television performances and productions emmys

EMO n type of music

EMODIN n type of chemical compound emodins

EMONG variant of ▸ among

EMONGES variant of ▸ among

EMONGST variant of ▸ amongst

EMOS ▸ emo

EMOTE vb display exaggerated emotion, as if acting emoted, emoter, emoters, emotes, emoting

EMOTION n

EMOTIVE adj

EMOVE vb cause to feel emotion emoved,

emoves, emoving

EMPAIRE variant of
  ▸ impair
EMPALE less common
spelling of ▸ impale
EMPALED ▸ empale
EMPALER ▸ empale
EMPALES ▸ empale
EMPANEL vb enter on a
list (names of persons
to be summoned for
jury service)
EMPARE variant of
  ▸ impair
EMPARED ▸ empare
EMPARES ▸ empare
EMPARL variant of
  ▸ imparl
EMPARLS ▸ emparl
EMPART variant of
  ▸ impart
EMPARTS ▸ empart
EMPATHY n ability to
understand someone
else's feelings
EMPAYRE variant of
  ▸ impair
EMPEACH variant of
  ▸ impeach
EMPERCE variant of
  > empierce
EMPEROR n
EMPERY n dominion or
power
EMPIGHT adj attached
or positioned
EMPIRE n empires
EMPIRIC n person who
relies on empirical
methods
EMPLACE vb put in
place or position
EMPLANE vb board or
put on board an

aeroplane
EMPLOY vb, n
EMPLOYE = employee
EMPLOYS ▸ employ
EMPLUME vb put a
plume on
EMPORIA > emporium
EMPOWER vb
EMPRESS n
EMPRISE n chivalrous or
daring enterprise
emprize
EMPT vb empty empted
EMPTIED, emptier,
empties, emptily
  ▸ empty
EMPTING ▸ empt
EMPTINS pl n liquid
leavening agent made
from potatoes
EMPTION n process of
buying something
EMPTS ▸ empt
EMPTY adj, vb, n
EMPUSA n goblin in
Greek mythology
empusas, empuse
EMPUSES ▸ empuse
EMPYEMA n collection
of pus in a body cavity
EMS ▸ em
EMU n
EMULATE vb emule
EMULED ▸ emule
EMULES ▸ emule
EMULGE vb remove
liquid from emulged,
emulges
EMULING ▸ emule
EMULOUS adj desiring
or aiming to equal or
surpass another
EMULSIN n enzyme that
is found in almonds

EMULSOR n device that
emulsifies
EMUNGE vb clean or
clear out emunged,
emunges
EMURE variant of
  ▸ immure
EMURED ▸ emure
EMURES ▸ emure
EMURING ▸ emure
EMUS ▸ emu
EMYD n freshwater
tortoise or terrapin
emyde
EMYDES ▸ emyde
EMYDS ▸ emyd
EMYS n freshwater
tortoise or terrapin
EN n unit of
measurement, half the
width of an em
ENABLE vb enabled,
enabler, enables
ENACT vb enacted,
enactor, enacts
ENAMEL n, vb enamels
ENAMINE n type of
unsaturated compound
ENAMOR = enamour
ENAMORS ▸ enamor
ENAMOUR vb inspire
with love
ENARCH variant of
  ▸ inarch
ENARM vb provide with
arms enarmed,
enarms
ENATE adj growing out
or outwards ▷ n
relative on the
mother's side enates
ENATIC adj related to
one's mother's side
ENATION ▸ enate

ENCAGE vb confine in or as in a cage **encaged, encages**

ENCALM vb becalm, settle **encalms**

ENCAMP vb **encamps**

ENCASE vb **encased, encases**

ENCASH vb exchange (a cheque) for cash

ENCAVE variant of ▸ **incave**

ENCAVED ▸ encave

ENCAVES ▸ encave

ENCHAFE vb heat up

ENCHAIN vb bind with chains

ENCHANT vb

ENCHARM vb enchant

ENCHASE less common word for ▸ **chase**

ENCHEER vb cheer up

ENCINA n type of oak **encinal, encinas**

ENCLASP vb clasp

ENCLAVE n, vb

ENCLOSE vb

ENCLOUD vb hide with clouds

ENCODE vb convert (a message) into code **encoded, encoder, encodes**

ENCOMIA > encomium

ENCORE interj, n, vb **encored, encores**

ENCRATY n control of one's desires, actions, etc

ENCRUST vb cover with a layer of something

ENCRYPT vb put (a message) into code

ENCYST vb enclose or

become enclosed by a cyst, thick membrane, or shell **encysts**

END n furthest point or part ▷ vb bring or come to a finish

ENDARCH adj having the first-formed xylem internal to that formed later

ENDART variant of ▸ **indart**

ENDARTS ▸ endart

ENDASH n short dash in punctuation

ENDEAR vb **endears**

ENDED ▸ end

ENDEMIC adj, n

ENDER ▸ end

ENDERON variant of ▸ **andiron**

ENDERS ▸ end

ENDEW variant of ▸ **endue**

ENDEWED ▸ endew

ENDEWS ▸ endew

ENDGAME n closing stage of a game of chess

ENDGATE n tailboard of a vehicle

ENDING n endings

ENDIRON variant of ▸ **andiron**

ENDITE variant of ▸ **indict**

ENDITED ▸ endite

ENDITES ▸ endite

ENDIVE n curly-leaved plant used in salads **endives**

ENDLANG variant of ▸ **endlong**

ENDLEAF n endpaper in

a book

ENDLESS adj

ENDLONG adv lengthways or on end

ENDMOST adj nearest the end

ENDNOTE n note at the end of a section of writing

ENDOGEN n plant that increases in size by internal growth

ENDOPOD n inner branch of a two-branched crustacean

ENDORSE vb

ENDOSS vb endorse

ENDOW vb **endowed, endower, endows**

ENDOZOA > endozoon

ENDPLAY n technique in card games ▷ vb force (an opponent) to make a particular lead near the end of a hand

ENDRIN n type of insecticide **endrins**

ENDS ▸ end

ENDSHIP n small village

ENDUE vb invest or provide, as with some quality or trait **endued, endues, enduing**

ENDURE vb **endured, endurer, endures**

ENDURO n long-distance race for vehicles **enduros**

ENDWAYS adv having the end forwards or upwards ▷ adj vertical or upright **endwise**

ENDYSES ▸ endysis

ENDYSIS n formation of new layers of integument after ecdysis

ENDZONE n (in American football) area at either end of the playing field

ENE variant of ▶ even

ENEMA n enemas, enemata

ENEMIES ▶ enemy

ENEMY n, adj

ENERGIC ▶ energy

ENERGID n nucleus and cytoplasm in a syncytium

ENERGY n

ENERVE vb enervate enerved, enerves

ENES ▶ ene

ENEW vb force a bird into water enewed, enewing, enews

ENFACE vb write, print, or stamp (something) on the face of (a document) enfaced, enfaces

ENFANT n French child enfants

ENFELON vb infuriate

ENFEOFF vb invest (a person) with possession of a freehold estate in land

ENFEVER vb make feverish

ENFILED adj passed through

ENFIRE vb set alight enfired, enfires

ENFIX variant of ▶ infix

ENFIXED ▶ enfix

ENFIXES ▶ enfix

ENFLAME variant of ▶ inflame

ENFLESH vb make flesh

ENFOLD vb enfolds

ENFORCE vb

ENFORM variant of ▶ inform

ENFORMS ▶ enform

ENFRAME vb put inside a frame

ENFREE vb release, make free enfreed, enfrees

ENFROZE > enfreeze

ENG another name for ▶ agma

ENGAGE vb, adj

ENGAGED adj

ENGAGEE adj (of a female artist) morally or politically committed to some ideology

ENGAGER ▶ engage

ENGAGES ▶ engage

ENGAOL vb put into gaol engaols

ENGILD vb cover with or as if with gold engilds, engilt

ENGINE n, vb engined, enginer, engines

ENGIRD vb surround engirds, engirt

ENGLISH vb put spin on a billiard ball

ENGLOBE vb surround as if in a globe

ENGLOOM vb make dull or dismal

ENGLUT vb devour ravenously engluts

ENGOBE n liquid put on pottery before glazing engobes

ENGORE vb pierce or wound engored, engores

ENGORGE vb clog with blood

ENGRACE vb give grace to

ENGRAFF variant of ▶ engraft

ENGRAFT vb graft (a shoot, bud, etc) onto a stock

ENGRAIL vb decorate or mark with small carved notches

ENGRAIN variant spelling of ▶ ingrain

ENGRAM n physical basis of an individual memory in the brain engrams

ENGRASP vb grasp or seize

ENGRAVE vb

ENGROSS vb

ENGS ▶ eng

ENGUARD vb protect or defend

ENGULF vb engulfs, engulph

ENHALO vb surround with or as if with a halo enhalos

ENIAC n early type of computer built in the 1940s eniacs

ENIGMA n enigmas

ENISLE vb put on or make into an island enisled, enisles

ENJAMB vb (of a line of verse) run over into the next line enjambs

ENJOIN vb enjoins
ENJOY vb enjoyed, enjoyer, enjoys
ENLACE vb bind or encircle with or as with laces enlaced, enlaces
ENLARD vb put lard on enlards
ENLARGE vb
ENLEVE adj having been abducted
ENLIGHT vb light up
ENLINK vb link together enlinks
ENLIST vb enlists
ENLIT ▶ enlight
ENLIVEN vb
ENLOCK vb lock or secure enlocks
ENMESH vb
ENMEW variant of ▶ emmew
ENMEWED ▶ enmew
ENMEWS ▶ enmew
ENMITY n
ENMOVE variant of ▶ emmove
ENMOVED ▶ enmove
ENMOVES ▶ enmove
ENNAGE n number of ens in printed matter ennages
ENNEAD n group or series of nine enneads
ENNOBLE vb
ENNOG n back alley ennogs
ENNUI n, vb ennuied, ennuis
ENNUYE adj bored
ENNUYED ▶ ennui
ENNUYEE = ennuye

ENODAL adj having no nodes
ENOKI variant of ▶ enokitake
ENOKIS ▶ enoki
ENOL n type of organic compound
ENOLASE n type of enzyme
ENOLIC ▶ enol
ENOLOGY usual US spelling of ▶ oenology
ENOLS ▶ enol
ENOMOTY n division of the Spartan army in ancient Greece
ENORM variant of ▶ enormous
ENOSES ▶ enosis
ENOSIS n union of Greece and Cyprus
ENOUGH adj, n, adv enoughs
ENOUNCE vb enunciate
ENOW archaic word for ▶ enough
ENOWS ▶ enow
ENPLANE vb board an aircraft
ENPRINT n standard photographic print
ENQUEUE vb add (an item) to a queue of computing tasks
ENQUIRE = inquire
ENQUIRY ▶ enquire
ENRACE vb bring in a race of people enraced, enraces
ENRAGE vb enraged, enrages
ENRANGE vb arrange, organize
ENRANK vb put in a row

enranks
ENRAPT ▶ enrapture
ENRHEUM vb pass a cold on to
ENRICH vb
ENRING vb put a ring round enrings
ENRIVEN adj ripped
ENROBE vb dress in or as if in a robe enrobed, enrober, enrobes
ENROL ▶ enroll
ENROLLS ▶ enroll
ENROLS ▶ enrol
ENROOT vb establish (plants) by fixing their roots in the earth enroots
ENROUGH vb roughen
ENROUND vb encircle
ENS n being or existence in the most general abstract sense
ENSATE adj shaped like a sword
ENSEAL vb seal up enseals
ENSEAM vb put a seam on enseams
ENSEAR vb dry ensears
ENSERF vb enslave enserfs
ENSEW variant of ▶ ensue
ENSEWED ▶ ensew
ENSEWS ▶ ensew
ENSHELL variant of ▶ inshell
ENSIGN n, vb ensigns
ENSILE vb store and preserve (green fodder) in an enclosed pit or silo ensiled, ensiles

ENSKIED ▸ ensky

ENSKIES ▸ ensky

ENSKY vb put in the sky **enskyed**

ENSLAVE vb

ENSNARE vb

ENSNARL vb become tangled in

ENSOUL vb endow with a soul **ensouls**

ENSTAMP vb imprint with a stamp

ENSTEEP vb soak in water

ENSTYLE vb give a name to

ENSUE vb **ensued, ensues**

ENSUING adj following subsequently or in order

ENSURE vb **ensured, ensurer, ensures**

ENSWEEP vb sweep across **enswept**

ENTAIL vb, n **entails**

ENTAME vb make tame **entamed, entames**

ENTASES ▸ entasis

ENTASIA = entasis

ENTASIS n slightly convex curve given to the shaft of a structure

ENTAYLE variant of ▸ entail

ENTENTE n

ENTER vb

ENTERA ▸ enteron

ENTERAL = enteric

ENTERED ▸ enter

ENTERER ▸ enter

ENTERIC adj intestinal ▷ n infectious disease of the intestines

ENTERON n alimentary canal

ENTERS ▸ enter

ENTETE adj obsessed **entetee**

ENTHRAL vb

ENTHUSE vb

ENTIA ▸ ens

| This means entities, and because of the common letters it uses is one of the most frequently played five-letter words, at least towards the end of the game.

ENTICE vb **enticed, enticer, entices**

ENTIRE adj, n **entires**

ENTITLE vb

ENTITY n

ENTOIL archaic word for ▸ ensnare

ENTOILS ▸ entoil

ENTOMB vb place (a corpse) in a tomb **entombs**

ENTOMIC adj denoting or relating to insects

ENTOPIC adj situated in its normal place or position

ENTOTIC adj of or relating to the inner ear

ENTOZOA > entozoon

ENTRAIL vb twist or entangle

ENTRAIN vb board or put aboard a train

ENTRALL variant of > **entrails**

ENTRANT n

ENTRAP vb trick into difficulty etc **entraps**

ENTREAT vb

ENTREE n dish served before a main course **entrees**

ENTREZ interj enter

ENTRIES ▸ entry

ENTRISM variant of > **entryism**

ENTRIST ▸ entryism

ENTROLD adj surrounded

ENTROPY n lack of organization

ENTRUST vb

ENTRY n, adj

ENTWINE vb

ENTWIST vb twist together or around

ENUF common intentional literary misspelling of ▸ enough

ENURE variant spelling of ▸ inure

ENURED ▸ enure

ENURES ▸ enure

ENURING ▸ enure

ENURN ▸ inurn

ENURNED ▸ inurned

ENURNS ▸ inurns

ENVAULT vb enclose in a vault; entomb

ENVELOP vb

ENVENOM vb fill or impregnate with venom

ENVIED, envier, enviers, envies ▸ envy

ENVIOUS adj

ENVIRO n environmentalist

ENVIRON vb encircle or surround

ENVIROS ▶ enviro

ENVOI = envoy

ENVOIS ▶ envoi

ENVOY n envoys

ENVY n, vb envying

ENWALL vb wall in **enwalls**

ENWHEEL archaic word for ▶ encircle

ENWIND vb wind or coil around **enwinds**

ENWOMB vb enclose in or as if in a womb **enwombs**

ENWOUND ▶ enwind

ENWRAP vb wrap or cover up **enwraps**

ENZIAN n gentian violet **enzians**

ENZONE vb enclose in a zone **enzoned, enzones**

ENZYM = enzyme

ENZYME n enzymes, **enzymic**

ENZYMS ▶ enzym

EOAN adj of or relating to the dawn

EOBIONT n hypothetical chemical precursor of a living cell

EOCENE adj of, denoting, or formed in the second epoch of the Tertiary period

EOLIAN adj of or relating to the wind

6-letter words tend to be among the least known and least used, because they leave you at the mercy of the tile bag without scoring that extra 50 points you would get for using all 7 letters. This word, meaning related to the wind, often comes in useful for dumping a surplus of vowels. And its alternative spelling **aeolian** is even better for this and what's more will get you a bonus!

EOLITH n stone used as a primitive tool in Eolithic times **eoliths**

EON n two or more eras

EONIAN adj of or relating to an eon

EONISM n adoption of female dress and behaviour by a male **eonisms**

EONS ▶ eon

EORL n Anglo-Saxon nobleman **eorls**

EOSIN n red crystalline water-insoluble derivative of fluorescein **eosine**

EOSINES ▶ eosine

EOSINIC ▶ eosin

EOSINS ▶ eosin

EOTHEN adv from the East

EPACRID n type of heath-like plant

EPACRIS n genus of the epacrids

EPACT n difference in time between the solar year and the lunar year **epacts**

EPAGOGE n inductive reasoning

EPARCH n bishop or metropolitan in charge of an eparchy **eparchs**

EPARCHY n diocese of the Eastern Christian Church

EPATANT adj startling or shocking

EPAULE n shoulder of a fortification **epaules**

EPAULET = epaulette

EPAXIAL adj above the axis

EPAZOTE n type of herb

EPEE n straight-bladed sword used in fencing

EPEEIST n one who uses or specializes in using an epee

EPEES ▶ epee

EPEIRA = epeirid

EPEIRAS ▶ epeira

EPEIRIC adj in, of, or relating to a continent

EPEIRID n type of spider

EPERDU adj distracted

EPERDUE adj distracted

EPERGNE n ornamental centrepiece for a table

EPHA = ephah

EPHAH n Hebrew unit of dry measure **ephahs**

EPHAS ▶ epha

EPHEBE n (in ancient Greece) youth about to enter full citizenship **ephebes, ephebi, ephebic**

EPHEBOI ▶ ephebos

EPHEBOS = ephebe

EPHEBUS = ephebe

EPHEDRA n gymnosperm shrub

EPHELIS n freckle

EPHOD n embroidered vestment worn by priests **ephods**

EPHOR n (in ancient Greece) one of a board of senior magistrates in any of several Dorian states **ephoral, ephori, ephors**

EPIBLEM n outermost cell layer of a root

EPIBOLY n process that occurs during gastrulation in vertebrates

EPIC n, adj **epical**

EPICARP n outermost layer of the pericarp of fruits

EPICEDE = epicedium

EPICENE adj having the characteristics of both sexes; hermaphroditic ▷ n epicene person or creature

EPICIER n grocer

EPICISM n style or trope characteristic of epics

EPICIST n writer of epics

EPICS ▷ epic

EPICURE n

EPIDERM = epidermis

EPIDOTE n green mineral

EPIGEAL adj of or relating to a form of seed germination **epigean, epigeic**

EPIGENE adj formed or taking place at or near the surface of the earth

EPIGON = epigone

EPIGONE n inferior follower or imitator **epigoni**

EPIGONS ▷ epigon

EPIGRAM n

EPIGYNY > epigynous

EPILATE vb remove hair from

EPILOG = epilogue

EPILOGS ▷ epilog

EPIMER n isomer

EPIMERE n dorsal part of the mesoderm of a vertebrate embryo

EPIMERS ▷ epimer

EPINAOI ▷ epinaos

EPINAOS n rear vestibule

EPISCIA n creeping plant

EPISODE n

EPISOME n unit of genetic material (DNA) in bacteria that can be replicated

EPISTLE n, vb

EPITAPH n, vb

EPITAXY n growth of a thin layer on the surface of a crystal

EPITHEM n external topical application

EPITHET n, vb

EPITOME n

EPITOPE n site on an antigen at which a specific antibody becomes attached

EPIZOA ▷ epizoon

EPIZOAN = epizoon

EPIZOIC adj (of an animal or plant) growing or living on

the exterior of a living animal

EPIZOON n animal that lives on the body of another animal

EPOCH n **epocha, epochal**

EPOCHAS ▷ epocha

EPOCHS ▷ epoch

EPODE n part of a lyric ode that follows the strophe and the antistrophe **epodes, epodic**

EPONYM n name derived from the name of a real or mythical person **eponyms**

EPONYMY n derivation of names of places, etc, from those of persons

EPOPEE n epic poem **epopees**

EPOPT n one initiated into mysteries **epopts**

EPOS n body of poetry in which the tradition of a people is conveyed **eposes**

EPOXIDE n chemical compound

EPOXIED ▷ epoxy

EPOXIES ▷ epoxy

EPOXY adj of or containing a specific type of chemical compound ▷ n epoxy resin ▷ vb glue with epoxy resin **epoxyed**

EPRIS adj enamoured **eprise**

EPSILON n fifth letter of the Greek alphabet

EPUISE adj exhausted
epuisee

EPULARY adj of or relating to feasting

EPULIS n swelling of the gum

EPURATE vb purify

EPYLLIA > epyllion

EQUABLE adj equably

EQUAL adj, n, vb equaled

EQUALI pl n pieces for a group of instruments of the same kind

EQUALLY ▶ equal

EQUALS ▶ equal

EQUANT n circle in which a planet was formerly believed to move equants

EQUATE vb equated, equates

EQUATOR n

EQUERRY n attendant to a member of a royal family

EQUID n any animal of the horse family equids

EQUINAL = equine

EQUINE adj, n equines

EQUINIA n glanders

EQUINOX n

EQUIP vb

EQUIPE n (esp in motor racing) team equipes

EQUIPS ▶ equip

EQUITES pl n cavalry

EQUITY n

ER interj sound made when hesitating in speech

ERA n eras

ERASE vb erased

ERASER n erasers

ERASES ▶ erase

ERASING ▶ erase

ERASION n act of erasing

> This means the state of being erased: not an exciting word, but its combination of common letters makes it one of the most frequently played of 7-letter bonus words.

ERASURE n erasing

ERATHEM n stratum of rocks representing a specific geological era

ERBIA n oxide of erbium erbias

ERBIUM n metallic element of the lanthanide series erbiums

ERE prep before ▷ vb plough

ERECT vb, adj erected

ERECTER = erector

ERECTLY ▶ erect

ERECTOR n any muscle that raises a part or makes it erect

ERECTS ▶ erect

ERED ▶ ere

ERELONG adv before long

EREMIC adj of or relating to deserts

EREMITE n Christian hermit

EREMURI > eremurus

ERENOW adv long

before the present

EREPSIN n mixture of proteolytic enzymes secreted by the small intestine

ERES ▶ ere

ERETHIC > erethism

EREV n day before erevs

ERF n plot of land marked off for building purposes

ERG = ergometer

ERGATE n worker ant ergates

ERGO = ergometer

ERGODIC adj of or relating to the probability that any state will recur

ERGON n work ergons

ERGOS ▶ ergo

ERGOT n fungal disease of cereal ergotic, ergots

ERGS ▶ erg

ERHU n Chinese two-stringed violin erhus

ERIACH = eric

ERIACHS ▶ eriach

ERIC n (in old Irish law) fine paid by a murderer to the family of his victim

ERICA n genus of plants including heathers ericas

ERICK = eric

ERICKS ▶ erick

ERICOID adj (of leaves) small and tough, resembling those of heather

ERICS ▶ eric
ERING ▶ ere
ERINGO = eryngo
ERINGOS ▶ eringo
ERINITE n arsenate of copper
ERINUS n type of plant
ERISTIC adj of, relating, or given to controversy or logical disputation ▷ n person who engages in logical disputes
ERK n aircraftman or naval rating erks
ERLANG n unit of traffic intensity in a telephone system erlangs
ERLKING n malevolent spirit who carries off children
ERM interj
ERMELIN n ermine
ERMINE n
ERMINED adj clad in the fur of the ermine
ERMINES ▶ ermine
ERN archaic variant of ▶ earn
ERNE n fish-eating (European) sea eagle
ERNED ▶ ern
ERNES ▶ erne
ERNING ▶ ern
ERNS ▶ ern
ERODE vb eroded, erodent, erodes, eroding
ERODIUM n type of geranium
EROS n lust
EROSE adj jagged or uneven, as though

gnawed or bitten erosely
EROSES ▶ eros
EROSION n erosive
EROTEMA n rhetorical question eroteme
EROTIC adj, n
EROTICA n
EROTICS ▶ erotic
EROTISE = erotize
EROTISM = eroticism
EROTIZE vb make erotic
ERR vb
ERRABLE adj capable of making a mistake
ERRANCY n state or an instance of erring or a tendency to err
ERRAND n errands
ERRANT adj behaving in a manner considered to be unacceptable ▷ n knight-errant errants
ERRATA ▶ erratum
ERRATAS informal variant of ▶ errata
ERRATIC adj, n
ERRATUM n error in writing or printing
ERRED ▶ err
ERRHINE adj causing nasal secretion ▷ n errhine drug or agent
ERRING ▶ err
ERRINGS ▶ err
ERROR n errors
ERRS ▶ err
ERS = ervil
ERSATZ adj made in imitation ▷ n ersatz substance or article
ERSES ▶ ers
ERST adv long ago
ERUCIC adj as in erucic

acid crystalline fatty acid
ERUCT vb belch eructed, eructs
ERUDITE adj, n
ERUGO n verdigris erugos
ERUPT vb erupted, erupts
ERUV n area within which certain activities forbidden to be done on the Sabbath are permitted eruvim, eruvin, eruvs
ERVEN ▶ erf
ERVIL n type of vetch ervils
ERYNGO n type of plant with toothed or lobed leaves eryngos
ES n letter S
ESCALOP another word for ▶ scallop
ESCAPE vb, n escaped
ESCAPEE n
ESCAPER ▶ escape
ESCAPES ▶ escape
ESCAR = esker
ESCARP n inner side of the ditch separating besiegers and besieged ▷ vb make into a slope escarps
ESCARS ▶ escar
ESCHAR n dry scab or slough eschars
ESCHEAT n possessions that become state property in the absence of an heir ▷ vb attain such property
ESCHEW vb eschews

ESCOLAR n slender spiny-finned fish

ESCORT n, vb escorts

ESCOT vb maintain escoted, escots

ESCRIBE vb make a mathematical drawing

ESCROC n conman escrocs

ESCROL = escroll

ESCROLL n scroll

ESCROLS ▶ escrol

ESCROW n item delivered to a third party pending fulfilment of a condition ▷ vb place (money, a document, etc) in escrow escrows

ESCUAGE (in medieval Europe) another word for ▶ scutage

ESCUDO n former monetary unit of Portugal escudos

ESERINE n crystalline alkaloid

ESES ▶ es

ESILE n vinegar esiles

ESKAR = esker

ESKARS ▶ eskar

ESKER n long ridge of gravel, sand, etc eskers

ESKIES ▶ esky

ESKY n portable insulated container

ESLOIN = eloign

ESLOINS ▶ esloin

ESLOYNE = eloign

ESNE n household slave

ESNECY n inheritance law

ESNES ▶ esne

ESOTERY ▶ esoteric

ESPADA n sword espadas

ESPANOL n Spanish person

ESPARTO n grass of S Europe and N Africa

ESPIAL n act or fact of being seen or discovered espials

ESPIED, espier, espiers, espies ▶ espy

ESPOUSE vb

ESPRIT n spirit, liveliness, or wit esprits

ESPY vb espying

ESQUIRE n courtesy title placed after a man's name ▷ vb escort

ESS n letter S

ESSAY n, vb essayed, essayer, essays

ESSE n existence

ESSENCE n

ESSES ▶ ess

ESSIVE n grammatical case essives

ESSOIN n excuse essoins, essoyne

EST n treatment intended to help people towards psychological growth

ESTATE n, vb estated, estates

ESTEEM n, vb esteems

ESTER n chemical compound esters

ESTHETE US spelling of ▶ aesthete

ESTIVAL usual US spelling of ▶ aestival

ESTOC n short stabbing sword estocs

ESTOILE n heraldic star with wavy points

ESTOP vb preclude by estoppel estops

ESTOVER = estovers

ESTRADE n dais or raised platform

ESTRAL US spelling of ▶ oestral

ESTRAY n stray domestic animal of unknown ownership ▷ vb stray estrays

ESTREAT n true copy of or extract from a court record ▷ vb send an extract of the court record

ESTREPE vb lay waste

ESTRICH n ostrich

ESTRIN US spelling of ▶ oestrin

ESTRINS ▶ estrin

ESTRIOL usual US spelling of ▶ oestriol

ESTRO n poetic inspiration

ESTRONE usual US spelling of ▶ oestrone

ESTROS ▶ estro

ESTROUS ▶ estrus

ESTRUAL ▶ estrus

ESTRUM usual US spelling of ▶ oestrum

ESTRUMS ▶ estrum

ESTRUS usual US spelling of ▶ oestrus

ESTS ▶ est

ESTUARY n

ET dialect past tense of ▶ eat

ETA n seventh letter in the Greek alphabet

ETACISM *n* pronunciation of eta as a long vowel sound

ETAERIO *n* aggregate fruit

> This strange-looking word is a type of fruit, and because it uses the commonest letters, is, along with **otarine**, the most frequently played of all bonus words.

ETAGE *n* floor in a multi-storey building

ETAGERE *n* stand with open shelves for displaying ornaments, etc

ETAGES ▶ etage

ETALAGE *n* display

ETALON *n* device used in spectroscopy **etalons**

ETAMIN = etamine

ETAMINE *n* cotton or worsted fabric of loose weave

ETAMINS ▶ etamin

ETAPE *n* public storehouse **etapes**

ETAS ▶ eta

ETAT *n* state

ETATISM = etatisme

ETATIST > etatisme

ETATS ▶ etat

ETCH *vb*

ETCHANT *n* any acid or corrosive used for etching

ETCHED, etcher, etchers, etches ▶ etch

ETCHING *n*

ETEN *n* giant **etens**

ETERNAL *adj, n* **eterne**

ETESIAN *adj* (of NW winds) recurring annually in the summer in the E Mediterranean ▷ *n* etesian wind

ETH = edh

ETHAL *n* cetyl alcohol **ethals**

ETHANAL *n* colourless volatile pungent liquid

ETHANE *n* odourless flammable gas **ethanes**

ETHANOL = alcohol

ETHE *adj* easy

ETHENE = ethylene

ETHENES ▶ ethene

ETHER *n* etheric, ethers

ETHIC *n* moral principle

ETHICAL *adj, n*

ETHICS *n*

ETHINYL = ethynyl

ETHION *n* type of pesticide **ethions**

ETHIOPS *n* dark-coloured chemical compound

ETHMOID *adj* denoting or relating to a specific bone of the skull ▷ *n* ethmoid bone

ETHNIC *adj, n* **ethnics**

ETHNOS *n* ethnic group

ETHOS *n* **ethoses**

ETHOXY ▶ ethoxyl

ETHOXYL *n* univalent radical

ETHS ▶ eth

ETHYL *adj* type of chemical hydrocarbon group **ethylic, ethyls**

ETHYNE another name for ▶ **acctylene**

ETHYNES ▶ ethyne

ETHYNYL *n* univalent radical

ETIC *adj* relating to linguistic terms analysed without regard to structural function

ETIOLIN *n* yellow pigment

ETNA *n* container used to heat liquids **etnas**

ETOILE *n* star **etoiles**

ETOURDI *adj* foolish

ETRENNE *n* New Year's gift

ETRIER *n* short portable ladder or set of webbing loops **etriers**

ETTIN *n* giant **ettins**

ETTLE *vb* intend **ettled, ettles, ettling**

ETUDE *n* short musical composition for a solo instrument **etudes**

ETUI *n* small usually ornamented case **etuis, etwee, etwees**

ETYMA ▶ etymon

ETYMIC ▶ etymon

ETYMON *n* earliest form of a word or morpheme from which another is derived **etymons**

ETYPIC *n* unable to conform to type

EUCAIN = eucaine

EUCAINE *n* crystalline optically active substance

EUCAINS ▶ eucain

EUCHRE n US and Canadian card game ▷ vb prevent (a player) from making his contracted tricks **euchred, euchres**

EUCLASE n brittle green gem

EUCRITE n type of stony meteorite

EUDEMON n benevolent spirit or demon

EUGARIE another name for ▶ **pipi**

EUGE interj well done!

EUGENIA n plant of the clove family

EUGENIC > **eugenics**

EUGENOL n oily liquid used in perfumery

EUGH archaic form of ▶ **yew**

EUGHEN archaic form of ▶ **yew**

EUGHS ▶ eugh

EUGLENA n type of freshwater unicellular organism

EUK vb itch **euked, euking, euks**

EULOGIA n blessed bread

This is one of the few 7-letter words that use all the vowels. What's more, it can take a plural in E as well as S, giving **eulogiae**, which can be great for getting you out of vowel trouble.

EULOGY n

EUMONG = eumung

EUMONGS ▶ eumong

EUMUNG n any of various Australian acacias **eumungs**

EUNUCH n **eunuchs**

EUOI n cry of Bacchic frenzy

This is a cry expressing Bacchic frenzy, and is forever coming in useful to dispose of a surplus of vowels. It has the less commonly played but still useful variants **evoe, evhoe** and **evohe**.

EUOUAE n musical term **euouaes**

This word is remarkable in containing no consonants. You will be surprised at how often you will be glad to play it!

EUPAD n antiseptic powder **eupads**

EUPEPSY = eupepsia

EUPHON n glass harmonica **euphons**

EUPHONY n pleasing sound

EUPHORY = euphoria

EUPHROE n wooden block through which the lines of a crowfoot are rove

EUPLOID adj having chromosomes in an exact multiple of the haploid number ▷ n euploid cell or individual

EUPNEA = eupnoea

EUPNEAS ▶ eupnea

EUPNEIC ▶ eupnoea

EUPNOEA n normal relaxed breathing

EUREKA n **eurekas**

EURIPI ▶ euripus

EURIPUS n strait or channel with a strong current or tide

EURO n

EUROKY n ability of an organism to live under different conditions

EUROPOP n type of pop music by European artists

EUROS ▶ euro

EURYOKY = euroky

EUSOL n solution of eupad in water **eusols**

EUSTACY > **eustatic**

EUSTASY > **eustatic**

EUSTELE n central cylinder of a seed plant

EUSTYLE n building with columns optimally spaced

EUTAXIA n condition of being easily melted

EUTAXY n good order

EUTEXIA = eutaxia

EUTROPY n chemical structure

EVACUEE n person evacuated from a place of danger

EVADE vb **evaded, evader, evaders, evades, evading**

EVANGEL n gospel of Christianity

EVANISH poetic word for ▸ **vanish**

EVASION n

EVASIVE adj

EVE n

EVEJAR n nightjar **evejars**

EVEN adj, adv, vb, n **evened, evener, eveners, evenest**

EVENING n, adj

EVENLY ▸ even

EVENS adv (of a bet) winning the same as the amount staked if successful

EVENT n, vb **evented**

EVENTER ▸ eventing

EVENTS ▸ event

EVER adv

EVERNET n hypothetical form of internet

EVERT vb turn (some bodily part) outwards or inside out **everted**

EVERTOR n any muscle that turns a part outwards

EVERTS ▸ evert

EVERY adj

EVES ▸ eve

EVET n eft **evets**

EVHOE interj cry of Bacchic frenzy

EVICT vb **evicted, evictee, evictor, evicts**

EVIDENT adj, n

EVIL n, adj, adv **eviler, evilest, eviller, evilly, evils**

EVINCE vb **evinced, evinces**

EVIRATE vb castrate

EVITATE archaic word for ▸ **avoid**

EVITE archaic word for ▸ **avoid**

EVITED ▸ evite

EVITES ▸ evite

EVITING ▸ evite

EVO informal word for ▸ **evening**

EVOCATE vb evoke

EVOE interj cry of Bacchic frenzy

EVOHE interj cry of Bacchic frenzy

EVOKE vb **evoked, evoker, evokers, evokes, evoking**

EVOLUE n colonial term for an African educated according to European principles **evolues**

EVOLUTE n geometric curve ▷ adj having the margins rolled outwards ▷ vb evolve

EVOLVE vb **evolved, evolver, evolves**

EVOS ▸ evo

EVOVAE n mnemonic used in sacred music **evovaes**

EVULSE vb extract by force **evulsed, evulses**

EVZONE n soldier in an elite Greek infantry regiment **evzones**

EWE n

EWER n **ewers**

EWES ▸ ewe

EWEST Scots word for ▸ **near**

EWFTES Spenserian plural of ▸ **eft**

EWGHEN archaic form of

▸ **yew**

EWHOW interj expression of pity or regret

EWK vb itch **ewked, ewking, ewks**

> Ewk is a dialect word for itch. It's a handy little word and a good one to remember in case you end up with both K and W, and remember that it's a verb so you can have **ewks, ewked** and **ewking**. It's also worth knowing its variants **euk, yeuk, youk, yuck** and **yuke**.

EWT archaic form of ▸ **newt**

EWTS ▸ ewt

EX prep not including ▷ n former husband, wife etc ▷ vb cross out or delete

EXABYTE n very large unit of computer memory

EXACT adj, vb

EXACTA n horse-racing bet **exactas**

EXACTED ▸ exact

EXACTER ▸ exact

EXACTLY adv, interj

EXACTOR ▸ exact

EXACTS ▸ exact

EXACUM n type of tropical plant **exacums**

EXALT vb

EXALTED adj

EXALTER ▸ exalt

EXALTS ▸ exalt

EXAM n

EXAMEN n examination of conscience **examens**

EXAMINE vb

EXAMPLE n

EXAMS ▸ exam

EXAPTED adj biologically adapted

EXARATE adj (of the pupa of some insects) having legs, wings, antennae, etc, free and movable

EXARCH n head of certain autonomous Orthodox Christian Churches ▸ adj (of a xylem strand) having the first-formed xylem external to that formed later **exarchs**

EXARCHY = exarchate

EXCAMB vb exchange **excambs**

EXCEED vb exceeds

EXCEL vb excels

EXCEPT prep, vb excepts

EXCERPT n, vb

EXCESS n, vb

EXCHEAT = escheat

EXCIDE vb cut out excided, excides

EXCIMER n excited dimer which would remain dissociated in the ground state

EXCIPLE n part of a lichen

EXCISE n, vb excised, excises

EXCITE vb

EXCITED adj

EXCITER n person or thing that excites

EXCITES ▸ excite

EXCITON n excited electron bound to the hole produced by its excitation

EXCITOR n type of nerve

EXCLAIM vb

EXCLAVE n territory owned by a country, but surrounded by another

EXCLUDE vb

EXCRETA n excrement

EXCRETE vb

EXCUDIT sentence substitute (named person) made this

EXCURSE vb wander

EXCUSAL ▸ excuse

EXCUSE n, vb excused, excuser, excuses

EXEAT n leave of absence from school or some other institution **exeats**

EXEC n executive **execs**

EXECUTE vb

EXED ▸ ex

EXEDRA n building, room, portico, or apse containing a continuous bench **exedrae**

EXEEM = exeme

EXEEMED ▸ exeem

EXEEMS ▸ exeem

EXEGETE n person who practises exegesis

EXEME vb set free exemed, exemes, exeming

EXCITED adj

EXEMPLA > exemplum

EXEMPLE = example

EXEMPT adj, vb, n exempts

EXEQUY n funeral rite
Meaning a funeral rite, this word combines X and Q. Even better is its plural **exequies**, which would earn an extra 50 points for using all your tiles.

EXERGUE n space on the reverse of a coin or medal

EXERGY n maximum amount of useful work obtainable from a system

EXERT vb exerted, exerts

EXES ▸ ex

EXEUNT vb (they) go out

EXHALE vb exhaled, exhales

EXHAUST vb, n

EXHEDRA = exedra

EXHIBIT vb, n

EXHORT vb exhorts

EXHUME vb exhumed, exhumer, exhumes

EXIES n hysterics

EXIGENT adj urgent ▸ n emergency

EXILE n, vb exiled, exiler, exilers, exiles, exilian, exilic, exiling

EXILITY n poverty or meagreness

EXINE n outermost coat of a pollen grain or a spore **exines**

EXING ▸ ex
EXIST *vb* existed, exists
EXIT *n, vb* exited, exiting, exits
EXO *informal word for* ▸ **excellent**
> Exo is an informal Australian way of saying excellent. This is a great little word as it allows you to combine X with two of the most common tiles in the game, E and O.
EXOCARP = epicarp
EXODE *n* exodus
EXODERM = ectoderm
EXODES ▸ exode
EXODIC ▸ exode
EXODIST ▸ exodus
EXODOI ▸ exodus
EXODOS *n* processional song performed at the end of a play
EXODUS *n*
EXOGAMY *n* act of marrying a person from another tribe, clan, etc
EXOGEN *n* type of plant exogens
EXOMION = exomis
EXOMIS *n* sleeveless jacket
EXON *n* one of the officers who command the Yeomen of the Guard **exonic, exons**
EXONYM *n* name given to a place by foreigners exonyms
EXOPOD = exopodite

EXOPODS ▸ exopod
EXORDIA ▸ exordium
EXOSMIC ▸ exosmosis
EXOTIC *adj, n*
EXOTICA *pl n* (collection of) exotic objects
EXOTICS ▸ exotic
EXOTISM ▸ exotic
EXPAND *vb* expands
EXPANSE *n*
EXPAT *n* short for expats
EXPECT *vb* expects
EXPEL *vb* expels
EXPEND *vb* expends
EXPENSE *n*
EXPERT *n, adj, vb* experts
EXPIATE *vb*
EXPIRE *vb* expired, expirer, expires
EXPIRY *n* end, esp of a contract period
EXPLAIN *vb*
EXPLANT *vb* transfer (living tissue) from its natural site to a new site or to a culture medium ▸ *n* piece of tissue treated in this way
EXPLODE *vb*
EXPLOIT *vb, n*
EXPLORE *vb*
EXPO *n* exposition, large public exhibition
EXPORT *n, vb* exports
EXPOS ▸ expo
EXPOSAL ▸ expose
EXPOSE *vb, n*
EXPOSED *adj* not concealed
EXPOSER ▸ expose
EXPOSES ▸ expose

EXPOSIT *vb* state
EXPOUND *vb*
EXPRESS *vb, adj, n, adv*
EXPUGN *vb* storm expugns
EXPULSE *vb* expel
EXPUNCT *vb* expunge
EXPUNGE *vb*
EXPURGE *vb* purge
EXSCIND *vb* cut off or out
EXSECT *vb* cut out exsects
EXSERT *vb* thrust out ▸ *adj* protruded or stretched out from (something) exserts
EXTANT *adj*
EXTASY = ecstasy
EXTATIC = ecstatic
EXTEND *vb* extends
EXTENSE *adj* extensive
EXTENT *n* extents
EXTERN *n* person with an official connection to an institution but does not reside in it externe, externs
EXTINCT *adj, vb*
EXTINE = exine
EXTINES ▸ extine
EXTIRP *vb* extirpate extirps
EXTOL *vb* extold, extoll
EXTOLLS ▸ extoll
EXTOLS ▸ extol
EXTORT *vb* extorts
EXTRA *adj, n, adv*
EXTRACT *vb, n*
EXTRAIT *n* extracts
EXTRAS ▸ extra
EXTREAT *n* extraction
EXTREMA > extremum
EXTREME *adj, n*

EXTRUDE vb

EXUDATE = exudation

EXUDE vb exuded, exudes, exuding

EXUL n exile exuls

EXULT vb exulted, exults

EXURB n residential area beyond suburbs

EXURBAN ▶ exurbia

EXURBIA n region outside the suburbs of a city

EXURBS ▶ exurb

EXUVIA n cast-off exoskeleton of animal exuviae, exuvial

EXUVIUM n cast-off exoskeleton of animal

EYALET n province of Ottoman Empire eyalets

EYAS n nestling hawk or falcon eyases, eyass

EYASSES ▶ eyass

EYE n, vb

EYEABLE adj pleasant to look at

EYEBALL n, vb

EYEBANK n place in which corneas are stored

EYEBAR n bar with flattened ends with holes for connecting pins eyebars

EYEBATH = eyecup

EYEBEAM n glance

EYEBOLT n type of threaded bolt

EYEBROW n, vb

EYECUP = eyebath

EYECUPS ▶ eyecup

EYED ▶ eye

EYEFOLD n fold of skin above eye

EYEFUL n view eyefuls

EYEHOLE n hole through which something is passed

EYEHOOK n hook attached to a ring at the extremity of a rope or chain

EYEING ▶ eye

EYELASH n

EYELESS ▶ eye

EYELET n, vb eyelets

EYELIAD = oeillade

EYELID n eyelids

EYELIFT n cosmetic surgery for eyes

EYELIKE ▶ eye

EYEN pl n eyes

EYER n someone who eyes eyers

EYES ▶ eye

EYESHOT n range of vision

EYESOME adj attractive

EYESORE n

EYESPOT n small area of pigment

EYEWASH n nonsense

EYEWEAR n spectacles; glasses

EYEWINK n wink of the eye; instant

EYING ▶ eye

EYLIAD = oeillade

EYLIADS ▶ eyliad

EYNE poetic plural of ▶ eye

EYOT n island eyots

EYRA n reddish-brown variety of the jaguarondi eyras

EYRE n obsolete circuit court eyres

EYRIE n eyries

EYRIR n Icelandic monetary unit

EYRY = eyrie**

Ff

F is a useful letter in Scrabble: it begins three two-letter words (**fa, fe** and **fy**). There are also quite a few words that combine **F** with **X** or **Z**, allowing high scores, particularly if you can hit a bonus square with them. **Fax, fix** and **fox** are good examples (13 points each), and don't forget **fez** and **fiz** (15 points each). **Fay, fey, fly, foy** and **fry** can also be used (9 each).

FA = fah

FAA *Scot word for* ▶ **fall**

FAAING ▶ faa

FAAN ▶ faa

FAAS ▶ faa

FAB *adj* excellent ▷ *n* fabrication **fabber, fabbest**

FABBIER ▶ fabby

FABBY = fab

FABLE *n, vb*

FABLED *adj*

FABLER ▶ fable

FABLERS ▶ fable

FABLES ▶ fable

FABLIAU *n* comic usually ribald verse tale

FABLING ▶ fable

FABRIC *n, vb* **fabrics**

FABS ▶ fab

FABULAR *adj* relating to fables

FACADE *n* **facades**

FACE *n, vb*

FACEBAR *n* wrestling hold

FACED ▶ face

FACEMAN *n* miner who works at the coalface **facemen**

FACER *n* difficulty or problem **facers**

FACES ▶ face

FACET *n, vb*

FACETE *adj* witty and humorous

FACETED ▶ facet

FACETS ▶ facet

FACEUP *adj* with the face or surface exposed

FACIA = fascia

FACIAE ▶ facia

FACIAL *adj, n* **facials**

FACIAS ▶ facia

FACIEND *n* multiplicand

FACIES *n* general form and appearance

FACILE *adj*

FACING *n* lining or covering for decoration or reinforcement **facings**

FACONNE *adj* denoting a fabric with the design woven in ▷ *n* such a fabric

FACT *n* factful

FACTICE *n* soft rubbery material

FACTION *n*

FACTIS *variant of* ▶ factice

FACTIVE *adj* giving rise to the presupposition that a sentence is true

FACTOID *n* piece of unreliable information believed to be true

FACTOR *n, vb* **factors**

FACTORY *n*

FACTS ▶ fact

FACTUAL *adj* concerning facts rather than opinions or theories

FACTUM *n* something done, deed **factums**

FACTURE *n* construction

FACULA n any of the bright areas on the sun's surface **faculae, facular**

FACULTY n

FAD n

FADABLE ▶ fade

FADAISE n silly remark

FADDIER ▶ faddy

FADDISH ▶ fad

FADDISM ▶ fad

FADDIST ▶ fad

FADDLE vb mess around, toy with **faddled, faddles**

FADDY adj

FADE vb, n faded, **fadedly**

FADEIN n gradual appearance of image on film **fadeins**

FADEOUT n gradual disappearance of image on film

FADER ▶ fade

FADERS ▶ fade

FADES ▶ fade

FADEUR n blandness, insipidness **fadeurs**

FADGE vb agree ▷ n package of wool in a wool-bale **fadged, fadges, fadging**

FADIER ▶ fady

FADIEST ▶ fady

FADING n variation in strength of received radio signals **fadings**

FADLIKE ▶ fad

FADO n type of melancholy Portuguese folk song **fados**

FADS ▶ fad

FADY adj faded

FAE Scot word for ▶ from

FAECAL adj of, relating to, or consisting of faeces

FAECES pl n

FAENA n a matador's final actions before the kill **faenas**

FAERIE n land of fairies

FAERIES ▶ faery

FAERY = faerie

FAFF vb dither or fuss **faffed, faffing, faffs**

FAG = faggot

FAGGED ▶ fag

FAGGING ▶ fag

FAGGOT n, vb faggots

FAGIN n criminal **fagins**

FAGOT = faggot

FAGOTED ▶ fagot

FAGOTER ▶ fagot

FAGOTS ▶ fagot

FAGOTTI ▶ fagotto

FAGOTTO n bassoon

FAGS ▶ fag

FAH n (in tonic sol-fa) fourth degree of any major scale

FAHLERZ n copper ore

FAHLORE n copper ore

FAHS ▶ fah

FAIBLE variant of ▶ foible

FAIBLES ▶ faible

FAIENCE n tin-glazed earthenware

FAIK vb grasp **faiked, faikes, faiking, faiks**

FAIL vb, n failed

FAILING n, prep

FAILLE n soft light ribbed fabric of silk, rayon, or taffeta **failles**

FAILS ▶ fail

FAILURE n

FAIN adv, adj **faine, fained, fainer**

FAINES ▶ faine

FAINEST ▶ fain

FAINING ▶ fain

FAINLY ▶ fain

FAINNE n badge worn by advocates of the Irish language **fainnes**

FAINS ▶ fainites

FAINT adj, vb, n **fainted, fainter, faintly, faints, fainty**

FAIR adj, adv, n, vb **faired, fairer, fairest**

FAIRIES ▶ fairy

FAIRILY ▶ fairy

FAIRING n structure fitted round part of a vehicle to reduce drag

FAIRISH adj moderately good, well, etc

FAIRLY adv moderately

FAIRS ▶ fair

FAIRWAY n

FAIRY n

FAITH n

FAITHED adj having faith or a faith

FAITHER Scot word for ▶ father

FAITHS ▶ faith

FAITOR n traitor, impostor **faitors**

FAITOUR n impostor

FAIX interj have faith

FAJITA ▶ fajitas

FAJITAS pl n Mexican dish

FAKE vb, n, adj faked

FAKEER = fakir

FAKERS ▶ fakeer

FAKER, fakers, fakery, fakes ▶ fake

FAKEY *adj, adv* (of a skateboarding or snowboarding manoeuvre) travelling backwards **fakie, fakier**

FAKIES ▶ fakie

FAKIEST ▶ fakey

FAKING ▶ fake

FAKIR *n* Muslim who spurns worldly possessions **fakirs**

FALAFEL *n* ball or cake made from chickpeas

FALAJ *n* kind of irrigation channel in ancient Oman

FALBALA *n* gathered flounce, frill, or ruffle

FALCADE *n* movement of a horse

FALCATE *adj* shaped like a sickle

FALCES ▶ falx

FALCON *n* **falcons**

FALCULA *n* sharp curved claw, esp of a bird

FALDAGE *n* feudal right

FALL *vb, n*

FALLACY *n*

FALLAL *n* showy ornament, trinket, or article of dress **fallals**

FALLEN ▶ fall

FALLER *n* any device that falls or operates machinery by falling **fallers**

FALLING ▶ fall

FALLOFF *n* decline or drop

FALLOUT *n, vb, sentence substitute*

FALLOW *adj, n, vb* **fallows**

FALLS ▶ fall

FALSE *adj, adv, vb* **falsed, falsely, falser**

FALSERS *n* colloquial term for false teeth

FALSES ▶ false

FALSEST ▶ false

FALSIE *n* pad used to enlarge breast shape **falsies**

FALSIFY *vb*

FALSING ▶ false

FALSISH ▶ false

FALSISM ▶ false

FALSITY *n* state of being false

FALTER *vb, n* **falters**

FALX *n* sickle-shaped anatomical structure

FAME *n, vb* **famed, fames**

FAMILLE *n* type of Chinese porcelain

FAMILY *n, adj*

FAMINE *n* **famines**

FAMING ▶ fame

FAMISH *vb* be or make very hungry or weak

FAMOUS *adj, vb*

FAMULI ▶ famulus

FAMULUS *n* (formerly) the attendant of a sorcerer or scholar

FAN *n, vb*

FANAL *n* lighthouse **fanals**

FANATIC *n, adj*

FANBASE *n* body of admirers

FANBOY *n* obsessive fan

of a subject or hobby **fanboys**

FANCIED *adj* imaginary

FANCIER *n* person interested in plants or animals

FANCIES ▶ fancy

FANCIFY *vb* make more beautiful

FANCILY ▶ fancy

FANCY *adj, n, vb*

FAND *vb* try **fanded, fanding**

FANDOM *n* collectively, the fans of a sport, pastime or person **fandoms**

FANDS ▶ fand

FANE *n* temple or shrine

FANEGA *n* Spanish unit of measurement **fanegas**

FANES ▶ fane

FANFARE *n, vb*

FANFIC *n* fiction based on work by other authors **fanfics**

FANFOLD *vb* fold (paper) like a fan

FANG *n, vb*

FANGA = **fanga**

FANGAS ▶ fanga

FANGED ▶ fang

FANGING ▶ fang

FANGLE *vb* fashion **fangled, fangles**

FANGO *n* mud from thermal springs in Italy **fangos**

FANGS ▶ fang

FANION *n* small flag used by surveyors **fanions**

FANJET = **turbofan**

FANJETS ▶ fanjet

FANK n sheep pen

FANKLE vb entangle ▷ n tangle **fankled, fankles**

FANKS ▶ fank

FANLIKE ▶ fan

FANNED ▶ fan

FANNEL n ecclesiastical vestment **fannell, fannels**

FANNER ▶ fan

FANNERS ▶ fan

FANNING ▶ fan

FANO = fanon

FANON n collar-shaped vestment **fanons**

FANOS ▶ fano

FANS ▶ fan

FANSITE n website aimed at fans of a celebrity, film, etc

FANSUB n fansubs

FANTAD n nervous, agitated state **fantads**

FANTAIL n

FANTASM archaic spelling of ▶ phantasm

FANTAST n dreamer or visionary

FANTASY n, adj, vb

FANTEEG n nervous, agitated state

FANTOD n crotchety or faddish behaviour **fantods**

FANTOM archaic spelling of ▶ phantom

FANTOMS ▶ fantom

FANUM n temple **fanums**

FANWISE adj like a fan

FANWORT n aquatic plant

FANZINE n magazine produced by fans

FAP adj drunk

FAQIR = fakir

> Meaning a Hindu ascetic, this is one of those invaluable words allowing you to play the Q without a U. It can also be spelt **fakeer, fakir** and **faquir**.

FAQIRS ▶ faqir

FAQUIR variant of ▶ faqir

FAQUIRS ▶ faquir

FAR adv, adj, vb

FARAD n unit of electrical capacitance

FARADAY n quantity of electricity

FARADIC adj of an intermittent asymmetric alternating current

FARADS ▶ farad

FARAND adj pleasant or attractive in manner or appearance

FARAWAY adj very distant

FARCE n, vb **farced**

FARCER = farceur

FARCERS ▶ farcer

FARCES ▶ farce

FARCEUR n writer of or performer in farces

FARCI adj (of food) stuffed **farcie**

FARCIED adj afflicted with farcy

FARCIES ▶ farcy

FARCIFY vb turn into a farce

FARCIN n equine disease

FARCING ▶ farce

FARCINS ▶ farcin

FARCY n form of glanders, a bacterial disease of horses

FARD n paint for the face, esp white paint ▷ vb paint (the face) with fard

FARDAGE n material laid beneath or between cargo

FARDED ▶ fard

FARDEL n bundle or burden **fardels**

FARDEN n farthing **fardens**

FARDING ▶ fard

FARDS ▶ fard

FARE n, vb

FAREBOX n box where money for bus fares is placed

FARED, farer, farers, fares ▶ fare

FARFAL = felafel

FARFALS ▶ farfal

FARFEL = felafel

FARFELS ▶ farfel

FARFET adj far-fetched

FARINA n flour or meal made from any kind of cereal grain **farinas**

FARING ▶ fare

FARINHA n cassava meal

FARL n thin cake of oatmeal, often triangular in shape **farle**

FARLES ▶ farle

FARLS ▶ farl

FARM n, vb

FARMED adj (of fish or game) reared on a farm

FARMER n person who owns or runs a farm **farmers**

FARMERY n farm buildings

FARMING n business or skill of agriculture

FARMOST ▶ far

FARMS ▶ farm

FARNESS ▶ far

FARO n gambling game **faros**

FARRAGO n jumbled mixture of things

FARRAND variant of ▶ farand

FARRANT variant of ▶ farand

FARRED ▶ far

FARREN n allotted ground **farrens**

FARRIER n

FARRING ▶ far

FARROW n, vb, adj **farrows**

FARRUCA n flamenco dance performed by men

FARS ▶ far

FARSE vb insert into **farsed, farses**

FARSIDE n part of the Moon facing away from the Earth

FARSING ▶ farse

FARTHEL = farl

FARTHER ▶ far

FARTLEK n in sport, another name for interval training

FAS ▶ fa

FASCES pl n (in ancient Rome) a bundle of rods containing an axe

FASCI ▶ fascio

FASCIA n outer surface of a dashboard **fasciae, fascial, fascias**

FASCINE n bundle of long sticks used in construction

FASCIO n political group

FASCIS ▶ fasci

FASCISM n

FASCIST n adherent or practitioner of fascism ▷ adj characteristic of or relating to fascism

FASH n worry ▷ vb trouble **fashed**

FASHERY n difficulty, trouble

FASHES ▶ fash

FASHING ▶ fash

FASHION n, vb

FAST adj, adv, vb, n **fasted**

FASTEN vb **fastens**

FASTER, fasters, fastest ▶ fast

FASTI pl n in ancient Rome, business days

FASTIE n deceitful act **fasties**

FASTING, fastish, fastly, fasts ▶ fast

FAT adj having excess flesh on the body ▷ n extra flesh on the body

FATAL adj

FATALLY adv resulting in death or disaster

FATBACK n fat from the

upper part of a side of pork

FATBIRD n nocturnal bird

FATE n, vb

FATED adj

FATEFUL adj

FATES ▶ fate

FATHEAD n stupid person

FATHER n, vb **fathers**

FATHOM n, vb **fathoms**

FATIDIC adj prophetic

FATIGUE n, vb

FATING ▶ fate

FATLESS ▶ fat

FATLIKE ▶ fat

FATLING n young farm animal fattened for killing

FATLY ▶ fat

FATNESS ▶ fat

FATS ▶ fat

FATSIA n type of shrub **fatsias**

FATTED ▶ fat

FATTEN vb **fattens**

FATTER ▶ fat

FATTEST ▶ fat

FATTIER ▶ fatty

FATTIES ▶ fatty

FATTILY ▶ fatty

FATTING ▶ fat

FATTISH ▶ fat

FATTISM n discrimination on the basis of weight **fattist**

FATTY adj containing fat ▷ n fat person

FATUITY n foolish thoughtlessness

FATUOUS adj

FATWA n religious decree issued by a

Muslim leader ▷ vb issue a fatwa **fatwah**

FATWAHS ▶ fatwah

FATWAS ▶ fatwa

FATWOOD n wood used for kindling

FAUCAL adj of or relating to the fauces **faucals**

FAUCES n area of the mouth

FAUCET n **faucets**

FAUCHON variant of ▶ fauchion

FAUCIAL = faucal

FAUGH interj exclamation of disgust, scorn, etc

FAULD n piece of armour **faulds**

FAULT n, vb faulted, **faults**

FAULTY adj

FAUN n (in Roman legend) mythological creature

FAUNA n **faunae, faunal, faunas, faunist**

FAUNS ▶ faun

FAUNULA n fauna of a small single environment **faunule**

FAUR Scot word for ▶ far

FAURD adj favoured

FAURER ▶ faur

FAUREST ▶ faur

FAUT Scot word for ▶ fault

FAUTED ▶ faut

FAUTING ▶ faut

FAUTOR n patron **fautors**

FAUTS ▶ faut

FAUVE adj of the style of the Fauve art

movement ▷ n member of the Fauve art movement **fauves, fauvism**

FAUVIST n artist following the Fauve style of painting

FAUX adj false

FAVA n type of bean **favas**

FAVE short for ▶ favourite

FAVEL adj (of a horse) dun-coloured

FAVELA n (in Brazil) a shanty or shantytown **favelas**

FAVELL variant of ▶ favel

FAVELLA n group of spores

FAVER ▶ fave

FAVES ▶ fave

FAVEST ▶ fave

FAVICON n icon displayed before a website's URL

FAVISM n type of anaemia **favisms**

FAVOR = favour

FAVORED ▶ favor

FAVORER ▶ favour

FAVORS = favours

FAVOSE = faveolate

FAVOUR n, vb

FAVOURS pl n sexual intimacy

FAVOUS adj resembling honeycomb

FAVRILE n type of iridescent glass

FAVUS n infectious fungal skin disease **favuses**

FAW n gypsy

> A **faw** is a gypsy, a good word for taking advantage of a nearby bonus square.

FAWN n, adj, vb **fawned, fawner, fawners**

FAWNIER ▶ fawny

FAWNING ▶ fawn

FAWNS ▶ fawn

FAWNY adj of a fawn colour

FAWS ▶ faw

FAX n, vb **faxed, faxes, faxing**

FAY n fairy or sprite ▷ adj of or resembling a fay ▷ vb fit or be fitted closely or tightly **fayed**

> A **fay** is a fairy but it can also be a verb, meaning to fit directly. It has a variant **fey**. Both are useful high-scoring short words.

FAYENCE variant of ▶ faience

FAYER ▶ fay

FAYEST ▶ fay

FAYING ▶ fay

FAYNE vb pretend **fayned, faynes, fayning**

FAYRE pseudo-archaic spelling of ▶ fair

FAYRES ▶ fayre

FAYS ▶ fay

FAZE vb

FAZED adj worried or disconcerted

FAZENDA n large estate or ranch

FAZES ▸ faze

FAZING ▸ faze

FE n

FEAGUE vb whip or beat **feagued, feagues**

FEAL vb conceal **fealed, fealing, feals**

FEALTY n (in feudal society) subordinate's loyalty

FEAR n, vb

FEARE n companion, spouse

FEARED ▸ fear

FEARER ▸ fear

FEARERS ▸ fear

FEARES ▸ feare

FEARFUL adj

FEARING ▸ fear

FEARS ▸ fear

FEART adj

FEASE vb perform an act **feased, feases, feasing**

FEAST n, vb **feasted, feaster, feasts**

FEAT n **feated, feater, featest**

FEATHER n, vb

FEATING ▸ feat

FEATLY ▸ feat

FEATOUS variant of > **feateous**

FEATS ▸ feat

FEATURE n, vb

FEAZE = feeze

FEAZED ▸ feaze

FEAZES ▸ feaze

FEAZING ▸ feaze

FEBRILE adj very active and nervous

FECAL = faecal

FECES = faeces

FECHT Scot word for ▸ **fight**

FECHTER ▸ fecht

FECHTS ▸ fecht

FECIAL adj heraldic **fecials**

FECIT vb (he or she) made it

FECULA n type of starch **feculae, feculas**

FECUND adj fertile

FED n

FEDARIE n accomplice

FEDAYEE n (in Arab states) a commando

FEDERAL adj, n

FEDEX vb send by FedEx **fedexed, fedexes**

FEDORA n man's soft hat with a brim **fedoras**

FEDS ▸ fee

FEE n, vb

FEEB n contemptible person

FEEBLE adj, vb **feebled, feebler, feebles, feebly**

FEEBS ▸ feeb

FEED vb, n

FEEDBAG n any bag in which feed for livestock is sacked

FEEDBOX n trough, manger

FEEDER n baby's bib **feeders**

FEEDING ▸ feed

FEEDLOT n area where livestock are fattened rapidly

FEEDS ▸ feed

FEEING ▸ fee

FEEL vb, n

FEELBAD n something inducing depression

FEELER n feelers

FEELESS ▸ fee

FEELING ▸ feel

FEELS ▸ feel

FEEN n in Irish dialect, an informal word for 'man' **feens**

FEER vb make a furrow **feered**

FEERIE n fairyland **feeries**

FEERIN n furrow

FEERING ▸ feer

FEERINS ▸ feerin

FEERS ▸ feer

FEES ▸ fee

FEESE vb perturb **feesed, feeses, feesing**

FEET ▸ foot

FEEZE vb beat ▷ n rush **feezed, feezes, feezing**

FEG = fig

FEGARY variant of ▸ **vagary**

FEGS ▸ feg

FEH ▸ fe

FEHM n medieval German court **fehme, fehmic**

FEHS ▸ feh

FEIGN vb **feigned, feigner, feigns**

FEIJOA n evergreen myrtaceous shrub of S America **feijoas**

FEINT n, vb, adj **feinted, feinter**

FEINTS pl n leavings of the second distillation of Scotch malt whisky

FEIRIE *adj* nimble **feirier**

FEIS *n* Irish music and dance festival

FEIST *n* small aggressive dog **feists**

FEISTY *adj* showing courage or spirit

FELAFEL = falafel

FELICIA *n* type of African herb

FELID *n* any animal belonging to the cat family **felids**

FELINE *adj, n* **felines**

FELL *vb, adj*

FELLA nonstandard variant of ▶ **fellow**

FELLAH *n* peasant in Arab countries **fellahs**

FELLAS ▶ **fella**

FELLATE *vb* perform fellatio on (a person)

FELLED ▶ **fell**

FELLER *n* person or thing that fells **fellers**

FELLEST ▶ **fell**

FELLIES ▶ **felly**

FELLING ▶ **fell**

FELLOE *n* (segment of) the rim of a wheel **felloes**

FELLOW *n, adj* **fellows**

FELLS ▶ **fell**

FELLY = **felloe**

FELON *n, adj*

FELONRY *n* felons collectively

FELONS ▶ **felon**

FELONY *n* serious crime

FELSIC *adj* relating to igneous rock

FELSITE *n* any fine-grained igneous rock

FELSPAR = feldspar

FELT *n, vb* **felted**

FELTER *vb* mat together **felters**

FELTIER ▶ **felt**

FELTING *n* felted material

FELTS ▶ **felt**

FELTY ▶ **felt**

FELUCCA *n* narrow lateen-rigged vessel

FELWORT *n* type of plant

FEM *n* passive homosexual

FEMAL *adj* effeminate ▷ *n* effeminate person

FEMALE *adj, n* **females**

FEMALS ▶ **femal**

FEME *n* woman or wife **femes**

FEMINAL *adj* feminine, female

FEMINIE *n* women collectively

FEMITER variant of ▶ **fumitory**

FEMME *n* woman or wife **femmes**

FEMMIER ▶ **femmy**

FEMMY *adj* markedly or exaggeratedly feminine

FEMORA ▶ **femur**

FEMORAL *adj* of the thigh

FEMS ▶ **fem**

FEMUR *n* **femurs**

FEN *n*

FENAGLE variant of ▶ **finagle**

FENCE *n, vb* **fenced**

FENCER *n* person who fights with a sword **fencers**

FENCES ▶ **fence**

FENCING *n*

FEND *vb, n* **fended**

FENDER *n* **fenders**

FENDIER ▶ **fendy**

FENDING ▶ **fend**

FENDS ▶ **fend**

FENDY *adj* thrifty

FENI *n* Goan alcoholic drink **fenis**

FENITAR variant of ▶ **fumitory**

FENKS *n* whale blubber

FENLAND ▶ **fen**

FENMAN ▶ **fen**

FENMEN ▶ **fen**

FENNEC *n* type of nocturnal desert fox **fennecs**

FENNEL *n* **fennels**

FENNIER ▶ **fenny**

FENNIES ▶ **fenny**

FENNISH ▶ **fen**

FENNY *adj* boggy or marshy ▷ *n* **feni**

FENS ▶ **fen**

FENT *n* piece of waste fabric **fents**

FENURON *n* type of herbicide

FEOD = feud

FEODAL ▶ **feod**

FEODARY ▶ **feod**

FEODS ▶ **feod**

FEOFF = fief

FEOFFED ▶ **feoff**

FEOFFEE *n* (in feudal society) a vassal granted a fief by his lord

FEOFFER ▶ **feoff**

FEOFFOR ▶ **feoff**

FEOFFS ▶ **feoff**

FER = far

FERAL *adj, n* **ferals**

FERBAM n powder used as a fungicide **ferbams**

FERE n companion ▷ adj fierce **ferer, feres, ferest**

FERIA n weekday on which no feast occurs **feriae**

FERIAL adj of or relating to a feria

FERIAS ▶ feria

FERINE = feral

FERITY ▶ feral

FERLIE ▶ ferly

FERLIED ▶ ferly

FERLIER ▶ ferly

FERLIES ▶ ferly

FERLY adj wonderful ▷ n wonder ▷ vb wonder

FERM variant of ▶ farm

FERMATA another word for ▶ pause

FERMATE ▶ fermata

FERMENT n, vb

FERMI n unit of length

FERMION n type of particle

FERMIS ▶ fermi

FERMIUM n chemical element

FERMS ▶ ferm

FERN n

FERNERY n place where ferns are grown

FERNIER ▶ fern

FERNING n production of a fern-like pattern

FERNS ▶ fern

FERNY ▶ fern

FERRATE n type of salt

FERREL variant of ▶ ferrule

FERRELS ▶ ferrel

FERRET n, vb ferrets,

ferrety

FERRIC adj of or containing iron

FERRIED ▶ ferry

FERRIES ▶ ferry

FERRITE n type of ceramic compound

FERROUS adj

FERRUGO n disease affecting plants

FERRULE n metal cap to strengthen the end of a stick ▷ vb equip (a stick, etc) with a ferrule

FERRUM Latin word for ▶ iron

FERRUMS ▶ ferrum

FERRY n, vb

FERTILE adj

FERULA n large Mediterranean plant **ferulae, ferulas**

FERULE = ferrule

FERULED ▶ ferule

FERULES ▶ ferule

FERVENT adj fervid

FERVOR = fervour

FERVORS ▶ fervor

FERVOUR n

FES ▶ fe

FESCUE n pasture and lawn grass with stiff narrow leaves **fescues**

FESS = fesse

FESSE n horizontal band across a shield

FESSED ▶ fesse

FESSES ▶ fesse

FESSING ▶ fess

FEST n event at which the emphasis is on a particular activity

FESTA n festival

FESTAL adj festive ▷ n

festivity **festals**

FESTAS ▶ festa

FESTER vb, n festers

FESTIER ▶ festy

FESTIVE adj

FESTOON vb, n

FESTS ▶ fest

FESTY adj dirty

FET vb fetch

FETA n white salty Greek cheese

FETAL adj of, relating to, or resembling a fetus

FETAS ▶ feta

FETCH vb, n fetched

FETCHER n person or animal that fetches

FETCHES ▶ fetch

FETE n, vb feted, fetes

FETIAL n ancient Roman herald ▷ adj of or relating to the fetiales **fetials**

FETICH = fetish

FETICHE variant of ▶ fetich

FETID adj fetider, fetidly

FETING ▶ fete

FETISH n

FETLOCK n

FETOR n offensive stale or putrid odour **fetors**

FETS ▶ fet

FETT variant of ▶ fet

FETTA variant of ▶ feta

FETTAS ▶ fetta

FETTED ▶ fet

FETTER n, vb fetters

FETTING ▶ fet

FETTLE = fettling

FETTLED ▶ fettle

FETTLER n person employed to maintain railway tracks

FETTLES ▸ fettle

FETTS ▸ fett

FETUS n fetuses

FETWA variant of ▸ fatwa

FETWAS ▸ fetwa

FEU n (in Scotland) type of rent

FEUAR n tenant of a feu feuars

FEUD n, vb

FEUDAL adj of or like feudalism

FEUDARY n holder of land through feudal right

FEUDED ▸ feud

FEUDING ▸ feud

FEUDIST n person who takes part in a feud or quarrel

FEUDS ▸ feud

FEUED ▸ feu

FEUING ▸ feu

FEUS ▸ feu

FEUTRE vb place in a resting position feutred, feutres

FEVER n, vb fevered, fevers

FEW adj as in the few

FEWER ▸ few

FEWEST ▸ few

FEWMET variant of ▸ fumet

FEWMETS ▸ fewmet

FEWNESS ▸ few

FEWS ▸ few

FEWTER variant of ▸ feutre

FEWTERS ▸ feutre

FEY adj, vb feyed, feyer, feyest, feying, feyly, feyness, feys

FEZ n fezes

FEZZED adj wearing a fez

FEZZES ▸ fez

FEZZY ▸ fez

FIACRE n small four-wheeled horse-drawn carriage fiacres

FIANCE n man engaged to be married

FIANCEE n woman who is engaged to be married

FIANCES ▸ fiance

FIAR n property owner

FIARS n legally fixed price of corn

FIASCHI ▸ fiasco

FIASCO n fiascos

FIAT n, vb fiated, fiating, fiats

FIAUNT n fiat fiaunts

FIB n, vb fibbed, fibber, fibbers, fibbery, fibbing

FIBER = fibre

FIBERED ▸ fibre

FIBERS ▸ fiber

FIBRATE n drug used to lower fat levels in the body

FIBRE n fibred, fibres

FIBRIL n small fibre fibrils

FIBRIN n fibrins

FIBRO n mixture of cement and asbestos fibre

FIBROID adj, n

FIBROIN n tough elastic protein

FIBROMA n type of benign tumour

FIBROS ▸ fibro

FIBROSE vb become fibrous

FIBROUS adj consisting of, containing, or resembling fibres

FIBS ▸ fib

FIBSTER n fibber

FIBULA n fibulae, fibular, fibulas

FICE n small aggressive dog fices

FICHE n film for storing publications in miniature fiches

FICHU n woman's shawl or scarf fichus

FICIN n enzyme ficins

FICKLE adj, vb fickled, fickler, fickles, fickly

FICO n worthless trifle ficoes, ficos

FICTILE adj moulded or capable of being moulded from clay

FICTION n

FICTIVE adj of, relating to, or able to create fiction

FICTOR n sculptor fictors

FICUS n type of plant ficuses

FID n spike for separating strands of rope in splicing

FIDDLE n, vb fiddled

FIDDLER n person who plays the fiddle

FIDDLES ▸ fiddle

FIDDLEY n area of a vessel

FIDDLY adj

FIDEISM n theological doctrine fideist

FIDES n faith or trust

FIDGE obsolete word for ▶ fidget

FIDGED ▶ fidge

FIDGES ▶ fidge

FIDGET vb, n fidgets, fidgety

FIDGING ▶ fidge

FIDIBUS n spill for lighting a candle or pipe

FIDO n generic term for a dog fidos

FIDS ▶ fid

FIE adj ▶ fey

FIEF n land granted by a lord in return for war service

FIEFDOM n (in Feudal Europe) the property owned by a lord

FIEFS ▶ fief

FIELD n, vb fielded

FIELDER n

FIELDS ▶ field

FIEND n fiends

FIENT n fiend fients

FIER = fere

FIERCE adj fiercer

FIERE ▶ fere

FIERES ▶ fere

FIERIER ▶ fiery

FIERILY ▶ fiery

FIERS ▶ fier

FIERY adj

FIEST ▶ fie

FIESTA n fiestas

FIFE n, vb fifed, fifer, fifers, fifes, fifing

FIFTEEN n, adj, determiner

FIFTH n, adj, adv fifthly, fifths

FIFTIES ▶ fifty

FIFTY n, adj, determiner

FIG n, vb figged

FIGGERY n adornment, ornament

FIGGING ▶ fig

FIGHT vb, n

FIGHTER n

FIGHTS ▶ fight

FIGMENT n

FIGO variant of ▶ fico

FIGOS ▶ figo

FIGS ▶ fig

FIGURAL adj composed of or relating to human or animal figures

FIGURE n, vb

FIGURED adj decorated with a design

FIGURER ▶ figure

FIGURES ▶ figure

FIGWORT n N temperate plant

FIKE vb fidget fiked

FIKERY n fuss

FIKES ▶ fike

FIKIER ▶ fiky

FIKIEST ▶ fiky

FIKING ▶ fike

FIKISH adj fussy

FIKY adj fussy

FIL = fils

FILA ▶ filum

FILABEG variant of ▶ filibeg

FILACER n formerly, English legal officer

FILAR adj of thread

FILAREE n type of storksbill, a weed

FILARIA n type of parasitic nematode worm

FILASSE n vegetable fibre such as jute

FILAZER variant of ▶ filacer

FILBERD variant of ▶ filbert

FILBERT n hazelnut

FILCH vb filched, filcher, filches

FILE n, vb filed

FILEMOT n type of brown colour

FILER ▶ file

FILERS ▶ file

FILES ▶ file

FILET variant of ▶ fillet

FILETED ▶ filet

FILETS ▶ filet

FILFOT variant of ▶ fylfot

FILFOTS ▶ filfot

FILIAL adj

FILIATE vb fix judicially the paternity of (a child)

FILIBEG n kilt worn by Scottish Highlanders

FILII ▶ filius

> This plural of **filius**, a Latin word for son, is the only 5-letter word that lets you get rid of three I's!

FILING ▶ file

FILINGS pl n

FILIUS n son

FILL vb

FILLE n girl

FILLED ▶ fill

FILLER n fillers

FILLES ▶ fille

FILLET n, vb fillets

FILLIES ▶ filly

FILLING n, adj

FILLIP n, vb fillips

FILLO variant of ▶ filo

FILLOS ▶ fillo

FILLS ▶ fill

FILLY n

FILM n, vb, adj

FILMDOM n cinema industry

FILMED ▶ film

FILMER n film-maker **filmers**

FILMI adj of or relating to Indian films

FILMIC adj of or suggestive of films or the cinema

FILMIER ▶ filmy

FILMILY ▶ filmy

FILMING ▶ film

FILMIS ▶ filmi

FILMISH ▶ film

FILMS ▶ film

FILMSET vb set (type matter) by filmsetting

FILMY adj

FILO n type of flaky Greek pastry in very thin sheets **filos**

FILOSE adj resembling a thread or threadlike process

FILS n monetary unit of Bahrain, Iraq, Jordan, and Kuwait

FILTER n, vb **filters**

FILTH n **filths**

FILTHY adj characterized by or full of filth ▷ adv extremely

FILTRE adj as in cafe filtre a strong black filtered coffee

FILUM n any threadlike structure or part

FIMBLE n male plant of the hemp **fimbles**

FIMBRIA n fringe or fringelike margin or border

FIN n, vb

FINABLE adj liable to a fine

FINAGLE vb get or achieve by craftiness or trickery

FINAL adj, n

FINALE n finales

FINALIS n musical finishing note

FINALLY adv

FINALS pl n deciding part of a competition

FINANCE vb, n

FINBACK another name for ▶ rorqual

FINCA n Spanish villa **fincas**

FINCH n

FINCHED adj with streaks or spots on the back

FINCHES ▶ finch

FIND vb discover by chance ▷ n person or thing found, esp when valuable

FINDER n small telescope fitted to a larger one **finders**

FINDING ▶ find

FINDRAM variant of ▶ finnan

FINDS ▶ find

FINE adj, n, vb **fined**

FINEER variant of ▶ veneer

FINEERS ▶ fineer

FINEISH ▶ fine

FINELY adv into small pieces

FINER ▶ fine

FINERS ▶ fine

FINERY n

FINES ▶ fine

FINESSE n, vb

FINEST ▶ fine

FINFISH n fish with fins, as opposed to shellfish

FINFOOT n type of aquatic bird

FINGAN variant of ▶ finjan

FINGANS ▶ fingan

FINGER n, vb **fingers**

FINI n end; finish

FINIAL n ornament at the apex of a gable or spire **finials**

FINICAL another word for ▶ finicky

FINICKY adj finikin

FINING n process of removing bubbles from molten glass **finings**

FINIS ▶ fini

FINISES ▶ finis

FINISH vb, n

FINITE adj, n finites

FINITO adj finished

FINJAN n small, handleless coffee cup **finjans**

FINK n strikebreaker ▷ vb inform (on someone), as to the police **finked, finking, finks**

FINLESS ▶ fin

FINLIKE ▶ fin

FINMARK n monetary unit of Finland

FINNAC variant of ▶ finnock

FINNACK *variant of* ▸ **finnock**

FINNACS ▸ **finnac**

FINNAN *n* smoked haddock **finnans**

FINNED ▸ **fin**

FINNER *another name for* ▸ **rorqual**

FINNERS ▸ **finner**

FINNIER ▸ **finny**

FINNING ▸ **fin**

FINNOCK *n* young sea trout on its first return to fresh water

FINNSKO *variant of* > **finnesko**

FINNY *adj* relating to or containing many fishes

FINO *n* very dry sherry **finos**

FINS ▸ **fin**

FINSKO *variant of* > **finnesko**

FIORD = **fjord**

FIORDS ▸ **fiord**

FIORIN *n* type of temperate perennial grass **fiorins**

FIPPLE *n* wooden plug forming a flue in the end of a pipe **fipples**

FIQH *n* Islamic jurisprudence **fiqhs**

FIQUE *n* hemp **fiques**

FIR *n*

FIRE *n, vb*

FIREARM *n*

FIREBOX *n* furnace chamber of a boiler in a steam locomotive

FIREBUG *n* person who deliberately sets fire to property

FIRED ▸ **fire**

FIREDOG *n* either of two metal stands supporing logs in a fire

FIREFLY *n*

FIRELIT *adj* lit by firelight

FIREMAN *n* **firemen**

FIREPAN *n* metal container for a fire in a room

FIREPOT *n* Chinese fondue-like cooking pot

FIRER ▸ **fire**

FIRERS ▸ **fire**

FIRES ▸ **fire**

FIRIE *n* in Australian English, informal word for a firefighter **firies**

FIRING *n* discharge of a firearm **firings**

FIRK *vb* beat **firked**

FIRKIN *n* small wooden barrel or similar container

FIRKING ▸ **firk**

FIRKINS ▸ **firkin**

FIRKS ▸ **firk**

FIRLOT *n* unit of measurement for grain **firlots**

FIRM *adj, adv, vb, n*

FIRMAN *n* edict of an Oriental sovereign **firmans**

FIRMED, firmer, firmers, firmest, firming, firmly, firms ▸ **firm**

FIRN *another name for* ▸ **neve**

FIRNS ▸ **firn**

FIRRIER ▸ **firry**

FIRRING *n* wooden battens used in building construction

FIRRY *adj* of, relating to, or made from fir trees

FIRS ▸ **fir**

FIRST *adj* earliest in time or order ▸ *n* person or thing coming before all others ▸ *adv* before anything else

FIRSTLY *adv* coming before other points, questions, etc

FIRSTS *pl n* saleable goods of the highest quality

FIRTH *n* narrow inlet of the sea, esp in Scotland **firths**

FIRWOOD *n* wood of the fir tree

FISC *n* state or royal treasury

FISCAL *adj, n* **fiscals**

FISCS ▸ **fisc**

FISGIG *variant of* ▸ **fishgig**

FISGIGS ▸ **fisgig**

FISH *n, vb* **fished**

FISHER *n* fisherman **fishers**

FISHERY *n*

FISHES ▸ **fish**

FISHEYE *n* type of lens

FISHFUL *adj* teeming with fish

FISHGIG *n* pole with barbed prongs for impaling fish

FISHIER ▸ **fishy**

FISHIFY *vb* change into fish

FISHILY ▸ fishy

FISHING n job or pastime of catching fish

FISHNET n open mesh fabric resembling netting

FISHWAY n fish ladder

FISHY adj

FISK vb frisk **fisked, fisking, fisks**

FISSATE ▸ fissate

FISSILE adj

FISSION n

FISSIVE ▸ fissile

FISSLE vb rustle **fissled, fissles**

FISSURE n, vb

FIST n, vb **fisted**

FISTFUL n quantity that can be held in a fist or hand

FISTIC adj of or relating to fisticuffs or boxing

FISTIER ▸ fist

FISTING ▸ fist

FISTS ▸ fist

FISTULA n long narrow ulcer

FISTY ▸ fist

FIT vb be appropriate or suitable for ▷ adj appropriate ▷ n way in which something fits

FITCH n fur of the polecat or ferret

FITCHE adj pointed **fitchee**

FITCHES ▸ fitch

FITCHET ▸ fitch

FITCHEW archaic name for ▸ polecat

FITCHY = fitche

FITFUL adj

FITLIER ▸ fitly

FITLY adv in a proper manner or place or at a proper time

FITMENT n accessory attached to a machine

FITNA n state of trouble or chaos **fitnas**

FITNESS n state of being fit

FITS ▸ fit

FITT n song **fitte**

FITTED ▸ fit

FITTER ▸ fit

FITTERS ▸ fit

FITTES ▸ fitte

FITTEST ▸ fit

FITTING ▸ fit

FITTS ▸ fitt

FIVE n, adj, determiner

FIVEPIN > fivepins

FIVER n five-pound note **fivers**

FIVES n ball game resembling squash

FIX vb, n **fixable**

FIXATE vb become or cause to become fixed **fixated, fixates**

FIXATIF variant of > fixative

FIXED adj attached or placed so as to be immovable **fixedly**

FIXER n solution used to make a photographic image permanent **fixers**

FIXES ▸ fix

FIXING n means of attaching one thing to another

FIXINGS pl n apparatus

or equipment

FIXIT n solution to a complex problem

FIXITY n

FIXIVE ▸ fix

FIXT adj fixed

FIXTURE n

FIXURE n firmness **fixures**

FIZ variant of ▸ fizz

FIZGIG vb inform on someone to the police **fizgigs**

FIZZ vb, n **fizzed**

FIZZEN variant of ▸ foison

FIZZENS ▸ fizzen

FIZZER n anything that fizzes **fizzers**

FIZZES ▸ fizz

FIZZGIG variant of ▸ fishgig

FIZZIER ▸ fizz

FIZZING ▸ fizz

FIZZLE vb, n **fizzled, fizzles**

FIZZY ▸ fizz

FJELD n high rocky plateau **fjelds**

FJORD n fjordic, fjords

FLAB n

FLABBY adj

FLABS ▸ flab

FLACCID adj

FLACK vb flutter **flacked**

FLACKER vb flutter like a bird

FLACKET n flagon

FLACKS ▸ flack

FLACON n small stoppered bottle or flask **flacons**

FLAFF vb flap **flaffed**

FLAFFER vb flutter
FLAFFS ▶ flaff
FLAG n, vb flagged, flagger
FLAGGY adj drooping
FLAGMAN n person who has charge of a flag flagmen
FLAGON n flagons
FLAGS ▶ flag
FLAIL vb, n flailed, flails
FLAIR n flairs
FLAK n
FLAKE n, vb flaked, flaker, flakers, flakes
FLAKEY = flaky
FLAKIER ▶ flaky
FLAKIES n dandruff
FLAKILY ▶ flaky
FLAKING ▶ flake
FLAKS ▶ flak
FLAKY adj like or made of flakes
FLAM n falsehood, deception, or sham ▷ vb cheat or deceive
FLAMBE vb cook or serve (food) in flaming brandy ▷ adj (of food) served in flaming brandy flambee, flambes
FLAME n, vb flamed
FLAMEN n (in ancient Rome) type of priest flamens
FLAMER ▶ flame
FLAMERS ▶ flame
FLAMES ▶ flame
FLAMFEW n fantastic trifle
FLAMIER ▶ flame
FLAMING adj burning

with flames ▷ adv extremely
FLAMM variant of ▶ flam
FLAMMED ▶ flam
FLAMMS ▶ flamm
FLAMS ▶ flam
FLAMY ▶ flame
FLAN n
FLANCH variant of ▶ flaunch
FLANES n arrows
FLANEUR n idler or loafer
FLANGE n, vb flanged, flanger, flanges
FLANK n, vb flanked
FLANKEN n cut of beef
FLANKER n one of a detachment of soldiers guarding the flanks
FLANKS ▶ flank
FLANNEL n, vb
FLANNEN adj made of flannel
FLANNIE ▶ flanny
FLANNY n shirt made of flannel
FLANS ▶ flan
FLAP vb, n flapped
FLAPPER n
FLAPPY adj loose
FLAPS ▶ flap
FLARE vb, n flared
FLARES pl n trousers with legs that widen below the knee
FLAREUP n outbreak of something
FLARIER ▶ flare
FLARING ▶ flare
FLARY ▶ flare
FLASER n type of sedimentary structure

in rock flasers
FLASH n, adj, vb flashed
FLASHER n man who exposes himself indecently
FLASHES ▶ flash
FLASHY adj
FLASK n
FLASKET n long shallow basket
FLASKS ▶ flask
FLAT adj, adv, n, vb
FLATBED n type of printing machine
FLATCAP n Elizabethan man's hat
FLATCAR n flatbed
FLATLET n small flat
FLATLY ▶ flat
FLATS ▶ flat
FLATTED ▶ flat
FLATTEN vb
FLATTER vb
FLATTIE n flat tyre
FLATTOP n informal name for an aircraft carrier
FLATTY n flat shoe
FLATUS n gas generated in the alimentary canal
FLAUGHT vb flutter
FLAUNCH n cement or mortar shaped to throw off water ▷ vb cause to slope in this manner
FLAUNE variant of ▶ flam
FLAUNES ▶ flaune
FLAUNT vb, n flaunts
FLAUNTY adj characterized by or inclined to ostentatious display

FLAUTA n tortilla rolled around a filling **flautas**

FLAVA n individual style **flavas**

FLAVIN n heterocyclic ketone **flavine, flavins**

FLAVONE n crystalline compound occurring in plants

FLAVOR = flavour

FLAVORS ▶ flavor

FLAVORY adj flavoursome

FLAVOUR n, adj

FLAW n, vb **flawed, flawier, flawing**

FLAWN variant of ▶ flam

FLAWNS ▶ flawn

FLAWS ▶ flaw

FLAWY ▶ flaw

FLAX n

FLAXEN adj

FLAXES ▶ flax

FLAXIER ▶ flaxy

FLAXY = flaxen

FLAY vb fley; **flayed, flayer, flayers, flaying, flay**

FLEA n

FLEABAG n dirty or unkempt person, esp a woman

FLEADH n festival of Irish music, dancing, and culture **fleadhs**

FLEAM n lancet used for letting blood **fleams**

FLEAPIT n shabby cinema or theatre

FLEAS ▶ flea

FLECHE n slender spire **fleches**

FLECK n, vb **flecked, flecker, flecks, flecky**

FLED ▶ flee

FLEDGE vb feed and care for (a young bird) until it is able to fly **fledged, fledges**

FLEDGY adj feathery or feathered

FLEE vb

FLEECE n, vb **fleeced, fleecer, fleeces**

FLEECH vb flatter

FLEECIE n person who collects fleeces for baling

FLEECY adj made of or like fleece ▷ n person who collects fleeces after shearing and prepares them for baling

FLEEING ▶ flee

FLEER vb grin or laugh at ▷ n derisory glance or grin **fleered, fleerer, fleers**

FLEES ▶ flee

FLEET n, adj, vb **fleeted, fleeter, fleetly, fleets**

FLEG vb scare **flegged, flegs**

FLEHMEN vb (of mammal) grimace

FLEME vb drive out **flemes**

FLEMING n inhabitant of Flanders or a Flemish-speaking Belgian

FLEMISH vb stow (a rope) in a Flemish coil

FLEMIT ▶ fleme

FLENCH = flense

FLENSE vb strip (a whale, seal, etc) of (its blubber or skin) **flensed, flenser, flenses**

FLESH n **fleshed**

FLESHER n person or machine that fleshes hides or skins

FLESHES ▶ flesh

FLESHLY adj carnal

FLESHY adj plump

FLETCH = fledge

FLETTON n type of brick

FLEURET = fleurette

FLEURON n decorative piece of pastry

FLEURY = flory

FLEW ▶ fly

FLEWED adj having large flews

FLEWS pl n upper lip of a bloodhound or similar dog

FLEX n, vb **flexed, flexes**

FLEXILE = flexible

FLEXING ▶ flex

FLEXION n act of bending a joint or limb

FLEXO n, adj, adv flexography

FLEXOR n type of muscle **flexors**

FLEXOS ▶ flexo

FLEXURE n act of flexing or the state of being flexed

FLEY vb be afraid or cause to be afraid **fleyed, fleying, fleys**

FLIC n French police officer

FLICK vb, n **flicked**

FLICKER vb, n

FLICKS ▶ flick

FLICS ▸ flic
FLIED, flier, fliers, flies, fliest ▸ fly
FLIGHT n, vb **flights**
FLIGHTY adj
FLIM n five-pound note
FLIMP vb steal **flimped, flimps**
FLIMS ▸ flim
FLIMSY adj, n
FLINCH = flense
FLINDER n fragment
FLING vb, n **flinger, flings**
FLINT n, vb **flinted, flints**
FLINTY adj
FLIP vb, n, adj **flipped**
FLIPPER n
FLIPPY adj (of clothes) moving to and fro as the wearer walks
FLIPS ▸ flip
FLIR n forward looking infrared radar **flirs**
FLIRT vb, n **flirted, flirter, flirts, flirty**
FLISK vb skip **flisked, flisks, flisky**
FLIT vb, n
FLITCH n side of pork salted and cured ▷ vb cut (a tree trunk) into flitches
FLITE vb scold or rail at ▷ n dispute or scolding **flited, flites, fliting**
FLITS ▸ flit
FLITT adj fleet
FLITTED ▸ flit
FLITTER ▸ flit
FLIVVER n old, cheap, or battered car
FLIX n fur ▷ vb have fur

flixed, flixes, flixing
FLOAT vb, n **floated**
FLOATEL = flotel
FLOATER n person or thing that floats
FLOATS pl n footlights
FLOATY adj filmy and light
FLOB vb **flobbed, flobs**
FLOC = flock
FLOCCED ▸ floc
FLOCCI ▸ floccus
FLOCCUS n downy or woolly covering ▷ adj (of a cloud) having the appearance of woolly tufts
FLOCK n, vb, adj **flocked, flocks, flocky**
FLOCS ▸ floc
FLOE n **floes**
FLOG vb **flogged, flogger, flogs**
FLOKATI n Greek hand-woven shaggy woollen rug
FLONG n material used for making moulds in stereotyping **flongs**
FLOOD n, vb **flooded, flooder, floods**
FLOOEY adj awry **flooie**
FLOOR n, vb **floored**
FLOORER n coup de grâce
FLOORS ▸ floor
FLOOSIE = floozy
FLOOSY variant of ▸ floosie
FLOOZIE = floozy
FLOOZY n disreputable woman
FLOP vb, n **flopped, flopper**

FLOPPY adj, n
FLOPS ▸ flop
FLOR n type of yeast
FLORA n **florae**
FLORAL adj, n **florals**
FLORAS ▸ flora
FLOREAT vb may (a person, institution, etc) flourish
FLORET n **florets**
FLORID adj
FLORIER ▸ flory
FLORIN n former British and Australian coin **florins**
FLORIST n
FLORS ▸ flor
FLORUIT prep (he or she) flourished in ▷ n such a period in a person's life
FLORULA n flora of a small single environment **florule**
FLORY adj containing a fleur-de-lys
FLOSH n hopper-shaped box **floshes**
FLOSS n, vb **flossed, flosser, flosses**
FLOSSIE variant of ▸ flossy
FLOSSY adj consisting of or resembling floss ▷ n floozy
FLOTA n formerly, Spanish commercial fleet
FLOTAGE n act or state of floating
FLOTANT adj in heraldry, flying in the air
FLOTAS ▸ flota
FLOTE n aquatic

perennial grass
FLOTEL n (in the oil industry) a rig or boat used as accommodation **flotels**
FLOTES ▶ flote
FLOTSAM n
FLOUNCE vb, n **flouncy**
FLOUR n, vb **floured, flours, floury**
FLOUSE vb splash **floused, flouses, floush**
FLOUT vb **flouted, flouter, flouts**
FLOW vb, n
FLOWAGE n act of overflowing or the state of having overflowed
FLOWED ▶ flow
FLOWER n, vb **flowers**
FLOWERY adj
FLOWING ▶ flow
FLOWN ▶ fly
FLOWS ▶ flow
FLOX adj as in flox silk type of silk
FLU n
FLUATE n fluoride **fluates**
FLUB vb bungle **flubbed, flubber**
FLUBDUB n bunkum
FLUBS ▶ flub
FLUE n
FLUED adj having a flue
FLUENCE ▶ fluency
FLUENCY n quality of being fluent
FLUENT adj, n **fluents**
FLUERIC adj of or relating to fluidics
FLUES ▶ flue
FLUEY adj involved in,

caused by, or like influenza
FLUFF n, vb **fluffed**
FLUFFER n person employed on a pornographic film set
FLUFFS ▶ fluff
FLUFFY adj of, resembling, or covered with fluff
FLUGEL n grand piano or harpsichord **flugels**
FLUID n, adj **fluidal**
FLUIDIC ▶ fluidics
FLUIDLY ▶ fluid
FLUIDS ▶ fluid
FLUIER ▶ fluey
FLUIEST ▶ fluey
FLUISH ▶ flu
FLUKE n, vb **fluked, flukes**
FLUKEY = fluky
FLUKIER ▶ fluky
FLUKILY ▶ fluky
FLUKING ▶ fluke
FLUKY adj done or gained by an accident
FLUME n narrow sloping channel for water ▶ vb transport (logs) in a flume **flumed, flumes, fluming**
FLUMMOX vb
FLUMP vb move or fall heavily **flumped, flumps**
FLUNG ▶ fling
FLUNK vb, n **flunked, flunker**
FLUNKEY = flunky
FLUNKIE = flunky
FLUNKS ▶ flunk
FLUNKY n servile person

FLUOR > fluorspar
FLUORIC adj of, concerned with, or produced from fluorine or fluorspar
FLUORID = fluoride
FLUORIN = fluorine
FLUORS ▶ fluor
FLURR vb scatter **flurred, flurrs**
FLURRY n, vb
FLUS ▶ flu
FLUSH vb, n, adj, adv **flushed, flusher, flushes**
FLUSHY adj ruddy
FLUSTER vb, n
FLUTE n, vb
FLUTED adj
FLUTER n craftsman who makes flutes or fluting **fluters**
FLUTES ▶ flute
FLUTEY ▶ flute
FLUTIER ▶ flute
FLUTINA n type of accordion
FLUTING n design of decorative grooves
FLUTIST = flautist
FLUTY ▶ flute
FLUVIAL adj
FLUX n, vb **fluxed, fluxes, fluxing**
FLUXION n rate of change of a function
FLUXIVE ▶ flux
FLUYT n Dutch sailing ship **fluyts**
FLY vb, n, adj **flyable**
FLYAWAY adj (of hair) very fine and soft ▶ n person who is frivolous

or flighty

FLYBACK n item of electrical equipment

FLYBANE n type of campion

FLYBELT n strip of tsetse-infested land

FLYBLEW ▷ flyblow

FLYBLOW vb contaminate ▷ n egg or young larva of a blowfly

FLYBOAT n any small swift boat

FLYBOOK n small case or wallet for storing artificial flies

FLYBOY n air force pilot flyboys

FLYBY n flight past a particular position or target flybys

FLYER ▷ fly

FLYERS ▷ fly

FLYEST ▷ fly

FLYHAND n device on a printing press

FLYING ▷ fly

FLYINGS ▷ fly

FLYLEAF n

FLYLESS ▷ fly

FLYMAN n stagehand flymen

FLYOFF n all water transferred from the earth to the atmosphere flyoffs

FLYOVER n

FLYPAST n ceremonial flight of aircraft over a given area

FLYPE vb fold back flyped, flypes, flyping

FLYSCH n type of

marine sedimentary facies

FLYTE = flite

FLYTED ▷ flyte

FLYTES ▷ flyte

FLYTIER n person who makes his own fishing flies

FLYTING ▷ flyte

FLYTRAP n any of various insectivorous plants

FLYWAY n usual route used by birds when migrating flyways

FOAL n, vb foaled, foaling, foals

FOAM n, vb foamed

FOAMER n (possibly obsessive) enthusiast foamers

FOAMIER ▷ foamy

FOAMILY ▷ foamy

FOAMING ▷ foam

FOAMS ▷ foam

FOAMY adj of, resembling, consisting of, or covered with foam

FOB n short watch chain ▷ vb cheat fobbed, fobbing, fobs

FOCAL adj of or at a focus focally

FOCI ▷ focus

FOCUS n, vb focused, focuser, focuses

FODDER n, vb fodders

FODGEL adj buxom

FOE n

FOEHN = fohn

FOEHNS ▷ foehn

FOEMAN n enemy in war foemen

FOEN ▷ foe

FOES ▷ foe

FOETAL = fetal

FOETID = fetid

FOETOR = fetor

FOETORS ▷ foetor

FOETUS = fetus

FOG n, vb

FOGASH n type of Hungarian pike perch

FOGBOW n faint arc of light sometimes seen in a fog bank fogbows

FOGDOG n spot sometimes seen in fog near the horizon fogdogs

FOGEY n fogeys

FOGGAGE n grass grown for winter grazing

FOGGED ▷ fog

FOGGER n device that generates a fog foggers

FOGGIER, foggily, fogging, foggy ▷ fog

FOGHORN n

FOGIE variant of ▷ fogey

FOGIES ▷ fogie

FOGLE n silk handkerchief fogles

FOGLESS ▷ fog

FOGMAN n person in charge of railway fog-signals fogmen

FOGOU n subterranean building found in Cornwall fogous

FOGRAM n fogey fograms

FOGS ▷ fog

FOGY = fogey

FOGYDOM ▷ fogy

FOGYISH ▸ fogy

FOGYISM ▸ fogy

FOH *interj* expression of disgust

FOHN *n* type of warm dry wind **fohns**

FOIBLE *n* **foibles**

FOID *n* rock-forming mineral similar to feldspar **foids**

FOIL *vb*, *n* foiled, foiling, foils

FOIN *n* thrust or lunge with a weapon ▸ *vb* thrust with a weapon **foined, foining, foins**

FOISON *n* plentiful supply or yield **foisons**

FOIST *vb* foisted, foister, foists

FOLACIN *n* folic acid

FOLATE *n* folic acid

FOLATES ▸ folic

FOLD *vb*, *n* folded

FOLDER *n* folders

FOLDING ▸ fold

FOLDOUT another name for ▸ gatefold

FOLDS ▸ fold

FOLDUP *n* something that folds up **foldups**

FOLEY *n* footsteps editor **foleys**

FOLIA ▸ folium

FOLIAGE *n*

FOLIAR *adj* of or relating to a leaf or leaves

FOLIATE *adj* relating to, possessing, or resembling leaves ▸ *vb* ornament with foliage or with leaf forms such as foils

FOLIC *adj* as in folic acid

any of a group of vitamins of the B complex

FOLIE *n* madness **folies**

FOLIO *n* sheet of paper folded in half to make two leaves of a book ▸ *adj* of or made in the largest book size, common esp in early centuries of European printing ▸ *vb* number the leaves of (a book) consecutively **folioed**

FOLIOLE *n* part of a compound leaf

FOLIOS ▸ folio

FOLIOSE *adj* (of a tree) leaf-bearing

FOLIOUS *adj* foliose

FOLIUM *n* plane geometrical curve **foliums**

FOLK *n*, *adj*

FOLKIE *n* devotee of folk music ▸ *adj* of or relating to folk music **folkier, folkies**

FOLKISH ▸ folk

FOLKMOT = folkmoot

FOLKS ▸ folk

FOLKSY *adj* simple and unpretentious

FOLKWAY singular form of ▸ folkways

FOLKY = folkie

FOLLES ▸ follis

FOLLIED ▸ folly

FOLLIES ▸ folly

FOLLIS *n* Roman coin

FOLLOW *vb* follows

FOLLY *n*, *vb*

FOMENT *vb* foments

FOMES *n* any material

that may harbour pathogens **fomite, fomites**

FOMITE ▸ fomes

FON *vb* compel

FOND *adj*, *n*, *vb*

FONDA *n* Spanish hotel

FONDANT *n* (sweet made from) flavoured paste of sugar and water ▸ *adj* (of a colour) soft

FONDAS ▸ fonda

FONDED, fonder, fondest, fonding ▸ fond

FONDLE *vb* fondled, fondler, fondles

FONDLY ▸ fond

FONDS ▸ fond

FONDU *n* ballet movement

FONDUE *n*, *vb* fondued, fondues

FONDUS ▸ fondu

FONE *variant of* ▸ foe

FONLY *adv* foolishly

FONNED ▸ fon

FONNING ▸ fon

FONS ▸ fon

FONT *n* fontal

FONTINA *n* mild Italian cheese

FONTLET ▸ font

FONTS ▸ font

FOOBAR = fubar

FOOD *n*

FOODFUL *adj* supplying abundant food

FOODIE *n* gourmet foodies

FOODISM *n* enthusiasm for and interest in good food

FOODS ▸ food

FOODY = foodie

FOOL n, vb **fooled**

FOOLERY n foolish behaviour

FOOLING ▸ fool

FOOLISH adj

FOOLS ▸ fool

FOOT n, vb

FOOTAGE n

FOOTBAG n type of sport

FOOTBAR n any bar used by footballers

FOOTBOY n boy servant

FOOTED ▸ foot

FOOTER n person who goes on foot ▷ vb potter **footers**

FOOTIE = footy

FOOTIER ▸ footy

FOOTIES ▸ footie

FOOTING n

FOOTLE vb loiter aimlessly ▷ n foolishness **footled, footler, footles**

FOOTMAN n footmen

FOOTPAD n highwayman, on foot rather than horseback

FOOTRA variant of ▸ foutra

FOOTRAS ▸ footra

FOOTS pl n sediment that accumulates at the bottom of a vessel

FOOTSIE n flirtation involving the touching together of feet **footsy**

FOOTWAY n way or path for pedestrians

FOOTY n football ▷ adj mean

FOOZLE vb bungle (a shot) ▷ n bungled shot

foozled, foozler, foozles

FOP n, vb

FOPLING n vain affected dandy

FOPPED ▸ fop

FOPPERY n clothes, affectations, etc, of or befitting a fop

FOPPING ▸ fop

FOPPISH ▸ fop

FOPS ▸ fop

FOR prep

FORA ▸ forum

FORAGE vb, n **foraged, forager, forages**

FORAM n marine protozoan

FORAMEN n natural hole

FORAMS ▸ foram

FORANE adj as in **vicar forane** type of Roman Catholic priest

FORAY n, vb **forayed, forayer, forays**

FORB n any herbaceous plant that is not a grass

FORBAD ▸ forbid

FORBADE ▸ forbid

FORBARE ▸ forbear

FORBEAR vb

FORBID vb forbids

FORBODE vb obsolete word meaning forbid ▷ n obsolete word meaning forbidding

FORBORE past tense of ▸ forbear

FORBS ▸ forb

FORBY adv besides **forbye**

FORCAT n convict or

galley slave **forcats**

FORCE n, vb

FORCED adj

FORCEPS pl n

FORCER forcers, **forces, forcing** ▸ force

FORD n, vb **forded**

FORDID ▸ fordo

FORDING ▸ ford

FORDO vb destroy **fordoes, fordone**

FORDS ▸ ford

FORE adj, n, interj

FOREARM n, vb

FOREBAY n reservoir or canal

FOREBY variant of ▸ forby

FOREBYE variant of ▸ forby

FORECAR n vehicle attached to a motorcycle

FOREDID ▸ foredo

FOREDO = fordo

FOREGO = forgo

FOREGUT n anterior part of the digestive tract of vertebrates

FOREIGN adj

FOREL n type of parchment

FORELAY archaic word for ▸ ambush

FORELEG n either of the front legs of an animal

FORELIE vb lie in front of

FORELS ▸ forel

FOREMAN n foremen

FOREPAW n either of the front feet of a land mammal

FORERAN ▸ forerun

FORERUN vb serve as a herald for

FORES ▸ fore

FORESAW ▸ foresee

FORESAY vb foretell

FORESEE vb

FOREST n, vb **forests**

FORETOP n platform at the top of the foremast

FOREVER adv

FOREX n foreign exchange **forexes**

FORFAIR vb perish

FORFEIT n, vb, adj

FORFEND vb protect or secure

FORFEX n pair of pincers, esp the paired terminal appendages of an earwig

FORGAT past tense of ▸ forget

FORGAVE ▸ forgive

FORGE n, vb **forged, forger, forgers**

FORGERY n

FORGES ▸ forge

FORGET vb **forgets**

FORGING n process of producing a metal component by hammering

FORGIVE vb

FORGO vb **forgoer, forgoes, forgone**

FORGOT past tense of ▸ forget

FORHENT variant of > forehent

FORHOO vb forsake **forhoos, forhow**

FORHOWS ▸ forhow

FORINT n standard monetary unit of Hungary **forints**

FORK n, vb

FORKED adj having a fork or forklike parts

FORKER ▸ fork

FORKERS ▸ fork

FORKFUL ▸ fork

FORKIER ▸ forky

FORKING ▸ fork

FORKS ▸ fork

FORKY adj forked

FORLANA n Venetian dance

FORLEND variant of > forelend

FORLENT ▸ forlend

FORLORN adj, n

FORM n, vb

FORMAL adj **formals**

FORMANT n any of several frequency ranges

FORMAT n, vb

FORMATE n type of salt or ester of formic acid ▷ vb fly aircraft in formation

FORMATS ▸ format

FORME n type matter assembled and ready for printing

FORMED ▸ form

FORMEE n type of heraldic cross

FORMER adj, n **formers**

FORMES ▸ forme

FORMFUL adj imaginative

FORMIC adj of, relating to, or derived from ants

FORMICA n tradename for any of various

laminated plastic sheets

FORMING ▸ form

FORMOL = formalin

FORMOLS ▸ formol

FORMS ▸ form

FORMULA n

FORMYL n of, consisting of, or containing the monovalent group HCO- **formyls**

FORNENT variant of > fornenst

FORNIX n any archlike structure

FORPET n quarter of a peck (measure) **forpets**

FORPINE vb waste away

FORPIT variant of ▸ forpet

FORPITS ▸ forpit

FORRAD adv forward

FORRAY archaic variant of ▸ foray

FORRAYS ▸ forray

FORREN adj foreign

FORRIT adv forward(s)

FORSAID ▸ forsay

FORSAKE vb

FORSAY vb renounce **forsays**

FORSLOE variant of ▸ forslow

FORSLOW vb hinder

FORSOOK past tense of ▸ forsake

FORT n, vb

FORTE n, adv

FORTED ▸ fort

FORTES ▸ fortis

FORTH adv, prep

FORTHY adv therefore

FORTIES ▸ forty
FORTIFY vb
FORTING ▸ fort
FORTIS adj (of a consonant) articulated with considerable muscular tension ▸ n type of consonantal pronunciation
FORTLET ▸ fort
FORTS ▸ fort
FORTUNE n, vb
FORTY n, adj, determiner
FORUM n forums
FORWARD = forwards
FORWARN archaic word for ▸ forbid
FORWENT past tense of ▸ forgo
FORWHY adv for what reason
FORWORN adj weary
FORZA n force
FORZATI ▸ forzato
FORZATO variant of > forzando
FORZE ▸ forza
FOSS = fosse
FOSSA n anatomical depression, trench, or hollow area **fossae, fossas**
FOSSATE adj having cavities or depressions
FOSSE n ditch or moat, esp one dug as a fortification
FOSSED adj having a ditch or moat
FOSSES ▸ fosse
FOSSICK vb
FOSSIL n, adj fossils
FOSSOR n grave digger **fossors**

FOSSULA n small fossa
FOSTER vb, adj fosters
FOTHER vb stop a leak in a ship's hull **fothers**
FOU adj full ▸ n bushel
FOUAT n succulent pink-flowered plant **fouats**
FOUD n sheriff in Orkney and Shetland
FOUDRIE n foud's district or office
FOUDS ▸ foud
FOUER ▸ fou
FOUEST ▸ fou
FOUET n archaic word for a whip **fouets**
FOUETTE n step in ballet
FOUGADE n booby-trapped pit or type of mine
FOUGHT ▸ fight
FOUGHTY adj musty
FOUL adj, n, vb
FOULARD n soft light fabric
FOULDER vb flash like lightning
FOULE n type of woollen cloth
FOULED ▸ foul
FOULER ▸ foul
FOULES ▸ foule
FOULEST ▸ foul
FOULIE n bad mood **foulies**
FOULING ▸ foul
FOULLY ▸ foul
FOULS ▸ foul
FOUMART former name for the ▸ polecat
FOUND vb founded
FOUNDER vb, n
FOUNDRY n

FOUNDS ▸ found
FOUNT = font
FOUNTS ▸ fount
FOUR n, adj, determiner
FOURGON n long covered wagon
FOURS ▸ four
FOURSES n snack eaten at four o'clock
FOURTH n, adj, adv fourths
FOUS ▸ fou
FOUSSA n Madagascan civet-like animal **foussas**
FOUSTY archaic variant of ▸ fusty
FOUTER = footer
FOUTERS ▸ fouter
FOUTH n abundance **fouths**
FOUTRA n fig; expression of contempt **foutras**
FOUTRE vb footer **foutred, foutres**
FOVEA n any small pit in the surface of a bodily organ or part **foveae, foveal, foveas, foveate**
FOVEOLA n small fovea **foveole**
FOWL n, vb fowled
FOWLER ▸ fowling
FOWLERS ▸ fowling
FOWLING n shooting or trapping of birds for sport or as a livelihood
FOWLPOX n viral infection of poultry and other birds
FOWLS ▸ fowl
FOWTH variant of

▸**fouth**

FOWTHS ▸ **fowth**

FOX n, vb **foxed, foxes**

FOXFIRE n glow emitted by certain fungi

FOXFISH n type of shark

FOXHOLE n small pit dug for protection

FOXHUNT n hunting of foxes with hounds ▷ vb hunt foxes with hounds

FOXIE n fox terrier

FOXIER ▸ **foxy**

FOXIES ▸ **foxie**

FOXIEST ▸ **foxy**

FOXILY ▸ **foxy**

FOXING n piece of leather used on part of the upper of a shoe **foxings**

FOXLIKE ▸ **fox**

FOXSHIP n cunning

FOXSKIN adj made from the skin of a fox ▷ n skin of a fox

FOXTAIL n type of grass

FOXTROT n ballroom dance with slow and quick steps ▷ vb perform this dance

FOXY adj of or like a fox, esp in craftiness

FOY n loyalty

This unusual word for loyalty can be a good scorer.

FOYBOAT n small rowing boat

FOYER n **foyers**

FOYLE variant of ▸ **foil**

FOYLED ▸ **foyle**

FOYLES ▸ **foyle**

FOYLING ▸ **foyle**

FOYNE variant of ▸ **foin**

FOYNED ▸ **foyne**

FOYNES ▸ **foyne**

FOYNING ▸ **foyne**

FOYS ▸ **foy**

FOZIER ▸ **fozy**

FOZIEST ▸ **fozy**

FOZY adj spongy

FRA n brother: a title given to an Italian monk or friar

FRAB vb nag **frabbed**

FRABBIT adj peevish

FRABS ▸ **frab**

FRACAS n

FRACK adj bold

FRACT vb break

FRACTAL n mathematically repeating structure ▷ adj of, relating to, or involving such a process

FRACTED ▸ **fract**

FRACTI ▸ **fractus**

FRACTS ▸ **fract**

FRACTUR variant of ▸ **fraktur**

FRACTUS n ragged-shaped cloud formation

FRAE Scot word for ▸ **from**

FRAENA ▸ **fraenum**

FRAENUM n fold of membrane or skin that supports an organ

FRAG vb kill or wound (a fellow soldier or superior officer) deliberately **fragged**

FRAGILE adj

FRAGOR n sudden sound **fragors**

FRAGS ▸ **frag**

FRAIL adj, n **frailer, frailly, frails**

FRAILTY n physical or moral weakness

FRAIM n stranger **fraims**

FRAISE n neck ruff worn during the 16th century ▷ vb provide a rampart with a palisade **fraised, fraises**

FRAKTUR n style of typeface

FRAME n, vb **framed, framer, framers, frames**

FRAMING n frame, framework, or system of frames

FRAMPAL = **frampold**

FRANC n

FRANCO adj post-free

FRANCS ▸ **franc**

FRANGER n condom

FRANION n lover, paramour

FRANK adj, n, vb **franked, franker**

FRANKLY adv in truth

FRANKS ▸ **frank**

FRANTIC adj

FRANZY adj irritable

FRAP vb lash down or together

FRAPE adj tightly bound

FRAPPE adj (of drinks) chilled ▷ n type of drink

FRAPPED ▸ **frap**

FRAPPEE ▸ **frappe**

FRAPPES ▸ **frappe**

FRAPS ▸ **frap**

FRAS ▸ **fra**

FRASS n refuse left by insects and insect larvae **frasses**

FRAT n member of a fraternity

FRATCH n quarrel

FRATCHY adj quarrelsome

FRATE n friar

FRATER n mendicant friar or a lay brother in a monastery or priory **fraters, fratery**

FRATI ▶ frate

FRATRY ▶ frater

FRATS ▶ frat

FRAU n married German woman

FRAUD n frauds

FRAUGHT adj, vb, n

FRAUS ▶ frau

FRAWZEY n celebration

FRAY n, vb frayed, fraying, frays

FRAZIL n small pieces of ice that form in turbulently moving water **frazils**

FRAZZLE n exhausted state ▷ vb tire out

FREAK n, adj, vb freaked, freaks

FREAKY adj weird, peculiar

FRECKLE n, vb freckly

FREE adj, vb

FREEBEE variant of ▶ freebie

FREEBIE n something provided without charge ▷ adj without charge

FREED ▶ free

FREEDOM n

FREEGAN n person who avoids buying consumer goods

FREEING ▶ free

FREELY ▶ free

FREEMAN n person who has been given the freedom of a city **freemen**

FREER n liberator **freers**

FREES ▶ free

FREESIA n

FREEST ▶ free

FREET n omen or superstition **freets**

FREETY adj superstitious

FREEWAY n

FREEZE vb, n

FREEZER n

FREEZES ▶ freeze

FREIGHT n, vb

FREIT variant of ▶ freet

FREITS ▶ freit

FREITY adj superstitious

FREMD adj, n alien or strange (person or thing) **fremds, fremit**

FREMITS ▶ fremit

FRENA ▶ frenum

FRENCH vb (of food) cut into thin strips

FRENNE variant of ▶ fremd

FRENNES ▶ frenne

FRENULA ▶ frenulum

FRENUM = fraenum

FRENUMS ▶ frenum

FRENZY n, vb

FRERE n friar **freres**

FRESCO n, vb frescos

FRESH adj, adv, vb freshed

FRESHEN vb

FRESHER n

FRESHES ▶ fresh

FRESHET n sudden overflowing of a river

FRESHIE n new Indian immigrant to the UK

FRESHLY ▶ fresh

FRESNEL n unit of frequency equivalent to 10^{12} hertz

FRET vb, n

FRETFUL adj irritable

FRETS ▶ fret

FRETSAW n fine saw with a narrow blade, used for fretwork

FRETTED ▶ fret

FRETTER ▶ fret

FRETTY adj decorated with frets

FRIABLE adj easily crumbled

FRIAND n small almond cake **friande, friands**

FRIAR n friarly, friars

FRIARY n house of friars

FRIB n piece of wool removed from a fleece during classing

FRIBBLE vb fritter away ▷ n wasteful or frivolous person or action ▷ adj frivolous

FRIBS ▶ frib

FRICHT vb frighten **frichts**

FRIDGE n, vb fridged, fridges

FRIED ▶ fry

FRIEND n, vb friends

FRIER = fryer

FRIERS ▶ frier

FRIES ▶ fry

FRIEZE n, vb friezed, friezes

FRIGATE n

FRIGHT n **frights**

FRIGID adj

FRIGOT variant of ▸ **frigate**

FRIGOTS ▸ **frigot**

FRIJOL n variety of bean **frijole**

FRILL n, vb **frilled, friller, frills**

FRILLY adj with a frill or frills

FRINGE n, vb, adj **fringed, fringes**

FRINGY adj having a fringe

FRIPON n rogue **fripons**

FRIPPER n dealer in old clothes

FRIPPET n frivolous or flamboyant young woman

FRIS ▸ **friska**

FRISBEE n tradename of a light plastic disc

FRISE n fabric with a long normally uncut nap used for upholstery and rugs

FRISEE n endive **frisees**

FRISES ▸ **fris**

FRISEUR n hairdresser

FRISK vb, n

FRISKA n (in Hungarian music) the fast movement of a piece **friskas**

FRISKED ▸ **frisk**

FRISKER ▸ **frisk**

FRISKET n part of a hand printing press

FRISKS ▸ **frisk**

FRISKY adj

FRISSON n shiver of fear or excitement

FRIST archaic word for ▸ postpone

FRISTED ▸ **frist**

FRISTS ▸ **frist**

FRISURE n styling the hair into curls

FRIT n basic materials for making glass, glazes for pottery, etc ▷ vb fuse (materials) in making frit

FRITES pl n chipped potatoes

FRITFLY n type of small black fly

FRITH = firth

FRITHS ▸ **frith**

FRITS ▸ **frit**

FRITT = frit

FRITTED ▸ **frit**

FRITTER n, vb

FRITTS ▸ **fritt**

FRITURE archaic word for ▸ **fritter**

FRITZ n as in **on the fritz** state of disrepair

FRIVOL vb behave frivolously **frivols**

FRIZ variant of ▸ **frizz**

FRIZE n coarse woollen fabric ▷ vb freeze **frized**

FRIZER n person who gives nap to cloth **frizers**

FRIZES ▸ **frize**

FRIZING ▸ **frize**

FRIZZ vb form (hair) into stiff wiry curls ▷ n hair that has been frizzed **frizzed, frizzer, frizzes**

FRIZZLE vb cook or heat until crisp and shrivelled ▷ n tight curl **frizzly**

FRIZZY adj

FRO adv away ▷ n afro

FROCK n, vb **frocked, frocks**

FROE n cutting tool **froes**

FROG n

FROGBIT n floating aquatic Eurasian plant

FROGEYE n plant disease

FROGGED adj decorated with frogging

FROGGY adj like a frog

FROGLET n young frog

FROGMAN n **frogmen**

FROGS ▸ **frog**

FROING n as in **wing and froing** going back and forth **froings**

FROISE n kind of pancake **froises**

FROLIC vb, n, adj **frolics**

FROM prep

FROMAGE n as in **fromage frais** low-fat soft cheese

FROND n

FRONDED adj having fronds

FRONDS ▸ **frond**

FRONS n plate on the head of some insects

FRONT n, adj, vb

FRONTAL adj of, at, or in the front ▷ n decorative hanging for the front of an altar

FRONTED ▸ **front**

FRONTER ▸ **front**

FRONTES ▸ **frons**

FRONTON n wall

against which pelota or jai alai is played

FRONTS ▶ front

FRORE adj very cold or frosty **froren, frorn, frorne**

FRORY adj frozen

FROS ▶ fro

FROSH n freshman **froshes**

FROST n, vb

FROSTED adj, n

FROSTS ▶ frost

FROSTY adj

FROTH n, vb frothed, **frother, froths, frothy**

FROUGHY adj rancid

FROUNCE vb wrinkle

FROUZY = frowzy

FROW ▶ froe

FROWARD adj obstinate

FROWIE variant of ▶ **froughy**

FROWIER ▶ frowie

FROWN vb, n frowned, **frowner, frowns**

FROWS ▶ frow

FROWST n hot and stale atmosphere ▷ vb abandon oneself to such an atmosphere **frowsts**

FROWSTY adj stale or musty

FROWSY = frowzy

FROWY variant of ▶ **froughy**

FROWZY adj dirty or unkempt

FROZE ▶ freeze

FROZEN ▶ freeze

FRUCTAN n type of polymer of fructose

FRUCTED adj fruit-bearing

FRUG vb perform the frug, a 1960s dance

FRUGAL adj

FRUGGED ▶ frug

FRUGS ▶ frug

FRUICT obsolete variant of ▶ **fruit**

FRUICTS ▶ fruict

FRUIT n, vb fruited

FRUITER n fruit grower

FRUITS ▶ fruit

FRUITY adj

FRUMP n, vb frumped

FRUMPLE vb wrinkle or crumple

FRUMPS ▶ frump

FRUMPY adj (of a woman, clothes, etc) dowdy or unattractive

FRUSH vb break into pieces frushed, **frushes**

FRUST n fragment

FRUSTA ▶ frustum

FRUSTS ▶ frust

FRUSTUM n part of a solid

FRUTEX n shrub

FRUTIFY vb malapropism for notify

FRY vb, n fryable

FRYER n person or thing that fries **fryers**

FRYING ▶ fry

FRYINGS ▶ fry

FRYPAN n long-handled shallow pan used for frying **frypans**

FUB vb cheat

FUBAR adj irreparably damaged or bungled

FUBBED ▶ fub

FUBBERY n cheating

FUBBIER ▶ fubby

FUBBING ▶ fub

FUBBY adj chubby

FUBS ▶ fub

FUBSIER ▶ fubsy

FUBSY adj short and stout

FUCHSIA n

FUCHSIN n greenish crystalline substance

FUCI ▶ fucus

FUCOID n type of seaweed **fucoids**

FUCOSE n aldose **fucoses**

FUCOUS = fucoidal

FUCUS n type of seaweed

FUCUSED adj archaic word meaning made up with cosmetics

FUCUSES ▶ fucus

FUD n rabbit's tail

FUDDIES ▶ fuddy

FUDDLE vb cause to be intoxicated or confused ▷ n confused state fuddled, **fuddler, fuddles**

FUDDY n old-fashioned person

FUDGE n, vb, interj fudged, fudges, **fudging**

FUDS ▶ fud

FUEHRER n leader: applied esp to Adolf Hitler

FUEL n, vb fueled, **fueler, fuelers, fueling, fuelled, fueller, fuels**

FUERO n Spanish code

of laws **fueros**

FUFF vb puff **fuffed**

FUFFIER ▸ fuffy

FUFFING ▸ fuff

FUFFS ▸ fuff

FUFFY adj puffy

FUG n, vb

FUGAL adj of, relating to, or in the style of a fugue **fugally**

FUGATO adj in the manner or style of a fugue ▷ n movement, section, or piece in this style **fugatos**

FUGGED, fuggier, fuggily, fugging, fuggy ▸ fug

FUGIE n runaway **fugies**

FUGIO n former US copper coin **fugios**

FUGLE vb act as a fugleman **fugled, fugles, fugling**

FUGS ▸ fug

FUGU n puffer fish

U is not normally a desirable letter to have on your rack unless you happen to have the Q, and two Us can be trouble. This Japanese fish can help you out.

FUGUE n, vb **fugued, fugues, fuguing**

FUGUIST n composer of fugues

FUGUS ▸ fug

FUHRER = **feuhrer**

FUHRERS ▸ fuhrer

FUJI n type of African music **fujis**

FULCRA ▸ fulcrum

FULCRUM n

FULFIL vb fulfill, **fulfils**

FULGENT adj shining brilliantly **fulgid**

FULGOR n brilliance **fulgors, fulgour**

FULHAM n loaded die **fulhams**

FULL adj, adv, vb

FULLAGE n price charged for fulling cloth

FULLAM variant of ▸ **fulham**

FULLAMS ▸ fullam

FULLAN variant of ▸ **fulham**

FULLANS ▸ fullan

FULLED ▸ full

FULLER n person who fulls cloth for his living ▷ vb forge (a groove) or caulk (a riveted joint) with a fuller **fullers**

FULLERY n place where fulling is carried out

FULLEST, fulling, fullish, fulls ▸ full

FULLY adv greatest degree or extent

FULMAR n Arctic sea bird **fulmars**

FULMINE vb fulminate

FULNESS ▸ full

FULSOME adj

FULVID variant of ▸ **fulvous**

FULVOUS adj of a dull brownish-yellow colour

FUM n phoenix, in Chinese mythology

FUMADO n salted,

smoked fish **fumados**

FUMAGE n hearth money **fumages**

FUMARIC adj as in fumaric acid colourless crystalline acid

FUMBLE vb, n fumbled, **fumbler, fumbles**

FUME vb

FUMED adj (of wood) having been exposed to ammonia fumes

FUMER ▸ fume

FUMERS ▸ fume

FUMES ▸ fume

FUMET n liquor from cooking fish, meat, or game **fumets, fumette**

FUMETTI ▸ fumetto

FUMETTO n speech balloon in a comic or cartoon

FUMIER, fumiest, fuming, fumous ▸ fume

FUMS ▸ fum

FUMULI ▸ fumulus

FUMULUS n smokelike cloud

FUMY ▸ fume

FUN n, vb

FUNCKIA n type of plant resembling the lily

FUNCTOR n performer of a function

FUND n, vb funded, **funder, funders**

FUNDI n

FUNDIC ▸ fundus

FUNDIE n fundamentalist

Christian **fundies**
FUNDING ▶ fund
FUNDIS ▶ fundi
FUNDS pl n money that is readily available
FUNDUS n base of an organ
FUNDY n fundamentalist
FUNEBRE adj funereal or mournful
FUNERAL n
FUNEST adj lamentable
FUNFAIR n
FUNFEST n enjoyable time
FUNG = funk
FUNGAL adj of, derived from, or caused by a fungus or fungi ▷ n fungus or fungal infection **fungals**
FUNGI ▶ fungus
FUNGIC ▶ fungus
FUNGO n in baseball, act of tossing and hitting the ball ▷ vb toss and hit a ball **fungoes**
FUNGOID adj resembling a fungus
FUNGOUS adj appearing and spreading quickly like a fungus
FUNGS ▶ fung
FUNGUS n
FUNICLE n stalk that attaches an ovule to the wall of the ovary
FUNK n, vb **funked, funker, funkers**
FUNKIA n hosta **funkias**
FUNKIER ▶ funky
FUNKILY ▶ funky

FUNKING ▶ funk
FUNKS ▶ funk
FUNKY adj (of music) having a strong beat
FUNNED ▶ fun
FUNNEL n, vb **funnels**
FUNNER ▶ fun
FUNNEST ▶ fun
FUNNIER ▶ funny
FUNNIES pl n comic strips in a newspaper
FUNNILY ▶ funny
FUNNING ▶ fun
FUNNY adj, n
FUNPLEX n large amusement centre
FUNS ▶ fun
FUNSTER n funnyman
FUR n, vb
FURAL n furfural **furals**
FURAN n colourless flammable toxic liquid heterocyclic compound **furane**
FURANES ▶ furane
FURANS ▶ furan
FURBISH vb
FURCA n any forklike structure, esp in insects **furcae, furcal**
FURCATE vb divide into two parts ▷ adj forked, branching
FURCULA n any forklike part or organ
FURDER = further
FUREUR n rage or anger **fureurs**
FURFAIR variant of ▶ furfur
FURFUR n scurf or scaling of the skin **furfurs**
FURIES ▶ fury

FURIOSO adv in a frantically rushing manner ▷ n passage or piece to be performed in this way
FURIOUS adj
FURKID n companion animal **furkids**
FURL vb, n
FURLANA variant of ▶ forlana
FURLED ▶ furl
FURLER ▶ furl
FURLERS ▶ furl
FURLESS ▶ fur
FURLING ▶ furl
FURLONG n
FURLS ▶ furl
FURMETY = frumenty
FURMITY = frumenty
FURNACE n, vb
FURNISH vb
FUROL variant of > furfural
FUROLE variant of > furfural
FUROLES ▶ furole
FUROLS ▶ furol
FUROR = furore
FURORE = furores
FURORS ▶ furor
FURPHY n rumour or fictitious story
FURR vb furrow
FURRED = furry
FURRIER n
FURRIES ▶ furry
FURRILY ▶ furry
FURRING ▶ fur
FURROW n, vb **furrows, furrowy**
FURRS ▶ furr
FURRY adj like or covered with fur or

something furlike ▷ *n* child's fur-covered toy animal

FURS ▶ fur

FURTH *adv* out

FURTHER *adv, adj, vb*

FURTIVE *adj*

FURY *n*

FURZE *n* gorse **furzes, furzier, furzy**

FUSAIN *n* fine charcoal pencil **fusains**

FUSAROL *variant of* > fusarole

FUSBALL > foosball

FUSC *adj* dark or dark-brown

FUSCOUS *adj* of a brownish-grey colour

FUSE *n, vb* **fused**

FUSEE *n* (in early clocks and watches) a spirally grooved spindle **fusees**

FUSEL *n* mixture of amyl alcohols, propanol, and butanol **fusels**

FUSES ▶ fuse

FUSHION *n* spirit

FUSIBLE *adj* capable of being melted **fusibly**

FUSIDIC *adj* as in **fusidic acid** kind of acid

FUSIL *n* light flintlock musket

FUSILE *adj* easily melted

FUSILLI *n* spiral-shaped pasta

FUSILS ▶ fusil

FUSING ▶ fuse

FUSION *n, adj* **fusions**

FUSS *n, vb* **fussed, fusser, fussers, fusses**

FUSSIER ▶ fussy

FUSSILY ▶ fussy

FUSSING ▶ fuss

FUSSPOT *n* person who is difficult to please and complains often

FUSSY *adj*

FUST *vb* become mouldy **fusted**

FUSTET *n* wood of the Venetian sumach shrub **fustets**

FUSTIAN *n* (formerly) a hard-wearing fabric of cotton mixed with flax or wool ▷ *adj* cheap

FUSTIC *n* large tropical American tree **fustics**

FUSTIER ▶ fusty

FUSTILY ▶ fusty

FUSTING ▶ fust

FUSTOC = fustic

FUSTOCS ▶ fustoc

FUSTS ▶ fust

FUSTY *adj*

FUSUMA *n* Japanese sliding door

FUTCHEL *n* timber support in a carriage

FUTHARC = futhark

FUTHARK *n* phonetic alphabet consisting of runes **futhorc, futhork**

FUTILE *adj* **futiler**

FUTON *n* Japanese-style bed **futons**

FUTSAL *n* form of association football **futsals**

FUTTOCK *n* one of the ribs in the frame of a wooden vessel

FUTURAL *adj* relating to the future

FUTURE *n, adj*

FUTURES *pl n* type of commodity trading

FUTZ *vb* fritter time away **futzed, futzes, futzing**

FUZE = fuse

FUZED ▶ fuze

FUZEE = fusee

FUZEES ▶ fuzee

FUZES ▶ fuze

FUZIL *variant of* ▶ fusil

FUZILS ▶ fuzil

FUZING ▶ fuze

FUZZ *n, vb*

FUZZBOX *n* device that distorts sound

FUZZED ▶ fuzz

FUZZES ▶ fuzz

FUZZIER ▶ fuzzy

FUZZILY ▶ fuzzy

FUZZING ▶ fuzz

FUZZLE *vb* make drunk **fuzzled, fuzzles**

FUZZY *adj*

FY *variant of* ▶ fie

FYCE *variant of* ▶ fice

FYCES ▶ fyce

FYKE *n* fish trap ▷ *vb* catch fish in this manner **fyked, fykes, fyking**

FYLE *variant of* ▶ file

FYLES ▶ fyle

FYLFOT *rare word for* > swastika

FYLFOTS ▶ fylfot

FYNBOS *n* area of low-growing, evergreen vegetation

FYRD *n* militia of an Anglo-Saxon shire **fyrds**

FYTTE *n* song **fyttes**

Gg

Only three two-letter words begin with **G** (**gi**, **go** and **gu**). Knowing these will save you worrying about other possibilities. There are quite a few short words beginning with **G** that use **Y**, which can prove very useful. These include **gay**, **gey**, **goy** and **guy** (7 points each), as well as **gym** and **gyp** (9 points each). And don't forget the very useful **gox** for 11 points.

GAB vb talk or chatter ▷ n mechanical device

GABBA n type of electronic dance music

GABBARD = gabbart

GABBART n Scottish sailing barge

GABBAS ▷ gabba

GABBED ▷ gab

GABBER ▷ gab

GABBERS ▷ gab

GABBIER ▷ gabby

GABBING ▷ gab

GABBLE vb, n gabbled, gabbler, gabbles

GABBRO n dark basic plutonic igneous rock gabbros

GABBY adj talkative

GABELLE n salt tax levied until 1790

GABFEST n prolonged gossiping or conversation

GABIES ▷ gaby

GABION n cylindrical metal container filled with stones **gabions**

GABLE n gabled, gables

GABLET n small gable gablets

GABLING ▷ gable

GABNASH n chatter

GABOON n dark wood gaboons

GABS ▷ gab

GABY n simpleton

GAD vb, n gadded, gadder, gadders

GADDI n cushion on an Indian prince's throne

GADDING ▷ gad

GADDIS ▷ gaddi

GADE = gad

GADES ▷ gade

GADFLY n fly that bites cattle

GADGE n man gadges

GADGET n gadgets, gadgety

GADGIE n fellow gadgies

GADI n Indian throne

GADID n type of marine fish **gadids**

GADIS ▷ gadi

GADJE = gadgie

GADJES ▷ gadje

GADJO ▷ gorgio

GADLING n vagabond

GADOID adj of the cod family of marine fishes ▷ n gadoid fish gadoids

GADROON n type of decorative moulding

GADS ▷ gad

GADSMAN n person who uses a gad when driving animals gadsmen

GADSO n archaic expression of surprise

GADWALL n type of duck related to the mallard

GAE Scot word for ▷ go

GAED ▷ gae

GAEING ▸ gae

GAEN ▸ gae

GAES ▸ gae

GAFF n stick with an iron hook for landing large fish ▸ vb hook or land (a fish) with a gaff

GAFFE n

GAFFED ▸ gaff

GAFFER n gaffers

GAFFES ▸ gaffe

GAFFING ▸ gaff

GAFFS ▸ gaff

GAG vb, n

GAGA adj

GAGAKU n type of traditional Japanese music gagakus

GAGE vb gauge ▸ n (formerly) an object thrown down as a challenge to fight gaged

GAGER = gauger

GAGERS ▸ gager

GAGES ▸ gage

GAGGED ▸ gag

GAGGER n person or thing that gags gaggers

GAGGERY n practice of telling jokes

GAGGING ▸ gag

GAGGLE n, vb gaggled, gaggles

GAGING ▸ gage

GAGMAN n person who writes gags for a comedian gagmen

GAGS ▸ gag

GAGSTER n standup comedian

GAHNITE n dark green mineral

GAID = gad

GAIDS ▸ gaid

GAIETY n

GAIJIN n (in Japan) a foreigner

GAILY adv

GAIN vb, n, adj gained

GAINER n person or thing that gains gainers

GAINEST ▸ gain

GAINFUL adj useful or profitable

GAINING ▸ gain

GAINLY adj graceful or well-formed ▸ adv conveniently or suitably

GAINS pl n profits or winnings

GAINSAY vb

GAINST short for ▸ against

GAIR n strip of green grass on a hillside gairs

GAIT n, vb

GAITA n type of bagpipe gaitas

GAITED ▸ gait

GAITER n gaiters

GAITING ▸ gait

GAITS ▸ gait

GAITT Scots word for ▸ gate

GAITTS ▸ gaitt

GAJO = gorgio

GAJOS ▸ gajo

GAK n gaks

GAL n girl

GALA n

GALABEA = djellaba

GALABIA = djellaba

GALAGE = galosh

GALAGES ▸ galage

GALAGO another name for ▸ bushbaby

GALAGOS ▸ galago

GALAH n galahs

GALANGA = galingale

GALANT n 18th-century style of music

GALANTY n as in galanty show pantomime shadow play

GALAS ▸ gala

GALATEA n strong twill-weave cotton fabric

GALAX n coltsfoot galaxes

GALAXY n

GALE n

GALEA n part or organ shaped like a helmet galeae, galeas, galeate

GALENA n soft bluish-grey mineral galenas, galenic

GALERE n group of people having a common interest galeres

GALES ▸ gale

GALETTE n type of savoury pancake

GALILEE n type of porch or chapel

GALIOT n small swift galley galiots

GALIPOT n resin obtained from several species of pine

GALL n, vb

GALLANT adj, n, vb

GALLATE n salt of gallic acid

GALLED ▸ gall

GALLEIN n type of dyestuff

GALLEON n

GALLERY n, vb

GALLET vb use mixture to support a roof-slate

GALLETA n low-growing, coarse grass

GALLETS ▸ gallet

GALLEY n galleys

GALLFLY n any of several small insects

GALLIC adj of or containing gallium in the trivalent state

GALLICA n variety of rose

GALLIED ▸ gally

GALLIES ▸ gally

GALLING adj annoying or bitterly humiliating

GALLIOT = galliot

GALLISE vb use method to increase the quantity of wine produced

GALLIUM n soft grey metallic element

GALLIZE = gallise

GALLNUT n type of plant gall that resembles a nut

GALLOCK adj left-handed

GALLON n gallons

GALLOON n narrow band of cord, gold braid, etc

GALLOOT = galloot

GALLOP n, vb gallops

GALLOUS adj of or containing gallium in the divalent state

GALLOW vb frighten

GALLOWS n

GALLS ▸ gall

GALLUS adj bold ▸ n suspender for trousers

GALLY vb frighten

GALOCHE = galosh

GALOOT n clumsy or uncouth person galoots

GALOP n 19th-century dance in quick duple time ▸ vb dance a galop galoped

GALOPIN n boy who ran errands for a cook

GALOPS ▸ galop

GALORE adv, adj, n galores

GALOSH n waterproof overshoe ▸ vb cover with galoshes **galoshe**

GALS ▸ gal

GALUMPH vb leap or move about clumsily

GALUT = galuth

GALUTH n exile of Jews from Palestine galuths

GALUTS ▸ galut

GALVO n instrument for measuring electric current galvos

GALYAC = galyak

GALYACS ▸ galyac

GALYAK n smooth glossy fur galyaks

GAM n school of whales ▸ vb (of whales) form a school

GAMA n tall perennial grass gamas

GAMASH n type of gaiter

GAMAY n red grape

variety, or the wine made from it **gamays**

GAMB n in heraldry, the whole foreleg of a beast

GAMBA n second-largest member of the viol family

GAMBADE = gambado

GAMBADO n leap or gambol; caper ▸ vb perform a gambado

GAMBAS ▸ gamba

GAMBE = gamb

GAMBES ▸ gambe

GAMBET n tattler gambets

GAMBIA = gambier

GAMBIAS ▸ gambia

GAMBIER n astringent resinous substance gambir

GAMBIRS ▸ gambir

GAMBIST n person who plays the (viola da) gamba

GAMBIT n, vb gambits

GAMBLE vb, n gambled, gambler, gambles

GAMBO n farm cart gamboes

GAMBOGE n gum resin

GAMBOL vb, n gambols

GAMBREL n hock of a horse or similar animal

GAMBS ▸ gamb

GAME n, vb, adj gamed

GAMELAN n type of percussion orchestra

GAMELY adv in a brave or sporting manner

GAMER n person who plays computer games gamers

GAMES ▸ game

GAMEST ▸ game

GAMESY adj sporty

GAMETAL ▸ gamete

GAMETE n **gametes**, **gametic**

GAMEY adj having the smell or flavour of game

GAMGEE n as in **gamgee tissue** type of wound-dressing

GAMIC adj (esp of reproduction) requiring the fusion of gametes

GAMIER ▸ gamey

GAMIEST ▸ gamey

GAMILY ▸ gamey

GAMIN n street urchin

GAMINE n slim boyish young woman **gamines**

GAMING n gambling **gamings**

GAMINS ▸ gamin

GAMMA n third letter of the Greek alphabet **gammas**

GAMME n musical scale

GAMMED ▸ gam

GAMMES ▸ gamme

GAMMING ▸ gam

GAMMOCK vb clown around

GAMMON n, vb **gammons**

GAMONE n chemical used by gametes during sexual reproduction **gamones**

GAMP n umbrella

GAMPISH adj bulging

GAMPS ▸ gamp

GAMS ▸ gam

GAMUT n **gamuts**

GAMY = gamey

GAN vb go

GANACHE n rich icing or filling

GANCH vb impale **ganched, ganches**

GANDER n, vb **ganders**

GANDY adj as in **gandy dancer** railway track maintenance worker

GANE = gangue

GANEF n unscrupulous opportunist **ganefs, ganev**

GANEVS ▸ ganev

GANG n, vb **ganged**

GANGER n foreman of a gang of labourers **gangers**

GANGING ▸ gang

GANGLIA ▸ ganglion

GANGLY = gangling

GANGREL n wandering beggar

GANGS ▸ gang

GANGSTA n member of a street gang

GANGUE n valueless material in an ore **gangues**

GANGWAY = gangplank

GANJA n highly potent form of cannabis **ganjah**

GANJAHS ▸ ganjah

GANJAS ▸ ganja

GANNED ▸ gan

GANNET n **gannets**

GANNING ▸ gan

GANOF = ganef

GANOFS ▸ ganof

GANOID adj of the scales of certain fishes ▷ n ganoid fish **ganoids**

GANOIN n the outer layer of fish scales **ganoine, ganoins**

GANS ▸ gan

GANSEY n jersey or pullover **ganseys**

GANT vb yawn **ganted, ganting**

GANTLET n section of a railway where two tracks overlap ▷ vb make railway tracks form a gantlet

GANTRY n

GANTS ▸ gant

GAOL = jail; **gaoled, gaoler, gaolers, gaoling, gaols**

GAP n

GAPE vb, n **gaped**

GAPER n person or thing that gapes **gapers**

GAPES n disease of young domestic fowl **gapier, gapiest**

GAPING adj wide open ▷ n state of having a gaping mouth **gapings**

GAPLESS ▸ gap

GAPO n forest near a river, flooded in the rainy season **gapos**

GAPOSIS n gap between closed fastenings on a garment

GAPPED ▸ gap

GAPPER n person taking a year out of education **gappers**

GAPPIER ▸ gap

GAPPING n

GAPPY ▸ gap

GAPS ▸ gap

GAPY ▸ gapes

GAR = garpike

GARAGE n, vb garaged, garages

GARAGEY adj (of music) in a garage style

GARB n, vb

GARBAGE n garbagy

GARBE n in heraldry, a wheat-sheaf

GARBED ▸ garb

GARBES ▸ garbe

GARBING ▸ garb

GARBLE vb jumble (a story, quotation, etc), esp unintentionally ▸ n act of garbling

GARBLED adj

GARBLER ▸ garble

GARBLES ▸ garble

GARBO n dustman

GARBOIL n confusion or disturbance

GARBOS ▸ garbo

GARBS ▸ garb

GARBURE n thick soup from Bearn in France

GARCON n waiter garcons

GARDA n member of the Irish police force gardai

GARDANT = guardant

GARDEN n, vb gardens

GARFISH n

GARGET n inflammation of the mammary gland gargets, gargety

GARGLE vb, n gargled, gargler, gargles

GARI n thinly sliced pickled ginger

GARIAL = gavial

GARIALS ▸ garial

GARIGUE n open shrubby vegetation of dry Mediterranean regions

GARIS ▸ gari

GARISH adj, vb

GARJAN = gurjun

GARJANS ▸ garjan

GARLAND n, vb

GARLIC n garlics

GARMENT n, vb

GARNER vb, n garners

GARNET n garnets

GARNI adj garnished

GARNISH vb, n

GAROTE = garrotte

GAROTED ▸ garote

GAROTES ▸ garote

GAROTTE = garrotte

GAROUPA in Chinese and SE Asian cookery, another name for ▸ groper

GARPIKE n primitive freshwater bony fish

GARRAN = garron

GARRANS ▸ garran

GARRE vb compel

GARRED ▸ gar

GARRES ▸ garre

GARRET n garrets

GARRING ▸ gar

GARRON n small sturdy pony garrons

GARROT n goldeneye duck

GARROTE = garrotte

GARROTS ▸ garrot

GARRYA n catkin-bearing evergreen shrub **garryas**

GARS ▸ gar

GART vb compel

GARTER n, vb garters

GARTH n courtyard surrounded by a cloister **garths**

GARUDA n Hindu god garudas

GARUM n fermented fish sauce garums

GARVEY n small flat-bottomed yacht garveys

GARVIE n sprat garvies

GARVOCK n sprat

GAS n, vb

GASAHOL n mixture of petrol and alcohol used as fuel

GASBAG n person who talks too much ▸ vb talk in a voluble way gasbags

GASCON n boaster gascons

GASEITY n state of being gaseous

GASEOUS adj

GASES ▸ gas

GASH vb, n, adj gashed, gasher, gashes, gashest

GASHFUL adj full of gashes

GASHING ▸ gash

GASHLY adv wittily

GASIFY vb change into a gas

GASKET n gaskets

GASKIN n lower part of a horse's thigh

GASKING = gasket

GASKINS ▸ gaskin

GASLESS ▸ gas

GASLIT adj lit by gas
GASMAN n man employed by a gas company **gasmen**
GASOHOL n mixture of petrol and ethyl alcohol
GASP vb, n **gasped**
GASPER n person who gasps **gaspers**
GASPIER, gasping, gasps, gaspy ▶ gasp
GASSED ▶ gas
GASSER n drilling or well that yields natural gas **gassers**
GASSES ▶ gas
GASSIER ▶ gassy
GASSILY ▶ gassy
GASSING ▶ gas
GASSY adj
GAST vb frighten **gasted, gaster, gasters, gasting**
GASTRAL adj relating to the stomach
GASTREA = gastraea
GASTRIC adj
GASTRIN n polypeptide hormone
GASTS ▶ gast
GAT n pistol or revolver
GATE n, vb
GATEAU n **gateaus, gateaux**
GATED ▶ gate
GATELEG adj (of a table) having a hinged leg that swings out
GATEMAN n gatekeeper **gatemen**
GATER variant of ▶ gator
GATERS ▶ gater
GATES ▶ gate

GATEWAY n
GATH n (in Indian music) second section of a raga
GATHER vb, n **gathers**
GATHS ▶ gath
GATING ▶ gate
GATINGS ▶ gate
GATLING n as in gatling gun kind of machinegun
GATOR shortened form of ▶ alligator
GATORS ▶ gator
GATS ▶ gat
GATVOL adj in South African English, fed up
GAU n district set up by the Nazi Party
GAUCHE adj **gaucher**
GAUCHO n S American cowboy **gauchos**
GAUCIE variant of ▶ gaucy
GAUCIER ▶ gaucy
GAUCY adj plump or jolly
GAUD n article of cheap finery ▷ vb decorate gaudily **gauded**
GAUDERY n cheap finery or display
GAUDGIE = gadgie
GAUDIER ▶ gaudy
GAUDIES ▶ gaudy
GAUDILY ▶ gaudy
GAUDING ▶ gaud
GAUDS ▶ gaud
GAUDY adj, n
GAUFER n wafer **gaufers**
GAUFFER = goffer
GAUFRE = gaufer
GAUFRES ▶ gaufre

GAUGE vb, n, adj **gauged**
GAUGER n person or thing that gauges **gaugers**
GAUGES ▶ gauge
GAUGING ▶ gauge
GAUJE = gadgie
GAUJES ▶ gauje
GAULT n stiff compact clay or thick heavy clayey soil
GAULTER n person who digs gault
GAULTS ▶ gault
GAUM vb understand **gaumed**
GAUMIER ▶ gaumy
GAUMING ▶ gaum
GAUMS ▶ gaum
GAUMY adj clogged
GAUN ▶ go
GAUNCH = ganch
GAUNT adj, vb **gaunted, gaunter, gauntly**
GAUNTRY = gantry
GAUNTS ▶ gaunt
GAUP = gawp; gauped, gauper, gaupers, gauping, gaups
GAUPUS = gawpus
GAUR n large wild member of the cattle tribe **gaurs**
GAUS ▶ gau
GAUSS n cgs unit of magnetic flux density **gausses**
GAUZE n **gauzes**
GAUZIER ▶ gauzy
GAUZILY ▶ gauzy
GAUZY adj
GAVAGE n forced feeding by means of a tube **gavages**

GAVE ▶ give

GAVEL n, vb gaveled, gavels

GAVIAL n as in false gavial small crocodile gavials

GAVOT = gavotte

GAVOTS ▶ gavot

GAVOTTE n old formal dance ▷ vb dance a gavotte

GAW n as in weather gaw partial rainbow

GAWCIER ▶ gawcy

GAWCY = gaucy

GAWD = gaud

GAWDS ▶ gawd

GAWK vb stare stupidly ▷ n clumsy awkward person gawked, gawker, gawkers

GAWKIER ▶ gawky

GAWKIES ▶ gawky

GAWKILY ▶ gawky

GAWKING ▶ gawk

GAWKISH = gawky

GAWKS ▶ gawk

GAWKY adj, n

GAWP vb gawped, gawper, gawpers, gawping, gawps

GAWPUS n silly person

GAWS ▶ gaw

GAWSIE = gaucy

GAWSIER ▶ gawsie

GAWSY = gaucy

GAY adj, n

GAYAL n type of ox gayals

GAYDAR n supposed ability of one homosexual person to know another gaydars

GAYER ▶ gay

GAYEST ▶ gay

GAYETY = gaiety

GAYLY ▶ gay

GAYNESS ▶ gay

GAYS ▶ gay

GAYSOME adj full of merriment

GAZABO n fellow or companion gazabos

GAZAL = ghazal

GAZALS ▶ gazal

GAZANIA n S African plant

GAZAR n type of silk cloth gazars

GAZE vb, n

GAZEBO n summerhouse with a good view gazebos

GAZED ▶ gaze

GAZEFUL adj gazing

GAZELLE n

GAZER ▶ gaze

GAZERS ▶ gaze

GAZES ▶ gaze

GAZETTE n, vb

GAZIER ▶ gazy

GAZIEST ▶ gazy

GAZING ▶ gaze

GAZINGS ▶ gaze

GAZON n sod used to cover a parapet in a fortification gazons

GAZOO n kazoo gazooka

GAZOON = gazon

GAZOONS ▶ gazoon

GAZOOS ▶ gazoo

GAZUMP vb, n gazumps

GAZY adj prone to gazing

GEAL vb congeal gealed, gealing

GEALOUS Spenserian spelling of ▶ jealous

GEALS ▶ geal

GEAN n white-flowered tree geans

GEAR n, vb

GEARBOX n

GEARE Spenserian spelling of ▶ jeer

GEARED ▶ gear

GEARES ▶ geare

GEARING n system of gears designed to transmit motion

GEARS ▶ gear

GEASON adj wonderful

GEAT n in casting, the channel which leads to a mould geats

GEBUR n tenant farmer geburs

GECK vb beguile gecked, gecking

GECKO n small tropical lizard geckoes, geckos

GECKS ▶ geck

GED Scots word for ▶ pike

GEDACT n flutelike stopped metal diapason organ pipe gedacts

GEDDIT interj exclamation meaning do you understand it?

GEDECKT = gedact

GEDS ▶ ged

GEE interj mild exclamation of surprise, admiration, etc ▷ vb move (an animal, esp a horse) ahead

GEEBUNG n Australian tree or shrub

GEECHEE n Black person from the southern states of the US

GEED ▸ gee

GEEGAW = gewgaw

GEEGAWS ▸ geegaw

GEEING ▸ gee

GEEK n geekdom

GEEKED adj highly excited

GEEKIER ▸ geek

GEEKS ▸ geek

GEEKY ▸ geek

GEELBEK n edible marine fish

GEEP n cross between a goat and a sheep **geeps**

GEES ▸ gee

GEESE ▸ goose

GEEST n area of heathland in N Germany and adjacent areas **geests**

GEEZ interj expression of surprise

GEEZAH variant spelling of ▸ geezer

GEEZAHS ▸ geezah

GEEZER n geezers

GEFILTE adj as in **gefilte fish** dish of fish stuffed with various ingredients

GEGGIE Scottish, esp Glaswegian, slang word for the ▸ mouth

GEGGIES ▸ geggie

GEISHA n geishas

GEIST n spirit geists

GEIT n border on clothing geits

GEL n, vb

GELABLE adj capable of

forming a gel

GELADA n NE African baboon **geladas**

GELANDE adj as in **gelande jump** jump made in downhill skiing

GELANT = gellant

GELANTS ▸ gelant

GELATE vb form a gel **gelated, gelates**

GELATI n layered dessert

GELATIN = gelatine

GELATIS ▸ gelati

GELATO n Italian frozen dessert, similar to ice cream **gelatos**

GELCAP n medicine enclosed in gelatine **gelcaps**

GELD vb castrate ▷ n tax on land in Anglo-Saxon and Norman England **gelded, gelder, gelders, gelding, gelds**

GELEE n jelly gelees

GELID adj very cold, icy, or frosty **gelider, gelidly**

GELLANT n compound that forms a solid structure

GELLED ▸ gel

GELLIES ▸ gelly

GELLING ▸ gel

GELLY = gelignite

GELS ▸ gel

GELT ▸ geld

GELTS ▸ geld

GEM n, vb

GEMCLIP n paperclip

GEMEL n in heraldry, parallel bars **gemels**

GEMFISH n Australian food fish with a delicate flavour

GEMINAL adj occurring in pairs

GEMINI n expression of surprise

GEMINY n pair

GEMLIKE ▸ gem

GEMMA n reproductive structure in liverworts, mosses, etc **gemmae**

GEMMAN dialect form of ▸ gentleman

GEMMATE adj (of some plants and animals) having gemmae ▷ vb produce or reproduce by gemmae

GEMMED ▸ gem

GEMMEN ▸ gemman

GEMMERY n gems collectively

GEMMIER ▸ gem

GEMMILY ▸ gem

GEMMING ▸ gem

GEMMULE n result of asexual reproduction by sponges

GEMMY ▸ gem

GEMONY = jiminy

GEMOT n (in Anglo-Saxon England) a legal or administrative assembly **gemote**

GEMOTES ▸ gemote

GEMOTS ▸ gemot

GEMS ▸ gem

GEMSBOK = oryx

GEN n, vb

GENA n cheek genal

GENAPPE *n* smooth worsted yarn used for braid, etc
GENAS ▸ gena
GENDER *n, vb* genders
GENE *n*
GENERA ▸ genus
GENERAL *adj, n, vb*
GENERIC *adj, n*
GENES ▸ gene
GENESES ▸ genesis
GENESIS *n*
GENET *n* type of agile catlike mammal
GENETIC *adj* of genes or genetics
GENETS ▸ genet
GENETTE = genet
GENEVA *n* gin genevas
GENIAL *adj*
GENIC *adj* of or relating to a gene or genes
GENIE *n* genies
GENII ▸ genius
GENIP = genipap
GENIPAP *n* evergreen Caribbean tree
GENIPS ▸ genip
GENISTA *n* any member of the broom family
GENITAL *adj* of the sexual organs or reproduction
GENITOR *n* biological father
GENIUS *n*
GENIZAH *n* repository for sacred objects which may not be destroyed genizot
GENLOCK *n* generator locking device
GENNED ▸ gen
GENNEL = ginnel

GENNELS ▸ gennel
GENNET *n* female donkey or ass gennets
GENNIES ▸ genny
GENNING ▸ gen
GENNY = genoa
GENOA *n* large triangular jib sail genoas
GENOISE *n* rich sponge cake
GENOM = genome
GENOME *n* genomes, genomic
GENOMS ▸ genom
GENRE *n* genres
GENRO *n* group of Japanese statesmen genros
GENS *n* (in ancient Rome) a group of aristocratic families
GENSENG = ginseng
GENT *n* gentleman
GENTEEL *adj*
GENTES ▸ gens
GENTIAN *n*
GENTIER ▸ genty
GENTIL *adj* gentle
GENTILE *n* non-Jewish person ▷ *adj* used to designate a place or the inhabitants of a place
GENTLE *adj, vb, n* gentled, gentler, gentles, gently
GENTOO *n* grey-backed penguin gentoos
GENTRY *n*
GENTS *n*
GENTY *adj* neat
GENU *n* any knee-like bend in a structure or

part **genua**
GENUINE *adj*
GENUS *n* genuses
GEO *n* (esp in Shetland) a small fjord or gully
GEODE *n* cavity within a rock mass or nodule geodes
GEODESY *n* study of the shape and size of the earth
GEODIC ▸ geode
GEODUCK *n* king clam
GEOFACT *n* rock shaped by natural forces
GEOGENY = geogony
GEOGONY *n* science of the earth's formation
GEOID *n* hypothetical surface geoidal, geoids
GEOLOGY *n*
GEOMANT *n* geomancer
GEORGIC *adj* agricultural ▷ *n* poem about rural or agricultural life
GEOS ▸ geo
GER *n* portable Mongolian dwelling
GERAH *n* ancient Hebrew unit of weight gerahs
GERBE = garbe
GERBERA *n* type of plant
GERBES ▸ garbe
GERBIL *n* gerbils
GERE *Spenserian spelling of* ▸ gear
GERENT *n* person who rules or manages gerents
GERENUK *n* slender antelope
GERES ▸ gear

GERLE *Spenserian spelling of* ▸ **girl**

GERLES ▸ **gerle**

GERM *n, vb*

GERMAIN = **germen**

GERMAN *n* type of dance ▷ *adj* having the same parents as oneself

GERMANE *adj*

GERMANS ▸ **german**

GERMED ▸ **germ**

GERMEN *n* cells that gives rise to the germ cells **germens**

GERMIER ▸ **germy**

GERMIN = **germen**

GERMINA ▸ **germen**

GERMING ▸ **germ**

GERMINS ▸ **germen**

GERMS ▸ **germ**

GERMY *adj* full of germs

GERNE *vb* grin **gerned, gernes, gerning**

GERS ▸ **ger**

GERT *adv* in dialect, great or very big

GERTCHA *interj* get out of here!

GERUND *n* noun formed from a verb **gerunds**

GESSE *Spenserian spelling of* ▸ **guess**

GESSED ▸ **gesse**

GESSES ▸ **gesse**

GESSING ▸ **gesse**

GESSO *n* plaster used for painting or in sculpture ▷ *vb* apply gesso to **gessoed, gessoes**

GEST *n* notable deed or exploit

GESTALT *n* perceptual pattern or structure

GESTANT *adj* laden

GESTAPO *n* any secret state police organization

GESTATE *vb* carry (young) in the uterus during pregnancy

GESTE = **gest**

GESTES ▸ **geste**

GESTIC *adj* consisting of gestures

GESTS ▸ **gest**

GESTURE *n, vb*

GET *vb* obtain or receive

GETA *n* type of Japanese wooden sandal

GETABLE ▸ **get**

GETAS ▸ **geta**

GETAWAY *n*

GETS ▸ **get**

GETTER *n* person or thing that gets ▷ *vb* remove (a gas) by the action of a getter **getters**

GETTING ▸ **get**

GETUP *n* outfit **getups**

GEUM *n* type of herbaceous plant **geums**

GEWGAW *n* showy but valueless trinket ▷ *adj* showy and valueless **gewgaws**

GEY *adv* extremely ▷ *adj* gallant

GEYAN *adv* somewhat

GEYER ▸ **gey**

GEYEST ▸ **gey**

GEYSER *n* **geysers**

GHARIAL = **gavial**

GHARRI = **gharry**

GHARRIS ▸ **gharri**

GHARRY *n* (in India)

horse-drawn vehicle

GHAST *vb* terrify **ghasted**

GHASTLY *adj, adv*

GHASTS ▸ **ghast**

GHAT *n* (in India) steps leading down to a river **ghats**

GHAUT *n* small cleft in a hill **ghauts**

GHAZAL *n* Arabic love poem **ghazals, ghazal**

GHAZELS ▸ **ghazel**

GHAZI *n* Muslim fighter against infidels **ghazies, ghazis**

GHEE *n* (in Indian cookery) clarified butter **ghees**

GHERAO *n* form of industrial action in India ▷ *vb* trap an employer in his office, to indicate the workforce's discontent **gheraos**

GHERKIN *n*

GHESSE *Spenserian spelling of* ▸ **guess**

GHESSED ▸ **ghesse**

GHESSES ▸ **ghesse**

GHEST ▸ **ghesse**

GHETTO *n, vb* **ghettos**

GHI = **ghee**

GHIBLI *n* fiercely hot wind of North Africa **ghiblis**

GHILGAI = **gilgai**

GHILLIE *n* type of tongueless shoe ▷ *vb* act as a g(h)illie

GHIS ▸ **ghi**

GHOST *n, vb* **ghosted**

GHOSTLY *adj* frightening

in appearance or effect **GHOSTS ▸ ghost**

GHOSTY *adj* pertaining to ghosts

GHOUL *n*

GHOULIE *n* goblin

GHOULS ▸ ghoul

GHRELIN *n*

GHUBAR *adj as in* **ghubar numeral** type of numeral

GHYLL = gill

GHYLLS ▸ ghyll

GI *n* white suit worn in martial arts

GIANT *n, adj*

GIANTLY *adj* giantlike

GIANTRY *n* collective term for giants

GIANTS ▸ giant

GIARDIA *n* species of parasite

GIB *n* metal wedge, pad, or thrust bearing ▷ *vb* fasten or supply with a gib **gibbed**

GIBBER *vb, n,* **gibbers**

GIBBET *n, vb* gibbets

GIBBING ▸ gib

GIBBON *n* gibbons

GIBBOSE = gibbous

GIBBOUS *adj* (of the moon) between half and fully illuminated

GIBE *vb, n* gibed

GIBEL *n* Prussian carp gibels

GIBER, gibers, gibes, gibing ▸ gibe

GIBLET ▸ giblets

GIBLETS *pl n*

GIBLI = ghibli

GIBLIS ▸ gibli

GIBS ▸ gib

GIBSON *n* martini garnished with onion **gibsons**

GIBUS *n* collapsible top hat **gibuses**

GID *n* disease of sheep

GIDDAP *interj* exclamation used to make a horse go faster

GIDDAY *interj*

GIDDIED, giddier, giddies, giddily ▸ giddy

GIDDY *adj, vb*

GIDDYAP = giddyup

GIDDYUP *interj* exclamation used to make a horse go faster

GIDGEE *n* small acacia tree **gidgees, gidjee**

GIDJEES ▸ gidjee

GIDS ▸ gid

GIE *Scot word for ▸ give*

GIED ▸ give

GIEING ▸ give

GIEN ▸ give

GIES ▸ give

GIF *obsolete word for ▸ if*

GIFT *n, vb*

GIFTED *adj*

GIFTEE *n* person given a gift **giftees**

GIFTING ▸ gift

GIFTS ▸ gift

GIG *n, vb*

GIGA = gigue

GIGABIT *n* unit of information in computing

GIGAS ▸ giga

GIGATON *n* unit of explosive force

GIGGED ▸ gig

GIGGING ▸ gig

GIGGIT *vb* move quickly **giggits**

GIGGLE *vb, n* giggled, giggler, giggles, giggly

GIGHE ▸ giga

GIGLET *n* flighty girl **giglets, giglot**

GIGLOTS ▸ giglot

GIGMAN *n* one who places great importance on respectability **gigmen**

GIGOLO *n* man paid by an older woman to be her escort or lover **gigolos**

GIGOT *n* leg of lamb or mutton **gigots**

GIGS ▸ gig

GIGUE *n* piece of music incorporated into the classical suite **gigues**

GILA *n* large venomous brightly coloured lizard **gilas**

GILBERT *n* unit of magnetomotive force

GILCUP = giltcup

GILCUPS ▸ gilcup

GILD *vb* gilded

GILDEN *adj* gilded

GILDER, gilders, gilding, gilds ▸ gild

GILET *n* waist- or hip-length garment **gilets**

GILGAI *n* natural water hole **gilgais**

GILGIE *n* type of freshwater crayfish **gilgies**

GILL *n, vb* gilled, giller,

gillers

GILLET n mare **gillets**

GILLIE n (in Scotland) attendant for hunting or fishing ▷ vb act as a gillie **gillied**

GILLIES ▶ **gilly**

GILLING ▶ **gill**

GILLION n (no longer in technical use) one thousand million

GILLNET n net designed to catch fish by the gills ▷ vb fish using a gillnet

GILLS pl n breathing organs in fish and other water creatures

GILLY vb act as a gillie

GILPEY n mischievous, frolicsome boy or girl **gilpeys, gilpies, gilpy**

GILT ▶ **gild**

GILTCUP n buttercup

GILTS ▶ **gild**

GIMBAL vb support on gimbals

GIMBALS pl n set of pivoted rings

GIMEL n third letter of the Hebrew alphabet **gimels**

GIMLET n, adj, vb **gimlets**

GIMMAL n ring composed of interlocking rings ▷ vb provide with gimmals **gimmals**

GIMME interj give me! ▷ n term used in shot putt

GIMMER n year-old ewe **gimmers**

GIMMES ▶ **gimme**

GIMMICK n, vb

GIMMIE n very short putt in golf **gimmies**

GIMMOR n mechanical device **gimmors**

GIN n, vb

GING n child's catapult

GINGAL n type of musket mounted on a swivel **gingall, gingals**

GINGE n person with ginger hair

GINGELI = **gingili**

GINGELY = **gingili**

GINGER n, adj, vb **gingers**

GINGERY adj like or tasting of ginger

GINGES ▶ **ginge**

GINGHAM n

GINGILI n oil obtained from sesame seeds

GINGIVA = **gum**

GINGKO = **ginkgo**

GINGKOS ▶ **gingko**

GINGLE = **jingle**

GINGLES ▶ **gingle**

GINGS ▶ **ging**

GINK n man or boy

GINKGO n ornamental Chinese tree **ginkgos**

GINKS ▶ **gink**

GINN = **jinn**

GINNED ▶ **gin**

GINNEL n narrow passageway between buildings **ginnels**

GINNER ▶ **gin**

GINNERS ▶ **gin**

GINNERY another word for > **ginhouse**

GINNIER ▶ **ginny**

GINNING ▶ **gin**

GINNY adj relating to

the spirit gin

GINS ▶ **gin**

GINSENG n (root of) a plant

GINSHOP n tavern

GIO = **geo**

GIOCOSO adv (of music) to be expressed joyfully or playfully

GIOS ▶ **gio**

GIP = **gyp**

GIPON another word for ▶ **jupon**

GIPONS ▶ **gipon**

GIPPED ▶ **gip**

GIPPER ▶ **gip**

GIPPERS ▶ **gip**

GIPPIES ▶ **gippy**

GIPPING ▶ **gip**

GIPPO ▶ **gippy**

GIPPOES ▶ **gippo**

GIPPOS ▶ **gippo**

GIPPY n starling

GIPS ▶ **gip**

GIPSEN obsolete word for ▶ **gypsy**

GIPSENS ▶ **gipsen**

GIPSIED ▶ **gipsy**

GIPSIES ▶ **gipsy**

GIPSY n, vb

GIRAFFE n

GIRASOL n type of opal

GIRD vb, n **girded**

GIRDER n **girders**

GIRDING ▶ **gird**

GIRDLE n, vb **girdled**

GIRDLER n person or thing that girdles

GIRDLES ▶ **girdle**

GIRDS ▶ **gird**

GIRKIN = **gherkin**

GIRKINS ▶ **girkin**

GIRL n

GIRLIE adj (of a

magazine, etc) featuring pictures of naked women ▷ n little girl

GIRLIER ▶ girly

GIRLIES ▶ girlie

GIRLISH adj of or like a girl in looks, behaviour, innocence, etc

GIRLOND obsolete word for ▶ garland

GIRLS ▶ girl

GIRLY = girlie

GIRN vb snarl **girned**

GIRNEL n large chest for storing meal **girnels**

GIRNER ▶ girn

GIRNERS ▶ girn

GIRNIE adj peevish **girnier**

GIRNING ▶ girn

GIRNS ▶ girn

GIRO n

GIROLLE n chanterelle mushroom

GIRON n part of a heraldic shield **gironic**

GIRONNY adj divided into segments from the fesse point

GIRONS ▶ giron

GIROS ▶ giro

GIROSOL = girasol

GIRR = gird

GIRRS ▶ girr

GIRSH n currency unit of Saudi Arabia **girshes**

GIRT vb gird; bind

GIRTED ▶ gird

GIRTH n, vb **girthed**, **girths**

GIRTING ▶ gird

GIRTS ▶ girt

GIS ▶ gi

GISARME n long-shafted battle-axe

GISMO = gizmo

GISMOS ▶ gizmo

GIST n **gists**

GIT n contemptible person ▷ vb dialect version of get

GITANA n female gypsy **gitanas**

GITANO n male gypsy **gitanos**

GITE n self-catering holiday cottage for let in France **gites**

GITS ▶ git

GITTED ▶ git

GITTERN n obsolete medieval instrument ▷ vb play the gittern

GITTIN n Jewish divorce

GITTING ▶ git

GIUST = joust

GIUSTED ▶ giust

GIUSTO adv as observed strictly

GIUSTS ▶ giust

GIVABLE ▶ give

GIVE vb, n

GIVED = gyved

GIVEN n **givens**

GIVER n **givers, gives, giving, givings ▶ give**

GIZMO n device **gizmos**

GIZZ n wig

GIZZARD n

GIZZEN vb (of wood) to warp **gizzens**

GIZZES ▶ gizz

GJETOST n type of Norwegian cheese

GJU n type of violin used in Shetland **gjus**

This unusual word for a Shetland fiddle is great for disposing of awkward letters for a good score.

GLACE adj preserved in a thick sugary syrup ▷ vb ice or candy (cakes, fruits, etc) **glaceed, glaces**

GLACIAL adj of ice or glaciers ▷ n ice age

GLACIER n

GLACIS n slight incline

GLAD adj, vb, n **gladded**

GLADDEN vb

GLADDER ▶ glad

GLADDIE = glad

GLADDON n stinking iris

GLADE n **glades**

GLADFUL adj full of gladness

GLADIER ▶ glade

GLADIUS n short sword used by Roman legionaries

GLADLY ▶ glad

GLADS ▶ glad

GLADY ▶ glade

GLAIK n prank

GLAIKET = glaikit

GLAIKIT adj foolish

GLAIKS ▶ glaik

GLAIR n white of egg ▷ vb apply glair to (something) **glaire, glaired**

GLAIRES ▶ glaire

GLAIRIN n viscous mineral deposit

GLAIRS ▶ glair

GLAIRY ▶ glair

GLAIVE archaic word for ▶ sword

GLAIVED adj armed with a sword

GLAIVES ▸ glaive

GLAM n magical illusion ▷ vb make oneself look glamorous **glammed**

GLAMMY adj glamorous

GLAMOR = glamour

GLAMORS ▸ glamor

GLAMOUR n, vb

GLAMS ▸ glam

GLANCE vb, n, glanced

GLANCER n log or pole used to protect trees from damage

GLANCES ▸ glance

GLAND n

GLANDES ▸ glans

GLANDS ▸ gland

GLANS n any small rounded body or glandlike mass

GLARE vb, n, adj

GLAREAL adj (of a plant) growing in cultivated land

GLARED ▸ glare

GLARES ▸ glare

GLARIER ▸ glare

GLARING adj

GLARY ▸ glare

GLASS n, vb glassed

GLASSEN adj glassy

GLASSES pl n

GLASSIE = glassy

GLASSY adj, n

GLAUM vb snatch glaumed, glaums

GLAUR n mud or mire glaurs, glaury

GLAZE vb, n, adj glazed

GLAZEN adj glazed

GLAZER ▸ glaze

GLAZERS ▸ glaze

GLAZES ▸ glaze

GLAZIER n

GLAZILY ▸ glaze

GLAZING n surface of a glazed object

GLAZY ▸ glaze

GLEAM n, vb gleamed

GLEAMER n mirror used to cheat in card games

GLEAMS ▸ gleam

GLEAMY ▸ gleam

GLEAN vb gleaned, gleaner, gleans

GLEAVE = sword

GLEAVES ▸ gleave

GLEBA n mass of spores glebae

GLEBE n land granted to a member of the clergy glebes

GLEBIER ▸ gleby

GLEBOUS adj gleby

GLEBY adj relating to a glebe

GLED n kite glede

GLEDES ▸ glede

GLEDGE vb glance sideways gledged, gledges

GLEDS ▸ gled

GLEE n, vb

GLEED n burning ember or hot coal gleeds

GLEEFUL adj merry or joyful

GLEEING ▸ glee

GLEEK vb jeer gleeked, gleeks

GLEEMAN n minstrel gleemen

GLEENIE n guinea fowl

GLEES ▸ glee

GLEET n stage of chronic gonorrhoea ▷ vb discharge pus gleeted, gleets, gleety

GLEG adj quick glegger, glegly

GLEI = gley

GLEIS ▸ glei

GLEN n

GLENOID adj resembling or having a shallow cavity ▷ n shallow cavity

GLENS ▸ glen

GLENT = glint

GLENTED ▸ glent

GLENTS ▸ glent

GLEY n bluish-grey compact sticky soil ▷ vb squint gleyed, gleying, gleys

GLIA n web of tissue that supports nerve cells

GLIADIN n protein of cereals with a high proline content

GLIAL ▸ glia

GLIAS ▸ glia

GLIB adj, vb glibbed, glibber, glibly, glibs

GLID adj moving smoothly and easily glidder

GLIDE vb, n glided

GLIDER n gliders

GLIDES ▸ glide

GLIDING n sport of flying gliders

GLIFF n slap gliffs

GLIFT n moment glifts

GLIKE = gleek

GLIKES ▸ glike

GLIM n light or lamp

GLIME vb glance sideways glimed,

gllmes, gliming

GLIMMER vb, n

GLIMPSE n, vb

GLIMS ▸ glim

GLINT vb, n glinted, glints, glinty

GLIOMA n tumour of the brain and spinal cord **gliomas**

GLIOSES ▸ gliosis

GLIOSIS n process leading to scarring in the nervous system

GLISK n glimpse **glisks**

GLISTEN vb, n

GLISTER archaic word for **▸ glitter**

GLIT n slimy matter

GLITCH n small problem that stops something from working **glitchy**

GLITS ▸ glit

GLITTER vb, n

GLITZ n ostentatious showiness ▷ vb make something more attractive **glitzed, glitzes**

GLITZY adj showily attractive

GLOAM n dusk **gloams**

GLOAT vb, n gloated, gloater, gloats

GLOB n rounded mass of thick fluid

GLOBAL adj

GLOBATE adj shaped like a globe

GLOBBY adj thick and lumpy

GLOBE n, vb globed, globes

GLOBI ▸ globus

GLOBIN n protein

component

GLOBING ▸ globe

GLOBINS ▸ globin

GLOBOID adj shaped approximately like a globe ▷ n globoid body

GLOBOSE adj spherical or approximately spherical ▷ n globose object **globous**

GLOBS ▸ glob

GLOBULE n

GLOBUS n any spherelike structure

GLOBY adj round

GLOCHID n barbed spine on a plant

GLODE ▸ glide

GLOGG n hot alcoholic mixed drink **gloggs**

GLOIRE n glory **gloires**

GLOM vb attach oneself to or associate oneself with

GLOMERA ▸ glomus

GLOMMED ▸ glom

GLOMS ▸ glom

GLOMUS n small anastomosis in an artery or vein

GLONOIN n nitroglycerin

GLOOM n, vb gloomed, glooms

GLOOMY adj

GLOOP vb cover with a viscous substance **glooped, gloops, gloopy**

GLOP vb cover with a viscous substance **glopped, gloppy, glops**

GLORIA n silk, wool, cotton, or nylon fabric

glorias

GLORIED ▸ glory

GLORIES ▸ glory

GLORIFY vb

GLORY n, vb

GLOSS n, vb

GLOSSA n paired tonguelike lobe in the labium of an insect **glossae, glossal, glossas**

GLOSSED ▸ gloss

GLOSSER ▸ gloss

GLOSSES ▸ gloss

GLOSSY adj, n

GLOST n lead glaze used for pottery **glosts**

GLOTTAL adj of the glottis

GLOTTIC adj of or relating to the tongue or the glottis

GLOTTIS n vocal cords and the space between them

GLOUT vb look sullen glouted, glouts

GLOVE n gloved

GLOVER n person who makes or sells gloves glovers

GLOVES ▸ glove

GLOVING ▸ glove

GLOW vb, n glowed

GLOWER n, vb glowers

GLOWFLY n firefly

GLOWING adj

GLOWS ▸ glow

GLOZE vb explain away ▷ n flattery or deceit **glozed, glozes, glozing**

GLUCAN n any polysaccharide

consisting of a polymer of glucose **glucans**

GLUCINA *n* oxide of glucinium

GLUCOSE *n*

GLUE *n, vb* **glued, glueing**

GLUEPOT *n* container for holding glue

GLUER, gluers, glues, gluey ▸ **glue**

GLUG *n* word representing a gurgling sound ▸ *vb* drink noisily, taking big gulps **glugged, glugs**

GLUIER, gluiest, gluily, gluing, gluish ▸ **glue**

GLUM *adj*

GLUME *n* one of a pair of dry membranous bracts in grasses **glumes**

GLUMLY ▸ **glum**

GLUMMER ▸ **glum**

GLUMPS *n* state of sulking

GLUMPY *adj* sullen

GLUMS *n* gloomy feelings

GLUNCH *vb* look sullen

GLUON *n* hypothetical particle **gluons**

GLURGE *n* stories supposed to be true but often fabricated **glurges**

GLUT *n, vb*

GLUTAEI > **glutaeus**

GLUTE *n* = **gluteus**

GLUTEAL ▸ **gluteus**

GLUTEI ▸ **gluteus**

GLUTEN *n* **glutens**

GLUTES ▸ **glute**

GLUTEUS *n* any of the three muscles of the buttock

GLUTS ▸ **glut**

GLUTTED ▸ **glut**

GLUTTON *n*

GLYCAN *n* polysaccharide **glycans**

GLYCIN = **glycine**

GLYCINE *n* nonessential amino acid

GLYCINS ▸ **glycin**

GLYCOL *n* another name (not in technical usage) for a diol **glycols**

GLYCOSE *n* any of various monosaccharides

GLYCYL *n* radical of glycine **glycyls**

GLYPH *n* carved channel or groove **glyphic, glyphs**

GLYPTAL *n* alkyd resin

GLYPTIC *adj* of or relating to engraving or carving

GNAMMA *variant of* ▸ **namma**

GNAR = **gnarl**

GNARL *n* any knotty protuberance or swelling on a tree ▸ *vb* knot or cause to knot

GNARLED *adj*

GNARLS ▸ **gnarl**

GNARLY *adj* good

GNARR = **gnarl**

GNARRED ▸ **gnar**

GNARRS ▸ **gnarr**

GNARS ▸ **gnar**

GNASH *vb, n* **gnashed**

GNASHER *n* tooth

GNASHES ▸ **gnash**

GNAT *n*

GNATHAL = **gnathic**

GNATHIC *adj* of or relating to the jaw

GNATS ▸ **gnat**

GNATTY *adj* infested with gnats

GNAW *vb, n* **gnawed, gnawer, gnawers, gnawing, gnawn, gnaws**

GNEISS *n* coarse-grained metamorphic rock

GNOCCHI *n* dumplings

GNOMAE ▸ **gnome**

GNOME *n* **gnomes**

GNOMIC *adj* of pithy sayings

GNOMISH ▸ **gnome**

GNOMIST *n* writer of pithy sayings

GNOMON *n* stationary arm on a sundial **gnomons**

GNOSES ▸ **gnosis**

GNOSIS *n* supposedly revealed knowledge of spiritual truths

GNOSTIC *adj* of, relating to, or possessing knowledge ▸ *n* one who knows

GNOW *n* Australian wild bird **gnows**

GNU *n* **gnus**

GO *vb* move to or from a place ▸ *n* attempt

GOA *n* Tibetan gazelle

GOAD *vb, n* **goaded, goading, goads**

GOAF *n* waste left in old

mine workings **goafs**
GOAL n, vb **goaled**
GOALIE n goalkeeper **goalies**
GOALING ▸ goal
GOALS ▸ goal
GOANNA n **goannas**
GOARY variant spelling of ▸ gory
GOAS ▸ goa
GOAT n
GOATEE n pointed tuft-like beard **goateed, goatees**
GOATIER ▸ goat

This means more like a goat: it may seem a silly sort of word but because it uses such common letters the chance to play it as a bonus comes up very frequently.

GOATISH adj of, like, or relating to a goat
GOATS ▸ goat
GOATY ▸ goat
GOB n, vb
GOBAN n board on which go is played **gobans**
GOBANG n Japanese board-game **gobangs**
GOBANS ▸ goban
GOBAR adj as in gobar numeral kind of numeral
GOBBED ▸ gob
GOBBET n lump, esp of food **gobbets**
GOBBI ▸ gobbo
GOBBIER ▸ gobby
GOBBING ▸ gob
GOBBLE vb, n, interj **gobbled**

GOBBLER n turkey
GOBBLES ▸ gobble
GOBBO n hunchback
GOBBY adj loudmouthed and offensive
GOBI n (in Indian cookery) cauliflower
GOBIES ▸ goby
GOBIID n member of the genus Gobius **gobiids**
GOBIOID n type of spiny-finned fish
GOBIS ▸ gobi
GOBLET n **goblets**
GOBLIN n **goblins**
GOBO n shield placed around a microphone **goboes**
GOBONEE = **gobony**
GOBONY adj in heraldry, composed of a row of small, alternately-coloured squares
GOBOS ▸ gobo
GOBS ▸ gob
GOBURRA n kookaburra
GOBY n small spiny-finned fish
GOD n, vb
GODDAM vb damn
GODDAMN interj oath expressing anger, surprise, etc ▸ vb damn extremely ▸ vb damn
GODDAMS ▸ goddam
GODDED ▸ god
GODDEN n evening greeting **goddens**
GODDESS n
GODDING ▸ god
GODET n triangular piece of material

inserted into a garment
GODETIA n plant with showy flowers
GODETS ▸ godet
GODHEAD n essential nature and condition of being a god
GODHOOD n state of being divine
GODLESS adj
GODLIER ▸ godly
GODLIKE adj resembling or befitting a god or God
GODLILY ▸ godly
GODLING n little god
GODLY adj
GODOWN n (in East Asia and India) warehouse **godowns**
GODROON = **gadroon**
GODS ▸ god
GODSEND n
GODSHIP n divinity
GODSLOT n time in a schedule for religious broadcasts
GODSO = **gadso**
GODSON n male godchild **godsons**
GODWARD adv towards God
GODWIT n shore bird with long legs and an upturned bill **godwits**
GOE = **go**
GOEL n in Jewish law, blood-avenger **goels**
GOER n person who attends something regularly **goers**
GOES ▸ go

GOEST vb archaic 2nd person sing present of go

GOETH vb archaic 3rd person sing present of go

GOETIC ▸ goety

GOETIES ▸ goety

GOETY n witchcraft

GOEY adj go-ahead

GOFER n employee or assistant performing menial tasks **gofers**

GOFF obsolete variant of ▸ golf

GOFFED ▸ goff

GOFFER vb press pleats into (a frill) ▸ n ornamental frill made by pressing pleats **goffers**

GOFFING ▸ goff

GOFFS ▸ goff

GOGGA n any small insect **goggas**

GOGGLE vb, n **goggled**

GOGGLER n big-eyed scad

GOGGLES ▸ goggle

GOGGLY ▸ goggle

GOGLET n long-necked water-cooling vessel **goglets**

GOGO n disco **gogos**

GOIER ▸ goey

GOIEST ▸ goey

GOING ▸ go

GOINGS ▸ go

GOITER = goitre

GOITERS ▸ goiter

GOITRE n goitred, **goitres**

GOJI > wolfberry

GOJIS ▸ goji

GOLD n, adj

GOLDARN euphemistic variant of ▸ goddamn

GOLDBUG n American beetle with a bright metallic lustre

GOLDEN adj, vb **goldens**

GOLDER ▸ gold

GOLDEST ▸ gold

GOLDEYE n N American fish

GOLDIER ▸ goldy

GOLDISH ▸ gold

GOLDS ▸ gold

GOLDURN variant of ▸ goddamn

GOLDY adj gold-like

GOLE obsolete spelling of ▸ goal

GOLEM n (in Jewish legend) artificially created human **golems**

GOLES ▸ gole

GOLF n, vb **golfed**

GOLFER n person who plays golf **golfers**

GOLFING ▸ golf

GOLFS ▸ golf

GOLIARD n one of a number of wandering scholars

GOLIAS vb behave outrageously

GOLIATH n giant

GOLLAN n yellow flower **golland, gollans**

GOLLAR = goller

GOLLARS ▸ gollar

GOLLER vb roar **gollers**

GOLLIED ▸ golly

GOLLIES ▸ golly

GOLLOP vb eat or drink (something) quickly or greedily **gollops**

GOLLY interj exclamation of mild surprise ▸ n short for golliwog: used chiefly by children ▸ vb spit

GOLOSH = galosh

GOLOSHE = galosh

GOLP = golpe

GOLPE n in heraldry, a purple circle **golpes**

GOLPS ▸ golp

GOMBEEN n usury

GOMBO = gumbo

GOMBOS ▸ gombo

GOMBRO = gumbo

GOMBROS ▸ gombro

GOMER n unwanted hospital patient

GOMERAL = gomeril

GOMEREL = gomeril

GOMERIL n slow-witted or stupid person

GOMERS ▸ gomer

GOMOKU another word for ▸ gobang

GOMOKUS ▸ gomoku

GOMPA n Tibetan monastery **gompas**

GOMUTI n E Indian feather palm **gomutis, gomuto**

GOMUTOS ▸ gomuto

GON n geometrical grade

GONAD n gonadal, gonadic, gonads

GONDOLA n

GONE ▸ go

GONEF = ganef

GONEFS ▸ gonef

GONER n person or thing beyond help or recovery **goners**

GONG n, vb **gonged, gonging, gongs**

GONGYO n Buddhist ceremony **gongyos**

GONIA ▸ **gonion**

GONIDIA > **gonidium**

GONIDIC = **gonidium**

GONIF = **ganef**

GONIFF = **ganef**

GONIFFS ▸ **goniff**

GONIFS ▸ **gonif**

GONION n point or apex of the angle of the lower jaw

GONIUM n immature reproductive cell

GONK n stuffed toy, often used as a mascot **gonks**

GONNA vb going to

GONOF = **ganef**

GONOFS ▸ **ganof**

GONOPH = **ganef**

GONOPHS ▸ **gonoph**

GONOPOD n either of the reproductive organs of insects

GONS ▸ **gon**

GONYS n lower outline of a bird's bill **gonyses**

GONZO adj wild or crazy

GOO n

GOOBER another name for ▸ **peanut**

GOOBERS ▸ **goober**

GOOBIES ▸ **gooby**

GOOBY n spittle

GOOD adj giving pleasure ▸ n benefit

GOODBY = **goodbye**

GOODBYE n, interj, sentence substitute

GOODBYS ▸ **goodby**

GOODIE = **goody**

GOODIER ▸ **goody**

GOODIES ▸ **goody**

GOODISH ▸ **good**

GOODLY adj considerable

GOODMAN n husband **goodmen**

GOODS ▸ **good**

GOODY n, interj, adj

GOOEY adj sticky and soft

GOOF n mistake ▸ vb make a mistake **goofed**

GOOFIER ▸ **goofy**

GOOFILY ▸ **goofy**

GOOFING ▸ **goof**

GOOFS ▸ **goof**

GOOFY adj silly or ridiculous

GOOG n egg

GOOGLE vb search on the internet using a search engine **googled, googles**

GOOGLY n ball that spins unexpectedly on the bounce

GOOGOL n number shown as one followed by 100 zeros **googols**

GOOGS ▸ **goog**

GOOIER ▸ **gooey**

GOOIEST ▸ **gooey**

GOOILY ▸ **gooey**

GOOKY adj sticky and messy

GOOL n corn marigold

GOOLD Scots word for ▸ **gold**

GOOLDS ▸ **goold**

GOOLS ▸ **gool**

GOOMBAH n patron or mentor

GOOMBAY n Bahamian

soft drink

GOON n stupid person

GOONDA n (in India) habitual criminal **goondas**

GOONEY n albatross **gooneys**

GOONIE Scots word for a ▸ **gown**

GOONIER ▸ **goon**

GOONIES ▸ **goonie**

GOONS ▸ **goon**

GOONY ▸ **goon**

GOOP n rude or ill-mannered person

GOOPED adj as in **gooped up** sticky with goop

GOOPIER ▸ **goop**

GOOPS ▸ **goop**

GOOPY ▸ **goop**

GOOR = **gur**

GOORAL n goral

GOORALS ▸ **gooral**

GOORIE ▸ **kuri**

GOORIES ▸ **goorie**

GOOROO = **guru**

GOOROOS ▸ **gooroo**

GOORS ▸ **goor**

GOORY ▸ **goor**

GOOS ▸ **goo**

GOOSE n, vb **goosed**

GOOSERY n place for keeping geese

GOOSES ▸ **goose**

GOOSEY = **goosy**

GOOSEYS ▸ **goosey**

GOOSIER ▸ **goosy**

GOOSIES ▸ **goosy**

GOOSING ▸ **goose**

GOOSY adj of or like a goose

GOPAK n Russian peasant dance **gopaks**

GOPHER n American burrowing rodent ▷ vb burrow **gophers**

GOPIK n money unit of Azerbaijan **gopiks**

GOPURA n gateway tower of an Indian temple **gopuram, gopuras**

GOR interj God!

GORA n (in Indian English) White or fair-skinned male

GORAL n small S Asian goat antelope **gorals**

GORAMY ▷ gourami

GORAS ▷ gora

GORCOCK n male of the red grouse

GORCROW n carrion crow

GORDITA n small thick tortilla

GORE n, vb gored, gores

GORGE n, vb gorged, gorger, gorgers, gorges

GORGET n collar-like piece of armour **gorgets**

GORGIA n improvised sung passage **gorgias**

GORGING ▷ gorge

GORGIO n word used by gypsies for a non-gypsy **gorgios**

GORGON n terrifying or repulsive woman **gorgons**

GORHEN n female red grouse **gorhens**

GORI n (in Indian English) White or fair-skinned female

GORIER ▷ gory

GORIEST ▷ gory

GORILLA n

GORILY ▷ gory

GORING ▷ gore

GORINGS ▷ gore

GORIS ▷ gori

GORM n foolish person ▷ vb understand

GORMAND = gourmand

GORMED ▷ gorm

GORMIER ▷ gormy

GORMING ▷ gorm

GORMS ▷ gorm

GORMY adj gormless

GORP = gawp

GORPED ▷ gawp

GORPING ▷ gawp

GORPS ▷ gawp

GORSE n

GORSEDD n meeting held daily before an eisteddfod

GORSES ▷ gorse

GORSIER ▷ gorse

GORSOON n young boy

GORSY ▷ gorse

GORY adj

GOS ▷ go

GOSH interj exclamation of mild surprise or wonder

GOSHAWK n large hawk

GOSHT n Indian meat dish **goshts**

GOSLET n pygmy goose **goslets**

GOSLING n

GOSPEL n, adj, vb **gospels**

GOSPODA > gospodin

GOSPORT n aeroplane communication device

GOSS vb spit

GOSSAN n oxidised portion of a mineral vein in rock **gossans**

GOSSE variant of ▷ gorse

GOSSED ▷ goss

GOSSES ▷ goss

GOSSIB n gossip **gossibs**

GOSSING ▷ goss

GOSSIP n, vb **gossips, gossipy**

GOSSOON n boy, esp a servant boy

GOSTER vb laugh uncontrollably **gosters**

GOT ▷ get

GOTCHA adj as in gotcha lizard Australian name for a crocodile **gotchas**

GOTH n aficionado of Goth music and fashion

GOTHIC adj of or relating to a literary style ▷ n family of heavy script typefaces **gothics**

GOTHITE = goethite

GOTHS ▷ goth

GOTTA vb got to

GOTTEN past participle of ▷ get

GOUACHE n (painting using) watercolours mixed with glue

GOUCH vb become drowsy or lethargic under the influence of narcotics **gouched, gouches**

GOUGE vb, n **gouged**

GOUGER n person or tool that gouges

GOUGERE n choux pastry flavoured with cheese

GOUGERS ▸ **gouger**

GOUGES ▸ **gouge**

GOUGING ▸ **gouge**

GOUJON n small strip of food **goujons**

GOUK = **gowk**

GOUKS ▸ **gouk**

GOULASH n

GOURA n large, crested ground pigeon found in New Guinea

GOURAMI n large SE Asian labyrinth fish

GOURAS ▸ **goura**

GOURD n

GOURDE n standard monetary unit of Haiti **gourdes**

GOURDS ▸ **gourd**

GOURDY adj (of horses) swollen-legged

GOURMET n

GOUSTY adj dismal

GOUT n

GOUTFLY n fly whose larvae infect crops

GOUTIER ▸ **gout**

GOUTILY ▸ **gout**

GOUTS ▸ **gout**

GOUTTE n heraldic device **gouttes**

GOUTY ▸ **gout**

GOV n boss

GOVERN vb, n **governs**

GOVS ▸ **gov**

GOWAN n any of various

flowers growing in fields **gowaned, gowans, gowany**

GOWD Scots word for ▸ **gold**

GOWDER ▸ **gowd**

GOWDEST ▸ **gowd**

GOWDS ▸ **gowd**

GOWF vb strike **gowfed, gowfer, gowfers, gowfing, gowfs**

GOWK n stupid person **gowks**

GOWL n substance in the corner of the eyes after sleep ▷ vb howl

GOWLAN = **gollan**

GOWLAND = **gollan**

GOWLANS ▸ **gowlan**

GOWLED ▸ **gowl**

GOWLING ▸ **gowl**

GOWLS ▸ **gowl**

GOWN n, vb

GOWNBOY n foundationer schoolboy who wears a gown

GOWNED ▸ **gown**

GOWNING ▸ **gown**

GOWNMAN n professional person who wears a gown **gownmen**

GOWNS ▸ **gown**

GOWPEN n pair of cupped hands **gowpens**

GOX n gaseous oxygen **goxes**

> Gox is gaseous oxygen, especially useful if you can use it to hit a bonus square.

GOYLE n ravine **goyles**

GOZZAN = **gossan**

GOZZANS ▸ **gozzan**

GRAAL n holy grail **graals**

GRAB vb, n **grabbed, grabber**

GRABBLE vb scratch or feel about with the hands

GRABBY adj greedy or selfish

GRABEN n elongated trough of land **grabens**

GRABS ▸ **grab**

GRACE n, vb **graced, graces**

GRACILE adj gracefully thin or slender

GRACING ▸ **grace**

GRACKLE n American songbird with a dark iridescent plumage

GRAD n graduate

GRADATE vb change or cause to change imperceptibly

GRADDAN vb dress corn

GRADE n, vb **graded**

GRADELY adj fine

GRADER n person or thing that grades **graders**

GRADES ▸ **grade**

GRADIN n ledge above or behind an altar **gradine**

GRADING ▸ **grade**

GRADINI ▸ **gradino**

GRADINO n step above an altar

GRADINS ▸ **gradin**

GRADS ▸ **grad**

GRADUAL adj, n

GRADUS n book of études or other musical exercises

GRAFF = graft

GRAFFED ▶ graff

GRAFFS ▶ graff

GRAFT n, vb grafted, grafter, grafts

GRAHAM n made of graham flour **grahams**

GRAIL n any desired ambition or goal **graile**

GRAILES ▶ graile

GRAILS ▶ grail

GRAIN n, vb

GRAINE n eggs of the silkworm

GRAINED ▶ grain

GRAINER ▶ grain

GRAINES ▶ graine

GRAINS ▶ grain

GRAINY adj

GRAIP n long-handled gardening fork **graips**

GRAITH vb clothe graiths

GRAKLE = grackle

GRAKLES ▶ grakle

GRAM n

GRAMA n type of grass

GRAMARY = gramarye

GRAMAS ▶ grama

GRAMASH n type of gaiter

GRAME n sorrow grames

GRAMMA n pasture grass of the South American plains

GRAMMAR n

GRAMMAS ▶ gramma

GRAMME ▶ gramme

GRAMMES ▶ gram

GRAMP n grandfather

GRAMPA variant of ▶ grandpa

GRAMPAS ▶ grampa

GRAMPS ▶ gramp

GRAMPUS n dolphin-like mammal

GRAMS ▶ gram

GRAN n

GRANA ▶ granum

GRANARY n

GRAND adj, n

GRANDAD n

GRANDAM n archaic word for grandmother

GRANDE feminine form of ▶ grand

GRANDEE n Spanish nobleman of the highest rank

GRANDER ▶ grand

GRANDLY ▶ grand

GRANDMA n

GRANDPA n grandfather

GRANDS ▶ grand

GRANFER n grandfather

GRANGE n country house with farm buildings

GRANGER n keeper or member of a grange

GRANGES ▶ grange

GRANITA n Italian iced drink

GRANITE n

GRANNAM n old woman

GRANNIE vb defeat without conceding a single point

GRANNOM n type of caddis fly esteemed as a bait by anglers

GRANNY n, vb

GRANOLA n muesli-like

breakfast cereal

GRANS ▶ gran

GRANT vb, n granted

GRANTEE n person to whom a grant is made

GRANTER ▶ grant

GRANTOR n person who makes a grant

GRANTS ▶ grant

GRANULE n small grain

GRANUM n membrane layers in a chloroplast

GRAPE n, vb graped

GRAPERY n building where grapes are grown

GRAPES n abnormal growth on the fetlock of a horse

GRAPEY ▶ grape

GRAPH n, vb graphed

GRAPHIC adj

GRAPHS ▶ graph

GRAPIER ▶ grape

GRAPING ▶ grape

GRAPLE = grapple

GRAPLES ▶ graple

GRAPLIN = grapnel

GRAPNEL n device with several hooks

GRAPPA n type of spirit grappas

GRAPPLE vb, n

GRAPY ▶ grape

GRASP vb, n grasped, grasper, grasps

GRASS n, vb grassed

GRASSER n police informant

GRASSES ▶ grass

GRASSUM n in Scots law, sum paid when taking a lease

GRASSY adj covered with, containing, or

GRASTE archaic past participle of ▶ grace
GRAT ▶ greet
GRATE vb, n grated
GRATER n graters
GRATES ▶ grate
GRATIFY vb, adj
GRATIN n crust of browned breadcrumbs
GRATINE adj cooked au gratin
GRATING adj, n
GRATINS ▶ gratin
GRATIS adj
GRAUNCH vb crush or destroy
GRAUPEL n soft hail or snow pellets
GRAV n unit of acceleration
GRAVE n, adj, vb, adv graved
GRAVEL n, vb gravels
GRAVELY ▶ grave
GRAVEN ▶ grave
GRAVER n any of various tools gravers
GRAVES ▶ grave
GRAVEST ▶ grave
GRAVID adj pregnant
GRAVIDA n pregnant woman
GRAVIES ▶ gravy
GRAVING ▶ grave
GRAVIS adj as in myasthenia gravis chronic muscle-weakening disease
GRAVITY n
GRAVLAX n dry-cured salmon
GRAVS ▶ grav
GRAVURE n method of

intaglio printing
GRAVY n
GRAY = grey
GRAYED ▶ gray
GRAYER ▶ gray
GRAYEST ▶ gray
GRAYFLY n trumpet fly
GRAYING ▶ gray
GRAYISH ▶ gray
GRAYLAG = greylag
GRAYLE n holy grail grayles
GRAYLY ▶ gray
GRAYOUT n impairment of vision due to lack of oxygen
GRAYS ▶ gray
GRAZE vb, n grazed, grazer, grazers, grazes
GRAZIER n person who feeds cattle for market
GRAZING n land on which grass for livestock is grown
GREASE n, vb greased
GREASER n mechanic, esp of motor vehicles
GREASES ▶ grease
GREASY adj covered with or containing grease ▷ n shearer
GREAT adj large in size or number ▷ n distinguished person
GREATEN vb make or become great
GREATER ▶ great
GREATLY ▶ great
GREATS ▶ great
GREAVE n piece of armour for the shin ▷ vb grieve greaved
GREAVES pl n residue

left after the rendering of tallow
GREBE n grebes
GREBO ▶ greebo
GREBOS ▶ grebo
GRECE n flight of steps greces, grecian
GRECISE = graecize
GRECIZE = graecize
GRECQUE n ornament of Greek origin
GREE n superiority or victory ▷ vb come or cause to come to agreement or harmony
GREEBO n unkempt or dirty-looking young man
GREECE = grece
GREECES ▶ greece
GREED n greeds
GREEDY adj
GREEING ▶ gree
GREEK vb represent text as grey lines on a computer screen greeked
GREEN adj, n, vb greened
GREENER n recent immigrant
GREENIE n conservationist
GREENLY ▶ green
GREENS ▶ green
GREENTH n greenness
GREENY ▶ green
GREES ▶ gree
GREESE = grece
GREESES ▶ greese
GREET vb, n greete, greeted
GREETER n person who

greets people
GREETES ▸ greete
GREETS ▸ greet
GREGALE n northeasterly wind occurring in the Mediterranean
GREGE vb make heavy
GREGO n short, thick jacket **gregos**
GREIGE adj (of a fabric or material) not yet dyed ▷ n unbleached or undyed cloth or yarn **greiges**
GREIN vb desire fervently **greined, greins**
GREISEN n light-coloured metamorphic rock
GREISLY = grisly
GREMIAL n type of cloth used in Mass
GREMLIN n imaginary being
GREMMIE n young surfer **gremmy**
GREN = grin
GRENADE n
GRENNED ▸ gren
GRENS ▸ gren
GRESE = grece
GRESES ▸ grese
GREVE = greave
GREVES ▸ greve
GREW vb shudder
GREWED ▸ grow
GREWING ▸ grow
GREWS ▸ grow
GREX n group of plants **grexes**
GREY adj, n, vb **greyed, greyer, greyest**

GREYHEN n female of the black grouse
GREYING ▸ grey
GREYISH ▸ grey
GREYLAG n large grey goose
GREYLY ▸ grey
GREYS ▸ grey
GRIBBLE n type of small marine crustacean
GRICE vb collect objects concerned with railways ▷ n object collected or place visited by a railway enthusiast **griced, gricer, gricers, grices, gricing**
GRID n **gridded**
GRIDDER n American football player
GRIDDLE n flat iron plate for cooking ▷ vb cook (food) on a griddle
GRIDE vb grate or scrape harshly ▷ n harsh or piercing sound **grided, grides, griding**
GRIDS ▸ grid
GRIECE = grece
GRIECED ▸ griece
GRIECES ▸ griece
GRIEF n
GRIEFER n online gamer who spoils the game for others on purpose
GRIEFS ▸ grief
GRIESIE = grisy
GRIESLY = grisy
GRIESY = grisy
GRIEVE vb, n **grieved, griever, grieves**
GRIFF n information

GRIFFE n carved ornament at the base of a column **griffes**
GRIFFIN n mythical monster **griffon**
GRIFFS ▸ griff
GRIFT vb swindle **grifted, grifter, grifts**
GRIG n lively person ▷ vb fish for grigs **grigged**
GRIGRI n African talisman, amulet, or charm **grigris**
GRIGS ▸ grig
GRIKE n fissure in rock **grikes**
GRILL n, n
GRILLE n
GRILLED adj cooked on a grill or gridiron
GRILLER ▸ grill
GRILLES ▸ grille
GRILLS ▸ grill
GRILSE n salmon on its first return from the sea to fresh water **grilses**
GRIM adj
GRIMACE n, vb
GRIME n, vb **grimed, grimes, grimier, grimily, griming**
GRIMLY ▸ grim
GRIMMER ▸ grim
GRIMY ▸ grime
GRIN vb, n
GRINCH n person whose attitude has a depressing effect
GRIND vb, n **grinder**
GRINDER n device for grinding substances
GRINDS ▸ grind
GRINNED ▸ grin
GRINNER ▸ grin

GRINS ▶ grin
GRIOT n (in W Africa)
member of a caste
recording tribal history
griots
GRIP n, vb
GRIPE vb complain
persistently ▷ n
complaint griped,
griper, gripers, gripes
GRIPEY adj causing
gripes gripier
GRIPING ▶ gripe
GRIPLE = gripple
GRIPMAN n cable-car
operator gripmen
GRIPPE former name for
> influenza
GRIPPED ▶ grip
GRIPPER ▶ grip
GRIPPES ▶ grippe
GRIPPLE adj greedy ▷ n
hook
GRIPPY adj having grip
GRIPS ▶ grip
GRIPT archaic variant of
▶ gripped
GRIPY = gripey
GRIS = grece
GRISE vb shudder grised
GRISELY = grisly
GRISES ▶ grise
GRISING ▶ grise
GRISKIN n lean part of a
loin of pork
GRISLED another word
for ▶ grizzled
GRISLY adj, n
GRISON n type of
mammal grisons
GRIST n
GRISTER n device for
grinding grain
GRISTLE n gristly

GRISTS ▶ grist
GRISY adj grim
GRIT n, vb, adj
GRITH n security or
peace guaranteed for
a period of time
griths
GRITS ▶ grit
GRITTED ▶ grit
GRITTER n vehicle that
spreads grit on the
roads
GRITTY adj courageous
and tough
GRIVET n E African
monkey grivets
GRIZE = grece
GRIZES ▶ grize
GRIZZLE vb, n
GRIZZLY n large
American bear ▷ adj
somewhat grey
GROAN n, vb groaned
GROANER n person or
thing that groans
GROANS ▶ groan
GROAT n fourpenny
piece
GROATS pl n hulled and
crushed grain of
various cereals
GROCER n grocers
GROCERY n
GROCKED ▶ grokked
GROCKLE n tourist in
SW England
GRODIER ▶ grody
GRODY adj unpleasant
GROG n, vb grogged
GROGGY adj
GROGRAM n coarse
fabric
GROGS ▶ grog
GROIN n, vb groined,

groins
GROK vb understand
completely and
intuitively
GROKED ▶ grokked
GROKING > grokking
GROKKED ▶ grok
GROKS ▶ grok
GROMA n Roman
surveying instrument
gromas
GROMET = grommet
GROMETS ▶ gromet
GROMMET n ring or
eyelet
GRONE obsolete word for
▶ groan
GRONED ▶ grone
GRONES ▶ grone
GRONING ▶ grone
GROOF n face, or front
of the body groofs
GROOLY adj gruesome
GROOM n, vb
groomed, groomer,
grooms
GROOVE n grooved
GROOVER n device that
makes grooves
GROOVES ▶ groove
GROOVY adj attractive
or exciting
GROPE vb, n groped
GROPER n type of large
fish of warm and
tropical seas gropers
GROPES ▶ grope
GROPING ▶ grope
GROSER n gooseberry
grosers, grosert,
groset
GROSETS ▶ groset
GROSS adj, n, vb, interj
grossed, grosser,

grosses, grossly

GROSZ n Polish monetary unit **grosze, groszy**

GROT n rubbish **grots**

GROTTO n **grottos**

GROTTY adj

GROUCH vb, n

GROUCHY adj bad-tempered

GROUF = **groof**

GROUFS ▶ **grouf**

GROUGH n natural channel or fissure in a peat moor **groughs**

GROUND n, adj, vb **grounds**

GROUP n, vb **grouped**

GROUPER n large edible sea fish

GROUPIE n ardent fan of a celebrity or of a sport or activity

GROUPS ▶ **group**

GROUPY = **groupie**

GROUSE n, vb, adj **groused, grouser, grouses**

GROUT n mortar ▷ vb fill up with grout **grouted, grouter**

GROUTS pl n sediment or grounds

GROUTY adj sullen or surly

GROVE n **groved**

GROVEL vb **grovels**

GROVES ▶ **grove**

GROVET n wrestling hold **grovets**

GROW vb

GROWER n person who grows plants **growers**

GROWING ▶ **grow**

GROWL vb, n **growled**

GROWLER n person, animal, or thing that growls

GROWLS ▶ **growl**

GROWLY ▶ **growl**

GROWN ▶ **grow**

GROWNUP n adult

GROWS ▶ **grow**

GROWTH n, adj **growths**

GROWTHY adj rapid-growing

GROYNE n **groynes**

GROZING adj as in **grozing iron** iron for smoothing joints between lead pipes

GRRL n as in **riot grrl** young woman who enjoys feminist punk rock **grrls**

> This slang term for a girl who likes loud rock music can come in useful when you are short of vowels. And it can also be spelt **grrrl**.

GRRRL n as in **riot grrrl** young woman who enjoys feminist punk rock **grrrls**

GRUB n, vb **grubbed**

GRUBBER n person who grubs

GRUBBLE = **grabble**

GRUBBY adj

GRUBS ▶ **grub**

GRUDGE vb, n, adj **grudged, grudger, grudges**

GRUE n shiver or shudder ▷ vb shiver or shudder **grued, grueing**

GRUEL n, vb **grueled, grueler, gruels**

GRUES ▶ **grue**

GRUFE = **groof**

GRUFES ▶ **grufe**

GRUFF adj, vb **gruffed, gruffer, gruffly, gruffs**

GRUFFY adj gruff

GRUFTED adj dirty

GRUGRU n tropical American palm **grugrus**

GRUING ▶ **grue**

GRUM adj surly

GRUMBLE vb, n **grumbly**

GRUME n clot **grumes**

GRUMLY ▶ **grum**

GRUMMER ▶ **grum**

GRUMMET = **grommet**

GRUMOSE = **grumous**

GRUMOUS adj (esp of plant parts) consisting of granular tissue

GRUMP n surly or bad-tempered person ▷ vb complain or grumble **grumped**

GRUMPH vb grunt **grumphs**

GRUMPHY = **grumphie**

GRUMPS ▶ **grump**

GRUMPY adj

GRUND n as in **grund mail** payment for right of burial

GRUNGE n style of rock music with a fuzzy guitar sound

GRUNGER n fan of grunge music

GRUNGES ▶ **grunge**

GRUNGEY adj messy or dirty

GRUNGY adj squalid or seedy

GRUNION n Californian marine fish that spawns on beaches

GRUNT vb, n grunted

GRUNTER n person or animal that grunts, esp a pig

GRUNTLE vb grunt or groan

GRUNTS ▶ grunt

GRUSHIE adj healthy and strong

GRUTCH vb grudge

GRUTTEN ▶ greet

GRUYERE n hard flat whole-milk cheese with holes

GRYCE = grice

GRYCES ▶ gryce

GRYDE = gride

GRYDED ▶ gryde

GRYDES ▶ gryde

GRYDING ▶ gryde

GRYESY adj grey

GRYFON = griffin

GRYFONS ▶ gryfon

GRYKE = grike

GRYKES ▶ gryke

GRYPE = gripe

GRYPES ▶ gripe

GRYPHON = griffin

GRYPT archaic form of ▶ gripped

GRYSBOK n small antelope

GRYSELY = grisly

GRYSIE = grisy

GU = gju

GUACO n any of several plants used as an antidote to snakebite **guacos**

GUAIAC = guaiacum

GUAIACS ▶ guaiacum

GUAN n type of bird of Central and S America

GUANA another word for ▶ iguana

GUANACO n S American animal related to the llama

GUANAS ▶ guana

GUANASE n type of enzyme

GUANAY n type of cormorant **guanays**

GUANGO n rain tree **guangos**

GUANIN = guanine

GUANINE n white almost insoluble compound **guanins**

GUANO n dried sea-bird manure **guanos**

GUANS ▶ guan

GUANXI n Chinese social concept **guanxis**

GUAR n Indian plant

GUARANA n type of shrub native to Venezuela

GUARANI n standard monetary unit of Paraguay

GUARD vb, n

GUARDED adj

GUARDEE n guardsman

GUARDER ▶ guard

GUARDS ▶ guard

GUARISH vb heal

GUARS ▶ guar

GUAVA n guavas

GUAYULE n bushy shrub of the southwestern US

GUB n white man ▷ vb

hit or defeat **gubbah**

GUBBAHS ▶ gubbah

GUBBED ▶ gub

GUBBING ▶ gub

GUBBINS n object of little or no value

GUBS ▶ gub

GUCK n slimy matter

GUCKIER ▶ gucky

GUCKS ▶ guck

GUCKY adj slimy and mucky

GUDDLE vb catch (fish) with the hands ▷ n muddle **guddled, guddles**

GUDE Scots word for ▶ good

GUDEMAN n male householder **gudemen**

GUDES n goods

GUDGEON n small freshwater fish ▷ vb trick or cheat

GUE = gju

GUELDER n as in **guelder rose** kind of shrub

GUENON n slender Old World monkey **guenons**

GUERDON n reward or payment ▷ vb give a guerdon to

GUEREZA n handsome colobus monkey

GUERITE n turret used by a sentry

GUES ▶ gue

GUESS vb, n guessed, guesser, guesses

GUEST n, vb guested

GUESTEN vb stay as a

guest in someone's house

GUESTS ▶ guest

GUFF n nonsense

GUFFAW n, vb **guffaws**

GUFFIE Scots word for
▶ **pig**

GUFFIES ▶ guffie

GUFFS ▶ guff

GUGA n gannet chick **gugas**

GUGGLE vb drink making a gurgling sound **guggled, guggles**

GUGLET = **goglet**

GUGLETS ▶ guglet

GUICHET n grating, hatch, or small opening in a wall

GUID Scot word for ▶ **good**

GUIDAGE n guidance

GUIDE n, vb **guided, guider, guiders, guides, guiding**

GUIDON n small pennant **guidons**

GUIDS n possessions

GUILD n

GUILDER n former monetary unit of the Netherlands

GUILDRY n in Scotland, corporation of merchants

GUILDS ▶ guild

GUILE n, vb **guiled**

GUILER n deceiver **guilers**

GUILES ▶ guile

GUILING ▶ guile

GUILT n **guilts**

GUILTY adj

GUIMP = **guimpe**

GUIMPE n short blouse worn under a pinafore dress ▷ vb make with gimp **guimped, guimpes**

GUIMPS ▶ guimp

GUINEA n **guineas**

GUIPURE n heavy lace

GUIRO n percussion instrument made from a hollow gourd **guiros**

GUISARD n guiser

GUISE n, vb **guised**

GUISER n mummer, esp at Christmas or Halloween revels **guisers**

GUISES ▶ guise

GUISING ▶ guise

GUITAR n **guitars**

GUIZER = **guiser**

GUIZERS ▶ guizer

GUL n design used in oriental carpets

GULA n gluttony

GULAG n forced-labour camp **gulags**

GULAR adj of or situated in the throat or oesophagus

GULAS ▶ gula

GULCH n deep narrow valley ▷ vb swallow fast **gulched, gulches**

GULDEN = **guilder**

GULDENS ▶ guilder

GULE Scots word for > **marigold**

GULES n red in heraldry

GULET n wooden Turkish sailing boat **gulets**

GULF n, vb **gulfed,**

gulfier, gulfing, gulfs, gulfy

GULL n, vb **gulled**

GULLER n deceiver **gullers**

GULLERY n breeding-place for gulls

GULLET n **gullets**

GULLEY = **gully**

GULLEYS ▶ gulley

GULLIED ▶ gully

GULLIES ▶ gully

GULLING ▶ gull

GULLISH adj stupid

GULLS ▶ gull

GULLY n, vb

GULP vb, n **gulped, gulper, gulpers**

GULPH archaic word for ▶ **gulf**

GULPHS ▶ gulph

GULPIER, gulping, gulps, gulpy ▶ gulp

GULS ▶ gul

GULY adj relating to gules

GUM n, vb

GUMBALL n round piece of chewing gum

GUMBO n mucilaginous pods of okra

GUMBOIL n abscess on the gum

GUMBOOT n

GUMBOS ▶ gumbo

GUMDROP n hard jelly-like sweet

GUMLESS ▶ gum

GUMLIKE ▶ gum

GUMLINE n line where gums meet teeth

GUMMA n rubbery tumour **gummas, gummata**

GUMMED ▶ gum

GUMMER n punch-cutting tool **gummers**

GUMMIER ▶ gummy

GUMMIES ▶ gummy

GUMMILY ▶ gummy

GUMMING ▶ gum

GUMMITE n orange or yellowish amorphous secondary mineral

GUMMOSE = gummous

GUMMOUS adj resembling or consisting of gum

GUMMY adj toothless ▷ n type of small crustacean-eating shark

GUMNUT n hardened seed container of the gumtree **gumnuts**

GUMP vb guddle **gumped, gumping, gumps**

GUMS ▶ gum

GUMSHOE n waterproof overshoe ▷ vb act stealthily

GUMTREE n

GUMWEED n any of several yellow-flowered plants

GUMWOOD = gumtree

GUN n, vb

GUNBOAT n

GUNDIES ▶ gundy

GUNDOG n dog trained to work with a hunter or gamekeeper **gundogs**

GUNDY n toffee

GUNFIRE n

GUNG adj as in gung ho extremely or excessively enthusiastic

about something

GUNGE n sticky unpleasant substance ▷ vb block or encrust with gunge **gunged, gunges, gungier, gunging, gungy**

GUNITE n mortar sprayed in a very dense concrete layer **gunites**

GUNK n slimy or filthy substance **gunkier, gunks, gunky**

GUNLESS ▶ gun

GUNLOCK n mechanism in some firearms

GUNMAN n armed criminal **gunmen**

GUNNAGE n number of guns carried by a warship

GUNNED ▶ gun

GUNNEL = gunwale

GUNNELS ▶ gunnel

GUNNEN ▶ gun

GUNNER n artillery soldier

GUNNERA n type of herbaceous plant

GUNNERS ▶ gunner

GUNNERY n use or science of large guns

GUNNIES ▶ gunny

GUNNING ▶ gun

GUNNY n strong coarse fabric used for sacks

GUNPLAY n use of firearms, as by criminals

GUNPORT n porthole or other opening for a gun

GUNROOM n the mess

allocated to junior officers

GUNS ▶ gun

GUNSEL n catamite **gunsels**

GUNSHIP n ship or helicopter armed with heavy guns

GUNSHOT n

GUNTER n type of gaffing **gunters**

GUNWALE n

GUNYAH n gunyahs

GUP n gossip

GUPPIES ▶ guppy

GUPPY n

GUPS ▶ gup

GUQIN n type of Chinese zither **guqins**

GUR n unrefined cane sugar

GURAMI = gourami

GURAMIS ▶ gurami

GURGE vb swallow up **gurged, gurges, gurging**

GURGLE n, vb **gurgled, gurgles**

GURGLET = goglet

GURJUN n S or SE Asian tree that yields a resin **gurjuns**

GURL vb snarl **gurled**

GURLET n type of pickaxe **gurlets**

GURLIER ▶ gurly

GURLING ▶ gurl

GURLS ▶ gurl

GURLY adj stormy

GURN variant spelling of ▶ girn

GURNARD n spiny armour-headed sea fish

GURNED ▶ gurn**

GURNET = gurnard

GURNETS ▶ gurnard

GURNEY n wheeled stretcher for transporting hospital patients **gurneys**

GURNING ▶ gurn

GURNS ▶ gurn

GURRAH n type of coarse muslin **gurrahs**

GURRIER n low-class tough ill-mannered person

GURRIES ▶ gurry

GURRY n dog-fight

GURS ▶ gur

GURSH n unit of currency in Saudi Arabia **gurshes**

GURU n

GURUDOM n state of being a guru

GURUISM ▶ guru

GURUS ▶ guru

GUS ▶ gu

GUSH vb, n gushed

GUSHER n spurting oil well **gushers**

GUSHES ▶ gush

GUSHIER ▶ gushy

GUSHILY ▶ gushy

GUSHING ▶ gush

GUSHY adj displaying excessive sentimentality

GUSLA n Balkan single-stringed musical instrument

GUSLAR n player of the gusla **guslars**

GUSLAS ▶ gusla

GUSLE = gusla

GUSLES ▶ gusle

GUSLI n Russian harp-like musical instrument **guslis**

GUSSET n, vb gussets

GUSSIE n young pig

GUSSIED ▶ gussy

GUSSIES ▶ gussy

GUSSY vb dress elaborately

GUST n, vb gusted

GUSTFUL adj tasty

GUSTIE adj tasty

GUSTIER ▶ gusty

GUSTILY ▶ gusty

GUSTING ▶ gust

GUSTO n gustoes, gustos

GUSTS ▶ gust

GUSTY adj blustery weather

GUT n, vb, adj

GUTCHER n grandfather

GUTFUL n bellyful gutfuls

GUTLESS adj cowardly

GUTLIKE ▶ gut

GUTROT n diarrhoea gutrots

GUTS vb gutsed

GUTSER n as in come a gutser fall heavily to the ground **gutsers**

GUTSES ▶ guts

GUTSFUL n bellyful

GUTSIER ▶ gutsy

GUTSILY ▶ gutsy

GUTSING ▶ guts

GUTSY adj courageous

GUTTA n small drop-like ornament **guttae, guttas**

GUTTATE adj covered with small drops or drop-like markings

▷ vb exude droplets of liquid

GUTTED ▶ gut

GUTTER n, vb gutters, guttery

GUTTIER ▶ gutty

GUTTIES ▶ gutty

GUTTING ▶ gut

GUTTLE vb eat greedily guttled, guttler, guttles

GUTTY n urchin or delinquent ▷ adj courageous

GUTZER n bad fall gutzers

GUV informal name for > governor

GUVS ▶ guv

GUY n, vb guyed, guying

GUYLE = guile; guyled, guyler, guylers, guyles

GUYLINE n guy rope

GUYLING ▶ guyle

GUYOT n flat-topped submarine mountain guyots

GUYS ▶ guy

GUYSE = guise

GUYSES ▶ guyse

GUZZLE vb guzzled

GUZZLER n person or thing that guzzles

GUZZLES ▶ guzzle

GWEDUC = geoduck

GWEDUCK = geoduck

GWEDUCS ▶ gweduck

GWINE dialect form of ▶ going

GWINIAD n powan

GWYNIAD n type of freshwater white fish

GYAL = gayal

GYALS ▶ gyal

GYBE *vb* (of a sail) swing suddenly from one side to the other ▷ *n* instance of gybing **gybed, gybes, gybing**

GYELD *n* guild **gyelds**

GYLDEN *adj* golden

GYM *n*

GYMBAL = gimbal

GYMBALS ▶ gymbal

GYMMAL = gimmal

GYMMALS ▶ gymmal

GYMNAST *n*

GYMNIC *adj* gymnastic

GYMPIE *n* tall tree with stinging hairs on its leaves **gympies**

GYMS ▶ gym

GYMSLIP *n* tunic or pinafore formerly worn by schoolgirls

GYNAE *adj* gynaecological ▷ *n* gynaecology **gynaes**

GYNECIA > gynecium

GYNECIC *adj* relating to the female sex

GYNIE *n* gynaecology **gynies**

GYNNEY *n* guinea hen **gynneys**

GYNNIES ▶ gynny

GYNNY = gynney

GYNY *n* gynaecology

GYOZA *n* Japanese fried dumpling **gyozas**

GYP *vb* swindle, cheat, or defraud ▷ *n* act of cheating

> This little word, meaning to swindle, can be useful when you are short of vowels.

GYPLURE *n* synthetic version of the gypsy moth sex pheromone

GYPPED ▶ gyp

GYPPER ▶ gyp

GYPPERS ▶ gyp

GYPPIE = gippy

GYPPIES ▶ gyppy

GYPPING ▶ gyp

GYPPY = gippy

GYPS ▶ gyp

GYPSIED ▶ gypsy

GYPSIES ▶ gypsy

GYPSTER *n* swindler

GYPSUM *n* gypsums

GYPSY *n, vb*

GYRAL *adj* having a circular, spiral, or rotating motion **gyrally**

GYRANT *adj* gyrating

GYRASE *n* topoisomerase enzyme **gyrases**

GYRATE *vb, adj*

gyrated, gyrates

GYRATOR *n* electronic circuit that inverts the impedance

GYRE *n* circular or spiral movement or path ▷ *vb* whirl **gyred**

GYRENE *n* nickname for a member of the US Marine Corps **gyrenes**

GYRES ▶ gyre

GYRI ▶ gyrus

GYRING ▶ gyre

GYRO *n* gyrocompass

GYROCAR *n* two-wheeled car

GYRON = giron

GYRONIC ▶ gyron

GYRONNY = gironny

GYRONS ▶ gyron

GYROS ▶ gyro

GYROSE *adj* marked with sinuous lines

GYROUS *adj* gyrose

GYRUS *n* convolution **gyruses**

GYTE *n* spoilt child **gytes**

GYTRASH *n* spirit that haunts lonely roads

GYTTJA *n* sediment on lake bottom **gyttjas**

GYVE *vb* shackle or fetter ▷ *n* fetters **gyved, gyves, gyving**

Hh

H forms a two-letter word in front of every vowel except **U** (and you can make **uh** with **U**), making it a versatile tile when you want to form words in more than one direction. It also goes with **M** to make **hm**. As **H** is worth 4 points on its own, you can earn some very high scores by doing this: even **ha**, **he**, **hi** and **ho** will give 5 points each. There are lots of good short words beginning with **H**, like **haw**, **hew**, **how**, **hay**, **hey** and **hoy** (9 each), while **hyp** can be useful if you are short of vowels. More high-scoring words with **H** include **haj**, **hex** and **hox** for 13 points each, and never forget the invaluable **zho** for 15 points.

HA *interj*

HAAF *n* fishing ground off the Shetland and Orkney Islands **haafs**

HAAR *n* cold sea mist or fog off the North Sea **haars**

HABDABS *n* highly nervous state

HABILE *adj* skilful

HABIT *n*, *vb*

HABITAN = **habitant**

HABITAT *n*

HABITED *adj* dressed in a habit

HABITS ▶ **habit**

HABITUE *n* frequent visitor to a place

HABITUS *n* general physical state

HABLE old form of ▶ **able**

HABOOB *n* sandstorm **haboobs**

HABU *n* large venomous snake **habus**

HACEK *n* pronunciation symbol in Slavonic language **haceks**

HACHIS *n* hash

HACHURE *n* shading drawn on a map to indicate steepness of a hill ▷ *vb* mark or show by hachures

HACK *vb*, *n*, *adj*

HACKBUT another word for ▶ **arquebus**

HACKED ▶ **hack**

HACKEE *n* chipmunk **hackees**

HACKER *n* **hackers**

HACKERY *n* journalism

HACKIE *n* US word meaning cab driver **hackies**

HACKING ▶ **hack**

HACKLE = **heckle**

HACKLED ▶ **hackle**

HACKLER ▶ **hackle**

HACKLES *pl n*

HACKLET *n* kittiwake

HACKLY *adj* rough or jagged

HACKMAN *n* taxi driver **hackmen**

HACKNEY *n* taxi ▷ *vb* make commonplace and banal by too frequent use

HACKS ▶ **hack**

HACKSAW *n*, *vb*

HAD *vb* Scots form of hold

HADAL *adj* denoting very deep zones of the oceans

HADARIM ▶ heder

HADAWAY *sentence substitute* exclamation urging the hearer to refrain from delay

HADDEN ▶ have

HADDEST = hadst

HADDIE *n* finnan haddock **haddies**

HADDING ▶ have

HADDOCK *n*

HADE *n* angle made to the vertical by the plane of a fault or vein ▷ *vb* incline from the vertical **haded**

HADEDAH *n* large grey-green S African ibis

HADES ▶ hade

HADING ▶ hade

HADITH *n* body of legend about Mohammed and his followers **hadiths**

HADJ = hajj

HADJEE = hadji

HADJEES ▶ hadjee

HADJES ▶ hadj

HADJI = hajji

HADJIS ▶ hadji

HADROME *n* part of xylem

HADRON *n* type of elementary particle **hadrons**

HADS ▶ have

HADST *singular form of the past tense (indicative mood) of* ▶ **have**

HAE *Scot variant of* ▶ **have**

HAED ▶ hae

HAEING ▶ hae

HAEM *n* red organic pigment containing ferrous iron

HAEMAL *adj* of the blood

HAEMIC = haematic

HAEMIN *n* haematin chloride **haemins**

HAEMOID = haematoid

HAEMONY *n* plant mentioned in Milton's poetry

HAEMS ▶ haem

HAEN ▶ hae

HAERES = heres

HAES ▶ hae

HAET *n* whit **haets**

HAFF *n* lagoon

HAFFET *n* side of head **haffets, haffit**

HAFFITS ▶ haffit

HAFFLIN = halfling

HAFFS ▶ haff

HAFIZ *n* title for a person who knows the Koran by heart **hafizes**

HAFNIUM *n* metallic element found in zirconium ores

HAFT *n* handle of an axe, knife, or dagger ▷ *vb* provide with a haft

HAFTARA = haftarah

HAFTED, hafter, hafters, hafting, hafts ▶ haft

HAG *n, vb*

HAGADIC > haggadic

HAGBOLT = hackbolt

HAGBORN *adj* born of a witch

HAGBUSH = arquebus

HAGBUT ▶ hagbut

HAGBUTS ▶ hagbut

HAGDEN = hackbolt

HAGDENS ▶ hagden

HAGDON = hackbolt

HAGDONS ▶ hagdon

HAGDOWN = hackbolt

HAGFISH *n* any of various primitive eel-like vertebrates

HAGG *n* boggy place

HAGGADA = haggadah

HAGGARD *adj,* n

HAGGED ▶ hag

HAGGING ▶ hag

HAGGIS *n*

HAGGISH ▶ hag

HAGGLE *vb* haggled, haggler, haggles

HAGGS ▶ hagg

HAGLET = hacklet

HAGLETS ▶ haglet

HAGLIKE ▶ hag

HAGRIDE *vb* torment or obsess **hagrode**

HAGS ▶ hag

HAH = ha

HAHA *n* wall or other boundary marker that is set in a ditch **hahas**

HAHNIUM *n* transuranic element

HAHS ▶ hah

HAICK = haik

HAICKS ▶ haick

HAIDUK *n* rural brigand **haiduks**

HAIK *n* Arab's outer garment **haika**

HAIKAI = haiku

HAIKS ▶ haik

HAIKU *n* Japanese verse form in 17 syllables **haikus**

HAIL n, vb, sentence substitute **hailed, hailer, hailers, hailier, hailing, hails, haily**

HAIMISH = **heimish**

HAIN vb Scots word meaning save

HAINCH Scots form of ▶ **haunch**

HAINED ▶ **hain**

HAINING ▶ **hain**

HAINS ▶ **hain**

HAINT = **haunt**

HAINTS ▶ **haint**

HAIQUE = **haik**

HAIQUES ▶ **haik**

HAIR n, vb

HAIRCAP n type of moss

HAIRCUT n

HAIRDO n **hairdos**

HAIRED adj with hair

HAIRIER ▶ **hairy**

HAIRIF another name for > **cleavers**

HAIRIFS ▶ **hairif**

HAIRING ▶ **hair**

HAIRNET n any of several kinds of light netting worn over the hair

HAIRPIN n

HAIRS ▶ **hair**

HAIRST Scots form of ▶ **harvest**

HAIRSTS ▶ **hairst**

HAIRY adj

HAITH interj Scots oath

HAJ = **hadj**

A **haj** is a Muslim pilgrimage to Mecca, and one of the key words to remember for using the J. It can also be spelt **hadj** or

hajj, and one who makes a haj is called a **hadjee, hadji, haji** or **hajji**.

HAJES ▶ **haj**

HAJI = **hajji**

HAJIS ▶ **haji**

HAJJ n

HAJJAH n Muslim woman who has made a pilgrimage to Mecca **hajjahs**

HAJJES ▶ **hajj**

HAJJI n Muslim who has made a pilgrimage to Mecca **hajjis**

HAKA n

HAKAM n text written by a rabbi **hakams**

HAKARI n Māori ritual feast **hakaris**

HAKAS ▶ **haka**

HAKE n

HAKEA n **hakeas**

HAKEEM = **hakim**

HAKEEMS ▶ **hakeem**

HAKES ▶ **hake**

HAKIM n Muslim judge, ruler, or administrator **hakims**

HAKU in New Zealand English, = kingfish

HAKUS ▶ **haku**

HALACHA n Jewish religious law **halakah, halakha**

HALAKIC ▶ **halakha**

HALAL n meat from animals slaughtered according to Muslim law ▷ adj of or relating to such meat ▷ vb kill (animals) in this way **HALALA** n money unit

in Saudi Arabia **halalah, halalas**

HALALAH ▶ **halal**

HALAVAH = **halvah**

HALBERD n halbert

HALCYON adj, n

HALE adj healthy, robust ▷ vb pull or drag **haled**

HALER = **heller**

HALERS ▶ **haler**

HALERU ▶ **haler**

HALES ▶ **hale**

HALEST ▶ **hale**

HALF n, adj, adv

HALFA n African grass **halfas**

HALFEN ▶ **half**

HALFLIN = **halfling**

HALFS ▶ **half**

HALFWAY adj

HALFWIT n

HALIBUT n

HALID = **halide**

HALIDE n binary compound **halides**

HALIDOM n holy place or thing

HALIDS ▶ **halid**

HALIMOT n court held by lord

HALING ▶ **hale**

HALITE n colourless or white mineral **halites**

HALITUS n vapour

HALL n

HALLAH variant spelling of ▶ **challah**

HALLAHS ▶ **hallah**

HALLAL = **halal**

HALLALI n bugle call

HALLALS ▶ **hallal**

HALLAN n partition in

cottage **hallans**
HALLEL n (in Judaism) section of the liturgy **hallels**
HALLIAN = **hallion**
HALLING n Norwegian country dance
HALLION n lout
HALLO = **halloo**
HALLOA = **halloo**
HALLOAS ► **halloa**
HALLOED ► **hallo**
HALLOES ► **hallo**
HALLOO interj shout used to call hounds at a hunt ▷ sentence substitute shout to attract attention, esp to call hounds at a hunt ▷ n shout of "halloo" ▷ vb shout (something) to (someone) **halloos**
HALLOS ► **hallo**
HALLOT ► **hallah**
HALLOTH = **challah**
HALLOW vb consecrate or set apart as being holy **hallows**
HALLS ► **hall**
HALLUX n first digit on the hind foot of an animal
HALLWAY n entrance area
HALLYON = **hallion**
HALM = **haulm**
HALMA n board game **halmas**
HALMS ► **halm**
HALO n, vb **haloed**, **haloes**
HALOGEN n
HALOID adj resembling

or derived from a halogen ▷ n compound containing halogen atoms in its molecules **haloids**
HALOING ► **halo**
HALON n any of a class of chemical compounds **halons**
HALOS ► **halo**
HALOUMI = **halloumi**
HALSE vb embrace **halsed**, **halser**, **halsers**, **halses**, **halsing**
HALT vb, n, adj **halted**
HALTER n, vb
HALTERE n one of a pair of modified hind wings in dipterous insects
HALTERS ► **halter**
HALTING ► **halt**
HALTS ► **halt**
HALUTZ variant spelling of ► **chalutz**
HALVA = **halvah**
HALVAH n E Mediterranean, Middle Eastern, or Indian sweetmeat **halvahs**
HALVAS ► **halva**
HALVE vb **halved**, **halver**, **halvers**, **halves**, **halving**
HALYARD n
HAM n, vb
HAMADA n rocky plateau in desert **hamadas**
HAMAL n (in Middle Eastern countries) a porter or servant **hamals**
HAMATE adj

hook-shaped ▷ n small bone in the wrist **hamates**
HAMAUL = **hamal**
HAMAULS ► **hamaul**
HAMBLE vb mutilate **hambled**, **hambles**
HAMBONE vb strike body to provide percussion
HAMBURG = **hamburger**
HAME n Scots word for home ▷ vb to home **hamed**, **hames**, **haming**
HAMLET n **hamlets**
HAMMADA = **hamada**
HAMMAL = **hamal**
HAMMALS ► **hammal**
HAMMAM n bathing establishment **hammams**
HAMMED ► **ham**
HAMMER n, vb **hammers**
HAMMIER ► **hammy**
HAMMILY ► **hammy**
HAMMING ► **ham**
HAMMOCK = **hummock**
HAMMY adj (of an actor) overacting or tending to overact
HAMOSE adj shaped like a hook **hamous**
HAMPER vb, n **hampers**
HAMS ► **ham**
HAMSTER n
HAMULAR = **hamulus**
HAMULI ► **hamulus**
HAMULUS n biological attribute
HAMZA n sign used in

Arabic to represent the glottal stop **hamzah**

HAMZAHS ▶ hamzah

HAMZAS ▶ hamza

HAN *archaic inflected form of* ▶ have

HANAP n medieval drinking cup

HANAPER n small wickerwork basket

HANAPS ▶ hanap

HANCE = haunch

HANCES ▶ hance

HANCH vb to try to bite **hanched, hanches**

HAND n, vb

HANDAX n small axe held in one hand

HANDBAG n

HANDCAR n small railway vehicle

HANDED ▶ hand

HANDER ▶ hand

HANDERS ▶ hand

HANDFED > handfeed

HANDFUL n

HANDGUN n firearm such as a pistol

HANDIER ▶ handy

HANDILY adv in a handy way or manner

HANDING ▶ hand

HANDISM n discrimination against left- or right-handed people

HANDJAR n Persian dagger

HANDLE n, vb handled

HANDLER n person who controls an animal

HANDLES ▶ handle

HANDOFF n (in rugby)

act of warding off an opposing player

HANDOUT n

HANDS ▶ hand

HANDSAW n any saw for use in one hand only

HANDSEL n gift for good luck ▷ vb give a handsel to (a person)

HANDSET n

HANDY adj

HANG vb

HANGAR n, vb hangars

HANGDOG adj, n

HANGED ▶ hang

HANGER n hangers

HANGI n

HANGING ▶ hang

HANGIS ▶ hangi

HANGMAN n man who executes people by hanging **hangmen**

HANGOUT n place where one lives or that one frequently visits

HANGS ▶ hang

HANGTAG n attached label

HANGUL n Korean language

HANGUP n emotional or psychological or problem **hangups**

HANIWA n Japanese funeral offering

HANJAR = hanjar

HANJARS ▶ hanjar

HANK n, vb hanked

HANKER vb hankers

HANKIE = hanky

HANKIES ▶ hanky

HANKING ▶ hank

HANKS ▶ hank

HANKY n

HANSA = hanse

HANSAS ▶ hansa

HANSE n medieval guild of merchants

HANSEL = handsel

HANSELS ▶ hansel

HANSES ▶ hanse

HANSOM n two-wheeled one-horse carriage **hansoms**

HANT = haunt

HANTED ▶ hant

HANTING ▶ hant

HANTLE n good deal **hantles**

HANTS ▶ hant

HANUMAN n type of monkey

HAO n monetary unit of Vietnam

HAOMA n type of ritual drink **haomas**

HAOS ▶ hao

HAP n luck ▷ vb cover up

HAPAX n word that appears once in a work of literature **hapaxes**

HAPKIDO n Korean martial art

HAPLESS adj

HAPLITE variant of ▶ aplite

HAPLOID adj denoting a cell or organism with unpaired chromosomes ▷ n haploid cell or organism

HAPLONT n organism with a haploid number of chromosomes

HAPLY archaic word for ▶ perhaps

HAPPED ▸ hap
HAPPEN vb happens
HAPPIED ▸ happy
HAPPIER ▸ happy
HAPPIES ▸ happy
HAPPILY ▸ happy
HAPPING ▸ hap
HAPPY adj feeling or causing joy ▷ vb make happy
HAPS ▸ hap
HAPTEN n incomplete antigen **haptene, haptens**
HAPTIC adj relating to or based on the sense of touch
HAPTICS n science of sense of touch
HAPU n subtribe
HAPUKA another name for ▸ groper
HAPUKAS ▸ hapuka
HAPUKU = hapuka
HAPUKUS ▸ hapuku
HAPUS ▸ hapu
HARAM n anything that is forbidden by Islamic law **harams**
HARASS vb
HARBOR = harbour
HARBORS ▸ harbor
HARBOUR n, vb
HARD adj, adv
HARDASS n tough person
HARDEN vb, n **hardens**
HARDER ▸ hard
HARDEST ▸ hard
HARDHAT n hat made of a hard material for protection ▷ adj typical of construction workers

HARDIER ▸ hardy
HARDIES ▸ hardy
HARDILY adv in a hardy manner
HARDISH ▸ hard
HARDLY adv
HARDMAN n tough, ruthless, or violent man **hardmen**
HARDOKE n burdock
HARDPAN n hard impervious layer of clay below the soil
HARDS pl n coarse fibres and other refuse from flax and hemp
HARDSET adj in difficulties
HARDTOP n car equipped with a metal or plastic roof
HARDY adj, n
HARE n, vb **hared**
HAREEM = harem
HAREEMS ▸ hareem
HARELD n long-tailed duck **harelds**
HARELIP n
HAREM n **harems**
HARES ▸ hare
HARIANA n Indian breed of cattle
HARICOT n variety of French bean
HARIJAN n member of an Indian caste
HARIM = harem
HARIMS ▸ harim
HARING ▸ hare
HARIRA n Moroccan soup **hariras**
HARISH adj like hare
HARISSA n hot paste
HARK vb **harked**

HARKEN = hearken
HARKENS ▸ harken
HARKING ▸ hark
HARKS ▸ hark
HARL = herl
HARLED ▸ harl
HARLING ▸ harl
HARLOT n, adj **harlots**
HARLS ▸ harl
HARM vb, n
HARMALA n African plant
HARMAN n constable **harmans**
HARMED ▸ harm
HARMEL = harmala
HARMELS ▸ harmel
HARMER ▸ harm
HARMERS ▸ harm
HARMFUL adj
HARMIN = harmalin
HARMINE = harmalin
HARMING ▸ harm
HARMINS ▸ harmin
HARMONY n
HARMOST n Spartan governor
HARMS ▸ harm
HARN n coarse linen
HARNESS n, vb
HARNS ▸ harn
HARO interj cry meaning alas **haros**
HAROSET n Jewish dish eaten at Passover
HARP n, vb **harped, harper, harpers**
HARPIES ▸ harpy
HARPIN n type of protein
HARPING ▸ harp
HARPINS = harpings
HARPIST ▸ harp
HARPOON n, vb

HARPS ▸ harp

HARPY n nasty or bad-tempered woman

HARRIED ▸ harry

HARRIER n cross-country runner

HARRIES ▸ harry

HARROW n implement used to break up lumps of soil ▹ vb draw a harrow over **harrows**

HARRY vb

HARSH adj, vb **hasped, hashing, hashes, hashier, hashing**

HARSHEN vb make harsh

HARSHER ▸ harsh

HARSHES ▸ harsh

HARSHLY ▸ harsh

HARSLET = haslet

HART n adult male deer

HARTAL n (in India) closing shops or suspending work **hartals**

HARTELY archaic spelling of ▸ heartily

HARTEN = hearten

HARTENS ▸ harten

HARTS ▸ hart

HARUMPH = harrumph

HARVEST n, vb

HAS ▸ have

HASBIAN n former lesbian

HASH n, vb **hashed, hashes, hashier, hashing**

HASHISH n

HASHY ▸ hash

HASK n archaic name for a basket for transporting fish **hasks**

HASLET n loaf of cooked minced pig's offal, eaten cold **haslets**

HASP n, vb **hasped, hasping, hasps**

HASS n as in **white hass** oatmeal pudding made with sheep's gullet

HASSAR n South American catfish **hassars**

HASSEL variant of ▸ hassle

HASSELS ▸ hassel

HASSES ▸ hass

HASSIUM n chemical element

HASSLE n, vb **hassled, hassles**

HASSOCK n

HAST singular form of the present tense (indicative mood) of ▸ have

HASTA Spanish for ▸ until

HASTATE adj shaped like a spear

HASTE n, vb **hasted**

HASTEN vb **hastens**

HASTES ▸ haste

HASTIER ▸ hasty

HASTILY ▸ hasty

HASTING ▸ haste

HASTY adj

HAT n, vb

HATABLE ▸ hate

HATBAND n band or ribbon around a hat

HATBOX n box or case for a hat or hats

HATCH vb, n **hatched**

HATCHEL = heckle

HATCHER ▸ hatch

HATCHES ▸ hatch

HATCHET n

HATE vb, n **hated**

HATEFUL adj

HATER ▸ hate

HATERS ▸ hate

HATES ▸ hate

HATFUL n amount a hat will hold **hatfuls**

HATH form of the present tense (indicative mood) of ▸ have

HATHA n as in **hatha yoga** form of yoga

HATING ▸ hate

HATLESS ▸ hat

HATLIKE ▸ hat

HATPEG n peg to hang hat on **hatpegs**

HATPIN n pin used to secure a woman's hat to her hair **hatpins**

HATRACK n rack for hanging hats on

HATRED n **hatreds**

HATS ▸ hat

HATSFUL ▸ hatful

HATTED ▸ hat

HATTER n person who makes and sells hats ▹ vb annoy **hatters**

HATTING ▸ hat

HATTOCK n small hat

HAUBERK n long sleeveless coat of mail

HAUBOIS n hautboy

HAUD Scot word for ▸ hold

HAUDING ▸ haud

HAUDS ▸ haud

HAUF Scot word for ▸ half

HAUFS ▸ hauf

HAUGH n low-lying often alluvial riverside

meadow **haughs**
HAUGHT = haughty
HAUGHTY adj
HAUL vb, n
HAULAGE n
HAULD Scots word for
▸ hold
HAULDS ▸ hauld
HAULED ▸ haul
HAULER = haulier
HAULERS ▸ hauler
HAULIER n firm or
person that transports
goods by road
HAULING ▸ haul
HAULM n stalks of
beans, peas, or
potatoes collectively
haulms
HAULMY adj having
haulms
HAULS ▸ haul
HAULST = halse
HAULT = haughty
HAUNCH n human hip
or fleshy hindquarter
of an animal ▷ vb cause
(an animal) to come
down on its haunches
HAUNT vb, n
HAUNTED adj
HAUNTER ▸ haunt
HAUNTS ▸ haunt
HAUSE = halse
HAUSED ▸ hause
HAUSEN n variety of
sturgeon **hausens**
HAUSES ▸ hause
HAUSING ▸ hause
HAUT = haughty
HAUTBOY n type of
strawberry
HAUTE adj French word
meaning high

HAUTEUR n
HAUYNE n blue mineral
containing calcium
hauynes
HAVARTI n Danish
cheese
HAVE vb possess, hold
HAVEN n, vb havened,
havens
HAVEOUR = havior
HAVER vb talk
nonsense ▷ n nonsense
havered
HAVEREL n fool
HAVERS ▸ haver
HAVES ▸ have
HAVING ▸ have
HAVINGS ▸ have
HAVIOR = haviour
HAVIORS ▸ havior
HAVIOUR n possession
HAVOC n, vb havocs
HAW n hawthorn berry
▷ vb make an
inarticulate utterance
HAWALA n Middle
Eastern system of
money transfer
hawalas
HAWBUCK n bumpkin
HAWED ▸ haw
HAWING ▸ haw
HAWK n, vb
HAWKBIT n any of three
perennial plants
HAWKED ▸ hawk
HAWKER n travelling
salesman **hawkers**
HAWKEY = hockey
HAWKEYS ▸ hawkey
HAWKIE n cow with
white stripe on face
hawkies
HAWKING another name

for ▸ **falconry**
HAWKISH adj favouring
the use of force rather
than diplomacy
HAWKIT adj having a
white streak
HAWKS ▸ hawk
HAWM vb be idle and
relaxed **hawmed,
hawming, hawms**
HAWS ▸ haw
HAWSE vb of boats,
pitch violently when at
anchor **hawsed**
HAWSER n hawsers
HAWSES ▸ hawse
HAWSING ▸ hawse
HAY n, vb
HAYBAND n rope made
by twisting hay
together
HAYBOX n airtight box
used to keep partially
cooked food warm
HAYCOCK n pile of hay
left until dry enough to
move
HAYED ▸ hay
HAYER n person who
makes hay **hayers**
HAYEY ▸ hay
HAYFORK n
long-handled fork
HAYIER ▸ hayey
HAYIEST ▸ hayey
HAYING ▸ hay
HAYINGS ▸ hay
HAYLAGE n type of hay
for animal fodder
HAYLE n welfare **hayles**
HAYLOFT n loft for
storing hay
HAYMOW n part of a
barn where hay is

stored **haymows**
HAYRACK n rack for
holding hay for feeding
to animals
HAYRAKE n large rake
used to collect hay
HAYRICK = haystack
HAYRIDE n pleasure trip
in hay wagon
HAYS ▶ hay
HAYSEED n seeds or
fragments of grass or
straw
HAYSEL n season for
making hay **haysels**
HAYWARD n parish
officer in charge of
enclosures and fences
HAYWIRE adj (of things)
not functioning
properly ▷ n wire for
binding hay
HAZAN = cantor
HAZANIM ▶ hazan
HAZANS ▶ hazan
HAZARD n, vb hazards
HAZE n, vb hazed
HAZEL n, adj hazelly,
hazels
HAZER ▶ haze
HAZERS ▶ haze
HAZES ▶ haze
HAZIER ▶ hazy
HAZIEST ▶ hazy
HAZILY ▶ hazy
HAZING ▶ haze
HAZINGS ▶ haze
HAZMAT n hazardous
material **hazmats**
HAZY adj
HAZZAN = cantor
HAZZANS ▶ hazzan
HE pron, n, interj
HEAD n upper or front

part of the body ▷ adj
chief, principal ▷ vb
be at the top or front
of
HEADAGE n payment to
farmer based on
animals owned
HEADED adj having a
head or heads
HEADEND n facility
from which cable
television is
transmitted
HEADER n headers
HEADFUL n amount
head will hold
HEADIER ▶ heady
HEADILY ▶ heady
HEADING = head
HEADMAN n chief or
leader **headmen**
HEADPIN another word
for ▶ kingpin
HEADRIG n edge of
ploughed field
HEADS adv with the
side of a coin with a
head on it uppermost
HEADSET n pair of
headphones
HEADWAY = headroom
HEADY adj
HEAL vb
HEALD = heddle
HEALDED ▶ heald
HEALDS ▶ heald
HEALED ▶ heal
HEALEE n person who is
being healed **healees**
HEALER n healers,
healing, heals ▶ heal
HEALTH n, interj
healths
HEALTHY adj

HEAME old form of
▶ home
HEAP n, vb heaped,
heaper, heapers
HEAPIER ▶ heapy
HEAPING adj (of a
spoonful) heaped
HEAPS ▶ heap
HEAPY adj having many
heaps
HEAR vb
HEARD = herd
HEARDS ▶ herd
HEARE old form of ▶ hair
HEARER ▶ hear
HEARERS ▶ hear
HEARES ▶ heare
HEARIE old form of
▶ hairy
HEARING ▶ hear
HEARKEN vb listen
HEARS ▶ hear
HEARSAY n
HEARSE n, vb hearsed,
hearses
HEARSY adj like a
hearse
HEART n, vb hearted
HEARTEN vb
HEARTH n hearths
HEARTLY adv vigorously
HEARTS n card game
HEARTY adj, n
HEAST = hest
HEASTE = hest
HEASTES ▶ heaste
HEASTS ▶ heast
HEAT vb, n
HEATED adj angry and
excited
HEATER n device for
supplying heat
heaters
HEATH n

HEATHEN n, adj
HEATHER n, adj
HEATHS ▸ heath
HEATHY ▸ heath
HEATING n
HEATS ▸ heat
HEAUME n large helmet reaching the shoulders heaumes
HEAVE vb, n heaved
HEAVEN n heavens
HEAVER ▸ heave
HEAVERS ▸ heave
HEAVES ▸ heave
HEAVIER ▸ heavy
HEAVIES ▸ heavy
HEAVILY ▸ heavy
HEAVING ▸ heave
HEAVY adj
HEBE n any of various flowering shrubs
HEBEN old form of ▸ ebony
HEBENON n source of poison
HEBENS ▸ heben
HEBES ▸ hebe
HEBETIC adj of or relating to puberty
HEBONA = hebenon
HEBONAS ▸ hebona
HECH interj expression of surprise
HECHT = hight
HECHTS ▸ hecht
HECK interj mild exclamation of surprise, irritation, etc ▸ n frame for obstructing the passage of fish in a river
HECKLE vb, n heckled, heckler, heckles
HECKS ▸ heck

HECTARE n
HECTIC adj, n hectics
HECTOR vb, n hectors
HEDDLE n frame on a loom ▸ vb pass thread through a heddle heddled, heddles
HEDER variant spelling of ▸ cheder
HEDERA ▸ ivy
HEDERAL ▸ hedera
HEDERAS ▸ hedera
HEDERS ▸ heder
HEDGE n, vb hedged, hedger, hedgers, hedges, hedgier, hedging, hedgy
HEDONIC ▸ hedonism
HEED n, vb heeded, heeder, heeders, heedful, heeding, heeds, heedy
HEEHAW interj representation of the braying sound of a donkey ▸ vb make braying sound heehaws
HEEL n, vb
HEELBAR n small shop where shoes are repaired
HEELED ▸ heel
HEELER ▸ heelers
HEELING ▸ heel
HEELS ▸ heel
HEELTAP n layer of leather, etc, in the heel of a shoe
HEEZE Scots word for ▸ hoist
HEEZED ▸ heeze
HEEZES ▸ heeze

HEEZIE n act of lifting heezies
HEEZING ▸ heeze
HEFT vb assess the weight of (something) by lifting ▸ n weight
HEFTE = heave
HEFTED ▸ heft
HEFTER ▸ heft
HEFTERS ▸ heft
HEFTIER ▸ hefty
HEFTILY ▸ hefty
HEFTING ▸ heft
HEFTS ▸ heft
HEFTY adj
HEGARI n African sorghum hegaris
HEGEMON n person in authority
HEGIRA n emigration escape or flight hegiras
HEGUMEN n head of a monastery of the Eastern Church
HEH interj exclamation of surprise or inquiry hehs
HEID Scot word for ▸ head
HEIDS ▸ heid
HEIFER n heifers
HEIGH = hey
HEIGHT n heighth, heights
HEIL vb give a German greeting heiled, heiling, heils
HEIMISH adj comfortable
HEINIE n buttocks heinies
HEINOUS adj
HEIR n, vb

HEIRDOM n succession by right of blood

HEIRED ▶ heir

HEIRESS n

HEIRING ▶ heir

HEIRS ▶ heir

HEISHI n Native American shell jewellery

HEIST n robbery ▷ vb steal or burgle **heisted, heister, heists**

HEITIKI n Māori neck ornament of greenstone

HEJAB = hijab

HEJABS ▶ hejab

HEJIRA = hegira

HEJIRAS ▶ hegira

HEJRA = hegira

HEJRAS ▶ hejra

HEKTARE = hectare

HELCOID adj having ulcers

HELD ▶ hold

HELE vb as in hele in insert (cuttings, etc) into soil **heled, heles**

HELIAC = heliacal

HELIAST n ancient Greek juror

HELIBUS n helicopter carrying passengers

HELICAL adj spiral

HELICES ▶ helix

HELICON n bass tuba

HELIMAN n helicopter pilot **helimen**

HELING ▶ hele

HELIO n instrument for sending messages in Morse code **helios**

HELIPAD n place for helicopters to land and take off

HELIUM n heliums

HELIX n helixes

HELL n, vb

HELLBOX n (in printing) container for broken type

HELLCAT n spiteful fierce-tempered woman

HELLED ▶ hell

HELLER n monetary unit of the Czech Republic and Slovakia

HELLERI n Central American fish

HELLERS ▶ heller

HELLERY n wild or mischievous behaviour

HELLIER n slater

HELLING ▶ hell

HELLION n rough or rowdy person, esp a child

HELLISH adj, adv

HELLO interj, n, sentence substitute, vb **helloed, helloes, hellos**

HELLOVA = helluva

HELLS ▶ hell

HELLUVA adj (intensifier)

HELM n, vb **helmed**

HELMER n film director **helmers**

HELMET n **helmets**

HELMING ▶ helm

HELMS ▶ helm

HELO n helicopter **helos**

HELOT n serf or slave

HELOTRY n serfdom or slavery

HELOTS ▶ helot

HELP vb, n helped, helper, helpers

HELPFUL adj

HELPING n

HELPS ▶ help

HELVE n handle of a hand tool such as an axe or pick ▷ vb fit a helve to (a tool) **helved, helves, helving**

HEM n, vb

HEMAGOG = hemagogue

HEMAL = haemal

HEMATAL = hemal

HEMATIC = haematic

HEMATIN = haematin

HEME = haem

HEMES ▶ heme

HEMIC > haematic

HEMIN = haemin

HEMINA n old liquid measure **heminas**

HEMINS ▶ hemin

HEMIOLA n rhythmic device

HEMIONE = hemionus

HEMIPOD = hemipode

HEMLINE n level to which the hem of a skirt hangs

HEMLOCK n

HEMMED ▶ hem

HEMMER n attachment on a sewing machine for hemming **hemmers**

HEMMING ▶ hem

HEMOID = haematoid

HEMP n hempen

HEMPIE variant of
▶ hempy

HEMPIER ▶ hempy

HEMPIES ▶ hempy

HEMPS ▶ hemp

HEMPY adj of or like
hemp ▷ n rogue

HEMS ▶ hem

HEN n, vb

HENBANE n poisonous
plant with sticky hairy
leaves

HENBIT n European
plant with small dark
red flowers **henbits**

HENCE adv, interj

HENCOOP n cage for
poultry

HEND vb seize **hended,
hending, hends**

HENGE n monument
from the Neolithic and
Bronze Ages **henges**

HENLEY n type of
sweater **henleys**

HENLIKE ▶ hen

HENNA n, vb **hennaed,
hennas**

HENNED ▶ hen

HENNER n challenge
henners

HENNERY n place or farm
for keeping poultry

HENNIER ▶ henny

HENNIES ▶ henny

HENNIN n former
women's hat

HENNING ▶ hen

HENNINS ▶ hennin

HENNISH ▶ hen

HENNY adj like hen ▷ n
cock that looks like hen

HENOTIC adj acting to
reconcile

HENPECK vb (of a
woman) to harass or
torment (a man)

HENRIES ▶ henry

HENRY n unit of
electrical inductance
henrys

HENS ▶ hen

HENT vb seize ▷ n
anything that has
been grasped, esp by
the mind **hented,
henting, hents**

HEP = hip

HEPAR n compound
containing sulphur

HEPARIN n
polysaccharide present
in most body tissues

HEPARS ▶ hepar

HEPATIC adj of the liver
▷ n any of various
drugs for use in
treating diseases of
the liver

HEPCAT n person who is
hep **hepcats**

HEPPER ▶ hep

HEPPEST ▶ hep

HEPS ▶ hep

HEPSTER = hipster

HEPT archaic spelling of
▶ **heaped**

HEPTAD n group or
series of seven
heptads

HEPTANE n alkane
found in petroleum

HEPTOSE n any
monosaccharide with
seven carbon atoms
per molecule

HER pron, adj, determiner

HERALD n, vb **heralds**

HERB n

HERBAGE n herbaceous
plants collectively

HERBAL adj of or
relating to herbs,
usually culinary or
medicinal herbs ▷ n
book describing and
listing the properties
of plants **herbals**

HERBAR = herbary

HERBARS ▶ herbary

HERBARY n herb garden

HERBED adj flavoured
with herbs

HERBIER ▶ herby

HERBIST = herbalist

HERBLET n little herb

HERBOSE = herbous

HERBOUS adj with
abundance of herbs

HERBS ▶ herb

HERBY adj abounding in
herbs

HERD n, vb

HERDBOY n boy who
looks after herd

HERDED ▶ herd

HERDEN n type of
coarse cloth **herdens**

HERDER = herdsman

HERDERS ▶ herder

HERDESS n female
herder

HERDIC n small
horse-drawn carriage
herdics

HERDING ▶ herd

HERDMAN = herdsman

HERDMEN ▶ herdman

HERDS ▶ herd

HERE adv, n

HEREAT adv because of
this

HEREBY adv

HEREDES ▸ heres

HEREIN adv

HEREOF adv of or concerning this

HEREON archaic word for > hereupon

HERES pl n ▸ here

HERESY n

HERETIC n person who holds unorthodox opinions

HERETO adv this place, matter, or document

HERIED ▸ hery

HERIES ▸ hery

HERIOT n (in medieval England) a death duty paid to the lord heriots

HERISSE adj with bristles

HERITOR n person who inherits

HERL n barb or barbs of a feather

HERLING n Scots word for a type of fish

HERLS ▸ herl

HERM n (in ancient Greece) a stone head of Hermes herma

HERMAE ▸ herma

HERMAI ▸ herma

HERMIT n hermits

HERMS ▸ herm

HERN archaic or dialect word for ▸ heron

HERNIA n herniae, hernial, hernias

HERNS ▸ hern

HERO n heroes

HEROIC adj

HEROICS pl n

extravagant behaviour

HEROIN n

HEROINE n

HEROINS ▸ heroin

HEROISE = heroize

HEROISM n

HEROIZE vb make into hero

HERON n

HERONRY n colony of breeding herons

HERONS ▸ heron

HEROON n temple or monument dedicated to hero heroons

HEROS ▸ hero

HERPES n

HERRIED ▸ herry

HERRIES ▸ herry

HERRING n

HERRY vb harry

HERS pron

HERSALL n rehearsal

HERSE n harrow

HERSED adj arranged like a harrow

HERSELF pron

HERSES ▸ herse

HERSHIP n act of plundering

HERTZ n hertzes

HERY vb praise herye

HERYED ▸ herye

HERYES ▸ herye

HERYING ▸ hery

HES ▸ he

HESP = hasp

HESPED ▸ hesp

HESPING ▸ hesp

HESPS ▸ hesp

HESSIAN n

HESSITE n black or grey metallic mineral

HEST archaic word for ▸ behest

HESTS ▸ hest

HET n short for heterosexual ▷ adj Scot word for hot

HETAERA n (esp in ancient Greece) a female prostitute hetaira

HETE = hight

HETERO n short for heterosexual heteros

HETES ▸ hete

HETH n eighth letter of the Hebrew alphabet

HETHER = hither

HETHS ▸ heth

HETING ▸ hete

HETMAN another word for ▸ ataman

HETMANS ▸ hetman

HETS ▸ het

HETTIE n hetties

HEUCH Scots word for ▸ crag

HEUCHS ▸ heuch

HEUGH ▸ heuch

HEUGHS ▸ heugh

HEUREKA = eureka

HEURISM n use of logic

HEVEA n rubber-producing South American tree heveas

HEW vb hewable, hewed, hewer, hewers

HEWGH interj sound made to imitate the flight of an arrow

HEWING, hewings, hewn, hews ▸ hew

HEX adj of or relating to hexadecimal notation

▷ *n* evil spell ▷ *vb* bewitch

> This word meaning to bewitch is a really useful one for using the X.

HEXACT *n* part of a sponge with six rays **hexacts**

HEXAD *n* group or series of six **hexade**

HEXADES ▶ hexade

HEXADIC ▶ hexad

HEXADS ▶ hexad

HEXAGON *n*

HEXANE *n* liquid alkane existing in five isomeric forms **hexanes**

HEXAPLA *n* edition of the Old Testament

HEXAPOD *n* six-footed arthropod

HEXARCH *adj* (of plant) with six veins

HEXED ▶ hex

HEXENE = hexylene

HEXENES ▶ hexene

HEXER ▶ hex

HEXEREI *n* witchcraft

HEXERS, hexes, hexing, hexings ▶ hex

HEXONE *n* colourless insoluble liquid ketone **hexones**

HEXOSAN *n* form of polysaccharide

HEXOSE *n* monosaccharide, such as glucose **hexoses**

HEXYL *adj* of or consisting of a specific group of atoms **hexylic, hexyls**

HEY *interj* expression of surprise or for catching attention ▷ *vb* perform a country dance

HEYDAY *n* heydays, heyday

HEYDEYS ▶ heydey

HEYDUCK = haiduk

HEYED ▶ hey

HEYING ▶ hey

HEYS ▶ hey

HI *interj*

HIANT *adj* gaping

HIATAL ▶ hiatus

HIATUS *n*

HIBACHI *n* portable brazier for heating and cooking food

HIC *interj* representation of the sound of a hiccup

HICATEE = hiccatee

HICCUP *n, vb* hiccups, hiccupy

HICK *n* unsophisticated country person

HICKEY *n* object or gadget **hickeys, hickie**

HICKIES ▶ hickie

HICKISH ▶ hick

HICKORY *n* N American nut-bearing tree

HICKS ▶ hick

HID ▶ hide

HIDABLE ▶ hide

HIDAGE *n* former tax on land **hidages**

HIDALGA *n* Spanish noblewoman

HIDALGO *n* member of the lower nobility in Spain

HIDDEN ▶ hide

HIDDER *n* young ram **hidders**

HIDE *vb, n* hided

HIDEOUS *adj*

HIDEOUT *n*

HIDER, hiders, hides, hiding, hidings ▶ hide

HIDLING *n* hiding place

HIDLINS = hidlings

HIE *vb* hurry **hied, hieing**

HIELAND *adj* characteristic of Highlanders

HIEMAL *less common word for* ▶ hibernal

HIEMS *n* winter

HIES ▶ hie

HIGGLE *less common word for* ▶ haggle

HIGGLED ▶ higgle

HIGGLER ▶ higgle

HIGGLES ▶ higgle

HIGH *adj* being a relatively great distance from top to bottom; tall ▷ *adv* at or to a height ▷ *n* high place or level ▷ *vb* hie

HIGHBOY *n* tall chest of drawers in two sections

HIGHED ▶ high

HIGHER *n* advanced level of the Scottish Certificate of Education ▷ *vb* raise up **highers**

HIGHEST ▶ high

HIGHING ▶ high

HIGHISH ▶ high

HIGHLY *adv*

HIGHMAN *n* dice weighted to make it

fall in particular way

highmen

HIGHS ▸ high

HIGHT vb archaic word for name or call **highted**

HIGHTH old form of **▸ height**

HIGHTHS ▸ highth

HIGHTOP n top of ship's mast

HIGHTS ▸ hight

HIGHWAY n

HIJAB n covering for the head and face **hijabs**

HIJACK vb, n **hijacks**

HIJINKS n lively enjoyment

HIJRA = hijrah

HIJRAH = hegira

HIJRAHS ▸ hijrah

HIJRAS ▸ hijra

HIKE n, vb **hiked, hiker, hikers, hikes, hiking**

HIKOI n walk or march, esp a Māori protest march ▹ vb take part in such a march **hikoied, hikois**

HILA ▸ hilum

HILAR ▸ hilus

HILCH vb hobble **hilched, hilches**

HILD = hold

HILDING n coward

HILI ▸ hilus

HILL n, vb **hilled, hiller, hillers, hillier, hilling**

HILLMEN = hillfolk

HILLO = hello

HILLOA = halloa

HILLOAS ▸ hilloa

HILLOCK n

HILLOED ▸ hillo

HILLOES ▸ hillo

HILLOS ▸ hillo

HILLS ▸ hill

HILLTOP n top of hill

HILLY ▸ hill

HILT n, vb **hilted, hilting, hilts**

HILUM n scar on a seed **hilus**

HIM pron, n

HIMATIA > himation

HIMS ▸ him

HIMSELF pron

HIN n Hebrew unit of capacity

HINAU n New Zealand tree **hinaus**

HIND adj, n

HINDER vb, adj **hinders**

HINDGUT n part of the vertebrate digestive tract

HINDLEG n back leg

HINDS ▸ hind

HING n asafoetida

HINGE n, vb **hinged**

HINGER n tool for making hinges **hingers**

HINGES ▸ hinge

HINGING ▸ hinge

HINGS ▸ hing

HINKIER ▸ hinky

HINKY adj strange

HINNIED ▸ hinny

HINNIES ▸ hinny

HINNY n offspring of a male horse and a female donkey ▹ vb whinny

HINS ▸ hin

HINT n, vb **hinted, hinter, hinters,**

hinting, hints

HIOI n New Zealand plant of the mint family **hiois**

HIP n, adj, interj

HIPBONE n either of the bones that form the sides of the pelvis

HIPLESS ▸ hip

HIPLIKE ▸ hip

HIPLINE n widest part of a person's hips

HIPLY ▸ hip

HIPNESS ▸ hip

HIPPED adj having a hip or hips

HIPPEN n baby's nappy **hippens**

HIPPER ▸ hip

HIPPEST ▸ hip

HIPPIC adj of horses

HIPPIE = hippy

HIPPIER ▸ hippy

HIPPIES ▸ hippy

HIPPIN = hippen

HIPPING = hippen

HIPPINS ▸ hippin

HIPPISH adj in low spirits

HIPPO n **hippos**

HIPPUS n spasm of eye

HIPPY n, adj

HIPS ▸ hip

HIPSHOT adj having a dislocated hip

HIPSTER n enthusiast of modern jazz

HIPT ▸ hip

HIRABLE ▸ hire

HIRAGE n fee for hiring **hirages**

HIRCINE adj of or like a goat, esp in smell

HIRE vb, n

HIREAGE = hirage
HIRED ▶ hire
HIREE n hired person
hirees
HIRER, hirers, hires,
hiring, hirings ▶ hire
HIRLING n Scots word
for a type of fish
HIRPLE vb limp ▷ n
limping gait hirpled,
hirples
HIRSEL vb sort into
groups hirsels
HIRSLE vb wriggle or
fidget hirsled, hirsles
HIRSTIE adj dry
HIRSUTE adj
HIRUDIN n
anticoagulant
HIS adj
HISH = hiss
HISHED ▶ hish
HISHES ▶ hish
HISHING ▶ hish
HISN dialect form of
▶ his
HISPID adj covered with
stiff hairs or bristles
HISS n, vb, interj hissed
HISSELF dialect form of
▶ himself
HISSER ▶ hiss
HISSERS ▶ hiss
HISSES ▶ hiss
HISSIER ▶ hissy
HISSIES ▶ hissy
HISSING ▶ hiss
HISSY n temper
tantrum ▷ adj sound
similar to a hiss
HIST interj exclamation
used to attract
attention ▷ vb make
hist sound histed

HISTIE = hirstie
HISTING ▶ hist
HISTOID adj (esp of a
tumour)
HISTONE n any of a
group of proteins
present in cell nuclei
HISTORY n
HISTRIO n actor
HISTS ▶ hist
HIT vb strike, touch
forcefully ▷ n hitting
HITCH n, vb hitched,
hitcher, hitches,
hitchy
HITHE n small harbour
HITHER adv, vb hithers
HITHES ▶ hithe
HITLESS ▶ hit
HITMAN n professional
killer hitmen
HITS ▶ hit
HITTER n boxer who has
a hard punch rather
than skill or finesse
hitters
HITTING ▶ hit
HIVE n, vb hived
HIVER n person who
keeps beehives hivers
HIVES n allergic reaction
HIVING ▶ hive
HIYA sentence substitute
informal term of
greeting
HIZEN n type of
Japanese porcelain
hizens
HIZZ = hiss
HIZZED ▶ hizz
HIZZES ▶ hizz
HIZZING ▶ hizz
HM interj sound made
to express hesitation

or doubt hmm
HOAED ▶ hoa
HOAGIE n sandwich
made with long bread
roll hoagies, hoagy
HOAING ▶ hoa
HOAR adj covered with
hoarfrost ▷ vb make
hoary
HOARD n, vb hoarded,
hoarder, hoards
HOARED ▶ hoar
HOARIER ▶ hoary
HOARILY ▶ hoary
HOARING ▶ hoar
HOARS ▶ hoar
HOARSE adj
HOARSEN vb make or
become hoarse
HOARSER ▶ hoarse
HOARY adj
HOAS ▶ hoa
HOAST n cough ▷ vb
cough hoasted,
hoasts
HOATZIN n South
American bird
HOAX n, vb hoaxed,
hoaxer, hoaxers,
hoaxes, hoaxing
HOB n, vb hobbed
HOBBER n machine
used in making gears
hobbers
HOBBIES ▶ hobby
HOBBING ▶ hob
HOBBISH adj like a
clown
HOBBIT n one of an
imaginary race of
half-size people
hobbits
HOBBLE vb, n hobbled,
hobbler, hobbles

HOBBY n

HOBDAY vb alleviate a breathing problem in certain horses **hobdays**

HOBJOB vb do odd jobs **hobjobs**

HOBLIKE b hob

HOBNAIL n short nail with a large head for protecting soles ▷ vb provide with hobnails

HOBNOB vb hobnobs

HOBO n, vb hobodom, hoboed, hoboes, hoboing, hoboism, hobos

HOBS b hob

HOC adj Latin for this

HOCK n, vb hocked, hocker, hockers

HOCKEY n hockeys

HOCKING b hock

HOCKLE vb spit hockled, hockles

HOCKS b hock

HOCUS vb take in hocused, hocuses

HOD n, vb

HODAD n person who pretends to be a surfer **hodaddy, hodads**

HODDED b hod

HODDEN n coarse homespun cloth **hoddens, hoddin**

HODDING b hod

HODDINS b hoddin

HODDLE vb waddle **hoddled, hoddles**

HODJA n respectful Turkish form of address **hodjas**

HODMAN n hod carrier **hodmen**

HODS b hod

HOE n, vb

HOECAKE n maize cake

HOED b hoe

HOEDOWN n boisterous square dance

HOEING, hoelike, hoer, hoers, hoes b hoe

HOG n, vb

HOGAN n wooden dwelling covered with earth hogans

HOGBACK n narrow ridge of steeply inclined rock strata

HOGEN n strong alcoholic drink hogens

HOGFISH n type of fish

HOGG = hog

HOGGED b hog

HOGGER b hog

HOGGERS b hog

HOGGERY n hogs collectively

HOGGET n young unsheared sheep hoggets

HOGGIN n finely sifted gravel hogging, hoggins

HOGGISH adj selfish, gluttonous, or dirty

HOGGS b hogg

HOGH n ridge of land

HOGHOOD n condition of being hog

HOGHS b hogh

HOGLIKE b hog

HOGMANE n short stiff mane

HOGNOSE n as in hognose snake puff adder

HOGNUT another name for ▷ pignut

HOGNUTS b hognut

HOGS b hog

HOGTIE vb tie together the legs or the arms and legs of hogtied, hogties

HOGWARD n person looking after hogs

HOGWASH n nonsense

HOGWEED n any of several umbelliferous plants

HOHA adj bored or annoyed

HOHED b hoh

HOHING b hoh

HOHS b hoh

HOI = hoy

HOICK vb raise abruptly and sharply hoicked

HOICKS interj cry used to encourage hounds to hunt ▷ vb shout hoicks

HOIDEN = hoyden

HOIDENS b hoiden

HOIK = hoick

HOIKED b hoik

HOIKING b hoik

HOIKS b hoik

HOISE = hoist

HOISED b hoise

HOISES b hoise

HOISIN n Chinese sweet spicy sauce

HOISING b hoise

HOISINS b hoisin

HOIST vb, n hoisted, hoister, hoists

HOKA n red cod hokas

HOKE vb overplay (a part, etc) hoked, hokes

HOKEY adj corny
HOKI n fish of New Zealand waters
HOKIER ▸ hokey
HOKIEST ▸ hokey
HOKILY ▸ hokey
HOKING ▸ hoke
HOKIS ▸ hoki
HOKKU = haiku
HOKONUI n illicit whisky
HOKUM n rubbish, nonsense **hokums**
HOLARD n amount of water contained in soil **holards**
HOLD vb, n
HOLDALL n
HOLDEN past participle of ▸ hold
HOLDER n person or thing that holds **holders**
HOLDING ▸ hold
HOLDOUT n (in US English) someone or thing that refuses to change
HOLDS ▸ hold
HOLDUP n robbery, esp an armed one **holdups**
HOLE n, vb **holed, holes**
HOLESOM = holesome
HOLEY adj full of holes **holeyer**
HOLIBUT = halibut
HOLIDAY n, vb
HOLIER ▸ holy
HOLIES ▸ holy
HOLIEST ▸ holy
HOLILY adv in a holy, devout, or sacred

manner
HOLING ▸ hole
HOLINGS ▸ hole
HOLISM n view that a whole is greater than the sum of its parts **holisms, holist, holists**
HOLK vb dig **holked, holking, holks**
HOLLA = hollo
HOLLAED ▸ holla
HOLLAND n coarse linen cloth, used esp for furnishing
HOLLAS ▸ holla
HOLLER n shout, yell ▸ vb shout or yell **hollers**
HOLLIES ▸ holly
HOLLO interj cry for attention, or of encouragement ▸ vb shout **holloa**
HOLLOAS ▸ holloa
HOLLOED ▸ hollo
HOLLOES ▸ hollo
HOLLOO = halloo
HOLLOOS ▸ holloo
HOLLOS ▸ hollo
HOLLOW adj, n, vb **hollows**
HOLLY n
HOLM n island in a river, lake, or estuary
HOLMIA n oxide of holmium **holmias**
HOLMIC adj of or containing holmium
HOLMIUM n
HOLMS ▸ holm
HOLON n autonomous self-reliant unit, esp in manufacturing

holonic, holons
HOLP past tense of ▸ help
HOLPEN past participle of ▸ help
HOLS pl n holidays
HOLSTER n, vb
HOLT n otter's lair **holts**
HOLY adj
HOLYDAM = halidom
HOLYDAY n day on which a religious festival is observed
HOM n sacred plant of the Parsees and ancient Persians **homa**
HOMAGE n, vb **homaged, homager, homages**
HOMAS ▸ homa
HOMBRE n slang word for ▸ man
HOMBRES ▸ hombre
HOMBURG n
HOME n, adj, adv, vb
HOMEBOY n close friend
HOMED ▸ home
HOMELY adj
HOMELYN n species of ray
HOMER n homing pigeon ▸ vb score a home run in baseball **homered**
HOMERIC adj grand or heroic
HOMERS ▸ homer
HOMES ▸ home
HOMEY = homy
HOMEYS ▸ homey
HOMIE short for ▸ homeboy
HOMIER ▸ homy

HOMIES ▶ homie
HOMIEST ▶ homy
HOMILY n
HOMINES ▶ homo
HOMING adj, n
homings
HOMINID n man or any
extinct forerunner
of man ▷ adj of or
belonging to this
family
HOMININ n member of
a zoological family
HOMINY n coarsely
ground maize
HOMME French word for
▶ man
HOMMES ▶ homme
HOMMOCK
= hummock
HOMMOS = hummus
HOMO n homogenized
milk
HOMOLOG
= homologue
HOMONYM n word that
is spelt the same as
another
HOMOS ▶ homo
HOMOSEX n sexual
activity between
homosexuals
HOMS ▶ hom
HOMY adj like a home
HON short for ▶ honey
HONAN n silk fabric of
rough weave honans
HONCHO n person in
charge ▷ vb supervise
or be in charge of
honchos
HOND old form of
▶ hand
HONDA n loop used to

make a lasso **hondas**
HONDLE vb negotiate
on price **hondled,
hondles**
HONDS ▶ hond
HONE vb, n **honed,
honer, honers,
hones**
HONEST adj
HONESTY n
HONEY n, vb **honeyed,
honeys**
HONG n (in China) a
factory, warehouse,
etc ▷ vb archaic form
of hang
HONGI n, vb **hongied,
hongies**
HONGING ▶ hong
HONGIS ▶ hongi
HONGS ▶ hong
HONIED ▶ honey
HONING ▶ hone
HONK n, vb **honked**
HONKER n person or
thing that honks
honkers
HONKING ▶ honk
HONKS ▶ honk
HONOR = honour
HONORED ▶ honour
HONOREE n honorand
HONORER ▶ honour
HONORS = honours
HONOUR n, vb **honours**
HONS ▶ hon
HOO interj expression of
joy, excitement, etc
HOOCH n alcoholic
drink, esp illicitly
distilled spirits
hooches
HOOCHIE n immoral
woman

HOOD n, vb
HOODED adj (of a
garment) having a
hood
HOODIA n any of
several southern
African succulent
plants **hoodias**
HOODIE n hooded
sweatshirt
HOODIER ▶ hood
HOODIES ▶ hoodie
HOODING ▶ hood
HOODLUM n violent
criminal, gangster
HOODMAN n
blindfolded person in
blindman's buff
hoodmen
HOODOO n (cause of)
bad luck ▷ vb bring bad
luck to **hoodoos**
HOODS ▶ hood
HOODY ▶ hood
HOOEY n nonsense
▷ interj nonsense
hooeys
HOOF n, vb
HOOFED adj having a
hoof or hoofs
HOOFER n professional
dancer **hoofers**
HOOFING ▶ hoof
HOOFROT n disease of
hoof
HOOFS ▶ hoof
HOOK n, vb
HOOKA = hookah
HOOKAH n oriental
pipe **hookahs**
HOOKAS ▶ hooka
HOOKED adj
HOOKER n prostitute
hookers

HOOKEY = hooky
HOOKEYS ▶ hookey
HOOKIER ▶ hooky
HOOKIES ▶ hooky
HOOKING ▶ hook
HOOKLET n little hook
HOOKS ▶ hook
HOOKUP n contact of an aircraft with the hose of a tanker aircraft **hookups**
HOOKY n truancy, usually from school ▷ adj hooklike
HOOLEY n lively party **hooleys, hoolie**
HOOLIER ▶ hooly
HOOLIES ▶ hoolie
HOOLOCK n Indian gibbon
HOOLY adj careful or gentle
HOON n loutish youth who drives irresponsibly ▷ vb drive irresponsibly **hooned, hooning, hoons**
HOOP n, vb **hooped**
HOOPER rare word for ▶ cooper
HOOPERS ▶ hooper
HOOPING ▶ hoop
HOOPLA n fairground game **hooplas**
HOOPOE n bird with a pinkish-brown plumage **hoopoes, hoopoo**
HOOPOOS ▶ hoopoo
HOOPS ▶ hoop
HOOR n unpleasant or difficult thing
HOORAH = hurrah
HOORAHS ▶ hoorah

HOORAY = hurrah
HOORAYS ▶ hooray
HOORD = hoard
HOORDS ▶ hoord
HOOROO = hurrah
HOORS ▶ hoor
HOOSGOW ▶ jail
HOOSH vb shoo away **hooshed, hooshes**
HOOT n, vb, interj
HOOTCH = hooch
HOOTED ▶ hoot
HOOTER n **hooters**
HOOTIER ▶ hoot
HOOTING ▶ hoot
HOOTS = hoot
HOOTY ▶ hoot
HOOVE ▶ heave
HOOVED ▶ hoove
HOOVEN ▶ hoove
HOOVER vb **hoovers**
HOOVES ▶ hoof
HOOVING ▶ hoove
HOP vb, n
HOPBIND n stalk of the hop **hopbine**
HOPDOG n species of caterpillar **hopdogs**
HOPE vb, n **hoped**
HOPEFUL adj having, expressing, or inspiring hope ▷ n person considered to be on the brink of success
HOPER ▶ hope
HOPERS ▶ hope
HOPES ▶ hope
HOPHEAD n heroin or opium addict
HOPING ▶ hope
HOPLITE n (in ancient Greece) a heavily armed infantryman
HOPPED ▶ hop

HOPPER n **hoppers**
HOPPIER ▶ hoppy
HOPPING ▶ hop
HOPPLE = hobble
HOPPLED ▶ hopple
HOPPLER ▶ hopple
HOPPLES ▶ hopple
HOPPUS adj as in **hoppus foot** unit of volume for round timber
HOPPY adj tasting of hops
HOPS ▶ hop
HOPSACK n roughly woven fabric
HOPTOAD n toad
HORA n traditional Israeli or Romanian circle dance **horah**
HORAHS ▶ horah
HORAL less common word for ▶ hourly
HORARY adj relating to the hours
HORAS ▶ hora
HORDE n, vb **horded**
HORDEIN n simple protein, rich in proline, that occurs in barley
HORDES ▶ horde
HORDING ▶ horde
HORDOCK = hardoke
HORE = hoar
HORIZON n
HORKEY = hockey
HORKEYS ▶ horkey
HORME n (in Jungian psychology) fundamental vital energy **hormes, hormic**
HORMONE n
HORN n, vb

HORNBUG n stag beetle

HORNED adj having a horn, horns, or hornlike parts

HORNER n dealer in horn **horners**

HORNET n **hornets**

HORNFUL n amount a horn will hold

HORNIER ► **horny**

HORNILY ► **horny**

HORNING ► **horn**

HORNISH adj like horn

HORNIST n horn player

HORNITO n small vent in volcano

HORNLET n small horn

HORNS ► **horn**

HORNY adj of or like horn

HOROEKA n New Zealand tree

HORRENT adj bristling

HORRID adj

HORRIFY vb

HORROR n, adj

HORRORS pl n fit of depression or anxiety ▷ interj expression of dismay, sometimes facetious

HORS adv as in **hors d'oeuvre** appetizer

HORSE n, vb **horsed, horses**

HORSEY adj

HORSIER ► **horsy**

HORSILY ► **horsy**

HORSING ► **horse**

HORSON = **whoreson**

HORSONS ► **horson**

HORST n ridge of land **horste**

HORSTES ► **horste**

HORSTS ► **horst**

HORSY = **horsey**

HOSANNA interj, n, vb

HOSE n, vb **hosed** ⸗

HOSEL n socket in head of golf club **hosels**

HOSEMAN n fireman in charge of hose **hosemen**

HOSEN ► **hose**

HOSER n person who swindles or deceives others **hosers**

HOSES ► **hose**

HOSEY vb claim possession **hoseyed, hoseys**

HOSIER n person who sells stockings, etc **hosiers**

HOSIERY n

HOSING ► **hose**

HOSPICE n

HOSS n horse **hosses**

HOST n, vb

HOSTA n ornamental plant

HOSTAGE n

HOSTAS ► **hosta**

HOSTED ► **host**

HOSTEL n, vb **hostels**

HOSTESS n, vb

HOSTIE n informal Australian word for an air hostess **hosties**

HOSTILE adj, n

HOSTING ► **host**

HOSTLER another name (esp Brit) for ► **ostler**

HOSTLY ► **host**

HOSTRY n lodging

HOSTS ► **host**

HOT adj

HOTBED n **hotbeds**

HOTBOX n closed room where marijuana is smoked

HOTCAKE n pancake

HOTCH vb jog **hotched, hotches**

HOTDOG vb perform a series of manoeuvres in skiing, etc **hotdogs**

HOTE ► **hight**

HOTEL n **hotels**

HOTEN ► **hight**

HOTFOOT adv, vb

HOTHEAD n

HOTLINE n direct telephone link for emergency use

HOTLINK n area on website connecting to another site

HOTLY ► **hot**

HOTNESS ► **hot**

HOTPOT n casserole topped with potatoes **hotpots**

HOTROD n car with a modified engine for increased power **hotrods**

HOTS pl n as in **the hots** feeling of lust

HOTSHOT n important person or expert, esp when showy

HOTSPOT n place where wireless broadband is provided

HOTSPUR n impetuous or fiery person

HOTTED ► **hot**

HOTTER vb simmer **hotters**

HOTTEST ► **hot**

HOTTIE n sexually

attractive person **hotties**

HOTTING n

HOTTISH adj fairly hot

HOTTY = hottie

HOUDAH = howdah

HOUDAHS ▶ houdah

HOUDAN n breed of light domestic fowl **houdans**

HOUF = howf

HOUFED ▶ houf

HOUFF = howf

HOUFFED ▶ houff

HOUFFS ▶ houff

HOUFING ▶ houf

HOUFS ▶ houf

HOUGH n in Scotland, a cut of meat corresponding to shin ▷ vb hamstring (cattle, horses, etc) **houghed, houghs**

HOUHERE n small evergreen New Zealand tree

HOUMMOS = hummus

HOUMOUS ▶ hummus

HOUMUS = hummus

HOUND n, vb hounded, hounder, hounds

HOUNGAN n voodoo priest

HOUR n

HOURI n any of the nymphs of paradise **houris**

HOURLY adv (happening) every hour ▷ adj of, occurring, or done once every hour ▷ n something that is done by the hour

HOURS pl n indefinite time

HOUSE n, vb, adj **housed**

HOUSEL vb give the Eucharist to (someone) **housels**

HOUSER ▶ house

HOUSERS ▶ house

HOUSES ▶ house

HOUSEY adj of or like house music **housier**

HOUSING n

HOUT = hoot

HOUTED ▶ hout

HOUTING n type of fish

HOUTS ▶ hout

HOVE ▶ heave

HOVEA n Australian plant with purple flowers **hoveas**

HOVED ▶ heave

HOVEL n, vb hoveled, hovels

HOVEN ▶ heave

HOVER vb, n hovered, hoverer, hovers

HOVES ▶ heave

HOVING ▶ heave

HOW adv, n, sentence substitute

HOWBE = howbeit

HOWBEIT adv in archaic usage, however

HOWDAH n canopied seat on an elephant's back **howdahs**

HOWDIE n midwife

HOWDIED ▶ howdy

HOWDIES ▶ howdy

HOWDY vb greet someone

HOWE n depression in the earth's surface

howes

HOWEVER adv

HOWF n haunt, esp a public house ▷ vb visit place frequently **howfed**

HOWFF vb visit place frequently **howffed, howffs**

HOWFING ▶ howf

HOWFS ▶ howf

HOWK vb dig (out or up) howked, howker, howkers, howking, howks

HOWL n, vb howled

HOWLER n howlers

HOWLET another word for ▶ owl

HOWLETS ▶ howlet

HOWLING adj great

HOWLS ▶ howl

HOWRE = hour

HOWRES ▶ howre

HOWS ▶ how

HOWSO = howsoever

HOWZAT ▶ how

HOWZIT informal word for ▶ hello

HOX vb hamstring hoxed, hoxes, hoxing This is a word found in Shakespeare's plays, and means to cut a horse's hamstring; it's one of the many short words with X that can get you a high score.

HOY interj cry used to attract someone's attention ▷ n freight barge ▷ vb drive animal with cry

HOYA *n* any of various E Asian or Australian plants **hoyas**

HOYDEN *n* wild or boisterous girl ▷ *vb* behave like a hoyden **hoydens**

HOYED ▷ **hoy**

HOYING ▷ **hoy**

HOYLE *n* archer's mark used as a target **hoyles**

HOYS ▷ **hoy**

HRYVNA *n* standard monetary unit of Ukraine **hryvnas**

HRYVNIA *n* money unit of Ukraine

HRYVNYA = **hryvna**

HUANACO = **guanaco**

HUB *n*

HUBBIES ▷ **hubby**

HUBBLY *adj* having an irregular surface

HUBBUB *n* **hubbubs**

HUBBY *n* husband

HUBCAP *n* metal disc that protects the hub of a wheel **hubcaps**

HUBRIS *n* pride, arrogance

HUBS ▷ **hub**

HUCK = **huckaback**

HUCKED ▷ **huck**

HUCKERY *adj* ugly

HUCKING ▷ **huck**

HUCKLE *n* hip or haunch ▷ *vb* force out or arrest roughly **huckled, huckles**

HUCKS ▷ **huck**

HUDDEN ▷ **haud**

HUDDLE *vb, n* **huddled, huddler, huddles**

HUDDUP *interj* get up

HUDNA *n* truce or ceasefire for a fixed duration **hudnas**

HUDUD *n* set of laws and punishments in the Koran **hududs**

HUE *n*

HUED *adj* having a hue or colour as specified

HUELESS ▷ **hue**

HUER *n* pilchard fisherman **huers**

HUES ▷ **hue**

HUFF *n, vb* **huffed**

HUFFER ▷ **huffing**

HUFFERS ▷ **huffing**

HUFFIER ▷ **huff**

HUFFILY ▷ **huff**

HUFFING *n* practice of inhaling fumes for intoxicating effects

HUFFISH ▷ **huff**

HUFFKIN *n* type of muffin

HUFFS ▷ **huff**

HUFFY ▷ **huff**

HUG *vb, n*

HUGE *adj*

HUGELY *adv* very much

HUGEOUS = **huge**

HUGER ▷ **huge**

HUGEST ▷ **huge**

HUGGED ▷ **hug**

HUGGER ▷ **hug**

HUGGERS ▷ **hug**

HUGGIER ▷ **huggy**

HUGGING ▷ **hug**

HUGGY *adj* sensitive and caring

HUGS ▷ **hug**

HUGY = **huge**

HUH *interj* exclamation

of derision or inquiry

HUHU *n* type of hairy New Zealand beetle **huhus**

HUI *n*

HUIA *n* extinct bird of New Zealand **huias**

HUIC *interj* in hunting, a call to hounds

HUIPIL *n* Mayan woman's blouse **huipils**

HUIS ▷ **hui**

HUITAIN *n* verse of eighteen lines

HULA *n* swaying Hawaiian dance **hulas**

HULE = **ule**

HULES ▷ **hule**

HULK *n, vb* **hulked**

HULKIER ▷ **hulky**

HULKING *adj* bulky, unwieldy

HULKS ▷ **hulk**

HULKY = **hulking**

HULL *n, vb* **hulled, huller, hullers**

HULLIER ▷ **hully**

HULLING ▷ **hull**

HULLO = **hello**

HULLOA = **halloa**

HULLOAS ▷ **hulloa**

HULLOED ▷ **hullo**

HULLOES ▷ **hullo**

HULLOO = **halloo**

HULLOOS ▷ **hulloo**

HULLOS ▷ **hullo**

HULLS ▷ **hull**

HULLY *adj* having husks

HUM *vb, n*

HUMA *n* mythical bird

HUMAN *adj, n*

HUMANE *adj* **humaner**

HUMANLY *adv* by

human powers or means

HUMANS ▸ human

HUMAS ▸ huma

HUMATE n decomposed plants used as fertilizer **humates**

HUMBLE adj, vb **humbled, humbler, humbles, humbly**

HUMBUG n, vb **humbugs**

HUMBUZZ n type of beetle

HUMDRUM adj, n

HUMECT vb make moist **humects**

HUMEFY = humify

HUMERAL adj of or relating to the humerus ▸ n silk shawl worn by a priest at High Mass; humeral veil

HUMERI ▸ humerus

HUMERUS n

HUMF = humph

HUMFED ▸ humf

HUMFING ▸ humf

HUMFS ▸ humf

HUMHUM n Indian cotton cloth **humhums**

HUMIC adj of, derived from, or resembling humus

HUMID adj **humider**

HUMIDEX n system of measuring discomfort

HUMIDLY ▸ humid

HUMIDOR n humid place for storing cigars, tobacco, etc

HUMIFY vb convert or

be converted into humus

HUMINT n human intelligence **humints**

HUMITE n mineral containing magnesium **humites**

HUMLIE n hornless cow **humlies**

HUMMAUM = hammam

HUMMED ▸ hum

HUMMEL adj (of cattle) hornless ▸ vb remove horns from **hummels**

HUMMER ▸ hum

HUMMERS ▸ hum

HUMMING ▸ hum

HUMMLE adj as in **humble bonnet** type of Scottish cap

HUMMOCK n, vb

HUMMUM = hammam

HUMMUMS
▸ hummum

HUMMUS n creamy dip

HUMOGEN n type of fertilizer

HUMOR = humour

HUMORAL adj denoting or relating to a type of immunity

HUMORED ▸ humor

HUMORS ▸ humor

HUMOUR n, vb **humours**

HUMOUS = humus

HUMP n, vb **humped**

HUMPEN n old German drinking glass **humpens**

HUMPER ▸ hump

HUMPERS ▸ hump

HUMPH interj

exclamation of annoyance or scepticism ▸ vb exclaim humph **humphed, humphs**

HUMPIER ▸ humpy

HUMPIES ▸ humpy

HUMPING ▸ hump

HUMPS ▸ hump

HUMPTY n low padded seat

HUMPY adj full of humps ▸ n primitive hut

HUMS ▸ hum

HUMUS n **humuses, humusy**

HUMVEE n military vehicle **humvees**

HUN n member of any of several nomadic peoples

HUNCH n, vb **hunched, hunches**

HUNDRED n, adj

HUNG ▸ hang

HUNGAN = houngan

HUNGANS ▸ hungan

HUNGER n, vb **hungers**

HUNGRY adj

HUNH = huh

HUNK n

HUNKER vb squat

HUNKERS pl n haunches

HUNKEY n person of Hungarian descent **hunkeys, hunkie**

HUNKIER ▸ hunky

HUNKS n crotchety old person **hunkses**

HUNKY adj excellent

HUNNISH ▸ hun

HUNS ▸ hun

HUNT vb, n

HUNTED adj harassed

and worn

HUNTER n person or animal that hunts wild animals **hunters**

HUNTING n pursuit and killing or capture of wild animals

HUNTS ▸ hunt

HUP vb cry used to get a horse to move

HUPIRO in New Zealand English, = stinkwood

HUPIROS ▸ hupiro

HUPPAH variant spelling of ▸ chuppah

HUPPAHS ▸ huppah

HUPPED ▸ hup

HUPPING ▸ hup

HUPPOT ▸ huppah

HUPPOTH ▸ huppot

HUPS ▸ hup

HURDEN = harden

HURDENS ▸ hurden

HURDIES pl n buttocks or haunches

HURDLE n, vb hurdled, hurdler, hurdles

HURDS = hards

HURL vb, n

HURLBAT = whirlbat

HURLED ▸ hurl

HURLER ▸ hurl

HURLERS ▸ hurl

HURLEY n another word for the game of hurling **hurleys**

HURLIES ▸ hurly

HURLING n Irish game like hockey

HURLS ▸ hurl

HURLY n wheeled barrow

HURRA = hurrah

HURRAED ▸ hurra

HURRAH interj exclamation of joy or applause ▷ n cheer of joy or victory ▷ vb shout "hurrah" **hurrahs**

HURRAS ▸ hurra

HURRAY = hurrah

HURRAYS ▸ hurray

HURRIED adj done quickly or too quickly

HURRIER ▸ hurry

HURRIES ▸ hurry

HURRY vb, n

HURST n wood **hursts**

HURT vb, n, adj hurter, hurters

HURTFUL adj unkind

HURTING ▸ hurt

HURTLE vb hurtled, hurtles

HURTS ▸ hurt

HUSBAND n, vb

HUSH vb, n, interj

HUSHABY interj used in quietening a baby or child to sleep ▷ n lullaby ▷ vb quieten to sleep

HUSHED ▸ hush

HUSHER = usher

HUSHERS ▸ husher

HUSHES ▸ hush

HUSHFUL adj quiet

HUSHIER ▸ hushy

HUSHING ▸ hush

HUSHY adj secret

HUSK n, vb husked, husker, huskers

HUSKIER ▸ husky

HUSKIES ▸ husky

HUSKILY ▸ husky

HUSKING ▸ husk

HUSKS ▸ husk

HUSKY adj, n

HUSO n sturgeon **husos**

HUSS n flesh of the European dogfish

HUSSAR n lightly armed cavalry soldier **hussars**

HUSSES ▸ huss

HUSSIES ▸ hussy

HUSSIF n sewing kit **hussifs**

HUSSY n

HUSTLE vb, n hustled, hustler, hustles

HUSWIFE = housewife

HUT n

HUTCH n, vb hutched, hutches

HUTCHIE n temporary shelter

HUTIA n rodent of West Indies **hutias**

HUTLIKE ▸ hut

HUTMENT n number or group of huts

HUTS ▸ hut

HUTTED ▸ hut

HUTTING ▸ hut

HUTZPA = hutzpah

HUTZPAH variant spelling of ▸ chutzpah

HUTZPAS ▸ hutzpa

HUZOOR n person of rank in India **huzoors**

HUZZA = huzzah

HUZZAED ▸ huzza

HUZZAH archaic word for ▸ hurrah

HUZZAHS ▸ huzzah

HUZZAS ▸ huzza

HUZZIES ▸ huzzy

HUZZY = hussy

HWAN another name for ▸ won

HWYL n emotional fervour, as in the recitation of poetry **hwyls**

This Welsh word can come in very useful for dealing with a consonant-heavy rack.

HYACINE = hyacinth
HYAENA = hyena
HYAENAS ▶ hyaena
HYAENIC ▶ hyaena
HYALIN n glassy translucent substance
HYALINE adj clear and translucent, with no fibres or granules ▷ n glassy transparent surface
HYALINS ▶ hyalin
HYALITE n clear and colourless variety of opal in globular form
HYALOID adj clear and transparent ▷ n delicate transparent membrane
HYBRID n, adj **hybrids**
HYBRIS = hubris
HYDATID n cyst containing tapeworm larvae
HYDRA n **hydrae**
HYDRANT n
HYDRAS ▶ hydra
HYDRASE n enzyme that removes water
HYDRATE n chemical compound of water with another substance ▷ vb treat or impregnate with water

HYDRIA n (in ancient Greece and Rome) a large water jar **hydriae**
HYDRIC adj of or containing hydrogen
HYDRID = hydroid
HYDRIDE n
HYDRIDS ▶ hydrid
HYDRO n hotel offering facilities for hydropathy ▷ adj short for hydroelectric
HYDROID adj of an order of colonial hydrozoan coelenterates ▷ n hydroid colony or individual
HYDROMA = hygroma
HYDROPS n anaemia in a fetus
HYDROS ▶ hydro
HYDROUS adj containing water
HYDROXY adj of a type of chemical compound
HYDYNE n type of rocket fuel **hydynes**
HYE = hie
HYED ▶ hye
HYEING ▶ hye
HYEN = hyena
HYENA n **hyenas, hyenic**
HYENINE adj of hyenas
HYENOID adj of or like hyenas
HYENS ▶ hyen
HYES ▶ hye
HYETAL adj of or relating to rain, rainfall, or rainy regions

HYGEIST = hygienist
HYGIENE n
HYGROMA n swelling soft tissue that occurs over a joint
HYING ▶ hie
HYKE = haik
HYKES ▶ hyke
HYLA n type of tropical American tree frog **hylas**
HYLDING = hilding
HYLE n wood
HYLEG n dominant planet when someone is born **hylegs**
HYLES ▶ hyle
HYLIC adj solid
HYLISM = hylicism
HYLISMS ▶ hylism
HYLIST ▶ hylism
HYLISTS ▶ hylism
HYLOIST n materialist
HYMEN n **hymenal**
HYMENIA ▶ hymenium
HYMENS ▶ hymen
HYMN n, vb
HYMNAL n book of hymns ▷ adj of, relating to, or characteristic of hymns **hymnals, hymnary**
HYMNED ▶ hymn
HYMNIC ▶ hymn
HYMNING ▶ hymn
HYMNIST n person who composes hymns
HYMNODY n composition or singing of hymns
HYMNS ▶ hymn
HYNDE = hind
HYNDES ▶ hynde

HYOID adj of or relating to the hyoid bone ▷ n horseshoe-shaped bone

HYOIDAL adj of or relating to the hyoid bone

HYOIDS ▶ hyoid

HYP n

HYPATE n string of lyre **hypates**

HYPE n intensive or exaggerated publicity or sales promotion ▷ vb promote (a product) using intensive or exaggerated publicity **hyped, hyper**

HYPERON n any baryon that is not a nucleon

HYPERS ▶ hype

HYPES ▶ hype

HYPHA n any of the filaments in the mycelium of a fungus

hyphae, hyphal

HYPHEN n, vb hyphens

HYPHIES ▶ hyphy

HYPHY n

HYPING ▶ hype

HYPINGS ▶ hype

HYPNIC n sleeping drug **hypnics**

HYPNOID adj of or relating to a state resembling sleep

HYPNONE n sleeping drug

HYPNUM n species of moss **hypnums**

HYPO vb inject with a hypodermic syringe **hypoed**

HYPOGEA > hypogeum

HYPOID adj as in hypoid gear type of gear

HYPOING ▶ hypo

HYPONEA = hypopnea

HYPONYM n word whose meaning is

included as part of another

HYPOS ▶ hypo

HYPOXIA n deficiency in oxygen delivery **hypoxic**

HYPPED ▶ hyp

HYPPING ▶ hyp

HYPS ▶ hyp

HYPURAL adj below the tail

HYRACES ▶ hyrax

HYRAX n type of hoofed rodent-like animal of Africa and Asia **hyraxes**

HYSON n Chinese green tea **hysons**

HYSSOP n sweet-smelling herb used in folk medicine **hyssops**

HYTE adj insane

HYTHE = hithe

HYTHES ▶ hythe

I i

The letter **I** can prove a difficult tile to use effectively in Scrabble. It's one of the most common tiles in the game, so you often end up with two or more on your rack, but it can be hard to get rid of. Where **I** does come in can be very useful, though, is in the number of everyday short words that can be formed from it, which are very helpful when you need to form short words in addition to the main word that you want to play. These words include **in**, **is**, **it** (2 points each), **id** (3) and **if** (5). Other handy words are **icy** (8), **ivy** (9) and **imp** (7). Don't forget the three-letter words that use **K**: **ilk**, **ink** and **irk** (7 each), while **iwi** for 6 points can be very useful in getting rid of a surplus of **I**s.

IAMB *n* metrical foot of two syllables
IAMBI ▶ iambus
IAMBIC *adj* written in a type of metrical unit ▷ *n* iambic foot, line, or stanza **iambics**
IAMBIST *n* one who writes iambs
IAMBS ▶ iamb
IAMBUS = iamb
IATRIC *adj* relating to medicine or physicians
IBADAH *n* following of Islamic beliefs and practices **ibadat**
IBERIS *n* plant with white or purple flowers
IBEX *n* wild goat **ibexes**, **ibices**

IBIDEM *adv* in the same place
IBIS *n* ibises
IBRIK ▶ cezve
IBRIKS ▶ ibrik
ICEBALL *n* ball of ice
ICEBERG *n*
ICEBOAT *n* boat that breaks up bodies of ice in water
ICEBOX *n*
ICECAP *n* icecaps
ICED *adj* covered with icing
ICEFALL *n* part of a glacier
ICELESS ▶ ice
ICELIKE ▶ ice
ICEMAN *n* person who sells or delivers

ice **icemen**
ICEPACK *n* bag or folded cloth containing ice
ICER *n* person who ices cakes **icers**
ICES ▶ ice
ICEWINE *n* dessert wine made from grapes that have frozen before being harvested
ICH *archaic form of* ▶ **eke**
A Shakespearean spelling of **eke**, this is a useful little word worth remembering because of its unusual combination of letters and relatively high score.

ICHABOD *interj* the glory has departed

ICHED ► ich

ICHES ► ich

ICHING ► ich

ICHNITE *n* trace fossil

ICHOR *n* fluid said to flow in the veins of the gods **ichors**

ICHS ► ich

ICHTHIC = ichthyic

ICHTHYS *n* early Christian emblem

ICICLE *n*

ICICLED *adj* covered with icicles

ICICLES ► icicle

ICIER ► icy

ICIEST ► icy

ICILY *adv* in an icy or reserved manner

ICINESS *n* condition of being icy or very cold

ICING *n* icings

ICK *interj* expression of disgust

> An interjection expressing disgust, this is one of the highest-scoring three-letter words beginning with I. It does not take an S, but it does take a Y to make **icky**.

ICKER *n* ear of corn **ickers**

ICKIER ► icky

ICKIEST ► icky

ICKILY ► icky

ICKLE *ironically childish word for* ► little

ICKLER ► ickle

ICKLEST ► ickle

ICKY *adj* sticky

ICON *n* icones

ICONIC *adj* relating to the character of an icon

ICONIFY *vb* render as an icon

ICONISE = iconize

ICONIZE *vb* render as an icon

ICONS ► icon

ICTAL ► ictus

ICTERIC ► icterus

ICTERID *n* bird of the oriole family

ICTERUS *n* yellowing of plant leaves

ICTIC ► ictus

ICTUS *n* metrical or rhythmic stress in verse feet **ictuses**

ICY *adj*

ID *n*

IDANT *n* chromosome **idants**

IDE *n* silver orfe fish

IDEA *n*, *vb*

IDEAL *adj*, *n* ideally, **ideals**

IDEAS ► idea

IDEATA ► ideatum

IDEATE *vb* form or have an idea of **ideated**, **ideates**

IDEATUM *n* objective reality

IDEE *n* idea **idees**

IDEM *adj* same

IDENT *n* short visual image that works as a logo

IDENTIC *adj* having the same intention regarding another power

IDENTS ► ident

IDES *n* specific date of each month in the Roman calendar

IDIOCY *n*

IDIOM *n* idioms

IDIOT *n*

IDIOTCY = idiocy

IDIOTIC *adj*

IDIOTS ► idiot

IDLE *adj*, *vb* idled

IDLER *n* person who idles **idlers**

IDLES, idlesse, idlest, idling, idly ► idle

IDOL *n*

IDOLA ► idolum

IDOLISE = idolize

IDOLISM ► idolize

IDOLIST ► idolize

IDOLIZE *vb*

IDOLON *n* mental image

IDOLS ► idol

IDOLUM *n* mental picture

IDS ► id

IDYL = idyll

IDYLIST = idyllist

IDYLL *n*

IDYLLIC *adj* of or relating to an idyll

IDYLLS ► idyll

IDYLS ► idyl

IF *n*

IFF *conj* in logic, a shortened form of if and only if

> This word is one of the highest-scoring three-letter words beginning with I, and of course provides a useful extension to **if**.

IFFIER ▸ iffy

IFFIEST ▸ iffy

IFFY *adj* doubtful, uncertain

IFS ▸ if

IFTAR *n* meal eaten by Muslims **iftars**

IGAD = egad

IGAPO *n* flooded forest **igapos**

IGARAPE *n* canoe route

IGG *vb* antagonize **igged, igging, iggs**

IGLOO *n* **igloos, iglu**

IGLUS ▸ iglu

IGNARO *n* ignoramus **ignaros**

IGNATIA *n* dried seed

IGNEOUS *adj*

IGNIFY *vb* turn into fire

IGNITE *vb* **ignited**

IGNITER *n* person or thing that ignites

IGNITES ▸ ignite

IGNITOR = igniter

IGNOBLE *adj* ignobly

IGNOMY *n* Shakespearean variant of ▸ **ignominy**

IGNORE *vb*, *n* **ignored, ignorer, ignores**

IGUANA *n* **iguanas, iguanid**

IHRAM *n* white robes worn by Muslim pilgrims to Mecca **ihrams**

IJTIHAD *n* effort of deriving a legal ruling from the Koran

IKAN *n* (in Malaysia) fish **ikans**

IKAT *n* method of creating patterns in fabric **ikats**

IKEBANA *n* Japanese art of flower arrangement

IKON = icon

IKONS ▸ ikon

ILEA ▸ ileum

> This is the plural of **ileum**, part of the small intestine, and is often useful as a rack-balancing play when you have too many vowels.

ILEAC *adj* of or relating to the ileum **ileal**

ILEITIS *n* inflammation of the ileum

ILEUM *n* lowest part of the small intestine

ILEUS *n* obstruction of the intestine **ileuses**

ILEX *n* any of a genus of trees or shrubs that includes holly **ilexes**

ILIA ▸ ilium

ILIAC *adj* of or relating to the ilium

ILIACUS *n* iliac

ILIAD *n* epic poem **iliads**

ILIAL ▸ ilium

ILICES ▸ ilex

ILIUM *n* part of the hipbone

ILK *n* type ▸ *determiner* each **ilka**

ILKADAY *n* every day

ILKS ▸ ilk

ILL *adj*, *n*, *adv*

ILLAPSE *vb* slide in

ILLEGAL *adj*, *n*

ILLER ▸ ill

ILLEST ▸ ill

ILLIAD *n* wink **illiads**

ILLICIT *adj*

ILLIPE *n* Asian tree **illipes**

ILLITE *n* clay mineral of the mica group **illites, illitic**

ILLNESS *n*

ILLOGIC *n* reasoning characterized by lack of logic

ILLS ▸ ill

ILLTH *n* condition of poverty or misery **illths**

ILLUDE *vb* trick or deceive **illuded, illudes**

ILLUME *vb* illuminate **illumed, illumes**

ILLUPI = illipe

ILLUPIS ▸ illupi

ILLUVIA > illuvium

ILLY *adv* badly

IMAGE *n*, *vb* **imaged**

IMAGER *n* device that produces images **imagers**

IMAGERY *n*

IMAGES ▸ image

IMAGINE *vb*, *sentence substitute*

IMAGING ▸ image

IMAGISM *n* poetic movement **imagist**

IMAGO *n* sexually mature adult insect **imagoes, imagos**

IMAM *n*

IMAMATE *n* region or territory governed by an imam

IMAMS ▸ imam

IMARET *n* (in Turkey) a hospice for pilgrims

or travellers **imarets**

IMARI n Japanese porcelain **imaris**

IMAUM = imam

IMAUMS ▸ imaum

IMBALM = embalm

IMBALMS ▸ imbalm

IMBAR vb bar in

IMBARK vb cover in bark **imbarks**

IMBARS ▸ imbar

IMBASE vb degrade **imbased, imbases**

IMBATHE vb bathe

IMBED = embed

IMBEDS ▸ imbed

IMBIBE vb imbibed, imbiber, imbibes

IMBIZO n meeting in S Africa **imbizos**

IMBLAZE vb depict heraldically

IMBODY = embody

IMBOSK vb conceal **imbosks**

IMBOSOM vb hold in one's heart

IMBOSS = emboss

IMBOWER vb enclose in a bower

IMBRAST Spenserian past participle of ▸ embrace

IMBREX n curved tile

IMBROWN vb make brown

IMBRUE vb stain, esp with blood **imbrued, imbrues**

IMBRUTE vb reduce to a bestial state

IMBUE vb fill or inspire with (ideals or principles) **imbued,**

imbues, imbuing

IMBURSE vb pay

IMID n immunomodulatory drug

IMIDE n any of a class of organic compounds **imides, imidic, imido**

IMIDS ▸ imid

IMINE n any of a class of organic compounds **imines, imino**

IMITANT = imitation

IMITATE vb

IMMANE adj monstrous

IMMASK vb disguise **immasks**

IMMENSE adj

IMMERGE archaic word for ▸ immerse

IMMERSE vb

IMMESH variant of ▸ enmesh

IMMEW vb confine **immewed, immews**

IMMIES ▸ immy

IMMIT vb insert **immits**

IMMIX vb mix in **immixed, immixes**

IMMORAL adj

IMMUNE adj, n **immunes**

IMMURE vb imprison **immured, immures**

IMMY n image-orthicon camera

IMP n, vb

IMPACT n, vb **impacts**

IMPAINT vb paint

IMPAIR vb **impairs**

IMPALA n southern African antelope **impalas**

IMPALE vb **impaled,**

impaler, impales

IMPANEL variant spelling (esp US) of ▸ empanel

IMPARK vb make into a park **imparks**

IMPARL vb parley **imparls**

IMPART vb **imparts**

IMPASSE n

IMPASTE vb apply paint thickly to

IMPASTO n, vb

IMPAVE vb set in a pavement **impaved, impaves**

IMPAVID adj fearless

IMPAWN vb pawn **impawns**

IMPEACH vb

IMPEARL vb adorn with pearls

IMPED ▸ imp

IMPEDE vb impeded, impeder, impedes

IMPEDOR n component that offers impedance

IMPEL vb **impels**

IMPEND vb be about to happen **impends**

IMPERIA > imperium

IMPERIL vb

IMPETUS n

IMPHEE n African sugar cane **imphees**

IMPI n group of Zulu warriors **impies**

IMPIETY n lack of respect or religious reverence

IMPING ▸ imp

IMPINGE vb

IMPINGS ▸ imp

IMPIOUS adj

IMPIS ▸ impi

IMPISH adj mischievous

IMPLANT n, vb

IMPLATE vb sheathe

IMPLEAD vb sue or prosecute **impled**

IMPLETE vb fill

IMPLEX n part of an arthropod

IMPLIED adj hinted at or suggested

IMPLIES ▸ imply

IMPLODE vb

IMPLORE vb

IMPLY vb

IMPONE vb impose imponed, impones

IMPORT vb, n imports

IMPOSE vb imposed, imposer, imposes

IMPOSEX n acquisition by female organisms of male characteristics

IMPOST n tax, esp a customs duty ▷ vb classify (imported goods) according to the duty payable on them **imposts**

IMPOT n slang term for the act of imposing **impots**

IMPOUND vb

IMPOWER less common spelling of ▸ empower

IMPREGN vb impregnate

IMPRESA n heraldic device **imprese**

IMPRESS vb, n

IMPREST n fund of cash used to pay incidental expenses

IMPRINT n, vb

IMPROV n improvisational comedy

IMPROVE vb

IMPROVS ▸ improv

IMPS ▸ imp

IMPUGN vb challenge the truth or validity of **impugns**

IMPULSE vb, n

IMPURE adj impurer

IMPUTE vb imputed, imputer, imputes

IMSHI interj go away! **imshy**

IN prep, adv, adj, n, vb

INANE adj, n inanely, inaner, inanes, inanest

INANGA n common type of New Zealand grass tree **inangas**

INANITY n lack of intelligence or imagination

INAPT adj not apt or fitting **inaptly**

INARCH vb graft (a plant)

INARM vb embrace inarmed, inarms

INBEING n existence in something else

INBENT adj bent inwards

INBOARD adj (of a boat's engine) inside the hull ▷ adv within the sides of a vessel or aircraft

INBORN adj

INBOUND vb pass into the playing area from outside it ▷ adj coming in

INBOX n inboxes

INBREAK n breaking in

INBRED n, adj inbreds

INBREED vb

INBRING vb bring in

INBUILT adj present from the start

INBURST n irruption

INBY adv into the house or an inner room ▷ adj located near or nearest to the house

INBYE adv near the house

INCAGE vb confine in or as in a cage **incaged, incages**

INCANT vb chant (a spell) **incants**

INCASE variant spelling of ▸ encase

INCASED ▸ incase

INCASES ▸ incase

INCAVE vb hide incaved, incaves

INCAVI ▸ incavo

INCAVO n incised part of a carving

INCEDE vb advance inceded, incedes

INCENSE vb, n

INCENT vb provide incentive **incents**

INCEPT vb (of organisms) to ingest (food) ▷ n rudimentary organ **incepts**

INCEST n incests

INCH n, vb

INCHASE = enchase

INCHED ▸ inch

INCHER n something

measuring given amount of inches **inchers**

INCHES ▸ inch

INCHING ▸ inch

INCHPIN n cervine sweetbread

INCIPIT n Latin introductory phrase

INCISAL adj relating to the cutting edge of incisors and cuspids

INCISE vb cut into with a sharp tool **incised, incises**

INCISOR n

INCITE vb **incited, inciter, incites**

INCIVIL archaic form of ▸ uncivil

INCLASP vb clasp

INCLE = inkle

INCLES ▸ incle

INCLINE vb, n

INCLIP vb embrace **inclips**

INCLOSE less common spelling of ▸ enclose

INCLUDE vb

INCOG n incognito **incogs**

INCOME n

INCOMER n person who comes to a place in which they were not born

INCOMES ▸ income

INCONIE adj fine or delicate

INCONNU n whitefish of Arctic waters

INCONY adj fine or delicate

INCROSS n variation

produced by inbreeding ▸ vb produce by inbreeding

INCRUST = encrust

INCUBI ▸ incubus

INCUBUS n (in folklore) type of demon

INCUDAL ▸ incus

INCUDES ▸ incus

INCULT adj (of land) uncultivated

INCUR vb incurs

INCURVE vb curve or cause to curve inwards

INCUS n bone in the ear of mammals

INCUSE vb design stamped or hammered onto a coin ▸ vb impress (a design) in a coin ▸ adj stamped or hammered onto a coin **incused, incuses**

INCUT adj cut or etched in

INDABA n (among South Africans) a meeting to discuss a serious topic **indabas**

INDAMIN = indamine

INDART vb dart in **indarts**

INDEED adv, interj

INDENE n colourless liquid hydrocarbon **indenes**

INDENT vb indents

INDEW = indue

INDEWED ▸ indew

INDEWS ▸ indew

INDEX n, vb indexal, indexed, indexer, indexes

INDIA n indias

INDICAN n compound secreted in the urine

INDICES plural of ▸ index

INDICIA > indicium

INDICT vb indicts

INDIE adj (of rock music) released by an independent record label ▸ n independent record company **indies**

INDIGEN = indigene

INDIGN adj undeserving

INDIGO adj, n indigos

INDITE vb write indited, inditer, indites

INDIUM n soft silvery-white metallic element **indiums**

INDOL = indole

INDOLE n crystalline heterocyclic compound **indoles**

INDOLS ▸ indol

INDOOR adj

INDOORS adj

INDORSE variant spelling of ▸ endorse

INDOW archaic variant of ▸ indow

INDOWED ▸ indow

INDOWS ▸ indow

INDOXYL n water-soluble crystalline compound

INDRAFT = indraught

INDRAWN adj drawn or pulled in

INDRI = indris

INDRIS n large lemuroid primate

INDUCE vb induced,

inducer, induces

INDUCT vb formally install (someone) in office **inducts**

INDUE variant spelling of ▶ endue

INDUED ▶ indue

INDUES ▶ indue

INDUING ▶ indue

INDULGE vb

INDULIN = induline

INDULT n type of faculty granted by the Holy See **indults**

INDUNA n (in South Africa) a Black African overseer **indunas**

INDUSIA ▶ indusium

INDWELL vb (of a spirit, principle, etc) to inhabit **indwelt**

INEARTH poetic word for ▶ bury

INEDITA pl n unpublished writings

INEPT adj **inepter, ineptly**

INERM adj without thorns

INERT n, adj **inerter**

INERTIA n

> This is not the easiest of words to see, but its combination of common letters makes it one of the most frequently played of 7-letter bonuses, while its plurals, which can be **inertiae** or **inertias**, are among the 8-letter bonus words that come up most often.

INERTLY ▶ inert

INERTS ▶ inert

INEXACT adj not exact or accurate

INFALL vb move towards (something) under the influence of gravity **infalls**

INFAME vb defame **infamed, infames**

INFAMY n

INFANCY n early childhood

INFANT n, adj

INFANTA n (formerly) daughter of a king of Spain or Portugal

INFANTE n (formerly) any son of a king of Spain or Portugal, except the heir to the throne

INFANTS ▶ infant

INFARCT n localized area of dead tissue ▶ vb obstruct the blood supply to part of a body

INFARE vb enter **infares**

INFAUNA n animals that live in ocean and river beds

INFAUST adj unlucky

INFECT vb, adj **infects**

INFEFT vb give possession of heritable property **infefts**

INFELT adj heartfelt

INFEOFF = enfeoff

INFER vb

INFERE adv together

INFERNO n

INFERS ▶ infer

INFEST vb infests

INFIDEL n person with no religion ▶ adj of unbelievers or unbelief

INFIELD n area of the field near the pitch

INFIGHT vb box at close quarters

INFILL vb fill in ▶ n act of filling or closing gaps in something **infills**

INFIMA ▶ infimum

INFIMUM n greatest lower bound

INFIRM vb, adj **infirms**

INFIX vb fix firmly in ▶ n affix inserted into the middle of a word **infixed, infixes**

INFLAME vb

INFLATE vb

INFLECT vb

INFLICT vb

INFLOW n something, such as liquid or gas, that flows in ▶ vb flow in **inflows**

INFLUX n

INFO n information

INFOLD variant spelling of ▶ enfold

INFOLDS ▶ infold

INFORCE = enforce

INFORM vb, adj **informs**

INFOS ▶ info

INFRA adv (esp in textual annotation) below

INFRACT vb violate or break (a law, an agreement, etc)

INFULA = infulae

INFULAE pl n two ribbons hanging from a bishop's mitre

INFUSE vb infused

INFUSER n any device used to make an infusion

INFUSES ▶ infuse

ING n meadow near a river

INGAN Scots word for ▶ onion

INGANS ▶ ingan

INGATE n entrance ingates

INGENER Shakespearean form of > engineer

INGENU n artless or inexperienced boy or young man

INGENUE n inexperienced girl or young woman

INGENUS ▶ ingenu

INGEST vb take (food or liquid) into the body

INGESTA pl n nourishment taken through the mouth

INGESTS ▶ ingest

INGINE n genius ingines

INGLE n fire in a room or a fireplace ingles

INGLOBE vb shape as a sphere

INGO n revelation ingoes, ingoing

INGOT n, vb ingoted, ingots

INGRAFT variant spelling of ▶ engraft

INGRAIN vb impress deeply on the mind or nature ▷ adj (of carpets) made of fibre that is dyed before being spun ▷ n carpet

made from ingrained yarn

INGRAM adj ignorant

INGRATE n ungrateful person ▷ adj ungrateful

INGRESS n entrance

INGROSS archaic form of ▶ engross

INGROUP n highly cohesive and relatively closed social group

INGROWN adj grown abnormally into the flesh

INGRUM adj ignorant

INGS ▶ ing

INGULF variant spelling of ▶ engulf

INGULFS ▶ ingulf

INGULPH archaic form of ▶ engulf

INHABIT vb

INHALE vb inhaled

INHALER n

INHALES ▶ inhale

INHAUL n line for hauling in a sail inhauls

INHAUST vb drink in

INHERCE = inhearse

INHERE vb be an inseparable part (of) inhered, inheres

INHERIT vb

INHIBIN n peptide hormone

INHIBIT vb

INHOOP vb confine inhoops

INHUMAN adj

INHUME vb inter inhumed, inhumer, inhumes

INIA ▶ inion

INION n most prominent point at the back of the head inions

INISLE vb put on or make into an island inisled, inisles

INITIAL adj, n, vb

INJECT vb injects

INJELLY vb place in jelly

INJERA n white Ethiopian flatbread, similar to a crepe injeras

INJOINT vb join

INJUNCT vb issue a legal injunction against (a person)

INJURE vb injured, injurer, injures

INJURY n

INK n, vb

INKBLOT n abstract patch of ink

INKED ▶ ink

INKER ▶ ink

INKERS ▶ ink

INKHORN n (formerly) a small portable container for ink

INKHOSI n Zulu clan chief

INKIER ▶ inky

INKIEST ▶ inky

INKING ▶ ink

INKJET adj of a method of printing

INKLE n kind of linen tape used for trimmings ▷ vb hint inkled, inkles

INKLESS ▶ ink

INKLIKE ▶ ink

INKLING n
INKOSI ▶ inkhosi
INKOSIS ▶ inkosi
INKPAD n pad used for rubber-stamping or fingerprinting **inkpads**
INKPOT n ink-bottle **inkpots**
INKS ▶ ink
INKSPOT n ink stain
INKWELL n
INKWOOD n type of tree
INKY adj dark or black
INLACE variant spelling of ▶ enlace
INLACED ▶ inlace
INLACES ▶ inlace
INLAID ▶ inlay
INLAND adv, adj, n **inlands**
INLAY n inlaid substance or pattern ▷ vb decorate by inserting wooden pieces **inlayer, inlays**
INLET n, vb **inlets**
INLIER n outcrop of rocks surrounded by younger rocks **inliers**
INLOCK vb lock up **inlocks**
INLY adv inwardly
INLYING adj situated within or inside
INMATE n **inmates**
INMESH variant spelling of ▶ enmesh
INMOST adj
INN n, vb
INNAGE n type of measurement **innages**

INNARDS pl n
INNATE adj
INNED ▶ inn
INNER adj, n **innerly, inners**
INNERVE vb supply with nervous energy
INNING n division of baseball match **innings**
INNIT interj isn't it
INNLESS adj without inns
INNS ▶ inn
INNYARD n courtyard of an inn
INOCULA > inoculum
INORB vb enclose in or as if in an orb **inorbed, inorbs**
INOSINE n type of molecule making up cell
INOSITE = inositol
INPHASE adj in the same phase
INPOUR vb pour in **inpours**
INPUT n, vb **inputs**
INQILAB n (in India, Pakistan, etc) revolution
INQUERE Spenserian form of ▶ inquire
INQUEST n
INQUIET vb disturb
INQUIRE vb
INQUIRY n question
INRO n Japanese seal-box
INROAD n invasion or hostile attack **inroads**
INRUN n slope down

which ski jumpers ski **inruns**
INRUSH n sudden and overwhelming inward flow
INS ▶ in
INSANE adj **insaner**
INSANIE n insanity
INSCAPE n essential inner nature of a person, etc
INSCULP vb engrave
INSEAM vb contain **inseams**
INSECT n **insects**
INSEEM vb cover with grease **inseems**
INSERT vb, n **inserts**
INSET n small picture inserted within a larger one ▷ vb place in or within ▷ adj decorated with something inserted **insets**
INSHELL vb retreat, as into a shell
INSHIP vb travel or send by ship **inships**
INSHORE adj, adv
INSIDE prep, adj, adv, n
INSIDER n
INSIDES ▶ inside
INSIGHT n
INSIGNE = insignia
INSINEW vb connect or strengthen, as with sinews
INSIPID adj
INSIST vb **insists**
INSNARE less common spelling of ▶ ensnare
INSOFAR adv to the extent

INSOLE n insoles
INSOOTH adv indeed
INSOUL variant of
► ensoul
INSOULS ► insoul
INSPAN vb harness
(animals) to (a vehicle)
inspans
INSPECT vb
INSPIRE vb
INSTAL = install
INSTALL vb
INSTALS ► instal
INSTANT n, adj
INSTAR vb decorate
with stars ▷ n stage in
the development of an
insect **instars**
INSTATE vb place in a
position or office
INSTEAD adv
INSTEP n insteps
INSTIL vb instill,
instils
INSULA n pyramid-
shaped area of the
brain **insulae**
INSULAR adj, n
INSULIN n
INSULSE adj stupid
INSULT vb, n insults
INSURE vb
INSURED adj covered by
insurance ▷ n those
covered by an
insurance policy
INSURER n person or
company that sells
insurance
INSURES ► insure
INSWEPT adj narrowed
towards the front
INSWING n movement
of a bowled ball

INTACT adj
INTAGLI > intaglio
INTAKE n intakes
INTEGER n
INTEL n US military
intelligence **intels**
INTENSE adj
INTENT n, adj intents
INTER vb
INTERIM adj, n, adv
INTERN vb, n interne,
interns
INTERS ► inter
INTHRAL archaic form of
► enthral
INTI n former monetary
unit of Peru
INTIL Scot form of
► into
INTIMA n innermost
layer of an organ or
part **intimae, intimal,
intimas**
INTIME adj intimate
INTINE n inner wall of a
pollen grain or a spore
intines
INTIRE archaic form of
► entire
INTIS ► inti
INTITLE archaic form of
► entitle
INTO prep
INTOED adj having
inward-turning toes
INTOMB = entomb
INTOMBS ► intomb
INTONE vb intoned,
intoner, intones
INTORT vb twist inward
intorts
INTOWN adj infield
INTRA prep within

INTRADA n prelude
INTRANT n one who
enters
INTREAT archaic spelling
of ► entreat
INTRO n introduction
INTROFY vb increase
the wetting properties
INTROIT n short prayer
said or sung
INTROLD variant of
► entrold
INTRON n stretch of
DNA **introns**
INTROS ► intro
INTRUDE vb
INTRUST = entrust
INTUIT vb know or
discover by intuition
intuits
INTURN n inward turn
inturns
INTUSE n contusion
intuses
INTWINE less common
spelling of ► entwine
INTWIST vb twist
together
INULA n plant of the
elecampane genus
inulas
INULASE n enzyme
INULIN n fructose
polysaccharide
inulins
INURE vb inured,
inures, inuring
INURN vb place (esp
cremated ashes) in an
urn **inurned, inurns**
INUST adj burnt in
INUTILE adj useless
INVADE vb invaded,
invader, invades

INVALID n, vb, adj

INVAR n alloy made from iron and nickel **invars**

INVEIGH vb criticize strongly

INVENIT sentence substitute (he or she) designed it

INVENT vb invents

INVERSE vb, adj, n

INVERT vb, n inverts

INVEST vb invests

INVEXED adj concave

INVIOUS adj without paths or roads

INVITAL adj not vital

INVITE vb, n invited

INVITEE n one who is invited

INVITER ▶ invite

INVITES ▶ invite

INVOICE n, vb

INVOKE vb invoked, invoker, invokes

INVOLVE vb

INWALL vb surround with a wall **inwalls**

INWARD adj, adv, n

INWARDS adv towards the inside or middle of something

INWEAVE vb weave together

INWICK vb perform a type of curling stroke **inwicks**

INWIND vb wind or coil around **inwinds**

INWIT n conscience

INWITS ▶ inwit

INWORK vb work in **inworks**

INWORN adj worn in

INWOUND ▶ inwind

INWOVE ▶ inweave

INWOVEN ▶ inweave

INWRAP less common spelling of ▶ enwrap

INWRAPS ▶ inwrap

INYALA n antelope **inyalas**

IO interj an exclamation ▷ n cry of "io"

IODATE = iodize

IODATED ▶ iodate

IODATES ▶ iodate

IODIC adj of or containing iodine

IODID = iodide

IODIDE n chemical compound **iodides**

IODIDS ▶ iodid

IODIN = iodine

IODINE n iodines

IODINS ▶ iodin

IODISE = iodize

IODISED ▶ iodise

IODISER ▶ iodise

IODISES ▶ iodise

IODISM n poisoning caused by iodine or its compounds **iodisms**

IODIZE vb treat with iodine **iodized, iodizer, iodizes**

IODOUS adj of or containing iodine

IODURET n iodide

IOLITE n grey or violet-blue dichroic mineral **iolites**

ION n

IONIC adj of or in the form of ions

IONICS pl n study of ions

IONISE = ionize

IONISED ▶ ionise

IONISER = ionizer

IONISES ▶ ionise

IONIUM n naturally occurring radioisotope of thorium **ioniums**

IONIZE vb change into ions **ionized**

IONIZER n person or thing that ionizes

IONIZES ▶ ionize

IONOGEN n compound that exists as ions when dissolved

IONOMER n type of thermoplastic

IONONE n yellowish liquid mixture **ionones**

IONS ▶ ion

IOS ▶ io

IOTA n iotas

> This word for a Greek letter is another of those that often come in handy when you are trying to rid your rack of too many vowels.

IPECAC n type of S American shrub **ipecacs**

IPOMOEA n convolvulaceous plant

IPPON n winning point awarded in a judo or karate competition **ippons**

IRACUND adj easily angered

IRADE n written edict of a Muslim ruler **irades**

IRATE adj **irately, irater, iratest**

IRE vb anger ▷ n anger **ired, ireful, ireless**
IRENIC adj tending to conciliate or promote peace
IRENICS n branch of theology
IRES ▶ ire
IRID n type of iris **iridal, irideal**
IRIDES ▶ iris
IRIDIAL ▶ irid
IRIDIAN ▶ irid
IRIDIC adj of or containing iridium
IRIDISE vb make iridescent
IRIDIUM n
IRIDIZE vb make iridescent
IRIDS ▶ irid
IRING ▶ ire
IRIS n, vb
IRISATE vb make iridescent
IRISED ▶ iris
IRISES ▶ iris
IRISING ▶ iris
IRITIC ▶ iritis
IRITIS n inflammation of the iris of the eye
  Since a plague of Is tends to afflict every Scrabble player's rack at regular intervals, it is well worth knowing words like this one, meaning inflammation of the iris, which use several of the wretched letter!
IRK vb **irked, irking, irks**

IRKSOME adj irritating, annoying
IROKO n tropical African hardwood tree **irokos**
IRON n, adj, vb
IRONE n fragrant liquid
  You may surprise your opponent by adding an E to **iron** if you know this word for a kind of aromatic oil.
IRONED ▶ iron
IRONER ▶ iron
IRONERS ▶ iron
IRONES ▶ irone
IRONIC adj using irony
IRONIER ▶ irony
IRONIES ▶ irony
IRONING n clothes to be ironed
IRONISE = ironize
IRONIST ▶ ironize
IRONIZE vb use or indulge in irony
IRONMAN n very strong man **ironmen**
IRONS ▶ iron
IRONY n, adj
IRREAL adj unreal
IRRUPT vb enter forcibly or suddenly **irrupts**
IS third person singular present tense of ▶ be
ISABEL n brown yellow colour **isabels**
ISAGOGE n academic introduction
ISATIN n yellowish-red crystalline compound **isatine, isatins**
ISBA n log hut **isbas**
ISCHIA ▶ ischium

ISCHIAL ▶ ischium
ISCHIUM n part of the hipbone
ISH n issue **ishes**
  An **ish** is a word for an issue in Scots law. If you have I, S and H on your rack, remember that as well as adding **ish** to the end of many words, you can also play those letters as a word in its own right.
ISIT sentence substitute expression used in response to a statement
ISLAND n, vb **islands**
ISLE vb, n **isled**
ISLEMAN n islander **islemen**
ISLES ▶ isle
ISLET n small island
ISLETED adj having islets
ISLETS ▶ islet
ISLING ▶ isle
ISM n doctrine, system, or practice
  While **ism** can be added to the ends of many words as a suffix, it's worth remembering as a word in its own right.
ISMATIC adj following fashionable doctrines
ISMS ▶ ism
ISNA vb is not **isnae**
ISO n short segment of film that can be

replayed easily

ISOAMYL *n as in* **isoamyl acetate** colourless volatile compound

ISOBAR *n* isobare, isobars

ISOBASE *n* line connecting points of equal land upheaval

ISOBATH *n* line showing equal depth of water

ISOCHOR *n* line showing equal pressure and temperature

ISODICA > **isodicon**

ISODOMA > **isodomon**

ISODONT *n* animal in which the teeth are of similar size

ISODOSE *n* dose of radiation applied in radiotherapy

ISOETES *n* quillwort

ISOFORM *n* protein similar in function but not form to another

ISOGAMY *n* fusion of similar gametes

ISOGENY > **isogenous**

ISOGON *n* equiangular polygon

ISOGONE = **isogonic**

ISOGONS > **isogon**

ISOGONY > **isogonic**

ISOGRAM = **isopleth**

ISOGRIV *n* line showing equal angular bearing

ISOHEL *n* line showing equal sunshine **isohels**

ISOHYET *n* line showing equal rainfall

ISOKONT = **isokontan**

ISOLATE *vb, n*

ISOLEAD *n* line on a ballistic graph

ISOLEX *n* line on map showing where a particular word is used

ISOLINE = **isopleth**

ISOLOG > **isologous**

ISOLOGS > **isologous**

ISOMER *n* compound that has the same molecular formula as another **isomere**, **isomers**

ISONOME *n* line on a map showing equal abundance of a species

ISONOMY *n* equality before the law of the citizens of a state

ISOPACH *n* line showing equal thickness

ISOPOD *n* type of crustacean ▷ *adj* of this type of crustacean **isopods**

ISOS ▶ **iso**

ISOSPIN *n* number used to classify elementary particles

ISOTACH *n* line showing equal wind speed

ISOTONE *n* atom with same number of neutrons as another

ISOTOPE *n* isotopy

ISOTRON *n* device for separating small quantities of isotopes

ISOTYPE *n* pictorial presentation of

statistical information

ISOZYME *n* variant of an enzyme

ISSEI *n* first-generation Japanese immigrant **isseis**

ISSUANT *adj* emerging or issuing

ISSUE *n, vb* issued, issuer, issuers, issues, issuing

ISTANA *n* (in Malaysia) a royal palace **istanas**

ISTHMI ▶ **isthmus**

ISTHMIC ▶ **isthmus**

ISTHMUS *n*

ISTLE *n* fibre obtained from various agave and yucca trees **istles**

IT *pron, n*

ITA *n* type of palm

ITACISM *n* pronunciation of the Greek letter eta

ITALIC *adj* (of printing type) sloping to the right ▷ *n* style of printing type **italics**

ITAS ▶ **ita**

ITCH *n, vb* itched, itches, itchier, itchily, itching, itchy

ITEM *n, adv, vb* itemed, iteming

ITEMISE = **itemize**

ITEMIZE *vb*

ITEMS ▶ **item**

ITERANT ▶ **iterate**

ITERATE *vb* repeat

ITERUM *adv* again

ITHER *Scot word for* ▶ **other**

ITS *pron, adj*

ITSELF *pron*

IURE adv by law
IVIED adj covered with ivy
IVIES ▶ ivy
IVORIED ▶ ivory
IVORIES pl n keys of a piano
IVORIST n worker in ivory
IVORY n, adj
IVRESSE n drunkenness
IVY n ivylike

IWI n
This Maori word for a tribe is a great one for getting rid of an awkward combination of letters.
IWIS archaic word for > **certainly**
IXIA n southern African plant **ixias**
IXODID n hard-bodied tick **ixodids**

IXORA n flowering shrub **ixoras**
IXTLE = istle
IXTLES ▶ ixtle
IZAR n long garment worn by Muslim women
IZARD n type of goat-antelope **izards**
IZARS ▶ izar
IZZARD n letter Z **izzards**
IZZAT n honour or prestige **izzats**

Jj

J, being worth 8 points on its own, is a good tile for scoring well with, especially as it combines well with **Z** to make **jiz** and with **X** to make great words like **jeux**, **jinx** and **jynx**. However, **J** is a difficult letter when it comes to making bonus words scoring that extra 50 points, so you will normally want to play it off fairly quickly. There are two two-letter words that begin with **J**: **ja** and **jo**. As **J** has such a high value, look out for double- and triple-letter squares when playing these. There are plenty of good three-letter words starting with **J**: **jab** (12 points), **jak** (14), **jam** (12), **jar** (10), **jaw** (13), **jay** (13), **jet** (10), **jib** (12), **jig** (11), **job** (12), **jog** (11), **jot** (10), **joy** (13), **jug** (11) and **jut** (10).

JA interj yes ▷ sentence substitute yes
JAB vb, n jabbed
JABBER vb, n jabbers
JABBING ▶ jab
JABBLE vb ripple jabbled, jabbles
JABERS interj Irish exclamation
JABIRU n jabirus
JABOT n frill or ruffle on the front of a blouse or shirt **jabots**
JABS ▶ jab
JACAL n Mexican daub hut **jacales, jacals**
JACAMAR n tropical American bird with an iridescent plumage
JACANA n long-legged long-toed bird **jacanas**

JACARE another name for ▶ cayman
JACARES ▶ jacare
JACCHUS n small monkey
JACENT adj lying
JACINTH another name for ▶ hyacinth
JACK n, vb
JACKAL n, vb jackals
JACKASS n fool
JACKDAW n
JACKED ▶ jack
JACKEEN n slick self-assertive lower-class Dubliner
JACKER n labourer jackers
JACKET n, vb jackets
JACKING ▶ jack
JACKLEG n unskilled

worker
JACKMAN n retainer jackmen
JACKPOT n
JACKS n type of game
JACOBIN n variety of fancy pigeon
JACOBUS n English gold coin
JACONET n light cotton fabric
JACUZZI n type of bath or pool
JADE n, adj, vb
JADED adj tired and unenthusiastic jadedly
JADEITE n usually green or white mineral
JADERY n shrewishness
JADES, jading, jadish,

jaditic ▸ jade

JAEGER n German or Austrian marksman **jaegers**

JAFFA n (in cricket) well-bowled ball **jaffas**

JAG n period of uncontrolled indulgence in an activity ▷ vb cut unevenly

JAGA n guard ▷ vb guard or watch **jagaed, jagaing, jagas**

JAGER ▸ jaeger

JAGERS ▸ jager

JAGG = jag

JAGGARY = jaggery

JAGGED ▸ jag

JAGGER n pedlar **jaggers**

JAGGERY n coarse brown sugar

JAGGIER ▸ jaggy

JAGGIES ▸ jaggy

JAGGING ▸ jag

JAGGS ▸ jagg

JAGGY adj prickly ▷ n jagged computer image

JAGHIR n Indian regional governance

JAGHIRE n Indian regional governance

JAGHIRS ▸ jaghir

JAGIR n Indian regional governance **jagirs**

JAGLESS ▸ jag

JAGRA n Hindu festival **jagras**

JAGS ▸ jag

JAGUAR n **jaguars**

JAI interj victory (to)

JAIL n, vb **jailed**

JAILER n **jailers**

JAILING ▸ jail

JAILOR = jailer

JAILORS ▸ jailor

JAILS ▸ jail

JAK ▸ jack

JAKE adj slang word meaning all right

JAKES n human excrement **jakeses**

JAKS ▸ jack

JALABIB ▸ jilbab

JALAP n Mexican convolvulaceous plant **jalapic**

JALAPIN n purgative resin

JALAPS ▸ jalap

JALOP = jalap

JALOPPY = jalopy

JALOPS ▸ jalop

JALOPY n old car

JALOUSE vb suspect

JAM vb, n

JAMAAT n **jamaats**

JAMADAR n Indian army officer

JAMB n, vb

JAMBART = greave

JAMBE = jamb

JAMBEAU another word for ▸ **greave**

JAMBED ▸ jamb

JAMBEE n light cane **jambees**

JAMBER = greave

JAMBERS ▸ jamber

JAMBES ▸ jambe

JAMBEUX ▸ jambeau

JAMBIER n greave

JAMBING ▸ jamb

JAMBIYA n curved dagger

JAMBO sentence substitute E African salutation

JAMBOK = sjambok

JAMBOKS ▸ jambok

JAMBONE n type of play in the card game euchre

JAMBOOL = jambolan

JAMBS ▸ jamb

JAMBU = jambolan

JAMBUL = jambolan

JAMBULS ▸ jambul

JAMBUS ▸ jambu

JAMDANI n patterned muslin

JAMES n jemmy **jameses**

JAMJAR n container for preserves **jamjars**

JAMLIKE, jammed, jammer, jammers ▸ jam

JAMMIER ▸ jammy

JAMMIES informal word for ▸ **pyjamas**

JAMMING ▸ jam

JAMMY adj lucky

JAMON n as in **jamon serrano** cured ham from Spain

JAMPAN n type of sedan chair used in India

JAMPANI = jampanee

JAMPANS ▸ jampan

JAMPOT n container for preserves **jampots**

JAMS ▸ jam

JANE n girl or woman **janes**

JANGLE vb, n **jangled, jangler, jangles**

JANGLY adj making a jangling sound

JANITOR n
JANIZAR = janissary
> This is an old word for a Turkish soldier, combining J and Z. If your opponent plays it, remember that you can add not only an S to it to form the plural, but also a Y, making the variant spelling **janizary**.

JANKER n device for transporting logs **jankers**
JANN n lesser jinn
JANNIES ▶ janny
JANNOCK = jonnock
JANNY n janitor
JANNS ▶ jann
JANSKY n unit of flux density **janskys**
JANTEE archaic version of ▶ jaunty
JANTIER ▶ janty
JANTIES ▶ janty
JANTY n petty officer ▷ adj (in archaic usage) jaunty
JAP vb splash
JAPAN n very hard varnish, usu black ▷ vb cover with this varnish ▷ adj relating to or varnished with **japans**
JAPE n joke or prank ▷ vb joke or jest (about) **japed, japer, japers, japery, japes, japing, japings**
JAPPED ▶ jap
JAPPING ▶ jap
JAPS ▶ jap

JAR n, vb **jarful**
JARFULS ▶ jarful
JARGON n, vb **jargons, jargony, jargoon**
JARHEAD n US Marine
JARINA n South American palm tree **jarinas**
JARK n seal or pass
JARKMAN n forger of passes or licences **jarkmen**
JARKS ▶ jark
JARL n Scandinavian chieftain or noble **jarldom, jarls**
JAROOL n Indian tree **jarools**
JARP vb strike or smash **jarped, jarping, jarps**
JARRAH n **jarrahs**
JARRED ▶ jar
JARRING ▶ jar
JARS ▶ jar
JARSFUL ▶ jarful
JARTA n heart **jartas**
JARUL variant of ▶ jarool
JARULS ▶ jarul
JARVEY n hackney coachman **jarveys, jarvie**
JARVIES ▶ jarvie
JASEY n wig **jaseys, jasies**
JASMIN = jasmine
JASMINE n
JASMINS ▶ jasmin
JASP another word for ▶ jasper
JASPE adj resembling jasper ▷ n subtly striped woven fabric
JASPER n variety of quartz **jaspers,**

jaspery
JASPES ▶ jaspe
JASPIS archaic word for ▶ jasper
JASPS ▶ jasp
JASS obsolete variant of ▶ jazz
JASSES ▶ jass
JASSID n leafhopper **jassids**
JASY n wig
JATAKA n text describing the birth of Buddha **jatakas**
JATO n jet-assisted takeoff **jatos**
JAUK vb dawdle **jauked, jauking, jauks**
JAUNCE vb prance **jaunced, jaunces, jaunse**
JAUNSED ▶ jaunse
JAUNSES ▶ jaunse
JAUNT n, vb **jaunted**
JAUNTEE old spelling of ▶ jaunty
JAUNTIE old spelling of ▶ jaunty
JAUNTS ▶ jaunt
JAUNTY adj, n
JAUP ▶ jarp
JAUPED ▶ jaup
JAUPING ▶ jaup
JAUPS ▶ jaup
JAVA n coffee or a variety of **javas**
JAVEL adj as in javel water bleach or disinfectant
JAVELIN n, vb
JAVELS ▶ javel
JAW n, vb
JAWAN n (in India) a soldier **jawans**

JAWARI n variety of sorghum **jawaris**

JAWBONE n lower jaw of a person or animal ▷ vb try to persuade by virtue of one's high office or position

JAWBOX n metal sink
> This Scots word for a sink combines the J and X, and of course its plural **jawboxes**, earning an extra 50 points, would be even better.

JAWED ▸ jaw

JAWFALL n depression

JAWHOLE n cesspit

JAWING, jawings, jawless, jawlike ▸ jaw

JAWLINE n outline of the jaw

JAWS ▸ jaw

JAY n

JAYBIRD n jay

JAYCEE n member of a Junior Chamber of Commerce **jaycees**

JAYGEE n lieutenant junior grade in the US army **jaygees**

JAYS ▸ jay

JAYVEE n junior varsity sports team **jayvees**

JAYWALK vb cross or walk in a street recklessly or illegally

JAZIES ▸ jazy

JAZY n wig
> This means a wig and is a wonderfully useful little word, combining J and Z for a high score.

JAZZ n, vb

JAZZBO n jazz musician or fan **jazzbos**

JAZZED, jazzer, jazzers, jazzes ▸ jazz

JAZZIER ▸ jazzy

JAZZILY ▸ jazzy

JAZZING ▸ jazz

JAZZMAN ▸ jazz

JAZZMEN ▸ jazz

JAZZY adj

JEALOUS adj

JEAN n tough twill-weave cotton fabric

JEANED adj wearing jeans

JEANS pl n

JEAT n jet **jeats**

JEBEL n hill or mountain in an Arab country **jebels**

JEDI n person claiming to live according to the Jedi philosophy **jedis**

JEE variant of ▸ gee

JEED ▸ jee

JEEING ▸ jee

JEEL vb make into jelly **jeeled**

JEELIE = jeely

JEELIED ▸ jeely

JEELIES ▸ jeely

JEELING ▸ jeel

JEELS ▸ jeel

JEELY n jelly ▷ vb make into jelly

JEEP n, vb **jeeped**

JEEPERS interj mild exclamation of surprise

JEEPING ▸ jeep

JEEPNEY n Filipino bus converted from a jeep

JEEPS ▸ jeep

JEER vb, n jeered, jeerer, jeerers, jeering, jeers

JEES ▸ jee

JEEZ interj expression of surprise or irritation

JEFE n (in Spanish-speaking countries) a military or political leader **jefes**

JEFF vb downsize or close down (an organization) **jeffed, jeffing, jeffs**

JEHAD = jihad

JEHADI = jihadi

JEHADIS ▸ jehadi

JEHADS ▸ jehad

JEHU n fast driver **jehus**

JEJUNA ▸ jejunum

JEJUNAL ▸ jejunum

JEJUNE adj simple or naive

JEJUNUM n

JELAB = jellaba

JELABS ▸ jelab

JELL vb

JELLABA n loose robe with a hood

JELLED ▸ jell

JELLIED ▸ jelly

JELLIES ▸ jelly

JELLIFY vb make into or become jelly

JELLING ▸ jell

JELLO n (in US English) type of dessert **jellos**

JELLS ▸ jell

JELLY n, vb

JEMADAR n native officer serving as a mercenary in India

JEMBE n hoe **jembes**

JEMIDAR = **jemadar**

JEMIMA n boot with elastic sides **jemimas**

JEMMIED ▶ jemmy

JEMMIER ▶ jemmy

JEMMIES ▶ jemmy

JEMMY n, vb, adj

JENNET n female donkey or ass **jennets**

JENNIES ▶ jenny

JENNY = **jennet**

JEOFAIL n oversight in legal pleading

JEON n Korean pancake

JEOPARD vb put in jeopardy

JERBIL variant spelling of ▶ **gerbil**

JERBILS ▶ jerbil

JERBOA n small mouselike rodent with long hind legs **jerboas**

JEREED = **jerid**

JEREEDS ▶ jereed

JERID n wooden javelin **jerids**

JERK vb, n **jerked, jerker, jerkers**

JERKIER ▶ jerky

JERKIES ▶ jerky

JERKILY ▶ jerky

JERKIN n

JERKING ▶ jerk

JERKINS ▶ jerkin

JERKS ▶ jerk

JERKY adj characterized by jerks ▷ n type of cured meat

JERQUE vb search for contraband **jerqued, jerquer, jerques**

To **jerque** is to search a vessel for stolen goods, and if you have

the right additional letters to make **jerqued, jerquer, jerques** or **jerquing**, using all your letters, you would get a really great score.

JERREED variant spelling of ▶ **jerid**

JERRID n blunt javelin **jerrids**

JERRIES ▶ jerry

JERRY short for ▶ **jeroboam**

JERSEY n **jerseys**

JESS n short leather strap used in falconry ▷ vb put jesses on (a hawk or falcon)

JESSAMY n fop

JESSE = **jess**

JESSED ▶ jess

JESSES ▶ jess

JESSIE n effeminate, weak, or cowardly boy or man **jessies**

JESSING ▶ jess

JEST vb, n **jested**

JESTEE n person about whom a joke is made **jestees**

JESTER n **jesters**

JESTFUL ▶ jest

JESTING ▶ jest

JESTS ▶ jest

JESUS n French paper size

JET n, vb

JETBEAD n ornamental shrub

JETE n dance step **jetes**

JETFOIL n type of

hydrofoil that is propelled by water jets

JETLAG n tiredness caused by crossing timezones in jet flight **jetlags**

JETLIKE ▶ jet

JETON n gambling chip **jetons**

JETPORT n airport for jet planes

JETS ▶ jet

JETSAM n **jetsams, jetsom**

JETSOMS ▶ jetsom

JETSON archaic form of ▶ **jetsam**

JETSONS ▶ jetson

JETTED ▶ jet

JETTIED ▶ jetty

JETTIER ▶ jetty

JETTIES ▶ jetty

JETTING ▶ jet

JETTON n counter or token **jettons**

JETTY n, adj, vb

JETWAY n tradename of device used in airports **jetways**

JEU n game

Jeu is the French word for game or play. The plural form, jeux, is a great little word, using both J and X, particularly if you can play it on a double- or triple-word square.

JEUNE adj young

JEUX ▶ jeu

JEWEL n, vb **jeweled**

JEWELER = **jeweller**

JEWELRY = **jewellery**

JEWELS ▶ jewel
JEWFISH n freshwater catfish
JEWIE n jewfish **jewies**
JEZAIL n Afghan musket **jezails**

> A **jezail** is a kind of Afghan musket, and if you have an S to go with it, earning the extra 50 points, so much the better.

JEZEBEL n shameless or scheming woman
JHALA n Indian musical style **jhalas**
JHATKA n slaughter of animals for food according to Sikh law **jhatkas**
JIAO n Chinese currency unit **jiaos**
JIB = jibe
JIBB = jibe
JIBBA n long, loose coat worn by Muslim men
JIBBAH = jubbah
JIBBAHS ▶ jibbah
JIBBAS ▶ jibba
JIBBED ▶ jibb
JIBBER variant of ▶ gibber
JIBBERS ▶ jibber
JIBBING ▶ jibb
JIBBONS pl n spring onions
JIBBOOM n spar forming an extension of the bowsprit
JIBBS ▶ jibb
JIBE vb, n **jibed, jiber, jibers, jibes, jibing**
JIBS ▶ jib
JICAMA n pale brown turnip **jicamas**

JIFF = jiffy
JIFFIES ▶ jiffy
JIFFS ▶ jiff
JIFFY n
JIG n, vb
JIGAJIG vb engage in sexual intercourse **jigajog**
JIGGED ▶ jig
JIGGER n small whisky glass ▷ vb interfere or alter **jiggers**
JIGGIER ▶ jiggy
JIGGING ▶ jig
JIGGISH ▶ jig
JIGGLE vb, n **jiggled, jiggles, jiggly**
JIGGY adj resembling a jig
JIGJIG variant of ▶ jigajig
JIGJIGS ▶ jigjig
JIGLIKE ▶ jig
JIGOT = gigot
JIGOTS ▶ jigot
JIGS ▶ jig
JIGSAW n, vb **jigsawn, jigsaws**
JIHAD n
JIHADI n person who takes part in a jihad **jihadis**
JIHADS ▶ jihad
JILBAB n long robe worn by Muslim women **jilbabs**
JILGIE n freshwater crayfish **jilgies**
JILL variant spelling of ▶ gill
JILLET n wanton woman **jillets**
JILLION n extremely large number or amount

JILLS ▶ jill
JILT vb, n **jilted, jilter, jilters, jilting, jilts**
JIMINY interj expression of surprise
JIMJAM ▶ jimjams
JIMJAMS pl n state of nervous tension, excitement, or anxiety
JIMMIE = jimmy
JIMMIED ▶ jimmy
JIMMIES ▶ jimmy
JIMMINY interj expression of surprise
JIMMY = jemmy
JIMP adj handsome **jimper, jimpest**
JIMPIER ▶ jimpy
JIMPLY adv neatly
JIMPSON ▶ jimson
JIMPY adj neat and tidy
JIMSON n as in **jimson weed** type of poisonous plant
JIN n Chinese unit of weight
JINGAL n swivel-mounted gun **jingall, jingals**
JINGKO = gingko
JINGLE n, vb **jingled, jingler, jingles**
JINGLET n sleigh-bell clapper
JINGLY ▶ jingle
JINGO n loud and bellicose patriot; chauvinism **jingoes**
JINJILI n type of sesame
JINK vb move quickly or jerkily in order to dodge someone ▷ n jinking movement **jinked**
JINKER n vehicle for

transporting timber
▷ *vb* carry or transport in a jinker **jinkers**

JINKING ▸ jink

JINKS ▸ jink

JINN ▸ jinni

JINNE *interj* South African exclamation

JINNEE = jinni

JINNI *n* spirit in Muslim mythology **jinnis, jinns**

JINS ▸ jin

JINX *n*, *vb* jinxed, jinxes, jinxing

JIPIJAPA = jipijapa

JIRBLE *vb* pour carelessly **jirbled, jirbles**

JIRD *n* gerbil **jirds**

JIRGA *n* Afghan council **jirgas**

JIRRE = jinne

JITNEY *n* small cheap bus **jitneys**

JITTER *vb* be anxious or nervous **jitters**

JITTERY *adj* nervous

JIVE *n*, *vb*

JIVEASS *adj* misleading or phoney

JIVED, jiver, jivers, jives, jivey, jivier, jiviest, jiving, jivy ▸ jive

JIZ *n* wig

When you find yourself with J and Z but nothing else that looks promising, there may well be an I on the board around which you can form **jiz**, which means a wig.

JIZZ *n* term for the characteristics that identify a particular species of bird or plant **jizzes**

JNANA *n* type of yoga **jnanas**

JO *n* Scots word for sweetheart

JOANNA *n* piano **joannas**

JOANNES = johannes

JOB *n*, *vb* jobbed

JOBBER *n* person who jobs **jobbers**

JOBBERY *n* practice of making private profit out of a public office

JOBBIE *n* piece of excrement **jobbies**

JOBBING *adj*, *n*

JOBE *vb* scold jobed, jobes, jobing

JOBLESS *pl n*, *adj*

JOBNAME *n* title of position

JOBS ▸ job

JOCK *n* athlete

JOCKEY *n*, *vb* jockeys

JOCKISH *adj* macho

JOCKO *n* chimpanzee **jockos**

JOCKS ▸ jock

JOCO *adj* relaxed

JOCOSE *adj*

JOCULAR *adj*

JOCUND *adj* merry or cheerful

JODEL = yodel

JODELS ▸ jodel

JODHPUR *n* as in jodhpur boots ankle-length leather

riding boots

JOE = jo

JOES ▸ joe

JOEY *n* joeys

JOG *vb*, *n* jogged

JOGGER *n* person who runs at a jog for exercise **joggers**

JOGGING ▸ jog

JOGGLE *vb*, *n* joggled, joggler, joggles

JOGS ▸ jog

JOGTROT *n* easy bouncy gait

JOHN *n* toilet

JOHNNIE = johnny

JOHNNY *n* chap

JOHNS ▸ john

JOIN *vb*, *n*

JOINDER *n* act of joining, esp in legal contexts

JOINED ▸ join

JOINER *n* joiners

JOINERY *n*

JOINING ▸ join

JOINS ▸ join

JOINT *adj*, *n*, *vb*

JOINTED *adj* having a joint or joints

JOINTER *n* tool for pointing mortar joints

JOINTLY ▸ joint

JOINTS ▸ joint

JOIST *n*, *vb* joisted, joists

JOJOBA *n* shrub of SW North America **jojobas**

JOKE *n*, *vb* joked

JOKER *n* jokers

JOKES ▸ joke

JOKEY *adj* intended as a joke **jokier, jokiest**

JOKILY ▸ joke

JOKING ▸ joke

JOKOL *Shetland word for* ▸ **yes**

JOKY = jokey

JOL *n* party ▸ *vb* have a good time

JOLE *vb* knock **joled, joles, joling, joll**

JOLLED ▸ jol

JOLLER *n* person who has a good time **jollers**

JOLLEY ▸ jolly

JOLLEYS ▸ jolley

JOLLIED ▸ jolly

JOLLIER *n* joker

JOLLIES ▸ jolly

JOLLIFY *vb* be or cause to be jolly

JOLLILY ▸ jolly

JOLLING ▸ jol

JOLLITY *n*

JOLLOP *n* cream or unguent **jollops**

JOLLS ▸ joll

JOLLY *adj, adv, vb, n* **jollyer**

JOLS ▸ jol

JOLT *n, vb* **jolted, jolter, jolters, joltier, joltily, jolting, jolts, jolty**

JOMO = zo

JOMON *n* particular era in Japanese history

JOMOS ▸ jomo

JONES *vb* desire **jonesed, joneses**

JONG *n* friend, often used in direct address **jongs**

JONNOCK *adj* genuine ▸ *adv* honestly

JONQUIL *n*

JONTIES ▸ jonty

JONTY *n* petty officer

JOOK *vb* poke or puncture (the skin) ▸ *n* jab or the resulting wound **jooked**

JOOKERY *n* mischief

JOOKING ▸ jook

JOOKS ▸ jook

JOR *n* movement in Indian music

JORAM ▸ jorum

JORAMS ▸ joram

JORDAN *n* chamber pot **jordans**

JORS ▸ jor

JORUM *n* large drinking bowl or vessel or its contents **jorums**

JOSEPH *n* woman's floor-length riding coat **josephs**

JOSH *vb* tease ▸ *n* teasing or bantering joke **joshed, josher, joshers, joshes, joshing**

JOSKIN *n* bumpkin **joskins**

JOSS *n* Chinese deity

JOSSER *n* simpleton **jossers**

JOSSES ▸ joss

JOSTLE *vb, n* **jostled, jostler, jostles**

JOT *vb, n*

JOTA *n* Spanish dance **jotas**

JOTS ▸ jot

JOTTED ▸ jot

JOTTER *n* **jotters**

JOTTIER ▸ jotty

JOTTING ▸ jot

JOTTY ▸ jot

JOTUN *n* giant **jotunn**

JOTUNNS ▸ jotunn

JOTUNS ▸ jotun

JOUAL *n* nonstandard variety of Canadian French **jouals**

JOUGS *pl n* iron ring for restraining an offender

JOUK *vb* duck or dodge ▸ *n* sudden evasive movement **jouked**

JOUKERY = jookery

JOUKING ▸ jouk

JOUKS ▸ jouk

JOULE *n, vb* **jouled, joules, jouling**

JOUNCE *vb* shake or jolt or cause to shake or jolt ▸ *n* jolting movement **jounced, jounces, jouncy**

JOUR *n* day

JOURNAL *n, vb*

JOURNEY *n, vb*

JOURNO *n* journalist **journos**

JOURS ▸ jour

JOUST *n, vb* **jousted, jouster, jousts**

JOVIAL *adj*

JOW *vb* ring (a bell)

JOWAR *n* variety of sorghum **jowari, jowaris, jowars**

JOWED ▸ jow

JOWING ▸ jow

JOWL *n, vb* **jowled**

JOWLER *n* dog with prominent jowls **jowlers**

JOWLIER, jowling, jowls, jowly

JOWS ▸ jow

JOY *n, vb*

JOYANCE *n* joyous feeling or festivity

JOYED ▸ joy
JOYFUL adj
JOYING ▸ joy
JOYLESS adj
JOYOUS adj
JOYPAD n computer games console **joypads**
JOYPOP vb take addictive drugs occasionally **joypops**
JOYRIDE n, vb **joyrode**
JOYS ▸ joy
JUBA n lively African-American dance **jubas**
JUBATE adj possessing a mane
JUBBAH n long loose outer garment with wide sleeves **jubbahs**
JUBE n **jubes**
JUBHAH = jubbah
JUBHAHS ▸ jubhah
JUBILE = jubilee
JUBILEE n
JUBILES ▸ jubile
JUCO n junior college in America **jucos**
JUD n large block of coal
JUDAS n peephole **judases**
JUDDER vb, n **judders**
JUDDERY adj shaky
JUDGE n, vb **judged, judger, judgers, judges, judging**
JUDIES ▸ judy
JUDO n
JUDOGI n white two-piece cotton costume **judogis**
JUDOIST ▸ judo
JUDOKA n competitor or expert in judo

Judokas
JUDOS ▸ judo
JUDS ▸ jud
JUDY n woman
JUG n, vb
JUGA ▸ jugum
JUGAL adj of or relating to the zygomatic bone ▷ n cheekbone **jugals**
JUGATE adj having parts arranged in pairs
JUGFUL = jug
JUGFULS ▸ jugful
JUGGED ▸ jug
JUGGING ▸ jug
JUGGINS n silly person
JUGGLE vb, n **juggled**
JUGGLER n person who juggles, esp a professional entertainer
JUGGLES ▸ juggle
JUGHEAD n clumsy person
JUGLET n small jug **juglets**
JUGS ▸ jug
JUGSFUL ▸ jugful
JUGULA ▸ jugulum
JUGULAR n
JUGULUM n lower throat
JUGUM n part of an insect's forewing **jugums**
JUICE n, vb **juiced**
JUICER n kitchen appliance **juicers**
JUICES ▸ juice
JUICIER ▸ juicy
JUICILY ▸ juicy
JUICING ▸ juice
JUICY adj
JUJITSU n

JUJU n W African magic charm or fetish
JUJUBE n chewy sweet made of flavoured gelatine **jujubes**
JUJUISM ▸ juju
JUJUIST ▸ juju
JUJUS ▸ juju
JUJUTSU = jujitsu
JUKE vb dance or play dance music
JUKEBOX n
JUKED ▸ juke
JUKES ▸ juke
JUKING ▸ juke
JUKSKEI n type of game
JUKU n Japanese martial art **jukus**
JULEP n sweet alcoholic drink **juleps**
JULIET n code word for the letter J **juliets**
JUMAR n climbing tool ▷ vb climb (up a fixed rope) using **jumars jumared, jumars**
JUMART n mythical offspring of a bull and a mare **jumarts**
JUMBAL = jumble
JUMBALS ▸ jumbal
JUMBIE n Caribbean ghost **jumbies**
JUMBLE n, vb **jumbled, jumbler, jumbles, jumbly**
JUMBO adj, n **jumbos**
JUMBUCK n
JUMBY n Caribbean ghost
JUMELLE n paired objects
JUMP vb, n **jumped**
JUMPER n **jumpers**
JUMPIER ▸ jumpy

JUMPILY ▶ jumpy
JUMPING ▶ jump
JUMPOFF *n* round in a showjumping contest
JUMPS ▶ jump
JUMPY *adj*
JUN *variant of* ▶ chon
JUNCATE = junket
JUNCO *n* North American bunting **juncoes, juncos**
JUNCUS *n* type of rush
JUNGLE *n*
JUNGLED *adj* covered with jungle
JUNGLES ▶ jungle
JUNGLI *n* uncultured person **junglis**
JUNGLY ▶ jungle
JUNIOR *adj, n* **juniors**
JUNIPER *n*
JUNK *n, vb* **junked**
JUNKER *n* (formerly) young German nobleman **junkers**
JUNKIE *n*
JUNKIER ▶ junky
JUNKIES ▶ junky
JUNKING ▶ junk
JUNKMAN *n* man who trades in discarded items **junkmen**
JUNKS ▶ junk
JUNKY *n* drug addict ▷ *adj* of low quality
JUNTA *n* **juntas, junto**

JUNTOS ▶ junto
JUPATI *n* type of palm tree **jupatis**
JUPE *n* sleeveless jacket **jupes**
JUPON *n* short sleeveless padded garment **jupons**
JURA ▶ jus
JURAL *adj* of or relating to law or to the administration of justice **jurally**
JURANT *n* person taking oath **jurants**
JURAT *n* statement at the foot of an affidavit **jurats**
JURE *adv* by legal right
JUREL *n* edible fish **jurels**
JURIDIC = juridical
JURIED ▶ jury
JURIES ▶ jury
JURIST *n* **jurists**
JUROR *n* **jurors**
JURY *n, adj, vb* **jurying**
JURYMAN *n* member of a jury, esp a man **jurymen**
JUS *n* right, power, or authority
JUSSIVE *n* mood of verbs used for giving orders; imperative
JUST *adv, adj, vb* **justed, juster, justers,**

justest
JUSTICE *n*
JUSTIFY *vb*
JUSTING ▶ joust
JUSTLE *less common word for* ▶ jostle
JUSTLED ▶ justle
JUSTLES ▶ justle
JUSTLY ▶ just
JUSTS ▶ joust
JUT *vb, n*
JUTE *n* **jutes**
JUTS ▶ jut
JUTTED ▶ jut
JUTTIED ▶ jutty
JUTTIES ▶ jutty
JUTTING ▶ jut
JUTTY *vb* project beyond
JUVE = juvenile
JUVENAL *variant spelling (esp US) of* ▶ juvenile
JUVES ▶ juve
JUVIE *n* juvenile detention centre **juvies**
JYMOLD *adj* having a hinge
JYNX *n* wryneck **jynxes**

This unusual word, another name for the bird known as a wryneck, is unique in combining J, Y and X without using any vowels.

Kk

Worth 5 points, **K** is a valuable tile to have in your rack. However, it's not the most useful tile for forming bonus words scoring that extra 50 points, so, as with the **J**, you will normally want to play it off fairly quickly. There are four two-letter words beginning with **K**: **ka**, **ki**, **ko** and **ky**. When it comes to three-letter words, remember **keg** (8 points), **ken** (7), **key** (10), **kex** (14), **kid** (8), **kin** (7), **kip** (9) and **kit** (7). Other three-letter words with **K** well worth remembering are **jak** (14) and **zek** (16).

KA *n* (in ancient Egypt) type of spirit ▷ *vb* (in archaic usage) help

KAAL *adj* naked

KAAMA *n* large African antelope with lyre-shaped horns **kaamas**

KAAS *n* Dutch cabinet or wardrobe

KAB *variant spelling of* ▷ **cab**

KABAB = kebab

KABABS ▷ **kabab**

KABADDI *n* type of game

KABAKA *n* any of the former rulers of the Baganda people **kabakas**

KABALA = kabbalah

KABALAS ▷ **kabala**

KABAR *archaic form of* ▷ **caber**

KABARS ▷ **kabar**

KABAYA *n* tunic **kabayas**

KABBALA = kabbalah

KABELE = kebele

KABELES ▷ **kabele**

KABIKI *n* fruit tree found in India **kabikis**

KABOB = kebab

KABOBS ▷ **kabob**

KABS ▷ **kab**

KABUKI *n* form of Japanese drama **kabukis**

KACCHA *n* trousers worn traditionally by Sikhs **kacchas**

KACHA *adj* crude **kachcha**

KACHERI = kachahri

KACHINA *n* type of supernatural being

KADDISH *n* ancient Jewish liturgical prayer

KADE = ked

KADES ▷ **kade**

KADI *variant spelling of* ▷ **cadi**

KADIS ▷ **kadi**

KAE *n* dialect word for jackdaw or jay ▷ *vb* (in archaic usage) help **kaed, kaeing, kaes**

KAF *n* letter of the Hebrew alphabet

KAFFIR *n* **kaffirs**

KAFILA *n* caravan **kafilas**

KAFIR = kaffir

KAFIRS ▷ **kafir**

KAFS ▷ **kaf**

KAFTAN *n* **kaftans**

KAGO *n* Japanese sedan chair

KAGOOL *variant spelling of* ▷ **cagoule**

KAGOOLS ▷ **kagool**

KAGOS ▷ **kago**

KAGOUL *variant spelling of* ▶ **cagoule**

KAGOULE = kagoul

KAGOULS ▶ kagoul

KAGU *n* crested nocturnal bird **kagus**

KAHAL *n* Jewish community **kahals**

KAHAWAI *n* food and game fish of New Zealand

KAHUNA *n* Hawaiian priest, shaman, or expert **kahunas**

KAI *n*

KAIAK = kayak

KAIAKED ▶ kaiak

KAIAKS ▶ kaiak

KAID *n* North African chieftain or leader **kaids**

KAIE *archaic form of* ▶ **key**

KAIES ▶ kaie

KAIF = kif

KAIFS ▶ kaif

KAIK = kainga

KAIKA = kainga

KAIKAI *n* food **kaikais**

KAIKAS ▶ kaika

KAIKS ▶ kaik

KAIL = kale

KAILS ▶ kail

KAIM = kame

KAIMS ▶ kaim

KAIN *variant spelling of* ▶ **cain**

KAING ▶ ka

KAINGA *n* (in New Zealand) a Māori village or small settlement **kaingas**

KAINIT = kainite

KAINITE *n* white mineral

KAINITS ▶ kainit

KAINS ▶ kain

KAIS ▶ kai

KAISER *n* German or Austro-Hungarian emperor **kaisers**

KAIZEN *n* type of philosophy **kaizens**

KAJAWAH *n* type of seat or panier used on a camel

KAJEPUT *n* variety of Australian melaleuca

KAKA *n* parrot of New Zealand

KAKAPO *n* nocturnal New Zealand parrot **kakapos**

KAKAS ▶ kaka

KAKI *n* Asian persimmon tree **kakis**

KAKODYL *variant spelling of* ▶ **cacodyl**

KAKURO *n* crossword-style puzzle with numbers **kakuros**

KALAM *n* discussion and debate **kalams**

KALE *n*

KALENDS = calends

KALES ▶ kale

KALI *another name for* ▶ **saltwort**

KALIAN *another name for* ▶ **hookah**

KALIANS ▶ kalian

KALIF *variant spelling of* ▶ **caliph**

KALIFS ▶ kalif

KALIMBA *n* musical instrument

KALIPH *variant spelling of* ▶ **caliph**

KALIPHS ▶ kaliph

KALIS ▶ kali

KALIUM *n* Latin for potassium **kaliums**

KALMIA *n* evergreen ericaceous shrub **kalmias**

KALONG *n* fruit bat **kalongs**

KALOOKI *n* card game **kalpa** *n* period in Hindu cosmology

KALPAC = calpac

KALPACS ▶ kalpac

KALPAK *variant spelling of* ▶ **calpac**

KALPAKS ▶ kalpak

KALPAS ▶ kalpa

KALPIS *n* Greek water jar

KALUKI ▶ kalooki

KALUKIS ▶ kaluki

KAM *Shakespearean word for* ▶ **crooked**

KAMA *n* large African antelope with lyre-shaped horns

KAMAHI *n* hardwood tree **kamahis**

KAMALA *n* East Indian tree **kamalas**

KAMAS ▶ kama

KAME *n* irregular mound of gravel, sand, etc

KAMEES ▶ kameez

KAMEEZ *n* long tunic

KAMELA = kamala

KAMELAS ▶ kamela

KAMERAD *interj* shout of surrender ▶ *vb* surrender

KAMES ▸ kame
KAMI n divine being or spiritual force in Shinto
KAMICHI n South American bird
KAMIK n traditional Inuit boot **kamiks**
KAMILA = kamala
KAMILAS ▸ kamila
KAMIS = kameez
KAMISES ▸ kamis
KAMME = kam
KAMPONG n (in Malaysia) village
KAMSEEN = khamsin
KAMSIN = kamseen
KAMSINS ▸ kamsin
KANA n Japanese syllabary
KANAE n grey mullet **kanaes**
KANAKA n Australian word for any native of the South Pacific **kanakas**
KANAS ▸ kana
KANBAN n just-in-time manufacturing process **kanbans**
KANDIES ▸ kandy
KANDY = candie
KANE n Hawaiian man or boy
KANEH n 6-cubit Hebrew measure **kanehs**
KANES ▸ kane
KANG n Chinese heatable platform
KANGA n piece of gaily decorated thin cotton cloth **kangas**
KANGHA n comb traditionally worn by

Sikhs **kanghas**
KANGS ▸ kang
KANJI n Japanese writing system **kanjis**
KANS n Indian wild sugar cane **kanses**
KANT archaic spelling of ▸ cant
KANTAR n unit of weight **kantars**
KANTED ▸ kant
KANTELA = kantele
KANTELE n Finnish stringed instrument
KANTEN = agar
KANTENS ▸ kanten
KANTHA n Bengali embroidered quilt **kanthas**
KANTING ▸ kant
KANTS ▸ kant
KANUKA n New Zealand myrtaceous tree **kanukas**
KANZU n long garment **kanzus**
KAOLIN n kaoline, **kaolins**
KAON n type of meson **kaonic, kaons**
KAPA n Hawaiian cloth made from beaten mulberry bark **kapas**
KAPH n 11th letter of the Hebrew alphabet **kaphs**
KAPOK n **kapoks**
KAPPA n tenth letter in the Greek alphabet **kappas**
KAPUKA = broadleaf
KAPUKAS ▸ kapuka
KAPUT adj ruined or broken **kaputt**

KARA n steel bangle traditionally worn by Sikhs
KARAISM n beliefs and doctrines of a Jewish sect
KARAIT ▸ krait
KARAITS ▸ krait
KARAKA n New Zealand tree **karakas**
KARAKIA n prayer
KARAKUL n sheep of central Asia
KARAMU n small New Zealand tree **karamus**
KARANGA n call or chant of welcome, sung by a female elder ▷ vb perform a karanga
KARAOKE n form of entertainment
KARAS ▸ kara
KARAT n measure of the proportion of gold in an alloy
KARATE n **karates**
KARATS ▸ karat
KARENGO n edible type of Pacific seaweed
KARITE n shea tree **karites**
KARK variant spelling of ▸ cark
KARKED ▸ kark
KARKING ▸ kark
KARKS ▸ kark
KARMA n **karmas, karmic**
KARN old word for ▸ cairn
KARNS ▸ karn
KARO n small New Zealand tree or shrub

KAROO n high arid plateau **karoos**

KARORO n large seagull **karoros**

KAROS ▶ **karo**

KAROSHI n (in Japan) death caused by overwork

KAROSS n type of blanket

KARRI n **karris**

KARROO = **karoo**

KARROOS ▶ **karroo**

KARSEY variant spelling of ▶ **khazi**

KARSEYS ▶ **karsey**

KARSIES ▶ **karsy**

KARST n geological term **karstic, karsts**

KARSY variant spelling of ▶ **khazi**

KART n light low-framed vehicle **karter, karters, karting, karts**

KARYON n nucleus of a cell **karyons**

KARZIES ▶ **karzy**

KARZY variant spelling of ▶ **khazi**

KAS ▶ **ka**

KASBAH n citadel of any of various North African cities **kasbahs**

KASHA n dish originating in Eastern Europe **kashas**

KASHER vb make fit for use **kashers**

KASHMIR variant spelling of > **cashmere**

KASHRUS = **kashrut**

KASHRUT = **kashruth**

KASME interj (in Indian English) I swear

KAT = **khat**

KATA n form of exercise

KATAL n SI unit of catalytic activity **katals**

KATANA n Japanese samurai sword **katanas**

KATAS ▶ **kata**

KATCINA variant spelling of ▶ **kachina**

KATHAK n form of dancing **kathaks**

KATHODE variant spelling of ▶ **cathode**

KATI variant spelling of ▶ **catty**

KATION variant spelling of ▶ **cation**

KATIONS ▶ **kation**

KATIPO n **katipos**

KATIS ▶ **kati**

KATORGA n type of labour camp

KATS ▶ **kat**

KATSURA n Asian tree

KATTI variant spelling of ▶ **catty**

KATTIS ▶ **katti**

KATYDID n large green grasshopper of N America

KAUGH = **kiaugh**

KAUGHS ▶ **kaugh**

KAUPAPA n strategy, policy, or cause

KAURI n

KAURIES ▶ **kaury**

KAURIS ▶ **kauri**

KAURU n edible stem of the cabbage tree **kaurus**

KAURY variant spelling of ▶ **kauri**

KAVA n Polynesian shrub

KAVAL n type of flute played in the Balkans **kavals**

KAVAS ▶ **kava**

KAVASS n armed Turkish constable

KAW variant spelling of ▶ **caw**

KAWA n protocol or etiquette **kawas**

KAWAU n New Zealand name for black shag **kawaus**

KAWED ▶ **kaw**

KAWING ▶ **kaw**

KAWS ▶ **kaw**

KAY n name of the letter K

KAYAK n, vb **kayaked, kayaker, kayaks**

KAYLE n one of a set of ninepins

KAYLES pl n ninepins

KAYLIED adj (in British slang) intoxicated or drunk

KAYO another term for > **knockout; kayoed, kayoes, kayoing, kayos**

KAYS ▶ **kay**

KAZI variant spelling of ▶ **khazi**

KAZIS ▶ **kazi**

KAZOO n musical instrument **kazoos**

KBAR n kilobar **kbars**

KEA n **keas**

KEASAR archaic variant of ▶ **kaiser**

KEASARS ▶ **keasar**

KEAVIE n archaic or dialect word for a type of crab **keavies**

KEB vb Scots word meaning miscarry or reject a lamb

KEBAB n, vb **kebabs**

KEBAR n Scots word for beam or rafter **kebars**

KEBBED ▸ keb

KEBBIE n Scots word for shepherd's crook **kebbies**

KEBBING ▸ keb

KEBBOCK n Scots word for a cheese **kebbuck**

KEBELE n Ethiopian local council **kebeles**

KEBLAH = **kiblah**

KEBLAHS ▸ keblah

KEBOB = **kebab**

KEBOBS ▸ kebob

KEBS ▸ keb

KECK vb retch or feel nausea **kecked, kecking**

KECKLE Scots variant of ▸ **cackle**

KECKLED ▸ keckle

KECKLES ▸ keckle

KECKS pl n trousers **keckses**

KECKSY n dialect word meaning hollow plant stalk

KED n as in **sheep ked** sheep tick

KEDDAH = **kheda**

KEDDAHS ▸ keddah

KEDGE vb move (a ship) using cable attached to an anchor ▸ n light anchor used for kedging **kedged**

KEDGER n small anchor **kedgers**

KEDGES ▸ kedge

KEDGIER ▸ kedgy

KEDGING ▸ kedge

KEDGY adj dialect word for happy or lively

KEDS ▸ ked

KEECH n old word for lump of fat **keeches**

KEEF = **kif**

KEEFS ▸ keef

KEEK Scot word for ▸ peep; **keeked, keeker, keekers, keeking, keeks**

KEEL n, vb

KEELAGE n fee charged by certain ports

KEELED ▸ keel

KEELER n bargeman **keelers**

KEELIE n kestrel **keelies**

KEELING ▸ keel

KEELMAN n bargeman **keelmen**

KEELS ▸ keel

KEELSON n part of a ship

KEEMA n (in Indian cookery) minced meat **keemas**

KEEN adj, vb, n **keened, keener, keeners, keenest, keening, keenly**

KEENO = **keno**

KEENOS ▸ keeno

KEENS ▸ keen

KEEP vb, n

KEEPER n **keepers**

KEEPING ▸ keep

KEEPNET n cylindrical net used to keep

fish alive

KEEPS ▸ keep

KEESTER = **keister**

KEET short for ▸ parakeet

KEETS ▸ keet

KEEVE n tub or vat **keeves**

KEF = **kif**

KEFFEL dialect word for ▸ horse

KEFFELS ▸ keffel

KEFIR n effervescent drink **kefirs**

KEFS ▸ kef

KEG n, vb

KEGELER = **kegler**

KEGGED, kegger, keggers, kegging ▸ keg

KEGLER n participant in a game of tenpin bowling **keglers**

KEGLING n bowling

KEGS ▸ keg

KEHUA n ghost or spirit **kehuas**

KEIGHT ▸ ketch

KEIR = kier

KEIREN n type of track cycling event **keirens**

KEIRIN n **keirins**

KEIRS ▸ keir

KEISTER n rump

KEITLOA n type of rhinoceros

KEKENO n New Zealand fur seal **kekenos**

KEKS = kecks

KEKSYE = kex

KEKSYES ▸ keksye

KELEP n large ant found in Central and South America **keleps**

KELIM = kilim

KELIMS ▶ kilim

KELL dialect word for ▶ hairnet

KELLAUT = khilat

KELLIES ▶ kelly

KELLS ▶ kell

KELLY n part of a drill system

KELOID n type of scar tissue **keloids**

KELP n, vb **kelped**

KELPER n Falkland Islander **kelpers**

KELPIE n

KELPIES ▶ kelpy

KELPING ▶ kelp

KELPS ▶ kelp

KELPY = kelpie

KELSON = keelson

KELSONS ▶ kelson

KELT n salmon that has recently spawned

KELTER = kilter

KELTERS ▶ kelter

KELTIE variant spelling of ▶ kelty

KELTIES ▶ kelty

KELTS ▶ kelt

KELTY n old Scots word for a drink imposed on someone not thought to be drinking enough

KELVIN n **kelvins**

KEMB old word for ▶ comb

KEMBED ▶ kemb

KEMBING ▶ kemb

KEMBLA n small change **kemblas**

KEMBO = kimbo

KEMBOED ▶ kembo

KEMBOS ▶ kembo

KEMBS ▶ kemb

KEMP n coarse hair or strand of hair ▶ vb dialect word meaning to compete or try to come first **kemped, kemper, kempers**

KEMPIER ▶ kempy

KEMPING ▶ kemp

KEMPLE n variable Scottish measure for hay or straw **kemples**

KEMPS ▶ kemp

KEMPT adj (of hair) tidy

KEMPY ▶ kemp

KEN vb know ▶ n range of knowledge or perception

KENAF another name for ▶ ambary

KENAFS ▶ kenaf

KENCH n bin for salting and preserving fish **kenches**

KENDO n Japanese sport of fencing using wooden staves **kendos**

KENNED ▶ ken

KENNEL n, vb **kennels**

KENNER ▶ ken

KENNERS ▶ ken

KENNET n old word for a small hunting dog **kennets**

KENNETT vb spoil or destroy ruthlessly

KENNING ▶ ken

KENO n game of chance similar to bingo **kenos**

KENOSES ▶ kenosis

KENOSIS n Christ's renunciation of certain divine attributes **kenotic**

KENS ▶ ken

KENT dialect word for ▶ punt

KENTE n brightly coloured handwoven cloth

KENTED ▶ kent

KENTES ▶ kente

KENTIA n plant name **kentias**

KENTING ▶ kent

KENTS ▶ kent

KEP vb catch

KEPHIR = kefir

KEPHIRS ▶ kephir

KEPI n French military cap with a flat top and a horizontal peak **kepis**

KEPPED, keppen, kepping, keppit, keps ▶ kep

KEPT ▶ keep

KERAMIC rare variant of ▶ ceramic

KERATIN n fibrous protein found in the hair and nails

KERB n, vb

KERBAYA n blouse worn by Malay women

KERBED ▶ kerb

KERBING n material used for a kerb

KERBS ▶ kerb

KERCHOO interj atishoo

KEREL n chap or fellow **kerels**

KERERU n New Zealand pigeon **kererus**

KERF n cut made by a saw, an axe, etc ▶ vb

cut **kerfed, kerfing, kerfs**
KERKIER ▶ kerky
KERKY adj stupid
KERMA n quantity of radiation **kermas**
KERMES n dried bodies of female scale insects
KERMESS = kermis
KERMIS n (formerly) annual country festival or carnival
KERN n projection of a printed character ▷ vb furnish (a typeface) with a kern **kerne**
KERNED ▶ kerne
KERNEL n, vb **kernels**
KERNES ▶ kerne
KERNING n provision of kerns in printing
KERNISH adj resembling an armed foot soldier or peasant
KERNITE n light soft colourless or white mineral
KERNS ▶ kern
KERO short for ▷ **kerosene**
KEROGEN n material that produces hydrocarbons when heated
KEROS ▶ kero
KERRIA n type of shrub with yellow flowers **kerrias**
KERRIES ▶ kerry
KERRY n breed of dairy cattle
KERSEY n smooth woollen cloth **kerseys**

KERVE dialect word for ▶ **carve**
KERVED ▶ kerve
KERVES ▶ kerve
KERVING ▶ kerve
KERYGMA n Christian gospel
KESAR old variant of ▶ **kaiser**
KESARS ▶ kesar
KESH n beard and uncut hair traditionally worn by Sikhs **keshes**
KEST old form of ▶ **cast**
KESTING ▶ kest
KESTREL n
KESTS ▶ kest
KET n dialect word for carrion
KETA n type of salmon **ketas**
KETCH n, vb **ketches**
KETCHUP n
KETE n basket woven from flax
KETENE n colourless irritating toxic gas **ketenes**
KETES ▶ kete
KETMIA n as in **bladder ketmia** plant with pale yellow flowers **ketmias**
KETO adj as in **keto form** form of tautomeric compounds
KETOL n nitrogenous substance **ketols**
KETONE n type of organic solvent ketones, ketonic
KETOSE n any monosaccharide that

contains a ketone group
KETOSES ▶ ketosis
KETOSIS n high concentration of ketone bodies in the blood **ketotic**
KETS ▶ ket
KETTLE n **kettles**
KETUBAH n Jewish marriage contract **ketubot**
KEVEL n strong bitt or bollard for securing heavy hawsers **kevels, kevil**
KEVILS ▶ kevil
KEWL nonstandard variant spelling of ▷ **cool**
KEWLER ▶ kewl
KEWLEST ▶ kewl
KEWPIE n type of brightly coloured doll **kewpies**
KEX n any of several hollow-stemmed umbelliferous plants **kexes**

This is another of the great high-scoring three-letter words that use X.

KEY n, adj, vb
KEYCARD n electronic card used as a key
KEYED ▶ key
KEYHOLE n opening for inserting a key into a lock
KEYING ▶ key
KEYINGS ▶ key
KEYLESS ▶ key
KEYLINE n outline image on artwork or

plans to show where it is to be placed

KEYNOTE adj central or dominating ▷ n dominant idea of a speech etc ▷ vb deliver a keynote address to (a political convention, etc)

KEYPAD n small panel with a set of buttons **keypads**

KEYPAL n person one regularly exchanges emails with for fun **keypals**

KEYRING adj of a type of computer drive

KEYS interj children's cry for truce

KEYSET n set of computer keys used for a particular purpose **keysets**

KEYSTER = keister

KEYWAY n engineering device **keyways**

KEYWORD n word or phrase used to find something on a computer

KGOTLA n (in South African English) meeting place **kgotlas**

KHADDAR n cotton cloth **khadi**

KHADIS ▶ khadi

KHAF n letter of the Hebrew alphabet **khafs**

KHAKI adj, n khakis

KHALAT = khilat

KHALATS ▶ khalat

KHALIF variant spelling of ▶ caliph

KHALIFA = caliph

KHALIFS ▶ khalif

KHAMSIN n hot southerly wind

KHAN n title of respect in Afghanistan and central Asia

KHANATE n territory ruled by a khan

KHANDA n khandas

KHANGA = kanga

KHANGAS ▶ khanga

KHANJAR n type of dagger

KHANS ▶ khan

KHANUM feminine form of ▶ khan

KHANUMS ▶ khanum

KHAPH n letter of the Hebrew alphabet **khaphs**

KHARIF n crop harvested at the beginning of winter **kharifs**

KHAT n white-flowered evergreen shrub **khats**

KHAYA n type of African tree

KHAYAL n kind of Indian classical vocal music **khayals**

KHAYAS ▶ khaya

KHAZEN = chazan

KHAZENS ▶ khazen

KHAZI n lavatory **khazis**

KHEDA n enclosure used to capture wild elephants **khedah**

KHEDAHS ▶ khedah

KHEDAS ▶ kheda

KHEDIVA n khedive's wife

KHEDIVE n viceroy of Egypt under Ottoman suzerainty

KHET n Thai district

KHETH = heth

KHETHS ▶ kheth

KHETS ▶ khet

KHI n letter of the Greek alphabet

> This is a letter of the Greek alphabet, also spelt **chi**. It is worth remembering as one of the higher-scoring three-letter words starting with K.

KHILAT n (in the Middle East) gift given to someone as a mark of honour **khilats**

KHILIM = kilim

KHILIMS ▶ khilim

KHIMAR n type of headscarf worn by Muslim women **khimars**

KHIRKAH n dervish's woollen or cotton outer garment

KHIS ▶ khi

KHODJA = khoja

KHODJAS ▶ khodja

KHOJA n teacher in a Muslim school **khojas**

KHOR n watercourse **khors**

KHOTBAH = khutbah

KHOTBEH = khutbah

KHOUM n Mauritanian monetary unit **khoums**

KHUD n Indian ravine **khuds**

KHURTA = kurta

KHURTAS ▶ khurta

KHUTBAH n sermon in a Mosque, especially on a Friday

KI n vital energy

KIAAT n tropical African leguminous tree **kiaats**

KIANG n variety of wild ass **kiangs**

KIAUGH n (in Scots) anxiety **kiaughs**

KIBBE n Middle Eastern dish **kibbeh**

KIBBEHS ▶ kibbeh

KIBBES ▶ kibbe

KIBBI = kibbe

KIBBIS ▶ kibbi

KIBBITZ = kibitz

KIBBLE n bucket used in wells or in mining for hoisting ▷ vb grind into small pieces **kibbled, kibbles**

KIBBUTZ n (in Israel)

KIBE n chilblain

KIBEI n someone of Japanese ancestry born in the US and educated in Japan **kibeis**

KIBES ▶ kibe

KIBITKA n (in Russia) covered sledge or wagon

KIBITZ vb interfere or offer unwanted advice

KIBLA = kiblah

KIBLAH n direction of Mecca **kiblahs**

KIBLAS ▶ kibla

KIBOSH vb put a stop to

KICK vb, n

KICKBOX vb box with hands and feet

KICKED ▶ kick

KICKER n person or thing that kicks **kickers**

KICKIER ▶ kicky

KICKING ▶ kick

KICKOFF n kick that starts a game of football

KICKOUT n (in basketball) instance of kicking the ball

KICKS ▶ kick

KICKUP n fuss **kickups**

KICKY adj excitingly unusual and different

KID n, vb, adj **kidded, kidder, kidders**

KIDDIE = kiddy

KIDDIED ▶ kiddy

KIDDIER n old word for a market trader

KIDDIES ▶ kiddy

KIDDING ▶ kid

KIDDISH ▶ kid

KIDDLE n device for catching fish in a river or in the sea **kiddles**

KIDDO n very informal term of address for a young person **kiddoes, kiddos**

KIDDUSH n (in Judaism) special blessing

KIDDY n affectionate word for a child ▷ vb tease or deceive

KIDEL = kiddle

KIDELS ▶ kidel

KIDGE dialect word for ▶ lively

KIDGIE adj dialect word for friendly and welcoming **kidgier**

KIDLET n humorous word for small child **kidlets**

KIDLIKE ▶ kid

KIDLING n young kid

KIDNAP vb kidnaps

KIDNEY n kidneys

KIDS ▶ kid

KIDSKIN n soft smooth leather

KIDULT n adult interested in entertainments intended for children ▷ adj aimed at or suitable for kidults, or both children and adults **kidults**

KIDVID n informal word for children's video or television **kidvids**

KIEF = kif

KIEFS ▶ kief

KIEKIE n climbing bush plant of New Zealand **kiekies**

KIER n vat in which cloth is bleached

KIERIE n South African cudgel **kieries**

KIERS ▶ kier

KIESTER = keister

KIEV n type of chicken dish

KIEVE = keeve

KIEVES ▶ kieve

KIEVS ▶ kiev

KIF n type of drug

KIFF adj South African slang for excellent

KIFS ▸ kif

KIGHT *n* archaic spelling of kite, the bird of prey **kights**

KIKOI *n* piece of cotton cloth **kikois**

KIKUMON *n* emblem of the imperial family of Japan

KIKUYU *n* type of grass **kikuyus**

KILD old spelling of ▸ **killed**

KILERG *n* 1000 ergs **kilergs**

KILEY = kylie

KILEYS ▸ kiley

KILIM *n* pileless woven rug **kilims**

KILL *vb*, *n*

KILLAS *n* Cornish clay slate

KILLCOW *n* important person

KILLDEE = killdeer

KILLED ▸ kill

KILLER *n* person or animal that kills, esp habitually **killers**

KILLICK *n* small anchor, esp one made of a heavy stone

KILLIE = killifish

KILLIES ▸ killie

KILLING *adj* very tiring ▷ *n* sudden financial success

KILLJOY *n* person who spoils others' pleasure

KILLOCK = killick

KILLS ▸ kill

KILLUT = khilat

KILLUTS ▸ killut

KILN *n*, *vb* kilned,

kilning, kilns

KILO *n*

KILOBAR *n* 1000 bars

KILOBIT *n* 1024 bits

KILORAD *n* 1000 rads

KILOS ▸ kilo

KILOTON *n* one thousand tons

KILP dialect form of ▸ **kelp**

KILPS ▸ kilp

KILT *n*, *vb* kilted

KILTER *n* working order or alignment **kilters**

KILTIE *n* someone wearing a kilt **kilties**

KILTING ▸ kilt

KILTS ▸ kilt

KILTY = kiltie

KIMBO *vb* place akimbo **kimboed, kimbos**

KIMCHEE = kimchi

KIMCHI *n* Korean dish **kimchis**

KIMMER = cummer

KIMMERS ▸ kimmer

KIMONO *n* kimonos

KIN *n*, *adj*

KINA *n* standard monetary unit of Papua New Guinea

KINARA *n* African candle holder **kinaras**

KINAS ▸ kina

KINASE *n* type of enzyme **kinases**

KINCHIN old slang word for ▸ **child**

KINCOB *n* fine silk fabric **kincobs**

KIND *adj*, *n*, *vb*

KINDA *adv* very informal shortening of kind of

KINDED ▸ kind

KINDER *adj* more kind ▷ *n* kindergarten or nursery school

KINDERS ▸ kind

KINDEST ▸ kind

KINDIE = kindy

KINDIES ▸ kindy

KINDING ▸ kind

KINDLE *vb* kindled, kindler, kindles

KINDLY *adj* having a warm-hearted nature ▷ *adv* in a considerate way

KINDRED *adj*, *n*

KINDS ▸ kind

KINDY *n* kindergarten

KINE *pl n* cows or cattle ▷ *n* Japanese pestle

KINEMA = cinema

KINEMAS ▸ kinema

KINES *n* ▸ **kine**

KINESES ▸ kinesis

KINESIC *adj* of or relating to kinesics

KINESIS *n* movement of an organism

KINETIC *adj*

KINETIN *n* plant hormone

KINFOLK another word for ▸ **kinsfolk**

KING *n*, *vb*

KINGCUP *n* yellow-flowered plant

KINGDOM *n*

KINGED ▸ king

KINGING ▸ king

KINGLE *n* Scots word for a type of hard rock **kingles**

KINGLET *n* king of a small or insignificant territory

KINGLY adj appropriate to a king ▷ adv in a manner appropriate to a king

KINGPIN n

KINGS ▶ king

KININ n type of polypeptide **kinins**

KINK n, vb **kinked**

KINKIER ▶ kinky

KINKILY ▶ kinky

KINKING ▶ kink

KINKLE n little kink **kinkles**

KINKS ▶ kink

KINKY adj

KINLESS adj without any relatives

KINO = keno

KINONE n benzoquinone **kinones**

KINOS ▶ kino

KINRED old form of ▶ kindred

KINREDS ▶ kinred

KINS ▶ kin

KINSHIP n

KINSMAN n relative **kinsmen**

KIORE n small brown rat native to New Zealand **kiores**

KIOSK n **kiosks**

KIP vb, n

KIPE n dialect word for a basket for catching fish **kipes**

KIPP uncommon variant of ▶ kip

KIPPA n skullcap worn by male Jews

KIPPAGE n Scots word for a state of anger or excitement

KIPPAS ▶ kippa

KIPPED ▶ kip

KIPPEN ▶ kep

KIPPER n, vb **kippers**

KIPPING ▶ kip

KIPPS ▶ kipp

KIPS ▶ kip

KIPSKIN = kip

KIPUNJI n Tanzanian species of monkey

KIR n drink made from dry white wine and cassis

KIRANA n **kiranas**

KIRBEH n leather bottle **kirbehs**

KIRBY n as in kirby grip type of hairgrip

KIRIMON n Japanese imperial crest

KIRK Scot word for ▶ church

KIRKED ▶ kirk

KIRKING ▶ kirk

KIRKMAN n member or strong upholder of the Kirk **kirkmen**

KIRKS ▶ kirk

KIRKTON n village or town with a parish church

KIRMESS = kermis

KIRN dialect word for ▶ churn

KIRNED ▶ kirn

KIRNING ▶ kirn

KIRNS ▶ kirn

KIRPAN n short sword traditionally carried by Sikhs **kirpans**

KIRRI n Hottentot stick **kirris**

KIRS ▶ kir

KIRSCH n cherry brandy

KIRTAN n devotional singing **kirtans**

KIRTLE n woman's skirt or dress ▷ vb dress with a kirtle **kirtled, kirtles**

KIS ▶ ki

KISAN n peasant or farmer **kisans**

KISH n graphite formed on the surface of molten iron **kishes**

KISHKA = kishke

KISHKAS ▶ kishka

KISHKE n stuffed beef or fowl intestine, boiled and roasted **kishkes**

KISMAT = kismet

KISMATS ▶ kismat

KISMET n fate or destiny **kismets**

KISS vb, n **kissed**

KISSEL n Russian dessert **kissels**

KISSER n mouth or face **kissers**

KISSES ▶ kiss

KISSIER ▶ kissy

KISSING ▶ kiss

KISSY adj showing exaggerated affection

KIST n large wooden chest ▷ vb place in a coffin **kisted, kistful, kisting, kists**

KIT n, vb

KITBAG n **kitbags**

KITCHEN n, vb

KITE n, vb **kited**

KITENGE n thick cotton cloth

KITER ▶ kite

KITERS ▶ kite

KITES ▶ kite

KITH *n* one's friends and acquaintances
KITHARA *variant of* ▸ cithara
KITHE ▸ kythe
KITHED ▸ kithe
KITHES ▸ kithe
KITHING ▸ kithe
KITHS ▸ kith
KITING ▸ kite
KITINGS ▸ kite
KITLING *dialect word for* ▸ kitten
KITS ▸ kit
KITSCH *n* art or literature with popular sentimental appeal ▸ *n* object or art that is tawdry, vulgarized, oversentimental or pretentious **kitschy**
KITSET ▸ kitsets
KITTED ▸ kit
KITTEL *n* white garment worn for certain Jewish rituals or burial **kittels**
KITTEN *n, vb* kittens, kitteny
KITTIES ▸ kitty
KITTING ▸ kit
KITTLE *adj* capricious and unpredictable ▸ *vb* be troublesome or puzzling to (someone) **kittled, kittler, kittles**
KITTLY *Scots word for* ▸ ticklish
KITTUL *n* type of palm from which jaggery sugar comes **kittuls**
KITTY *n*
KITUL ▸ kittul

KITULS ▸ kitul
KIVA *n* large room in a Pueblo Indian village **kivas**
KIWI *n* kiwis
KLANG *n* (in music) kind of tone **klangs**
KLAP *vb* slap or spank **klapped, klaps**
KLATCH *n* gathering, especially over coffee **klatsch**
KLAVERN *n* local Ku Klux Klan group
KLAVIER = clavier
KLAXON *n* loud horn used on emergency vehicles ▸ *vb* hoot with a klaxon **klaxons**
KLEAGLE *n* person with a particular rank in the Ku Klux Klan
KLEENEX *n* tradename for a kind of tissue
KLEPHT *n* group of Greeks **klephts**
KLEPTO *n* compulsive thief **kleptos**
KLETT *n* lightweight climbing boot **kletts**
KLEZMER *n* Jewish folk musician
KLICK *n* kilometre **klicks**
KLIEG *n as in* **klieg light** intense carbon-arc light
KLIK *US military slang word for* ▸ kilometre
KLIKS ▸ klik
KLINKER *n* type of brick used in paving
KLIPDAS *n* rock hyrax
KLISTER *n* type of ski

dressing for improving grip on snow
KLONG *n* type of canal in Thailand **klongs**
KLOOCH = kloochman
KLOOF *n* kloofs
KLOOTCH = kloochman
KLUDGE *n* untidy solution ▸ *vb* cobble something together **kludged, kludges, kludgey, kludgy, kluge**
KLUGED ▸ kluge
KLUGES ▸ kluge
KLUGING ▸ kluge
KLUTZ *n* clumsy or stupid person **klutzes, klutzy**
KNACK *n, vb*
KNACKED *adj* broken or worn out
KNACKER *n* buyer of old horses for killing ▸ *vb* exhaust
KNACKS ▸ knack
KNACKY *adj* old or dialect word for cunning or artful
KNAG *n* knot in wood
KNAGGY *adj* knotty
KNAGS ▸ knag
KNAIDEL = kneidel
KNAP *n* crest of a hill ▸ *vb* hit, hammer, or chip **knapped, knapper**
KNAPPLE *old word for* ▸ nibble
KNAPS ▸ knap
KNAR *old spelling of* ▸ gnar
KNARL *old spelling of* ▸ gnarl
KNARLS ▸ knarl

KNARLY = gnarly

KNARRED ▶ knar

KNARRY ▶ knar

KNARS ▶ knar

KNAUR *variant form of* ▶ knur

KNAURS ▶ knaur

KNAVE n

KNAVERY n dishonest behaviour

KNAVES ▶ knave

KNAVISH ▶ knave

KNAWE = knawel

KNAWEL n type of Old World plant **knawels**

KNAWES ▶ knawe

KNEAD vb kneaded, kneader, kneads

KNEE n, vb

KNEECAP *nontechnical name for* ▶ patella

KNEED ▶ knee

KNEEING ▶ knee

KNEEL vb, n kneeled, kneeler, kneels

KNEEPAD n protective covering for the knee

KNEEPAN *another word for* ▶ patella

KNEES ▶ knee

KNEIDEL n (in Jewish cookery) small dumpling

KNELL n, vb knelled, knells

KNELT ▶ kneel

KNESSET n parliament or assembly

KNEVELL vb old Scots word meaning beat

KNEW ▶ know

KNICKER n woman's or girl's undergarment

KNICKS pl n knickers

KNIFE n, vb knifed, knifer, knifers, knifes, knifing

KNIGHT n, vb knights

KNISH n type of dish knishes

KNIT vb, n

KNITCH *dialect word for* ▶ bundle

KNITS ▶ knit

KNITTED ▶ knit

KNITTER ▶ knit

KNITTLE n old word for string or cord

KNIVE *rare variant of* ▶ knife

KNIVED ▶ knive

KNIVES ▶ knife

KNIVING ▶ knive

KNOB n, vb knobbed

KNOBBER n two-year-old male deer

KNOBBLE n small knob
▷ vb dialect word meaning strike

KNOBBLY adj covered with small bumps

KNOBBY ▶ knob

KNOBS ▶ knob

KNOCK vb, n knocked

KNOCKER n

KNOCKS ▶ knock

KNOLL n, vb knolled, knoller, knolls, knolly

KNOP n knob, esp an ornamental one knopped, knops

KNOSP n budlike architectural feature knosps

KNOT n, vb knots, knotted, knotter

KNOTTY adj full of knots

KNOUT n stout whip
▷ vb whip knouted, knouts

KNOW vb be or feel certain of the truth of (information etc)

KNOWE = knoll

KNOWER ▶ know

KNOWERS ▶ know

KNOWES ▶ knowe

KNOWHOW n ingenuity, knack, or skill

KNOWING, known, knowns, knows
▶ know

KNUB *dialect word for* ▶ knob

KNUBBLE vb dialect word for beat or pound using one's fists

KNUBBLY adj having small lumps or protuberances

KNUBBY adj knub

KNUBS ▶ knub

KNUCKLE n knuckly

KNUR n knot or protuberance in a tree trunk or in wood

KNURL n small ridge, often one of a series
▷ vb impress with a series of fine ridges or serrations knurled, knurls

KNURLY *rare word for* ▶ gnarled

KNURR = knur

KNURRS ▶ knur

KNURS ▶ knur

KNUT n dandy knuts

KO n (in New Zealand) traditional digging tool

KOA *n* Hawaiian leguminous tree

KOALA *n* koalas

KOAN *n* (in Zen Buddhism) problem that admits no logical solution **koans**

KOAS ▶ koa

KOB *n* any of several species of antelope

KOBAN *n* old oval-shaped Japanese gold coin **kobang**

KOBANGS ▶ kobang

KOBANS ▶ koban

KOBO *n* Nigerian monetary unit

KOBOLD *n* mischievous household sprite **kobolds**

KOBOS ▶ kobo

KOBS ▶ kob

KOCHIA *n* any of several plants whose foliage turns dark red **kochias**

KOEKOEA *n* long-tailed cuckoo of New Zealand

KOEL *n* any of several parasitic cuckoos **koels**

KOFF *n* Dutch masted merchant vessel **koffs**

KOFTA *n* Indian dish **koftas**

KOFTGAR *n* (in India) person skilled at inlaying steel with gold

KOGAL *n* (in Japan) trendy teenage girl **kogals**

KOHA *n* gift or donation, esp of cash

KOHANIM ▶ kohen

KOHAS ▶ koha

KOHEN *n* member of the Jewish priestly caste

KOHL *n* cosmetic powder **kohls**

KOI *n* any of various ornamental forms of the common carp

KOINE *n* common language among speakers of different languages **koines**

KOIS ▶ koi

KOJI *n* Japanese steamed rice **kojis**

KOKA *n* former type of score in judo

KOKAKO *n* type of crow **kokakos**

KOKANEE *n* type of freshwater salmon

KOKAS ▶ koka

KOKER *n* Guyanese sluice **kokers**

KOKIRI *n* type of rough-skinned New Zealand triggerfish **kokiris**

KOKOBEH *adj* (of certain fruit) having a rough skin

KOKOPU *n* any of several small freshwater fish of New Zealand **kokopus**

KOKOWAI *n* type of clay

KOKRA *n* type of wood **kokras**

KOKUM *n* tropical tree **kokums**

KOLA *n* as in kola nut caffeine-containing seed used in medicine and soft drinks

KOLACKY *n* sweet bun with a fruit, jam, or nut filling

KOLAS ▶ kola

KOLBASI = kolbassi

KOLHOZ = kolkhoz

KOLHOZY = kolkhoz

KOLKHOS = kolkhoz

KOLKHOZ *n* (formerly) collective farm in the Soviet Union **kolkoz**

KOLKOZY = kolkoz

KOLO *n* Serbian folk dance **kolos**

KOMATIK *n* type of sledge

KOMBU *n* dark brown seaweed **kombus**

KON *old word for* ▶ know

KONAKI = koneke

KONAKIS = konaki

KONBU = kombu

KONBUS ▶ konbu

KOND = kon

KONDO *n* (in Uganda) thief or armed robber **kondos**

KONEKE *n* type of farm vehicle **konekes**

KONFYT *n* South African fruit preserve **konfyts**

KONGONI *n* E African hartbeest

KONINI *n* edible dark purple berry **koninis**

KONK = conk

KONKED ▶ konk

KONKING ▶ konk

KONKS ▶ konk

KONNING ▶ kon

KONS ▶ kon

KOODOO = kudu

KOODOOS ▶ koodoo

KOOK n eccentric person ▷ vb dialect word for vanish **kooked**
KOOKIE = kooky
KOOKIER ▶ kooky
KOOKILY ▶ kooky
KOOKING ▶ kook
KOOKS ▶ kook
KOOKY adj crazy, eccentric, or foolish
KOOLAH old form of ▶ koala
KOOLAHS ▶ koolah
KOORI n Australian Aborigine **koories, kooris**
KOP n prominent isolated hill or mountain in southern Africa
KOPECK n former Russian monetary unit **kopecks, kopek**
KOPEKS ▶ kopek
KOPH n 19th letter in the Hebrew alphabet **kophs**
KOPIYKA n monetary unit of Ukraine **kopiyok**
KOPJE n small hill **kopjes**
KOPPA n consonantal letter in the Greek alphabet **koppas**
KOPPIE = kopje
KOPPIES ▶ koppie
KOPS ▶ kop
KOR n ancient Hebrew unit of capacity
KORA n West African instrument
KORAI ▶ kore
KORARI n native New

Zealand flax plant **koraris**
KORAS ▶ kora
KORAT n as in korat cat rare blue-grey breed of cat **korats**
KORE n ancient Greek statue of a young woman wearing clothes
KORERO n talk or discussion ▷ vb speak or converse **koreros**
KORES ▶ kore
KORKIR n variety of lichen used in dyeing **korkirs**
KORMA n type of mild Indian dish **kormas**
KORO n elderly Māori man
KORORA n small New Zealand penguin **kororas**
KOROS ▶ koro
KOROWAI n decorative woven cloak worn by a Māori chief
KORS ▶ kor
KORU n stylized curved pattern used esp in carving
KORUN ▶ koruna
KORUNA n standard monetary unit of the Czech Republic and Slovakia **korunas, koruny**
KORUS ▶ koru
KOS n Indian unit of distance **koses**
KOSHER adj, n, vb **koshers**
KOSMOS variant form of

▶ cosmos
KOSS = kos
KOSSES ▶ koss
KOTARE n small greenish-blue kingfisher **kotares**
KOTO n Japanese stringed instrument **kotos**
KOTOW = kowtow
KOTOWED ▶ kotow
KOTOWER ▶ kotow
KOTOWS ▶ kotow
KOTUKU n type of white heron **kotukus**
KOTWAL n senior police officer or magistrate in an Indian town **kotwals**
KOULAN = kulan
KOULANS ▶ koulan
KOUMIS, koumiss, koumys, koumyss = kumiss
KOUPREY n large wild SE Asian ox
KOURA n New Zealand freshwater crayfish **kouras**
KOUROI ▶ kouros
KOUROS n ancient Greek statue of a young man
KOUSSO n Abyssinian tree **koussos**
KOW old variant of ▶ cow
This dialect variant of cow scores well for a three-letter word, and can be a good one to form when playing in more than one direction.

KOWHAI n kowhais

KOWS ▸ kow

KOWTOW vb, n kowtows

KRAAL n, adj, vb kraaled, kraals

KRAB = karabiner

KRABS ▸ krab

KRAFT n strong wrapping paper krafts

KRAIT n brightly coloured venomous snake of S and SE Asia kraits

KRAKEN n legendary sea monster krakens

KRANG n dead whale from which the blubber has been removed krangs

KRANS n sheer rock face kranses, krantz, kranz, kranzes

KRATER = crater

KRATERS ▸ krater

KRAUT n sauerkraut krauts

KREEP n lunar substance kreeps

KREESE = kris

KREESED ▸ kreese

KREESES ▸ kreese

KREMLIN n citadel of any Russian city

KRENG = krang

KRENGS ▸ kreng

KREUZER = kreutzer

KREWE n club taking part in New Orleans carnival parade krewes

KRILL n small shrimplike sea creature krills

KRIMMER n tightly curled light grey fur

KRIS n type of Malayan and Indonesian knife ▸ vb stab or slash with a kris krised, krises, krising

KRONA n standard monetary unit of Sweden

KRONE n standard monetary unit of Norway and Denmark kronen, kroner

KRONOR ▸ krona

KRONUR ▸ krona

KROON n standard monetary unit of Estonia krooni, kroons

KRUBI n aroid plant with an unpleasant smell krubis, krubut

KRUBUTS ▸ krubut

KRULLER variant spelling of ▸ cruller

KRUMPER > krumping

KRUNK n style of hip-hop music

KRUNKED ▸ crunked

KRUNKS ▸ krunk

KRYPSES ▸ krypsis

KRYPSIS n idea that Christ made secret use of his divine attributes

KRYPTON n

KRYTRON n type of fast electronic gas-discharge switch

KSAR old form of ▸ tsar

KSARS ▸ ksar

KUCCHA = kaccha

KUCCHAS ▸ kuccha

KUCHCHA = kacha

KUCHEN n breadlike cake kuchens

KUDLIK n Inuit soapstone seal-oil lamp kudliks

KUDO variant of ▸ kudos

KUDOS n kudoses

KUDU n kudus

KUDZU n hairy leguminous climbing plant kudzus

KUE n name of the letter Q

KUEH n (in Malaysia) any cake of Malay, Chinese, or Indian origin

KUES ▸ kue

KUFI n cap for Muslim man kufis

KUFIYAH = keffiyeh

KUGEL n baked pudding in traditional Jewish cooking kugels

KUIA n Māori female elder or elderly woman kuias

KUKRI n heavy, curved knife used by Gurkhas kukris

KUKU n mussel kukus

KULA n ceremonial gift exchange among islanders in the W Pacific

KULAK n (formerly) property-owning Russian peasant kulaki, kulaks

KULAN n Asiatic wild ass kulans

KULAS ▸ kula

KULBASA ▷ kielbasa

KULFI n Indian dessert **kulfis**

KULTUR n German civilization **kulturs**

KUMARA n **kumaras**

KUMARI n (in Indian English) maiden **kumaris**

KUMERA n **kumara**

KUMERAS ▷ kumera

KUMISS n drink made from fermented mare's or other milk

KUMITE n freestyle sparring or fighting **kumites**

KUMMEL n German liqueur **kummels**

KUMQUAT n

KUMYS = kumiss

KUMYSES ▷ kumys

KUNA n standard monetary unit of Croatia **kune**

KUNJOOS adj (in Indian English) mean or stingy

KUNKAR n type of limestone **kunkars, kunkur**

KUNKURS ▷ kunkur

KUNZITE n variety of the mineral spodumene

KURBASH vb whip with a hide whip

KURGAN n Russian burial mound **kurgans**

KURI n mongrel dog **kuris**

KURRE old variant of ▷ **cur**

KURRES ▷ kurre

KURSAAL n public room

at a health resort

KURTA n long loose garment **kurtas**

KURU n degenerative disease of the nervous system **kurus**

> This word for a kind of sickness found in New Guinea can give you something to laugh about when you have two Us to dispose of.

KURVEY vb (in old South African English) transport goods by ox cart **kurveys**

KUSSO variant spelling of ▷ **kousso**

KUSSOS ▷ kusso

KUTA n (in Indian English) male dog **kutas**

KUTCH = catechu

KUTCHA adj makeshift or not solid

KUTCHES ▷ kutch

KUTI n (in Indian English) female dog or bitch **kutis**

KUTU n body louse **kutus**

KUVASZ n breed of dog from Hungary

KUZU = kudzu

> A Japanese climbing plant, this can be a great word for getting a high score out of a difficult rack.

KUZUS ▷ kuzu

KVAS = kvass

KVASES ▷ kvas

KVASS n alcoholic drink **kvasses**

KVELL vb US word meaning be happy **kvelled, kvells**

KVETCH vb complain or grumble

KVETCHY adj tending to grumble or complain

KWACHA n standard monetary unit of Zambia **kwachas**

KWAITO n type of South African pop music **kwaitos**

KWANZA n standard monetary unit of Angola **kwanzas**

KWELA n type of pop music **kwelas**

KY pl n Scots word for cows

KYACK n type of panier **kyacks**

KYAK = kayak

KYAKS ▷ kyak

KYANG = kiang

KYANGS ▷ kyang

KYANISE = kyanize

KYANITE n grey, green, or blue mineral

KYANIZE vb treat (timber) with corrosive sublimate

KYAR = coir

KYARS ▷ kyar

KYAT n standard monetary unit of Myanmar **kyats**

KYBO n temporary lavatory used when camping **kybos**

KYBOSH = kibosh

KYDST ▷ kythe

KYE n Korean fundraising meeting **kyes**

KYLE n narrow strait or channel **kyles**

KYLICES ▶ kylix

KYLIE n type of boomerang **kylies**

KYLIKES ▶ kylix

KYLIN n (in Chinese art) mythical animal **kylins**

KYLIX n drinking vessel used in ancient Greece

KYLOE n breed of beef cattle **kyloes**

KYND old variant of ▶ kind

KYNDE old variant of ▶ kind

KYNDED ▶ kynd

KYNDES ▶ kynde

KYNDING ▶ kynd

KYNDS ▶ kynd

KYNE pl n archaic word for cows

KYOGEN n type of Japanese drama **kyogens**

KYPE n hook on the lower jaw of a mature male salmon **kypes**

KYRIE n type of prayer **kyries**

KYTE n belly **kytes**

KYTHE vb appear **kythed, kythes, kything**

KYU n (in judo) one of the five student grades **kyus**

This means a novice grade in judo, and its unusual combination of letters makes it a useful word to remember when you have an unpromising set of letters on your rack.

LI

L can be a difficult letter to use well, especially when you need to play short words. Just three two-letter words begin with **L**: **la, li** and **lo**. Knowing this will save you valuable time in a game, especially when you are trying to fit words into a crowded board. There aren't very many three-letter words either, but don't forget common words like **lab** (5 points), **law** (6), **lay** (6), **low** (6) and **lye** (6). Try to remember the three-letter words that combine **L** with **X**: **lax, lex, lox** and **lux** (10 points each). These are particularly useful towards the end of a game if you have an **X** but little opportunity to play it. There is also the very useful **luz** for 12 points.

LA n exclamation of surprise or emphasis ▷ n the sixth note of the musical scale

LAAGER n (in Africa) a camp defended by a circular formation of wagons ▷ vb form (wagons) into a laager **laagers**

LAARI = **lari**

LAARIS ▶ **laari**

LAB n

LABARA ▶ **labarum**

LABARUM n standard carried in Christian processions

LABDA = **lambda**

LABDAS ▶ **labda**

LABEL n, vb **labeled, labeler**

LABELLA > **labellum**

LABELS ▶ **label**

LABIA ▶ **labium**

LABIAL adj of the lips ▷ n speech sound that involves the lips **labials**

LABIATE n plant with square stems, aromatic leaves, and a two-lipped flower ▷ adj of this family

LABILE adj (of a compound) prone to chemical change

LABIS n cochlear **labises**

LABIUM n lip or liplike structure

LABLAB n twining leguminous plant

lablabs

LABOR = **labour**

LABORED = **laboured**

LABORER = **labourer**

LABORS ▶ **labor**

LABOUR n, vb **labours**

LABRA ▶ **labrum**

LABRAL adj of or like a lip

LABRET n piece of bone or shell **labrets**

LABRID = **labroid**

LABRIDS ▶ **labrid**

LABROID n type of fish ▷ adj of or relating to such fish

LABROSE adj thick-lipped

LABRUM n lip or liplike part **labrums**

LABRYS n type of axe

LABS ▶ lab

LAC = lakh

LACE n, vb **laced, lacer, lacers, laces**

LACET n braidwork **lacets**

LACEY ▶ lacy

LACHES n unreasonable delay in pursuing a legal remedy

LACIER ▶ lacy

LACIEST ▶ lacy

LACILY ▶ lacy

LACING ▶ lace

LACINGS ▶ lace

LACINIA n narrow fringe on petal

LACK n, vb **lacked**

LACKER variant spelling of ▶ lacquer

LACKERS ▶ lacker

LACKEY n, vb **lackeys**

LACKING ▶ lack

LACKS ▶ lack

LACMUS n old form of litmus

LACONIC adj

LACQUER n, vb

LACQUEY = lackey

LACS ▶ lac

LACTAM n any of a group of inner amides **lactams**

LACTARY adj relating to milk

LACTASE n any of a group of enzymes that hydrolyse lactose to glucose and galactose

LACTATE vb, n

LACTEAL adj of or like milk ▷ n any of the lymphatic vessels that convey chyle from the

small intestine to the blood

LACTEAN another word for ▶ lacteous

LACTIC adj of or derived from milk

LACTONE n any of a class of organic compounds

LACTOSE n

LACUNA n gap or missing part, esp in a document or series **lacunae, lacunal**

LACUNAR n ceiling, soffit, or vault having coffers ▷ adj having a lacuna

LACUNAS ▶ lacuna

LACUNE n hiatus **lacunes**

LACY adj fine, like lace

LAD n

LADANUM = labdanum

LADDER n, vb **ladders, laddery**

LADDIE n **laddies**

LADDISH adj behaving in a macho or immature manner

LADDISM n laddish attitudes and behaviour

LADE vb put cargo on board ▷ n watercourse **laded**

LADEN adj, vb **ladened, ladens**

LADER ▶ lade

LADERS ▶ lade

LADES ▶ lade

LADETTE n young woman who behaves like a young man

LADHOOD ▶ lad

LADIES n women's public toilet

LADIFY = ladyfy

LADING ▶ lade

LADINGS ▶ lade

LADINO n Italian variety of white clover **ladinos**

LADLE n, vb **ladled**

LADLER n person who serves with a ladle **ladlers**

LADLES ▶ ladle

LADLING ▶ ladle

LADRON = ladrone

LADRONE n thief

LADRONS ▶ ladron

LADS ▶ lad

LADY n, adj

LADYBOY n transvestite or transsexual from the Far East

LADYBUG = ladybird

LADYCOW another word for ▶ ladybird

LADYFLY another word for ▶ ladybird

LADYFY vb make a lady of (someone)

LADYISH ▶ lady

LADYISM ▶ lady

LADYKIN n endearing form of lady

LAER another word for ▶ laager

LAERED ▶ laer

LAERING ▶ laer

LAERS ▶ laer

LAESIE old form of ▶ lazy

LAETARE n fourth Sunday of Lent

LAEVO adj on the left

LAG vb, n

LAGAN n goods or wreckage on the sea bed **lagans**

LAGENA n bottle with a narrow neck **lagenas**

LEGEND = lagan

LAGENDS ▶ lagend

LAGER n, vb **lagered, lagers**

LAGGARD n, adj

LAGGED ▶ lag

LAGGEN n spar of a barrel **laggens**

LAGGER n person who lags pipes **laggers**

LAGGIN = laggen

LAGGING ▶ lag

LAGGINS ▶ laggin

LAGOON n **lagoons**

LAGS ▶ lag

LAGUNA n lagoon **lagunas**

LAGUNE = lagoon

LAGUNES ▶ lagune

LAH n (in tonic sol-fa) sixth degree of any major scale

LAHAR n landslide of volcanic debris and water **lahars**

LAHS ▶ lah

LAIC adj laical ▷ n layman

LAICAL adj secular

LAICH n low-lying piece of land **laichs**

LAICISE = laicize

LAICISM ▶ laic

LAICITY n state of being laical

LAICIZE vb remove ecclesiastical status from

LAICS ▶ laic

LAID Scots form of ▶ load

LAIDED ▶ laid

LAIDING ▶ laid

LAIDLY adj very ugly

LAIDS ▶ laid

LAIGH adj low-lying ▷ n area of low-lying ground **laigher, laighs**

LAIK vb play (a game, etc)

LAIKA n type of small dog **laikas**

LAIKED, laiker, laikers, laiking, laiks ▶ laik

LAIN ▶ lie

LAIPSE vb beat soundly **laipsed, laipses**

LAIR n, vb

LAIRAGE n accommodation for farm animals

LAIRD n

LAIRDLY adj pertaining to laird(s)

LAIRDS ▶ laird

LAIRED ▶ lair

LAIRIER ▶ lairy

LAIRING ▶ lair

LAIRISE = lairize

LAIRIZE vb show off

LAIRS ▶ lair

LAIRY adj gaudy or flashy

LAISSE n type of rhyme scheme **laisses**

LAITH Scots form of ▶ loath

LAITHLY = laidly

LAITIES ▶ laity

LAITY n

LAKE n, vb

LAKEBED n bed of lake

LAKED ▶ lake

LAKELET n small lake

LAKER n lake cargo vessel **lakers**

LAKES ▶ lake

LAKH n (in India) 100 000, esp referring to this sum of rupees **lakhs**

LAKIER ▶ laky

LAKIEST ▶ laky

LAKIN short form of ▶ ladykin

LAKING ▶ lake

LAKINGS ▶ lake

LAKINS ▶ lakin

LAKISH adj similar to poetry of Lake poets

LAKSA n (in Malaysia) Chinese dish of rice noodles in curry or hot soup **laksas**

LAKY adj of the reddish colour of the pigment lake

LALANG n coarse weedy Malaysian grass **lalangs**

LALDIE n great gusto **laldies, laldy**

LALIQUE n ornamental glass

LALL vb make bad 'l' or 'r' sounds

LALLAN n literary version of the English spoken in Lowland Scotland **lalland, lallans**

LALLED ▶ lall

LALLING ▶ lall

LALLS ▶ lall

LAM vb attack vigorously

LAMA n **lamas**

LAMB n, vb

LAMBADA n erotic Brazilian dance

LAMBAST vb beat or thrash

LAMBDA n 11th letter of the Greek alphabet **lambdas**

LAMBED ▶ lamb

LAMBENT adj (of a flame) flickering softly

LAMBER n person that attends to lambing ewes **lambers**

LAMBERT n cgs unit of illumination, equal to 1 lumen per square centimetre

LAMBIE = lambkin

LAMBIER ▶ lamby

LAMBIES ▶ lambie

LAMBING n birth of lambs at the end of winter

LAMBKIN n young lamb

LAMBOYS n skirt-like piece of armour made from metal strips

LAMBS ▶ lamb

LAMBY adj lamb-like

LAME adj, vb, n

LAMED n 12th letter in the Hebrew alphabet **lamedh**

LAMEDHS ▶ lamedh

LAMEDS ▶ lamed

LAMELLA n thin layer, plate, etc, like the calcified layers of which bone is formed

LAMELY ▶ lame

LAMENT vb, n laments

LAMER ▶ lame

LAMES ▶ lame

LAMEST ▶ lame

LAMETER Scots form of ▶ lamiger

LAMIA n female monster with a snake's body and a woman's head and breasts **lamiae, lamias**

LAMIGER n disabled person

LAMINA n thin plate, esp of bone or mineral **laminae**

LAMINAL n consonant articulated with blade of tongue

LAMINAR ▶ lamina

LAMINAS ▶ lamina

LAMING ▶ lame

LAMININ n type of protein

LAMISH adj rather lame

LAMITER = lameter

LAMMED ▶ lam

LAMMER Scots word for ▶ amber

LAMMERS ▶ lammer

LAMMIE = lammy

LAMMIES ▶ lammy

LAMMING ▶ lam

LAMMY n thick woollen jumper

LAMP n, vb

LAMPAD n candlestick **lampads**

LAMPAS n swelling of the mucous membrane of the hard palate of horses

LAMPED ▶ lamp

LAMPER n lamprey

LAMPERN n migratory European lamprey

LAMPERS ▶ lamper

LAMPING ▶ lamp

LAMPION n oil-burning lamp

LAMPLIT adj lit by lamps

LAMPOON n, vb

LAMPREY n

LAMPS ▶ lamp

LAMPUKA = lampuki

LAMPUKI n type of fish

LAMS ▶ lam

LAMSTER n fugitive

LANA n wood from genipap tree

LANAI Hawaiian word for ▶ veranda

LANAIS ▶ lanai

LANAS ▶ lana

LANATE adj having or consisting of a woolly covering of hairs **lanated**

LANCE n, vb lanced

LANCER n formerly, cavalry soldier armed with a lance

LANCERS n quadrille for eight or sixteen couples

LANCES ▶ lance

LANCET n lancets

LANCH obsolete form of ▶ launch

LANCHED ▶ lanch

LANCHES ▶ lanch

LANCING ▶ lance

LAND n, vb

LANDAU n landaus

LANDE n type of moorland in SW France

LANDED adj

LANDER n spacecraft which lands on a planet or other body **landers**

LANDES ▶ lande

LANDING n

LANDLER n Austrian country dance

LANDMAN n person who lives and works on land **landmen**

LANDS pl n holdings in land

LANE n

LANELY Scots form of ▸ **lonely**

LANES ▸ **lane**

LANEWAY n lane

LANG Scot word for ▸ **long**

LANGAHA n type of Madagascan snake

LANGAR n dining hall in a gurdwara **langars**

LANGEST ▸ **lang**

LANGLEY n unit of solar radiation

LANGREL = **langrage**

LANGUE n language considered as an abstract system

LANGUED adj having a tongue

LANGUES ▸ **langue**

LANGUET n anything resembling a tongue

LANGUID adj

LANGUOR n

LANGUR n type of arboreal Old World monkey **langurs**

LANIARD = **lanyard**

LANIARY adj adapted for tearing ▸ n tooth adapted for tearing

LANITAL n fibre used in production of synthetic wool

LANK adj, vb **lanked, lanker, lankest**

LANKIER ▸ **lanky**

LANKILY ▸ **lanky**

LANKING ▸ **lank**

LANKLY ▸ **lank**

LANKS ▸ **lank**

LANKY adj

LANNER n large falcon **lanners**

LANOLIN n

LANOSE = **lanate**

LANT n stale urine

LANTANA n

LANTERN n, vb

LANTS ▸ **lant**

LANUGO n layer of fine hairs, esp the covering of the human fetus before birth **lanugos**

LANX n dish; plate

LANYARD n

LAOGAI n forced labour camp in China **laogais**

LAP n, vb

LAPDOG n **lapdogs**

LAPEL n **lapeled, lapels**

LAPFUL = **lap**

LAPFULS ▸ **lapful**

LAPHELD adj small enough to be used on one's lap

LAPIDES ▸ **lapis**

LAPILLI ▸ **lapillus**

LAPIN n castrated rabbit **lapins**

LAPIS n as in **lapis lazuli** brilliant blue mineral gemstone **lapises**

LAPJE = **lappie**

LAPJES ▸ **lapje**

LAPPED ▸ **lap**

LAPPEL = **lapel**

LAPPELS ▸ **lappel**

LAPPER n one that laps ▸ vb curdle **lappers**

LAPPET n small hanging flap **lappets**

LAPPIE n rag **lappies**

LAPPING ▸ **lap**

LAPS ▸ **lap**

LAPSANG n Chinese tea

LAPSE n, vb **lapsed, lapser, lapsers, lapses, lapsing**

LAPSUS n lapse or error

LAPTOP adj small enough to fit on a user's lap ▸ n small computer **laptops**

LAPTRAY n tray with a cushioned underside

LAPWING n

LAPWORK n work with lapping edges

LAR n boy or young man

LARCENY n

LARCH n

LARCHEN adj of larch

LARCHES ▸ **larch**

LARD n, vb **larded**

LARDER n **larders**

LARDIER ▸ **lardy**

LARDING ▸ **lard**

LARDON n strip or cube of fat or bacon used in larding meat **lardons, lardoon**

LARDS ▸ **lard**

LARDY adj fat

LARE another word for ▸ **lore**

LAREE n Asian fish-hook **larees**

LARES ▸ **lare**

LARGE adj great in size, number ▸ n formerly, musical note

LARGELY adv

LARGEN another word for
▸ **enlarge**

LARGENS ▸ **largen**

LARGER ▸ **large**

LARGES ▸ **large**

LARGESS = **largesse**

LARGEST ▸ **large**

LARGISH adj fairly large

LARGO adv in a slow
and dignified manner
▷ n performance piece
in a slow manner
largos

LARI n monetary unit of
Georgia

LARIAT n lasso ▷ vb
tether with lariat
lariats

LARINE adj of, relating
to, or resembling a gull

LARIS ▸ **lari**

LARK n, vb **larked,
larker, larkers**

LARKIER ▸ **larky**

LARKING ▸ **lark**

LARKISH ▸ **lark**

LARKS ▸ **lark**

LARKY adj frolicsome

LARMIER n pouch
under lower eyelid of
deer

LARN vb learn

LARNAX n terracotta
coffin

LARNED ▸ **larn**

LARNEY n white person
▷ adj (of clothes) smart
larneys, larnier

LARNING ▸ **larn**

LARNS ▸ **larn**

LAROID adj relating to
Larus genus of gull
family

LARRUP vb beat or flog

larrups

LARS ▸ **lar**

LARUM archaic word for
▸ **alarm**

LARUMS ▸ **larum**

LARVA n **larvae, larval,
larvas**

LARVATE adj masked;
concealed

LARYNX n

LAS ▸ **la**

LASAGNA = **lasagne**

LASAGNE n

LASCAR n East Indian
seaman **lascars**

LASE vb to be capable
of acting as a laser
lased

LASER n **lasers**

LASES ▸ **lase**

LASH n, vb **lashed,
lasher, lashers,
lashes, lashing**

LASHINS variant of
> **lashings**

LASHKAR n troop of
Indian men with
weapons

LASING ▸ **lase**

LASINGS ▸ **lase**

LASKET n loop at the
foot of a sail onto
which an extra sail
may be fastened
laskets

LASQUE n flat-cut
diamond **lasques**

LASS n **lasses**

LASSI n cold drink made
of yoghurt or
buttermilk, flavoured
with sugar, salt, or
spice

LASSIE n **lassies**

LASSIS ▸ **lassi**

LASSO n, vb

LASSOCK another word
for ▸ **lass**

**LASSOED, lassoer,
lassoes, lassos**
▸ **lasso**

LASSU n slow part of
csárdás folk dance
lassus

LAST adv coming at the
end or after all others
▷ adj only remaining
▷ n last person or thing
▷ vb continue

LASTAGE n space for
storing goods in ship

LASTED ▸ **last**

LASTER ▸ **last**

LASTERS ▸ **last**

LASTING adj remaining
effective for a long
time ▷ n strong
durable fabric used for
shoe uppers, etc

LASTLY adv at the end
or at the last point

LASTS ▸ **last**

LAT n former coin of
Latvia

LATAH n psychological
condition **latahs**

LATAKIA n Turkish
tobacco

LATCH n, vb **latched,
latches**

LATCHET n shoe
fastening

LATE adj, adv

LATED archaic word for
▸ **belated**

LATEEN adj of a rig with
a triangular sail bent
to a yard hoisted to the

head of a low mast

lateens

LATELY *adv*

LATEN *vb* become or cause to become late

LATENCE ▶ latent

LATENCY ▶ latent

LATENED ▶ laten

LATENS ▶ laten

LATENT *adj*, *n* **latents**

LATER *adv* afterwards

LATERAD *adv* towards the side

LATERAL *adj*, *n*, *vb*

LATEST *n* the most recent news **latests**

LATEX *n* **latexes**

LATH *n*, *vb*

LATHE *n*, *vb* **lathed**

LATHEE – lathi

LATHEES ▶ lathee

LATHEN *adj* covered with laths

LATHER *n*, *vb* **lathers**, **lathery**

LATHES ▶ lathe

LATHI *n* long heavy wooden stick used as a weapon in India

LATHIER ▶ lathy

LATHING ▶ lathe

LATHIS ▶ lathi

LATHS ▶ lath

LATHY *adj* resembling a lath, esp in being tall and thin

LATI ▶ lat

LATICES ▶ latex

LATIGO *n* strap on horse's saddle **latigos**

LATILLA *n* stick making up part of ceiling

LATINA *n* US female of Latin American origin

latinas

LATINO *n* US male of Latin American origin

latinos

LATISH *adv* rather late ▷ *adj* rather late

LATITAT *n* writ presuming that person accused was hiding

LATKE *n* crispy Jewish pancake **latkes**

LATOSOL *n* type of deep, well-drained soil

LATRANT *adj* barking

LATRIA *n* adoration that may be offered to God alone **latrias**

LATRINE *n*

LATRON *n* bandit **latrons**

LATS ▶ lat

LATTE *n* coffee with hot milk

LATTEN *n* metal or alloy, esp brass, made in thin sheets **lattens**

LATTER *adj*

LATTES ▶ latte

LATTICE *n*, *vb*

LATTIN *n* brass alloy beaten into a thin sheet **lattins**

LATU ▶ lat

LAUAN *n* type of wood used in furniture-making **lauans**

LAUCH Scots form of ▶ laugh

LAUCHS ▶ lauch

LAUD *vb*, *n* **lauded**, **lauder**, **lauders**, **lauding**

LAUDS *n* traditional morning prayer of the

Western Church

LAUF *n* run in bobsleighing **laufs**

LAUGH *vb* make sounds with the voice expressing amusement ▷ *n* act of laughing **laughed**, **laugher**, **laughs**

LAUGHY *adj* laughing a lot

LAUNCE old form of ▶ lance

LAUNCED ▶ launce

LAUNCES ▶ launce

LAUNCH *vb*, *n*

LAUND *n* open grassy space

LAUNDER *vb*, *n*

LAUNDRY *n*

LAUNDS ▶ laund

LAURA *n* group of monastic cells **laurae**, **lauras**

LAUREL *n*, *vb* **laurels**

LAURIC *adj* as in **lauric acid** dodecanoic acid

LAURYL *n* as in **lauryl alcohol** crystalline solid used to make detergents **lauryls**

LAUWINE *n* avalanche

LAV short for ▶ lavatory

LAVA *n*

LAVABO *n* ritual washing of priest's hands at Mass **lavabos**

LAVAGE *n* washing out of a hollow organ **lavages**

LAVAS ▶ lava

LAVASH *n* Armenian flat bread

LAVE archaic word for ▸ wash

LAVED ▸ lave

LAVEER vb (in sailing) tack **laveers**

LAVER n priest's waterbasin for ritual ablutions **lavers**

LAVES ▸ lave

LAVING ▸ lave

LAVISH adj, vb

LAVOLT = lavolta

LAVOLTA n old Italian dance ▷ vb dance the lavolta

LAVOLTS ▸ lavolt

LAVRA = laura

LAVRAS ▸ lavra

LAVROCK = laverock

LAVS ▸ lav

LAVVIES ▸ lavvy

LAVVY n lavatory

LAW n, vb, adj

LAWBOOK n book on subject of law

LAWED ▸ law

LAWER ▸ law

LAWEST ▸ law

LAWFARE n use of the law by a country against its enemies

LAWFUL adj allowed by law

LAWIN n bill or reckoning

LAWINE n avalanche **lawines**

LAWING ▸ lawin

LAWINGS ▸ lawing

LAWINS ▸ lawin

LAWK interj used to show surprise **lawks**

LAWLAND = lowland

LAWLESS adj

LAWLIKE ▸ law

LAWMAN n officer of the law **lawmen**

LAWN n

LAWNED adj having a lawn

LAWNIER ▸ lawn

LAWNS ▸ lawn

LAWNY ▸ lawn

LAWS ▸ law

LAWSUIT n

LAWYER n, vb **lawyers**

LAX adj, n

LAXATOR n muscle that loosens body part

LAXER ▸ lax

LAXES ▸ lax

LAXEST ▸ lax

LAXISM ▸ laxist

LAXISMS ▸ laxist

LAXIST n lenient or tolerant person **laxists**

LAXITY ▸ lax

LAXLY ▸ lax

LAXNESS ▸ lax

LAY ▸ lie

LAYAWAY n merchandise reserved for future delivery

LAYBACK n technique for climbing cracks ▷ vb use layback technique

LAYDEEZ pl n jocular spelling of ladies

LAYED ▸ lay

LAYER n, vb **layered, layers**

LAYETTE n

LAYIN n basketball score

LAYING ▸ lay

LAYINGS ▸ lay

LAYINS ▸ layin

LAYLOCK old form of ▸ lilac

LAYMAN n **laymen**

LAYOFF n act of suspending employees **layoffs**

LAYOUT n **layouts**

LAYOVER n break in a journey

LAYS ▸ lie

LAYTIME n time allowed for loading cargo

LAYUP n period of incapacity through illness **layups**

LAZAR archaic word for ▸ leper

LAZARET = lazaretto

LAZARS ▸ lazar

LAZE vb, n **lazed, lazes**

LAZIED adj lazier, lazies, laziest, lazily ▸ lazy

LAZING ▸ laze

LAZO another word for ▸ lasso; **lazoed, lazoes, lazoing, lazos**

LAZULI n lapis lazuli **lazulis**

LAZY vb, adj **lazying, lazyish**

LAZZI ▸ lazzo

LAZZO n comic routine in the commedia dell'arte

LEA n meadow

LEACH vb, n **leached, leacher, leaches**

LEACHY adj porous

LEAD vb, n, adj

LEADED adj (of windows) made from many small panes of glass held together by lead strips

LEADEN adj, vb **leadens**

LEADER n leaders
LEADIER ▶ leady
LEADING ▶ lead
LEADMAN n man who leads leadmen
LEADOFF n initial move
LEADS ▶ lead
LEADY adj like lead
LEAF n, vb
LEAFAGE n leaves of plants
LEAFBUD n bud producing leaves rather than flowers
LEAFED ▶ leaf
LEAFERY n foliage
LEAFIER ▶ leafy
LEAFING ▶ leaf
LEAFLET n, vb
LEAFS ▶ leaf
LEAFY adj covered with leaves
LEAGUE n leagued
LEAGUER vb harass; beset ▷ n encampment, esp of besiegers
LEAGUES ▶ league
LEAK n, vb
LEAKAGE n
LEAKED ▶ leak
LEAKER ▶ leak
LEAKERS ▶ leak
LEAKIER ▶ leaky
LEAKILY ▶ leaky
LEAKING ▶ leak
LEAKS ▶ leak
LEAKY adj leaking
LEAL adj loyal lealer, lealest, leally, lealty
LEAM vb shine leamed, leaming, leams
LEAN vb, adj, n leaned, leaner, leaners,

leanest, leaning, leanly, leans, leant, leany
LEAP vb, n leaped, leaper, leapers, leaping, leaps, leapt
LEAR vb instruct leare, leared
LEARES ▶ leare
LEARIER ▶ leary
LEARING ▶ lear
LEARN vb learned
LEARNER n someone who is learning something
LEARNS ▶ learn
LEARNT ▶ learn
LEARS ▶ lear
LEARY = leery
LEAS ▶ lea
LEASE n, vb leased, leaser, leasers, leases
LEASH n, vb leashed, leashes
LEASING ▶ lease
LEASOW vb pasture leasowe, leasows
LEAST n, adj, adv leasts
LEASURE old form of ▶ leisure
LEAT n trench or ditch that conveys water to a mill wheel
LEATHER n, adj, vb
LEATS ▶ leat
LEAVE vb, n
LEAVED adj with leaves
LEAVEN n, vb leavens
LEAVER ▶ leave
LEAVERS ▶ leave
LEAVES ▶ leaf
LEAVIER ▶ leavy
LEAVING ▶ leave
LEAVY = leafy

LEAZE = lease
LEAZES ▶ leaze
LEBBEK n type of timber tree lebbeks
LEBEN n semiliquid food made from curdled milk lebens
LECCIES ▶ leccy
LECCY n electricity
LECH vb behave lecherously ▷ n lecherous act
LECHAIM interj drinking toast ▷ n drink for a toast
LECHED ▶ lech
LECHER n man who has or shows excessive sexual desire ▷ vb behave lecherously lechers
LECHERY n unrestrained and promiscuous sexuality
LECHES ▶ lech
LECHING ▶ lech
LECHWE n African antelope lechwes
LECTERN n
LECTIN n type of protein lectins
LECTION n variant reading of a passage in a text
LECTOR n university lecturer lectors
LECTURE n, vb
LECTURN old form of ▶ lectern
LECYTHI > lecythus
LED ▶ lead
LEDDEN n language; speech leddens
LEDGE n ledged

LEDGER n, vb **ledgers**
LEDGES ▸ **ledge**
LEDGIER ▸ **ledge**
LEDGY ▸ **ledge**
LEDUM n evergreen shrub **ledums**
LEE n, vb
LEEAR Scots form of ▸ **liar**
LEEARS ▸ **leear**
LEECH n, vb **leeched**
LEECHEE = **litchi**
LEECHES ▸ **leech**
LEED ▸ **lee**
LEEING ▸ **lee**
LEEK n **leeks**
LEEP vb boil; scald **leeped, leeping, leeps**
LEER vb, n **leered**
LEERIER ▸ **leery**
LEERILY ▸ **leery**
LEERING ▸ **leer**
LEERS ▸ **leer**
LEERY adj
LEES pl n
LEESE old form of ▸ **loose**
LEESES ▸ **leese**
LEESING ▸ **leese**
LEET n shortlist
LEETLE form of ▸ **little**
LEETS ▸ **leet**
LEEWARD n, adv, adj
LEEWAY n **leeways**
LEEZE adj as in **leeze me** Scots for lief is me, an expression of affection
LEFT adj, n
LEFTE old past tense of ▸ **lift**
LEFTER ▸ **left**
LEFTEST ▸ **left**
LEFTIE ▸ **lefty**
LEFTIES ▸ **lefty**
LEFTISH ▸ **left**

LEFTISM ▸ **leftist**
LEFTIST adj, n
LEFTS ▸ **left**
LEFTY n left-winger
LEG n
LEGACY n
LEGAL adj, n **legally, legals**
LEGATE n, vb **legated**
LEGATEE n recipient of a legacy
LEGATES ▸ **legate**
LEGATO adv smoothly ▷ n playing with no gaps between notes
LEGATOR n person who gives a legacy or makes a bequest
LEGATOS ▸ **legato**
LEGEND n **legends**
LEGER variant of ▸ **ledger**
LEGERS ▸ **leger**
LEGES ▸ **lex**
LEGGE vb lighten or lessen
LEGGED ▸ **leg**
LEGGER n man who moves barge through tunnel using legs **leggers**
LEGGES ▸ **legge**
LEGGIE n leg spin bowler
LEGGIER ▸ **leggy**
LEGGIES ▸ **leggie**
LEGGIN = **legging**
LEGGING n extra outer covering for the lower leg
LEGGINS ▸ **leggin**
LEGGISM n blacklegging
LEGGY adj
LEGHORN n Italian

wheat straw woven into hats
LEGIBLE adj **legibly**
LEGION n, adj **legions**
LEGIST n legal mind **legists**
LEGIT n legitimate drama ▷ adj legitimate
LEGITIM n inheritance due to children from father
LEGITS ▸ **legit**
LEGLAN ▸ **leglin**
LEGLANS ▸ **leglan**
LEGLEN ▸ **leglin**
LEGLENS ▸ **leglen**
LEGLESS adj without legs
LEGLET n leg jewellery **leglets**
LEGLIKE ▸ **leg**
LEGLIN n milk-pail **leglins**
LEGMAN n newsman who reports from the scene **legmen**
LEGONG n Indonesian dance **legongs**
LEGROOM n space to move one's legs comfortably
LEGS ▸ **leg**
LEGSIDE n part of a cricket field to the left of a right-handed batsman as he faces the bowler
LEGUAAN n S African lizard **leguan**
LEGUANS ▸ **leguan**
LEGUME n **legumes**
LEGUMIN n protein from leguminous plants
LEGWEAR n clothing for legs

LEGWORK n work that involves travelling on foot or as if on foot

LEHAIM = lechaim

LEHAIMS ▶ lehaim

LEHAYIM = lehaim

LEHR n long tunnel-shaped oven used for annealing glass **lehrs**

LEHUA n flower of Hawaii **lehuas**

LEI ▶ leu

LEIDGER = ledger

LEIGER = ledger

LEIGERS ▶ leiger

LEIPOA n Australian bird **leipoas**

LEIR = lear

LEIRED ▶ leir

LEIRING ▶ leir

LEIRS ▶ leir

LEIS ▶ leu

LEISH adj agile **leisher**

LEISLER n small bat

LEISTER n pronged fishing spear ▷ vb spear with a leister

LEISURE n, vb

LEK n bird display area ▷ vb gather at lek

LEKE old form of ▶ leak

LEKKED ▶ lek

LEKKER adj

LEKKING ▶ lek

LEKS ▶ lek

LEKU ▶ lek

LEKVAR n prune or apricot pie filling **lekvars**

LEKYTHI ▶ lekythos

LEMAN n beloved **lemans**

LEME = leam

LEMED ▶ leme

LEMEL n metal filings **lemels**

LEMES ▶ leme

LEMING ▶ leme

LEMMA n word in its citation form **lemmas, lemmata**

LEMMING n

LEMON n, adj, vb **lemoned, lemons**

LEMONY adj like a lemon

LEMPIRA n monetary unit of Honduras

LEMUR n

LEMURES pl n spirits of the dead

LEMURS ▶ lemur

LEND vb **lender, lenders, lending, lends**

LENES ▶ lenis

LENG vb linger ▷ adj long **lenged, lenger, lengest, lenging, lengs**

LENGTH n **lengths**

LENGTHY adj

LENIENT adj, n

LENIFY vb make lenient

LENIS adj pronounced with little muscular tension ▷ n consonant like this

LENITE vb undergo lenition **lenited, lenites**

LENITY n mercy or clemency

LENO n weave in which the warp yarns are twisted in pairs between the weft **lenos**

LENS n lense

LENSED adj incorporating a lens

LENSES ▶ lens

LENSING n materials which colour and diffuse light

LENSMAN n camera operator **lensmen**

LENT ▶ lend

LENTEN adj of or relating to Lent

LENTI ▶ lento

LENTIC adj of, relating to, or inhabiting still water

LENTIGO technical name for a ▶ freckle

LENTIL n lentils

LENTISC ▶ lentisk

LENTISK n mastic tree

LENTO adv slowly ▷ n movement or passage performed slowly

LENTOID adj lentiform ▷ n lentiform object

LENTOR n lethargy **lentors**

LENTOS ▶ lento

LENTOUS adj lethargic

LENVOY another word for ▶ envoy

LENVOYS ▶ lenvoy

LEONE n monetary unit of Sierra Leone **leones**

LEONINE adj

LEOPARD n

LEOTARD n

LEP dialect word for ▶ leap

LEPER n lepers

LEPID adj amusing

LEPORID adj of the family of mammals including rabbits and hares ▷ n any animal belonging to this family

LEPPED ▶ lep

LEPPING ▶ lep

LEPRA n leprosy **lepras**

LEPROSE adj having or denoting a whitish scurfy surface

LEPROSY n

LEPROUS adj having leprosy

LEPS ▶ lep

LEPT ▶ leap

LEPTA ▶ lepton

LEPTIN n protein that regulates the amount of fat in the body **leptins**

LEPTOME n tissue of plant conducting food

LEPTON n any of a group of elementary particles with weak interactions **leptons**

LEQUEAR = lacunar

LERE = lear

LERED ▶ lere

LERES ▶ lere

LERING ▶ lere

LERP n crystallized honeydew **lerps**

LESBIAN n, adj

LESBIC adj relating to lesbians

LESION n, vb **lesions**

LESS n, adj, pron, adv, prep

LESSEE n **lessees**

LESSEN vb **lessens**

LESSER adj

LESSES ▶ less

LESSON n, vb **lessons**

LESSOR n **lessors**

LEST conj, vb **lested, lesting, lests**

LET n, vb

LETCH = lech

LETCHED ▶ letch

LETCHES ▶ letch

LETDOWN n

LETHAL adj, n **lethals**

LETHE n forgetfulness **lethean**

LETHEE n life-blood **lethees**

LETHES ▶ lethe

LETHIED adj forgetful

LETS ▶ let

LETTED ▶ let

LETTER n, vb

LETTERN another word for ▶ lectern

LETTERS pl n literary knowledge

LETTING ▶ let

LETTRE n letter **lettres**

LETTUCE n

LETUP n lessening or abatement **letups**

LEU n monetary unit of Romania

LEUCH ▶ lauch

LEUCHEN ▶ lauch

LEUCIN = leucine

LEUCINE n essential amino acid

LEUCINS ▶ leucin

LEUCITE n grey or white mineral

LEUCO n as in leuco base colourless compound

LEUCOMA n white opaque scar of the cornea

LEUD Scots word for ▶ breadth

LEUDES ▶ leud

LEUDS ▶ leud

LEUGH ▶ lauch

LEUGHEN ▶ lauch

LEUKOMA = leucoma

LEUKON n white blood cell count **leukons**

LEV n monetary unit of Bulgaria **leva**

LEVANT n leather made from the skins of goats, sheep, or seals ▷ vb bolt or abscond **levants**

LEVATOR n muscle that raises a part of the body

LEVE adj darling ▷ adv gladly

LEVEE n, vb **leveed, levees**

LEVEL adj, vb, n **leveled**

LEVELER = leveller

LEVELLY ▶ level

LEVELS ▶ level

LEVER n, vb **levered**

LEVERET n

LEVERS ▶ lever

LEVES ▶ leve

LEVIED, levier, leviers, levies ▶ levy

LEVIN archaic word for > lightning

LEVINS ▶ levin

LEVIS n jeans

LEVITE n Christian clergyman **levites, levitic**

LEVITY n

LEVO adj anticlockwise

LEVULIN n substance obtained from certain bulbs

LEVY vb, n **levying**

LEW adj tepid

LEWD *adj* lewder,
lewdest, lewdly
LEWDSBY *another word
for* ▸ lewdster
LEWIS *n* lifting device
for heavy stone or
concrete blocks
lewises
LEWISIA *n* type of herb
LEX *n* system or body of
laws
LEXEME *n* minimal
meaningful unit of
language lexemes,
lexemic
LEXES ▸ lex
LEXICA ▸ lexicon
LEXICAL *adj* relating to
the vocabulary of a
language
LEXICON *n*
LEXIS *n* totality of
vocabulary in a
language lexises
LEY *n* land under grass
leys
LI *n* Chinese
measurement of
distance
LIABLE *adj*
LIAISE *vb* liaised, liaises
LIAISON *n*
LIANA *n* lianas, liane
LIANES ▸ liane
LIANG *n* Chinese unit of
weight liangs
LIANOID ▸ liana
LIAR *n*
LIARD *adj* grey ▷ *n*
former small coin
liards
LIARS ▸ liar
LIART *Scots form of*
▸ liard

LIAS *n* lowest series of
rocks of the Jurassic
system liases
LIATRIS *n* North
American plant with
white flowers
LIB *n* informal word for
liberation ▷ *vb* geld
LIBANT *adj* touching
lightly
LIBATE *vb* offer as gift to
the gods libated,
libates
LIBBARD *another word
for* ▸ leopard
LIBBED ▸ lib
LIBBING ▸ lib
LIBEL *n, vb* libeled
LIBELEE = libellee
LIBELER ▸ libel
LIBELS ▸ libel
LIBER *n* tome or book
LIBERAL *adj, n*
LIBERO *another name for*
▸ sweeper
LIBEROS ▸ libero
LIBERS ▸ liber
LIBERTY *n*
LIBIDO *n* libidos
LIBKEN *n* lodging
libkens
LIBLAB *n* 19th century
British liberal liblabs
LIBRA *n* ancient Roman
unit of weight librae
LIBRARY *n*
LIBRAS ▸ libra
LIBRATE *vb* oscillate or
waver
LIBRI ▸ liber
LIBS ▸ lib
LICE ▸ louse
LICENCE *n, vb*
LICENSE *vb*

LICENTE *adj* permitted;
allowed
LICH *n* dead body
LICHEE = litchi
LICHEES ▸ lichee
LICHEN *n, vb* lichens
LICHES ▸ lich
LICHI = litchi
LICHIS ▸ litchi
LICHT *Scot word for*
▸ light
LICHTED ▸ licht
LICHTER ▸ licht
LICHTLY *vb* treat
discourteously
LICHTS ▸ licht
LICHWAY *n* path used
to carry coffin into
church
LICIT *adj* lawful,
permitted licitly
LICK *vb, n* licked, licker,
lickers
LICKING *n* beating
LICKS ▸ lick
LICTOR *n* one of a group
of ancient Roman
officials lictors
LID *n*
LIDAR *n* radar-type
instrument lidars
LIDDED ▸ lid
LIDDING ▸ lids
LIDGER *variant form of*
▸ ledger
LIDGERS ▸ ledger
LIDLESS *adj* having no
lid or top
LIDO *n* open-air centre
for swimming and
water sports lidos
LIDS ▸ lid
LIE *vb, n*
LIED *n* setting for solo

voice and piano of a poem **lieder**

LIEF adv gladly ▷ adj ready ▷ n beloved person **liefer, liefest, liefly, liefs**

LIEGE adj, n

LIEGER = ledger

LIEGERS ▶ lieger

LIEGES ▶ liege

LIEN n right to hold another's property until a debt is paid

LIENAL adj of or relating to the spleen

LIENS ▶ lien

LIER n person who lies down

LIERNE n short secondary rib that connects intersections of the primary ribs **liernes**

LIERS ▶ lier

LIES ▶ lie

LIEU n **lieus**

LIEVE = leve

LIEVER ▶ lieve

LIEVES ▶ lieve

LIEVEST ▶ lieve

LIFE n

LIFEFUL adj full of life

LIFER n **lifers**

LIFES pl n as in **still lifes** paintings or drawings of inanimate objects

LIFEWAY n way of life

LIFT vb, n

LIFTBOY n person who operates a lift

LIFTED, lifter, lifters, lifting ▶ lift

LIFTMAN = liftboy

LIFTMEN ▶ liftman

LIFTOFF n, vb

LIFTS ▶ lift

LIFULL obsolete form of ▶ lifeful

LIG n function with free entertainment and refreshments ▷ vb attend such a function

LIGAN = lagan

LIGAND n atom, molecule, radical, or ion forming a complex with a central atom **ligands**

LIGANS ▶ ligan

LIGASE n any of a class of enzymes **ligases**

LIGATE vb tie up or constrict (something) with a ligature **ligated, ligates**

LIGER n hybrid offspring of a female tiger and a male lion **ligers**

LIGGE obsolete form of ▶ lie

LIGGED ▶ lig

LIGGER ▶ lig

LIGGERS ▶ lig

LIGGES ▶ ligge

LIGGING ▶ lig

LIGHT n, adj, vb, adv **lighted**

LIGHTEN vb

LIGHTER n, vb

LIGHTLY adv in a light way ▷ vb belittle

LIGHTS ▶ light

LIGNAGE another word for ▶ lineage

LIGNAN n beneficial substance found in plants **lignans**

LIGNE n unit of measurement **lignes**

LIGNIFY vb become woody with the deposition of lignin in cell walls

LIGNIN n complex polymer occurring in certain plant cell walls making the plant rigid **lignins**

LIGNITE n

LIGNOSE n explosive compound

LIGNUM n wood **lignums**

LIGROIN n volatile fraction of petroleum

LIGS ▶ lig

LIGULA = ligule

LIGULAE ▶ ligula

LIGULAR ▶ ligula

LIGULAS ▶ ligula

LIGULE n membranous outgrowth between the leaf blade and sheath **ligules**

LIGURE n any of the 12 precious stones used in the breastplates of high priests **ligures**

LIKABLE adj likably

LIKE adj similar ▷ vb find enjoyable ▷ n favourable feeling, desire, or preference **liked**

LIKELY adj, adv

LIKEN vb likened, **likens**

LIKER, likers, likes, likest ▶ like

LIKIN n historically, Chinese tax

LIKING n **likings**

LIKINS ▶ likin
LIKUTA n coin in Zaïre
LILAC n, adj lilacs
LILIED adj decorated with lilies
LILIES ▶ lily
LILL obsolete form of ▶ loll
LILLED ▶ lill
LILLING ▶ lill
LILLS ▶ lill
LILO n inflatable mattress lilos
LILT n, vb lilted, lilting, lilts
LILY n
LIMA n type of edible bean
LIMACEL n small shell inside some kinds of slug
LIMACES ▶ limax
LIMACON n heart-shaped curve
LIMAIL = lemel
LIMAILS ▶ limail
LIMAN n lagoon limans
LIMAS ▶ lima
LIMAX n slug
LIMB n, vb
LIMBA n type of African tree limbas
LIMBATE adj having an edge or border of a different colour from the rest
LIMBEC obsolete form of ▶ alembic
LIMBECK obsolete form of ▶ alembic
LIMBECS ▶ limbec
LIMBED ▶ limb
LIMBER vb, adj, n limbers

LIMBI ▶ limbus
LIMBIC ▶ limbus
LIMBIER ▶ limby
LIMBING ▶ limb
LIMBO n limbos
LIMBOUS adj with overlapping edges
LIMBS ▶ limb
LIMBUS n border
LIMBY adj with long legs, stem, branches, etc
LIME n, vb, adj
LIMEADE n drink made from sweetened lime juice and plain or carbonated water
LIMED ▶ lime
LIMELIT > limelight
LIMEN another term for > threshold
LIMENS ▶ limen
LIMEPIT n pit containing lime in which hides are placed to remove the hair
LIMES n fortified boundary of the Roman Empire
LIMEY n, adj limeys
LIMIER ▶ limy
LIMIEST ▶ limy
LIMINA ▶ limen
LIMINAL adj relating to the point (or threshold) beyond which a sensation becomes too faint to be experienced
LIMING ▶ lime
LIMINGS ▶ lime
LIMIT n, vb
LIMITED adj, n
LIMITER n electronic circuit whose

amplitude is limited to some fixed value above which the peaks become flattened
LIMITES ▶ limes
LIMITS ▶ limit
LIMMA n semitone limmas
LIMMER n scoundrel limmers
LIMN vb represent in drawing or painting limned, limner, limners
LIMNIC adj relating to lakes
LIMNING ▶ limn
LIMNS ▶ limn
LIMO short for > limousine
LIMOS ▶ limo
LIMOSES ▶ limosis
LIMOSIS n excessive hunger
LIMOUS adj muddy
LIMP vb, n, adj
LIMPA n type of rye bread limpas
LIMPED, limper, limpers, limpest ▶ limp
LIMPET n, adj limpets
LIMPID adj
LIMPING ▶ limp
LIMPKIN n rail-like wading bird
LIMPLY ▶ limp
LIMPS ▶ limp
LIMPSEY = limpsy
LIMPSY adj limpsy
LIMULI ▶ limulus
LIMULUS n horseshoe crab
LIMY adj of, like, or smeared with birdlime

LIN vb cease

LINABLE ▶ line

LINAC n linear accelerator **linacs**

LINAGE n number of lines in written or printed matter **linages**

LINALOL = linalool

LINCH n ledge **linches, linchet**

LINCTUS n

LIND variant of ▶ linden

LINDANE n white poisonous crystalline powder

LINDEN n large tree with heart-shaped leaves and fragrant yellowish flowers **lindens**

LINDIES ▶ lindy

LINDS ▶ lind

LINDY n lively dance

LINE n, vb

LINEAGE n

LINEAL adj in direct line of descent

LINEAR adj

LINEATE adj marked with lines

LINECUT n method of relief printing

LINED ▶ line

LINEMAN = linesman

LINEMEN ▶ lineman

LINEN n linens, lineny

LINER n liners

LINES ▶ line

LINEUP n row or arrangement of people or things **lineups**

LINEY ▶ line

LING n slender food fish

LINGA = lingam

LINGAM n (in Sanskrit)

masculine gender **lingams**

LINGAS ▶ linga

LINGCOD n type of food fish

LINGEL n shoemaker's thread **lingels**

LINGER vb lingers

LINGIER ▶ lingy

LINGLE = lingel

LINGLES = lingle

LINGO n lingoes

LINGOT n ingot **lingots**

LINGS ▶ ling

LINGUA n any tongue-like structure **linguae**

LINGUAL adj of the tongue ▷ n lingual consonant

LINGUAS ▶ lingua

LINGULA n small tongue

LINGY adj heather-covered

LINHAY n farm building with an open front **linhays**

LINIER ▶ line

LINIEST ▶ line

LININ n network of viscous material in the nucleus of a cell that connects the chromatin granules

LINING n linings

LININS ▶ linin

LINISH vb polish metal

LINK n, vb

LINKAGE n act of linking or the state of being linked

LINKBOY n (formerly) a boy who carried a torch for pedestrians

in dark streets

LINKED ▶ link

LINKER n person or thing that links **linkers**

LINKIER ▶ linky

LINKING ▶ link

LINKMAN = linkboy

LINKMEN ▶ linkman

LINKROT n

LINKS ▶ link

LINKUP n establishing of a union between objects, groups, organizations, etc **linkups**

LINKY adj (of countryside) consisting of links

LINN n waterfall or a pool at the foot of it

LINNED ▶ lin

LINNET n linnets

LINNEY = linhay

LINNEYS ▶ linney

LINNIES ▶ linny

LINNING ▶ lin

LINNS ▶ linn

LINNY = linhay

LINO = linoleum

LINOCUT n

LINOS ▶ lino

LINS ▶ lin

LINSANG n any of several forest-dwelling viverrine mammals

LINSEED n seed of the flax plant

LINSEY n type of cloth **linseys**

LINT n, vb

LINTED adj having lint

LINTEL n lintels

LINTER n machine for stripping the short

LOME *vb* cover with lome **lomed**

LOMEIN *n* Chinese dish **lomeins**

LOMENT *n* pod of certain leguminous plants

LOMENTA ▸ **lomentum**

LOMENTS ▸ **loment**

LOMES ▸ **lome**

LOMING ▸ **lome**

LOMPISH another word for ▸ **lumpish**

LONE *adj*

LONELY *adj*

LONER *n* **loners**

LONG *adj* having length ▷ *adv* for a certain time ▷ *vb* have a strong desire (for)

LONGA *n* long note

LONGAN *n* sapindaceous tree of tropical and subtropical Asia **longans**

LONGAS ▸ **longa**

LONGBOW *n*

LONGE *n* rope used in training a horse ▷ *vb* train using a longe

LONGED ▸ **long**

LONGER *n* line of barrels on a ship **longers**

LONGES ▸ **longe**

LONGEST ▸ **long**

LONGIES *n* long johns

LONGING *n, adj*

LONGISH *adj* rather long

LONGLY ▸ **long**

LONGS *pl n* full-length trousers

LOO *n, vb*

LOOBIER ▸ **looby**

LOOBIES ▸ **looby**

LOOBILY ▸ **looby**

LOOBY *adj* foolish ▷ *n* foolish or stupid person

LOOED ▸ **loo**

LOOEY *n* lieutenant **looeys**

LOOF *n* part of ship's side

LOOFA = **loofah**

LOOFAH *n* **loofahs**

LOOFAS ▸ **loofa**

LOOFFUL *n* handful

LOOFS ▸ **loof**

LOOIE = **looey**

LOOIES ▸ **looie**

LOOING ▸ **loo**

LOOK *vb* direct the eyes or attention (towards) ▷ *n* instance of looking **looked**

LOOKER *n* person who looks **lookers**

LOOKING ▸ **look**

LOOKISM *n* discrimination because of appearance **lookist**

LOOKOUT *n, vb*

LOOKS ▸ **look**

LOOKUP *n* act of looking up informatiion **lookups**

LOOM *n, vb* **loomed, looming, looms**

LOON *n* diving bird

LOONEY = **loony**

LOONEYS ▸ **loony**

LOONIE *n* Canadian dollar coin

LOONIER ▸ **loony**

LOONIES ▸ **loony**

LOONILY ▸ **loony**

LOONING *n* cry of the loon

LOONS ▸ **loon**

LOONY *adj, n*

LOOP *n, vb* **looped**

LOOPER *n* person or thing that loops or makes loops **loopers**

LOOPIER ▸ **loopy**

LOOPILY ▸ **loopy**

LOOPING ▸ **loop**

LOOPS ▸ **loop**

LOOPY *adj* slightly mad or crazy

LOOR ▸ **lief**

LOORD obsolete word for ▸ **lout**

LOORDS ▸ **loord**

LOOS ▸ **loo**

LOOSE *adj, adv, vb* **loosed, loosely**

LOOSEN *vb* **loosens**

LOOSER ▸ **loose**

LOOSES ▸ **loose**

LOOSEST ▸ **loose**

LOOSIE *n* informal word for loose forward

LOOSIES *pl n* cigarettes sold individually

LOOSING *n* celebration of one's 21st birthday

LOOT *vb, n* **looted**

LOOTEN *Scots past form of* ▸ **let**

LOOTER, looters, looting, loots ▸ **loot**

LOOVES ▸ **loof**

LOP *vb, n*

LOPE *vb, n* **loped, loper, lopers, lopes, loping**

LOPPED ▸ **lop**

LOPPER *n* tool for lopping ▷ *vb* curdle **loppers**

LOPPIER ▸ **loppy**

LOPPIES ▸ **loppy**

LOPPING ▶ lop
LOPPY adj floppy ▷ n ranch hand
LOPS ▶ lop
LOQUAT n ornamental evergreen rosaceous tree **loquats**
LOR interj exclamation of surprise or dismay
LORAL adj of part of side of bird's head
LORAN n radio navigation system operating over long distances **lorans**
LORATE adj like a strap
LORCHA n junk-rigged vessel **lorchas**
LORD n, vb **lorded**
LORDING n gentleman
LORDKIN n little lord
LORDLY adj, adv
LORDOMA = lordosis
LORDS ▶ lord
LORDY interj exclamation of surprise or dismay
LORE n
LOREAL adj concerning or relating to lore
LOREL another word for ▶ losel
LORELS ▶ lorel
LORES ▶ lore
LORETTE n concubine
LORGNON n monocle or pair of spectacles
LORIC ▶ lorica
LORICA n hard outer covering of rotifers, ciliate protozoans, and similar organisms **loricae, lorics**
LORIES ▶ lory

LORIMER n (formerly) a person who made bits and spurs **loriner**
LORING n teaching **lorings**
LORIOT n golden oriole (bird) **loriots**
LORIS n any of several prosimian primates **lorises**
LORN adj forsaken or wretched
LORRELL obsolete word for ▶ losel
LORRIES ▶ lorry
LORRY n
LOS n approval
LOSABLE ▶ loose
LOSE vb **losed**
LOSEL n worthless person ▷ adj worthless **losels**
LOSEN ▶ loose
LOSER n person or thing that loses **losers**
LOSES ▶ loose
LOSH interj lord
LOSING ▶ lose
LOSINGS pl n losses
LOSS n losses
LOSSIER ▶ lossy
LOSSY adj designed to have a high attenuation
LOST adj
LOT pron, n, vb
LOTA n globular water container **lotah**
LOTAHS ▶ lotah
LOTAS ▶ lota
LOTE another word for ▶ lotus
LOTES ▶ lote
LOTH = loath

LOTHER ▶ loth
LOTHEST ▶ loth
LOTI n monetary unit of Lesotho
LOTIC adj of communities living in rapidly flowing water
LOTION n lotions
LOTO = lotto
LOTOS = lotus
LOTOSES ▶ lotos
LOTS ▶ lot
LOTTE n type of fish
LOTTED ▶ lot
LOTTER n someone who works an allotment **lotters**
LOTTERY n
LOTTES ▶ lotte
LOTTING ▶ lot
LOTTO n game of chance **lottos**
LOTUS n lotuses
LOU Scot word for ▶ love
LOUCHE adj shifty **loucher**
LOUD adj
LOUDEN vb make louder **loudens**
LOUDER ▶ loud
LOUDEST ▶ loud
LOUDISH adj fairly loud
LOUDLY ▶ loud
LOUED ▶ lou
LOUGH n loughs
LOUIE = looey
LOUIES ▶ louie
LOUING ▶ lou
LOUIS n former French gold coin
LOUMA n market in developing countries **loumas**
LOUN = lown

LOUND = loun
LOUNDED ▸ lound
LOUNDER vb beat severely
LOUNDS ▸ lound
LOUNED ▸ loun
LOUNGE n, vb lounged
LOUNGER n comfortable sometimes adjustable couch or extending chair designed for someone to relax in
LOUNGES ▸ lounge
LOUNGEY n suggestive of a lounge bar or easy-listening music
LOUNGY adj casual; relaxed
LOUNING ▸ loun
LOUNS ▸ loun
LOUP Scot word for ▸ leap
LOUPE n magnifying glass used by jewellers, horologists, etc
LOUPED, loupen ▸ loup
LOUPES ▸ loupe
LOUPING, loupit, loups ▸ loup
LOUR vb, n
LOURE n slow, former French dance
LOURED ▸ lour
LOURES ▸ loure
LOURIE n
LOURIER ▸ loury
LOURIES ▸ lourie
LOURING ▸ lour
LOURS ▸ lour
LOURY adj sombre
LOUS ▸ lou
LOUSE n, vb loused
LOUSER n mean nasty

person **lousers**
LOUSES ▸ louse
LOUSIER ▸ lousy
LOUSILY ▸ lousy
LOUSING ▸ louse
LOUSY adj
LOUT n, vb louted, louting
LOUTISH adj of a lout
LOUTS ▸ lout
LOUVAR n large silvery whalelike scombroid fish **louvars**
LOUVER = louvre
LOUVERS ▸ louver
LOUVRE n
LOUVRED adj having louvres
LOUVRES ▸ louvre
LOVABLE adj lovably
LOVAGE n European plant used for flavouring food **lovages**
LOVAT n yellowish-or bluish-green mixture in tweeds **lovats**
LOVE vb, n
LOVEBUG n small US flying insect
LOVED ▸ love
LOVELY adj, n
LOVER n
LOVERED adj having a lover
LOVERLY adj loverlike
LOVERS ▸ lover
LOVES ▸ love
LOVEY another word for ▸ love
LOVEYS ▸ lovey
LOVING adj lovings
LOW adj, adv, n, vb
LOWAN n type of

Australian bird **lowans**
LOWBALL vb deliberately under-charge
LOWBORN adj of ignoble or common parentage
LOWBOY n lowboys
LOWBRED = lowborn
LOWBROW adj, n
LOWDOWN n inside info
LOWE variant of ▸ low
LOWED ▸ low
LOWER adj, vb lowered, lowers
LOWERY adj sombre
LOWES ▸ lowe
LOWEST, lowing, lowings, lowish ▸ low
LOWLAND n low-lying country ▷ adj of a lowland or lowlands
LOWLIER ▸ lowly
LOWLIFE n member or members of the underworld
LOWLILY ▸ lowly
LOWLY adj, adv
LOWN vb calm lowned
LOWNDED ▸ lownd
LOWNDS ▸ lownd
LOWNE = loon
LOWNED ▸ lown
LOWNES ▸ lowne
LOWNESS ▸ low
LOWNING ▸ lown
LOWNS ▸ lown
LOWP = loup
LOWPED ▸ lowp
LOWPING ▸ lowp
LOWPS ▸ lowp
LOWRIE another name for ▸ lory
LOWRIES ▸ lowry

LOWRY another name for ▶ lory

LOWS ▶ low

LOWSE vb release or loose ▷ adj loose **lowsed, lowser, lowses, lowsest, lowsing, lowsit**

LOWT = lout

LOWTED ▶ lowt

LOWTING ▶ lowt

LOWTS ▶ lowt

LOWVELD n low ground in S Africa

LOX vb load fuel tanks of spacecraft with liquid oxygen ▷ n kind of smoked salmon **loxed, loxes, loxing**

A good word when you have an X to dispose of.

LOXYGEN n liquid oxygen

LOY n narrow spade with a single footrest

LOYAL adj loyaler, **loyally**

LOYALTY n quality of being loyal

LOYS ▶ loy

LOZELL obsolete form of ▶ losel

LOZELLS ▶ lozell

LOZEN n window pane

LOZENGE n

LOZENGY adj divided by diagonal lines to form a lattice

LOZENS ▶ lozen

LUACH n Jewish calendar

LUAU n feast of Hawaiian food **luaus**

LUBBARD = lubber

LUBBER n big, awkward, or stupid person **lubbers**

LUBE n lubricating oil ▷ vb lubricate with oil **lubed, lubes**

LUBFISH n type of fish

LUBING ▶ lube

LUBRA n lubras

LUBRIC adj slippery

LUCARNE n type of dormer window

LUCE another name for ▶ pike

LUCENCE ▶ lucent

LUCENCY ▶ lucent

LUCENT adj brilliant

LUCERN = lucerne

LUCERNE n

LUCERNS ▶ lucern

LUCES ▶ luce

LUCHOT ▶ luach

LUCHOTH ▶ luach

LUCID adj lucider, **lucidly**

LUCIFER n friction match

LUCIGEN n type of lamp

LUCITE n type of transparent acrylic-based plastic **lucites**

LUCK n, vb lucked

LUCKEN adj shut

LUCKIE = lucky

LUCKIER ▶ lucky

LUCKIES ▶ luckie

LUCKILY ▶ lucky

LUCKING ▶ luck

LUCKS ▶ luck

LUCKY adj, n

LUCRE n lucres

LUCUMA n S American tree **lucumas**

LUCUMO n Etruscan king **lucumos**

LUD n lord ▷ interj exclamation of dismay or surprise

LUDE n slang word for drug for relieving anxiety **ludes**

LUDIC adj playful

LUDO n game played with dice and counters on a board **ludos**

LUDS ▶ lud

LUDSHIP ▶ lud

LUES n any venereal disease **luetic, luetics**

LUFF vb sail (a ship) towards the wind ▷ n leading edge of a fore-and-aft sail

LUFFA = loofah

LUFFAS ▶ luffa

LUFFED ▶ luff

LUFFING ▶ luff

LUFFS ▶ luff

LUG vb, n

LUGE n racing toboggan ▷ vb ride on a luge **luged, lugeing**

LUGER n pistol lugers

LUGES ▶ luge

LUGGAGE n

LUGGED ▶ lug

LUGGER n small working boat with an oblong sail **luggers**

LUGGIE n wooden bowl **luggies**

LUGGING ▶ lug

LUGHOLE informal word for ▶ ear

LUGING ▶ luge

LUGINGS ▶ luge

LUGS ▶ lug

LUGSAIL n four-sided sail

LUGWORM n large worm used as bait

LUIT Scots past form of ► let

LUITEN ► let

LUKE variant of > lukewarm

LULIBUB obsolete form of > lollipop

LULL vb, n

LULLABY n, vb

LULLED, luller, lullers, lulling, lulls ► lull

LULU n person or thing deemed to be outstanding **lulus**

LUM n chimney

LUMA n monetary unit of Armenia **lumas**

LUMBAGO n

LUMBANG n type of tree

LUMBAR adj, n **lumbars**

LUMBER n, vb **lumbers**

LUMEN n lumenal, **lumens, lumina, luminal**

LUMINE vb illuminate **lumined, lumines**

LUMME interj exclamation of surprise or dismay

LUMMIER ► lummy

LUMMOX n clumsy person

LUMMY interj exclamation of surprise ► adj excellent

LUMP n, vb **lumped**

LUMPEN adj stupid or unthinking ► n member of underclass **lumpens**

LUMPER n stevedore **lumpers**

LUMPIER ► lumpy

LUMPILY ► lumpy

LUMPING ► lump

LUMPISH adj stupid or clumsy

LUMPKIN n lout

LUMPS ► lump

LUMPY adj full of lumps

LUMS ► lum

LUNA n large American moth

LUNACY n

LUNAR adj, n **lunars**

LUNARY n moonwort herb

LUNAS ► luna

LUNATE adj shaped like a crescent ► n crescent-shaped bone forming part of the wrist **lunated, lunates**

LUNATIC adj, n

LUNCH n, vb **lunched, luncher, lunches**

LUNE ► lunette

LUNES ► lune

LUNET n small moon or satellite **lunets**

LUNETTE n anything that is shaped like a crescent

LUNG n

LUNGAN = longan

LUNGANS ► lungan

LUNGE n, vb **lunged**

LUNGEE = lungi

LUNGEES ► lungee

LUNGER ► lunge

LUNGERS ► lunge

LUNGES ► lunge

LUNGFUL ► lung

LUNGI n cotton cloth worn as a loincloth,

sash, or turban

LUNGIE n guillemot **lungies**

LUNGING ► lunge

LUNGIS ► lungi

LUNGS ► lung

LUNGYI = lungi

LUNGYIS ► lungyi

LUNIER ► luny

LUNIES ► luny

LUNIEST ► luny

LUNK n awkward person

LUNKER n very large fish **lunkers**

LUNKS ► lunk

LUNT vb produce smoke **lunted, lunting, lunts**

LUNULA n white area at base of the fingernail **lunulae**

LUNULAR = lunulate

LUNULE = lunula

LUNULES ► lunule

LUNY = loony

LUNYIE = lungie

LUNYIES ► lunyie

LUPANAR n brothel

LUPIN n

LUPINE adj like a wolf ► n lupin **lupines**

LUPINS ► lupin

LUPOID adj suffering from lupus

LUPOUS adj relating to lupus

LUPPEN Scots past form of ► leap

LUPULIN n resinous powder extracted from the female flowers of the hop plant

LUPUS n ulcerous skin disease **lupuses**

LUR n large bronze musical horn

LURCH vb, n lurched

LURCHER n crossbred dog trained to hunt silently

LURCHES ▶ lurch

LURDAN n stupid or dull person ▷ adj dull or stupid **lurdane, lurdans, lurden**

LURDENS ▶ lurden

LURE vb, n lured, lurer, lurers, lures

LUREX n thin glittery thread **lurexes**

LURGI ▶ lurgy

LURGIES ▶ lurgy

LURGIS ▶ lurgi

LURGY n any undetermined illness

LURID adj lurider, luridly

LURING ▶ lure

LURINGS ▶ luring

LURK vb lurked, lurker, lurkers

LURKING adj lingering

LURKS ▶ lurk

LURRIES ▶ lurry

LURRY n confused jumble

LURS ▶ lur

LURVE n love **lurves**

LUSER n humorous term for computer user **lusers**

LUSH adj, n, vb lushed

LUSHER adj more lush ▷ n drunkard **lushers**

LUSHES ▶ lush

LUSHEST ▶ lush

LUSHIER ▶ lushy

LUSHING ▶ lush

LUSHLY ▶ lush

LUSHY adj slightly intoxicated

LUSK vb lounge around **lusked, lusking**

LUSKISH adj lazy

LUSKS ▶ lusk

LUST n, vb lusted

LUSTER ▶ lustre

LUSTERS ▶ luster

LUSTFUL adj

LUSTICK obsolete word for ▶ lusty

LUSTIER ▶ lusty

LUSTILY ▶ lusty

LUSTING ▶ lust

LUSTRA ▶ lustrum

LUSTRAL adj of or relating to a ceremony of purification

LUSTRE n, vb lustred, lustres

LUSTRUM n period of five years

LUSTS ▶ lust

LUSTY adj

LUSUS n freak, mutant **lususes**

LUTE n, vb

LUTEA adj yellow

LUTEAL adj relating to the development of the corpus luteum

LUTED ▶ lute

LUTEIN n xanthophyll pigment **luteins**

LUTEOUS adj of a greenish-yellow colour

LUTER n lute player **luters**

LUTES ▶ lute

LUTEUM adj yellow

LUTFISK = lutefisk

LUTHERN another name for ▶ dormer

LUTHIER n lute-maker

LUTING n cement and clay **lutings**

LUTIST = lutenist

LUTISTS ▶ lutist

LUTITE another name for ▶ pelite

LUTITES ▶ lutite

LUTTEN ▶ loot

LUTZ n skating jump **lutzes**

LUV n love

LUVS ▶ love

LUVVIE n person who is involved in acting or the theatre

LUVVIES ▶ luvvie

LUVVY = luvvie

LUX n unit of illumination

| One of the key words using X.

LUXATE vb put (a shoulder, knee, etc) out of joint **luxated, luxates**

LUXE n as in de luxe rich **luxes**

LUXURY n, adj

LUZ n supposedly indestructible bone of the human body

| This very unusual word is very useful for playing the Z.

LUZERN n alfalfa **luzerns**

LUZZES ▶ luz

LWEI n Angolan monetary unit **lweis**

LYAM n leash **lyams**

LYARD = liard

LYART = liard
LYASE n any enzyme that catalyses the separation of two parts of a molecule **lyases**
LYCEA ▶ lyceum
LYCEE n secondary school **lycees**
LYCEUM n public building for concerts **lyceums**
LYCH = lich
LYCHEE = litchi
LYCHEES ▶ lychee
LYCHES ▶ lych
LYCHNIS n plant with red, pink, or white flowers
LYCOPOD n type of moss
LYCRA n type of elastic fabric used for tight-fitting garments **lycras**
LYDDITE n explosive consisting chiefly of fused picric acid
LYE n caustic solution **lyes**
LYFULL obsolete form of ▶ lifeful
LYING ▶ lie
LYINGLY ▶ lie
LYINGS ▶ lie
LYM obsolete form of

▶ lyam
LYME n as in lyme grass type of perennial dune grass **lymes**
LYMITER = limiter
LYMPH n
LYMPHAD n ancient rowing boat
LYMPHS n lymph
LYMS ▶ lym
LYNAGE obsolete form of ▶ lineage
LYNAGES ▶ lynage
LYNCEAN adj of a lynx
LYNCH vb lynched, lyncher, lynches
LYNCHET n ridge formed by ploughing a hillside
LYNE n flax lynes
LYNX n lynxes
LYOPHIL = lyophilic
LYRA n as in lyra viol lutelike musical instrument
LYRATE adj shaped like a lyre **lyrated**
LYRE n lyres
LYRIC adj, n lyrical
LYRICON n wind synthesizer
LYRICS ▶ lyric
LYRISM n art or technique of playing the lyre **lyrisms**
LYRIST = lyricist

LYRISTS ▶ lyrist
LYSATE n material formed by lysis **lysates**
LYSE vb undergo lysis **lysed**
LYSES ▶ lysis
LYSIN n antibodies that dissolute cells against which they are directed
LYSINE n essential amino acid that occurs in proteins **lysines**
LYSING ▶ lyse
LYSINS ▶ lysin
LYSIS n destruction of cells by a lysin
LYSOGEN n lysis-inducing agent
LYSOL n antiseptic solution **lysols**
LYSSA less common word for ▶ rabies
LYSSAS ▶ lyssa
LYTE vb dismount lyted, lytes
LYTHE n type of fish lythes
LYTIC adj relating to, causing, or resulting from lysis
LYTING ▶ lyte
LYTTA n mass of cartilage under the tongue in carnivores **lyttae, lyttas**

Mm

M is a very useful letter when you need to form short words as it starts a two-letter word with every vowel, as well as with **Y** and with another **M**. Remembering this allows you to use **M** effectively when you're forming a word parallel to, and in contact with, a word that is already on the board. **M** also combines well with **X** and **Z**, so there is a lot of potential for high-scoring words. Keep **max, mix** and **mux** (12 points each) in mind, as well as **miz** and **muz** (14 each). It's also worth remembering the three-letter words ending in **W**: **maw, mew** and **mow** (8 points each). **Myc** is another useful word to remember when you are short of vowels.

MA *n* mother
MAA *vb* (of goats) bleat **maaed, maaing**
MAAR *n* coneless volcanic crater **maare, maars**
MAAS *n* thick soured milk **maases**
MAATJES *n* pickled herring
MABE *n* type of pearl
MABELA *n* ground kaffir corn **mabelas**
MABES ▶ mabe
MAC *n*
MACABER = macabre
MACABRE *adj*
MACACO *n* type of lemur **macacos**
MACADAM *n* road surface

MACAQUE *n* monkey of Asia and Africa
MACAW *n* large tropical American parrot **macaws**
MACCHIA *n* thicket in Italy **macchie**
MACE *n, vb* **maced**
MACER *n* macebearer, esp (in Scotland) an official who acts as usher in a court of law
MACERAL *n* any of the organic units that constitute coal
MACERS ▶ macer
MACES ▶ mace
MACH *n* ratio of the speed of a body in a particular medium to the speed of sound in

that medium
MACHAIR *n* (in the western Highlands of Scotland) a strip of sandy, grassy, land
MACHAN *n* (in India) a raised platform used in tiger hunting **machans**
MACHE *n* papier-mâché
MACHER *n* important or influential person **machers**
MACHES ▶ mache
MACHETE *n*
MACHI *n as in* **machi chips** in Indian English, fish and chips
MACHINE *n, vb*
MACHO *adj, n* **machos**

MACHREE n Irish form of address meaning my dear

MACHS ▶ mach

MACHZOR n Jewish prayer book

MACING ▶ mace

MACK = mac

MACKLE n blurred impression ▷ vb mend hurriedly or in a makeshift way **mackled, mackles**

MACKS ▶ mack

MACLE n crystal consisting of two parts **macled, macles**

MACON n wine from the Mâcon area **macons**

MACOYA n South American tree **macoyas**

MACRAME n ornamental work of knotted cord **macrami**

MACRO n close-up lens

MACRON n mark placed over a letter to represent a long vowel **macrons**

MACROS ▶ macro

MACS ▶ mac

MACULA n small spot like a freckle **maculae, macular, maculas**

MACULE = mackle

MACULED ▶ macule

MACULES ▶ macule

MACUMBA n religious cult in Brazil

MAD adj, vb

MADAFU n coconut milk **madafus**

MADAM n, vb

MADAME n French title equivalent to Mrs

MADAMED ▶ madam

MADAMES ▶ madame

MADAMS ▶ madam

MADCAP adj foolish or reckless ▷ n impulsive or reckless person **madcaps**

MADDED ▶ mad

MADDEN vb **maddens**

MADDER n type of rose

MADDERS ▶ madam

MADDEST ▶ mad

MADDING ▶ mad

MADDISH ▶ mad

MADDOCK = mattock

MADE ▶ make

MADEFY vb make moist

MADEIRA n kind of rich sponge cake

MADGE n type of hammer **madges**

MADID adj wet

MADISON n type of cycle relay race

MADLING n insane person

MADLY adv

MADMAN n person who is insane **madmen**

MADNESS n insanity

MADONNA n picture or statue of the Virgin Mary

MADOQUA n Ethiopian antelope

MADRAS n medium-hot curry

MADRASA = madrasah

MADRE Spanish word for ▶ mother

MADRES ▶ madre

MADRONA n N American evergreen tree or shrub **madrone, madrono**

MADS ▶ mad

MADTOM n species of catfish **madtoms**

MADURO adj (of cigars) dark and strong ▷ n cigar of this type **maduros**

MADWORT n low-growing Eurasian plant with small blue flowers

MADZOON = matzoon

MAE adj more

MAELID n mythical spirit of apple **maelids**

MAENAD n female disciple of Dionysus, the Greek god of wine **maenads**

MAERL n type of red coralline algae **maerls**

MAES ▶ mae

MAESTRI ▶ maestro

MAESTRO n outstanding musician or conductor

MAFFIA = mafia

MAFFIAS ▶ maffia

MAFFICK vb celebrate extravagantly and publicly

MAFFLED adj baffled

MAFFLIN n half-witted person

MAFIA n international secret organization founded in Sicily **mafias**

MAFIC n minerals present in igneous rock **mafics**

MAFIOSI ▸ mafioso

MAFIOSO n member of the Mafia

MAFTED adj suffering under oppressive heat

MAFTIR n final section of the weekly Torah reading **maftirs**

MAG vb talk ▸ n talk

MAGALOG = magalogue

MAGE archaic word for ▸ **magician**

MAGENTA adj, n

MAGES ▸ mage

MAGG = mag

MAGGED ▸ mag

MAGGIE n magpie **maggies**

MAGGING ▸ mag

MAGGOT n maggots

MAGGOTY adj relating to, resembling, or ridden with maggots

MAGGS ▸ magg

MAGI ▸ magus

MAGIAN ▸ magus

MAGIANS ▸ magus

MAGIC n, vb, adj magical, magics

MAGILP = megilp

MAGILPS ▸ magilp

MAGISM = magus

MAGISMS ▸ magus

MAGLEV n type of high-speed train **maglevs**

MAGMA n magmas, magmata

MAGNATE n

MAGNES n magnetic iron ore

MAGNET n

MAGNETO n

MAGNETS ▸ magnet

MAGNIFY vb

MAGNON n short for Cro-Magnon **magnons**

MAGNOX n alloy used in fuel elements of some nuclear reactors

MAGNUM n large wine bottle holding about 1.5 litres **magnums**

MAGNUS adj as in **magnus hitch** knot similar to a clove hitch but having one more turn

MAGOT n Chinese or Japanese figurine in a crouching position, usually grotesque **magots**

MAGPIE n magpies

MAGS ▸ mag

MAGSMAN n raconteur **magsmen**

MAGUEY n tropical American agave plant **magueys**

MAGUS n Zoroastrian priest of the ancient Medes and Persians

MAGYAR adj of or relating to a style of sleeve

MAHA n as in **maha yoga** form of yoga

MAHATMA n person revered for holiness and wisdom

MAHEWU n (in South Africa) fermented liquid mealie-meal porridge **mahewus**

MAHJONG n game of Chinese origin, using tiles

MAHMAL n litter used in Muslim ceremony **mahmals**

MAHOE n New Zealand tree **mahoes**

MAHONIA n Asian and American evergreen shrub

MAHOUT n (in India and the East Indies) elephant driver or keeper **mahouts**

MAHSEER n large freshwater Indian fish **mahsir**

MAHSIRS ▸ mahsir

MAHUA n Indian tree

MAHUANG n herbal medicine from shrub

MAHUAS ▸ mahua

MAHWA = mahua

MAHWAS ▸ mahwa

MAHZOR = machzor

MAHZORS ▸ mahzor

MAID n, vb

MAIDAN n (in Pakistan, India, etc) open area **maidans**

MAIDED ▸ maid

MAIDEN n, adj maidens

MAIDING ▸ maid

MAIDISH ▸ maid

MAIDISM n pellagra

MAIDS ▸ maid

MAIGRE adj not containing meat ▸ n species of fish **maigres**

MAIHEM = mayhem

MAIHEMS ▸ maihem

MAIK n old halfpenny

MAIKO n apprentice geisha **maikos**

MAIKS ▶ **maik**

MAIL n, vb

MAILBAG n large bag for transporting or delivering mail

MAILBOX n box into which letters and parcels are delivered

MAILCAR = **mailcoach**

MAILE n halfpenny

MAILED ▶ **mail**

MAILER n person who addresses or mails letters, etc **mailers**

MAILES ▶ **maile**

MAILING ▶ **mail**

MAILL n Scots word meaning rent

MAILLOT n tights worn for ballet, gymnastics, etc

MAILLS ▶ **maill**

MAILMAN n postman **mailmen**

MAILS ▶ **mail**

MAILVAN n vehicle used to transport post

MAIM vb, n maimed, maimer, maimers, maiming, maims

MAIN adj, n, vb mained, mainer, mainest, maining

MAINLY adv

MAINOR n act of doing something **mainors, mainour**

MAINS ▶ **main**

MAINTOP n top or platform at the head of the mainmast

MAIR Scots form of ▶ **more**

MAIRE n New Zealand tree **maires**

MAIRS ▶ **mair**

MAISE n measure of herring **maises**

MAIST Scot word for ▶ **most**

MAISTER Scots word for ▶ **master**

MAISTRY ▶ **maister**

MAISTS ▶ **maist**

MAIZE n maizes

MAJAGUA = **mahoe**

MAJESTY n

MAJLIS n (in Arab countries) an assembly

MAJOR adj, n, vb

MAJORAT n estate, the right to which is that of the first born child of a family

MAJORED ▶ **major**

MAJORLY adv very

MAJORS ▶ **major**

MAK Scot word for ▶ **make**

MAKABLE ▶ **make**

MAKAR = **maker**

MAKARS ▶ **makar**

MAKE vb, n

MAKER n person or company that makes something **makers**

MAKES ▶ **make**

MAKEUP n cosmetics applied to the face **makeups**

MAKI n in Japanese cuisine, rice and other ingredients wrapped in a short seaweed roll

MAKING ▶ **make**

MAKINGS pl n potentials, qualities, or materials

MAKIS ▶ **maki**

MAKO n powerful shark of the Atlantic and Pacific Oceans **makos**

MAKS ▶ **mak**

MAKUTA plural of ▶ **likuta**

MAKUTU n Polynesian witchcraft ▷ vb cast a spell on **makutus**

MAL n illness

MALA n string of beads or knots, used in praying and meditating

MALACCA n stem of the rattan palm

MALACIA n softening of an organ or tissue

MALADY n

MALAISE n

MALAM = **mallam**

MALAMS ▶ **malam**

MALANGA = **cocoyam**

MALAR n cheekbone ▷ adj of or relating to the cheek or cheekbone

MALARIA n

MALARKY = **malarkey**

MALARS ▶ **malar**

MALAS ▶ **mala**

MALATE n any salt or ester of malic acid **malates**

MALAX vb soften **malaxed, malaxes**

MALE adj, n

MALEATE n any salt or ester of maleic acid

MALEFIC adj causing evil

MALEIC adj as in **maleic acid** colourless soluble crystalline substance

MALES ▸ male

MALFED adj having malfunctioned

MALGRE = maugre

MALGRED ▸ malgre

MALGRES ▸ malgre

MALI n member of an Indian caste

MALIBU n as in **malibu board** lightweight surfboard

MALIC adj as in **malic acid** colourless crystalline compound occurring in apples

MALICE n, vb maliced, malices

MALICHO n mischief

MALIGN vb, adj maligns

MALIK n person of authority in India maliks

MALINE n stiff net malines

MALIS ▸ mali

MALISM n belief that evil dominates world malisms

MALISON archaic or poetic word for ▸ **curse** malist

MALKIN archaic or dialect name for a ▸ **cat**

MALKINS ▸ malkin

MALL n street or shopping area closed to vehicles ▷ vb maul

MALLAM n (in W Africa) expert in the Koran mallams

MALLARD n

MALLED ▸ mall

MALLEE n mallees

MALLEI ▸ malleus

MALLET n mallets

MALLEUS n small bone in the middle ear

MALLING ▸ mall

MALLOW n plant with pink or purple flowers mallows

MALLS ▸ mall

MALM n soft greyish limestone that crumbles easily

MALMAG n Asian monkey malmags

MALMIER ▸ malmy

MALMS ▸ malm

MALMSEY n sweet Madeira wine

MALMY adj looking like malm

MALODOR = malodour

MALONIC adj as in **malonic acid** colourless crystalline compound

MALOTI plural of ▸ **loti**

MALS ▸ mal

MALT n, vb

MALTASE n enzyme that hydrolyses maltose to glucose

MALTED ▸ malt

MALTEDS ▸ malt

MALTESE adj as in **maltese cross** cross-shaped part of a film projector

MALTHA n any of various naturally occurring mixtures of hydrocarbons malthas

MALTIER ▸ malty

MALTING n building in which malt is made or stored

MALTMAN = maltster

MALTMEN ▸ maltman

MALTOL n food additive maltols

MALTOSE n sugar formed by the action of enzymes on starch

MALTS ▸ malt

MALTY adj of, like, or containing malt

MALVA n mallow plant malvas

MALWA n Ugandan drink brewed from millet

MALWARE n computer program designed to cause damage to a system

MALWAS ▸ malwa

MAM = mother

MAMA n mother

MAMAGUY vb deceive or tease ▷ n deception or flattery

MAMAKAU = mamaku

MAMAKO = mamaku

MAMAKOS ▸ mamako

MAMAKU n tall edible New Zealand tree fern mamakus

MAMAS ▸ mama

MAMBA n deadly S African snake mambas

MAMBO n Latin American dance resembling the rumba ▷ vb perform this dance **mamboed, mamboes, mambos**

MAMEE = **mamey**

MAMEES ▷ **mamee**

MAMELON n small rounded hillock

MAMEY n tropical tree **mameyes, mameys**

MAMIE n tropical tree **mamies**

MAMILLA n nipple or teat

MAMLUK = **mameluke**

MAMLUKS ▷ **mamluk**

MAMMA n buxom and voluptuous woman **mammae**

MAMMAL n mammals

MAMMARY adj

MAMMAS ▷ **mamma**

MAMMATE adj having breasts

MAMMATI > **mammatus**

MAMMEE = **mamey**

MAMMEES ▷ **mammee**

MAMMER vb hesitate **mammers**

MAMMET = **maumet**

MAMMETS ▷ **mammet**

MAMMEY = **mamey**

MAMMEYS ▷ **mammey**

MAMMIE = **mammy**

MAMMIES ▷ **mammy**

MAMMOCK n fragment ▷ vb tear or shred

MAMMON n wealth regarded as a source of evil **mammons**

MAMMOTH n, adj

MAMMY n Black woman employed as a nurse or servant to a White family

MAMPARA n foolish person, idiot

MAMPOER n home-distilled brandy

MAMS ▷ **mam**

MAMZER n child of an incestuous or adulterous union **mamzers**

MAN n, vb

MANA n

MANACLE vb, n

MANAGE vb **managed**

MANAGER n

MANAGES ▷ **manage**

MANAIA n figure in Māori carving **manaias**

MANAKIN = **manikin**

MANANA n tomorrow ▷ adv tomorrow **mananas**

MANAS ▷ **mana**

MANAT n standard monetary unit of Azerbaijan

MANATEE n large tropical plant-eating aquatic mammal **manati**

MANATIS ▷ **manati**

MANATS ▷ **manat**

MANATU n large flowering deciduous New Zealand tree **manatus**

MANAWA in New Zealand, = **mangrove**

MANAWAS ▷ **manawa**

MANCALA n African and Asian board game

MANCHE n long sleeve **manches**

MANCHET n type of bread

MANCUS n former English coin

MAND ▷ **man**

MANDALA n circular design symbolizing the universe

MANDATE n, vb

MANDI n (in India) a big market

MANDIOC = **manioc**

MANDIR n **mandira, mandirs**

MANDIS ▷ **mandi**

MANDOLA n early type of mandolin

MANDOM n mankind **mandoms**

MANDORA n ancestor of mandolin

MANDREL n shaft on which work is held in a lathe **mandril**

MANE n **maned**

MANEGE n art of training horses and riders ▷ vb train horse **maneged, maneges**

MANEH = **mina**

MANEHS ▷ **maneh**

MANENT ▷ **manet**

MANES pl n spirits of the dead, often revered as minor deities

MANET vb theatre direction, remain on stage

MANFUL adj determined and brave

MANG vb speak

MANGA n type of Japanese comic book

MANGABY = mangabey

MANGAL n Turkish brazier **mangals**

MANGAS ▶ manga

MANGE n skin disease of domestic animals

MANGEAO n small New Zealand tree with glossy leaves

MANGED ▶ mange

MANGEL n Eurasian variety of the beet plant **mangels**

MANGER n mangers

MANGES ▶ mange

MANGEY = mangy

MANGIER ▶ mangy

MANGILY ▶ mangy

MANGING ▶ mang

MANGLE vb, n mangled, mangler, mangles

MANGO n mangoes

MANGOLD n type of root vegetable

MANGOS ▶ mango

MANGS ▶ mang

MANGY adj

MANHOLE n

MANHOOD n

MANHUNT n organized search, usu by police, for a wanted man

MANI n place to pray

MANIA n

MANIAC n maniacs

MANIAS ▶ mania

MANIC adj, n manics

MANIES ▶ many

MANIHOC variation of ▶ manioc

MANIHOT n tropical American plant

MANIKIN n little man or dwarf

MANILA n strong brown paper used for envelopes **manilas**

MANILLA n early currency in W Africa in the form of a small bracelet

MANILLE n (in ombre and quadrille) the second best trump

MANIOC = cassava

MANIOCA = manioc

MANIOCS ▶ manioc

MANIPLE n (in ancient Rome) a unit of 120 to 200 foot soldiers

MANIS n pangolin

MANITO = manitou

MANITOS ▶ manito

MANITOU n (among the Algonquian Indians) a deified spirit or force manitu

MANITUS ▶ manitu

MANJACK n single individual

MANKIER ▶ manky

MANKIND n

MANKINI n

MANKY adj worthless, rotten, or in bad taste

MANLESS ▶ man

MANLIER ▶ manly

MANLIKE adj resembling or befitting a man

MANLILY ▶ manly

MANLY adj

MANMADE adj made or produced by man

MANNA n

MANNAN n drug derived from mannose mannans

MANNAS ▶ manna

MANNED ▶ man

MANNER n

MANNERS pl n person's social conduct

MANNING ▶ man

MANNISH adj (of a woman) like a man

MANNITE = mannitol

MANNOSE n hexose sugar

MANO n stone for grinding grain

MANOAO n New Zealand shrub manoaos

MANOR n manors

MANOS ▶ mano

MANPACK n load carried by one person

MANQUE adj would-be

MANRED n homage manreds, manrent

MANROPE n rope railing

MANS ▶ man

MANSARD n type of sloping roof

MANSE n house provided for a minister in some religious denominations manses

MANSION n

MANTA n type of large ray with very wide winglike pectoral fins mantas

MANTEAU n cloak or mantle
MANTEEL n cloak
MANTEL n structure round a fireplace ▷ vb construct a mantel **mantels**
MANTES ▶ mantis
MANTIC adj of or relating to divination and prophecy
MANTID = mantis
MANTIDS ▶ mantid
MANTIES ▶ manty
MANTIS n carnivorous insect like a grasshopper
MANTLE = mantel
MANTLED ▶ mantle
MANTLES ▶ mantle
MANTLET = mantelet
MANTO = manteau
MANTOES ▶ manto
MANTOS ▶ manto
MANTRA n mantram
MANTRAP n snare for catching people, esp trespassers
MANTRAS ▶ mantra
MANTRIC ▶ mantra
MANTUA n loose gown of the 17th and 18th centuries **mantuas, manty**
MANUAL adj, n **manuals, manuary**
MANUKA n New Zealand tree **manukas**
MANUL n Asian wildcat **manuls**
MANUMEA n pigeon of Samoa
MANUMIT vb free from slavery

MANURE n, vb **manured, manurer, manures**
MANUS n wrist and hand
MANWARD adv towards humankind
MANWISE adv in human way
MANY adj, n
MANYATA = manyatta
MAOMAO n fish of New Zealand seas **maomaos**
MAORMOR = mormaor
MAP n, vb
MAPAU n small New Zealand tree **mapaus**
MAPLE n **maples**
MAPLESS, maplike, mapped, mapper, mappers ▶ map
MAPPERY n making of maps
MAPPING ▶ map
MAPPIST ▶ map
MAPS ▶ map
MAPWISE adv like map
MAQUI n Chilean shrub
MAQUILA n US-owned factory in Mexico
MAQUIS n French underground movement in World War II
MAR vb, n
MARA n harelike S American rodent
MARABI n kind of music popular in S African townships in the 1930s **marabis**
MARABOU n large black-and-white

African stork
MARACA n shaken percussion instrument **maracas**
MARAE n **maraes**
MARAH n bitterness **marahs**
MARANTA n tropical American plant
MARARI n eel-like blennoid food fish **mararis**
MARAS ▶ mara
MARASCA n European cherry tree with red acid-tasting fruit
MARAUD vb wander or raid in search of plunder **marauds**
MARBLE n, vb **marbled, marbler**
MARBLES n game in which marble balls are rolled at one another
MARBLY ▶ marble
MARC n remains of grapes or other fruit that have been pressed for wine-making
MARCATO adj (of notes) heavily accented ▷ adv with each note heavily accented ▷ n heavily accented note
MARCEL n hairstyle characterized by repeated regular waves ▷ vb make such waves in (the hair) **marcels**
MARCH vb, n **marched**
MARCHEN n German story

MARCHER n person who marches

MARCHES ▶ march

MARCONI vb communicate by wireless

MARCS ▶ marc

MARD ▶ mar

MARDIED ▶ mardy

MARDIER ▶ mardy

MARDIES ▶ mardy

MARDY adj (of a child) spoilt ▷ vb behave in mardy way

MARE n

MAREMMA n marshy unhealthy region near the shore, esp in Italy **maremme**

MARENGO adj browned in oil and cooked with tomatoes, mushrooms, garlic, wine, etc

MARERO n **mareros**

MARES ▶ mare

MARG short for **▶ margarine**

MARGAY n feline mammal of Central and S America **margays**

MARGE n margarine

MARGES ▶ marge

MARGIN n, vb margins

MARGOSA n Indian tree

MARGS ▶ marg

MARIA ▶ mare

MARID n spirit in Muslim mythology **marids**

MARIES ▶ mary

MARIMBA n Latin

American percussion instrument

MARINA n marinas

MARINE adj, n

MARINER n

MARINES ▶ marine

MARISH n marsh

MARITAL adj

MARK n line, dot, scar, etc visible on a surface ▷ vb make a mark on

MARKA n unit of currency introduced as an interim currency in Bosnia-Herzegovina **markas**

MARKED adj

MARKER n object used to show the position of something **markers**

MARKET n, vb markets

MARKHOR n large wild Himalayan goat

MARKING n arrangement of colours on an animal or plant

MARKKA n former standard monetary unit of Finland **markkaa, markkas**

MARKMAN n person owning land **markmen**

MARKS ▶ mark

MARKUP n percentage or amount added to the cost of a commodity to provide the seller with a profit and to cover overheads, costs, etc **markups**

MARL n soil formed of clay and lime, used as

fertilizer ▷ vb fertilize (land) with marl

MARLE ▶ marvel

MARLED ▶ marl

MARLES ▶ marle

MARLIER ▶ marly

MARLIN = marline

MARLINE n light rope, usually tarred, made of two strands laid left-handed **marling**

MARLINS ▶ marlin

MARLITE n type of marl that contains clay and calcium carbonate

MARLS ▶ marl

MARLY adj marl-like

MARM = madam

MARMEM n as in **marmem alloy** type of alloy

MARMITE n large cooking pot

MARMOSE n South American opossum

MARMOT n burrowing rodent **marmots**

MARMS ▶ marm

MARON n freshwater crustacean **marons**

MAROON adj, vb, n **maroons**

MAROR n Jewish ceremonial dish of bitter herbs **marors**

MARPLOT n person interfering with plot

MARQUE n brand of product, esp of a car

MARQUEE n

MARQUES ▶ marque

MARQUIS n

MARRAM n as in **marram grass** any of several grasses that grow on sandy shores **marrams**

MARRANO n Spanish or Portuguese Jew of the late Middle Ages who was converted to Christianity

MARRED ▶ mar

MARRELS = merils

MARRER ▶ mar

MARRERS ▶ mar

MARRI n W Australian eucalyptus

MARRIED ▶ marry

MARRIER ▶ marry

MARRIES ▶ marry

MARRING ▶ marry

MARRIS ▶ marri

MARRON n large edible sweet chestnut **marrons**

MARROW n, vb **marrows, marrowy**

MARRUM = marram

MARRUMS ▶ marrum

MARRY vb, interj

MARS ▶ mar

MARSALA n dark sweet dessert wine made in Sicily

MARSE = master

MARSES ▶ marse

MARSH n

MARSHAL n, vb

MARSHES ▶ marsh

MARSHY adj of, involving, or like a marsh

MART n market ▷ vb sell or trade **marted**

MARTEL n hammer-shaped weapon ▷ vb use such a weapon **martels**

MARTEN n weasel-like animal **martens**

MARTEXT n preacher who makes many mistakes

MARTIAL adj

MARTIAN n inhabitant of Mars

MARTIN n bird with a slightly forked tail

MARTING ▶ mart

MARTINI n cocktail of vermouth and gin

MARTINS ▶ martin

MARTLET n footless bird often found in coats of arms

MARTS ▶ mart

MARTYR n, vb **martyrs**

MARTYRY n shrine or chapel erected in honour of a martyr

MARVEL vb, n **marvels**

MARVER vb roll molten glass on slab **marvers**

MARVIER ▶ marvy

MARVY shortened form of > marvelous

MARY n woman

MARYBUD n bud of marigold

MAS ▶ ma

MASA n Mexican maize dough

MASALA n mixture of spices ground into a paste ▷ adj spicy **masalas**

MASAS ▶ masa

MASCARA n

MASCLE n charge consisting of a lozenge with a lozenge-shaped hole in the middle **mascled, mascles**

MASCON n any of several lunar regions of high gravity **mascons**

MASCOT n **mascots**

MASCULY ▶ mascle

MASE vb function as maser **mased**

MASER n device for amplifying microwaves **masers**

MASES ▶ mase

MASH n, vb **mashed, masher, mashers, mashes**

MASHIE n former golf club, used for approach shots

MASHIER ▶ mashy

MASHIES ▶ mashie

MASHING ▶ mash

MASHLAM = maslin

MASHLIM = maslin

MASHLIN = maslin

MASHLUM = maslin

MASHMAN n brewery worker **mashmen**

MASHUA n South American plant **mashuas**

MASHUP n piece of music in which a producer or DJ blends together two or more tracks **mashups**

MASHY adj like mash

MASING ▶ mase

MASJID n mosque

MASJIDS ▶ masjid

MASK n, vb

MASKED adj disguised or covered by or as if by a mask

MASKEG n North American bog **maskegs**

MASKER n person who wears a mask or takes part in a masque **maskers**

MASKING n act or practice of masking

MASKS ▶ mask

MASLIN n mixture of wheat, rye or other grain **maslins**

MASON n, vb **masoned**

MASONIC adj

MASONRY n

MASONS ▶ mason

MASQUE n 16th–17th-century form of dramatic entertainment

MASQUER = masker

MASQUES ▶ masque

MASS n, adj, vb

MASSA old fashioned variant of ▶ master

MASSAGE n, vb

MASSAS ▶ massa

MASSE n billiard stroke that makes the ball move in a curve around another ball

MASSED ▶ mass

MASSES pl n body of common people

MASSEUR n

MASSIER ▶ massy

MASSIF n **massifs**

MASSING ▶ mass

MASSIVE adj, n **massy**

MAST n

MASTABA n mud-brick superstructure above tombs in ancient Egypt

MASTED ▶ mast

MASTER n, vb **masters**

MASTERY n

MASTFUL ▶ mast

MASTIC n gum obtained from certain trees **mastich, mastics**

MASTIER ▶ mast

MASTIFF n large dog

MASTING ▶ mast

MASTIX n type of gum

MASTOID n projection of the bone behind the ear ▷ adj shaped like a nipple or breast

MASTS ▶ mast

MASTY ▶ mast

MASU n Japanese salmon

MASULA = masoolah

MASULAS ▶ masula

MASUS ▶ masu

MAT n, vb, adj

MATADOR n

MATAI n New Zealand tree, the wood of which is used for timber for building **matais**

MATATA = fernbird

MATATAS ▶ matata

MATATU n type of shared taxi used in Kenya **matatus**

MATCH n, vb **matched, matcher, matches**

MATCHET = machete

MATCHUP n sports match

MATE n, vb **mated**

MATELOT n sailor

MATER n mother: often used facetiously **maters**

MATES ▶ mate

MATEY adj friendly or intimate ▷ n friend or fellow: usually used in direct address **mateys**

MATH = mathematics

MATHS = mathematics

MATICO n Peruvian shrub **maticos**

MATIER ▶ maty

MATIES ▶ maty

MATIEST ▶ maty

MATILDA n bushman's swag

MATILY ▶ maty

MATIN adj of or relating to matins **matinal**

MATINEE n

MATING ▶ mate

MATINGS ▶ mate

MATINS pl n

MATIPO n New Zealand shrub **matipos**

MATJES = maatjes

MATLESS ▶ mat

MATLO = matelot

MATLOS ▶ matlo

MATLOW = matelot

MATLOWS ▶ matlow

MATOKE n (in Uganda) the flesh of bananas, boiled and mashed as a food **matokes, matooke**

MATRASS n long-necked glass flask

MATRES ▶ mater

MATRIC n matriculation

MATRICE = matrix

MATRICS ▶ matric

MATRIX n

MATRON n matrons

MATROSS n gunner's assistant

MATS ▶ mat

MATSAH = matzo

MATSAHS ▶ matsah

MATSURI n Japanese religious ceremony

MATT adj matte

MATTED ▶ mat

MATTER n, vb matters

MATTERY adj discharging pus

MATTES ▶ matte

MATTIE n young herring matties

MATTIFY vb make (the skin of the face) less oily or shiny using cosmetics

MATTIN = matin

MATTING ▶ mat

MATTINS = matins

MATTOCK n large pick with one of its blade ends flattened for loosening soil

MATTOID n person displaying eccentric behaviour and mental characteristics

MATTS ▶ matt

MATURE adj, vb matured, maturer, matures

MATWEED n grass found on moors

MATY = matey

MATZA = matzo

MATZAH = matzo

MATZAHS ▶ matzah

MATZAS ▶ matza

MATZO n large very thin biscuit of unleavened bread matzoh

MATZOHS ▶ matzoh

MATZOON n fermented milk product similar to yogurt

MATZOS ▶ matzo

MATZOT ▶ matzo

MATZOTH ▶ matzoh

MAUBIES ▶ mauby

MAUBY n Caribbean bittersweet drink

MAUD n shawl or rug of grey wool plaid

MAUDLIN adj

MAUDS ▶ maud

MAUGER = maugre

MAUGRE prep in spite of
▷ vb behave spitefully towards maugred, maugres

MAUL vb, n mauled, mauler

MAULERS pl n hands

MAULGRE = maugre

MAULING ▶ maul

MAULS ▶ maul

MAULVI n expert in Islamic law maulvis

MAUMET n false god maumets

MAUN dialect word for
▶ must

MAUND n unit of weight used in Asia
▷ vb beg maunded

MAUNDER vb talk or act aimlessly or idly

MAUNDS ▶ maund

MAUNDY n ceremonial washing of the feet of poor people

MAUNGY adj (esp of a child) sulky, bad-tempered, or peevish

MAUNNA vb Scots term meaning must not

MAURI n soul mauris

MAUT = mahout

MAUTHER n girl

MAUTS ▶ maut

MAUVAIS adj bad

MAUVE adj, n

MAUVEIN = mauveine

MAUVER ▶ mauve

MAUVES ▶ mauve

MAUVEST ▶ mauve

MAUVIN = mauveine

MAUVINE = mauveine

MAUVINS ▶ mauvin

MAVEN n expert or connoisseur mavens

MAVIE n type of thrush mavies

MAVIN = maven

MAVINS ▶ mavin

MAVIS n song thrush mavises

MAW n animal's mouth, throat, or stomach
▷ vb eat or bite mawed

MAWGER adj (of persons or animals) thin or lean

MAWING ▶ maw

MAWK n maggot mawkier

MAWKIN n slovenly woman mawkins

MAWKISH adj

MAWKS ▶ mawk

MAWKY ▶ mawk

MAWMET = maumet

MAWMETS ▶ mawmet

MAWN ▶ maw

MAWPUS = mopus

MAWR ▶ mauther

MAWRS ▶ mawr

MAWS ▶ maw

MAWSEED n poppy seed

MAWTHER = mauther

MAX vb reach the full extent **maxed, maxes**

> Max is a short form of **maximum**, and can also be a verb giving **maxed, maxes** and **maxing**. Another of the key words using X, and it can be extended to **maxi**.

MAXI adj (of a garment) very long ▷ n type of large racing yacht

MAXILLA n upper jawbone of a vertebrate

MAXIM n

MAXIMA ▶ maximum

MAXIMAL adj maximum ▷ n maximum

MAXIMIN n highest of a set of minimum values

MAXIMS ▶ maxim

MAXIMUM n, adj

MAXIMUS n method rung on twelve bells

MAXING ▶ max

MAXIS ▶ maxi

MAXIXE n Brazilian dance in duple time **maxixes**

MAXWELL n cgs unit of magnetic flux

MAY vb

MAYA n illusion, esp the material world of the senses regarded as illusory **mayan, mayas**

MAYBE adv, sentence substitute **maybes**

MAYBIRD n American songbird

MAYBUSH n flowering shrub

MAYDAY n international radiotelephone distress signal **maydays**

MAYED ▶ may

MAYEST = mayst

MAYFLY n short-lived aquatic insect

MAYHAP archaic word for ▶ perhaps

MAYHEM n mayhems

MAYING ▶ may

MAYINGS ▶ maying

MAYO n mayonnaise

MAYOR n mayoral, mayors

MAYOS ▶ mayo

MAYPOLE n pole set up for dancing round on the first day of May to celebrate spring

MAYPOP n American wild flower **maypops**

MAYS ▶ may

MAYST singular form of the present tense of ▶ may

MAYSTER = master

MAYVIN = maven

MAYVINS ▶ mayvin

MAYWEED n widespread Eurasian weedy plant

MAZARD = mazer

MAZARDS ▶ mazard

MAZE n mazed

MAZEDLY adv in a bewildered way

MAZEFUL ▶ maze

MAZER n large hardwood drinking bowl **mazers**

MAZES ▶ maze

MAZEY adj dizzy

MAZHBI n low-caste Sikh **mazhbis**

MAZIER ▶ mazy

MAZIEST ▶ mazy

MAZILY ▶ mazy

MAZING ▶ maze

MAZOUT = mazut

MAZOUTS ▶ mazout

MAZUMA n money **mazumas**

MAZURKA n lively Polish dance

MAZUT n residue left after distillation of petrol **mazuts**

MAZY adj of or like a maze

MAZZARD = mazard

MBIRA n African musical instrument **mbiras**

ME n, pron

MEACOCK n timid person

MEAD n alcoholic drink made from honey

MEADOW n meadows, meadowy

MEADS ▶ mead

MEAGER = meagre

MEAGRE adj, n meagrer, meagres

MEAL n, vb mealed

MEALER n person eating but not lodging

at boarding house
mealers
MEALIE n
MEALIER ▶ mealy
MEALIES South African
word for ▶ maize
MEALING ▶ meal
MEALS ▶ meal
MEALY adj resembling
meal
MEAN vb, adj, n
MEANDER vb, n
MEANE vb moan
meaned
MEANER ▶ mean
MEANERS ▶ mean
MEANES ▶ meane
MEANEST ▶ mean
MEANIE n unkind or
miserly person
MEANIES ▶ meany
MEANING n what
something means
MEANLY ▶ mean
MEANS ▶ mean
MEANT ▶ mean
MEANY = meanie
MEARE ▶ mere
MEARES ▶ meare
MEARING adj forming
boundary
MEASE vb assuage
**meased, meases,
measing**
MEASLE vb infect with
measles
MEASLED adj (of cattle,
sheep, or pigs) infested
with tapeworm larvae
MEASLES n
MEASLY adj
MEASURE n, vb
MEAT n
MEATAL ▶ meatus

MEATAXE n meat
cleaver
MEATED adj fattened
MEATH = mead
MEATHE = mead
MEATHES ▶ meathe
MEATHS ▶ meath
MEATIER ▶ meaty
MEATILY ▶ meaty
MEATMAN n meat seller
meatmen
MEATS ▶ meat
MEATUS n natural
opening or channel
MEATY adj (tasting) of
or like meat
MEAWES = mews
MEAZEL = mesel
MEAZELS ▶ meazel
MEBOS n South African
dish of dried apricots
meboses
MECCA n place that
attracts many visitors
meccas
MECK = maik
MECKS ▶ meck
MECONIC adj derived
from poppies
MECONIN n substance
found in opium
MED n doctor
MEDACCA n Japanese
freshwater fish
medaka
MEDAKAS ▶ medaka
MEDAL n, vb medaled
MEDALET n small medal
MEDALS ▶ medal
MEDDLE vb meddled,
meddler, meddles
MEDEVAC n evacuation
of casualties ▷ vb
transport (a wounded

or sick person) to
hospital
MEDFLY n
Mediterranean fruit fly
MEDIA n
MEDIACY n quality or
state of being mediate
MEDIAD adj situated
near the median line
or plane of an
organism
MEDIAE ▶ medium
MEDIAL adj of or in the
middle ▷ n speech
sound between being
fortis and lenis
medials
MEDIAN n, adj medians
MEDIANT n third degree
of a major or minor
scale
MEDIAS ▶ medium
MEDIATE vb, adj
MEDIC n
MEDICAL adj, n
MEDICK n type of small
leguminous plant with
yellow or purple
flowers **medicks**
MEDICO n doctor or
medical student
medicos
MEDICS ▶ medic
MEDIGAP n private
health insurance
MEDII ▶ medius
MEDINA n ancient
quarter of North
African city **medinas**
MEDIUM adj, n
MEDIUMS pl n
medium-dated
gilt-edged securities
MEDIUS n middle finger

MEDIVAC variant spelling of ▶ **medevac**

MEDLAR n apple-like fruit of a small tree **medlars**

MEDLE = **meddle**

MEDLED ▶ **medle**

MEDLES ▶ **medle**

MEDLEY n, adj **medleys**

MEDLING ▶ **medle**

MEDRESA > **madrasa**

MEDRESE = **madrasah**

MEDS ▶ **med**

MEDULLA n marrow, pith, or inner tissue

MEDUSA n jellyfish **medusae, medusal, medusan, medusas**

MEE n Malaysian noodle dish

MEED n recompense **meeds**

MEEK adj

MEEKEN vb make meek **meekens**

MEEKER ▶ **meek**

MEEKEST ▶ **meek**

MEEKLY ▶ **meek**

MEEMIE n hysterical person **meemies**

MEER = **mere**

MEERCAT = **meerkat**

MEERED ▶ **meer**

MEERING ▶ **meer**

MEERKAT n S African mongoose

MEERS ▶ **meer**

MEES ▶ **mee**

MEET vb, n, adj **meeter, meeters, meetest, meeting, meetly, meets**

MEFF dialect word for ▶ **tramp**

MEFFS ▶ **meff**

MEG short for > **megabyte**

MEGA adj extremely good, great, or successful

MEGABAR n unit of million bars

MEGABIT n one million bits

MEGAFOG n amplified fog signal

MEGAHIT n great success

MEGAPOD = **megapode**

MEGARA ▶ **megaron**

MEGARAD n unit of million rads

MEGARON n tripartite rectangular room, found in Bronze Age Greece and Asia Minor

MEGASS another name for ▶ **bagasse**

MEGASSE = **megass**

MEGATON n

MEGILLA = **megillah**

MEGILP n oil-painting medium of linseed oil mixed with mastic varnish or turpentine **megilph, megilps**

MEGOHM n one million ohms **megohms**

MEGRIM n caprice

MEGRIMS n fit of depression

MEGS ▶ **meg**

MEH interj

MEHNDI n (esp in India) the practice of painting designs on the hands, feet, etc using henna **mehndis**

MEIKLE adj Scots word meaning large

MEIN Scots word for ▶ **moan**

MEINED ▶ **mein**

MEINEY = **meiny**

MEINEYS ▶ **meiny**

MEINIE = **meiny**

MEINIES ▶ **meiny**

MEINING ▶ **mein**

MEINS ▶ **mein**

MEINT = **ming**

MEINY n retinue or household

MEIOSES ▶ **meiosis**

MEIOSIS ▶ **meiotic**

MEISHI n business card in Japan **meishis**

MEISTER n person who excels at a particular activity

MEITH n landmark **meiths**

MEJLIS = **majlis**

MEKKA = **mecca**

MEKKAS ▶ **mekka**

MEL n pure form of honey

MELA n Asian cultural or religious fair or festival

MELAMED n Hebrew teacher

MELANGE n mixture

MELANIC adj relating to melanism or melanosis ▷ n darker form of creature

MELANIN n dark pigment found in the hair, skin, and eyes

MELANO n person with abnormally dark skin **melanos**

MELAS ▶ **mela**

MELBA adj relating to a type of dessert sauce or toast

MELD vb merge or blend ▷ n act of melding **melded, melder, melders, melding, melds**

MELEE n noisy confused fight or crowd **melees**

MELENA n excrement or vomit stained by blood **melenas**

MELIC adj (of poetry, esp ancient Greek lyric poems) intended to be sung ▷ n type of grass

MELICK n either of two pale green perennial grasses **melicks**

MELICS ▶ **melic**

MELIK = **malik**

MELIKS ▶ **melik**

MELILOT n plant with small white or yellow fragrant flowers

MELISMA n expressive vocal phrase or passage consisting of several notes sung to one syllable

MELL vb mix

MELLAY = **melee**

MELLAYS ▶ **mellay**

MELLED ▶ **mell**

MELLING ▶ **mell**

MELLITE n soft yellow mineral

MELLOW adj, vb **mellows, mellowy**

MELLS ▶ **mell**

MELODIA = **melodica**

MELODIC adj

MELODY n

MELOID n type of long-legged beetle **meloids**

MELON n melons

MELS ▶ **mel**

MELT vb, n

MELTAGE n process or result of melting or the amount melted

MELTED ▶ **melt**

MELTEMI n northerly wind in the northeast Mediterranean

MELTER ▶ **melt**

MELTERS ▶ **melt**

MELTIER ▶ **melty**

MELTING ▶ **melt**

MELTITH n meal

MELTON n heavy smooth woollen fabric with a short nap, used esp for overcoats **meltons**

MELTS ▶ **melt**

MELTY adj tending to melt

MEM n 13th letter in the Hebrew alphabet, transliterated as m

MEMBER n, adj **members**

MEMBRAL adj of limbs

MEME n idea or element of social behaviour

MEMENTO n

MEMES ▶ **meme**

MEMETIC adj of or relating to a meme

MEMO n

MEMOIR n biography or historical account based on personal knowledge

MEMOIRS pl n

MEMORY n

MEMOS ▶ **memo**

MEMS ▶ **mem**

MEN ▶ **man**

MENACE n, vb **menaced, menacer, menaces**

MENAD = **maenad**

MENADS ▶ **menad**

MENAGE old form of ▶ **manage**

MENAGED ▶ **menage**

MENAGES ▶ **menage**

MENAZON n type of insecticide

MEND vb, n **mended, mender, menders**

MENDIGO n Spanish beggar or vagrant

MENDING n something to be mended, esp clothes

MENDS ▶ **mend**

MENE Scots form of ▶ **moan**

MENED ▶ **mene**

MENEER n S African title of address **meneers**

MENES ▶ **mene**

MENFOLK pl n men collectively, esp the men of a particular family

MENG vb mix **menge, menged**

MENGES ▶ **menge**

MENGING ▶ **meng**

MENGS ▶ **meng**

MENHIR n single upright prehistoric stone **menhirs**

MENIAL adj, n **menials**

MENING ▸ mene

MENINX n one of three membranes that envelop the brain and spinal cord

MENISCI > meniscus

MENO adv musical instruction indicating 'less'

MENORAH n

MENSA n faint constellation in the S hemisphere

MENSAE n star of the mensa constellation

MENSAL adj monthly

MENSAS ▸ mensa

MENSCH n decent person **menschy**

MENSE vb grace **mensed**

MENSES n menstruation

MENSH vb mention **menshed**

MENSHEN n Chinese door god

MENSHES ▸ mensh

MENSING ▸ mense

MENSUAL = mensal

MENT = ming

MENTA ▸ mentum

MENTAL adj

MENTEE n person trained by mentor **mentees**

MENTHOL n

MENTION vb, n

MENTO n Jamaican song

MENTOR n, vb **mentors**

MENTOS ▸ mento

MENTUM ▸ chin

MENU n

MENUDO n Mexican soup **menudos**

MENUS ▸ menu

MENYIE = meinie

MENYIES ▸ menyie

MEOU = meow

MEOUED ▸ meou

MEOUING ▸ meou

MEOUS ▸ meou

MEOW vb (of a cat) to make a characteristic crying sound ▸ interj imitation of this sound **meowed, meowing, meows**

MERANTI n wood from any of several Malaysian trees

MERC n mercenary

MERCAT Scots word for ▸ **market**

MERCATS ▸ mercat

MERCER n dealer in textile fabrics and fine cloth **mercers, mercery**

MERCES ▸ merc

MERCH n merchandise **merches**

MERCHET n (in feudal England) fine paid by tenant to his lord for allowing the marriage of his daughter

MERCIES ▸ mercy

MERCIFY vb show mercy to

MERCS ▸ merc

MERCURY n

MERCY n

MERDE French word for ▸ **excrement**

MERDES ▸ merde

MERE adj, n, vb

MERED adj forming a boundary

MEREL = meril

MERELL = meril

MERELLS = merils

MERELS ▸ merils

MERELY adv only

MERER ▸ mere

MERES ▸ mere

MEREST ▸ mere

MERFOLK n mermaids and mermen

MERGE vb **merged**

MERGEE n business taken over by merger **mergees**

MERGER n combination of business firms into one **mergers**

MERGES ▸ merge

MERGING ▸ merge

MERI n Māori war club

MERIL n counter used in merils

MERILS n old board game

MERING ▸ mere

MERINGS ▸ mering

MERINO n **merinos**

MERIS ▸ meri

MERISES ▸ merisis

MERISIS n growth by division of cells

MERISM n duplication of biological parts **merisms**

MERIT n, vb **merited, merits**

MERK n old Scots coin

MERKIN n artificial hairpiece for the pudendum **merkins**

MERKS ▸ merk

MERL = **merle**

MERLE adj (of a dog, esp a collie) having a bluish-grey coat with speckles or streaks of black **merles**

MERLIN n small falcon

MERLING n whiting

MERLINS ▸ merlin

MERLON n solid upright section in a crenellated battlement **merlons**

MERLOT n type of black grape **merlots**

MERLS ▸ merl

MERMAID n

MERMAN n male counterpart of the mermaid **mermen**

MEROME = **merosome**

MEROMES ▸ merome

MERONYM n part of something used to refer to the whole

MEROPIA n partial blindness **meropic**

MERRIER ▸ merry

MERRIES ▸ merry

MERRILY ▸ merry

MERRY adj, n

MERSE n low level ground by a river or shore **merses**

MERSION n dipping in water

MES ▸ me

MESA n flat-topped hill found in arid regions

MESAIL n visor **mesails**

MESAL = **mesial**

MESALLY ▸ mesal

MESARCH adj (of a xylem strand) having the first-formed xylem surrounded by that formed later, as in fern stems

MESAS ▸ mesa

MESCAL n spineless globe-shaped cactus **mescals**

MESCLUM = **mesclun**

MESCLUN n type of green salad

MESE n middle string on lyre

MESEEMS vb it seems to me

MESEL n leper

MESELED adj afflicted by leprosy

MESELS ▸ mesel

MESES ▸ mese

MESETA n plateau in Spain **mesetas**

MESH n, vb, adj **meshed, meshes, meshier, meshing**

MESHUGA adj crazy

MESHY ▸ mesh

MESIAD adj relating to or situated at the middle or centre

MESIAL another word for ▸ **medial**

MESIAN = **mesial**

MESIC ▸ meson

MESNE adj (in law) intermediate or intervening **mesnes**

MESON n elementary atomic particle **mesonic, mesons**

MESQUIN adj mean

MESQUIT = **mesquite**

MESS n, vb

MESSAGE n, vb

MESSAN Scots word for ▸ **dog**

MESSANS ▸ messan

MESSED ▸ mess

MESSES ▸ mess

MESSIAH n exceptional or hoped for liberator **messias**

MESSIER ▸ messy

MESSILY ▸ messy

MESSING ▸ mess

MESSMAN n sailor working in ship's mess **messmen**

MESSY adj dirty, confused, or untidy

MESTEE = **mustee**

MESTEES ▸ mestee

MESTER n master: used as a term of address for a man who is the head of a house **mesters**

MESTESO n Spanish music genre

MESTINO n person of mixed race

MESTIZA ▸ mestizo

MESTIZO n person of mixed parentage

MESTO adj sad

MESTOM = **mestome**

MESTOME n conducting tissue associated with parenchyma

MESTOMS ▸ mestom

MET n meteorology

META adj in a self-parodying style

METAGE n official measuring of weight or contents **metages**

METAL n, adj, vb **metaled**

METALLY adj like metal

METALS ▶ metal

METAMER n any of two or more isomeric compounds exhibiting metamerism

METATAG n element of HTML code used by search engines to index pages

METATE n stone for grinding grain on **metates**

METAYER n farmer who pays rent in kind

METAZOA > metazoan

METCAST n weather forecast

METE vb, n **meted**

METEOR n **meteors**

METEPA n type of pesticide **metepas**

METER = **metre**

METERED ▶ meter

METERS ▶ meter

METES ▶ mete

METH n variety of amphetamine

METHANE n

METHINK = **methinks**

METHO n methylated spirits

METHOD n **methods**

METHOS ▶ metho

METHOXY n steroid drug

METHS n

METHYL n compound containing a saturated hydrocarbon group of atoms **methyls**

METIC n (in ancient Greece) alien having some rights of citizenship

METICAL n money unit in Mozambique

METICS ▶ metic

METIER n profession or trade **metiers**

METIF n person of mixed race **metifs**

METING ▶ mete

METIS n person of mixed parentage **metisse**

METOL n organic substance used as a photographic developer **metols**

METONYM n word used in a metonymy

METOPAE ▶ metope

METOPE n square space between two triglyphs in a Doric frieze **metopes**

METOPIC adj of or relating to the forehead

METOPON n painkilling drug

METRE n, vb **metred**, **metres**

METRIC adj

METRICS n art of using poetic metre

METRIFY vb render into poetic metre

METRING ▶ metre

METRIST n person skilled in the use of poetic metre

METRO n **metros**

METS ▶ met

METTLE n

METTLED adj spirited, courageous, or valiant

METTLES ▶ mettle

METUMP n band for carrying a load or burden **metumps**

MEU another name for ▶ spignel

MEUS ▶ meu

MEUSE n gap through which an animal passed ▷ vb to go through this gap **meused**, **meuses**, **meusing**

MEVE = move

MEVED ▶ meve

MEVES ▶ meve

MEVING ▶ meve

MEVROU n S African title of address **mevrous**

MEW n, vb **mewed**, **mewing**

MEWL vb (esp of a baby) to cry weakly ▷ n weak or whimpering cry **mewled**, **mewler**, **mewlers**, **mewling**, **mewls**

MEWS ▶ meuse

MEWSED ▶ mews

MEWSES ▶ mews

MEWSING ▶ mews

MEYNT ▶ ming

MEZAIL = mesail

MEZAILS ▶ mezail

MEZCAL variant spelling of ▶ mescal

MEZCALS ▶ mezcal

MEZE n type of hors d'oeuvre **mezes**

MEZQUIT = mesquite

| A **mezquit** is a kind of American tree, and makes a great bonus

to play. Remember also that it takes an E to form the variant spelling **mezquite**.

MEZURA = mezuza

MEZUZAH *n* piece of parchment inscribed with biblical passages

MEZUZAS ▶ mezuza

MEZUZOT ▶ mezuzah

MEZZ = mezzanine

MEZZE = meze

MEZZES ▶ mezze

MEZZO *adv* moderately **mezzos**

MGANGA *n* witch doctor **mgangas**

MHO *former name for* ▶ siemens

MHORR *n* African gazelle **mhorrs**

MHOS ▶ mho

MI *n* (in tonic sol-fa) the third degree of any major scale

MIAOU = meow

MIAOUED ▶ miaou

These 7-letter words using all of the vowels are not easy to see on your rack, but they come in useful so often that it's well worth paying them special attention.

MIAOUS ▶ miaou

MIAOW = meow

MIAOWED ▶ miaow

MIAOWS ▶ miaow

MIASM = miasma

MIASMA *n* miasmal, miasmas, miasmic

MIASMS ▶ miasm

MIAUL = meow

MIAULED ▶ miaul

MIAULS ▶ miaul

MIB *n* marble used in games **mibs**

MIBUNA *n* type of Japanese leafy vegetable **mibunas**

MIC *n* microphone

MICA *n* micas

MICATE *vb* add mica to **micated, micates**

MICE ▶ mouse

MICELL = micelle

MICELLA = micelle

MICELLE *n* charged aggregate of molecules of colloidal size in a solution

MICELLS ▶ micell

MICH = mitch; **miched, micher, michers, miches, miching**

MICHAEL *n as in* take the michael *teasing*

MICHE = mich

MICHT *n* Scots word for might **michts**

MICKERY *n* waterhole, esp in a dry riverbed

MICKEY *n* young bull ▷ *vb* drug person's drink **mickeys**

MICKIES ▶ micky

MICKLE *adj* large or abundant ▷ *adv* much ▷ *n* great amount **mickler, mickles**

MICKY = mickey

MICO *n* marmoset **micos**

MICRA ▶ micron

MICRIFY *vb* make very small

MICRO *n* small computer

MICROBE *n*

MICROHM *n* millionth of ohm

MICRON *n* microns

MICROS ▶ micro

MICS ▶ mic

MICTION *n* urination

MID *adj* intermediate, middle ▷ *n* middle ▷ *prep* amid

MIDAIR *n* some point above ground level, in the air **midairs**

MIDBAND *adj* using a range of frequencies between narrowband and broadband

MIDCAP *adj* (of investments) involving medium-sized amounts of capital

MIDCULT *n* middlebrow culture

MIDDAY *n* **middays**

MIDDEN *n* dunghill or rubbish heap **middens**

MIDDEST *adj* in middle

MIDDIE *n* glass or bottle containing 285ml of beer

MIDDIES ▶ middy

MIDDLE *adj, n, vb* **middled**

MIDDLER *n* pupil in middle years at school

MIDDLES ▶ middle

MIDDY *n* middle-sized glass of beer

MIDGE *n* **midges**

MIDGET *n, adj* **midgets**

MIDGIE *n* informal word for a small winged

biting insect such as the midge or sandfly

MIDGIER ▶ midge

MIDGIES ▶ midgie

MIDGUT n middle part of the digestive tract **midguts**

MIDGY ▶ midge

MIDI adj (of a skirt, coat, etc) reaching to below the knee or midcalf ▷ n skirt, coat, etc reaching to below the knee or midcalf

MIDIRON n golf club used for medium-length approach shots

MIDIS ▶ midi

MIDLAND n middle part of a country

MIDLEG n middle of leg **midlegs**

MIDLIFE n middle age

MIDLINE n line at middle of something

MIDLIST n books in publisher's range that sell reasonably well

MIDMOST adv in the middle or midst ▷ n the middle or midst

MIDNOON n noon

MIDRASH n homily on a Jewish scriptural passage

MIDRIB n main vein of a leaf **midribs**

MIDRIFF n

MIDS ▶ mid

MIDSHIP adj in, of, or relating to the middle of a vessel ▷ n middle of a vessel

MIDSIZE adj medium-sized

MIDSOLE n layer between the inner and the outer sole of a shoe

MIDST See ▶ amid

MIDSTS ▶ midst

MIDTERM n middle of a term in a school, university, etc

MIDTOWN n centre of a town

MIDWAY adv, adj, n **midways**

MIDWEEK n middle of the week

MIDWIFE n, vb

MIDWIVE vb act as midwife

MIDYEAR n middle of the year

MIELIE = mealie

MIELIES ▶ mielie

MIEN n person's bearing, demeanour, or appearance **miens**

MIEVE = move

MIEVED ▶ mieve

MIEVES ▶ mieve

MIEVING ▶ mieve

MIFF vb take offence or offend ▷ n petulant mood **miffed**

MIFFIER ▶ miffy

MIFFILY ▶ miffy

MIFFING ▶ miff

MIFFS ▶ miff

MIFFY adj easily upset **mifty**

MIG n marble used in games **migg**

MIGGLE n US word for playing marble **miggles**

MIGGS ▶ migg

MIGHT ▶ may

MIGHTS ▶ may

MIGHTST ▶ may

MIGHTY adj, adv

MIGNON adj small and pretty ▷ n tender boneless cut of meat **mignons**

MIGRANT n person or animal that moves from one place to another ▷ adj moving from one place to another

MIGRATE vb

MIGS ▶ mig

MIHA n young fern frond which has not yet opened **mihas**

MIHI n Māori ceremonial greeting ▷ vb greet **mihied, mihiing, mihis**

MIHRAB n niche in a mosque showing the direction of Mecca **mihrabs**

MIKADO n Japanese emperor **mikados**

MIKE n miked, mikes, miking

MIKRA ▶ mikron

MIKRON n micron

MIKRONS ▶ mikron

MIKVAH n pool used for ritual purification **mikvahs, mikvah**

MIKVEHS ▶ mikveh

MIKVOS ▶ mikveh

MIKVOT ▶ mikveh **mikvoth**

MIL n unit of length equal to one thousandth of an inch

MILADI = **milady**

MILADIS ▸ miladi

MILADY n (formerly) a continental title for an English gentlewoman

MILAGE = **mileage**

MILAGES ▸ milage

MILCH adj (of a cow) giving milk

MILCHIG = **milchik**

MILCHIK adj containing or used in the preparation of milk products

MILD adj, n, vb **milded**

MILDEN vb make or become mild or milder **mildens**

MILDER ▸ mild

MILDEST ▸ mild

MILDEWS ▸ mildew

MILDEWY ▸ mildew

MILDING ▸ mild

MILDLY ▸ mild

MILDS ▸ mild

MILE n

MILEAGE n

MILER n athlete, horse, etc, that specializes in races of one mile **milers**

MILES ▸ mile

MILFOIL = **yarrow**

MILIA ▸ milium

MILIARY adj resembling or relating to millet seeds

MILIEU n **milieus, milieux**

MILITAR = **military**

MILITIA n

MILIUM n pimple

MILK n, vb **milked**

MILKEN adj of or like milk

MILKER n cow, goat, etc, that yields milk **milkers**

MILKIER ▸ milky

MILKILY ▸ milky

MILKING ▸ milk

MILKMAN n man who delivers milk to people's houses **milkmen, milko**

MILKOS ▸ milko

MILKS ▸ milk

MILKSOP n feeble man

MILKY adj

MILL n, vb

MILLAGE adj American tax rate calculated in thousandths per dollar

MILLDAM n dam built to raise the water level to turn a millwheel

MILLE French word for ▸ **thousand**

MILLED adj crushed or ground in a mill

MILLER n **millers**

MILLES ▸ mille

MILLET n **millets**

MILLIER n metric weight of million grams

MILLIME = **millieme**

MILLINE n measurement of advertising space

MILLING n act or process of grinding, cutting, pressing, or crushing in a mill

MILLION n

MILLRUN = **millrace**

MILLS ▸ mill

MILNEB n type of pesticide **milnebs**

MILO n variety of sorghum with heads of yellow or pinkish seeds

MILOR = **milord**

MILORD n (formerly) a continental title used for an English gentleman **milords**

MILORS ▸ milor

MILOS ▸ milo

MILPA n form of subsistence agriculture in Mexico **milpas**

MILREIS n former monetary unit of Portugal and Brazil

MILS ▸ mil

MILSEY n milk strainer **milseys**

MILT n sperm of fish ▷ vb fertilize (the roe of a female fish) with milt, esp artificially **milted**

MILTER n male fish that is mature and ready to breed **milters**

MILTIER ▸ milty

MILTING ▸ milt

MILTS ▸ milt

MILTY adj full of milt

MILTZ = **miltz**

MILTZES ▸ miltz

MILVINE adj of kites and related birds

MIM adj prim, modest, or demure

MIMBAR n pulpit in mosque **mimbars**

MIME n, vb **mimed**

MIMEO vb mimeograph **mimeoed, mimeos**

MIMER ▸ mime

MIMERS ▸ mime

MIMES ▸ mime

MIMESES ▸ mimesis

MIMESIS *n* imitative representation of nature or human behaviour

MIMETIC *adj* imitating or representing something

MIMIC *vb, n, adj* mimical

MIMICRY *n* act or art of copying or imitating closely

MIMICS ▸ mimic

MIMING ▸ mime

MIMMER ▸ mim

MIMMEST ▸ mim

MIMMICK = minnick

MIMOSA *n* shrub with fluffy yellow flowers and sensitive leaves **mimosae, mimosas**

MIMSEY ▸ mimsy

MIMSIER ▸ mimsy

MIMSY *adj* prim, underwhelming, and ineffectual

MIMULUS *n* plants cultivated for their yellow or red flowers

MINA *n* ancient unit of weight and money, used in Asia Minor

MINABLE ▸ mine

MINAE ▸ mina

MINAR *n* tower

MINARET *n*

MINARS ▸ minar

MINAS ▸ mina

MINBAR ▸ mimbar

MINBARS ▸ minbar

MINCE *vb, n* minced

MINCER *n* mincers

MINCES ▸ mince

MINCEUR *adj* (of food) low-fat

MINCIER ▸ mincy

MINCING *adj* affected in manner

MINCY *adj* effeminate

MIND *n, vb*

MINDED *adj* having an inclination as specified

MINDER *n* aide or bodyguard **minders**

MINDFUL *adj*

MINDING ▸ mind

MINDS ▸ mind

MINDSET *n* ideas and attitudes with which a person approaches a situation

MINE *pron, n, vb* mined

MINEOLA = minneola

MINER *n* person who works in a mine

MINERAL *n, adj*

MINERS ▸ miner

MINES ▸ mine

MINETTE *n* type of rock

MINEVER ▸ miniver

MING *vb* mix minged

MINGIER ▸ mingy

MINGING *adj* unattractive or unpleasant

MINGLE *vb* mingled, mingler, mingles

MINGS ▸ ming

MINGY *adj* miserly

MINI ▸ minidress

MINIATE *vb* paint with minium

MINIBAR *n* selection of drinks and confectionery provided in a hotel room

MINIBUS *n*

MINICAB *n* ordinary car used as a taxi

MINICAM *n* portable television camera

MINICAR *n* small car

MINICOM *n* device allowing typed telephone messages to be sent and received

MINIER ▸ miny

MINIEST ▸ miny

MINIFY *vb* minimize or lessen the size or importance of (something)

MINIKIN *n* small, dainty, or affected person or thing ▷ *adj* dainty, prim, or affected

MINILAB *n* equipment for processing photographic film

MINIM *n, adj*

MINIMA ▸ minimum

MINIMAL *adj, n*

MINIMAX *n* lowest of a set of maximum values ▷ *vb* make maximum as low as possible

MINIMS ▸ minim

MINIMUM *n, adj*

MINIMUS *adj* youngest: used after the surname of a schoolboy with elder brothers at the same school

MINING *n* act, process, or industry of extracting coal or ores from the earth **minings**

MINION n, adj **minions**
MINIS ▸ mini
MINISH vb diminish
MINISKI n short ski
MINIUM n bright red poisonous insoluble oxide of lead **miniums**
MINIVAN n small van, esp one with seats in the back for carrying passengers
MINIVER n white fur, used in ceremonial costumes
MINIVET n brightly coloured tropical Asian cuckoo shrike
MINK n
MINKE n as in **minke whale** type of small whalebone whale or rorqual **minkes**
MINKS ▸ mink
MINNICK vb behave in fussy way
MINNIE n mother **minnies**
MINNOCK = minnick
MINNOW n **minnows**
MINNY = minnie
MINO = mynah
MINOR adj, n, vb
MINORCA n breed of light domestic fowl
MINORED ▸ minor
MINORS ▸ minor
MINOS ▸ mino
MINSTER n cathedral or large church
MINT n, vb
MINTAGE n process of minting
MINTED, minter, minters, mintier,

minting, mints,
minty ▸ mint
MINUEND n number from which another number is to be subtracted
MINUET n **minuets**
MINUS adj, n, prep **minuses**
MINUTE n, vb, adj **minuted, minuter**
MINUTES pl n official record of the proceedings of a meeting or conference
MINUTIA singular noun of > minutiae
MINX n bold or flirtatious girl **minxes, minxish**
MINY adj of or like mines
MINYAN n number of persons required by Jewish law to be present for a religious service **minyans**
MIOCENE adj of, denoting, or formed in the fourth epoch of the Tertiary period
MIOMBO n (in E Africa) a dry wooded area with sparse deciduous growth **miombos**
MIOSES ▸ miosis
MIOSIS n excessive contraction of the pupil of the eye, as in response to drugs **miotic, miotics**
MIPS n unit used to express the speed of

a computer's central processing unit
MIR n peasant commune in prerevolutionary Russia
MIRABLE adj wonderful
MIRACLE n
MIRADOR n window, balcony, or turret
MIRAGE n **mirages**
MIRBANE n substance used in perfumes
MIRCHI Indian English word for > hot
MIRE n, vb **mired, mires**
MIREX n type of insecticide **mirexes**
MIRI ▸ mir
MIRIER ▸ mire
MIRIEST ▸ mire
MIRIFIC adj achieving wonderful things
MIRIN n Japanese rice wine
MIRING ▸ mire
MIRINS ▸ mirin
MIRITI n South American palm **miritis**
MIRK n = murk; **mirker, mirkest, mirkier, mirkily, mirks, mirky**
MIRLIER ▸ mirly
MIRLY = marly
MIRO n tall New Zealand tree **miros**
MIRROR n, vb **mirrors**
MIRS ▸ mir
MIRTH n **mirths**
MIRV n missile that has several warheads, each one being directed to different enemy targets ▷ vb arm with

mirvs **mirved, mirving, mirvs**

MIRY ▷ mire

MIRZA n title of respect placed before the surname of a distinguished man **mirzas**

MIS ▷ mi

MISACT vb act wrongly **misacts**

MISADD vb add badly **misadds**

MISAIM vb aim badly **misaims**

MISALLY vb form unsuitable alliance

MISATE ▷ miseat

MISAVER vb claim wrongly

MISBIAS vb prejudice wrongly

MISBILL vb present inaccurate bill

MISBIND vb bind wrongly

MISBORN adj abortive

MISCALL vb call by the wrong name

MISCAST vb cast (a role or actor) inappropriately

MISCH adj as in **misch metal** alloy of cerium and other rare earth metals

MISCITE vb cite wrongly

MISCODE vb code wrongly

MISCOIN vb coin wrongly

MISCOOK vb cook badly

MISCOPY vb copy badly

MISCUE n faulty stroke in snooker, etc ▷ vb make a miscue **miscued, miscues**

MISCUT n cut wrongly **miscuts**

MISDATE vb date (a letter, event, etc) wrongly

MISDEAL vb deal out cards incorrectly ▷ n faulty deal

MISDEED n

MISDEEM vb form bad opinion of

MISDIAL vb dial telephone number incorrectly

MISDID ▷ misdo

MISDIET n wrong diet

MISDO vb do badly or wrongly **misdoer, misdoes**

MISDONE adj done badly

MISDRAW vb draw poorly **misdrew**

MISE n issue in the obsolete writ of right

MISEASE n unease

MISEAT vb eat unhealthy food **miseats**

MISEDIT vb edit badly

MISER n

MISERE n call in solo whist and other card games declaring a hand that will win no tricks **miseres**

MISERLY adj of or resembling a miser

MISERS ▷ miser

MISERY n

MISES ▷ mise

MISFALL vb happen as piece of bad luck

MISFARE vb get on badly

MISFED ▷ misfeed

MISFEED vb feed wrongly

MISFELL ▷ misfall

MISFILE vb file (papers, records, etc) wrongly

MISFIRE vb, n

MISFIT n, vb misfits

MISFORM vb form badly

MISGAVE ▷ misgive

MISGIVE vb make or be apprehensive or suspicious

MISGO vb go wrong way **misgoes, misgone**

MISGREW ▷ misgrow

MISGROW vb grow in unsuitable way

MISHAP n, vb mishaps

MISHAPT = misshapen

MISHEAR vb hear (what someone says) wrongly

MISHIT n faulty shot, kick, or stroke ▷ vb hit or kick a ball with a faulty stroke **mishits**

MISHMEE n root of Asian plant

MISHMI n evergreen perennial plant **mishmis**

MISJOIN vb join badly

MISKAL n unit of weight in Iran **miskals**

MISKEEP vb keep wrongly

MISKEN vb be unaware of **miskens, miskent**

MISKEPT ▶ miskeep

MISKEY vb key wrongly **miskeys**

MISKICK vb fail to kick properly

MISKNEW vb
▶ **misknow**

MISKNOW vb have wrong idea about

MISLAID ▶ mislay

MISLAIN ▶ mislay

MISLAY vb mislays

MISLEAD vb misled

MISLIE vb lie wrongly **mislies**

MISLIKE vb dislike ▷ n dislike or aversion

MISLIT > mislight

MISLIVE vb live wickedly

MISLUCK vb have bad luck

MISMADE ▶ mismake

MISMAKE vb make badly

MISMARK vb mark wrongly

MISMATE vb mate wrongly

MISMEET vb fail to meet **mismet**

MISMOVE vb move badly

MISNAME vb name badly

MISO n thick brown salty paste made from soya beans **misos**

MISPAGE vb page wrongly

MISPART vb part wrongly

MISPEN vb write wrongly **mispens**

MISPLAN vb plan badly or wrongly

MISPLAY vb play badly or wrongly in games or sports ▷ n wrong or unskilful play

MISPLED > misplead

MISRATE vb rate wrongly

MISREAD vb misinterpret (a situation etc)

MISRELY vb rely wrongly

MISRULE vb govern inefficiently or unjustly ▷ n inefficient or unjust government

MISS vb, n

MISSA n Roman Catholic mass **missae**

MISSAID ▶ missay

MISSAL n book containing the prayers and rites of the Mass **missals**

MISSAW ▶ missee

MISSAY vb say wrongly **missays**

MISSEAT vb seat wrongly

MISSED ▶ miss

MISSEE vb see wrongly

MISSEEM vb be unsuitable for

MISSEEN ▶ missee

MISSEES ▶ missee

MISSEL adj as in missel thrush large European thrush

MISSELL vb sell (a product, esp a financial one) misleadingly

MISSELS ▶ missel

MISSEND vb send

wrongly **missent**

MISSES ▶ miss

MISSET vb set wrongly **missets**

MISSHOD adj badly shod

MISSIER ▶ missy

MISSIES ▶ missy

MISSILE n

MISSING adj

MISSION n, vb

MISSIS = missus

MISSISH adj like a schoolgirl

MISSIVE n, adj

MISSOLD ▶ missell

MISSORT vb sort wrongly

MISSOUT n someone who has been overlooked

MISSTEP n false step ▷ vb take a false step

MISSTOP vb stop wrongly

MISSUIT vb be unsuitable for

MISSUS n one's wife or the wife of the person addressed or referred to

MISSY n affectionate or disparaging form of address to a girl ▷ adj missish

MIST n, vb

MISTAKE n, vb

MISTAL n cow shed **mistals**

MISTBOW = fogbow

MISTED ▶ mist

MISTELL vb tell wrongly

MISTEND vb tend wrongly

MISTER *n, vb*

MISTERM *vb* term badly

MISTERS ▸ mister

MISTERY = mystery

MISTEUK *Scots variant of* ▸ **mistook**

MISTFUL ▸ mist

MISTICO *n* small Mediterranean sailing ship

MISTIER ▸ misty

MISTILY ▸ misty

MISTIME *vb* do (something) at the wrong time

MISTING *n* application of a fake suntan by spray

MISTLE = mizzle

MISTLED ▸ mistle

MISTLES ▸ mistle

MISTOLD ▸ mistell

MISTOOK *past tense of* ▸ **mistake**

MISTRAL *n* strong dry northerly wind of S France

MISTS ▸ mist

MISTUNE *vb* fail to tune properly

MISTY *adj*

MISTYPE *vb* type badly

MISUSE *n, vb* misused

MISUSER *n* abuse of some right, privilege, office, etc

MISUSES ▸ misuse

MISUST ▸ misuse

MISWEEN *vb* assess wrongly

MISWEND *vb* become lost **miswent**

MISWORD *vb* word badly

MISWRIT ▸ miswrite

MISYOKE *vb* join wrongly

MITCH *vb* play truant from school **mitched, mitches**

MITE *n*

MITER = mitre

MITERED ▸ miter

MITERER ▸ miter

MITERS ▸ miter

MITES ▸ mite

MITHER *vb* fuss over or moan about something **mithers**

MITIER ▸ mity

MITIEST ▸ mity

MITIS *n* malleable iron **mitises**

MITOGEN *n* any agent that induces mitosis

MITOSES ▸ mitosis

MITOSIS *n* mitotic

MITRAL *adj* of or like a mitre

MITRE *n, vb* mitred, mitres, mitring

MITSVAH = mitzvah

MITT = mitten

MITTEN *n* mittens

MITTS ▸ mitt

MITUMBA *n* used clothes imported for sale in African countries

MITY *adj* having mites

MITZVAH *n* commandment or precept, esp one found in the Bible

MIURUS *n* type of rhythm in poetry

MIX *vb, n* mixable

MIXDOWN *n* (in sound recording) the transfer of a multitrack master mix to two-track stereo tape

MIXED *adj* mixedly

MIXEN *n* dunghill mixens

MIXER *n* mixers

MIXES ▸ mix

MIXIBLE ▸ mix

MIXIER ▸ mix

MIXIEST ▸ mix

MIXING ▸ mix

MIXT ▸ mix

MIXTE *adj* of or denoting a type of bicycle frame in which angled twin lateral tubes run back to the rear axle

MIXTION *n* amber-based mixture used in making gold leaf

MIXTURE *n*

MIXUP *n* something that is mixed up mixups

MIXY *adj* mixed

MIZ *shortened form of* ▸ **misery**

> **Miz** is an informal short form of **misery**, very useful as a Z word. But you'll need a blank tile for the second Z if you want to form the plural **mizzes**.

MIZEN = mizzen

MIZENS ▸ mizen

MIZMAZE *n* maze

MIZUNA *n* Japanese variety of lettuce mizunas

MIZZ = miz

MIZZEN n sail set on a mizzenmast ▷ adj of or relating to any kind of gear used with a mizzenmast mizzens

MIZZES ▶ miz

MIZZLE vb decamp mizzled, mizzles, mizzly

MIZZY adj as in mizzy maze dialect expression meaning state of confusion

MM interj

MNA = mina

MNAS ▶ mna

MNEME n ability to retain memory mnemes, mnemic

MNEMON n unit of memory mnemons

MO n moment

MOA n

MOAI n any of the gigantic carved stone figures found on Easter Island (Rapa Nui)

MOAN n, vb moaned, moaner, moaners, moanful, moaning, moans

MOAS ▶ moa

MOAT n, vb moated, moating, moats

MOB n, vb mobbed, mobber, mobbers

MOBBIE = mobby

MOBBIES ▶ mobby

MOBBING ▶ mob

MOBBISH ▶ mob

MOBBISM n behaviour as mob

MOBBLE = moble

MOBBLED ▶ mobble

MOBBLES ▶ mobble

MOBBY n West Indian drink

MOBCAP n woman's 18th-century cotton cap mobcaps

MOBCAST vb

MOBE n mobile phone mobes

MOBEY ▶ moby

MOBEYS ▶ mobey

MOBIE n mobile phone

MOBIES ▶ moby

MOBILE adj, n mobiles

MOBLE vb muffle mobled, mobles, mobling

MOBLOG n blog recorded in the form of mobile phone calls, text messages, and photographs moblogs

MOBS ▶ mob

MOBSMAN n person in mob mobsmen

MOBSTER n member of a criminal organization

MOBY n mobile phone

MOC shortening of ▷ moccasin

MOCCIES pl n informal Australian word for moccasins

MOCH n spell of humid weather

MOCHA n kind of strong dark coffee mochas

MOCHELL = much

MOCHIE adj damp or humid mochier

MOCHILA n South American shoulder bag

MOCHS ▶ moch

MOCHY = mochie

MOCK vb, adj, n

MOCKADO n imitation velvet

MOCKAGE = mockery

MOCKED ▶ mock

MOCKER vb dress up mockers

MOCKERY n

MOCKING ▶ mock

MOCKNEY n person who affects a cockney accent ▷ adj denoting an affected cockney accent or a person who has one

MOCKS ▶ mock

MOCKUP n working full-scale model of a machine, apparatus, etc, for testing, research, etc mockups

MOCOCK n Native American birchbark container mococks

MOCS ▶ moc

MOCUCK = mocock

MOCUCKS ▶ mocuck

MOD n member of a group of fashionable young people, orig. in the 1960s ▷ vb modify (a piece of software or hardware)

MODAL adj of or relating to mode or manner ▷ n modal word modally, modals

MODDED ▶ mod vb

MODDER n person who modifies a piece of hardware or software **modders**

MODDING n

MODE n, adj, vb

MODEL n, adj, vb **modeled, modeler**

MODELLI ▶ **modello**

MODELLO n artist's preliminary sketch or model

MODELS ▶ **model**

MODEM n, vb **modemed, modems**

MODENA n popular variety of domestic fancy pigeon **modenas**

MODER n intermediate layer in humus

MODERN adj, n

MODERNE n style of architecture and design of the late 1920s and 1930s ▷ adj of or relating to this style of architecture and design

MODERNS ▶ **modern**

MODERS ▶ **moder**

MODES ▶ **mode**

MODEST adj

MODESTY n quality or condition of being modest

MODGE vb do shoddily **modged, modges, modging**

MODI ▶ **modus**

MODICA ▶ **modicum**

MODICUM n

MODIFY vb

MODII ▶ **modius**

MODIOLI ▶ **modiolus**

MODISH adj in fashion

MODIST n follower of fashion

MODISTE n fashionable dressmaker or milliner

MODISTS ▶ **modist**

MODIUS n ancient Roman quantity measure

MODS ▶ **mod**

MODULAR adj of, consisting of, or resembling a module or modulus ▷ n thing comprised of modules

MODULE n **modules**

MODULI ▶ **modulus**

MODULO adv with reference to modulus

MODULUS n coefficient expressing a specified property

MODUS n way of doing something

MOE adv, n

MOELLON n rubble

MOER n in South Africa, slang word for the womb ▷ vb in South Africa, attack (someone or something) violently **moered, moering, moers**

MOES ▶ **moe**

MOFETTE n opening in a region of nearly extinct volcanic activity, through which gases pass

MOFFIE n homosexual ▷ adj homosexual **moffies**

MOG vb go away

MOGGAN n stocking without foot **moggans**

MOGGED ▶ **mog**

MOGGIE = **moggy**

MOGGIES ▶ **moggy**

MOGGING ▶ **mog**

MOGGY n cat

MOGHUL n mogul

MOGHULS ▶ **moghul**

MOGS ▶ **mog**

MOGUL n important or powerful person

MOGULED adj having moguls

MOGULS ▶ **mogul**

MOHAIR n **mohairs**

MOHALIM = **mohelim**

MOHAWK n half turn from either edge of either skate to the corresponding edge of the other skate **mohawks**

MOHEL n man qualified to conduct circumcisions **mohelim, mohels**

MOHICAN n punk hairstyle

MOHR n = **mhorr**

MOHRS ▶ **mohr**

MOHUA n small New Zealand bird **mohuas**

MOHUR n former Indian gold coin worth 15 rupees **mohurs**

MOI ▶ **me**

MOIDER = **moither**

MOIDERS ▶ **moider**

MOIDORE n former Portuguese gold coin

MOIETY n half

MOIL vb moisten or soil or become moist,

soiled, etc ▷ n toil
**moiled, moiler,
moilers, moiling,
moils**
MOINEAU n small
fortification

> Meaning part of a
> fortification, this is
> another of those very
> useful 7-letter vowel
> dumps.

MOIRA n fate **moirai**
MOIRE adj having a
watered or wavelike
pattern ▷ n any fabric
that has such a
pattern **moires**
MOISER n informer
moisers
MOIST adj, vb **moisted**
MOISTEN vb
MOISTER ▶ moist
MOISTLY ▶ moist
MOISTS ▶ moist
MOIT = mote
MOITHER vb bother or
bewilder
MOITS ▶ moit
MOJARRA n tropical
American sea fish
MOJITO n rum-based
cocktail **mojitos**
MOJO n charm or magic
spell **mojoes, mojos**
MOKE n donkey **mokes**
MOKI n edible sea fish
of New Zealand
MOKIHI n Māori raft
mokihis
MOKIS ▶ moki
MOKO n Māori tattoo
or tattoo pattern
MOKORO n (in
Botswana) the

traditional dugout
canoe of the people of
the Okavango Delta
mokoros
MOKOS ▶ moko
MOKSHA n freedom
from the endless cycle
of transmigration into
a state of bliss **mokshas**
MOL n
MOLA another name for
▶ sunfish
MOLAL adj of or
consisting of a
solution containing
one mole of solute per
thousand grams of
solvent
MOLAR n, adj **molars**
MOLAS ▶ mola
MOLASSE n soft
sediment produced
by the erosion of
mountain ranges after
the final phase of
mountain building
MOLD = mould
MOLDED ▶ mold
MOLDER = moulder
MOLDERS ▶ molder
MOLDIER ▶ moldy
MOLDING = moulding
MOLDS ▶ mold
MOLDY = mouldy
MOLE n **moles**
MOLEST vb **molests**
MOLIES ▶ moly
MOLIMEN n effort
needed to perform
bodily function
MOLINE adj (of a cross)
having arms of equal
length, forked and
curved back at the

ends ▷ n moline cross
molines
MOLINET n stick for
whipping chocolate
MOLL n gangster's
female accomplice
MOLLA = mollah
MOLLAH = mullah
MOLLAHS ▶ mollah
MOLLAS ▶ molla
MOLLIE = molly
MOLLIES ▶ molly
MOLLIFY vb
MOLLS ▶ moll
MOLLUSC n mollusk
MOLLY n American
freshwater fish
MOLOCH n spiny
Australian
desert-living lizard
molochs
MOLOSSI > molossus
MOLS ▶ mol
MOLT = moult
MOLTED ▶ molt
MOLTEN ▶ melt
MOLTER ▶ molt
MOLTERS ▶ molt
MOLTING ▶ molt
MOLTO adv very
MOLTS ▶ molt
MOLY n mythical magic
herb
MOM = mother
MOME n fool
MOMENT n
MOMENTA
> momentum
MOMENTO = memento
MOMENTS ▶ moment
MOMES ▶ mome
MOMI = mom
MOMISM n excessive
domination of a child

by his or her mother **momisms**

MOMMA = mamma

MOMMAS ▷ momma

MOMMET = mammet

MOMMETS ▷ mommet

MOMMIES ▷ mommy

MOMMY = mom

MOMS ▷ mom

MOMSER = momzer

MOMSERS ▷ momser

MOMUS n person who ridicules **momuses**

MOMZER = mamzer

MOMZERS ▷ momzer

MON dialect variant of ▷ man

MONA n W African guenon monkey

MONACID = monoacid

MONACT adj (of sponge) with mono-spiked structures in skeleton

MONAD n any fundamental singular metaphysical entity **monadal**

MONADES ▷ monas

MONADIC adj being or relating to a monad

MONADS ▷ monad

MONAL n S Asian pheasant **monals**

MONARCH n

MONARDA n mintlike N American plant

MONAS = monad

MONASES ▷ monas

MONAUL = monal

MONAULS ▷ monaul

MONAXON n type of sponge

MONDAIN n man who moves in fashionable society ▷ adj characteristic of fashionable society

MONDE n French word meaning world or society **mondes**

MONDIAL adj of or involving the whole world

MONDO n Buddhist questioning technique **mondos**

MONEME less common word for ▷ morpheme

MONEMES ▷ moneme

MONER n hypothetical simple organism **monera**

MONERAN n type of bacterium

MONERON = moner

MONETH = month

MONETHS ▷ moneth

MONEY n

MONEYED adj

MONEYER n person who coins money

MONEYS ▷ money

MONGED adj under the influence of drugs

MONGER n trader or dealer ▷ vb deal in **mongers, mongery**

MONGO = mungo

MONGOE = mongo

MONGOES ▷ mongoe

MONGOS ▷ mongo

MONGREL n, adj

MONGST short for ▷ amongst

MONIAL n mullion **monials**

MONIE Scots word for ▷ many

MONIED = moneyed

MONIES ▷ money

MONIKER n person's name or nickname

MONILIA n type of fungus

MONISH = admonish

MONISM n doctrine that reality consists of only one basic substance or element **monisms, monist, monists**

MONITOR n, vb

MONK n

MONKEY n, vb **monkeys**

MONKISH adj of, relating to, or resembling a monk or monks

MONKS ▷ monk

MONO n

MONOAO n New Zealand plant with rigid leaves **monoaos**

MONOCLE n

MONOCOT n type of flowering plant with a single embryonic seed leaf

MONODIC ▷ monody

MONODY n (in Greek tragedy) an ode sung by a single actor

MONOECY = monoecism

MONOFIL n synthetic thread or yarn composed of a single strand rather than twisted fibres

MONOLOG = monologue

MONOMER n compound whose molecules can join together to form a polymer

MONONYM n person who is famous enough to be known only by one name

MONOPOD = monopode

MONOS ▶ mono

MONOSES ▶ monosis

MONOSIS n abnormal separation

MONOSKI n wide ski on which the skier stands with both feet ▷ vb ski on a monoski

MONOSY = monosis

MONS ▶ mon

MONSOON n

MONSTER n, adj, vb

MONTAGE n, vb

MONTAN adj as in montan wax hard wax obtained from lignite and peat

MONTANE n area of mountain dominated by vegetation ▷ adj of or inhabiting mountainous regions

MONTANT n vertical part in woodwork

MONTE n gambling card game of Spanish origin

MONTEM n former money-raising practice at Eton school montems

MONTERO n round cap with a flap at the back

worn by hunters

MONTES ▶ monte

MONTH n

MONTHLY adj, adv, n

MONTHS ▶ month

MONTIES ▶ monty

MONTRE n pipes of organ montres

MONTURE n mount or frame

MONTY n complete form of something

MONURON n type of weedkiller

MONY Scot word for ▶ many

MOO n, vb, interj

MOOBS pl n

MOOCH vb mooched, moocher, mooches

MOOD n

MOODIED, moodier, moodies, moodily ▶ moody

MOODS ▶ mood

MOODY adj, vb

MOOED ▶ moo

MOOI adj pleasing or nice

MOOING ▶ moo

MOOKTAR = mukhtar

MOOL = mould

MOOLA = moolah

MOOLAH slang word for ▶ money

MOOLAHS ▶ moolah

MOOLAS ▶ moola

MOOLED ▶ mool

MOOLEY = mooly

MOOLEYS ▶ mooley

MOOLI n type of large white radish

MOOLIES ▶ mooly

MOOLING ▶ mool

MOOLIS ▶ mooli

MOOLOO n person from the Waikato mooloos

MOOLS ▶ mool

MOOLVI = moolvie

MOOLVIE n (esp in India) Muslim learned man

MOOLVIS ▶ moolvi

MOOLY = muley

MOON n, vb

MOONBOW n rainbow made by moonlight

MOONED adj decorated with a moon

MOONER ▶ moon

MOONERS ▶ moon

MOONEYE n N American large-eyed freshwater fish

MOONG n as in moong bean kind of bean

MOONIER ▶ moony

MOONIES ▶ moony

MOONILY ▶ moony

MOONING ▶ moon

MOONISH ▶ moon

MOONLET n small moon

MOONLIT adj illuminated by the moon

MOONS ▶ moon

MOONSET n moment when the moon disappears below the horizon

MOONY adj dreamy or listless ▷ n crazy or foolish person

MOOP = moup

MOOPED ▶ moop

MOOPING ▶ moop

MOOPS ▶ moop

MOOR n, vb
MOORAGE n place for mooring a vessel
MOORED ▸ moor
MOORHEN n
MOORIER ▸ moor
MOORILL n disease of cattle on moors
MOORING n
MOORISH adj of or relating to the Moor people of North Africa
MOORLOG n rotted wood below the surface of a moor
MOORMAN n person living on a moor **moormen**
MOORS ▸ moor
MOORVA = murva
MOORVAS ▸ moorva
MOORY ▸ moor
MOOS ▸ moo
MOOSE n
MOOT adj, vb, n mooted, mooter, mooters, mootest, mooting
MOOTMAN n person taking part in a moot **mootmen**
MOOTS ▸ moot
MOOVE = move
MOOVED ▸ moove
MOOVES ▸ moove
MOOVING ▸ moove
MOP n, vb
MOPANE = mopani
MOPANES ▸ mopane
MOPANI n S African tree that is highly resistant to drought **mopanis**
MOPE vb, n
MOPED n mopeds
MOPER ▸ mope

MOPERS ▸ mope
MOPERY n gloominess
MOPES ▸ mope
MOPEY ▸ mope
MOPHEAD n person with shaggy hair
MOPIER ▸ mope
MOPIEST ▸ mope
MOPILY ▸ mopy
MOPING ▸ mope
MOPISH ▸ mope
MOPOKE n mopokes
MOPPED ▸ mop
MOPPER ▸ mop
MOPPERS ▸ mop
MOPPET = poppet
MOPPETS ▸ moppet
MOPPIER ▸ moppy
MOPPING ▸ mop
MOPPY adj drunk
MOPS ▸ mop
MOPSIES ▸ mopsy
MOPSY n untidy or dowdy person
MOPUS n person who mopes **mopuses**
MOPY ▸ mope
MOR n layer of acidic humus formed in cool moist areas
MORA n quantity of a short syllable in verse **morae**
MORAINE n accumulated mass of debris deposited by a glacier
MORAL adj, n, vb
MORALE n morales
MORALL = mural
MORALLS ▸ morall
MORALLY ▸ moral
MORALS ▸ moral
MORAS ▸ mora

MORASS n morassy
MORAT n drink containing mulberry juice **morats**
MORAY n large voracious eel **morays**
MORBID adj
MORBUS n disease
MORCEAU n fragment or morsel
MORCHA n (in India) hostile demonstration **morchas**
MORDANT adj, n, vb
MORDENT n melodic ornament in music
MORE adj, adv, pron
MOREEN n heavy, usually watered, fabric of wool or wool and cotton **moreens**
MOREISH adj (of food) causing a desire for more
MOREL n edible mushroom with a pitted cap
MORELLE n nightshade
MORELLO n variety of small very dark sour cherry
MORELS ▸ morel
MORENDO adv (in music) dying away
MORES pl n
MORGAN n American breed of small compact saddle horse **morgans**
MORGAY n small dogfish **morgays**
MORGEN n South African unit of area **morgens**

MORGUE = mortuary
MORGUES ▶ morgue
MORIA n folly **morias**
MORICHE = miriti
MORION n 16th-century helmet with a brim and wide comb **morions**
MORISCO n morris dance
MORISH = moreish
MORKIN n animal dying in accident **morkins**
MORLING n sheep killed by disease
MORMAOR n former high-ranking Scottish nobleman
MORN n morning
MORNAY adj served with a cheese sauce **mornays**
MORNE = mourn
MORNED ▶ morne
MORNES ▶ morne
MORNING n
MORNS ▶ morn
MOROCCO n goatskin leather
MORON n moronic, **morons**
MOROSE adj **moroser**
MORPH n phonological representation of a morpheme ▶ vb undergo or cause to undergo morphing **morphed**
MORPHEW n blemish on skin
MORPHIA = morphine
MORPHIC adj as in **morphic resonance** idea that an event can

lead to similar events in the future through a telepathic effect
MORPHIN variant form of > morphine
MORPHO n type of butterfly **morphos**
MORPHS ▶ morph
MORRA = mora
MORRAS ▶ morra
MORRELL n tall SW Australian eucalypt with pointed buds
MORRHUA n cod
MORRICE = morris
MORRION = morion
MORRIS vb perform morris dance
MORRO n rounded hill or promontory **morros**
MORROW n next day **morrows**
MORS ▶ mor
MORSAL ▶ morsure
MORSE n clasp or fastening on a cope
MORSEL n, vb **morsels**
MORSES ▶ morse
MORSURE n bite
MORT n call blown on a hunting horn to signify the death of the animal hunted
MORTAL adj, n **mortals**
MORTAR n, vb **mortars**
MORTARY adj of or like mortar
MORTICE = mortise
MORTIFY vb
MORTISE n slot cut into a piece of wood, stone, etc ▶ vb cut a slot in (a piece of wood, stone, etc)

MORTS ▶ mort
MORULA n solid ball of cells resulting from cleavage of a fertilized ovum **morulae, morular, morulas**
MORWONG n food fish of Australasian coastal waters
MORYAH interj exclamation of annoyance, disbelief, etc
MOS ▶ mo
MOSAIC n **mosaics**
MOSE vb have glanders **mosed**
MOSELLE n German white wine from the Moselle valley
MOSES ▶ mose
MOSEY vb walk in a leisurely manner **moseyed, moseys**
MOSH n dance performed to loud rock music ▶ vb dance in this manner
MOSHAV n cooperative settlement in Israel
MOSHED, mosher, moshers, moshes, moshing ▶ mosh
MOSING ▶ mose
MOSK = mosque
MOSKS ▶ mosk
MOSQUE n **mosques**
MOSS n, vb **mossed, mosser, mossers, mosses**
MOSSIE n common sparrow

MOSSIER ▸ moss
MOSSIES ▸ mossie
MOSSING ▸ moss
MOSSO *adv* to be performed with rapidity
MOSSY ▸ moss
MOST *n, adj, adv*
MOSTE ▸ mote
MOSTEST ▸ most
MOSTLY *adv*
MOSTS ▸ most
MOT *n* girl or young woman, esp one's girlfriend
MOTE *n* tiny speck ▷ *vb* may or might
MOTED *adj* containing motes
MOTEL *n* motels
MOTEN ▸ mote
MOTES ▸ mote
MOTET *n* short sacred choral song **motets, motett, motetts**
MOTEY *adj* containing motes
MOTH *n*
MOTHED *adj* damaged by moths
MOTHER *n, adj, vb* **mothers, mothery**
MOTHIER ▸ mothy
MOTHS ▸ moth
MOTHY *adj* ragged
MOTIER ▸ motey
MOTIEST ▸ motey
MOTIF *n*
MOTIFIC *adj* causing motion
MOTIFS ▸ motif
MOTILE *adj* capable of independent movement ▷ *n* person whose mental imagery

strongly reflects movement **motiles**
MOTION *n, vb* motions
MOTIVE *n, adj, vb* **motived, motives**
MOTIVIC *adj* of musical motif
MOTLEY *adj, n* motleys, motlier
MOTMOT *n* tropical American bird with a long tail and blue and brownish-green plumage **motmots**
MOTOR *n, vb, adj* **motored, motoric, motors, motory**
MOTS ▸ mot
MOTSER *n* large sum of money, esp a gambling win **motsers**
MOTT *n* clump of trees
MOTTE *n* mound on which a castle was built **mottes**
MOTTIER ▸ motty
MOTTIES ▸ motty
MOTTLE *vb* colour with streaks or blotches of different shades ▷ *n* mottled appearance, as of the surface of marble **mottled**
MOTTLER *n* paintbrush for mottled effects
MOTTLES ▸ mottle
MOTTO *n*
MOTTOED *adj* having motto
MOTTOES ▸ motto
MOTTOS ▸ motto
MOTTS ▸ mott
MOTTY *n* target at which coins are aimed

in pitch-and-toss ▷ *adj* containing motes
MOTUCA *n* Brazilian fly motucas
MOTZA = motser
MOTZAS ▸ motza
MOU *Scots word for* **▸ mouth**
MOUCH = mooch
MOUCHED ▸ mouch
MOUCHER ▸ mouch
MOUCHES ▸ mouch
MOUE *n* disdainful or pouting look **moues**
MOUFLON *n* wild mountain sheep of Corsica and Sardinia
MOUGHT ▸ mote
MOUILLE *adj* palatalized, as in the sounds represented by Spanish ll or ñ
MOUJIK = muzhik
MOUJIKS ▸ moujik
MOULAGE *n* mould making
MOULD *n, vb* moulded
MOULDER *vb* decay into dust ▷ *n* person who moulds or makes moulds
MOULDS ▸ mould
MOULDY *adj* stale or musty
MOULIN *n* vertical shaft in a glacier **moulins**
MOULS *Scots word for* **▸ mould**
MOULT *vb, n* moulted
MOULTEN *adj* having moulted
MOULTER ▸ moult
MOULTS ▸ moult
MOUND *n, vb*

mounded, mounds

MOUNT vb, n

MOUNTED adj riding horses

MOUNTER ▶ mount

MOUNTS ▶ mount

MOUP n nibble mouped, mouping, moups

MOURN vb mourned

MOURNER n

MOURNS ▶ mourn

MOUS ▶ mou

MOUSAKA = moussaka

MOUSE n, vb moused

MOUSER n cat used to catch mice mousers

MOUSERY n place infested with mice

MOUSES ▶ mouse

MOUSEY = mousy

MOUSIE n little mouse

MOUSIER ▶ mousy

MOUSIES ▶ mousie

MOUSILY ▶ mousy

MOUSING n device for closing off a hook

MOUSLE vb handle roughly mousled, mousles

MOUSME n Japanese girl mousmee, mousmes

MOUSSE n, vb moussed, mousses

MOUST = must

MOUSTED ▶ moust

MOUSTS ▶ moust

MOUSY adj

MOUTAN n variety of peony moutans

MOUTER = multure

MOUTERS ▶ mouter

MOUTH n, vb mouthed,

mouther, mouths

MOUTHY adj bombastic

MOUTON n sheepskin processed to resemble the fur of another animal moutons

MOVABLE adj, n movably

MOVE vb change in place or position ▷ n moving moved

MOVER n person or animal that moves in a particular way movers

MOVES ▶ move

MOVIE n cinema film movies

MOVING adj

MOVIOLA n viewing machine used in cutting and editing film

MOW vb, n

MOWA = mahua

MOWAS ▶ mowa

MOWBURN vb heat up in mow

MOWDIE Scot words for ▶ mole

MOWDIES ▶ mowdie

MOWED ▶ mow

MOWER ▶ mow

MOWERS ▶ mow

MOWING ▶ mow

MOWINGS ▶ mow

MOWN ▶ mow

MOWRA = mahua

MOWRAS ▶ mowra

MOWS ▶ mow

MOXA n downy material obtained from various plants moxas

MOXIE n courage,

nerve, or vigour moxies

MOY n coin

MOYA n mud emitted from a volcano moyas

MOYITY = moiety

MOYL = moyle

MOYLE vb toil moyled, moyles, moyling

MOYLS ▶ moyl

MOYS ▶ moy

MOZ n hex

| This unusual word, Australian slang for bad luck, is another of the very useful short words that use the Z, and it can be extended to **moze** or **mozo**.

MOZE vb give nap to mozed

MOZES ▶ moz

MOZETTA = mozzetta

MOZETTE ▶ mozzetta

MOZING ▶ moze

MOZO n porter in southwest USA mozos

MOZZ = moz

MOZZES ▶ mozz

MOZZIE = mossie

MOZZIES ▶ mozzie

MOZZLE n luck mozzles

MPRET n former Albanian ruler mprets

MRIDANG n drum used in Indian music

MU n 12th letter in the Greek alphabet

MUCATE n salt of mucic acid mucates

MUCH adj, n, adv muchel, muchell

MUCHELS ▶ muchel

MUCHES ▶ much

MUCHLY ▶ much

MUCHO adv Spanish for very

MUCIC adj as in **mucic acid** colourless crystalline solid carboxylic acid

MUCID adj mouldy, musty, or slimy

MUCIGEN n substance present in mucous cells that is converted into mucin

MUCIN n any of a group of nitrogenous mucoproteins occurring in saliva, skin, tendon, etc **mucins**

MUCK n **mucked**

MUCKER n person who shifts broken rock or waste ▷ vb hoard **muckers**

MUCKIER ▶ mucky

MUCKILY ▶ mucky

MUCKING ▶ muck

MUCKLE = mickle

MUCKLES ▶ muckle

MUCKS ▶ muck

MUCKY adj dirty or muddy

MUCLUC = mukluk

MUCLUCS ▶ mucluc

MUCOID adj of the nature of or resembling mucin ▷ n substance like mucin **mucoids**

MUCOR n type of fungus **mucors**

MUCOSA n mucus-secreting

membrane that lines body cavities **mucosae, mucosal, mucosas**

MUCOSE = mucous

MUCOUS adj of, resembling, or secreting mucus

MUCRO n short pointed projection from certain parts or organs **mucros**

MUCUS n **mucuses**

MUD n, vb

MUDBATH n medicinal bath in heated mud

MUDBUG n crayfish **mudbugs**

MUDCAP vb use explosive charge in blasting **mudcaps**

MUDCAT n any of several large North American catfish **mudcats**

MUDDED ▶ mud

MUDDER n horse that runs well in mud **mudders**

MUDDIED ▶ muddy

MUDDIER ▶ muddy

MUDDIES ▶ muddy

MUDDILY ▶ muddy

MUDDING ▶ mud

MUDDLE vb, n **muddled**

MUDDLER n person who muddles or muddles through

MUDDLES ▶ muddle

MUDDLY ▶ muddle

MUDDY adj, vb

MUDEJAR n Spanish Moor ▷ adj of or relating to a style of

architecture

MUDEYE n larva of the dragonfly **mudeyes**

MUDFISH n fish that lives at the muddy bottoms of rivers, lakes, etc

MUDFLAP n flap above wheel to deflect mud

MUDFLAT n tract of low muddy land

MUDFLOW n flow of soil mixed with water down a steep unstable slope

MUDGE vb speak vaguely **mudged, mudger, mudgers, mudges, mudging**

MUDHEN n water bird living in muddy place **mudhens**

MUDHOLE n hole with mud at bottom

MUDHOOK n anchor

MUDIR n local governor

MUDIRIA n province of mudir

MUDIRS ▶ mudir

MUDLARK n street urchin ▷ vb play in mud

MUDPACK n cosmetic paste applied to the face

MUDRA n hand movement in Hindu religious dancing **mudras**

MUDROCK n type of sedimentary rock

MUDROOM n room where muddy shoes may be left

MUDS ▶ mud

MUDSCOW n boat for travelling over mudflats

MUDSILL n support for building at or below ground

MUDWORT n plant growing in mud

MUEDDIN = muezzin

MUESLI ▶ mueslis

MUEZZIN n official who summons Muslims to prayer

MUFF n tube-shaped covering to keep the hands warm ▷ vb bungle (an action) **muffed**

MUFFIN n

MUFFING ▶ muff

MUFFINS ▶ muffin

MUFFISH ▶ muff

MUFFLE vb, n muffled

MUFFLER n scarf

MUFFLES ▶ muffle

MUFFS ▶ muff

MUFLON = moufflon

MUFLONS ▶ muflon

MUFTI n muftis

MUG n, vb mugful

MUGFULS ▶ mugful

MUGG = mug

MUGGA n Australian eucalyptus tree

MUGGAR = mugger

MUGGARS ▶ muggar

MUGGAS ▶ mugga

MUGGED ▶ mug

MUGGEE n mugged person **muggees**

MUGGER n person who commits robbery with violence **muggers**

MUGGIER ▶ muggy

MUGGILY ▶ muggy

MUGGING ▶ mug

MUGGINS n stupid or gullible person

MUGGISH = muggy

MUGGS ▶ mug

MUGGUR = mugger

MUGGURS ▶ muggur

MUGGY adj

MUGHAL = mogul

MUGHALS ▶ mughal

MUGS ▶ mug

MUGSHOT n police photograph of person's face

MUGWORT n N temperate herbaceous plant with aromatic leaves

MUGWUMP n neutral or independent person

MUHLIES ▶ muhly

MUHLY n American grass

MUID n former French measure of capacity **muids**

MUIL = mule

MUILS ▶ muil

MUIR = moor

MUIRS ▶ muir

MUIST = must

MUISTED ▶ muist

MUISTS ▶ muist

MUJIK = muzhik

MUJIKS ▶ mujik

MUKHTAR n lawyer in India

MUKLUK n soft boot, usually of sealskin **mukluks**

MUKTUK n thin outer skin of the beluga, used as food **muktuks**

MULATTA n female mulatto

MULATTO n child of one Black and one White parent ▷ adj of a light brown colour

MULCH n, vb mulched, mulches

MULCT vb cheat or defraud ▷ n fine or penalty **mulcted, mulcts**

MULE n, vb muled

MULES vb surgically remove folds of skin from a sheep **mulesed, muleses**

MULETA n small cape attached to a stick used by a matador **muletas**

MULEY adj (of cattle) having no horns ▷ n any hornless cow **muleys**

MULGA n mulgas

MULING ▶ mule

MULISH adj

MULL vb, n

MULLA = mullah

MULLAH n Muslim scholar, teacher, or religious leader **mullahs**

MULLAS ▶ mulla

MULLED ▶ mull

MULLEIN n type of European plant **mullen**

MULLENS ▶ mullen

MULLER n flat heavy implement used to grind material ▷ vb beat up or defeat thoroughly **mullers**

MULLET n mullets
MULLEY = muley
MULLEYS ▶ mulley
MULLING ▶ mull
MULLION n vertical dividing bar in a window ▷ vb furnish with mullions
MULLITE n colourless mineral
MULLOCK n waste material from a mine
MULLS ▶ mull
MULMUL n muslin mulmull, mulmuls
MULSE n drink containing honey mulses
MULSH = mulch
MULSHED ▶ mulsh
MULSHES ▶ mulsh
MULTUM n substance used in brewing multums
MULTURE n fee formerly paid to a miller for grinding grain ▷ vb take multure
MUM n, vb
MUMBLE vb, n mumbled, mumbler, mumbles, mumbly
MUMM = mum
MUMMED ▶ mum
MUMMER n actor in a traditional English folk play mummers
MUMMERY n performance by mummers
MUMMIA n mummified flesh used as medicine mummias
MUMMIED ▶ mummy

MUMMIES ▶ mummy
MUMMIFY vb preserve a body as a mummy
MUMMING ▶ mum
MUMMOCK = mammock
MUMMS ▶ mumm
MUMMY n, vb
MUMP vb be silent mumped, mumper, mumpers, mumping
MUMPISH ▶ mumps
MUMPS n
MUMS ▶ mum
MUMSIER ▶ mumsy
MUMSY adj out of fashion
MUMU n oven in Papua New Guinea mumus
MUN = maun
MUNCH vb munched, muncher, munches
MUNDANE adj
MUNDIC n iron pyrites mundics
MUNDIFY vb cleanse
MUNG vb process (computer data)
MUNGA n army canteen mungas
MUNGE vb modify a password into an unguessable state
MUNGED ▶ mung
MUNGES ▶ mung
MUNGING ▶ mung
MUNGO n cheap felted fabric made from waste wool mungoes, mungos
MUNGS ▶ mung
MUNI n municipal radio broadcast

MUNIFY vb fortify
MUNIS ▶ muni
MUNITE vb strengthen munited, munites
MUNNION archaic word for ▶ mullion
MUNS ▶ mun
MUNSHI n secretary in India munshis
MUNSTER variant of > muenster
MUNTIN n supporting or strengthening bar munting, muntins
MUNTJAC n small Asian deer muntjak
MUNTRIE n Australian shrub with green-red edible berries
MUON n elementary particle with a mass 207 times that of an electron muonic
MUONIUM n form of hydrogen
MUONS ▶ muon
MUPPET n stupid person muppets
MURA n group of people living together in Japanese countryside
MURAENA n moray eel
MURAGE n tax levied for the construction or maintenance of town walls murages
MURAL n, adj
MURALED ▶ muralled
MURALS ▶ mural
MURAS ▶ mura
MURDER n, vb murders
MURE archaic or literary word for ▶ immure
MURED ▶ mure

MUREIN n polymer found in cells **mureins**

MURENA = mauraena

MURENAS ▶ murena

MURES ▶ mure

MUREX n marine gastropod formerly used as a source of purple dye **murexes**

MURGEON vb grimace at

MURIATE obsolete name for a ▶ chloride

MURICES ▶ murex

MURID n animal of mouse family **murids**

MURINE n animal belonging to the family that includes rats and mice **murines**

MURING ▶ mure

MURK n thick darkness ▷ adj dark or gloomy **murker, murkest**

MURKIER ▶ murky

MURKILY ▶ murky

MURKISH ▶ murk

MURKLY ▶ murk

MURKS ▶ murk

MURKY adj

MURL vb crumble

MURLAIN n type of basket **murlan**

MURLANS ▶ murlan

MURLED ▶ murl

MURLIER ▶ murl

MURLIN = murlain

MURLING ▶ murl

MURLINS ▶ murlin

MURLS ▶ murl

MURLY ▶ murl

MURMUR vb, n **murmurs**

MURPHY dialect or informal word for ▶ potato

MURR n former name for a cold

MURRA = murrhine

MURRAGH n type of large caddis fly

MURRAIN n cattle plague

MURRAM n type of gravel **murrams**

MURRAS ▶ murra

MURRAY n large Australian freshwater fish **murrays**

MURRE n type of guillemot

MURREE n native Australian **murrees**

MURREN = murrain

MURRENS ▶ murren

MURRES ▶ murre

MURREY adj mulberry colour **murreys**

MURRHA = murra

MURRHAS ▶ murrha

MURRI = murree

MURRIES ▶ murry

MURRIN = murrain

MURRINE = murrhine

MURRINS ▶ murrin

MURRION = murrain

MURRIS ▶ murri

MURRS ▶ murr

MURRY = moray

MURTHER = murder

MURTI n image of a deity, which itself is considered divine **murtis**

MURVA n type of hemp **murvas**

MUS ▶ mu

MUSANG n catlike animal of Malaysia **musangs**

MUSAR n rabbinic literature concerned with ethics **musars**

MUSCA n small constellation in the S hemisphere **muscae**

MUSCAT = muscatel

MUSCATS ▶ muscat

MUSCID n type of fly **muscids**

MUSCLE n, vb **muscled, muscles, muscly**

MUSCOID adj of family of plants

MUSCONE = muskone

MUSCOSE adj like moss

MUSCOVY adj as in **muscovy duck** a kind of duck

MUSE vb, n **mused, museful, muser, musers, muses**

MUSET = musit

MUSETS ▶ muset

MUSETTE n type of bagpipe formerly popular in France

MUSEUM n **museums**

MUSH n, interj, vb

MUSHA interj Irish exclamation of surprise

MUSHED, musher, mushers, mushes ▶ mush

MUSHIER ▶ mushy

MUSHILY ▶ mushy

MUSHING ▶ mush

MUSHY adj

MUSIC n, vb

MUSICAL adj, n

MUSICK = music
MUSICKS ▶ musick
MUSICS ▶ music
MUSIMON = mouflon
MUSING ▶ muse
MUSINGS ▶ muse
MUSIT n gap in fence **musits**
MUSIVE adj mosaic
MUSJID = masjid
MUSJIDS ▶ musjid
MUSK n, vb musked
MUSKEG n area of undrained boggy land **muskegs**
MUSKET n muskets
MUSKIE n large North American freshwater game fish **muskier, muskies**
MUSKILY ▶ musky
MUSKING ▶ musk
MUSKIT = mesquite
MUSKITS ▶ muskit
MUSKLE = mussel
MUSKLES ▶ muskle
MUSKONE n substance in musk
MUSKOX n large Canadian mammal
MUSKRAT n
MUSKS ▶ musk
MUSKY = muskie
MUSLIN n muslins
MUSMON = musimon
MUSMONS ▶ musmon
MUSO n musician who is concerned with technique rather than content or expression **musos**
MUSPIKE n Canadian freshwater fish

MUSROL n part of bridle **musrols**
MUSS vb make untidy ▷ n state of disorder **musse, mussed**
MUSSEL n mussels
MUSSES ▶ muss
MUSSIER ▶ mussy
MUSSILY ▶ mussy
MUSSING ▶ muss
MUSSY adj untidy or disordered
MUST vb, n
MUSTANG n
MUSTARD n, adj
MUSTED ▶ must
MUSTEE n offspring of a White and a quadroon **mustees**
MUSTER vb, n musters
MUSTH n state of frenzied sexual excitement in the males of certain large mammals **musths**
MUSTIER ▶ musty
MUSTILY ▶ musty
MUSTING ▶ must
MUSTS ▶ must
MUSTY adj
MUT another word for ▶ em
MUTABLE adj liable to change **mutably**
MUTAGEN n any substance that can induce genetic mutation
MUTANDA > mutandum
MUTANT n mutated animal, plant, etc ▷ adj of or resulting from mutation **mutants**

MUTASE n type of enzyme mutases
MUTATE vb mutated, mutates
MUTCH n close-fitting linen cap ▷ vb cadge mutched, mutches
MUTE adj, n, vb
MUTED adj mutedly
MUTELY, muter, mutes, mutest ▶ mute
MUTI n
MUTINE vb mutiny mutined, mutines
MUTING ▶ mute
MUTINY n, vb
MUTIS ▶ muti
MUTISM n state of being mute mutisms
MUTON n part of gene mutons
MUTS ▶ mut
MUTT n mongrel dog
MUTTER vb, n mutters
MUTTON n muttons, muttony
MUTTS ▶ mutt
MUTUAL adj, n mutuals
MUTUCA = motuca
MUTUCAS ▶ mutuca
MUTUEL n system of betting mutuels
MUTULAR ▶ mutule
MUTULE n flat block in a Doric cornice mutules
MUTUUM n contract for loan of goods mutuums
MUUMUU n loose brightly-coloured dress worn by women in Hawaii muumuus

MUX vb spoil **muxed, muxes, muxing**
This word meaning to spoil or botch is very useful not only because it contains an X, but because its verb forms can enable you to clear your rack of unpromising letters.

MUZAKY adj having a bland sound

MUZHIK n Russian peasant, esp under the tsars **muzhiks, muzjik**

MUZJIKS ▶ muzjik

MUZZ vb make (something) muzzy **muzzed, muzzes**

MUZZIER ▶ muzzy

MUZZILY ▶ muzzy

MUZZING ▶ muzz

MUZZLE n, vb **muzzled, muzzler, muzzles**

MUZZY adj

MVULE n tropical African tree **mvules**

MWAH interj

MWALIMU n teacher

MY adj, interj

MYAL ▶ myalism

MYALGIA n a pain in a muscle or a group of muscles **myalgic**

MYALISM n kind of witchcraft **myalist**

MYALL n Australian acacia with hard scented wood **myalls**

MYASES ▶ myasis

MYASIS ▶ myiasis

MYC n oncogene that aids the growth of tumorous cells

MYCELE n microscopic spike-like structure in mucus **myceles**

MYCELIA ▶ mycelium

MYCELLA n blue-veined Danish cream cheese

MYCETES n fungus

MYCOSES ▶ mycosis

MYCOSIS n any infection or disease caused by fungus **mycotic**

MYCS ▶ myc

MYELIN n white tissue forming an insulating sheath around certain nerve fibres **myeline, myelins**

MYELOID adj of or relating to the spinal cord or the bone marrow

MYELOMA n tumour of the bone marrow

MYELON n spinal cord **myelons**

MYGALE n large American spider **mygales**

MYIASES ▶ myiasis

MYIASIS n infestation of the body by the larvae of flies

MYLAR n tradename for a kind of strong polyester film **mylars**

MYLODON n prehistoric giant sloth

MYNA ▶ **mynah**

MYNAH n tropical Asian starling which can mimic human speech **mynahs**

MYNAS ▶ myna

MYNHEER n Dutch title of address

MYOGEN n albumin found in muscle **myogens**

MYOGRAM n tracings of muscular contractions

MYOID adj like muscle

MYOLOGY n study of the structure and diseases of muscles

MYOMA n benign tumour composed of muscle tissue **myomas, myomata**

MYOPE n any person afflicted with myopia **myopes**

MYOPIA n **myopias**

MYOPIC n shortsighted person **myopics**

MYOPIES ▶ myopy

MYOPS ▶ myope

MYOPY ▶ myopia

MYOSES ▶ myosis

MYOSIN n protein found in muscle **myosins**

MYOSIS = miosis

MYOSOTE = myosotis

MYOTIC = miosis

MYOTICS ▶ miosis

MYOTOME n any segment of embryonic mesoderm that develops into skeletal muscle

MYOTUBE n cylindrical cell in muscle

MYRBANE = mirbane

MYRIAD adj, n **myriads**

MYRICA n dried root bark of the wax myrtle, used as a tonic and to treat diarrhoea **myricas**

MYRINGA n eardrum

MYRRH n myrrhic

MYRRHOL n oil of myrrh

MYRRHS ▸ myrrh

MYRTLE n flowering evergreen shrub **myrtles**

MYSELF pron

MYSID n small shrimplike crustacean **mysids**

MYSOST n Norwegian cheese **mysosts**

MYSPACE vb

MYSTERY n

MYSTIC n, adj **mystics**

MYSTIFY vb

MYTH n

MYTHI ▸ mythus

MYTHIC = mythical

MYTHIER ▸ mythy

MYTHISE = mythize

MYTHISM = mythicism

MYTHIST ▸ mythism

MYTHIZE = mythicize

MYTHOI ▸ mythos

MYTHOS n beliefs of a specific group or society

MYTHS ▸ myth

MYTHUS = mythos

MYTHY adj of or like myth

MYXO n viral disease of rabbits

MYXOID adj containing mucus

MYXOMA n tumour composed of mucous connective tissue **myxomas**

MYXOS ▸ myxo

MZEE n old person ▷ adj advanced in years **mzees**

MZUNGU n White person **mzungus**

Nn

Along with **R** and **T**, **N** is one of the most common consonants in Scrabble. As you'll often have it on your rack, it's well worth learning what **N** can do in different situations. **N** is useful when you need short words, as it begins two-letter words with every vowel except **I**, and with **Y** as well. There are plenty of three-letter words starting with **N**, but there aren't many high-scoring ones apart from **nix** and **nox** for 10 points each and **nek** for 7 points. Remember words like **nab** (5 points), **nag** (4), **nap** (5), **nay** (6), **new** (6), **nib** (5), **nob** (5), **nod** (4) and **now** (6).

NA = nae

NAAM = nam

NAAMS ▶ naam

NAAN *n* slightly leavened flat Indian bread **naans**

NAARTJIE = naartjie

NAB *vb* arrest (someone) **nabbed**

NABBER *n* thief **nabbers**

NABBING ▶ nab

NABE *n* Japanese hotpot **nabes**

NABIS *n* Parisian art movement

NABK *n* edible berry **nabks**

NABLA another name for ▶ del

NABLAS ▶ nabla

NABOB = nawab

NABOBS ▶ nabob

NABS ▶ nab

NACARAT *n* red-orange colour

NACELLE *n* streamlined enclosure on an aircraft

NACH *n* Indian dance

NACHAS *n* pleasure

NACHE *n* rump **naches**

NACHO *n* snack of a piece of tortilla with a topping **nachos**

NACKET *n* light lunch, snack **nackets**

NACRE *n* mother of pearl **nacred, nacres**

NACRITE *n* mineral

NACROUS ▶ nacre

NADA *n* nothing **nadas**

NADIR *n* nadiral, nadirs

NADORS *n* thirst brought on by excess of alcohol

NAE *Scot word for* ▶ no

NAEBODY *Scots variant of* ▶ nobody

NAEVE *n* birthmark

NAEVES ▶ naevus

NAEVI ▶ naevus

NAEVOID ▶ naevus

NAEVUS *n* birthmark or mole

NAFF *adj* lacking quality or taste ▷ *vb* go away **naffed, naffer, naffest, naffing, naffly, naffs**

NAG *vb, n*

NAGA *n* cobra

NAGANA *n* disease of all domesticated animals of central and southern Africa **naganas**

NAGAPIE n bushbaby

NAGARI n scripts for writing several languages of India **nagaris**

NAGAS ▸ naga

NAGGED ▸ nag

NAGGER ▸ nag

NAGGERS ▸ nag

NAGGIER ▸ nag

NAGGING ▸ nag

NAGGY ▸ nag

NAGMAAL n Communion

NAGOR another name for > reedbuck

NAGORS ▸ nagor

NAGS ▸ nag

NAH = no

NAHAL n agricultural settlement run by an Israeli military youth organization **nahals**

NAIAD n nymph living in a lake or river **naiades, naiads**

NAIANT adj swimming

NAIF less common word for ▸ naive

NAIFER ▸ naif

NAIFEST ▸ naif

NAIFLY ▸ naif

NAIFS ▸ naif

NAIK n chief **naiks**

NAIL n, vb **nailed, nailer, nailers**

NAILERY n nail factory

NAILING ▸ nail

NAILS ▸ nail

NAILSET n punch for driving down the head of a nail

NAIN adj own

NAIRA n standard monetary unit of Nigeria, divided into 100 kobo **nairas**

NAIRU n Non-Accelerating Inflation Rate of Unemployment **nairus**

NAIVE adj, n **naively, naiver, naives, naivest**

NAIVETE variant of ▸ naivety

NAIVETY n state or quality of being naive

NAIVIST ▸ naive

NAKED adj **nakeder, nakedly**

NAKER n small kettledrum used in medieval music **nakers**

NAKFA n standard currency unit of Eritrea **nakfas**

NALA n ravine **nalas**

NALED n type of insecticide **naleds**

NALLA n ravine **nallah**

NALLAHS ▸ nallah

NALLAS ▸ nalla

NAM n distraint

NAMABLE ▸ name

NAMASTE n Indian greeting

NAME n, vb **named**

NAMELY adv

NAMER ▸ name

NAMERS ▸ name

NAMES ▸ name

NAMETAG n identification badge

NAMING ▸ name

NAMINGS ▸ name

NAMMA adj as in **namma hole** Australian word for a natural well in rock

NAMS ▸ nam

NAMU n black New Zealand sandfly **namus**

NAN n grandmother **nana**

NANAS ▸ nana

NANDIN n type of shrub

NANDINA n type of shrub

NANDINE n African palm civet

NANDINS ▸ nandin

NANDOO ▸ nandu

NANDOOS ▸ nandoo

NANDU n type of ostrich **nandus**

NANE Scot word for ▸ none

NANG adj

NANISM n dwarfism **nanisms**

NANITE n microscopically small machine or robot **nanites**

NANKEEN n hard-wearing buff-coloured cotton fabric **nankin**

NANKINS ▸ nankin

NANNA = nan

NANNAS ▸ nanna

NANNIE = nanny

NANNIED ▸ nanny

NANNIES ▸ nanny

NANNY n, vb

NANOBE n microbe that is smaller than the smallest known bacterium **nanobes**

NANOBOT n microscopically small robot

NANODOT n microscopic cluster of atoms used to store data in a computer chip

NANOOK n polar bear **nanooks**

NANS ▸ nan

NANUA = moki

NANUAS ▸ nanua

NAOI ▸ naos
The plural of **naos**, the inner cell of a temple. A very useful word for ridding your rack of unwanted vowels.

NAOS n ancient classical temple **naoses**

NAP n, vb

NAPA n type of leather

NAPALM n, vb **napalms**

NAPAS ▸ napa

NAPE n, vb **naped**

NAPERY n household linen, esp table linen

NAPES ▸ nape

NAPHTHA n liquid mixture used as a solvent and in petrol

NAPHTOL = naphthol

NAPING ▸ nape

NAPKIN = nappy

NAPKINS ▸ napkin

NAPLESS adj threadbare

NAPOO vb kill **napooed, napoos**

NAPPA n soft leather **nappas**

NAPPE n mass of rock that has been thrust from its original position by earth movements

NAPPED ▸ nap

NAPPER n person or thing that raises the nap on cloth **nappers**

NAPPES ▸ nappe

NAPPIE = nappy

NAPPIER ▸ nappy

NAPPIES ▸ nappy

NAPPING ▸ nap

NAPPY n, adj

NAPRON = apron

NAPRONS ▸ napron

NAPS ▸ nap

NARAS = narras

NARASES ▸ naras

NARC n narcotics agent

NARCEEN = narceine

NARCEIN = narceine

NARCISM n exceptional admiration for oneself

NARCIST n narcissist

NARCO n officer working in the area of anti-drug operations

NARCOMA n coma caused by intake of narcotic drugs

NARCOS n drug smugglers

NARCOSE = narcosis

NARCS ▸ narc

NARD n any of several plants with aromatic roots ▷ vb anoint with nard oil **narded, nardine, narding**

NARDOO n cloverlike fern which grows in swampy areas **nardoos**

NARDS ▸ nard

NARE n nostril

NARES pl n nostrils

NARGILE = narghile

NARGILY = narghile

NARIAL adj of or relating to the nares

NARIC ▸ nare

NARINE = narial

NARIS ▸ nares

NARK vb annoy ▷ n informer or spy **narked**

NARKIER ▸ narky

NARKING ▸ nark

NARKS ▸ nark

NARKY adj irritable or complaining

NARRAS n type of shrub

NARRATE vb

NARRE adj nearer

NARROW adj, vb

NARROWS pl n narrow part of a strait, river, or current

NARTHEX n portico at the west end of a basilica or church

NARTJIE = naartjie
This word for a small sweet orange is one to look out for when you have the J with the good letters of 'retain'. And it has alternative spellings **naartje** and **naartjie**.

NARWAL = narwhal

NARWALS ▸ narwal

NARWHAL n arctic whale with a long spiral tusk

NARY adv not

NAS vb has not

NASAL adj, n nasally, nasals

NASARD n organ stop nasards

NASCENT adj starting to grow or develop

NASHGAB n chatter

NASHI n fruit of the Japanese pear nashis

NASIAL ▶ nasion

NASION n craniometric point where the top of the nose meets the ridge of the forehead nasions

NASTIC adj (of movement of plants) independent of the direction of the external stimulus

NASTIER ▶ nasty

NASTIES ▶ nasty

NASTILY ▶ nasty

NASTY adj, n

NASUTE n type of termite nasutes

NAT n supporter of nationalism

NATAL adj

NATANT adj (of aquatic plants) floating on the water

NATCH sentence substitute naturally ▶ n notch natches

NATES pl n buttocks

NATHEMO ▶ nathemore

NATION n nations

NATIS ▶ nates

NATIVE adj, n natives

NATRIUM obsolete name for ▶ sodium

NATRON n whitish or yellow mineral natrons

NATS ▶ nat

NATTER vb, n natters

NATTERY adj irritable

NATTIER ▶ natty

NATTILY ▶ natty

NATTY adj smart and spruce

NATURA n nature naturae

NATURAL adj, n

NATURE n

NATURED adj having a certain disposition

NATURES ▶ nature

NAUCH = nautch

NAUCHES ▶ nauch

NAUGHT n, adv naughts

NAUGHTY adj, n

NAUNT n aunt naunts

NAUPLII ▶ nauplius

NAUSEA n nauseas

NAUTCH n intricate traditional Indian dance

NAUTIC = nautical

NAUTICS ▶ nautic

NAUTILI ▶ nautilus

NAVAID n navigational aid navaids

NAVAL adj navally

NAVAR n system of air navigation

NAVARCH n admiral

NAVARHO n aircraft navigation system

NAVARIN n stew of mutton or lamb with root vegetables

NAVARS ▶ navar

NAVE n

NAVEL n navels

NAVES ▶ nave

NAVETTE n gem cut

NAVEW another name for ▶ turnip

NAVEWS ▶ navew

NAVIES ▶ navy

NAVVIED ▶ navvy

NAVVIES ▶ navvy

NAVVY n, vb

NAVY n, adj

NAW = no

NAWAB n (formerly) a Muslim ruler or landowner in India nawabs

NAY interj, n, adv, sentence substitute nays

NAYSAID ▶ naysay

NAYSAY vb say no naysays

NAYWARD n towards denial

NAYWORD n proverb

NAZE n flat marshy headland nazes

NAZI n person who thinks or acts in a brutal or dictatorial way

NAZIFY vb make nazi in character

NAZIR n Muslim official nazirs

NAZIS ▶ nazi

NE conj nor

NEAFE ▶ nieve

NEAFES ▶ neafe

NEAFFE ▶ nieve

NEAFFES ▶ neaffe

NEAL = anneal

NEALED ▶ neal

NEALING ▶ neal

NEALS ▶ neal

NEANIC adj of or relating to the early stages in a life cycle

NEAP adj of, relating to, or constituting a neap tide ▷ vb be grounded by a neap tide **neaped, neaping, neaps**

NEAR adj, vb, prep, adv, n

NEARBY adj, adv

NEARED, nearer, nearest, nearing ▶ near

NEARLY adv

NEARS ▶ near

NEAT adj, n

NEATEN vb make neat **neatens**

NEATER ▶ neat

NEATEST ▶ neat

NEATH short for ▶ beneath

NEATLY ▶ neat

NEATNIK n very neat and tidy person

NEATS ▶ neat

NEB n beak of a bird or the nose of an animal ▷ vb look around nosily **nebbed**

NEBBICH = nebbish

NEBBING ▶ neb

NEBBISH n unfortunate simpleton

NEBBUK n type of shrub **nebbuks, nebbuk**

NEBECKS ▶ nebeck

NEBEK = nebbuk

NEBEKS ▶ nebeck

NEBEL n Hebrew musical instrument **nebels**

NEBISH = nebbish

NEBRIS n fawn-skin

NEBS ▶ neb

NEBULA n nebulae, nebular, nebulas

NEBULE n cloud **nebules**

NEBULY adj wavy

NECK n, vb necked, necker, neckers

NECKING n activity of kissing and embracing passionately

NECKLET n ornament worn round the neck

NECKS ▶ neck

NECKTIE = tie

NECROSE vb cause or undergo necrosis

NECTAR n nectars

NECTARY n structure secreting nectar in a plant

NEDDIER ▶ neddy

NEDDIES ▶ neddy

NEDDISH ▶ neddy

NEDDY n donkey ▷ adj of or relating to neds

NEE prep indicating the maiden name of a married woman ▷ adj indicating the maiden name of a married woman

NEED vb n needed, needer, needers

NEEDFUL adj necessary or required

NEEDIER ▶ needy

NEEDILY ▶ needy

NEEDING ▶ need

NEEDLE n, vb needled

NEEDLER n needle maker

NEEDLES ▶ needle

NEEDLY ▶ needle

NEEDS adv necessarily ▷ pl n what is required

NEEDY adj

NEELD = needle

NEELDS ▶ neeld

NEELE = needle

NEELES ▶ neele

NEEM n type of large Indian tree **neemb**

NEEMBS ▶ neemb

NEEMS ▶ neem

NEEP dialect name for ▶ turnip

NEEPS ▶ neep

NEESE = neeze

NEESED ▶ neese

NEESES ▶ neese

NEESING ▶ neese

NEEZE vb sneeze **neezed, neezes, neezing**

NEF n church nave

NEFAST adj wicked

NEFS ▶ nef

NEG n photographic negative

NEGATE vb negated, negater, negates

NEGATON = negatron

NEGATOR ▶ negate

NEGLECT vb, n

NEGLIGE variant of ▶ negligee

NEGRONI n type of cocktail

NEGS ▶ neg

NEGUS n hot drink of port and lemon juice **neguses**

NEIF = nieve

NEIFS ▶ neif

NEIGH n, vb neighed, neighs

NEINEI n type of plant **neineis**

NEIST Scots variant of ▶ **next**

NEITHER pron, adj

NEIVE = **nieve**

NEIVES ▶ **neive**

NEK n mountain pass **neks**

NEKTON n free-swimming animals in the middle depths of a sea or lake **nektons**

NELIES = **nelis**

NELIS n type of pear

NELLIE n effeminate man **nellies**

NELLY n as in **not on your nelly** not under any circumstances

NELSON n type of wrestling hold **nelsons**

NELUMBO n type of aquatic plant

NEMA n filament **nemas**

NEMATIC adj having a mesomorphic state in which a linear orientation of the molecules causes anisotropic properties

NEMESES ▶ **nemesis**

NEMESIA n type of southern African plant

NEMESIS n retribution or vengeance

NEMN vb name **nemned, nemning, nemns**

NEMORAL adj of a wood

NEMPT adj named

NENE n rare black-and-grey short-winged Hawaiian goose **nenes**

NEOCON n supporter of conservative politics **neocons**

NEOGENE adj of, denoting, or formed during the Miocene and Pliocene epochs

NEOLITH n Neolithic stone implement

NEOLOGY = **neologism**

NEON n, adj

NEONATE n newborn child

NEONED adj lit with neon

NEONS ▶ **neon**

NEOSOUL n soul music combined with other genres

NEOTENY n persistence of larval or fetal features in the adult form of an animal

NEOTYPE n specimen selected to replace a type specimen that has been lost or destroyed

NEP n catmint

NEPER n unit expressing the ratio of two quantities **nepers**

NEPETA = **catmint**

NEPETAS ▶ **nepeta**

NEPHEW n **nephews**

NEPHRIC adj renal

NEPHRON n

urine-secreting tubule in the kidney

NEPIT n **nepits**

NEPOTIC ▶ **nepotism**

NEPS ▶ **nep**

NERAL n isomer of citral **nerals**

NERD n boring person obsessed with a particular subject

NERDIC ▶ **geekspeak**

NERDICS ▶ **nerdic**

NERDIER, nerdish, nerds, nerdy ▶ **nerd**

NEREID n sea nymph in Greek mythology **nereids**

NEREIS n type of marine worm

NERINE n type of S African plant related to the amaryllis **nerines**

NERITE n type of sea snail **nerites**

NERITIC adj of or formed in shallow seas near a coastline

NERK n fool

NERKA n type of salmon **nerkas**

NERKS ▶ **nerk**

NEROL n scented liquid

NEROLI n brown oil used in perfumery **nerolis**

NEROLS ▶ **nerol**

NERTS interj nuts **nertz**

NERVAL ▶ **nerve**

NERVATE adj (of leaves) with veins

NERVE n, vb **nerved, nerver, nervers, nerves**

NERVIER ▶ nervy

NERVILY ▶ nervy

NERVINE adj having a soothing effect upon the nerves ▷ n nervine drug or agent

NERVING ▶ nerve

NERVOUS adj

NERVULE n small vein

NERVURE n stiff rod in an insect's wing

NERVY adj excitable or nervous

NESH adj sensitive to the cold nesher, neshest

NESS n headland, cape nesses

NEST n, vb nested, nester, nesters, nestful, nesting

NESTLE vb nestled, nestler, nestles

NESTOR n wise old man nestors

NESTS ▶ nest

NET n, vb, adj

NETBALL n

NETE n lyre string netes

NETFUL ▶ net

NETFULS ▶ net

NETHEAD n expert on the internet

NETHER adj lower

NETIZEN n person who regularly uses the internet

NETLESS ▶ net

NETLIKE ▶ net

NETOP n friend netops

NETROOT n

NETS ▶ net

NETSUKE n (in Japan) a carved ornamental toggle

NETT = net

NETTED ▶ net

NETTER n person that makes nets netters

NETTIE n enthusiastic user of the internet

NETTIER ▶ net

NETTIES ▶ netty

NETTING ▶ net

NETTLE n, vb nettled, nettler, nettles, nettly

NETTS ▶ nett

NETTY n lavatory, originally an earth closet

NETWORK n, vb

NEUK Scot word for ▶ nook

NEUKS ▶ neuk

NEUM = neume

NEUME n notational symbol neumes, neumic

NEUMS ▶ neum

NEURAL adj of a nerve or the nervous system

NEURINE n poisonous alkaloid

NEURISM n nerve force

NEURITE n biological cell component

NEUROID adj nervelike

NEUROMA n any tumour composed of nerve tissue

NEURON = neurone

NEURONE n

NEURONS ▶ neuron

NEURULA n stage of embryonic development

NEUSTIC ▶ neuston

NEUSTON n organisms that float on the surface of open water

NEUTER adj, vb, n neuters

NEUTRAL adj, n

NEUTRON n

NEVE n mass of porous ice, formed from snow

NEVEL vb beat with the fists nevels

NEVER adv, sentence substitute, interj

NEVES ▶ neve

NEVI ▶ nevus

NEVOID ▶ naevus

NEVUS = naevus

NEW adj not existing before ▷ adv recently ▷ vb make new

NEWBIE n person new to a job, club, etc newbies

NEWBORN adj, n

NEWCOME > newcomer

NEWED ▶ new

NEWEL n post at the top or bottom of a flight of stairs

NEWELL n new thing newells

NEWELS ▶ newel

NEWER ▶ new

NEWEST ▶ new

NEWIE n fresh idea or thing newies

NEWING ▶ new

NEWISH adj fairly new

NEWLY adv

NEWMOWN adj freshly cut

NEWNESS ▶ new

NEWS n, vb

NEWSBOY n boy who sells or delivers newspapers

NEWSED ▸ news

NEWSES ▸ news

NEWSIE = newsy

NEWSIER ▸ newsy

NEWSIES ▸ newsie

NEWSING ▸ news

NEWSMAN n male newsreader or reporter **newsmen**

NEWSY adj full of news ▷ n newsagent

NEWT n

NEWTON n newtons

NEWTS ▸ newt

NEXT adv immediately following ▷ n next person or thing **nextly, nexts**

NEXUS n connection or link **nexuses**

NGAI n

NGAIO n small New Zealand tree **ngaios**

NGANA = nagana

NGANAS ▸ ngana

NGARARA n lizard found in New Zealand

NGATI n (occurring as part of the tribe name) a tribe or clan **ngatis**

NGOMA n type of drum **ngomas**

NGWEE n Zambian monetary unit

NHANDU n type of spider **nhandus**

NIACIN n niacins

NIB n, vb nibbed, nibbing

NIBBLE vb, n nibbled

NIBBLER n person,

animal, or thing that nibbles

NIBBLES ▸ nibble

NIBLICK n former golf club giving a great deal of lift

NIBLIKE ▸ nib

NIBS ▸ nib

NICAD n rechargeable dry-cell battery **nicads**

NICE adj pleasant niceish, nicely, nicer, nicest

NICETY n

NICHE n, adj, vb niched

NICHER vb snigger nichers

NICHES ▸ niche

NICHING ▸ niche

NICHT Scot word for ▸ night

NICHTS ▸ nicht

NICISH ▸ nice

NICK vb, n

NICKAR n hard seed nickars

NICKED ▸ nick

NICKEL n, vb nickels

NICKER n pound sterling ▷ vb (of a horse) to neigh softly **nickers**

NICKING ▸ nick

NICKLE = nickel

NICKLED ▸ nickle

NICKLES ▸ nickle

NICKS ▸ nick

NICKUM n mischievous person **nickums**

NICOISE adj prepared with tomatoes, black olives, garlic and anchovies

NICOL n device for producing

plane-polarized light **nicols**

NICOTIN = nicotine

NICTATE = nictitate

NID = nide

NIDAL ▸ nidus

NIDATE vb undergo nidation **nidated, nidates**

NIDDICK n nape of the neck

NIDE vb nest **nided, nides**

NIDGET n fool **nidgets**

NIDI ▸ nidus

NIDIFY vb (of a bird) to make or build a nest

NIDING n coward **nidings**

NIDOR n cooking smell **nidors**

NIDS ▸ nid

NIDUS n nest in which insects or spiders deposit their eggs **niduses**

NIE archaic spelling of ▸ nigh

NIECE n nieces

NIED ▸ nie

NIEF = nieve

NIEFS ▸ nief

NIELLI ▸ niello

NIELLO n black compound of sulphur and silver, lead, or copper ▷ vb decorate or treat with niello **niellos**

NIES ▸ nie

NIEVE n closed hand **nieves**

NIFE n earth's core **nifes**

NIFF n stink ▷ vb stink niffed

NIFFER vb barter **niffers**
NIFFIER ▸ niff
NIFFING ▸ niff
NIFFS ▸ niff
NIFFY ▸ niff
NIFTIER ▸ nifty
NIFTIES ▸ nifty
NIFTILY ▸ nifty
NIFTY adj, n
NIGELLA n type of Mediterranean plant
NIGGARD n stingy person ▷ adj miserly ▷ vb act in a niggardly way
NIGGLE vb, n niggled, niggler, niggles, niggly
NIGH prep near ▷ adv nearly ▷ adj near ▷ vb approach nighed, nigher, nighest, nighing, nighly, nighs
NIGHT n, adj
NIGHTED adj darkened
NIGHTIE = nightgown
NIGHTLY adv, adj
NIGHTS adv at night or on most nights
NIGHTY = nightie
NIGIRI n small oval block of cold rice, wasabi and fish nigiris
NIGRIFY vb blacken
NIHIL n nil nihils
NIHONGA n Japanese form of painting
NIKAB = niqab
NIKABS ▸ nikab
NIKAH n Islamic marriage contract nikahs
NIKAU n palm tree native to New Zealand

nikaus
NIL n
NILGAI n large Indian antelope nilgais
NILGAU = nilghau
NILGAUS ▸ nilgau
NILGHAI = nilgai
NILGHAU = nilgai
NILL vb be unwilling nilled, nilling, nills
NILS ▸ nil
NIM n game involving removing one or more small items from several rows or piles ▷ vb steal
NIMB n halo nimbed
NIMBI ▸ nimbus
NIMBLE adj nimbler, nimbly
NIMBS ▸ nimb
NIMBUS ▸ n
NIMIETY rare word for ▸ excess
NIMIOUS ▸ nimiety
NIMMED ▸ nim
NIMMER ▸ nim
NIMMERS ▸ nim
NIMMING ▸ nim
NIMONIC adj as in nimonic alloy type of nickel-based alloy
NIMPS adj easy
NIMROD n hunter nimrods
NIMS ▸ nim
NINCOM = nicompoop
NINCOMS ▸ nincom
NINCUM = nicompoop
NINCUMS ▸ nincum
NINE n
NINEPIN n skittle used in ninepins

NINES ▸ nine
NINETY n, determiner
NINJA n person skilled in ninjutsu ninjas
NINNIES ▸ ninny
NINNY n stupid person
NINON n fine strong silky fabric ninons
NINTH n (of) number nine in a series ▷ adj coming after the eighth ▷ adv after the eighth ninthly, ninths
NIOBATE n type of salt crystal
NIOBIC adj of or containing niobium in the pentavalent state
NIOBITE another name for ▸ columbite
NIOBIUM n white metallic element
NIOBOUS adj of or containing niobium in the trivalent state
NIP vb, n
NIPA n palm tree of S and SE Asia nipas
NIPPED ▸ nip
NIPPER n, vb
NIPPERS pl n instrument or tool for pinching or squeezing
NIPPIER ▸ nippy
NIPPILY ▸ nippy
NIPPING ▸ nip
NIPPLE n, vb nippled, nipples
NIPPY adj
NIPS ▸ nip
NIPTER n type of religious ceremony nipters

NIQAB n type of veil worn by some Muslim women **niqabs**

> One of those invaluable words allowing you to play the Q without a U. It can also be spelt **nikab**.

NIRL vb shrivel **nirled**

NIRLIE variant of ▶ **nirly**

NIRLIER ▶ **nirly**

NIRLING ▶ **nirl**

NIRLIT ▶ **nirl**

NIRLS ▶ **nirl**

NIRLY adj shrivelled

NIRVANA n

NIS n friendly goblin

NISEI n native-born citizen of the US or Canada whose parents were Japanese **niseis**

NISGUL n smallest and weakest bird in a brood of chickens **nisguls**

NISH n nothing **nishes**

NISI adj (of a court order) coming into effect on a specified date

NISSE = nis

NISSES ▶ **nisse**

NISUS n impulse towards or striving after a goal

NIT n

NITE variant of ▶ **night**

NITER = nitre

NITERIE n nightclub

NITERS ▶ **niter**

NITERY ▶ **nite**

NITES ▶ **nite**

NITHER vb shiver **nithers**

NITHING n coward

NITID adj bright

NITINOL n metal alloy

NITON less common name for ▶ **radon**

NITONS ▶ **niton**

NITPICK vb criticize unnecessarily

NITRATE n, vb

NITRE n potassium nitrate **nitres**

NITRIC adj of or containing nitrogen

NITRID = nitride

NITRIDE n compound of nitrogen ▷ vb make into a nitride

NITRIDS ▶ **nitrid**

NITRIFY vb treat or cause to react with nitrogen

NITRIL = nitrile

NITRILE n any one of a particular class of organic compounds

NITRILS ▶ **nitril**

NITRITE n salt or ester of nitrous acid

NITRO n nitroglycerine **nitros**

NITROSO adj of a particular monovalent group

NITROUS adj derived from or containing nitrogen in a low valency state

NITROX n mixture of nitrogen and oxygen used in diving

NITRY adj nitrous

NITRYL n chemical compound **nitryls**

NITS ▶ **nit**

NITTIER ▶ **nitty**

NITTY adj infested with nits

NITWIT n stupid person **nitwits**

NIVAL adj of or growing in or under snow

NIVEOUS adj resembling snow, esp in colour

NIX sentence substitute be careful! watch out! ▷ n rejection or refusal ▷ vb veto, deny, reject, or forbid (plans, suggestions, etc)

> This is a handy little word, combining X with two of the most common tiles in the game.

NIXE n water sprite

NIXED ▶ **nix**

NIXER n spare-time job **nixers**

NIXES ▶ **nix**

NIXIE n female water sprite, usually unfriendly to humans **nixies**

NIXING ▶ **nix**

NIXY = nixie

NIZAM n (formerly) a Turkish regular soldier **nizams**

NKOSI n term of address to a superior **nkosis**

NO interj, adj, adv, n

NOAH n shark **noahs**

NOB n person of wealth or social distinction **nobbier, nobbily**

NOBBLE vb attract the attention of **nobbled, nobbler, nobbles**

NOBBUT adv nothing but

NOBBY ▶ nob

NOBLE adj, n nobler, nobles, noblest, nobly

NOBODY pron, n

NOBS ▶ nob

NOCAKE n Indian meal made from dried corn nocakes

NOCENT n guilty person nocents

NOCHEL ▶ notchel

NOCHELS ▶ nochel

NOCK n notch on an arrow or a bow for the bowstring ▷ vb fit (an arrow) on a bowstring nocked

NOCKET = nacket

NOCKETS ▶ nocket

NOCKING ▶ nock

NOCKS ▶ nock

NOCTUA n type of moth noctuas

NOCTUID n type of nocturnal moth ▷ adj of or relating to this type of moth

NOCTULE n any of several large Old World insectivorous bats

NOCTURN n any of the main sections of the office of matins

NOCUOUS adj harmful

NOD vb, n

NODAL adj of or like a node nodally

NODATED adj knotted

NODDED ▶ nod

NODDER ▶ nod

NODDERS ▶ nod

NODDIER ▶ noddy

NODDIES ▶ noddy

NODDING ▶ nod

NODDLE n head ▷ vb nod (the head), as through drowsiness noddled, noddles

NODDY n tropical tern with a dark plumage ▷ adj very easy to use or understand

NODE n nodes

NODI ▶ nodus

NODICAL adj of or relating to the nodes of a celestial body

NODOSE adj having nodes or knotlike swellings nodous

NODS ▶ nod

NODULAR ▶ nodule

NODULE n noduled, nodules

NODUS n problematic idea, situation, etc

NOEL n Christmas noels

NOES ▶ no

NOESES ▶ noesis

NOESIS n exercise of reason

NOETIC adj of or relating to the mind

NOG = nogging

NOGAKU n Japanese style of drama

NOGG = nog

NOGGED adj built with timber and brick

NOGGIN n head

NOGGING n short horizontal timber member

NOGGINS ▶ noggin

NOGGS ▶ nogg

NOGS ▶ nog

NOH n stylized classic drama of Japan

NOHOW adv under any conditions

NOIL n short or knotted fibres that are separated from the long fibres by combing

NOILIER ▶ noily

NOILS ▶ noil

NOILY ▶ noil

NOINT vb anoint nointed

NOINTER n mischievous child

NOINTS ▶ noint

NOIR adj (of a film) showing characteristics of a film noir, in plot or style ▷ n film noir noirish, noirs

NOISE n noised, noises

NOISIER ▶ noisy

NOISILY ▶ noisy

NOISING

NOISOME adj (of smells) offensive

NOISY adj

NOLE = noll

NOLES ▶ nole

NOLL n head nolls

NOLO vb as in nolo contendere plea indicating that the defendant does not wish to contest the case nolos

NOM n name

NOMA n gangrenous inflammation of the mouth

NOMAD n nomade

NOMADES ▶ nomade

NOMADIC adj relating to or characteristic of nomads

NOMADS ▶ nomad

NOMADY n practice of living like nomads

NOMARCH n head of an ancient Egyptian nome

NOMAS ▶ noma

NOMBLES variant spelling of ▶ numbles

NOMBRIL n point on a shield

NOME n any of the former provinces of modern Greece

NOMEN n ancient Roman's second name

NOMES ▶ nome

NOMIC adj normal or habitual

NOMINA ▶ nomen

NOMINAL adj, n

NOMINEE n candidate

NOMISM n adherence to laws as a primary exercise of religion nomisms

NOMOI ▶ nomos

NOMOS n convention

NOMS ▶ nom

NON adv not

NONA n sleeping sickness

NONACID adj not acid ▷ n nonacid substance

NONAGE n state of being under full legal age nonaged, nonages

NONAGON n geometric figure with nine sides

NONANE n type of chemical compound nonanes

NONART n something that does not constitute art nonarts

NONARY adj based on the number nine

NONAS ▶ nones

NONBANK n business or institution that is not a bank but provides similar services

NONBODY n nonphysical nature of a person

NONBOOK n book with little substance

NONCASH adj other than cash

NONCE n present time or occasion nonces

NONCOLA n soft drink other than cola

NONCOM n person not involved in combat noncoms

NONCORE adj not central or essential

NONDRIP adj (of paint) specially formulated to minimize dripping during application

NONDRUG adj not involving the use of drugs

NONE pron

NONEGO n everything that is outside one's conscious self nonegos

NONES n (in the Roman calendar) the ninth day before the ides of each month

NONET n piece of music composed for a group of nine instruments nonets, nonette, nonetti, nonetto

NONFACT n event or thing not provable

NONFAN n person who is not a fan nonfans

NONFARM adj not connected with a farm

NONFAT adj fat free

NONFOOD n item that is not food

NONFUEL adj not relating to fuel

NONG n stupid or incompetent person

NONGAME adj not pursued for competitive sport purposes

NONGAY n person who is not gay nongays

NONGS ▶ nong

NONHEME adj of dietary iron, obtained from vegetable foods

NONHERO n person who is not a hero

NONHOME adj not of the home

NONI n tree of SE Asia and the Pacific islands

NONIRON adj not requiring ironing

NONIS ▶ noni

NONJURY n trial without a jury

NONLIFE n matter which is not living

NONMAN n being that is not a man
NONMEAT adj not containing meat
NONMEN ▷ nonman
NONNEWS adj not concerned with news
NONNIES ▷ nonny
NONNY n meaningless word
NONOILY adj not oily
NONORAL adj not oral
NONPAID adj without payment
NONPAR adj nonparticipating
NONPAST n grammatical term
NONPEAK n period of low demand
NONPLAY n social behaviour that is not classed as play
NONPLUS vb put at a loss ▷ n state of utter perplexity prohibiting action or speech
NONPOOR adj not poor
NONPROS vb enter a judgment of non prosequitur
NONSELF n foreign molecule in the body
NONSKED n non-scheduled aeroplane
NONSKID adj designed to reduce skidding
NONSLIP adj designed to prevent slipping
NONSTOP adv, adj, n
NONSUCH = nonesuch
NONSUIT n order of a judge dismissing a suit

▷ vb order the dismissal of the suit of (a person)
NONTAX n tax that has little real effect
NONUPLE adj ninefold ▷ n ninefold number
NONUSE n failure to use **nonuser, nonuses**
NONWAGE adj not part of wages
NONWAR n state of nonviolence **nonwars**
NONWOOL adj not wool
NONWORD n series of letters not recognised as a word
NONWORK adj not involving work
NONYL n type of chemical **nonyls**
NONZERO adj not equal to zero
NOO n type of Japanese musical drama
NOOB ▷ newbie
NOOBS ▷ noob
NOODGE vb annoy persistently **noodged, noodges**
NOODLE n, vb **noodled, noodles**
NOOGIE n act of inflicting pain by rubbing head hard **noogies**
NOOIT interj South African exclamation of surprise
NOOK n **nooks**
NOOLOGY n study of intuition
NOON n, vb
NOONDAY adj happening at noon ▷ n

middle of the day
NOONED ▷ noon
NOONER n sexual encounter during a lunch hour **nooners**
NOONING n midday break for rest or food
NOONS ▷ noon
NOOP n point of the elbow **noops**
NOOSE n **noosed**
NOOSER n person who uses a noose **noosers**
NOOSES ▷ noose
NOOSING ▷ noose
NOPAL n type of cactus **nopales, nopals**
NOPE interj no
NOPLACE = nowhere
NOR prep
NORDIC adj of competitions in cross-country racing and ski-jumping
NORI n edible seaweed
NORIA n water wheel with buckets attached to its rim **norias**
NORIMON n Japanese passenger vehicle
NORIS ▷ nori
NORITE n variety of gabbro **norites, noritic**
NORK n female breast **norks**
NORLAND n north part of a country or the earth
NORM n
NORMA n norm or standard
NORMAL adj, n **normals**

NORMAN n post used for winding on a ship **normans**

NORMAS ▸ **norma**

NORMED n mathematical term

NORMS ▸ **norm**

NORSEL vb fit with short lines for fastening hooks **norsels**

NORTENA = **norteno**

NORTENO n type of Mexican music

NORTH n, adj, adv, vb **northed**

NORTHER n wind or storm from the north ▸ vb move north

NORTHS ▸ **north**

NORWARD = **northward**

NOS ▸ **no**

NOSE n, vb

NOSEAN n type of mineral **noseans**

NOSEBAG n bag containing feed fastened round a horse's head

NOSED ▸ **nose**

NOSEGAY n small bunch of flowers

NOSER n strong headwind **nosers**

NOSES ▸ **nose**

NOSEY adj prying or inquisitive ▸ n nosey person **noseys**

NOSH n food ▸ vb eat **noshed, nosher, noshers**

NOSHERY n restaurant or other place where food is served

NOSHES ▸ **nosh**

NOSHING ▸ **nosh**

NOSIER, nosies, nosiest, nosily ▸ **nosy**

NOSING n edge of a step or stair tread **nosings**

NOSODE n homeopathic remedy **nosodes**

NOSTOC n type of bacterium occurring in moist places **nostocs**

NOSTOI ▸ **nostos**

NOSTOS n story of a return home

NOSTRIL n

NOSTRO adj as in **nostro account** bank account conducted by a British bank with a foreign bank

NOSTRUM n quack medicine

NOSY adj

NOT adv

NOTA ▸ **notum**

NOTABLE adj, n

NOTABLY adv particularly or especially

NOTAEUM n back of a bird's body

NOTAIRE ▸ **notum**

NOTAL ▸ **notum**

NOTANDA > **notandum**

NOTARY n

NOTATE vb write (esp music) in notation **notated, notates**

NOTCH n, vb **notched**

NOTCHEL vb refuse to pay another person's debts

NOTCHER n person who cuts notches

NOTCHES ▸ **notch**

NOTCHY adj (of a motor vehicle gear mechanism) requiring careful gear-changing

NOTE n, vb

NOTED adj **notedly**

NOTELET n small folded card with a design on the front

NOTEPAD n number of sheets of paper fastened together

NOTER n person who takes notes **noters**

NOTES pl n short descriptive or summarized jottings

NOTHER = other

NOTHING pron, adv, n

NOTICE n, vb noticed

NOTICER n person who takes notice

NOTICES ▸ **notice**

NOTIFY vb

NOTING ▸ **note**

NOTION n

NOTIONS pl n pins, cotton, ribbon, and similar wares used for sewing

NOTITIA n register or list, esp of ecclesiastical districts

NOTOUR adj notorious

NOTT = not

NOTUM n cuticular plate on an insect

NOUGAT n **nougats**

NOUGHT n **noughts**

NOUL = **noll**

NOULD vb would not **noulde**

NOULE = noll
NOULES ▸ noule
NOULS ▸ noul
NOUMENA
> noumenon
NOUN n nounal
NOUNIER ▸ nouny
NOUNS ▸ noun
NOUNY adj nounlike
NOUP n steep headland
noups
NOURICE n nurse
NOURISH vb
NOURSLE vb nurse
NOUS n common sense
NOUSELL vb foster
NOUSES ▸ nous
NOUSLE vb nuzzle
nousled, nousles
NOUT = nought
NOUVEAU adj having
recently become the
thing specified
NOVA n novae
NOVALIA n newly
reclaimed land
NOVAS ▸ nova
NOVATE vb substitute
one thing in place of
another
NOVATED adj as in
novated lease
Australian system of
employer-aided car
purchase
NOVATES ▸ novate
NOVEL n, adj
NOVELLA n short novel
novelle
NOVELLY ▸ novel
NOVELS ▸ novel
NOVELTY n
NOVENA n set of
prayers or services on

nine consecutive days
novenae, novenas
NOVICE n novices
NOVITY n novelty
NOVUM n game played
with dice novums
NOW adv
NOWAY adv in no
manner ▸ sentence
substitute used to make
an emphatic refusal,
denial etc noways
NOWED adj knotted
NOWHERE adv, n
NOWISE another word for
▸ noway
NOWL n crown of the
head nowls
NOWN = own
NOWNESS ▸ nown
NOWS ▸ now
NOWT n nothing
NOWTIER ▸ nowty
nowts
NOWTY adj
bad-tempered
NOWY adj having a
small projection at
the centre (of a cross)
NOX n nitrogen oxide

> Meaning nitrogen
oxide, this is another
of those very useful
short words
containing X.

NOXAL adj relating to
damage done by
something belonging
to another
NOXES ▸ nox
NOXIOUS adj
NOY vb harrass
NOYADE n execution by
drowning noyades

NOYANCE n nuisance
NOYAU n brandy-based
liqueur noyaus
NOYED ▸ noy
NOYES archaic form of
▸ noise
NOYESES ▸ noyes
NOYING ▸ noy
NOYOUS ▸ noy
NOYS ▸ noy
NOYSOME ▸ noy
NOZZER n new recruit
(in the Navy) nozzers
NOZZLE n nozzles
NTH adj of an
unspecified number

> A good word to
remember for
awkward situations
on the board, as it's
one of very few
three-letter words
that doesn't contain
a vowel.

NU n 13th letter in the
Greek alphabet
NUANCE n, vb nuanced,
nuances
NUB n, vb nubbed
NUBBIER ▸ nubby
NUBBIN n something
small or undeveloped,
esp a fruit or ear of corn
NUBBING ▸ nub
NUBBINS ▸ nubbin
NUBBLE n small lump
nubbled, nubbles,
nubbly
NUBBY adj having small
lumps or
protuberances
NUBIA n fleecy scarf for
the head, worn by
women nubias

NUBILE adj
NUBS ▸ nub
NUBUCK n type of leather with a velvety finish **nubucks**
NUCELLI > nucellus
NUCHA n back or nape of the neck **nuchae**
NUCHAL n scale on a reptile's neck **nuchals**
NUCLEAL ▸ nucleus
NUCLEAR adj
NUCLEI ▸ nucleus
NUCLEIC adj as in **nucleic acid** type of complex compound that is a vital constituent of living cells
NUCLEIN n protein that occurs in the nuclei of living cells
NUCLEON n proton or neutron
NUCLEUS n
NUCLIDE n species of atom characterized by its atomic number and its mass number
NUCULE n small seed **nucules**
NUDDIES ▸ nuddy
NUDDY n as in **in the nuddy** in the nude
NUDE adj, n **nudely, nuder, nudes, nudest**
NUDGE vb, n **nudged, nudger, nudgers, nudges, nudging**
NUDIE n film, show, or magazine depicting nudity **nudies**
NUDISM n practice of not wearing clothes

nudisms, nudist, nudists
NUDITY n state or fact of being nude
NUDNICK = nudnik
NUDNIK n boring person **nudniks**
NUDZH = nudge
NUDZHED ▸ nudzh
NUDZHES ▸ nudzh
NUFF slang form of ▸ **enough**
NUFFIN slang form of ▸ **nothing**
NUFFINS ▸ nuffin
NUFFS ▸ nuff
NUGAE n jests
NUGGAR n sailing boat used to carry cargo on the Nile **nuggars**
NUGGET n, vb **nuggets**
NUGGETY adj of or resembling a nugget
NUKE vb attack with nuclear weapons ▸ n nuclear weapon **nuked, nukes, nuking**
NULL adj, vb
NULLA = nullah
NULLAH n stream or drain **nullahs**
NULLAS ▸ nulla
NULLED ▸ null
NULLIFY vb
NULLING n knurling
NULLITY n state of being null
NULLS ▸ null
NUMB adj, vb
NUMBAT n numbats
NUMBED ▸ numb
NUMBER n, vb numbers
NUMBEST ▸ numb
NUMBING ▸ numb

NUMBLES pl n animal organs, cooked for food
NUMBLY ▸ numb
NUMBS ▸ numb
NUMDAH n coarse felt made esp in India **numdahs**
NUMEN n deity or spirit presiding over a thing or place
NUMERAL n, adj
NUMERIC n number or numeral
NUMINA plural of ▸ **numen**
NUMMARY adj of or relating to coins
NUMNAH = numdah
NUMNAHS ▸ numnah
NUMPTY n stupid person
NUN n
NUNATAK n isolated mountain peak projecting through glacial ice
NUNCIO n pope's ambassador **nuncios**
NUNCLE archaic or dialect word for ▸ **uncle**
NUNCLES ▸ nuncle
NUNDINE n market day
NUNHOOD n condition, practice, or character of a nun
NUNLIKE ▸ nun
NUNNERY n convent
NUNNISH ▸ nun
NUNNY n as in **nunny bag** small sealskin haversack used in Canada
NUNS ▸ nun
NUNSHIP ▸ nun

NUPTIAL *adj* relating to marriage
NUR *n* wooden ball
NURAGHE *n* Sardinian round tower **nuraghi**
NURD = **nerd**
NURDIER ▸ **nerd**
NURDISH ▸ **nerd**
NURDLE *vb* score runs in cricket by soft deflections **nurdled, nurdles**
NURDS ▸ **nurd**
NURDY ▸ **nurd**
NURHAG *n* Sardinian round tower **nurhags**
NURL *variant of* ▸ **knurl**
NURLED ▸ **nurl**
NURLING ▸ **nurl**
NURLS ▸ **nurl**
NURR *n* wooden ball **nurrs**
NURS ▸ **nur**
NURSE *n, vb* **nursed**
NURSER *n* person who treats something carefully **nursers**
NURSERY *n*
NURSES ▸ **nurse**
NURSING *n*
NURSLE *vb* nuzzle **nursled, nursles**
NURTURE *n, vb*
NUS ▸ **nu**
NUT *n, vb*
NUTANT *adj* having the apex hanging down
NUTATE *vb* nod **nutated, nutates**

NUTGALL *n* nut-shaped gall caused by gall wasps on the oak and other trees
NUTJOB *n* crazy person **nutjobs**
NUTLET *n* portion of a fruit that fragments when mature **nutlets**
NUTLIKE ▸ **nut**
NUTMEAL *n* type of grain
NUTMEAT *n* kernel of a nut
NUTMEG *n, vb* **nutmegs**
NUTPICK *n* tool used to dig the meat from nuts
NUTRIA *n* fur of the coypu **nutrias**
NUTS ▸ **nut**
NUTTED ▸ **nut**
NUTTERY *n* place where nut trees grow
NUTTIER ▸ **nutty**
NUTTILY ▸ **nutty**
NUTTING *n* act of gathering nuts
NUTTY *adj*
NUTWOOD *n* any of various nut-bearing trees, such as walnut
NUZZER *n* present given to a superior in India **nuzzers**
NUZZLE *vb* **nuzzled**
NUZZLER *n* person or thing that nuzzles
NUZZLES ▸ **nuzzle**
NY = **nigh**

NYAFF *n* small or contemptible person ▷ *vb* yelp like a small dog **nyaffed, nyaffs**
NYALA *n* spiral-horned southern African antelope **nyalas**
NYANZA *n* (in E Africa) a lake **nyanzas**
NYAS *n* young hawk **nyases**
NYBBLE *n* small byte **nybbles**
NYE *n* flock of pheasants ▷ *vb* near **nyed, nyes, nying**
NYLGHAI = **nilgai**
NYLGHAU = **nilgai**
NYLON *n*
NYLONS *pl n* stockings made of nylon
NYMPH *n*
NYMPHA *n* either one of the labia minora **nymphae**
NYMPHAL ▸ **nymph**
NYMPHET *n* sexually precocious young girl
NYMPHIC ▸ **nymph**
NYMPHLY ▸ **nymph**
NYMPHO *n* nymphomaniac **nymphos**
NYMPHS ▸ **nymph**
NYS ▸ **ny**
NYSSA *n* type of tree **nyssas**

Oo

With eight **O**s in the bag, you're likely to have at least one on your rack during a game. There are plenty of good two-letter words starting with **O**. It's worth knowing that **O** will form a two-letter word in front of every other vowel except **A**, as well as in front of **Y**. **O** also combines well with **X**, with **ox** (9 points) as the obvious starting point, and several words that refer to **oxygen** (17), including **oxo** (10) and **oxy** (13). Don't forget the short everyday words that begin with **O**. While **on** and **or** (2 each) won't earn you many points, they can be very helpful when you are trying to score in more than one direction at a time. **Of** and **oh** (5 each) can also prove very useful.

OAF *n* oafish, oafs

OAK *n*

OAKED *adj* relating to wine that is stored for a time in oak barrels prior to bottling

OAKEN *adj* made of the wood of the oak

OAKER = ochre

OAKERS ▶ oaker

OAKIER ▶ oaky

OAKIES ▶ oaky

OAKIEST ▶ oaky

OAKLIKE ▶ oak

OAKLING *n* young oak

OAKMOSS *n* type of lichen

OAKS ▶ oak

OAKUM *n* fibre obtained by unravelling old rope **oakums**

OAKY *adj* hard like the wood of an oak ▷ *n* ice cream

OAR *n, vb*

OARAGE *n* use or number of oars **oarages**

OARED *adj* equipped with oars

OARFISH *n* very long ribbonfish with long slender ventral fins

OARIER ▶ oary

OARIEST ▶ oary

OARING ▶ oar

OARLESS ▶ oar

OARLIKE ▶ oar

OARLOCK *n* swivelling device that holds an oar in place

OARS ▶ oar

OARSMAN *n* person who rows **oarsmen**

OARWEED *n* type of brown seaweed

OARY *adj* of or like an oar

OASES ▶ oasis

OASIS *n*

OAST *n* oven for drying hops **oasts**

OAT *n*

OATCAKE *n* thin flat biscuit of oatmeal

OATEN *adj* made of oats or oat straw

OATER *n* film about the American Wild West **oaters**

OATH *n* oaths

OATIER ▶ oaty

OATIEST ▶ oaty

OATLIKE ▶ oat
OATMEAL n, adj
OATS ▶ oat
OATY adj of, like, or containing oats
OAVES ▶ oaf
OB n expression of opposition
OBA n (in W Africa) a Yoruba chief or ruler
OBANG n former Japanese coin **obangs**
OBAS ▶ oba
OBCONIC adj shaped like a cone and attached at the pointed end
OBDURE vb make obdurate **obdured, obdures**
OBE n ancient Laconian village
OBEAH vb cast spell on **obeahed, obeahs**
OBECHE n African tree **obeches**
OBEISM n belief in obeah **obeisms**
OBELI ▶ obelus
OBELIA n type of jellyfish **obelias**
OBELION n area of skull
OBELISE = obelize
OBELISK n
OBELISM n practice of marking passages in text
OBELIZE vb mark (a word or passage) with an obelus
OBELUS n mark used to indicate spurious words or passages

OBENTO n Japanese lunch box **obentos**
OBES ▶ obe
OBESE adj obesely, obeser, obesest, obesity
OBEY vb obeyed, obeyer, obeyers, obeying, obeys
OBI n broad sash tied in a large flat bow at the back ▷ vb bewitch
OBIA = obeah
OBIAS ▶ obia
OBIED, obiing, obiism, obiisms ▶ obi
OBIIT vb died
OBIS ▶ obi
OBIT n memorial service
OBITAL adj of obits
OBITER adv by the way
OBITS ▶ obit
OBITUAL adj of obits
OBJECT n, vb
OBJET n object **objets**
OBJURE vb put on oath objured, objures
OBLAST n administrative division of the constituent republics of Russia **oblasti, oblasts**
OBLATE adj (of a sphere) flattened at the poles ▷ n person dedicated to a monastic or religious life **oblates**
OBLIGE vb obliged
OBLIGEE n person in whose favour an obligation, contract, or bond is created
OBLIGER ▶ oblige

OBLIGES ▶ oblige
OBLIGOR n person who binds himself by contract
OBLIQUE adj, n, vb
OBLONG adj, n oblongs
OBLOQUY n verbal abuse
OBO n ship carrying oil and ore
OBOE n oboes, oboist, oboists
OBOL = obolus
OBOLARY adj very poor
OBOLE n former weight unit in pharmacy oboles
OBOLI ▶ obolus
OBOLS ▶ obol
OBOLUS n Greek unit of weight
OBOS ▶ obo
OBOVATE adj (of a leaf) shaped like the longitudinal section of an egg with the narrower end at the base
OBOVOID adj (of a fruit) egg-shaped with the narrower end at the base
OBS ▶ ob
OBSCENE adj
OBSCURE adj, vb
OBSEQUY singular of > obsequies
OBSERVE vb
OBSESS vb preoccupy (someone) compulsively
OBSIGN vb confirm obsigns
OBTAIN vb obtains

OBTECT adj (of a pupa) encased in a hardened secretion

OBTEND vb put forward **obtends**

OBTEST vb beg (someone) earnestly **obtests**

OBTRUDE vb push oneself or one's ideas on others

OBTUND vb deaden or dull **obtunds**

OBTUSE adj **obtuser**

OBVERSE n, adj

OBVERT vb deduce the obverse of (a proposition) **obverts**

OBVIATE vb

OBVIOUS adj

OCA n any of various South American herbaceous plants

OCARINA n small oval wind instrument

OCAS ▶ oca

OCCAM n computer programming language **occams**

OCCAMY n type of alloy

OCCIES ▶ occy

OCCIPUT n back of the head

OCCLUDE vb obstruct

OCCULT adj, vb **occults**

OCCUPY vb

OCCUR vb **occurs**

OCCY n as in **all over the occy** dialect expression meaning in every direction

OCEAN n

OCEANIC adj of or relating to the ocean

OCEANID n ocean nymph in Greek mythology

OCEANS ▶ ocean

OCELLAR ▶ ocellus

OCELLI ▶ ocellus

OCELLUS n simple eye of insects and some other invertebrates

OCELOID adj of or like an ocelot

OCELOT n ocelots

OCH interj expression of surprise, annoyance, or disagreement

OCHE n (in darts) mark behind which a player must stand

OCHER = ochre

OCHERED ▶ ocher

OCHERS ▶ ocher

OCHERY ▶ ocher

OCHES ▶ oche

OCHONE interj expression of sorrow or regret

OCHRE n, adj, vb

OCHREA n cup-shaped structure that sheathes the stems of certain plants **ochreae**

OCHRED, ochres, ochrey, ochring, ochroid, ochrous, ochry ▶ ochre

OCICAT n breed of cat with a spotted coat **ocicats**

OCKER n uncultivated or boorish Australian **ockers**

OCREA = ochrea

OCREAE ▶ ocrea

OCREATE adj

possessing an ocrea

OCTA = okta

OCTAD n group or series of eight **octadic, octads**

OCTAGON n

OCTAL n number system with a base 8 **octals**

OCTAN n illness that occurs weekly

OCTANE n octanes

OCTANOL n alcohol containing eight carbon atoms

OCTANS ▶ octan

OCTANT n any of the eight parts into which the three planes containing the Cartesian coordinate axes divide space **octants**

OCTAPLA n book with eight texts

OCTAS ▶ octa

OCTAVAL ▶ octave

OCTAVE n, adj octaves

OCTAVO n book size in which the sheets are folded into eight leaves **octavos**

OCTET n octets, octett, octette

OCTETTS ▶ octett

OCTOFID adj divided into eight

OCTOPI ▶ octopus

OCTOPOD n type of mollusc ▶ adj of these molluscs

OCTOPUS n

OCTROI n duty on various goods brought

into certain European towns **octrois**

OCTUOR n octet **octuors**

OCTUPLE n quantity or number eight times as great as another ▷ adj eight times as much or as many ▷ vb multiply by eight

OCTUPLY adv by eight times

OCTYL n group of atoms **octyls**

OCULAR adj relating to the eyes or sight ▷ n lens in an optical instrument **oculars**

OCULATE adj possessing eyes

OCULI ▶ oculus

OCULIST n

OCULUS n round window

OD n hypothetical force

ODA n room in a harem **odah**

ODAHS ▶ odah

ODAL = udal

ODALISK = odalisque

ODALLER ▶ odal

ODALS ▶ odal

ODAS ▶ oda

ODD adj

ODDBALL n eccentric person ▷ adj strange or peculiar

ODDER ▶ odd

ODDEST ▶ odd

ODDISH ▶ odd

ODDITY n

ODDLY ▶ odd

ODDMENT n odd piece or thing

ODDNESS ▶ odd

ODDS pl n probability of something happening

ODDSMAN n umpire **oddsmen**

ODE n

ODEA ▶ odeum

ODEON = odeum

ODEONS ▶ odeon

ODES ▶ ode

ODEUM n ancient building for musical performances **odeums**

ODIC ▶ od

ODIOUS adj

ODISM ▶ od

ODISMS ▶ od

ODIST ▶ od

ODISTS ▶ od

ODIUM n widespread dislike **odiums**

ODONATE n dragonfly or related insect

ODONTIC adj of teeth

ODOR = odour

ODORANT n something with a strong smell

ODORATE adj having a strong smell

ODORED ▶ odoured

ODORFUL = odourful

ODORISE = odorize

ODORIZE vb give an odour to

ODOROUS adj having or emitting a characteristic smell

ODORS ▶ odor

ODOUR n

ODOURED adj having odour

ODOURS ▶ odour

ODS ▶ od

ODSO n cry of suprise

ODYL = od

ODYLE = od

ODYLES ▶ odyle

ODYLISM ▶ odyl

ODYLS ▶ odyl

ODYSSEY n

ODZOOKS interj cry of surprise

OE n grandchild

OECIST n colony founder **oecists**

OEDEMA n oedemas

OEDIPAL adj relating to a complex whereby a male child wants to replace his father

OENOMEL n drink made of wine and honey

OERSTED n cgs unit of magnetic field strength

OES ▶ oe

OESTRAL ▶ oestrus

OESTRIN obsolete term for ▷ oestrogen

OESTRUM = oestrus

OESTRUS n regularly occurring period of fertility in female mammals

OEUVRE n work of art, literature, music, etc **oeuvres**

OF prep

OFF prep, adv, adj, n, vb

OFFAL n offals

OFFBEAT adj unusual or eccentric ▷ n any of the normally unaccented beats in a bar

OFFCAST n cast-off

OFFCUT n piece remaining after the required parts have been cut out **offcuts**

OFFED ▶ off

OFFENCE n

OFFEND vb offends

OFFENSE = offence

OFFER vb, n offered

OFFEREE n person to whom an offer is made

OFFERER ▶ offer

OFFEROR ▶ offer

OFFERS ▶ offer

OFFHAND adj, adv

OFFICE n

OFFICER n, vb

OFFICES ▶ office

OFFIE n off-licence offies

OFFING n offings

OFFISH adj aloof or distant in manner

OFFKEY adj out of tune

OFFLINE adj

OFFLOAD vb pass responsibility to someone else

OFFPEAK adj relating to times outside periods of intensive use

OFFPUT n act of putting off offputs

OFFRAMP n road allowing traffic to leave a motorway

OFFS ▶ off

OFFSCUM n scum

OFFSET vb, n offsets

OFFSIDE adv, n

OFFTAKE n act of taking off

OFFY ▶ offie

OFLAG n prisoner-of-war camp for officers in World War II oflags

OFT adv often

OFTEN adv oftener

OFTER ▶ oft

OFTEST ▶ oft

OGAM = ogham

OGAMIC ▶ ogam

OGAMS ▶ ogam

OGDOAD n group of eight ogdoads

OGEE n moulding having a cross section in the form of a letter S

OGEED adj (of an arch or moulding) having an ogee

OGEES ▶ ogee

OGGIN n sea oggins

OGHAM n ancient writing system used by the Celts oghamic, oghams

OGIVAL ▶ ogive

OGIVE n diagonal rib or groin of a Gothic vault ogives

OGLE vb, n ogled, ogler, oglers, ogles, ogling, oglings

OGMIC ▶ ogam

OGRE n ogreish, ogreism, ogres, ogress, ogrish, ogrism, ogrisms

OH interj exclamation of surprise, pain, etc ▷ vb say oh ohed

OHIA n Hawaiian plant ohias

OHING ▶ oh

OHM n

OHMAGE n electrical resistance in ohms ohmages

OHMIC adj of or relating to a circuit element

OHMS ▶ ohm

OHO n exclamation expressing surprise, exultation, or derision

OHONE = ochone

OHS ▶ oh

OI interj shout to attract attention ▷ n grey-faced petrel

OIDIA ▶ oidium

OIDIOID ▶ oidium

OIDIUM n type of fungal spore

OIKIST = oecist

OIKISTS ▶ oikist

OIL n, vb

OILBIRD n type of nocturnal gregarious cave-dwelling bird

OILCAMP n camp for oilworkers

OILCAN n container with a long nozzle for applying oil to machinery oilcans

OILCUP n cup-shaped oil reservoir in a machine providing continuous lubrication for a bearing oilcups

OILED ▶ oil

OILER n person, device, etc, that lubricates or supplies oil oilers

OILERY n oil business

OILGAS n gaseous mixture of hydrocarbons used as a fuel

OILHOLE n hole for oil

OILIER ▶ oily

OILIEST ▶ oily

OILILY ▶ oily

OILING ▶ oil

OILLET = eyelet

OILLETS ▶ oillet

OILMAN n person who owns or operates oil wells oilmen

OILNUT n nut from which oil is extracted oilnuts

OILS ▶ oil

OILSEED n seed from which oil is extracted

OILSKIN n

OILWAY n channel for oil oilways

OILY adj

OINK n grunt of a pig or an imitation of this ▷ interj imitation or representation of the grunt of a pig ▷ vb make noise of pig oinked, oinking, oinks

OINOMEL = oenomel

OINT vb anoint ointed, ointing, oints

OIS ▶ oi

OJIME n Japanese bead used to secure cords ojimes

OKA n unit of weight used in Turkey

OKAPI n African animal related to the giraffe but with a shorter neck okapis

OKAS ▶ oka

OKAY adj, vb, n, interj okayed, okaying, okays

OKE = oka

OKEH = okay

OKEHS ▶ okeh

OKES ▶ oke

OKIMONO n Japanese ornamental item

OKRA n okras

OKTA n unit used in meteorology to measure cloud cover oktas

OLD adj having lived or existed for a long time ▷ n earlier or past time

OLDE adj old-world or quaint, used facetiously

OLDEN adj, vb oldened, oldens

OLDER adj having lived or existed longer

OLDEST ▶ old

OLDIE n old but popular song or film oldies

OLDISH ▶ old

OLDNESS ▶ old

OLDS ▶ old

OLDSTER n older person

OLDWIFE n any of various fishes, esp the menhaden or the alewife

OLDY = oldie

OLE interj exclamation of approval or encouragement customary at bullfights ▷ n cry of olé

OLEA ▶ oleum

OLEARIA n daisy bush

OLEATE n any salt or ester of oleic acid oleates

OLEFIN = olefine

OLEFINE another name for ▶ alkene

OLEFINS ▶ olefin

OLEIC adj as in oleic acid colourless oily liquid used in making soap

OLEIN another name for ▶ triolein

OLEINE = olein

OLEINES ▶ oleine

OLEINS ▶ olein

OLENT adj having smell

OLEO n as in oleo oil oil extracted from beef fat oleos

OLES ▶ ole

OLESTRA n trademark term for an artificial fat

OLEUM n type of sulphuric acid oleums

OLFACT vb smell something olfacts

OLICOOK n doughnut

OLID adj foul-smelling

OLIGIST n type of iron ore

OLINGO n South American mammal olingos

OLIO n dish of many different ingredients olios

OLITORY n kitchen garden

OLIVARY adj shaped like an olive

OLIVE n, adj

OLIVER n as in Bath oliver type of unsweetened biscuit olivers

OLIVES ▶ olive

OLIVET n button shaped like olive olivets

OLIVINE n olive-green mineral of the olivine group

OLLA n cooking pot

OLLAMH n old Irish term for a wise man **ollamhs**

OLLAS ▶ olla

OLLAV = ollamh

OLLAVS ▶ ollav

OLLER n waste ground **ollers**

OLLIE n type of skateboarding jump **ollies**

OLM n pale blind eel-like salamander **olms**

OLOGIES ▶ ology

OLOGIST n scientist

OLOGOAN vb complain loudly without reason

OLOGY n science or other branch of knowledge

OLOROSO n golden-coloured sweet sherry

OLPAE ▶ olpe

OLPE n ancient Greek jug **olpes**

OLYCOOK = olykoek

OLYKOEK n American type of doughnut

OM n sacred syllable in Hinduism

OMASA ▶ omasum

OMASAL ▶ omasum

OMASUM n compartment in the stomach of a ruminant animal

OMBER = ombre

OMBERS ▶ omber

OMBRE n 18th-century card game **ombres**

OMBU n South American tree **ombus**

OMEGA n last letter in the Greek alphabet **omegas**

OMELET = omelette

OMELETS ▶ omelet

OMEN n, vb omened, omening, omens

OMENTA ▶ omentum

OMENTAL ▶ omentum

OMENTUM n double fold of the peritoneum

OMER n ancient Hebrew unit of dry measure **omers**

OMERTA n conspiracy of silence **omertas**

OMICRON n 15th letter in the Greek alphabet

OMIGOD interj exclamation of surprise, pleasure, dismay, etc

OMIKRON = omicron

OMINOUS adj

OMIT vb omits, omitted, omitter

OMLAH n staff team in India **omlahs**

OMMATEA > ommateum

OMNEITY n state of being all

OMNIANA n miscellaneous collection

OMNIBUS n, adj

OMNIETY = omneity

OMNIFIC adj creating all things

OMNIFY vb make something universal

OMNIUM n total value **omniums**

OMOV n voting system in which each voter has one vote to cast **omovs**

OMPHALI > omphalos

OMRAH n Muslim noble **omrahs**

OMS ▶ om

ON prep, adv, adj, n, vb

ONAGER n wild ass of Persia **onagers, onagri**

ONANISM n withdrawal in sexual intercourse before ejaculation **onanist**

ONBEAT n first and third beats in a bar of four-four time **onbeats**

ONBOARD adj on a ship or other craft

ONCE adv, n

ONCER n (formerly) a one-pound note **oncers**

ONCES ▶ once

ONCET dialect form of ▶ once

ONCOGEN n substance causing tumours to form

ONCOME n act of coming on **oncomes**

ONCOST = overheads

ONCOSTS ▶ oncost

ONCUS = onkus

ONDATRA = musquash

ONDINE = undine

ONDINES ▶ undine

ONDING Scots word for ▶ onset

ONDINGS ▶ onding
ONE adj, n, pron
ONEFOLD adj simple
ONEIRIC adj of or relating to dreams
ONELY = only
ONENESS n
ONER n single continuous action
ONERIER ▶ onery
ONEROUS adj
ONERS ▶ oner
ONERY = ornery
ONES ▶ one
ONESELF pron
ONETIME adj at some time in the past
ONEYER old form of ▶ one
ONEYERS ▶ oneyer
ONEYRE ▶ oneyer
ONEYRES ▶ oneyre
ONFALL n attack or onset **onfalls**
ONFLOW n flowing on **onflows**
ONGOING adj
ONIE variant spelling of ▶ ony
ONION n, vb **onioned, onions, oniony**
ONIRIC = oneiric
ONIUM n as in **onium compound** type of chemical salt **oniums**
ONKUS adj bad
ONLAY n artificial veneer for a tooth **onlays**
ONLIEST = only
ONLINE adj
ONLINER n person who uses the internet regularly

ONLOAD vb load files on to a computer **onloads**
ONLY adj, adv
ONNED ▶ on
ONNING ▶ on
ONO n Hawaiian fish **onos**
ONRUSH n forceful forward rush or flow
ONS ▶ on
ONSET n **onsets**
ONSHORE adv towards the land
ONSIDE adv (of a player in various sports) in a legal position ▷ adj taking one's part or side ▷ n part of cricket field where a batsman stands **onsides**
ONST = once
ONSTAGE adj visible by audience
ONSTEAD Scots word for ▷ **farmstead**
ONTIC adj having real existence
ONTO prep
ONUS n **onuses**
ONWARD = onwards
ONWARDS adv
ONY Scots word for ▶ **any**
ONYCHA n part of mollusc **onychas**
ONYCHIA n inflammation of the nails or claws of animals
ONYMOUS adj (of a book) bearing its author's name
ONYX n **onyxes**

OO Scots word for ▶ **wool**
OOBIT n hairy caterpillar **oobits**
OOCYST n type of zygote **oocysts**
OOCYTE n immature female germ cell that gives rise to an ovum **oocytes**
OODLES pl n great quantities **oodlins**
OOF n money **oofier, oofiest, oofs**
OOFTISH n money
OOFY ▶ oof
OOGAMY n type of sexual reproduction
OOGENY n oogenesis
OOGONIA ▶ oogonium
OOH interj exclamation of surprise, pleasure, pain, etc ▷ vb say ooh **oohed, oohing, oohs**
OOIDAL adj shaped like egg
OOLAKAN = eulachon
OOLITE n limestone made up of tiny grains of calcium carbonate **oolites**
OOLITH n tiny spherical grain of sedimentary rock **ooliths**
OOLITIC ▶ oolite
OOLOGIC ▶ oology
OOLOGY n study of birds' eggs
OOLONG n kind of dark tea **oolongs**
OOM n title of respect used to refer to an elderly man
OOMIAC = umiak

OOMIACK = umiak

OOMIACS ▷ oomiac

OOMIAK = umiak

OOMIAKS ▷ umiak

OOMPAH *n* representation of the sound made by a deep brass instrument ▷ *vb* make the noise of a brass instrument **oompahs**

OOMPH *n* enthusiasm, vigour, or energy **oomphs**

OOMS ▷ oom

OON *Scots word for* ▷ oven

OONS ▷ oon

OONT *n* camel **oonts**

OOP *vb Scots word meaning to bind* **ooped**

OOPHYTE *n* gametophyte in mosses, liverworts, and ferns

OOPING ▷ oop

OOPS *interj* exclamation of surprise or apology

OOR *Scots form of* ▷ our

OORALI *n* member of Indian people **ooralis**

OORIAL *n* Himalayan sheep **oorials**

OORIE *adj Scots word meaning shabby* **oorier, ooriest**

> This Scots word is one of the classic 5-letter vowel dumps. It has almost equally useful variants **ourie** and **owrie**.

OOS ▷ oo

OOSE *n* dust **ooses, oosier, oosiest**

OOSPERM *n* fertilized ovum

OOSPORE *n* thick-walled sexual spore

OOSY ▷ oose

OOT *Scots word for* ▷ out

OOTHECA *n* capsule containing eggs

OOTID *n* immature female gamete that develops into an ovum **ootids**

OOTS ▷ oot

OOZE *vb, n* **oozed, oozes**

OOZIER ▷ oozy

OOZIEST ▷ oozy

OOZILY ▷ oozy

OOZING ▷ ooze

OOZY *adj* moist or dripping

OP *n* operation

OPACIFY *vb* become or make opaque

OPACITY *n* state or quality of being opaque

OPACOUS = opaque

OPAH *n* large soft-finned deep-sea fish **opahs**

OPAL *n*

OPALED *adj* made like opal

OPALINE *adj* opalescent ▷ *n* opaque or semiopaque whitish glass

OPALS ▷ opal

OPAQUE *adj, n, vb* **opaqued, opaquer, opaques**

OPCODE *n* computer code containing operating instructions **opcodes**

OPE *archaic or poetic word for* ▷ open

OPED ▷ ope

OPEN *adj, vb, n* **opened**

OPENER *n* tool for opening cans and bottles **openers**

OPENEST ▷ open

OPENING *n, adj*

OPENLY ▷ open

OPENS ▷ open

OPEPE *n* African tree **opepes**

OPERA *n*

OPERAND *n* quantity, variable, or function upon which an operation is performed

OPERANT *adj* producing effects ▷ *n* person or thing that operates

OPERAS ▷ opera

OPERATE *vb*

OPERON *n* group of adjacent genes in bacteria **operons**

OPEROSE *adj* laborious

OPES ▷ ope

OPHITE *n* any of several greenish mottled rocks **ophites**

OPHITIC *adj* having small elongated feldspar crystals enclosed

OPHIURA *n* sea creature like a starfish

OPIATE *n, adj, vb* **opiated, opiates**

OPINE vb express an opinion **opined, opines**

OPING ▶ **ope**

OPINING ▶ **opine**

OPINION n

OPIOID n substance that resembles morphine **opioids**

OPIUM n **opiums**

OPORICE n former medicine made from fruit

OPOSSUM n

OPPIDAN adj of a town ▷ n person living in a town

OPPO n counterpart in another organization **oppos**

OPPOSE vb **opposed, opposer, opposes**

OPPRESS vb control by cruelty or force

OPPUGN vb call into question **oppugns**

OPS ▶ **op**

OPSIN n type of protein **opsins**

OPSONIC ▶ **opsonin**

OPSONIN n constituent of blood serum

OPT vb

OPTANT n person who opts **optants**

OPTED ▶ **opt**

OPTER ▶ **opt**

OPTERS ▶ **opt**

OPTIC adj

OPTICAL adj

OPTICS n

OPTIMA ▶ **optimum**

OPTIMAL adj best or most favourable

OPTIME n mathematics student at Cambridge University **optimes**

OPTIMUM n, adj

OPTING ▶ **opt**

OPTION n, vb **options**

OPTS ▶ **opt**

OPULENT adj

OPULUS n flowering shrub

OPUNTIA n type of cactus

OPUS n

OPUSCLE = opuscule

OPUSES ▶ **opus**

OQUASSA n American trout

OR prep, adj, n

ORA ▶ **os**

ORACH = orache

ORACHE n type of plant **oraches**

ORACIES ▶ **oracy**

ORACLE n, vb **oracled, oracles**

ORACY n capacity to use speech

ORAD adv towards the mouth

ORAL adj, n

ORALISM n oral method of communicating with deaf people **oralist**

ORALITY n state of being oral

ORALLY ▶ **oral**

ORALS ▶ **oral**

ORANG n orangutan

ORANGE n, adj **oranger, oranges, orangey**

ORANGS ▶ **orang**

ORANGY ▶ **orange**

ORANT n artistic representation of worshipper **orants**

ORARIA ▶ **orarium**

ORARIAN n person who lives on the coast

ORARION n garment worn by Greek clergyman

ORARIUM n handkerchief

ORATE vb make or give an oration **orated, orates, orating**

ORATION n

ORATOR n **orators**

ORATORY n

ORATRIX n female orator

ORB n, vb **orbed**

ORBIER ▶ **orby**

ORBIEST ▶ **orby**

ORBING ▶ **orb**

ORBIT n, vb **orbita**

ORBITAL adj, n

ORBITAS ▶ **orbita**

ORBITED ▶ **orbit**

ORBITER n spacecraft or satellite designed to orbit a planet without landing on it

ORBITS ▶ **orbit**

ORBITY n bereavement

ORBLESS ▶ **orb**

ORBS ▶ **orb**

ORBY adj orb-shaped

ORC n any of various whales, such as the killer and grampus

ORCA n killer whale **orcas**

ORCEIN n brown crystalline material **orceins**

ORCHARD n orchat

ORCHATS ▶ **orchat**

ORCHEL = orchil
ORCHELS ▸ orchel
ORCHID n orchids
ORCHIL n any of various lichens **orchils**
ORCHIS n type of orchid
ORCIN = orcinol
ORCINE = orcinol
ORCINES ▸ orcine
ORCINOL n colourless crystalline water-soluble solid
ORCINS ▸ orcin
ORCS ▸ orc
ORD n pointed weapon
ORDAIN vb ordains
ORDEAL n ordeals
ORDER n, vb ordered, orderer
ORDERLY adj, n, adv
ORDERS ▸ order
ORDINAL adj denoting a certain position in a sequence of numbers ▸ n book containing the forms of services for the ordination of ministers
ORDINAR Scots word for ▸ ordinary
ORDINEE n person being ordained
ORDINES ▸ ordo
ORDO n religious order ordos
ORDS ▸ ord
ORDURE n ordures
ORE n
OREAD n mountain nymph **oreades, oreads**
ORECTIC adj of or relating to the desires
OREGANO n

OREIDE = oroide
OREIDES ▸ oreide
ORES ▸ ore
OREWEED n seaweed
OREXIN n hormone that promotes wakefulness and stimulates the appetite **orexins**
OREXIS n appetite
ORF n infectious disease of sheep
ORFE n small slender European fish **orfes**
ORFRAY = orphrey
ORFRAYS ▸ orfray
ORFS ▸ orf
ORGAN n
ORGANA ▸ organon
ORGANDY = organdie
ORGANIC adj, n
ORGANON n system of logical or scientific rules
ORGANS ▸ organ
ORGANUM = organon
ORGANZA n
ORGASM n, vb orgasms
ORGEAT n drink made with orange flower water **orgeats**
ORGIA = orgy
ORGIAC ▸ orgy
ORGIAS ▸ orgia
ORGIAST n participant in orgy
ORGIC ▸ orgy
ORGIES ▸ orgy
ORGONE n substance claimed to be needed for sexual activity and mental health **orgones**
ORGUE n number of

stakes lashed together **orgues**
ORGY n
ORIBI n small African antelope **oribis**
ORIEL n oriels
ORIENCY n state of being orient
ORIENT vb, n, adj orients
ORIFEX = orifice
ORIFICE n
ORIGAMI n
ORIGAN another name for ▸ marjoram
ORIGANE = origan
ORIGANS ▸ origan
ORIGIN n origins
ORIHOU n small New Zealand tree **orihous**
ORIOLE n tropical or American songbird **orioles**
ORISHA n any of the minor gods or spirits of traditional Yoruba religion **orishas**
ORISON another word for ▸ prayer
ORISONS ▸ orison
ORIXA n orisha
ORIXAS ▸ orixa
ORLE n border around a shield
ORLEANS n type of fabric
ORLES ▸ orle
ORLON n crease-resistant acrylic fibre or fabric **orlons**
ORLOP n (in a vessel with four or more decks) the lowest deck **orlops**

ORMER n edible marine mollusc **ormers**

ORMOLU n ormolus

ORNATE adj **ornater**

ORNERY adj stubborn or vile-tempered

ORNIS less common word for > avifauna

ORNISES ▸ ornis

OROGEN n part of earth subject to orogeny **orogens**

OROGENY n formation of mountain ranges

OROIDE n alloy containing copper, tin, and other metals **oroides**

OROLOGY = orography

OROPESA n float used in minesweeping

OROTUND adj (of the voice) resonant and booming

ORPHAN n, vb **orphans**

ORPHIC adj mystical or occult

ORPHISM n style of abstract art

ORPHREY n richly embroidered band or border

ORPIN = orpine

ORPINE n type of plant **orpines**

ORPINS ▸ orpin

ORRA adj odd or unmatched

ORRAMAN n man who does odd jobs **orramen**

ORRERY n mechanical model of the solar system

ORRICE = orris

ORRICES ▸ orrice

ORRIS n kind of iris **orrises**

ORS ▸ or

ORT n fragment

ORTHIAN adj having high pitch

ORTHO n type of photographic plate . **orthos**

ORTHROS n canonical hour in the Greek Church

ORTS pl n scraps or leavings

ORVAL n plant of sage family **orvals**

ORYX n **oryxes**

ORZO n pasta in small grain shapes **orzos**

OS n mouth or . mouthlike part or opening **osar**

OSCAR n cash **oscars**

OSCHEAL adj of scrotum

OSCINE n songbird ▸ adj of songbirds **oscines**

OSCULA ▸ osculum

OSCULAR adj of or relating to an osculum

OSCULE n small mouth or opening **oscules**

OSCULUM n mouthlike aperture

OSE = esker

OSES ▸ ose

OSETRA n type of caviar **osetras**

OSHAC n plant smelling of ammonia **oshacs**

OSIER n

OSIERED adj covered with osiers

OSIERS ▸ osier

OSIERY n work done with osiers

OSMATE n salt of osmic acid **osmates**

OSMATIC adj relying on sense of smell

OSMIATE = osmate

OSMIC adj of or containing osmium in a high valence state

OSMICS n science of smell

OSMIOUS = osmous

OSMIUM n heaviest known metallic element **osmiums**

OSMOL = osmole

OSMOLAL ▸ osmole

OSMOLAR adj containing one osmole per litre

OSMOLE n unit of osmotic pressure **osmoles**

OSMOLS ▸ osmol

OSMOSE vb undergo or cause to undergo osmosis **osmosed, osmoses**

OSMOSIS n osmotic

OSMOUS adj of or containing osmium in a low valence state

OSMUND = osmunda

OSMUNDA n type of fern

OSMUNDS ▸ osmund

OSPREY n **ospreys**

OSSA ▸ os

OSSEIN n protein that forms the organic matrix of bone **osseins**

OSSELET n growth on knee of horse

OSSEOUS adj consisting of or like bone

OSSETER n sturgeon

OSSETRA = osetra

OSSIA conj (in music) or

OSSICLE n small bone, esp one of those in the middle ear

OSSIFIC adj making something turn to bone

OSSIFY vb

OSSUARY n any container for the burial of human bones, such as an urn or vault

OSTEAL adj of or relating to bone or to the skeleton

OSTENT n appearance **ostents**

OSTEOID adj of or resembling bone ▷ n bony deposit

OSTEOMA n tumour composed of bone or bonelike tissue

OSTIA ▶ ostium

OSTIAL ▶ ostium

OSTIARY another word for ▶ porter

OSTIATE adj having ostium

OSTIOLE n pore in the reproductive bodies of certain algae and fungi

OSTIUM n pore in sponges through which water enters the body

OSTLER n stableman at an inn **ostlers**

OSTMARK n currency of the former East Germany

OSTOMY n surgically made opening

OSTOSES ▶ ostosis

OSTOSIS n formation of bone

OSTRACA > ostracon

OSTRAKA > ostrakon

OSTRICH n

OTAKU n Japanese computer geeks

OTALGIA technical name for ▶ earache

OTALGIC ▶ otalgia

OTALGY = otalgia

OTARIES ▶ otary

OTARINE ▶ otary

This means like an otary or eared seal, and is perhaps the most commonly played of all 7-letter bonus words, so well worth learning for that extra 50 points it can give you.

OTARY n seal with ears

OTHER adj, n others

OTIC adj of or relating to the ear

OTIOSE adj not useful

OTITIC ▶ otitis

OTITIS n inflammation of the ear

OTOCYST n embryonic structure in vertebrates that develops into the inner ear

OTOLITH n granule of calcium carbonate in the inner ear of vertebrates

OTOLOGY n branch of medicine concerned with the ear

OTTAR variant of ▶ attar

OTTARS ▶ ottar

OTTAVA n interval of an octave **ottavas**

OTTER n, vb ottered, otters

OTTO another name for ▶ attar

OTTOMAN n

OTTOS ▶ otto

OU interj expressing concession ▷ n man, bloke, or chap

OUABAIN n poisonous white crystalline glycoside

OUAKARI n South American monkey

OUBAAS n man in authority

OUBIT n hairy caterpillar **oubits**

OUCH interj, n, vb ouched, ouches, ouching

OUCHT Scots word for > anything

OUCHTS ▶ oucht

OUD n Arabic stringed musical instrument **ouds**

OUENS ▶ ou

OUGHLY variant of ▶ ugly

OUGHT vb, n oughted, oughts

OUGLIE variant of ▶ ugly

OUGLIED ▶ ouglie

OUGLIES ▶ ouglie

OUGUIYA n standard monetary unit of Mauritania

OUIJA n tradename for a board through which spirits supposedly answer questions **ouijas**

OUK Scots word for ▶ week

OUKS ▶ ouk

OULAKAN = eulachon

OULD Scots or Irish form of ▶ old

OULDER ▶ ould

OULDEST ▶ ould

OULK Scots form of ▶ week

OULKS ▶ oulk

OULONG = oolong

OULONGS ▶ oolong

OUMA n grandmother, often as a title with a surname **oumas**

OUNCE n ounces

OUNDY adj wavy

OUP = oop

OUPA n grandfather, often as a title with a surname **oupas**

OUPED ▶ oup

OUPH = oaf

OUPHE = oaf

OUPHES ▶ ouphe

OUPHS ▶ ouph

OUPING ▶ oup

OUPS ▶ oup

OUR adj, determiner

OURALI n plant from which curare comes **ouralis**

OURANG = orang

OURANGS ▶ ourang

OURARI = ourali

OURARIS ▶ ourari

OUREBI = oribi

OUREBIS ▶ ourebi

OURIE = oorie

OURIER ▶ ourie

OURIEST ▶ ourie

OURN dialect form of ▶ our

OURS pron

OURSELF pron formal word for myself used by monarchs

OUS = ou

OUSEL = ouzel

OUSELS ▶ ousel

OUST vb ousted

OUSTER n act of forcing someone out of a position **ousters**

OUSTING ▶ oust

OUSTITI n device for opening locked door

OUSTS ▶ oust

OUT adj, vb

OUTACT vb surpass in acting **outacts**

OUTADD vb beat or surpass at adding **outadds**

OUTAGE n period of power failure **outages**

OUTASK vb declare wedding banns **outasks**

OUTATE ▶ outeat

OUTBACK n

OUTBAKE vb bake more or better than

OUTBAR vb keep out

OUTBARK vb bark more or louder than

OUTBARS ▶ outbar

OUTBAWL vb bawl more or louder than

OUTBEAM vb beam more or brighter than

OUTBEG vb beg more or better than **outbegs**

OUTBID vb outbids

OUTBOX vb surpass in boxing

OUTBRAG vb brag more or better than

OUTBRED > outbreed

OUTBULK vb exceed in bulk

OUTBURN vb burn longer or brighter than

OUTBUY vb buy more than **outbuys**

OUTBY adv outside **outbye**

OUTCALL n visit to customer's home by professional

OUTCAST n, adj

OUTCHID > outchide

OUTCITY n anywhere outside a city's confines

OUTCOME n

OUTCOOK vb cook more or better than

OUTCROP n, vb

OUTCROW vb exceed in crowing

OUTCRY n, vb

OUTDARE vb be more brave than

OUTDATE vb make or become old-fashioned or obsolete

OUTDID ▶ outdo

OUTDO vb outdoer, outdoes, outdone

OUTDOOR adj

OUTDRAG vb beat in drag race

OUTDRAW vb draw (a gun) faster than **outdrew**

OUTDROP = outcrop

OUTDUEL vb defeat in duel

OUTDURE vb last longer than

OUTEARN vb earn more than

OUTEAT vb eat more than **outeats**

OUTECHO vb echo more than

OUTED ▷ out

OUTEDGE n furthest limit

OUTER adj, n outers

OUTFACE vb subdue or disconcert by staring

OUTFALL n mouth of a river or drain

OUTFAST vb fast longer than

OUTFAWN vb exceed in fawning

OUTFEEL vb exceed in feeling **outfelt**

OUTFIND vb exceed in finding

OUTFIRE vb exceed in firing

OUTFISH vb catch more fish than

OUTFIT n, vb outfits

OUTFLEW ▷ outfly

OUTFLOW n anything that flows out, such as liquid or money ▷ vb flow faster than

OUTFLY vb fly better or faster than

OUTFOOL vb be more foolish than

OUTFOOT vb (of a boat) to go faster than (another boat)

OUTFOX vb defeat or foil by being more cunning

OUTGAIN vb gain more than

OUTGAS vb undergo the removal of adsorbed or absorbed gas from solids

OUTGATE n way out

OUTGAVE ▷ outgive

OUTGAZE vb gaze beyond

OUTGIVE vb exceed in giving

OUTGLOW vb glow more than

OUTGNAW vb exceed in gnawing

OUTGO vb exceed or outstrip ▷ n cost **outgoer, outgoes, outgone**

OUTGREW ▷ outgrow

OUTGRIN vb exceed in grinning

OUTGROW vb

OUTGUN vb surpass in fire power **outguns**

OUTGUSH vb gush out

OUTHAUL n line or cable for tightening the foot of a sail

OUTHEAR vb exceed in hearing

OUTHER = other

OUTHIRE vb hire out

OUTHIT vb hit something further than (someone else) **outhits**

OUTHOWL vb exceed in howling

OUTHUNT vb exceed in hunting

OUTHYRE = outhire

OUTING n outings

OUTJEST vb exceed in jesting

OUTJET n projecting part **outjets**

OUTJINX vb exceed in jinxing

> If someone else plays jinx, you can outjinx them by adding O, U and T! And if you can form the whole word using all of your letters, you'll get a 50-point bonus.

OUTJUMP vb jump higher or farther than

OUTJUT vb jut out ▷ n projecting part **outjuts**

OUTKEEP vb beat or surpass at keeping **outkept**

OUTKICK vb exceed in kicking

OUTKILL vb exceed in killing

OUTKISS vb exceed in kissing

OUTLAID ▷ outlay

OUTLAIN ▷ outlay

OUTLAND adj outlying or distant ▷ n outlying areas of a country or region

OUTLASH n sudden attack

OUTLAST vb

OUTLAW n, vb outlaws

OUTLAY n, vb outlays

OUTLEAD vb be better leader than

OUTLEAP vb leap higher or farther than

OUTLED ▸ outlead

OUTLER n farm animal kept out of doors **outlers**

OUTLET n **outlets**

OUTLIE vb lie outside a particular place **outlied**

OUTLIER n outcrop of rocks that is entirely surrounded by older rocks

OUTLIES ▸ outlie

OUTLINE n, vb

OUTLIVE vb

OUTLOOK n, vb

OUTLOVE vb surpass in loving

OUTMAN vb surpass in manpower **outmans**

OUTMODE vb make unfashionable

OUTMOST another word for ▸ **outermost**

OUTMOVE vb move faster or better than

OUTNAME vb be more notorious than

OUTNESS n state or quality of being external

OUTPACE vb

OUTPART n remote region

OUTPASS vb exceed in passing

OUTPEEP vb peep out

OUTPEER vb surpass

OUTPITY vb exceed in pitying

OUTPLAN vb exceed in planning

OUTPLAY vb

OUTPLOD vb exceed in plodding

OUTPLOT vb exceed in plotting

OUTPOLL vb win more votes than

OUTPORT n isolated fishing village, esp in Newfoundland

OUTPOST n

OUTPOUR n act of flowing or pouring out ▸ vb pour or cause to pour out freely or rapidly

OUTPRAY vb exceed in praying

OUTPULL vb exceed in pulling

OUTPUSH vb exceed in pushing

OUTPUT n, vb **outputs**

OUTRACE vb surpass in racing

OUTRAGE n, vb

OUTRAN ▸ outrun

OUTRANG ▸ outring

OUTRANK vb be of higher rank than (someone)

OUTRATE vb offer better rate than

OUTRAVE vb outdo in raving

OUTRE adj shockingly eccentric

OUTREAD vb outdo in reading

OUTRED vb be redder than **outreds**

OUTRIDE vb outdo by riding faster, farther, or better than ▸ n extra unstressed syllable within a metrical foot

OUTRIG vb supply with outfit **outrigs**

OUTRING vb exceed in ringing

OUTRO n instrumental passage that concludes a piece of music

OUTROAR vb roar louder than

OUTROCK vb outdo in rocking

OUTRODE ▸ outride

OUTROLL vb exceed in rolling

OUTROOP n auction

OUTROOT vb root out

OUTROPE = outroop

OUTROS ▸ outro

OUTROW vb outdo in rowing **outrows**

OUTRUN vb run faster than

OUTRUNG ▸ outring

OUTRUNS ▸ outrun

OUTRUSH n flowing or rushing out ▸ vb rush out

OUTS ▸ out

OUTSAID ▸ outsay

OUTSAIL vb sail better than

OUTSANG ▸ outsing

OUTSAT ▸ outsit

OUTSAW ▸ outsee

OUTSAY vb say something out loud **outsays**

OUTSEE vb exceed in seeing **outseen, outsees**

OUTSELL vb be sold in greater quantities than

OUTSERT n another word for ▸ wraparound

OUTSET n outsets

OUTSHOT n projecting part

OUTSIDE adv, adj, n

OUTSIN vb sin more than

OUTSING vb sing better or louder than

OUTSINS ▸ outsin

OUTSIT vb sit longer than outsits

OUTSIZE adj, n

OUTSOAR vb fly higher than

OUTSOLD ▸ outsell

OUTSOLE n outermost sole of a shoe

OUTSPAN vb

OUTSPED ▸ outspeed

OUTSTAY vb

OUTSTEP vb step farther than

OUTSULK vb outdo in sulking

OUTSUM vb add up to more than outsums

OUTSUNG ▸ outsing

OUTSWAM ▸ outswim

OUTSWIM vb outdo in swimming outswum

OUTTAKE n unreleased take from a recording session, film, or TV programme ▸ vb take out

OUTTALK vb talk more, longer, or louder than (someone)

OUTTASK vb assign task to staff outside

organization

OUTTELL vb make known outtold

OUTTOOK ▸ outtake

OUTTOP vb rise higher than outtops

OUTTROT vb exceed at trotting

OUTTURN = output

OUTVIE vb outdo in competition outvied, outvies

OUTVOTE vb defeat by getting more votes than

OUTWAIT vb wait longer than

OUTWALK vb walk farther or longer than

OUTWAR vb surpass or exceed in warfare

OUTWARD = outwards

OUTWARS ▸ outwar

OUTWASH n gravel carried and deposited by water from melting glaciers

OUTWEAR vb use up or destroy by wearing

OUTWEED vb root out

OUTWEEP vb outdo in weeping

OUTWELL vb pour out

OUTWENT ▸ outgo

OUTWEPT ▸ outweep

OUTWICK vb move one curling stone by striking with another

OUTWILE vb surpass in cunning

OUTWILL vb demonstrate stronger will than

OUTWIN vb get out of

OUTWIND vb unwind

OUTWING vb surpass in flying

OUTWINS ▸ outwin

OUTWISH vb surpass in wishing

OUTWIT vb

OUTWITH prep outside

OUTWITS ▸ outwit

OUTWON ▸ outwin

OUTWORE ▸ outwear

OUTWORK n defences which lie outside main defensive works ▸ vb work better, harder, etc, than

OUTWORN adj

OUTWRIT ▸ outwrite

OUTYELL vb outdo in yelling

OUTYELP vb outdo in yelping

OUVERT adj open ouverte

OUVRAGE n work

OUVRIER n worker

OUZEL n type of bird ouzels

OUZO n strong aniseed-flavoured spirit from Greece ouzos

OVA ▸ ovum

OVAL adj, n ovality, ovally, ovals

OVARIAL ▸ ovary

OVARIAN ▸ ovary

OVARIES ▸ ovary

OVARY n

OVATE adj shaped like an egg ▸ vb give ovation ovated, ovately, ovates, ovating

OVATION n

OVATOR ▸ ovate

OVATORS ▸ ovate

OVEL *n* mourner, esp during the first seven days after a death **ovels**

OVEN *n*, *vb* ovened, ovening, ovens

OVER *adv*, *adj*, *n*, *vb*

OVERACT *vb*

OVERAGE *adj*, *n*

OVERALL *adv*, *n*, *adj*

OVERAPT *adj* tending excessively

OVERARM *adv*, *adj*, *vb*

OVERATE ▸ overeat

OVERAWE *vb*

OVERBED *adj* fitting over bed

OVERBET *vb* bet too much

OVERBID *vb* bid for more tricks than one can expect to win ▷ *n* bid higher than someone else's bid

OVERBIG *adj* too big

OVERBUY *vb* buy too much or too many

OVERBY *adv* Scots expression meaning over the road or across the way

OVERCOY *adj* too modest

OVERCUT *vb* cut too much

OVERDID ▸ overdo

OVERDO *vb*

OVERDOG *n* person or side in an advantageous position

OVERDRY *vb* dry too much

OVERDUB *vb* add (new sounds) to a tape so that the old and the new sounds can be heard ▷ *n* sound or series of sounds added by this method

OVERDUE *adj*

OVERDYE *vb* dye (a fabric, yarn, etc) excessively

OVEREAT *vb* eat more than is necessary or healthy

OVERED ▸ over

OVEREGG *vb* exaggerate absurdly

OVEREYE *vb* survey

OVERFAR *adv* too far

OVERFAT *adj* too fat

OVERFED ▸ overfeed

OVERFIT *adj* too fit

OVERFLY *vb* fly over (a territory) or past (a point)

OVERGET *vb* overtake

OVERGO *vb* go beyond

OVERGOT ▸ overget

OVERHIT *vb* hit too strongly

OVERHOT *adj* too hot

OVERING ▸ over

OVERJOY *vb* give great delight to

OVERLAP *vb*, *n*

OVERLAX *adj* too lax

OVERLAY *vb*, *n*

OVERLET *vb* let to too many

OVERLIE *vb* lie on or cover (something or someone)

OVERLIT ▸ overlight

OVERLY *adv*

OVERMAN *vb* provide with too many staff ▷ *n* man who oversees others **overmen**

OVERMIX *vb* mix too much

OVERNET *vb* cover with net

OVERNEW *adj* too new

OVERPAY *vb* pay (someone) at too high a rate

OVERPLY *vb* ply too much

OVERRAN ▸ overrun

OVERRED *vb* paint over in red

OVERREN = overrun

OVERRUN *vb*, *n*

OVERS ▸ over

OVERSAD *adj* too sad

OVERSAW ▸ oversee

OVERSEA = overseas

OVERSEE *vb*

OVERSET *vb* disturb or upset

OVERSEW *vb* sew (two edges) with stitches that pass over them both

OVERSOW *vb* sow again after first sowing

OVERSUP *vb* sup too much

OVERT *adj*

OVERTAX *vb*

OVERTIP *vb* give too much money as a tip

OVERTLY ▸ overt

OVERTOP *vb* exceed in height

OVERUSE *vb* use excessively ▷ *n* excessive use

OVERWET vb make too wet

OVIBOS n type of ox

OVICIDE n killing of sheep

OVIDUCT n

OVIFORM adj shaped like an egg

OVINE adj of or like a sheep ▷ n member of sheep family **ovines**

OVIPARA n all oviparous animals

OVISAC n capsule or sac in which egg cells are produced **ovisacs**

OVIST n person believing ovum contains all subsequent generations **ovists**

OVOID adj egg-shaped ▷ n something that is ovoid

OVOIDAL adj ovoid ▷ n something that is ovoid

OVOIDS ▶ ovoid

OVOLI ▶ ovolo

OVOLO n type of convex moulding **ovolos**

> Two Os on your rack can normally be dealt with; three is a bit much, but this word for a moulding can handle them. Note that the plural can be **ovolos** or **ovoli**.

OVONIC adj using particular electronic storage batteries

OVONICS n science of ovonic equipment

OVULAR ▶ ovule

OVULARY ▶ ovule

OVULATE vb

OVULE n plant part that contains the egg cell **ovules**

OVUM n

OW interj exclamation of pain

OWCHE = ouch

OWCHES ▶ owche

OWE vb owed

OWELTY n equality, esp in financial transactions

OWER Scots word for ▶ over

OWERBY adv over there

OWES ▶ owe

OWING ▶ owe

OWL n, vb owled

OWLER vb smuggler **owlers**

OWLERY n place where owls live

OWLET n young or nestling owl **owlets**

OWLIER ▶ owly

OWLIEST ▶ owly

OWLING ▶ owl

OWLISH adj like an owl

OWLLIKE ▶ owl

OWLS ▶ owl

OWLY = owlish

OWN adj used to emphasize possession ▷ pron thing(s) belonging to a particular person ▷ vb possess

OWNABLE adj able to be owned

OWNED ▶ own

OWNER n owners

OWNING ▶ own

OWNS ▶ own

OWRE = ower

OWRELAY Scots form of ▶ overlay

OWRES ▶ owre

OWRIE = oorie

OWRIER ▶ owrie

OWRIEST ▶ owrie

OWSE Scots form of ▶ ox

OWSEN Scots word for ▶ oxen

OWT dialect word for > anything

OWTS ▶ owt

OX n

OXALATE n salt or ester of oxalic acid ▷ vb treat with oxalate

OXALIC adj as in **oxalic acid** poisonous acid found in many plants

OXALIS n type of plant

OXAZINE n type of chemical compound

OXBLOOD n dark reddish-brown colour ▷ adj of this colour

OXBOW n piece of wood fitted around the neck of a harnessed ox **oxbows**

OXCART n cart pulled by ox **oxcarts**

OXEN ▶ ox

OXER n high fence **oxers**

OXES ▶ ox

OXEYE n daisy-like flower **oxeyes**

OXFORD n type of stout laced shoe with a low heel **oxfords**

OXGANG n old measure of farmland **oxgangs, oxgate**

OXGATES ▸ oxgate

OXHEAD *n* head of an ox **oxheads**

OXHEART *n* heart-shaped cherry

OXHIDE *n* leather made from the hide of an ox **oxhides**

OXID = oxide

OXIDANT *n*

OXIDASE *n* enzyme that brings about oxidation

OXIDATE *another word for ▸* oxidize

OXIDE *n* oxides, oxidic

OXIDISE = oxidize

OXIDIZE *vb*

OXIDS ▸ oxid

OXIES ▸ oxy

OXIM = oxime

OXIME *n* type of chemical compound **oximes**

OXIMS ▸ oxim

OXLAND = oxgang

OXLANDS ▸ oxland

OXLIKE ▸ ox

OXLIP *n* type of woodland plant **oxlips**

OXO *n as in* oxo acid acid that contains oxygen

OXONIUM *n as in* oxonium compound

type of salt derived from an organic ether

OXSLIP = oxlip

OXSLIPS ▸ oxslip

OXTAIL *n* oxtails

OXTER *n* armpit ▷ *vb* grip under arm **oxtered, oxters**

OXY ▸ ox

OXYACID *n* any acid that contains oxygen

OXYGEN *n* oxygens

OXYMEL *n* mixture of vinegar and honey **oxymels**

OXYMORA > oxymoron

OXYNTIC *adj* of or denoting stomach cells that secrete acid

OXYPHIL *n* type of cell found in glands

OXYSALT *n* any salt of an oxyacid

OXYSOME *n* group of molecules

OXYTONE *adj* having an accent on the final syllable ▷ *n* oxytone word

OY *n* grandchild **oye**

OYER *n* (in the 13th century) an assize **oyers**

OYES – oyez

OYESES ▸ oyes

OYESSES ▸ oyes

OYEZ *interj* shouted three times by a public crier calling for attention ▷ *n* such a cry **oyezes**

OYS ▸ oy

OYSTER *n, vb* oysters

OZAENA *n* inflammation of nasal mucous membrane **ozaenas**

OZALID *n* method of duplicating writing or illustrations **ozalids**

OZEKI *n* sumo wrestling champion **ozekis**

OZONATE *vb* add ozone to

OZONE *n* ozones, ozonic

OZONIDE *n* type of unstable explosive compound

OZONISE = ozonize

OZONIZE *vb* convert (oxygen) into ozone

OZONOUS ▸ ozone

OZZIE *n* hospital **ozzies**

Pp

P forms a two-letter word in front of every vowel except **U**, which makes it very useful for joining a new word to one already on the board. It also forms several three-letter words with **X**: **pax, pix, pox** (12 points each) and **pyx** (15). Other three-letter words with **P** well worth remembering are **zap, zep** and **zip** for 14 points each and **jap** for 12 points.

PA n

PAAL n stake driven into the ground **paals**

PAAN n leaf of the betel tree **paans**

PABLUM = pabulum

PABLUMS ▶ pablum

PABULAR ▶ pabulum

PABULUM n food

PAC n soft shoe

PACA n large burrowing rodent

PACABLE adj easily appeased

PACAS ▶ paca

PACE n, vb, prep **paced**

PACEMAN n pacemen

PACER n horse trained to move at a special gait, esp for racing **pacers**

PACES ▶ pace

PACEWAY n racecourse for trotting and pacing

PACEY adj fast-moving, quick, lively

PACHA = pasha

PACHAK n fragrant roots of Asian plant **pachaks**

PACHAS ▶ pacha

PACHISI n Indian game resembling backgammon

PACHUCO n young Mexican living in the US

PACIER ▶ pacy

PACIEST ▶ pacy

PACIFIC adj tending to bring peace

PACIFY vb

PACING ▶ pace

PACK vb, n

PACKAGE = packet

PACKED adj

PACKER n person or company who packs goods **packers**

PACKET n, vb **packets**

PACKING n material, such as paper or plastic, used to protect packed goods

PACKLY ▶ pack

PACKMAN n person carrying pack **packmen**

PACKS ▶ pack

PACKWAX n neck ligament

PACKWAY n path for pack animals

PACO n S American mammal **pacos**

PACS ▶ pac

PACT n

PACTA ▶ pactum

PACTION vb concur with

PACTS ▶ pact

PACTUM n pact

PACY = pacey

PAD n, vb

PADANG n (in Malaysia) playing field **padangs**

PADAUK n tropical African or Asian tree **padauks**

PADDED ▷ pad
PADDER n highwayman who robs on foot **padders**
PADDIES ▷ paddy
PADDING ▷ pad
PADDLE n, vb paddled, **paddler, paddles**
PADDOCK n, vb
PADDY n
PADELLA n type of candle
PADI = paddy
PADIS ▷ padi
PADKOS n snacks and provisions for a journey
PADLE another name for > lumpfish
PADLES ▷ padle
PADLOCK n, vb
PADMA n type of lotus **padmas**
PADNAG n ambling horse **padnags**
PADOUK = padauk
PADOUKS ▷ padouk
PADRE n padres, padri
PADRONE n owner or proprietor of an inn, esp in Italy **padroni**
PADS ▷ pad
PADSAW n small narrow saw used for cutting curves **padsaws**
PADSHAH = padishah
PAEAN n song of triumph or thanksgiving **paeans**
PAEDO n paedos
PAELLA n Spanish dish of rice, chicken, shellfish, and vegetables **paellas**

PAENULA n ancient Roman cloak
PAEON n metrical foot of four syllables **paeonic, paeons**
PAEONY = peony
PAESAN n fellow countryman
PAESANI ▷ paesano
PAESANO n Italian-American man
PAESANS ▷ paesan
PAGAN adj, n pagans
PAGE n, vb
PAGEANT n
PAGEBOY n type of hairstyle
PAGED ▷ page
PAGEFUL n amount (of text, etc) that a page will hold
PAGER n small electronic device, capable of receiving short messages **pagers**
PAGES ▷ page
PAGINAL adj page-for-page
PAGING ▷ page
PAGINGS ▷ page
PAGLE = paigle
PAGLES ▷ pagle
PAGOD n oriental idol
PAGODA n pagodas
PAGODS ▷ pagod
PAGRI n type of turban **pagris**
PAGURID = pagurian
PAH = pa
PAHLAVI n Iranian coin
PAHS ▷ pah
PAID ▷ pay
PAIDLE Scots variant of ▷ paddle

PAIDLES ▷ paidle
PAIGLE n cowslip **paigles**
PAIK vb thump or whack **paiked, paiking, paiks**
PAIL n pailful
PAILLON n thin leaf of metal
PAILS ▷ pail
PAIN n, vb
PAINCH Scots variant of ▷ paunch
PAINED adj having or suggesting pain or distress
PAINFUL adj
PAINIM n heathen or pagan **painims**
PAINING ▷ pain
PAINS pl n care or trouble
PAINT n, vb painted
PAINTER n
PAINTS ▷ paint
PAINTY ▷ paint
PAIOCK obsolete word for ▷ peacock
PAIOCKE obsolete word for ▷ peacock
PAIOCKS ▷ paiock
PAIR n, vb paire, paired, pairer
PAIRES ▷ paire
PAIREST ▷ pair
PAIRIAL variant of ▷ prial
PAIRING ▷ pair
PAIRS ▷ pair
PAIS n country
PAISA n monetary unit of Bangladesh, Bhutan, India, Nepal, and Pakistan
PAISAN n fellow countryman

PAISANA n female peasant

PAISANO n friend

PAISANS ▶ paisan

PAISAS ▶ paisa

PAISE ▶ paisa

PAISLEY n pattern of small curving shapes with intricate detailing

PAJAMA = pyjama

PAJAMAS ▶ pajama

PAJOCK obsolete word for ▶ peacock

PAJOCKE obsolete word for ▶ peacock

PAJOCKS ▶ pajock

PAKAHI n acid land that is unsuitable for cultivation **pakahis**

PAKAPOO n Chinese lottery

PAKEHA n pakehas

PAKFONG = packfong

PAKIHI n area of swampy infertile land **pakihis**

PAKKA variant of ▶ pukka

PAKOKO n small freshwater fish **pakokos**

PAKORA n fried battered pieces of vegetable, chicken, etc **pakoras**

PAKTONG = pakthong

PAL n, vb

PALABRA n word

PALACE n

PALACED adj having palaces

PALACES ▶ palace

PALADIN n knight who did battle for a monarch

PALAGI n palagis

PALAIS n dance hall

PALAMA n webbing on bird's feet **palamae**

PALAPA n open-sided tropical building **palapas**

PALAS n East Indian tree **palases**

PALATAL adj of or relating to the palate ▷ n bony plate that forms the palate

PALATE n, vb palated, palates

PALAY n type of rubber **palays**

PALAZZI ▶ palazzo

PALAZZO n Italian palace

PALE adj, vb, n

PALEA n bract in a grass spikelet **paleae, paleal**

PALEATE adj having scales

PALED, palely, paler, pales, palest ▶ pale

PALET n perpendicular band on escutcheon

PALETOT n loose outer garment

PALETS ▶ palet

PALETTE n

PALFREY n light saddle horse, esp ridden by women

PALIER ▶ paly

PALIEST ▶ paly

PALIKAR n Greek soldier

PALING n wooden or metal post used in fences **palings**

PALINKA n type of apricot brandy

PALISH adj rather pale

PALKEE n covered Oriental litter **palkees, palki**

PALKIS ▶ palki

PALL n, vb

PALLA n ancient Roman cloak **pallae**

PALLAH n S African antelope **pallahs**

PALLED ▶ pall

PALLET = palette

PALLETS = pallet

PALLIA ▶ pallium

PALLIAL adj relating to cerebral cortex

PALLID adj

PALLIED ▶ pally

PALLIER ▶ pally

PALLIES ▶ pally

PALLING ▶ pall

PALLIUM n garment worn by men in ancient Greece or Rome

PALLONE n Italian ball game

PALLOR n pallors

PALLS ▶ pall

PALLY adj on friendly terms ▷ vb as in **pally up** become friends with

PALM n, vb

PALMAR adj of or relating to the palm of the hand

PALMARY adj worthy of praise

PALMATE adj

PALMED ▶ palm

PALMER n medieval pilgrim **palmers**

PALMFUL n amount that can be held in the palm of a hand

PALMIE n palmtop computer

PALMIER ▸ palmy

PALMIES ▸ palmie

PALMIET n South African rush

PALMING ▸ palm

PALMIST > palmistry

PALMS ▸ palm

PALMTOP adj small enough to be held in the hand ▸ n computer small enough to be held in the hand

PALMY adj successful, prosperous and happy

PALMYRA n tall tropical Asian palm

PALOLO n polychaete worm of the S Pacific Ocean **palolos**

PALOOKA n stupid or clumsy boxer or other person

PALP n sensory appendage in crustaceans and insects ▸ vb feel **palpal**

PALPATE vb examine (an area of the body) by touching ▸ adj of, relating to, or possessing a palp or palps

PALPED ▸ palp

PALPI ▸ palpus

PALPING ▸ palp

PALPS ▸ palp

PALPUS = palp

PALS ▸ pal

PALSHIP n state of being pals

PALSIED ▸ palsy

PALSIER ▸ palsy

PALSIES ▸ palsy

PALSY n, vb, adj

PALTER vb act or talk insincerely **palters**

PALTRY adj

PALUDAL adj of, relating to, or produced by marshes

PALUDIC adj of malaria

PALY adj vertically striped

PAM n knave of clubs

PAMPA n grassland area

PAMPAS pl n pampean

PAMPER vb

PAMPERO n dry cold wind in South America

PAMPERS ▸ pamper

PAMPOEN n pumpkin

PAMS ▸ pam

PAN n, vb

PANACEA n

PANACHE n

PANADA n mixture used as a thickening in cookery **panadas**

PANAMA n hat made of plaited leaves **panamas**

PANARY n storehouse for bread

PANAX n genus of perennial herbs **panaxes**

PANCAKE n, vb

PANCE n pansy **pances**

PANCHAX n brightly coloured tropical Asian cyprinodont fish

PAND n valance

PANDA n

PANDANI n tropical tree

PANDAR vb act as a pimp **pandars**

PANDAS ▸ panda

PANDECT n treatise covering all aspects of a particular subject

PANDER vb, n panders

PANDIED ▸ pandy

PANDIES ▸ pandy

PANDIT = pundit

PANDITS ▸ pundit

PANDOOR = pandour

PANDORA n handsome red sea bream

PANDORE another word for ▸ bandore

PANDOUR n one of an 18th-century force of Croatian soldiers

PANDS ▸ pand

PANDURA n ancient stringed instrument

PANDY n (in schools) stroke on the hand with a strap as a punishment ▸ vb punish with such strokes

PANE n, adj paned

PANEER n soft white cheese, used in Indian cookery **paneers**

PANEITY n state of being bread

PANEL n, vb, adj paneled, panels

PANES ▸ pane

PANFISH n small food fish

PANFRY vb fry in a pan

PANFUL ▸ pan

PANFULS ▸ pan

PANG n, vb

PANGA n broad heavy knife of E Africa, used as a tool or weapon

PANGAMY n unrestricted mating

PANGAS ▸ panga

PANGED ▸ pang

PANGEN = pangene

PANGENE n hypothetical particle of protoplasm

PANGENS ▸ pangen

PANGING ▸ pang

PANGRAM n sentence incorporating all the letters of the alphabet

PANGS ▸ pang

PANIC n, vb, adj panick

PANICKS ▸ panick

PANICKY ▸ panic

PANICLE n loose, irregularly branched cluster of flowers

PANICS ▸ panic

PANICUM n type of grass

PANIER = pannier

PANIERS ▸ panier

PANIM n heathen or pagan panims

PANING ▸ pane

PANINI n panino

PANINIS ▸ panini

PANINO n Italian sandwich

PANISC n faun; attendant of Pan paniscs, panisk

PANISKS ▸ panisk

PANKO n flaky breadcrumbs used in Japanese cookery pankos

PANNAGE n pasturage for pigs, esp in a forest

PANNE n lightweight velvet fabric

PANNED ▸ pan

PANNER ▸ pan

PANNERS ▸ pan

PANNES ▸ panne

PANNICK old spelling of the noun ▸ panic

PANNIER ▸ pan

PANNING ▸ pan

PANNOSE adj like felt

PANNUS n inflammatory fleshy lesion on the surface of the eye

PANOCHA n coarse grade of sugar made in Mexico

PANOCHE n type of dark sugar

PANOPLY n

PANPIPE n wind instrument

PANS ▸ pan

PANSIED adj covered with pansies

PANSIES ▸ pansy

PANSY n

PANT vb, n panted

PANTER n person who pants panters

PANTHER n

PANTIE = panty

PANTIES pl n women's underpants

PANTILE n roofing tile with an S-shaped cross section ▸ vb tile roof with pantiles

PANTINE n pasteboard puppet

PANTING ▸ pant

PANTLER n pantry servant

PANTO = pantomime

PANTON n type of horseshoe pantons

PANTOS ▸ panto

PANTOUM n verse form

PANTRY n

PANTS pl n

PANTUN n Malayan poetry pantuns

PANTY n woman's undergarment

PANZER n German tank panzers

PAOLI ▸ paolo

PAOLO n Italian silver coin

PAP n, vb

PAPA n father

PAPABLE adj suitable for papacy

PAPACY n

PAPADAM variant of > poppadom

PAPADOM variant of > poppadom

PAPADUM variant of > poppadom

PAPAIN n enzyme in the unripe fruit of the papaya papains

PAPAL adj of the pope papally

PAPAS ▸ papa

PAPAUMA n New Zealand word for broadleaf

PAPAW = papaya

PAPAWS ▸ papaw

PAPAYA n papayan, papayas

PAPE n spiritual father

PAPER n, vb papered, paperer, papers

PAPERY adj like paper, esp in thinness, flimsiness, or dryness

PAPES ▶ pape
PAPHIAN n prostitute
PAPILIO n butterfly
PAPILLA n small projection of tissue
PAPOOSE n Native American child
PAPPED ▶ pap
PAPPI ▶ pappus
PAPPIER ▶ pappy
PAPPIES ▶ pappy
PAPPING ▶ pap
PAPPOSE ▶ pappus
PAPPOUS ▶ pappus
PAPPUS n ring of hairs surrounding the fruit in composite plants
PAPPY adj resembling pap
PAPRICA = paprika
PAPRIKA n
PAPS ▶ pap
PAPULA = papule
PAPULAE ▶ papula
PAPULAR ▶ papule
PAPULE n small solid usually round elevation of the skin papules
PAPYRAL ▶ papyrus
PAPYRI ▶ papyrus
PAPYRUS n
PAR n, vb
PARA n paratrooper
PARABEN n
PARABLE n, vb
PARACME n phase where fever lessens
PARADE n, vb paraded, parader, parades
PARADOR n state-run hotel in Spain
PARADOS n bank behind a trench or other fortification
PARADOX n
PARAE n type of fish
PARAFLE = paraffle
PARAGE n type of feudal land tenure **parages**
PARAGON n, vb
PARAMO n high plateau in the Andes **paramos**
PARANG n knife used by the Dyaks of Borneo **parangs**
PARANYM n euphemism
PARAPET n, vb
PARAPH n flourish after a signature ▶ vb embellish signature **paraphs**
PARAS ▶ para
PARASOL n
PARATHA n (in Indian cookery) flat unleavened bread
PARAZOA > parazoan
PARBAKE vb partially bake
PARBOIL vb
PARCEL n, vb parcels
PARCH vb make very hot and dry **parched, parches**
PARD n leopard or panther
PARDAH = purdah
PARDAHS ▶ pardah
PARDAL variant spelling of ▶ pardale
PARDALE n leopard
PARDALS ▶ pardal
PARDED adj having spots
PARDEE adv certainly **pardi, pardie**
PARDINE adj spotted

PARDNER n friend or partner: used as a term of address
PARDON vb, n, interj, sentence substitute **pardons**
PARDS ▶ pard
PARDY = pardee
PARE vb pared
PAREIRA n root of a South American climbing plant
PARELLA n type of lichen **parelle**
PARENT n, vb parents
PAREO = pareu
PAREOS ▶ pareu
PARER ▶ pare
PARERA n New Zealand duck **pareras**
PARERGA > parergon
PARERS ▶ pare
PARES ▶ pare
PARESES ▶ paresis
PARESIS n incomplete or slight paralysis of motor functions **paretic**
PAREU n Polynesian skirt or loincloth **pareus**
PAREV adj containing neither meat nor milk products **pareve**
PARFAIT n dessert consisting of layers of ice cream, fruit, and sauce
PARGANA n Indian sub-district
PARGE vb coat with plaster **parged, parges**
PARGET n plaster, mortar, etc, used to

line chimney flues or cover walls ▷ vb cover or decorate with parget **pargets**

PARGING ▶ parge

PARGO n sea bream **pargos**

PARIAH n pariahs

PARIAL n pair royal of playing cards **parials**

PARIAN n type of marble or porcelain **parians**

PARIES n wall of an organ or bodily cavity

PARING n piece pared off **parings**

PARIS n type of herb **parises**

PARISH n

PARISON n unshaped mass of glass

PARITOR n official who summons witnesses

PARITY n

PARK n, vb

PARKA n

PARKADE n building used as a car park

PARKAS ▶ parka

PARKED ▶ park

PARKEE n Eskimo outer garment **parkees**

PARKER ▶ park

PARKERS ▶ park

PARKI variant of ▶ parka

PARKIE n park keeper

PARKIER ▶ parky

PARKIES ▶ parkie

PARKIN n moist spicy ginger cake

PARKING ▶ park

PARKINS ▶ parkin

PARKIS ▶ parki

PARKISH adj like a park

PARKLY adj having many parks or resembling a park

PARKOUR n sport of running in urban areas over obstacles

PARKS ▶ park

PARKWAY n wide road planted with trees, turf, etc

PARKY adj (of the weather) chilly

PARLAY vb stake (winnings from one bet) on a subsequent wager ▷ n bet in which winnings are parlayed **parlays**

PARLE vb speak **parled, parles**

PARLEY n meeting between opponents to discuss terms ▷ vb have a parley **parleys**

PARLIES pl n small Scottish biscuits

PARLING ▶ parle

PARLOR = parlour

PARLORS ▶ parlor

PARLOUR n

PARLOUS adj, adv

PARLY n short form of parliament

PARODIC ▶ parody

PARODOI n path leading to Greek theatre

PARODOS n ode sung by Greek chorus

PARODY n, vb

PAROL n (formerly) pleadings in an action when presented by word of mouth ▷ adj (of a contract, lease, etc) not made under seal

PAROLE n, vb paroled, parolee, paroles

PAROLS ▶ parol

PARONYM n cognate word

PARORE n type of fish found around Australia and New Zealand **parores**

PAROTIC adj situated near the ear

PAROTID adj relating to or situated near the parotid gland ▷ n parotid gland

PAROTIS n parotid gland

PAROUS adj having given birth

PARP vb make a honking sound

PARPANE n parapet on bridge

PARPED ▶ parp

PARPEN = parpend

PARPEND = perpend

PARPENS ▶ parpen

PARPENT n parapet on bridge

PARPING ▶ parp

PARPS ▶ parp

PARQUET n, vb

PARR n salmon up to two years of age

PARRA n tourist or non-resident on a beach

PARRAL = parrel

PARRALS ▶ parral

PARRAS ▶ parra

PARRED ▶ par

PARREL n ring that holds the jaws of a boom to the mast **parrels**

PARRIED ▶ parry

PARRIER ▶ parry

PARRIES ▶ parry

PARRING ▶ par

PARROCK vb put (an animal) in a paddock

PARROT n, vb **parrots**

PARROTY adj like a parrot; chattering

PARRS ▶ parr

PARRY vb, n

PARS ▶ par

PARSE vb

PARSEC n unit of astronomical distance **parsecs**

PARSED ▶ parse

PARSER n program that interprets input to a computer **parsers**

PARSES ▶ parse

PARSING ▶ parse

PARSLEY n, n

PARSNEP = parsnip

PARSNIP n

PARSON n **parsons**

PART n, vb

PARTAKE vb

PARTAN Scottish word for ▶ crab

PARTANS ▶ partan

PARTED adj divided almost to the base

PARTER n thing that parts **parters**

PARTI n concept of architectural design

PARTIAL adj, n, vb

PARTIED ▶ party

PARTIER n person who parties

PARTIES ▶ party

PARTIM adv in part

PARTING = part

PARTIS ▶ parti

PARTITA n type of suite

PARTITE adj composed of or divided into a specified number of parts

PARTLET n woman's garment

PARTLY adv

PARTNER n, vb

PARTON n hypothetical elementary particle **partons**

PARTOOK ▶ partake

PARTS pl n abilities or talents

PARTURE n departure

PARTWAY adv some of the way

PARTY n, vb, adj

PARTYER n person who parties

PARULIS another name for ▶ gumboil

PARURA = parure

PARURAS ▶ parura

PARURE n set of jewels or other ornaments **parures**

PARVE = parev

PARVENU n person newly risen to a position of power or wealth ▷ adj of or characteristic of a parvenu

PARVIS n court or portico in front of a building, esp a church

parvise

PARVO n disease of cattle and dogs **parvos**

PAS n dance step or movement, esp in ballet

PASCAL n unit of pressure **pascals**

PASCHAL adj of the Passover or Easter ▷ n Passover or Easter

PASCUAL adj relating to pasture

PASE n movement of the cape or muleta by a matador

PASEAR vb go for a rambling walk **pasears**

PASELA = bonsela

PASELAS ▶ pasela

PASEO n bullfighters' procession **paseos**

PASES ▶ pase

PASH n infatuation ▷ vb throw or be thrown and break or be broken to bits

PASHA n high official of the Ottoman Empire **pashas**

PASHED ▶ pash

PASHES ▶ pash

PASHIM ▶ pashm

PASHIMS ▶ pashm

PASHING ▶ pash

PASHKA n rich Russian dessert **pashkas**

PASHM n underfur of various Tibetan animals, esp goats, used for cashmere shawls **pashms**

PASPIES ▶ paspy

PASPY n piece of music in triple time

PASQUIL n abusive lampoon or satire ▷ vb ridicule with pasquil

PASS vb, n

PASSADE n act of moving back and forth in the same place

PASSADO n forward thrust with sword

PASSAGE n, vb

PASSANT adj (of a heraldic beast) walking

PASSATA n sauce made from sieved tomatoes

PASSE adj out-of-date

PASSED ▷ pass

PASSEE adj out of fashion

PASSEL n group or quantity of no fixed number **passels**

PASSER n person or thing that passes **passers**

PASSES ▷ pass

PASSIM adv everywhere, throughout

PASSING adj, n

PASSION n, vb

PASSIVE adj, n

PASSKEY n private key

PASSMAN n student who passes without honours **passmen**

PASSOUT n (in ice hockey) pass by an attacking player from behind the opposition goal line

PASSUS n division or section of a poem, story, etc

PAST adj, n, adv, prep

PASTA n pastas

PASTE n, vb pasted

PASTEL n, adj pastels

PASTER n person or thing that pastes

PASTERN n part of a horse's foot

PASTERS ▷ paster

PASTES ▷ paste

PASTEUP n material pasted on a sheet of paper or board

PASTIE n decorative cover for nipple

PASTIER ▷ pasty

PASTIES ▷ pasty

PASTIL = pastille

PASTILS ▷ pastil

PASTILY ▷ pasty

PASTIME n

PASTINA n small pieces of pasta

PASTING n heavy defeat

PASTIS n anise-flavoured alcoholic drink

PASTOR n, vb pastors

PASTRY n

PASTS ▷ past

PASTURE n, vb

PASTY adj, n

PAT vb, n, adj

PATACA n monetary unit of Macao patacas

PATAGIA > patagium

PATAKA n building on stilts, used for storing provisions patakas

PATAMAR n type of boat

PATBALL n game like squash but using hands

PATCH n, vb patched, patcher, patches

PATCHY adj

PATE n head pated

PATELLA n

PATEN n plate used for the bread at Communion

PATENCY n condition of being obvious

PATENS ▷ paten

PATENT n, adj, vb patents

PATER n father

PATERA n shallow ancient Roman bowl paterae

PATERS ▷ pater

PATES ▷ pate

PATH n, vb pathed

PATHIC n catamite ▷ adj of or relating to a catamite **pathics**

PATHING ▷ path

PATHOS n

PATHS ▷ path

PATHWAY n

PATIBLE adj endurable

PATIENT adj, n, vb

PATIKI n New Zealand sand flounder or dab patikis

PATIN = paten

PATINA n patinae, patinas

PATINE vb cover with patina patined, patines

PATINS ▷ patin

PATIO n patios

PATKA n head covering worn by Sikh men patkas

PATLY adv fitly

PATNESS n appropriateness

PATOIS n

PATONCE adj (of cross) with limbs which broaden from centre

PATRIAL n (in Britain, formerly) person with a right to live in the United Kingdom

PATRICK n former Irish coin

PATRICO n fraudulent priest

PATRIOT n

PATROL n, vb patrols

PATRON n patrons

PATROON n Dutch land-holder in New Netherland and New York

PATS ▸ pat

PATSIES ▸ patsy

PATSY n person who is easily cheated, victimized, etc

PATTE n band keeping belt in place

PATTED ▸ pat

PATTEE adj (of a cross) having triangular arms widening outwards

PATTEN n wooden clog or sandal ▷ vb wear pattens **pattens**

PATTER vb, n

PATTERN n, vb

PATTERS ▸ patter

PATTES ▸ patte

PATTIE = patty

PATTIES ▸ patty

PATTING ▸ pat

PATTLE dialect for ▸ paddle

PATTLES ▸ pattle

PATTY n small flattened cake of minced food

PATU n short Māori club, now used ceremonially

PATULIN n toxic antibiotic

PATUS ▸ patu

PATY adj (of cross) having arms of equal length

PATZER n novice chess player **patzers**

PAUA n edible shellfish of New Zealand **pauas**

PAUCAL n grammatical number for words in contexts where a few of their referents are described ▷ adj relating to or inflected for this number **paucals**

PAUCITY n

PAUGHTY Scots word for ▸ haughty

PAUL = pawl

PAULIN n tarpaulin **paulins**

PAULS ▸ paul

PAUNCE n pansy **paunces**

PAUNCH n, vb

PAUNCHY adj having a protruding belly or abdomen

PAUPER n, vb paupers

PAUSAL ▸ pause

PAUSE vb, n paused, pauser, pausers, pauses, pausing

PAV short for ▸ pavlova

PAVAGE n tax towards paving streets **pavages**

PAVAN = pavane

PAVANE n slow and stately dance **pavanes**

PAVANS ▸ pavan

PAVE vb, n paved

PAVED adj (of jewels) set close together

PAVEN = pavane

PAVENS ▸ paven

PAVER ▸ pave

PAVERS ▸ pave

PAVES ▸ pave

PAVID adj fearful

PAVIN = pavane

PAVING n paved surface ▷ adj of or for a paved surface or pavement **pavings**

PAVINS ▸ pavin

PAVIOR = paviour

PAVIORS ▸ pavior

PAVIOUR n person who lays paving

PAVIS n large square shield **pavise**

PAVISER n soldier holding pavise

PAVISES ▸ pavise

PAVISSE = pavis

PAVLOVA n meringue cake topped with whipped cream and fruit

PAVONE n peacock **pavones**

PAVS ▸ pav

PAW n, vb

PAWA old word for ▸ peacock

PAWAS ▸ pawa

PAWAW vb recite N American incantation **pawawed, pawaws**

PAWED ▸ paw

PAWER n person or animal that paws **pawers**

PAWING ▸ paw

PAWK Scots word for ▸ trick

PAWKIER ▸ pawky

PAWKILY ▸ pawky

PAWKS ▸ pawk

PAWKY adj having or characterized by a dry wit

PAWL n pivoted lever shaped to engage with a ratchet **pawls**

PAWN vb, n **pawnage**

PAWNCE old word for ▸ pansy

PAWNCES ▸ pawnce

PAWNED ▸ pawn

PAWNEE n one who accepts goods in pawn **pawnees**

PAWNER n one who pawns his or her possessions **pawners**

PAWNING ▸ pawn

PAWNOR = pawner

PAWNORS ▸ pawnor

PAWNS ▸ pawn

PAWPAW = papaw

PAWPAWS ▸ pawpaw

PAWS ▸ paw

PAX n peace ▷ interj call signalling a desire to end hostilities **paxes**

> Latin for peace, this is yet another of those very useful short words containing X.

PAXIUBA n tropical tree

PAXWAX n strong ligament in the neck of many mammals

PAY vb, n

PAYABLE adj **payably**

PAYBACK n return on an investment

PAYDAY n day on which wages or salaries are paid **paydays**

PAYED ▸ pay

PAYEE n **payees**

PAYER n person who pays **payers**

PAYFONE US spelling of ▸ payphone

PAYING ▸ pay

PAYINGS ▸ pay

PAYLIST n list of people to be paid

PAYLOAD n

PAYMENT n

PAYNIM n heathen or pagan **paynims**

PAYOFF n final settlement, esp in retribution **payoffs**

PAYOLA n bribe to promote a commercial product **payolas**

PAYOR = payer

PAYORS ▸ payor

PAYOUT n sum of money paid out **payouts**

PAYROLL n

PAYS ▸ pay

PAYSAGE n landscape

PAYSD Spenserian form of ▸ poised

PAYSLIP n note of payment given to employee

PAZAZZ = pizzazz

PAZZAZZ = pizzazz

PE n 17th letter of the Hebrew alphabet, transliterated as p

PEA n

PEACE n **peaced, peaces**

PEACH n, adj, vb **peached, peacher, peaches**

PEACHY adj of or like a peach, esp in colour or texture

PEACING ▸ peace

PEACOAT n woollen jacket

PEACOCK n, vb

PEACOD = peapod

PEACODS ▸ peacod

PEAFOWL n peacock or peahen

PEAG n (formerly) money used by North American Indians **peage**

PEAGES ▸ peage

PEAGS ▸ peag

PEAHEN ▸ peacock

PEAHENS ▸ peacock

PEAK n, vb, adj

PEAKED adj having a peak

PEAKIER ▸ peak

PEAKING ▸ peak

PEAKISH adj sickly

PEAKS ▸ peak

PEAKY ▸ peak

PEAL n, vb **pealed**

PEALIKE ▸ pea

PEALING ▸ peal

PEALS ▸ peal

PEAN = peen

PEANED ▸ pean

PEANING ▸ pean

PEANS ▸ pean

PEANUT n **peanuts**

PEAPOD n pod of the pea plant **peapods**

PEAR n

PEARCE old spelling of
▶ **pierce**

PEARCED ▶ pearce

PEARCES ▶ pearce

PEARE obsolete spelling
of ▶ **pear**

PEARES ▶ peare

PEARL = purl

PEARLED ▶ pearl

PEARLER n person who
dives for or trades in
pearls ▷ adj excellent

PEARLIN n type of lace
used to trim clothes

PEARLS ▶ pearl

PEARLY adj resembling
a pearl, esp in lustre
▷ n London
costermonger who
wears pearl buttons

PEARS ▶ pear

PEARST archaic variant
of ▶ **pierced**

PEART adj lively
pearter, peartly

PEAS ▶ pea

PEASANT n

PEASCOD = cod

PEASE n archaic or
dialect word for pea
▷ vb appease **peased,
peasen, peases,
peasing, peason**

PEAT n

PEATARY n area covered
with peat **peatery**

PEATIER ▶ peat

PEATMAN n person who
collects peat **peatmen**

PEATS ▶ peat

PEATY ▶ peat

PEAVEY n wooden lever
used for handling logs
peaveys

PEAVIES ▶ peavy

PEAVY = peavey

PEAZE = pease

PEAZED ▶ peaze

PEAZES ▶ peaze

PEAZING ▶ peaze

PEBA n type of
armadillo **pebas**

PEBBLE n, vb **pebbled,
pebbles, pebbly**

PEBRINE n disease of
silkworms

PEC n pectoral muscle

PECAN n pecans

PECCANT adj guilty of
an offence

PECCARY n piglike
animal of American
forests

PECCAVI n confession of
guilt

PECH Scottish word for
▶ **pant**

PECHAN Scots word for
▶ **stomach**

PECHANS ▶ pechan

PECHED ▶ pech

PECHING ▶ pech

PECHS ▶ pech

PECK vb, n

PECKE n quarter of
bushel

PECKED ▶ peck

PECKES ▶ pecke

PECKIER ▶ pecky

PECKING ▶ peck

PECKISH adj

PECKS ▶ peck

PECKY adj discoloured

PECS pl n pectoral
muscles

PECTASE n enzyme
occurring in certain
ripening fruits

PECTATE n salt or ester
of pectic acid

PECTEN n comblike
structure in the eye of
birds and reptiles
pectens

PECTIC ▶ pectin

PECTIN n pectins

PECTISE = pectize

PECTIZE vb change into
a jelly

PECTOSE n insoluble
carbohydrate found in
unripe fruit

PECULIA ▶ peculium

PED n pannier

PEDAGOG
= pedagogue

PEDAL n, vb, adj
pedaled, pedaler

PEDALO n
pedal-operated
pleasure craft **pedalos**

PEDALS ▶ pedal

PEDANT n pedants

PEDATE adj (of a plant
leaf) divided into
several lobes arising at
a common point

PEDDER old form of
▶ **pedlar**

PEDDERS ▶ pedder

PEDDLE vb peddled

PEDDLER = pedlar

PEDDLES ▶ peddle

PEDES ▶ pes

PEDESES ▶ pedesis

PEDESIS n random
motion of small
particles

PEDETIC adj of feet

PEDICAB n pedal-
operated tricycle,
available for hire

PEDICEL n stalk bearing a single flower of an inflorescence

PEDICLE n any small stalk

PEDLAR n person who sells goods from door to door **pedlars**

PEDLARY = pedlery

PEDLER = pedlar

PEDLERS ▶ pedler

PEDLERY n business of pedler

PEDOCAL n type of soil that is rich in lime

PEDRAIL n device replacing wheel on rough surfaces

PEDRERO n type of cannon

PEDRO n card game **pedros**

PEDS ▶ ped

PEEBEEN n type of large evergreen

PEECE obsolete variant of ▶ piece

PEECES ▶ peece

PEEK n, vb

PEEKABO = peekaboo

PEEKED ▶ peek

PEEKING ▶ peek

PEEKS ▶ peek

PEEL vb, n **peeled**

PEELER n device for peeling vegetables, fruit, etc **peelers**

PEELING n strip that has been peeled off

PEELS ▶ peel

PEEN n end of a hammer head opposite the striking face ▷ vb strike with

the peen of a hammer **peened**

PEENGE vb complain **peenged, peenges**

PEENING ▶ peen

PEENS ▶ peen

PEEOY n homemade firework **peeoys**

PEEP vb, n

PEEPE old spelling of ▶ pip

PEEPED ▶ peep

PEEPER n person who peeps **peepers**

PEEPES archaic spelling of ▶ peeps

PEEPING ▶ peep

PEEPS ▶ peep

PEEPUL n Indian moraceous tree **peepuls**

PEER n, vb

PEERAGE n

PEERED ▶ peer

PEERESS n (in Britain) woman holding the rank of a peer

PEERIE n spinning top ▷ adj small **peerier, peeries**

PEERING ▶ peer

PEERS ▶ peer

PEERY n child's spinning top

PEEVE vb irritate or annoy ▷ n something that irritates **peeved**

PEEVER n hopscotch **peevers**

PEEVES ▶ peeve

PEEVING ▶ peeve

PEEVISH adj

PEEWEE = pewee

PEEWEES ▶ pewee

PEEWIT = lapwing

PEEWITS ▶ peewit

PEG n, vb

PEGASUS n winged horse

PEGBOX n part of stringed instrument that holds tuning pegs

PEGGED ▶ peg

PEGGIES ▶ peggy

PEGGING ▶ peg

PEGGY n type of small warbler

PEGH variant of ▶ pech

PEGHED ▶ pegh

PEGHING ▶ pegh

PEGHS ▶ pegh

PEGLESS ▶ peg

PEGLIKE ▶ peg

PEGS ▶ peg

PEH ▶ pe

PEHS ▶ peh

PEIN = peen

PEINCT vb paint **peincts**

PEINED ▶ pein

PEINING ▶ pein

PEINS ▶ pein

PEISE = peize

PEISED ▶ peise

PEISES ▶ peise

PEISHWA n Indian leader

PEISING ▶ peise

PEIZE vb weight or poise **peized, peizes, peizing**

PEKAN n large North American marten **pekans**

PEKE n Pekingese dog

PEKEPOO = peekapoo

PEKES ▶ peke

PEKIN n silk fabric **pekins**

PEKOE n high-quality

tea **pekoes**
PEL n pixel
PELA n insect living on wax
PELAGE n coat of a mammal, consisting of hair, wool, fur, etc **pelages**
PELAGIC adj of or relating to the open sea ▷ n any pelagic creature
PELAS ▶ pela
PELE Spenserian variant of ▶ **peal**
PELES ▶ pele
PELF n money or wealth **pelfs**
PELHAM n horse's bit for a double bridle **pelhams**
PELICAN n
PELISSE n cloak or loose coat which is usually fur-trimmed
PELITE n any argillaceous rock such as shale **pelites, pelitic**
PELL n hide of an animal
PELLACH = pellack
PELLACK n porpoise
PELLET n, vb **pellets**
PELLOCK n porpoise
PELLS ▶ pell
PELLUM n dust **pellums**
PELMA n sole of the foot **pelmas**
PELMET n **pelmets**
PELOID n mud used therapeutically **peloids**
PELON adj hairless

PELORIA n abnormal production of flowers in a plant **peloric**
PELORUS n sighting device
PELORY n floral mutation
PELOTA n game where players propel a ball against a wall **pelotas**
PELOTON n main field of riders in a road race
PELS ▶ pel
PELT vb, n
PELTA n small ancient shield **peltae, peltas**
PELTAST n (in ancient Greece) lightly armed foot soldier
PELTATE adj (of leaves) having the stalk attached to the centre of the lower surface
PELTED ▶ pelt
PELTER vb
PELTERS ▶ pelt
PELTING ▶ pelt
PELTRY n pelts of animals collectively
PELTS ▶ pelt
PELVES ▶ pelvis
PELVIC adj of, near, or relating to the pelvis ▷ n pelvic bone **pelvics**
PELVIS n
PEMBINA n type of cranberry
PEMICAN = pemmican
PEMPHIX n type of crustacean
PEN n, vb
PENAL adj **penally**
PENALTY n
PENANCE n, vb

PENANG variant of ▶ **pinang**
PENANGS ▶ penang
PENATES pl n household gods
PENCE ▶ penny
PENCEL n small pennon **pencels**
PENCES ▶ penny
PENCIL n, vb **pencils**
PEND vb await judgment or settlement ▷ n archway or vaulted passage
PENDANT n
PENDED ▶ pend
PENDENT adj hanging ▷ n pendant
PENDING prep, adj
PENDS ▶ pend
PENDU adj in informal Indian English, culturally backward
PENDULE n type of climbing manoeuvre
PENE variant of ▶ **peen**
PENED ▶ pene
PENES ▶ penis
PENFOLD = pinfold
PENFUL n contents of pen **penfuls**
PENGO n former monetary unit of Hungary **pengos**
PENGUIN n
PENI old spelling of ▶ **penny**
PENIAL ▶ penis
PENICIL n small pad for wounds
PENIE old spelling of ▶ **penny**
PENIES ▶ penie

PENILE *adj* of or relating to the penis

PENILL ▶ penillion

PENING ▶ pene

PENIS *n* penises

PENK *n* small fish penks

PENLITE = penlight

PENMAN *n* person skilled in handwriting penmen

PENNA *n* large feather pennae

PENNAL *n* first-year student of Protestant university pennals

PENNAME *n* author's pseudonym

PENNANT = pendant

PENNATE *adj* having feathers, wings, or winglike structures

PENNE *n* pasta in the form of short tubes

PENNED ▶ pen

PENNER *n* person who writes penners

PENNES ▶ penne

PENNI *n* former Finnish monetary unit pennia

PENNIED *adj* having money

PENNIES ▶ penny

PENNILL *n* stanza in a Welsh poem

PENNINE *n* mineral found in the Pennine Alps

PENNING ▶ pen

PENNIS ▶ penni

PENNON *n* triangular or tapering flag pennons

PENNY *n*

PENOCHE *n* type of fudge

PENS ▶ pen

PENSEE *n* thought put down on paper pensees

PENSEL = pencel

PENSELS ▶ pensel

PENSIL = pencel

PENSILE *adj* designating or building a hanging nest

PENSILS ▶ pensil

PENSION *n, vb*

PENSIVE *adj*

PENSTER *n* writer

PENSUM *n* school exercise pensums

PENT *n* penthouse

PENTACT *n* sponge spicule with five rays

PENTAD *n* group or series of five pentads

PENTANE *n* alkane hydrocarbon with three isomers

PENTENE *n* colourless flammable liquid alkene

PENTHIA *n* child born fifth

PENTICE *vb* accommodate in a penthouse pentise

PENTITI ▶ pentito

PENTITO *n* criminal who offers information to the police

PENTODE *n* electronic valve having five electrodes

PENTOSE *n* monosaccharide containing five atoms of carbon per molecule

PENTS ▶ pent

PENTYL *n* one of a

particular chemical group pentyls

PENUCHE = panocha

PENUCHI = panocha

PENULT *n* last syllable but one in a word penults

PENURY *n*

PEON *n* Spanish-American farm labourer or unskilled worker

PEONAGE *n* state of being a peon

PEONES ▶ peon

PEONIES ▶ peony

PEONISM = peonage

PEONS ▶ peon

PEONY *n*

PEOPLE *pl n, vb* peopled

PEOPLER *n* settler

PEOPLES ▶ people

PEP *n* high spirits, energy, or enthusiasm ▶ *vb* liven by imbuing with new vigour

PEPFUL *adj* full of vitality

PEPINO *n* purple-striped yellow fruit pepinos

PEPLA ▶ peplum

PEPLOS *n* part of a woman's attire in ancient Greece peplum

PEPLUMS ▶ peplum

PEPLUS = peplos

PEPO *n* fruit such as the melon, squash, cucumber, or pumpkin pepos

PEPPED ▶ pep

PEPPER *n, vb* peppers

PEPPERY *adj* tasting of pepper

PEPPIER ▸ peppy

PEPPILY ▸ peppy

PEPPING ▸ pep

PEPPY *adj* full of vitality

PEPS ▸ pep

PEPSIN *n* enzyme produced in the stomach **pepsine, pepsins**

PEPTALK *n* talk meant to inspire ▸ *vb* give a peptalk to

PEPTIC *adj* relating to digestion or the digestive juices ▸ *n* substance that aids digestion **peptics**

PEPTID *variant of* ▸ peptide

PEPTIDE *n* organic chemical compound

PEPTIDS ▸ peptid

PEPTISE = peptize

PEPTIZE *vb* disperse into a colloidal state

PEPTONE *n* any of a group of organic compounds

PER *prep*

PERACID *n* acid in which the element forming the acid radical exhibits its highest valency

PERAEA ▸ peraeon

PERAEON ▸ pereion

PERAI *another name for* ▸ piranha

PERAIS ▸ perai

PERCALE *n* close-textured woven cotton fabric

PERCASE *adv* perchance

PERCE *obsolete word for* ▸ pierce

PERCED ▸ perce

PERCEN ▸ perce

PERCENT *n* percentage or proportion

PERCEPT *n* concept that depends on recognition of some external object or phenomenon

PERCES ▸ perce

PERCH *n, vb* **perched, percher, perches**

PERCINE *adj* of perches

PERCING ▸ perce

PERCOCT *adj* well-cooked

PERCOID *n* type of spiny-finned teleost fish

PERCUSS *vb* strike sharply, rapidly, or suddenly

PERDIE *adv* certainly

PERDU *adj* (of a soldier) placed on hazardous sentry duty ▸ *n* soldier placed on hazardous sentry duty **perdue**

PERDUES ▸ perdue

PERDURE *vb* last for long time

PERDUS ▸ perdu

PERDY *adv* certainly

PERE *n* addition to a French surname to specify the father

PEREA ▸ pereon

PEREGAL *adj* equal ▸ *n* equal

PEREIA ▸ pereion

PEREION *n* thorax of some crustaceans

PEREIRA *n* bark of a South American

apocrynaceous tree

PERENTY = perentie

PEREON ▸ pereion

PEREONS ▸ pereon

PERES ▸ pere

PERFAY *interj* by my faith

PERFECT *adj, n, vb* **perfet**

PERFIDY *n* perfidious act

PERFIN *former name for* ▸ spif

PERFING *n* practice of taking early retirement from the police force

PERFINS ▸ perfin

PERFORM *vb*

PERFUME *n, vb*

PERFUMY *adj* like perfume

PERFUSE *vb* permeate through or over

PERGOLA *n* framework of trellis supporting climbing plants

PERHAPS *adv, sentence substitute, n*

PERI *n* (in Persian folklore) one of a race of beautiful supernatural beings

PERIAPT *n* charm or amulet

PERICON *n* Argentinian dance

PERIDIA > peridium

PERIDOT *n* pale green transparent gemstone

PERIGEE *n* point in the orbit of the moon or a satellite that is nearest the earth

PERIGON *n* angle of 360°

PERIL *n, vb* **periled**

PERILLA n type of mint
PERILS ▷ peril
PERINEA ▷ perineum
PERIOD n, adj, vb **periods**
PERIOST n thick fibrous two-layered membrane covering the surface of bones
PERIQUE n strong highly-flavoured tobacco
PERIS ▷ peri
PERISH vb
PERITI ▷ peritus
PERITUS n Catholic theology consultant
PERIWIG = peruke
PERJINK adj prim or finicky
PERJURE vb render (oneself) guilty of perjury
PERJURY n
PERK n, adj, vb **perked**
PERKIER ▷ perky
PERKILY ▷ perky
PERKIN = parkin
PERKING ▷ perk
PERKINS ▷ perk
PERKISH adj perky
PERKS ▷ perk
PERKY adj lively or cheerful
PERLITE n variety of obsidian
PERLOUS = perilous
PERM n, vb permed
PERMIAN adj of, denoting, or formed in the last period of the Palaeozoic era
PERMIE n person, esp an office worker,

employed by a firm on a permanent basis **permies**
PERMING ▷ perm
PERMIT vb, n **permits**
PERMS ▷ perm
PERMUTE vb change the sequence of
PERN n type of buzzard
PERNIO n chilblain
PERNOD n aniseed-flavoured aperitif from France **pernods**
PERNS ▷ pern
PEROGI n type of Polish dumpling
PERONE n fibula **perones**
PERORAL adj administered through mouth
PEROXID variant of > peroxide
PEROXO n type of acid
PEROXY adj containing the peroxide group
PERP n someone who has committed a crime
PERPEND n large stone that passes through a wall from one side to the other ▷ vb ponder **perpent**
PERPLEX vb
PERPS ▷ perp
PERRIER n short mortar
PERRIES ▷ perry
PERRON n external flight of steps **perrons**
PERRY n alcoholic drink made from fermented pears
PERSALT n any salt of a peracid

PERSANT adj piercing
PERSE old variant of ▷ pierce
PERSES ▷ perse
PERSICO = persicot
PERSING ▷ perse
PERSIST vb
PERSON n
PERSONA n
PERSONS ▷ person
PERSPEX n any of various clear acrylic resins
PERST adj perished
PERSUE obsolete form of ▷ pursue
PERSUED ▷ persue
PERSUES ▷ persue
PERT adj, n
PERTAIN vb
PERTAKE obsolete form of ▷ partake
PERTER ▷ pert
PERTEST ▷ pert
PERTLY ▷ pert
PERTOOK ▷ pertake
PERTS ▷ pert
PERTURB vb
PERTUSE adj having holes
PERUKE n wig for men worn in the 17th and 18th centuries
PERUKED adj wearing wig
PERUKES ▷ peruke
PERUSAL ▷ peruse
PERUSE vb perused, peruser, peruses
PERV n pervert ▷ vb give a person an erotic look
PERVADE vb
PERVE = perv
PERVED ▷ perv
PERVERT vb, n

PERVES ▶ perv

PERVIER ▶ pervy

PERVING ▶ perv

PERVS ▶ perv

PERVY adj perverted

PES n animal part corresponding to the foot

PESADE n position in which the horse stands on the hind legs with the forelegs in the air pesades

PESANT obsolete spelling of ▶ peasant

PESANTE adv to be performed clumsily

PESANTS ▶ pesant

PESAUNT obsolete spelling of ▶ peasant

PESETA n pesetas

PESEWA n Ghanaian monetary unit pesewas

PESHWA = peishwa

PESHWAS ▶ peshwa

PESKIER ▶ pesky

PESKILY ▶ pesky

PESKY adj troublesome

PESO n pesos

PESSARY n

PESSIMA n lowest point

PEST n

PESTER n pesters

PESTFUL adj causing annoyance

PESTIER ▶ pesty

PESTLE n, vb pestled, pestles

PESTO n sauce for pasta pestos

PESTS ▶ pest

PESTY adj persistently annoying

PET n, adj, vb

PETAL n petaled, petals

PETAR obsolete variant of ▶ petard

PETARA n clothes basket petaras

PETARD n petards

PETARS ▶ petar

PETARY n weapon for hurling stones

PETASOS = petasus

PETASUS n broad-brimmed hat worn by the ancient Greeks

PETCOCK n small valve

PETER vb fall (off) in volume, intensity, etc, and finally cease ▷ n act of petering petered, peters

PETHER old variant of ▶ pedlar

PETHERS ▶ pether

PETIOLE n stalk which attaches a leaf to a plant

PETIT adj of little or lesser importance

PETITE adj, n petites

PETNAP vb steal pet petnaps

PETRALE n type of sole

PETRARY n weapon for hurling stones

PETRE = saltpetre

PETREL n petrels

PETRES ▶ petre

PETRI n as in petri dish shallow glass dish used for cultures of bacteria

PETRIFY vb

PETROL n, vb petrols

PETROUS adj denoting the dense part of the temporal bone around the inner ear

PETS ▶ pet

PETSAI n Chinese cabbage petsais

PETTED ▶ pet

PETTER ▶ pet

PETTERS ▶ pet

PETTI ▶ petto

PETTIER ▶ petty

PETTIES ▶ petti

PETTILY ▶ petty

PETTING ▶ pet

PETTISH adj peevish or fretful

PETTLE vb pat animal pettled, pettles

PETTO n breast of animal

PETTY adj

PETUNIA n

PEW n

PEWEE n small N American flycatcher pewees

PEWIT another name for ▶ lapwing

PEWITS ▶ pewit

PEWS ▶ pew

PEWTER n pewters

PEYOTE another name for ▶ mescal

PEYOTES ▶ peyote

PEYOTL = peyote

PEYOTLS ▶ peyotl

PEYSE vb weight or poise peysed, peyses, peysing

PEYTRAL = peytrel

PEYTREL n breastplate of horse's armour

PEZANT obsolete spelling of ▸ **peasant**

PEZANTS ▸ **pezant**

PFENNIG n

PFFT interj sound indicating sudden disappearance of something

PFUI interj phooey

PHACOID adj lentil- or lens-shaped

PHAEIC adj (of animals) having dusky coloration **phaeism**

PHAETON n light four-wheeled horse-drawn carriage

PHAGE n parasitic virus that destroys its host **phages**

PHALANX n

PHALLI ▸ **phallus**

PHALLIC adj of or resembling a phallus

PHALLIN n poisonous substance from mushroom

PHALLUS n

PHANG old variant spelling of ▸ **fang**

PHANGED ▸ **phang**

PHANGS ▸ **phang**

PHANTOM n, adj

PHARAOH n

PHARE n beacon tower **phares**

PHARM vb redirect (a website user) to another, bogus website

PHARMA n pharmaceutical companies considered together as an industry **pharmas**

PHARMED ▸ **pharm**

PHARMS ▸ **pharm**

PHAROS n lighthouse

PHARYNX n

PHASE n, vb phaseal, phased, phases, phasic

PHASING n effect achieved by varying the phase relationship of two similar audio signals

PHASIS another word for ▸ **phase**

PHASMID n stick insect or leaf insect

PHASOR n rotating vector representing a quantity that varies sinusoidally **phasors**

PHAT adj terrific

PHATIC adj (of speech) used to express sociability rather than specific meaning

PHATTER ▸ **phat**

PHEAZAR old variant of ▸ **vizier**

PHEER = fere

PHEERE = fere

PHEERES ▸ **pheere**

PHEERS ▸ **pheer**

PHEESE vb worry pheesed, pheeses, pheeze

PHEEZED ▸ **pheeze**

PHEEZES ▸ **pheeze**

PHELLEM technical name for ▸ **cork**

PHENATE n ester or salt of phenol

PHENE n genetically determined characteristic of organism **phenes**

PHENIC adj of phenol

PHENIX = phoenix

PHENOL n chemical used in disinfectants and antiseptics **phenols**

PHENOM n person or thing of outstanding abilities **phenoms**

PHENOXY modifier as in **phenoxy resin** any of a class of resins derived from polyhydroxy ethers

PHENYL n chemical substance **phenyls**

PHEON n barbed iron head of dart **pheons**

PHESE ▸ **pheese**

PHESED ▸ **phese**

PHESES ▸ **phese**

PHESING ▸ **phese**

PHEW interj exclamation of relief, surprise, etc

PHI n 21st letter in the Greek alphabet

PHIAL n, vb phials

PHILTER n drink supposed to arouse love, desire, etc ▸ vb arouse sexual or romantic feelings by means of a philter

PHILTRA > philtrum

PHILTRE n magic drink supposed to arouse love in the person who drinks it ▸ vb mix with love potion

PHIS ▸ phi
PHIZ n face or a facial expression **phizes, phizog**
PHIZOGS ▸ phizog
PHIZZES ▸ phiz
PHLEGM n phlegms, phlegmy
PHLOEM n plant tissue that acts as a path for the distribution of food **phloems**
PHLOMIS n plant of Phlomis genus
PHLOX n phloxes
PHO n Vietnamese noodle soup
PHOBIA n phobias
PHOBIC adj of, relating to, or arising from a phobia ▸ n person suffering from a phobia **phobics**
PHOBISM n phobia **phobist**
PHOCA n genus of seals **phocae, phocas**
PHOCINE adj of, relating to, or resembling a seal
PHOEBE n greyish-brown North American flycatcher **phoebes**
PHOEBUS n sun
PHOENIX n
PHOH variant of ▸ foh
PHOLAS n type of bivalve mollusc
PHON n unit of loudness
PHONAL adj relating to voice

PHONATE vb articulate speech sounds
PHONE vb, n phoned
PHONEME n one of the set of speech sounds in a language
PHONER n person making a telephone call **phoners**
PHONES ▸ phone
PHONEY adj, n, vb phoneys
PHONIC ▸ phonics
PHONICS n method of teaching people to read
PHONIED, phonier, phonies, phonily ▸ phony
PHONING ▸ phone
PHONO n phonograph
PHONON n quantum of vibrational energy **phonons**
PHONOS ▸ phono
PHONS ▸ phon
PHONY vb fake
PHOOEY interj exclamation of scorn or contempt
PHORATE n type of insecticide
PHORESY n association in which one animal clings to another to ensure movement from place to place
PHOS ▸ pho
PHOSSY adj as in **phossy jaw** gangrenous condition of the lower jawbone

PHOT n unit of illumination
PHOTIC adj of or concerned with light
PHOTICS n science of light
PHOTISM n sensation of light or colour caused by stimulus of another sense
PHOTO n, vb photoed
PHOTOG n photograph **photogs**
PHOTON n quantum of electromagnetic radiation energy **photons**
PHOTOS ▸ photo
PHOTS ▸ phot
PHPHT interj expressing irritation or reluctance
PHRASAL adj of, relating to, or composed of phrases
PHRASE n, vb phrased, phraser, phrases
PHRASY adj containing phrases
PHRATRY n group of people within a tribe who have a common ancestor
PHREAK vb hack into a telecommunications system **phreaks**
PHRENIC adj of or relating to the diaphragm ▸ n (a nerve, blood vessel, etc) located in the diaphragm
PHRENSY obsolete spelling of ▸ frenzy

PHT = phpht
It is easy to overlook this little word, that may offer a way out when your rack seems hopelessly clogged with consonants.

PHUT vb make muffled explosive sound **phuts, phutted**

PHWOAH ▸ phwoar

PHWOAR interj expression of sexual interest or attraction

PHYLA ▸ phylum

PHYLAE ▸ phyle

PHYLAR ▸ phylum

PHYLE n tribe or clan of an ancient Greek people **phylic**

PHYLLID n leaf of a liverwort or moss

PHYLLO variant of ▸ filo

PHYLLOS ▸ phyllo

PHYLON n tribe

PHYLUM n major taxonomic division of animals and plants

PHYSED n physical education **physeds**

PHYSES ▸ physis

PHYSIC n medicine or drug, esp a cathartic or purge ▷ vb treat (a patient) with medicine

PHYSICS n

PHYSIO n physiotherapy **physios**

PHYSIS n part of bone responsible for lengthening

PHYTANE n hydrocarbon found in fossilised plant remains

PHYTIN n substance from plants used as an energy supplement **phytins**

PHYTOID adj resembling plant

PHYTOL n alcohol used to synthesize some vitamins **phytols**

PHYTON n unit of plant structure **phytons**

PI n, vb.

PIA n innermost of the three membranes that cover the brain and the spinal cord

PIAFFE n passage done on the spot ▷ vb strut on the spot **piaffed, piaffer, piaffes**

PIAL adj relating to pia mater

PIAN n contagious tropical skin disease

PIANI ▸ piano

PIANIC adj of piano

PIANINO n small upright piano

PIANISM n technique, skill, or artistry in playing the piano

PIANIST n person who plays the piano

PIANO n, adv **pianos**

PIANS ▸ pian

PIARIST n member of a Roman religious order

PIAS ▸ pia

PIASABA = piassava

PIASAVA = piassava

PIASTER = piastre

PIASTRE n standard monetary unit of South Vietnam

PIAZZA n **piazzas, piazze**

PIBAL n method of measuring wind **pibals**

PIBROCH n form of bagpipe music

PIC n photograph or illustration

PICA n abnormal craving to ingest substances

PICACHO n pointed solitary mountain

PICADOR n mounted bullfighter with a lance

PICAL adj relating to pica

PICAMAR n hydrocarbon extract of beechwood tar

PICANTE adj spicy

PICARA n female adventurer **picaras**

PICARO n roguish adventurer **picaros**

PICAS ▸ pica

PICCATA adj sautéed and served in a lemon sauce

PICCIES ▸ piccy

PICCOLO n

PICCY n picture or photograph

PICE n former Indian coin worth one sixty-fourth of a rupee

PICENE n type of hydrocarbon **picenes**

PICEOUS adj of, relating to, or resembling pitch

PICINE adj relating to woodpeckers

PICK vb, n

PICKAX = pickaxe

PICKAXE n, vb

PICKED ▶ pick

PICKEER vb make raid for booty

PICKER n person or thing that picks **pickers**

PICKERY n petty theft

PICKET n, vb **pickets**

PICKIER ▶ picky

PICKILY ▶ picky

PICKIN n small child

PICKING ▶ pick

PICKINS ▶ pickin

PICKLE n, vb

PICKLED adj

PICKLER ▶ pickle

PICKLES ▶ pickle

PICKMAW n type of gull

PICKOFF n baseball play

PICKS ▶ pick

PICKUP n small truck with an open body and low sides **pickups**

PICKY adj fussy

PICNIC n, vb **picnics**

PICOLIN variant of > picoline

PICONG n any teasing or satirical banter **picongs**

PICOT n any of pattern of small loops, as on lace ▷ vb decorate material with small loops

PICOTE adj (of material) picoted

PICOTED ▶ picot

PICOTEE n type of carnation

PICOTS ▶ picot

PICQUET vb provide early warning of attack

PICRA n powder of aloes and canella **picras**

PICRATE n any salt or ester of picric acid

PICRIC adj as in **picric acid** toxic sparingly soluble crystalline yellow acid

PICRITE n coarse-grained ultrabasic igneous rock

PICS ▶ pic

PICTURE n, vb

PICUL n unit of weight, used in China, Japan, and SE Asia

PICULET n small tropical woodpecker with a short tail

PICULS ▶ picul

PIDDLE vb urinate **piddled, piddler, piddles**

PIDDLY adj trivial

PIDDOCK n marine bivalve that bores into rock, clay, or wood

PIDGEON variant of ▶ pidgin

PIDGIN n pidgins

PIE n

PIEBALD adj, n

PIECE n pieced

PIECEN vb join broken threads **piecens**

PIECER n person who mends, repairs, or joins something **piecers**

PIECES ▶ piece

PIECING ▶ piece

PIED ▶ pi

PIEDISH n container for baking pies

PIEFORT = piedfort

PIEHOLE n person's mouth

PIEING ▶ pie

PIEMAN n seller of pies **piemen**

PIEND n salient angle **piends**

PIER n

PIERAGE n accommodation for ships at piers

PIERCE vb pierced, piercer, pierces

PIERID n type of butterfly **pierids**

PIERIS n American or Asiatic shrub

PIEROGI n Polish dumpling

PIERROT n clown or masquerader with a whitened face

PIERS ▶ pier

PIERST archaic spelling of ▶ pierced

PIERT n small plant with small greenish flowers **pierts**

PIES ▶ pie

PIET n magpie

PIETA n sculpture, painting, or drawing of the dead Christ, supported by the Virgin Mary **pietas**

PIETIES ▶ piety

PIETISM n exaggerated piety **pietist**

PIETS ▶ piet

PIETY n

PIEZO adj piezoelectric

PIFFERO n small rustic flute

PIFFLE n, vb **piffled**
PIFFLER n talker of nonsense
PIFFLES ▶ piffle
PIG n, vb
PIGBOAT n submarine
PIGEON n, vb pigeons
PIGFACE n creeping succulent plant
PIGFEED n food for pigs
PIGFISH n grunting fish of the North American Atlantic coast
PIGGED ▶ pig
PIGGERY n place for keeping and breeding pigs
PIGGIE = piggy
PIGGIER ▶ piggy
PIGGIES ▶ piggy
PIGGIN n small wooden bucket or tub
PIGGING ▶ pig
PIGGINS ▶ piggin
PIGGISH adj like a pig, esp in appetite or manners
PIGGY n child's word for a pig ▷ adj like a pig
PIGHT vb pierce **pighted**
PIGHTLE n small enclosure
PIGHTS ▶ pight
PIGLET n piglets
PIGLIKE ▶ pig
PIGLING n young pig
PIGMEAN = pygmaean
PIGMEAT less common name for ▶ pork
PIGMENT n, vb
PIGMIES ▶ pigmy
PIGMOID adj of pygmies
PIGMY = pygmy

PIGNOLI = pignolia
PIGNORA ▶ pignus
PIGNUS n pawn or pledge
PIGNUT n bitter nut of hickory trees **pignuts**
PIGOUT n binge **pigouts**
PIGPEN = pigsty
PIGPENS ▶ pigpen
PIGS ▶ pig
PIGSKIN n skin of the domestic pig ▷ adj made of pigskin
PIGSNEY = pigsny
PIGSNIE = pigsny
PIGSNY n former pet name for girl
PIGSTY = pigpen
PIGTAIL n
PIGWASH n wet feed for pigs
PIGWEED n coarse North American weed
PIING ▶ pi
PIKA n burrowing mammal
PIKAKE n type of Asian vine **pikakes**
PIKAS ▶ pika
PIKAU n pack, knapsack, or rucksack **pikaus**
PIKE n, vb, adj **piked**
PIKELET n small thick pancake
PIKEMAN n (formerly) soldier armed with a pike **pikemen**
PIKER n shirker **pikers**
PIKES ▶ pike
PIKI n bread made from blue cornmeal
PIKING ▶ pike
PIKINGS ▶ pike

PIKIS ▶ piki
PIKUL = picul
PIKULS ▶ pikul
PILA n pillar-like anatomical structure
PILAF = pilau
PILAFF = pilau
PILAFFS ▶ pilaff
PILAFS ▶ pilaf
PILAO = pilau
PILAOS ▶ pilao
PILAR adj relating to hair
PILAU n Middle Eastern dish **pilaus, pilaw**
PILAWS ▶ pilaw
PILCH n outer garment, originally one made of skin
PILCHER n scabbard for sword
PILCHES ▶ pilch
PILCORN n type of oat
PILCROW n paragraph mark
PILE n, vb
PILEA n plant which releases a cloud of pollen when shaken **pileas**
PILEATE adj (of birds) having a crest
PILED ▶ pile
PILEI ▶ pileus
PILEOUS adj hairy
PILER n placer of things on pile **pilers**
PILES pl n swollen veins in the rectum, haemorrhoids
PILEUM n top of a bird's head
PILEUP n multiple collision of vehicles **pileups**

PILEUS n upper cap-shaped part of a mushroom

PILFER vb pilfers

PILFERY n theft

PILGRIM n

PILI n Philippine tree with edible seeds resembling almonds

PILING n act of driving piles pilings

PILINUT n type of nut found in the Philippines

PILIS ▶ pili

PILL n, vb

PILLAGE vb, n

PILLAR n, vb pillars

PILLAU = pilau

PILLAUS ▶ pillau

PILLBOX n small box for pills

PILLED ▶ pill

PILLIE n pilchard pillies

PILLING ▶ pill

PILLION n, adv, vb

PILLOCK n stupid or annoying person

PILLORY n, vb

PILLOW n, vb pillows, pillowy

PILLS ▶ pill

PILOSE adj covered with fine soft hairs

PILOT n, adj, vb piloted

PILOTIS pl n posts raising a building up from the ground

PILOTS ▶ pilot

PILOUS = pilose

PILOW = pilau

PILOWS ▶ pilow

PILSNER n type of pale beer with a strong flavour of hops

PILULA n pill pilulae

PILULAR ▶ pilule

PILULAS ▶ pilula

PILULE n small pill pilules

PILUM n ancient Roman javelin

PILUS ▶ pili

PILY adj like wool or pile

PIMA n type of cotton pimas

PIMENT n wine flavoured with spices

PIMENTO = pimiento

PIMENTS ▶ piment

PIMP n, vb pimped, pimping

PIMPLE n pimpled, pimples, pimply

PIMPS ▶ pimp

PIN n, vb

PINA n cone of silver amalgam

PINANG n areca tree pinangs

PINAS ▶ pina

PINATA n papier-mâché party decoration filled with sweets pinatas

PINBALL vb

PINBONE n part of sirloin

PINCASE n case for holding pins

PINCER vb grip with pincers

PINCERS pl n

PINCH vb, n pinched, pincher, pinches

PINDAN n desert region of Western Australia pindans

PINDARI n former irregular Indian

horseman

PINDER n person who impounds pinders

PINDOWN n wrestling manoeuvre

PINE n, vb

PINEAL adj resembling a pine cone ▷ n pineal gland pineals

PINED ▶ pine

PINENE n isomeric terpene found in many essential oils pinenes

PINERY n place, esp a hothouse, where pineapples are grown

PINES ▶ pine

PINESAP n red herb of N America

PINETA ▶ pinetum

PINETUM n area of land where pine trees are grown

PINEY ▶ pine

PINFALL another name for ▶ fall

PINFISH n small porgy of the Atlantic

PINFOLD n pound for stray cattle ▷ vb gather or confine in or as if in a pinfold

PING n short high-pitched sound ▷ vb make such a noise pinged

PINGER n device, esp a timer, that makes a pinging sound pingers

PINGING ▶ ping

PINGLE vb enclose small area of ground pingled, pingler, pingles

PINGO n mound of earth or gravel formed in Arctic regions **pingoes, pingos**

PINGS ▷ ping

PINGUID adj fatty, oily, or greasy

PINGUIN = penguin

PINHEAD n head of a pin

PINHOLE n small hole made with or as if with a pin

PINIER ▷ piny

PINIES ▷ piny

PINIEST ▷ piny

PINING ▷ pine

PINION n, vb **pinions**

PINITE n greyish-green or brown mineral **pinites**

PINITOL n compound found in pinewood

PINK n, adj, vb **pinked**

PINKEN vb turn pink **pinkens**

PINKER n something that pinks **pinkers**

PINKEST ▷ pink

PINKEY n type of ship

PINKEYE n acute inflammation of the conjunctiva of the eye

PINKEYS ▷ pinkey

PINKIE n little finger

PINKIER ▷ pinky

PINKIES ▷ pinkie

PINKING ▷ pink

PINKISH ▷ pink

PINKLY ▷ pink

PINKO n person regarded as mildly left-wing **pinkoes, pinkos**

PINKS ▷ pink

PINKY adj of a pink colour

PINNA n external part of the ear

PINNACE n ship's boat

PINNAE ▷ pinna

PINNAL ▷ pinna

PINNAS ▷ pinna

PINNATE adj (of compound leaves) having leaflets growing opposite each other in pairs

PINNED ▷ pin

PINNER n person or thing that pins **pinners**

PINNET n pinnacle **pinnets**

PINNIE = pinny

PINNIES ▷ pinnie

PINNING ▷ pin

PINNOCK n small bird

PINNOED adj held or bound by the arms

PINNULA = pinnule

PINNULE n lobe of a leaflet of a pinnate compound leaf

PINNY informal or child's name for ▷ pinafore

PINOCLE = pinochle

PINOLE n flour made in the southwestern United States **pinoles**

PINON n low-growing pine **pinones, pinons**

PINOT n any of several grape varieties **pinots**

PINS ▷ pin

PINT n

PINTA n pint of milk

PINTADA = pintado

PINTADO n species of seagoing petrel

PINTAIL n greyish-brown duck with a pointed tail

PINTANO n tropical reef fish

PINTAS ▷ pinta

PINTLE n pin or bolt forming the pivot of a hinge **pintles**

PINTO adj marked with patches of white ▷ n pinto horse **pintoes, pintos**

PINTS ▷ pint

PINUP n picture of a sexually attractive person **pinups**

PINWALE n fabric with narrow ridges

PINWEED n herb with tiny flowers

PINWORK n (in needlepoint lace) fine raised stitches

PINWORM n parasitic nematode worm

PINXIT vb (he or she) painted (it)

PINY variant of ▷ peony

PINYIN n system of romanized spelling for the Chinese language

PINYON n low-growing pine **pinyons**

PIOLET n type of ice axe **piolets**

PION n type of subatomic particle

PIONED adj abounding in marsh marigolds

PIONEER n, vb **pioner**

PIONERS ▶ pioner
PIONEY = peony
PIONEYS ▶ pioney
PIONIC ▶ pion
PIONIES ▶ piony
PIONING n work of pioneers
PIONS ▶ pion
PIONY = peony
PIOPIO n New Zealand thrush, thought to be extinct **piopios**
PIOSITY n grandiose display of piety
PIOTED adj pied
PIOUS adj piously
PIOY variant of ▶ **peeoy**
PIOYE variant of ▶ **peeoy**
PIOYES ▶ pioye
PIOYS ▶ pioy
PIP n, vb
PIPA n tongueless S American toad
PIPAGE n pipes collectively **pipages**
PIPAL = peepul
PIPALS ▶ pipal
PIPAS ▶ pipa
PIPE n, vb
PIPEAGE = pipage
PIPED ▶ pipe
PIPEFUL ▶ pipe
PIPER n
PIPERIC ▶ piperine
PIPERS ▶ piper
PIPES ▶ pipe
PIPET = pipette
PIPETS ▶ pipet
PIPETTE n, vb
PIPI n edible mollusc often used as bait
PIPIER ▶ pipe
PIPIEST ▶ pipe

PIPING n pipings
PIPIS ▶ pipi
PIPIT n pipits
PIPKIN = piggin
PIPKINS ▶ pipkin
PIPLESS ▶ pip
PIPPED ▶ pip
PIPPIER ▶ pippy
PIPPIN n
PIPPING ▶ pip
PIPPINS ▶ pippin
PIPPY adj containing many pips
PIPS ▶ pip
PIPUL n Indian fig tree **pipuls**
PIPY ▶ pipe
PIQUANT adj
PIQUE n, vb piqued, piques
PIQUET n card game for two ▷ vb play game of piquet **piquets**
PIQUING ▶ pique
PIR n Sufi master
PIRACY n
PIRAGUA = pirogue
PIRAI n large S American fish **pirais**
PIRANA = piranha
PIRANAS ▶ pirana
PIRANHA n
PIRATE n, vb pirated, pirates, piratic
PIRAYA = pirai
PIRAYAS ▶ piraya
PIRL n ripple in water **pirls**
PIRN n reel or bobbin
PIRNIE n stripy nightcap **pirnies**
PIRNIT adj striped
PIRNS ▶ pirn
PIROG n large pie filled

with meat, vegetables, etc
PIROGEN n turnovers made from kneaded dough
PIROGHI ▶ pirog
PIROGI ▶ pirog
PIROGUE n any of various kinds of dugout canoes
PIROJKI = piroshki
PIROQUE = pirogue
PIRS ▶ pir
PIS ▶ pi
PISCARY n place where fishing takes place
PISCINA n stone basin where water used at Mass is poured away
PISCINE n pond or pool
PISCO n S American brandy **piscos**
PISE n rammed earth or clay used to make floors or walls **pises**
PISH interj exclamation of impatience or contempt ▷ vb make this exclamation at (someone or something) **pished**
PISHEOG ▶ pishogue
PISHER n Yiddish term for small boy **pishers**
PISHES ▶ pish
PISHING ▶ pish
PISHOGE ▶ pishogue
PISKIES ▶ pisky
PISKY n Cornish fairy
PISMIRE archaic or dialect word for ▶ ant
PISO n peso of the Philippines **pisos**
PISTE n ski slope **pistes**

PISTIL n pistils
PISTOL n, vb
PISTOLE n gold coin formerly used in Europe
PISTOLS ▶ pistol
PISTON n pistons
PISTOU n French sauce **pistous**
PIT n, vb
PITA n any of several agave plants yielding a strong fibre
PITAPAT adv with quick light taps ▷ n such taps ▷ vb make quick light taps or beats
PITARA variant of ▶ petara
PITARAH variant of ▶ petara
PITARAS ▶ pitara
PITAS ▶ pita
PITAYA = pitahaya
PITAYAS ▶ pitaya
PITCH vb, n pitched
PITCHER n
PITCHES ▶ pitch
PITCHY adj full of or covered with pitch
PITEOUS adj
PITFALL n
PITH n, vb
PITHEAD n top of a mine shaft and the buildings and hoisting gear around it
PITHED ▶ pith
PITHFUL ▶ pith
PITHIER ▶ pithy
PITHILY ▶ pithy
PITHING ▶ pith
PITHOI ▶ pithos
PITHOS n large ceramic

container for oil or grain
PITHS ▶ pith
PITHY adj
PITIED, pitier, pitiers, pities ▶ pity
PITIETH vb as in it **pitieth me** archaic inflection of 'pity'
PITIFUL adj
PITMAN n coal miner ▷ n connecting rod (in a machine) **pitmans, pitmen**
PITON n metal spike used in climbing to secure a rope **pitons**
PITS ▶ pit
PITSAW n large saw formerly used for cutting logs into planks **pitsaws**
PITTA n small brightly coloured ground-dwelling tropical bird **pittas**
PITTED ▶ pit
PITTEN adj having been put
PITTER vb make pattering sound **pitters**
PITTING ▶ pit
PITTITE n occupant of a theatre pit
PITUITA n thick nasal secretion
PITUITE n mucus
PITURI n Australian solanaceous shrub **pituris**
PITY n, vb **pitying**
PIU adv more (quickly,

softly, etc)
PITHS ▶ pith
PIUM n stinging insect **piums**
PIUPIU n skirt worn by Māoris on ceremonial occasions **piupius**
PIVOT n, vb
PIVOTAL adj of crucial importance
PIVOTED ▶ pivot
PIVOTER ▶ pivot
PIVOTS ▶ pivot
PIX less common spelling of ▶ pyx
PIXEL n any of a number of very small picture elements **pixels**
PIXES ▶ pix
PIXIE n
PIXIES ▶ pixy
PIXY = pixie
PIXYISH ▶ pixy
PIZAZZ = pizzazz
PIZAZZY ▶ pizazz
PIZE vb strike (someone a blow) **pized, pizes, pizing**
PIZZA n pizzas
PIZZAZ = pzazz
PIZZAZZ n attractive combination of energy and style
PIZZLE n penis of an animal, esp a bull **pizzles**
PLAAS n farm **plaases**
PLACARD n, vb
PLACATE vb
PLACCAT variant of ▶ placket
PLACE n, vb
PLACEBO n
PLACED ▶ place

PLACER *n* surface sediment containing particles of gold or some other valuable mineral **placers**

PLACES ▶ place

PLACET *n* vote or expression of assent **placets**

PLACID *adj*

PLACING *n* method of issuing securities to the public using an intermediary

PLACIT *n* decree or dictum

PLACITA ▶ placitum

PLACITS ▶ placit

PLACK *n* small former Scottish coin

PLACKET *n* opening at the waist of a dress or skirt for buttons or zips or for access to a pocket

PLACKS ▶ plack

PLACOID *adj* platelike or flattened ▷ *n* fish with placoid scales

PLAFOND *n* ceiling, esp one having ornamentation

PLAGAL *adj* (of a cadence) progressing from the subdominant to the tonic chord

PLAGE *n* bright patch in the sun's chromosphere **plages**

PLAGIUM *n* crime of kidnapping

PLAGUE *n, vb* plagued, plaguer, plagues

PLAGUEY = plaguy

PLAGUY *adj* disagreeable or vexing ▷ *adv* disagreeably or annoyingly

PLAICE *n* plaices

PLAID *n, vb* plaided, plaids

PLAIN *adj, n, adv, vb* plained, plainer, plainly

PLAINS *pl n* extensive tracts of flat treeless countryside

PLAINT *n* complaint or lamentation **plaints**

PLAIT *n, vb* plaited, plaiter, plaits

PLAN *n, vb*

PLANAR *adj* of or relating to a plane

PLANATE *adj* having been flattened

PLANCH *vb* cover with planks **planche**

PLANE *n, adj, vb* planed

PLANER *n* machine with a cutting tool that makes repeated horizontal strokes **planers**

PLANES ▶ plane

PLANET *n* planets

PLANING ▶ plane

PLANISH *vb* give a smooth surface to (a metal)

PLANK *n, vb* planked, planks

PLANNED ▶ plan

PLANNER *n* person who makes plans

PLANS ▶ plan

PLANT *n, vb*

PLANTA *n* sole of foot **plantae**

PLANTAR *adj* of, relating to, or occurring on the sole of the foot

PLANTAS ▶ planta

PLANTED ▶ plant

PLANTER *n* owner of a plantation

PLANTS ▶ plant

PLANULA *n* free-swimming larva of hydrozoan coelenterates

PLANURY *another name for* ▶ planury

PLANXTY *n* Celtic melody for harp

PLAP = plop

PLAPPED ▶ plap

PLAPS ▶ plap

PLAQUE *n* plaques

PLASH = pleach

PLASHED ▶ plash

PLASHER *n* type of farm tool

PLASHES ▶ plash

PLASHET *n* small pond

PLASHY *adj* wet or marshy

PLASM = plasma

PLASMA *n* plasmas, plasmic

PLASMID *n* small circle of bacterial DNA

PLASMIN *n* proteolytic enzyme that causes fibrinolysis in blood clots

PLASMON *n* sum total of plasmagenes in a cell

PLASMS ▶ plasm

PLAST *archaic past participle of* ▶ place

PLASTE archaic past participle of ▸ **place**

PLASTER n, vb

PLASTIC n, adj

PLASTID n small particle in the cells of plants and some animals

PLAT n small area of ground

PLATAN n plane tree **platane, platans**

PLATE n, vb

PLATEAU n, vb

PLATED adj

PLATEN n roller of a typewriter, against which the paper is held **platens**

PLATER n person or thing that plates **platers**

PLATES ▸ **plate**

PLATIER ▸ **platy**

PLATIES ▸ **platy**

PLATINA n alloy of platinum and several other metals

PLATING n coating of metal

PLATOON n, vb

PLATS ▸ **plat**

PLATTED ▸ **plat**

PLATTER n

PLATY adj of, relating to, or designating rocks the constituents of which occur in flaky layers ▸ n brightly coloured freshwater fish

PLATYPI > **platypus**

PLATYS ▸ **platy**

PLAUDIT n expression of enthusiastic approval

PLAY vb, n

PLAYA n (in the US) temporary lake in a desert basin

PLAYACT vb pretend or make believe

PLAYAS ▸ **playa**

PLAYBOY n

PLAYDAY n day given to play

PLAYED ▸ **play**

PLAYER n person who plays a game or sport **players**

PLAYFUL adj

PLAYING ▸ **play**

PLAYLET n short play

PLAYOFF n extra contest to decide the winner when two or more competitors are tied

PLAYPEN n

PLAYS ▸ **play**

PLAZA n **plazas**

PLEA n, vb

PLEACH vb interlace the stems or boughs of (a tree or hedge)

PLEAD vb **pleaded, pleader, pleads**

PLEAED ▸ **plea**

PLEAING ▸ **plea**

PLEAS ▸ **plea**

PLEASE vb, adv **pleased, pleaser, pleases**

PLEAT n, vb **pleated**

PLEATER n attachment on a sewing machine that makes pleats

PLEATS ▸ **pleat**

PLEB n common vulgar person

PLEBBY adj common or vulgar

PLEBE n member of the lowest class at the US Naval Academy or Military Academy

PLEBEAN old variant of > **plebeian**

PLEBES ▸ **plebe**

PLEBIFY vb make plebeian

PLEBS n common people

PLECTRA ▸ **plectrum**

PLECTRE variant of > **plectrum**

PLED ▸ **plead**

PLEDGE n, vb **pledged**

PLEDGEE n person to whom a pledge is given

PLEDGER = **pledgor**

PLEDGES ▸ **pledge**

PLEDGET n small flattened pad of wool, cotton, etc

PLEDGOR n person who gives or makes a pledge

PLEIAD n brilliant or talented group, esp one with seven members **pleiads**

PLENA ▸ **plenum**

PLENARY adj, n

PLENCH n tool combining wrench and pliers

PLENIPO n plenipotentiary diplomat

PLENISH vb fill, stock, or resupply

PLENISM n philosophical theory **plenist**

PLENTY n, adj, adv

PLENUM n enclosure containing gas at a high pressure **plenums**

PLEON n abdomen of crustacean

PLEONAL adj of the abdomen of a crustacean

PLEONIC ▸ pleon

PLEONS ▸ pleon

PLEOPOD another name for **▸ swimmeret**

PLERION n filled-centre supernova remnant

PLEROMA n abundance

PLEROME n central column in growing stem or root

PLESH n small pool **pleshes**

PLESSOR = plexor

PLEUCH = pleugh

PLEUCHS ▸ pleuch

PLEUGH Scottish word for **▸ plough**

PLEUGHS ▸ pleugh

PLEURA, pleurae, pleural, pleuras ▸ pleuron

PLEURON n part of the cuticle of arthropods

PLEW n (formerly in Canada) beaver skin used as a standard unit of value in the fur trade **plews**

PLEX n shortening of multiplex

PLEXAL ▸ plexus

PLEXES ▸ plex

PLEXOR n small hammer with a rubber head **plexors**

PLEXURE n act of weaving together

PLEXUS n complex network of nerves or blood vessels

PLIABLE adj pliably

PLIANCY ▸ pliant

PLIANT adj

PLICA n folding over of parts, such as a fold of skin, muscle, peritoneum, etc **plicae, plical**

PLICATE adj having or arranged in parallel folds or ridges ▷ vb arrange into parallel folds

PLIE n classic ballet practice posture with back erect and knees bent

PLIED ▸ ply

PLIER n person who plies a trade

PLIERS pl n

PLIES ▸ ply

PLIGHT n plights

PLIM vb swell with water **plimmed, plims**

PLIMSOL = plimsole

PLING n (in computer jargon) an exclamation mark **plings**

PLINK n short sharp often metallic sound ▷ vb make such a noise **plinked, plinker, plinks**

PLINKY adj (of a sound) short, sharp, and often metallic

PLINTH n plinths

PLISKIE n practical joke **plisky**

PLISSE n fabric with a wrinkled finish, achieved by treatment involving caustic soda **plisses**

PLOAT vb thrash **ploated, ploats**

PLOD vb, n plodded

PLODDER n person who plods

PLODGE vb wade in water, esp the sea ▷ n act of wading **plodged, plodges**

PLODS ▸ plod

PLOIDY n number of copies of set of chromosomes in cell

PLONG obsolete variant of **▸ plunge**

PLONGD ▸ plong

PLONGE ▸ plunge

PLONGED ▸ plonge

PLONGES ▸ plonge

PLONGS ▸ plong

PLONK vb, n, interj **plonked**

PLONKER n stupid person

PLONKO n alcoholic, esp one who drinks wine **plonkos**

PLONKS ▸ plonk

PLONKY ▸ plonk

PLOOK = plouk

PLOOKIE = plouky

PLOOKS ▸ plook

PLOOKY ▸ plook

PLOP n, vb, interj **plopped, plops**

PLOSION n sound of an abrupt break or closure, esp the audible release of a stop

PLOSIVE adj pronounced with a sudden release of breath ▷ n plosive consonant

PLOT n, vb plotful, plots, plotted

PLOTTER ▷ plouter

PLOTTIE n hot spiced drink

PLOTTY adj intricately plotted

PLOTZ vb faint or collapse plotzed, plotzes

PLOUGH n, vb ploughs

PLOUK n pimple ploukie, plouks, plouky

PLOUTER = plowter

PLOVER n plovers, plovery

PLOW = plough

PLOWBOY = ploughboy

PLOWED, plower, plowers, plowing ▷ plow

PLOWMAN = ploughman

PLOWMEN ▷ plowman

PLOWS ▷ plow

PLOWTER vb work or play in water or mud ▷ n act of plowtering

PLOY n, vb ployed, ploying, ploys

PLU = plew

PLUCK n, vb plucked, plucker, plucks

PLUCKY adj brave

PLUE = plew

PLUES ▷ plue

PLUFF vb expel in puffs pluffed, pluffs, pluffy

PLUG n, vb plugged, plugger

PLUGOLA n plugging of products on television

PLUGS ▷ plug

PLUM n, adj

PLUMAGE n

PLUMATE adj of, relating to, or possessing one or more feathers or plumes

PLUMB vb, adv, n plumbed

PLUMBER n

PLUMBIC adj of or containing lead in the tetravalent state

PLUMBS ▷ plumb

PLUMBUM n obsolete name for lead (the metal)

PLUMCOT n hybrid of apricot and plum

PLUME n, vb plumed

PLUMERY n plumes collectively

PLUMES ▷ plume

PLUMIER ▷ plumy

PLUMING ▷ plume

PLUMIST n person who makes plumes

PLUMMER ▷ plum

PLUMMET vb, n

PLUMMY adj of, full of, or like plums

PLUMOSE = plumate

PLUMOUS adj having plumes or feathers

PLUMP adj, vb, n, adv plumped

PLUMPEN vb make or become plump

PLUMPER n pad carried in the mouth by actors to round out the cheeks

PLUMPIE = plumpy

PLUMPLY ▷ plump

PLUMPS ▷ plump

PLUMPY adj plump

PLUMS ▷ plum

PLUMULA n down feather

PLUMULE n embryonic shoot of seed-bearing plants

PLUMY adj like a feather

PLUNDER vb, n

PLUNGE vb, n plunged

PLUNGER n

PLUNGES ▷ plunge

PLUNK vb pluck the strings of (a banjo etc) to produce a twanging sound ▷ n act or sound of plunking ▷ interj exclamation imitative of the sound of something plunking ▷ adv exactly plunked, plunker, plunks

PLUNKY adj sounding like plucked banjo string

PLURAL adj, n plurals

PLURRY euphemism for ▷ bloody

PLUS vb

PLUSAGE = plussage

PLUSED ▷ plus

PLUSES ▷ plus

PLUSH n, adj plusher, plushes, plushly, plushy

PLUSING ▷ plus

PLUSSED ▸ plus
PLUSSES ▸ plus
PLUTEAL ▸ pluteus
PLUTEI ▸ pluteus
PLUTEUS n larva of sea urchin
PLUTON n any mass of igneous rock that has solidified below the surface of the earth **plutons**
PLUVIAL adj of or caused by the action of rain ▸ n of or relating to rainfall or precipitation
PLUVIAN n crocodile bird
PLUVIUS adj as in **pluvius insurance** insurance against rain
PLY vb, n
PLYER n person who plies trade **plyers**
PLYING ▸ ply
PLYWOOD n
PNEUMA n person's vital spirit, soul, or creative energy **pneumas**
PO n chamber pot
POA n type of grass
POACH vb **poached**
POACHER n person who catches animals illegally on someone else's land
POACHES ▸ poach
POACHY adj (of land) wet and soft
POAKA n type of stilt (bird) native to New Zealand **poakas**
POAKE n waste matter

from tanning of hides **poakes**
POAS ▸ poa
POBLANO n variety of chilli pepper
POBOY n New Orleans sandwich **poboys**
POCHARD n European diving duck
POCHAY n closed horse-drawn four-wheeled coach **pochays**
POCHOIR n print made from stencils
POCK n pus-filled blister resulting from smallpox ▸ vb mark with scars
POCKARD variant of ▸ pochard
POCKED ▸ pock
POCKET n, vb, adj **pockets**
POCKIER ▸ pock
POCKIES pl n woollen mittens
POCKILY ▸ pock
POCKING ▸ pock
POCKPIT n mark left on skin after a pock has gone
POCKS ▸ pock
POCKY ▸ pock
POCO adv little
POCOSEN = pocosin
POCOSIN n swamp in US upland coastal region **pocoson**
POD n, vb
PODAGRA n gout of the foot or big toe
PODAL adj relating to feet

PODALIC adj relating to feet
PODCAST n audio file able to be downloaded and listened to on a computer or MP3 player ▸ vb make available in this format
PODDED ▸ pod
PODDIE n user of or enthusiast for the iPod, a portable digital music player
PODDIER ▸ poddy
PODDIES ▸ poddy
PODDING ▸ pod
PODDLE vb move or travel in a leisurely manner **poddled, poddles**
PODDY n, adj
PODESTA n (in modern Italy) subordinate magistrate in some towns
PODEX n posterior **podexes**
PODGE n short chubby person **podges**
PODGIER ▸ podgy
PODGILY ▸ podgy
PODGY adj
PODIA ▸ podium
PODIAL ▸ podium
PODITE n crustacean leg **podites**
PODITIC adj similar to the limb segment of an arthropod
PODIUM n **podiums**
PODLEY n young coalfish **podleys**
PODLIKE ▸ pod
PODS ▸ pod

PODSOL = podzol

PODSOLS ▶ podsol

PODZOL n type of soil characteristic of coniferous forest regions **podzols**

POEM n poems

POEP n emission of gas from the anus **poeps**

POESIED ▶ poesy

POESIES ▶ poesy

POESY n poetry ▷ vb write poems

POET n

POETESS n female poet

POETIC adj

POETICS n principles and forms of poetry or the study of these

POETISE = poëticize

POETIZE = poëticize

POETRY n

POETS ▶ poet

POFFLE n small piece of land **poffles**

POGEY n financial or other relief given to the unemployed by the government **pogeys**

POGGE n European marine scorpaenoid fish **pogges**

POGIES ▶ pogy

POGO vb jump up and down in one spot **pogoed, pogoer, pogoers, pogoing**

POGONIA n orchid with pink or white fragrant flowers

POGONIP n icy winter fog

POGOS ▶ pogo

POGROM n organized persecution and massacre ▷ vb carry out a pogrom **pogroms**

POGY = pogey

POH interj exclamation expressing contempt or disgust

POHIRI variant spelling of ▶ powhiri

POHIRIS ▶ pohiri

POI n ball of woven flax swung rhythmically by Māori women during poi dances

POILU n infantryman in the French Army **poilus**

POINADO old variant of ▶ poniard

POIND vb take (property of a debtor) in execution or by way of distress **poinded, poinder, poinds**

POINT n, vb

POINTE n tip of the toe

POINTED adj

POINTEL n engraver's tool

POINTER n

POINTES ▶ pointe

POINTS ▶ point

POINTY adj having a sharp point or points

POIS ▶ poi

POISE n, vb

POISED adj

POISER n balancing organ of some insects **poisers**

POISES ▶ poise

POISHA n monetary unit of Bangladesh

POISING ▶ poise

POISON n, vb poisons

POISSON n fish

POITIN variant spelling of ▶ poteen

POITINS ▶ poitin

POITREL n breastplate of horse's armour

POKABLE ▶ poke

POKAL n tall drinking cup **pokals**

POKE vb, n poked

POKEFUL n contents of small bag

POKER n pokers

POKES ▶ poke

POKEY = pokie

POKEYS ▶ pokey

POKIE n poker machine

POKIER, pokies, pokiest, pokily ▶ poky

POKING ▶ poke

POKY adj

POL n political campaigner

POLACCA = polacre

POLACRE n three-masted sailing vessel

POLAR adj, n

POLARON n kind of electron

POLARS ▶ polar

POLDER n, vb polders

POLE n, vb

POLEAX = poleaxe

POLEAXE vb, n

POLECAT n

POLED ▶ pole

POLEIS ▶ polis

POLEMIC n, adj

POLENTA n thick porridge made in Italy, usually from maize

POLER n person or thing that poles, esp a punter **polers**
POLES ▸ pole
POLEY adj (of cattle) hornless or polled ▸ n animal with horns removed
POLEYN n piece of armour for protecting the knee **poleyns**
POLICE n, vb **policed**
POLICER n computer device controlling use
POLICES ▸ police
POLICY n
POLIES ▸ poly
POLING ▸ pole
POLINGS ▸ pole
POLIO n **polios**
POLIS n ancient Greek city-state **polises**
POLISH vb, n
POLITE adj **politer**
POLITIC adj
POLITY n politically organized state, church, or society
POLJE n large elliptical depression in karst regions **poljes**
POLK vb dance a polka
POLKA n, vb **polkaed**, **polkas**
POLKED ▸ polk
POLKING ▸ polk
POLKS ▸ polk
POLL n, vb
POLLACK n food fish related to the cod, found in northern seas
POLLAN n whitefish that occurs in lakes in

Northern Ireland **pollans**
POLLARD n animal that has shed its horns or has had them removed ▸ vb cut off the top of (a tree) to make it grow bushy
POLLAXE = poleaxe
POLLED adj (of animals, esp cattle) having the horns cut off or being naturally hornless
POLLEE ▸ poll
POLLEES ▸ poll
POLLEN n, vb **pollens**
POLLENT adj strong
POLLER ▸ poll
POLLERS ▸ poll
POLLEX n first digit of the forelimb of amphibians, reptiles, birds, and mammals
POLLICY obsolete spelling of ▸ policy
POLLIES ▸ polly
POLLING n casting or registering of votes at an election
POLLIST n one advocating the use of polls
POLLMAN n one passing a degree without honours **pollmen**
POLLOCK = pollack
POLLS ▸ poll
POLLUTE vb
POLLY n politician
POLO n
POLOIST n devotee of polo
POLONIE = polony

POLONY n bologna sausage
POLOS ▸ polo
POLS ▸ pol
POLT n thump or blow ▸ vb strike **polted**, **polting**, **polts**
POLY n polytechnic
POLYACT adj (of a sea creature) having many tentacles or limb-like protrusions
POLYCOT n plant that has or appears to have more than two cotyledons
POLYENE n organic chemical compound
POLYGAM n plant of the Polygamia class
POLYGON n
POLYMER n
POLYNIA = polynya
POLYNYA n stretch of open water surrounded by ice **polynyi**
POLYOL n type of alcohol **polyols**
POLYOMA n type of tumour caused by virus
POLYP n polype
POLYPED = polypod
POLYPES ▸ polype
POLYPI ▸ polypus
POLYPOD adj (esp of insect larvae) having many legs or similar appendages ▸ n animal of this type
POLYPS ▸ polyp
POLYPUS = polyp
POLYS ▸ poly

POLYZOA n small mosslike aquatic creatures

POMACE n apple pulp left after pressing for juice **pomaces**

POMADE n perfumed oil put on the hair to make it smooth and shiny ▷ vb put pomade on **pomaded, pomades**

POMATO n hybrid of tomato and potato

POMATUM = pomade

POMBE n any alcoholic drink **pombes**

POME n fleshy fruit of the apple and related plants

POMELO n edible yellow fruit, like a grapefruit **pomelos**

POMEROY n bullet used to down airships

POMES ▶ pome

POMFRET n small black rounded liquorice sweet

POMMEE adj (of cross) having end of each arm ending in disk

POMMEL = pummel

POMMELE adj having a pommel

POMMELS ▶ pommel

POMO n postmodernism **pomos**

POMP n

POMPANO n deep-bodied carangid food fish

POMPELO n large Asian citrus fruit

POMPEY vb mollycoddle **pompeys**

POMPIER adj slavishly conventional

POMPION n pumpkin

POMPOM n decorative ball of tufted wool, silk, etc **pompoms, pompon**

POMPONS ▶ pompon

POMPOON = pompom

POMPOUS adj

POMPS ▶ pomp

POMROY variant of ▶ pomeroy

POMROYS ▶ pomroy

POMS ▶ pom

PONCEAU n scarlet red

PONCHO n loose circular cloak with a hole for the head **ponchos**

POND n, vb

PONDAGE n water held in reservoir

PONDED ▶ pond

PONDER vb **ponders**

PONDING ▶ pond

PONDOK n (in southern Africa) crudely made house or shack **pondoks**

PONDS ▶ pond

PONE n bread made of maize

PONENT adj westerly

PONES ▶ pone

PONEY = pony

PONEYS ▶ poney

PONG n, vb

PONGA n tall New Zealand tree fern **pongas**

PONGED ▶ pong

PONGEE n thin plain-weave silk fabric **pongees**

PONGID n primate of the family which includes the gibbons and the great apes **pongids**

PONGIER ▶ pong

PONGING ▶ pong

PONGO n anthropoid ape, esp an orang-utan or (formerly) a gorilla **pongoes, pongos**

PONGS ▶ pong

PONGY ▶ pong

PONIARD n small slender dagger ▷ vb stab with a poniard

PONIED ▶ pony

PONIES ▶ pony

PONK n evil spirit ▷ vb stink **ponked, ponking, ponks**

PONS n bridge of connecting tissue

PONT n (in South Africa) river ferry

PONTAGE n tax paid for repairing bridge

PONTAL adj of or relating to the pons

PONTES ▶ pons

PONTIC adj of or relating to the pons

PONTIE = ponty

PONTIES ▶ ponty

PONTIFF n

PONTIFY vb speak or behave in a pompous or dogmatic manner

PONTIL = punty

PONTILE adj relating to pons ▷ n metal bar used in glass-making

PONTILS ▶ pontil

PONTINE adj of or relating to bridges

PONTON variant of ▶ pontoon

PONTONS ▶ ponton

PONTOON n, vb

PONTS ▶ pont

PONTY n rod used for shaping molten glass

PONY n, vb ponying

PONZU n type of Japanese dipping sauce ponzus

POO vb defecate

POOCH n slang word for dog ▷ vb bulge or protrude pooched, pooches

POOD n unit of weight, used in Russia

POODLE n poodles

POODS ▶ pood

POOED ▶ poo

POOGYE n Hindu nose-flute poogyes

POOH interj exclamation of disdain, contempt, or disgust ▷ vb make such an exclamation poohed, poohing, poohs

POOING ▶ poo

POOJA variant of ▶ puja

POOJAH variant of ▶ puja

POOJAHS ▶ poojah

POOJAS ▶ pooja

POOK vb pluck

POOKA n malevolent Irish spirit pookas

POOKING ▶ pook

POOKIT ▶ pook

POOKS ▶ pook

POOL n, vb pooled

POOLER n person taking part in pool poolers

POOLING ▶ pool

POOLS pl n organized nationwide gambling pool

POON n SE Asian tree

POONAC n coconut residue poonacs

POONS ▶ poon

POOP n raised part at the back of a sailing ship ▷ vb (of a wave or sea) break over the stern of (a vessel) pooped

POOPER n as in party pooper person who spoils other people's enjoyment poopers

POOPING ▶ poop

POOPS ▶ poop

POOR adj poorer, poorest

POORI n unleavened Indian bread pooris

POORISH ▶ poor

POORLY adv, adj

POORT n (in South Africa) steep narrow mountain pass poorts

POOS ▶ poo

POOT vb break wind pooted, pooter, pooters, pooting

POOTLE vb travel or go in a relaxed or leisurely manner pootled, pootles

POOTS ▶ poot

POP vb, n, adj

POPADUM = poppadom

POPCORN n

POPE n bishop of Rome as head of the Roman Catholic Church

POPEDOM n office or dignity of a pope

POPERA n music drawing on opera or classical music and aiming for popular appeal poperas

POPERIN n kind of pear

POPES ▶ pope

POPETTE n young female fan or performer of pop music

POPEYED adj staring in astonishment

POPGUN n toy gun that fires a pellet or cork by means of compressed air popguns

POPJOY vb amuse oneself popjoys

POPLAR n poplars

POPLIN n ribbed cotton material poplins

POPOVER n individual Yorkshire pudding, often served with roast beef

POPPA = papa

POPPAS ▶ poppa

POPPED ▶ pop

POPPER n poppers

POPPET n term of affection for a small child or sweetheart poppets

POPPIED adj covered with poppies

POPPIER ▶ poppy

POPPIES ▶ poppy

POPPING ▶ pop
POPPISH adj like pop music
POPPIT n bead used to form necklace **poppits**
POPPLE vb (of boiling water or a choppy sea) to heave or toss **poppled, popples**
POPPLY adj covered in small bumps
POPPY n, adj
POPRIN = **poperin**
POPS ▶ pop
POPSIE = **popsy**
POPSIES ▶ popsy
POPSOCK n women's knee-length nylon stocking
POPSTER n pop star
POPSY n attractive young woman
POPULAR adj, n
PORAE n large edible sea fish of New Zealand waters **poraes**
PORAL adj relating to pores
PORANGI adj crazy
PORCH n **porches**
PORCINE adj of or like a pig
PORCINI ▶ porcino
PORCINO n edible woodland fungus
PORE n, vb **pored**
PORER n person who pores
PORERS ▶ pore
PORES ▶ pore
PORGE vb cleanse (slaughtered animal) ceremonially **porged, porges**

PORGIE = **porgy**
PORGIES ▶ porgy
PORGING ▶ porge
PORGY n any of various sparid fishes
PORIER ▶ pory
PORIEST ▶ pory
PORIFER n type of invertebrate
PORINA n larva of a moth which causes damage to grassland **porinas**
PORING ▶ pore
PORISM n type of mathematical proposition **porisms**
PORK vb, n **porked**
PORKER n pig raised for food **porkers**
PORKIER ▶ porky
PORKIES ▶ porky
PORKING ▶ pork
PORKPIE n hat with a round flat crown and a brim that can be turned up or down
PORKS ▶ pork
PORKY adj of or like pork ▷ n lie
PORLOCK vb interrupt or intrude at an awkward moment
PORN n pornography
PORNIER ▶ porny
PORNO = **porn**
PORNOS ▶ porno
PORNS ▶ porn
PORNY adj pornographic
POROSE adj pierced with small pores
POROSES ▶ porosis
POROSIS n porous

condition of bones
POROUS adj
PORPESS n type of fish
PORRECT adj extended forwards ▷ vb stretch forward
PORRIGO n disease of the scalp
PORT = **porthole**
PORTA n aperture in an organ
PORTAGE n (route for) transporting boats overland ▷ vb transport (boats) in this way
PORTAL n **portals**
PORTAS ▶ porta
PORTATE adj diagonally athwart escutcheon
PORTED ▶ port
PORTEND vb be a sign of
PORTENT n
PORTER n, vb **porters**
PORTESS variant of > portesse
PORTHOS = **portesse**
PORTICO n
PORTIER ▶ port
PORTING ▶ port
PORTION n, vb
PORTLY adj
PORTMAN n inhabitant of port **portmen**
PORTOUS variant of > portesse
PORTRAY vb
PORTS ▶ port
PORTY adj like port
PORY adj containing pores
POS ▶ po
POSABLE ▶ pose

POSADA n inn in a Spanish-speaking country **posadas**

POSAUNE n organ chorus reed

POSE vb, n **posed**

POSER n **posers**

POSES ▶ **pose**

POSEUR n person who behaves in an affected way to impress others **poseurs**

POSEUSE n female poseur

POSEY adj (of a place) for, characteristic of, or full of posers

POSH adj, adv, vb **poshed, posher, poshes, poshest, poshing, poshly**

POSHO n corn meal **poshos**

POSIER ▶ **posy**

POSIES ▶ **posy**

POSIEST ▶ **posy**

POSING ▶ **pose**

POSINGS ▶ **pose**

POSIT vb lay down as a basis for argument ▶ n fact, idea, etc, that is posited **posited**

POSITIF n (on older organs) manual controlling soft stops

POSITON n part of chromosome

POSITS ▶ **posit**

POSNET n small basin or dish **posnets**

POSOLE n hominy **posoles**

POSS vb wash (clothes) by agitating them with

a long rod, pole, etc

POSSE n group of men organized to maintain law and order

POSSED ▶ **poss**

POSSER n short stick used for stirring clothes in a washtub **possers**

POSSES ▶ **posse**

POSSESS vb

POSSET n drink of hot milk curdled with ale, beer, etc, flavoured with spices ▶ vb treat with a posset **possets**

POSSIE n place **possies**

POSSING ▶ **poss**

POSSUM vb **possums**

POST n, vb

POSTAGE n

POSTAL adj of a Post Office or the mail-delivery service ▶ n postcard **postals**

POSTBAG n postman's bag

POSTBOX n

POSTBOY n man or boy who brings the post. round to offices

POSTBUS n vehicle carrying the mail that also carries passengers

POSTDOC n postdoctoral degree

POSTED ▶ **post**

POSTEEN n Afghan leather jacket

POSTER n, vb

POSTERN n small back door or gate ▶ adj situated at the rear or the side

POSTERS ▶ **poster**

POSTFIX vb add or append at the end of something

POSTIE n postman **posties**

POSTIL n commentary or marginal note, as in a Bible ▶ vb annotate (a biblical passage) **postils**

POSTIN variant of ▶ **posteen**

POSTING n job to which someone is assigned

POSTINS ▶ **postin**

POSTMAN n **postmen**

POSTOP n person recovering from surgery **postops**

POSTS ▶ **post**

POSTTAX adj of the period after tax is paid

POSTURE n, vb

POSTWAR adj occurring or existing after a war

POSY n

POT n, vb

POTABLE adj drinkable ▶ n something fit to drink

POTAE n hat **potaes**

POTAGE n thick soup

POTAGER n small kitchen garden

POTAGES ▶ **potage**

POTALE n residue from a grain distillery, used as animal feed **potales**

POTAMIC adj of or relating to rivers

POTASH n, vb

POTASS abbreviated form of ▶ **potassium**

POTASSA n potassium oxide

POTATO n

POTBOIL vb boil in a pot

POTBOY n (esp formerly) youth or man employed at a public house to serve beer, etc potboys

POTCH n inferior quality opal used in jewellery for mounting precious opals

POTCHE vb stab potched, potcher

POTCHES ▶ potch

POTE vb push poted

POTEEN n (in Ireland) illegally made alcoholic drink poteens

POTENCE = potency

POTENCY n state or quality of being potent

POTENT adj, n potents

POTES ▶ pote

POTFUL n amount held by a pot potfuls

POTGUN n pot-shaped mortar potguns

POTHEAD n habitual user of cannabis

POTHEEN rare variant of ▶ poteen

POTHER n fuss or commotion ▷ vb make or be troubled or upset

POTHERB n plant whose leaves, flowers, or stems are used in cooking

POTHERS ▶ pother

POTHERY adj stuffy

POTHOLE n

POTHOOK n S-shaped hook for suspending a pot over a fire

POTHOS n climbing plant

POTICHE n tall vase or jar that narrows towards the neck

POTIN n bronze alloy with high tin content

POTING ▶ pote

POTINS ▶ potin

POTION n potions

POTJIE n potjies

POTLACH = potlatch

POTLIKE ▶ pot

POTLINE n row of electrolytic cells for reducing metals

POTLUCK n

POTMAN = potboy

POTMEN ▶ potman

POTOO n nocturnal tropical bird potoos

POTOROO n Australian leaping rodent

POTPIE n meat and vegetable stew with a pie crust on top potpies

POTS ▶ pot

POTSHOP n public house

POTSHOT n shot taken without careful aim

POTSIE = potsy

POTSIES ▶ potsy

POTSY n hopscotch

POTT old variant of ▶ pot

POTTAGE n thick soup or stew

POTTED ▶ pot

POTTEEN = poteen

POTTER = putter

POTTERS ▶ potter

POTTERY n

POTTIER ▶ potty

POTTIES ▶ potty

POTTING ▶ pot

POTTLE n liquid measure equal to half a gallon pottles

POTTO n short-tailed prosimian primate pottos

POTTS ▶ pott

POTTY adj, n

POTZER = patzer

POTZERS ▶ potzer

POUCH n, vb pouched, pouches, pouchy

POUDER obsolete spelling of ▶ powder

POUDERS ▶ pouder

POUDRE old spelling of ▶ powder

POUDRES ▶ poudre

POUF n large solid cushion used as a seat ▷ vb pile up hair into rolled puffs poufed, pouff, pouffe

POUFFED ▶ pouffe

POUFFES ▶ pouffe

POUFFS ▶ pouff

POUFING ▶ pouf

POUFS ▶ pouf

POUK Scots variant of ▶ poke

POUKE n mischievous spirit poukes

POUKING ▶ pouk

POUKIT ▶ pouk

POUKS ▶ pouk

POULARD n hen that has been spayed for fattening

POULDER obsolete spelling of ▶ **powder**

POULDRE archaic spelling of ▶ **powder**

POULE n fowl suitable for slow stewing **poules**

POULP n octopus **poulpe**

POULPES ▶ **poulpe**

POULPS ▶ **poulp**

POULT n young of a gallinaceous bird

POULTER n poultry dealer

POULTRY n

POULTS ▶ **poult**

POUNCE vb, n pounced, pouncer, pounces

POUNCET n box with a perforated top used for perfume

POUND n, vb

POUNDAL n fps unit of force

POUNDED ▶ **pound**

POUNDER ▶ **pound**

POUNDS ▶ **pound**

POUPE vb make sudden blowing sound pouped, poupes, pouping, poupt

POUR vb poured, pourer, pourers

POURIE n jug pouries

POURING ▶ **pour**

POURS ▶ **pour**

POURSEW obsolete spelling of ▶ **pursue**

POURSUE obsolete spelling of ▶ **pursue**

POUSADA n traditional Portuguese hotel

POUSSE = pease

POUSSES ▶ **pousse**

POUSSIE old variant of ▶ **pussy**

POUSSIN n young chicken reared for eating

POUT vb, n pouted

POUTER n pigeon that can puff out its crop pouters

POUTFUL adj tending to pout

POUTHER Scots variant of ▶ **powder**

POUTIER ▶ **pout**

POUTINE n dish of chipped potatoes topped with cheese and sauce

POUTING ▶ **pout**

POUTS ▶ **pout**

POUTY ▶ **pout**

POVERTY n

POW interj exclamation to indicate that a collision or explosion has taken place ▷ n head or a head of hair

POWAN n type of freshwater whitefish occurring in some Scottish lakes powans

POWDER n, vb powders, powdery

POWER n, vb powered, powers

POWHIRI n Māori ceremony of welcome, esp to a marae

POWIN n peacock powins, pown

POWND obsolete spelling of ▶ **pound**

POWNDED ▶ **pownd**

POWNDS ▶ **pownd**

POWNEY old Scots spelling of ▶ **pony**

POWNEYS ▶ **powney**

POWNIE old Scots spelling of ▶ **pony**

POWNIES ▶ **pownie**

POWNS ▶ **pown**

POWNY old Scots spelling of ▶ **pony**

POWRE obsolete spelling of ▶ **power**

POWRED ▶ **powre**

POWRES ▶ **powre**

POWRING ▶ **powre**

POWS ▶ **pow**

POWTER vb scrabble about powters

POWWAW interj expression of disbelief or contempt

POWWOW n talk or conference ▷ vb hold a powwow powwows

POX n disease in which skin pustules form ▷ vb infect with pox poxed, poxes

POXIER ▶ **poxy**

POXIEST ▶ **poxy**

POXING ▶ **pox**

POXY adj having or having had syphilis

POYNANT old variant of ▶ **poignant**

POYNT obsolete spelling of ▶ **point**

POYNTED ▶ **poynt**

POYNTS ▶ **poynt**

POYOU n type of armadillo poyous

POYSE obsolete variant of ▶ **poise**

POYSED ▶ poyse

POYSES ▶ poyse

POYSING ▶ poyse

POYSON obsolete spelling of ▶ poison

POYSONS ▶ poyson

POZ adj positive

Poz is an old-fashioned short form of positive, and one of the most frequently played short Z words.

POZOLE = posole

POZOLES ▶ pozole

POZZ adj positive

POZZIES ▶ pozzy

POZZY = possie

PRAAM ▶ pram

PRAAMS ▶ praam

PRABBLE variant of ▶ brabble

PRACTIC adj practical ▷ n practice

PRAD n horse **prads**

PRAESES n Roman governor

PRAETOR n (in ancient Rome) senior magistrate ranking just below the consuls

PRAHU = proa

PRAHUS ▶ prahu

PRAIRIE n

PRAISE vb, n praised, praiser, praises

PRAJNA n wisdom or understanding prajnas

PRALINE n sweet made of nuts and caramelized sugar

PRAM n prams

PRANA n cosmic energy

believed to come from the sun **pranas**

PRANCE vb, n pranced, prancer, prances

PRANCK obsolete variant of ▶ prank

PRANCKE obsolete variant of ▶ prank

PRANCKS ▶ pranck

PRANG n crash in a car or aircraft ▷ vb crash or damage (an aircraft or car) pranged, prangs

PRANK n, vb pranked

PRANKLE obsolete variant of ▶ prance

PRANKS ▶ prank

PRANKY ▶ prank

PRAO = proa

PRAOS ▶ prao

PRASE n light green translucent variety of chalcedony prases

PRAT n stupid person

PRATE vb talk idly and at length ▷ n chatter prated, prater, praters, prates

PRATIE n potato praties

PRATING ▶ prate

PRATS ▶ prat

PRATT n buttocks ▷ vb hit on the buttocks pratted

PRATTLE vb, n

PRATTS ▶ pratt

PRATY obsolete variant of ▶ pretty

PRAU = proa

PRAUNCE obsolete variant of ▶ prance

PRAUS ▶ prau

PRAVITY n moral

degeneracy

PRAWLE n Shakespearian spelling of "brawl" prawles

PRAWLIN variant of ▶ praline

PRAWN n, vb prawned, prawner, prawns

PRAXES ▶ praxis

PRAXIS n practice as opposed to theory

PRAY vb, adv, interj prayed

PRAYER n prayers

PRAYING ▶ pray

PRAYS ▶ pray

PRE prep before

PREACE obsolete variant of ▶ press

PREACED ▶ preace

PREACES ▶ preace

PREACH vb

PREACHY adj inclined to or marked by preaching

PREACT vb act beforehand preacts

PREAGED adj treated to appear older

PREAMP n electronic amplifier preamps

PREANAL adj situated in front of anus

PREARM vb arm beforehand prearms

PREASE vb crowd or press preased, preases

PREASSE obsolete spelling of ▶ press

PREAVER vb aver in advance

PREBADE ▶ prebid

PREBAKE vb bake

before further cooking

PREBEND n allowance paid to a canon or member of the cathedral chapter

PREBID vb bid beforehand **prebids**

PREBILL vb issue an invoice before the service has been provided

PREBIND vb bind a book in a hard-wearing binding

PREBOIL vb boil beforehand

PREBOOK vb book well in advance

PREBOOM adj of the period before an economic boom

PREBORN adj unborn

PREBUY vb buy in advance **prebuys**

PRECAST adj cast in a particular form before being used ▷ vb cast (concrete) in a particular form before use

PRECAVA n superior vena cava

PRECEDE vb

PRECENT vb issue a command or law

PRECEPT n

PRECES pl n prayers

PRECESS vb undergo or cause to undergo precession

PRECIPE n type of legal document

PRECIS n short written summary of a longer

piece ▷ vb make a precis of

PRECISE adj

PRECODE vb code beforehand

PRECOOK vb cook (food) beforehand

PRECOOL vb cool in advance

PRECOUP adj of the period before a coup

PRECURE vb cure in advance

PRECUT vb cut in advance **precuts**

PREDATE vb occur at an earlier date than

PREDAWN n period before dawn

PREDIAL = praedial

PREDICT vb

PREDIED ▷ predy

PREDIES ▷ predy

PREDIVE adj happening before a dive

PREDOOM vb pronounce (someone or something's) doom beforehand

PREDRY vb dry beforehand

PREDUSK n period before dawn

PREDY vb prepare for action

PREE vb try or taste **preed**

PREEDIT vb edit beforehand

PREEING ▷ pree

PREEMIE n premature infant

PREEMPT vb acquire in advance of or to the

exclusion of others

PREEN vb, n preened, preener, preens

PREES ▷ pree

PREEVE old form of ▷ prove

PREEVED ▷ preeve

PREEVES ▷ preeve

PREFAB n, vb prefabs

PREFACE n, vb

PREFADE vb fade beforehand

PREFARD vb old form of preferred

PREFECT n

PREFER vb prefers

PREFILE vb file beforehand

PREFIRE vb fire beforehand

PREFIX n, vb

PREFORM vb form beforehand

PREFUND vb pay for in advance

PREGAME adj of the period before a sports match ▷ vb in such a period

PREGGY informal word for > **pregnant**

PREHEAT vb heat (an oven, grill, pan, etc) beforehand

PREHEND vb take hold of

PREIF old form of ▷ proof

PREIFE old form of ▷ proof

PREIFES ▷ preife

PREIFS ▷ preif

PREJINK variant of ▷ perjink

PRELACY n office or status of a prelate

PRELATE n

PRELATY n prelacy

PRELAW adj before taking up study of law

PRELECT vb lecture or discourse in public

PRELIFE n life lived before one's life on earth

PRELIM n event which precedes another

PRELIMS pl n pages of a book which come before the main text

PRELOAD vb load beforehand

PRELUDE n, vb

PRELUDI > preludio

PREM n informal word for a premature infant

PREMADE adj made in advance

PREMAN n hominid

PREMEAL adj of the period before a meal

PREMED n premedical student premeds

PREMEET adj happening before a meet

PREMEN > preman

PREMIA > premium

PREMIE = preemie

PREMIER n, adj

PREMIES > premie

PREMISE n, vb premiss

PREMIUM n

PREMIX vb mix beforehand premixt

PREMOLD vb mold in advance

PREMOLT adj happening in the period before an animal molts

PREMOVE vb prompt to action

PREMS > prem

PREMUNE adj having immunity to a disease as a result of latent infection

PREMY variant of > preemie

PRENAME n forename

PRENEED adj

PRENOON adj of the period before noon

PRENT Scots variant of > print

PRENTED > prent

PRENTS > prent

PRENUP n prenuptial agreement prenups

PRENZIE adj Shakespearian word supposed by some to mean "princely"

PREON n (in particle physics) hypothetical subcomponent of a quark preons

PREOP n patient being prepared for surgery preops

PREORAL adj situated in front of mouth

PREP vb prepare

PREPACK vb pack in advance of sale

PREPAID > prepay

PREPARE vb

PREPAVE vb pave beforehand

PREPAY vb pay for in advance prepays

PREPILL adj of the period before the contraceptive pill became available

PREPLAN vb plan beforehand

PREPONE vb bring forward to an earlier time

PREPOSE vb place before

PREPPED > prep

PREPPIE = preppy

PREPPY adj denoting a fashion style of neat, understated clothes ▷ n person exhibiting such style

PREPREG n material already impregnated with synthetic resin

PREPS > prep

PREPUCE n foreskin

PREPUPA n insect in stage of life before pupa

PREQUEL n film or book about an earlier stage of a story

PRERACE adj of the period before a race

PRERIOT adj of the period before a riot

PREROCK adj of the era before rock music

PRERUPT adj abrupt

PRESA n musical sign or symbol to indicate the entry of a part

PRESAGE vb, n

PRESALE n practice of arranging the sale of a product before it is available

PRESE > presa

PRESELL vb promote in advance of appearance

PRESENT adj, n, vb

PRESES variant of
▶ **praeses**

PRESET vb set a timer so
that equipment starts
to work at a specific
time ▷ adj (of
equipment) with the
controls set in advance
▷ n control that is used
to set initial conditions
presets

PRESHIP vb ship in
advance

PRESHOW vb show in
advance

PRESIDE vb

PRESIFT vb sift
beforehand

PRESOAK vb soak
beforehand

PRESOLD ▶ presell

PRESONG adj of the
period before a song is
sung

PRESORT vb sort in
advance

PRESS vb, n pressed,
presser, presses

PRESSIE informal word
for ▶ present

PRESSOR n something
that produces an
increase in blood
pressure

PREST adj prepared for
action or use ▷ n loan
of money ▷ vb give as
a loan prested,
prester

PRESTO adv very quickly
▷ n passage to be played
very quickly prestos

PRESTS ▶ prest

PRESUME vb

PRETAPE vb tape in
advance

PRETAX adj before tax

PRETEEN n boy or girl
approaching his or her
teens

PRETELL vb predict

PRETEND vb, adj

PRETERM n premature
baby

PRETEST vb test
(something) before
presenting it to its
intended public or
client ▷ n act or
instance of pretesting

PRETEXT n, vb

PRETOLD ▶ pretell

PRETOR = praetor

PRETORS ▶ pretor

PRETRIM vb trim in
advance

PRETTY adj, adv, vb

PRETYPE vb type in
advance

PRETZEL n brittle salted
biscuit

PREVAIL vb

PREVE vb prove
preved

PREVENE vb come
before

PREVENT vb

PREVERB n particle
preceding root of verb

PREVES ▶ preve

PREVIEW n, vb

PREVING ▶ preve

PREVISE vb predict or
foresee

PREVUE = preview

PREVUED ▶ prevue

PREVUES ▶ prevue

PREWAR adj relating to
the period before a
war, esp before World
War I or II

PREWARM vb warm
beforehand

PREWARN vb warn in
advance

PREWASH vb give a
preliminary wash to
(clothes) ▷ n
preliminary wash

PREWIRE vb wire
beforehand

PREWORK vb work in
advance

PREWORN adj (of
clothes) second-hand

PREWRAP vb wrap in
advance

PREWYN obsolete
spelling of ▶ prune

PREWYNS ▶ prewyn

PREX = prexy

PREXES ▶ prex

PREXIES ▶ prexy

PREXY n US college
president

PREY n, vb preyed,
preyer, preyers

PREYFUL adj rich in
prey

PREYING ▶ prey

PREYS ▶ prey

PREZ n president
prezes

PREZZIE = pressie

PRIAL n pair royal of
cards prials

PRIAPI ▶ priapus

PRIAPIC adj phallic

PRIAPUS n
representation of the
penis

PRIBBLE variant of
▶ **prabble**

PRICE n, vb priced,
pricer, pricers, prices

PRICEY adj

PRICIER ▶ pricy

PRICILY ▶ pricey

PRICING ▶ price

PRICK vb, n pricked

PRICKER n person or
thing that pricks

PRICKET n male deer in
the second year of life

PRICKLE n, vb

PRICKLY adj having
prickles

PRICKS ▶ prick

PRICKY adj covered
with pricks

PRICY = pricey

PRIDE n prided, prides

PRIDIAN adj relating to
yesterday

PRIDING ▶ pride

PRIED ▶ pry

PRIEF obsolete variant of
▶ **proof**

PRIEFE obsolete variant
of ▶ **proof**

PRIEFES ▶ priefe

PRIEFS ▶ prief

PRIER n person who
pries priers

PRIES ▶ pry

PRIEST n, vb priests

PRIEVE obsolete variant
of ▶ **proof**

PRIEVED ▶ prieve

PRIEVES ▶ prieve

PRIG n prigged

PRIGGER n thief

PRIGS ▶ prig

PRILL vb convert
(a material) into a

granular free-flowing
form ▷ n prilled
material **prilled, prills**

PRIM adj, vb

PRIMA = primo

PRIMACY n

PRIMAGE n tax added to
customs duty

PRIMAL adj

PRIMARY adj, n

PRIMAS ▶ prima

PRIMATE n

PRIME adj, n, vb primed,
primely

PRIMER n

PRIMERO n 16th- and
17th-century card
game

PRIMERS ▶ primer

PRIMES ▶ prime

PRIMEUR n anything
(esp fruit) produced
early

PRIMI ▶ primo

PRIMINE n integument
surrounding an
ovule or the outer
of two such
integuments

PRIMING = primer

PRIMLY ▶ prim

PRIMMED ▶ prim

PRIMMER ▶ prim

PRIMO n upper or
right-hand part in a
piano duet **primos**

PRIMP vb tidy (one's hair
or clothes) fussily
primped, primps

PRIMS ▶ prim

PRIMSIE Scots variant of
▶ **prim**

PRIMULA n type of
primrose with brightly

coloured flowers

PRIMUS n presiding
bishop in the Synod

PRIMY adj prime

PRINCE vb princed,
princes

PRINCOX n pert youth

PRINK vb dress (oneself)
finely prinked,
prinker, prinks

PRINT vb, n printed

PRINTER n person or
company engaged in
printing

PRINTS ▶ print

PRION n dovelike petrel
with a serrated bill
prions

PRIOR adj, n priorly,
priors

PRIORY n

PRISAGE n customs
duty levied until 1809
upon wine imported
into England

PRISE = pry

PRISED ▶ prise

PRISER ▶ prise

PRISERE n primary sere
or succession from
bare ground to the
community climax

PRISERS ▶ prise

PRISES ▶ prise

PRISING ▶ prise

PRISM n prisms, prismy

PRISON n, vb prisons

PRISS n prissy person
▷ vb act prissily
prissed, prisses

PRISSY adj prim,
correct, and easily
shocked ▷ n prissy
person

PRITHEE *interj* pray thee

PRIVACY *n* condition of being private

PRIVADO *n* close friend

PRIVATE *adj, n*

PRIVET *n* privets

PRIVIER ▸ privy

PRIVIES ▸ privy

PRIVILY *adv* in a secret way

PRIVITY *n* legally recognized relationship between two parties

PRIVY *adj, n*

PRIZE *n, adj, vb* prized

PRIZER *n* contender for prize **prizers**

PRIZES ▸ prize

PRIZING ▸ prize

PRO *prep, n, adv*

PROA *n* canoe-like boat used in the South Pacific **proas**

PROB *n* problem

PROBALL *adj* believable

PROBAND *n* first patient to be investigated in a family study

PROBANG *n* long flexible rod used to apply medication

PROBATE *n* process of proving the validity of a will ▸ *vb* establish officially the authenticity and validity of (a will)

PROBE *vb, n* probed, prober, probers, probes, probing

PROBIT *n* statistical measurement **probits**

PROBITY *n* honesty, integrity

PROBLEM *n, adj*

PROBS ▸ prob

PROCARP *n* female reproductive organ in red algae

PROCEED *vb*

PROCESS *n, vb*

PROCTAL *adj* relating to the rectum

PROCTOR *n* university worker who enforces discipline ▸ *vb* invigilate (an examination)

PROCURE *vb*

PROD *vb, n* prodded, prodder

PRODIGY *n*

PRODRUG *n* compound that is metabolized in the body to produce an active drug

PRODS ▸ prod

PRODUCE *vb, n*

PRODUCT *n*

PROEM *n* introduction or preface **proems**

PROETTE *n* female golfing professional

PROF *short for* ▸ professor

PROFACE *interj* much good may it do you

PROFANE *adj, vb*

PROFESS *vb*

PROFFER *vb, n*

PROFILE *n, vb*

PROFIT *n, vb* profits

PROFS ▸ prof

PROFUSE *adj*

PROG *vb* prowl about for or as if for food or

plunder ▸ *n* food obtained by begging

PROGENY *n*

PROGGED ▸ prog

PROGGER *n* fan of progressive rock

PROGRAM = programme

PROGS ▸ prog

PROGUN *adj* in favour of public owning firearms

PROIGN = proin

PROIGNS ▸ proign

PROIN *vb* trim or prune **proine, proined**

PROINES ▸ proine

PROINS ▸ proin

PROJECT *n, vb*

PROJET *n* draft of a proposed treaty **projets**

PROKE *vb* thrust or poke **proked, proker, prokers, prokes, proking**

PROLAN *n* constituent of human pregnancy urine **prolans**

PROLATE *adj* having a polar diameter which is longer than the equatorial diameter ▸ *vb* pronounce or utter

PROLE *old form of* ▸ prowl

PROLED ▸ prole

PROLEG *n* appendage on abdominal segment of a caterpillar **prolegs**

PROLER *n* prowler **prolers**

PROLES ▶ prole

PROLINE n nonessential amino acid that occurs in protein

PROLING ▶ prole

PROLIX adj (of speech or a piece of writing) overlong and boring

PROLL vb prowl or search **prolled, proller, prolls**

PROLOG = prologue

PROLOGS ▶ prolog

PROLONG vb

PROM n

PROMINE n substance promoting cell growth

PROMISE vb, n

PROMMER n spectator at promenade concert

PROMO vb promote (something) **promoed, promos**

PROMOTE vb

PROMPT vb, adj, adv, n **prompts**

PROMS ▶ prom

PRONAOI ▶ pronaos

PRONAOS n inner area of the portico of a classical temple

PRONATE vb turn (a limb, hand, or foot) so that the palm or sole is directed downwards

PRONE n pronely, proner, prones, pronest

PRONEUR n flatterer

PRONG n, vb pronged, prongs

PRONK vb jump straight up **pronked, pronks**

PRONOTA > pronotum

PRONOUN n

PRONTO adv at once

PROO interj (to a horse) stop!

PROOF n, adj, vb proofed

PROOFER n reader of proofs

PROOFS ▶ proof

PROOTIC n bone in front of ear

PROP vb, n

PROPAGE vb propagate

PROPALE vb publish (something)

PROPANE n

PROPEL vb propels

PROPEND vb be inclined or disposed

PROPENE n colourless gaseous alkene obtained by cracking petroleum

PROPER adj, n propers

PROPHET n

PROPINE vb drink a toast to

PROPJET another name for > turboprop

PROPMAN n member of the stage crew in charge of the stage props **propmen**

PROPONE vb propose or put forward, esp before a court

PROPOSE vb

PROPPED ▶ prop

PROPRIA > proprium

PROPS ▶ prop

PROPYL n of, consisting of, or containing the monovalent group of atoms C_3H_7-

PROPYLA > propylon

PROPYLS ▶ propyl

PRORATE vb divide, assess, or distribute (something) proportionately

PRORE n forward part of ship prores

PROS ▶ pro

PROSAIC adj

PROSE n, vb

PROSECT vb dissect a cadaver for a public demonstration

PROSED ▶ prose

PROSER n writer of prose prosers

PROSES ▶ prose

PROSIER ▶ prosy

PROSIFY vb write prose

PROSILY ▶ prosy

PROSING ▶ prose

PROSIT interj good health! cheers!

PROSO n millet

PROSODY n study of poetic metre and techniques

PROSOMA n head and thorax of an arachnid

PROSOS ▶ proso

PROSPER vb

PROSS n prostitute prosses

PROSSIE n prostitute

PROST = prosit

PROSTIE n prostitute

PROSY adj dull and long-winded

PROTEA n

PROTEAN adj constantly changing ▷ n creature that can change shape

PROTEAS ▶ protea

PROTECT vb

PROTEGE n person who is protected and helped by another

PROTEI ▶ proteus

PROTEID n protein

PROTEIN n

PROTEND vb hold out or stretch

PROTEST n, vb

PROTEUS n aerobic bacterium

PROTHYL variant of ▶ protyle

PROTIST n organism belonging to the protozoans, unicellular algae, and simple fungi

PROTIUM n most common isotope of hydrogen

PROTO n as in proto team relating to a team of people trained to deal with underground rescues, etc

PROTON n protons

PROTORE n primary mineral deposit

PROTYL = protyle

PROTYLE n hypothetical primitive substance

PROTYLS ▶ protyl

PROUD adj prouder, proudly

PROUL variant of ▶ prowl

PROULED ▶ proul

PROULER Scots variant of ▶ prowler

PROULS ▶ proul

PROVAND n food

PROVANT adj supplied with provisions

PROVE vb proved, proven

PROVEND = provand

PROVER ▶ prove

PROVERB n, vb

PROVERS ▶ prove

PROVES ▶ prove

PROVIDE vb

PROVINE vb plant branch of vine in ground for propagation

PROVING ▶ prove

PROVISO n

PROVOKE vb

PROVOST n

PROW n, adj

PROWAR adj in favour of or supporting war

PROWER ▶ prow

PROWESS n

PROWEST ▶ prow

PROWL vb, n prowled, prowler, prowls

PROWS ▶ prow

PROXIES ▶ proxy

PROXIMO adv in or during the next or coming month

PROXY n

PROYN obsolete spelling of ▶ prune

PROYNE obsolete spelling of ▶ prune

PROYNED ▶ proyn

PROYNES ▶ proyne

PROYNS ▶ proyn

PRUDE n

PRUDENT adj

PRUDERY ▶ prude

PRUDES ▶ prude

PRUDISH ▶ prude

PRUH variant of ▶ proo

PRUINA n woolly white covering on some lichens pruinas

PRUINE obsolete spelling of ▶ prune

PRUINES ▶ pruine

PRUNE n, vb pruned, pruner, pruners, prunes, pruning

PRUNT n glass ornamentation prunted, prunts

PRUNUS n type of ornamental tree or shrub

PRURIGO n chronic inflammatory disease of the skin

PRUSIK n sliding knot used in climbing ▷ vb climb (up a rope) using prusiks prusiks

PRUSSIC adj as in prussic acid weakly acidic extremely poisonous aqueous solution of hydrogen cyanide

PRUTA = prutah

PRUTAH n former Israeli coin prutot, prutoth

PRY vb, n

PRYER = prier

PRYERS ▶ pryer

PRYING ▶ pry

PRYINGS ▶ pry

PRYS old variant of ▶ price

PRYSE old variant of ▶ price

PRYSED ▶ pryse

PRYSES ▶ pryse

PRYSING ▶ pryse

PRYTHEE = prithee

PSALM n, vb psalmed, psalmic, psalms

PSALTER n book containing a version of Psalms

PSALTRY = psaltery

PSAMMON n microscopic life forms living between grains of sand

PSCHENT n ancient Egyptian crown

PSEUD n pretentious person

PSEUDO n pretentious person pseudos

PSEUDS ▸ pseud

PSHAW n exclamation of disgust, impatience, disbelief, etc ▸ vb make this exclamation pshawed, pshaws

PSI n 23rd letter of the Greek alphabet

PSION n type of elementary particle

PSIONIC > psionics

PSIONS ▸ psion

PSIS ▸ psi

PSOAE ▸ psoas

PSOAI ▸ psoas

PSOAS n either of two muscles of the loins that aid in flexing and rotating the thigh psoases, psoatic

PSOCID n tiny wingless insect psocids

PSORA n itching skin complaint psoras, psoric

PSST interj sound made to attract someone's attention, esp without others noticing

PST interj sound made to attract someone's attention

You would need to be fairly desperate to use good letters to play this exclamation, but sometimes with no vowels on your rack things can be that desperate.

PSYCH vb psychoanalyse psyche, psyched, psyches

PSYCHIC adj, n

PSYCHS ▸ psych

PSYLLA = psyllid

PSYLLAS ▸ psylla

PSYLLID n type of insect of the family which comprises the jumping plant lice

PSYOP n psychological operation psyops

PSYWAR n psychological warfare psywars

PTARMIC n material that causes sneezing

PTERIA ▸ pterion

PTERIN n compound such as folic acid pterins

PTERION n point on the side of the skull where a number of bones meet

PTEROIC adj as in pteroic acid a kind of acid found in spinach

PTERYLA n any of the tracts of skin that bear contour feathers

PTISAN n grape juice drained off without pressure ptisans

PTOMAIN = ptomaine

PTOOEY interj imitation of the sound of spitting

PTOSES ▸ ptosis

PTOSIS n prolapse or drooping of a part, esp the eyelid ptotic

PTUI ▸ ptooey

PTYALIN n amylase secreted in the saliva of man and other animals

PTYXES ▸ ptyxis

PTYXIS n folding of a leaf in a bud

PUB n, vb pubbed, pubbing

PUBCO n company operating a chain of pubs pubcos

PUBE n pubic hair

PUBERAL adj relating to puberty

PUBERTY n

PUBES ▸ pube

PUBIC adj

PUBIS n one of the three sections of the hipbone that forms part of the pelvis pubises

PUBLIC adj of or concerning the people as a whole ▸ n community, people in general publics

PUBLISH vb

PUBS ▸ pub
PUCAN *n* traditional Connemara open sailing boat **pucans**
PUCCOON *n* N American plant that yields a red dye
PUCE *adj*, *n*
PUCELLE *n* maid or virgin
PUCER ▸ puce
PUCES ▸ puce
PUCEST ▸ puce
PUCK *n* mischievous or evil spirit ▷ *vb* strike (the ball) in hurling
PUCKA = pukka
PUCKED ▸ puck
PUCKER *vb*, *n* **puckers**
PUCKERY *adj* (of wine) high in tannins
PUCKING ▸ puck
PUCKISH ▸ puck
PUCKLE *n* early type of machine gun **puckles**
PUCKOUT *n*
PUCKS ▸ puck
PUD *short for* ▸ pudding
PUDDEN *dialect spelling of* ▸ pudding
PUDDENS ▸ pudden
PUDDER *vb* make bother or fuss **pudders**
PUDDIES ▸ puddy
PUDDING *n*
PUDDLE *n*, *vb* **puddled, puddler, puddles, puddly**
PUDDOCK = paddock
PUDDY *n* paw
PUDENCY *n* modesty, shame, or prudishness
PUDENDA > **pudendum**
PUDENT *adj* lacking in ostentation; humble

PUDGE = podge
PUDGES ▸ pudge
PUDGIER ▸ pudgy
PUDGILY ▸ pudgy
PUDGY *adj* podgy
PUDIC > pudendum
PUDOR *n* sense of shame **pudors**
PUDS ▸ pud
PUDSEY *variant of* ▸ pudsy
PUDSIER ▸ pudsy
PUDSY *adj* plump
PUDU *n* diminutive Andean antelope **pudus**
PUEBLO *n* communal village of flat-roofed houses **pueblos**
PUER *vb* steep hides in an alkaline substance from the dung of dogs **puered**
PUERILE *adj*
PUERING ▸ puer
PUERS ▸ puer
PUFF *n*, *vb* **puffed**
PUFFER *n* person or thing that puffs **puffers**
PUFFERY *n* exaggerated praise, esp in publicity or advertising
PUFFIER ▸ puffy
PUFFILY ▸ puffy
PUFFIN *n*
PUFFING ▸ puff
PUFFINS ▸ puffin
PUFFS ▸ puff
PUFFY *adj* short of breath
PUG *n*, *vb*
PUGAREE = puggree
PUGGED ▸ pug

PUGGERY = puggree
PUGGIE *n* Scottish word for fruit machine
PUGGIER ▸ puggy
PUGGIES ▸ puggie
PUGGING ▸ pug
PUGGISH ▸ pug
PUGGLE *vb* stir up by poking **puggled, puggles**
PUGGREE *n* scarf, usually pleated, around the crown of some hats, esp sun helmets **puggry**
PUGGY *adj* sticky, claylike ▷ *n* term of endearment
PUGH *interj* exclamation of disgust
PUGIL *n* pinch or small handful **pugils**
PUGMARK *n* trail of an animal
PUGREE = puggree
PUGREES ▸ puggree
PUGS ▸ pug
PUH *interj* exclamation expressing contempt or disgust
PUHA *n* sow thistle **puhas**
PUIR *Scottish word for* ▸ poor
PUIRER ▸ puir
PUIREST ▸ puir
PUISNE *adj* (esp of a subordinate judge) of lower rank ▷ *n* judge of lower rank **puisnes**
PUISNY *adj* younger or inferior
PUJA *n* pujah
PUJAHS ▸ pujah

PUJARI n Hindu priest **pujaris**

PUJAS ▶ puja

PUKA in New Zealand English, = broadleaf

PUKAS ▶ puka

PUKATEA n aromatic New Zealand tree

PUKE vb, n **puked**

PUKEKO n brightly coloured New Zealand wading bird **pukekos**

PUKER n person who vomits **pukers**

PUKES ▶ puke

PUKEY adj of or like vomit **pukier, pukiest**

PUKING ▶ puke

PUKKA adj properly done, constructed, etc

PUKU n belly or stomach **pukus**

PUKY ▶ pukey

PUL n Afghan monetary unit

PULA n standard monetary unit of Botswana

PULAO = pilau

PULAOS ▶ pulao

PULAS ▶ pula

PULDRON = pauldron

PULE vb whine or whimper **puled, puler, pulers, pules**

PULI ▶ pul

PULIER ▶ puly

PULIEST ▶ puly

PULIK ▶ pul

PULING ▶ pule

PULINGS ▶ pule

PULIS ▶ pul

PULK ▶ pulka

PULKA n reindeer-drawn sleigh **pulkas, pulkha**

PULKHAS ▶ pulkha

PULKS ▶ pulk

PULL vb, n **pulled, puller, pullers**

PULLET n **pullets**

PULLEY n **pulleys**

PULLI ▶ pullus

PULLING ▶ pull

PULLMAN n luxurious railway coach, esp a sleeping car

PULLOUT n removable section of a magazine, etc

PULLS ▶ pull

PULLUP n exercise in which the body is raised by the arms pulling on a horizontal bar **pullups**

PULLUS n technical term for a chick or young bird

PULMO n lung

PULP n, vb **pulpal, pulped, pulper, pulpers**

PULPIER ▶ pulpy

PULPIFY vb reduce to pulp

PULPILY ▶ pulpy

PULPING ▶ pulp

PULPIT n **pulpits**

PULPOUS n soft and yielding

PULPS ▶ pulp

PULPY adj having a soft or soggy consistency

PULQUE n light alcoholic drink from Mexico **pulques**

PULS ▶ pul

PULSANT adj vibrant

PULSAR n **pulsars**

PULSATE vb

PULSE n, vb **pulsed**

PULSER n thing that pulses **pulsers**

PULSES ▶ pulse

PULSING ▶ pulse

PULSION n act of driving forward

PULTAN n native Indian regiment **pultans, pulton**

PULTONS ▶ pulton

PULTOON = pultan

PULTUN = pultan

PULTUNS ▶ pultun

PULTURE n food and drink claimed by foresters

PULU n substance used for stuffing cushions **pulus**

PULVER vb make into powder **pulvers**

PULVIL vb apply perfumed powder **pulvils**

PULVINI > pulvinus

PULWAR n light Indian river boat **pulwars**

PULY adj whiny

PUMA n **pumas**

PUMELO = pomelo

PUMELOS ▶ pumelo

PUMICE n, vb **pumiced, pumicer, pumices**

PUMIE n small stone **pumies**

PUMMEL vb

PUMMELO = pomelo

PUMMELS ▶ pummel

PUMP n, vb **pumped, pumper, pumpers, pumping**

PUMPION archaic word for ▶ pumpkin

PUMPKIN n

PUMPS ▶ pump

PUMY adj large and round

PUN n, vb

PUNA n high cold dry plateau, esp in the Andes

PUNALUA n marriage between the sisters of one family to the brothers of another

PUNAS ▶ puna

PUNCE n kick ▷ vb kick **punced, punces**

PUNCH vb, n **punched, puncher, punches**

PUNCHY adj

PUNCING ▶ punce

PUNCTA ▶ punctum

PUNCTO n tip of a fencing sword **punctos**

PUNCTUM n tip or small point

PUNDIT n **pundits**

PUNG n horse-drawn sleigh with a boxlike body on runners

PUNGA variant spelling of ▶ ponga

PUNGAS ▶ punga

PUNGENT adj

PUNGLE vb make payment **pungled, pungles**

PUNGS ▶ pung

PUNIER ▶ puny

PUNIEST ▶ puny

PUNILY ▶ puny

PUNISH vb

PUNJI n sharpened bamboo stick **punjis**

PUNK n, adj

PUNKA n fan made of a palm leaf or leaves **punkah**

PUNKAHS ▶ punkah

PUNKAS ▶ punka

PUNKER ▶ punk

PUNKERS ▶ punk

PUNKEST ▶ punk

PUNKEY n small winged insect **punkeys, punkie**

PUNKIER ▶ punky

PUNKIES ▶ punkie

PUNKIN = pumpkin

PUNKINS ▶ punkin

PUNKISH ▶ punk

PUNKS ▶ punk

PUNKY adj of punk music

PUNNED ▶ pun

PUNNER ▶ pun

PUNNERS ▶ pun

PUNNET n **punnets**

PUNNIER ▶ punny

PUNNING ▶ pun

PUNNY adj of puns

PUNS ▶ pun

PUNSTER n person who is fond of making puns

PUNT n, vb **punted**

PUNTEE = punty

PUNTEES ▶ puntee

PUNTER n **punters**

PUNTIES ▶ punty

PUNTING ▶ punt

PUNTO n hit in fencing **puntos**

PUNTS ▶ punt

PUNTY n long iron rod used in the finishing process of glass-blowing

PUNY adj

PUP n, vb

PUPA n **pupae, pupal**

PUPARIA ▶ puparium

PUPAS ▶ pupa

PUPATE vb (of an insect larva) to develop into a pupa **pupated, pupates**

PUPFISH n type of small fish

PUPIL n **pupilar, pupils**

PUPPED ▶ pup

PUPPET n **puppets**

PUPPIED ▶ puppy

PUPPIES ▶ puppy

PUPPING ▶ pup

PUPPY n, vb

PUPS ▶ pup

PUPU n Hawaiian dish

PUPUNHA n fruit of a type of palm tree

PUPUS ▶ pupu

PUR = purr

PURANA n type of Sanskrit sacred writing **puranas, puranic**

PURDA = purdah

PURDAH n **purdahs**

PURDAS ▶ purda

PURE adj, vb **pured**

PUREE n smooth thick pulp of cooked and sieved fruit, vegetables, meat, or fish ▷ vb make (cooked foods) into a puree **pureed, purees**

PURELY adv

PURER ▶ pure

PURES ▶ pure

PUREST ▶ pure

PURFLE n ruffled or curved ornamental band ▷ vb decorate with such a band or bands **purfled, purfler, purfles, purfly**

PURGE vb, n **purged, purger, purgers, purges, purging**

PURI n unleavened flaky Indian bread, that is deep-fried in ghee and served hot

PURIFY vb

PURIN = purine

PURINE n colourless crystalline solid that can be prepared from uric acid **purines**

PURING ▶ pure

PURINS ▶ purin

PURIRI n forest tree of New Zealand **puriris**

PURIS ▶ puri

PURISM n strict insistence on the correct usage or style **purisms, purist, purists**

PURITAN n, adj

PURITY n state or quality of being pure

PURL n, vb **purled**

PURLER n headlong or spectacular fall **purlers**

PURLIEU n land on the edge of a royal forest

PURLIN n horizontal beam that supports the rafters of a roof **purline**

PURLING ▶ purl

PURLINS ▶ purlin

PURLOIN vb

PURLS ▶ purl

PURPIE old Scots word for ▶ purslane

PURPIES ▶ purpie

PURPLE n, adj, vb **purpled, purpler, purples, purply**

PURPORT vb, n

PURPOSE n

PURPURA n blood disease causing purplish spots

PURPURE n purple

PURPY variant of ▶ purpie

PURR vb, n **purred, purring, purrs**

PURS ▶ pur

PURSE n, vb **pursed**

PURSER n **pursers**

PURSES ▶ purse

PURSEW archaic spelling of ▶ pursue

PURSEWS ▶ pursew

PURSIER ▶ pursy

PURSILY ▶ pursy

PURSING ▶ purse

PURSUAL n act of pursuit

PURSUE vb **pursued, pursuer, pursues**

PURSUIT n pursuing

PURSY adj short-winded

PURTIER ▶ purty

PURTY adj pretty

PURVEY vb supply (provisions) ▷ n food and drink laid on at a wedding reception, etc **purveys**

PURVIEW n scope or range of activity or outlook

PUS n **puses**

PUSH vb, n

PUSHED adj short of

PUSHER n **pushers**

PUSHES ▶ push

PUSHFUL ▶ push

PUSHIER ▶ pushy

PUSHILY ▶ pushy

PUSHING prep, adj, adv

PUSHPIN n pin with a small ball-shaped head

PUSHPIT n safety rail at the stern of a boat

PUSHROD n metal rod transmitting motion in an engine

PUSHUP n exercise in which the body is alternately raised from and lowered to the floor by the arms **pushups**

PUSHY adj

PUSLE old spelling of ▶ puzzle

PUSLED ▶ pusle

PUSLES ▶ pusle

PUSLEY = purslane

PUSLEYS ▶ pusley

PUSLIKE ▶ pus

PUSLING ▶ pusle

PUSS = pussy

PUSSEL n slatternly woman **pussels**

PUSSER n naval purser **pussers**

PUSSES ▶ puss

PUSSIER ▶ pussy

PUSSIES ▶ pussy

PUSSLEY n weedy trailing herb **pussly**

PUSSY n, adj

PUSTULE n pimple containing pus

PUT vb, n

PUTAMEN n hard endocarp or stone of fruit

PUTCHER n trap for catching salmon

PUTCHUK = pachak

PUTDOWN n snub or insult

PUTEAL n enclosure around a well **puteals**

PUTELI n (in India) type of boat **putelis**

PUTID adj having an unpleasant odour

PUTLOCK = putlog

PUTLOG n short horizontal beam that with others supports the floor planks of a scaffold **putlogs**

PUTOFF n pretext or delay **putoffs**

PUTOIS n brush to paint pottery

PUTON n hoax or piece of mockery **putons**

PUTOUT n baseball play in which the batter or runner is put out **putouts**

PUTREFY vb

PUTRID adj

PUTS ▶ put

PUTSCH n sudden violent attempt to remove a government from power

PUTT n, vb **putted**

PUTTEE n strip of cloth worn round about the leg **puttees**

PUTTEN old Scots past participle of ▶ put

PUTTER n golf club for putting ▷ vb busy oneself in a desultory though agreeable manner **putters**

PUTTI ▶ putto

PUTTIE = puttee

PUTTIED ▶ putty

PUTTIER n glazier

PUTTIES ▶ putty

PUTTING ▶ put

PUTTO n representation of a small boy

PUTTOCK n type of bird of prey

PUTTS ▶ putt

PUTTY n, vb

PUTURE n claim of foresters for food **putures**

PUTZ n despicable or stupid person ▷ vb waste time **putzed, putzes, putzing**

PUY n small volcanic cone **puys**

PUZEL = pucelle

PUZELS ▶ puzel

PUZZEL n prostitute **puzzels**

PUZZLE vb, n **puzzled**

PUZZLER n person or thing that puzzles

PUZZLES ▶ puzzle

PYA n monetary unit of Myanmar worth one hundredth of a kyat

PYAEMIA n blood poisoning with pus-forming microorganisms in the blood **pyaemic**

PYAS ▶ pya

PYAT n magpie ▷ adj pied **pyats**

PYCNIC = pyknic

PYCNITE n variety of topaz

PYCNON old word for > semitone

PYCNONS ▶ pycnon

PYE = pie

PYEBALD = piebald

PYEING ▶ pye

PYEMIA = pyaemia

PYEMIAS ▶ pyaemia

PYEMIC = pyaemia

PYES ▶ pye

PYET = pyat

PYETS ▶ pyet

PYGAL n rear part **pygals**

PYGARG n type of horned mammal **pygargs**

PYGIDIA > pygidium

PYGMEAN ▶ pygmy

PYGMIES ▶ pygmy

PYGMOID adj of or like pygmies

PYGMY n, adj

PYIC adj relating to pus

PYIN n constituent of pus **pyins**

PYJAMA = pyjamas

PYJAMAS pl n

PYKNIC adj (of a physical type) characterized by a broad squat fleshy physique with a large chest and abdomen ▷ n person with this physical type **pyknics**

PYLON n **pylons**

PYLORI ▶ pylorus

PYLORIC ▶ pylorus

PYLORUS *n* small circular opening at the base of the stomach

PYNE *archaic variant of* ▶ **pine**

PYNED ▶ **pyne**

PYNES ▶ **pyne**

PYNING ▶ **pyne**

PYOID *adj* resembling pus

PYONER *old variant of* ▶ **pioneer**

PYONERS ▶ **pyoner**

PYOSES ▶ **pyosis**

PYOSIS *n* formation of pus

PYOT = **pyat**

PYOTS ▶ **pyot**

PYRAL ▶ **pyre**

PYRALID *n* tropical moth **pyralis**

PYRAMID *n, vb*

PYRAMIS *n* pyramid-shaped structure

PYRAN *n* unsaturated heterocyclic organic compound **pyrans**

PYRE *n*

PYRENE *n* solid polynuclear aromatic hydrocarbon extracted from coal tar **pyrenes**

PYRES ▶ **pyre**

PYRETIC *adj* of, relating to, or characterized by fever

PYREX *n* tradename for glass used in cookery and chemical apparatus **pyrexes**

PYREXIA *technical name for* ▶ **fever**

PYREXIC ▶ **pyrexia**

PYRIC *adj* of or relating to burning

PYRIDIC > **pyridine**

PYRITE *n* yellow mineral consisting of iron sulphide in cubic crystalline form **pyrites, pyritic**

PYRO *n* pyromaniac

PYROGEN *n* any of a group of substances that cause a rise in temperature in an animal body

PYROLA *n* evergreen perennial **pyrolas**

PYRONE *n* type of heterocyclic compound **pyrones**

PYROPE *n* deep yellowish-red garnet used as a gemstone **pyropes, pyropus**

PYROS ▶ **pyro**

PYROSES ▶ **pyrosis**

PYROSIS *technical name for* ▶ **heartburn**

PYRRHIC *n* metrical foot of two short or unstressed syllables ▷ *adj* of or relating to such a metrical foot

PYRROL = **pyrrole**

PYRROLE *n* colourless insoluble toxic liquid

PYRROLS ▶ **pyrrol**

PYRUVIC *adj as in* **pyruvic acid** colourless pleasant-smelling liquid

PYTHIUM *n* type of fungi

PYTHON *n* pythons

PYURIA *n* any condition characterized by the presence of pus in the urine **pyurias**

PYX *n* any receptacle for the Eucharistic Host ▷ *vb* put (something) in a pyx **pyxed, pyxes** This word can also be spelt **pix**. It's a great word to know as it can earn a good score from a rack that is short of vowels.

PYXIDES ▶ **pyxis**

PYXIDIA > **pyxidium**

PYXIE *n* creeping evergreen shrub of the eastern US **pyxies**

PYXING ▶ **pyx**

PYXIS = **pyxidium**

PZAZZ = **pizzazz**

PZAZZES ▶ **pzazz**

Qq

With a value of 10 points, **Q** can help you to some good scores, but it can also be a very awkward tile, making it difficult to get bonus words scoring that extra 50 points, and you will normally want to play it off quickly. Often you will not have a **U** to go with it, so it's a good idea to remember the short words beginning with **Q** that don't need a **U**. This is easy, as there's only one two-letter word starting with Q: **qi** (11 points). There are four three-letter words, only one of which needs a U: **qua** (12). The other three are **qat**, **qin** and **qis** (12 each). If you do have a **U**, remember **quiz** (22), which is a very useful word, and can take an **S** at the front to make **squiz** (12 points). Don't forget **quartz** (24) either, while the useful **suq** (12 points) is easily overlooked.

QABALA = kabbalah

QABALAH = kabbalah

QABALAS ▸ qabala

QADI *variant spelling of* ▸ **cadi**

QADIS ▸ qadi

QAID *n* chief **qaids**
An Arabic word, this and its variant **qadi** are two of the most frequently played words in Scrabble. There are also alternative spellings **cadi, caid, kadi** and **kaid**.

QANAT *n* underground irrigation channel **qanats**

This word comes up many times as one of the words allowing you to play the Q without a U.

QASIDA *n* Arabic verse form **qasidas**

QAT *variant spelling of* ▸ **khat**
The leaves of this shrub are chewed as a stimulant, and it's certainly been a stimulus for Scrabble, being one of the three three-letter words that can be played without a U: the others are **qin** and **qis**.

QATS ▸ qat

QAWWAL *n* qawwali singer

QAWWALI *n* Islamic religious song, esp in Asia

QAWWALS ▸ qawwal

QI *variant of* ▸ **chi**

QIBLA *variant of* ▸ **kiblah**
The direction in which Muslims turn to pray, a useful word allowing the Q to be played without the U. It can also be spelt **keblah, kibla** and **kiblah**.

QIBLAS ▸ qibla

QIGONG *n* system of breathing and exercise **qigongs**

QIN *n* Chinese stringed

instrument related to the zither

> This Chinese musical instrument is another indispensable word as, like **qat**, it combines Q with two of the most common letters in the game.

QINDAR n Albanian monetary unit **qindars**

QINS ▸ qin

QINTAR = qindar

QINTARS ▸ qintar

QIS ▸ qi

QIVIUT n soft muskox wool **qiviuts**

QOPH variant of ▸ **koph**

> A letter of the Hebrew alphabet, also spelt **koph**. The Hebrew alphabet, like the Greek alphabet, is well worth studying from the Scrabble point of view, as it gives us many other useful short words like **ayin**, **beth**, **heth**, **kaph** and **lamedh**.

QOPHS ▸ qoph

QORMA variant spelling of ▸ **korma**

QORMAS ▸ qorma

QUA prep in the capacity of

> This is the only three-letter word beginning with Q that needs a U. It is played so often that it is well worth mastering all the hooks to this: it takes A at the front to make

aqua and D, G, I, T and Y at the back to make **quad**, **quag**, **quai**, **quat** and **quay**.

QUACK vb, n **quacked**, **quacker**, **quackle**, **quacks**, **quacky**

QUAD n

QUADDED adj formed of multiple quads

QUADRAT n area marked out for study of the plants in the surrounding area

QUADRIC adj having or characterized by an equation of the second degree ▷ n quadric curve, surface, or function

QUADS ▸ quad

QUAERE n query or question ▷ interj ask or inquire ▷ vb ask **quaered**, **quaeres**

QUAFF vb **quaffed**, **quaffer**, **quaffs**

QUAG another word for > quagmire

QUAGGA n recently extinct zebra **quaggas**

QUAGGY adj resembling a marsh or quagmire

QUAGS ▸ quag

QUAHAUG = quahog

QUAHOG n edible clam **quahogs**

QUAI = quay

QUAICH n small shallow drinking cup **quaichs**, **quaigh**

QUAIGHS ▸ quaigh

QUAIL n, vb **quailed**, **quails**

QUAINT adj

QUAIR n book **quairs**

QUAIS ▸ quai

QUAKE vb, n **quaked**, **quaker**, **quakers**, **quakes**

QUAKIER ▸ quaky

QUAKILY ▸ quaky

QUAKING ▸ quake

QUAKY adj inclined to quake

QUALE n essential property or quality **qualia**

QUALIFY vb

QUALITY n, adj

QUALM n **qualms**, **qualmy**

QUAMASH another name for ▸ camass

QUANGO n **quangos**

QUANNET n flat file with handle at one end

QUANT n long pole for propelling a boat ▷ vb propel (a boat) with a quant

QUANTA ▸ quantum

QUANTAL adj of or relating to a quantum or an entity that is quantized

QUANTED ▸ quant

QUANTIC n mathematical function

QUANTS ▸ quant

QUANTUM n, adj

QUARE adj remarkable or strange **quarer**, **quarest**

QUARK n **quarks**

> This subatomic particle appears in the Scrabble cloud-

chamber fairly often, and when it does, remember that you can put an S on the front of it to make **squark**.

QUARREL n, vb
QUARRY n, vb
QUART n
QUARTAN adj (esp of a malarial fever) occurring every third day ⊳ n quartan malaria
QUARTE n fourth of eight basic positions from which a parry or attack can be made in fencing
QUARTER n, vb, adj
QUARTES ▶ quarte
QUARTET n
QUARTIC n biquadratic equation
QUARTO n book size in which the sheets are folded into four leaves quartos
QUARTS ▶ quart
QUARTZ n quartzy
QUASAR n quasars
QUASH vb quashed, quasher, quashes
QUASI adv as if
QUASS variant of ▶ kvass
QUASSES ▶ quass
QUASSIA n tropical American tree
QUASSIN n bitter crystalline substance
QUAT n spot
QUATCH vb move
QUATE n fortune
QUATRE n playing card with four pips **quatres**
QUATS ▶ quat

QUAVER vb, n quavers, quavery
QUAY n
QUAYAGE n system of quays
QUAYD archaic past participle of ▶ quail
a Spenserian word meaning daunted, that makes a surprising hook for quay.
QUAYS ▶ quay
QUAZZY adj unwell
QUBIT n quantum bit qubits
QUBYTE n unit of eight qubits **qubytes**
QUEACH n thicket
QUEACHY adj unwell
QUEAN n boisterous, impudent, or disreputable woman **queans**
QUEASY adj queazy
QUEBEC n quebecs
QUEECHY = queachy
QUEEN n, vb queened
QUEENIE n scallop
QUEENLY adj resembling or appropriate to a queen ⊳ adv in a manner appropriate to a queen
QUEENS ▶ queen
QUEENY adj effeminate
QUEER adj, n, vb queered, queerer, queerly, queers
QUEEST n wood pigeon queests
QUEINT = quaint
QUELCH = squelch
QUELEA n East African weaver bird queleas

QUELL vb quelled, queller, quells
QUEME vb please quemed, quemes, queming
QUENA n Andean flute quenas
QUENCH vb
QUEP interj expression of derision
QUERIDA n sweetheart
QUERIED ▶ query
QUERIER ▶ query
QUERIES ▶ query
QUERIST n person who makes inquiries or queries
QUERN n stone hand mill for grinding corn querns
QUERY n, vb
QUEST n, vb quested, quester
QUESTOR = quaestor
QUESTS ▶ quest
QUETCH vb move
QUETHE vb say quethes
QUETSCH n plum brandy
QUETZAL n crested bird of Central and N South America
This is a great word if you can get the tiles for it, so it's well worth remembering both spellings – it can also be **quezal** – and the four plural forms, which are **quetzals** or **quetzales** and **quezals** or **quezales**.
QUEUE n, vb queued, queuer, queuers, queues, queuing

QUEY n young cow

QUEYN n girl **queynie, queyns**

QUEYS ▸ **quey**

QUEZAL = **quetzal**

QUEZALS ▸ **quezal**

QUIBBLE vb, n **quiblin**

QUICH vb move

QUICHE n

QUICHED ▸ **quich**

QUICHES ▸ **quiche**

QUICK adj, n, adv

QUICKEN vb make or become faster ▸ n rowan tree

QUICKER ▸ **quick**

QUICKIE n anything done or made hurriedly ▸ adj made or done rapidly

QUICKLY ▸ **quick**

QUICKS ▸ **quick**

QUICKY n hastily arranged divorce

QUID n

QUIDAM n specified person **quidams**

QUIDDIT = **quiddity**

QUIDDLE vb waste time

QUIDS ▸ **quid**

QUIESCE vb quieten

QUIET adj, n, vb **quieted**

QUIETEN vb

QUIETER ▸ **quiet**

QUIETLY ▸ **quiet**

QUIETS ▸ **quiet**

QUIETUS n release from life

QUIFF n tuft of hair brushed up above the forehead **quiffs**

QUIGHT vb quit **quights**

QUILL n, vb

QUILLAI another name

for > **soapbark**

QUILLED ▸ **quill**

QUILLET n quibble or subtlety

QUILLON n either half of the extended crosspiece of a sword or dagger

QUILLS ▸ **quill**

QUILT n, vb **quilted, quilter, quilts**

QUIN short for > **quintuplet**

QUINA n quinine

QUINARY adj consisting of fives or by fives ▸ n set of five

QUINAS ▸ **quina**

QUINATE adj arranged in or composed of five parts

QUINCE n **quinces**

QUINCHE vb move

QUINE variant of ▸ **quean**

QUINELA = **quinella**

QUINES ▸ **quine**

QUINIC adj as in **quinic acid** white crystalline soluble optically active carboxylic acid

QUINIE n girl **quinies**

QUININ = **quinine**

QUININA = **quinine**

QUININE n

QUININS ▸ **quinin**

QUINNAT n Pacific salmon

QUINO = **keno**

QUINOA n type of grain high in nutrients **quinoas**

QUINOID = **quinonoid**

QUINOL n white crystalline soluble

phenol used as a photographic developer **quinols**

QUINONE n yellow crystalline water-soluble unsaturated ketone

QUINOS ▸ **quino**

QUINS ▸ **quin**

QUINSY n inflammation of the throat or tonsils

QUINT = **quin**

QUINTA n Portuguese vineyard where grapes for wine or port are grown

QUINTAL n unit of weight

QUINTAN adj (of a fever) occurring every fourth day ▸ n quintan fever

QUINTAR n Albanian unit of currency

QUINTAS ▸ **quinta**

QUINTE n fifth of eight basic positions from which a parry or attack can be made in fencing **quintes**

QUINTET n

QUINTIC adj of or relating to the fifth degree ▸ n mathematical function

QUINTIN = **quintain**

QUINTS ▸ **quint**

QUINZE n card game where players aim to score 15 **quinzes**

> Deriving from the French word for fifteen, this makes a high-scoring word that you may well

get to play, and if you can use all your tiles to form the plural, you'll get a 50-point bonus.

QUIP *n, vb*
QUIPO = quipu
QUIPOS ▶ quipo
QUIPPED ▶ quip
QUIPPER ▶ quip
QUIPPU = quipu
QUIPPUS ▶ quippu
QUIPPY ▶ quip
QUIPS ▶ quip
QUIPU *n* device of the Incas used to record information using knotted cords **quipus**
QUIRE *n* set of 24 or 25 sheets of paper ▶ *vb* arrange in quires **quired, quires, quiring**
QUIRK *n, vb* **quirked, quirks, quirky**
QUIRT *n* whip with a leather thong at one end ▶ *vb* strike with a quirt **quirted, quirts**
QUIST *n* wood pigeon **quists**
QUIT *vb, adj*
QUITCH *vb* move
QUITE *archaic form of* ▶ quit
QUITED ▶ quite
QUITES ▶ quite
QUITING ▶ quite
QUITS ▶ quite
QUITTAL *n* repayment of an action with a similar action
QUITTED ▶ quit
QUITTER *n* person who lacks perseverance

QUITTOR *n* infection of the cartilages on the side of a horse's foot
QUIVER *vb, n* **quivers, quivery**
QUIXOTE *n* impractical idealist

Using the Q and X, this word for an impractical dreamer has a reasonable chance of coming up, so keeping an eye open for it is not that quixotic!

QUIZ *n, vb* **quizzed, quizzer, quizzes**
QUOAD *adv* as far as
QUOD *n* jail ▶ *vb* say **quodded**
QUODLIN *n* cooking apple
QUODS ▶ quod
QUOHOG *n* edible clam **quohogs**
QUOIF *vb* arrange (the hair) **quoifed, quoifs**
QUOIN *n* external corner of a building ▶ *vb* wedge **quoined, quoins**
QUOIST *n* wood pigeon **quoists**
QUOIT *n* large ring used in the game of quoits ▶ *vb* throw as a quoit **quoited, quoiter**
QUOITS *n* game in which quoits are tossed at a stake in the ground
QUOKKA *n* small Australian wallaby **quokkas**

QUOLL *n* Australian catlike carnivorous marsupial **quolls**
QUOMODO *n* manner
QUONDAM *adj* of an earlier time
QUONK *vb* make an accidental noise while broadcasting **quonked, quonks**
QUOOKE *archaic past participle of* ▶ quake
QUOP *vb* pulsate or throb **quopped, quops**
QUORATE *adj* having or being a quorum
QUORUM *n* **quorums**
QUOTA *n* **quotas**
QUOTE *vb, n, interj* **quoted, quoter, quoters, quotes**
QUOTH *vb*
QUOTHA *interj* expression of mild sarcasm, used in picking up a word or phrase used by someone else
QUOTING ▶ quote
QUOTUM = quota
QUOTUMS ▶ quotum
QURSH = qurush
QURSHES ▶ qurush
QURUSH *n* Saudi Arabian currency unit
QUYTE = quit
QUYTED ▶ quyte
QUYTES ▶ quyte
QUYTING ▶ quyte
QWERTY *n* standard English-language typewriter or computer keyboard **qwertys**

Rr

R is one of the most common consonants in Scrabble, along with **N** and **T**. Despite this, however, there is only one two-letter word beginning with **R**: **re** (2 points). This is worth remembering, as you won't need to waste time trying to think of others. There are some good three-letter words with **R**, however, some of which are quite unusual: **raj**, **rax**, **rex** (10 each), **rez** and **riz** (12 each). Also, don't forget common words like **raw**, **ray** and **row** (6 each).

RABANNA *n* Madagascan woven raffia

RABAT *vb* rotate so that the plane rotated coincides with another

RABATO *n* wired or starched collar **rabatos**

RABATS ▶ rabat

RABATTE = rabat

RABBET *n* recess cut into a surface ▶ *vb* cut or form a rabbet in (timber) **rabbets**

RABBI *n* **rabbies**, **rabbin**

RABBINS ▶ rabbin

RABBIS ▶ rabbi

RABBIT *n, vb*

RABBITO = rabbitoh

RABBITS ▶ rabbit

RABBITY *adj* rabbitlike

RABBLE *n, vb* **rabbled**

RABBLER *n* device for stirring, mixing, or skimming a molten charge in a furnace

RABBLES ▶ rabble

RABBONI *n* very respectful Jewish title or form of address

RABI *n* (in Pakistan, India, etc) a crop that is harvested at the end of winter

RABIC ▶ rabies

RABID *adj* **rabider**, **rabidly**

RABIES *n*

RABIS ▶ rabi

RACA *adj* biblical word meaning worthless or empty-headed

RACCOON *n*

RACE *n, vb* **raced**

RACEME *n* cluster of flowers along a central stem, as in the foxglove

RACEMED *adj* with or in racemes

RACEMES ▶ raceme

RACEMIC *adj* being a mixture of equal amounts of enantiomers

RACER *n* person, animal, or machine that races **racers**

RACES ▶ race

RACEWAY *n* racetrack, esp one for banger racing

RACH *n* scent hound **rache, raches**

RACHET = ratchet

RACHETS ▶ rachet

RACHIAL ▶ rachis

RACHIS *n* main axis or stem of an inflorescence or compound leaf

RACIAL *adj*

RACIER ▶ racy

RACIEST ▸ racy
RACILY ▸ racy
RACING *adj* denoting or associated with horse races ▷ *n* practice of engaging in contests of speed **racings**
RACINO *n* combined racetrack and casino **racinos**
RACISM *n* racisms, racist, racists
RACK *n, vb* racked, racker, rackers
RACKET *n, vb*
RACKETS *n* ball game played in a paved walled court
RACKETT *n* early double-reeded wind instrument
RACKETY *adj* involving noise, commotion and excitement
RACKFUL ▸ rack
RACKING ▸ rack
RACKLE *adj* dialect word meaning rash
RACKS ▸ rack
RACLOIR *n* scraper
RACON *n* radar beacon **racons**
RACOON = raccoon
RACOONS ▸ racoon
RACQUET = racket
RACY *adj*
RAD *n, vb, adj*
RADAR *n* radars
RADDED, radder, raddest, radding ▸ rad
RADDLE = ruddle
RADDLED *adj* (of a

person) unkempt or run-down in appearance
RADDLES ▸ raddle
RADE (*in Scots dialect*) *past tense of* ▸ ride
RADGE *adj* angry or uncontrollable ▷ *n* person acting in such a way **radger, radges, radgest**
RADIAL *adj, n*
RADIALE *n* bone in the wrist
RADIALS ▸ radial
RADIAN *n* radians
RADIANT *adj, n*
RADIATA *adj as in* radiata pine type of pine tree
RADIATE *vb, adj*
RADICAL *adj, n*
RADICEL *n* very small root
RADICES ▸ radix
RADICLE *n*
RADII ▸ radius
RADIO *n, vb, adj* radioed, radios
RADISH *n*
RADIUM *n* radiums
RADIUS *n*
RADIX *n* any number that is the base of a number system or of a system of logarithms **radixes**
RADOME *n* protective housing for a radar antenna **radomes**
RADON *n* radons
RADS ▸ rad
RADULA *n* horny tooth-bearing strip on

the tongue of molluscs **radulae, radular, radulas**
RAFALE *n* burst of artillery fire **rafales**
RAFF *n* rubbish
RAFFIA *n* raffias
RAFFISH *adj*
RAFFLE *n, vb* raffled, raffler, raffles
RAFFS ▸ raff
RAFT *n, vb* rafted
RAFTER *n, vb* rafters
RAFTING ▸ raft
RAFTMAN = raftsman
RAFTMEN ▸ raftsman
RAFTS ▸ raft
RAG *n, vb, adj*
RAGA *n* pattern of melody and rhythm in Indian music **ragas**
RAGBAG *n* confused assortment, jumble **ragbags**
RAGBOLT *n* bolt that has angled projections on it
RAGDE *archaic past form of* ▸ rage
RAGE *n, vb* raged
RAGEE = ragi
RAGEES ▸ ragee
RAGEFUL, rager, ragers, rages ▸ rage
RAGG = ragstone
RAGGA *n* dance-oriented style of reggae **raggas**
RAGGED ▸ rag
RAGGEDY *adj* somewhat ragged
RAGGEE = ragi
RAGGEES ▸ raggee

RAGGERY n rags

RAGGIER ▶ raggy

RAGGIES ▶ raggy

RAGGING ▶ rag

RAGGLE n thin groove cut in stone or brickwork ▷ vb cut a raggle in **raggled, raggles**

RAGGS ▶ ragg

RAGGY adj raglike ▷ n cereal grass cultivated in Africa and Asia for its edible grain

RAGI n cereal grass cultivated in Africa and Asia for its edible grain

RAGING ▶ rage

RAGINGS ▶ rage

RAGINI n Indian musical form related to a raga **raginis**

RAGIS ▶ ragi

RAGLAN adj, n **raglans**

RAGMAN n rag-and-bone man **ragmans, ragmen**

RAGMENT n statute, roll, or list

RAGOUT n richly seasoned stew of meat and vegetables ▷ vb make into a ragout **ragouts**

RAGS ▶ rag

RAGTAG n disparaging term for common people **ragtags**

RAGTIME n

RAGTOP n informal word for a car with a folding or removable roof **ragtops**

RAGU n Italian meat and tomato sauce

RAGULED = raguly

RAGULY adj (in heraldry) having toothlike or stublike projections

RAGUS ▶ ragu

RAGWEED n any of several plants

RAGWORK n weaving or needlework using rags

RAGWORM n type of worm that lives chiefly in burrows in sand or mud

RAGWORT n plant with ragged leaves and yellow flowers

RAH informal US word for ▶ cheer

RAHED ▶ rah

RAHING ▶ rah

RAHS ▶ rah

RAHUI n Māori prohibition **rahuis**

RAI n type of Algerian popular music

RAIA = rayah

RAIAS ▶ raia

RAID n, vb **raided, raider, raiders, raiding, raids**

RAIK n wander ▷ vb wander **raiked, raiking, raiks**

RAIL n, vb

RAILAGE n cost of transporting goods by rail

RAILBED n ballast layer supporting the sleepers of a railway track

RAILBUS n buslike vehicle for use on railway lines

RAILCAR n passenger-carrying railway vehicle consisting of a single coach

RAILE archaic spelling of ▶ rail

RAILED ▶ rail

RAILER ▶ rail

RAILERS ▶ rail

RAILES ▶ raile

RAILING n

RAILLY old word for ▶ mock

RAILMAN n railway employee **railmen**

RAILS ▶ rail

RAILWAY n

RAIMENT n

RAIN n, vb

RAINBOW n

RAINE archaic spelling of ▶ reign

RAINED ▶ rain

RAINES ▶ raine

RAINIER ▶ rainy

RAINILY ▶ rainy

RAINING ▶ rain

RAINOUT n radioactive fallout or atmospheric pollution carried to the earth by rain

RAINS ▶ rain

RAINY adj characterized by a large rainfall

RAIRD = reird

RAIRDS ▶ raird

RAIS ▶ rai

RAISE vb, n **raised, raiser, raisers, raises**

RAISIN n

RAISING n rule that moves a constituent from an embedded clause into the main clause

RAISINS ▶ raisin

RAISINY ▶ raisin

RAIT = ret

RAITA n Indian dish of chopped cucumber, mint, etc, in yogurt **raitas**

RAITED ▶ rait

RAITING ▶ rait

RAITS ▶ rait

RAIYAT = ryot

RAIYATS ▶ raiyat

RAJ n (in India) government

This Indian word for rule or empire is one of the essential short words that use a J. Remember that it can extended to **raja**.

RAJA = rajah

RAJAH n rajahs

RAJAS ▶ raja

RAJES ▶ raj

RAKE n, vb raked

RAKEE = raki

RAKEES ▶ rakee

RAKEOFF n share of profits, esp one that is illegal or given as a bribe

RAKER n person who rakes **rakers**

RAKERY n rakish behaviour

RAKES ▶ rake

RAKI n strong spirit distilled from grain

RAKIA n strong fruit-based alcoholic drink popular in the Balkans **rakias, rakija**

RAKIJAS ▶ rakija

RAKING n (in rugby) offence of scraping an opponent with the studs **rakings**

RAKIS ▶ raki

RAKISH adj

RAKSHAS = rakshasa

RAKU n type of Japanese pottery **rakus**

RALE n abnormal coarse crackling sound heard on auscultation of the chest **rales**

RALLIED ▶ rally

RALLIER ▶ rally

RALLIES ▶ rally

RALLINE adj relating to a family of birds that includes the rails, crakes, and coots

RALLY n, vb rallied

RALLYES ▶ rallye

RAM n, vb

RAMADA n outdoor eating area with roof but open sides **ramadas**

RAMAKIN = ramekin

RAMAL adj relating to a branch or branches

RAMATE adj with branches

RAMBLA n dried-up riverbed **ramblas**

RAMBLE vb, n rambled

RAMBLER n person who rambles

RAMBLES ▶ ramble

RAMCAT n dialect word for a male cat **ramcats**

RAMEAL = ramal

RAMEE = ramie

RAMEES ▶ ramee

RAMEKIN n small ovenproof dish for a single serving of food

RAMEN n Japanese dish consisting of a clear broth containing thin white noodles **ramens**

RAMENTA > ramentum

RAMEOUS = ramal

RAMET n any of the individuals in a group of clones **ramets**

RAMI = ramie

RAMIE n woody Asian shrub with broad leaves **ramies**

RAMIFY vb become complex

RAMILIE = ramillie

RAMIN n swamp-growing tree found in Malaysia and Indonesia **ramins**

RAMIS ▶ rami

RAMJET n type of jet engine **ramjets**

RAMMED ▶ ram

RAMMEL n discarded or waste matter **rammels**

RAMMER ▶ ram

RAMMERS ▶ ram

RAMMIER ▶ rammish

RAMMIES ▶ rammish

RAMMING ▶ ram

RAMMISH adj like a ram, esp in being lustful or foul-smelling

RAMMLE n collection of items saved in case they become useful **rammles**

RAMMY n noisy disturbance or free-for-all ▷ vb make a rammy

RAMONA = sagebrush

RAMONAS ▶ ramona

RAMOSE adj having branches **ramous**

RAMP n, vb

RAMPAGE vb

RAMPANT adj

RAMPART n, vb

RAMPED ▶ ramp

RAMPER ▶ ramp

RAMPERS ▶ ramp

RAMPICK = rampike

RAMPIKE n US or dialect word for a dead tree

RAMPING ▶ ramp

RAMPION n European and Asian plant

RAMPIRE archaic variant of ▶ rampart

RAMPOLE = rampike

RAMPS ▶ ramp

RAMROD n, adj, vb **ramrods**

RAMS ▶ ram

RAMSON n type of garlic **ramsons**

RAMSTAM adv headlong ▷ adj headlong

RAMTIL n African plant grown in India esp for its oil **ramtils**

RAMULAR adj relating to a branch or branches

RAMULI ▶ ramulus

RAMULUS n small branch

RAMUS n barb of a bird's feather

RAN ▶ run

RANA n genus of frogs **ranas**

RANCE Scots word for ▷ prop

RANCED ▶ rance

RANCEL vb (in Shetland and Orkney) carry out a search **rancels**

RANCES ▶ rance

RANCH n, vb **ranched**

RANCHER n person who owns, manages, or works on a ranch

RANCHES ▶ ranch

RANCHO n hut or group of huts for housing ranch workers **ranchos**

RANCID adj

RANCING ▶ rance

RANCOR = rancour

RANCORS ▶ rancor

RANCOUR n

RAND n, vb

RANDAN n boat rowed by three people **randans**

RANDED ▶ rand

RANDEM adv with three horses harnessed together as a team ▷ n carriage or team of horses so driven **randems**

RANDIE = randy

RANDIER ▶ randy

RANDIES ▶ randy

RANDILY ▶ randy

RANDING ▶ rand

RANDOM adj, n **randoms, randon**

RANDONS ▶ randon

RANDS ▶ rand

RANDY adj sexually aroused ▷ n rude or reckless person

RANEE = rani

RANEES ▶ ranee

RANG ▶ ring

RANGE n, vb **ranged**

RANGER n **rangers**

RANGES ▶ range

RANGI n sky

RANGIER ▶ rangy

RANGILY ▶ rangy

RANGING ▶ range

RANGIS ▶ rangi

RANGOLI n traditional Indian ground decoration

RANGY adj having long slender limbs

RANI n wife or widow of a rajah

RANID n frog **ranids**

RANINE adj relating to frogs

RANIS ▶ rani

RANK n, vb, adj **ranke, ranked**

RANKER n soldier in the ranks **rankers**

RANKES ▶ ranke

RANKEST ▶ rank

RANKING adj prominent ▷ n position on a scale

RANKISH adj old word meaning rather rank

RANKISM n discrimination against people on the grounds of rank

RANKLE vb rankled, rankles
RANKLY ▶ rank
RANKS ▶ rank
RANPIKE = rampike
RANSACK vb
RANSEL = rancel
RANSELS ▶ ransel
RANSOM n, vb ransoms
RANT vb, n ranted, ranter, ranters, ranting, rants
RANULA n saliva-filled cyst that develops under the tongue
RANULAR adj of a cyst under the tongue
RANULAS ▶ ranula
RANZEL = rancel
RANZELS ▶ ranzel
RAOULIA n flowering plant of New Zealand
RAP vb, n
RAPE vb, n raped, raper, rapers, rapes
RAPHAE ▶ raphe
RAPHE n elongated ridge of conducting tissue along the side of certain seeds raphes
RAPHIA = raffia
RAPHIAS ▶ raphia
RAPHIDE n needle-shaped crystal that occurs in many plant cells raphis
RAPID adj rapider, rapidly
RAPIDS pl n part of a river with a fast turbulent current
RAPIER n rapiers
RAPINE n pillage or

plundering **rapines**
RAPING ▶ rape
RAPINI pl n type of leafy vegetable
RAPIST n person who commits rape **rapists**
RAPLOCH n Scots word for homespun woollen material ▷ adj Scots word meaning coarse or homemade
RAPPE n Arcadian dish of grated potatoes and pork or chicken
RAPPEE n moist English snuff of the 18th and 19th centuries **rappees**
RAPPEL n (formerly) a drumbeat to call soldiers to arms ▷ vb abseil **rappels**
RAPPEN n Swiss coin equal to one hundredth of a franc
RAPPER n something used for rapping, such as a knocker on a door **rappers**
RAPPES ▶ rappe
RAPPING ▶ rap
RAPPINI ▶ rapini
RAPPORT n
RAPS ▶ rap
RAPT adj raptly
RAPTOR n any bird of prey **raptors**
RAPTURE n, vb
RARE adj, vb
RAREBIT n as in Welsh rarebit dish made from melted cheese served on toast
RARED ▶ rare

RAREE n as in raree show street show or carnival
RAREFY vb make or become rarer or less dense
RARELY adv seldom
RARER ▶ rare
RARES ▶ rare
RAREST ▶ rare
RARIFY = rarefy
RARING adj
RARITY n
RARK vb as in rark up informal New Zealand expression meaning reprimand severely **rarked, rarking, rarks**
RAS n headland
RASBORA n often brightly coloured tropical fish
RASCAL n, adj rascals
RASCHEL n type of loosely knitted fabric
RASE = raze; rased, raser, rasers, rases
RASH adj, n, vb rashed
RASHER n rashers
RASHES ▶ rash
RASHEST ▶ rash
RASHIE n protective shirt worn by surfers rashies
RASHING ▶ rash
RASHLY ▶ rash
RASING ▶ rase
RASP n, vb rasped, rasper, raspers
RASPIER ▶ raspy
RASPING adj (esp of a noise) harsh or grating
RASPISH ▶ rasp
RASPS ▶ rasp

RASPY = rasping

RASSE n small S Asian civet **rasses**

RASSLE dialect variant of ▶ wrestle

RASSLED ▶ rassle

RASSLES ▶ rassle

RAST archaic past form of ▶ race

RASTA adj of a member of a particular Black religious movement

RASTER n image consisting of rows of pixel information ▷ vb turn a digital image into a large picture **rasters**

RASTRUM n pen for drawing the five lines of a musical stave simultaneously

RASURE n scraping **rasures**

RAT n, vb

RATA n New Zealand hard-wood forest tree

RATABLE adj able to be rated or evaluated **ratably**

RATAFEE = ratafia

RATAFIA n

RATAL n amount on which rates are assessed ▷ adj of or relating to rates (local taxation) **ratals**

RATAN = rattan

RATANS ▶ ratan

RATANY n flowering desert shrub

RATAS ▶ rata

RATATAT n sound of knocking on a door

RATBITE n as in ratbite fever acute infectious disease that can be caught from rats

RATCH = ratchet

RATCHED ▶ ratch

RATCHES ▶ ratch

RATCHET n, vb

RATE n, vb rated

RATEEN = ratine

RATEENS ▶ rateen

RATEL n large African and S Asian musteline mammal **ratels**

RATER ▶ rate

RATERS ▶ rate

RATES pl n (in some countries) a tax on property levied by a local authority

RATFINK n contemptible or undesirable person

RATFISH n deep-sea fish with a whiplike tail

RATH = rathe

RATHA n (in India) a four-wheeled carriage drawn by horses or bullocks **rathas**

RATHE adj blossoming or ripening early in the season

RATHER adv, interj, sentence substitute

RATHEST adv dialect or archaic word meaning soonest

RATHOLE n rat's hiding place or burrow

RATHS ▶ rath

RATIFY vb

RATINE n coarse loosely woven cloth **ratines**

RATING n ratings

RATIO n

RATION n, vb

RATIONS pl n fixed daily allowance of food

RATIOS ▶ ratio

RATITE adj (of flightless birds) having a breastbone that lacks a keel ▷ n bird that belongs to this group **ratites**

RATLIKE ▶ rat

RATLIN = ratline

RATLINE n light line tied across the shrouds of a sailing vessel

RATLING n young rat

RATLINS ▶ ratlin

RATO = ratu

RATOO = ratu

RATOON n new shoot that grows from near the root or crown of crop plants ▷ vb propagate by such a growth **ratoons**

RATOOS ▶ ratoo

RATOS ▶ rato

RATPACK n members of the press who pursue celebrities

RATS ▶ rat

RATTAIL n type of fish

RATTAN n climbing palm with jointed stems used for canes **rattans**

RATTED ▶ rat

RATTEEN = ratine

RATTEN vb sabotage or steal tools in order to disrupt the work of **rattens**

RATTER n dog or cat that catches and kills rats **ratters**

RATTERY n rats' dwelling area

RATTIER ▸ ratty

RATTILY ▸ ratty

RATTING ▸ rat

RATTISH adj of, resembling, or infested with rats

RATTLE vb, n **rattled**

RATTLER n something that rattles

RATTLES ▸ rattle

RATTLIN = ratline

RATTLY adj having a rattle

RATTON n dialect word for a little rat **rattons**

RATTOON = ratoon

RATTRAP n device for catching rats

RATTY adj

RATU n title used by Fijian chiefs or nobles **ratus**

RAUCID adj raucous

RAUCITY ▸ raucous

RAUCLE adj Scots word for rough or tough **raucler**

RAUCOUS adj

RAUGHT archaic past form of ▸ reach

RAUN n fish roe or spawn

RAUNCH n lack of polish or refinement ▷ vb behave in a raunchy manner

RAUNCHY adj earthy, sexy

RAUNGE archaic word for ▸ range

RAUNGED ▸ raunge

RAUNGES ▸ raunge

RAUNS ▸ raun

RAUPATU n confiscation or seizure of land

RAUPO n New Zealand bulrush **raupos**

RAURIKI n any of various plants with prickly leaves

RAV n Hebrew word for rabbi

RAVAGE vb, n **ravaged, ravager, ravages**

RAVE vb, n **raved**

RAVEL vb tangle or become entangled ▷ n tangle or complication **raveled, raveler**

RAVELIN n outwork having two embankments at a salient angle

RAVELLY ▸ ravel

RAVELS ▸ ravel

RAVEN n, adj, vb **ravened, ravener, ravens**

RAVER n person who leads a wild or uninhibited social life **ravers**

RAVES ▸ rave

RAVIN archaic spelling of ▸ raven

RAVINE n

RAVINED ▸ ravin

RAVINES ▸ ravine

RAVING adj, n **ravings**

RAVINS ▸ ravin

RAVIOLI n

RAVISH vb

RAVS ▸ rav

RAW as in **in the raw** adj

RAWARU n New Zealand name for blue cod **rawarus**

RAWBONE archaic variant of ▸ rawboned

RAWER ▸ raw

RAWEST ▸ raw

RAWHEAD n bogeyman

RAWHIDE n untanned hide ▷ vb whip

RAWIN n monitoring of winds in the upper atmosphere using radar and a balloon

RAWING (in dialect) = rowen

RAWINGS ▸ rawing

RAWINS ▸ rawin

RAWISH ▸ raw

RAWLY ▸ raw

RAWN (in dialect) = rowen

RAWNESS ▸ raw

RAWNS ▸ rawn

RAWS ▸ raw

RAX vb stretch or extend ▷ n act of stretching or straining **raxed, raxes, raxing**

A dialect word meaning to stretch or strain, and one of the essential short words to know for using the X.

RAY n, vb

RAYA = rayah

RAYAH n (formerly) a non-Muslim subject of the Ottoman Empire **rayahs**

RAYAS ▸ raya

RAYED ▸ ray

RAYING ▸ ray
RAYLE archaic spelling of ▸ **rail**
RAYLED ▸ rayle
RAYLES ▸ rayle
RAYLESS adj dark
RAYLET n small ray raylets
RAYLIKE adj resembling a ray
RAYLING ▸ rayle
RAYNE archaic spelling of ▸ **reign**
RAYNES ▸ rayne
RAYON n rayons
RAYS ▸ ray
RAZE vb razed
RAZEE n sailing ship that has had its upper deck or decks removed ▷ vb remove the upper deck or decks of (a sailing ship) razeed, razees
RAZER, razers, razes, razing ▸ raze
RAZOO n imaginary coin razoos
RAZOR n, vb razored, razors
RAZURE = rasure
RAZURES ▸ razure
RAZZ vb make fun of razzed, razzes
RAZZIA n raid for plunder or slaves razzias
RAZZING ▸ razz
RAZZLE n as in on the razzle out enjoying oneself or celebrating razzles
RE prep concerning ▷ n the second note of the

musical scale
REACH vb, n reached, reacher, reaches
REACT vb reacted
REACTOR n
REACTS ▸ react
READ vb, n
READAPT vb adapt again
READD vb add again readded, readds
READER n readers
READIED ▸ ready
READIER ▸ ready
READIES pl n ready money
READILY adv
READING ▸ read
README n document which accompanies computer files or software
READMIT vb let (a person, country, etc) back in to a place or organization
READOPT vb adopt again
READORN vb adorn again
READOUT n act of retrieving information from a computer memory or storage device
READS ▸ read
READY adj, vb
REAFFIX vb affix again
REAGENT n
REAGIN n type of antibody that is formed against an allergen reagins
REAK = reck

REAKED ▸ reak
REAKING ▸ reak
REAKS ▸ reak
REAL adj, n realer, reales, realest
REALGAR n rare orange-red soft mineral
REALIA pl n real-life facts and material used in teaching
REALIGN vb change or put back to a new or former place or position
REALISE = realize
REALISM n
REALIST n person who accepts events, etc, as they are
REALITY n
REALIZE vb
REALLIE old or dialect variant of ▸ **really**
REALLOT vb allot again
REALLY adv, interj, vb
REALM n realms
REALO n member of the German Green party with moderate views realos

> A **realo** is a member of the less radical section of the German Green party. It is important to know not because it scores well, but because it provides an easily overlooked 'hook', by allowing you to add O to **real**.

REALS ▸ real
REALTER vb alter again

REALTIE n archaic word meaning sincerity

REALTOR n estate agent

REALTY n immovable property

REAM n, vb

REAME archaic variant of ▶ realm

REAMED ▶ ream

REAMEND vb amend again

REAMER n tool used for smoothing the bores of holes accurately to size **reamers**

REAMES ▶ reame

REAMIER ▶ reamy

REAMING ▶ ream

REAMS ▶ ream

REAMY Scots for ▶ creamy

REAN = reen

REANNEX vb annex again

REANS ▶ rean

REAP vb reaped

REAPER n person who reaps or machine for reaping **reapers**

REAPING ▶ reap

REAPPLY vb put or spread (something) on again

REAPS ▶ reap

REAR n, vb reared, rearer, rearers

REARGUE vb argue again

REARING ▶ rear

REARISE vb arise again

REARLY old word for ▶ early

REARM vb rearmed, rearms

REAROSE ▶ rearise

REARS ▶ rear

REASON n, vb reasons

REAST = reest

REASTED ▶ reast

REASTS ▶ reast

REASTY adj (in dialect) rancid

REATA n lasso reatas

REATE n type of crowfoot **reates**

REAVAIL vb avail again

REAVE vb carry off (property, prisoners, etc) by force **reaved, reaver, reavers, reaves, reaving**

REAVOW vb avow again reavows

REAWAKE vb awake again **reawoke**

REB n Confederate soldier in the American Civil War

REBACK vb provide with a new back, backing, or lining **rebacks**

REBADGE vb relaunch (a product) under a new name, brand, or logo

REBAIT vb bait again rebaits

REBAR n rod providing reinforcement in concrete structures rebars

REBATE n, vb rebated, rebater, rebates

REBATO = rabato

REBATOS ▶ rebato

REBBE n individual's chosen spiritual mentor **rebbes**

REBEC n medieval stringed instrument resembling the violin rebeck

REBECKS ▶ rebeck

REBECS ▶ rebec

REBEGAN ▶ rebegin

REBEGIN vb begin again rebegun

REBEL vb, n, adj rebels

REBID vb bid again rebids

REBILL vb bill again rebills

REBIND vb bind again rebinds

REBIRTH n revival or renaissance

REBIT ▶ rebite

REBITE vb (in printing) to give another application of acid rebites

REBLEND vb blend again **reblent**

REBLOOM vb bloom again

REBOANT adj resounding or reverberating

REBOARD vb board again

REBODY vb give a new body to

REBOIL vb boil again reboils

REBOOK vb book again rebooks

REBOOT vb shut down and then restart (a computer system) reboots

REBOP = bebop

REBOPS ▶ rebop

REBORE n boring of a cylinder to restore its true shape ▷ vb carry out this process **rebored, rebores**

REBORN adj active again after a period of inactivity

REBOUND vb, n

REBOZO n long scarf covering the shoulders and head **rebozos**

REBRACE vb brace again

REBRAND vb change or update the image of (an organization or product)

REBRED ▶ rebreed

REBREED vb breed again

REBS ▶ reb

REBUFF vb, n **rebuffs**

REBUILD vb **rebuilt**

REBUKE vb, n **rebuked, rebuker, rebukes**

REBURY vb bury again

REBUS n puzzle consisting of pictures and symbols representing words or syllables **rebuses**

REBUT vb **rebuts**

REBUY vb buy again **rebuys**

REC n short for recreation

RECAL = recall

RECALL vb, n **recalls, recals**

RECANE vb cane again **recaned, recanes**

RECANT vb **recants**

RECAP vb, n **recaps**

RECARRY vb carry again

RECAST vb organize or set out in a different way **recasts**

RECATCH vb catch again

RECCE vb reconnoitre ▷ n reconnaissance **recced, recceed, recces**

RECCIED ▶ reccy

RECCIES ▶ reccy

RECCO = recce

RECCOS ▶ recco

RECCY = recce

RECEDE vb receded, recedes

RECEIPT n, vb

RECEIVE vb

RECENCY ▶ recent

RECENSE vb revise

RECENT adj

RECEPT n idea or image formed in the mind by repeated experience **recepts**

RECESS n, vb

RECHART vb chart again

RECHATE = recheat

RECHEAT n (in a hunt) sounding of the horn to call back the hounds ▷ vb sound the horn to call back the hounds

RECHECK vb check again

RECHEW vb chew again **rechews**

RECHIE adj smoky

RECHIP vb put a new chip into (a stolen mobile phone) so it can be reused **rechips**

RECHOSE ▶ rechoose

RECIPE n **recipes**

RECIT n narrative

RECITAL n

RECITE vb **recited, reciter, recites**

RECITS ▶ recit

RECK vb mind or care about (something)

RECKAN adj strained, tormented, or twisted

RECKED ▶ reck

RECKING ▶ reck

RECKON vb **reckons**

RECKS ▶ reck

RECLAD vb cover in a different substance **reclads**

RECLAIM vb, n

RECLAME n public acclaim or attention

RECLASP vb clasp again

RECLEAN vb clean again

RECLIMB vb climb again

RECLINE vb

RECLOSE vb close again

RECLUSE n, adj

RECOAL vb supply or be supplied with fresh coal **recoals**

RECOAT vb coat again **recoats**

RECOCK vb cock again **recocks**

RECODE vb put into a new code **recoded, recodes**

RECOIL vb, n **recoils**

RECOIN vb coin again **recoins**

RECOLOR vb give a new colour to

RECOMB vb comb again **recombs**

RECON vb make a preliminary survey **recons**

RECOOK vb cook again **recooks**

RECOPY vb copy again

RECORD n, vb **records**

RECORK vb cork again **recorks**

RECOUNT vb

RECOUP vb

RECOUPE vb (in law) keep back or withhold **RECOUPS** ▶ recoup

RECOURE archaic variant of ▶ recover

RECOVER vb **recover**

RECOYLE archaic spelling of ▶ recoil

RECREATE vb crate again

RECROSS vb move or go across (something) again

RECROWN vb crown again

RECRUIT vb, n

RECS ▶ rec

RECTA ▶ rectum

RECTAL adj of the rectum

RECTI ▶ rectus

RECTIFY vb

RECTION n (in grammar) the determination of the form of one word by another word

RECTO n right-hand page of a book

RECTOR n rectors

RECTORY n

RECTOS ▶ recto

RECTRIX n any of the large stiff feathers of a bird's tail

RECTUM n rectums

RECTUS n straight muscle

RECUILE archaic variant of ▶ recoil

RECULE archaic variant of ▶ recoil

RECULED ▶ recule

RECULES ▶ recule

RECUR vb

RECURE vb archaic word for cure or recover **recured, recures**

RECURS ▶ recur

RECURVE vb curve or bend (something) back or down

RECUSAL n withdrawal of a judge from a case

RECUSE vb (in law) object to or withdraw (a judge) **recused, recuses**

RECUT vb cut again **recuts**

RECYCLE vb, n

RED adj, n

REDACT vb compose or draft (an edict, proclamation, etc) **redacts**

REDAN n fortification of two parapets at a salient angle **redans**

REDATE vb change date of **redated, redates**

REDBACK n

REDBAIT vb harass those with leftwing leanings

REDBAY n type of tree **redbays**

REDBIRD n type of bird, the male of which has bright red plumage

REDBONE n type of American dog

REDBUD n American tree with heart-shaped leaves **redbuds**

REDBUG another name for ▶ chigger

REDBUGS ▶ redbug

REDCAP n military policeman **redcaps**

REDCOAT n British soldier

REDD vb bring order to ▷ n act or an instance of redding **redded**

REDDEN vb **reddens**

REDDER ▶ redd

REDDERS ▶ redd

REDDEST ▶ red

REDDIER ▶ reddy

REDDING ▶ redd

REDDISH adj somewhat red

REDDLE = ruddle

REDDLED ▶ reddle

REDDLES ▶ reddle

REDDS ▶ redd

REDDY adj reddish

REDE n advice or counsel ▷ vb advise

REDEAL vb deal again **redeals, redealt**

REDEAR n variety of sunfish with a red flash above the gills **redears**

REDED ▶ rede

REDEEM vb **redeems**

REDEFY vb defy again

REDENY vb deny again

REDES ▶ rede

REDEYE n inferior whiskey **redeyes**

REDFIN n any of various small fishes with reddish fins that are popular aquarium fishes **redfins**

REDFISH n male salmon that has recently spawned

REDFOOT n fatal disease of newborn lambs

REDHEAD n person with reddish hair

REDIA n parasitic larva of flukes **rediae**

REDIAL vb dial (a telephone number) again **redials**

REDIAS ▶ redia

REDID ▶ redo

REDING ▶ rede

REDIP vb dip again **redips, redipt**

REDLINE vb refuse a loan to (a person or country) because of the presumed risks involved

REDLY ▶ red

REDNESS ▶ red

REDO vb do over again in order to improve ▷ n instance of redoing something

REDOCK vb dock again **redocks**

REDOES ▶ redo

REDOING ▶ redo

REDON vb don again

REDONE ▶ redon

REDONS ▶ redon

REDOS ▶ redo

REDOUBT n small fort defending a hilltop or pass ▷ vb fear

REDOUND vb cause advantage or disadvantage (to)

REDOUT n reddened vision caused by a rush of blood to the head **redouts**

REDOWA n Bohemian folk dance similar to the waltz **redowas**

REDOX n chemical reaction in which one substance is reduced and the other is oxidized **redoxes**

REDPOLL n mostly grey-brown finch with a red crown and pink breast

REDRAFT vb write a second copy of (a letter, proposal, essay, etc) ▷ n second draft

REDRAW vb draw or draw up (something) again or differently **redrawn, redraws**

REDREAM vb dream again

REDRESS vb, n

REDREW ▶ redraw

REDRIED ▶ redry

REDRIES ▶ redry

REDRILL vb drill again

REDRIVE vb drive again

REDROOT n yellow-flowered bog plant whose roots yield a red dye

REDROVE ▶ redrive

REDRY vb dry again

REDS ▶ red

REDSEAR = redshort

REDTAIL n variety of bird with red colouring on its tail

REDTOP n sensationalist tabloid newspaper **redtops**

REDUB vb fix or repair **redubs**

REDUCE vb reduced

REDUCER n chemical solution used to lessen the density of a negative or print

REDUCES ▶ reduce

REDUIT n fortified part from which a garrison may fight on once an enemy has taken outworks **reduits**

REDUX adj brought back or returned

REDWARE another name for ▶ kelp

REDWING n small European thrush

REDWOOD n

REDYE vb dye again **redyed, redyes**

REE n Scots word for walled enclosure

REEARN vb earn again **reearns**

REEBOK = rhebok

REEBOKS ▶ reebok

REECH vb (in dialect) smoke **reeched, reeches**

REECHIE = reechy

REECHO vb echo again

REECHY adj (in dialect) smoky

REED n

REEDBED n area of wetland with reeds growing in it

REEDE obsolete variant of ▶ **red**

REEDED ▶ **reed**

REEDEN adj of or consisting of reeds

REEDER n thatcher **reeders**

REEDES ▶ **reede**

REEDIER ▶ **reedy**

REEDIFY vb edify again or rebuild

REEDILY ▶ **reedy**

REEDING n set of small semicircular architectural mouldings

REEDIT vb edit again **reedits**

REEDMAN n musician who plays a wind instrument that has a reed **reedmen**

REEDS ▶ **reed**

REEDY adj harsh and thin in tone

REEF n, vb **reefed**

REEFER n **reefers**

REEFIER ▶ **reefy**

REEFING ▶ **reef**

REEFS ▶ **reef**

REEFY adj with reefs

REEJECT vb eject again

REEK vb, n **reeked, reeker, reekers**

REEKIE = **reeky**

REEKIER ▶ **reek**

REEKING ▶ **reek**

REEKS ▶ **reek**

REEKY adj steamy or smoky

REEL n, vb

REELECT vb elect again

REELED, reeler, reelers, reeling ▶ **reel**

REELMAN n (formerly) member of a beach life-saving team operating a winch **reelmen**

REELS ▶ **reel**

REEMIT vb emit again **reemits**

REEN n ditch, esp a drainage channel

REENACT vb enact again

REENDOW vb endow again

REENJOY vb enjoy again

REENS ▶ **reen**

REENTER vb enter again

REENTRY n return of a spacecraft into the earth's atmosphere

REEQUIP vb equip again

REERECT vb erect again

REES ▶ **ree**

REEST vb (esp of horses) to be noisily uncooperative **reested, reests**

REESTY = **reasty**

REEVE n local representative of the king in a shire until the early 11th century ▷ vb pass (a rope or cable) through an eye or other narrow opening **reeved, reeves, reeving**

REEVOKE vb evoke again

REEXPEL vb expel again

REF n referee in sport

▷ vb referee

REFACE vb repair or renew the facing of (a wall) **refaced, refaces**

REFALL vb fall again **refalls**

REFECT vb archaic word for restore or refresh with food and drink **refects**

REFED ▶ **refeed**

REFEED vb feed again **refeeds**

REFEEL vb feel again **refeels**

REFEL vb refute

REFELL ▶ **refall**

REFELS ▶ **refel**

REFELT ▶ **refeel**

REFENCE vb fence again

REFER vb

REFEREE n, vb

REFERS ▶ **refer**

REFFED ▶ **ref**

REFFING ▶ **ref**

REFIGHT vb fight again ▷ n second or new fight

REFILE vb file again **refiled, refiles**

REFILL vb fill again ▷ n second or subsequent filling **refills**

REFILM vb film again **refilms**

REFIND vb find again **refinds**

REFINE vb

REFINED adj

REFINER n person, device, or substance that removes impurities, etc

REFINES ▶ **refine**

REFIRE vb fire again **refired, refires**

REFIT vb make ready for use again by repairing or re-equipping ▷ n repair or re-equipping for further use **refits**

REFIX vb fix again **refixed, refixes**

REFLAG vb flag again **reflags**

REFLATE vb inflate or be inflated again

REFLECT vb

REFLET n iridescent glow or lustre, as on ceramic ware **reflets**

REFLEW ▶ refly

REFLEX n, adj, vb

REFLIES ▶ refly

REFLOAT vb float again

REFLOOD vb flood again

REFLOW vb flow again

REFLOWN ▶ refly

REFLOWS ▶ reflow

REFLUX vb boil in a vessel attached to a condenser, so that the vapour condenses and flows back in ▷ n act of refluxing

REFLY vb fly again

REFOCUS vb focus again or anew

REFOLD vb fold again **refolds**

REFOOT vb foot again **refoots**

REFORGE vb forge again

REFORM n, vb **reforms**

REFOUND vb found again

REFRACT vb change the course of (light etc) passing from one medium to another

REFRAIN n, vb

REFRAME vb support or enclose (a picture, photograph, etc) in a new or different frame

REFRESH vb

REFRIED ▶ refry

REFRIES ▶ refry

REFRONT vb put a new front on

REFROZE > refreeze

REFRY vb fry again

REFS ▶ ref

REFT ▶ reave

REFUEL vb **refuels**

REFUGE n, vb **refuged**

REFUGEE n

REFUGES ▶ refuge

REFUGIA > refugium

REFUND vb, n **refunds**

REFUSAL n

REFUSE vb, n **refused, refuser, refuses**

REFUTAL n act or process of refuting

REFUTE vb **refuted, refuter, refutes**

REG n large expanse of stony desert terrain

REGAIN vb, n **regains**

REGAL adj, n

REGALE vb, n **regaled, regaler, regales**

REGALIA pl n

REGALLY ▶ regal

REGALS ▶ regal

REGAR = regur

REGARD vb, n **regards**

REGARS ▶ regar

REGATTA n

REGAUGE vb gauge again

REGAVE ▶ regive

REGEAR vb readjust **regears**

REGENCE old variant of ▶ regency

REGENCY n

REGENT n, adj **regents**

REGES ▶ rex

REGEST n archaic word for register **regests**

REGGAE n **reggaes**

REGGO = rego

REGGOS ▶ reggo

REGIE n government-directed management or government monopoly **regies**

REGIFT vb give (a previously received gift) to someone else **regifts**

REGILD vb gild again **regilds, regilt**

REGIME n

REGIMEN n prescribed system of diet etc

REGIMES ▶ regime

REGINA n queen **reginae**

REGINAL adj queenly

REGINAS ▶ regina

REGION n **regions**

REGIUS adj as in regius professor Crown-appointed holder of a university chair

REGIVE vb give again or back **regiven, regives**

REGLAZE vb glaze again

REGLET n flat narrow architectural moulding **reglets**

REGLOSS vb gloss again or give a new gloss to

REGLOW vb glow again **reglows**

REGLUE vb glue again **reglued, reglues**

REGMA n type of fruit with cells that break open and break away when ripe **regmata**

REGNA ▶ regnum

REGNAL adj of a sovereign, reign, or kingdom

REGNANT adj reigning

REGNUM n reign or rule

REGO n registration of a motor vehicle

REGORGE vb vomit up

REGOS ▶ rego

REGOSOL n type of azonal soil

REGRADE vb grade again

REGRAFT vb graft again

REGRANT vb grant again

REGRATE vb buy up (commodities) in advance so as to raise their price for resale

REGREDE vb go back

REGREEN vb green again

REGREET vb greet again or return greetings of

REGRESS vb, n **regrets**

REGRET vb, n **regrets**

REGREW ▶ regrow

REGRIND vb grind again

REGROOM vb groom again

REGROUP vb reorganize (military forces) after an attack or a defeat

REGROW vb grow or be grown again after having been cut or having died or withered **regrown, regrows**

REGS ▶ reg

REGULA n rule **regulae**

REGULAR adj, n

REGULI ▶ regulus

REGULO n any of a number of temperatures to which a gas oven may be set **regulos**

REGULUS n impure metal forming beneath the slag during the smelting of ores

REGUR n black loamy Indian soil **regurs**

REH n (in India) salty surface crust on the soil

REHAB vb help (a person) to readapt to society or a new job ▷ n treatment or help given to an addict, etc **rehabs**

REHANG vb hang again **rehangs**

REHASH vb, n

REHEAR vb hear again **reheard, rehears**

REHEAT vb heat or be heated again **reheats**

REHEEL vb put a new heel or new heels on **reheels**

REHEM vb hem again **rehems**

REHINGE vb put a new hinge or new hinges on

REHIRE vb hire again **rehired, rehires**

REHOME vb find a new home for (esp a pet) **rehomed, rehomes**

REHOUSE vb

REHS ▶ reh

REHUNG ▶ rehang

REI n name for a former Portuguese coin

REIF n Scots word meaning robbery or plunder

REIFIED ▶ reify

REIFIER ▶ reify

REIFIES ▶ reify

REIFS ▶ reif

REIFY vb consider or make (an abstract idea or concept) real or concrete

REIGN n, vb **reigned, reigns**

REIK Scots word for ▶ **smoke**

REIKI n form of therapy to encourage healing or restore wellbeing **reikis**

REIKS ▶ reik

REIMAGE vb image again

REIN vb

REINCUR vb incur again

REINDEX vb index again

REINED ▶ rein

REINING ▶ rein

REINK vb ink again **reinked, reinks**

REINS pl n narrow straps attached to a bit to guide a horse

REINTER vb inter again

REIRD Scots word for ▸ **din**

REIRDS ▸ **reird**

REIS ▸ **rei**

REISES ▸ **rei**

REISSUE n book, record, etc, that is released again after being unavailable ▸ vb release (a book, record, etc) again after a period of unavailability

REIST = **reest**

REISTED ▸ **reist**

REISTS ▸ **reist**

REITBOK = **reedbuck**

REITER n soldier in the German cavalry **reiters**

REIVE vb go on a plundering raid **reived, reiver, reivers, reives, reiving**

REJECT vb, n **rejects**

REJIG vb re-equip (a factory or plant) ▸ n act or process of rejigging **rejigs**

REJOICE vb

REJOIN vb **rejoins**

REJON n bullfighting lance

REJONEO n bullfighting activity in which a mounted bullfighter spears the bull with lances

REJONES ▸ **rejon**

REJOURN vb archaic word meaning postpone or adjourn

REJUDGE vb judge again

REKE = **reck**

REKED ▸ **reke**

REKES ▸ **reke**

REKEY vb key again **rekeyed, rekeys**

REKING ▸ **reke**

REKNIT vb knit again **reknits**

REKNOT vb knot again **reknots**

RELABEL vb label again

RELACE vb lace again **relaced, relaces**

RELACHE n break

RELAID ▸ **relay**

RELAND vb land again **relands**

RELAPSE vb, n

RELATA ▸ **relatum**

RELATE vb

RELATED adj

RELATER ▸ **relate**

RELATES ▸ **relate**

RELATOR n person who relates a story

RELATUM n one of the objects between which a relation is said to hold

RELAX vb **relaxed**

RELAXER n person or thing that relaxes

RELAXES ▸ **relax**

RELAXIN n hormone secreted during pregnancy

RELAY n, vb **relayed, relays**

RELEARN vb learn (something previously known) again

RELEASE vb, n

RELEND vb lend again **relends**

RELENT vb **relents**

RELET vb let again **relets**

RELEVE n dance move in which heels are off the ground **releves**

RELIANT > **reliance**

RELIC n **relics**

RELICT n relic **relicts**

RELIDE archaic past form of ▸ **rely**

RELIE archaic spelling of ▸ **rely**

RELIED ▸ **rely**

RELIEF n **reliefs**

RELIER ▸ **rely**

RELIERS ▸ **rely**

RELIES ▸ **rely**

RELIEVE vb

RELIEVO = **relief**

RELIGHT vb ignite or cause to ignite again

RELINE vb line again or anew **relined, relines**

RELINK vb link again **relinks**

RELIQUE archaic spelling of ▸ **relic**

RELISH vb, n

RELIST vb list again **relists**

RELIT ▸ **relight**

RELIVE vb **relived**

RELIVER vb deliver up again

RELIVES ▸ **relive**

RELLENO n Mexican dish of stuffed vegetable

RELLIE n relative

RELLIES pl n relatives or relations

RELLISH (in music) variant of ▸ **relish**

RELOAD vb put fresh ammunition into (a firearm) **reloads**

RELOAN vb loan again **reloans**

RELOCK vb lock again **relocks**

RELOOK vb look again **relooks**

RELUCT vb struggle or rebel **relucts**

RELUME vb light or brighten again **relumed, relumes**

RELY vb relying

REM n dose of ionizing radiation

REMADE n object that has been reconstructed from original materials **remades**

REMAIL vb mail again **remails**

REMAIN vb remains

REMAINS pl n relics, esp of ancient buildings

REMAKE vb make again in a different way ▷ n new version of an old film **remaker, remakes**

REMAN vb man again or afresh

REMAND vb remands

REMANET n something left over

REMANIE n fragments and fossils of older origin found in a more recent deposit

REMANS ▶ reman

REMAP vb map again **remaps**

REMARK vb, n remarks

REMARRY vb

REMATCH n second or return game or contest between two players ▷ vb match (two contestants) again

REMATE vb mate again ▷ n finishing pass in bullfighting **remated, remates**

REMBLAI n earth used for an embankment or rampart

REMBLE dialect word for ▶ remove

REMBLED ▶ remble

REMBLES ▶ remble

REMEAD archaic or dialect word for ▶ remedy

REMEADS ▶ remead

REMEDE archaic or dialect word for ▶ remedy

REMEDED ▶ remede

REMEDES ▶ remede

REMEDY n, vb

REMEET vb meet again **remeets**

REMEID archaic or dialect word for ▶ remedy

REMEIDS ▶ remeid

REMELT vb melt again **remelts**

REMEN n ancient Egyptian measurement unit

REMEND vb mend again **remends**

REMENS ▶ remen

REMERCY vb archaic word for thank

REMERGE vb merge again

REMET ▶ remeet

REMEX n any of the large flight feathers of a bird's wing **remiges**

REMIND vb reminds

REMINT vb mint again **remints**

REMISE vb give up or relinquish (a right, claim, etc) ▷ n second thrust made on the same lunge after the first has missed **remised, remises**

REMISS adj

REMIT vb, n remits

REMIX vb change the relative prominence of each performer's part of (a recording) ▷ n remixed version of a recording **remixed, remixes, remixt**

REMNANT n, adj

REMODEL vb give a different shape or form to ▷ n something that has been remodelled

REMOLD US spelling of ▶ remould

REMOLDS ▶ remold

REMORA n spiny-finned fish **remoras, remorid**

REMORSE n

REMOTE adj, n remoter, remotes

REMOUD Spenserian variant of ▶ removed

REMOULD vb, n

REMOUNT vb get on (a horse, bicycle, etc) again ▷ n fresh horse

REMOVAL *n*

REMOVE *vb, n*

REMOVED *adj*

REMOVER ▶ remove

REMOVES ▶ remove

REMS ▶ rem

REMUAGE *n* process of turning wine bottles to let the sediment out

REMUDA *n* stock of horses enabling riders to change mounts **remudas**

REMUEUR *n* person carrying out remuage

REN *archaic variant of* ▶ run

RENAGUE = renege

RENAIL *vb* nail again **renails**

RENAL *adj*

RENAME *vb* renamed, **renames**

RENAY *vb* archaic word meaning renounce **renayed, renays**

REND *vb* tear or wrench apart **rended**

RENDER *vb, n* **renders**

RENDING ▶ rend

RENDS ▶ rend

RENEGE *vb* reneged, **reneger, reneges, renegue**

RENEST *vb* nest again or form a new nest **renests**

RENEW *vb*

RENEWAL *n* act of renewing or state of being renewed

RENEWED ▶ renew

RENEWER ▶ renew

RENEWS ▶ renew

RENEY = renay

RENEYED ▶ reney

RENEYS ▶ reney

RENGA *n* type of collaborative poetry found in Japan **rengas**

RENIED ▶ reny

RENIES ▶ reny

RENIG = renege

RENIGS ▶ renig

RENIN *n* enzyme secreted by the kidneys **renins**

RENK *adj* unpleasant **renker, renkest**

RENNASE = rennin

RENNE *archaic variant of* ▶ run

RENNED ▶ ren

RENNES ▶ renne

RENNET *n* rennets

RENNIN *n* enzyme that occurs in gastric juice

RENNING ▶ ren

RENNINS ▶ rennin

RENOWN *n* widespread good reputation ▷ *vb* make famous **renowns**

RENS ▶ ren

RENT *n* payment made by a tenant to a landlord or owner of a property ▷ *vb* grant the right to use one's property for payment

RENTAL *n, adj* **rentals**

RENTE *n* annual income from capital investment

RENTED ▶ rent

RENTER *n* person who lets his property in return for rent **renters**

RENTES ▶ rente

RENTIER *n* person who lives off unearned income such as rents or interest

RENTING ▶ rent

RENTS ▶ rent

RENVOI *n* referring of a dispute to a jurisdiction other than that in which it arose **renvois, renvoy**

RENVOYS ▶ renvoy

RENY = renay

RENYING ▶ reny

REO *n* New Zealand language

REOCCUR *vb* happen, take place, or come about again

REOFFER *vb* offer again

REOIL *vb* oil again **reoiled, reoils**

REOPEN *vb* open again after a period of being closed or suspended **reopens**

REORDER *vb* change the order of

REOS ▶ reo

REP *n, vb*

REPACK *vb* place or arrange (articles) in (a container) again or in a different way **repacks**

REPAID ▶ repay

REPAINT *vb* apply a new or fresh coat of paint

REPAIR *vb, n* **repairs**

REPAND *adj* having a wavy margin

REPANEL *vb* panel again or anew

REPAPER vb paper again or afresh

REPARK vb park again **reparks**

REPASS vb pass again

REPAST n, vb **repasts**

REPATCH vb patch again

REPAVE vb pave again **repaved, repaves**

REPAY vb **repays**

REPEAL vb, n **repeals**

REPEAT vb, n **repeats**

REPEG vb peg again **repegs**

REPEL vb **repels**

REPENT vb, adj **repents**

REPERK vb perk again **reperks**

REPIN vb pin again

REPINE vb fret or complain **repined, repiner, repines**

REPINS ▶ **repin**

REPIQUE n score of 30 in the card-game piquet ▷ vb score a repique against (someone)

REPLA ▶ **replum**

REPLACE vb

REPLAN vb plan again **replans**

REPLANT vb plant again

REPLATE vb plate again

REPLAY n, vb **replays**

REPLEAD vb plead again **repled**

REPLETE adj, vb

REPLEVY vb recover possession of (goods) by replevin

REPLICA n

REPLIED ▶ **reply**

REPLIER ▶ **reply**

REPLIES ▶ **reply**

REPLOT vb plot again **replots**

REPLOW vb plow again **replows**

REPLUM n internal separating wall in some fruits

REPLUMB vb plumb again

REPLY vb, n

REPO n act of repossessing

REPOINT vb repair the joints of (brickwork, masonry, etc) with mortar or cement

REPOLL vb poll again **repolls**

REPOMAN n man employed to repossess goods in cases of non-payment **repomen**

REPONE vb restore (someone) to his former status, office, etc **reponed, repones**

REPORT vb, n **reports**

REPOS ▶ **repo**

REPOSAL n repose

REPOSE n, vb **reposed, reposer, reposes**

REPOSIT vb put away, deposit, or store up

REPOST vb post again **reposts**

REPOT vb put (a house plant) into a new usually larger pot **repots**

REPOUR vb pour back or again **repours**

REPOWER vb put new engine in

REPP = **rep**

REPPED ▶ **rep**

REPPING ▶ **rep**

REPPS ▶ **repp**

REPRESS vb

REPRICE vb price again

REPRIME vb prime again

REPRINT vb, n

REPRISE n repeating of an earlier theme ▷ vb repeat an earlier theme

REPRIVE archaic spelling of > **reprieve**

REPRIZE archaic spelling of ▶ **reprise**

REPRO n imitation or facsimile of a work of art; reproduction

REPROBE vb probe again

REPROOF n, vb

REPROS ▶ **repro**

REPROVE vb

REPRYVE archaic spelling of > **reprieve**

REPS ▶ **rep**

REPTANT adj creeping, crawling, or lying along the ground

REPTILE n, adj

REPUGN vb oppose or conflict (with) **repugns**

REPULP vb pulp again **repulps**

REPULSE vb, n

REPUMP vb pump again **repumps**

REPUNIT n any number that consists entirely

of the same repeated digits

REPURE vb archaic word meaning make pure again **repured, repures**

REPUTE n, vb

REPUTED adj

REPUTES ▶ repute

REQUERE archaic variant of ▶ require

REQUEST vb, n

REQUIEM n

REQUIN n type of shark **requins**

REQUIRE vb

REQUIT vb quit again

REQUITE vb return to someone (the same treatment or feeling as received)

REQUITS ▶ requit

REQUOTE vb quote again

RERACK vb rack again **reracks**

RERAIL vb put back on a railway line **rerails**

RERAISE vb raise again

RERAN ▶ rerun

REREAD vb read (something) again **rereads**

REREDOS n ornamental screen behind an altar

REREMAI n New Zealand word for the basking shark

RERENT vb rent again **rerents**

RERIG vb rig again **rerigs**

RERISE vb rise again **rerisen, rerises**

REROLL vb roll again **rerolls**

REROOF vb put a new roof or roofs on **reroofs**

REROSE ▶ rerise

REROUTE vb

RERUN n film or programme that is broadcast again, repeat ▷ vb put on (a film or programme) again **reruns**

RES informal word for ▶ residence

RESAID ▶ resay

RESAIL vb sail again **resails**

RESALE n selling of something purchased earlier **resales**

RESAT ▶ resit

RESAW vb saw again **resawed, resawn, resaws**

RESAY vb say again or in response **resays**

RESCALE vb resize

RESCIND vb

RESCORE vb score afresh

RESCUE vb, n **rescued, rescuer, rescues**

RESEAL vb close or secure tightly again **reseals**

RESEAT vb show (a person) to a new seat **reseats**

RESEAU n mesh background to a lace or other pattern **reseaus, reseaux**

RESECT vb cut out part of (a bone, an organ,

or other structure or part) **resects**

RESEDA n plant that has small spikes of grey-green flowers ▷ adj of a greyish-green colour **resedas**

RESEE vb see again

RESEED vb form seed and reproduce naturally, forming a constant plant population **reseeds**

RESEEK vb seek again **reseeks**

RESEEN ▶ resee

RESEES ▶ resee

RESEIZE vb seize again

RESELL vb sell (something) one has previously bought **resells**

RESEND vb send again **resends**

RESENT vb resents

RESERVE vb, n

RESES ▶ res

RESET vb set again (a broken bone, matter in type, a gemstone, etc) ▷ n act or an instance of setting again **resets**

RESEW vb sew again **resewed, resewn, resews**

RESH n 20th letter of the Hebrew alphabet

RESHAPE vb shape (something) again or differently

RESHAVE vb shave again

RESHES ▶ resh

RESHINE vb shine again

RESHIP vb ship again **reships**

RESHOD ▶ reshoe

RESHOE vb put a new shoe or shoes on **reshoed, reshoes**

RESHONE ▶ reshine

RESHOOT vb shoot again **reshot**

RESHOW vb show again **reshown, reshows**

RESIANT archaic word for ▶ resident

RESID n residual oil left over from the petroleum distillation process

RESIDE vb resided, resider, resides

RESIDS ▶ resid

RESIDUA ▶ residuum

RESIDUE n

RESIFT vb sift again **resifts**

RESIGHT vb sight again

RESIGN vb resigns

RESILE vb spring or shrink back **resiled, resiles**

RESILIN n substance found in insect bodies

RESIN n, vb resined

RESINER n applier or collector of resin

RESINS ▶ resin

RESINY adj resembling, containing or covered with resin

RESIST vb, n resists

RESIT vb take (an exam) again ▷ n exam that has to be taken again

RESITE vb move to a different site **resited,**

resites

RESITS ▶ resit

RESIZE vb change size of **resized, resizes**

RESKEW archaic spelling of ▶ rescue

RESKEWS ▶ reskew

RESKILL vb train (workers) to acquire new skills

RESKUE archaic spelling of ▶ rescue

RESKUED ▶ reskue

RESKUES ▶ reskue

RESLATE vb slate again

RESMELT vb smelt again

RESOAK vb soak again **resoaks**

RESOD vb returf **resods**

RESOJET n type of jet engine

RESOLD ▶ resell

RESOLE vb put a new sole or new soles on **resoled, resoles**

RESOLVE vb, n

RESORB vb absorb again **resorbs**

RESORT vb, n resorts

RESOUND vb

RESOW vb sow again **resowed, resown, resows**

RESPACE vb change the spacing of

RESPADE vb dig over

RESPEAK vb speak further

RESPECT n, vb

RESPELL vb spell again **respelt**

RESPIRE vb

RESPITE n, vb

RESPLIT vb split again

RESPOKE ▶ respeak

RESPOND vb, n

RESPOOL vb rewind onto spool

RESPOT vb (in billiards) replace on one of the spots **respots**

RESPRAY n new coat of paint applied to a car, van, etc ▷ vb spray (a car, wheels, etc) with a new coat of paint

REST n, vb

RESTACK vb stack again

RESTAFF vb staff again

RESTAGE vb produce or perform a new production of (a play)

RESTAMP vb stamp again

RESTART vb commence (something) or set (something) in motion again ▷ n act or an instance of starting again

RESTATE vb state or affirm (something) again or in a different way

RESTED ▶ rest

RESTEM vb stem again **restems**

RESTER ▶ rest

RESTERS ▶ rest

RESTFUL adj

RESTIER ▶ resty

RESTIFF = restive

RESTING ▶ rest

RESTIVE adj

RESTO n restored antique, vintage car, etc

RESTOCK vb replenish stores or supplies

RESTOKE vb stoke again

RESTORE vb

RESTOS ▶ resto

RESTS ▶ rest

RESTUDY vb study again

RESTUFF vb put new stuffing in

RESTUMP vb provide with new stumps

RESTY adj restive

RESTYLE vb style again

RESULT n, vb results

RESUME vb, n resumed, resumer, resumes

RESURGE vb rise again from or as if from the dead

RET vb moisten or soak (flax, hemp, jute, etc) to facilitate separation of fibres

RETABLE n ornamental screenlike structure above and behind an altar

RETACK vb tack again retacks

RETAG vb tag again retags

RETAIL n, adj, adv, vb retails

RETAIN vb retains

Perhaps the most important word in Scrabble, because its letters combine with every other letter apart from A, Q, V, X, Y and Z to form a 7-letter bonus word that will score you an extra 50 points, so if you have these six

letters on your rack you know that a bonus is either available or very close. And if you have an S as well, so much the better, because not only does this rack offer you 11 different words to choose from, but if none of those can be fitted in then RETAINS combines with every other letter except for Q, V, X, Y and Z to form at least one eight-letter word.

RETAKE vb recapture ▷ n act of rephotographing a scene retaken, retaker, retakes

RETALLY vb count up again

RETAMA n type of shrub retamas

RETAPE vb tape again retaped, retapes

RETARD vb, n retards

RETASTE vb taste again

RETAX vb tax again retaxed, retaxes

RETCH vb, n retched, retches

RETE n any network of nerves or blood vessels

RETEACH vb teach again

RETEAM vb team up again reteams

RETEAR vb tear again retears

RETELL vb relate (a story, etc) again or differently retells

RETEM n type of shrub retems

RETENE n yellow crystalline hydrocarbon found in tar oils retenes

RETEST vb test (something) again or differently retests

RETHINK vb, n

RETIA ▶ rete

RETIAL ▶ rete

RETIARY adj of, relating to, or resembling a net or web

RETICLE n network of fine lines, wires, etc, used in optical instruments

RETIE vb tie again retied, reties

RETILE vb put new tiles in or on retiled, retiles

RETIME vb time again or alter time of retimed, retimes

RETINA n retinae

RETINAL adj of or relating to the retina ▷ n aldehyde form of the polyene retinol

RETINAS ▶ retina

RETINE n chemical found in body cells that slows cell growth and division retines

RETINOL n another name for vitamin A and rosin oil

RETINT vb tint again or change tint of **retints**

RETINUE n

RETIRAL n act of retiring from office, one's work, etc

RETIRE vb

RETIRED adj having retired from work etc

RETIREE n person who has retired from work

RETIRER ▶ retire

RETIRES ▶ retire

RETITLE vb give a new title to

RETOLD ▶ retell

RETOOK ▶ retake

RETOOL vb replace, re-equip, or rearrange the tools in (a factory, etc) **retools**

RETORE ▶ retear

RETORN ▶ retear

RETORT vb, n **retorts**

RETOTAL vb add up again

RETOUCH vb

RETOUR vb (in Scottish law) to return as heir **retours**

RETRACE vb

RETRACK vb track again

RETRACT vb

RETRAIN vb train to do a new or different job

RETRAIT archaic form of ▶ retreat

RETRAL adj at, near, or towards the back

RETRATE archaic form of ▶ retreat

RETREAD n, vb

RETREAT vb, n

RETREE n imperfectly made paper **retrees**

RETRIAL n second trial of a case or defendant in a court of law

RETRIED ▶ retry

RETRIES ▶ retry

RETRIM vb trim again **retrims**

RETRO adj associated with or revived from the past ▷ n a retro style of art

RETROD ▶ retread

RETROS ▶ retro

RETRY vb try again (a case already determined)

RETS ▶ ret

RETSINA n Greek wine flavoured with resin

RETTED ▶ ret

RETTERY n flax-retting place

RETTING ▶ ret

RETUND vb weaken or blunt **retunds**

RETUNE vb tune (a musical instrument) differently or again **retuned, retunes**

RETURF vb turf again **returfs**

RETURN vb, n, adj **returns**

RETUSE adj having a rounded apex and a central depression

RETWIST vb twist again

RETYING ▶ retie

RETYPE vb type again **retyped, retypes**

REUNIFY vb bring together again something previously divided

REUNION n

REUNITE vb

REURGE vb urge again **reurged, reurges**

REUSE vb use again ▷ n act of using something again **reused, reuses, reusing**

REUTTER vb utter again

REV n, vb

REVALUE vb

REVAMP vb, n **revamps**

REVEAL vb, n **reveals**

REVEL vb, n **reveled, reveler**

REVELRY n festivity

REVELS ▶ revel

REVENGE n, vb

REVENUE n

REVERB n electronic device that creates artificial acoustics ▷ vb reverberate **reverbs**

REVERE vb revered, **reverer, reveres**

REVERIE n

REVERS n

REVERSE vb, n, adj

REVERSI n game played on a draughtboard

REVERSO another name for ▶ verso

REVERT vb **reverts**

REVERY = reverie

REVEST vb restore (former power, authority, status, etc, to a person) **revests**

REVET vb face (a wall or embankment) with stones **revets**

REVEUR n daydreamer **reveurs**

REVEUSE n female daydreamer

REVIE vb archaic cards term meaning challenge by placing a larger stake **revied, revies**

REVIEW n, vb reviews

REVILE vb be abusively scornful of **reviled, reviler, reviles**

REVISAL ▶ revise

REVISE vb, n revised, reviser, revises

REVISIT vb visit again

REVISOR ▶ revise

REVIVAL n reviving or renewal

REVIVE vb revived, reviver, revives

REVIVOR n means of reviving a lawsuit that has been suspended

REVOICE vb utter again

REVOKE vb, n revoked, revoker, revokes

REVOLT n, vb revolts

REVOLVE vb, n

REVOTE vb decide or grant again by a new vote revoted, revotes

REVS ▶ rev

REVUE n revues, revuist

REVVED ▶ rev

REVVING ▶ rev

REVYING ▶ revie

REW archaic spelling of ▶ rue

REWAKE vb awaken again rewaked

REWAKEN vb awaken again

REWAKES ▶ rewake

REWAN archaic past form of ▶ rewin

REWARD n, vb rewards

REWARM vb warm again rewarms

REWASH vb wash again

REWATER vb water again

REWAX vb wax again rewaxed, rewaxes

REWEAR vb wear again rewears

REWEAVE vb weave again

REWED vb wed again reweds

REWEIGH vb weigh again

REWELD vb weld again rewelds

REWET vb wet again rewets

REWIDEN vb widen again

REWIN vb win again

REWIND vb rewinds

REWINS ▶ rewin

REWIRE vb provide (a house, engine, etc) with new wiring rewired, rewires

REWOKE ▶ rewake

REWOKEN ▶ rewake

REWON ▶ rewin

REWORD vb alter the wording of rewords

REWORE ▶ rewear

REWORK vb improve or bring up to date reworks

REWORN ▶ rewear

REWOUND ▶ rewind

REWOVE ▶ reweave

REWOVEN ▶ reweave

REWRAP vb wrap again rewraps, rewrapt

REWRITE vb, n rewrote

REWS ▶ rew

REWTH archaic variant of ▶ ruth

REWTHS ▶ rewth

REX n king rexes

> **Rex** is a Latin word for **king**, a very commonly played X word.

REXINE n tradename for a form of artificial leather **rexines**

REYNARD n fox

REZ n informal word for an instance of reserving; reservation

> **Rez** is a short informal word for **reservation**, and is one of the most commonly played Z words.

REZERO vb reset to zero rezeros

REZONE vb zone again rezoned, rezones

REZZES ▶ rez

RHABDOM n rodlike structures found in the eye of insects

RHABDUS n sponge spicule

RHACHIS = rachis

RHAMNUS n buckthorn

RHANJA n Indian English word for a male lover **rhanjas**

RHAPHAE ▶ rhaphe

RHAPHE n raphe

RHAPHES ▶ rhaphe

RHAPHIS = raphide

RHATANY n South American leguminous shrub

RHEA n rheas

RHEBOK n woolly brownish-grey southern African antelope **rheboks**

RHEME n constituent of a sentence that adds most new information **rhemes**

RHENIUM n silvery-white metallic element with a high melting point

RHESUS n

RHETOR n teacher of rhetoric **rhetors**

RHEUM n watery discharge from the eyes or nose

RHEUMED adj rheumy

RHEUMIC adj of or relating to rheum

RHEUMS ▶ rheum

RHEUMY adj of the nature of rheum

RHEXES ▶ rhexis

RHEXIS n rupture

RHIES ▶ rhy

RHIME old spelling of ▶ rhyme

RHIMES ▶ rhime

RHINAL adj of or relating to the nose

RHINE n dialect word for a ditch **rhines**

RHINO n rhinos

RHIZIC adj of or relating to the root of an equation

RHIZINE = rhizoid

RHIZOID n hairlike structure in mosses, ferns, and related plants

RHIZOMA = rhizome

RHIZOME n

RHIZOPI > rhizopus

RHO n 17th letter in the Greek alphabet

It's useful to remember words that start with RH, as they can come in useful. If you or someone else plays rho, which is a Greek letter, remember that it can be expanded to, for example, **rhody, rhomb, rhodium, rhombus** or **rhomboid**.

RHODIC adj of or containing rhodium, esp in the tetravalent state

RHODIE = rhody

RHODIES ▶ rhody

RHODIUM n

RHODORA n type of shrub

RHODOUS adj of or containing rhodium (but proportionally more than a rhodic compound)

RHODY n rhododendron

RHOMB = rhombus

RHOMBI ▶ rhombus

RHOMBIC adj relating to or having the shape of a rhombus

RHOMBOI ▶ rhombos

RHOMBOS n wooden slat attached to a thong that makes a roaring sound when the thong is whirled

RHOMBS ▶ rhomb

RHOMBUS n

RHONCHI > rhonchus

RHONE = rone

RHONES ▶ rhone

RHOS ▶ rho

RHOTIC adj denoting or speaking a dialect of English in which postvocalic r s are pronounced

RHUBARB n, interj, vb

RHUMB n as in **rhumb line** imaginary line on the surface of a sphere that intersects all meridians at the same angle

RHUMBA = rumba

RHUMBAS ▶ rhumba

RHUMBS ▶ rhumb

RHUS n genus of shrubs and small trees **rhuses**

RHY archaic spelling of ▶ rye

This alternative spelling of **rye** can come in useful when you are short of vowels.

RHYME n, vb rhymed

RHYMER = rhymester

RHYMERS ▶ rhymer

RHYMES ▶ rhyme

RHYMING ▶ rhyme

RHYMIST ▶ rhyme

RHYNE = rhine

RHYNES ▶ rhyne

RHYTA ▶ rhyton

RHYTHM n

RHYTHMI ▶ rhythmus

RHYTHMS ▶ rhythm

RHYTINA n type of sea cow

RHYTON n (in ancient Greece) horn-shaped drinking vessel **rhytons**

RIA n long narrow inlet of the seacoast

RIAD n traditional Moroccan house with an interior garden **riads**

RIAL n standard monetary unit of Iran **rials**

RIALTO n market or exchange **rialtos**

RIANCY ▶ riant

RIANT adj laughing **riantly**

RIAS ▶ ria

RIATA = reata

RIATAS ▶ riata

RIB n, vb

RIBA n (in Islam) interest or usury

RIBALD adj, n ribalds

RIBAND n ribbon awarded for some achievement **ribands**

RIBAS ▶ riba

RIBAUD archaic variant of ▶ ribald

RIBAUDS ▶ ribaud

RIBBAND = riband

RIBBED ▶ rib

RIBBER n someone who ribs **ribbers**

RIBBIER ▶ ribby

RIBBING ▶ rib

RIBBON n, vb ribbons, ribbony

RIBBY adj with noticeable ribs

RIBCAGE n

RIBES n genus of shrubs that includes currants

RIBEYE n beefsteak cut from the outer side of the rib section **ribeyes**

RIBIBE n rebeck ribibes, ribible

RIBIER n variety of grape **ribiers**

RIBLESS ▶ rib

RIBLET n small rib riblets

RIBLIKE ▶ rib

RIBOSE n pentose sugar that occurs in RNA and riboflavin **riboses**

RIBS ▶ rib

RIBSTON n variety of apple

RIBWORK n work or structure involving ribs

RIBWORT n Eurasian plant with lancelike ribbed leaves

RICE n, vb riced

RICER n kitchen utensil through which soft foods are pressed to form a coarse mash **ricers**

RICES ▶ rice

RICEY adj resembling or containing rice

RICH adj, vb riched

RICHEN vb enrich richens

RICHER ▶ rich

RICHES pl n wealth

RICHEST ▶ rich

RICHING ▶ rich

RICHLY adv

RICHT adj, adv, n, vb right **richted, richter, richts**

RICIER ▶ ricy

RICIEST ▶ ricy

RICIN n highly toxic protein, a lectin, derived from castor-oil seeds

RICING ▶ rice

RICINS ▶ ricin

RICINUS n genus of plants

RICK n, vb ricked

RICKER n young kauri tree of New Zealand **rickers**

RICKET n mistake

RICKETS n

RICKETY adj

RICKEY n cocktail consisting of gin or vodka, lime juice, and soda water, served iced **rickeys**

RICKING ▶ rick

RICKLE n unsteady or shaky structure **rickles**

RICKLY adj archaic word for run-down or rickety

RICKS ▶ rick

RICKSHA = rickshaw

RICOTTA n soft white unsalted Italian cheese made from sheep's milk

RICRAC = rickrack

RICRACS ▶ ricrac

RICTAL ▶ rictus

RICTUS n gape or cleft of an open mouth or beak

RICY = ricey

RID vb

RIDABLE ▶ ride

RIDDED ▶ rid

RIDDEN ▶ ride

RIDDER ▶ rid

RIDDERS ▶ rid

RIDDING ▶ rid

RIDDLE n, vb **riddled, riddler, riddles**

RIDE vb, n

RIDENT adj laughing, smiling, or gay

RIDER n **ridered, riders**

RIDES ▶ ride

RIDGE n, vb **ridged**

RIDGEL = ridgeling

RIDGELS ▶ ridgel

RIDGER n plough used to form furrows and ridges **ridgers**

RIDGES ▶ ridge

RIDGIER ▶ ridge

RIDGIL = ridgeling

RIDGILS ▶ ridgil

RIDGING ▶ ridge

RIDGY ▶ ridge

RIDING ▶ ride

RIDINGS ▶ ride

RIDLEY n marine turtle **ridleys**

RIDOTTO n entertainment with music and dancing, often in masquerade

RIDS ▶ rid

RIEL n standard monetary unit of Cambodia **riels**

RIEM n strip of hide

RIEMPIE n leather thong or lace used mainly to make chair seats

RIEMS ▶ riem

RIEVE n archaic word

for rob or plunder

RIEVER n archaic word for robber or plunderer **rievers**

RIEVES ▶ rieve

RIEVING ▶ rieve

RIF vb lay off

RIFE adj **rifely, rifer, rifest**

RIFF n short repeated melodic figure ▷ vb play or perform riffs in jazz or rock music

RIFFAGE n (in jazz or rock music) act or an instance of playing a short series of chords

RIFFED ▶ riff

RIFFING ▶ riff

RIFFLE vb, n **riffled**

RIFFLER n file with a curved face for filing concave surfaces

RIFFLES ▶ riffle

RIFFOLA n use of an abundance of dominant riffs

RIFFS ▶ riff

RIFLE n, vb **rifled, rifler, riflers**

RIFLERY n rifle shots

RIFLES ▶ rifle

RIFLING n cutting of spiral grooves on the inside of a firearm's barrel

RIFLIP n genetic difference between two individuals **riflips**

RIFS ▶ rif

RIFT n, vb **rifte, rifted, riftier, rifting, rifts, rifty**

RIG vb, n

RIGG n type of fish

RIGGALD = ridgeling

RIGGED ▶ rig

RIGGER n workman who rigs vessels, etc **riggers**

RIGGING ▶ rig

RIGGISH adj dialect word meaning wanton

RIGGS ▶ rigg

RIGHT adj just ▷ adv correctly ▷ n claim, title, etc allowed or due ▷ vb bring or come back to a normal or correct state **righted**

RIGHTEN vb set right

RIGHTER ▶ right

RIGHTLY adv in accordance with the true facts or justice

RIGHTO interj expression of agreement or compliance

RIGHTS ▶ right

RIGHTY n informal word for a right-winger

RIGID adj, adv, n **rigider, rigidly, rigids**

RIGLIN = ridgeling

RIGLING = ridgeling

RIGLINS ▶ riglin

RIGOL n (in dialect) ditch or gutter **rigoll**

RIGOLLS ▶ rigoll

RIGOLS ▶ rigol

RIGOR = rigour

RIGORS ▶ rigor

RIGOUR n **rigours**

RIGOUT n person's clothing **rigouts**

RIGS ▸ rig

RIKISHA = rickshaw

RIKISHI n sumo wrestler

RIKSHAW = rickshaw

RILE vb riled, riles

RILEY adj cross or irritable **rilier, riliest**

RILIEVI ▸ rilievo

RILIEVO = relief

RILING ▸ rile

RILL n small stream ▷ vb trickle **rille, rilled**

RILLES ▸ rille

RILLET n little rill **rillets**

RILLING ▸ rill

RILLS ▸ rill

RIM n, vb

RIMA n long narrow opening **rimae**

RIMAYE n crevasse at the head of a glacier **rimayes**

RIME = rhyme

RIMED ▸ rime

RIMER = rhymester

RIMERS ▸ rimer

RIMES ▸ rime

RIMFIRE adj (of a cartridge) having the primer in the rim of the base ▷ n cartridge of this type

RIMIER ▸ rimy

RIMIEST ▸ rimy

RIMING ▸ rime

RIMLAND n area situated on the outer edges of a region

RIMLESS ▸ rim

RIMMED ▸ rim

RIMMER n tool for shaping the edge of something **rimmers**

RIMMING ▸ rim

RIMOSE adj (esp of plant parts) having the surface marked by a network of intersecting cracks **rimous**

RIMPLE vb crease or wrinkle **rimpled, rimples**

RIMROCK n rock forming the boundaries of a sandy or gravelly alluvial deposit

RIMS ▸ rim

RIMSHOT n deliberate simultaneous striking of skin and rim of drum

RIMU n rimus

RIMY adj coated with rime

RIN Scots variant of ▸ run

RIND n, vb rinded

RINDIER ▸ rindy

RINDING ▸ rind

RINDS ▸ rind

RINDY adj with a rind or rindlike skin

RINE archaic variant of ▸ rind

RINES ▸ rine

RING vb, n

RINGBIT n type of bit worn by a horse

RINGED ▸ ring

RINGENT adj (of the corolla of plants) consisting of two gaping lips

RINGER n ringers

RINGGIT n standard monetary unit of Malaysia

RINGING ▸ ring

RINGLET n

RINGMAN n (in dialect) ring finger **ringmen**

RINGS ▸ ring

RINGTAW n game in which the aim is to knock marbles out of a ring

RINGWAY n bypass

RINK n, vb rinked, rinking, rinks

RINNING ▸ rin

RINS ▸ rin

RINSE vb, n rinsed, rinser, rinsers, rinses, rinsing

RIOJA n red or white Spanish wine with a vanilla bouquet and flavour **riojas**

RIOT n, vb rioted, rioter, rioters, rioting

RIOTISE n archaic word for riotous behaviour and excess **riotize**

RIOTOUS adj

RIOTRY n riotous behaviour

RIOTS ▸ riot

RIP vb, n

RIPCORD n

RIPE adj, vb

RIPECK = ryepeck

RIPECKS ▸ ripeck

RIPED ▸ ripe

RIPELY ▸ ripe

RIPEN vb ripened, ripener, ripens

RIPER adj more ripe ▷ n old Scots word meaning plunderer **ripers**

RIPES ▸ ripe

RIPEST ▶ ripe

RIPIENI ▶ ripieno

RIPIENO n (in baroque concertos and concerti grossi) the full orchestra

RIPING ▶ ripe

RIPOFF n grossly overpriced article **ripoffs**

RIPOST = riposte

RIPOSTE n, vb

RIPOSTS ▶ ripost

RIPP n old Scots word for a handful of grain

RIPPED ▶ rip

RIPPER n rippers

RIPPIER n archaic word for fish seller

RIPPING ▶ rip

RIPPLE n, vb rippled, rippler, ripples

RIPPLET n tiny ripple

RIPPLY ▶ ripple

RIPPS ▶ ripp

RIPRAP vb deposit broken stones in or on **ripraps**

RIPS ▶ rip

RIPSAW n handsaw for cutting along the grain of timber ▶ vb saw with a ripsaw **ripsawn, ripsaws**

RIPSTOP n tear-resistant cloth

RIPT archaic past form of ▶ rip

RIPTIDE n stretch of turbulent water in the sea

RISE vb, n risen

RISER n risers

RISES ▶ rise

RISHI n Indian seer or sage **rishis**

RISIBLE adj causing laughter, ridiculous **risibly**

RISING ▶ rise

RISINGS ▶ rise

RISK n, vb risked, risker, riskers, riskful

RISKIER ▶ risky

RISKILY ▶ risky

RISKING ▶ risk

RISKS ▶ risk

RISKY adj full of risk, dangerous

RISORII ▶ risorius

RISOTTO n

RISP n Scots word meaning rasp **risped, risping, risps**

RISQUE n risk **risques**

RISSOLE n

RISTRA n string of dried chilli peppers **ristras**

RISUS n involuntary grinning expression **risuses**

RIT vb Scots word for cut or slit

RITARD n (in music) a slowing down **ritards**

RITE n rites

RITS ▶ rit

RITT = rit

RITTED ▶ rit

RITTER n knight or horseman **ritters**

RITTING ▶ rit

RITTS ▶ ritt

RITUAL n, adj rituals

RITZ modifier as in put on the ritz assume a superior air or make an ostentatious display **ritzes**

RITZIER ▶ ritzy

RITZILY ▶ ritzy

RITZY adj luxurious or elegant

RIVA n rock cleft

RIVAGE n bank, shore, or coast **rivages**

RIVAL n, adj, vb rivaled

RIVALRY n

RIVALS ▶ rival

RIVAS ▶ riva

RIVE vb split asunder **rived**

RIVEL vb archaic word meaning wrinkle **rivels**

RIVEN ▶ rive

RIVER n

RIVERED adj with a river or rivers

RIVERET n archaic word for rivulet or stream

RIVERS ▶ river

RIVERY adj riverlike

RIVES ▶ rive

RIVET n, vb riveted, riveter, rivets

RIVIERA n coastline resembling the Meditteranean Riviera

RIVIERE n necklace of diamonds which gradually increase in size

RIVING ▶ rive

RIVLIN n Scots word for rawhide shoe **rivlins**

RIVO interj (in the past) an informal toast

RIVULET n

RIYAL n standard monetary unit of Qatar, divided into 100 dirhams **riyals**

RIZ (in some dialects) past form of ▶ rise
This unusual past tense of **rise** is one of the essential Z words.

RIZA n partial icon cover made from precious metal

RIZARD n redcurrant **rizards**

RIZAS ▶ riza

RIZZAR n Scots word for red currant ▷ vb Scots word for sun-dry **rizzars**

RIZZART n Scots word for red currant

RIZZER = rizzar

RIZZERS ▶ rizzer

RIZZOR vb dry **rizzors**

ROACH n, vb

ROACHED adj arched convexly, as the back of certain breeds of dog, such as the whippet

ROACHES ▶ roach

ROAD n

ROADBED n material used to make a road

ROADEO n competition testing driving skills **roadeos**

ROADIE n person who transports and sets up equipment for a band **roadies**

ROADING n road building

ROADMAN n someone involved in road repair or construction **roadmen**

ROADS ▶ road

ROADWAY n part of a road used by vehicles

ROAM vb, n roamed, roamer, roamers, roaming, roams

ROAN adj, n roans

ROAR vb, n roared, roarer, roarers

ROARIE Scots word for ▶ noisy

ROARIER ▶ roary

ROARING ▶ roar

ROARS ▶ roar

ROARY adj roarlike or tending to roar

ROAST vb, n, adj roasted

ROASTER n person or thing that roasts

ROASTS ▶ roast

ROATE archaic form of ▶ rote

ROATED ▶ roate

ROATES ▶ roate

ROATING ▶ roate

ROB vb

ROBALO n tropical fish robalos

ROBAND n piece of marline used for fastening a sail to a spar **robands**

ROBBED ▶ rob

ROBBER ▶ rob

ROBBERS ▶ rob

ROBBERY n stealing of property from a person by using or threatening to use force

ROBBIN = roband

ROBBING ▶ rob

ROBBINS ▶ robbin

ROBE n, vb robed, robes

ROBIN n

ROBING ▶ robe

ROBINGS ▶ robe

ROBINIA n type of leguminous tree

ROBINS ▶ robin

ROBLE n oak tree robles

ROBOT n robotic, robotry, robots

ROBS ▶ rob

ROBUST adj

ROBUSTA n species of coffee tree

ROC n monstrous bird of Arabian mythology

ROCH = rotch

ROCHES ▶ rotch

ROCHET n white surplice with tight sleeves, worn by Church dignitaries **rochets**

ROCK n, vb, adj

ROCKABY = rockabye

ROCKED ▶ rock

ROCKER n rockers

ROCKERY n

ROCKET n, vb rockets

ROCKIER ▶ rocky

ROCKILY ▶ rocky

ROCKING ▶ rock

ROCKLAY = rokelay

ROCKOON n rocket fired from a balloon at high altitude

ROCKS ▶ rock

ROCKY adj

ROCOCO adj (of furniture, architecture, etc) having much elaborate decoration ▷ n style of architecture and decoration characterized by elaborate ornamentation **rococos**

ROCQUET n another name for the salad plant rocket

ROCS ▶ roc

ROD n, vb rodded, rodding

RODE vb (of the male woodcock) to perform a display flight **roded**

RODENT n rodents

RODEO n, vb rodeoed, rodeos

RODES ▶ rode

RODEWAY archaic spelling of ▶ roadway

RODING ▶ rode

RODINGS ▶ rode

RODLESS ▶ rod

RODLIKE ▶ rod

RODMAN n someone who uses or fishes with a rod **rodmen**

RODS ▶ rod

RODSMAN = rodman

RODSMEN ▶ rodsman

RODSTER n angler

ROE n

ROEBUCK n male of the roe deer

ROED adj with roe inside

ROEMER n drinking glass, typically having an ovoid bowl on a short stem **roemers**

ROES ▶ roe

ROESTI ▶ rosti

ROESTIS ▶ roesti

ROGALLO n flexible fabric delta wing

ROGNON n isolated rock outcrop on a glacier **rognons**

ROGUE n, adj, vb rogued

ROGUER n rogue roguers

ROGUERY n dishonest or immoral behaviour

ROGUES ▶ rogue

ROGUING ▶ rogue

ROGUISH adj roguy

ROIL vb make (a liquid) cloudy or turbid by stirring up dregs or sediment **roiled**

ROILIER ▶ roily

ROILING ▶ roil

ROILS ▶ roil

ROILY adj cloudy or muddy

ROIN = royne

ROINED ▶ roin

ROINING ▶ roin

ROINISH = roynish

ROINS ▶ roin

ROIST archaic variant of ▶ roister

ROISTED ▶ roist

ROISTER vb make merry noisily or boisterously

ROISTS ▶ roist

ROJAK n (in Malaysia) a salad dish served in chilli sauce **rojaks**

ROJI n Japanese tea garden or its path of stones **rojis**

ROK = roc

> Rok is an alternative spelling of roc, the mythical bird. Other spellings are ruc and rukh.

ROKE vb (in dialect)

steam or smoke **roked**

ROKELAY n type of cloak

ROKER n variety of ray rokers

ROKES ▶ roke

ROKIER ▶ roky

ROKIEST ▶ roky

ROKING ▶ roke

ROKKAKU n hexagonal Japanese kite

ROKS ▶ rok

ROKY adj (in dialect) steamy or smoky

ROLAG n roll of carded wool ready for spinning **rolags**

ROLE n roles

ROLF vb massage following a particular technique **rolfed, rolfer, rolfers, rolfing, rolfs**

ROLL vb, n

ROLLBAR n bar that reinforces the frame of a car

ROLLED ▶ roll

ROLLER n rollers

ROLLICK vb behave in a boisterous manner ▷ n boisterous or carefree escapade

ROLLING ▶ roll

ROLLMOP n herring fillet rolled round onion slices and pickled

ROLLOCK = rowlock

ROLLOUT n presentation to the public of a new aircraft, product, etc; launch

ROLLS ▸ roll

ROLLTOP n as in **rolltop desk** desk having a slatted wooden panel that can be pulled down over the writing surface

ROLLWAY n incline down which logs are rolled

ROM n male gypsy

ROMA n gypsy

ROMAGE archaic variant of ▸ **rummage**

ROMAGES ▸ romage

ROMAIKA n Greek dance

ROMAINE n usual US and Canadian name for 'cos' (lettuce)

ROMAJI n Roman alphabet as used to write Japanese **romajis**

ROMAL = **rumal**

ROMALS ▸ romal

ROMAN adj in or relating to the vertical style of printing type used for most printed matter ▸ n roman type

ROMANCE n, vb

ROMANO n hard light-coloured sharp-tasting cheese **romanos**

ROMANS ▸ roman

ROMANZA n short instrumental piece of song-like character

ROMAUNT n verse romance

ROMCOM n comedy based around the romantic relationships of the characters **romcoms**

ROMEO n ardent male lover **romeos**

ROMNEYA n bushy type of poppy

ROMP vb, n **romped**

ROMPER n playful or boisterous child

ROMPERS pl n

ROMPING ▸ romp

ROMPISH ▸ romp

ROMPS ▸ romp

ROMS ▸ rom

RONDE n round dance

RONDEAU n poem with the opening words of the first line used as a refrain

RONDEL n rondeau with a two-line refrain appearing twice or three times **rondels**

RONDES ▸ ronde

RONDINO n short rondo

RONDO n **rondos**

RONDURE n circle or curve

RONE n drainpipe or gutter for carrying rainwater from a roof

RONEO vb duplicate (a document) from a stencil ▸ n document reproduced by this process **roneoed, roneos**

RONES ▸ rone

RONG archaic past participle of ▸ **ring**

RONIN n lordless samurai, esp one whose feudal lord had been deprived of his territory **ronins**

RONIONS ▸ ronion

RONNE archaic form of ▸ **run**

RONNEL n type of pesticide **ronnels**

RONNIE n Dublin slang word for moustache **ronnies**

RONNING ▸ ronne

RONT archaic variant of ▸ **runt**

RONTE archaic variant of ▸ **runt**

RONTES ▸ ronte

RONTGEN variant spelling of > **roentgen**

RONTS ▸ ront

RONZ n rest of New Zealand

RONZER n New Zealand word for a New Zealander not from Auckland **ronzers**

ROO n

ROOD n Cross **roods**

ROOF n, vb **roofed, roofer, roofers**

ROOFIE n tablet of sedative drug

ROOFIER ▸ roofy

ROOFIES ▸ roofie

ROOFING n

ROOFS ▸ roof

ROOFTOP n

ROOFY adj with roofs

ROOIBOS n tea prepared from the dried leaves of an African plant

ROOIKAT n South African lynx

ROOK n, vb **rooked**

ROOKERY n
ROOKIE n new recruit
ROOKIER ▶ rooky
ROOKIES ▶ rookie
ROOKING ▶ rook
ROOKISH ▶ rook
ROOKS ▶ rook
ROOKY adj abounding in rooks
ROOM n, vb roomed, roomer, roomers
ROOMFUL n number or quantity sufficient to fill a room
ROOMIE n roommate
ROOMIER ▶ roomy
ROOMIES ▶ roomie
ROOMILY ▶ roomy
ROOMING ▶ room
ROOMS ▶ room
ROOMY adj spacious
ROON n Scots word for shred or strip roons
ROOP = roup
ROOPED ▶ roop
ROOPIER ▶ roopy
ROOPING ▶ roop
ROOPIT = roopy
ROOPS ▶ roop
ROOPY adj (in dialect) hoarse
ROOS ▶ roo
ROOSA n type of grass roosas
ROOSE vb flatter roosed, rooser, roosers, rooses, roosing
ROOST n, vb roosted
ROOSTER n
ROOSTS ▶ roost
ROOT n, vb
ROOTAGE n root system
ROOTCAP n layer of cells at root tip

ROOTED, rooter, rooters, rootier
▶ root
ROOTIES ▶ rooty
ROOTING ▶ root
ROOTKIT n
ROOTLE = root
ROOTLED ▶ rootle
ROOTLES ▶ rootle
ROOTLET n small root or branch of a root
ROOTS adj (of popular music) going back to the origins of a style rootsy
ROOTY adj rootlike ▷ n (in military slang) bread
ROPABLE adj capable of being roped
ROPE n roped
ROPER n someone who makes ropes ropers
ROPERY n place where ropes are made
ROPES ▶ rope
ROPEWAY n type of aerial lift
ROPEY adj
ROPIER ▶ ropy
ROPIEST ▶ ropy
ROPILY ▶ ropy
ROPING ▶ rope
ROPINGS ▶ rope
ROPY = ropey
ROQUE n game developed from croquet roques
ROQUET vb drive one's ball against (another person's ball) in croquet ▷ n act of roqueting roquets
RORAL archaic word for

▶ dewy
RORE archaic spelling of
▶ roar
RORES ▶ rore
RORIC = roral
RORID = roral
RORIE = roary
RORIER ▶ rory
RORIEST ▶ rory
RORQUAL n toothless whale with a dorsal fin
RORT n dishonest scheme ▷ vb take unfair advantage of something rorted
RORTER n small-scale confidence trickster rorters
RORTIER, rorting, rorts, rorty ▶ rort
RORY adj dewy
ROSACE another name for ▶ rosette
ROSACEA n chronic inflammatory disease affecting the skin of the face
ROSACES ▶ rosace
ROSAKER archaic word for ▶ realgar
ROSALIA n melody which is repeated but at a higher pitch each time
ROSARIA > rosarium
ROSARY n
ROSBIF n term used in France for an English person rosbifs
ROSCID adj dewy
ROSCOE slang word for
▶ gun
ROSCOES ▶ roscoe
ROSE ▶ rise

ROSEAL adj rosy or roselike

ROSEATE adj rose-coloured

ROSEBAY n as in **rosebay willowherb** perennial plant with spikes of deep pink flowers

ROSEBUD n rose which has not yet fully opened

ROSED ▶ rise

ROSEHIP n berry-like fruit of a rose plant

ROSELLA n

ROSELLE n Indian flowering plant

ROSEOLA n feverish condition of young children caused by the human herpes virus

ROSERY n bed or garden of roses

ROSES ▶ rise

ROSET n Scots word meaning rosin ▷ vb rub rosin on **roseted, rosets**

ROSETTE n

ROSETTY ▶ roset

ROSETY ▶ roset

ROSHI n teacher of Zen Buddhism **roshis**

ROSIED ▶ rosy

ROSIER archaic word for > rosebush

ROSIERE archaic word for > rosebush

ROSIERS ▶ rosier

ROSIES ▶ rosy

ROSIEST ▶ rosy

ROSILY ▶ rosy

ROSIN n resin used for treating the bows of

violins etc ▷ vb apply rosin to **rosined**

ROSINER n strong alcoholic drink

ROSING ▶ rise

ROSINOL n yellowish fluorescent oily liquid obtained from certain resins

ROSINS ▶ rosin

ROSINY ▶ rosin

ROSIT ▶ roset

ROSITED ▶ rosit

ROSITS ▶ rosit

ROSOLIO n type of cordial

ROSSER n bark-removing machine **rossers**

ROST archaic spelling of ▶ roast

ROSTED ▶ rost

ROSTER n, vb **rosters**

ROSTI n cheese-topped fried Swiss dish of grated potato

ROSTING ▶ rost

ROSTIS ▶ rosti

ROSTRA ▶ rostrum

ROSTRAL adj of or like a beak or snout

ROSTRUM n

ROSTS ▶ rost

ROSULA n rosette **rosulas**

ROSY adj, vb **rosying**

ROT vb, n

ROTA n

ROTAL adj of or relating to wheels or rotation

ROTAN another name for ▶ rattan

ROTANS ▶ rotan

ROTARY adj, n

ROTAS ▶ rota

ROTATE vb, adj **rotated, rotates**

ROTATOR n person, device, or part that rotates or causes rotation

ROTCH n little auk **rotche, rotches, rotchie**

ROTE n, vb **roted, rotes**

ROTGUT n alcoholic drink of inferior quality **rotguts**

ROTHER dialect word for ▶ ox

ROTHERS ▶ rother

ROTI n (in India and the Caribbean) a type of unleavened bread

ROTIFER n minute aquatic multicellular invertebrate

ROTING ▶ rote

ROTIS ▶ roti

ROTL n unit of weight used in Muslim countries **rotls**

ROTO n printing process using a cylinder etched with many small recesses in a rotary press

ROTOLO n (in Italian cuisine) a roll **rotolos**

ROTON n quantum of vortex motion **rotons**

ROTOR n **rotors**

ROTOS ▶ roto

ROTS ▶ rot

ROTTAN n (in dialect) a rat **rottans**

ROTTE n ancient stringed instrument

ROTTED ▸ rot

ROTTEN *adj, adv, n* **rottens**

ROTTER *n* despicable person **rotters**

ROTTES ▸ rotte

ROTTING ▸ rot

ROTULA *n* kneecap **rotulae, rotulas**

ROTUND *adj, vb*

ROTUNDA *n* circular building or room, esp with a dome

ROTUNDS ▸ rotund

ROUBLE *n* roubles

ROUCHE = **ruche**

ROUCHES ▸ rouche

ROUCOU another name for ▸ **annatto**

ROUCOUS ▸ roucou

ROUE *n* man given to immoral living

ROUEN *n* breed of duck **rouens**

ROUES ▸ roue

ROUGE *n, vb* **rouged, rouges**

ROUGH *adj, vb, n* **roughed**

ROUGHEN *vb*

ROUGHER *n* person that does the rough preparatory work on something ▹ *adj* more rough

ROUGHIE *n* small food fish found in Australian waters

ROUGHLY *adv* without being exact or fully authenticated

ROUGHS ▸ rough

ROUGHT *archaic past form of* ▸ **reach**

ROUGHY *spelling variant of* ▸ **roughie**

ROUGING ▸ rouge

ROUILLE *n* kind of sauce

ROUL *archaic form of* ▸ **roll**

ROULADE *n* slice of meat rolled and cooked

ROULE *archaic form of* ▸ **roll**

ROULEAU *n* roll of paper containing coins

ROULES ▸ roule

ROULS ▸ roul

ROUM *archaic spelling of* ▸ **room**

ROUMING *n* pasture given for an animal

ROUMS ▸ roum

ROUNCE *n* handle that is turned to move paper and plates on a printing press **rounces**

ROUNCY *archaic word for* ▸ **horse**

ROUND *adj, prep, vb, n*

ROUNDED *adj*

ROUNDEL = **roundelay**

ROUNDER *n* run round all four bases after one hit in rounders

ROUNDLE = **roundel**

ROUNDLY *adv*

ROUNDS ▸ round

ROUNDUP *n*

ROUP *n* any of various chronic respiratory diseases of birds, esp poultry ▹ *vb* sell by auction **rouped**

ROUPET *adj* Scots word meaning hoarse or croaky

ROUPIER, roupily,

rouping ▸ roup

ROUPIT = **roupet**

ROUPS, roupy ▸ roup

ROUSANT *adj* (in heraldry) rising

ROUSE = **reveille**

ROUSED ▸ rouse

ROUSER *n* person or thing that rouses people **rousers**

ROUSES ▸ rouse

ROUSING *adj* lively, vigorous

ROUST *vb* rout or stir, as out of bed **rousted**

ROUSTER *n* unskilled labourer on an oil rig

ROUSTS ▸ roust

ROUT *n, vb*

ROUTE *n, vb* **routed**

ROUTER *n* device that allows data to be moved between points on a network **routers**

ROUTES ▸ route

ROUTH *n* abundance ▹ *adj* abundant

ROUTHIE *adj* abundant, plentiful, or well filled

ROUTHS ▸ routh

ROUTINE *n, adj*

ROUTING ▸ rout

ROUTOUS ▸ rout

ROUTS ▸ rout

ROUX ▸ roux

ROVE ▸ reeve

ROVED ▸ reeve

ROVEN ▸ reeve

ROVER *n* wanderer, traveller **rovers**

ROVES ▸ reeve

ROVING ▸ rove

ROVINGS ▸ rove

ROW *n, vb* **rowable**

ROWAN n rowans
ROWBOAT n small boat propelled by one or more pairs of oars
ROWDIER ▸ rowdy
ROWDIES ▸ rowdy
ROWDILY ▸ rowdy
ROWDY adj, n
ROWED ▸ row
ROWEL n small spiked wheel on a spur ▷ vb goad (a horse) using a rowel **roweled, rowels**
ROWEN another word for > aftermath
ROWENS ▸ rowen
ROWER n rowers, rowing, rowings ▸ row
ROWLOCK n
ROWME archaic variant of ▸ room
ROWMES ▸ rowme
ROWND archaic variant of ▸ round
ROWNDED ▸ rownd
ROWNDS ▸ rownd
ROWOVER n act of winning a rowing race unopposed
ROWS ▸ row
ROWT archaic variant of ▸ rout
ROWTED ▸ rowt
ROWTH = routh
ROWTHS ▸ rowth
ROWTING ▸ rowt
ROWTS ▸ rowt
ROYAL adj, n
ROYALET n minor king
ROYALLY ▸ royal
ROYALS ▸ royal
ROYALTY n
ROYNE archaic word for ▸ gnaw

ROYNED ▸ royne
ROYNES ▸ royne
ROYNING ▸ royne
ROYNISH archaic word for ▸ mangy
ROYST = roist
ROYSTED ▸ royst
ROYSTER = roister
ROYSTS ▸ royst
ROZELLE = roselle
ROZET = roset
ROZETED ▸ rozet
ROZETS ▸ rozet
ROZIT = roset
ROZITED ▸ rozit
ROZITS ▸ rozit
ROZZER n policeman **rozzers**
RUANA n woollen wrap resembling a poncho **ruanas**
RUB vb, n
RUBABOO n soup or stew made by boiling pemmican with, if available, flour and vegetables
RUBACE = rubasse
RUBACES ▸ rubace
RUBAI n verse form of Persian origin consisting of four-line stanzas
RUBASSE n type of quartz containing red haematite
RUBATI ▸ rubato
RUBATO n (with) expressive flexibility of tempo ▷ adv be played with a flexible tempo **rubatos**
RUBBED ▸ rub
RUBBER n, adj, vb

rubbers
RUBBERY adj
RUBBET old Scots past form of ▸ rob
RUBBIDY = rubbity
RUBBIES ▸ rubby
RUBBING ▸ rub
RUBBISH n
RUBBIT old Scots past form of ▸ rob
RUBBITY n pub
RUBBLE n, vb rubbled, rubbles, rubbly
RUBBY n rubbing alcohol, esp when mixed with cheap wine for drinking
RUBDOWN n act of drying or cleaning vigorously
RUBEFY vb make red
RUBEL n currency unit of Belarus
RUBELLA n
RUBELS ▸ rubel
RUBEOLA technical name for ▸ measles
RUBICON n point of no return ▷ vb (in bezique) to beat before the loser has managed to gain as many as 1000 points
RUBIDIC > rubidium
RUBIED, rubier, rubies, rubiest ▸ ruby
RUBIFY = rubefy
RUBIGO old Scots word for ▸ penis
RUBIGOS ▸ rubigo
RUBIN archaic word for ▸ ruby
RUBINE archaic word for ▸ ruby

RUBINES ▸ rubine
RUBINS ▸ rubin
RUBIOUS adj of the colour ruby
RUBLE = rouble
RUBLES ▸ ruble
RUBOFF n resulting effect on something else; consequences **ruboffs**
RUBOUT n killing or elimination **rubouts**
RUBRIC n, adj **rubrics**
RUBS ▸ rub
RUBUS n fruit-bearing genus of shrubs
RUBY n, adj, vb **rubying**
RUC = roc
RUCHE n pleat or frill of lace etc as a decoration ▸ vb put a ruche on **ruched, ruches**
RUCHING n material used for a ruche
RUCK n rough crowd of common people ▸ vb wrinkle or crease **rucked, rucking, ruckle**
RUCKLED ▸ ruckle
RUCKLES ▸ ruckle
RUCKMAN n person who plays in the ruck **ruckmen**
RUCKS ▸ ruck
RUCKUS n uproar
RUCOLA n another name for the salad plant rocket **rucolas**
RUCS ▸ ruc
RUCTION n
RUD n red or redness ▸ vb redden

RUDAS n Scots word for a coarse, rude old woman **rudases**
RUDD n European freshwater fish
RUDDED ▸ rud
RUDDER n **rudders**
RUDDIED, ruddier, ruddies, ruddily ▸ ruddy
RUDDING ▸ rud
RUDDLE n red ochre, used esp to mark sheep ▸ vb mark (sheep) with ruddle **ruddled, ruddles**
RUDDOCK dialect name for the ▸ **robin**
RUDDS ▸ rud
RUDDY adj, adv, vb
RUDE archaic spelling of ▸ **rood**
RUDELY ▸ rude
RUDER ▸ rude
RUDERAL n plant that grows on waste ground ▸ adj growing in waste places
RUDERY ▸ rude
RUDES ▸ rude
RUDESBY n archaic word for rude person
RUDEST ▸ rude
RUDIE n member of a youth movement originating in the 1960s **rudies**
RUDISH adj somewhat rude
RUDS ▸ rud
RUE vb feel regret for ▸ n plant with evergreen bitter leaves **rued**

RUEDA n type of Cuban round dance **ruedas**
RUEFUL adj
RUEING ▸ rue
RUEINGS ▸ rue
RUELLE n area between bed and wall **ruelles**
RUELLIA n genus of plants
RUER ▸ rue
RUERS ▸ rue
RUES ▸ rue
RUFF n, vb
RUFFE n European freshwater fish
RUFFED ▸ ruff
RUFFES ▸ ruffe
RUFFIAN n, vb
RUFFIN archaic name for ▸ **ruffe**
RUFFING ▸ ruff
RUFFINS ▸ ruffin
RUFFLE vb, n **ruffled**
RUFFLER n person or thing that ruffles
RUFFLES ▸ ruffle
RUFFLY adj ruffled
RUFFS ▸ ruff
RUFIYAA n standard monetary unit of the Maldives
RUFOUS adj reddish-brown
RUG n, vb
RUGA n fold, wrinkle, or crease **rugae**
RUGAL adj (in anatomy) with ridges or folds
RUGATE = rugose
RUGBIES ▸ rugby
RUGBY n
RUGGED adj
RUGGER = rugby
RUGGERS ▸ rugger

RUGGIER ▶ ruggy

RUGGING ▶ rug

RUGGY adj (in dialect) rough or rugged

RUGLIKE ▶ rug

RUGOLA n another name for the salad plant rocket **rugolas**

RUGOSA n any of various shrubs descended from a particular type of wild rose **rugosas**

RUGOSE adj wrinkled **rugous**

RUGS ▶ rug

RUIN vb, n

RUINATE vb archaic word for bring or come to ruin

RUINED ▶ ruin

RUINER ▶ ruin

RUINERS ▶ ruin

RUING ▶ rue

RUINGS ▶ rue

RUINING ▶ ruin

RUINOUS adj

RUINS ▶ ruin

RUKH = roc

RUKHS ▶ rukh

RULABLE ▶ rule

RULE n, vb **ruled**

RULER n, vb **rulered, rulers**

RULES ▶ rule

RULESSE adj archaic word meaning ruleless or without rules

RULIER ▶ ruly

RULIEST ▶ ruly

RULING n formal decision ▷ adj controlling or exercising authority **rulings**

RULLION n Scots word for rawhide shoe

RULLOCK = rowlock

RULY adj orderly

RUM n, adj

RUMAKI n savoury of chicken liver and sliced water chestnut wrapped in bacon **rumakis**

RUMAL n handkerchief or type of cloth **rumals**

RUMBA n lively ballroom dance of Cuban origin ▷ vb dance the rumba **rumbaed, rumbas**

RUMBLE vb, n **rumbled, rumbler, rumbles**

RUMBLY adj rumbling or liable to rumble

RUMBO n rum-based cocktail **rumbos**

RUME archaic form of ▶ rheum

RUMEN n first compartment of the stomach of ruminants **rumens**

RUMES ▶ rume

RUMINA ▶ rumen

RUMINAL ▶ rumen

RUMKIN n archaic term for a drinking vessel **rumkins**

RUMLY ▶ rum

RUMMAGE vb, n

RUMMER ▶ rum

RUMMERS ▶ rum

RUMMEST ▶ rum

RUMMIER ▶ rummy

RUMMIES ▶ rummy

RUMMILY ▶ rummy

RUMMISH adj rather

strange, peculiar or odd

RUMMY n, adj

RUMNESS ▶ rum

RUMOR = rumour

RUMORED ▶ rumor

RUMORS ▶ rumor

RUMOUR n, vb **rumours**

RUMP n, vb **rumped**

RUMPIES ▶ rumpy

RUMPING ▶ rump

RUMPLE vb, n **rumpled, rumples, rumply**

RUMPS ▶ rump

RUMPUS n

RUMPY n tailless Manx cat ▷ adj with a large or noticeable rump

RUMS ▶ rum

RUN vb move with a more rapid gait than walking ▷ n act or spell of running

RUNANGA n Māori assembly or council

RUNAWAY n

RUNBACK n (in tennis) the areas behind the baselines of the court

RUNCH n another name for white charlock **runches**

RUND = roon

RUNDALE n system of land tenure in Ireland

RUNDLE n rung of a ladder

RUNDLED adj rounded

RUNDLES ▶ rundle

RUNDLET n liquid measure, generally about 15 gallons

RUNDOWN adj, n

RUNDS ▶ rund
RUNE *n* any character of the earliest Germanic alphabet
RUNED *n* with runes on
RUNES ▶ rune
RUNFLAT *adj* having a safety feature that prevents tyres becoming dangerous when flat
RUNG ▶ ring
RUNGS ▶ ring
RUNIC ▶ rune
RUNKLE *vb* (in dialect) crease or wrinkle **runkled, runkles**
RUNLESS ▶ run
RUNLET *n* cask for wine, beer, etc **runlets**
RUNNEL *n* small brook **runnels**
RUNNER *n* **runners**
RUNNET *dialect word for* ▶ **rennet**
RUNNETS ▶ runnet
RUNNIER ▶ runny
RUNNING ▶ run
RUNNY *adj*
RUNOFF *n* extra race to decide the winner after a tie **runoffs**
RUNOUT *n* dismissal of a batsman by running him out **runouts**
RUNOVER *n* incident in which someone is run over by a vehicle
RUNRIG = **rundale**
RUNRIGS ▶ runrig
RUNS ▶ run
RUNT *n*
RUNTED *adj* stunted
RUNTIER ▶ runt

RUNTISH ▶ runt
RUNTS ▶ runt
RUNTY ▶ runt
RUNWAY *n* **runways**
RUPEE *n* **rupees**
RUPIA *n* type of skin eruption
RUPIAH *n* standard monetary unit of Indonesia **rupiahs**
RUPIAS ▶ rupia
RUPTURE *n, vb*
RURAL *adj, n* **rurally, rurals**
RURBAN *adj* part country, part urban
RURP *n* very small piton **rurps**
RURU *another name for* ▶ **mopoke**
RURUS ▶ ruru
RUSA *n* type of deer with a mane
RUSALKA *n* water nymph or spirit
RUSAS ▶ rusa
RUSCUS *n* type of shrub
RUSE *n* **ruses**
RUSH *vb, n, adj* **rushed**
RUSHEE *n* someone interested in gaining fraternity or sorority membership **rushees**
RUSHEN *adj* made of rushes
RUSHER ▶ rush
RUSHERS ▶ rush
RUSHES *pl n* (in film-making) the initial prints of a scene or scenes before editing
RUSHIER ▶ rushy
RUSHING ▶ rush
RUSHY *adj* full of rushes

RUSINE *adj* of or relating to rusa deer
RUSK *n* **rusks**
RUSMA *n* Turkish depilatory **rusmas**
RUSSE *adj* as in **charlotte russe** cold dessert made from cream, etc, surrounded by sponge fingers
RUSSEL *n* type of woollen fabric **russels**
RUSSET *adj, n, vb* **russets, russety**
RUSSIA *n* Russia leather **russias**
RUSSIFY *vb* cause to become Russian in character
RUSSULA *n* type of fungus, typically of toadstool shape
RUST *n, adj, vb* **rusted**
RUSTIC *adj, n* **rustics**
RUSTIER ▶ rusty
RUSTILY ▶ rusty
RUSTING ▶ rust
RUSTLE *n, vb* **rustled**
RUSTLER *n* cattle thief
RUSTLES ▶ rustle
RUSTRE *n* (in heraldry) lozenge with a round hole in the middle showing the background colour **rustred, rustres**
RUSTS ▶ rust
RUSTY *adj*
RUT *n, vb*
RUTH *n* pity
RUTHFUL *adj* full of or causing sorrow or pity
RUTHS ▶ ruth

RUTILE n black, yellowish, or reddish-brown mineral **rutiles**

RUTIN n bioflavonoid found in various plants including rue **rutins**

RUTS ▶ rut

RUTTED ▶ rut

RUTTER n (in history) type of cavalry soldier **rutters**

RUTTIER ▶ rutty

RUTTILY ▶ rutty

RUTTING ▶ rut

RUTTISH adj (of an animal) in a condition of rut

RUTTY adj full of ruts or holes

RYA n type of rug originating in Scandinavia

RYAL n one of several old coins **ryals**

RYAS ▶ rya

RYBAT n polished stone piece forming the side of a window or door **rybats**

RYE n

RYEPECK n punt-mooring pole

RYES ▶ rye

RYFE archaic variant of ▶ **rife**

RYKE Scots variant of ▶ **reach**

RYKED ▶ ryke

RYKES ▶ ryke

RYKING ▶ ryke

RYMME = rim

RYMMED ▶ rymme

RYMMES ▶ rymme

RYMMING ▶ rymme

RYND n (in milling) crossbar piece forming part of the support structure of the upper millstone **rynds**

RYOKAN n traditional Japanese inn **ryokans**

RYOT n (in India) a peasant or tenant farmer **ryots**

RYPE n ptarmigan

RYPECK = ryepeck

RYPECKS ▶ rypeck

RYPER ▶ rype

Ss

S begins only four two-letter words, **sh** (5 points), **si**, **so** and **st** (2 each). These are easy to remember, and it's worth noting that two of them, **sh** and **st**, don't use any vowels. Interestingly, there are quite a few three-letter words beginning with **S** that don't contain vowels, some of which give good scores. These are **shh** (9), **shy** (9), **sky** (10), **sly** (6), **sny** (6), **spy** (6), **sty** (6), **swy** (9) and **syn** (6). **S** also forms a number of three-letter words with **X**. These are easy to remember as they use every vowel except **U**: **sax**, **sex**, **six** and **sox** (10 each). When it comes to **Z**, you will find **saz**, **sez** and **soz** (12 each) very useful, and the same applies to **suq** (12 points).

SAAG n (in Indian cookery) spinach **saags**

SAB n person engaged in direct action to prevent a targeted activity taking place ▷ vb take part in such action

SABAL n variety of palm tree **sabals**

SABATON n foot covering in suit of armour

SABAYON n dessert or sweet sauce made with egg yolks, sugar, and wine

SABBAT n midnight meeting of witches

SABBATH n period of rest

SABBATS ▶ sabbat

SABBED ▶ sab

SABBING ▶ sab

SABE n very informal word meaning sense or savvy ▷ vb very informal word meaning know or savvy **sabed, sabeing**

SABELLA n marine worm

SABER = sabre

SABERED ▶ saber

SABERS ▶ saber

SABES ▶ sabe

SABHA n set of Muslim prayer beads **sabhas**

SABIN n unit of acoustic absorption

SABINE variant of ▶ savin

SABINES ▶ sabine

SABINS ▶ sabin

SABIR n member of ancient Turkic people **sabirs**

SABKHA n flat coastal plain with a salt crust, common in Arabia

SABKHAH n sabkha

SABKHAS ▶ sabkha

SABKHAT n sabkha

SABLE n, adj **sabled, sables, sabling**

SABOT n wooden shoe traditionally worn by peasants in France **sabots**

SABRA n native-born Israeli Jew **sabras**

SABRE n, vb **sabred, sabres,**

SABREUR n person wielding sabre

SABRING ▸ sabre

SABS ▸ sab

SABURRA n granular deposit

SAC n

SACATON n coarse grass of the southwestern US and Mexico

SACBUT n medieval trombone **sacbuts**

SACCADE n movement of the eye when it makes a sudden change of fixation, as in reading

SACCATE adj in the form of a sac

SACCOI ▸ saccos

SACCOS n bishop's garment in the Orthodox Church

SACCULE n small sac

SACCULI ▸ sacculus

SACELLA ▸ sacellum

SACHEM = sagamore

SACHEMS ▸ sachem

SACHET n sachets

SACK n, vb

SACKAGE n act of sacking a place

SACKBUT n medieval form of trombone

SACKED, sacker, sackers, sackful ▸ sack

SACKING n rough woven material used for sacks

SACKS ▸ sack

SACLESS adj old word meaning unchangeable

SACLIKE ▸ sac

SACQUE = sack

SACQUES ▸ sacque

SACRA ▸ sacrum

SACRAL adj of or associated with sacred rites ▷ n sacral vertebra **sacrals**

SACRED adj

SACRIFY vb old form of sacrifice

SACRING n act or ritual of consecration

SACRIST = sacristan

SACRUM n wedge-shaped bone at the base of the spine **sacrums**

SACS ▸ sac

SAD adj, vb **sadded**

SADDEN vb **saddens**

SADDER ▸ sad

SADDEST ▸ sad

SADHU = sadhu

SADDHUS ▸ saddhu

SADDIE ▸ saddo n

SADDIES ▸ saddie

SADDING ▸ sad

SADDISH ▸ sad

SADDLE n, vb **saddled**

SADDLER n

SADDLES ▸ saddle

SADDO vb make sad ▷ n socially inadequate or pathetic person **saddoes, saddos**

SADE = sadhe

SADES ▸ sade

SADHANA n one of a number of spiritual practices which lead to perfection

SADHE n 18th letter in the Hebrew alphabet **sadhes**

SADHU n Hindu wandering holy man

SADI variant of ▸ sadhe

SADIRON n heavy iron pointed at both ends, for pressing clothes

SADIS ▸ sadi

SADISM n sadisms, sadist, sadists

SADLY ▸ sad

SADNESS ▸ sad

SADO variant of ▸ chado

SADOS ▸ sado

SADS ▸ sad

SADZA n southern African porridge **sadzas**

SAE Scot word for ▸ so

SAETER n upland pasture in Norway **saeters**

SAFARI n, vb safaris

SAFE adj, n, vb safed, safely, safer, safes, safest

SAFETY n, vb

SAFING ▸ safe

SAFFIAN n leather tanned with sumach and usually dyed a bright colour

SAFFRON n, adj

SAFROL n oily liquid obtained from sassafras

SAFROLE n colourless or yellowish oily water-insoluble liquid

SAFROLS ▸ safrol

SAFT Scot word for ▸ soft

SAFTER ▸ saft

SAFTEST ▸ saft

SAG vb, n

SAGA n

SAGAMAN n person reciting Norse sagas **sagamen**

SAGAS ▸ saga

SAGATHY n type of light fabric

SAGBUT n medieval trombone **sagbuts**

SAGE n, adj **sagely**

SAGENE n fishing net **sagenes**

SAGER ▸ sage

SAGES ▸ sage

SAGEST ▸ sage

SAGGAR n box in which fragile ceramic wares are placed for protection ▷ vb put in a saggar

SAGGARD n saggar

SAGGARS ▸ saggar

SAGGED ▸ sag

SAGGER = saggar

SAGGERS ▸ sagger

SAGGIER ▸ saggy

SAGGING ▸ sag

SAGGY adj tending to sag

SAGIER ▸ sagy

SAGIEST ▸ sagy

SAGITTA n sine of an arc

SAGO n

SAGOIN n South American monkey **sagoins**

SAGOS ▸ sago

SAGOUIN n South American monkey **sagouins**

SAGRADA adj as in cascara sagrada dried bark of the cascara buckthorn

SAGS ▸ sag

SAGUARO n giant cactus of desert regions

SAGUIN n South American monkey **saguins**

SAGUM n Roman soldier's cloak

SAGY adj like or containing sage

SAHEB = sahib

SAHEBS ▸ saheb

SAHIB n Indian term of address placed after a man's name as a mark of respect

SAHIBA n respectful Indian term of address for woman

SAHIBAH n sahiba

SAHIBAS ▸ sahiba

SAHIBS ▸ sahib

SAHIWAL n breed of cattle in India

SAHUARO = saguaro

SAI n South American monkey

SAIC n boat of eastern Mediterranean

SAICE = syce

SAICES ▸ saice

SAICK n boat of eastern Mediterranean **saicks**

SAICS ▸ saic

SAID = sayyid

SAIDEST ▸ say

SAIDS ▸ said

SAIDST ▸ say

SAIGA n either of two antelopes of the plains of central Asia **saigas**

SAIKEI n Japanese ornamental miniature landscape **saikeis**

SAIL n, vb **sailed**

SAILER n vessel, esp one equipped with sails, with specified sailing characteristics **sailers**

SAILING n practice, art, or technique of sailing a vessel

SAILOR n **sailors**

SAILS ▸ sail

SAIM Scots word for ▸ lard

SAIMIN n Hawaiian dish of noodles **saimins**

SAIMIRI n South American monkey

SAIMS ▸ saim

SAIN vb make the sign of the cross over so as to bless or protect from evil or sin

SAINE vb old form of say

SAINED ▸ sain

SAINING ▸ sain

SAINS ▸ sain

SAINT n, vb

SAINTED adj formally recognized by a Christian Church as a saint

SAINTLY adj

SAINTS ▸ saint

SAIQUE n boat in eastern Mediterranean **saiques**

SAIR Scot word for ▸ sore; **saired, sairer, sairest, sairing, sairs**

SAIS ▸ sai

SAIST ▸ say

SAITH form of the present tense (indicative mood) of ▸ say

SAITHE *n* dark-coloured food fish found in northern seas **saithes**

SAITHS ▸ saith

SAIYID *n* Muslim descended from Mohammed's grandson **saiyids**

SAJOU *n* South American monkey **sajous**

SAKAI *n* Malaysian aborigine **sakais**

SAKE *n*

SAKER *n* large falcon of E Europe and central Asia

SAKERET *n* male saker

SAKERS ▸ saker

SAKES ▸ sake

SAKI = sake

SAKIA *n* water wheel in Middle East **sakias**

SAKIEH *n* water wheel in Middle East **sakiehs**

SAKIS ▸ saki

SAKIYEH *n* water wheel in Middle East

SAKKOI ▸ sakkos

SAKKOS *n* bishop's garment in Orthodox Church

SAKSAUL *n* Asian tree

SAL *pharmacological term for ▸* **salt**

SALAAM *n* low bow of greeting among Muslims ▸ *vb* make a salaam **salaams**

SALABLE = saleable

SALABLY > saleably

SALAD *n*

SALADE = sallet

SALADES ▸ salade

SALADS ▸ salad

SALAL *n* North American shrub **salals**

SALAMI *n* salamis

SALAMON *n* word used in old oaths

SALARY *n, vb*

SALBAND *n* coating of mineral

SALCHOW *n* type of figure-skating jump

SALE *n*

SALEP *n* dried ground starchy tubers of various orchids **saleps**

SALES ▸ sale

SALET ▸ sallet

SALETS ▸ salet

SALEWD ▸ salue

SALFERN *n* plant of borage family

SALIC *adj* (of rocks and minerals) having a high content of silica and alumina

SALICES ▸ salix

SALICET *n* soft-toned organ stop

SALICIN *n* colourless or white crystalline water-soluble glucoside

SALIENT *adj, n*

SALIFY *vb* treat, mix with, or cause to combine with a salt

SALIGOT *n* water chestnut

SALINA *n* salt marsh, lake, or spring **salinas**

SALINE *adj, n* **salines**

SALIVA *n* salival, salivas

SALIX *n* plant or tree of willow family

SALL *archaic form of ▸* **shall**

SALLAD *old spelling of ▸* **salad**

SALLADS ▸ sallad

SALLAL *n* North American shrub **sallals**

SALLE *n* hall

SALLEE *n* SE Australian eucalyptus **sallees**

SALLES ▸ salle

SALLET *n* light round helmet **sallets**

SALLIED ▸ sally

SALLIER ▸ sally

SALLIES ▸ sally

SALLOW *adj, vb, n* **sallows, sallowy**

SALLY *n, vb*

SALMI *n* ragout of game stewed in a rich brown sauce **salmis**

SALMON *n, adj* **salmons**

SALMONY *adj* of or like a salmon

SALOL *n* white sparingly soluble crystalline compound **salols**

SALON *n* salons

SALOON *n* saloons

SALOOP *n* infusion of aromatic herbs or other plant parts formerly used as a tonic or cure **saloops, salop**

SALOPS ▸ salop

SALP *n* minute animal floating in sea

SALPA *n* any of various minute floating

animals of warm oceans **salpae, salpas**

SALPIAN n minute animal floating in sea

SALPID n minute animal floating in sea **salpids**

SALPINX n Fallopian tube or Eustachian tube

SALPS ▶ salp

SALS ▶ sal

SALSA n lively Puerto Rican dance ▷ vb dance the salsa **salsaed, salsas**

SALSE n volcano expelling mud **salses**

SALSIFY n Mediterranean plant with a long white edible root

SALT n, vb

SALTANT adj (of an organism) differing from others of its species because of a saltation ▷ n saltant organism

SALTATE vb go through saltation

SALTATO n saltando

SALTBOX n box for salt with a sloping lid

SALTCAT n salty medicine for pigeons

SALTED adj seasoned, preserved, or treated with salt

SALTER n person who deals in or manufactures salt

SALTERN n place where salt is obtained from

pools of evaporated sea water

SALTERS ▶ salter

SALTEST ▶ salt

SALTIE n saltwater crocodile

SALTIER ▶ saltire

SALTIES ▶ saltie

SALTILY ▶ salty

SALTINE n salty biscuit

SALTING n area of low ground regularly inundated with salt water

SALTIRE n diagonal cross on a shield

SALTISH ▶ salt

SALTLY ▶ salt

SALTO n daring jump ▷ vb perform a daring jump **saltoed, saltos**

SALTPAN n shallow basin containing salt from an evaporated salt lake

SALTS ▶ salt

SALTUS n break in the continuity of a sequence

SALTY adj

SALUE vb old word meaning salute **salued, salues, saluing**

SALUKI n type of tall hound with a smooth coat **salukis**

SALUTE n, vb **saluted, saluter, salutes**

SALVAGE n, vb

SALVE n, vb **salved**

SALVER = salvor

SALVERS ▶ salver

SALVES ▶ salve

SALVETE n Latin greeting

SALVIA n plant with blue or red flowers **salvias**

SALVING ▶ salve

SALVO n, vb **salvoed, salvoes**

SALVOR n person instrumental in salvaging a vessel or its cargo **salvors**

SALVOS ▶ salvo

SALWAR n as in salwar kameez long tunic worn over a pair of baggy trousers **salwars**

SAM vb collect

SAMA n Japanese title of respect

SAMAAN n South American tree **samaans**

SAMADHI n state of deep meditative contemplation

SAMAN n South American tree **samans**

SAMARA n dry indehiscent one-seeded fruit **samaras**

SAMAS ▶ sama

SAMBA n, vb **sambaed**

SAMBAL n Malaysian dish **sambals**

SAMBAR n S Asian deer with three-tined antlers **sambars**

SAMBAS ▶ samba

SAMBHAR n Indian dish

SAMBHUR n Asian deer

SAMBUCA n Italian liqueur

SAMBUKE n ancient Greek stringed instrument

SAMBUR = sambar

SAMBURS ▶ sambur

SAME adj, n

SAMECH n letter in Hebrew alphabet **samechs**

SAMEK variant of ▶ samekh

SAMEKH n 15th letter in the Hebrew alphabet **samekhs**

SAMEKS ▶ samek

SAMEL adj of brick, not sufficiently fired

SAMELY adj the same

SAMEN old Scots form of ▶ same

SAMES ▶ same

SAMEY adj monotonous

SAMFOO n style of casual dress worn by Chinese women **samfoos**

SAMFU n Chinese female outfit **samfus**

SAMIEL = simoom

SAMIELS ▶ samiel

SAMIER ▶ samey

SAMIEST ▶ samey

SAMISEN n Japanese plucked stringed instrument with a long neck

SAMITE n heavy fabric of silk used in the Middle Ages **samites**

SAMITHI = samiti

SAMITI n (in India) an association, esp one formed to organize

political activity **samitis**

SAMLET n young salmon **samlets**

SAMLOR n motor vehicle in Thailand **samlors**

SAMMED ▶ sam

SAMMIES ▶ sammy

SAMMING ▶ sam

SAMMY n (in South Africa) an Indian fruit and vegetable vendor

SAMOSA n samosas

SAMOVAR n

SAMOYED n Siberian breed of dog with a tightly curled tail

SAMP n crushed maize used for porridge

SAMPAN n sampans

SAMPI n old Greek number character

SAMPIRE n samphire

SAMPIS ▶ sampi

SAMPLE n, vb sampled

SAMPLER n

SAMPLES ▶ sample

SAMPS ▶ samp

SAMS ▶ sam

SAMSARA n endless cycle of birth, death, and rebirth

SAMSHOO n Chinese alcoholic drink

SAMSHU n alcoholic drink made from fermented rice **samshus**

SAMURAI n

SAN n sanatorium

SANCAI n glaze in Chinese pottery **sancais**

SANCHO n African stringed instrument **sanchos**

SANCTA ▶ sanctum

SANCTUM n sacred place

SAND n, vb

SANDAL n, vb **sandals**

SANDBAG n, vb

SANDBAR n ridge of sand in a river or sea, often exposed at low tide

SANDBOX n container on a locomotive from which sand is released onto the rails

SANDBOY n as in **happy as a sandboy** very happy or high-spirited

SANDBUR n variety of wild grass

SANDDAB n type of small Pacific flatfish

SANDED ▶ sand

SANDEK n man who holds a baby being circumcised **sandeks**

SANDER n power tool for smoothing surfaces **sanders**

SANDFLY n any of various small mothlike flies

SANDHI n modification of a word under the influence of an adjacent word **sandhis**

SANDHOG n person who works in underground or underwater construction projects

SANDIER ▶ sandy
SANDING ▶ sand
SANDLOT n area of vacant ground used for children's games
SANDMAN n (in folklore) a magical person supposed to put children to sleep **sandmen**
SANDPIT n shallow pit or container holding sand for children to play in
SANDS ▶ sand
SANDY adj
SANE adj, vb **saned, sanely, saner, sanes, sanest**
SANG Scots word for ▶ **song**
SANGA n Ethiopian ox
SANGAR n breastwork of stone or sods **sangars**
SANGAS ▶ sanga
SANGEET n Indian pre-wedding celebration
SANGER n sandwich **sangers**
SANGH n Indian union or association
SANGHA n Buddhist monastic order or community **sanghas**
SANGHAT n local Sikh community or congregation
SANGHS ▶ sangh
SANGO = sanger
SANGOMA n witch doctor or herbalist
SANGOS ▶ sango

SANGRIA n Spanish drink of red wine and fruit
SANGS ▶ sang
SANICLE n type of plant with clusters of small white flowers
SANIES n thin greenish foul-smelling discharge from a wound, etc
SANIFY vb make healthy
SANING ▶ sane
SANIOUS ▶ sanies
SANITY n
SANJAK n (in the Turkish Empire) a subdivision of a vilayet **sanjaks**
SANK ▶ sink
SANKO n African stringed instrument **sankos**
SANNIE Scots word for > **sandshoe**
SANNIES ▶ sannie
SANNOP n Native American married man **sannops**
SANNUP n Native American married man **sannups**
SANPAN n sampan **sanpans**
SANPRO n sanitary-protection products, collectively **sanpros**
SANS archaic word for ▶ **without**
SANSA n African musical instrument
SANSAR n name of a wind that blows in

Iran **sansars**
SANSAS ▶ sansa
SANSEI n American whose parents were Japanese immigrants **sanseis**
SANT n devout person in India
SANTAL n sandalwood **santals**
SANTERA n priestess of santeria
SANTERO n priest of santeria
SANTIMI ▶ santims
SANTIMS n money unit in Latvia **santimu**
SANTIR n Middle Eastern stringed instrument **santirs**
SANTO n saint or representation of one
SANTOL n fruit from Southeast Asia **santols**
SANTON n French figurine **santons**
SANTOOR = santir
SANTOS ▶ santo
SANTOUR n Middle Eastern stringed instrument
SANTS ▶ sant
SANTUR n Middle Eastern stringed instrument **santurs**
SANYASI = sannyasi
SAOLA n small, very rare bovine mammal of Vietnam and Laos **saolas**
SAOUARTI n tropical American tree
SAP n, vb

SAPAJOU n capuchin monkey

SAPAN n tropical tree **sapans**

SAPEGO n skin disease

SAPELE n type of W African tree **sapeles**

SAPFUL adj full of sap

SAPHEAD n simpleton, idiot, or fool

SAPHENA n either of two large superficial veins of the legs

SAPID adj having a pleasant taste

SAPIENS adj relating to or like modern human beings

SAPIENT adj wise, shrewd ▷ n wise person

SAPLESS ▶ sap

SAPLING ▶ sap

SAPONIN n any of a group of plant glycosides

SAPOR n quality in a substance that is perceived by the sense of taste **sapors**

SAPOTA = sapodilla

SAPOTAS ▶ sapota

SAPOTE n Central American tree **sapotes**

SAPOUR variant of ▶ sapor

SAPOURS ▶ sapour

SAPPAN n tropical tree **sappans**

SAPPED ▶ sap

SAPPER n soldier in an engineering unit **sappers**

SAPPHIC adj lesbian ▷ n verse written in a particular form

SAPPIER ▶ sappy

SAPPILY ▶ sappy

SAPPING ▶ sap

SAPPLE vb Scots word meaning wash in water **sappled, sapples**

SAPPY adj (of plants) full of sap

SAPROBE n organism that lives on decaying organisms

SAPS ▶ sap

SAPSAGO n hard greenish Swiss cheese

SAPWOOD n soft wood, just beneath the bark in tree trunks, that consists of living tissue

SAR n marine fish ▷ vb Scots word meaning savour

SARAFAN n Russian woman's cloak

SARAN n any one of a class of thermoplastic resins

SARANGI n stringed instrument of India played with a bow

SARANS ▶ saran

SARAPE n serape **sarapes**

SARCASM n (use of) bitter or wounding ironic language

SARCINA n type of bacterium

SARCODE n material making up living cell

SARCOID adj of, relating

to, or resembling flesh ▷ n tumour resembling a sarcoma

SARCOMA n malignant tumour beginning in connective tissue

SARCOUS adj (of tissue) muscular or fleshy

SARD n orange, red, or brown variety of chalcedony

SARDANA n Catalan dance

SARDAR n title used before the name of Sikh men **sardars**

SARDEL n small fish **sardels**

SARDINE n, vb

SARDIUS = sard

SARDS ▶ sard

SARED ▶ sar

SAREE = sari

SAREES ▶ saree

SARGE n sergeant **sarges**

SARGO = sargus

SARGOS variant of ▶ sargus

SARGUS n species of sea fish

SARI n

SARIN n chemical used in warfare as a lethal nerve gas producing asphyxia

SARING ▶ sar

SARINS ▶ sarin

SARIS ▶ sari

SARK n shirt or (formerly) chemise

SARKIER ▶ sarky

SARKILY ▶ sarky

SARKING n flat

planking supporting the roof cladding of a building

SARKS ▶ sark

SARKY adj sarcastic

SARMENT n thin twig

SARMIE n **sarmies**

SARNEY n sandwich **sarneys**

SARNIE n sandwich **sarnies**

SAROD n Indian stringed musical instrument

SARODE n Indian stringed instrument **sarodes**

SARODS ▶ sarod

SARONG n **sarongs**

SARONIC ▶ saros

SAROS n cycle in which eclipses of the sun and moon occur in the same sequence **saroses**

SARS ▶ sar

SARSAR = **sansar**

SARSARS ▶ sarsar

SARSDEN n sarsen

SARSEN n boulder of silicified sandstone **sarsens**

SARSNET n type of silk

SARTOR humorous or literary word for ▶ **tailor**

SARTORS ▶ sartor

SARUS n Indian bird of crane family **saruses**

SASER n device for amplifying ultrasound **sasers**

SASH n, vb

SASHAY vb move or walk in a casual or a showy manner **sashays**

SASHED ▶ sash

SASHES ▶ sash

SASHIMI n Japanese dish of thin fillets of raw fish

SASHING ▶ sash

SASIN another name for ▶ **blackbuck**

SASINE n granting of legal possession of feudal property **sasines**

SASINS ▶ sasin

SASS n insolent or impudent talk or behaviour ▶ vb talk or answer back in such a way

SASSABY n African antelope of grasslands and semideserts

SASSE n old word meaning canal lock

SASSED ▶ sass

SASSES ▶ sass

SASSIER ▶ sassy

SASSIES ▶ sassy

SASSILY ▶ sassy

SASSING ▶ sass

SASSY adj insolent, impertinent ▶ n W African leguminous tree with poisonous bark

SASTRA = **shastra**

SASTRAS ▶ sastra

SAT ▶ sit

SATAI = **satay**

SATAIS ▶ satai

SATANG n monetary unit of Thailand worth one hundredth of a baht **satangs**

SATANIC adj

SATARA n type of cloth **sataras**

SATAY n Indonesian and Malaysian dish **satays**

SATCHEL n

SATE vb satisfy (a desire or appetite) fully **sated**

SATEEN n glossy linen or cotton fabric, woven in such a way that it resembles satin **sateens**

SATEM adj denoting or belonging to a particular group of Indo-European languages

SATES ▶ sate

SATI n Indian widow suicide

SATIATE vb

SATIETY n feeling of having had too much

SATIN n, adj, vb **satined**

SATINET n thin or imitation satin

SATING ▶ sate

SATINS ▶ satin

SATINY ▶ satin

SATIRE n **satires**

SATIRIC = **satirical**

SATIS ▶ sati

SATISFY vb

SATIVE adj old word meaning cultivated

SATORI n state of sudden indescribable intuitive enlightenment **satoris**

SATRAP n (in ancient Persia) a provincial governor or subordinate ruler **satraps**

SATRAPY n province, office, or period of rule of a satrap

SATSUMA n

SATYR n woodland god, part man, part goat

SATYRA n female satyr

SATYRAL n mythical beast in heraldry

SATYRAS ▶ satyra

SATYRIC ▶ satyr

SATYRID n butterfly with typically brown or dark wings with paler markings

SATYRS ▶ satyr

SAU archaic past tense of ▶ see

SAUBA n South American ant **saubas**

SAUCE n, vb **sauced**

SAUCER n **saucers**

SAUCES ▶ sauce

SAUCH n sallow or willow **sauchs**

SAUCIER n chef who makes sauces

SAUCILY ▶ saucy

SAUCING ▶ sauce

SAUCY adj

SAUGER n small North American pikeperch **saugers**

SAUGH = sauch

SAUGHS ▶ saugh

SAUGHY adj Scots word meaning made of willow

SAUL Scots word for ▶ soul

SAULGE n old word for sage plant **saulges**

SAULIE n Scots word meaning professional mourner **saulies**

SAULS ▶ saul

SAULT n waterfall in Canada **saults**

SAUNA n, vb **saunaed, saunas**

SAUNT Scots form of ▶ saint

SAUNTED ▶ saunt

SAUNTER vb, n

SAUNTS ▶ saunt

SAUREL n type of mackerel **saurels**

SAURIAN n

SAURIES ▶ saury

SAUROID adj like a lizard

SAURY n type of fish of tropical and temperate seas

SAUSAGE n

SAUT Scot word for ▶ salt

SAUTE vb fry quickly in a little fat ▷ n dish of sautéed food ▷ adj sautéed until lightly brown

SAUTED ▶ saut

SAUTEED ▶ saute

SAUTES ▶ saute

SAUTING ▶ saut

SAUTOIR n necklace or pendant

SAUTS ▶ saut

SAV short for ▶ saveloy

SAVABLE ▶ save

SAVAGE adj, n **savaged, savager, savages**

SAVANNA n

SAVANT n learned person **savante, savants**

SAVARIN n type of cake

SAVATE n form of boxing in which blows may be delivered with the feet **savates**

SAVE vb, n, prep **saved**

SAVELOY n spicy smoked sausage

SAVER ▶ save

SAVERS ▶ save

SAVES ▶ save

SAVEY vb understand **saveyed, saveys**

SAVIN n small spreading juniper bush of Europe, N Asia, and North America **savine**

SAVINES ▶ savine

SAVING n, prep, adj **savings**

SAVINS ▶ savin

SAVIOR = saviour

SAVIORS ▶ savior

SAVIOUR n

SAVOR = savour

SAVORED ▶ savor

SAVORER ▶ savor

SAVORS ▶ savor

SAVORY = savoury

SAVOUR vb, n **savours**

SAVOURY adj, n

SAVOY n variety of cabbage **savoys**

SAVS ▶ sav

SAVVEY vb understand **savveys**

SAVVIED, savvier, savvies, savvily ▶ savvy

SAVVY vb understand ▷ n understanding, intelligence ▷ adj shrewd

SAW n, vb

SAWAH n paddyfield **sawahs**

SAWBILL n type of hummingbird

SAWBUCK n sawhorse, esp one having an X-shaped supporting structure

SAWDER n flattery ▷ vb flatter **sawders**

SAWDUST n, vb

SAWED ▶ saw

SAWER ▶ saw

SAWERS ▶ saw

SAWFISH n fish with a long toothed snout

SAWFLY n any of various hymenopterous insects

SAWING ▶ saw

SAWINGS ▶ saw

SAWLIKE ▶ saw

SAWLOG n log suitable for sawing **sawlogs**

SAWMILL n

SAWN past participle of ▶ saw

SAWPIT n pit above which a log is sawn into planks **sawpits**

SAWS ▶ saw

SAWYER n person who saws timber for a living **sawyers**

SAX = saxophone

SAXAUL n Asian tree **saxauls**

SAXE adj as in saxe blue light greyish-blue colour

SAXES ▶ sax

SAXHORN n valved brass instrument used

chiefly in brass and military bands

SAXONY n fine 3-ply yarn used for knitting and weaving

SAXTUBA n bass saxhorn

SAY vb speak or utter ▷ n right or chance to speak **sayable**

SAYED = sayyid

SAYEDS ▶ sayed

SAYER ▶ say

SAYERS ▶ say

SAYEST ▶ say

SAYID = sayyid

SAYIDS ▶ sayid

SAYING ▶ say

SAYINGS ▶ say

SAYNE ▶ say

SAYS ▶ say

SAYST ▶ say

SAYYID n Muslim claiming descent from Mohammed's grandson Husain **sayyids**

SAZ n Middle Eastern stringed instrument

> This musical instrument is one of the most frequently played Z words.

SAZERAC n mixed drink of whisky, Pernod, syrup, bitters, and lemon

SAZES ▶ saz

SAZHEN n Russian measure of length **sazhens**

SAZZES ▶ saz

SBIRRI ▶ sbirro

SBIRRO n Italian police officer

SCAB n, vb scabbed

SCABBLE vb shape (stone) roughly

SCABBY adj covered with scabs

SCABIES n

SCABID adj having a rough or scaly surface

SCABS ▶ scab

SCAD n any of various carangid fishes

SCADS pl n large amount or number

SCAFF n Scots word meaning food

SCAFFIE n Scots word meaning street cleaner

SCAFFS ▶ scaff

SCAG n tear in a garment or piece of cloth ▷ vb make a tear in (cloth) **scagged**

SCAGLIA n type of limestone

SCAGS ▶ scag

SCAIL vb Scots word meaning disperse **scailed, scails**

SCAITH vb old word meaning injure **scaiths**

SCALA n passage inside the cochlea

SCALADE short for > escalade

SCALADO = scalade

SCALAE ▶ scala

SCALAGE n percentage deducted from the price of goods liable to shrink or leak

SCALAR adj having magnitude but no direction ▷ n quantity that has magnitude but not direction

SCALARE another name for ▷ **angelfish**

SCALARS ▶ scalar

SCALD = skald

SCALDED ▶ scald

SCALDER ▶ scald

SCALDIC ▶ skald

SCALDS ▶ scald

SCALE n, vb scaled

SCALENE adj

SCALENI > scalenus

SCALER n person or thing that scales scalers

SCALES ▶ scale

SCALEUP n increase

SCALIER ▶ scaly

SCALING ▶ scaling

SCALL n disease of the scalp characterized by itching and scab formation scalled

SCALLOP n, vb

SCALLS ▶ scall

SCALLY n rascal

SCALP n, vb scalped

SCALPEL n

SCALPER ▶ scalp

SCALPS ▶ scalp

SCALY adj

SCAM n dishonest scheme ▷ vb swindle (someone) by means of a trick

SCAMBLE vb scramble

SCAMEL n Shakespearian word of uncertain meaning scamels

SCAMMED ▶ scam

SCAMMER n person who perpetrates a scam

SCAMP n mischievous child ▷ vb perform without care scamped

SCAMPER vb, n

SCAMPI pl n scampis

SCAMPS ▶ scamp

SCAMS ▶ scam

SCAMTO n argot of urban South African Blacks scamtos

SCAN vb, n scand

SCANDAL n, vb

SCANDIA n scandium oxide

SCANDIC adj of or containing scandium

SCANNED ▶ scan

SCANNER n

SCANS ▶ scan

SCANT adj, vb, adv scanted, scanter

SCANTLE vb stint

SCANTLY ▶ scant

SCANTS ▶ scant

SCANTY adj

SCAPA variant of ▶ scarper

SCAPAED ▶ scapa

SCAPAS ▶ scapa

SCAPE n leafless stalk in plants ▷ vb archaic word for escape scaped, scapes

SCAPI ▶ scapus

SCAPING ▶ scape

SCAPOSE ▶ scape

SCAPPLE vb shape roughly

SCAPULA n

SCAPUS n flower stalk

SCAR n, vb

SCARAB n sacred beetle of ancient Egypt scarabs

SCARCE adj scarcer

SCARE vb, n, adj scared, scarer, scarers, scares

SCAREY adj frightening

SCARF n, vb scarfed, scarfer, scarfs

SCARIER ▶ scary

SCARIFY vb scratch or cut slightly all over

SCARILY ▶ scary

SCARING ▶ scare

SCARLET n, adj, vb

SCARP n, vb

SCARPA vb run away scarpas

SCARPED ▶ scarp

SCARPER vb, n

SCARPH vb join with scarf joint scarphs

SCARPS ▶ scarp

SCARRE n Shakespearian word of unknown meaning

SCARRED ▶ scar

SCARRES ▶ scarre

SCARRY ▶ scar

SCARS ▶ scar

SCART vb scratch or scrape ▷ n scratch or scrape scarted

SCARTH Scots word for > cormorant

SCARTHS ▶ scarth

SCARTS ▶ scart

SCARVES ▶ scarf

SCARY adj

SCAT vb go away ▷ n jazz singing using improvised vocal

sounds instead of words

SCATCH = stilt

SCATH vb old word meaning injure

SCATHE vb attack with severe criticism ▷ n harm **scathed, scathes**

SCATHS ▶ scath

SCATOLE n substance found in coal

SCATS ▶ scat

SCATT n old word meaning tax ▷ vb tax

SCATTED ▶ scat

SCATTER vb, n

SCATTS ▶ scatt

SCATTY adj

SCAUD Scot word for ▶ scald

SCAUDED ▶ scaud

SCAUPER ▶ scorper

SCAUPS ▶ scaup

SCAUR = scar

SCAURED ▶ scaur

SCAURS ▶ scaur

SCAURY n young seagull

SCAVAGE n old word meaning toll

SCAW n headland **scaws**

SCAZON n metre in poetry **scazons**

SCEAT n Anglo-Saxon coin

SCEATT n Anglo-Saxon coin

SCEDULE old spelling of > schedule

SCENA n scene in an opera, usually longer than a single aria

SCENARY n scenery

SCENAS ▶ scena

SCEND vb (of a vessel) to surge upwards in a heavy sea ▷ n upward heaving of a vessel pitching **scended, scends**

SCENE n, vb **scened**

SCENERY n

SCENES ▶ scene

SCENIC adj, n **scenics**

SCENING ▶ scene

SCENT n, vb **scented, scents**

SCEPSIS n doubt

SCEPTER = sceptre

SCEPTIC n, adj

SCEPTRE n, vb

SCEPTRY adj having sceptre

SCERNE vb old word meaning discern **scerned, scernes**

SCHANSE n stones heaped to shelter soldier in battle

SCHANZE n stones heaped to shelter soldier in battle

SCHAPPE n yarn or fabric made from waste silk

SCHAV n Polish soup **schavs**

SCHELLY n freshwater whitefish of the English Lake District

SCHELM n South African word meaning rascal **schelms**

SCHEMA n schemas

SCHEME n, vb schemed, schemer, schemes

SCHERZI ▶ scherzo

SCHERZO n brisk lively piece of music

SCHISM n

SCHISMA n musical term

SCHISMS ▶ schism

SCHIST n crystalline rock which splits into layers **schists**

SCHLEP vb drag or lug (oneself or an object) with difficulty ▷ n stupid or clumsy person

SCHLEPP vb schlep

SCHLEPS ▶ schlep

SCHLICH n finely crushed ore

SCHLOCK n goods or produce of cheap or inferior quality ▷ adj cheap, inferior, or trashy

SCHLOSS n castle

SCHLUB n coarse or contemptible person **schlubs**

SCHLUMP vb move in lazy way

SCHMALZ = schmaltz

SCHMEAR n situation, matter, or affair ▷ vb spread or smear

SCHMECK n taste

SCHMEER = schmear

SCHMELZ n ornamental glass

SCHMICK adj (in Australia) excellent, elegant, or stylish

SCHMO n dull, stupid, or boring person

SCHMOCK n stupid person

SCHMOE n stupid person

SCHMOES ▶ schmo

SCHMOOS variant of > schmoose

SCHMOOZ n chat

SCHMOS ▶ schmo

SCHMUCK n stupid or contemptible person

SCHNAPS = schnapps

SCHNELL adj German word meaning quick

SCHNOOK n stupid or gullible person

SCHNORR vb beg

SCHNOZ n nose

SCHNOZZ n nose

SCHOLAR n

SCHOLIA > scholium

SCHOOL n, vb

SCHOOLE n old form of shoal

SCHOOLS ▶ school

SCHORL n type of black tourmaline **schorls**

SCHOUT n council officer in Netherlands **schouts**

SCHRIK variant of ▶ skrik

SCHRIKS ▶ schrik

SCHROD n young cod **schrods**

SCHTICK = shtick

SCHTIK n schtick **schtiks**

SCHTOOK n trouble

SCHTOOM adj silent

SCHTUCK n trouble

SCHTUM adj silent or dumb

SCHUIT n Dutch boat with flat bottom **schuits**

SCHUL = shul

SCHULN ▶ schul

SCHULS ▶ schul

SCHUSS n straight high-speed downhill run ▷ vb perform a schuss

SCHUYT n Dutch boat with flat bottom **schuyts**

SCHWA n vowel representing the sound in unstressed syllables **schwas**

SCIARID n small fly

SCIATIC adj of the hip ▷ n sciatic part of the body

SCIENCE n

SCIENT adj old word meaning scientific

SCILLA n plant with small bell-shaped flowers **scillas**

SCIOLTO adv musical direction meaning freely

SCION n scions

SCIROC n hot Mediterranean wind **scirocs**

SCIRRHI ▶ scirrhus

SCISSEL n waste metal left over from sheet metal after discs have been punched out of it

SCISSIL n scissel

SCISSOR vb cut (an object) with scissors

SCIURID n squirrel or related rodent

SCLAFF vb cause (the club) to hit (the ground behind the ball) when making a stroke ▷ n sclaffing stroke or shot **sclaffs**

SCLATE vb Scots word meaning slate **sclates**

SCLAVE n old form of slave **sclaves**

SCLERA n tough white substance that forms the outer covering of the eyeball **sclerae, scleral, scleras**

SCLERE n supporting anatomical structure **scleres**

SCLIFF n Scots word for small piece **scliffs**

SCLIM n Scots word meaning climb **sclims**

SCODIER ▶ scody

SCODY adj unkempt

SCOFF vb, n **scoffed, scoffer, scoffs**

SCOG vb shelter **scogged, scogs**

SCOLD vb, n **scolded, scolder, scolds**

SCOLEX n headlike part of a tapeworm

SCOLIA ▶ scolion

SCOLION n ancient Greek drinking song

SCOLLOP variant of ▶ scallop

SCONCE n bracket on a wall for holding candles or lights ▷ vb challenge (a fellow student) to drink a large quantity of beer **sconced, sconces**

SCONE n scones

SCOOBY n clue; notion

SCOOCH vb compress one's body into smaller space

SCOOG vb shelter **scooged, scoogs**

SCOOP n, vb **scooped, scooper, scoops**

SCOOSH vb squirt ▷ n squirt or rush of liquid

SCOOT vb leave or move quickly ▷ n act of scooting

SCOOTCH = **scooch**

SCOOTED ▷ scoot

SCOOTER n

SCOOTS ▷ scoot

SCOP n (in Anglo-Saxon England) a bard or minstrel

SCOPA n tuft of hairs on the abdomen or hind legs of bees **scopae**

SCOPATE adj having tuft

SCOPE n, vb **scoped, scopes, scoping**

SCOPS ▷ scop

SCOPULA n small tuft of dense hairs on the legs and chelicerae of some spiders

SCORCH vb burn on the surface ▷ n slight burn

SCORE n, vb **scored, scorer, scorers, scores**

SCORIA n mass of solidified lava containing many cavities **scoriac, scoriae**

SCORIFY vb remove (impurities) from

metals by forming scoria

SCORING n act or practice of scoring

SCORN n, vb **scorned, scorner, scorns**

SCORPER n kind of fine chisel with a square or curved tip

SCORSE vb exchange **scorsed, scorser, scorses**

SCOT n payment or tax

SCOTCH vb, n

SCOTER n type of sea duck **scoters**

SCOTIA n deep concave moulding **scotias**

SCOTOMA n blind spot

SCOTOMY n dizziness

SCOTS ▷ scot

SCOTTIE n type of small sturdy terrier

SCOUG vb shelter **scouged, scougs**

SCOUP vb Scots word meaning jump **scouped, scoups**

SCOUR vb, n **scoured, scours**

SCOURGE n, vb

SCOURIE n young seagull

SCOURS ▷ scour

SCOURSE vb exchange

SCOUSE n stew made from left-over meat

SCOUSER n inhabitant of Liverpool

SCOUSES ▷ scouse

SCOUT n, vb **scouted, scouter**

SCOUTH n Scots word meaning plenty of

scope **scouths**

SCOUTS ▷ scout

SCOW n unpowered barge used for carrying freight ▷ vb transport by scow

SCOWDER vb Scots word meaning scorch

SCOWED ▷ scow

SCOWING ▷ scow

SCOWL n, vb **scowled**

SCOWLER n person who scowls

SCOWLS ▷ scowl

SCOWP vb Scots word meaning jump **scowped, scowps**

SCOWRER n old word meaning hooligan

SCOWRIE n young seagull

SCOWS ▷ scow

SCOWTH n Scots word meaning plenty of scope **scowths**

SCOZZA n rowdy person, esp one who drinks a lot of alcohol **scozzas**

SCRAB vb scratch **scrabs**

SCRAE Scots word for ▷ scree

SCRAES ▷ scrae

SCRAG n thin end of a neck of mutton ▷ vb wring the neck of

SCRAGGY adj

SCRAGS ▷ scrag

SCRAICH vb Scots word meaning scream

SCRAIGH vb Scots word meaning scream

SCRAM vb, n

SCRAMB vb scratch with nails or claws **scrambs**

SCRAMS ▶ scram

SCRAN n food

SCRANCH vb crunch

SCRANNY adj scrawny

SCRANS ▶ scran

SCRAP n, vb

SCRAPE vb, n, scraped, scraper, scrapes

SCRAPIE n disease of sheep and goats

SCRAPPY adj

SCRAPS ▶ scrap

SCRAT vb scratch

SCRATCH vb, n, adj

SCRATS ▶ scrat

SCRAUCH vb squawk

SCRAUGH vb squawk

SCRAW n sod from the surface of a peat bog or from a field

SCRAWL vb, n scrawls, scrawly

SCRAWM vb dialect word meaning scratch **scrawms**

SCRAWNY adj

SCRAWP vb scratch (the skin) to relieve itching **scrawps**

SCRAWS ▶ scraw

SCRAY n tern

SCRAYE n tern **scrayes**

SCRAYS ▶ scray

SCREAK vb screech or creak ▷ n screech or creak **screaks, screaky**

SCREAM vb, n

SCREAMO n

SCREAMS ▶ scream

SCREE n

SCREECH n, vb

SCREED n long tedious piece of writing ▷ vb rip **screeds**

SCREEN n, vb **screens**

SCREES ▶ scree

SCREET vb shed tears ▷ n act or sound of crying **screets**

SCREEVE vb write

SCREICH = screigh

SCREIGH Scot word for ▶ screech

SCREW n, vb

SCREWED adj fastened by a screw or screws

SCREWER ▶ screw

SCREWS ▶ screw

SCREWUP n something done badly

SCREWY adj crazy or eccentric

SCRIBAL ▶ scribe

SCRIBE n, vb scribed

SCRIBER n pointed steel tool used to score materials as a guide to cutting, etc

SCRIBES ▶ scribe

SCRIECH vb Scots word meaning screech

SCRIED ▶ scry

SCRIENE n old form of screen

SCRIES ▶ scry

SCRIEVE vb Scots word meaning write

SCRIKE vb old word meaning shriek **scriked, scrikes**

SCRIM n open-weave muslin or hessian fabric

SCRIMP vb scrimps, scrimpy

SCRIMS ▶ scrim

SCRINE n old form of shrine **scrines**

SCRIP n certificate representing a claim to stocks or shares **scrips**

SCRIPT n, vb **scripts**

SCRITCH vb screech

SCRIVE Scots word for ▶ write

SCRIVED ▶ scrive

SCRIVES ▶ scrive

SCROBE n groove **scrobes**

SCROD n young cod or haddock **scrods**

SCROG n Scots word meaning small tree

SCROGGY variant of > scroggie

SCROGS ▶ scrog

SCROLL n, vb **scrolls**

SCROME vb crawl or climb **scromed, scromes**

SCROOCH vb scratch (the skin) to relieve itching

SCROOGE variant of ▶ scrouge

SCROOP vb emit a grating or creaking sound ▷ n such a sound **scroops**

SCRORP n deep scratch or weal **scrorps**

SCROTA ▶ scrotum

SCROTAL ▶ scrotum

SCROTUM n

SCROUGE vb crowd or press

SCROW n scroll

SCROWL vb old form of scroll

SCROWLE vb old form of scroll

SCROWLS ▶ scrowl

SCROWS ▶ scrow

SCROYLE n old word meaning wretch

SCRUB vb, n, adj

SCRUBBY adj covered with scrub

SCRUBS ▶ scrub

SCRUFF = scum

SCRUFFS ▶ scruff

SCRUFFY adj

SCRUM n, vb

SCRUMMY adj delicious

SCRUMP vb steal (apples) from an orchard or garden **scrumps**

SCRUMPY n rough dry cider

SCRUMS ▶ scrum

SCRUNCH vb crumple or crunch or be crumpled or crunched ▷ n act or sound of scrunching

SCRUNT n Scots word meaning stunted thing **scrunts, scrunty**

SCRUPLE n, vb

SCRUTO n trapdoor on stage **scrutos**

SCRUZE vb old word meaning squeeze **scruzed, scruzes**

SCRY vb divine, esp by crystal gazing **scryde, scryer, scryers, scrying**

SCRYNE n old form of shrine **scrynes**

SCUBA n apparatus used in diving ▷ vb dive using scuba equipment **scubaed, scubas**

SCUCHIN n old form of scutcheon

SCUD vb, n **scudded, scudder**

SCUDDLE vb scuttle

SCUDI ▶ scudo

SCUDLER n Scots word meaning leader of festivities

SCUDO n any of several former Italian coins

SCUDS ▶ scud

SCUFF vb, n **scuffed**

SCUFFER n type of sandal

SCUFFLE vb, n

SCUFFS ▶ scuff

SCUFT n dialect word meaning nape of neck **scufts**

SCUG vb shelter **scugged, scugs**

SCUL n old form of school

SCULCH n rubbish

SCULK vb old form of skulk **sculked, sculker, sculks**

SCULL n, vb

SCULLE n old form of school

SCULLED ▶ scull

SCULLER ▶ scull

SCULLES ▶ sculle

SCULLS ▶ scull

SCULP variant of > sculpture

SCULPED ▶ sculp

SCULPIN n type of fish of the family which includes bullheads and sea scorpions

SCULPS ▶ sculp

SCULPT = sculpture

SCULPTS ▶ sculpt

SCULS ▶ scul

SCULTCH = sculch

SCUM n, vb

SCUMBER vb old word meaning defecate

SCUMBLE vb soften or blend (an outline or colour) with a thin upper coat of opaque colour ▷ n upper layer of colour applied in this way

SCUMMED ▶ scum

SCUMMER ▶ scum

SCUMMY adj of, resembling, consisting of, or covered with scum

SCUMS ▶ scum

SCUNGE vb borrow ▷ n dirty or worthless person **scunged, scunges**

SCUNGY adj

SCUNNER vb feel aversion ▷ n strong aversion

SCUP n common sparid fish of American coastal regions of the Atlantic

SCUPPER vb, n

SCUPS ▶ scup

SCUR n small unattached growth of horn at the site of a normal horn in cattle

SCURF n **scurfs, scurfy**

SCURRED ▶ scur

SCURRIL adj old word meaning vulgar

SCURRY vb, n

SCURS ▸ scur

SCURVY n, adj

SCUSE shortened form of ▸ excuse

SCUSED ▸ scuse

SCUSES ▸ scuse

SCUSING ▸ scuse

SCUT n short tail of the hare, rabbit, or deer

SCUTA ▸ scutum

SCUTAGE n payment to a lord from his vassal in lieu of military service

SCUTAL ▸ scute

SCUTATE adj (of animals) having or covered with large bony or horny plates

SCUTCH vb separate the fibres from the woody part of (flax) by pounding ▷ n tool used for this

SCUTE n horny or chitinous plate that makes up part of the exoskeleton in armadillos, etc scutes

SCUTS ▸ scut

SCUTTER informal word for ▸ scurry

SCUTTLE n, vb

SCUTUM n middle of three plates into which the notum of an insect's thorax is divided

SCUZZ n dirt scuzzes

SCUZZY adj unkempt, dirty, or squalid

SCYBALA ▸ scybalum

SCYE n Scots word meaning sleeve-hole scyes

SCYPHI ▸ scyphus

SCYPHUS n ancient Greek two-handled drinking cup

SCYTALE n coded message in ancient Sparta

SCYTHE n, vb scythed, scyther, scythes

SDAINE vb old form of disdain sdained, sdaines

SDAYN vb old form of disdain sdayned, sdayns

SDEIGN vb old form of disdain

SDEIGNE vb old form of disdain

SDEIGNS ▸ sdeign

SDEIN vb old form of disdain sdeined, sdeins

SEA n

SEABAG n canvas bag for holding a sailor's belongings seabags

SEABANK n sea shore

SEABED n bottom of sea seabeds

SEABIRD n bird that lives on the sea

SEABOOT n sailor's waterproof boot

SEACOCK n valve in the hull of a vessel below the water line

SEADOG another word for ▸ fogbow

SEADOGS ▸ seadog

SEAFOLK n people who sail sea

SEAFOOD n edible saltwater fish or shellfish

SEAFOWL n seabird

SEAGIRT adj surrounded by the sea

SEAGULL n skua

SEAHAWK n skua

SEAHOG n porpoise seahogs

SEAKALE n European coastal plant

SEAL n, vb

SEALANT n any substance used for sealing

SEALCH Scots word for ▸ seal

SEALCHS ▸ sealch

SEALED adj (of a road) having a hard surface

SEALER n person or thing that seals sealers

SEALERY n occupation of hunting seals

SEALGH Scots word for ▸ seal

SEALGHS ▸ sealgh

SEALIFT vb transport by ship

SEALINE n company running regular sailings

SEALING ▸ seal

SEALS ▸ seal

SEALWAX n sealing wax

SEAM n, vb

SEAMAID n mermaid

SEAMAN n

SEAMARK n conspicuous object on a shore used as a guide

SEAME n old word meaning grease

SEAMED ▶ seam

SEAMEN ▶ seaman

SEAMER n bowler who makes the ball bounce on its seam **seamers**

SEAMES ▶ seame

SEAMIER ▶ seamy

SEAMING ▶ seam

SEAMS ▶ seam

SEAMSET n tool for flattening seams in metal

SEAMY adj

SEAN vb fish with seine net

SEANCE n seances

SEANED ▶ sean

SEANING ▶ sean

SEANS ▶ sean

SEAPORT n town or city with a harbour for boats and ships

SEAR vb, n, adj

SEARAT n pirate **searats**

SEARCE vb sift **searced, searces**

SEARCH vb, n

SEARE adj old word meaning dry and withered

SEARED, searer, searest, searing, sears ▶ sear

SEAS ▶ sea

SEASE vb old form of seize **seased, seases**

SEASICK adj

SEASIDE n

SEASING ▶ sease

SEASON n, vb seasons

SEASURE n old form

of seizure

SEAT n, vb seated

SEATER n person or thing that seats **seaters**

SEATING n, adj

SEATS ▶ seat

SEAWALL n wall built to prevent encroachment or erosion by the sea

SEAWAN n shell beads used by certain North American Indians as money **seawans**

SEAWANT n Native American name for silver coins

SEAWARD = seawards

SEAWARE n any of numerous large coarse seaweeds

SEAWAY n waterway giving access to an inland port **seaways**

SEAWEED n

SEAWIFE n variety of sea fish

SEAWORM n marine worm

SEAZE vb old form of seize **seazed, seazes, seazing**

SEBACIC adj derived from sebacic acid, a white crystalline acid **sebasic**

SEBATE n salt of sebacic acid **sebates**

SEBIFIC adj producing fat

SEBUM n oily substance secreted by the sebaceous glands **sebums**

SEBUNDY n irregular soldier in India

SEC = secant

SECANT n (in trigonometry) the ratio of the length of the hypotenuse to the length of the adjacent side **secants**

SECCO n wall painting done on dried plaster with tempera **seccos**

SECEDE vb seceded, seceder, secedes

SECERN vb (of a gland or follicle) to secrete **secerns**

SECESH n secessionist in US Civil War

SECH n hyperbolic secant **sechs**

SECKEL variant of ▶ seckle

SECKELS ▶ seckel

SECKLE n type of pear **seckles**

SECLUDE vb keep (a person) from contact with others

SECO adj (of wine) dry

SECONAL n tradename for secobarbitol

SECOND adj, n, vb

SECONDE n second of eight positions from which a parry or attack can be made in fencing

SECONDI ▶ secondo

SECONDO n left-hand part in a piano duet

SECONDS ▶ second

SECPAR n distance unit in astronomy **secpars**

SECRECY n state of being secret

SECRET adj, n

SECRETA n secretions

SECRETE vb

SECRETS ▶ secret

SECS ▶ sec

SECT n

SECTARY n member of a sect

SECTILE adj able to be cut smoothly

SECTION n, vb

SECTOR n, vb sectors

SECTS ▶ sect

SECULAR adj, n

SECULUM n age in astronomy

SECUND adj having or designating parts arranged on or turned to one side of the axis

SECURE adj, vb secured, securer, secures

SED old spelling of ▶ said

SEDAN = saloon

SEDANS ▶ sedan

SEDARIM ▶ seder

SEDATE adj, vb sedated, sedater, sedates

SEDENT adj seated

SEDER n Jewish ceremonial meal held on the first night or first two nights of Passover seders

SEDES Latin word for ▶ seat

SEDGE n

SEDGED adj having sedge

SEDGES ▶ sedge

SEDGIER ▶ sedge

SEDGY ▶ sedge

SEDILE n seat for clergy in church

SEDILIA n group of three seats where the celebrant and ministers sit during High Mass

SEDUCE vb seduced

SEDUCER n person who entices, allures, or seduces

SEDUCES ▶ seduce

SEDUM n rock plant sedums

SEE vb perceive with the eyes or mind ▷ n diocese of a bishop seeable

SEED n, vb

SEEDBED n area of soil prepared for the growing of seedlings before they are transplanted

SEEDBOX n part of plant that contains seeds

SEEDED ▶ seed

SEEDER n person or thing that seeds seeders

SEEDIER ▶ seedy

SEEDILY ▶ seedy

SEEDING ▶ seed

SEEDLIP n basket holding seeds to be sown

SEEDMAN n seller of seeds seedmen

SEEDPOD n carpel enclosing the seeds of a flowering plant

SEEDS ▶ seed

SEEDY adj

SEEING ▶ see

SEEINGS ▶ see

SEEK vb seeker, seekers, seeking, seeks

SEEL vb sew up the eyelids of (a hawk or falcon) so as to render it quiet and tame

SEELD adj old word meaning rare

SEELED ▶ seel

SEELIE pl n good benevolent fairies

SEELIER ▶ seel

SEELING ▶ seel

SEELS ▶ seel

SEELY adj old word meaning happy

SEEM vb seemed, seemer, seemers

SEEMING adj, n

SEEMLY adj, adv

SEEMS ▶ seem

SEEN ▶ see

SEEP vb, n

SEEPAGE n act or process of seeping

SEEPED ▶ seep

SEEPIER ▶ seepy

SEEPING ▶ seep

SEEPS ▶ seep

SEEPY adj tending to seep

SEER n seeress, seers

SEES ▶ see

SEESAW n, vb seesaws

SEETHE vb, n seethed, seether, seethes

SEEWING n suing

SEFER n scrolls of the Law

SEG n metal stud on shoe sole

SEGAR n cigar **segars**

SEGETAL adj (of weeds) growing amongst crops

SEGGAR n box in which pottery is baked **seggars**

SEGHOL n pronunciation mark in Hebrew **seghols**

SEGMENT n, vb

SEGNI ▶ segno

SEGNO n sign at the beginning or end of a section directed to be repeated **segnos**

SEGO n American variety of lily

SEGOL variant of ▶ seghol

SEGOLS ▶ segol

SEGOS ▶ sego

SEGS ▶ seg

SEGUE vb proceed from one section or piece of music to another without a break ▷ n practice or an instance of playing music in this way **segued, segues**

SEHRI n meal eaten before sunrise by Muslims fasting during Ramadan **sehris**

SEI n type of rorqual

SEICHE n periodic oscillation of the surface of an enclosed or semienclosed body of water **seiches**

SEIDEL n vessel for drinking beer **seidels**

SEIF n long ridge of blown sand in a desert **seifs**

SEIK Scot word for ▶ sick

SEIKER ▶ seik

SEIKEST ▶ seik

SEIL vb dialect word meaning strain **seiled, seiling, seils**

SEINE n large fishing net that hangs vertically from floats ▷ vb catch (fish) using this net **seined, seiner, seiners, seines, seining**

SEIR n fish of Indian seas **seirs**

SEIS ▶ sei

SEISE vb put into legal possession of (property, etc) **seised, seiser, seisers, seises**

SEISIN n feudal possession of an estate in land

SEISING ▶ seise

SEISINS ▶ seisin

SEISM n earthquake

SEISMAL adj of earthquakes

SEISMIC adj

SEISMS ▶ seism

SEISOR n person who takes seisin **seisors**

SEISURE n act of seisin

SEITAN = seitan

SEITANS ▶ seitan

SEITEN n gluten from wheat **seitens**

SEITIES ▶ seity

SEITY n selfhood

SEIZE vb seized, seizer, seizers, seizes

SEIZIN = seisin

SEIZING n binding used for holding together two ropes, two spars, etc

SEIZINS ▶ seizin

SEIZOR n person who takes seisin **seizors**

SEIZURE n

SEJANT adj (of a beast) shown seated **sejeant**

SEKOS n holy place **sekoses**

SEKT n German sparkling wine **sekts**

SEL Scot word for ▶ self

SELAH n Hebrew word of unknown meaning occurring in the Old Testament psalms **selahs**

SELD adj old word meaning rare

SELDOM adv

SELE n old word meaning happiness

SELECT vb, adj

SELECTA n disc jockey

SELECTS ▶ select

SELENIC adj of or containing selenium, esp in the hexavalent state

SELES ▶ sele

SELF n, pron, vb

SELFDOM n selfhood

SELFED ▶ self

SELFING ▶ self

SELFISH adj

SELFISM n emphasis on self **selfist**

SELFS ▶ self

SELKIE = silkie

SELKIES ▶ selkie

SELL *vb, n*

SELLA *n* area of bone in body **sellae, sellas**

SELLE *n* old word meaning seat

SELLER *n* person who sells **sellers**

SELLES ▸ selle

SELLING *n*

SELLOFF *n* act of selling cheaply

SELLOUT *n*

SELLS ▸ sell

SELS ▸ sel

SELSYN = synchro

SELSYNS ▸ selsyn

SELTZER *n* natural effervescent water containing minerals

SELVA *n* dense equatorial forest

SELVAGE *n, vb*

SELVAS ▸ selva

SELVES ▸ self

SEMATIC *adj* acting as a warning, esp to potential predators

SEMBLE *vb* seem **sembled, sembles**

SEME *adj* dotted (with) **semee**

SEMEED *adj* seme

SEMEIA ▸ semeion

SEMEION *n* unit of metre in ancient poetry

SEMEME *n* meaning of a morpheme **sememes, sememic**

SEMEN *n* semens

SEMES ▸ seme

SEMI *n* semidetached house

SEMIDRY *adj* partly dry

SEMIE *n* historical name for a student in second year at a Scottish university **semies**

SEMIFIT *adj* not fully fit

SEMILOG *adj* semilogarithmic

SEMIMAT *adj* semimatt

SEMINA ▸ semen

SEMINAL *adj*

SEMINAR *n*

SEMIPED *n* measure in poetic metre

SEMIPRO *n* semiprofessional

SEMIRAW *adj* not fully cooked or processed

SEMIS ▸ semi

SEMISES ▸ semi

SEMITAR *old spelling of* > **scimitar**

SEMMIT *n* vest **semmits**

SEMPER *adv* Latin word meaning always

SEMPLE *adj* Scots word meaning simple **sempler**

SEMPRE *adv* (preceding a tempo or dynamic marking) always

SEMSEM *n* sesame **semsems**

SEN *n* monetary unit of Brunei, Cambodia, Indonesia, Malaysia, and formerly of Japan

SENA *n* (in India) the army

SENARII ▸ senarius

SENARY *adj* of or relating to the number six

SENAS ▸ sena

SENATE *n* main

governing body at some universities **senates**

SENATOR *n*

SEND *vb*

SENDAL *n* fine silk fabric used for ceremonial clothing, etc **sendals**

SENDED *vb* old word meaning sent

SENDER ▸ send

SENDERS ▸ send

SENDING ▸ send

SENDOFF *n* demonstration of good wishes at a person's departure ▸ *vb* dispatch (something, such as a letter)

SENDS ▸ send

SENDUP *n* parody or imitation **sendups**

SENE *n* money unit in Samoa

SENECA *variant of* > **senega**

SENECAS ▸ seneca

SENECIO *n* type of plant of the genus which includes groundsels and ragworts

SENEGA *n* milkwort plant of the eastern US **senegas**

SENES ▸ sene

SENGI *n* African shrew

SENHOR *n* Portuguese term of address for man

SENHORA *n* Portuguese term of address for woman

SENHORS ▸ senhor

SENILE *adj, n* **seniles**

SENIOR adj, n **seniors**

SENITI n money unit in Tonga

SENNA n tropical plant **sennas**

SENNET n fanfare: used as a stage direction in Elizabethan drama **sennets**

SENNIT n flat braided cordage used on ships **sennits**

SENOPIA n short-sightedness in old age

SENOR n Spanish term of address equivalent to sir or Mr

SENORA n Spanish term of address equivalent to madam or Mrs **senoras**

SENORES ► **senor**

SENORS ► **senor**

SENRYU n Japanese short poem

SENS ► **sen**

SENSA ► **sensum**

SENSATE adj perceived by the senses ▷ vb make sensate

SENSE n, vb **sensed**

SENSEI n martial arts teacher **senseis**

SENSES ► **sense**

SENSI = **sensei**

SENSILE adj capable of feeling

SENSING ► **sense**

SENSIS ► **sensi**

SENSISM n theory that ideas spring from senses **sensist**

SENSOR n **sensors**

SENSORY adj

SENSUAL adj

SENSUM n sensation detached from the information it conveys

SENT n former monetary unit of Estonia

SENTE n money unit in Lesotho

SENTED ► **send**

SENTI ► **sent**

SENTIMO n money unit in Philippines

SENTING ► **send**

SENTRY n

SENTS ► **sent**

SENVIES ► **senvy**

SENVY n mustard

SENZA prep without

SEPAD vb suppose **sepads**

SEPAL n leaflike division of the calyx of a flower **sepaled, sepals**

SEPHEN n stingray **sephens**

SEPIA n, adj **sepias**

SEPIC adj of sepia

SEPIOST n cuttlefish bone

SEPIUM n cuttlefish bone **sepiums**

SEPMAG adj designating a film, etc for which the sound is recorded on separate magnetic material

SEPOY n (formerly) Indian soldier in the service of the British **sepoys**

SEPPUKU n Japanese ritual suicide

SEPS n species of lizard

SEPSES ► **sepsis**

SEPSIS n poisoning caused by pus-forming bacteria

SEPT n clan, esp in Ireland or Scotland

SEPTA ► **septum**

SEPTAGE n waste removed from septic tank

SEPTAL adj of or relating to a septum

SEPTATE adj divided by septa

SEPTET n group of seven performers **septets**

SEPTIC adj, n **septics**

SEPTIME n seventh of eight basic positions from which a parry can be made in fencing

SEPTS ► **sept**

SEPTUM n dividing partition between two cavities in the body **septums**

SEPTUOR n group of seven musicians

SEQUEL n

SEQUELA n disease related to or arising from a pre-existing disease

SEQUELS ► **sequel**

SEQUENT adj following in order or succession ▷ n something that follows

SEQUIN n, vb **sequins**

SEQUOIA n giant Californian coniferous tree

This word for a redwood tree is one of the most

frequently played bonuses using the Q, a great one to remember as it also clears out a surplus of vowels.

SER *n* unit of weight used in India

SERA ► serum

SERAC *n* pinnacle of ice among crevasses on a glacier, usually on a steep slope **seracs**

SERAFIN *n* old silver coin of Goa

SERAI *n* (in the East) a caravanserai or inn

SERAIL = seraglio

SERAILS ► serail

SERAIS ► serai

SERAL ► sere

SERANG *n* native captain of a crew of sailors in the East Indies **serangs**

SERAPE *n* blanket-like shawl often of brightly-coloured wool **serapes**

SERAPH *n* seraphs

SERDAB *n* secret chamber in an ancient Egyptian tomb **serdabs**

SERE *adj* dried up or withered ▷ *n* series of changes occurring in the ecological succession of a particular community ▷ *vb* sear **sered**

SEREIN *n* fine rain falling from a clear sky after sunset **sereins**

SERENE *adj, vb* serened, serener, serenes

SERER ► sere

SERES ► sere

SEREST ► sere

SERF *n* serfage, serfdom, serfish, serfs

SERGE *n*

SERGED *adj* with sewn seam

SERGER *n* sewing machine attachment for finishing seams **sergers**

SERGES ► serge

SERGING *n* type of sewing

SERIAL *n, adj* serials

SERIATE *adj* forming a series ▷ *vb* form into a series

SERIC *adj* of silk

SERICIN *n* gelatinous protein found on the fibres of raw silk

SERICON *n* solution used in alchemy

SERIEMA *n* either of two cranelike South American birds

SERIES *n*

SERIF *n* small line at the extremities of a main stroke in a type character

SERIFED *adj* having serifs

SERIFS ► serif

SERIN *n* any of various small yellow-and-brown finches

SERINE *n* sweet-tasting amino acid **serines**

SERING ► sere

SERINGA *n* any of several trees that yield rubber

SERINS ► serin

SERIOUS *adj* giving cause for concern

SERIPH = serif

SERIPHS ► seriph

SERK *Scots word for* ► shirt

SERKALI *n* government in Africa

SERKS ► serk

SERMON *n, vb* sermons

SERON *n* crate serons

SEROON *n* crate seroons

SEROPUS *n* liquid consisting of serum and pus

SEROSA *n* one of the thin membranes surrounding the embryo in an insect's egg **serosae, serosal, serosas**

SEROUS *adj* of, containing, or like serum

SEROVAR *n* subdivision of species

SEROW *n* either of two antelopes of mountainous regions of S and SE Asia **serows**

SERPENT *n*

SERPIGO *n* any progressive skin eruption

SERR *vb* press close together

SERRA *n* sawlike part or organ **serrae**

SERRAN n species of fish

SERRANO n type of Spanish ham

SERRANS ▶ serran

SERRAS ▶ serra

SERRATE adj (of leaves) having a margin of forward pointing teeth ▷ vb make serrate

SERRATI ▶ serratus

SERRE vb press close together **serred, serres**

SERRIED adj

SERRIES ▶ serry

SERRING ▶ serre

SERRS ▶ serr

SERRY vb close together

SERS ▶ ser

SERUEWE vb old word meaning survey

SERUM n serumal, serums

SERVAL n feline African mammal **servals**

SERVANT n, vb

SERVE vb, n served

SERVER n servers

SERVERY n room from which food is served

SERVES ▶ serve

SERVEWE vb old word meaning survey

SERVICE n, adj, vb

SERVILE adj, n

SERVING n

SERVLET n small program that runs on a web server

SERVO n servomechanism ▷ adj of a servomechanism **servos**

SESAME n sesames

SESE interj exclamation found in Shakespeare

SESELI n garden plant seselis

SESEY interj exclamation found in Shakespeare

SESH short for ▶ session

SESHES ▶ sesh

SESS n old word meaning tax

SESSA interj exclamation found in Shakespeare

SESSES ▶ sess

SESSILE adj (of flowers or leaves) having no stalk

SESSION n

SESTET n last six lines of a sonnet **sestets**

SESTETT n group of six

SESTINA n elaborate verse form of Italian origin

SESTINE n poem of six lines

SESTON n type of plankton **sestons**

SET vb, n, adj

SETA n bristle or bristle-like appendage **setae, setal**

SETBACK n

SETLINE n any of various types of fishing line

SETNESS n ▶ set

SETOFF n counterbalance setoffs

SETON n surgical thread inserted below the skin **setons**

SETOSE adj covered with setae

SETOUS ▶ seta

SETOUT n beginning or outset setouts

SETS ▶ set

SETT n badger's burrow

SETTEE n settees

SETTER n, vb setters

SETTING ▶ set

SETTLE vb, n settled

SETTLER n

SETTLES ▶ settle

SETTLOR n person who settles property on someone

SETTS ▶ sett

SETUALE n valerian

SETULE n small bristle setules

SETUP n way in which anything is organized or arranged **setups**

SETWALL n wallian

SEVEN n, adj, determiner

SEVENS n Rugby Union match or series of matches played with seven players on each side

SEVENTH n, adj, adv

SEVENTY n, adj, determiner

SEVER vb

SEVERAL adj, n

SEVERE adj

SEVERED ▶ sever

SEVERER ▶ severe

SEVERS ▶ sever

SEVERY n part of vaulted ceiling

SEVICHE n Mexican fish dish

SEVRUGA n species of sturgeon

SEW vb sewable

SEWAGE n sewages

SEWAN n seawan

SEWANS ▶ sewan

SEWAR n Asian dagger **sewars**

SEWED ▶ sew

SEWEL n scarecrow **sewels**

SEWEN = sewin

SEWENS ▶ sewen

SEWER n, vb sewered, sewers

SEWIN n sea trout

SEWING ▶ sew

SEWINGS ▶ sew

SEWINS ▶ sewin

SEWN ▶ sew

SEWS ▶ sew

SEX n, vb, adj

SEXED adj having a specified degree of sexuality

SEXER n person checking sex of chickens **sexers**

SEXES ▶ sex

SEXFID adj split into six

SEXFOIL n flower with six petals or leaves

SEXIER ▶ sexy

SEXIEST ▶ sexy

SEXILY ▶ sexy

SEXING ▶ sex

SEXINGS ▶ sexing

SEXISM n sexisms, sexist, sexists

SEXLESS adj

SEXPERT n person who professes a knowledge of sexual matters

SEXPOT n person

considered as sexually very attractive **sexpots**

SEXT n fourth of the seven canonical hours of the divine office

SEXTAIN = sestina

SEXTAN adj (of a fever) marked by paroxysms that recur after an interval of five days

SEXTANS n Roman coin

SEXTANT n

SEXTET n sextets

SEXTETT n sextet

SEXTILE n value of a variable dividing its distribution into six groups with equal frequencies

SEXTO = sixmo

SEXTON n sextons

SEXTOS ▶ sexto

SEXTS ▶ sext

SEXTUOR n sextet

SEXUAL adj

SEXY adj

SEY n Scots word meaning part of cow carcase

SEYEN n old form of scion **seyens**

SEYS ▶ sey

SEYSURE n old form of seizure

SEZ vb informal spelling of 'says'

> **Sez** is a short informal form of **says**, very useful for disposing of the Z.

SFERICS = spherics

SFUMATO n gradual transition between

areas of different colour in painting

SH interj

SHA interj be quiet

SHABASH interj (in Indian English) bravo or well done

SHABBLE n Scots word meaning old sword

SHABBY adj

SHACK n, vb shacked

SHACKLE n, vb

SHACKO = shako

SHACKOS ▶ shacko

SHACKS ▶ shack

SHAD n herring-like fish

SHADE n, vb shaded, shader, shaders

SHADES pl n gathering darkness at nightfall

SHADFLY American name for ▶ mayfly

SHADIER ▶ shady

SHADILY ▶ shady

SHADING n graded areas of tone indicating light and dark in a painting or drawing

SHADOOF n mechanism for raising water

SHADOW n, vb shadows

SHADOWY adj

SHADS ▶ shad

SHADUF = shadoof

SHADUFS ▶ shaduf

SHADY adj

SHAFT n, vb shafted, shafter, shafts

SHAGGY adj

SHAH n formerly, ruler of Iran

SHAHADA n Islamic declaration of faith

SHAHDOM ▶ shah

SHAHEED ▶ shahid

SHAHID n Muslim martyr **shahids**

SHAHS ▶ shah

SHAIKH n sheikh **shaikhs**

SHAIRD n Scots word meaning shred **shairds**

SHAIRN Scots word for ▶ dung

SHAIRNS ▶ shairn

SHAITAN n (in Muslim countries) an evil spirit

SHAKE vb, n

SHAKED vb old form of shook

SHAKEN ▶ shake

SHAKER n container in which drinks are mixed or from which powder is shaken **shakers**

SHAKES ▶ shake

SHAKEUP n radical reorganization

SHAKIER ▶ shaky

SHAKILY ▶ shaky

SHAKING ▶ shake

SHAKO n tall cylindrical peaked military hat with a plume **shakoes, shakos**

SHAKT vb old form of shook

SHAKUDO n Japanese alloy of copper and gold

SHAKY adj

SHALE n **shaled, shales, shaley, shalier, shaling**

SHALL vb

SHALLI n type of fabric **shallis**

SHALLON n American shrub

SHALLOP n light boat used for rowing in shallow water

SHALLOT n

SHALLOW adj, n, vb

SHALM n old woodwind instrument **shalms**

SHALOM n Jewish greeting meaning 'peace be with you' **shaloms**

SHALOT n shallot **shalots**

SHALT singular form of the present tense (indicative mood) of ▶ **shall**

SHALWAR n pair of loose-fitting trousers tapering to a narrow fit around the ankles

SHALY ▶ shale

SHAM n, adj, vb

SHAMA n Indian songbird

SHAMAL n hot northwesterly wind **shamals**

SHAMAN n priest of shamanism **shamans**

SHAMAS ▶ shama

SHAMBA n (in E Africa) any field used for growing crops **shambas**

SHAMBLE vb, n **shambly**

SHAME n, vb **shamed**

SHAMER n cause of shame

SHAMERS ▶ shame

SHAMES ▶ shame

SHAMINA n wool blend of pashm and shahtoosh

SHAMING ▶ shame

SHAMMAS = shammes

SHAMMED ▶ sham

SHAMMER ▶ sham

SHAMMES n official acting as the beadle, sexton, and caretaker of a synagogue **shammos**

SHAMMY n piece of chamois leather ▷ vb rub with a shammy

SHAMOIS n chamois

SHAMOS = shammes

SHAMOY n chamois ▷ vb rub with a shamoy **shamoys**

SHAMPOO n, vb

SHAMS ▶ sham

SHAMUS n police or private detective

SHAN variant of ▶ **shand**

SHAND n old word meaning fake coin

SHANDRY n light horse-drawn cart

SHANDS ▶ shand

SHANDY n

SHANK n, vb **shanked, shanks**

SHANNY n European blenny of rocky coastal waters

SHANS ▶ shan

SHANTEY = shanty

SHANTI n peace **shantih, shantis**

SHANTY n

SHAPE n, vb shaped

SHAPELY adj

SHAPEN vb old form of shaped

SHAPER ▶ shape

SHAPERS ▶ shape

SHAPES ▶ shape

SHAPEUP n system of hiring dockers for a day's work

SHAPING ▶ shape

SHAPS n leather over-trousers worn by cowboys

SHARD n

SHARDED adj old word meaning hidden under dung

SHARDS ▶ shard

SHARE n, vb shared, sharer, sharers, shares

SHARIA n body of doctrines that regulate the lives of Muslims shariah, sharias

SHARIAT n Islamic religious law

SHARIF = sherif

SHARIFS ▶ sharif

SHARING ▶ share

SHARK n, vb sharked

SHARKER n shark hunter

SHARKS ▶ shark

SHARN Scots word for ▶ dung

SHARNS ▶ sharn

SHARNY ▶ sharn

SHARON n as in sharon fruit persimmon

SHARP adj, adv, n, vb sharped

SHARPEN vb

SHARPER n person who cheats

SHARPIE n member of a teenage group having short hair and distinctive clothes

SHARPLY ▶ sharp

SHARPS ▶ sharp

SHARPY n swindler

SHASH vb old form of sash shashed, shashes

SHASLIK n type of kebab

SHASTER = shastra

SHASTRA n any of the sacred writings of Hinduism

SHATTER vb, n

SHAUGH n old word meaning small wood shaughs

SHAUL vb old form of shawl shauled, shauls

SHAVE vb, n shaved

SHAVEN adj

SHAVER n shavers

SHAVES ▶ shaul

SHAVIE n Scots word meaning trick shavies

SHAVING ▶ shave

SHAW n small wood ▷ vb show shawed, shawing

SHAWL n, vb shawled, shawls

SHAWM n medieval form of the oboe with a conical bore and flaring bell shawms, shawn

SHAWS ▶ shaw

SHAY dialect word for ▶ chaise

SHAYA n Indian plant shayas

SHAYS ▶ shay

SHAZAM interj magic slogan

SHCHI n Russian cabbage soup shchis

SHE pron, n

SHEA n tropical African tree

SHEAF n, vb sheafed, sheafs, sheafy

SHEAL vb old word meaning shell shealed, sheals

SHEAR vb, n sheared, shearer, shears

SHEAS ▶ shea

SHEATH n

SHEATHE vb

SHEATHS ▶ sheath

SHEATHY ▶ sheathe

SHEAVE vb gather or bind into sheaves ▷ n wheel with a grooved rim sheaved

SHEAVES ▶ sheaf

SHEBANG n situation, matter, or affair

SHEBEAN = shebeen

SHEBEEN n place where alcohol is sold illegally ▷ vb run a shebeen

SHED n, vb shedded

SHEDDER n person or thing that sheds

SHEDFUL n quantity or amount contained in a shed

SHEDS ▶ shed

SHEEL vb old word meaning shell sheeled, sheels

SHEEN n, adj, vb **sheened, sheens**

SHEEP n

SHEEPLE pl n people who follow the majority in matters of opinion, taste, etc

SHEEPO n person employed to bring sheep to the catching pen in a shearing shed **sheepos**

SHEEPY ▶ sheep

SHEER adj, adv, vb, n **sheered, sheerer, sheerly, sheers**

SHEESH interj exclamation of surprise or annoyance

SHEESHA n Oriental water-pipe for smoking tobacco

SHEET n, vb **sheeted, sheeter, sheets, sheety**

SHEEVE n part of mine winding gear **sheeves**

SHEHITA n slaughter of animal according to Jewish religious law

SHEIK n sheikh

SHEIKH n Arab chief

SHEIKHA n chief wife of sheikh

SHEIKHS ▶ sheikh

SHEIKS ▶ sheik

SHEILA n girl or woman **sheilas**

SHEITAN n Muslim demon

SHEKEL n monetary unit of Israel **shekels**

SHELF n, vb **shelfed, shelfs, shelfy**

SHELL n, vb

SHELLAC n resin used in varnishes ▷ vb coat with shellac

SHELLED, sheller, shells, shelly ▶ shell

SHELTA n secret language used by some traveling people in Britain and Ireland **sheltas**

SHELTER n, vb

SHELTIE n small dog similar to a collie **shelty**

SHELVE vb **shelved, shelver**

SHELVES ▶ shelf

SHELVY adj having shelves

SHEMALE n male who has acquired female physical characteristics through surgery

SHEND vb put to shame **shends, shent**

SHEOL n hell **sheols**

SHEQEL = shekel

SHEQELS ▶ sheqel

SHERANG n person in charge

SHERBET n

SHERD = shard

SHERDS ▶ sherd

SHERE old spelling of ▶ sheer

SHEREEF = sherif

SHERIA = sharia

SHERIAS ▶ sheria

SHERIAT n Muslim religious law

SHERIF n descendant of Mohammed

through his daughter Fatima

SHERIFF n

SHERIFS ▶ sherif

SHEROOT n cheroot

SHERPA n official who assists at a summit meeting **sherpas**

SHERRIS n old form of sherry

SHERRY n

SHES ▶ she

SHET vb old form of shut **shets**

SHEUCH n ditch or trough ▷ vb dig **sheuchs, sheugh**

SHEUGHS ▶ sheugh

SHEVA n mark in Hebrew writing **shevas**

SHEW archaic spelling of ▶ show

SHEWED ▶ shew

SHEWEL n old word meaning scarecrow **shewels**

SHEWER, shewers, shewing, shewn, shews ▶ shew

SHH interj sound made to ask for silence

SHIAI n judo contest **shiais**

SHIATSU n type of massage

SHIATZU = shiatsu

SHIBAH n Jewish period of mourning **shibahs**

SHICKER n alcoholic drink

SHIDDER n old word meaning female animal

SHIED ▷ shy

SHIEL vb sheal

SHIELD n, vb shields

SHIELED ▷ shiel

SHIELS ▷ shiel

SHIER n horse that shies habitually **shiers**

SHIES ▷ shy

SHIEST ▷ shy

SHIFT vb, n shifted, shifter, shifts

SHIFTY adj

SHIKAR n hunting, esp big-game hunting ▷ vb hunt (game, esp big game)

SHIKARI n (in India) a hunter

SHIKARS ▷ shikar

SHIKKER n Yiddish term for drunk person

SHILL n confidence trickster's assistant ▷ vb act as a shill shilled, shills

SHILPIT adj puny

SHILY ▷ shy

SHIM n thin strip of material placed between two close surfaces to fill a gap ▷ vb fit or fill up with a shim

SHIMAAL n hot Middle Eastern wind

SHIMMED ▷ shim

SHIMMER n, vb

SHIMMEY n chemise

SHIMMY n American ragtime dance ▷ vb dance the shimmy

SHIMS ▷ shim

SHIN n, vb

SHINDIG n

SHINDY n quarrel or commotion **shindys**

SHINE vb, n shined

SHINER n black eye shiners

SHINES ▷ shine

SHININESS ▷ shiny

SHINGLE n, vb shingly

SHINIER ▷ shiny

SHINIES ▷ shiny

SHINILY ▷ shiny

SHINING ▷ shine

SHINJU n (formerly, in Japan) a ritual double suicide of lovers **shinjus**

SHINKIN n worthless person

SHINNE n old form of chin

SHINNED ▷ shin shinnes

SHINNEY vb climb with hands and legs

SHINNY = shinty

SHINS ▷ shin

SHINTY n game like hockey ▷ vb play shinty

SHINY adj

SHIP n, vb

SHIPFUL n amount carried by ship

SHIPLAP n method of constructing ship hull

SHIPMAN n master or captain of a ship shipmen

SHIPPED ▷ ship

SHIPPEN n dialect word for cattle shed

SHIPPER n person or company that ships

SHIPPIE n prostitute who solicits at a port

SHIPPO n Japanese enamel work

SHIPPON n dialect word for cattle shed

SHIPPOS ▷ shippo

SHIPS ▷ ship

SHIPWAY n structure on which a vessel is built, then launched

SHIR n gathering in material

SHIRE n, vb shired, shires, shiring

SHIRK vb, n shirked, shirker, shirks

SHIRR vb gather (fabric) into parallel rows to decorate a dress, etc ▷ n series of gathered rows decorating a dress, etc

SHIRRA old Scots word for ▶ sheriff

SHIRRAS ▷ shirra

SHIRRED ▷ shirr

SHIRRS ▷ shirr

SHIRS ▷ shir

SHIRT n, vb shirted, shirts

SHIRTY adj

SHISH adj as in shish kebab dish of meat and vegetables grilled on skewers

SHISHA = hookah

SHISHAS ▷ shisha

SHISO n Asian plant with aromatic leaves shisos

SHIST n schist shists

SHITAKE = shiitake

SHITTAH n tree mentioned in the Old Testament **shittim**

SHITZU n breed of small dog with long, silky fur **shitzus**

SHIUR n lesson in which a passage of the Talmud is studied **shiurim**

SHIV variant spelling of ▸ chiv

SHIVA variant of ▸ shivah

SHIVAH n Jewish period of formal mourning **shivahs**

SHIVAS ▸ shiva

SHIVE n flat cork or bung for wide-mouthed bottles

SHIVER vb, n **shivers**

SHIVERY adj

SHIVES ▸ shive

SHIVITI n Jewish decorative plaque with religious message

SHIVOO n Australian word meaning rowdy party **shivoos**

SHIVS ▸ shiv

SHIVVED ▸ shiv

SHLEP vb schlep

SHLEPP vb schlep **shlepps**

SHLEPS ▸ shlep

SHLOCK n something of poor quality **shlocks, shlocky**

SHLUB = schlub

SHLUBS ▸ shlub

SHLUMP vb move in lazy way **shlumps, shlumpy**

SHMALTZ n schmaltz

SHMATTE n rag

SHMEAR n set of things **shmears**

SHMEK n smell **shmeks**

SHMO = schmo

SHMOCK n despicable person **shmocks**

SHMOES ▸ shmo

SHMOOSE variant of > schmooze

SHMOOZE variant of > schmooze

SHMOOZY adj talking casually, gossipy

SHMUCK n despicable person

SHMUCKS ▸ schmuck

SHNAPPS = schnapps

SHNAPS n schnaps

SHNOOK n stupid person **shnooks**

SHOAL n, vb, adj **shoaled, shoaler, shoals**

SHOALY adj shallow

SHOAT n piglet that has recently been weaned **shoats**

SHOCHET n (in Judaism) a person licensed to slaughter animals and birds

SHOCK vb, n, adj **shocked**

SHOCKER n person or thing that shocks or horrifies

SHOCKS ▸ shock

SHOD ▸ shoe

SHODDEN vb old form of shod

SHODDY adj, n

SHODER n skins used in making gold leaf **shoders**

SHOE n, vb

SHOEBOX n cardboard box for shoes

SHOED ▸ shoe

SHOEING ▸ shoe

SHOEPAC n waterproof boot

SHOER n person who shoes horses **shoers**

SHOES ▸ shoe

SHOFAR n ram's horn sounded in Jewish synagogue **shofars**

SHOG vb shake **shogged**

SHOGGLE vb shake **shoggly**

SHOGI n Japanese chess **shogis**

SHOGS ▸ shog

SHOGUN n Japanese chief military commander **shoguns**

SHOJI n Japanese rice-paper screen in a sliding wooden frame **shojis**

SHOLA n Indian plant **sholas**

SHOLOM n Hebrew greeting **sholoms**

SHONE ▸ shine

SHONEEN n Irishman who imitates English ways

SHONKY adj unreliable or unsound

SHOO interj, vb **shooed**

SHOOFLY n as in **shoofly pie** US dessert similar to treacle tart

SHOOGIE vb Scots word meaning swing

SHOOGLE vb shake, sway, or rock back and forth ⊳ n rocking motion **shoogly**

SHOOING ▶ shoo

SHOOK n set of parts ready for assembly **shooks**

SHOOL dialect word for ▶ shovel

SHOOLE dialect word for ▶ shovel

SHOOLED ▶ shool

SHOOLES ▶ shoole

SHOOLS ▶ shool

SHOON plural of ▶ shoe

SHOORA = shura

SHOORAS ▶ shoora

SHOOS ▶ shoo

SHOOT vb, n

SHOOTER n person or thing that shoots

SHOOTS ▶ shoot

SHOP n, vb

SHOPBOT n

SHOPBOY n boy working in shop

SHOPE n old form of shape

SHOPFUL n amount stored in shop

SHOPHAR = shofar

SHOPMAN n man working in shop **shopmen**

SHOPPE old-fashioned spelling of ▶ shop

SHOPPED ▶ shop

SHOPPER n person who buys goods in a shop

SHOPPES ▶ shoppe

SHOPPY adj of a shop

SHOPS ▶ shop

SHORAN n short-range radar system **shorans**

SHORE n, vb shored, shorer, shorers, shores, shoring

SHORL n black mineral **shorls**

SHORN past participle of ▶ shear

SHORT adj not long ⊳ adv abruptly ⊳ n drink of spirits ⊳ vb short-circuit **shorted**

SHORTEN vb

SHORTER ▶ short

SHORTIA n American flowering plant

SHORTIE n person or thing that is extremely short

SHORTLY adv

SHORTS pl n trousers reaching the top of the thigh or partway to the knee

SHORTY = shortie

SHOT vb load with shot

SHOTE = shoat

SHOTES ▶ shote

SHOTGUN n, adj, vb

SHOTS ▶ shot

SHOTT n shallow temporary salt lake or marsh in the North African desert

SHOTTE n old form of shoat

SHOTTED ▶ shot

SHOTTEN adj (of fish, esp herring) having recently spawned

SHOTTES ▶ shotte

SHOTTLE n small drawer

SHOTTS ▶ shott

SHOUGH n old word meaning lapdog **shoughs**

SHOULD ▶ shall

SHOUSE n toilet ⊳ adj unwell or in poor spirits **shouses**

SHOUT n, vb shouted, shouter, shouts

SHOUTY adj characterized by or involving shouting

SHOVE vb, n shoved

SHOVEL n, vb shovels

SHOVER ▶ shove

SHOVERS ▶ shove

SHOVES ▶ shove

SHOVING n act of pushing hard

SHOW vb make, be, or become noticeable or visible ⊳ n public exhibition

SHOWBIZ n entertainment industry including theatre, films, and TV

SHOWBOX n box containing showman's material

SHOWD vb rock or sway to and fro ⊳ n rocking motion **showded, showds**

SHOWED ▶ show

SHOWER n, vb showers, showery

SHOWGHE n old word meaning lapdog

SHOWIER ▶ showy

SHOWILY ▶ showy

SHOWING ▶ show

SHOWMAN n man skilled at presenting

anything spectacularly **showmen**

SHOWN ▶ show

SHOWOFF n person who makes a vain display of himself or herself

SHOWS ▶ show

SHOWY adj

SHOYU n Japanese variety of soy sauce **shoyus**

SHRANK ▶ shrink

SHRED n, vb **shreddy, shreds**

SHREEK old spelling of ▶ **shriek**

SHREEKS ▶ shreek

SHREIK old spelling of ▶ **shriek**

SHREIKS ▶ shreik

SHREW n, vb

SHREWD adj

SHREWED ▶ shrew

SHREWS ▶ shrew

SHRI n Indian title of respect

SHRIECH old spelling of ▶ **shriek**

SHRIEK n, vb **shrieks, shrieky**

SHRIEVE archaic word for ▶ **sheriff**

SHRIFT n **shrifts**

SHRIGHT n old word meaning shriek

SHRIKE n songbird with a heavy hooked bill ▷ vb archaic word for shriek **shriked, shrikes**

SHRILL adj, vb **shrills, shrilly**

SHRIMP n, vb **shrimps, shrimpy**

SHRINAL ▶ shrine

SHRINE n, vb **shrined, shrines**

SHRINK vb, n **shrinks**

SHRIS ▶ shri

SHRITCH vb old word meaning shriek

SHRIVE vb hear the confession of (a penitent) **shrived**

SHRIVEL vb

SHRIVEN ▶ shrive

SHRIVER ▶ shrive

SHRIVES ▶ shrive

SHROFF n (in China and Japan) expert employed to identify counterfeit money ▷ vb test (money) and separate out the counterfeit and base **shroffs**

SHROOM n slang for magic mushroom ▷ vb take magic mushrooms **shrooms**

SHROUD n, vb **shrouds, shroudy**

SHROVE vb dialect word meaning to observe Shrove-tide **shroved, shroves**

SHROW vb old form of shrew

SHROWD adj old form of shrewd

SHROWED ▶ shrow

SHROWS ▶ shrow

SHRUB n, vb

SHRUBBY adj consisting of, planted with, or abounding in shrubs

SHRUBS ▶ shrub

SHRUG vb, n **shrugs**

SHRUNK ▶ shrink

SHTCHI n Russian cabbage soup **shtchis**

SHTETEL n Jewish community in Eastern Europe

SHTETL n Jewish community in Eastern Europe **shtetls**

SHTICK n comedian's routine **shticks, shticky**

SHTIK n shtick **shtiks**

SHTOOK n trouble **shtooks**

SHTOOM adj silent

SHTUCK n trouble **shtucks**

SHTUM adj silent

SHTUMM adj silent

SHTUP vb have sex (with) **shtups**

SHUCK n outer covering of something ▷ vb remove the shucks from **shucked, shucker**

SHUCKS pl n something of little value ▷ interj exclamation of disappointment, annoyance, etc

SHUDDER vb, n

SHUFFLE vb, n

SHUFTI = **shufty**

SHUFTIS ▶ shufti

SHUFTY n look

SHUGGY n swing, as at a fairground

SHUL Yiddish word for ▶ **synagogue**

SHULE vb saunter **shuled, shules, shuling**

SHULN ▸ shul

SHULS ▸ shul

SHUN vb **shunned, shunner, shuns**

SHUNT vb, n **shunted**

SHUNTER n small railway locomotive used for manoeuvring coaches

SHUNTS ▸ shunt

SHURA n consultative council or assembly **shuras**

SHUSH interj be quiet! ▸ vb quiet by saying 'shush' **shushed, shusher, shushes**

SHUT vb

SHUTE variant of ▸ **chute**

SHUTED ▸ shute

SHUTES ▸ shute

SHUTEYE n sleep

SHUTING ▸ shute

SHUTOFF n device that shuts something off

SHUTOUT n game in which the opposing team does not score

SHUTS ▸ shut

SHUTTER n, vb

SHUTTLE n, vb

SHWA = schwa

SHWAS ▸ shwa

SHY adj, vb, n **shyer, shyers, shyest, shying, shyish**

SHYLOCK vb lend money at an exorbitant rate of interest

SHYLY ▸ shy

SHYNESS ▸ shy

SHYPOO n liquor of poor quality **shypoos**

SHYSTER n person who uses discreditable or unethical methods

SI = te

SIAL n silicon-rich and aluminium-rich rocks of the earth's continental upper crust **sialic**

SIALID n species of fly **sialids**

SIALOID adj resembling saliva

SIALON n type of ceramic **sialons**

SIALS ▸ sial

SIAMANG n large black gibbon

SIAMESE variant of ▸ **siameze**

SIAMEZE vb join together

SIB n blood relative

SIBB n sib **sibbs**

SIBLING n

SIBS ▸ sib

SIBSHIP n group of children of the same parents

SIBYL n (in ancient Greece and Rome) prophetess **sibylic, sibyls**

SIC adv, vb

SICCAN adj Scots word meaning such

SICCAR adj sure

SICCED ▸ sic

SICCING ▸ sic

SICCITY n dryness

SICE = syce

SICES ▸ sice

SICH adj old form

of such

SICHT Scot word for ▸ **sight**

SICHTED ▸ sicht

SICHTS ▸ sicht

SICK adj, n, vb

SICKBAY n room for the treatment of sick people

SICKBED n

SICKED ▸ sick

SICKEE n person off work through illness **sickees**

SICKEN vb **sickens**

SICKER ▸ sick

SICKEST ▸ sick

SICKIE n day of sick leave from work **sickies**

SICKING ▸ sick

SICKISH ▸ sick

SICKLE n, vb **sickled, sickles**

SICKLY adj, adv, vb

SICKO n person who is mentally disturbed or perverted ▸ adj perverted or in bad taste **sickos**

SICKOUT n industrial action in which all workers report sick simultaneously

SICKS ▸ sick

SICLIKE adj Scots word meaning suchlike

SICS ▸ sic

SIDA n Australian hemp plant **sidas**

SIDDHA n (in Hinduism) person who has achieved perfection **siddhas**

SIDDHI n (in Hinduism) power attained with perfection **siddhis**

SIDDUR n Jewish prayer book **siddurs**

SIDE n, adj

SIDEARM n weapon worn on belt

SIDEBAR n small newspaper article beside larger one

SIDECAR n

SIDED ► side

SIDEMAN n member of a dance band or a jazz group other than the leader **sidemen**

SIDER n one who sides with another

SIDERAL adj from the stars

SIDERS ► sider

SIDES ► side

SIDEWAY variant of ► sideways

SIDH pl n fairy people

SIDHA n (in Hinduism) person who has achieved perfection **sidhas**

SIDHE pl n inhabitants of fairyland

SIDING n sidings

SIDLE vb, n sidled, sidler, sidlers, sidles, sidling

SIECLE n century, period, or era **siecles**

SIEGE n, vb sieged

SIEGER n person who besieges **siegers**

SIEGES ► siege

SIEGING ► siege

SIELD adj provided with a ceiling

SIEMENS n SI unit of electrical conductance

SIEN n old word meaning scion

SIENITE n type of igneous rock

SIENNA n reddish- or yellowish-brown pigment made from natural earth **siennas**

SIENS ► sien

SIENT n old word meaning scion **sients**

SIERRA n range of mountains in Spain or America with jagged peaks **sierran, sierras**

SIES interj

SIESTA n siestas

SIETH n old form of scythe **sieths**

SIEUR n French word meaning lord **sieurs**

SIEVE n, vb sieved

SIEVERT n derived SI unit of dose equivalent, equal to 1 joule per kilogram

SIEVES ► sieve

SIEVING ► sieve

SIF adj South African slang for disgusting

SIFAKA n either of two large rare arboreal lemuroid primates **sifakas**

SIFFLE vb whistle siffled, siffles

SIFREI ► sefer

SIFT vb sifted, sifter, sifters, sifting, sifts

SIGANID n tropical fish

SIGH n, vb sighed, sigher, sighers, sighful, sighing, sighs

SIGHT n, vb

SIGHTED adj

SIGHTER n any of six practice shots allowed to each competitor in a tournament

SIGHTLY adj pleasing or attractive to see

SIGHTS ► sight

SIGIL n seal or signet **sigils**

SIGLA n list of symbols used in a book **siglas**

SIGLOI ► siglos

SIGLOS n silver coin of ancient Persia

SIGLUM n symbol used in book

SIGMA n 18th letter in the Greek alphabet **sigmas**

SIGMATE adj shaped like the Greek letter sigma or the Roman S ► n sigmate thing ► vb add a sigma

SIGMOID adj shaped like the letter S ► n S-shaped bend in the final portion of the large intestine

SIGN n, vb

SIGNA pl n symbols

SIGNAGE n signs collectively

SIGNAL n, adj, vb signals

SIGNARY n set of symbols

SIGNED ► sign

SIGNEE n person signing document **signees**

SIGNER n person who signs something **signers**

SIGNET n small seal used to authenticate documents ▶ vb stamp or authenticate with a signet **signets**

SIGNEUR old spelling of ▶ senior

SIGNIFY vb

SIGNING n system of communication using hand and arm movements

SIGNIOR = signor

SIGNOR n Italian term of address equivalent to sir or Mr

SIGNORA n Italian term of address equivalent to madam or Mrs

SIGNORE n Italian man: a title of respect equivalent to sir **signori**

SIGNORS ▶ signor

SIGNORY = seigniory

SIGNS ▶ sign

SIJO n Korean poem **sijos**

SIK adj excellent

SIKA n Japanese forest-dwelling deer **sikas**

SIKE n small stream

SIKER adj old spelling of sicker

SIKES ▶ sike

SILAGE n, vb **silaged, silages**

SILANE n gas containing silicon **silanes**

SILD n any of various small young herrings **silds**

SILE vb pour with rain **siled**

SILEN n god of woodland

SILENCE n, vb

SILENE n type of plant with mostly red or pink flowers, often grown as a garden plant **silenes**

SILENI ▶ silenus

SILENS ▶ silen

SILENT adj, n **silents**

SILENUS n woodland deity

SILER n strainer **silers**

SILES ▶ sile

SILESIA n twill-weave fabric of cotton or other fibre

SILEX n type of heat-resistant glass made from fused quartz **silexes**

SILICA n **silicas**

SILICIC adj of, concerned with, or containing silicon or an acid obtained from silicon

SILICLE = silicula

SILICON n, adj

SILING ▶ sile

SILIQUA n long dry dehiscent fruit of cruciferous plants such as the wallflower **silique**

SILK n, vb **silked**

SILKEN adj, vb **silkens**

SILKIE n Scots word for a seal

SILKIER ▶ silky

SILKIES ▶ silkie

SILKILY ▶ silky

SILKING ▶ silk

SILKS ▶ silk

SILKY adj

SILL n

SILLER n silver ▶ adj silver **sillers**

SILLIER ▶ silly

SILLIES ▶ silly

SILLILY ▶ silly

SILLOCK n young coalfish

SILLS ▶ sill

SILLY adj, n

SILO n, vb **siloed, siloing, silos**

SILPHIA > silphium

SILT n, vb **silted, siltier, silting, silts, silty**

SILURID n type of freshwater fish of the family which includes catfish

SILVA = sylva

SILVAE ▶ silva

SILVAN = sylvan

SILVANS ▶ silvan

SILVAS ▶ silva

SILVER n, adj, vb

SILVERN adj silver

SILVERS ▶ silver

SILVERY adj

SILVEX n type of weedkiller

SILVICS n study of trees

SIM n computer game that simulates an activity

SIMA n silicon-rich and magnesium-rich rocks of the earth's oceanic crust

SIMAR variant spelling of ▶ cymar

SIMARRE n woman's loose gown

SIMARS ▸ simar

SIMATIC ▸ sima

SIMAS ▸ sima

SIMBA E African word for ▸ lion

SIMBAS ▸ simba

SIMI n East African sword

SIMIAL adj of apes

SIMIAN n, adj simians

SIMILAR adj

SIMILE n similes

SIMILOR n alloy used in cheap jewellery

SIMIOID adj of apes

SIMIOUS adj of apes

SIMIS ▸ simi

SIMITAR = scimitar

SIMKIN word used in India for ▸ champagne

SIMKINS ▸ simkin

SIMLIN n American variety of squash plant simlins

SIMMER vb, n simmers

SIMNEL n as in simnel cake fruit cake with marzipan eaten at Easter simnels

SIMONY n practice of buying or selling Church benefits

SIMOOM n hot suffocating sand-laden desert wind simooms, simoon

SIMOONS ▸ simoon

SIMORG n bird in Persian myth simorgs

SIMP short for ▸ simpleton

SIMPAI n Indonesian monkey simpais

SIMPER vb, n simpers

SIMPKIN word used in India for ▸ champagne

SIMPLE adj, n, vb simpled, simpler, simples

SIMPLEX adj permitting the transmission of signals in only one direction in a radio circuit ▷ n simple not a compound word

SIMPLY adv

SIMPS ▸ simp

SIMS ▸ sim

SIMUL adj simultaneous ▷ n simultaneous broadcast

SIMULAR n person or thing that simulates or imitates ▷ adj fake

SIMULS ▸ simul

SIMURG n bird in Persian myth

SIMURGH n bird in Persian myth

SIMURGS ▸ simurg

SIN n, vb

SINCE prep, adv

SINCERE adj

SIND variant of ▸ syne

SINDED ▸ sind

SINDING ▸ sind

SINDON n type of cloth sindons

SINDS ▸ sind

SINE ▸ syne

SINED ▸ sine

SINES ▸ sine

SINEW n, vb

SINEWED adj having sinews

SINEWS ▸ sinew

SINEWY adj

SINFUL adj

SING vb, n

SINGE vb, n singed

SINGER n person who sings, esp professionally singers

SINGES ▸ singe

SINGING ▸ sing

SINGLE adj, n, vb singled

SINGLES pl n match played with one person on each side

SINGLET n

SINGLY adv

SINGS ▸ sing

SINGULT n old word meaning sob

SINH n hyperbolic sine sinhs

SINICAL ▸ sine

SINING ▸ sine

SINK vb, n

SINKAGE n act of sinking or degree to which something sinks or has sunk

SINKER n weight for a fishing line sinkers

SINKIER ▸ sinky

SINKING ▸ sink

SINKS ▸ sink

SINKY adj giving underfoot

SINLESS adj free from sin or guilt

SINNED ▸ sin

SINNER n, vb

SINNERS ▸ sin

SINNET n braided rope sinnets

SINNING ▸ sin

SINOPIA n pigment made from iron ore sinopie

SINOPIS n pigment made from iron ore

SINS ▸ sin

SINSYNE adv Scots word meaning since

SINTER n whitish porous incrustation deposited from hot springs ▸ vb form large particles from (powders) by heating or pressure **sinters, sintery**

SINUATE vb sinuous

SINUOSE adj sinuous

SINUOUS adj

SINUS n **sinuses**

SIP vb, n

SIPE vb soak **siped, sipes**

SIPHON n, vb **siphons**

SIPING ▸ sipe

SIPPED ▸ sip

SIPPER ▸ sip

SIPPERS ▸ sip

SIPPET n small piece of toast eaten with soup or gravy **sippets**

SIPPING ▸ sip

SIPPLE vb sip **sippled, sipples**

SIPPY adj as in sippy cup infant's drinking cup with a tight-fitting lid and perforated spout

SIPS ▸ sip

SIR n, vb

SIRCAR n government in India **sircars**

SIRDAR n = sardar

SIRDARS ▸ sirdar

SIRE n, vb **sired**

SIREE emphasized form of ▸ sir

SIREES ▸ siree

SIREN n sirenic, sirens

SIRES ▸ sire

SIRGANG n Asian bird

SIRI n betel

SIRIH n betel **sirihs**

SIRING ▸ sire

SIRINGS ▸ siring

SIRIS ▸ siri

SIRKAR n government in India **sirkars**

SIRLOIN n

SIRNAME vb old form of surname

SIROC n sirocco

SIROCCO n hot wind blowing from N Africa into S Europe

SIROCS ▸ siroc

SIROSET adj of the chemical treatment of woollen fabrics to give a permanent-press effect

SIRRA disrespectful form of ▸ sir

SIRRAH n contemptuous term used in addressing a man or boy **sirrahs**

SIRRAS ▸ sirra

SIRRED ▸ sir

SIRREE n form of 'sir' used for emphasis **sirrees**

SIRRING ▸ sir

SIRS ▸ sir

SIRTUIN n protein that regulates cell metabolism and ageing

SIRUP = syrup

SIRUPED ▸ sirup

SIRUPS ▸ sirup

SIRUPY ▸ sirup

SIS n

SISAL n **sisals**

SISES ▸ sis

SISKIN n yellow-and-black finch **siskins**

SISS shortening of ▸ sister

SISSES ▸ siss

SISSIER ▸ sissy

SISSIES ▸ sissy

SISSOO n Indian tree **sissoos**

SISSY n, adj

SIST vb Scottish law term meaning stop **sisted**

SISTER n, adj, vb **sisters**

SISTING ▸ sist

SISTRA ▸ sistrum

SISTRUM n musical instrument of ancient Egypt consisting of a metal rattle

SISTS ▸ sist

SIT vb

SITAR n **sitars**

SITCOM n **sitcoms**

SITE n, vb **sited**

SITELLA n type of small generally black-and-white bird

SITES ▸ site

SITFAST n sore on a horse's back caused by rubbing of the saddle

SITH archaic word for ▸ since

SITHE vb old form of scythe **sithed**

SITHEE interj look here! listen!

SITHEN adv old word meaning since

SITHENS adv old word meaning since

SITHES ▶ sithe

SITHING ▶ sithe

SITING ▶ site

SITKA modifier as in sitka spruce tall North American spruce tree

SITREP n military situation report sitreps

SITS ▶ sit

SITTAR n sitar sittars

SITTEN adj dialect word for in the saddle

SITTER n baby-sitter sitters

SITTINE adj of nuthatch bird family

SITTING ▶ sit

SITUATE vb place ▷ adj (now used esp in legal contexts) situated

SITULA n bucket-shaped container situlae

SITUP n exercise in which the body is brought into a sitting position situps

SITUS n position or location situses

SITZ n as in sitz bath bath in which the buttocks and hips are immersed in hot water

SIVER = syver

SIVERS ▶ siver

SIWASH vb (in the Pacific Northwest) to camp out with only natural shelter

SIX n

SIXAIN n stanza or poem of six lines

SIXAINE n six-line stanza of poetry

SIXAINS ▶ sixain

SIXER = six

SIXERS ▶ sixer

SIXES ▶ six

SIXFOLD adj having six times as many or as much ▷ adv by six times as many or as much

SIXMO n book size resulting from folding a sheet of paper into six leaves sixmos

SIXTE n sixth of eight basic positions from which a parry or attack can be made in fencing

SIXTEEN n, adj, determiner

SIXTES ▶ sixte

SIXTH n, adj, adv sixthly, sixths

SIXTIES ▶ sixty

SIXTY n, adj

SIZABLE adj sizably

SIZAR n undergraduate receiving a maintenance grant from the college sizars

SIZE n, vb

SIZED adj of a specified size

SIZEISM n discrimination on the basis of a person's size sizeist

SIZEL n scrap metal clippings sizels

SIZER, sizers, sizes, sizier, siziest, sizing,

sizings ▶ size

SIZISM n discrimination against people because of weight sizisms, sizist, sizists

SIZY ▶ size

SIZZLE vb, n sizzled

SIZZLER n something that sizzles

SIZZLES ▶ sizzle

SJAMBOK n, vb

SJOE interj South African exclamation of surprise, admiration, exhaustion, etc

SKA n type of West Indian pop music of the 1960s

SKAG = scag

SKAGS ▶ skag

SKAIL vb Scots word meaning disperse skailed, skails

SKAITH vb Scots word meaning injure skaiths

SKALD n (in ancient Scandinavia) a bard or minstrel skaldic, skalds

SKANK n fast dance to reggae music ▷ vb perform this dance skanked, skanker, skanks

SKANKY adj dirty or unattractive

SKART Scots word for > cormorant

SKARTH Scots word for > cormorant

SKARTHS ▶ skarth

SKARTS ▶ skart

SKAS ▶ ska

SKAT n three-handed card game using 32 cards

SKATE n, vb skate

SKATER n person who skates **skaters**

SKATES ▶ skate

SKATING ▶ skate

SKATOL n skatole

SKATOLE n white or brownish crystalline solid

SKATOLS ▶ skatol

SKATS ▶ skat

SKATT n dialect word meaning throw **skatts**

SKAW variant of ▶ scaw

SKAWS ▶ skaw

SKEAN n kind of double-edged dagger

SKEANE = skein

SKEANES ▶ skeane

SKEANS ▶ skean

SKEAR dialect form of ▶ scare

SKEARED ▶ skear

SKEARS ▶ skear

SKEARY dialect form of ▶ scary

SKEE variant spelling of ▶ ski

SKEED ▶ skee

SKEEF adj, adv South African slang for at an oblique angle

SKEEING ▶ skee

SKEELY adj Scots word meaning skilful

SKEEN n type of ibex **skeens**

SKEER dialect form of ▶ scare

SKEERED ▶ skeer

SKEERS ▶ skeer

SKEERY dialect form of ▶ scary

SKEES ▶ skee

SKEET n form of clay-pigeon shooting

SKEETER informal word for ▶ mosquito

SKEETS ▶ skeet

SKEG n reinforcing brace between the after end of a keel and the rudderpost

SKEGG n skeg

SKEGGER n young salmon

SKEGGS ▶ skegg

SKEGS ▶ skeg

SKEIGH adj Scots word meaning shy

SKEIN n, vb skeined, skeins

SKELDER vb beg

SKELF n splinter of wood, esp when embedded accidentally in the skin **skelfs**

SKELL n homeless person

SKELLIE adj skelly

SKELLS ▶ skell

SKELLUM n rogue

SKELLY n whitefish of certain lakes in the Lake District ▷ vb look sideways or squint ▷ adj cross-eyed

SKELM n villain or crook **skelms**

SKELP vb slap ▷ n slap **skelped**

SKELPIT vb Scots word meaning skelped

SKELPS ▶ skelp

SKELTER vb scurry

SKELUM n Scots word meaning rascal **skelums**

SKEN vb squint or stare

SKENE n Scots word meaning dagger **skenes**

SKENNED ▶ sken

SKENS ▶ sken

SKEO n Scots dialect word meaning hut **skeos**

SKEP n beehive, esp one constructed of straw ▷ vb gather into a hive

SKEPFUL n amount skep will hold

SKEPPED ▶ skep

SKEPS ▶ skep

SKEPSIS n doubt

SKEPTIC = sceptic

SKER vb scour **skerred**

SKERRY n rocky island or reef

SKERS ▶ sker

SKET vb splash (water)

SKETCH n, vb

SKETCHY adj

SKETS ▶ sket

SKETTED ▶ sket

SKEW vb, adj, n skewed

SKEWER n, vb skewers

SKEWEST ▶ skew

SKEWING ▶ skew

SKEWS ▶ skew

SKI n, vb skiable

SKIBOB n vehicle made of two short skis for gliding down snow slopes **skibobs**

SKID vb, n skidded, skidder

SKIDDOO vb go away quickly

SKIDDY ▶ skid

SKIDLID n crash helmet

SKIDOO n snowmobile ▷ vb travel on a skidoo **skidoos**

SKIDPAN n area made slippery so that vehicle drivers can practise controlling skids

SKIDS ▶ skid

SKIDWAY n platform on which logs ready for sawing are piled

SKIED ▶ sky

SKIER ▶ ski

SKIERS ▶ ski

SKIES ▶ sky

SKIEY adj of the sky **skieyer**

SKIFF n, vb **skiffed**

SKIFFLE n style of popular music of the 1950s ▷ vb play this style of music

SKIFFS ▶ skiff

SKIING ▶ ski

SKIINGS ▶ ski

SKILFUL adj

SKILL n

SKILLED adj

SKILLET n

SKILLS ▶ skill

SKILLY n thin soup or gruel ▷ adj skilled

SKIM vb, n **skimmed**

SKIMMER n person or thing that skims

SKIMMIA n shrub of S and SE Asia

SKIMP vb skimped, **skimps**

SKIMPY adj

SKIMS ▶ skim

SKIN n, vb

SKINFUL n sufficient alcoholic drink to make one drunk

SKINK n type of lizard with reduced limbs and smooth scales ▷ vb serve a drink **skinked, skinker, skinks**

SKINNED ▶ skin

SKINNER n person who prepares or deals in animal skins

SKINNY adj, n

SKINS ▶ skin

SKINT adj skinter

SKIO n Scots dialect word meaning hut **skios**

SKIP vb, n **skipped**

SKIPPER vb, n

SKIPPET n small round box for preserving a document or seal

SKIPPY adj in high spirits

SKIPS ▶ skip

SKIRL n sound of bagpipes ▷ vb (of bagpipes) to give out a shrill sound **skirled, skirls**

SKIRR vb move, run, or fly rapidly ▷ n whirring or grating sound, as of the wings of birds in flight **skirred**

SKIRRET n umbelliferous Old World plant

SKIRRS ▶ skirr

SKIRT n, vb **skirted**

SKIRTER n man who skirts fleeces

SKIRTS ▶ skirt

SKIS ▶ ski

SKIT n

SKITCH vb (of a dog) to attack

SKITE n, vb **skited, skites, skiting**

SKITS ▶ skit

SKITTER vb move or run rapidly or lightly

SKITTLE n, vb

SKIVE vb skived

SKIVER n tanned outer layer split from a skin ▷ vb cut leather **skivers**

SKIVES ▶ skive

SKIVIE adj old Scots word meaning disarranged **skivier**

SKIVING ▶ skive

SKIVVY n female servant who does menial work ▷ vb work as a skivvy

SKIVY ▶ skive

SKIWEAR n clothes for skiing in

SKLATE Scots word for slate

SKLATED ▶ sklate

SKLATES ▶ sklate

SKLENT Scots word for slant

SKLENTS ▶ sklent

SKLIFF n Scots word meaning little piece **skliffs**

SKLIM vb Scots word meaning climb **sklims**

SKOAL = skol

SKOALED ▶ skoal

SKOALS ▶ skoal

SKOFF vb eat greedily **skoffed, skoffs**

SKOL *sentence substitute* good health! (a drinking toast) ▷ *vb* down (an alcoholic drink) in one go

SKOLIA ▸ skolion

SKOLION *n* ancient Greek drinking song

SKOLLED ▸ skol

SKOLLIE = skolly

SKOLLY *n* hooligan, usually one of a gang

SKOLS ▸ skol

SKOOKUM *adj* strong or brave

SKOOL *ironically illiterate or childish spelling of* ▸ school

SKOOLS ▸ skool

SKOOSH *vb* Scots word meaning squirt

SKORT *n* pair of shorts with a front panel which gives the appearance of a skirt **skorts**

SKOSH *n* little bit **skoshes**

SKRAN *n* food **skrans**

SKREEGH *vb* Scots word meaning screech **skreens**

SKREEN *n* screen **skreens**

SKREIGH *vb* Scots word meaning screech

SKRIECH *vb* Scots word meaning screech

SKRIED ▸ skry

SKRIEGH *vb* Scots word meaning screech

SKRIES ▸ skry

SKRIK *n* South African word meaning fright

SKRIKE *vb* cry **skriked, skrikes**

SKRIKS ▸ skrik

SKRIMP *vb* steal apples **skrimps**

SKRONK *n* type of dissonant, grating popular music **skronks**

SKRUMP *vb* steal apples **skrumps**

SKRY *vb* try to tell future **skryer, skryers, skrying**

SKUA *n* large predatory gull **skuas**

SKUDLER *n* Scots word meaning leader of festivities

SKUG *vb* shelter **skugged, skugs**

SKULK *vb, n* **skulked, skulker, skulks**

SKULL *n, vb* **skulled, skulls**

SKULPIN *n* North American fish

SKUMMER *vb* defecate

SKUNK *n, vb* **skunked, skunks, skunky**

SKURRY *vb* scurry

SKUTTLE *vb* scuttle

SKY *n, vb*

SKYBORN *adj* born in heaven

SKYBOX *n* luxurious suite high up in the stand of a sports stadium

SKYCAP *n* luggage porter at American airport **skycaps**

SKYCLAD *adj* naked

SKYDIVE *vb* take part in skydiving **skydove**

SKYED ▸ sky

SKYER *n* cricket ball hit up into air **skyers**

SKYEY *adj* of the sky

SKYF *n* South African slang for a cigarette or substance for smoking ▷ *vb* smoke a cigarette **skyfed, skyfing, skyfs**

SKYHOME *n* Australian slang for a sub-penthouse flat in a tall building

SKYHOOK *n* hook hung from helicopter

SKYIER ▸ skyey

SKYIEST ▸ skyey

SKYING ▸ sky

SKYISH ▸ sky

SKYJACK *vb* hijack (an aircraft)

SKYLAB *n* orbiting space station **skylabs**

SKYLARK *n* lark that sings while soaring at a great height ▷ *vb* play or frolic

SKYLESS *adj* having no sky

SKYLIKE ▸ sky

SKYLINE *n*

SKYLIT *adj* having skylight

SKYMAN *n* paratrooper **skymen**

SKYPHOI ▸ skyphos

SKYPHOS *n* ancient Greek drinking cup

SKYR *n* Scandinavian cheese

SKYRE *vb* Scots word meaning shine **skyred, skyres, skyring**

SKYRS ▸ skyr

SKYSAIL *n* square sail set above the royal on a square-rigger
SKYSURF *vb* perform freefall aerobatics
SKYTE *vb* Scots word meaning slide **skyted, skytes, skyting**
SKYWALK *n* tightrope walk at great height
SKYWARD *adj* towards the sky ▷ *adv* towards the sky
SKYWAY *n* air route **skyways**
SLAB *n, vb* **slabbed**
SLABBER *vb* dribble from the mouth
SLABBY ▸ **slab**
SLABS ▸ **slab**
SLACK = **slake**
SLACKED ▸ **slack**
SLACKEN *vb*
SLACKER *n* person who evades work or duty
SLACKLY ▸ **slack**
SLACKS *pl n* casual trousers
SLADANG *n* Malayan tapir
SLADE *n* little valley **slades**
SLAE Scots word for ▸ **sloe**
SLAES ▸ **slae**
SLAG *n, vb* **slagged, slaggy, slags**
SLAID *vb* Scots word for 'slid'
SLAIN ▸ **slay**
SLAINTE *interj* cheers!
SLAIRG Scots word for ▸ **spread**
SLAIRGS ▸ **slairg**

SLAKE *vb* **slaked, slaker, slakers, slakes, slaking**
SLALOM *n, vb* **slaloms**
SLAM *vb, n* **slammed**
SLAMMER *n* prison
SLAMS ▸ **slam**
SLANDER *n, vb*
SLANE *n* spade for cutting turf **slanes**
SLANG *n, vb* **slanged**
SLANGER *n* street vendor
SLANGS ▸ **slang**
SLANGY ▸ **slang**
SLANK dialect word for ▸ **lank**
SLANT *vb, n* **slanted**
SLANTER ▸ **slinter**
SLANTLY ▸ **slant**
SLANTS ▸ **slant**
SLANTY *adj* slanting
SLAP *n, vb* **slapped, slapper, slaps**
SLART *vb* spill (something) **slarted, slarts**
SLASH *vb, n* **slashed**
SLASHER *n* machine used for cutting scrub or undergrowth in the bush
SLASHES ▸ **slash**
SLAT *n, vb*
SLATCH *n* slack part of rope
SLATE *n, vb, adj* **slated**
SLATER *n* person trained in laying roof slates **slaters**
SLATES ▸ **slate**
SLATEY *adj* slightly mad
SLATHER *vb* spread quickly or lavishly

SLATIER ▸ **slaty**
SLATING *n* act or process of laying slates
SLATS ▸ **slat**
SLATTED ▸ **slat**
SLATTER *vb* be slovenly
SLATY *adj* consisting of or resembling slate
SLAVE *n, vb* **slaved**
SLAVER *n, vb* **slavers**
SLAVERY *n* state or condition of being a slave
SLAVES ▸ **slave**
SLAVEY *n* female general servant **slaveys**
SLAVING ▸ **slave**
SLAVISH *adj*
SLAW short for > coleslaw
SLAWS ▸ **slaw**
SLAY *vb* **slayed, slayer, slayers, slaying, slays**
SLEAVE *n* tangled thread ▷ *vb* disentangle (twisted thread, etc) **sleaved, sleaves**
SLEAZE *n* behaviour considered dishonest or disreputable **sleazes**
SLEAZO *n* sleazy person
SLEAZY *adj*
SLEB *n* celebrity **slebs**
SLED = **sledge**
SLEDDED ▸ **sled**
SLEDDER ▸ **sled**
SLEDED ▸ **sled**
SLEDGE *n, vb* **sledged, sledger, sledges**
SLEDS ▸ **sled**
SLEE Scots word for ▸ **sly**
SLEECH *n* slippery mud **sleechy**

SLEEK adj, vb **sleeked**
SLEEKEN vb make sleek
SLEEKER ▶ sleek
SLEEKIT adj smooth
SLEEKLY ▶ sleek
SLEEKS ▶ sleek
SLEEKY ▶ sleek
SLEEP n, vb
SLEEPER n
SLEEPRY Scots word for
▶ sleepy
SLEEPS ▶ sleep
SLEEPY adj
SLEER ▶ slee
SLEEST ▶ slee
SLEET n, vb **sleeted,**
sleets, sleety
SLEEVE n **sleeved**
SLEEVER n old beer
measure
SLEEVES ▶ sleeve
SLEEZY adj sleazy
SLEIDED adj old word
meaning separated
SLEIGH = sledge
SLEIGHS ▶ sleigh
SLEIGHT n skill or
cunning
SLENDER adj
SLENTER = slinter
SLEPT ▶ sleep
SLEUTH n, vb **sleuths**
SLEW vb **slewed,**
slewing, slews
SLEY n weaver's tool for
separating threads
sleys
SLICE n, vb **sliced, slicer,**
slicers, slices, slicing
SLICK adj, n, vb **slicked**
SLICKEN vb make
smooth
SLICKER n sly or
untrustworthy person

SLICKLY ▶ slick
SLICKS ▶ slick
SLID ▶ slide
SLIDDEN ▶ slide
SLIDDER vb slip
SLIDE vb, n **slided,**
slider, sliders, slides,
sliding
SLIER ▶ sly
SLIEST ▶ sly
SLIEVE n Irish mountain
slieves
SLIGHT adj, n, vb **slights**
SLILY ▶ sly
SLIM adj, vb
SLIME n, vb **slimed,**
slimes
SLIMIER ▶ slimy
SLIMILY ▶ slimy
SLIMING ▶ slime
SLIMLY ▶ slim
SLIMMED ▶ slim
SLIMMER ▶ slim
SLIMPSY adj thin and
flimsy
SLIMS ▶ slim
SLIMSY adj frail
SLIMY adj
SLING n, vb **slinger,**
slings
SLINK vb, n **slinked,**
slinker, slinks
SLINKY adj
SLINTER n dodge, trick,
or stratagem
SLIOTAR n ball used in
hurling
SLIP vb, n
SLIPE n wool removed
from the pelt of a
slaughtered sheep ▷ vb
remove skin **sliped,**
slipes, sliping
SLIPOUT n instance of

slipping out
SLIPPED ▶ slip
SLIPPER n, vb
SLIPPY adj slippery
SLIPS ▶ slip
SLIPT vb old form of
slipped
SLIPUP n mistake or
mishap **slipups**
SLIPWAY n
SLISH n old word
meaning cut **slishes**
SLIT vb, n
SLITHER vb, n
SLITS, slitted, slitter,
slitty ▶ slit
SLIVE vb slip **slived,**
sliven
SLIVER n, vb **slivers**
SLIVES ▶ slive
SLIVING ▶ slive
SLOAN n severe
telling-off **sloans**
SLOB n
SLOBBER vb, n
SLOBBY ▶ slob
SLOBS ▶ slob
SLOCKEN vb Scots word
meaning slake
SLOE n **sloes**
SLOG vb, n
SLOGAN n **slogans**
SLOGGED ▶ slog
SLOGGER ▶ slog
SLOGS ▶ slog
SLOID n Swedish
woodwork **sloids**
SLOJD n Swedish
woodwork **slojds**
SLOKEN vb Scots word
meaning slake **slokens**
SLOOM n slumber
sloomed, slooms,
sloomy

SLOOP n sloops

SLOOSH vb wash with water

SLOOT n ditch for irrigation or drainage **sloots**

SLOP vb, n

SLOPE vb, n sloped, sloper, slopers, slopes, slopier, sloping

SLOPPED ▶ slop

SLOPPY adj

SLOPS ▶ slop

SLOPY ▶ slope

SLORM vb wipe carelessly **slormed, slorms**

SLOSH vb, n sloshed, sloshes, sloshy

SLOT n, vb

SLOTH n, vb slothed, sloths

SLOTS ▶ slot

SLOTTED ▶ slot

SLOTTER ▶ slot

SLOUCH vb, n

SLOUCHY adj slouching

SLOUGH n, vb

SLOUGHI n N African breed of dog resembling a greyhound

SLOUGHS ▶ slough

SLOUGHY ▶ slough

SLOVE ▶ slive

SLOVEN n habitually dirty or untidy person **slovens**

SLOW adj, adv, vb slowed, slower, slowest, slowing, slowish, slowly, slows

SLOYD n Swedish woodwork **sloyds**

SLUB n lump in yarn or fabric ▷ vb draw out and twist (a sliver of fibre) before spinning ▷ adj (of material) having an irregular appearance **slubb, slubbed**

SLUBBER vb smear

SLUBBS ▶ slubb

SLUBBY ▶ slub

SLUBS ▶ slub

SLUDGE n, vb sludged, sludges

SLUDGY adj consisting of, containing, or like sludge

SLUE = slew

SLUED ▶ slue

SLUEING ▶ slue

SLUES ▶ slue

SLUFF = slough

SLUFFED ▶ sluff

SLUFFS ▶ sluff

SLUG n, vb slugged

SLUGGER n (esp in boxing, baseball, etc) a person who strikes hard

SLUGS ▶ slug

SLUICE n, vb sluiced, sluices, sluicy

SLUING ▶ slue

SLUIT n water channel in South Africa **sluits**

SLUM n, vb

SLUMBER n, vb

SLUMBRY = slumbery

SLUMGUM n material left after wax is extracted from honeycomb

SLUMISM n existence of slums

SLUMMED ▶ slum

SLUMMER ▶ slum

SLUMMY ▶ slum

SLUMP vb, n slumped, slumps

SLUMPY adj boggy

SLUMS ▶ slum

SLUNG ▶ sling

SLUNK ▶ slink

SLUR vb, n

SLURB n suburban slum **slurban, slurbs**

SLURP vb, n slurped, slurper, slurps

SLURPY adj making a slurping noise

SLURRED ▶ slur

SLURRY n, vb

SLURS ▶ slur

SLUSE = sluice

SLUSES ▶ sluice

SLUSH n, vb slushed, slushes

SLUSHY adj of, resembling, or consisting of slush ▷ n unskilled kitchen assistant

SLUTCH n mud slutchy

SLY adj slyer, slyest, slyish, slyly, slyness

SLYPE n covered passageway in a church **slypes**

SMA Scots word for ▶ small

SMAAK vb South African slang for like or love smaaked, smaaks

SMACK vb, n, adv smacked

SMACKER n loud kiss

SMACKS ▸ smack

SMAIK n Scots word meaning rascal **smaiks**

SMALL adj not large in size, number, or amount ▷ n narrow part of the lower back ▷ adv into small pieces ▷ vb make small **smalled, smaller, smalls**

SMALM = smarm

SMALMED ▸ smalm

SMALMS ▸ smalm

SMALMY = smarmy

SMALT n type of silica glass coloured deep blue with cobalt oxide

SMALTI ▸ smalto

SMALTO n coloured glass, etc, used in mosaics **smaltos**

SMALTS ▸ smalt

SMARAGD n any green gemstone, such as the emerald

SMARM vb bring (oneself) into favour (with) ▷ n obsequious flattery **smarmed, smarms**

SMARMY adj

SMART adj, vb, n, adv **smarted**

SMARTEN vb

SMARTER ▸ smart

SMARTIE = smarty

SMARTLY ▸ smart

SMARTS pl n know-how, intelligence, or wits

SMARTY n would-be clever person

SMASH vb, n, adv

SMASHED adj

SMASHER n attractive person or thing

SMASHES ▸ smash

SMASHUP n bad collision of cars

SMATCH less common word for ▸ **smack**

SMATTER n smattering ▷ vb prattle

SMAZE n smoky haze, less damp than fog **smazes**

SMEAR vb, n smeared, smearer, smears

SMEARY adj smeared, dirty

SMEATH n duck **smeaths**

SMECTIC adj (of a substance) existing in state in which the molecules are oriented in layers

SMEDDUM n any fine powder

SMEE n duck

SMEECH Southwest English dialect form of ▸ **smoke**

SMEEK vb smoke **smeeked**

SMEEKS ▸ smeech

SMEES ▸ smee

SMEETH n duck **smeeths**

SMEGMA n whitish sebaceous secretion that accumulates beneath the prepuce **smegmas**

SMEIK ▸ smeke

SMEIKED ▸ smeked

SMEIKS ▸ smeik

SMEKE n smoke ▷ vb smoke smeked, smekes, smeking

SMELL vb, n smelled, smeller, smells

SMELLY adj

SMELT vb extract metal from an ore

SMELTED ▸ smelt

SMELTER n industrial plant where smelting is carried out

SMELTS ▸ smell

SMERK = smirk

SMERKED ▸ smerk

SMERKS ▸ smerk

SMEUSE n way through hedge **smeuses**

SMEW n duck of N Europe and Asia **smews**

SMICKER vb look at someone amorously

SMICKET n smock

SMICKLY adv amorously

SMIDDY Scots word for ▸ **smithy**

SMIDGE n very small amount or part

SMIDGEN n very small amount or part

SMIDGES ▸ smidge

SMIDGIN = smidgen

SMIGHT = smite

SMIGHTS ▸ smight

SMILAX n type of climbing shrub

SMILE n, vb smiled, smiler, smilers, smiles

SMILET n little smile **smilets**

SMILEY n symbol depicting a smile or

other facial expression, used in e-mail ⊳ *adj* cheerful **smileys, smilier**

SMILING ▶ smile

SMIR *n* drizzly rain ⊳ *vb* drizzle lightly

SMIRCH *n* stain ⊳ *vb* disgrace

SMIRK *n, vb* smirked, smirker, smirks, smirky

SMIRR = smir

SMIRRED ▶ smirr

SMIRRS ▶ smirr

SMIRRY ▶ smirr

SMIRS ▶ smir

SMIT ▶ smite

SMITE *vb* smiter, smiters, smites

SMITH *n, vb* smithed, smiths

SMITHY *n, vb*

SMITING ▶ smite

SMITS ▶ smit

SMITTED ▶ smit

SMITTEN ▶ smite

SMITTLE *adj* infectious

SMOCK *n, vb* smocked, smocks

SMOG *n* smoggy, smogs

SMOILE = smile

SMOILED ▶ smoile

SMOILES ▶ smoile

SMOKE *n, vb* smoked

SMOKEHO ▶ smoko

SMOKER *n* person who habitually smokes tobacco **smokers**

SMOKES ▶ smoke

SMOKEY ▶ smoky

SMOKIE *n* smoked haddock

SMOKIER ▶ smoky

SMOKIES ▶ smoky

SMOKILY ▶ smoky

SMOKING ▶ smoke

SMOKO *n* short break from work for tea or a cigarette **smokos**

SMOKY *adj, n*

SMOLDER = smoulder

SMOLT *n* young salmon at the stage when it migrates to the sea **smolts**

SMOOCH *vb* kiss and cuddle ⊳ *n* smooching

SMOOCHY *adj* romantic

SMOODGE = smooch

SMOOGE = smooch

SMOOGED ▶ smooge

SMOOGES ▶ smooge

SMOOR *vb* Scots word meaning put out fire **smoored, smoors**

SMOOSH *vb* paint to give softened look

SMOOT *vb* work as printer **smooted**

SMOOTH *adj, vb, adv, n* smooths

SMOOTHY = smoothie

SMOOTS ▶ smoot

SMORE = smoor

SMORED ▶ smore

SMORES ▶ smore

SMORING ▶ smore

SMOTE ▶ smite

SMOTHER *vb*

SMOUCH *vb* kiss

SMOUSE *vb* South African word meaning peddle **smoused, smouser, smouses**

SMOUT *n* child or undersized person ⊳ *vb* creep or sneak **smouted, smouts, smowt**

SMOWTS ▶ smowt

SMOYLE = smile

SMOYLED ▶ smoyle

SMOYLES ▶ smoyle

SMRITI *n* class of Hindu sacred literature **smritis**

SMUDGE *vb, n* smudged, smudger, smudges

SMUDGY *adj* smeared, blurred, or soiled, or likely to become so

SMUG *adj, vb* smugged, smugger

SMUGGLE *vb*

SMUGLY ▶ smug

SMUGS ▶ smug

SMUR = smir

SMURRED ▶ smur

SMURRY ▶ smur

SMURS ▶ smur

SMUSH *vb* crush smushed, smushes

SMUT *n, vb*

SMUTCH *vb* smudge ⊳ *n* mark **smutchy**

SMUTS ▶ smut

SMUTTED ▶ smut

SMUTTY ▶ smut

SMYTRIE *n* Scots word meaning collection

SNAB = snob

SNABBLE = snaffle

SNABS ▶ snab

SNACK *n, vb* snacked, snacker, snacks

SNAFFLE *n* jointed bit for a horse ⊳ *vb* steal

SNAFU *n* confusion or chaos regarded as the

normal state ▷ adj confused or muddled up, as usual ▷ vb throw into chaos **snafued, snafus**

SNAG n, vb snagged

SNAGGY adj having sharp protuberances

SNAGS ▶ snag

SNAIL n, vb snailed, snails, snaily

SNAKE n, vb snaked, snakes

SNAKEY = snaky

SNAKIER ▶ snaky

SNAKILY ▶ snaky

SNAKING ▶ snake

SNAKISH ▶ snake

SNAKY adj twisted or winding

SNAP vb, n, adj, adv snapped

SNAPPER n, vb

SNAPPY adj

SNAPS ▶ snap

SNAPTIN n container for food

SNAR = snarl

SNARE n, vb snared, snarer, snarers, snares

SNARIER ▶ snare

SNARING ▶ snare

SNARK n imaginary creature in Lewis Carroll's poetry **snarks**

SNARKY adj unpleasant and scornful

SNARL vb, n snarled, snarler, snarls, snarly

SNARRED ▶ snar

SNARS ▶ snar

SNARY ▶ snare

SNASH vb Scots word meaning speak cheekily **snashed, snashes**

SNASTE n candle wick **snastes**

SNATCH vb, n

SNATCHY adj disconnected or spasmodic

SNATH n handle of a scythe **snathe**

SNATHES ▶ snathe

SNATHS ▶ snath

SNAW Scots variant of ▶ snow

SNAWED ▶ snaw

SNAWING ▶ snaw

SNAWS ▶ snaw

SNAZZY adj

SNEAD n scythe handle **sneads**

SNEAK vb, n, adj sneaked

SNEAKER n

SNEAKS ▶ sneak

SNEAKY ▶ sneak

SNEAP vb nip **sneaped, sneaps**

SNEATH = snath

SNEATHS ▶ sneath

SNEB = snib

SNEBBE = snub

SNEBBED ▶ sneb

SNEBBES ▶ snebbe

SNEBS ▶ sneb

SNECK n small squared stone used in a rubble wall to fill spaces between stones ▷ vb fasten (a latch) **snecked, snecks**

SNED vb prune or trim **snedded, sneds**

SNEE vb cut **sneed, sneeing**

SNEER n, vb sneered, sneerer, sneers

SNEERY adj contemptuous or scornful

SNEES ▶ snee

SNEESH n Scots word meaning pinch of snuff

SNEEZE vb, n sneezed, sneezer, sneezes, sneezy

SNELL adj biting ▷ vb attach hook to fishing line **snelled, sneller, snells, snelly**

SNIB n catch of a door or window ▷ vb bolt or fasten (a door) **snibbed, snibs**

SNICK n (make) a small cut or notch ▷ vb make a small cut or notch in (something) **snicked**

SNICKER ▶ snigger

SNICKET n passageway between walls or fences

SNICKS ▶ snick

SNIDE adj, n, vb snided, snidely, snider, snides, snidest, snidey

SNIDIER ▶ snidey

SNIDING ▶ snide

SNIES ▶ sny

SNIFF vb, n sniffed

SNIFFER n device for detecting hidden substances such as drugs

SNIFFLE *vb, n* sniffly

SNIFFS ▸ sniff

SNIFFY *adj* contemptuous or scornful

SNIFT = sniff

SNIFTED ▸ snift

SNIFTER *n* small quantity of alcoholic drink ▹ *vb* sniff

SNIFTS ▸ snift

SNIFTY *adj* slang word meaning excellent

SNIG *vb* drag (a felled log) by a chain or cable snigged

SNIGGER *n, vb*

SNIGGLE *vb* fish for eels by dangling or thrusting a baited hook into cavities ▹ *n* baited hook used for sniggling eels

SNIGLET *n* invented word

SNIGS ▸ snig

SNIP *vb, n, interj*

SNIPE *n, vb* sniped

SNIPER *n* person who shoots at someone from cover snipers

SNIPES ▸ snipe

SNIPIER ▸ snipy

SNIPING ▸ snipe

SNIPPED ▸ snip

SNIPPER ▸ snip

SNIPPET *n*

SNIPPY *adj* scrappy

SNIPS ▸ snip

SNIPY *adj* like a snipe

SNIRT *n* Scots word meaning suppressed laugh

SNIRTLE *vb* Scots word meaning snicker

SNIRTS ▸ snirt

SNIT *n* fit of temper

SNITCH *vb* act as an informer ▹ *n* informer

SNITCHY *adj* bad-tempered or irritable

SNITS ▸ snit

SNIVEL *vb, n* snivels

SNOB *n* snobby, snobs

SNOD *vb* Scots word meaning make tidy snodded, snodder, snoddit, snods

SNOEK *n* edible marine fish snoeks

SNOEP *adj* mean or tight-fisted

SNOG *vb* kiss and cuddle ▹ *n* act of kissing and cuddling snogged, snogs

SNOKE = snook

SNOKED ▸ snoke

SNOKES ▸ snoke

SNOKING ▸ snoke

SNOOD *n* pouch loosely holding a woman's hair at the back ▹ *vb* hold (the hair) in a snood snooded, snoods

SNOOK *n* any of several large game fishes ▹ *vb* lurk snooked

SNOOKER *n, vb*

SNOOKS ▸ snook

SNOOL *vb* Scots word meaning dominate snooled, snools

SNOOP *vb, n* snooped

SNOOPER *n*

SNOOPS ▸ snoop

SNOOPY ▸ snoop

SNOOT *n* nose ▹ *vb* look contemptuously at snooted, snoots

SNOOTY *adj*

SNOOZE *vb, n* snoozed, snoozer, snoozes

SNOOZLE *vb* cuddle and sleep

SNOOZY ▸ snooze

SNORE *vb, n* snored, snorer, snorers, snores, snoring

SNORKEL *n, vb*

SNORT *vb, n* snorted

SNORTER *n* person or animal that snorts

SNORTS ▸ snort

SNORTY ▸ snort

SNOT *n, vb*

SNOTRAG *n* handkerchief

SNOTS ▸ snot

SNOTTED ▸ snot

SNOTTER *vb* breathe through obstructed nostrils

SNOTTIE *n* midshipman

SNOTTY *adj* covered with mucus from the nose

SNOUT *n, vb* snouted, snouts, snouty

SNOW *n, vb*

SNOWCAP *n* cap of snow on top of a mountain

SNOWCAT *n* tracked vehicle for travelling over snow

SNOWED *adj* under the influence of narcotic drugs

SNOWIER ▸ snowy

SNOWILY ▸ snowy

SNOWING ▶ snow
SNOWISH adj like snow
SNOWK = snook
SNOWKED ▶ snowk
SNOWKS ▶ snowk
SNOWMAN n snowmen
SNOWS ▶ snow
SNOWY adj covered with or abounding in snow
SNUB vb, n, adj
SNUBBE n stub
SNUBBED ▶ snub
SNUBBER ▶ snub
SNUBBES ▶ snubbe
SNUBBY ▶ snub
SNUBFIN adj as in snubfin dolphin Australian dolphin with a small dorsal fin
SNUBS ▶ snub
SNUCK past tense and past participle of ▶ sneak
SNUDGE vb be miserly snudged, snudges
SNUFF n, vb snuffed, snuffer
SNUFFLE vb, n snuffly
SNUFFS ▶ snuff
SNUFFY adj of, relating to, or resembling snuff
SNUG adj, n, vb snugged, snugger
SNUGGLE vb, n
SNUGLY ▶ snug
SNUGS ▶ snug
SNUSH vb take snuff snushed, snushes
SNUZZLE vb root in ground
SNY = snye

A side channel of a river, that can be

useful when you are short of vowels. And note that it can be extended to form snye.

SNYE n side channel of a river snyes
SO adv, interj, n
SOAK vb, n
SOAKAGE n process or a period in which a permeable substance is soaked in a liquid
SOAKED, soaken, soaker, soakers, soaking, soaks ▶ soak
SOAP n, vb
SOAPBOX n crate used as a platform for speech-making ▶ vb deliver a speech from a soapbox
SOAPED ▶ soap
SOAPER n soap opera soapers
SOAPIE n soap opera
SOAPIER ▶ soapy
SOAPIES ▶ soapie
SOAPILY ▶ soapy
SOAPING ▶ soap
SOAPS ▶ soap
SOAPY adj covered with soap
SOAR vb, n
SOARE n young hawk
SOARED, soarer, soarers ▶ soar
SOARES ▶ soare
SOARING, soars ▶ soar
SOAVE n dry white Italian wine soaves
SOB vb, n
SOBA n (in Japanese cookery) noodles

made from buckwheat flour **sobas**
SOBBED, sobber, sobbers, sobbing ▶ sob
SOBEIT conj provided that
SOBER adj, vb sobered, soberer, soberly, sobers
SOBFUL adj tearful
SOBOLE n creeping underground stem that produces roots and buds **soboles**
SOBS ▶ sob
SOC n feudal right to hold court
SOCA n mixture of soul and calypso music
SOCAGE n tenure of land by certain services **socager, socages**
SOCAS ▶ soca
SOCCAGE = socage
SOCCER n soccers
SOCIAL adj, n socials
SOCIATE n associate
SOCIETY n
SOCK n, vb socked
SOCKET n, vb sockets
SOCKEYE n Pacific salmon with red flesh
SOCKING ▶ sock
SOCKMAN = socman
SOCKMEN ▶ sockman
SOCKO adj excellent
SOCKS ▶ sock
SOCLE another name for ▶ plinth
SOCLES ▶ socle
SOCMAN n tenant holding land by socage **socmen**

SOCS ▸ soc

SOD *n, vb*

SODA *n*

SODAIC *adj* containing soda

SODAIN = **sudden**

SODAINE = **sudden**

SODAS ▸ soda

SODDED ▸ sod

SODDEN *adj, vb* **soddens**

SODDIER ▸ soddy

SODDIES ▸ soddy

SODDING ▸ sod

SODDY *adj* covered with turf

SODGER *dialect variant of* ▸ **soldier**

SODGERS ▸ sodger

SODIC *adj* containing sodium

SODIUM *n* **sodiums**

SODOM *n* person who performs sodomy **sodoms**

SODOMY *n* anal intercourse

SODS ▸ sod

SOEVER *adv* in any way at all

SOFA *n*

SOFABED *n* sofa that converts into a bed

SOFAR *n* system for determining a position at sea **sofars**

SOFAS ▸ sofa

SOFFIT *n* underside of a part of a building or a structural component **soffits**

SOFT *adj, adv, vb*

SOFTA *n* Muslim student of divinity and jurisprudence **softas**

SOFTED ▸ soft

SOFTEN *vb* **softens**

SOFTER ▸ soft

SOFTEST ▸ soft

SOFTIE *n* person who is easily upset

SOFTIES ▸ softy

SOFTING ▸ soft

SOFTISH ▸ soft

SOFTLY ▸ soft

SOFTS ▸ soft

SOFTY = **softie**

SOG *vb* soak

SOGER = **sodger**

SOGERS ▸ soger

SOGGED ▸ sog

SOGGIER ▸ soggy

SOGGILY ▸ soggy

SOGGING ▸ sog

SOGGY *adj*

SOGS ▸ sog

SOH *n* (in tonic sol-fa) fifth degree of any major scale

SOHO *interj* exclamation announcing the sighting of a hare

SOHS ▸ soh

SOHUR ▸ suhur

SOHURS ▸ suhur

SOIGNE *adj* well-groomed, elegant **soignee**

SOIL *n, vb*

SOILAGE *n* green fodder

SOILED, soilier, soiling, soils ▸ soil

SOILURE *n* act of soiling or the state of being soiled

SOILY ▸ soil

SOIREE *n* **soirees**

SOJA = **soya**

SOJAS ▸ soja

SOJOURN *vb, n*

SOKAH = **soca**

SOKAHS ▸ sokah

SOKAIYA *n* Japanese extortionist

SOKE *n* right to hold a local court

SOKEMAN = **socman**

SOKEMEN ▸ sokeman

SOKEN *n* feudal district **sokens**

SOKES ▸ soke

SOKOL *n* Czech gymnastic association **sokols**

SOL *n* liquid colloidal solution

SOLA ▸ solum

SOLACE *vb, n* **solaced, solacer, solaces**

SOLAH *n* Indian plant **solahs**

SOLAN *archaic name for* ▸ **gannet**

SOLAND *n* solan goose **solands**

SOLANIN = **solanine**

SOLANO *n* hot wind in Spain **solanos**

SOLANS ▸ solan

SOLANUM *n* any plant of the genus that includes the potato

SOLAR *adj*

SOLARIA > **solarium**

SOLARS ▸ solum

SOLAS ▸ solum

SOLATE *vb* change from gel to liquid **solated, solates**

SOLATIA > **solatium**

SOLD n obsolete word for salary

SOLDADO n soldier

SOLDAN archaic word for ▸ sultan

SOLDANS ▸ soldan

SOLDE n wages

SOLDER n, vb solders

SOLDES ▸ solde

SOLDI ▸ soldo

SOLDIER n, vb

SOLDO n former Italian copper coin

SOLDS ▸ sold

SOLE adj, n, vb soled

SOLEI ▸ soleus

SOLEIN = sullen

SOLELY adv

SOLEMN adj

SOLER = sole

SOLERA n system for aging sherry and other fortified wines **soleras**

SOLERET n armour for foot

SOLERS ▸ soler

SOLES ▸ sole

SOLEUS n muscle in calf of leg

SOLFEGE variant of ▸ solfeggio

SOLGEL adj changing between sol and gel

SOLI adv to be performed by or with soloists

SOLICIT vb

SOLID adj, n solider

SOLIDI ▸ solidus

SOLIDLY ▸ solid

SOLIDS ▸ solid

SOLIDUM n part of pedestal

SOLIDUS = slash

SOLING ▸ sole

SOLION n amplifier used in chemistry **solions**

SOLIPED n animal whose hooves are not cloven

SOLITO adv musical instruction meaning play in usual manner

SOLITON n type of isolated particle-like wave

SOLIVE n type of joist **solives**

SOLLAR n archaic word meaning attic **sollars, soller**

SOLLERS ▸ soller

SOLO n, adj, adv, vb soloed, soloing

SOLOIST n

SOLON n US congressman **solons**

SOLOS ▸ solo

SOLS ▸ sol

SOLUBLE adj, n solubly

SOLUM n upper layers of the soil profile **solums**

SOLUNAR adj relating to sun and moon

SOLUS adj alone

SOLUTAL adj relating to a solute

SOLUTE n, adj solutes

SOLVATE vb undergo, cause to undergo, or partake in solvation

SOLVE vb solved

SOLVENT adj, n

SOLVER, solvers, solves, solving ▸ solve

SOM n currency of Kyrgyzstan and Uzbekistan

SOMA n body of an organism as distinct from the germ cells

SOMAN n compound developed as a nerve gas **somans**

SOMAS ▸ soma

SOMATA ▸ soma

SOMATIC adj of the body, as distinct from the mind

SOMBER adj (in the US) sombre ▹ vb (in the US) make sombre **sombers**

SOMBRE adj, vb sombred, sombrer, sombres

SOME adj, pron, adv, determiner

SOMEDAY adv at some unspecified time in the future

SOMEHOW adv

SOMEONE pron, n

SOMEWAY adv in some unspecified manner

SOMEWHY adv for some reason

SOMITAL ▸ somite

SOMITE n segment of mesoderm in vertebrate embryos somites, somitic

SOMNIAL adj of dreams

SOMONI n monetary unit of Tajikistan

SOMS ▸ som

SOMY ▸ som

SON n

SONANCE ▸ sonant

SONANCY ▶ sonant
SONANT n voiced sound able to form a syllable or syllable nucleus ▷ adj denoting a voiced sound like this **sonants**
SONAR n sonars
SONATA n sonatas
SONCE n Scots word meaning good luck **sonces**
SONDAGE n deep trial trench for inspecting stratigraphy
SONDE n rocket, balloon, or probe used for observing in the upper atmosphere
SONDELI n Indian shrew
SONDER n yacht category **sonders**
SONDES ▶ sonde
SONE n subjective unit of loudness
SONERI n Indian cloth of gold **soneris**
SONES ▶ sone
SONG n
SONGFUL adj tuneful
SONGKOK n (in Malaysia and Indonesia) a kind of oval brimless hat, resembling a skull
SONGMAN n singer **songmen**
SONGS ▶ song
SONHOOD ▶ son
SONIC adj
SONICS n study of mechanical vibrations in matter
SONLESS ▶ son

SONLIKE ▶ son
SONLY adj like a son
SONNE = son
SONNES ▶ sonne
SONNET n, vb sonnets
SONNIES ▶ sonny
SONNY n term of address to a boy
SONOVOX n device used to alter sound of human voice in music recordings
SONS ▶ son
SONSE = sonce
SONSES ▶ sonse
SONSHIP ▶ son
SONSIE = sonsy
SONSIER ▶ sonsy
SONSY adj plump
SONTAG n type of knitted women's cape **sontags**
SONTIES n Shakespearian oath
SOOEY interj call used to summon pigs
SOOGEE vb clean ship using a special solution **soogeed, soogees, soogie**
SOOGIED ▶ soogie
SOOGIES ▶ soogie
SOOJEY = soogee
SOOJEYS ▶ soojey
SOOK n baby ▷ vb suck **sooked, sooking, sooks**
SOOL vb incite (a dog) to attack **soole, sooled**
SOOLES ▶ soole
SOOLING ▶ sool
SOOLS ▶ sool
SOOM Scots word for

▶ swim
SOOMED ▶ soom
SOOMING ▶ soom
SOOMS ▶ soom
SOON adv
SOONER adv rather ▷ n idler or shirker **sooners**
SOONEST adv as soon as possible
SOOP Scots word for ▶ sweep
SOOPED ▶ soop
SOOPING ▶ soop
SOOPS ▶ soop
SOOT n, vb
SOOTE n sweet
SOOTED ▶ soot
SOOTES ▶ soot
SOOTH n truth or reality ▷ adj true or real
SOOTHE vb soothed
SOOTHER vb
SOOTHES ▶ soothe
SOOTHLY ▶ sooth
SOOTHS ▶ sooth
SOOTIER ▶ sooty
SOOTILY ▶ sooty
SOOTING ▶ soot
SOOTS ▶ soot
SOOTY adj covered with soot
SOP n, vb
SOPH shortened form of ▶ sophomore
SOPHIES ▶ sophy
SOPHISM n argument that seems reasonable but is actually false and misleading
SOPHIST n person who uses clever but invalid arguments
SOPHS ▶ soph

SOPHY n title of the Persian monarchs

SOPITE vb lull to sleep **sopited, sopites**

SOPOR n abnormally deep sleep **sopors**

SOPPED ▶ sop

SOPPIER ▶ soppy

SOPPILY ▶ soppy

SOPPING ▶ sop

SOPPY adj

SOPRA adv musical instruction meaning above

SOPRANI ▶ soprano

SOPRANO n, adj

SOPS ▶ sop

SORA n North American rail with a yellow bill

SORAGE n first year in hawk's life **sorages**

SORAL ▶ sorus

SORAS ▶ sora

SORB n any of various related trees, esp the mountain ash ▷ vb absorb or adsorb

SORBATE n salt of sorbic acid

SORBED ▶ sorb

SORBENT ▶ sorb

SORBET = sherbet

SORBETS ▶ sorbet

SORBIC ▶ sorb

SORBING ▶ sorb

SORBITE n mineral found in steel

SORBO n as in sorbo rubber spongy form of rubber

SORBOSE n sugar derived from the berries of the mountain ash

SORBS ▶ sorb

SORBUS n rowan or related tree

SORCERY n

SORD n flock of mallard ducks

SORDA n deaf woman

SORDES pl n dark incrustations on the lips and teeth of patients with prolonged fever

SORDID adj

SORDINE = sordino

SORDINI ▶ sordino

SORDINO n mute for a stringed or brass musical instrument

SORDO n deaf man

SORDOR n sordidness **sordors**

SORDS ▶ sord

SORE adj, n, adv, vb **sored**

SOREDIA > soredium

This is the plural of **soredium**, a reproductive body in lichens. It is a very frequently played bonus, and it has a 'twin' **roadies**. It is a good idea to become familiar with at least the higher probability twin sevens and eights, since the thought of one will often prompt the other, and it may well be that one twin will fit on the board where the other would not.

SOREE = sora

SOREES ▶ soree

SOREHON n old Irish feudal right

SOREL variant of ▶ sorrel

SORELL = sorel

SORELLS ▶ sorell

SORELS ▶ sorel

SORELY adv greatly

SORER ▶ sore

SORES ▶ sore

SOREST ▶ sore

SOREX n shrew or related animal **sorexes**

SORGHO = sorgo

SORGHOS ▶ sorgho

SORGHUM n

SORGO n any of several varieties of sorghum that have watery sweet juice **sorgos**

SORI ▶ sorus

SORING ▶ sore

SORINGS ▶ sore

SORITES n type of syllogism in which only the final conclusion is stated **soritic**

SORN vb obtain food, etc, from another person by presuming on his or her generosity **sorned, sorner**

SORNERS ▶ sore

SORNING ▶ sorn

SORNS ▶ sorn

SOROBAN n Japanese abacus

SOROCHE n altitude sickness

SORORAL adj of sister

SOROSES ▶ sorosis

SOROSIS n fleshy multiple fruit

SORRA Irish word for ▶ sorrow

SORRAS ▶ sorra

SORREL n sorrels

SORRIER ▶ sorry

SORRILY ▶ sorry

SORROW n, vb sorrows

SORRY adj, interj

SORT n, vb

SORTA adv phonetic representation of 'sort of'

SORTAL n type of logical or linguistic concept sortals

SORTED interj exclamation of satisfaction, approval, etc ▷ adj possessing the desired recreational drugs

SORTER ▶ sort

SORTERS ▶ sort

SORTES n divination by opening book at random

SORTIE n, vb sortied, sorties

SORTING ▶ sort

SORTS ▶ sort

SORUS n cluster of sporangia on the undersurface of certain fern leaves

SOS ▶ so

SOSATIE n skewer of curried meat pieces

SOSS vb make dirty or muddy sossed, sosses, sossing

SOT n habitual drunkard ▷ adv indeed: used to contradict a negative statement ▷ vb be a drunkard

SOTH archaic variant of ▶ sooth

SOTHS ▶ soth

SOTOL n American plant related to agave sotols

SOTS, sotted, sotting, sottish ▶ sot

SOU n former French coin

SOUARI n tree of tropical America souaris

SOUBISE n purée of onions mixed into a thick white sauce and served over eggs, fish, etc

SOUCAR n Indian banker soucars

SOUCE = souse; souced, souces, soucing, souct

SOUDAN obsolete variant of ▶ sultan

SOUDANS ▶ soudan

SOUFFLE n light fluffy dish made with beaten egg whites ▷ adj made light and puffy

SOUGH vb (of the wind) make a sighing sound ▷ n soft continuous murmuring sound soughed, soughs

SOUGHT ▶ seek

SOUK = sook

SOUKED ▶ souk

SOUKING ▶ souk

SOUKOUS n style of African popular music

SOUKS ▶ souk

SOUL n

SOULDAN = soldan

SOULED adj having soul

SOULFUL adj

SOULS ▶ soul

SOUM vb decide how many animals can graze particular pasture soumed, souming, soums

SOUND n something heard, noise ▷ vb make or cause to make a sound ▷ adj in good condition ▷ adv soundly sounded

SOUNDER n device formerly used to convert electric signals into sounds

SOUNDLY ▶ sound

SOUNDS ▶ sound

SOUP n, vb

SOUPCON n small amount

SOUPED ▶ soup

SOUPER n person dispensing soup soupers

SOUPFIN n Pacific requiem shark valued for its fins

SOUPIER ▶ soupy

SOUPING ▶ soup

SOUPLE = supple

SOUPLED ▶ souple

SOUPLES ▶ souple

SOUPS ▶ soup

SOUPY adj having the appearance or consistency of soup
SOUR adj, vb
SOURCE n, vb sourced, sources
SOURED, sourer, sourest, souring, sourish, sourly ▶ sour
SOUROCK n Scots word for sorrel plant
SOURS ▶ sour
SOURSE ▶ source
SOURSES ▶ sourse
SOURSOP n small West Indian tree
SOUS ▶ sou
SOUSE vb, n soused, souses, sousing
SOUSLIK = suslik
SOUT = soot
SOUTANE n Roman Catholic priest's cassock
SOUTAR = souter
SOUTARS ▶ soutar
SOUTER n shoemaker or cobbler **souters**
SOUTH n, adj, adv, vb southed
SOUTHER n strong wind or storm from the south ▷ vb turn south
SOUTHS ▶ south
SOUTS ▶ sout
SOV shortening of ▶ sovereign
SOVIET n formerly, elected council in the USSR ▷ adj of the former USSR **soviets**
SOVKHOZ n large mechanized farm in former USSR

SOVRAN literary word for ▶ sovereign
SOVRANS ▶ sovran
SOVS ▶ sov
SOW vb, n sowable
SOWANS = sowens
SOWAR n Indian cavalryman
SOWARRY = sowarree
SOWARS ▶ sowar
SOWBACK another name for ▶ hogback
SOWCAR ▶ soucar
SOWCARS ▶ sowcar
SOWCE ▶ souse
SOWCED ▶ sowce
SOWCES ▶ sowce
SOWCING ▶ sowce
SOWDER ▶ sawder n
SOWDERS ▶ sowder
SOWED ▶ sow
SOWENS n pudding made from oatmeal husks steeped and boiled
SOWER ▶ sow
SOWERS ▶ sow
SOWF = sowth
SOWFED ▶ sowf
SOWFF = sowth
SOWFFED ▶ sowff
SOWFFS ▶ sowff
SOWFING ▶ sowf
SOWFS ▶ sowf
SOWING ▶ sow
SOWINGS ▶ sow
SOWL ▶ sole
SOWLE ▶ sole
SOWLED ▶ sowl
SOWLES ▶ sowle
SOWLING ▶ sowl
SOWLS ▶ sowl
SOWM ▶ soum
SOWMED ▶ sowm

SOWMING ▶ sowm
SOWMS ▶ sowm
SOWN ▶ sow
SOWND vb wield sownded, sownds
SOWNE = sound
SOWNES ▶ sowne
SOWP n spoonful **sowps**
SOWS ▶ sow
SOWSE ▶ souse
SOWSED ▶ sowse
SOWSES ▶ sowse
SOWSING ▶ sowse
SOWSSE ▶ souse
SOWSSED ▶ sowsse
SOWSSES ▶ sowsse
SOWTER ▶ souter
SOWTERS ▶ sowter
SOWTH vb Scots word meaning whistle sowthed, sowths
SOX pl n informal spelling of 'socks'
This informal word for **socks** is one of the key short words to remember for using the X.
SOY as in soy sauce salty dark brown sauce made from soya beans
SOYA n soyas
SOYBEAN n soya bean
SOYLE n body soyles
SOYMILK n milk substitute made from soya
SOYS ▶ soy
SOYUZ n Russian spacecraft soyuzes
SOZ interj
SOZIN n form of protein sozine

SOZINES ▸ sozine
SOZINS ▸ sozin
SOZZLE vb make wet
SOZZLED adj drunk
SOZZLES ▸ sozzle
SOZZLY adj wet
SPA n, vb
SPACE n, vb **spaced**
SPACER n piece of material used to create or maintain a space between two things **spacers**
SPACES ▸ space
SPACEY adj vague and dreamy, as if under the influence of drugs
SPACIAL = spatial
SPACIER ▸ spacey
SPACING n arrangement of letters, words, etc. on a page in order to achieve legibility
SPACKLE vb fill holes in plaster
SPACY = spacey
SPADE n **spaded, spader, spaders, spades**
SPADGER n sparrow
SPADING ▸ spade
SPADIX n spike of small flowers on a fleshy stem
SPADO n neutered animal **spadoes, spados**
SPAE vb foretell (the future) **spaed, spaeing**
SPAEMAN n man who foretells future **spaemen**
SPAER ▸ spae

SPAERS ▸ spae
SPAES ▸ spae
SPAG vb (of a cat) to scratch (a person) with the claws ▷ n Australian offensive slang for an Italian **spagged, spags**
SPAHEE = spahi
SPAHEES ▸ spahee
SPAHI n (formerly) an irregular cavalryman in the Turkish armed forces **spahis**
SPAIL Scots word for **▸ spall**
SPAILS ▸ spail
SPAIN variant of **▸ spane**
SPAINED ▸ spain
SPAING ▸ spa
SPAINGS ▸ spa
SPAINS ▸ spain
SPAIRGE Scots word for **▸ sparge**
SPAIT ▸ spate
SPAITS ▸ spait
SPAKE past tense of **▸ speak**
SPALD = spauld
SPALDS ▸ spald
SPALE Scots word for **▸ spall**
SPALES ▸ spale
SPALL n splinter or chip of ore, rock, or stone ▷ vb split or cause to split into such fragments
SPALLE = spauld
SPALLED ▸ spall
SPALLER ▸ spall
SPALLES ▸ spalle
SPALLS ▸ spall

SPALT vb split **spalted, spalts**
SPAM vb, n
SPAMBOT n computer program that sends spam
SPAMMED ▸ spam
SPAMMER ▸ spam
SPAMMIE n love bite
SPAMMY adj bland
SPAMS ▸ spam
SPAN n, vb
SPANCEL n length of rope for hobbling an animal ▷ vb hobble (an animal) with a loose rope
SPANDEX n type of synthetic stretch fabric made from polyurethane fibre
SPANE vb Scots word meaning wean **spaned, spanes**
SPANG adv exactly, firmly, or straight ▷ vb dash **spanged**
SPANGLE n, vb **spangly**
SPANGS ▸ spang
SPANIEL n
SPANING ▸ spane
SPANK vb, n **spanked**
SPANKER n fore-and-aft sail or a mast that is aftermost in a sailing vessel
SPANKS ▸ spank
SPANNED ▸ span
SPANNER n
SPANS ▸ span
SPAR n, vb
SPARD ▸ spare
SPARE adj, n, vb **spared, sparely, sparer,**

sparers, spares, sparest

SPARGE vb sprinkle or scatter (something) **sparged, sparger, sparges**

SPARID n type of marine percoid fish ▷ adj of or belonging to this family of fish **sparids**

SPARING adj

SPARK n, vb

SPARKE n weapon

SPARKED ▶ spark

SPARKER ▶ spark

SPARKES ▶ sparke

SPARKIE n electrician

SPARKLE vb, n

SPARKLY adj sparkling ▷ n sparkling thing

SPARKS n electrician

SPARKY adj lively

SPAROID = sparid

SPARRE = spar

SPARRED ▶ spar

SPARRER ▶ spar

SPARRES ▶ sparre

SPARROW n

SPARRY adj (of minerals) containing, relating to, or resembling spar

SPARS ▶ spar

SPARSE adj **sparser**

SPART n esparto

SPARTAN adj, n

SPARTH n type of battle-axe **sparthe, sparths**

SPARTS ▶ spart

SPAS ▶ spa

SPASM n, vb **spasmed, spasmic, spasms**

SPAT vb have a quarrel

SPATE n **spates**

SPATHAL ▶ spathe

SPATHE n large sheathlike leaf enclosing a flower cluster **spathed, spathes**

SPATHIC adj (of minerals) resembling spar

SPATIAL adj

SPATS ▶ spat

SPATTED ▶ spat

SPATTEE n type of gaiter

SPATTER vb, n

SPATULA n

SPATULE n spatula

SPATZLE = spaetzle

SPAUL = spauld

SPAULD n shoulder **spaulds**

SPAULS ▶ spaul

SPAVIE Scots variant of ▶ spavin

SPAVIES ▶ spavie

SPAVIET adj Scots word meaning spavined

SPAVIN n enlargement of the hock of a horse by a bony growth **spavins**

SPAW = spa

SPAWL vb spit **spawled, spawls**

SPAWN n, vb **spawned, spawner, spawns**

SPAWNY adj like spawn

SPAWS ▶ spaw

SPAY vb

SPAYAD n male deer **spayads, spayd**

SPAYDS ▶ spayd

SPAYED ▶ spay

SPAYING ▶ spay

SPAYS ▶ spay

SPAZA adj as in **spaza shop** South African slang for a small shop in a township

SPEAK vb

SPEAKER n

SPEAKS ▶ speak

SPEAL = spule

SPEALS ▶ speal

SPEAN = spane

SPEANED ▶ spean

SPEANS ▶ spean

SPEAR n, vb **speared, spearer, spears, speary**

SPEAT = spate

SPEATS ▶ speat

SPEC vb specced

SPECCY n person wearing spectacles

SPECIAL adj, n, vb

SPECIE n coins as distinct from paper money

SPECIES n

SPECIFY vb

SPECK n, vb specked

SPECKLE n, vb

SPECKS ▶ speck

SPECKY = speccy

SPECS pl n spectacles

SPECTER = spectre

SPECTRA ▷ spectrum

SPECTRE n

SPECULA > speculum

SPED ▶ speed

SPEECH n, vb

SPEED n, vb **speeded, speeder**

SPEEDO n speedometer **speedos**

SPEEDS ▶ speed

SPEEDUP n acceleration

SPEEDY adj

SPEEL n splinter of wood ▷ vb Scots meaning climb **speeled, speeler, speels**

SPEER = **speir**

SPEERED ▶ **speer**

SPEERS ▶ **speer**

SPEIL dialect word for ▶ **climb**

SPEILED ▶ **speil**

SPEILS ▶ **speil**

SPEIR vb ask **speired, speirs**

SPEISE = **speiss**

SPEISES ▶ **speise**

SPEISS n compounds formed from ores containing arsenic or antimony are smelted

SPEK n bacon, fat, or fatty pork used for larding venison or other game **speks**

SPELD vb Scots word meaning spread **spelded, spelder**

SPELDIN n fish split and dried

SPELDS ▶ **speld**

SPELEAN = **spelaean**

SPELK n splinter of wood **spelks**

SPELL vb, n **spelled**

SPELLER n person who spells words in the manner specified

SPELLS ▶ **spell**

SPELT ▶ **spell**

SPELTER n impure zinc, usually containing about 3 per cent of

lead and other impurities

SPELTS ▶ **spell**

SPELTZ n wheat variety

SPELUNK vb explore caves

SPENCE n larder or pantry

SPENCER n short fitted coat or jacket

SPENCES ▶ **spence**

SPEND vb

SPENDER n person who spends money in a manner specified

SPENDS ▶ **spend**

SPENDY adj expensive

SPENSE = **spence**

SPENSES ▶ **spense**

SPENT ▶ **spend**

SPEOS n (esp in ancient Egypt) a temple or tomb cut into a rock face **speoses**

SPERM n

SPERMIC = **spermatic**

SPERMS ▶ **sperm**

SPERRE vb bolt **sperred, sperres**

SPERSE vb disperse **spersed, sperses, sperst**

SPERTHE = **sparth**

SPET = **spit**

SPETCH n piece of animal skin

SPETS ▶ **spet**

SPEUG n sparrow **speugs**

SPEW vb, n **spewed, spewer, spewers**

SPEWIER ▶ **spewy**

SPEWING ▶ **spew**

SPEWS ▶ **spew**

SPEWY adj marshy

SPHAER = **sphere**

SPHAERE = **sphere**

SPHAERS ▶ **sphaere**

SPHEAR = **sphere**

SPHEARE = **sphere**

SPHEARS ▶ **sphear**

SPHENE n brown, yellow, green, or grey lustrous mineral **sphenes**

SPHENIC adj having the shape of a wedge

SPHERAL adj of or shaped like a sphere

SPHERE n, vb **sphered, spheres**

SPHERIC = **spherical**

SPHERY adj resembling a sphere

SPHINX n

SPHYNX n breed of cat

SPIAL n observation **spials**

SPICA n spiral bandage formed by a series of overlapping figure-of-eight turns **spicae, spicas**

SPICATE adj having, arranged in, or relating to spikes

SPICE n, vb **spiced, spicer, spicers**

SPICERY n spices collectively

SPICES ▶ **spice**

SPICEY = **spicy**

SPICIER ▶ **spicy**

SPICILY ▶ **spicy**

SPICING ▶ **spice**

SPICULA > **spiculum**

SPICULE n small slender pointed structure or crystal

SPICY adj

SPIDER n spiders

SPIDERY adj

SPIE = spy

SPIED ▶ spy

SPIEGEL n manganese-rich pig iron

SPIEL n speech made to persuade someone to do something ▷ vb deliver a prepared spiel **spieled, spieler, spiels**

SPIER variant of ▶ speir

SPIERED ▶ spier

SPIERS ▶ spier

SPIES ▶ spy

SPIF n postage stamp perforated with the initials of a firm to avoid theft by employees

SPIFF vb make smart **spiffed, spiffs**

SPIFFY adj smart ▷ n smart thing or person ▷ vb smarten

SPIFS ▶ spif

SPIGHT = spite

SPIGHTS ▶ spight

SPIGNEL n European umbelliferous plant

SPIGOT n stopper for, or tap fitted to, a cask **spigots**

SPIKE n, vb spiked, spiker, spikes

SPIKERY n High-Church Anglicanism

SPIKES ▶ spike

SPIKEY = spiky

SPIKIER ▶ spiky

SPIKILY ▶ spiky

SPIKING ▶ spike

SPIKY adj

SPILE n heavy timber stake or pile ▷ vb provide or support with a spile **spiled, spiles, spiling**

SPILITE n type of igneous rock

SPILL vb, n spilled, spiller, spills, spilt

SPILTH n something spilled **spilths**

SPIM n unsolicited communications received via an instant-messaging system **spims**

SPIN vb, n

SPINA n spine

SPINACH n

SPINAE ▶ spina

SPINAGE = spinach

SPINAL adj, n spinals

SPINAR n fast-spinning star **spinars**

SPINAS ▶ spina

SPINATE adj having a spine

SPINDLE n, vb

SPINDLY adj

SPINE n spined

SPINEL n any of a group of hard glassy minerals of variable colour **spinels**

SPINES ▶ spine

SPINET n spinets

SPINIER ▶ spiny

SPINK n finch spinks

SPINNER n bowler who makes the ball change direction when it bounces

SPINNET = spinet

SPINNEY n spinny

SPINODE another name for ▶ cusp

SPINOFF n development derived incidentally from an existing enterprise

SPINONE n as in Italian spinone wiry-coated gun dog **spinoni**

SPINOR n type of mathematical object **spinors**

SPINOSE adj (esp of plants) bearing many spines

SPINOUS adj resembling a spine or thorn

SPINOUT n spinning skid that causes a car to run off the road

SPINS ▶ spin

SPINTO n lyrical singing voice **spintos**

SPINULA n small spine

SPINULE n very small spine, thorn, or prickle

SPINY adj

SPIRAEA n plant with small white or pink flowers

SPIRAL n, vb, adj spirals

SPIRANT n fricative consonant

SPIRE n, vb

SPIREA = spiraea

SPIREAS ▶ spirea

SPIRED ▶ spire

SPIREM = spireme

SPIREME n tangled mass of chromatin threads

SPIREMS ▸ spirem
SPIRES ▸ spire
SPIRIC n type of curve spirics
SPIRIER ▸ spire
SPIRING ▸ spire
SPIRIT n, vb spirits
SPIRITY adj spirited
SPIROID adj resembling a spiral or displaying a spiral form
SPIRT ▸ spurt
SPIRTED ▸ spirt
SPIRTLE = spurtle
SPIRTS ▸ spirt
SPIRULA n tropical cephalopod mollusc
SPIRY ▸ spire
SPIT vb, n
SPITAL n hospital, esp for the needy sick spitals
SPITE n, vb spited, spites, spiting
SPITS, spitted, spitten, spitter ▸ spit
SPITTLE n
SPITZ n stockily built dog with a tightly curled tail spitzes
SPIV n smartly dressed man who makes a living by shady dealings spivs, spivvy
SPLAKE n type of hybrid trout bred by Canadian zoologists splakes
SPLASH vb, n
SPLASHY adj having irregular marks
SPLAT n wet slapping sound ▷ vb make wet slapping sound

SPLATCH vb splash
SPLATS ▸ splat
SPLAY vb, adj, n splayed, splays
SPLEEN n spleens, spleeny
SPLENIA > splenium
SPLENIC adj of, relating to, or in the spleen
SPLENII > splenius
SPLENT = splint
SPLENTS ▸ splent
SPLICE vb spliced, splicer, splices
SPLIFF n cannabis, used as a drug spliffs
SPLINE n type of narrow key around a shaft that fits into a corresponding groove ▷ vb provide (a shaft, part, etc) with splines splined, splines
SPLINT n, vb splints
SPLISH vb splash
SPLIT vb, n splits
SPLODGE n, vb splodgy
SPLOG n spam blog splogs
SPLOOSH vb splash or cause to splash about uncontrollably ▷ n instance or sound of splooshing
SPLORE n revel splores
SPLOSH vb scatter (liquid) vigorously about in blobs ▷ n instance or sound of sploshing
SPLOTCH vb splash, daub
SPLURGE vb, n splurgy
SPOD adj boring,

unattractive, or overstudious spoddy
SPODE n type of English china or porcelain spodes
SPODIUM n black powder
SPODS ▸ spod
SPOFFY = spoffish
SPOIL vb spoiled
SPOILER n device on an aircraft or car to increase drag
SPOILS ▸ spoil
SPOILT ▸ spoil
SPOKE n radial member of a wheel ▷ vb equip with spokes spoked
SPOKEN ▸ speak
SPOKES ▸ spoke
SPOKING ▸ spoke
SPONDEE n metrical foot of two long syllables
SPONDYL n vertebra
SPONGE n, vb sponged
SPONGER n person who sponges on others
SPONGES ▸ sponge
SPONGIN n fibrous horny protein in sponges
SPONGY adj
SPONSAL n marriage
SPONSON n outboard support for a gun enabling it to fire fore and aft
SPONSOR n, vb
SPOOF n, vb spoofed, spoofer, spoofs, spoofy
SPOOK n, vb spooked, spooks

SPOOKY adj

SPOOL n, vb spooled, spooler, spools

SPOOM vb sail fast before wind spoomed, spooms

SPOON n, vb spooned

SPOONEY = spoony

SPOONS ▶ spoon

SPOONY adj foolishly or stupidly amorous ▷ n fool or silly person, esp one in love

SPOOR n, vb spoored, spoorer, spoors

SPOOT n razor shell spoots

SPORAL ▶ spore

SPORE n, vb spored, spores, sporing

SPORK n spoon-shaped piece of cutlery with tines like a fork sporks

SPOROID adj of or like a spore

SPORRAN n

SPORT n, vb sported, sporter

SPORTIF adj sporty

SPORTS adj of or used in sports ▷ n meeting held at a school or college for competitions in athletic events

SPORTY adj, n

SPORULE n spore, esp a very small spore

SPOSH n slush sposhes, sposhy

SPOT n; vb

SPOTLIT ▶ spotlight

SPOTS ▶ spot

SPOTTED ▶ spot

SPOTTER n

SPOTTIE n young deer of up to three months of age

SPOTTY adj

SPOUSAL n marriage ceremony ▷ adj of or relating to marriage

SPOUSE n, vb spoused, spouses

SPOUT vb, n spouted, spouter, spouts, spouty

SPRACK adj vigorous

SPRAD ▶ spread

SPRAG n device used to prevent a vehicle from running backwards on an incline ▷ vb use sprag to prevent vehicle from moving sprags

SPRAID vb chapped

SPRAIN vb, n sprains

SPRAINT n piece of otter's dung

SPRANG n branch sprangs

SPRAT n sprats

SPRAWL vb, n sprawls, sprawly

SPRAY n, vb sprayed, sprayer, sprayey, sprays

SPREAD vb, n, adj spreads

SPREAGH n cattle raid

SPREAZE = spreathe

SPRED = spread

SPREDD = spread

SPREDDE = spread

SPREDDS ▶ spredd

SPREDS ▶ spred

SPREE n, vb speed, sprees

SPREEZE = spreathe

SPRENT > sprinkle

SPREW = sprue

SPREWS ▶ sprew

SPRIER ▶ spry

SPRIEST ▶ spry

SPRIG n, vb spriggy

SPRIGHT = sprite

SPRIGS ▶ sprig

SPRING vb, n

SPRINGE n type of snare for catching small wild animals or birds ▷ vb set such a snare

SPRINGS ▶ spring

SPRINGY adj

SPRINT n, vb sprints

SPRIT n small spar set diagonally across a sail to extend it

SPRITE n sprites

SPRITS ▶ sprit

SPRITZ vb spray liquid

SPROD n young salmon sprods

SPROG n child sprogs

SPRONG ▶ spring

SPROUT vb, n sprouts

SPRUCE n, adj spruced, sprucer, spruces, sprucy

SPRUE n vertical channel in a mould sprues

SPRUG n sparrow sprugs

SPRUIK vb speak in public (used esp of a showman or salesman) spruiks

SPRUIT n small tributary stream or

watercourse **sprults**
SPRUNG ▸ spring
SPRUSH Scots form of
▸ spruce
SPRY adj **spryer,
spryest, spryly**
SPUD n, vb **spudded,
spudder**
SPUDDLE n feeble
movement
SPUDDY adj short and
fat
SPUDS ▸ spud
SPUE = spew; **spued,
spueing, spuer,
spuers, spues**
SPUG = spuggy
SPUGGY n house
sparrow
SPUGS ▸ spug
SPUING ▸ spue
SPULE Scots word for
▸ shoulder
SPULES ▸ spule
SPULYE = spuilzie
SPULYED ▸ spulye
SPULYES ▸ spulye
SPULYIE = spuilzie
SPULZIE = spuilzie
SPUME vb, n **spumed,
spumes**
SPUMIER ▸ spumy
SPUMING ▸ spume
SPUMONE n creamy
Italian ice cream
spumoni
SPUMOUS ▸ spume
SPUMY ▸ spume
SPUN ▸ spin
SPUNGE = sponge
SPUNGES ▸ spunge
SPUNK n, vb **spunked**
SPUNKIE n
will-o'-the-wisp

SPUNKS ▸ spunk
SPUNKY ▸ spunk
SPUR n, vb
SPURGE n plant with
milky sap **spurges**
SPURIAE n type of bird
feathers
SPURN vb, n
SPURNE vb spur
SPURNED ▸ spurn
SPURNER ▸ spurn
SPURNES ▸ spurne
SPURNS ▸ spurn
SPURRED ▸ spur
SPURRER ▸ spur
SPURREY n any of
several low-growing
European plants
SPURRY n spurrey ▷ adj
resembling a spur
SPURS ▸ spur
SPURT vb, n **spurted,
spurter**
SPURTLE n wooden
spoon for stirring
porridge
SPURTS ▸ spurt
SPURWAY n path used
by riders
SPUTA ▸ sputum
SPUTNIK n
SPUTTER n, vb
SPUTUM n
SPY n, vb
SPYAL n spy **spyals**
SPYCAM n camera used
for covert surveillance
spycams
SPYHOLE n small hole in
a door, etc through
which one may watch
secretly
SPYING ▸ spy
SPYINGS ▸ spy

SPYRE = spire
SPYRES ▸ spyre
SPYWARE n software
used to gain
information about a
computer user
SQUAB n young bird yet
to leave the nest ▷ adj
(of birds) recently
hatched and still
unfledged ▷ vb fall
squabby, **squabs**
SQUACCO n S European
heron
SQUAD n, vb
SQUADDY = squaddie
SQUADS ▸ squad
SQUAIL vb throw sticks
at squails
SQUALID adj
SQUALL n, vb **squalls,
squally**
SQUALOR n
SQUAMA n scale or
scalelike structure
squamae, **squame**
SQUAMES ▸ squame
SQUARE n, adj, vb, adv
**squared, squarer,
squares**
SQUARK n hypothetical
boson partner of a
quark **squarks**
SQUASH vb, n
SQUASHY adj
SQUAT vb, n, adj
squatly, squats
SQUATTY adj short and
broad
SQUAWK n, vb
squawks, squawky
SQUEAK n, vb **squeaks,
squeaky**
SQUEAL n, vb **squeals**

SQUEEZE *vb, n* **squeezy**

SQUEG *vb* oscillate **squegs**

SQUELCH *vb, n*

SQUIB *n* **squibs**

SQUID *n, vb*

SQUIDGE *vb* squash

SQUIDGY *adj* soft, moist, and squashy

SQUIDS ▸ squid

SQUIER = squire

SQUIERS ▸ squier

SQUIFF = squiffy

SQUIFFY *adj* slightly drunk

SQUILL *n* Mediterranean plant of the lily family

SQUILLA *n* type of mantis shrimp

SQUILLS ▸ squill

SQUINCH *n* small arch across an internal corner of a tower ▸ *vb* squeeze

SQUINNY *vb* squint ▸ *adj* squint

SQUINT *vb, n, adj* **squints, squinty**

SQUINY = squinny

SQUIRE *n, vb* **squired, squires**

SQUIRM *vb, n* **squirms**

SQUIRMY *adj* moving with a wriggling motion

SQUIRR = skirr

SQUIRRS ▸ squirr

SQUIRT *vb, n* **squirts**

SQUISH *n* a soft squelching sound ▸ *vb* crush (something) with a soft squelching sound

SQUISHY *adj* soft and yielding to the touch

SQUIT *n* insignificant person

SQUITCH *n* couch grass

SQUITS ▸ squit

SQUIZ *n* look or glance, esp an inquisitive one
The word *quiz* comes up surprisingly often, so it is useful to remember that you can put an S on the front of it to form this Australian slang word for a quick look.

SQUOOSH *vb* squash **squush**

SRADDHA *n* Hindu offering to ancestor

SRADHA = sradha

SRADHAS ▸ sradha

SRI *n* title of respect used when addressing a Hindu **sris**

ST *interj* exclamation to attract attention

STAB *vb, n* **stabbed, stabber**

STABILE *n* stationary abstract construction, usually of wire, metal, wood, etc ▸ *adj* fixed

STABLE *n, vb, adj* **stabled**

STABLER *n* stable owner

STABLES ▸ stable

STABLY ▸ stable

STABS ▸ stab

STACHYS *n* type of plant of the genus which includes lamb's ears and betony

STACK *n, vb* **stacked, stacker**

STACKET *n* fence of wooden posts

STACKS ▸ stack

STACKUP *n* number of aircraft waiting to land

STACTE *n* one of several sweet-smelling spices used in incense **stactes**

STADDA *n* type of saw **staddas**

STADDLE *n* type of support or prop

STADE = stadium

STADES ▸ stade

STADIA *n* instrument used in surveying

STADIAL *n* stage in development of glacier

STADIAS ▸ stadia

STADIUM *n*

STAFF *n, vb* **staffed**

STAFFER *n* member of staff, esp, in journalism, of editorial staff

STAFFS ▸ staff

STAG *n, adv, vb*

STAGE *n, vb* **staged**

STAGER *n* person of experience **stagers**

STAGERY *n* theatrical effects or techniques

STAGES ▸ stage

STAGEY = stagy

STAGGED ▸ stag

STAGGER *vb, n*

STAGGIE *n* little stag

STAGGY ▸ stag

STAGIER ▸ stagy

STAGILY ▶ stagy
STAGING n temporary support used in building
STAGS ▶ stag
STAGY adj too theatrical or dramatic
STAID adj staider, staidly
STAIG Scots variant of ▶ stag
STAIGS ▶ staig
STAIN vb, n stained, stainer, stains
STAIR n
STAIRED adj having stairs
STAIRS pl n flight of steps between floors, usu indoors
STAITH = staithe
STAITHE n wharf
STAITHS ▶ staith
STAKE n, vb staked, stakes, staking
STALAG n German prisoner-of-war camp stalags
STALE adj, vb, n staled, stalely, staler, stales, stalest, staling
STALK n, vb stalked, stalker
STALKO n idle gentleman
STALKS ▶ stalk
STALKY adj like a stalk
STALL n, vb stalled, stalls
STAMEN n stamens
STAMINA n
STAMMEL n coarse woollen cloth in former use for

undergarments
STAMMER vb, n
STAMNOI ▶ stamnos
STAMNOS n ancient Greek jar
STAMP n, vb stamped, stamper, stamps
STANCE n stances
STANCH vb stem the flow of (a liquid, esp blood) ▷ adj loyal and dependable
STANCK adj faint
STAND vb, n
STANDBY n person or thing that is ready for use
STANDEE n person who stands
STANDEN ▶ stand
STANDER ▶ stand
STANDS ▶ stand
STANDUP n comedian who performs solo
STANE Scot word for ▶ stone
STANED ▶ stane
STANES ▶ stane
STANG vb sting stanged, stangs
STANIEL n kestrel
STANINE n scale of nine levels
STANING ▶ stane
STANK vb dam
STANKED ▶ stink
STANKS ▶ stink
STANNEL = staniel
STANNIC adj of or containing tin, esp in the tetravalent state
STANNUM n tin (the metal)
STANOL n drug taken to

prevent heart disease stanols
STANYEL = staniel
STANZA n stanzas
STANZE = stanza
STANZES ▶ stanze
STANZO = stanza
STANZOS ▶ stanzo
STAP = stop
STAPES n stirrup-shaped bone in the middle ear of mammals
STAPH n staphylococcus staphs
STAPLE n, vb, adj stapled
STAPLER n
STAPLES ▶ staple
STAPPED ▶ stap
STAPPLE = stopple
STAPS ▶ stap
STAR n, vb, adj
STARCH n, vb, adj
STARCHY adj containing starch
STARDOM n status of a star in the entertainment or sports world
STARE vb, n stared, starer, starers, stares
STARETS n Russian holy man
STARETZ = staretz
STARING ▶ stare
STARK adj, adv, vb starked
STARKEN vb become or make stark
STARKER ▶ stark
STARKLY ▶ stark
STARKS ▶ stark

STARLET n young actress presented as a future star

STARLIT = starlight

STARN = stern

STARNED ▶ starn

STARNIE n Scots word for little star

STARNS ▶ starn

STARR n (in Judaism) release from a debt

STARRED ▶ star

STARRS ▶ starr

STARRY adj

STARS ▶ star

START vb take the first step, begin ▶ n first part of something **started**

STARTER n

STARTLE vb

STARTLY = startlish

STARTS ▶ start

STARTSY ▶ starets

STARTUP n business enterprise that has been launched recently

STARVE vb starved, starver, starves

STASES ▶ stasis

STASH vb, n stashed, stashes

STASHIE = stushie

STASIMA > stasimon

STASIS n stagnation in the normal flow of bodily fluids

STAT n statistic

STATAL adj of a federal state

STATANT adj (of an animal) in profile with all four feet on the ground

STATE n, adj, vb

STATED adj (esp of a sum) determined by agreement

STATELY adj, adv

STATER n any of various usually silver coins of ancient Greece **staters**

STATES ▶ state

STATIC adj, n

STATICE n plant name formerly used for both thrift and sea lavender

STATICS n study of the forces producing a state of equilibrium

STATIM adv right away

STATIN n type of drug that lowers the levels of low-density lipoproteins in the blood

STATING ▶ state

STATINS ▶ statin

STATION n, vb

STATISM n theory or practice of concentrating economic and political power in the state

STATIST n advocate of statism ▶ adj of, characteristic of, advocating, or relating to statism

STATIVE adj denoting a verb describing a state rather than an activity, act, or event ▶ n stative verb

STATOR n stationary part of a rotary machine or device **stators**

STATS ▶ stat

STATTO n person preoccupied with the facts and figures of a subject **stattos**

STATUA = statue

STATUAS ▶ statua

STATUE n

STATUED adj decorated with or portrayed in a statue or statues

STATUES ▶ statue

STATURE n

STATUS n

STATUSY adj conferring or having status

STATUTE n

STAUN Scot word for ▶ stand

STAUNCH = stanch

STAUNS ▶ staun

STAVE = staff

STAVED ▶ stave

STAVES ▶ stave

STAVING ▶ stave

STAW Scots form of ▶ stall

STAWED ▶ staw

STAWING ▶ staw

STAWS ▶ staw

STAY vb, n stayed

STAYER n person or thing that stays **stayers**

STAYING ▶ stay

STAYNE ▶ stain

STAYNED ▶ stayne

STAYNES ▶ stayne

STAYRE ▶ stair

STAYRES ▶ stayre

STAYS pl n old-fashioned corsets with bones in them

STEAD n, vb steaded, steads

STEADY adj, vb, adv
STEAK n steaks
STEAL vb
STEALE n handle
STEALED ▸ steal
STEALER n person who steals something
STEALES = steale
STEALS ▸ steal
STEALT ▸ steal
STEALTH n, adj, vb
STEAM n, vb steamed
STEAMER n, vb
STEAMIE n public wash house
STEAMS ▸ steam
STEAMY adj full of steam
STEAN n earthenware vessel
STEANE = steen
STEANED ▸ steane
STEANES ▸ steane
STEANS ▸ stean
STEAR = steer
STEARD ▸ stear
STEARE = steer
STEARED ▸ steare
STEARES ▸ steare
STEARIC adj of or relating to suet or fat
STEARIN n colourless crystalline ester of glycerol and stearic acid
STEARS ▸ stear
STED = stead
STEDD = stead
STEDDE = stead
STEDDED ▸ sted
STEDDES ▸ stedde
STEDDS ▸ stedd
STEDDY = steady
STEDE = stead

STEDED ▸ stede
STEDES ▸ stede
STEDING ▸ stede
STEDS ▸ sted
STEED = stead
STEEDED ▸ steed
STEEDS ▸ steed
STEEDY = steady
STEEK vb Scots word meaning shut steeked, steekit, steeks
STEEL n, vb steeld, steeled
STEELIE n steel ball bearing used as marble
STEELS pl n shares and bonds of steel companies
STEELY ▸ steel
STEEM variant of ▸ esteem
STEEMED ▸ steem
STEEMS ▸ steem
STEEN vb line with stone steened, steens
STEEP adj, vb, n steeped
STEEPEN vb become steep or steeper
STEEPER ▸ steep
STEEPLE n spire
STEEPLY ▸ steep
STEEPS ▸ steep
STEEPUP adj very steep
STEEPY ▸ steep
STEER vb, n steered, steerer, steers
STEERY n commotion
STEEVE n spar having a pulley block at one end ▸ vb stow (cargo) securely in the hold of

a ship steeved, steever, steeves
STEIL = steal
STEILS ▸ steil
STEIN = steen
STEINED ▸ stein
STEINS ▸ stein
STELA = stele
STELAE ▸ stele
STELAI ▸ stele
STELAR ▸ stele
STELE n upright stone slab or column decorated with figures or inscriptions stelene, steles, stelic
STELL n shelter for cattle or sheep built on moorland or hillsides ▸ vb position or place
STELLA n star or something star-shaped
STELLAR adj
STELLAS ▸ stella
STELLED ▸ stell
STELLIO n as in stellio lizard denoting type of lizard
STELLS ▸ stell
STEM vb, n
STEMBOK = steenbok
STEME = steam
STEMED ▸ steme
STEMES ▸ steme
STEMING ▸ steme
STEMLET n little stem
STEMMA n family tree stemmas
STEMME archaic variant of ▸ stem
STEMMED ▸ stem
STEMMER ▸ stem
STEMMES ▸ stemme

STEMMY adj (of wine) young and raw

STEMPEL n timber support **stemple**

STEMS ▶ stem

STEMSON n curved timber at the bow of a wooden vessel

STEN vb stride

STENCH n, vb **stenchy**

STENCIL n, vb

STEND vb Scots word meaning bound **stended, stends**

STENGAH = stinger

STENNED ▶ sten

STENO n stenographer

STENOKY n survival dependent on conditions remaining within a narrow range of variables

STENOS ▶ steno

STENS ▶ sten

STENT n surgical implant used to keep an artery open ▷ vb assess **stented**

STENTOR n person with an unusually loud voice

STENTS ▶ stent

STEP vb, n

STEPNEY n spare wheel

STEPPE n

STEPPED ▶ step

STEPPER n person or animal that steps, esp a horse or a dancer

STEPPES ▶ steppe

STEPS ▶ step

STEPSON n

STEPT ▶ step

STERE n unit used to

measure volumes of stacked timber

STEREO n, adj, vb **stereos**

STERES ▶ stere

STERIC adj of or caused by the spatial arrangement of atoms in a molecule

STERILE adj

STERLET n small sturgeon of N Asia and E Europe

STERN adj, n, vb

STERNA ▶ sternum

STERNAL ▶ sternum

STERNED, sterner, sternly, sterns ▶ stern

STERNUM n

STEROID n

STEROL n natural insoluble alcohol such as cholesterol and ergosterol **sterols**

STERTOR n laborious or noisy breathing

STERVE = starve

STERVED ▶ sterve

STERVES ▶ sterve

STET interj instruction to ignore an alteration previously made ▷ vb indicate to a printer that deleted matter is to be kept ▷ n mark indicating that deleted matter is to be kept **stets**

STETSON n cowboy hat

STETTED ▶ stet

STEVEN n voice **stevens**

STEW n, vb

STEWARD n, vb

STEWBUM n drunkard

STEWED adj (of food) cooked by stewing

STEWER, stewers, stewier, stewing ▶ stew

STEWPAN n pan used for making stew

STEWPOT n pot used for making stew

STEWS ▶ stew

STEWY ▶ stew

STEY adj Scots word meaning steep **steyer, steyest**

STHENIA n abnormal strength

STHENIC adj abounding in energy or bodily strength

STIBBLE Scots form of ▶ **stubble**

STIBIAL ▶ stibium

STIBINE n colourless slightly soluble poisonous gas

STIBIUM obsolete name for > **antimony**

STICH n line of poetry **stichic**

STICHOI ▶ stichos

STICHOS n line of poem

STICHS ▶ stich

STICK n, vb **sticked**

STICKER n

STICKIT Scots form of ▶ **stuck**

STICKLE vb dispute stubbornly, esp about minor points

STICKS ▶ stick

STICKUM n adhesive

STICKUP n robbery at gun-point

STICKY adj, vb, n
STIDDIE = stithy
STIE = sty
STIED ▸ sty
STIES ▸ sty
STIEVE = steeve
STIEVER ▸ stieve
STIFF adj, n, adv, vb
  stiffed
STIFFEN vb
STIFFER ▸ stiff
STIFFLY ▸ stiff
STIFFS ▸ stiff
STIFFY n erection of the
  penis
STIFLE vb, n stifled,
  stifler, stifles
STIGMA n
STIGMAL adj of part of
  insect wing
STIGMAS ▸ stigma
STIGME n dot in Greek
  punctuation **stigmes**
STILB n unit of
  luminance **stilbs**
STILE = style
STILED ▸ stile
STILES ▸ stile
STILET = stylet
STILETS ▸ stilet
STILING ▸ stile
STILL adv, adj, n, vb
  stilled, stiller, stills
STILLY adv quietly or
  calmly ▸ adj still, quiet,
  or calm
STILT n, vb
STILTED adj
STILTER ▸ stilt
STILTS ▸ stilt
STILTY ▸ stilt
STIM n very small
  amount
STIME = styme

STIMED ▸ stime
STIMES ▸ stime
STIMIE = stymie
STIMIED ▸ stimie
STIMIES ▸ stimie
STIMING ▸ stime
STIMS ▸ stim
STIMULI > stimulus
STIMY = stymie
STING vb, n stinged
STINGER n person,
  plant, animal, etc, that
  stings or hurts
STINGO n strong
  alcohol **stingos**
STINGS ▸ sting
STINGY adj, n
STINK n, vb
STINKER n difficult or
  unpleasant person or
  thing
STINKO adj drunk
STINKS ▸ stink
STINKY adj having a foul
  smell
STINT vb, n stinted,
  stinter, stints, stinty
STIPA n variety of grass
  stipas
STIPE n stalk in plants
  that bears
  reproductive
  structures
STIPED = stipitate
STIPEL n small paired
  leaflike structure at
  the base of certain
  leaflets **stipels**
STIPEND n
STIPES n second
  maxillary segment in
  insects and crustaceans
STIPPLE vb paint, draw,
  or engrave using dots

▸ n technique of
  stippling
STIPULE n small paired
  usually leaflike
  outgrowth occurring
  at the base of a leaf or
  its stalk
STIR vb, n
STIRE = steer
STIRED ▸ stire
STIRES ▸ stire
STIRING ▸ stire
STIRK n heifer of 6 to 12
  months old **stirks**
STIRP = stirps
STIRPES ▸ stirps
STIRPS n line of
  descendants from an
  ancestor
STIRRA = sirra
STIRRAH = sirrah
STIRRAS ▸ stirra
STIRRE = steer
STIRRED ▸ stir
STIRRER n person who
  deliberately causes
  trouble
STIRRES ▸ stirre
STIRRUP n
STIRS ▸ stir
STISHIE = stushie
STITCH n, vb
STITHY n forge or anvil
  ▸ vb forge on an anvil
STIVE vb stifle **stived**
STIVER n former Dutch
  coin worth **stivers**
STIVES ▸ stive
STIVIER ▸ stivy
STIVING ▸ stive
STIVY adj stuffy
STOA n covered walk
  that has a colonnade
  on one or both sides

stoae, stoai, stoas

STOAT n stoats

STOB = stab

STOBBED ▸ stob

STOBIE adj as in **stobie pole** steel and concrete pole for supporting electricity wires

STOBS ▸ stob

STOCK n, adj, vb stocked, stocker

STOCKS pl n instrument of punishment in which an offender was locked

STOCKY adj

STODGE n heavy starchy food ▸ vb stuff (oneself or another) with food stodged

STODGER n dull person

STODGES ▸ stodge

STODGY adj

STOEP n verandah stoeps

STOGEY = stogy

STOGEYS ▸ stogey

STOGIE = stogy

STOGIES ▸ stogy

STOGY n any long cylindrical inexpensive cigar

STOIC n, adj

STOICAL adj suffering great difficulties without showing one's feelings

STOICS ▸ stoic

STOIT vb bounce stoited

STOITER vb stagger

STOITS ▸ stoit

STOKE vb

STOKED adj very pleased

STOKER n person employed to tend a furnace on a ship or train powered by steam stokers

STOKES n cgs unit of kinematic viscosity

STOKING ▸ stoke

STOKVEL n (in S Africa) informal savings pool or syndicate

STOLE n long scarf or shawl

STOLED adj wearing a stole

STOLEN ▸ steal

STOLES ▸ stole

STOLID adj

STOLLEN n rich sweet bread containing nuts, raisins, etc

STOLN ▸ steal

STOLON n long horizontal stem that grows along the surface of the soil stolons

STOMA n

STOMACH n, vb

STOMACK n as in **have a stomack** (in E Africa) be pregnant

STOMAL ▸ stoma

STOMAS ▸ stoma

STOMATA ▸ stoma

STOMATE n opening on leaf through which water evaporates

STOMIA ▸ stomium

STOMIUM n part of the sporangium of ferns that ruptures to release the spores

STOMP vb, n stomped

STOMPER n song with a strong beat

STOMPIE n cigarette butt

STOMPS ▸ stomp

STOND = stand

STONDS ▸ stond

STONE n, vb

STONED adj

STONEN adj of stone

STONER n device for removing stones from fruit

STONERN = stonen

STONERS ▸ stoner

STONES ▸ stone

STONEY = stony

STONG ▸ sting

STONIED, stonier, stonies, stonily ▸ stony

STONING ▸ stone

STONISH = astonish

STONK vb bombard (soldiers, buildings, etc) with artillery ▸ n concentrated bombardment stonked

STONKER vb destroy

STONKS ▸ stonk

STONN = stun

STONNE = stun

STONNED ▸ stonne

STONNES ▸ stonne

STONNS ▸ stonn

STONY adj, vb

STOOD ▸ stand

STOODEN ▸ stand

STOOGE n, vb stooged, stooges

STOOK n number of

sheaves set upright in a field to dry ▷ *vb* set up (sheaves) in stooks **stooked, stooker**

STOOKIE *n* stucco

STOOKS ▶ **stook**

STOOL *n*, *vb* **stooled**

STOOLIE *n* police informer

STOOLS ▶ **stool**

STOOP *vb*

STOOPE = **stoup**

STOOPED ▶ **stoop**

STOOPER ▶ **stoop**

STOOPES ▶ **stoope**

STOOPS ▶ **stoop**

STOOR = **stour**

STOORS ▶ **stoor**

STOOZE *vb* borrow money cheaply and invest it to make a profit **stoozed**

STOOZER *n* person who stoozes

STOOZES ▶ **stooze**

STOP *vb*, *n*

STOPE *n* steplike excavation made in a mine to extract ore ▷ *vb* mine (ore, etc) by cutting stopes **stoped**

STOPER *n* drill used in mining **stopers**

STOPES ▶ **stope**

STOPGAP *n*

STOPING *n* process by which country rock is broken up and engulfed by magma

STOPOFF *n* break in a journey

STOPPED ▶ **stop**

STOPPER *n*, *vb* **stopple**

STOPS ▶ **stop**

STOPT ▶ **stop**

STORAGE *n*

STORAX *n* type of tree or shrub with white flowers

STORE *vb*, *n* **stored, storer, storers**

STORES *pl n* supply of food and essentials for a journey

STOREY *n* **storeys**

STORGE *n* affection **storges**

STORIED ▶ **story**

STORIES ▶ **story**

STORING ▶ **store**

STORK *n* **storks**

STORM *n*, *vb* **stormed**

STORMER *n* outstanding example of its kind

STORMS ▶ **storm**

STORMY *adj* characterized by storms

STORY *n*, *vb*

STOSS *adj* (of the side of a hill) facing the onward flow of a glacier ▷ *n* hillside facing glacier flow **stosses**

STOT *n* bullock ▷ *vb* bounce or cause to bounce

STOTIN *n* monetary unit of Slovenia **stotins**

STOTS ▶ **stot**

STOTT = **stot**

STOTTED ▶ **stot**

STOTTER = **stot**

STOTTIE *n* wedge of bread cut from a flat round loaf

STOTTS ▶ **stott**

STOTTY *n* type of flat, round loaf made in NE England

STOUN = **stun**

STOUND *n* short while ▷ *vb* ache **stounds**

STOUNS ▶ **stoun**

STOUP *n* small basin for holy water **stoups**

STOUR *n* turmoil or conflict **stoure**

STOURES ▶ **stoure**

STOURIE = **stoury**

STOURS ▶ **stour**

STOURY *adj* dusty

STOUSH *vb* hit or punch (someone) ▷ *n* fighting or violence

STOUT *adj*, *n*

STOUTEN *vb* make or become stout

STOUTER ▶ **stout**

STOUTH *n* Scots word meaning theft **stouths**

STOUTLY ▶ **stout**

STOUTS ▶ **stout**

STOVE *n*, *vb* **stoved**

STOVER *n* fodder **stovers**

STOVES ▶ **stove**

STOVIES *pl n* potatoes stewed with onions

STOVING ▶ **stove**

STOW *vb*

STOWAGE *n* space or charge for stowing goods

STOWED, stower, stowers, stowing ▶ **stow**

STOWN ▶ **steal**

STOWND ▶ **stound**

STOWNDS ▶ **stownd**

STOWP = stoup

STOWPS ▶ stowp

STOWRE = stour

STOWRES ▶ stowre

STOWS ▶ stow

STRACK vb archaic past tense form of strike

STRAD n violin made by Stradivarius **strads**

STRAE Scots form of ▶ straw

STRAES ▶ strae

STRAFE vb attack (an enemy) with machine guns from the air ▷ n act or instance of strafing **strafed, strafer, strafes, straff**

STRAFFS ▶ straff

STRAG n straggler **strags**

STRAIK Scots word for ▶ stroke

STRAIKS ▶ straik

STRAIN vb, n **strains**

STRAINT n pressure

STRAIT n, adj, vb **straits**

STRAK vb archaic past tense form of strike

STRAKE n curved metal plate forming part of the close rim on a wooden wheel

STRAKED adj having a strake

STRAKES ▶ strake

STRAMP Scots variant of ▶ tramp

STRAMPS ▶ stramp

STRAND vb, n **strands**

STRANG dialect variant of ▶ strong

STRANGE adj, n

STRAP n, vb

STRAPPY adj having straps

STRAPS ▶ strap

STRASS another word for ▶ paste

STRATA ▶ stratum

STRATAL ▶ stratum

STRATAS ▶ stratum

STRATH n flat river valley **straths**

STRATI ▶ stratus

STRATUM n

STRATUS n grey layer cloud

STRAW n, vb **strawed**

STRAWEN adj of straw

STRAWN ▶ strew

STRAWS ▶ straw

STRAWY adj containing straw, or like straw in colour or texture

STRAY vb, adj, n **strayed, strayer, strays**

STRAYVE vb wander aimlessly

STREAK n, vb **streaks**

STREAKY adj marked with streaks

STREAM n, vb **streams**

STREAMY adj (of an area, land, etc) having many streams

STREEK Scots word for ▶ stretch

STREEKS ▶ streek

STREEL n slovenly woman ▷ vb trail **streels**

STREET n, vb **streets**

STREETY adj of streets

STRENE = strain

STRENES ▶ strene

STREP n streptococcus

streps

STRESS n, vb

STRETCH vb, n

STRETTA = stretto

STRETTE ▶ stretta

STRETTI ▶ stretto

STRETTO n (in a fugue) the close overlapping of two parts or voices

STREW vb **strewed, strewer, strewn, strews**

STREWTH interj expression of surprise or alarm

STRIA n scratch or groove on the surface of a rock crystal **striae**

STRIATA > striatum

STRIATE adj marked with striae ▷ vb mark with striae

STRICH n screech owl

STRICK n any bast fibres preparatory to being made into slivers **stricks**

STRICT adj

STRIDE vb, n **strider, strides**

STRIDOR n high-pitched whistling sound made during respiration

STRIFE n **strifes**

STRIFT n struggle **strifts**

STRIG vb remove stalk from

STRIGA = stria

STRIGAE ▶ striga

STRIGIL n curved blade used to scrape the body after bathing

STRIGS ▶ strig

STRIKE *vb, n*
STRIKER *n*
STRIKES ▸ strike
STRIM *vb* cut (grass) using a strimmer **strims**
STRING *n, vb* **strings**
STRINGY *adj*
STRIP *vb, n*
STRIPE *n, vb*
STRIPED *adj* marked or decorated with stripes
STRIPER *n* officer who has a stripe or stripes on his uniform
STRIPES ▸ stripe
STRIPEY = stripy
STRIPS ▸ strip
STRIPT ▸ strip
STRIPY *adj* marked by or with stripes
STRIVE *vb* **strived, striven, striver, strives**
STROAM *vb* wander **stroams**
STROBE *n* high intensity flashing beam of light ▷ *vb* give the appearance of slow motion by using a strobe **strobed, strobes**
STROBIC *adj* spinning or appearing to spin
STROBIL *n* scaly multiple fruit
STRODE ▸ stride
STRODLE = straddle
STROKE *vb, n* **stroked**
STROKEN ▸ strike
STROKER ▸ stroke
STROKES ▸ stroke
STROLL *vb, n* **strolls**

STROMA *n* gel-like matrix of chloroplasts and certain cells **stromal**
STROMB *n* shellfish like a whelk **strombs**
STROND = strand
STRONDS ▸ strond
STRONG *adj* having physical power
STROOK ▸ strike
STROOKE ▸ stroke
STROP *n* leather strap for sharpening razors ▷ *vb* sharpen (a razor, etc) on a strop
STROPHE *n* movement made by chorus during a choral ode
STROPPY *adj*
STROPS ▸ strop
STROUD *n* coarse woollen fabric **strouds**
STROUP *Scots word for* ▸ **spout**
STROUPS ▸ stroup
STROUT *vb* bulge **strouts**
STROVE ▸ strive
STROW *archaic variant of* ▸ **strew; strowed, strower, strown, strows**
STROY *archaic variant of* ▸ **destroy**
STROYED ▸ stroy
STROYER ▸ stroy
STROYS ▸ stroy
STRUCK ▸ strike
STRUDEL *n* thin sheet of filled dough rolled up and baked
STRUM *vb*
STRUMA *n* abnormal

enlargement of the thyroid gland **strumae, strumas**
STRUMS ▸ strum
STRUNG ▸ string
STRUNT *Scots word for* ▸ **strut**
STRUNTS ▸ strunt
STRUT *vb, n* **struts**
STUB *n, vb* **stubbed**
STUBBIE = stubby
STUBBLE *n* **stubbly**
STUBBY *adj, n*
STUBS ▸ stub
STUCCO *n, vb* **stuccos**
STUCK ▸ stucks
STUD *n, vb* **studded**
STUDDEN ▸ stand
STUDDIE *Scots word for* ▸ **anvil**
STUDDLE *n* post
STUDE *vb* past tense and past participle of staun (Scots form of stand)
STUDENT *n*
STUDIED *adj* carefully practised
STUDIER ▸ study
STUDIES ▸ study
STUDIO *n* **studios**
STUDLY *adj* strong and virile
STUDS ▸ stud
STUDY *vb, n*
STUFF *n, vb* **stuffed, stuffer, stuffs**
STUFFY *adj*
STUGGY *adj* stout
STUIVER = stiver
STULL *n* timber prop or platform in a stope **stulls**
STULM *n* shaft **stulms**
STUM *n* partly

fermented wine added to fermented wine as a preservative ▷ vb preserve (wine) by adding stum

STUMBLE vb, n

STUMBLY adj tending to stumble

STUMER n forgery or cheat **stumers**

STUMM = **shtoom**

STUMMED ▷ **stum**

STUMMEL n bowl of pipe

STUMP n, vb **stumped, stumper, stumps**

STUMPY adj, n

STUMS ▷ **stum**

STUN vb, n

STUNG ▷ **sting**

STUNK ▷ **stink**

STUNNED ▷ **stun**

STUNNER n beautiful person or thing

STUNS ▷ **stun**

STUNT vb, n **stunted, stunts**

STUPA n domed edifice housing Buddhist or Jain relics **stupas**

STUPE n hot damp cloth applied to the body to relieve pain ▷ vb treat with a stupe **stuped**

STUPEFY vb make insensitive or lethargic

STUPENT adj astonished

STUPES ▷ **stupe**

STUPID adj, n **stupids**

STUPING ▷ **stupe**

STUPOR n **stupors**

STURDY adj, n

STURE = **stoor**

STURMER n type of

eating apple with pale green skin

STURNUS n bird of starling family

STURT vb bother **sturted, sturts**

STUSHIE n commotion, rumpus, or row

STUTTER vb, n

STY vb

STYE n **styed, styes**

STYGIAN adj dark, gloomy, or hellish

STYING ▷ **sty**

STYLAR ▷ **stylus**

STYLATE adj having style

STYLE n, vb **styled, stylee**

STYLEES ▷ **stylee**

STYLER ▷ **style**

STYLERS ▷ **style**

STYLES ▷ **style**

STYLET n wire to stiffen a flexible cannula or catheter **stylets**

STYLI ▷ **stylus**

STYLIE adj fashion-conscious **stylier**

STYLING ▷ **style**

STYLISE ▷ **stylize**

STYLISH adj

STYLIST n hairdresser

STYLITE n one of a class of recluses who in ancient times lived on the top of high pillars

STYLIZE vb cause to conform to an established stylistic form

STYLO n type of fountain pen

STYLOID adj resembling a stylus ▷ n spiny growth

STYLOPS n type of insect that lives as a parasite in other insects

STYLOS ▷ **stylo**

STYLUS n

STYME vb peer **stymed, stymes**

STYMIE vb

STYMIED ▷ **stymy**

STYMIES ▷ **stymy**

STYMING ▷ **styme stymy**

STYMY = **stymie**

STYPSIS n action, application, or use of a styptic

STYPTIC adj (drug) used to stop bleeding ▷ n styptic drug

STYRAX n type of tropical or subtropical tree

STYRE = **stir**

STYRED ▷ **styre**

STYRENE n colourless oily volatile flammable water-insoluble liquid

STYRES ▷ **styre**

STYRING ▷ **styre**

STYTE vb bounce **styted, stytes, styting**

SUABLE adj liable to be sued in a court **suably**

SUASION n persuasion **suasive, suasory**

SUAVE adj **suavely, suaver, suavest, suavity**

SUB n subeditor ▷ vb act

SUBA *n* shepherd's cloak
SUBACID *adj* (esp of some fruits) moderately acid or sour
SUBACT *vb* subdue **subacts**
SUBADAR *n* chief native officer of a company of Indian soldiers in the British service **subah**
SUBAHS ▸ subah
SUBALAR *adj* below a wing
SUBAQUA *adj* of or relating to underwater sport
SUBAREA *n* area within a larger area
SUBARID *adj* receiving slightly more rainfall than arid regions
SUBAS ▸ suba
SUBATOM *n* part of an atom
SUBBASE = subbass
SUBBASS another name for ▸ bourdon
SUBBED ▸ sub
SUBBIE *n* subcontractor **subbies**
SUBBING ▸ sub
SUBBY ▸ subbie
SUBCELL *n* cell within a larger cell
SUBCLAN *n* clan within a larger clan
SUBCODE *n* computer tag identifying data
SUBCOOL *vb* make colder
SUBCULT *n* cult within larger cult
SUBDEAN *n* deputy of

dean
SUBDEB *n* young woman who is not yet a debutante **subdebs**
SUBDEW = subdue
SUBDEWS ▸ subdew
SUBDUAL ▸ subdue
SUBDUCE *vb* withdraw
SUBDUCT *vb* draw or turn (the eye, etc) downwards
SUBDUE *vb*
SUBDUED *adj*
SUBDUER ▸ subdue
SUBDUES ▸ subdue
SUBECHO *n* echo resonating more quietly than another echo
SUBEDAR = subadar
SUBEDIT *vb* edit and correct (written or printed material)
SUBER *n* cork
SUBERIC = suberose
SUBERIN *n* fatty or waxy substance that is present in the walls of cork cells
SUBERS ▸ suber
SUBFEU *vb* grant feu to vassal **subfeus**
SUBFILE *n* file within another file
SUBFIX *n* suffix
SUBFUSC *adj* devoid of brightness or appeal ▸ *n* (at Oxford University) formal academic dress **subfusk**
SUBGOAL *n* secondary goal
SUBGUM *n* Chinese dish **subgums**
SUBHA *n* string of beads

used in praying and meditating **subhas**
SUBHEAD *n* heading of a subsection in a printed work
SUBIDEA *n* secondary idea
SUBITEM *n* item that is less important than another item
SUBITO *adv* (preceding or following a dynamic marking, etc) suddenly
SUBJECT *n, adj, vb*
SUBJOIN *vb* add or attach at the end of something spoken, written, etc
SUBLATE *vb* deny
SUBLET *vb, n* **sublets**
SUBLIME *adj, vb*
SUBLINE *n* secondary headline
SUBLOT *n* subdivision of a lot **sublots**
SUBMAN *n* primitive form of human **submen**
SUBMENU *n* further list of options within computer menu
SUBMISS *adj* docile
SUBMIT *vb* **submits**
SUBNET *n* part of network **subnets**
SUBORAL *adj* not quite oral
SUBORN *vb* bribe or incite (a person) to commit a wrongful act **suborns**
SUBOVAL *adj* not quite oval
SUBPAR *adj* not up to

standard

SUBPART *n* part within another part

SUBPENA = subpoena

SUBPLOT *n* secondary plot in a novel, play, or film

SUBRACE *n* race of people considered to be inferior

SUBRENT *n* rent paid to renter who rents to another

SUBRING *n* mathematical ring that is a subset of another ring

SUBRULE *n* rule within a rule

SUBS ► sub

SUBSALE *n* sale carried out within the process of a larger sale

SUBSEA *adj* undersea

SUBSECT *n* sect within a larger sect

SUBSERE *n* secondary sere arising when the progress of a sere has been interrupted

SUBSET *n* subsets

SUBSIDE *vb*

SUBSIDY *n*

SUBSIST *vb*

SUBSITE *n* location within a website

SUBSOIL *n*, *vb*

SUBSONG *n* subdued form of birdsong modified from the full territorial song

SUBSUME *vb*

SUBTACK *Scots word for* > sublease

SUBTASK *n* task that is part of a larger task

SUBTAXA > subtaxon

SUBTEEN *n* young person who has not yet become a teenager

SUBTEND *vb* be opposite (an angle or side)

SUBTEST *n* test that is part of larger test

SUBTEXT *n* underlying theme in a piece of writing

SUBTIL ► subtle

SUBTILE *rare spelling of* ► subtle

SUBTLE *adj* subtler, subtly

SUBTONE *n* subdivision of a tone

SUBTYPE *n* secondary or subordinate type or genre

SUBUNIT *n* distinct part or component of something larger

SUBURB *n* suburbs

SUBVENE *vb* happen in such a way as to be of assistance

SUBVERT *vb*

SUBWAY *n*, *vb* subways

SUBZERO *adj* lower than zero

SUBZONE *n* subdivision of a zone

SUCCADE *n* piece of candied fruit

SUCCAH = sukkah

SUCCAHS ► succah

SUCCEED *vb*

SUCCES *French word for* ► success

SUCCESS *n*

SUCCI ► succus

SUCCISE *adj* ending abruptly, as if cut off

SUCCOR = succour

SUCCORS ► succor

SUCCORY *another name for* ► chicory

SUCCOS ► succoth

SUCCOSE ► succus

SUCCOT = sukkoth

SUCCOTH *variant of* ► sukkoth

SUCCOUR *n*, *vb*

SUCCOUS ► succus

SUCCUBA ► succubus

SUCCUBI ► succubus

SUCCUMB *vb*

SUCCUS *n* fluid

SUCCUSS *vb* shake (a patient) to detect the sound of fluid in a cavity

SUCH *adj*, *pron*

SUCK *vb*, *n* sucked

SUCKEN *Scots word for* > district

SUCKENS ► sucken

SUCKER *n*, *vb* suckers

SUCKET = succade

SUCKETS ► sucket

SUCKIER ► sucky

SUCKING *adj* not yet weaned

SUCKLE *vb* suckled, suckler, suckles

SUCKS *interj* expression of disappointment

SUCKY *adj* despicable

SUCRASE *another name for* > invertase

SUCRE *n* former standard monetary unit of Ecuador

SUCRES ► sucre

SUCRIER *n* small

container for sugar at table

SUCROSE = sugar

SUCTION n, vb

SUD singular of ▶ suds

SUDAMEN n small cavity in the skin

SUDARIA > sudarium

SUDARY = sudarium

SUDATE vb sweat **sudated, sudates**

SUDD n floating masses of reeds and weeds on the White Nile

SUDDEN adj suddens

SUDDER n supreme court in India **sudders**

SUDDS ▶ sudd

SUDOR technical name for ▶ sweat

SUDORAL ▶ sudor

SUDORS ▶ sudor

SUDS pl n, vb **sudsed**

SUDSER n soap opera **sudsers**

SUDSES, sudsier, sudsing, sudsy ▶ suds

SUE vb **sueable, sued**

SUEDE n, vb **sueded, suedes, sueding**

SUENT adj smooth

SUER ▶ sue

SUERS ▶ sue

SUES ▶ sue

SUET n **suetier, suets, suetty, suety**

SUFFARI = safari

SUFFECT adj additional

SUFFER vb **suffers**

SUFFETE n official in ancient Carthage

SUFFICE vb

SUFFIX n, vb

SUFFUSE vb

SUG vb sell a product while pretending to conduct market research

SUGAN n straw rope **sugans**

SUGAR n, vb

SUGARED adj made sweeter or more appealing with or as with sugar

SUGARER ▶ sugar

SUGARS ▶ sugar

SUGARY adj of, like, or containing sugar

SUGGED ▶ sug

SUGGING n practice of selling products under the pretence of conducting market research

SUGH = sough

SUGHED ▶ sugh

SUGHING ▶ sugh

SUGHS ▶ sugh

SUGO n Italian pasta sauce **sugos**

SUGS ▶ sug

SUHUR n meal eaten before sunrise by Muslims fasting during Ramadan **suhurs**

SUI adj of itself

SUICIDE n, vb

SUID n pig or related animal **suidian, suids**

SUING ▶ sue

SUINGS ▶ sue

SUINT n water-soluble substance found in the fleece of sheep **suints**

SUIPLAP n South African slang for a drunkard

SUIT n, vb

SUITE n

SUITED ▶ suit

SUITER n piece of luggage for carrying suits and dresses **suiters**

SUITES ▶ suite

SUITING n fabric used for suits

SUITOR n, vb **suitors**

SUITS ▶ suit

SUIVEZ vb musical direction meaning follow

SUJEE = soogee

SUJEES ▶ sujee

SUK = souk

SUKH = souk

SUKHS ▶ sukh

SUKKAH n structure in which orthodox Jews eat and sleep during Sukkoth **sukkahs**

SUKKOS = sukkoth

SUKKOT = sukkoth

SUKKOTH n eight-day Jewish harvest festival

SUKS ▶ suk

SUKUK n sukuks

SULCAL ▶ sulcus

SULCATE adj marked with longitudinal parallel grooves

SULCI ▶ sulcus

SULCUS n linear groove, furrow, or slight depression

SULDAN = sultan

SULDANS ▶ suldan

SULFA = sulpha

SULFAS ▶ sulfa

SULFATE = sulphate

SULFID = sulphide

SULFIDE = sulphide
SULFIDS ▶ sulfid
SULFITE = sulphite
SULFO = sulphonic
SULFONE = sulphone
SULFUR variant of ▶ sulphul
SULFURS ▶ sulfur
SULFURY ▶ sulfur
SULK vb, n sulked, sulker
SULKERS ▶ sulker
SULKIER ▶ sulky
SULKIES ▶ sulky
SULKILY ▶ sulky
SULKING ▶ sulk
SULKS ▶ sulk
SULKY adj, n
SULLAGE n filth or waste, esp sewage
SULLEN adj, n sullens
SULLIED ▶ sully
SULLIES ▶ sully
SULLY vb, n
SULPH n amphetamine sulphate
SULPHA n any of a group of sulphonamides that prevent the growth of bacteria **sulphas**
SULPHID = sulphide
SULPHS ▶ sulph
SULPHUR n, vb
SULTAN n
SULTANA n
SULTANS ▶ sultan
SULTRY adj
SULU n type of sarong worn in Fiji **sulus**
SUM n, vb
SUMAC = sumach
SUMACH n type of temperate or subtropical shrub or small tree **sumachs**
SUMACS ▶ sumac
SUMATRA n violent storm blowing from the direction of Sumatra
SUMLESS adj uncountable
SUMMA n compendium of theology, philosophy, or canon law **summae**
SUMMAND n number or quantity forming part of a sum
SUMMAR Scots variant of ▶ summer
SUMMARY n, adj
SUMMAS ▶ summa
SUMMAT pron something ▶ n impressive or important person or thing
SUMMATE vb add up
SUMMATS ▶ summat
SUMMED ▶ sum
SUMMER n, vb summers, summery
SUMMING ▶ sum
SUMMIST n writer of summae
SUMMIT n, vb summits
SUMMON vb
SUMMONS n, vb
SUMO n Japanese style of wrestling **sumoist, sumos**
SUMP n
SUMPH n stupid person **sumphs**
SUMPIT n Malay blowpipe **sumpits**
SUMPS ▶ sump

SUMPTER n packhorse, mule, or other beast of burden
SUMS ▶ sum
SUMY pl n the monetary units of Uzbekistan
SUN n, vb
SUNBACK adj (of dress) cut low at back
SUNBAKE vb sunbathe, esp in order to become tanned ▶ n period of sunbaking
SUNBATH n exposure of the body to the sun to get a suntan
SUNBEAM n
SUNBEAT adj exposed to sun
SUNBED n machine for giving an artificial tan **sunbeds**
SUNBELT n southern states of the US
SUNBIRD n type of small songbird with a bright plumage in the males
SUNBOW n bow of colours produced when sunlight shines through spray **sunbows**
SUNBURN n, vb
SUNDAE n sundaes
SUNDARI n Indian tree
SUNDECK n upper open deck on a passenger ship
SUNDER vb break apart **sunders**
SUNDEW n type of bog plant with leaves covered in sticky hairs **sundews**

SUNDIAL n

SUNDOG n small rainbow or halo near the horizon **sundogs**

SUNDOWN = sunset

SUNDRA = sundari

SUNDRAS ▸ sundra

SUNDRI = sundari

SUNDRIS ▸ sundri

SUNDRY adj

SUNFAST adj not fading in sunlight

SUNFISH n large sea fish with a rounded body

SUNG ▸ sing

SUNGAR = sangar

SUNGARS ▸ sungar

SUNGLOW n pinkish glow often seen in the sky before sunrise or after sunset

SUNHAT n hat that shades the face and neck from the sun **sunhats**

SUNI n S African dwarf antelope **sunis**

SUNK n bank or pad

SUNKEN adj

SUNKET n something good to eat **sunkets**

SUNKIE n little stool **sunkies**

SUNKS ▸ sunk

SUNLAMP n lamp that generates ultraviolet rays

SUNLAND n sunny area

SUNLESS adj without sun or sunshine

SUNLIKE ▸ sun

SUNLIT ▸ sunlight

SUNN n leguminous plant of the East

Indies

SUNNA n body of traditional Islamic law **sunnah**

SUNNAHS ▸ sunnah

SUNNAS ▸ sunna

SUNNED ▸ sun

SUNNIER ▸ sunny

SUNNIES pl n pair of sunglasses

SUNNILY ▸ sunny

SUNNING ▸ sun

SUNNS ▸ sunn

SUNNY adj

SUNRAY n ray of light from the sun **sunrays**

SUNRISE n

SUNROOF n

SUNROOM n room or glass-enclosed porch designed to display beautiful views

SUNS ▸ sun

SUNSET n sunsets

SUNSPOT n

SUNSTAR n type of starfish with up to 13 arms

SUNSUIT n child's outfit consisting of a brief top and shorts or a short skirt

SUNTAN n suntans

SUNTRAP n very sunny sheltered place

SUNUP = sunrise

SUNUPS ▸ sunup

SUNWARD = sunwards

SUNWISE adv moving in the same direction as the sun

SUP = supine

SUPAWN = suppawn

SUPAWNS ▸ supawn

SUPE n superintendent

SUPER adj, n, interj, vb

SUPERB adj

SUPERED ▸ super

SUPERS ▸ super

SUPES ▸ supe

SUPINE adj, n supines

SUPLEX n type of wrestling hold

SUPPAWN n kind of porridge

SUPPED ▸ sup

SUPPER n, vb suppers

SUPPING ▸ sup

SUPPLE adj, vb suppled, suppler, supples

SUPPLY vb, n, adj, adv

SUPPORT vb, n

SUPPOSE vb

SUPRA adv above, esp referring to earlier parts of a book etc

SUPREMA ▸ supremum

SUPREME adj, n

SUPREMO n person in overall authority

SUPS ▸ sup

SUQ = souk

This unusual word for an Arab market-place is easy to overlook because we tend not to think of words ending in Q. It can also be spelt **sook**, **souk**, **suk** or **sukh**.

SUQS ▸ suq

SUR prep above

SURA n any of the 114 chapters of the Koran

SURAH n twill-weave fabric of silk or rayon, used for dresses, blouses, etc **surahs**

SURAL adj of or relating to the calf of the leg

SURAMIN n drug used in treating sleeping sickness

SURANCE = assurance

SURAS ▸ sura

SURAT n cotton fabric from Surat in India **surats**

SURBASE n uppermost part, such as a moulding, of a pedestal, base, or skirting

SURBATE vb make feet sore through walking

SURBED vb put something on its edge **surbeds**

SURBET ▸ surbate

SURCOAT n tunic worn by a knight over his armour

SURCULI ▸ surculus

SURD n number that cannot be expressed in whole numbers ▷ adj of or relating to a surd

SURDITY n deafness

SURDS ▸ surd

SURE adj, interj, vb **sured**

SURELY adv

SURER ▸ sure

SURES ▸ sure

SUREST ▸ sure

SURETY n, vb

SURF n, vb

SURFACE n, vb

SURFED ▸ surf

SURFEIT n, vb

SURFER ▸ surfing

SURFERS ▸ surfing

SURFIE n young person whose main interest is in surfing

SURFIER ▸ surf

SURFIES ▸ surfie

SURFING n

SURFMAN n sailor skilled in sailing through surf **surfmen**

SURFS ▸ surf

SURFY ▸ surf

SURGE n, vb **surged**, **surgent**

SURGEON n

SURGER ▸ surge

SURGERS ▸ surge

SURGERY n

SURGES, **surgier**, **surging**, **surgy** ▸ surge

SURIMI n blended seafood product made from precooked fish **surimis**

SURING ▸ sure

SURLIER ▸ surly

SURLILY ▸ surly

SURLOIN ▸ sirloin

SURLY adj

SURMISE n, vb

SURNAME n, vb

SURPASS vb

SURPLUS n, adj, vb

SURRA n tropical febrile disease of animals **surras**

SURREAL adj, n

SURREY n light four-wheeled horse-drawn carriage **surreys**

SURTAX n, vb

SURTOUT n man's overcoat resembling a frock coat

SURVEIL = surveille

SURVEY vb, n **surveys**

SURVIEW vb survey

SURVIVE vb

SUS = suss

SUSES ▸ sus

SUSHI n Japanese dish of small cakes of cold rice with a topping of raw fish **sushis**

SUSLIK n central Eurasian ground squirrel **susliks**

SUSPECT vb, adj, n

SUSPEND vb

SUSPENS = suspense

SUSPIRE vb sigh or utter with a sigh

SUSS vb attempt to work out (a situation, etc), using one's intuition ▷ n sharpness of mind **sussed**, **susses**, **sussing**

SUSTAIN vb, n

SUSU n (in the Caribbean) savings fund shared by friends **susus**

SUTILE adj involving sewing

SUTLER n merchant who accompanied an army in order to sell provisions **sutlers**, **sutlery**

SUTOR n cobbler **sutors**

SUTRA n Sanskrit sayings or collections of sayings **sutras**

SUTTA n Buddhist scripture **suttas**

SUTTEE n custom whereby a widow burnt herself on her husband's funeral pyre **suttees**

SUTTLE vb work as sutler **suttled, suttles**

SUTTLY ▸ subtle

SUTURAL ▸ suture

SUTURE n, vb **sutured, sutures**

SVARAJ = swaraj

SVELTE adj **svelter**

SWAB n, vb **swabbed**

SWABBER n person who uses a swab

SWABBIE = swabby

SWABBY n seaman

SWABS ▸ swab

SWACK adj flexible

SWACKED adj in a state of intoxication, stupor, or euphoria induced by drugs or alcohol

SWAD n loutish person

SWADDIE = swaddy

SWADDLE vb wrap (a baby) in swaddling clothes ▷ n swaddling clothes

SWADDY n private soldier

SWADS ▸ swaddle

SWAG n, vb

SWAGE n shaped tool or die used in forming cold metal by hammering ▷ vb form (metal) with a swage **swaged, swager, swagers, swages**

SWAGGED ▸ swag

SWAGGER vb, n, adj **swaggie**

SWAGING ▸ swage

SWAGMAN n swagmen

SWAGS ▸ swag

SWAIL = swale

SWAILS ▸ swail

SWAIN n suitor **swains**

SWALE n moist depression in a tract of land ▷ vb sway **swaled, swales, swalier, swaling**

SWALLET n hole where water goes underground

SWALLOW vb, n

SWALY ▸ swale

SWAM ▸ swim

SWAMI n Hindu religious teacher **swamies, swamis**

SWAMP n, vb **swamped**

SWAMPER n person who lives or works in a swampy region

SWAMPS ▸ swamp

SWAMPY ▸ swamp

SWAMY = swami

SWAN n, vb

SWANG ▸ swing

SWANK vb show off or boast ▷ n showing off or boasting **swanked, swanker**

SWANKEY = swanky

SWANKIE = swanky

SWANKS ▸ swank

SWANKY adj, n

SWANNED ▸ swan

SWANNIE n (in NZ) type of all-weather heavy woollen shirt

SWANNY adj swanlike

SWANPAN n Chinese abacus

SWANS ▸ swan

SWAP vb, n **swapped, swapper, swaps, swapt**

SWARAJ n (in British India) self-government

SWARD n stretch of short grass ▷ vb cover or become covered with grass **swarded, swards**

SWARDY adj covered with sward

SWARE ▸ swear

SWARF n material removed by cutting tools in the machining of metals, stone, etc ▷ vb faint **swarfed, swarfs**

SWARM n, vb **swarmed, swarmer, swarms**

SWART adj swarthy **swarth**

SWARTHS ▸ swarth

SWARTHY adj

SWARTY ▸ swart

SWARVE = swarf

SWARVED ▸ swarf

SWARVES ▸ swarf

SWASH n rush of water up a beach following each break of the waves ▷ vb wash or move with noisy splashing **swashed**

SWASHER n braggart

SWASHES ▸ swash

SWASHY adj slushy

SWAT vb, n

SWATCH n sample of cloth

SWATH n width of one sweep of a scythe or of the blade of a mowing machine

SWATHE vb, n swathed, swather, swathes

SWATHS ▸ swath

SWATHY ▸ swath

SWATS ▸ swat

SWATTED ▸ swat

SWATTER n device for killing insects ▷ vb splash

SWATTY ▸ swotty

SWAY vb, n swayed, swayer, swayers, swayful, swaying

SWAYL = sweal

SWAYLED ▸ swayl

SWAYLS ▸ swayl

SWAYS ▸ sway

SWAZZLE n small metal instrument used to produce a shrill voice

SWEAL vb scorch swealed, sweals

SWEAR vb

SWEARD = sword

SWEARDS ▸ sweard

SWEARER ▸ swear

SWEARS ▸ swear

SWEARY adj using swear-words

SWEAT n, vb

SWEATED adj made by exploited labour

SWEATER n

SWEATS ▸ sweat

SWEATY adj

SWEDE n swedes

SWEDGER n Scots dialect word for sweet

SWEE vb sway sweed, sweeing

SWEEL = sweal

SWEELED ▸ sweel

SWEELS ▸ sweel

SWEENEY n police flying squad

SWEENY n wasting of the shoulder muscles of a horse

SWEEP vb, n

SWEEPER n device used to sweep carpets

SWEEPS ▸ sweep

SWEEPY ▸ sweep

SWEER variant of ▸ sweir

SWEERED ▸ sweer

SWEERS ▸ sweer

SWEERT ▸ sweer

SWEES ▸ swee

SWEET adj, n, vb sweeted

SWEETEN vb

SWEETER ▸ sweet

SWEETIE n lovable person

SWEETLY ▸ sweet

SWEETS ▸ sweet

SWEETY = sweetie

SWEIR vb swear ▷ adj lazy sweired, sweirer, sweirs, sweirt

SWELL vb, n, adj swelled, sweller, swells

SWELT vb die swelted

SWELTER vb, n

SWELTRY adj sultry

SWELTS ▸ swelt

SWEPT ▸ sweep

SWERF = swarf

SWERFED ▸ swerf

SWERFS ▸ swerf

SWERVE vb, n swerved, swerver, swerves

SWEVEN n vision or dream swevens

SWEY = swee

SWEYED ▸ swey

SWEYING ▸ swey

SWEYS ▸ swey

SWIDDEN n area of land where slash-and-burn techniques are used

SWIES ▸ swy

SWIFT adj, n, adv, vb swifted

SWIFTER n line run around the ends of capstan bars

SWIFTIE n trick, ruse, or deception

SWIFTLY ▸ swift

SWIFTS ▸ swift

SWIFTY = swiftie

SWIG n, vb swigged, swigger, swigs

SWILER n (in Newfoundland) a seal hunter swilers

SWILL vb, n swilled, swiller, swills

SWIM vb, n swimmer

SWIMMY adj dizzy

SWIMS ▸ swim

SWINDGE = swinge

SWINDLE vb, n

SWINE n

SWINERY n pig farm

SWINES ▸ swine

SWING vb, n

SWINGBY n act of spacecraft passing close to planet

SWINGE vb beat, flog, or punish swinged

SWINGER n person regarded as being modern and lively

SWINGES ▸ swinge

SWINGLE n flat-bladed wooden instrument used for beating and scraping flax ▷ vb use a swingle on

SWINGS ▶ swing

SWINGY adj lively and modern

SWINISH ▶ swine

SWINK vb toil or drudge ▷ n toil or drudgery **swinked, swinker, swinks**

SWINNEY variant of ▶ sweeny

SWIPE vb, n **swiped, swiper, swipers**

SWIPES pl n beer, esp when poor or weak

SWIPEY adj drunk **swipier**

SWIPING ▶ swipe

SWIPLE ▶ swipple

SWIPLES ▶ swiple

SWIPPLE n part of a flail that strikes the grain

SWIRE n neck swires

SWIRL vb, n **swirled, swirls, swirly**

SWISH vb, n, adj **swished, swisher, swishes**

SWISHY adj moving with a swishing sound

SWISS n type of muslin **swisses**

SWITCH n, vb **switchy**

SWITH adv swiftly **swithe**

SWITHER vb hesitate or be indecisive ▷ n state of hesitation or uncertainty

SWITHLY ▶ swith

SWITS = switch

SWITSES ▶ swits

SWIVE vb have sexual intercourse with (a person) **swived**

SWIVEL vb, n **swivels**

SWIVES ▶ swive

SWIVET n nervous state **swivets**

SWIVING ▶ swive

SWIZ n swindle or disappointment **swizz**

SWIZZED ▶ swizz

SWIZZES ▶ swizz

SWIZZLE n unshaken cocktail ▷ vb stir a swizzle stick in (a drink)

SWOB less common word for ▶ swab

SWOBBED ▶ swob

SWOBBER ▶ swob

SWOBS ▶ swob

SWOFFER > swoffing

SWOLLEN ▶ swell

SWOLN ▶ swell

SWOON n, vb **swooned, swooner, swoons**

SWOONY adj romantic or sexy

SWOOP vb, n **swooped, swooper, swoops, swoopy**

SWOOSH vb make a swirling or rustling sound when moving or pouring out ▷ n swirling or rustling sound or movement

SWOP = swap; **swopped, swopper, swops, swopt**

SWORD n, vb **sworded**

SWORDER n fighter with sword

SWORDS ▶ sword

SWORE ▶ swear

SWORN ▶ swear

SWOT vb, n **swots, swotted, swotter**

SWOTTY adj given to studying hard, esp to the exclusion of other activities

SWOUN = swoon

SWOUND = swoon

SWOUNDS less common spelling of ▶ zounds

SWOUNE = swoon

SWOUNED = swoon

SWOUNES ▶ swoune

SWOUNS ▶ swoun

SWOWND = swoon

SWOWNDS = swoon

SWOWNE = swoon

SWOWNES ▶ swowne

SWOZZLE = swazzle

SWUM ▶ swim

SWUNG ▶ swing

SWY n Australian gambling game involving two coins

> A type of card-game, that can be useful in helping you to clear a difficult rack.

SYBBE = sib

SYBBES ▶ sybbe

SYBIL = sibyl

SYBILS ▶ sybil

SYBO n spring onion **syboe**

SYBOES ▶ syboe

SYBOTIC adj of a swineherd

SYBOW = sybo

SYBOWS ▶ sybow

SYCE n (formerly, in

India) a servant employed to look after horses, etc

SYCEE n silver ingots formerly used as a medium of exchange in China **sycees**

SYCES ▶ syce

SYCONIA > syconium

SYCOSES ▶ sycosis

SYCOSIS n chronic inflammation of the hair follicles

SYE vb strain **syed, syeing**

SYEN = scion

SYENITE n light-coloured coarse-grained plutonic igneous rock

SYENS ▶ syen

SYES ▶ sye

SYKE = sike

SYKER adv surely

SYKES ▶ syke

SYLI n Finnish unit of volume **sylis**

SYLLABI > syllabus

SYLLOGE n collection or summary

SYLPH n sylphic

SYLPHID n little sylph

SYLPHS ▶ sylph

SYLPHY ▶ sylph

SYLVA n trees growing in a particular region **sylvae**

SYLVAN adj, n sylvans

SYLVAS ▶ sylva

SYLVIA n songbird sylvias

SYLVIN = sylvite

SYLVINE = sylvite

SYLVINS ▶ sylvin

SYLVITE n soluble

colourless, white, or coloured mineral

SYMAR = cymar

SYMARS ▶ symar

SYMBION = symbiont

SYMBIOT = symbiont

SYMBOL n, vb

SYMBOLE = cymbal

SYMBOLS ▶ symbol

SYMITAR = scimitar

SYMPTOM n

SYN Scots word for ▶ since

SYNAGOG = synagogue

SYNANON n type of therapy given to drug addicts

SYNAPSE n, vb

SYNAPTE n litany in Greek Orthodox Church

SYNAXES ▶ synaxis

SYNAXIS n early Christian meeting

SYNC n synchronization ▷ vb synchronize

SYNCARP n fleshy multiple fruit

SYNCED ▶ sync

SYNCH = sync

SYNCHED ▶ synch

SYNCHRO n type of electrical device

SYNCHS ▶ synch

SYNCING ▶ sync

SYNCOM n communications satellite in stationary orbit **syncoms**

SYNCOPE n omission of one or more sounds or letters from the middle of a word

SYNCS ▶ sync

SYND = syne

SYNDED ▶ synd

SYNDET n synthetic detergent **syndets**

SYNDIC n business or legal agent of some institutions **syndics**

SYNDING ▶ synd

SYNDS ▶ synd

SYNE vb rinse ▷ n rinse ▷ adv since **syned**

SYNERGY n

SYNES ▶ syne

SYNESES ▶ synesis

SYNESIS n grammatical construction in which the form of a word is conditioned by the meaning

SYNFUEL n synthetic fuel

SYNGAMY n sexual reproduction

SYNGAS n mixture of carbon monoxide and hydrogen

SYNING ▶ syne

SYNOD n

SYNODAL adj of or relating to a synod ▷ n money paid to a bishop by less senior members of the clergy at a synod

SYNODIC adj involving conjunction of the same star, planet, or satellite

SYNODS ▶ synod

SYNONYM n

SYNOVIA n clear thick fluid that lubricates the body joints

SYNROC n

titanium-ceramic substance that can incorporate nuclear waste in its crystals **synrocs**

SYNTAGM = syntagma

SYNTAN n synthetic tanning substance **syntans**

SYNTAX n

SYNTENY n presence of two or more genes on the same chromosome

SYNTH n type of electrophonic musical instrument operated by a keyboard and pedals

SYNTHON n molecule used in synthesis

SYNTHS ▶ synth

SYNTONY n matching of frequencies

SYNURA n variety of microbe **synurae**

SYPE = sipe

SYPED ▶ sype

SYPES ▶ sype

SYPH shortening of > **syphilis**

SYPHER vb lap (a chamfered edge) in order to form a flush surface **syphers**

SYPHON = siphon

SYPHONS ▶ syphon

SYPHS ▶ syph

SYPING ▶ sype

SYRAH n type of French red wine **syrahs**

SYREN = siren

SYRENS ▶ syren

SYRETTE n small disposable syringe

SYRINGA n mock orange or lilac

SYRINGE n, vb

SYRINX n vocal organ of a bird

SYRPHID n type of fly

SYRTES ▶ syrtis

SYRTIS n area of quicksand

SYRUP n, vb **syruped,**

syrups

SYRUPY adj thick and sweet

SYSOP n person who runs a system or network **sysops**

SYSTEM n **systems**

SYSTOLE n regular contraction of the heart as it pumps blood

SYSTYLE n building with different types of columns

SYTHE = sith

SYTHES ▶ sythe

SYVER n street drain or the grating over it **syvers**

SYZYGAL ▶ syzygy

SYZYGY n position of a celestial body when sun, earth, and the body are in line

Tt

T is one of the most common consonants in Scrabble. There are only four two-letter words that begin with **T**, but they are easy to remember as there is one for every vowel except **U**. Like **S**, **T** begins a number of three-letter words that don't use vowels, which are well worth remembering. These are: **thy** (6 points), **try** (6), **tsk** (7), **twp** (8) and **tyg** (7). There are also some useful three-letter words using **X**: **tax**, **tex**, **tix** and **tux** (10 each). If you have an **X** during a game, remember words like **text** (11), **texts** (12), **textile** (14), **textual** (14) and **texture** (14). The last three of these have seven letters, and so will earn you 50-point bonuses if you use all your tiles to form them. Other threes well worth remembering are **taj** (10) and **tik** (7).

TA *interj* thank you ▷ *n* thank you

TAAL *n* language: usually, by implication, Afrikaans **taals**

TAATA *child's word for* ▷ **father**

> This East African word for a father is one of those short words that can help you dispose of a surplus of As.

TAATAS ▷ **taata**

TAB *n, vb*

TABANID *n* stout-bodied fly

TABARD *n* short sleeveless tunic decorated with a coat of arms, worn in medieval times **tabards**

TABARET *n* hard-wearing fabric of silk or similar cloth with stripes of satin or moire

TABBED ▷ **tab**

TABBIED ▷ **tabby**

TABBIES ▷ **tabby**

TABBING ▷ **tab**

TABBIS *n* silken cloth

TABBY *vb, n*

TABEFY *vb* emaciate or become emaciated

TABER *old variant of* ▷ **tabor**

TABERD = **tabard**

TABERDS ▷ **taberd**

TABERED ▷ **taber**

TABERS ▷ **taber**

TABES *n* wasting of a bodily organ or part **tabetic**

TABETIC *adj* emaciated

TABI *n* thick-soled Japanese sock, worn with sandals

TABID *adj* emaciated

TABINET *n* type of tabbied fabric

TABLA *n* one of a pair of Indian drums played with the hands **tablas**

TABLE *n, vb*

TABLEAU *n*

TABLED ▷ **table**

TABLES ▷ **table**

TABLET *n, vb* **tablets**

TABLIER n (formerly) part of a dress resembling an apron

TABLING ▸ table

TABLOID n

TABOO n, adj, vb tabooed, taboos

TABOR vb tabored, taborer

TABORET n low stool, originally in the shape of a drum taborin

TABORS ▸ tabor

TABOUHI = tabbouleh

TABOUR = tabor

TABOURS ▸ tabour

TABRERE = tabor

TABRET n smaller version of a tabor tabrets

TABS ▸ tab

TABU = taboo

TABUED ▸ tabu

TABUING ▸ tabu

TABULA n tablet for writing on tabulae

TABULAR adj

TABULI variant of
> tabbouleh

TABULIS ▸ tabuli

TABUN n organic compound used as a lethal nerve gas tabuns

TABUS ▸ tabu

TACAN n electronic ultrahigh-frequency navigation system for aircraft tacans

TACE n tasset

TACES ▸ tace

TACET n musical direction indicating that an instrument or

singer does not take part

TACH n device for measuring speed

TACHE n buckle, clasp, or hook taches

TACHINA n as in tachina fly bristly fly

TACHISM = tachisme

TACHIST ▸ tachism

TACHO = tachogram

TACHOS ▸ tacho

TACHS ▸ tach

TACHYON n hypothetical elementary particle

TACIT adj tacitly

TACK n, vb tacked, tacker, tackers

TACKET n nail, esp a hobnail tackets, tackety

TACKEY ▸ tacky

TACKIER ▸ tacky

TACKIES pl n

TACKIFY vb give (eg rubber) a sticky feel

TACKILY ▸ tacky

TACKING ▸ tack

TACKLE vb, n tackled, tackler, tackles

TACKS ▸ tack

TACKY adj

TACNODE n point at which two branches of a curve have a common tangent

TACO n tortilla fried until crisp, served with a filling tacos

TACRINE n drug used to treat Alzheimer's disease

TACT n tactful

TACTIC n

TACTICS n art of directing military forces in battle

TACTILE adj

TACTION n act of touching

TACTISM another word for ▸ taxis

TACTS ▸ tact

TACTUAL adj caused by touch

TAD n small bit or piece

TADDIE short for
▸ tadpole

TADDIES ▸ taddie

TADPOLE n

TADS ▸ tad

TAE Scots form of the verb
▸ toe

TAED ▸ tae

TAEDIUM archaic spelling of ▸ tedium

TAEING ▸ tae

TAEL n unit of weight, used in the Far East taels

TAENIA n (in ancient Greece) a narrow fillet or headband for the hair taeniae, taenias

TAES ▸ tae

TAFFETA = taffety

TAFFIA = tafia

TAFFIAS ▸ taffia

TAFFIES ▸ taffy

TAFFY = toffee

TAFIA n type of rum, esp from Guyana or the Caribbean tafias

TAG n, vb

TAGETES n any of a genus of plants with yellow or orange flowers

TAGGANT n microscopic material added to substance to identify it

TAGGED ▸ tag

TAGGEE n one who has been made to wear a tag **taggees**

TAGGER n one who marks with a tag **taggers**

TAGGIER ▸ taggy

TAGGING ▸ tag

TAGGY adj (of wool, hair, etc) matted

TAGINE n large, heavy N African cooking pot with a conical lid **tagines**

TAGLESS adj having no tag

TAGLIKE adj resembling a tag

TAGLINE n funny line of joke

TAGMA n distinct region of the body of an arthropod **tagmata**

TAGMEME n class of speech elements all of which may fulfil the same grammatical role

TAGRAG = ragtag

TAGRAGS ▸ tagrag

TAGS ▸ tag

TAGUAN n nocturnal flying squirrel of the East Indies **taguans**

TAHA n type of South African bird **tahas**

TAHINA = tahini

TAHINAS ▸ tahina

TAHINI n paste made from ground sesame seeds **tahinis**

TAHR n goatlike mammal of mountainous regions of S and SW Asia **tahrs**

TAHSIL n administrative division of a zila in certain states in India **tahsils**

TAI n type of sea bream

TAIAHA n carved weapon in the form of a staff, now used in Māori ceremonial oratory **taiahas**

TAIGA n belt of coniferous forest **taigas**

TAIGLE vb entangle or impede **taigled, taigles**

TAIHOA interj hold on! no hurry!

TAIKO n large Japanese drum **taikos**

TAIL n, adj, vb

TAILARD n one having a tail

TAILED ▸ tail

TAILER n one that tails **tailers**

TAILFAN n fanned structure at the hind end of a lobster

TAILFIN n decorative projection at back of car

TAILFLY n in angling, the lowest fly on a wet-fly cast

TAILING n part of a beam, rafter, projecting brick or stone, etc, embedded in a wall

TAILLE n (in France before 1789) a tax levied by a king or overlord on his subjects **tailles**

TAILLIE n (in law) the limitation of an estate or interest to a person and the heirs of his body

TAILOR n, vb **tailors**

TAILS adv with the side of a coin that does not have a portrait of a head on it uppermost

TAILYE = taillie

TAILYES ▸ tailye

TAILZIE = taillie

TAIN n tinfoil used in backing mirrors **tains**

TAINT vb, n tainted, **taints**

TAIPAN n **taipans**

TAIRA = tayra

TAIRAS ▸ taira

TAIS ▸ tai

TAISCH n (in Scotland) apparition of a person whose death is imminent **taish**

TAISHES ▸ taish

TAIT = tate

TAITS ▸ tait

TAIVER = taver

TAIVERS ▸ taiver

TAIVERT adj Scots word meaning confused or bewildered

TAJ n tall conical cap worn as a mark of distinction by Muslims **tajes**

▌ This word for a Muslim's cap is one

of the key words to remember for using the J.

TAJINE = tagine

TAJINES ▸ tajine

TAK Scots variant spelling of ▸ take

TAKA n standard monetary unit of Bangladesh, divided into 100 paise

TAKABLE ▸ take

TAKAHE n very rare flightless New Zealand bird **takahes**

TAKAS ▸ taka

TAKE vb remove from a place ▹ n one of a series of recordings from which the best will be used **taken**

TAKEOFF n act or process of making an aircraft airborne

TAKEOUT n shop or restaurant that sells such food

TAKER n person who agrees to take something that is offered **takers**

TAKES ▸ take

TAKEUP n claiming or acceptance of something that is due or available **takeups**

TAKHI n type of wild Mongolian horse **takhis, taki**

TAKIER ▸ taky

TAKIEST ▸ taky

TAKIN n bovid mammal of mountainous regions of S Asia

TAKING ▸ take

TAKINGS ▸ take

TAKINS ▸ takin

TAKIS ▸ taki

TAKKIES = tackies

TAKS ▸ tak

TAKY adj appealing

TALA n standard monetary unit of Samoa, divided into 100 sene

TALAK = talaq

TALAKS ▸ talak

TALANT old variant of ▸ talent

TALANTS ▸ talant

TALAQ n Muslim form of divorce **talaqs**

> In Islamic law, a word for divorce: easy to miss because one tends not to think of words ending in Q.

TALAR n ankle-length robe

TALARIA pl n winged sandals, such as those worn by Hermes

TALARS ▸ talar

TALAS ▸ tala

TALAUNT old variant of ▸ talon

TALAYOT n ancient Balearic stone tower

TALBOT n ancient breed of large hound **talbots**

TALC n, vb, adj **talced**

TALCIER ▸ talcy

TALCING ▸ talc

TALCKED ▸ talcky

TALCKY = talcy

TALCOSE ▸ talc

TALCOUS ▸ talc

TALCS ▸ talc

TALCUM n white, grey, brown, or pale green mineral **talcums**

TALCY adj like, containing, or covered in talc

TALE n

TALEA n rhythmic pattern in certain mediaeval choral compositions **taleae**

TALEFUL adj having many tales

TALENT n **talents**

TALER = thaler

TALERS ▸ taler

TALES n group of persons summoned to fill vacancies on a jury panel

TALI ▸ talus

TALION n principle of making punishment correspond to the crime **talions**

TALIPAT = talipot

TALIPED adj having a club foot ▹ n club-footed person

TALIPES n congenital deformity of the foot by which it is twisted in any of various positions

TALIPOT n palm tree of the East Indies

TALK vb, n

TALKBOX n voice box

TALKED ▸ talk

TALKER ▸ talk

TALKERS ▸ talk

TALKIE n early film with a soundtrack

TALKIER ▸ talky

TALKIES ▸ talkie

TALKING *n* speech; the act of speaking

TALKS ▸ talk

TALKY *adj* containing too much dialogue or inconsequential talk

TALL *adj*

TALLAGE *n* tax levied on Crown lands and royal towns ▸ *vb* levy a tax (upon)

TALLAT = **tallet**

TALLATS ▸ tallat

TALLBOY *n*

TALLENT *n* plenty

TALLER ▸ tall

TALLEST ▸ tall

TALLET *n* loft **tallets**

TALLIED ▸ tally

TALLIER ▸ tally

TALLIES ▸ tally

TALLIS *variant of* ▸ **tallith**

TALLISH *adj* quite tall

TALLIT *variant of* ▸ **tallith**

TALLITH *n* shawl worn by Jewish males during religious services

TALLITS ▸ tallith

TALLOL *n* oily liquid used for making soaps, lubricants, etc **tallols**

TALLOT = **tallet**

TALLOTS ▸ tallot

TALLOW *n, vb* tallows, tallowy

TALLS ▸ tall

TALLY *vb, n*

TALLYHO *n* cry to encourage hounds when the quarry is sighted ▸ *vb* make the cry of tallyho

TALMA *n* short cloak **talmas**

TALMUD *n* primary source of Jewish religious law, consisting of the Mishnah and the Gemara **talmuds**

TALON *n* taloned, talons

TALOOKA = **taluk**

TALPA *n* sebaceous cyst talpae, talpas

TALUK *n* subdivision of a district **taluka**

TALUKAS ▸ taluka

TALUKS ▸ taluk

TALUS *n* bone of the ankle that articulates with the leg bones to form the ankle joint **taluses**

TALWEG = **thalweg**

TALWEGS ▸ talweg

TAM *n* type of hat

TAMABLE ▸ tame

TAMAL = **tamale**

TAMALE *n* Mexican dish of minced meat wrapped in maize husks and steamed **tamales**

TAMALS ▸ tamal

TAMANDU = **tamandua**

TAMANU *n* poon tree tamanus

TAMARA *n* powder consisting of cloves, cinnamon, fennel, coriander, etc

TAMARAO = **tamarau**

TAMARAS ▸ tamara

TAMARAU *n* small rare member of a cattle tribe in the Philippines

TAMARI *n* Japanese variety of soy sauce

TAMARIN *n* small monkey of South and Central America

TAMARIS ▸ tamari

TAMASHA *n* (in India) a show

TAMBAC = **tombac**

TAMBACS ▸ tambac

TAMBAK = **tombac**

TAMBAKS ▸ tambak

TAMBALA *n* unit of Malawian currency

TAMBER = **timbre**

TAMBERS ▸ tamber

TAMBOUR *n* embroidery frame consisting of two hoops ▸ *vb* embroider (fabric or a design) on a tambour

TAMBUR *n* old Turkish stringed instrument

TAMBURA *n* Middle-Eastern stringed instrument with a long neck

TAMBURS ▸ tambur

TAME *adj, vb* tamed

TAMEIN *n* Burmese skirt tameins

TAMELY, tamer, tamers, tames, tamest ▸ tame

TAMIN *n* thin woollen fabric **tamine**

TAMINES ▸ tamine

TAMING *n* act of making

(something) tame

tamings

TAMINS ▸ tamin

TAMIS = tammy

TAMISE n type of thin cloth

TAMISES ▸ tamis

TAMMAR n small scrub wallaby **tammars**

TAMMIE n short for tam-o'-shanter, a traditional Scottish hat

TAMMIED ▸ tammy

TAMMIES ▸ tammy

TAMMY n glazed woollen or mixed fabric ▷ vb strain (sauce, soup, etc) through a tammy

TAMP vb pack down by repeated taps

TAMPALA n Asian plant, eaten as food

TAMPAN n biting mite **tampans**

TAMPED ▸ tamp

TAMPER vb, n **tampers**

TAMPING adj very angry ▷ n act or instance of tamping

TAMPION n plug placed in a gun's muzzle to keep out moisture and dust

TAMPON n, vb **tampons**

TAMPS ▸ tamp

TAMS ▸ tam

TAN n, vb, adj

TANA n small Madagascan lemur

TANADAR n commanding officer of an Indian police station

TANAGER n American songbird with a short thick bill

TANAGRA n type of tanager

TANAS ▸ tana

TANBARK n bark of certain trees, esp the oak and hemlock, used as a source of tannin

TANDEM n **tandems**

TANDOOR n type of Indian clay oven

TANE old Scottish variant of ▸ **taken**

TANG n, vb

TANGA n triangular loincloth worn by indigenous peoples in tropical America **tangas**

TANGED ▸ tang

TANGELO n hybrid produced by crossing a tangerine tree with a grapefruit tree

TANGENT n

TANGHIN n poison formerly used in Madagascar to determine the guilt of crime suspects

TANGI n Māori funeral ceremony

TANGIE n water spirit of Orkney, appearing as a figure draped in seaweed, or as a seahorse

TANGIER ▸ tangy

TANGIES ▸ tangie

TANGING ▸ tang

TANGIS ▸ tangi

TANGLE n, vb **tangled,**

tangler, tangles, tangly

TANGO n, vb tangoed, tangos

TANGRAM n type of Chinese puzzle

TANGS ▸ tang

TANGUN n small and sturdy Tibetan pony **tanguns**

TANGY adj having a pungent, fresh, or briny flavour or aroma

TANH n hyperbolic tangent **tanhs**

TANIST n heir apparent of a Celtic chieftain **tanists**

TANIWHA n

TANK n, vb

TANKA n Japanese verse form consisting of five lines

TANKAGE n capacity or contents of a tank or tanks

TANKARD n

TANKAS ▸ tanka

TANKED ▸ tank

TANKER n **tankers**

TANKFUL n quantity contained in a tank

TANKIA n type of boat used in Canton **tankias**

TANKIES ▸ tanky

TANKING n heavy defeat

TANKINI n swimming costume consisting of a camisole top and bikini briefs

TANKS ▸ tank

TANKY n die-hard communist

TANLING n suntanned person

TANNA n Indian police station or army base

TANNAGE n act or process of tanning

TANNAH = tanna

TANNAHS ▸ tannah

TANNAS ▸ tanna

TANNATE n any salt or ester of tannic acid

TANNED ▸ tan

TANNER ▸ tan

TANNERS ▸ tan

TANNERY ▸ tan

TANNEST ▸ tan

TANNIC adj of, containing, or produced from tannin or tannic acid

TANNIE n in S Africa, title of respect used to refer to an elderly woman **tannies**

TANNIN n

TANNING ▸ tan

TANNINS ▸ tannin

TANNISH ▸ tan

TANNOY n sound-amplifying apparatus used as a public-address system ▸ vb announce (something) using a Tannoy system **tannoys**

TANREC = tenrec

TANRECS ▸ tanrec

TANS ▸ tan

TANSIES ▸ tansy

TANSY n yellow-flowered plant

TANTARA n blast, as on a trumpet or horn

TANTI adj old word for worthwhile

TANTIVY adv at full speed ▸ interj hunting cry, esp at full gallop

TANTO adv too much

TANTONY n runt

TANTRA n sacred books of Tantrism **tantras, tantric**

TANTRUM n

TANUKI n animal similar to a raccoon, found in Japan **tanukis**

TANYARD n part of a tannery

TAO n (in Confucian philosophy) the correct course of action

TAONGA n treasure **taongas**

TAOS ▸ tao

TAP vb, n

TAPA n inner bark of the paper mulberry

TAPALO n Latin American scarf, often patterned and brightly coloured **tapalos**

TAPAS pl n (in Spanish cookery) light snacks or appetizers

TAPE n, vb **taped**

TAPEN adj made of tape

TAPER n, adj tapered, taperer, tapers, tapes ▸ tape

TAPET n example of tapestry

TAPETA ▸ tapetum

TAPETAL ▸ tapetum

TAPETI n forest rabbit of Brazil **tapetis**

TAPETS ▸ tapet

TAPETUM n layer of nutritive cells that surrounds developing spore cells

TAPHOLE n hole in a furnace for running off molten metal or slag

TAPING ▸ tape

TAPIOCA n

TAPIR n tapirs

TAPIS n tapestry or carpeting **tapises**

TAPIST n person who records read out printed matter in an audio format **tapists**

TAPLASH n dregs of beer

TAPPA = tapa

TAPPAS ▸ tappa

TAPPED ▸ tap

TAPPER n person who taps **tappers**

TAPPET n **tappets**

TAPPICE vb hide

TAPPING ▸ tap

TAPPIT adj crested; topped

TAPROOM n public bar in a hotel or pub

TAPROOT n

TAPS ▸ tap

TAPSMAN n old word for a barman **tapsmen**

TAPSTER n barman

TAPSTRY adj relating to tapestry

TAPU adj sacred ▸ n Māori religious or superstitious restriction on something ▸ vb put a tapu on something tapued, tapuing, tapus

TAR n, vb

TARA = taro

TARAIRE n type of New Zealand tree

TARAMA n cod roe taramas

TARAMEA n variety of New Zealand speargrass

TARAND n northern animal of legend, now supposed to have been the reindeer tarands

TARAS ▶ tara

TARBOY n boy who applies tar to the skin of sheep cut during shearing tarboys

TARBUSH = tarboosh

TARCEL = tarcel

TARCELS ▶ tarcel

TARDIED, tardier, tardies, tardily ▶ tardy

TARDIVE adj tending to develop late

TARDO adj (of music) slow; to be played slowly

TARDY adj, vb

TARDYON n particle travelling slower than the speed of light

TARE n weight of the wrapping or container of goods ▷ vb weigh (a package, etc) in order to calculate the amount of tare **tared, tares**

TARGA n as in targa top denotes removable hard roof on a car

TARGE vb interrogate targed, targes

TARGET n, vb targets

TARGING ▶ targe

TARIFF n, vb tariffs

TARING ▶ tare

TARINGS ▶ tare

TARMAC See also ▶ macadam

TARMACS ▶ tarmac

TARN n

TARNAL adj damned ▷ adv extremely

TARNISH vb, n

TARNS ▶ tarn

TARO n plant with a large edible rootstock

TAROC old variant of ▶ tarot

TAROCS ▶ taroc

TAROK old variant of ▶ tarot

TAROKS ▶ tarok

TAROS ▶ taro

TAROT n, adj tarots

TARP informal word for ▶ tarpaulin

TARPAN n European wild horse common in prehistoric times tarpans

TARPON n large silvery clupeoid game fish found in warm Atlantic waters tarpons

TARPS ▶ tarp

TARRAS = trass

TARRE vb old word meaning to provoke or goad

TARRED ▶ tar

TARRES ▶ tarre

TARRIED ▶ tarry

TARRIER ▶ tarry

TARRIES ▶ tarry

TARRING ▶ tar

TARROCK n seabird

TARROW vb exhibit reluctance tarrows

TARRY vb, n, adj

TARS ▶ tar

TARSAL adj of the tarsus or tarsi ▷ n tarsal bone tarsals

TARSEAL n

TARSEL = tercel

TARSELS ▶ tarsel

TARSI ▶ tarsus

TARSIA another term for ▶ intarsia

TARSIAS ▶ tarsia

TARSIER n small nocturnal primate of the E Indies, which has very large eyes

TARSUS n

TART n, adj, vb

TARTAN n

TARTANA n small Mediterranean sailing boat **tartane**

TARTANS ▶ tartan

TARTAR n

TARTARE n mayonnaise sauce mixed with hard-boiled egg yolks, herbs, etc

TARTARS ▶ tartar

TARTED ▶ tart

TARTER ▶ tart

TARTEST ▶ tart

TARTIER ▶ tarty

TARTILY ▶ tarty

TARTINE n slice of bread with butter or jam spread on it

TARTING ▶ tart

TARTISH ▸ tart

TARTLET n individual pastry case with a filling of fruit or other sweet or savoury mixture

TARTLY ▸ tart

TARTS ▸ tart

TARTUFE = tartuffe

TARTUFO n Italian mousse-like chocolate dessert

TARTY adj provocative in a cheap and bawdy way

TARWEED n resinous Californian plant

TARZAN n man with great physical strength **tarzans**

TAS ▸ tass

TASAR = tussore

TASARS ▸ tasar

TASBIH n form of Islamic prayer **tasbihs**

TASER vb use a Taser stun gun on (someone) **tasered, tasers**

TASH vb stain or besmirch **tashed, tashes, tashing**

TASK n, vb

TASKBAR n area of computer screen showing what programs are running

TASKED, tasker, taskers, tasking, tasks ▸ task

TASLET = tasset

TASLETS ▸ taslet

TASS n cup, goblet, or glass

TASSE = tasset

TASSEL n, vb tassell, tassels

TASSES ▸ tasse

TASSET n piece of armour to protect the thigh **tassets**

TASSIE = tass

TASSIES ▸ tassie

TASTE n, vb tasted

TASTER n person employed to test the quality of food or drink by tasting it **tasters**

TASTES ▸ taste

TASTIER ▸ tasty

TASTILY ▸ tasty

TASTING ▸ taste

TASTY adj

TAT n tatty or tasteless article(s) ▸ vb make (something) by tatting

TATAMI n thick rectangular mat of woven straw **tatamis**

TATAR n brutal person **tatars**

TATE n small tuft of fibre

TATER n potato **taters**

TATES ▸ tate

TATH vb (of cattle) to defecate **tathed, tathing, taths**

TATIE = tattie

TATIES ▸ tatie

TATLER old variant of ▸ tattler

TATLERS ▸ tatler

TATOU n armadillo

TATOUAY n large armadillo of South America

TATOUS ▸ tatou

TATS ▸ tat

TATSOI n variety of Chinese cabbage **tatsois**

TATT = tat

TATTED ▸ tat

TATTER vb make or become torn **tatters**

TATTERY = tattered

TATTIE Scot or dialect word for ▸ potato

TATTIER ▸ tatty

TATTIES ▸ tattie

TATTILY ▸ tatty

TATTING ▸ tat

TATTLE n, vb tattled

TATTLER n person who tattles

TATTLES ▸ tattle

TATTOO n, vb tattoos, tattow

TATTOWS ▸ tattow

TATTS ▸ tatt

TATTY adj

TATU old variant of ▸ tattoo

TATUED ▸ tatu

TATUING ▸ tatu

TATUS ▸ tatu

TAU n 19th letter in the Greek alphabet

TAUBE n type of German aeroplane **taubes**

TAUGHT ▸ teach

TAUHINU New Zealand name for ▸ poplar

TAUHOU = silvereye

TAUHOUS ▸ tauhou

TAUIWI n Māori term for the non-Māori people of New Zealand **tauiwis**

TAULD vb old Scots variant of told

TAUNT vb, n, adj **taunted, taunter, taunts**

TAUON n negatively charged elementary particle **tauons**

TAUPATA n New Zealand shrub or tree

TAUPE adj brownish-grey ▷ n brownish-grey colour **taupes**

TAUPIE = **tawpie**

TAUPIES ▶ **taupie**

TAUREAN adj born under or characteristic of Taurus

TAURINE adj of, relating to, or resembling a bull ▷ n substance obtained from the bile of animals

TAUS ▶ **tau**

TAUT adj, vb

TAUTAUG = **tautog**

TAUTED ▶ **taut**

TAUTEN vb **tautens**

TAUTER ▶ **taut**

TAUTEST ▶ **taut**

TAUTING ▶ **taut**

TAUTIT adj Scots word meaning tangled

TAUTLY ▶ **taut**

TAUTOG n large dark-coloured wrasse, used as a food fish **tautogs**

TAUTS ▶ **taut**

TAV n 23rd and last letter in the Hebrew alphabet

TAVA n thick Indian frying pan **tavah**

TAVAHS ▶ **tavah**

TAVAS ▶ **tava**

TAVER vb wander about **tavered**

TAVERED ▶ **taver**

TAVERN n

TAVERNA n (in Greece) a guesthouse that has its own bar

TAVERNS ▶ **tavern**

TAVERS ▶ **taver**

TAVERT adj bewildered or confused

TAVS ▶ **tav**

TAW vb convert skins into leather

TAWA n tall timber tree from New Zealand

TAWAI n New Zealand beech **tawais**

TAWAS ▶ **tawa**

TAWDRY adj, n

TAWED ▶ **taw**

TAWER ▶ **taw**

TAWERS ▶ **taw**

TAWERY n place where tawing is carried out

TAWHAI = **tawai**

TAWHAIS ▶ **tawhai**

TAWHIRI n small New Zealand tree with wavy green glossy leaves

TAWIE adj easily persuaded or managed **tawier, tawiest**

TAWING ▶ **taw**

TAWINGS ▶ **taw**

TAWNEY = **tawny**

TAWNEYS ▶ **tawney**

TAWNIER ▶ **tawny**

TAWNIES ▶ **tawny**

TAWNILY ▶ **tawny**

TAWNY adj, n

TAWPIE n foolish or maladroit girl **tawpies**

TAWS = **tawse**

TAWSE n leather strap with one end cut into thongs ▷ vb punish (someone) with or as if with a tawse **tawsed, tawses, tawsing**

TAWT = taut; **tawted, tawtie, tawtier, tawting, tawts**

TAX n, vb

TAXA ▶ **taxon**

TAXABLE adj capable of being taxed ▷ n person, income, property, etc, that is subject to tax **taxably**

TAXED ▶ **tax**

TAXEME n any element of speech that may differentiate meaning **taxemes, taxemic**

TAXER ▶ **tax**

TAXERS ▶ **tax**

TAXES ▶ **tax**

TAXI n, vb **taxicab, taxied**

TAXIES ▶ **taxis**

TAXIING ▶ **taxi**

TAXIMAN n taxi driver **taximen**

TAXING adj demanding, onerous

TAXINGS ▶ **tax**

TAXIS n movement of a cell or organism in response to an external stimulus ▷ n ancient Greek army unit

TAXITE n type of volcanic rock **taxites, taxitic**

TAXIWAY n marked path along which aircraft taxi to or from a runway, parking area, etc

TAXLESS ▶ tax

TAXMAN n collector of taxes **taxmen**

TAXOL n trademarked anti-cancer drug **taxols**

TAXON n any taxonomic group or rank **taxons**

TAXOR ▶ tax

TAXORS ▶ tax

TAXPAID adj (of taxable products, esp wine) having had the applicable tax paid already

TAXUS n genus of conifers

TAXWISE adv regarding tax

TAXYING ▶ taxi

TAY Irish dialect word for ▶ tea

TAYRA n large arboreal mammal of Central and South America **tayras**

TAYS ▶ tay

TAZZA n wine cup with a shallow bowl and a circular foot **tazzas**, **tazze**

TCHICK vb make a clicking noise with the tongue **tchicks**

TE n (in tonic sol-fa) seventh degree of any major scale

TEA n, vb

TEABAG n porous bag of tea leaves for infusion **teabags**

TEABOWL n small bowl used (instead of a teacup) for serving tea

TEABOX n box for storing tea

TEACAKE n

TEACART n trolley from which tea is served

TEACH vb

TEACHER n

TEACHES ▶ teach

TEACHIE old form of ▶ tetchy

TEACUP n cup out of which tea may be drunk **teacups**

TEAD old word for ▶ torch

TEADE = tead

TEADES ▶ teade

TEADS ▶ tead

TEAED ▶ tea

TEAGLE vb raise or hoist using a tackle **teagled**, **teagles**

TEAING ▶ tea

TEAK n **teaks**

TEAL n

TEALIKE adj resembling tea

TEALS ▶ teal

TEAM n, vb **teamed**, **teamer**, **teamers**, **teaming**, **teams**

TEAPOT n **teapots**

TEAPOY n small table or stand with a tripod base **teapoys**

TEAR n, vb **teared**, **tearer**, **tearers**

TEARFUL adj

TEARGAS n gas or vapour that makes the eyes smart and water

▷ vb deploy teargas against

TEARIER ▶ teary

TEARILY ▶ teary

TEARING ▶ tear

TEAROOM = teashop

TEARS ▶ tear

TEARY adj characterized by, covered with, or secreting tears

TEAS ▶ tea

TEASE vb, n **teased**

TEASEL n plant with prickly leaves and flowers ▷ vb tease (a fabric) **teasels**

TEASER n annoying or difficult problem **teasers**

TEASES ▶ tease

TEASHOP n restaurant where tea and light refreshments are served

TEASING ▶ tease

TEAT n **teated**

TEATIME n late afternoon

TEATS ▶ teat

TEAWARE n implements for brewing and serving tea

TEAZE old variant of ▶ tease

TEAZED ▶ teaze

TEAZEL = teasel

TEAZELS ▶ teazel

TEAZES ▶ teaze

TEAZING ▶ teaze

TEAZLE = teasel

TEAZLED ▶ teazle

TEAZLES ▶ teazle

TEBBAD n sandstorm **tebbads**

TEC *short for* ▷ **detective**

TECH *n*

TECHED *adj* showing slight insanity

TECHIE *n* person who is skilled in the use of technology ▷ *adj* relating to or skilled in the use of technology

TECHIER ▶ **techy**

TECHIES ▶ **techie**

TECHILY ▶ **techy**

TECHNIC *another word for* ▷ **technique**

TECHNO *n* type of electronic dance music with a very fast beat **technos**

TECHS ▶ **tech**

TECHY = **techie**

TECKEL *n* dachshund **teckels**

TECS ▶ **tec**

TECTA ▶ **tectum**

TECTAL ▶ **tectum**

TECTITE = **tektite**

TECTRIX *another name for* ▶ **covert**

TECTUM *n* any roof-like structure in the body **tectums**

TED *vb* shake out (hay), so as to dry it **tedded**

TEDDER *n* machine equipped with a series of small rotating forks for tedding hay **tedders**

TEDDIE = **teddy**

TEDDIES ▶ **teddy**

TEDDING ▶ **ted**

TEDDY *n*

TEDIER ▶ **tedy**

TEDIEST ▶ **tedy**

TEDIOUS *adj*

TEDIUM *n* **tediums**

TEDS ▶ **ted**

TEDY = **tedious**

TEE *n, vb* **teed, teeing**

TEEK *adj* in Indian English, well

TEEL = **sesame**

TEELS ▶ **teel**

TEEM *vb* **teemed, teemer, teemers, teemful, teeming, teems**

TEEN *n* affliction or woe ▷ *n* **teenager** ▷ *vb* set alight

TEENAGE *adj, n*

TEEND = **tind**

TEENDED ▶ **teend**

TEENDS ▶ **teend**

TEENE = **teen**

TEENED ▶ **teen**

TEENER ▶ **teen**

TEENERS ▶ **teen**

TEENES ▶ **teene**

TEENFUL ▶ **teen**

TEENIER ▶ **teeny**

TEENING ▶ **teen**

TEENS ▶ **teen**

TEENSY = **teeny**

TEENTSY = **teeny**

TEENTY = **teeny**

TEENY *adj* extremely small

TEEPEE = **tepee**

TEEPEES ▶ **tepee**

TEER *vb* smear; daub **teered, teering, teers**

TEES ▶ **tee**

TEETER *vb* **teeters**

TEETH ▶ **tooth**

TEETHE *vb* **teethed**

TEETHER *n* object for an infant to bite on during teething

TEETHES ▶ **teethe**

TEF *n* annual grass, of NE Africa, grown for its grain **teff**

TEFFS ▶ **teff**

TEFLON *n* substance used in nonstick cooking vessels **teflons**

TEFS ▶ **tef**

TEG *n* two-year-old sheep **tegg**

TEGGS ▶ **tegg**

TEGMEN *n* either of the leathery forewings of the cockroach and related insects **tegmina**

TEGS ▶ **teg**

TEGU *n* large South American lizard

TEGUA *n* type of moccasin **teguas**

TEGULA *n* one of a pair of coverings of the forewings of certain insects **tegulae**

TEGULAR *adj* of, relating to, or resembling a tile or tiles

TEGUMEN = **tegmen**

TEGUS ▶ **tegu**

TEHR = **tahr**

TEHRS ▶ **tehr**

TEHSIL *n* administrative region in some S Asian countries **tehsils**

TEIID *n* member of the Teiidae family of lizards **teiids**

TEIL *n* lime tree **teils**

TEIN *n* monetary unit of Kazakhstan

TEIND *Scot and northern English word for* ▶ **tithe**

TEINDED ▶ **teind**

TEINDS ▶ **teind**

TEINS ▶ **tein**

TEKKIE *variant of* ▶ **techie**

TEKKIES ▶ **tekkie**

TEKTITE *n* small dark glassy object found in several areas around the world

TEL = **tell**

TELA *n* any delicate tissue or weblike structure **telae**

TELAMON *n* column in the form of a male figure

TELARY *adj* capable of spinning a web

TELCO *n* telecommunications company **telcos**

TELD = **tauld**

TELE = **telly**

TELECOM *n* telecommunications

TELEDU *n* badger of SE Asia and Indonesia **teledus**

TELEFAX *another word for* ▶ **fax**

TELEGA *n* rough four-wheeled cart used in Russia **telegas**

TELEMAN *n* noncommissioned officer in the US navy **telemen**

TELEOST *n* bony fish with rayed fins and a swim bladder ▷ *adj* of, relating to, or belonging to this type of fish

TELEPIC *n* feature-length film made for television

TELERAN *n* electronic navigational aid

TELERGY *n* name for the form of energy supposedly transferred during telepathy

TELES ▶ **tele**

TELESES ▶ **telesis**

TELESIS *n* purposeful use of natural and social processes to obtain specific social goals

TELESM *n* talisman **telesms**

TELETEX *n* international means of communicating text between a variety of terminals

TELEX *n, vb* telexed, telexes

TELFER *n* overhead transport system **telfers**

TELFORD *n* road built using a method favoured by Thomas Telford

TELIA ▶ **telium**

TELIAL ▶ **telium**

TELIC *adj* directed or moving towards some goal

TELIUM *n* spore-producing body of some rust fungi in which the teliospores are formed

TELL *vb* make known in words ▷ *n* large mound resulting from the accumulation of rubbish

TELLAR = **tiller**

TELLARS ▶ **tellar**

TELLEN ▶ **tellin**

TELLENS ▶ **tellen**

TELLER *n, vb* **tellers**

TELLIES ▶ **telly**

TELLIN *n* slim marine bivalve molluscs that live in intertidal sand

TELLING ▶ **tell**

TELLINS ▶ **tellin**

TELLS ▶ **tell**

TELLUS *n* earth

TELLY *n* **tellys**

TELNET *n* system allowing remote access to other computers on the same network ▷ *vb* use a telnet system **telnets**

TELOI ▶ **telos**

TELOME *n* fundamental unit of a plant's structure **telomes, telomic**

TELOS *n* objective; ultimate purpose

TELPHER = **telferage**

TELS ▶ **tel**

TELSON *n* segment of the body of crustaceans and arachnids **telsons**

TELT = **tauld**

TEMBLOR n earthquake or earth tremor

TEME old variant of ▸ **team**

TEMED ▸ **teme**

TEMENE ▸ **temenos**

TEMENOS n sacred area, esp one surrounding a temple

TEMES ▸ **teme**

TEMP = temporary

TEMPED ▸ **temp**

TEMPEH n fermented soya beans **tempehs**

TEMPER n, adj

TEMPERA n

TEMPERS ▸ **temper**

TEMPEST n, vb

TEMPI ▸ **tempo**

TEMPING ▸ **temp**

TEMPLAR n lawyer who has chambers in the Inner or Middle Temple in London

TEMPLE n templed, temples

TEMPLET = template

TEMPO n

TEMPORE adv in the time of

TEMPOS ▸ **tempo**

TEMPS ▸ **temp**

TEMPT vb tempted, tempter, tempts

TEMPURA n Japanese dish of seafood or vegetables dipped in batter and deep-fried

TEMS = temse

TEMSE vb sieve temsed, temses, temsing

TEN n, adj

TENABLE adj tenably

TENACE n holding of two nonconsecutive high cards of a suit, such as the ace and queen **tenaces**

TENAIL = tenaille

TENAILS ▸ **tenail**

TENANCY n temporary possession of property owned by somebody else

TENANT n, vb tenants

TENCH n tenches

TEND vb tended

TENDENZ = tendency

TENDER adj, vb, n tenders

TENDING ▸ **tend**

TENDON n tendons

TENDRE n care tendres

TENDRIL n

TENDRON n shoot

TENDS ▸ **tend**

TENDU n position in ballet tendus

TENE = teen

TENES ▸ **tene**

TENET n tenets

TENFOLD n one tenth

TENGE n standard monetary unit of Kazakhstan tenges

TENIA = taenia

TENIAE ▸ **tenia**

This plural of *tenia*, a kind of hair-ribbon, is another of those 6-letter words which come in useful for dumping a surplus of vowels.

TENIAS ▸ **tenia**

TENIOID ▸ **tenia**

TENNE n tawny colour

TENNER n tenners

TENNES ▸ **tenne**

TENNIES ▸ **tenny**

TENNIS n

TENNIST n tennis player

TENNO n formal title of the Japanese emperor tennos

TENNY = tenne

TENON n, vb tenoned, tenoner, tenons

TENOR n, adj tenors, tenour

TENOURS ▸ **tenour**

TENPIN n one of the pins used in tenpin bowling tenpins

TENREC n small mammal resembling hedgehogs or shrews tenrecs

TENS ▸ **ten**

TENSE adj, vb, n tensed, tensely, tenser, tenses, tensest

TENSILE adj

TENSING ▸ **tense**

TENSION n, vb tensity

TENSIVE adj of or causing tension or strain

TENSON n type of French lyric poem tensons

TENSOR n any muscle that can cause a part to become firm or tense tensors

TENT n, vb

TENTAGE n tents collectively

TENTED ▸ **tent**

TENTER ▸ **tent**

TENTERS ▸ **tent**

TENTFUL n number of people or objects that can fit in a tent

TENTH n (of) number ten in a series ▷ adj coming after the ninth in numbering or counting order, position, time, etc ▷ adv after the ninth person, position, event, etc **tenthly, tenths**

TENTIE adj wary **tentier**

TENTIGO n morbid preoccupation with sex

TENTING ▶ tent

TENTS ▶ tent

TENTY = tentie

TENUE n deportment

TENUES ▶ tenuis

TENUIS n (in the grammar of classical Greek) any of the voiceless stops

TENUITY ▶ tenuous

TENUOUS adj

TENURE n, vb

TENURED adj having tenure of office

TENURES ▶ tenure

TENUTI ▶ tenuto

TENUTO adv (of a note) to be held for or beyond its full time value ▷ vb note sustained thus **tenutos**

TENZON = tenson

TENZONS ▶ tenzon

TEOPAN n enclosure surrounding a teocalli **teopans**

TEPA n type of tree native to South America

TEPAL n subdivisions of a perianth **tepals**

TEPAS ▶ tepa

TEPEE ▶ tepees

TEPEFY vb make or become tepid

TEPHRA n solid matter ejected during a volcanic eruption **tephras**

TEPID adj **tepider, tepidly**

TEPOY = teapoy

TEPOYS ▶ tepoy

TEQUILA n

TERAI n felt hat with a wide brim worn in subtropical regions **terais**

TERAOHM n unit of resistance equal to 10^{12} ohms

TERAPH n household god or image venerated by ancient Semitic peoples

TERAS n monstrosity; teratism **terata**

TERBIA n amorphous white insoluble powder **terbias**

TERBIC ▶ terbium

TERBIUM n rare metallic element

TERCE n third of the seven canonical hours of the divine office

TERCEL n male falcon or hawk, esp as used in falconry **tercels**

TERCES ▶ terce

TERCET n group of three lines of verse that rhyme together **tercets**

TERCIO n regiment of Spanish or Italian infantry **tercios**

TEREBIC adj as in **terebic acid** white crystalline carboxylic acid produced by the action of nitric acid on turpentine

TEREBRA n ancient Roman device used for boring holes in defensive walls

TEREDO n marine mollusc that bores into and destroys submerged timber **teredos**

TEREFA = tref

TEREFAH = tref

TEREK n type of sandpiper **tereks**

TERES n shoulder muscle

TERETE adj (esp of plant parts) smooth and usually cylindrical and tapering **teretes**

TERF old variant of ▶ turf

TERFE old variant of ▶ turf

TERFES ▶ terfe

TERFS ▶ terf

TERGA ▶ tergum

TERGAL ▶ tergum

TERGITE n constituent part of a tergum

TERGUM n cuticular plate covering the

dorsal surface of a body segment of an arthropod

TERM n, vb **termed**

TERMER = termor

TERMERS ▶ termer

TERMING ▶ term

TERMINI ▶ terminus

TERMITE n

TERMLY n publication issued once a term

TERMOR n person who holds an estate for a term of years or until he dies **termors**

TERMS ▶ term

TERN n **ternal**

TERNARY adj, n

TERNATE adj (esp of a leaf) consisting of three leaflets or other parts

TERNE n alloy of lead containing tin and antimony ▶ vb coat with this alloy **terned, ternes, terning**

TERNION n group of three

TERNS ▶ tern

TERPENE n unsaturated hydrocarbon found in the essential oils of many plants

TERRA n (in legal contexts) earth or land

TERRACE n, vb

TERRAE ▶ terra

TERRAIN = terrane

TERRANE n series of rock formations

TERRAS = trass

TERREEN old variant of ▶ tureen

TERRENE adj of or relating to the earth ▶ n land

TERRET n ring on a harness saddle through which the reins are passed **terrets**

TERRIER n

TERRIES ▶ terry

TERRIFY vb

TERRINE n earthenware dish with a lid

TERRIT = terret

TERRITS ▶ territ

TERROIR n combination of factors that gives a wine its distinctive character

TERROR n **terrors**

TERRY n

TERSE adj **tersely, terser, tersest**

TERSION n action of rubbing off or wiping

TERTIA = tercio

TERTIAL = tertiary

TERTIAN adj (of a fever or the symptoms of a disease) occurring every other day ▶ n tertian fever or symptoms

TERTIAS ▶ tertia

TERTIUM adj as in tertium quid unknown or indefinite thing related in some way to two known or definite things, but distinct from both

TERTIUS n third (in a group)

TERTS n card game

using 32 cards

TES ▶ te

TESLA n derived SI unit of magnetic flux density **teslas**

TESSERA n small square tile used in mosaics

TEST vb, n

TESTA n hard outer layer of a seed

TESTACY ▶ testate

TESTAE ▶ testa

TESTATE adj having left a valid will ▶ n person who dies and leaves a legally valid will

TESTE n witness

TESTED ▶ test

TESTEE n person subjected to a test **testees**

TESTER n person or thing that tests or is used for testing

TESTERN vb give (someone) a teston

TESTERS ▶ tester

TESTES ▶ testis

TESTIER ▶ testy

TESTIFY vb

TESTILY ▶ testy

TESTING ▶ test

TESTIS = testicle

TESTON n French silver coin of the 16th century **testons, testoon**

TESTRIL = testrill

TESTS ▶ test

TESTUDO n protective cover used by the ancient Roman army

TESTY adj

TET = teth

TETANAL ▶ tetanus

TETANIC adj of, relating to, or producing tetanus or the spasms of tetanus ▷ n tetanic drug or agent

TETANUS n

TETANY n abnormal increase in the excitability of nerves and muscles

TETCHED = **teched**

TETCHY adj

TETE n elaborate hairstyle **tetes**

TETH n ninth letter of the Hebrew alphabet

TETHER n, vb tethers

TETHS ▶ teth

TETOTUM = **teetotum**

TETRA n brightly coloured tropical freshwater fish

TETRACT n sponge spicule with four rays

TETRAD n group or series of four **tetrads**

TETRAS ▶ tetra

TETRI n currency unit of Georgia **tetris**

TETRODE n electronic valve having four electrodes

TETRYL n yellow crystalline explosive solid used in detonators **tetryls**

TETS ▶ tet

TETTER n blister or pimple ▷ vb cause a tetter to erupt (on) **tetters**

TETTIX n cicada

TEUCH Scots variant of ▶ tough

TEUCHAT Scots variant of ▶ tewit

TEUCHER ▶ teuch

TEUGH = **teuch**

TEUGHER ▶ teugh

TEUGHLY ▶ teugh

TEW vb work hard

TEWART = **tuart**

TEWARTS ▶ tewart

TEWED ▶ tew

TEWEL n horse's rectum **tewels**

TEWHIT = **tewit**

TEWHITS ▶ tewhit

TEWING ▶ tew

TEWIT n lapwing **tewits**

TEWS ▶ tew

TEX n unit of weight used to measure yarn density

TEXAS n structure on the upper deck of a paddle-steamer **texases**

TEXES ▶ tex

TEXT n, vb **texted**

TEXTER n person who communicates by text messaging **texters**

TEXTILE n, adj

TEXTING ▶ text

TEXTS ▶ text

TEXTUAL adj of, based on, or relating to, a text or texts

TEXTURE n, vb

THACK Scots word for ▶ thatch

THACKED ▶ thack

THACKS ▶ thack

THAE Scots word for ▶ those

THAGI = **thuggee**

THAGIS ▶ thagi

THAIM Scots variant of ▶ them

THAIRM n catgut **thairms**

THALAMI > thalamus

THALE n as in **thale cress** cruciferous wall plant

THALER n former German, Austrian, or Swiss silver coin **thalers**

THALI n meal consisting of several small dishes accompanied by rice, bread, etc

THALIAN adj of or relating to comedy

THALIS ▶ thali

THALLI ▶ thallus

THALLIC adj of or containing thallium

THALLUS n undifferentiated vegetative body of algae, fungi, and lichens

THALWEG n longitudinal outline of a riverbed from source to mouth

THAN prep, n

THANA = **tana**

THANAGE n state of being a thane

THANAH = **tana**

THANAHS ▶ thanah

THANAS ▶ thana

THANE n Anglo-Saxon or medieval Scottish nobleman **thanes**

THANG n thing

THANGKA n (in Tibetan Buddhism) a religious painting on a scroll

THANGS ▶ thang

THANK vb thanked

THANKEE interj thank you

THANKER ▶ thank

THANKIT adj as in be thankit thank God

THANKS pl n, interj

THANNA = tana

THANNAH = tana

THANNAS ▶ thanna

THANS ▶ than

THAR = tahr

THARM n stomach tharms

THARS ▶ thar

THAT pron

THATCH n, vb

THATCHT old variant of > thatched

THATCHY ▶ thatch

THAW vb, n thawed, thawer, thawers

THAWIER ▶ thawy

THAWING ▶ thaw

THAWS ▶ thaw

THAWY adj tending to thaw

THE determiner

THEATER = theatre

THEATRE n

THEAVE n young ewe theaves

THEBE n inner satellite of Jupiter discovered in 1979 thebes

THECA n enclosing organ, cell, or spore case thecae, thecal, thecate

THEE pron, vb theed, theeing

THEEK Scots variant of ▶ thatch

THEEKED ▶ theek

THEEKS ▶ theek

THEELIN trade name for ▶ estrone

THEELOL n estriol

THEES ▶ thee

THEFT n thefts

THEGN = thane

THEGNLY ▶ thegn

THEGNS ▶ thegn

THEIC n person who drinks excessive amounts of tea theics

THEIN old variant of ▶ thane

THEINE another name for > caffeine

THEINES ▶ theine

THEINS ▶ thein

THEIR determiner

THEIRS pron

THEISM n belief in a God or gods theisms, theist, theists

THELF n old contraction of "the element" thelves

THEM pron

THEMA n theme themata

THEME n, vb themed, themes, theming

THEN adv, pron, adj, n

THENAGE old variant of ▶ thanage

THENAL adj of or relating to the thenar

THENAR n palm of the hand ▷ adj of or relating to the palm or the region at the base of the thumb thenars

THENCE adv

THENS ▶ then

THEOCON n

THEOLOG = theologue

THEORBO n obsolete form of the lute, having two necks

THEOREM n

THEORIC n theory; conjecture

THEORY n

THEOW n slave in Anglo-Saxon Britain theows

THERAPY n

THERE adv, n

THEREAT adv at that point or time

THEREBY adv

THEREIN adv in or into that place or thing

THEREOF adv of or concerning that or it

THEREON archaic word for > thereupon

THERES ▶ there

THERETO adv that or it

THERIAC n ointment or potion used as an antidote to a poison

THERIAN n animal of the class Theria, a subclass of mammals

THERM n

THERMAE pl n public baths or hot springs, esp in ancient Greece or Rome

THERMAL adj, n

THERME old variant of ▶ therm

THERMEL n type of thermometer using thermoelectric current

THERMES ▶ therme

THERMIC = thermal

THERMIT variant of
> thermite

THERMOS n trademark
for a stoppered
vacuum flask

THERMS ▸ therm

THEROID adj of, relating
to, or resembling a
beast

THESE determiner

THESES ▸ thesis

THESIS n

THESP short for
> thespian

THESPS ▸ thesp

THETA n eighth letter of
the Greek alphabet
thetas

THETCH old variant
spelling of ▸ thatch

THETE n member of the
lowest order of
freeman in ancient
Athens **thetes**

THETHER old variant of
▸ thither

THETIC adj (in classical
prosody) of, bearing,
or relating to a
metrical stress

THEURGY n intervention
of a divine or
supernatural agency in
the affairs of man

THEW n muscle, esp if
strong or
well-developed

THEWED adj strong;
muscular

**THEWES, thewier,
thews, thewy**
▸ thew

THEY pron

THIAMIN = thiamine

THIASUS n people
gathered to sing and
dance in honour of
a god

THIAZIN = thiazine

THIAZOL = thiazole

THIBET n coloured
woollen cloth **thibets**

THIBLE n stick for
stirring porridge
thibles

THICK adj, vb **thicked**

THICKEN vb

THICKER ▸ thick

THICKET n

THICKLY ▸ thick

THICKS ▸ thick

THIEF n

THIEVE vb steal
thieved, thieves

THIG vb beg **thigger,
thiggit**

THIGH n

THIGHED adj having
thighs

THIGHS ▸ thigh

THIGS ▸ thig

THILK pron that same

THILL another word for
▸ shaft

THILLER n horse that
goes between the
thills of a cart

THILLS ▸ thill

THIMBLE n, vb

THIN adj not thick ▷ vb
make or become thin
▷ adv in order to
produce something
thin

THINE adj (something)
of or associated with
you (thou) ▷ pron
something belonging
to you (thou)
▷ determiner of,
belonging to, or
associated in some
way with you (thou)

THING n things

THINGY adj existing in
reality; actual

THINK vb consider,
judge, or believe
thinker, thinks

THINLY thinned,
thinner, thins ▸ thin

THIO adj of, or relating
to, sulphur

THIOL n any of a class of
sulphur-containing
organic compounds
thiolic, thiols

THIONIC adj of, relating
to, or containing
sulphur

THIONIN = thionine

THIONYL n of,
consisting of, or
containing the
divalent group SO

THIR Scots word for
▸ these

THIRAM n antifungal
agent **thirams**

THIRD adj, n, adv, vb
**thirded, thirdly,
thirds**

THIRL vb bore or drill
thirled, thirls

THIRST n, vb **thirsts**

THIRSTY adj feeling a
desire to drink

THIRTY n, adj, determiner

THIS pron, adj

THISTLE n **thistly**

THITHER adv to or towards
that place

THIVEL = thible

THIVELS ▸ thivel

THO *short for* ▸ **though**

THOFT n bench (in a boat) upon which a rower sits **thofts**

THOLE n wooden pin set in the side of a rowing boat to serve as a fulcrum for rowing ▷ vb bear or put up with **tholed, tholes**

THOLI ▸ tholus

THOLING ▸ thole

THOLOI ▸ tholos

THOLOS n beehive-shaped tomb associated with Mycenaean Greece

THOLUS n domed tomb

THON *Scot word for* ▸ **yon**

THONDER *Scot word for* ▸ **yonder**

THONG n

THONGED adj fastened with a thong

THONGS ▸ thong

THORAX n

THORIA ▸ thorium

THORIAS ▸ thorium

THORIC ▸ thorium

THORITE n yellow, brownish, or black radioactive mineral

THORIUM n

THORN n, vb thorned, thorns

THORNY adj

THORO *(nonstandard)* variant spelling of ▸ **thorough**

THORON n radioisotope of radon that is a decay product of thorium **thorons**

THORP n small village **thorpe**

THORPES ▸ thorpe

THORPS ▸ thorp

THOSE determiner

THOTHER pron old contraction of *the other*

THOU pron, n, vb thoued

THOUGH adv

THOUGHT ▸ think

THOUING ▸ thou

THOUS ▸ thou

THOWEL old variant of ▸ **thole**

THOWELS ▸ thowel

THOWL old variant of ▸ **thole**

THOWLS ▸ thowel

THRAE = frae

THRALL n state of being in the power of another person ▷ vb enslave or dominate **thralls**

THRANG n throng ▷ vb throng ▷ adj crowded **thrangs**

THRASH vb, n

THRAVE n twenty-four sheaves of corn **thraves**

THRAW vb twist (something); make something thrawn **thrawed**

THRAWN adj crooked or twisted

THRAWS ▸ thraw

THREADS slang word for ▸ **clothes**

THREADY adj of, relating to, or resembling a thread or threads

THREAP vb scold **threaps**

THREAT n threats

THREAVE = thrave

THREE n, adj, determiner

THREEP = threap

THREEPS ▸ threep

THREES ▸ three

THRENE n dirge; threnody **threnes**

THRENOS n threnody; lamentation

THRESH vb, n

THRETTY nonstandard variant of ▸ **thirty**

THREW ▸ throw

THRICE adv

THRID old variant of ▸ **thread**

THRIDS ▸ thrid

THRIFT n thrifts

THRIFTY adj

THRILL n, vb thrills

THRILLY adj causing thrills

THRIMSA = thrymsa

THRIP ▸ thrips

THRIPS n small slender-bodied insect with piercing mouthparts that feeds on plant sap

THRIST old variant of ▸ **thirst**

THRISTS ▸ thrist

THRISTY ▸ thrist

THRIVE vb thrived, thriven, thriver, thrives

THRO = through

THROAT n, vb throats

THROATY adj

THROB vb, n **throbs**

THROE n pang or pain ▷ n endure throes **throed**

THROES pl n

THROMBI > thrombus

THRONE n, vb **throned, thrones**

THRONG vb, n, adj **throngs**

THROUGH prep, adj

THROVE > thrive

THROW vb, n

THROWE old variant of ▷ throe

THROWER > throw

THROWES > throwe

THROWN > throw

THROWS > throw

THRU = through

THRUM vb strum rhythmically but without expression ▷ n in textiles, unwoven ends of wap thread

THRUMMY adj made of thrums

THRUMS > thrum

THRUPUT n quantity of raw material or information processed in a given period

THRUSH n

THRUST vb, n **thrusts**

THRUTCH n narrow, fast-moving stream ▷ vb thrust

THRUWAY n thoroughfare

THRYMSA n gold coin used in Anglo-Saxon England

THUD n, vb **thudded, thuds**

THUG n

THUGGEE n methods and practices of the thugs of India

THUGGO n tough and violent person **thuggos**

THUGS > thug

THUJA n coniferous tree of North America and East Asia **thujas**

THULIA n oxide of thulium **thulias**

THULITE n rose-coloured zoisite sometimes incorporated into jewellery

THULIUM n malleable ductile silvery-grey element

THUMB n, vb **thumbed, thumbs**

THUMBY adj clumsy; uncoordinated

THUMP n, vb **thumped, thumper, thumps**

THUNDER n, vb

THUNK another word for ▷ thud

THUNKED > thunk

THUNKS > thunk

THURIFY vb burn incense near or before an altar, shrine, etc

THURL = thirl

THURLS > thirl

THUS adv, n **thuses**

THUSLY adv in such a way; thus

THUYA = thuja

THUYAS > thuya

THWACK n, vb, interj **thwacks**

THWAITE n piece of land cleared from forest or reclaimed from wasteland

THWART vb, n, adj, adv **thwarts**

THY adj, determiner

THYINE adj of or relating to the sandarac tree

THYLOSE old variant of ▷ tylosis

THYME n **thymes, thymey**

THYMI > thymus

THYMIC adj of or relating to the thymus

THYMIER > thyme

THYMINE n white crystalline pyrimidine base found in DNA

THYMOL n substance obtained from thyme **thymols**

THYMUS n

THYMY > thyme

THYROID n (of) a gland in the neck controlling body growth ▷ adj of or relating to the thyroid gland

THYRSE n type of inflorescence, occurring in the lilac and grape **thyrses**

THYRSI > thyrsus

THYRSUS = thyrse

THYSELF pron reflexive form of thou

TI = te

TIAN n traditional French vegetable stew or earthenware dish it is cooked in **tians**

TIAR = tiara
TIARA n tiaraed, tiaras
TIARS ▸ tiar
TIBIA n tibiae, tibial, tibias
TIC n
TICAL n former standard monetary unit of Thailand **ticals**
TICCA adj acquired for temporary use in exchange for payment
TICCED ▸ tic
TICCING ▸ tic
TICE vb tempt or allure; entice **ticed, tices**
TICH = titch
TICHES ▸ tich
TICHIER ▸ tichy
TICHY = titchy
TICING ▸ tice
TICK n, vb ticked
TICKEN = ticking
TICKENS ▸ ticken
TICKER n heart **tickers**
TICKET n, vb
TICKETS pl n death or ruin
TICKEY n South African threepenny piece **tickeys**
TICKIES ▸ ticky
TICKING n
TICKLE vb, n tickled
TICKLER n difficult or delicate problem
TICKLES ▸ tickle
TICKLY ▸ tickle
TICKS ▸ tick
TICKY = tickey
TICS ▸ tic
TICTAC ▸ ticktack
TICTACS ▸ tictac
TICTOC ▸ ticktock

TICTOCS ▸ tictoc
TID n girl
TIDAL adj tidally
TIDBIT ▸ titbit
TIDBITS ▸ tidbit
TIDDIER ▸ tiddy
TIDDIES ▸ tiddy
TIDDLE vb busy oneself with inconsequential tasks **tiddled**
TIDDLER n
TIDDLES ▸ tiddle
TIDDLEY = tiddly
TIDDLY adj, n
TIDDY n four of trumps in the card game gleek
TIDE n, vb tided
TIDERIP = riptide
TIDES ▸ tide
TIDEWAY n strong tidal current or its channel, esp the tidal part of a river
TIDIED, tidier, tidiers, tidies, tidiest, tidily ▸ tidy
TIDING ▸ tide
TIDINGS pl n
TIDS ▸ tid
TIDY adj, vb, n tidying
TIE vb, n
TIEBACK n length of cord, ribbon, or other fabric used for tying a curtain to one side
TIED ▸ tie
TIEING ▸ tie
TIELESS ▸ tie
TIEPIN n ornamental pin used to pin the two ends of a tie to a shirt **tiepins**
TIER n, vb
TIERCE = terce

TIERCED adj (of a shield) divided into three sections of similar size but different colour
TIERCEL ▸ tercel
TIERCES ▸ tierce
TIERCET ▸ tercet
TIERED ▸ tier
TIERING ▸ tier
TIERS ▸ tier
TIES ▸ tie
TIETAC n fastener for holding a tie in place **tietack, tietacs**
TIFF n, vb
TIFFANY n sheer fine gauzy fabric
TIFFED ▸ tiff
TIFFIN n (in India) a light meal, esp at midday ▷ vb take tiffin
TIFFING ▸ tiff
TIFFINS ▸ tiffin
TIFFS ▸ tiff
TIFOSI ▸ tifoso
TIFOSO n fanatical fan (esp an Italian F1 fan)
TIFT Scots variant of ▸ tift
TIFTED ▸ tift
TIFTING ▸ tift
TIFTS ▸ tift
TIG n child's game
TIGE n trunk of an architectural column
TIGER n
TIGERLY adj of or like a tiger
TIGERS ▸ tiger
TIGERY ▸ tiger
TIGES ▸ tige
TIGGED ▸ tig
TIGGING ▸ tig

TIGHT adj, adv

TIGHTEN vb

TIGHTER ▸ tight

TIGHTLY ▸ tight

TIGHTS pl n

TIGLIC adj as in **tiglic acid** syrupy liquid or crystalline colourless unsaturated carboxylic acid

TIGLON = tigon

TIGLONS ▸ tiglon

TIGON n hybrid offspring of a male tiger and a female lion **tigons**

TIGRESS n female tiger

TIGRINE adj of, characteristic of, or resembling a tiger

TIGRISH ▸ tiger

TIGROID adj resembling a tiger

TIGS ▸ tig

TIK n South African slang term for crystal meth

TIKA = tikka

TIKANGA n Māori ways or customs

TIKAS ▸ tika

TIKI n, vb tikied, tikiing, tikis

TIKKA adj marinated in spices and dry-roasted ▸ n act of marking a tikka on the forehead **tikkas**

TIKS ▸ tik

TIL another name for ▸ sesame

TILAK n coloured spot or mark worn by Hindus **tilaks**

TILAPIA n type of fish

TILBURY n light two-wheeled horse-drawn open carriage

TILDE n tildes

TILE n, vb tiled, tiler, tilers

TILERY n place where tiles are produced

TILES ▸ tile

TILING n tiles collectively **tilings**

TILL prep, vb, n

TILLAGE n act, process, or art of tilling

TILLED ▸ till

TILLER n, vb

TILLERS ▸ till

TILLIER ▸ till

TILLING ▸ till

TILLITE n rock formed from hardened till

TILLS ▸ till

TILLY ▸ till

TILS ▸ til

TILT vb, n tilted, tilter, tilters

TILTH n (condition of) land that has been tilled **tilths**

TILTING ▸ tilt

TILTS ▸ tilt

TIMARAU = tamarau

TIMBAL n type of kettledrum

TIMBALE n mixture of meat, fish, etc, in a rich sauce

TIMBALS ▸ timbal

TIMBER n, adj, vb, interj timbers, timbery

TIMBO n Amazonian vine from which a useful insecticide can be derived **timbos**

TIMBRAL adj relating to timbre

TIMBRE n

TIMBREL n tambourine

TIMBRES ▸ timbre

TIME n past, present, and future as a continuous whole ▸ vb note the time taken by **timed**

TIMELY adj, adv

TIMEOUS adj in good time

TIMEOUT n in sport, interruption in play during which players rest, etc

TIMER n timers

TIMES ▸ time

TIMID adj timider, timidly

TIMING n timings

TIMIST n one concerned with time **timists**

TIMOLOL n relaxant medicine used (for example) to reduce blood pressure

TIMON n apparatus by which a vessel is steered **timons**

TIMOTHY n as in **timothy grass** perennial grass of temperate regions

TIMOUS = timeous

TIMPANA n traditional Maltese baked pasta and pastry dish

TIMPANI pl n

TIMPANO n kettledrum

TIMPS = timpani

TIN *n, vb*

TINA *n*

TINAJA *n* large jar for cooling water **tinajas**

TINAMOU *n* type of bird of Central and S America

TINAS ▸ tina

TINCAL another name for ▸ **borax**

TINCALS ▸ tincal

TINCHEL *n* in Scotland, a circle of deer hunters who gradually close in on their quarry

TINCT *vb* tint ▷ *adj* tinted or coloured **tincted, tincts**

TIND *vb* set alight

TINDAL *n* petty officer **tindals**

TINDED ▸ tind

TINDER *n* **tinders, tindery**

TINDING ▸ tind

TINDS ▸ tind

TINE *n, vb*

TINEA *n* any fungal skin disease, esp ringworm **tineal, tineas**

TINED ▸ tine

TINEID *n* type of moth of the family which includes the clothes moths **tineids**

TINES ▸ tine

TINFOIL *n*

TINFUL *n* contents of a tin or the amount a tin will hold **tinfuls**

TING = thing

TINGE *n, vb* tinged, tinges, tinging

TINGLE *n, vb* tingled, tingler, tingles, tingly

TINGS ▸ ting

TINHORN *n* cheap pretentious person, esp a gambler with extravagant claims ▷ *adj* cheap and showy

TINIER ▸ tiny

TINIES *pl n* small children

TINIEST ▸ tiny

TINILY ▸ tiny

TINING ▸ tine

TINK shortened form of ▸ **tinker**

TINKED ▸ tink

TINKER *n, vb* **tinkers**

TINKING ▸ tink

TINKLE *vb, n* tinkled

TINKLER = tinker

TINKLES ▸ tinkle

TINKLY ▸ tinkle

TINKS ▸ tink

TINLIKE ▸ tin

TINMAN *n* one who works with tin or tin plate **tinmen**

TINNED ▸ tin

TINNER *n* tin miner **tinners**

TINNIE = tinny

TINNIER ▸ tinny

TINNIES ▸ tinny

TINNILY ▸ tinny

TINNING ▸ tin

TINNY *adj, n*

TINPOT *adj, n* tinpots

TINS ▸ tin

TINSEL *n, adj, vb* tinsels, tinsey

TINSEYS ▸ tinsey

TINT *n, vb*

TINTACK *n* tin-plated tack

TINTED ▸ tint

TINTER ▸ tint

TINTERS ▸ tint

TINTIER ▸ tinty

TINTING ▸ tint

TINTS ▸ tint

TINTY *adj* having many tints

TINTYPE another name for ▸ **ferrotype**

TINWARE *n* objects made of tin plate

TINWORK *n* objects made of tin

TINY *adj*

TIP *n, vb*

TIPCART *n* cart that can be tipped to empty out its contents

TIPCAT *n* game in which a piece of wood is tipped in the air with a stick **tipcats**

TIPI *variant spelling of* ▸ **tepee**

TIPIS ▸ tipi

TIPLESS ▸ tip

TIPOFF *n* warning or hint, esp given confidentially **tipoffs**

TIPPED ▸ tip

TIPPEE *n* person who receives a tip, esp regarding share prices **tippees**

TIPPER *n* person who gives or leaves a tip **tippers**

TIPPET *n* scarflike piece of fur **tippets**

TIPPIER ▸ tippy

TIPPING ▸ tip

TIPPLE *vb, n* tippled, tippler, tipples

TIPPY adj extremely fashionable or stylish
TIPS ▸ tip
TIPSIER ▸ tipsy
TIPSIFY vb make tipsy
TIPSILY ▸ tipsy
TIPSTER n person who sells tips about races
TIPSY adj
TIPT ▸ tip
TIPTOE vb tiptoed, tiptoes
TIPTOP adj of the highest quality or condition ▸ adv of the highest quality or condition ▸ n best in quality **tiptops**
TIPULA n crane fly **tipulas**
TIPUNA n ancestor **tipunas**
TIRADE n tirades
TIRAGE n drawing of wine from a barrel prior to bottling **tirages**
TIRASSE n mechanism in an organ connecting two pedals
TIRE vb
TIRED adj tireder, tiredly
TIRES ▸ tire
TIRING ▸ tire
TIRINGS ▸ tire
TIRITI n another name for the Treaty of Waitangi

A Maori word for treaty. Any 6-letter word that lets you get rid of three Is can't be bad! **tiritis**

TIRL vb turn **tirled, tirling, tirls**
TIRO = tyro
TIROES ▸ tiro
TIRONIC variant of ▸ tyronic
TIROS ▸ tiro
TIRR vb strip or denude **tirred, tirring**
TIRRIT n panic; scare **tirrits**
TIRRS ▸ tirr
TIS ▸ ti
TISANE n infusion of dried or fresh leaves or flowers **tisanes**
TISICK n splutter; cough **tisicks**
TISSUAL adj relating to tissue
TISSUE n, vb tissued, tissues, tissuey
TISWAS n state of anxiety or excitement
TIT n, vb
TITAN n person who is huge, strong, or very important
TITANIA ▸ titanium
TITANIC adj
TITANIS n large predatory flightless prehistoric bird
TITANS ▸ titan
TITBIT n titbits
TITCH n small person **titches**
TITCHY adj very small
TITE adj immediately
TITELY adv immediately
TITER = titre
TITERS ▸ titer
TITFER n hat titfers
TITHE n, vb tithed,

tither, tithers, tithes, tithing
TITI n small omnivorous monkey
TITIAN n titians
TITIS ▸ titi
TITLARK another name for ▸ pipit
TITLE n, vb
TITLED adj
TITLER n one who writes titles
TITLERS ▸ title
TITLES ▸ title
TITLING ▸ title
TITLIST n titleholder
TITMAN n (of pigs) the runt of a litter **titmen**
TITMICE ▸ titmouse
TITMOSE old spelling of ▸ titmouse
TITOKI n New Zealand evergreen tree with a spreading crown and glossy green leaves **titokis**
TITRANT n solution in a titration that is added to a measured quantity of another solution
TITRATE vb measure the volume or concentration of (a solution) by titration
TITRE n concentration of a solution as determined by titration **titres**
TITS ▸ tit
TITTED ▸ tit
TITTER vb, n titters
TITTIE n sister; young woman **titties**
TITTING ▸ tit

TITTISH *adj* testy

TITTLE *n* very small amount ▷ *vb* chatter; tattle **tittled, tittles**

TITTUP *vb* prance or frolic ▷ *n* caper **tittups**

TITTUPY *adj* spritely; lively

TITTY = **tittie**

TITULAR *adj, n*

TITULE = **title**

TITULED ▶ **titule**

TITULES ▶ **titule**

TITULI ▶ **titulus**

TITULUS *n* sign attached to the top of the crucifixion

TITUP = **tittup**

TITUPED ▶ **titup**

TITUPS ▶ **titup**

TITUPY = **tittupy**

TIVY = **tantivy**

TIX *pl n* tickets

> **Tix** is an informal word for **tickets**, and one of the key short words for using the X.

TIYIN *n* monetary unit of Uzbekistan and Kyrgyzstan **tiyins**

TIZWAS = **tiswas**

TIZZ = **tizzy**

TIZZES ▶ **tizz**

TIZZIES ▶ **tizzy**

TIZZY *n* confused or agitated state

TMESES ▶ **tmesis**

TMESIS *n* interpolation of a word between the parts of a compound word

TO *prep, adv*

TOAD *n*

TOADIED ▶ **toady**

TOADIES ▶ **toady**

TOADISH ▶ **toad**

TOADS ▶ **toad**

TOADY *n, vb*

TOAST *n, vb* toasted, toaster

TOASTIE = **toasty**

TOASTS ▶ **toast**

TOASTY *n* toasted sandwich ▷ *adj* tasting or smelling like toast

TOAZE *variant spelling of* ▶ **toze**

TOAZED ▶ **toaze**

TOAZES ▶ **toaze**

TOAZING ▶ **toaze**

TOBACCO *n*

TOBIES ▶ **toby**

TOBY *n* water stopcock at the boundary of a street and house section

TOC *n* in communications code, signal for letter t

TOCCATA *n* rapid piece of music for a keyboard instrument **toccate**

TOCHER *n* dowry ▷ *vb* give a dowry to **tochers**

TOCK *n* sound made by a clock ▷ *vb* (of a clock) make such a sound **tocked**

TOCKIER ▶ **tocky**

TOCKING ▶ **tock**

TOCKS ▶ **tock**

TOCKY *adj* muddy

TOCO *n* punishment **tocos**

TOCS ▶ **toc**

TOCSIN *n* warning signal **tocsins**

TOD *n* unit of weight, used for wool, etc ▷ *vb* produce a tod

TODAY *n, adv* todays

TODDE = **tod**

TODDED ▶ **todde**

TODDES ▶ **todde**

TODDIES ▶ **toddy**

TODDING ▶ **tod**

TODDLE *vb, n* toddled

TODDLER *n*

TODDLES ▶ **toddle**

TODDY *n*

TODIES ▶ **tody**

TODS ▶ **tod**

TODY *n* small bird of the Caribbean

TOE *n, vb*

TOEA *n* monetary unit of Papua New Guinea **toeas**

> This monetary unit of Papua New Guinea is very often played to rid the rack of a surplus of vowels.

TOEBIE *n* South African slang for sandwich **toebies**

TOECAP *n* strengthened covering for the toe of a shoe **toecaps**

TOECLIP *n* clip on a bicycle pedal into which the toes are inserted to prevent the foot from slipping

TOED ▶ **toe**

TOEHOLD *n*

TOEIER ▸ toey This is the comparative of **toey**, Australian slang for nervous or edgy, and can come in useful for dumping a surplus of vowels.

TOEIEST ▸ toey

TOEING ▸ toe

TOELESS *adj* not having toes

TOELIKE ▸ toe

TOENAIL *n* thin hard clear plate covering part of the upper surface of the end of each toe ▹ *vb* join (beams) by driving nails obliquely

TOES ▸ toe

TOESHOE *n* ballet pump with padded toes

TOETOE = toitoi

TOETOES ▸ toetoe

TOEY *adj* (of a person) nervous or anxious

TOFF *n*

TOFFEE *n* toffees

TOFFIER ▸ toffy

TOFFIES ▸ toffy

TOFFISH *adj* belonging to or characteristic of the upper class

TOFFS *adj* like a toff

TOFFY = toffee

TOFORE *prep* before

TOFT *n* homestead **tofts**

TOFU *n* soft food made from soya-bean curd **tofus**

TOFUTTI *n* tradename for nondairy, soya-based food products

TOG *n* unit for measuring the insulating power of duvets ▹ *vb* dress oneself

TOGA *n, vb* togae, togaed, togas

TOGATE *adj* clad in a toga **togated**

TOGE old variant of ▸ toga

TOGED ▸ toge

TOGES ▸ toge

TOGGED ▸ tog

TOGGER *vb* play football ▹ *n* football player **toggers**

TOGGERY *n* clothes

TOGGING ▸ tog

TOGGLE *n, vb* toggled, toggler, toggles

TOGS ▸ tog

TOGUE *n* large North American freshwater game fish **togues**

TOHEROA *n* large edible mollusc of New Zealand

TOHO *n* (to a hunting dog) an instruction to stop

TOHUNGA *n* Māori priest

TOIL *n, vb*

TOILE *n* transparent linen or cotton fabric

TOILED ▸ toil

TOILER ▸ toil

TOILERS ▸ toil

TOILES ▸ toile

TOILET *n, vb* toilets

TOILFUL = toilsome

TOILING ▸ toil

TOILS ▸ toil

TOING *n as in* toing and froing state of going back and forth **toings**

TOISE *n* obsolete French unit of length roughly equal to 2m

TOISECH = toiseach

TOISES ▸ toise

TOISON *n* fleece toisons

TOIT *vb* walk or move in an unsteady manner, as from old age **toited, toiting**

TOITOI *n* tall grasses with feathery fronds **toitois**

TOITS ▸ toit

TOKAMAK *n* reactor used in thermonuclear experiments

TOKAY *n* small gecko of S and SE Asia, having a retractile claw at the tip of each digit **tokays**

TOKE *n* draw on a cannabis cigarette ▹ *vb* take a draw on a cannabis cigarette **toked**

TOKEN *n, adj* tokened, tokens

TOKER, tokers, tokes, toking ▸ toke

TOKO = toco

TOKOMAK *variant spelling of* ▸ tokamak

TOKOS ▸ toko

TOLA *n* unit of weight, used in India

TOLAN *n* white crystalline derivative of acetylene **tolane**

TOLANES ▸ tolane

TOLANS ▸ tolan

TOLAR n standard monetary unit of Slovenia **tolarji, tolars**

TOLAS ▸ tola

TOLD ▸ tell

TOLE = toll

TOLED ▸ tole

TOLEDO n type of sword originally made in Toledo **toledos**

TOLES ▸ tole

TOLIDIN = tolidine

TOLING ▸ tole

TOLINGS ▸ tole

TOLL vb, n **tollage**

TOLLBAR n bar blocking passage of a thoroughfare, raised on payment of a toll

TOLLED ▸ toll

TOLLER ▸ toll

TOLLERS ▸ toller

TOLLEY n large shooting marble used in a game of marbles **tolleys**

TOLLIE = tolly

TOLLIES ▸ tolly

TOLLING ▸ toll

TOLLMAN n man who collects tolls **tollmen**

TOLLS ▸ toll

TOLLWAY n road on which users must pay tolls to travel

TOLLY n castrated calf

TOLSEL n tolbooth **tolsels**

TOLSEY n tolbooth

TOLSEYS > tolbooth

TOLT n type of obsolete English writ

TOLTER vb struggle or move with difficulty, as in mud **tolters**

TOLTS ▸ tolt

TOLU n sweet-smelling balsam obtained from a South American tree

TOLUATE n any salt or ester of any of the three isomeric forms of toluic acid

TOLUENE n colourless volatile flammable liquid obtained from petroleum and coal tar

TOLUIC adj as in **toluic acid** white crystalline derivative of toluene

TOLUID n white crystalline derivative of glycocoll **toluide, toluids**

TOLUOL another name for ▸ **toluene**

TOLUOLE another name for ▸ **toluene**

TOLUOLS ▸ toluol

TOLUS ▸ tolu

TOLUYL n of, consisting of, or containing any of three groups derived from a toluic acid **toluyls**

TOLYL n of, consisting of, or containing any of three isomeric groups, $CH_3C_6H_4$-, derived from toluene **tolyls**

TOLZEY n tolbooth **tolzeys**

TOM n, adj, vb

TOMAN n gold coin formerly issued in Persia **tomans**

TOMATO n

TOMB n

TOMBAC n any of various brittle alloys containing copper and zinc **tomback, tombacs, tombak**

TOMBAKS ▸ tombak

TOMBAL adj like or relating to a tomb

TOMBED ▸ tomb

TOMBIC adj of or relating to tombs

TOMBING ▸ tomb

TOMBOC n weapon **tombocs**

TOMBOLA n

TOMBOLO n narrow bar linking a small island with another island or the mainland

TOMBOY n **tomboys**

TOMBS ▸ tomb

TOMCAT vb (of a man) to be promiscuous **tomcats**

TOMCOD n small fish resembling the cod **tomcods**

TOME n

TOMENTA > tomentum

TOMES ▸ tome

TOMFOOL n fool ▸ vb act the fool

TOMIA ▸ tomium

TOMIAL ▸ tomium

TOMIUM n sharp edge of a bird's beak

TOMMIED ▸ tommy

TOMMIES ▸ tommy

TOMMY n, vb

TOMO n shaft formed by the action of water on limestone or volcanic rock **tomos**

TOMPION = tampion
TOMPON = tampon
TOMPONS ▸ tompon
TOMS ▸ tom
TOMTIT n small European bird that eats insects and seeds **tomtits**
TON n
TONAL adj **tonally**
TONANT adj very loud
TONDI ▸ tondo
TONDINI ▸ tondino
TONDINO n small tondo
TONDO n circular easel painting or relief carving **tondos**
TONE n, vb
TONEARM = pickup
TONED ▸ tone
TONEME n phoneme that is distinguished from another phoneme only by its tone **tonemes, tonemic**
TONEPAD n keypad used to transmit information
TONER n cosmetic applied to the skin to reduce oiliness **toners**
TONES ▸ tone
TONETIC adj (of a language) distinguishing words by tone as well as by other sounds
TONETTE n small musical instrument resembling a recorder
TONEY variant spelling of ▸ tony
TONG vb gather or seize with tongs ▸ n

(formerly) a Chinese secret society
TONGA n light two-wheeled vehicle used in rural areas of India **tongas**
TONGED ▸ tong
TONGER n one who uses tongs to gather oysters **tongers**
TONGING ▸ tong
TONGMAN another word for ▸ tonger
TONGMEN ▸ tongman
TONGS pl n
TONGUE n, vb **tongued, tongues**
TONIC n, adj **tonics**
TONIER ▸ tony
TONIES ▸ tony
TONIEST ▸ tony
TONIGHT n, adv
TONING ▸ tone
TONINGS ▸ tone
TONISH ▸ ton
TONITE n explosive used in quarrying **tonites**
TONK vb strike with a heavy blow ▸ n effete or effeminate man
TONKA n as in tonka bean tall leguminous tree of tropical America
TONKED, tonker, tonkers, tonking, tonks ▸ tonk
TONLET n skirt of a suit of armour, consisting of overlapping metal bands **tonlets**
TONNAG n type of (usually tartan) shawl
TONNAGE n

TONNAGS ▸ tonnag
TONNE ▸ ton
TONNEAU n detachable cover to protect the rear part of an open car
TONNELL old spelling of ▸ tunnel
TONNER n something that weighs one ton
TONNERS ▸ tonne
TONNES ▸ tonne
TONNISH ▸ ton
TONS ▸ ton
TONSIL n **tonsils**
TONSOR n barber **tonsors**
TONSURE n, vb
TONTINE n type of annuity scheme
TONUS n normal tension of a muscle at rest **tonuses**
TONY adj stylish or distinctive ▸ n stylish or distinctive person
TOO adv
TOOART variant spelling of ▸ tuart
TOOARTS ▸ tooart
TOOK ▸ take
TOOL n, vb
TOOLBAG n bag for storing or carrying tools
TOOLBAR n row or column of selectable buttons displayed on a computer screen
TOOLBOX n box for storing or carrying tools
TOOLED ▸ tool
TOOLER ▸ tool
TOOLERS ▸ tool
TOOLIE n toolies

TOOLING n any decorative work done with a tool

TOOLKIT n set of tools designed to be used together or for a particular purpose

TOOLMAN n person who works with tools toolmen

TOOLS ▸ tool

TOOLSET n set of tools associated with a computer application

TOOM vb empty (something) ▸ adj empty toomed, toomer, toomest, tooming, tooms

TOON n large tree of the East Indies and Australia

TOONIE n Canadian two-dollar coin toonies

TOONS ▸ toon

TOORIE n tassel or bobble on a bonnet toories

TOOSHIE adj angry

TOOT n, vb tooted, tooter, tooters

TOOTH n

TOOTHED adj having a tooth or teeth

TOOTHS ▸ tooth

TOOTHY adj having or showing numerous, large, or prominent teeth

TOOTING ▸ toot

TOOTLE vb hoot softly or repeatedly ▸ n soft hoot or series of hoots tootled, tootler,

tootles

TOOTS Scots version of ▸ tut

TOOTSED ▸ toots

TOOTSES ▸ toots

TOOTSIE = tootsy

TOOTSY = toots

TOP n, adj, vb

TOPARCH n ruler of a small state or realm

TOPAZ n semiprecious stone in various colours topazes

TOPCOAT n overcoat

TOPE vb drink alcohol regularly ▸ n small European shark toped

TOPEE n lightweight hat worn in tropical countries topees

TOPEK = tupik

TOPEKS ▸ topek

TOPER ▸ tope

TOPERS ▸ tope

TOPES ▸ tope

TOPFUL variant spelling of ▸ topfull

TOPFULL adj full to the top

TOPH n variety of sandstone tophe

TOPHES ▸ tophe

TOPHI ▸ tophus

TOPHS ▸ toph

TOPHUS n deposit of sodium urate in the helix of the ear or surrounding a joint

TOPI = topee

TOPIARY n, adj

TOPIC n

TOPICAL adj

TOPICS ▸ topic

TOPING ▸ tope

TOPIS ▸ topi

TOPKICK n (formerly) sergeant

TOPKNOT n crest, tuft, decorative bow, etc, on the top of the head

TOPLESS adj (of a costume or woman) with no covering for the breasts

TOPLINE vb headline; be the main focus of a newspaper story

TOPMAN n sailor positioned in the rigging of the topsail

TOPMAST n mast next above a lower mast on a sailing vessel

TOPMEN ▸ topman

TOPMOST adj

TOPO n picture of a mountain with details of climbing routes superimposed on it topoi

TOPONYM n name of a place

TOPOS ▸ topo

TOPPED ▸ top

TOPPER n top hat toppers

TOPPIER ▸ toppy

TOPPING ▸ top

TOPPLE vb toppled, topples

TOPPY adj (of audio reproduction) having too many high-frequency sounds

TOPS ▸ top

TOPSAIL n square sail carried on a yard set on a topmast

TOPSIDE n lean cut of beef from the thigh containing no bone

TOPSMAN n chief drover **topsmen**

TOPSOIL n, vb

TOPSPIN n spin imparted to make a ball bounce or travel exceptionally far, high, or quickly

TOPWORK vb graft shoots or twigs onto the main branches of (a tree)

TOQUE = **tuque**

TOQUES ▶ **toque**

TOQUET = **toque**

TOQUETS ▶ **toquet**

TOR n

TORA variant spelling of ▶ **torah**

TORAH n whole body of traditional Jewish teaching **torahs**

TORAN n (in Indian architecture) an archway **torana**

TORANAS ▶ **torana**

TORANS ▶ **toran**

TORAS ▶ **tora**

TORC = **torque**

TORCH n, vb **torched**, **torcher**, **torches**

TORCHON n as in **torchon lace** coarse linen or cotton lace with a simple openwork pattern

TORCHY adj sentimental; maudlin; characteristic of a torch song

TORCS ▶ **torc**

TORDION n old triple-time dance for two people

TORE = **torus**

TORERO n bullfighter, esp one on foot **toreros**

TORES ▶ **tore**

TORGOCH n type of char

TORI ▶ **torus**

TORIC adj of, relating to, or having the form of a torus **torics**

TORIES ▶ **tory**

TORII n gateway, esp one at the entrance to a Japanese Shinto temple

TORMENT vb, n

TORMINA n complaints

TORN ▶ **tear**

TORNADE = **tornado**

TORNADO n

TORO n bull

TOROID n surface generated by rotating a closed plane curve about a coplanar line that does not intersect it **toroids**

TOROS ▶ **toro**

TOROSE adj (of a cylindrical part) having irregular swellings

TOROT ▶ **torah**

TOROTH ▶ **torah**

TOROUS = **torose**

TORPEDO n, vb

TORPEFY vb make torpid

TORPID adj

TORPIDS n series of boat races held at Oxford University

TORPOR n **torpors**

TORQUE n force causing rotation ▷ vb apply torque to (something) **torqued**, **torquer**

TORQUES n distinctive band of hair, feathers, skin, or colour around the neck of an animal

TORR n unit of pressure

TORREFY vb dry (drugs, ores, etc) by subjection to intense heat

TORRENT n, adj

TORRET = **terret**

TORRETS ▶ **torret**

TORRID adj

TORRIFY = **torrefy**

TORRS ▶ **torr**

TORS ▶ **tor**

TORSADE n ornamental twist or twisted cord, as on hats

TORSE = **torso**

TORSEL n wooden beam along the top of a wall **torsels**

TORSES ▶ **torse**

TORSI ▶ **torso**

TORSION n twisting of a part by equal forces being applied at both ends but in opposite directions

TORSIVE adj twisted

TORSK n fish with a single long dorsal fin **torsks**

TORSO n **torsos**

TORT n civil wrong or injury for which damages may be claimed

TORTA n (in mining) a flat circular pile of

silver ore **tortas**

TORTE n rich cake, originating in Austria **torten, tortes**

TORTILE adj twisted or coiled

TORTIVE adj twisted

TORTONI n rich ice cream often flavoured with sherry

TORTRIX n type of moth

TORTS ▶ **tort**

TORTURE vb, n

TORULA n species of fungal microorganisms **torulae, torulas**

TORULI ▶ **torulus**

TORULIN n vitamin found in yeast

TORULUS n socket in an insect's head in which its antenna is attached

TORUS n large convex moulding approximately semicircular in cross section, esp one used on the base of a classical column

TORY n ultraconservative or reactionary person ▷ adj ultraconservative or reactionary

TOSA n large reddish dog, originally bred for fighting **tosas**

TOSE ▶ **toze**

TOSED ▶ **tose**

TOSES ▶ **tose**

TOSH n nonsense ▷ vb tidy or trim

TOSHACH n military leader of a clan

TOSHED, tosher, toshers, toshes ▶ **tosh**

TOSHIER ▶ **toshy**

TOSHING ▶ **tosh**

TOSHY adj neat; trim

TOSING ▶ **tose**

TOSS vb, n **tossed, tossen, tosses**

TOSSIER ▶ **tossy**

TOSSILY ▶ **tossy**

TOSSING ▶ **toss**

TOSSUP n instance of tossing up a coin **tossups**

TOSSY adj impudent

TOST old past participle of ▶ **toss**

TOSTADA n crispy deep-fried tortilla topped with meat, cheese, and refried beans **tostado**

TOT n, vb

TOTABLE ▶ **tote**

TOTAL n, adj, vb **totaled, totally, totals**

TOTANUS another name for ▶ **redshank**

TOTARA n tall coniferous forest tree of New Zealand **totaras**

TOTE vb, n **toted**

TOTEM n **totemic, totems**

TOTER ▶ **tote**

TOTERS ▶ **tote**

TOTES ▶ **tote**

TOTHER n other

TOTIENT n quantity of numbers less than,

and sharing no common factors with, a number

TOTING ▶ **tote**

TOTS ▶ **tot**

TOTTED ▶ **tot**

TOTTER vb, n **totters, tottery**

TOTTIE adj very small

TOTTIER ▶ **totty**

TOTTIES ▶ **totty**

TOTTING ▶ **tot**

TOTTY n people, esp women, collectively considered as sexual objects ▷ adj very small

TOUCAN n **toucans**

TOUCH vb, n, adj

TOUCHE interj acknowledgment of a remark or witty reply

TOUCHED adj emotionally moved

TOUCHER ▶ **touch**

TOUCHES ▶ **touch**

TOUCHUP n renovation or retouching, as of a painting

TOUCHY adj

TOUGH adj, n **toughed**

TOUGHEN vb make or become tough or tougher

TOUGHER ▶ **tough**

TOUGHIE n person who is tough

TOUGHLY ▶ **tough**

TOUGHS ▶ **tough**

TOUGHY = **toughie**

TOUK = **tuck**

TOUKED ▶ **touk**

TOUKING ▶ **touk**

TOUKS ▶ **touk**

TOUN n town **touns**

TOUPEE n

TOUPEED adj wearing a toupee

TOUPEES ▶ toupee

TOUPET = toupee

TOUPETS ▶ toupet

TOUR n, adj

TOURACO n brightly coloured crested arboreal African bird

TOURED ▶ tour

TOURER n large open car with a folding top **tourers**

TOURIE = toorie

TOURIES ▶ tourie

TOURING ▶ tour

TOURISM n

TOURIST n, adj

TOURNEY n knightly tournament ▶ vb engage in a tourney

TOURS ▶ tour

TOUSE vb tangle, ruffle, or disarrange; treat roughly **toused, touser, tousers, touses**

TOUSIER ▶ tousy

TOUSING ▶ touse

TOUSLE vb make (hair or clothes) ruffled and untidy ▶ n disorderly, tangled, or rumpled state **tousled, tousles**

TOUSTIE adj irritable; testy

TOUSY adj tousled

TOUT vb, n **touted, touter, touters**

TOUTIE adj childishly irritable or sullen **toutier**

TOUTING ▶ tout

TOUTS ▶ tout

TOUZE variant spelling of ▶ touse

TOUZED ▶ touze

TOUZES ▶ touze

TOUZIER ▶ touzy

TOUZING ▶ touze

TOUZLE rare spelling of ▶ tousle

TOUZLED ▶ touzle

TOUZLES ▶ touzle

TOUZY variant spelling of ▶ tousy

TOW vb, n **towable**

TOWAGE n charge made for towing **towages**

TOWARD = towards

TOWARDS prep

TOWAWAY n vehicle which has been towed away

TOWBAR n **towbars**

TOWBOAT n another word for tug (the boat)

TOWED ▶ tow

TOWEL n, vb **toweled, towels**

TOWER n, vb

TOWERED adj having a tower or towers

TOWERS ▶ tower

TOWERY adj with towers

TOWHEAD n often disparaging term for a person with blond or yellowish hair

TOWHEE n N American brownish-coloured sparrow **towhees**

TOWIE n truck used for towing

TOWIER ▶ tow

TOWIES ▶ towie

TOWIEST, towing, towings ▶ tow

TOWKAY n sir **towkays**

TOWLINE = towrope

TOWMON = towmond

TOWMOND n old word for year

TOWMONS ▶ towmon

TOWMONT = towmond

TOWN n

TOWNEE = townie

TOWNEES ▶ townee

TOWNIE n often disparaging term for a resident in a town

TOWNIER ▶ towny

TOWNIES ▶ towny

TOWNISH ▶ town

TOWNLET n small town

TOWNLY adj characteristic of a town

TOWNS ▶ town

TOWNY adj characteristic of a town

TOWPATH n

TOWROPE n rope or cable used for towing a vehicle or vessel

TOWS ▶ tow

TOWSACK n sack made from tow

TOWSE = touse; **towsed, towser, towsers, towses**

TOWSIER ▶ towsy

TOWSING ▶ towse

TOWSY = tousy

TOWT vb sulk **towted, towting, towts**

TOWY ▶ tow

TOWZE = touse

TOWZED ▶ towze

TOWZES ▸ towze
TOWZIER ▸ towzy
TOWZING ▸ towze
TOWZY = tousy
TOXAEMIA = toxaemia
TOXEMIC ▸ toxaemia
TOXIC *adj, n*
TOXICAL *adj* toxic
TOXICS ▸ toxic
TOXIN *n* toxine
TOXINES ▸ toxine
TOXINS ▸ toxine
TOXOID *n* toxin that has been treated to reduce its toxicity **toxoids**
TOY *n, adj, vb* toyed, toyer, toyers
TOYETIC *adj*
TOYING ▸ toy
TOYINGS ▸ toy
TOYISH *adj* resembling a toy
TOYLESS ▸ toy
TOYLIKE ▸ toy
TOYLSOM *old spelling of* ▸ **toilsome**
TOYMAN *n* man who sells toys **toymen**
TOYO *n* Japanese straw-like material made out of rice paper and used to make hats
TOYON *n* shrub related to the rose **toyons**
TOYOS ▸ toyo
TOYS ▸ toy
TOYSHOP *n* shop selling toys
TOYSOME *adj* playful
TOYTOWN *adj* having an unreal and picturesque appearance

TOZE *vb* tease out; (of wool, etc) card **tozed, tozes**
TOZIE *n* type of shawl **tozies**
TOZING ▸ toze
TRABS *pl n* training shoes
TRACE *vb, n* traced
TRACER *n* projectile which leaves a visible trail **tracers**
TRACERY *n*
TRACES ▸ trace
TRACEUR *n* parkour participant
TRACHEA *n*
TRACHLE *vb* (of hair, clothing, etc) make untidy
TRACING *n* traced copy
TRACK *n, vb* tracked, tracker, tracks
TRACT *n, vb* tracted
TRACTOR *n*
TRACTS ▸ tract
TRACTUS *n* anthem sung in some RC masses
TRAD *n* traditional jazz, as revived in the 1950s
TRADE *n, vb, adj* traded
TRADER *n* traders
TRADES ▸ trade
TRADING ▸ trade
TRADS ▸ trad
TRADUCE *vb*
TRAFFIC *n, vb*
TRAGAL ▸ tragus
TRAGEDY *n*
TRAGI ▸ tragus
TRAGIC *adj, n* tragics
TRAGULE *n* mouse deer

TRAGUS *n* fleshy projection that partially covers the entrance to the external ear
TRAIK *vb* trudge; trek with difficulty **traiked, traikit, traiks**
TRAIL *n, vb* trailed
TRAILER *n, vb*
TRAILS ▸ trail
TRAIN *vb, n* trained
TRAINEE *n, adj*
TRAINER *n* person who trains an athlete or sportsman
TRAINS ▸ train
TRAIPSE *vb, n*
TRAIT *n*
TRAITOR *n*
TRAITS ▸ trait
TRAJECT *vb* transport or transmit
TRAM = trammel
TRAMCAR = tram
TRAMEL *variant spelling of* ▸ **trammel**
TRAMELL *variant spelling of* ▸ **trammel**
TRAMELS ▸ tramel
TRAMMED ▸ tram
TRAMMEL *n, vb*
TRAMMIE *n* conductor or driver of a tram
TRAMP *vb, n* tramped
TRAMPER *n* person who tramps
TRAMPET *variant spelling of* ▸ **trampette**
TRAMPLE *vb, n*
TRAMPS ▸ tramp
TRAMPY *adj* (of woman) disreputable
TRAMS ▸ tram

TRAMWAY = tramline

TRANCE *n*, *vb* tranced, trances

TRANCEY *adj* (of music) characteristic of the trance sub-genre

TRANCHE *n* portion of something large

TRANECT *n* ferry

TRANGAM *n* bauble or trinket

TRANGLE *n* (in heraldry) a small fesse

TRANK *n* short form of tranquillizer: drug that calms a person **tranks**

TRANKUM *n* trankum

TRANNIE *n* transistor radio **tranny**

TRANQ *n* **trank**

> Short for tranquilliser; another of those useful words allowing you to play the Q without a U.

TRANQS ▶ **tranq**

TRANS *n* short from of translation

TRANSE *n* way through; passage **transes**

TRANSIT *n*, *vb*

TRANSOM *n* horizontal bar across a window

TRANT *vb* travel from place to place selling goods **tranted, tranter, trants**

TRAP *n*, *vb*

TRAPAN = **trepan**

TRAPANS ▶ **trapan**

TRAPE = **traipse**

TRAPED ▶ **trape**

TRAPES = **traipse**

TRAPEZE *n*, *vb*

TRAPING ▶ **trape**

TRAPPED ▶ **trap**

TRAPPER *n*

TRAPPY *adj* having many traps

TRAPS ▶ **trap**

TRAPT *old past participle of* ▶ **trap**

TRASH *n*, *vb*

TRASHED *adj* drunk

TRASHER ▶ **trash**

TRASHES ▶ **trash**

TRASHY *adj*

TRASS *n* variety of the volcanic rock tuff **trasses**

TRAT *n* type of fishing line holding a series of baited hooks **trats**

TRATT *short for* > **trattoria**

TRATTS ▶ **tratt**

TRAUMA *n* **traumas**

TRAVAIL *n*, *vb*

TRAVE *n* stout wooden cage in which difficult horses are shod

TRAVEL *vb*, *n* **travels**

TRAVES ▶ **trave**

TRAVIS ▶ **treviss**

TRAVOIS *n* sled used for dragging logs

TRAWL *n*, *vb* **trawled**

TRAWLER *n*

TRAWLEY = **trolley**

TRAWLS ▶ **trawl**

TRAY *n*

TRAYBIT *n* threepenny bit

TRAYFUL *n* as many or as much as will fit on a tray

TRAYNE *old spelling of* ▶ **train**

TRAYNED ▶ **train**

TRAYNES ▶ **trayne**

TRAYS ▶ **tray**

TREACLE *n*, *vb* **treacly**

TREAD *vb*, *n* **treaded, treader**

TREADLE *n*, *vb*

TREADS ▶ **tread**

TREAGUE *n* agreement to stop fighting

TREASON *n*

TREAT *vb*, *n* **treated, treater, treats**

TREATY *n*

TREBLE *adj*, *n*, *vb* **trebled, trebles, trebly**

TRECK = **trek**

TRECKED ▶ **treck**

TRECKS ▶ **treck**

TREDDLE *variant spelling of* ▶ **treadle**

TREE *n* **treed, treeing**

TREEN *adj* made of wood ▷ *n* art of making treenware **treens**

TREES ▶ **tree**

TREETOP *n* top of a tree

TREEWAX *n* yellowish wax secreted by an oriental scale insect

TREF *adj* in Judaism, ritually unfit to be eaten **trefa, trefah**

TREFOIL *n*

TREHALA *n* edible sugary substance from the cocoon of an Asian weevil

TREIF = **tref**

TREIFA = **tref**

TREILLE *another word for* ▶ **trellis**

TREK n, vb **trekked,
trekker, treks**

TRELLIS n, vb

TREMA n mark placed over vowel to indicate it is to be pronounced separately **tremas**

TREMBLE vb, n **trembly**

TREMIE n metal hopper and pipe used to distribute freshly mixed concrete underwater **tremies**

TREMOLO n

TREMOR n, vb **tremors**

TRENAIL = **treenail**

TRENCH n, adj, vb

TREND n, vb **trended, trends**

TRENDY n, adj

TRENISE n one of the figures in a quadrille

TRENTAL n mass said in remembrance of a person 30 days after his or her death

TREPAN = **trephine**

TREPANG n any of various large sea cucumbers

TREPANS ▶ **trepan**

TREPID adj **trembling**

TRES adj very

TRESS n lock of hair, esp a long lock of woman's hair ▶ vb arrange in tresses

TRESSED adj having a tress or tresses as specified

TRESSEL variant spelling of ▶ **trestle**

TRESSES ▶ **tress**

TRESSY ▶ **tress**

TREST old variant of ▶ **trestle**

TRESTLE n

TRESTS ▶ **trest**

TRET n (formerly) allowance granted for waste due to transportation **trets**

TREVET = **trivet**

TREVETS ▶ **trevet**

TREVIS variant spelling of ▶ **treviss**

TREVISS n partition in a stable for keeping animals apart

TREW old variant spelling of ▶ **true**

TREWS pl n close-fitting tartan trousers

TREY n any card or dice throw with three spots

TREYBIT = **traybit**

TREYS ▶ **trey**

TREZ = **trey**

TREZES ▶ **trez**

TRIABLE adj liable to be tried judicially

TRIAC n device for regulating the amount of reacting current allowed to reach a circuit

TRIACID adj (of a base) capable of reacting with three molecules of a monobasic acid

TRIACS ▶ **triac**

TRIACT adj having three rays

TRIAD n

TRIADIC n something that has the characteristics of a triad

TRIADS ▶ **triad**

TRIAGE n sorting emergency patients into categories of priority ▶ vb sort (patients) into categories of priority **triaged, triages**

TRIAL n **trials**

TRIARCH n one of three rulers of a triarchy

TRIATIC n rope between a ship's mastheads

TRIAXON another name for ▶ **triaxial**

TRIAZIN = **triazine**

TRIBADE n lesbian, esp one who practises tribadism

TRIBAL adj of or denoting a tribe or tribes ▶ n member of a tribal community **tribals**

TRIBBLE n frame for drying paper

TRIBE n **tribes**

TRIBLET n spindle or mandrel used in making rings, tubes, etc

TRIBUNE n

TRIBUTE n

TRICAR n car with three wheels **tricars**

TRICE n, vb **triced**

TRICEP = **triceps**

TRICEPS n

TRICES ▶ **trice**

TRICING ▶ **trice**

TRICK n, vb **tricked, tricker**

TRICKIE Scots form of ▶ **tricky**

TRICKLE vb, n **trickly**

TRICKS ▸ **trick**

TRICKSY adj playing tricks habitually

TRICKY adj

TRICLAD n type of worm having a tripartite intestine

TRICORN n cocked hat with opposing brims turned back and caught in three places ▹ adj having three horns or corners

TRICOT n thin rayon or nylon fabric knitted or resembling knitting, used for dresses, etc **tricots**

TRIDARN n sideboard with three levels

TRIDE old spelling of the past tense of ▸ **try**

TRIDENT n, adj

TRIDUAN adj three days long

TRIDUUM n period of three days for prayer before a feast

TRIE old spelling of ▸ **try**

TRIED ▸ **try**

TRIELLA n bet on the winners of three nominated horse races

TRIENE n chemical compound containing three double bonds **trienes**

TRIENS n Byzantine gold coin worth one third of a solidus

TRIER n person or thing that tries **triers**

TRIES ▸ **try**

TRIFF adj terrific; very good indeed **triffer**

TRIFFIC adj terrific; very good indeed

TRIFFID n fictional plant that could kill humans

TRIFID adj divided or split into three parts or lobes

TRIFLE n, vb **trifled, trifler, trifles**

TRIFOLD less common word for ▸ **triple**

TRIFOLY = **trefoil**

TRIFORM adj having three parts

TRIG adj neat or spruce ▹ vb make or become spruce

TRIGAMY n condition of having three spouses

TRIGGED ▸ **trig**

TRIGGER n, vb

TRIGLOT n person who can speak three languages

TRIGLY ▸ **trig**

TRIGO n wheat field

TRIGON n (in classical Greece or Rome) a triangular harp or lyre **trigons**

TRIGOS ▸ **trigo**

TRIGRAM n three-letter inscription

TRIGS ▸ **trig**

TRIJET n jet with three engines **trijets**

TRIKE n tricycle **trikes**

TRILBY n **trilbys**

TRILD old past tense of ▸ **trill**

TRILITH = **trilithon**

TRILL n, vb **trilled, triller**

TRILLO n (in music) a trill

TRILLS ▸ **trill**

TRILOBE n three-lobed thing

TRILOGY n

TRIM adj, vb, n

TRIMER n polymer or a molecule of a polymer consisting of three identical monomers **trimers**

TRIMIX n gas mixture of nitrogen, helium and oxygen used by deep-sea divers

TRIMLY, trimmed, trimmer, trims ▸ **trim**

TRIMTAB n small control surface to enable the pilot to balance an aircraft

TRIN n triplet

TRINAL ▸ **trine**

TRINARY adj made up of three parts

TRINDLE vb move heavily on (or as if on) wheels

TRINE n aspect of 120° between two planets, an orb of 8° being allowed ▹ adj of or relating to a trine ▹ vb put in a trine aspect **trined, trines**

TRINGLE n slim rod

TRINING ▸ **trine**

TRINITY n

TRINKET n, vb

TRINKUM n trinket or bauble

TRINS ▸ trin

TRIO n

TRIODE n electronic valve having three electrodes, a cathode, an anode, and a grid **triodes**

TRIOL n any of a class of alcohols that have three hydroxyl groups per molecule

TRIOLET n verse form of eight lines

TRIOLS ▸ triol

TRIONES n seven stars of the constellation Ursa Major

TRIONYM another name for > **trinomial**

TRIOR old form of ▸ **trier**

TRIORS ▸ trior

TRIOS ▸ trio

TRIOSE n simple monosaccharide produced by the oxidation of glycerol **trioses**

TRIOXID n = trioxide

TRIP n, vb

TRIPACK n pack of three

TRIPART adj composed of three parts

TRIPE n

TRIPERY n place where tripe is prepared

TRIPES ▸ tripe

TRIPEY ▸ tripe

TRIPIER ▸ tripe

TRIPLE adj, vb, n **tripled, triples**

TRIPLET n

TRIPLEX n building

divided into three separate dwellings

TRIPLY vb give a reply to a duply

TRIPOD n **tripods**

TRIPODY n metrical unit consisting of three feet

TRIPOLI n lightweight porous siliceous rock

TRIPOS n final examinations for an honours degree at Cambridge University

TRIPPED ▸ trip

TRIPPER n

TRIPPET n any mechanism that strikes or is struck at regular intervals, as by a cam

TRIPPLE vb canter

TRIPPY adj suggestive of or resembling the effect produced by a hallucinogenic drug

TRIPS ▸ trip

TRIPSES ▸ tripsis

TRIPSIS n act of kneading the body to promote circulation, suppleness, etc

TRIPTAN n drug used to treat migraine

TRIPY ▸ tripe

TRIREME n ancient Greek warship with three rows of oars on each side

TRISECT vb divide into three parts, esp three equal parts

TRISEME n metrical foot of a length equal to

three short syllables

TRISHAW another name for > **rickshaw**

TRISMIC ▸ trismus

TRISMUS n state of being unable to open the mouth

TRISOME n chromosome occurring three times (rather than twice) in a cell

TRISOMY n condition of having one chromosome represented three times

TRIST variant spelling of ▸ **triste**

TRISTE adj sad

TRISUL n trident symbol of Siva **trisula, trisuls**

TRITE adj, n tritely, **triter, trites, tritest**

TRITIDE n tritium compound

TRITIUM n radioactive isotope of hydrogen

TRITOMA another name for > **kniphofia**

TRITON n any of various chiefly tropical marine gastropod molluscs

TRITONE n musical interval consisting of three whole tones

TRITONS ▸ triton

TRIUMPH n, vb

TRIUNE adj constituting three things in one ▸ n group of three **triunes**

TRIVET n **trivets**

TRIVIA pl n

TRIVIAL adj

TRIVIUM n (in medieval learning) the lower division of the seven liberal arts

TRIZONE n area comprising three zones

TROAD = trod

TROADE = trod

TROADES ▶ troade

TROADS ▶ troad

TROAK old form of ▶ truck

TROAKED ▶ troak

TROAKS ▶ troak

TROAT vb (of a rutting buck) to call or bellow **troated, troats**

TROCAR n surgical instrument for removing fluid from bodily cavities **trocars**

TROCHAL adj shaped like a wheel

TROCHAR old variant spelling of ▶ trocar

TROCHE another name for ▶ lozenge

TROCHEE n metrical foot of one long and one short syllable

TROCHES ▶ troche

TROCHI ▶ trochus

TROCHIL ▶ trochilus

TROCHUS n hoop (used in exercise)

TROCK = truck

TROCKED ▶ trock

TROCKEN adj dry (used of wine)

TROCKS ▶ trock

TROD vb past participle of tread ▷ n path

TRODDEN ▶ tread

TRODE = trod

TRODES ▶ trode

TRODS ▶ trod

TROELIE = troolie

TROELY = troolie

TROFFER n fixture for holding and reflecting light from a fluorescent tube

TROG vb walk, esp aimlessly or heavily **trogged**

TROGGS n loyalty; fidelity

TROGON n bird of tropical and subtropical America, Africa, and Asia **trogons**

TROGS ▶ trog

TROIKA n troikas

TROILUS n type of large butterfly

TROIS Scots form of ▶ troy

TROKE = truck

TROKED ▶ troke

TROKES ▶ troke

TROKING ▶ troke

TROLAND n unit of light intensity in the eye

TROLL n, vb trolled, troller

TROLLEY n, vb

TROLLS ▶ troll

TROLLY = trolley

TROMINO n shape made from three squares, each joined to the next along one full side

TROMMEL n revolving cylindrical sieve used to screen crushed ore

TROMP vb trample

TROMPE n apparatus for supplying the blast of air in a forge

TROMPED ▶ tromp

TROMPES ▶ trompe

TROMPS ▶ tromp

TRON n public weighing machine

TRONA n greyish mineral that occurs in salt deposits **tronas**

TRONC n pool into which waiters, waitresses, hotel workers, etc, pay their tips **troncs**

TRONE = tron

TRONES ▶ trone

TRONK n jail tronks

TRONS ▶ tron

TROOLIE n large palm leaf

TROOP n, vb trooped

TROOPER n

TROOPS ▶ troop

TROOZ = trews

TROP adv too, too much

TROPE n figure of speech ▷ vb use tropes (in speech or writing) **troped, tropes**

TROPHI pl n collective term for the mandibles and other parts of an insect's mouth

TROPHIC adj of or relating to nutrition

TROPHY n, adj, vb

TROPIC n either of two lines of latitude at 23½°N (tropic of Cancer) or 23½°S (tropic of Capricorn) **tropics**

TROPIN n adrenal androgen

TROPINE n white crystalline poisonous alkaloid

TROPING ▶ trope

TROPINS ▶ tropin

TROPISM n tropist

TROPPO adv too much ▷ adj mentally affected by a tropical climate

TROT vb, n

TROTH n, vb trothed, troths

TROTS ▶ trot

TROTTED ▶ trot

TROTTER n

TROTYL n yellow solid used chiefly as a high explosive trotyls

TROUBLE n, vb

TROUCH n rubbish

TROUGH n, vb troughs

TROULE old variant of ▶ troll

TROULED ▶ troule

TROULES ▶ troule

TROUNCE vb

TROUPE n, vb trouped

TROUPER n member of a troupe

TROUPES ▶ troupe

TROUSE pl n close-fitting breeches worn in Ireland

TROUSER adj of trousers ▷ vb take (something, esp money), often surreptitiously or unlawfully ▷ n of or relating to trousers

TROUSES ▶ trouse

TROUT n, vb trouter, trouts, trouty

TROVE n as in treasure-trove valuable articles found hidden in the earth

TROVER n act of assuming proprietary rights over goods or property belonging to another trovers

TROVES ▶ trove

TROW vb think, believe, or trust trowed

TROWEL n, vb trowels

TROWING ▶ trow

TROWS ▶ trow

TROWTH variant spelling of ▶ troth

TROWTHS ▶ trowth

TROY n as in troy weight system of weights used for precious metals and gemstones, based on the grain, which is identical to the avoirdupois grain troys

TRUANCY ▶ truant

TRUANT n, adj, vb truants

TRUCAGE n art forgery

TRUCE n, vb truced, truces, trucial, trucing

TRUCK n, vb trucked

TRUCKER n truck driver

TRUCKIE n truck driver

TRUCKLE vb yield weakly or give in ▷ n small wheel

TRUCKS ▶ truck

TRUDGE vb, n trudged

TRUDGEN n type of swimming stroke

TRUDGER ▶ trudge

TRUDGES ▶ trudge

TRUE adj trued, trueing

TRUEMAN n honest person truemen

TRUER ▶ true

TRUES ▶ true

TRUEST ▶ true

TRUFFE rare word for ▶ truffle

TRUFFES ▶ truffe

TRUFFLE n, vb

TRUG n long shallow basket used by gardeners

TRUGO n game similar to croquet trugos

TRUGS ▶ trug

TRUING ▶ true

TRUISM n truisms

TRULL n prostitute trulls

TRULY adv in a true manner

TRUMEAU n section of a wall or pillar between two openings

TRUMP adj, vb, pl n trumped

TRUMPET n, vb

TRUMPS ▶ trump

TRUNCAL adj of or relating to the trunk

TRUNDLE vb, n

TRUNK n, vb trunked

TRUNKS pl n shorts worn by a man for swimming

TRUNNEL = treenail

TRUSS vb, n trussed, trusser, trusses

TRUST vb, n, adj **trusted**

TRUSTEE n, vb

TRUSTER ▶ **trust**

TRUSTOR n person who sets up a trust

TRUSTS ▶ **trust**

TRUSTY adj, n

TRUTH n **truths**

TRUTHY adj truthful

TRY vb, n

TRYE adj very good; select

TRYER variant of ▶ **trier**

TRYERS ▶ **tryer**

TRYING ▶ **try**

TRYINGS ▶ **try**

TRYKE variant spelling of ▶ **trike**

TRYKES ▶ **tryke**

TRYMA n drupe produced by the walnut and similar plants **trymata**

TRYOUT n trial or test, as of an athlete or actor **tryouts**

TRYP n parasitic protozoan

TRYPAN modifier as in **trypan blue** dye used for staining cells in biological research

TRYPS ▶ **tryp**

TRYPSIN n enzyme occurring in pancreatic juice **tryptic**

TRYSAIL n small fore-and-aft sail on a sailing vessel

TRYST n, vb **tryste, trysted, tryster**

TRYSTES ▶ **tryste**

TRYSTS ▶ **tryst**

TSADDIK variant of ▶ **zaddik**

TSADDIQ variant of ▶ **zaddik**

TSADE variant spelling of ▶ **sadhe**

TSADES ▶ **tsade**

TSADI variant of ▶ **sadhe**

TSADIS ▶ **tsadi**

TSAMBA n Tibetan dish made from roasted barley and tea **tsambas**

TSANTSA n shrunken head of an enemy kept as a trophy

TSAR n **tsardom**

TSARINA n

TSARISM n system of government by a tsar **tsarist**

TSARS ▶ **tsar**

TSATSKE variant of ▶ **tchotchke**

TSETSE n any of various bloodsucking African flies **tsetses**

TSIGANE variant of ▶ **tzigane**

TSIMMES variant spelling of ▶ **tzimmes**

TSK vb utter the sound "tsk", usu in disapproval **tsked, tsking, tsks, tsktsk**

| This can occasionally be useful because it enables you to play K without using vowels. |

TSKTSKS ▶ **tsktsk**

TSOORIS variant of ▶ **tsuris**

TSORES variant of ▶ **tsuris**

TSORIS variant of ▶ **tsuris**

TSOTSI n Black street thug or gang member **tsotsis**

TSOURIS variant of ▶ **tsuris**

TSUBA n sword guard of a Japanese sword **tsubas**

TSUNAMI n

TSURIS n grief or strife

TUAN n lord **tuans**

TUART n eucalyptus tree of Australia **tuarts**

TUATARA n tuatera

TUATH n territory of an ancient Irish tribe **tuaths**

TUATUA n edible marine bivalve of New Zealand waters **tuatuas**

TUB n, vb

TUBA n tubae

TUBAGE n insertion of a tube **tubages**

TUBAIST ▶ **tuba**

TUBAL adj of or relating to a tube

TUBAR another word for ▶ **tubular**

TUBAS ▶ **tuba**

TUBATE less common word for ▶ **tubular**

TUBBED ▶ **tub**

TUBBER ▶ **tub**

TUBBERS ▶ **tub**

TUBBIER ▶ **tubby**

TUBBING ▶ **tub**

TUBBISH adj fat

TUBBY adj

TUBE n **tubed**

TUBEFUL n quantity (of something) that a tube can hold

TUBER n tubers

TUBES ▸ tube

TUBFAST n period of fasting and sweating in a tub, intended as a cure for disease

TUBFISH another name for ▸ gurnard

TUBFUL n amount a tub will hold tubfuls

TUBIFEX n type of small reddish freshwater worm

TUBING n length of tube tubings

TUBIST ▸ tuba

TUBISTS ▸ tuba

TUBLIKE ▸ tub

TUBS ▸ tub

TUBULAR adj

TUBULE n any small tubular structure tubules

TUBULIN n protein forming the basis of microtubules

TUCHUN n (formerly) a Chinese military governor or warlord tuchuns

TUCK vb, n tucked

TUCKER n, vb tuckers

TUCKET n flourish on a trumpet tuckets

TUCKING ▸ tuck

TUCKS ▸ tuck

TUFA n tufas

TUFF n porous rock formed from volcanic dust or ash

TUFFE old form of ▸ tuft

TUFFES ▸ tuffe

TUFFET n small mound or seat tuffets

TUFFS ▸ tuff

TUFOLI n type of tubular pasta

TUFT n, vb

TUFTED adj having a tuft or tufts

TUFTER n, tufters, tuftier, tuftily, tufting, tufts, tufty ▸ tuft

TUG vb, n, tugboat, tugged, tugger, tuggers, tugging

TUGHRA n Turkish Sultan's official emblem tughras

TUGHRIK n = tugrik

TUGLESS ▸ tug

TUGRA n = tughra

TUGRAS ▸ tugra

TUGRIK n standard monetary unit of Mongolia tugriks

TUGS ▸ tug

TUI n New Zealand honeyeater that mimics human speech and the songs of other birds

TUILLE n (in a suit of armour) hanging plate protecting the thighs tuilles

TUILYIE vb fight tuilzie

TUINA n form of massage originating in China tuinas

TUIS ▸ tui

TUISM n practice of putting the interests of another before one's own **tuisms**

TUITION n

TUKTOO = tuktu

TUKTOOS ▸ tuktoo

TUKTU (in Canada) another name for ▸ caribou

TUKTUS ▸ tuktu

TULADI n large trout found in Canada and northern US **tuladis**

TULBAN old form of ▸ turban

TULBANS ▸ tulban

TULCHAN n skin of a calf placed next to a cow to induce it to give milk

TULE n type of bulrush found in California **tules**

TULIP n tulips

TULLE n tulles

TULPA n being or object created through willpower and visualization techniques **tulpas**

TULWAR n Indian sabre **tulwars**

TUM informal or childish word for ▸ stomach

TUMBLE vb, n tumbled

TUMBLER n

TUMBLES ▸ tumble

TUMBREL n tumbril

TUMEFY vb make or become tumid

TUMESCE vb swell

TUMID adj (of an organ or part of the body) enlarged or swollen **tumidly**

TUMMIES ▸ tummy

TUMMLER n entertainer employed to encourage audience participation

TUMMY n

TUMOR = tumour

TUMORAL ▶ tumour

TUMORS ▶ tumor

TUMOUR n tumours

TUMP n small mound or clump ▷ vb make a tump around **tumped**

TUMPHY n dolt; fool

TUMPIER, tumping, tumps, tumpy ▶ tump

TUMS ▶ tum

TUMSHIE n turnip

TUMULAR adj of, relating to, or like a mound

TUMULI ▶ tumulus

TUMULT n, vb tumults

TUMULUS n

TUN n, vb

TUNA n

TUNABLE adj able to be tuned **tunably**

TUNAS ▶ tuna

TUND vb beat: strike tunded, tunding

TUNDISH n type of funnel

TUNDRA n tundras

TUNDS ▶ tund

TUNDUN n wooden instrument used by Native Australians in religious rites tunduns

TUNE n, vb tuned

TUNEFUL adj

TUNER n tuners

TUNES ▶ tune

TUNEUP n adjustments made to an engine to improve its performance **tuneups**

TUNG n as in tung oil fast-drying oil obtained from the seeds of a central Asian tree **tungs**

TUNIC n

TUNICA n tissue forming a layer or covering of an organ or part **tunicae**

TUNICIN n cellulose-like substance found in tunicates

TUNICLE n vestment worn at High Mass and other religious ceremonies

TUNICS ▶ tunic

TUNIER ▶ tuny

TUNIEST ▶ tuny

TUNING n set of pitches to which the open strings of a guitar, violin, etc, are tuned **tunings**

TUNNAGE = tonnage

TUNNED ▶ tun

TUNNEL n, vb tunnels

TUNNIES ▶ tunny

TUNNING ▶ tun

TUNNY = tuna

TUNS ▶ tun

TUNY adj having an easily discernable melody

TUP n male sheep ▷ vb cause (a ram) to mate with a ewe

TUPEK = tupik

TUPEKS ▶ tupek

TUPELO n large tree of deep swamps and rivers of the southern US **tupelos**

TUPIK n tent of seal or caribou skin used for shelter by the Inuit in summer **tupiks**

TUPLE n row of values in a relational database **tuples**

TUPPED ▶ tup

TUPPING ▶ tup

TUPS ▶ tup

TUPUNA = tipuna

TUPUNAS ▶ tupuna

TUQUE n knitted cap with a long tapering end **tuques**

TURACIN n red pigment found in touraco feathers

TURACO = touraco

TURACOS ▶ turaco

TURACOU variant of ▶ touraco

TURBAN n turband, turbans, turbant

TURBARY n land where peat or turf is cut or has been cut

TURBETH variant of ▶ turpeth

TURBID adj

TURBINE n

TURBIT n crested breed of domestic pigeon

TURBITH variant of ▶ turpeth

TURBITS ▶ turbit

TURBO n

TURBOND old variant of ▶ turban

TURBOS ▶ turbo

TURBOT n turbots

TURDINE adj of, relating to, or characteristic of thrushes

TURDION variant of ▸ tordion

TURDOID = turdine

TUREEN n tureens

TURF n, vb turfed

TURFEN adj made of turf

TURFIER ▸ turfy

TURFING ▸ turf

TURFITE = turfman

TURFMAN n person devoted to horse racing turfmen

TURFS ▸ turf

TURFSKI n ski down a grassy hill on skis modified with integral wheels

TURFY adj of, covered with, or resembling turf

TURGENT obsolete word for ▸ turgid

TURGID old

TURGITE n red or black mineral consisting of hydrated ferric oxide

TURGOR n normal rigid state of a cell turgors

TURION n perennating bud produced by many aquatic plants turions

TURISTA n traveller's diarrhoea

TURKEY n turkeys

TURKIES old form of > turquoise

TURKIS old form of > turquoise

TURKOIS old form of > turquoise

TURM n troop of horsemen turme

TURMES ▸ turme

TURMOIL n, vb

TURMS ▸ turm

TURN vb, n

TURNDUN another name for ▸ tundun

TURNED ▸ turn

TURNER n person or thing that turns turners

TURNERY n objects made on a lathe

TURNING n

TURNIP n, vb turnips

TURNIPY adj like a turnip

TURNKEY n, adj

TURNOFF n road or other way branching off from the main

TURNON n something sexually exciting turnons

TURNOUT n

TURNS ▸ turn

TURNUP n the turned-up fold at the bottom of some trouser legs turnups

TURPETH n convolvulaceous plant of the East Indies, having roots with purgative properties

TURPS n

TURRET n turrets

TURTLE n turtled, turtler, turtles

TURVES ▸ turf

TUSCHE n substance used in lithography for drawing the design tusches

TUSH interj exclamation of disapproval or contempt ▷ n small tusk ▷ vb utter the interjection "tush" tushed

TUSHERY n use of affectedly archaic language in novels, etc

TUSHES ▸ tush

TUSHIE n pair of buttocks tushies

TUSHING ▸ tush

TUSHKAR variant of ▸ tuskar

TUSHKER variant of ▸ tuskar

TUSHY = tushie

TUSK n, vb

TUSKAR n peat-cutting spade tuskars

TUSKED ▸ tusk

TUSKER n any animal with prominent tusks, esp a wild boar or elephant tuskers

TUSKIER, tusking, tusks, tusky ▸ tusk

TUSSAC modifier as in tussac grass kind of grass

TUSSAH = tussore

TUSSAHS ▸ tussah

TUSSAL ▸ tussis

TUSSAR variant of ▸ tussore

TUSSARS ▸ tussar

TUSSEH variant of ▸ tussore

TUSSEHS ▸ tusseh

TUSSER = tussore

TUSSERS ▶ tusser

TUSSES ▶ tussis

TUSSIS *technical name for a* ▶ **cough**

TUSSIVE ▶ tussis

TUSSLE *vb, n* tussled, tussles

TUSSOCK *n*

TUSSOR *variant of* ▶ tussore

TUSSORE *n* strong coarse brownish Indian silk obtained from the cocoons of an Oriental saturniid silkworm

TUSSORS ▶ tussor

TUSSUCK *variant of* ▶ tussock

TUSSUR = tussore

TUSSURS ▶ tussur

TUT *interj* an exclamation of mild disapproval, or surprise ▷ *vb* express disapproval by the exclamation of "tut-tut." ▷ *n* payment system based on measurable work done

TUTANIA *n* alloy of low melting point used mostly for decorative purposes

TUTEE *n* one who is tutored, esp in a university **tutees**

TUTELAR = tutelary

TUTENAG *n* zinc alloy

TUTMAN *n* one who does tutwork **tutmen**

TUTOR *n, vb* tutored, tutors

TUTOYED *adj* addressed in a familiar way

TUTOYER *vb* speak to someone on familiar terms

TUTRESS = tutoress

TUTRIX *n* female tutor; tutoress

TUTS *Scots version of* ▶ tut

TUTSAN *n* woodland shrub of Europe and W Asia **tutsans**

TUTSED ▶ tuts

TUTSES ▶ tuts

TUTSING ▶ tuts

TUTTED ▶ tut

TUTTI *adv* be performed by the whole orchestra or choir ▷ *n* piece of tutti music

TUTTIES ▶ tutty

TUTTING ▶ tut

TUTTIS ▶ tutti

TUTTY *n* finely powdered impure zinc oxide

TUTU *n*

TUTUED *adj* wearing tutu

TUTUS ▶ tutu

TUTWORK *n* work paid using a tut system

TUX *short for* ▶ **tuxedo**

> Tux is a short form of **tuxedo**, and is a very commonly played X word.

TUXEDO *n* tuxedos

TUXES ▶ tux

TUYER *variant of* ▶ tuyere

TUYERE *n* water-cooled nozzle through which

air is blown into a cupola, blast furnace, or forge **tuyeres**

TUYERS ▶ tuyer

TUZZ *n* tuft or clump of hair **tuzzes**

TWA *Scots word for* ▶ **two**

TWADDLE *n, vb* twaddly

TWAE = twa

TWAES ▶ twae

TWAFALD *Scots variant of* ▶ **twofold**

TWAIN *n* twains

TWAITE *n* herring-like food fish **twaites**

TWAL *n* twelve twals

TWANG *n, vb* twanged, twanger

TWANGLE *vb* make a continuous loose twanging sound

TWANGS ▶ twang

TWANGY ▶ twang

TWANK *vb* make a sharply curtailed twang

TWANKAY *n* variety of Chinese green tea

TWANKS ▶ twank

TWANKY = twankay

TWAS ▶ twa

TWASOME = twosome

TWATTLE *rare word for* ▶ **twaddle**

TWAY *old variant of* ▶ **twain**

TWAYS ▶ tway

TWEAK *vb, n* tweaked

TWEAKER *n* engineer's small screwdriver

TWEAKS ▶ tweak

TWEAKY ▶ tweak

TWEE adj

TWEED n

TWEEDLE vb improvise aimlessly on a musical instrument

TWEEDS ▷ tweed

TWEEDY adj of or made of tweed

TWEEL variant of ▷ **twill**

TWEELED ▷ tweel

TWEELS ▷ tweel

TWEELY ▷ twee

TWEEN = between

TWEENER = tweenager

TWEENIE = tweeny

TWEENS ▷ tween

TWEENY n maid who assists both cook and housemaid

TWEER variant of ▷ **twire**

TWEERED ▷ tweer

TWEERS ▷ tweer

TWEEST ▷ twee

TWEET vb, interj tweeted

TWEETER n loudspeaker reproducing high-frequency sounds

TWEETS ▷ tweet

TWEEZE vb take hold of or pluck (hair, small objects, etc) with or as if with tweezers tweezed

TWEEZER = tweezers tweezes

TWELFTH n (of) number twelve in a series ▷ adj of or being number twelve in a series

TWELVE n, adj, determiner twelves

TWENTY n, adj, determiner

TWERP n silly person twerps, twerpy

TWIBIL = twibill

TWIBILL n mattock with a blade shaped like an adze on one end and like an axe at the other

TWIBILS ▷ twibill

TWICE adv

TWICER n someone who does something twice twicers

TWIDDLE vb, n twiddly

TWIER variant of ▷ **tuyere**

TWIERS ▷ twier

TWIFOLD variant of ▷ **twofold**

TWIG n, vb twigged

TWIGGEN adj made of twigs

TWIGGER ▷ twig

TWIGGY adj of or relating to a twig or twigs

TWIGHT old variant of ▷ **twit**

TWIGHTS ▷ twight

TWIGLET n small twig

TWIGLOO n temporary shelter made from twigs, branches, leaves, etc

TWIGS ▷ twig

TWILIT ▷ twilight

TWILL n, adj, vb twilled, twills

TWILLY n machine having revolving spikes for opening and cleaning raw textile fibres

TWILT variant of ▷ **quilt**

TWILTED ▷ twilt

TWILTS ▷ twilt

TWIN n, vb

TWINE n, vb twined, twiner, twiners, twines

TWINGE n, vb twinged, twinges

TWINIER ▷ twine

TWINING ▷ twine

TWINJET n jet aircraft with two engines

TWINK n white correction fluid for deleting written text ▷ vb twinkle twinked

TWINKIE n stupid person

TWINKLE vb, n twinkly

TWINKS ▷ twink

TWINNED ▷ twin

TWINS ▷ twin

TWINSET n

TWINTER n animal that is 2 years old

TWINY ▷ twine

TWIRE vb look intently at with (or as if with) difficulty twired, twires, twiring

TWIRL vb, n twirled, twirler, twirls, twirly

TWIRP = twerp

TWIRPS ▷ twirp

TWIRPY ▷ twirp

TWISCAR variant of ▷ **tuskar**

TWIST vb, n twisted

TWISTER n

TWISTOR n variable corresponding to the coordinates of a point in space and time

TWISTS ▶ twist

TWISTY ▶ twist

TWIT vb, n

TWITCH vb, n

TWITCHY adj nervous, worried, and ill-at-ease

TWITE n N European finch with a brown streaked plumage **twites**

TWITS ▶ twit

TWITTED ▶ twit

TWITTEN n narrow alleyway

TWITTER vb, n

TWIXT = betwixt

TWIZZLE vb spin around

TWO n

TWOCCER ▶ twoccing

TWOCKER ▶ twoccing

TWOER n (in a game) something that scores two **twoers**

TWOFER n single ticket allowing the buyer entrance to two events **twofers**

TWOFOLD adj, adv, n

TWONESS n state or condition of being two

TWONIE = toonie

TWONIES ▶ twonie

TWOONIE variant of ▶ toonie

TWOS ▶ two

TWOSOME n

TWP adj stupid

> This Welsh word for stupid is useful because it contains no vowels, and can thus help you when you have an awkward rack full of consonants.

TWYER n tuyere

TWYERE variant of ▶ tuyere

TWYERES ▶ twyere

TWYERS ▶ twyer

TWYFOLD adj twofold

TYCHISM n theory that chance is an objective reality at work in the universe

TYCOON n tycoons

TYDE old variant of the past participle of ▶ tie

TYE n trough used in mining to separate valuable material from dross ▶ vb (in mining) isolate valuable material from dross using a tye **tyed**

TYEE n large northern Pacific salmon **tyees**

TYEING, tyer, tyers, tyes ▶ tye

TYG n mug with two handles **tygs**

> This old word for a two-handled drinking cup is another key word to know for situations when you are short of vowels.

TYIN variant of ▶ tyiyn

TYING ▶ tie

TYIYN n money unit of Kyrgyzstan **tyiyns**

TYLER variant of ▶ tiler

TYLERS ▶ tyler

TYLOPOD n mammal with padded feet, such as a camel or llama

TYLOSES ▶ tylosis

TYLOSIN n broad spectrum antibiotic

TYLOSIS n bladder-like outgrowth from certain cells in woody tissue

TYLOTE n knobbed sponge spicule **tylotes**

TYMBAL = timbal

TYMBALS ▶ tymbal

TYMP n blast furnace outlet through which molten metal flows

TYMPAN = tympanum

TYMPANA > tympanum

TYMPANI = timpani

TYMPANO ▶ tympani

TYMPANS ▶ tympan

TYMPANY n distention of the abdomen

TYMPS ▶ tymp

TYND variant of ▶ tind

TYNDE variant of ▶ tind

TYNE variant of ▶ tine

TYNED variant of ▶ tyne

TYNES ▶ tyne

TYNING ▶ tyne

TYPABLE ▶ type

TYPAL rare word for ▶ typical

TYPE n, vb

TYPEBAR n one of the bars in a typewriter that carry the type and are operated by keys

TYPED ▶ type

TYPES ▶ type

TYPESET vb

TYPEY variant of ▶ typy

TYPHOID adj

TYPHON n whirlwind **typhons**

TYPHOON *n*
TYPHOSE *adj* relating to typhoid
TYPHOUS ▶ typhus
TYPHUS *n*
TYPIC = typical
TYPICAL *adj*
TYPIER ▶ typy
TYPIEST ▶ typy
TYPIFY *vb*
TYPING *n* typings
TYPIST *n* typists
TYPO *n* typographical error typos
TYPP *n* unit of thickness of yarn typps
TYPTO *vb* learn Greek conjugations typtoed, typtos
TYPY *adj* (of an animal) typifying the breed
TYRAN *vb* act as a tyrant tyraned, tyranne
TYRANNY *n*

TYRANS ▶ tyran
TYRANT *n*, *vb* tyrants
TYRE *n*, *vb* tyred, tyres, tyring
TYRO *n* tyroes, tyrones, tyronic, tyros
TYSTIE *n* black guillemot tysties
TYTE variant spelling of ▶ tite
TYTHE variant of ▶ tithe
TYTHED ▶ tythe
TYTHES ▶ tythe
TYTHING ▶ tythe
TZADDI ▶ sadhe
TZADDIK variant of ▶ zaddik
TZADDIQ variant of ▶ zaddik

An unlikely word from Judaism, meaning a person of great piety, but offering a great score played as a bonus.

TZADDIS ▶ tzaddi
TZAR = tsar
TZARDOM ▶ tzar
TZARINA variant of ▶ tsarina
TZARISM variant of ▶ tsarism
TZARIST ▶ tzarism
TZARS ▶ tzar
TZETSE variant of ▶ tsetse
TZETSES ▶ tzetse
TZETZE variant of ▶ tsetse
TZETZES ▶ tzetze
TZIGANE *n* type of Gypsy music tzigany
TZIMMES *n* traditional Jewish stew
TZITZIS variant of > tsitsith
TZITZIT variant of ▶ tzitzit
TZURIS variant of ▶ tsuris

Uu

U can be a difficult tile to use effectively. Although there are quite a few two-letter words beginning with **U**, most of them are quite unusual, and so difficult to remember. Only **up** (4 points) and **us** (2) are immediately obvious, so it's well worth learning words like **ug** (3), **uh** (5), **um** (4), and **un**, **ur** and **ut** (2 each). Three-letter words beginning with **U** can also be difficult to remember. If you are trying to use a **Q**, **X** or **Z**, bear in mind that there aren't any valid three-letter words with these letters that start with **U**. Knowing this can save you valuable time. It's also helpful to remember that there aren't any particularly high-scoring two- or three-letter words starting with **U**, the best being **uke** (7 points) and **uva** (6 points). If you have a surplus of **U**s, it is well worth remembering **ulu**, **umu** and **utu**, which score only 3 points but should improve your rack.

UAKARI n type of monkey **uakaris**

UBEROUS adj abundant

UBERTY n abundance

UBIETY n condition of being in a particular place

UBIQUE adv everywhere

UBUNTU n quality of compassion and humanity **ubuntus**

UCKERS n type of naval game

UDAL n form of freehold possession of land used in Orkney and Shetland

UDALLER n person possessing a udal

UDALS ▶ udal

UDDER n uddered, udders

UDO n stout perennial plant of Japan and China

UDON n (in Japanese cookery) large noodles made of wheat flour **udons**

UDOS ▶ udo

UDS interj God's or God save

UEY n u-turn **ueys**

UFO n flying saucer

UFOLOGY n study of UFOs

UFOS ▶ ufo

UG vb hate

UGALI n type of stiff porridge **ugalis**

UGGED ▶ ug

UGGING ▶ ug

UGH interj exclamation of disgust ▷ n sound made to indicate disgust **ughs**

> Together with **uke**, this is the highest-scoring three-letter word starting with U.

UGLIED, uglier, uglies, ugliest ▸ ugly

UGLIFY vb make or become ugly or more ugly

UGLILY ▸ ugly

UGLY adj, vb **uglying**

UGS ▸ ug

UGSOME adj loathsome

UH interj used to express hesitation

UHLAN n member of a body of lancers first employed in the Polish army **uhlans**

UHURU n national independence **uhurus**

> You won't often have three Us on your rack, but when you do this Swahili word for freedom may get you out of trouble. The only other 5-letter word containing three Us is **urubu**, a kind of vulture.

UILLEAN adj as in **uillean pipes** bagpipes developed in Ireland

UJAMAA n as in **ujamaa village** communally organized village in Tanzania **ujamaas**

UKASE n (in imperial Russia) a decree from the tsar **ukases**

UKE short form of ▸ **ukulele**

> Together with ugh, this is the highest-scoring three-letter word starting with U.

UKELELE = ukulele

UKES ▸ uke

UKULELE n

ULAMA n body of Muslim scholars or religious leaders **ulamas**

ULAN = uhlan

ULANS ▸ ulan

ULCER n, vb **ulcered, ulcers**

ULE n rubber tree

ULEMA = ulama

ULEMAS ▸ ulema

ULES ▸ ule

ULEX n variety of shrub **ulexes**

ULEXITE n type of mineral

ULICES ▸ ulex

ULICON = eulachon

ULICONS ▸ ulicon

ULIKON = eulachon

ULIKONS ▸ ulikon

ULITIS n gingivitis

ULLAGE n volume by which a liquid container falls short of being full ▸ vb create ullage in **ullaged, ullages**

ULLING n process of filling **ullings**

ULMIN n substance found in decaying vegetation **ulmins**

ULNA n

ULNAD adv towards the ulna

ULNAE ▸ ulna

ULNAR ▸ ulna

ULNARE n bone in the wrist **ulnaria**

ULNAS ▸ ulna

ULOSES ▸ ulosis

ULOSIS n formation of a scar

ULPAN n Israeli study centre **ulpanim**

ULSTER n man's heavy double-breasted overcoat **ulsters**

ULTIMA n final syllable of a word **ultimas**

ULTIMO adv in or during the previous month

ULTION n vengeance **ultions**

ULTRA n person who has extreme or immoderate beliefs or opinions ▸ adj extreme or immoderate, esp in beliefs or opinions **ultras**

ULU n type of knife

ULULANT ▸ ululate

ULULATE vb howl or wail

ULUS ▸ ulu

ULVA n genus of seaweed **ulvas**

ULYIE Scots variant of ▸ **oil**

ULYIES ▸ ulyie

ULZIE Scots variant of ▸ **oil**

ULZIES ▸ ulzie

UM interj representation of a common sound made when hesitating in speech ▸ vb hesitate while speaking

UMAMI n savoury flavour **umamis**

UMBEL n umbrella-like flower cluster

UMBELED = umbelled

UMBELS ▸ umbel

UMBER adj, n, vb
umbered, umbers,
umbery

UMBLE adj as in **umble
pie** (formerly) a pie
made from the heart,
entrails, etc, of a deer

UMBLES another term for
▶ numbles

UMBO n small hump
projecting from the
centre of the cap in
certain mushrooms
umbonal, umbones,
umbonic, umbos

UMBRA n shadow, esp
the shadow cast by
the moon onto the
earth during a solar
eclipse **umbrae**

UMBRAGE n, vb

UMBRAL ▶ umbra

UMBRAS ▶ umbra

UMBRE = umbrette

UMBREL n umbrella
umbrels

UMBRERE n helmet visor

UMBRES ▶ umbre

UMBRIL = umbrere

UMBRILS ▶ umbril

UMBROSE = umbrous

UMBROUS adj shady

UMFAZI n African
married woman
umfazis

UMIAC variant of
▶ umiak

UMIACK variant of
▶ umiak

UMIACKS ▶ umiack

UMIACS ▶ umiac

UMIAK n Inuit boat
made of skins **umiaks,
umiaq**

UMIAQS ▶ umiaq

UMLAUT n, vb umlauts

UMLUNGU n White
man: used esp as a
term of address

UMM = um

UMMA n Muslim
community ummah

UMMAHS ▶ ummah

UMMAS ▶ umma

UMMED ▶ um

UMMING ▶ um vb

UMP short for ▶ umpire

UMPED ▶ ump

UMPH = humph

UMPIE informal word for
▶ umpire

UMPIES ▶ umpy

UMPING ▶ ump

UMPIRE n, vb umpired,
umpires

UMPS ▶ ump

UMPTEEN adj,
determiner umpty

UMPY = umpie

UMRA n pilgrimage to
Mecca that can be
made at any time of
the year umrah

UMRAHS ▶ umrah

UMRAS ▶ umra

UMS ▶ um

UMU n type of oven
umus

UMWELT n
environmental factors
affecting the
behaviour of an animal
or individual umwelts

UMWHILE = umquhile

UN pron spelling of 'one'
intended to reflect a
dialectal or informal
pronunciation

UNABLE adj

UNACTED adj not acted
or performed

UNADDED adj not
added

UNADEPT adj not adept

UNADULT adj not
mature

UNAGED adj not old

UNAGILE adj not agile

UNAGING = unageing

UNAI = unau

UNAIDED adv, adj

UNAIMED adj not
aimed or specifically
targeted

UNAIRED adj not aired

UNAIS ▶ unai

UNAKIN adj not related

UNAKING Shakespearean
form of ▶ unaching

UNAKITE n type of
mineral

UNALIKE adj not similar

UNALIST n priest
holding only one
benefice

UNALIVE adj unaware

UNAPT adj not suitable
or qualified unaptly

UNARM less common
word for ▶ disarm

UNARMED adj

UNARMS ▶ unarm

UNARY adj consisting
of, or affecting, a
single element or
component

UNASKED adv without
being asked to do
something ▶ adj (of a
question) not asked,
although sometimes
implied

UNAU n two-toed sloth **unaus**

UNAWAKE adj not awake

UNAWARE adj, adv

UNAWED adj not awed

UNAXED adj not axed

UNBAG vb take out of a bag **unbags**

UNBAKED adj not having been baked

UNBALE vb remove from bale **unbaled, unbales**

UNBAN vb stop banning or permit again **unbans**

UNBAR vb take away a bar or bars from

UNBARE vb expose **unbared, unbares**

UNBARK vb strip bark from **unbarks**

UNBARS ▸ unbar

UNBASED adj not having a base

UNBATED adj (of a sword, lance, etc) not covered with a protective button

UNBE vb make non-existent

UNBEAR vb release (horse) from the bearing rein **unbears**

UNBED vb remove from bed **unbeds**

UNBEEN ▸ unbe

UNBEGET vb deprive of existence

UNBEGOT adj unbegotten

UNBEGUN adj not commenced

UNBEING n non-existence

UNBELT vb unbuckle the belt of (a garment) **unbelts**

UNBEND vb become less strict or more informal in one's attitudes or behaviour **unbends**

UNBENT adj not bent or bowed

UNBIAS vb free from prejudice

UNBID = unbidden

UNBIND vb set free from bonds or chains **unbinds**

UNBITT vb remove (cable) from the bitts **unbitts**

UNBLENT = unblended

UNBLESS vb deprive of a blessing

UNBLEST = unblessed

UNBLIND vb rid of blindness

UNBLOCK vb remove a blockage from

UNBLOWN adj (of a flower) still in the bud

UNBOLT vb unfasten a bolt of (a door) **unbolts**

UNBONE vb remove bone from

UNBONED adj (of meat, fish, etc) not having had the bones removed

UNBONES ▸ unbone

UNBOOT vb remove boots from **unboots**

UNBORE adj unborn

UNBORN adj

UNBORNE adj not borne

UNBOSOM vb relieve (oneself) of (secrets or feelings) by telling someone

UNBOUND adj (of a book) not bound within a cover

UNBOWED adj not giving in or submitting

UNBOX vb empty a box **unboxed, unboxes**

UNBRACE vb remove tension or strain from

UNBRAID vb remove braids from

UNBRAKE vb stop reducing speed by releasing brake

UNBRED adj not taught or instructed

UNBROKE = unbroken

UNBUILD vb destroy **unbuilt**

UNBULKY adj not bulky

UNBURNT adj not burnt

UNBURY vb unearth

UNBUSY adj not busy

UNCAGE vb release from a cage

UNCAGED adj at liberty

UNCAGES ▸ uncage

UNCAKE vb remove compacted matter from **uncaked, uncakes**

UNCANNY adj

UNCAP vb remove a cap or top from (a container)

UNCAPE vb remove the cape from **uncaped, uncapes**

UNCAPS ▶ uncap
UNCARED adj as in uncared for not cared (for)
UNCART vb remove from a cart **uncarts**
UNCASE vb display uncased, **uncases**
UNCAST adj not cast
UNCATE = uncinate
UNCE = ounce
UNCEDED adj not ceded
UNCES ▶ unce
UNCHAIN vb remove a chain or chains from
UNCHAIR vb unseat from chair
UNCHARM vb disenchant
UNCHARY adj not cautious
UNCHECK vb remove check mark from
UNCHIC adj not chic
UNCHILD vb deprive of children
UNCHOKE vb unblock
UNCI ▶ uncus
UNCIA n twelfth part **unciae**
UNCIAL adj of a writing style used in manuscripts of the third to ninth centuries ▷ n uncial letter or manuscript **uncials**
UNCINAL = uncinate
UNCINI ▶ uncinus
UNCINUS n small hooked structure
UNCITED adj not quoted
UNCIVIL adj
UNCLAD adj having no clothes on

UNCLAMP vb remove clamp from
UNCLASP vb unfasten the clasp of (something)
UNCLE n, vb
UNCLEAN adj
UNCLEAR adj
UNCLED ▶ uncle
UNCLEFT adj not cleft
UNCLES ▶ uncle
UNCLEW vb undo **unclews**
UNCLING ▶ uncle
UNCLIP vb remove clip from **unclips, unclipt**
UNCLOAK vb remove cloak from
UNCLOG vb remove an obstruction from (a drain, etc) **unclogs**
UNCLOSE vb open or cause to open
UNCLOUD vb clear clouds from
UNCO adj awkward ▷ n awkward or clumsy person
UNCOCK vb remove from a cocked position **uncocks**
UNCODED adj not coded
UNCOER ▶ unco
UNCOES ▶ unco
UNCOEST ▶ unco
UNCOIL vb unwind or untwist **uncoils**
UNCOLT vb divest of a horse **uncolts**
UNCOMFY adj not comfortable
UNCOMIC adj not comical

UNCOOL adj unsophisticated
UNCOPE vb unmuzzle **uncoped, uncopes**
UNCORD vb release from cords **uncords**
UNCORK vb remove the cork from (a bottle) **uncorks**
UNCOS ▶ unco
UNCOUTH adj
UNCOVER vb
UNCOWL vb remove hood from **uncowls**
UNCOY adj not modest
UNCRATE vb remove from a crate
UNCRAZY adj not crazy
UNCROSS vb cease to cross
UNCROWN vb take the crown from
UNCTION n
UNCUFF vb remove handcuffs from **uncuffs**
UNCURB vb remove curbs from (a horse) **uncurbs**
UNCURED adj not cured
UNCURL vb move or cause to move out of a curled or rolled up position **uncurls**
UNCURSE vb remove curse from
UNCUS n hooked part or process, as in the human cerebrum
UNCUT adj not shortened or censored
UNCUTE adj not cute
UNDAM vb free from a dam **undams**

UNDATE *vb* remove date from

UNDATED *adj* (of a manuscript, letter, etc) not having an identifying date

UNDE = undee

UNDEAD *adj* alive

UNDEAF *vb* restore hearing to **undeafs**

UNDEALT *adj* not dealt (with)

UNDEAR *adj* not dear

UNDECK *vb* remove decorations from **undecks**

UNDEE *adj* wavy

UNDEIFY *vb* strip of the status of a deity

UNDER *adv, prep*

UNDERDO *vb* do (something) inadequately

UNDERGO *vb*

UNDERN *n* time between sunrise and noon **underns**

UNDID ▶ undo

UNDIES *pl n* underwear, esp women's

UNDIGHT *vb* remove

UNDINE *n* female water spirit **undines**

UNDO *vb*

UNDOCK *vb* take out of a dock **undocks**

UNDOER ▶ undo

UNDOERS ▶ undo

UNDOES ▶ undo

UNDOING *n*

UNDONE *adj* not done or completed

UNDRAPE *vb* remove drapery from

UNDRAW *vb* open (curtains) **undrawn, undraws**

UNDRESS *vb, n, adj*

UNDREST = undressed

UNDREW ▶ undraw

UNDRIED *adj* not dried

UNDRUNK *adj* not drunk

UNDUE *adj*

UNDUG *adj* not having been dug

UNDULAR > undulate

UNDULY *adv* excessively

UNDY = undee

UNDYED *adj* not dyed

UNDYING *adj*

UNEAGER *adj* nonchalant

UNEARED *adj* not ploughed

UNEARTH *vb*

UNEASE ▶ uneasy

UNEASES ▶ uneasy

UNEASY *adj*

UNEATEN *adj* (of food) not having been consumed

UNEATH *adv* not easily

UNEDGE *vb* take the edge off **unedged, unedges**

UNENDED *adj* without end

UNEQUAL *adj, n*

UNETH = uneath

UNEVEN *adj*

UNEYED *adj* unseen

UNFACT *n* event or thing not provable **unfacts**

UNFADED *adj* not faded

UNFAIR *adj, vb* **unfairs**

UNFAITH *n* lack of faith

UNFAKED *adj* not faked

UNFAMED *adj* not famous

UNFANCY *vb* consider (a sportsperson or team) unlikely to win or succeed

UNFAZED *adj* not disconcerted

UNFED *adj* not fed

UNFEED *adj* unpaid

UNFELT *adj* not felt

UNFENCE *vb* remove a fence from

UNFEUED *adj* not feued

UNFILDE *archaic form of* ▶ unfiled

UNFILED *adj* not filed

UNFINE *adj* not fine

UNFIRED *adj* not fired

UNFIRM *adj* soft or unsteady

UNFIT *adj, vb*

UNFITLY *adv* in an unfit way

UNFITS ▶ unfit

UNFIX *vb* unfasten, detach, or loosen

UNFIXED *adj* not fixed

UNFIXES ▶ unfix

UNFIXT = unfixed

UNFLESH *vb* remove flesh from

UNFLUSH *vb* lose the colour caused by flushing

UNFOLD *vb* **unfolds**

UNFOND *adj* not fond

UNFOOL *vb* undeceive **unfools**

UNFORM *vb* make formless **unforms**

UNFOUND *adj* not found

UNFREE vb remove freedom from **unfreed, unfrees**

UNFROCK vb deprive (a priest in holy orders) of his or her priesthood

UNFROZE > unfreeze

UNFUMED adj not fumigated

UNFUNNY adj not funny

UNFURL vb unroll or unfold **unfurls**

UNFUSED adj not fused

UNFUSSY adj not characterized by overelaborate detail

UNGAG vb restore freedom of speech to **ungags**

UNGAIN adj inconvenient

UNGATED adj without gate

UNGAZED adj as in **ungazed at/ungazed upon** not gazed (at or upon)

UNGEAR vb disengage **ungears**

UNGET vb get rid of **ungets**

UNGILD vb remove gilding from **ungilds, ungilt**

UNGIRD vb remove belt from **ungirds**

UNGIRT adj not belted

UNGIRTH vb release from a girth

UNGLAD adj not glad

UNGLOVE vb remove glove(s)

UNGLUE vb remove adhesive from

unglued, unglues

UNGOD vb remove status of being a god from

UNGODLY adj

UNGODS ▶ ungod

UNGORD > ungored

UNGORED adj not gored

UNGOT = ungotten

UNGOWN vb remove gown (from) **ungowns**

UNGREEN adj not environmentally friendly

UNGROWN adj not fully developed

UNGUAL adj of, relating to, or affecting the fingernails or toenails

UNGUARD vb expose (to attack)

UNGUENT n ointment

UNGUES ▶ unguis

UNGUIS n nail, claw, or hoof, or the part of the digit giving rise to it

UNGULA n truncated cone, cylinder, etc **ungulae, ungular**

UNGULED adj hoofed

UNGUM vb remove adhesive from **ungums**

UNGYVE vb release from shackles **ungyved, ungyves**

UNHABLE = unable

UNHAIR vb remove the hair from (a hide) **unhairs**

UNHAND vb release from one's grasp **unhands**

UNHANDY adj not skilful with one's hands

UNHANG vb take down from hanging position **unhangs**

UNHAPPY adj, vb

UNHARDY adj fragile

UNHASP vb unfasten **unhasps**

UNHASTY adj not speedy

UNHAT vb doff one's hat **unhats**

UNHEAD vb remove the head from **unheads**

UNHEAL vb expose **unheals**

UNHEARD adj not listened to

UNHEART vb discourage

UNHEEDY adj not heedful

UNHELE = unheal

UNHELED ▶ unhele

UNHELES ▶ unhele

UNHELM vb remove the helmet of (oneself or another) **unhelms**

UNHERST archaic past form of > unhearse

UNHEWN adj not hewn

UNHINGE vb

UNHIP adj not at all fashionable or up to date

UNHIRED adj not hired

UNHITCH vb unfasten or detach

UNHIVE vb remove from a hive **unhived, unhives**

UNHOARD vb remove from a hoard

UNHOLY adj immoral or wicked

UNHOOD vb remove hood from **unhoods**

UNHOOK vb unfasten the hooks of (a garment) **unhooks**

UNHOOP vb remove hoop(s) from **unhoops**

UNHOPED adj unhoped-for

UNHORSE vb knock or throw from a horse

UNHOUSE vb remove from a house

UNHUMAN adj inhuman or not human

UNHUNG ▶ **unhang**

UNHURT adj not injured in an accident, attack, etc

UNHUSK vb remove the husk from **unhusks**

UNI n (in informal English) university

UNIBODY adj of a vehicle in which frame and body are one unit

UNIBROW n informal word for eyebrows that meet above the nose

UNICITY n oneness

UNICORN n

UNIDEAL adj not ideal

UNIFACE n type of tool

UNIFIC adj unifying

UNIFIED ▶ **unify**

UNIFIER ▶ **unify**

UNIFIES ▶ **unify**

UNIFORM n, adj, vb

UNIFY vb

UNION n, adj **unions**

UNIPED n person or thing with one foot **unipeds**

UNIPOD n one-legged support, as for a camera **unipods**

UNIQUE n uniquer, uniques

UNIS ▶ **uni**

UNISEX adj, n

UNISIZE adj in one size only

UNISON n **unisons**

UNIT n **unitage, unital**

UNITARD n all-in-one skintight suit

UNITARY adj consisting of a single undivided whole

UNITE vb, n

UNITED adj produced by two or more people or things in combination

UNITER ▶ **unite**

UNITERS ▶ **unite**

UNITES ▶ **unite**

UNITIES ▶ **unity**

UNITING ▶ **unite**

UNITION n joining

UNITISE = **unitize**

UNITIVE adj tending to unite or capable of uniting

UNITIZE vb convert (an investment trust) into a unit trust

UNITS ▶ **unit**

UNITY n

UNJADED adj not jaded

UNJAM vb remove blockage from **unjams**

UNJOINT vb disjoint

UNJUST adj

UNKED adj alien

UNKEMPT adj

UNKEND = **unkenned**

UNKENT = **unkenned**

UNKEPT adj not kept

UNKET = **unked**

UNKID = **unked**

UNKIND adj

UNKING vb strip of sovereignty **unkings**

UNKINK vb straighten out **unkinks**

UNKISS vb cancel (a previous action) with a kiss

UNKNIT vb make or become undone, untied, or unravelled **unknits**

UNKNOT vb disentangle or undo a knot or knots in **unknots**

UNKNOWN adj, n

UNLACE vb loosen or undo the lacing of (shoes, garments, etc)

UNLACED adj not laced

UNLACES ▶ **unlace**

UNLADE less common word for ▶ **unload**

UNLADED ▶ **unlade**

UNLADEN adj not laden

UNLADES ▶ **unlade**

UNLAID ▶ **unlay**

UNLASH vb untie or unfasten

UNLAST archaic variant of ▶ **unlaced**

UNLASTE archaic variant of ▶ **unlaced**

UNLATCH vb open or unfasten or come open or unfastened by

the lifting or release of
a latch

UNLAW *vb* penalize
unlawed, unlaws

UNLAY *vb* untwist (a
rope or cable) to
separate its strands
unlays

UNLEAD *vb* strip off lead
unleads

UNLEAL *adj*
treacherous

UNLEARN *vb* try to
forget something
learnt or to discard
accumulated
knowledge

UNLEASH *vb*

UNLED *adj* not led

UNLESS *conj, prep*

UNLET *adj* not rented

UNLEVEL *adj* not level
▷ *vb* make unbalanced

UNLICH *Spenserian form
of* ▶ **unlike**

UNLID *vb* remove lid
from **unlids**

UNLIKE *adj, prep, n*

UNLIKED *adj* not liked

UNLIKES ▶ **unlike**

UNLIME *vb* detach
unlimed, unlimes

UNLINE *vb* remove the
lining from

UNLINED *adj* not having
any lining

UNLINES ▶ **unline**

UNLINK *vb* undo or
break the link or links between
unlinks

UNLIT *adj*

UNLIVE *vb* live so as to
nullify, undo, or live
down (past events or

times) **unlived,
unlives**

UNLOAD *vb* unloads

UNLOBED *adj* without
lobes

UNLOCK *vb* unlocks

UNLOOSE *vb* set free or
release

UNLORD *vb* remove
from position of being
lord **unlords**

UNLOST *adj* not lost

UNLOVE *vb* stop loving

UNLOVED *adj* not loved
by anyone

UNLOVES ▶ **unlove**

UNLUCKY *adj*

UNMACHO *adj* not
macho

UNMADE *adj*

UNMAKE *vb* undo or
destroy **unmaker,
unmakes**

UNMAN *vb* cause to lose
courage or nerve

UNMANLY *adj*

UNMANS ▶ **unman**

UNMARD = **unmarred**

UNMARRY *vb* divorce

UNMASK *vb* remove the
mask or disguise from
unmasks

UNMATED *adj* not
mated

UNMEANT *adj*
unintentional

UNMEEK *adj* not
submissive

UNMEET *adj* not meet

UNMERRY *adj* not
merry

UNMESH *vb* release
from mesh

UNMET *adj* unfulfilled

UNMETED *adj*
unmeasured

UNMEW *vb* release from
confinement
unmewed, unmews

UNMINED *adj* not
mined

UNMIRY *adj* not
swampy

UNMITER = **unmitre**

UNMITRE *vb* divest of a
mitre

UNMIX *vb* separate
**unmixed, unmixes,
unmixt**

UNMOLD = **unmould**

UNMOLDS ▶ **unmould**

UNMOOR *vb* weigh the
anchor or drop the
mooring of (a vessel)
unmoors

UNMORAL *adj* outside
morality

UNMOULD *vb* change
shape of

UNMOUNT *vb* dismount

UNMOVED *adj*

UNMOWN *adj* not mown

UNNAIL *vb* unfasten by
removing nails **unnails**

UNNAMED *adj* not
mentioned by name

UNNEATH *adj* archaic
word for underneath

UNNERVE *vb*

UNNEST *vb* remove
from a nest **unnests**

UNNOBLE *vb* strip of
nobility

UNNOISY *adj* quiet

UNNOTED *adj* not noted

UNOAKED *adj* (of wine)
not matured in an oak
barrel

UNOFTEN adv infrequently

UNOILED adj not lubricated with oil

UNOPEN adj not open

UNORDER vb cancel an order

UNOWED = unowned

UNOWNED adj not owned

UNPACED adj without the aid of a pacemaker

UNPACK vb unpacks

UNPAGED adj (of a book) having no page numbers

UNPAID adj

UNPAINT vb remove paint from

UNPANEL vb unsaddle

UNPAPER vb remove paper from

UNPARED adj not pared

UNPAVED adj not covered in paving

UNPAY vb undo unpays

UNPEG vb remove the peg or pegs from, as to unfasten unpegs

UNPEN vb release from a pen unpens, unpent

UNPERCH vb remove from a perch

UNPICK vb unpicks

UNPILE vb remove from a pile unpiled, unpiles

UNPIN vb remove a pin or pins from

UNPINKT = unpinked

UNPINS ▶ unpin

UNPLACE = displace

UNPLAIT vb remove plaits from

UNPLUG vb unplugs

UNPLUMB vb remove lead from

UNPLUME vb remove feathers from

UNPOPE vb strip of popedom unpoped, unpopes

UNPOSED adj not posed

UNPRAY vb withdraw (a prayer) unprays

UNPROP vb remove support from unprops

UNPURE = impure

UNPURSE vb relax (lips) from pursed position

UNQUEEN vb depose from the position of queen

UNQUIET adj, n, vb

UNQUOTE interj expression used to indicate the end of a quotation ▶ vb close (a quotation), esp in printing

UNRACED adj not raced

UNRAKE vb unearth through raking

UNRAKED adj not raked

UNRAKES ▶ unrake

UNRATED adj not rated

UNRAVEL vb

UNRAZED adj not razed

UNREAD adj (of a book or article) not yet read

UNREADY adj not ready or prepared

UNREAL adj

UNREAVE vb unwind

UNRED = unread

UNREDY = unready

UNREEL vb unwind from a reel unreels

UNREEVE vb withdraw

(a rope) from a block, thimble, etc

UNREIN vb free from reins unreins

UNRENT adj not torn

UNREST n unrests

UNRID adj unridden

UNRIG vb strip (a vessel) of standing and running rigging

UNRIGHT n wrong

UNRIGS ▶ unrig

UNRIMED = unrhymed

UNRIP vb rip open

UNRIPE adj not fully matured unriper

UNRIPS ▶ unrip

UNRISEN adj not risen

UNRIVEN adj not torn apart

UNRIVET vb remove rivets from

UNROBE = disrobe

UNROBED ▶ unrobe

UNROBES ▶ unrobe

UNROLL vb unrolls

UNROOF vb remove the roof from unroofs

UNROOST vb remove from a perch

UNROOT less common word for ▶ uproot

UNROOTS ▶ unroot

UNROPE vb release from a rope unroped, unropes

UNROUGH adj not rough

UNROUND vb release (lips) from a rounded position

UNROVE ▶ unreeve

UNROVEN ▶ unreeve

UNROYAL adj not royal

UNRUDE adj not rude

UNRUFFE = unrough

UNRULE n lack of authority

UNRULED adj not ruled

UNRULES ▸ unrule

UNRULY adj

UNS ▸ un

UNSAFE adj dangerous **unsafer**

UNSAID adj not said or expressed

UNSAINT vb remove status of being a saint from

UNSATED adj not sated

UNSAVED adj not saved

UNSAWED = unsawn

UNSAWN adj not cut with a saw

UNSAY vb retract or withdraw (something said or written) **unsays**

UNSCALE = descale

UNSCARY adj not scary

UNSCREW vb

UNSEAL vb unseals

UNSEAM vb open or undo the seam of **unseams**

UNSEAT vb unseats

UNSEEL vb undo seeing **unseels**

UNSEEN adj, adv, n **unseens**

UNSELF vb remove self-centredness from n lack of self **unselfs**

UNSELL vb speak unfavourably and off-puttingly of (something or someone) **unsells**

UNSENSE vb remove sense from

UNSENT adj not sent

UNSET adj not yet solidified or firm ▸ vb displace **unsets**

UNSEW vb undo stitching of **unsewed, unsewn, unsews**

UNSEX vb deprive (a person) of the attributes of his or her sex **unsexed, unsexes**

UNSEXY adj not sexually attractive

UNSHALE vb expose

UNSHAPE vb make shapeless

UNSHARP adj not sharp

UNSHED adj not shed

UNSHELL vb remove from a shell

UNSHENT adj undamaged

UNSHEWN adj unshown

UNSHIFT vb release the shift key on a keyboard

UNSHIP vb be or cause to be unloaded, discharged, or disembarked from a ship **unships**

UNSHOD adj not wearing shoes

UNSHOE vb remove shoes from

UNSHOED = unshod

UNSHOES ▸ unshoe

UNSHOOT *Shakespearean variant of* ▸ **unshout**

UNSHORN adj not cut

UNSHOT adj not shot

UNSHOUT vb revoke (an earlier statement) by shouting a contrary one

UNSHOWN adj not shown

UNSHOWY adj not showy

UNSHUT vb open **unshuts**

UNSIGHT vb obstruct vision of

UNSINEW vb weaken

UNSIZED adj not made or sorted according to size

UNSLAIN adj not killed

UNSLICK adj not slick

UNSLING vb remove or release from a slung position **unsling**

UNSMART adj not smart

UNSMOTE = unsmitten

UNSNAG vb remove snags from **unsnags**

UNSNAP vb unfasten (the snap or catch) of (something) **unsnaps**

UNSNARL vb free from a snarl or tangle

UNSNECK vb unlatch

UNSOBER adj not sober

UNSOD = unsodden

UNSOFT adj hard

UNSOLD adj not sold

UNSOLID adj not solid

UNSONCY = unsonsy

UNSONSY adj unfortunate

UNSOOTE adj not sweet

UNSOUL vb cause to be soulless **unsouls**

UNSOUND adj

UNSOWED = unsown

UNSOWN adj not sown

UNSPAR vb open unspars

UNSPEAK obsolete word for ▸ unsay

UNSPED adj not achieved

UNSPELL vb release from a spell

UNSPENT adj not spent

UNSPIDE = unspied

UNSPIED adj unnoticed

UNSPILT adj not spilt

UNSPLIT adj not split

UNSPOKE ▸ unspeak

UNSPOOL vb unwind from spool

UNSPUN adj not spun

UNSTACK vb remove from a stack

UNSTAID adj not staid

UNSTATE vb deprive of state

UNSTEEL vb make (the heart, feelings, etc) more gentle or compassionate

UNSTEP vb remove (a mast) from its step unsteps

UNSTICK vb free or loosen (something stuck)

UNSTOCK vb remove stock from

UNSTOP vb remove the stop or stopper from unstops

UNSTOW vb remove from storage unstows

UNSTRAP vb undo the straps fastening (something) in position

UNSTRIP vb strip

UNSTUCK adj

UNSTUFT = unstuffed

UNSTUNG adj not stung

UNSUIT vb make unsuitable unsuits

UNSUNG adj

UNSUNK adj not sunken

UNSUNNY adj not sunny

UNSURE adj

UNSURED adj not assured

UNSURER ▸ unsure

UNSWEAR vb retract or revoke (a sworn oath)

UNSWEET adj not sweet

UNSWEPT adj not swept

UNSWORE ▸ unswear

UNSWORN ▸ unswear

UNTACK vb remove saddle and harness, etc, from untacks

UNTAKEN adj not taken

UNTAME vb undo the taming of

UNTAMED adj not brought under human control

UNTAMES ▸ untame

UNTAX vb stop taxing

UNTAXED adj not subject to taxation

UNTAXES ▸ untax

UNTEACH vb cause to disbelieve (teaching)

UNTEAM vb disband a team unteams

UNTENT vb remove from a tent untents

UNTENTY adj inattentive

UNTHAW = thaw

UNTHAWS ▸ unthaw

UNTHINK vb reverse one's opinion about

UNTIDY adj, vb

UNTIE vb untied, unties

UNTIL prep

UNTILE vb strip tiles from untiled, untiles

UNTIMED adj not timed

UNTIN vb remove tin from untins

UNTIRED adj not tired

UNTO prep

UNTOLD adj

UNTOMB vb exhume untombs

UNTONED adj not toned

UNTORN adj not torn

UNTRACE vb remove traces from

UNTRACK vb remove from track

UNTREAD vb retrace (a course, path, etc)

UNTRIDE = untried

UNTRIED adj

UNTRIM vb deprive of elegance or adornment untrims

UNTROD ▸ untread

UNTRUE adj untruer, untruly

UNTRUSS vb release from or as if from a truss

UNTRUST n mistrust

UNTRUTH n

UNTUCK vb become or cause to become loose or not tucked in untucks

UNTUNE vb make out of tune untuned, untunes

UNTURF vb remove turf from **unturfs**

UNTURN vb turn in a reverse direction **unturns**

UNTWINE vb untwist, unravel, and separate

UNTWIST vb twist apart and loosen

UNTYING ▶ untie

UNURGED adj not urged

UNUSED adj

UNUSUAL adj

UNVAIL = unveil

UNVAILE = unveil

UNVAILS ▶ unvail

UNVEIL vb unveils

UNVEXED adj not annoyed **unvext**

UNVISOR vb remove visor from

UNVITAL adj not vital

UNVOCAL adj not vocal

UNVOICE vb pronounce without vibration of the vocal cords

UNWAGED adj (of a person) not having a paid job

UNWAKED = unwakened

UNWARE = unaware

UNWARES = unawares

UNWARIE = unwary

UNWARY adj

UNWATER vb dry out

UNWAXED adj not treated with wax

UNWAYED adj having no routes

UNWEAL n ill or sorrow **unweals**

UNWEARY adj not weary

UNWEAVE vb undo (weaving)

UNWED adj not wed

UNWELDY = unwieldy

UNWELL adj

UNWEPT adj not wept for or lamented

UNWET adj not wet

UNWHIPT = unwhipped

UNWHITE adj not white

UNWILL vb will the reversal of (something that has already occurred) **unwills**

UNWIND vb unwinds

UNWIPED adj not wiped

UNWIRE vb remove wiring from **unwired, unwires**

UNWISE adj unwiser

UNWISH vb retract or revoke (a wish)

UNWIST adj unknown

UNWIT vb divest of wit

UNWITCH vb release from witchcraft

UNWITS ▶ unwit

UNWITTY adj not clever and amusing

UNWIVE vb remove a wife from **unwived, unwives**

UNWOMAN vb remove womanly qualities from

UNWON adj not won

UNWONT adj unaccustomed

UNWOOED adj not wooed

UNWORK vb destroy (work previously done) **unworks**

UNWORN adj not having deteriorated through use or age

UNWORTH n lack of value

UNWOUND past tense and past participle of ▶ unwind

UNWOVE ▶ unweave

UNWOVEN ▶ unweave

UNWRAP vb unwraps

UNWRITE vb cancel (what has been written) **unwrote**

UNWRUNG adj not twisted

UNYOKE vb release (an animal, etc) from a yoke **unyoked, unyokes**

UNYOUNG adj not young

UNZIP vb unfasten the zip of (a garment) **unzips**

UNZONED adj not divided into zones

UP adv, adj, vb

UPAS n large Javan tree with whitish bark and poisonous milky sap **upases**

UPBEAR vb sustain **upbears**

UPBEAT adj cheerful and optimistic ▷ n unaccented beat **upbeats**

UPBIND vb bind up **upbinds**

UPBLEW ▶ upblow

UPBLOW vb inflate **upblown, upblows**

UPBOIL vb boil up **upboils**

UPBORE ▸ upbear
UPBORNE adj held up
UPBOUND adj travelling upwards
UPBOW n stroke of the bow from its tip to its nut on a stringed instrument **upbows**
UPBRAID vb scold or reproach
UPBRAST = upburst
UPBRAY vb shame **upbrays**
UPBREAK vb escape upwards
UPBRING vb rear
UPBROKE ▸ upbreak
UPBUILD vb build up **upbuilt**
UPBURST vb burst upwards
UPBY = upbye
UPBYE adv yonder
UPCAST n material cast or thrown up ▷ adj directed or thrown upwards ▷ vb throw or cast up **upcasts**
UPCATCH vb catch up
UPCHEER vb cheer up
UPCHUCK vb vomit
UPCLIMB vb ascend
UPCLOSE vb close up
UPCOAST adv up the coast
UPCOIL vb make into a coil **upcoils**
UPCOME vb come up **upcomes**
UPCOURT adv up basketball court
UPCURL vb curl up **upcurls**

UPCURVE vb curve upwards
UPDART vb dart upwards **updarts**
UPDATE vb, n **updated, updater, updates**
UPDIVE vb leap upwards **updived, updives**
UPDO n type of hairstyle **updos**
UPDOVE ▸ updive
UPDRAFT n upwards air current
UPDRAG vb drag up **updrags**
UPDRAW vb draw up **updrawn, updraws, updrew**
UPDRIED ▸ updry
UPDRIES ▸ updry
UPDRY vb dry up
UPEND vb upended, **upends**
UPFIELD adj in sport, away from the defending team's goal
UPFILL vb fill up **upfills**
UPFLING vb throw upwards
UPFLOW vb flow upwards **upflows**
UPFLUNG ▸ upfling
UPFOLD vb fold up **upfolds**
UPFRONT adj open and frank ▷ adv (of money) paid out at the beginning of a business arrangement
UPFURL vb roll up **upfurls**
UPGANG n climb **upgangs**

UPGAZE vb gaze upwards **upgazed, upgazes**
UPGIRD vb belt up **upgirds, upgirt**
UPGO vb ascend **upgoes, upgoing, upgone**
UPGRADE vb
UPGREW ▸ upgrow
UPGROW vb grow up **upgrown, upgrows**
UPGUSH vb flow upwards
UPHAND adj lifted by hand
UPHANG vb hang up **uphangs**
UPHAUD Scots variant of ▸ uphold
UPHAUDS ▸ uphaud
UPHEAP vb computing term **upheaps**
UPHEAVE vb heave or rise upwards
UPHELD ▸ uphold
UPHILD archaic past form of ▸ uphold
UPHILL adj, adv, n **uphills**
UPHOARD vb hoard up
UPHOIST vb raise
UPHOLD vb upholds
UPHOORD vb heap up
UPHOVE ▸ upheave
UPHROE variant spelling of ▸ euphroe
UPHROES ▸ uphroe
UPHUNG ▸ uphang
UPHURL vb throw upwards **uphurls**
UPJET vb stream upwards **upjets**
UPKEEP n **upkeeps**
UPKNIT vb bind **upknits**

UPLAID ▸ uplay

UPLAND adj, n **uplands**

UPLAY vb stash **uplays**

UPLEAD vb lead upwards **upleads**

UPLEAN vb lean on something **upleans, upleant**

UPLEAP vb jump upwards **upleaps, upleapt**

UPLED ▸ uplead

UPLIFT vb raise or lift up ▸ n act or process of improving moral, social, or cultural conditions ▸ adj (of a bra) designed to lift and support the breasts **uplifts**

UPLIGHT n lamp or wall light designed or positioned to cast its light upwards ▸ vb light in an upward direction

UPLINK n transmitter that sends signals up to a communications satellite ▸ vb send (data) to a communications satellite **uplinks**

UPLIT ▸ uplight

UPLOAD vb uploads

UPLOCK vb lock up **uplocks**

UPLOOK vb look up **uplooks**

UPLYING adj raised

UPMAKE vb make up **upmaker, upmakes**

UPMOST another word for ▸ **uppermost**

UPO prep upon

UPON prep **up**

UPPED ▸ up

UPPER adj, n **uppers**

UPPILE vb pile up **uppiled, uppiles**

UPPING ▸ up

UPPINGS ▸ up

UPPISH adj snobbish, arrogant, or presumptuous

UPPITY adj snobbish, arrogant, or presumptuous

UPPROP vb support **upprops**

UPRAISE vb lift up

UPRAN ▸ uprun

UPRATE vb raise the value, rate, or size of, upgrade **uprated, uprates**

UPREACH vb reach up

UPREAR vb lift up **uprears**

UPREST n uprising **uprests**

UPRIGHT adj, adv, n, vb

UPRISAL ▸ uprise

UPRISE vb rise up **uprisen, upriser, uprises**

UPRIST = uprest

UPRISTS ▸ uprist

UPRIVER adv towards or near the source of a river ▸ n area located upstream

UPROAR n, vb **uproars**

UPROLL vb roll up **uprolls**

UPROOT vb **uproots**

UPROSE ▸ uprise

UPROUSE vb rouse or stir up

UPRUN vb run up **upruns**

UPRUSH n upward rush, as of consciousness ▸ vb rush upwards

UPRYST = uprest

UPS ▸ up

UPSCALE adj of or for the upper end of an economic or social scale ▸ vb upgrade

UPSEE n drunken revel **upsees**

UPSELL vb persuade a customer to buy a more expensive or additional item **upsells**

UPSEND vb send up **upsends, upsent**

UPSET adj, vb, n **upsets**

UPSEY = upsee

UPSEYS ▸ upsey

UPSHIFT vb move up (a gear)

UPSHOOT vb shoot upwards

UPSHOT n **upshots**

UPSIDE n upper surface or part **upsides**

UPSIES ▸ upsy

UPSILON n 20th letter in the Greek alphabet

UPSIZE vb increase in size **upsized, upsizes**

UPSKILL vb improve the aptitude for work of (a person)

UPSLOPE adv up a or the slope

UPSOAR vb soar up **upsoars**

UPSOLD ▶ upsell

UPSPAKE ▶ upspeak

UPSPEAK *vb* speak with rising intonation

UPSPEAR *vb* grow upwards in a spear-like manner

UPSPOKE ▶ upspeak

UPSTAGE *adj, vb, adv, n*

UPSTAIR ▶ upstairs

UPSTAND *vb* rise

UPSTARE *vb* stare upwards

UPSTART *n, vb*

UPSTATE *adv* towards, in, from, or relating to the outlying or northern sections of a state ▷ *n* outlying, esp northern, sections of a state

UPSTAY *vb* support **upstays**

UPSTEP *n* type of vocal intonation **upsteps**

UPSTIR *vb* stir up ▷ *n* commotion **upstirs**

UPSTOOD ▶ upstand

UPSURGE *n, vb*

UPSWAY *vb* swing in the air **upsways**

UPSWEEP *vb* curve or sweep upwards ▷ *vb* sweep, curve, or brush to be swept, curved, or brushed upwards

UPSWELL *vb* swell up or cause to swell up

UPSWEPT ▶ upsweep

UPSWING *n* recovery period in the trade cycle ▷ *vb* swing or move up **upswung**

UPSY = upsee

UPTA = upter

UPTAK = uptake

UPTAKE *n, vb* uptaken, uptakes

UPTAKS ▶ uptak

UPTALK *n* style of speech in which every sentence ends with a rising tone ▷ *vb* talk in this manner **uptalks**

UPTEAR *vb* tear up **uptears**

UPTEMPO *adj* fast ▷ *n* uptempo piece

UPTER *adj* of poor quality

UPTHREW ▶ upthrow

UPTHROW *n* upward movement of rocks on one side of a fault plane relative to rocks on the other side ▷ *vb* throw upwards

UPTICK *n* rise or increase **upticks**

UPTIE *vb* tie up **uptied, upties**

UPTIGHT *adj*

UPTILT *vb* tilt up **uptilts**

UPTIME *n* time during which a machine, such as a computer, actually operates **uptimes**

UPTOOK ▶ uptake

UPTORE ▶ uptear

UPTORN ▶ uptear

UPTOSS *vb* throw upwards

UPTOWN *adv* towards, in, or relating to some part of a town that is away from the centre ▷ *n* such a part of town, esp a residential

part **uptowns**

UPTRAIN *vb* train up

UPTREND *n* upward trend

UPTURN *n, vb* upturns

UPTYING ▶ uptie

UPVALUE *vb* raise the value of

UPWAFT *vb* waft upwards **upwafts**

UPWARD = upwards

UPWARDS *adv*

UPWELL *vb* well up **upwells**

UPWENT ▶ upgo

UPWHIRL *vb* spin upwards

UPWIND *adv* into or against the wind ▷ *adj* going against the wind ▷ *vb* wind up **upwinds, upwound**

UPWRAP *vb* wrap up **upwraps**

UR *interj* hesitant utterance used to fill gaps in talking

URACHI ▶ urachus

URACHUS *n* cord of tissue connected to the bladder

URACIL *n* pyrimidine present in all living cells **uracils**

URAEI ▶ uraeus

URAEI This plural of **uraeus**, an Egyptian symbol of kingship, is very useful for dumping a surplus of vowels.

URAEMIA *n* accumulation of waste products in the blood **uraemic**

URAEUS n sacred serpent of ancient Egypt

URALI n type of plant **uralis**

URALITE n mineral that replaces pyroxene in some rocks

URANIA n uranium dioxide

URANIAN adj heavenly

URANIAS ▸ urania

URANIC adj of or containing uranium, esp in a high valence state

URANIDE n any element having an atomic number greater than that of protactinium

URANIN n type of alkaline substance **uranins**

URANISM n homosexuality

URANITE n any of various minerals containing uranium, esp torbernite or autunite

URANIUM n

URANOUS adj of or containing uranium, esp in a low valence state

URANYL n of, consisting of, or containing the divalent ion UO_2^{2+} or the group $-UO_2$ **uranyls**

URAO n type of mineral **uraos**

URARE = urali

URARES ▸ urare

URARI = urali

URARIS ▸ urari

URASE = urease

URASES ▸ urase

URATE n any salt or ester of uric acid **urates, uratic**

URB n urban area

URBAN adj

URBANE adj **urbaner**

URBIA n urban area **urbias**

URBS ▸ urb

URCEOLI > urceolus

URCHIN n urchins

URD n type of plant with edible seeds

URDE adj (in heraldry) having points **urdee**

URDS ▸ urd

URDY n heraldic line pattern

URE = aurochs

UREA n white soluble crystalline compound found in urine **ureal, ureas**

UREASE n enzyme that converts urea to ammonium carbonate **ureases**

UREDIA ▸ uredium

UREDIAL ▸ uredium

UREDINE ▸ uredo

UREDIUM n spore-producing body of some rust fungi in which uredospores are formed

UREDO less common name for > urticaria

UREDOS ▸ uredo

UREIC ▸ urea

UREIDE n any of a class of organic compounds

derived from urea **ureides**

UREMIA = uraemia

UREMIAS ▸ uremia

UREMIC ▸ uraemia

URENA n plant genus **urenas**

URENT adj burning

URES ▸ ure

URESES ▸ uresis

URESIS n urination

URETER n ureters

URETHAN = urethane

URETHRA n

URETIC adj of or relating to the urine

URGE n, vb urged

URGENCE ▸ urgent

URGENCY ▸ urgent

URGENT adj

URGER, urgers, urges, urging, urgings ▸ urge

URIAL n type of sheep **urials**

URIC adj of or derived from urine

URICASE n type of enzyme

URIDINE n nucleoside present in all living cells in a combined form, esp in RNA

URINAL n urinals

URINANT adj having the head downwards

URINARY adj of urine or the organs that secrete and pass urine ▸ n reservoir for urine

URINATE vb

URINE n, vb urined, urines, urining

URINOSE = urinous

URINOUS adj of, resembling, or containing urine

URITE n part of the abdomen **urites**

URMAN n forest **urmans**

URN n, vb urnal, urned

URNFUL n capacity of an urn **urnfuls**

URNING n homosexual man **urnings**

URNLIKE ▶ urn

URNS ▶ urn

URODELE n amphibian of the order which includes the salamanders and newts

UROLITH n calculus in the urinary tract

UROLOGY n branch of medicine concerned with the urinary system and its diseases

UROMERE n part of the abdomen

UROPOD n paired appendage forming part of the tailfan in lobsters **uropods**

UROSES ▶ urosis

UROSIS n urinary disease

UROSOME n abdomen of arthropods

URP dialect word for ▶ vomit

URPED ▶ urp

URPING ▶ urp

URPS ▶ urp

URSA n she-bear **ursae**

URSID n meteor **ursids**

URSINE adj of or like a bear

URSON n type of porcupine **ursons**

URTEXT n earliest form of a text **urtexts**

URTICA n type of nettle **urticas**

URUBU n type of bird **urubus**

URUS another name for the ▶ aurochs

URUSES ▶ urus

URVA n Indian mongoose **urvas**

US pron

USABLE adj able to be used **usably**

USAGE n

USAGER n person who has the use of something in trust **usagers**

USAGES ▶ usage

USANCE n period of time permitted for the redemption of foreign bills of exchange **usances, usaunce**

USE vb, n

USEABLE ▶ usable

USEABLY ▶ usable

USED adj

USEFUL adj, n **usefuls**

USELESS adj

USER n continued exercise, use, or enjoyment of a right, esp in property **users**

USES ▶ use

USHER n, vb ushered, **ushers**

USING ▶ use

USNEA n type of lichen **usneas**

USQUE n whisky **usques**

USTION n burning **ustions**

USUAL adj, adv

USUALLY adv most often, in most cases

USUALS ▶ usual

USUCAPT > usucapion

USURE vb be involved in usury **usured**

USURER n person who lends funds at an exorbitant rate of interest **usurers**

USURES ▶ usure

USURESS n female usurer

USURIES ▶ usury

USURING ▶ usure

USUROUS ▶ usury

USURP vb usurped, usurper, usurps

USURY n practice of lending money at an extremely high rate of interest

USWARD adv towards us **uswards**

UT n syllable used in the fixed system of solmization for the note C

UTA n side-blotched lizard

UTAS n eighth day of a festival **utases**

UTE = utility

UTENSIL n

UTERI ▶ uterus

UTERINE adj of or affecting the womb

UTERUS *n*
UTES ▸ ute
UTILE *obsolete word for* ▸ **useful**
UTILISE = utilize
UTILITY *n, adj*
UTILIZE *vb*
UTIS *n* uproar **utises**
UTMOST *n, adj* **utmosts**
UTOPIA *n* real or imaginary society, place, state, etc, considered to be perfect or ideal
UTOPIAN *adj* of or relating to a perfect or ideal existence ▸ *n*

idealistic social reformer
UTOPIAS ▸ utopia
UTOPISM ▸ utopia
UTOPIST ▸ utopia
UTRICLE *n* larger of the two parts of the membranous labyrinth of the internal ear
UTS ▸ ut
UTTER *vb, adj* **uttered, utterer**
UTTERLY *adv* extrremely
UTTERS ▸ utter
UTU *n* reward **utus**
UVA *n* grape or fruit resembling this **uvae, uvas**

UVEA *n* part of the eyeball consisting of the iris, ciliary body, and choroid **uveal, uveas**
UVEITIC ▸ uveitis
UVEITIS *n* inflammation of the uvea
UVEOUS ▸ uvea
UVULA *n* uvulae
UVULAR *adj* of or relating to the uvula ▸ *n* uvular consonant **uvulars**
UVULAS ▸ uvula
UXORIAL *adj* of or relating to a wife

Vv

If you have a **V** on your rack, the first thing to remember is that there are no valid two-letter words beginning with **V**. In fact, there are no two-letter words that end in **V** either, so you can't form any two-letter words using **V**. Remembering this will stop you wasting time trying to think of some. While **V** is useless for two-letter words, it does start some good short three-letter words. **Vex** and **vox** (13 points each) are the best of these, while **vaw, vow** and **vly** (9 each) are also useful.

VAC vb clean with a vacuum cleaner

> Meaning to clean with a vacuum cleaner, this can be a useful short word for dealing with that awkward letter V.

VACANCE n vacant period
VACANCY n unfilled job
VACANT adj
VACATE vb **vacated, vacates**
VACATUR n annulment
VACCINA = vaccinia
VACCINE n
VACKED ▶ vac
VACKING ▶ vac
VACS ▶ vac
VACUA ▶ vacuum
VACUATE vb empty
VACUIST n person believing in the existence of vacuums in nature
VACUITY n absence of intelligent thought or ideas
VACUOLE n
VACUOUS adj
VACUUM n, vb **vacuums**
VADE vb fade **vaded, vades, vading**
VADOSE adj of or derived from water occurring above the water table
VAE = voe
VAES ▶ vae
VAG n vagrant
VAGAL adj of, relating to, or affecting the vagus nerve **vagally**
VAGARY n
VAGGED ▶ vag
VAGGING ▶ vag
VAGI ▶ vagus

VAGILE adj able to move freely
VAGINA n **vaginae, vaginal, vaginas**
VAGITUS n new-born baby's cry
VAGRANT n, adj **vagrom**
VAGS ▶ vag
VAGUE adj, vb **vagued, vaguely, vaguer, vagues, vaguest, vaguing**
VAGUS n tenth cranial nerve, which supplies the heart, lungs, and viscera
VAHANA n vehicle **vahanas**
VAHINE n Polynesian woman **vahines**
VAIL vb lower (something, such as a weapon), esp as a sign of deference or

VANILLA n, adj

VANISH vb, n

VANITAS n type of Dutch painting

VANITY n

VANLOAD n amount van will carry

VANMAN n man in control of a van **vanmen**

VANNED ▶ van

VANNER n horse used to pull delivery vehicles **vanners**

VANNING ▶ van

VANPOOL n van-sharing group

VANS ▶ van

VANT archaic word for ▶ vanguard

VANTAGE n state, position, or opportunity offering advantage ▶ vb benefit

VANTS ▶ vant

VANWARD adv in or towards the front

VAPID adj vapider, vapidly

VAPOR = vapour

VAPORED ▶ vapor

VAPORER ▶ vapor

VAPORS ▶ vapor

VAPORY ▶ vapour

VAPOUR n, vb vapours, vapoury

VAQUERO n cattlehand

VAR n unit of reactive power of an alternating current

VARA n unit of length used in Spain, Portugal, and South America

VARAN n type of lizard **varans**

VARAS ▶ vara

VARDIES ▶ vardy

VARDY n verdict

VARE n rod

VAREC n ash obtained from kelp **varech**

VARECHS ▶ varech

VARECS ▶ varec

VARES ▶ vare

VAREUSE n type of coat

VARIA n collection or miscellany, esp of literary works

VARIANT adj, n

VARIAS ▶ varia

VARIATE n random variable or a numerical value taken by it ▶ vb vary

VARICES ▶ varix

VARIED ▶ vary

VARIER n person who varies **variers**

VARIES ▶ vary

VARIETY n

VARIOLA n smallpox

VARIOLE n any of the rounded masses that make up the rock variolite

VARIOUS adj

VARIX n tortuous dilated vein

VARLET n menial servant **varlets**

VARMENT = varmint

VARMINT n irritating or obnoxious person or animal

VARNA n any of the four Hindu castes **varnas**

VARNISH n, vb

VAROOM = vroom

VAROOMS = varoom

VARROA n small parasite **varroas**

VARS ▶ var

VARSAL adj universal

VARSITY n university

VARUS adj denoting a deformity of a limb ▷ n abnormal position of a limb **varuses**

VARVE n typically thin band of sediment deposited annually in glacial lakes

VARVED adj having layers of sedimentary deposit

VARVEL n piece of falconry equipment **varvels**

VARVES ▶ varve

VARY vb varying

VAS n vessel or duct that carries a fluid **vasa, vasal**

VASCULA > vasculum

VASE n vases

VASSAIL archaic variant of ▶ vassal

VASSAL n, adj, vb **vassals**

VAST adj, n vaster, vastest

VASTIER ▶ vasty

VASTITY ▶ vast

VASTLY ▶ vast

VASTS ▶ vast

VASTY archaic or poetic word for ▶ vast

VAT n, vb

VATABLE adj subject to VAT

VATFUL n amount enough to fill a vat **vatfuls**

VATIC adj of, relating to, or characteristic of a prophet **vatical**

VATMAN n Customs and Excise employee **vatmen**

VATS ▶ vat

VATTED ▶ vat

VATTER n person who works with vats; blender **vatters**

VATTING ▶ vat

VATU n standard monetary unit of Vanuatu **vatus**

VAU = vav

VAUCH vb move fast **vauched, vauches**

VAUDOO = voodoo

VAUDOOS ▶ vaudoo

VAUDOUX = voodoo

VAULT n, vb **vaulted, vaulter, vaults**

VAULTY adj arched

VAUNCE ▶ advance

VAUNCED ▶ vaunce

VAUNCES ▶ vaunce

VAUNT vb describe or display (success or possessions) boastfully ▶ n boast **vaunted, vaunter**

VAUNTIE = vaunty

VAUNTS ▶ vaunt

VAUNTY adj proud

VAURIEN n rascal

VAUS ▶ vau

VAUT ▶ vault

VAUTE ▶ vault

VAUTED ▶ vaute

VAUTES ▶ vaute

VAUTING ▶ vaut

VAUTS ▶ vaut

VAV n sixth letter of the Hebrew alphabet

It is surprising how often one wants to get rid of two Vs, and when one does, this word, the name of a Hebrew letter, fits the bill nicely. It has an equally useful variant **vaw**.

VAVS ▶ vav

VAW n Hebrew letter

VAWARD n vanguard **vawards**

VAWNTIE ▶ vaunt

VAWS ▶ vaw

VAWTE ▶ vault

VAWTED ▶ vawte

VAWTES ▶ vawte

VAWTING ▶ vawte

VEAL n, vb

VEALE ▶ veil

VEALED ▶ veal

VEALER n young bovine animal of up to 14 months old grown for veal **vealers**

VEALES ▶ veale

VEALIER, vealing, veals, vealy ▶ veal

VEDALIA n Australian ladybird which is a pest of citrus fruits

VEDETTE n small patrol vessel

VEDUTA n painting of a town or city **vedute**

VEE n letter 'v'

VEEJAY n video jockey **veejays**

VEENA = vina

VEENAS ▶ veena

VEEP n vice president

VEEPEE n vice president **veepees**

VEEPS ▶ veep

VEER vb, n **veered**

VEERIES ▶ veery

VEERING ▶ veer

VEERS ▶ veer

VEERY n tawny brown North American thrush

VEES ▶ vee

VEG n vegetable or vegetables ▶ vb relax

Veg is a short form of **vegetable**. If someone plays this, remember that you can add an A or O to it to form **vega** or **vego**.

VEGA n tobacco plantation

VEGAN n, adj

VEGANIC adj farmed without the use of animal products or byproducts

VEGANS ▶ vegan

VEGAS ▶ vega

VEGES ▶ veg

VEGETAL adj of or relating to plant life ▶ n vegetable

VEGETE adj lively

VEGGED ▶ veg

VEGGES ▶ veg

VEGGIE n vegetable ▷ adj vegetarian **veggies**

VEGGING ▶ veg

VEGIE = veggie

VEGIES ▶ vegie

VEGO adj vegetarian ▷ n vegetarian **vegos**

VEHICLE n

VEHM n type of medieval German court **vehme, vehmic**

VEIL n, vb

VEILED adj disguised

VEILER ▶ veil

VEILERS ▶ veil

VEILIER ▶ veil

VEILING n veil or the fabric used for veils

VEILS ▶ veil

VEILY ▶ veil

VEIN n, vb **veinal, veined**

VEINER n wood-carving tool **veiners**

VEINIER ▶ vein

VEINING n pattern or network of veins or streaks

VEINLET n any small vein or venule

VEINOUS ▶ vein

VEINS ▶ vein

VEINULE less common spelling of ▶ **venule**

VEINY ▶ vein

VELA ▶ velum

VELAMEN n thick layer of dead cells that covers the aerial roots of certain orchids

VELAR adj of, relating to, or attached to a velum ▷ n velar sound

VELARIA ▶ velarium

VELARIC ▶ velar

VELARS ▶ velar

VELATE adj having or covered with velum **velated**

VELCRO n tradename for a fastening consisting of two strips of nylon fabric that are pressed together **velcros**

VELD n velds, veldt

VELDTS ▶ veldt

VELE = veil

VELES ▶ vele

VELETA = valeta

VELETAS ▶ veleta

VELIGER n free-swimming larva of many molluscs

VELITES pl n light-armed troops in ancient Rome, drawn from the poorer classes

VELL vb cut turf

VELLET n velvet **vellets**

VELLON n silver and copper alloy used in old Spanish coins **vellons**

VELLS ▶ vell

VELLUM n, adj **vellums**

VELLUS n as in vellus hair short fine unpigmented hair covering the human body

VELOCE adv be played rapidly

VELOUR n **velours**

VELOUTE n rich white sauce or soup made from stock, egg yolks,

and cream

VELUM n any of various membranous structures

VELURE n velvet or a similar fabric ▷ vb cover with velure **velured, velures**

VELVET n, vb **velvets, velvety**

VENA n vein in the body **venae**

VENAL adj **venally**

VENATIC adj of, relating to, or used in hunting

VENATOR n hunter

VEND vb sell

VENDACE n either of two small whitefish occurring in lakes in Scotland and NW England

VENDAGE n vintage

VENDED ▶ vend

VENDEE n person to whom something, esp real property, is sold **vendees**

VENDER = vendor

VENDERS ▶ vender

VENDING ▶ vend

VENDIS = vendace

VENDISS = vendace

VENDOR n **vendors**

VENDS ▶ vend

VENDUE n public sale **vendues**

VENEER n, vb **veneers**

VENEFIC adj having poisonous effects

VENENE n medicine from snake venom **venenes**

VENERER n hunter

VENERY n pursuit of sexual gratification

VENEWE = venue

VENEWES ▶ venewe

VENEY n thrust **veneys**

VENGE vb avenge **venged, venger, vengers, venges, venging**

VENIAL adj

VENIN n any of the poisonous constituents of animal venoms **venine**

VENINES ▶ venine

VENINS ▶ venin

VENIRE n list from which jurors are selected **venires**

VENISON n

VENITE n musical setting for the 95th psalm **venites**

VENNEL n lane **vennels**

VENOM n, vb venomed, venomer, venoms

VENOSE adj having veins

VENOUS adj

VENT n, vb

VENTAGE n small opening

VENTAIL n (in medieval armour) a covering for the lower part of the face

VENTANA n window

VENTED ▶ vent

VENTER ▶ vent

VENTERS ▶ vent

VENTIGE = ventage

VENTIL n valve on a musical instrument **ventils**

VENTING ▶ vent

VENTOSE adj full of wind

VENTRAL adj relating to the front of the body ▷ n ventral fin

VENTRE = venture

VENTRED ▶ ventre

VENTRES ▶ ventre

VENTS ▶ vent

VENTURE n, vb

VENTURI n tube used to control the flow of fluid

VENUE n venues

VENULAR ▶ venule

VENULE n any of the small branches of a vein **venules**

VENUS n type of marine bivalve mollusc **venuses**

VERA adj as in aloe vera plant substance used in skin and hair preparations

VERANDA n

VERB n

VERBAL adj, n, vb verbals

VERBENA n plant with sweet-smelling flowers

VERBID n any nonfinite form of a verb or any nonverbal word derived from a verb **verbids**

VERBIFY another word for ▶ verbalize

VERBILE n person who is best stimulated by words

VERBING n use of nouns as verbs

VERBOSE adj

VERBS ▶ verb

VERD adj as in verd antique dark green mottled impure variety of serpentine marble

VERDANT adj

VERDET n type of verdigris **verdets**

VERDICT n

VERDIN n small W North American tit having grey plumage with a yellow head **verdins**

VERDIT = verdict

VERDITE n type of rock used in jewellery

VERDITS ▶ verdit

VERDOY n floral or leafy shield decoration

VERDURE n flourishing green vegetation

VERGE n, vb verged

VERGER n vergers

VERGES ▶ verge

VERGING ▶ verge

VERGLAS n thin film of ice on rock

VERIDIC = veridical

VERIER ▶ very

VERIEST ▶ very

VERIFY vb

VERILY adv in truth

VERISM n extreme naturalism in art or literature

VERISMO n school of composition that originated in Italian opera

VERISMS ▶ verism

VERIST ▶ verism

VERISTS ▶ verism

VERITAS n truth

VERITE adj involving a high degree of realism or naturalism ▷ n this kind of realism in film **verites**

VERITY n

VERLAN n variety of French slang in which the syllables are inverted **verlans**

VERLIG adj enlightened

VERMAL ▷ vermis

VERMEIL n gilded silver, bronze, or other metal, used esp in the 19th century ▷ vb decorate with vermeil ▷ adj vermilion **vermell**

VERMES ▷ vermis

VERMIAN ▷ vermis

VERMIL = vermeil

VERMILS ▷ vermeil

VERMILY ▷ vermeil

VERMIN pl n vermins, verminy

VERMIS n middle lobe connecting the two halves of the cerebellum

VERMUTH = vermouth

VERNAL adj occurring in spring **vernant**

VERNIER n movable scale on a measuring instrument for taking readings in fractions

VERNIX n white substance covering the skin of a foetus

VERONAL n long-acting barbiturate used medically

VERRA Scot word for

▷ **very**

VERREL n ferrule verrels

VERREY = vair

VERRUCA n verruga

VERRY = vair

VERS n verse

VERSAL n embellished letter **versals**

VERSANT n side or slope of a mountain or mountain range

VERSE n, vb

VERSED adj

VERSER n versifier versers

VERSES ▷ verse

VERSET n short, often sacred, verse **versets**

VERSIFY vb write in verse

VERSIN = versine

VERSINE n mathematical term

VERSING ▷ verse

VERSINS ▷ versin

VERSION n

VERSO n left-hand page of a book **versos**

VERST n unit of length used in Russia **verste**

VERSTES ▷ verste

VERSTS ▷ verste

VERSUS prep

VERSUTE adj cunning

VERT n right to cut green wood in a forest ▷ vb turn **verted**

VERTEX n

VERTIGO n

VERTING ▷ vert

VERTS ▷ vert

VERTU = virtu

VERTUE = virtu

VERTUES ▷ virtue

VERTUS ▷ vertu

VERVAIN n plant with spikes of blue, purple, or white flowers

VERVE n

VERVEL = varvel

VERVELS ▷ vervel

VERVEN = vervain

VERVENS ▷ verven

VERVES ▷ verve

VERVET n variety of a South African guenon monkey **vervets**

VERY adv, adj

VESICA n bladder vesicae

VESICAL adj of or relating to a vesica, esp the urinary bladder

VESICLE n sac or small cavity, esp one containing fluid

VESPA n type of wasp vespas

VESPER n evening prayer, service, or hymn

VESPERS pl n

VESPID n insect of the family that includes the common wasp and hornet ▷ adj of or belonging to this family **vespids**

VESPINE adj of, relating to, or resembling a wasp or wasps

VESPOID adj like a wasp

VESSAIL archaic variant of ▷ **vessel**

VESSEL n, adj vessels

VEST n, vb

VESTA n short friction match, usually of wood

VESTAL adj pure, chaste ▷ n chaste woman **vestals**

VESTAS ▸ vesta

VESTED adj having an existing right to the immediate or future possession of property

VESTEE n person having a vested interest in something **vestees**

VESTIGE n

VESTING ▸ vest

VESTRAL ▸ vestry

VESTRY n

VESTS ▸ vest

VESTURE n garment or something that seems like a garment ▷ vb clothe

VET vb, n

VETCH n vetches

VETCHY adj consisting of vetches

VETERAN n, adj

VETIVER n tall hairless grass of tropical and subtropical Asia

VETKOEK n South African cake

VETO n, vb vetoed, vetoer, vetoers, vetoes, vetoing

VETS, vetted, vetter, vetters ▸ vet

VETTING n as in positive vetting

VETTURA n Italian mode of transport

VEX vb

VEXED adj vexedly

VEXER ▸ vex

VEXERS ▸ vex

VEXES ▸ vex

VEXIL = vexillum

VEXILLA > vexillum

VEXILS > vexil

VEXING ▸ vex

VEXINGS ▸ vex

VEXT = vexed

VEZIR = vizier

VEZIRS > vezir

VIA prep, n

VIABLE adj viably

VIADUCT n

VIAE ▸ via

VIAL n, vb vialed, vialful, vialing, vialled, vials

VIAND n type of food, esp a delicacy **viands**

VIAS ▸ via

VIATIC = viatical

VIATICA > viaticum

VIATOR n traveller viators

VIBE n feeling or flavour of the kind specified

VIBES pl n

VIBEX n mark under the skin

VIBEY adj lively and vibrant

VIBICES ▸ vibex

VIBIER ▸ vibey

VIBIEST ▸ vibey

VIBIST n person who plays a vibraphone in a jazz band or group vibists

VIBRANT adj, n

VIBRATE vb

VIBRATO n

VIBRIO n curved or spiral rodlike bacterium vibrion, vibrios

VIBS pl n type of climbing shoes

VICAR n vicarly, vicars

VICARY n office of a vicar

VICE n, adj, vb, prep viced

VICEROY n

VICES ▸ vice

VICHIES ▸ vichy

VICHY n French mineral water

VICIATE = vitiate

VICINAL adj neighbouring

VICING ▸ vice

VICIOUS adj

VICOMTE n French nobleman

VICTIM n victims

VICTOR n victors

VICTORY n

VICTRIX = victress

VICTUAL vb supply with or obtain victuals

VICUGNA = vicuna

VICUNA n S American animal like the llama vicunas

VID = video

VIDAME n French nobleman vidames

VIDE interj look

VIDENDA > videndum

VIDEO vb, adj, n videoed, videos

VIDETTE = vedette

VIDICON n small television camera tube used in closed-circuit television

VIDIMUS *n* inspection

VIDS ▸ vid

VIDUAGE *n* widows collectively

VIDUAL *adj* widowed

VIDUITY *n* widowhood

VIDUOUS *adj* empty

VIE *vb* vied

VIELLE *n* stringed musical instrument vielles

VIENNA *n* as in vienna loaf, vienna steak associated with Vienna

VIER ▸ vie

VIERS ▸ vie

VIES ▸ vie

VIEW *n, vb* viewed

VIEWER *n* viewers

VIEWIER ▸ viewy

VIEWING *n* act of watching television

VIEWLY *adj* pleasant on the eye

VIEWS ▸ view

VIEWY *adj* having fanciful opinions or ideas

VIFDA = vivda

VIFDAS ▸ vifda

VIG *n* interest on a loan that is paid to a moneylender

VIGA *n* rafter vigas

VIGIA *n* navigational hazard whose existence has not been confirmed vigias

VIGIL *n* vigils

VIGOR ▸ vigour

VIGORO *n* women's game similar to cricket vigoros

VIGORS ▸ vigor

VIGOUR *n* physical or mental energy vigours

VIGS ▸ vig

VIHARA *n* a type of Buddhist temple viharas

VIHUELA *n* obsolete plucked stringed instrument of Spain

VIKING *n* Dane, Norwegian, or Swede who raided by sea between the 8th and 11th centuries vikings

VILAYET *n* major administrative division of Turkey

VILD = vile

VILDE = vile

VILDLY ▸ vild

VILE *adj* vilely, viler, vilest

VILIACO *n* scoundrel viliago

VILIFY *vb*

VILL *n* township

VILLA *n* villae

VILLAGE *n*

VILLAIN *n* villein

VILLAN = villein

VILLANS ▸ villan

VILLANY = villainy

VILLAR ▸ villa

VILLAS ▸ villa

VILLEIN *n* peasant bound in service to his lord

VILLI ▸ villus

VILLOSE = villous

VILLOUS *adj* (of plant parts) covered with long hairs

VILLS ▸ vill

VILLUS *n*

VIM *n* force, energy This word can be helpful when you're stuck with unpromising letters, and gives a reasonable score for a three-letter word.

VIMANA *n* Indian mythological chariot of the gods vimanas

VIMEN *n* long flexible shoot that occurs in certain plants vimina, viminal

VIMS ▸ vim

VIN *n* French wine

VINA *n* stringed musical instrument related to the sitar

VINAL *n* type of manmade fibre vinals

VINAS ▸ vina

VINASSE *n* residue left in a still after distilling spirits, esp brandy

VINCA *n* type of trailing plant with blue flowers vincas

VINCULA ▸ vinculum

VINE *n, vb*

VINEAL *adj* relating to wines

VINED ▸ vine

VINEGAR *n, vb*

VINER *n* vinedresser viners

VINERY *n* hothouse for growing grapes

VINES ▸ vine

VINEW *vb* become mouldy vinewed, vinews

VINIC adj of, relating to, or contained in wine

VINIER ▶ vine

VINIEST ▶ vine

VINIFY vb convert into wine

VINING ▶ vine

VINO n wine vinos

VINOUS adj of or characteristic of wine

VINS ▶ vin

VINT vb sell (wine)

VINTAGE n, adj, vb

VINTED ▶ vint

VINTING ▶ vint

VINTNER n dealer in wine

VINTRY n place where wine is sold

VINTS ▶ vint

VINY ▶ vine

VINYL n, adj vinylic, vinyls

VIOL n

VIOLA n violas

VIOLATE vb, adj

VIOLD archaic or poetic past form of ▶ vial

VIOLENT adj, vb

VIOLER n person who plays the viol violers

VIOLET n, adj violets

VIOLIN n violins

VIOLIST n person who plays the viola

VIOLONE n double-bass member of the viol family

VIOLS ▶ viol

VIPER n vipers

VIRAGO n aggressive woman viragoes

VIRAL adj of or caused by a virus virally

VIRANDA = veranda

VIRANDO = veranda

VIRE vb turn vired

VIRELAI = virelay

VIRELAY n old French verse form

VIREMIA = viraemia

VIREMIC ▶ viremia

VIRENT adj green

VIREO n American songbird vireos

VIRES ▶ vire

VIRETOT n as in on the viretot in a rush

VIRGA n wisps of rain or snow that evaporate before reaching the earth virgas

VIRGATE adj long, straight, and thin ▷ n obsolete measure of land area

VIRGE n rod

VIRGER n rod-bearer virgers

VIRGES ▶ virge

VIRGIN n, adj, vb virgins

VIRGULE another name for ▶ slash

VIRID adj verdant

VIRILE adj

VIRING ▶ vire

VIRINO n entity postulated to be the causative agent of BSE virinos

VIRION n virus in infective form, consisting of an RNA particle within a protein covering virions

VIRL = ferrule

VIRLS ▶ virl

VIROID n any of various infective RNA particles viroids

VIROSE adj poisonous

VIROSES ▶ virosis

VIROSIS n viral disease

VIROUS ▶ virose

VIRTU n taste or love for curios or works of fine art

VIRTUAL adj

VIRTUE n virtues

VIRTUS ▶ virtu

VIRUS n viruses

VIS n power, force, or strength

VISA n, vb visaed

VISAGE n visaged, visages

VISAING ▶ visa

VISARD = vizard

VISARDS ▶ visard

VISAS ▶ visa

VISCERA pl n

VISCID adj sticky

VISCIN n sticky substance found on plants viscins

VISCOID adj (of a fluid) somewhat viscous

VISCOSE = viscous

VISCOUS adj

VISCUM n shrub genus viscums

VISCUS n internal organ

VISE vb advise or award a visa to ▷ n (in US English) vice **vised, viseed, viseing, vises**

VISHING n telephone scam used to gain access to credit card numbers or bank details

VISIBLE adj, n visibly

VISIE = vizy; visied, visier, visiers, visies

VISILE n person best stimulated by vision visiles

VISING ▸ vise

VISION n, vb visions

VISIT vb, n

VISITE n type of cape

VISITED ▸ visit

VISITEE n person who is visited

VISITER variant of ▸ visitor

VISITES ▸ visite

VISITOR n person who visits a person or place

VISITS ▸ visit

VISIVE adj visual

VISNE n neighbourhood visnes

VISNOMY n method of judging character from facial features

VISON n type of mink visons

VISOR n, vb visored, visors

VISTA n, vb vistaed, vistal, vistas, visto

VISTOS ▸ visto

VISUAL adj, n visuals

VITA n curriculum vitae vitae

VITAL adj, n vitally, vitals

VITAMER n type of chemical

VITAMIN n

VITAS ▸ vita

VITE adv musical direction

VITELLI ▸ vitellus

VITESSE n speed

VITEX n type of herb vitexes

VITIATE vb

VITIOUS adj mistaken

VITRAGE n light fabric

VITRAIL n stained glass

VITRAIN n type of coal

VITRAUX ▸ vitrail

VITREUM n vitreous body

VITRIC adj of, relating to, resembling, or having the nature of glass

VITRICS n glassware

VITRIFY vb change or be changed into glass or a glassy substance

VITRINE n glass display case or cabinet for works of art, curios, etc

VITRIOL n, vb

VITTA n tubelike cavity containing oil that occurs in the fruits of certain plants vittae, vittate

VITTLE obsolete or dialect spelling of ▸ victual

VITTLED ▸ vittle

VITTLES obsolete or dialect spelling of ▸ victuals

VITULAR = vituline

VIVA interj, n, vb

VIVACE adj, adv (to be performed) in a lively manner ▷ n piece of music to be performed in this way vivaces

VIVAED ▸ viva

VIVAING ▸ viva

VIVARIA ▸ vivarium

VIVARY n = vivarium

VIVAS ▸ viva

VIVAT interj long live ▷ n expression of acclamation vivats

VIVDA n method of drying meat vivdas

VIVE interj long live

VIVELY adv in a lively manner

VIVENCY n physical or mental energy

VIVER n fish pond

VIVERRA n civet genus

VIVERS ▸ viver

VIVES n disease found in horses

VIVID adj vivider, vividly

VIVIFIC adj giving life

VIVIFY vb animate, inspire

VIVO adv with life and vigour

VIVRES n provisions

VIXEN n vixenly, vixens

VIZARD n means of disguise ▷ vb conceal by means of a disguise vizards

VIZIED ▸ vizy

VIZIER n high official in certain Muslim countries viziers

VIZIES ▸ vizy

VIZIR = vizier

VIZIRS ▸ vizir

VIZOR = visor

VIZORED ▸ vizor

VIZORS ▸ vizor

VIZSLA n breed of Hungarian hunting dog vizslas

VIZY vb look vizying, vizzie

VIZZIED ▸ vizzie

VIZZIES ▸ vizzie

VLEI n area of low marshy ground **vleis**

VLIES ▸ vly

VLOG n

VLOGGER n person who keeps a video blog

VLOGS ▸ vlog

VLY = **vlei**

This word for low-lying wet ground can be useful when you are short of vowels. It can also be spelt **vlei**.

VOAR n spring **voars**

VOCAB n vocabulary

VOCABLE n word regarded simply as a sequence of letters or spoken sounds ▸ adj capable of being uttered **vocably**

VOCABS ▸ vocab

VOCAL adj, n

VOCALIC adj of, relating to, or containing a vowel or vowels

VOCALLY ▸ vocal

VOCALS ▸ vocal

VOCES ▸ vox

VOCODER n type of synthesizer that uses the human voice as an oscillator

VOCULAR ▸ vocule

VOCULE n faint noise made when articulating certain sounds **vocules**

VODCAST vb

VODDIES ▸ voddy

VODDY n vodka

VODKA n vodkas

VODOU variant of ▸ **voodoo**

This West Indian word for a kind of black magic may indeed work magic on an unpromising rack. And it has a host of variants, though few people will remember them all: **vaudoo, vaudoux, vodoun, vodun, voudon, voudou** and **vodoun**!

VODOUN ▸ vodun

VODOUNS ▸ vodoun

VODOUS ▸ vodou

VODUN n voodoo **voduns**

VOE n (in Orkney and Shetland) a small bay or narrow creek

VOEMA n vigour or energy **voemas**

VOES ▸ voe

VOGIE adj conceited **vogier, vogiest**

VOGUE n, adj, vb vogued, voguer, voguers, vogues, voguey, voguier

VOGUING ▸ vogueing

VOGUISH ▸ vogue

VOICE n, vb

VOICED adj articulated with accompanying vibration of the vocal cords

VOICER, voicers, voices, voicing ▸ voice

VOID adj, n, vb

VOIDED adj (of a design) with a hole in the centre of the same shape as the design

VOIDEE n light meal eaten before bed **voidees**

VOIDER, voiders, voiding, voids ▸ void

VOILA interj word used to express satisfaction

VOILE n light semitransparent fabric **voiles**

VOIP n voips

VOITURE n type of vehicle

VOIVODE n type of military leader

VOL n heraldic wings

VOLA n palm of hand or sole of foot

VOLABLE adj quick-witted

VOLAE ▸ vola

VOLAGE adj changeable

VOLANT adj in a flying position

VOLANTE n Spanish horse carriage

VOLAR adj of or relating to the palm of the hand or the sole of the foot

VOLARY n large bird enclosure

VOLATIC adj flying

VOLCANO n

VOLE n, vb voled

VOLENS adj as in nolens volens whether willing or unwilling

VOLERY = volary

VOLES ▸ vole

VOLET n type of veil **volets**

VOLING ▷ **vole**

VOLK n people or nation, esp the nation of Afrikaners **volks**

VOLLEY n, vb **volleys**

VOLOST n (in the former Soviet Union) a rural soviet **volosts**

VOLPINO n Italian breed of dog

VOLS ▷ **vol**

VOLT n, vb

VOLTA n quick-moving Italian dance

VOLTAGE n

VOLTAIC adj producing an electric current

VOLTE = volt

VOLTED ▷ **volt** vb

VOLTES ▷ **volte**

VOLTI adv musical direction

VOLTING ▷ **volt** vb

VOLTS ▷ **volt**

VOLUBIL = voluble

VOLUBLE adj volubly

VOLUME n, vb volumed, volumes

VOLUSPA n Icelandic mythological poem

VOLUTE n spiral or twisting turn, form, or object ▷ adj having the form of a volute voluted, volutes

VOLUTIN n granular substance found in cells

VOLVA n cup-shaped structure that sheathes the base of the stalk of certain

mushrooms **volvae, volvas, volvate**

VOLVE vb turn over **volved, volves, volving**

VOLVOX n freshwater protozoan

VOLVULI > volvulus

VOMER n thin flat bone separating the nasal passages in mammals **vomers**

VOMICA n pus-containing cavity **vomicae, vomicas**

VOMIT vb, n vomited, vomiter

VOMITO n form of yellow fever **vomitos**

VOMITS ▷ **vomit**

VOMITUS n matter that has been vomited

VONGOLE pl n (in Italian cookery) clams

VOODOO n, adj, vb **voodoos**

VOR vb (in dialect) warn

VORAGO n chasm

VORANT adj devouring

VORLAGE n skiing position

VORPAL adj sharp

VORRED ▷ **vor**

VORRING ▷ **vor**

VORS ▷ **vor**

VORTEX n

VOSTRO adj as in vostro account bank account held by a foreign bank with a British bank

VOTABLE ▷ **vote**

VOTARY n person dedicated to religion or to a cause ▷ adj

ardently devoted to the services or worship of God

VOTE n, vb voted

VOTEEN n devotee **voteens**

VOTER n person who can or does vote **voters**

VOTES ▷ **vote**

VOTING ▷ **vote**

VOTINGS ▷ **vote**

VOTIVE adj done or given to fulfil a vow ▷ n votive offering **votives**

VOTRESS > votaress

VOUCH vb, n vouched

VOUCHEE n person summoned to court to defend a title

VOUCHER n, vb

VOUCHES ▷ **vouch**

VOUDON variant of ▷ voodoo

VOUDONS ▷ **voudon**

VOUDOU = voodoo

VOUDOUN variant of ▷ voodoo

VOUDOUS ▷ **voudou**

VOUGE n form of pike used by foot soldiers in the 14th century and later **vouges**

VOULGE n type of medieval weapon **voulges**

VOULU adj deliberate

VOUVRAY n dry white French wine

VOW n, vb vowed

VOWEL n, vb vowelly, vowels

VOWER ▷ **vow**

VOWERS ▷ **vow**

VOWESS n nun

VOWING ▶ vow

VOWLESS ▶ vow

VOWS ▶ vow

VOX n voice or sound
Along with **vex**, this Latin word for voice is the highest-scoring three-letter word beginning with V.

VOXEL n term used in computing imaging **voxels**

VOYAGE n, vb voyaged, voyager, voyages

VOYEUR n voyeurs

VOZHD n Russian leader **vozhds**
This unlikely looking word is Russian for a chief or leader, and may provide a great score from an apparently difficult rack.

VRAIC n type of seaweed **vraics**

VRIL n life force **vrils**

VROOM interj exclamation imitative of a car engine revving up ▷ vb move noisily and at high speed **vroomed, vrooms**

VROT adj South African slang for rotten

VROU n Afrikaner woman, esp a married woman **vrous**

VROUW n woman **vrouws, vrow**
The heart of any Scrabble player sinks to see a combination of U, V and W on the rack, as there are relatively few words that use even two of these letters. But **vrouw**, a word of Dutch origin for a woman or goodwife, may get you out of the mess.

VROWS ▶ vrow

VUG n small cavity in a rock or vein, usually lined with crystals **vugg, vuggier**
This unusual word of Cornish origin, meaning a cavity in rock, is another that can be useful when you have an uninspiring combination of letters. And it has a variant **vugh** and can be extended to **vuggy** or **vughy**.

VUGGS ▶ vugg

VUGGY ▶ vug

VUGH = vug

VUGGS ▶ vugg

VUGGY ▶ vug

VUGHIER ▶ vugh

VUGHS ▶ vugh

VUGHY ▶ vugh

VUGS ▶ vug

VULCAN n blacksmith **vulcans**

VULGAR adj, n **vulgars**

VULGATE n commonly recognized text or version ▷ adj generally accepted

VULGO adv generally

VULGUS n the common people

VULN vb wound **vulned, vulning, vulns**

VULPINE adj of or like a fox

VULTURE n

VULTURN n type of turkey

VULVA n **vulvae, vulval, vulvar, vulvas, vulvate**

VUM vb swear **vummed, vumming, vums**

VUTTIER ▶ vutty

VUTTY adj dirty

VYING ▶ vie

VYINGLY ▶ vie

VYINGS ▶ vie

Ww

W, like **V**, can be an awkward tile to handle, but at least there are two two-letter words that begin with **W**: **we** and **wo** (5 points each) and two that end with **W**: **aw** and **ow** (5 points each). There are lots of everyday three-letter words that earn good scores: **wiz** (15), **wax** (13) with its two old-fashioned variants **wex** and **wox** (also 13 each) and **way**, **who**, **why**, **wow** and **wry** (9 each). Don't forget **wok** (10) either, which can be as useful on the Scrabble board as in the kitchen!

WAAC *n* (formerly) member of the Women's Auxiliary Army Corp **waacs**

WAB ▶ **web** *n*

WABAIN = ouabain

WABAINS ▶ wabain

WABBIT *adj* weary

WABBLE = wobble; wabbled, wabbler, wabbles, wabbly

WABOOM another word for > wagenboom

WABOOMS ▶ waboom

WABSTER *Scots form of* ▶ webster

WACK *n* friend

WACKE *n* any of various soft earthy rocks that resemble or are derived from basaltic rocks

WACKER = wack

WACKERS ▶ wacker

WACKES ▶ wacke

WACKEST ▶ wack

WACKIER ▶ wacky

WACKILY ▶ wacky

WACKO *adj* mad or eccentric ▷ *n* mad or eccentric person wackos

WACKS ▶ wack

WACKY *adj*

WAD *n, vb*

WADABLE ▶ wade

WADD = wad

WADDED ▶ wad

WADDER ▶ wad

WADDERS ▶ wad

WADDIE = waddy

WADDIED ▶ waddy

WADDIES ▶ waddy

WADDING ▶ wad

WADDLE *vb, n* waddled, waddler, waddles, waddly

WADDS ▶ wadd

WADDY *n, vb*

WADE *vb, n* waded

WADER ▶ wade

WADERS *pl n* long waterproof boots which completely cover the legs

WADES ▶ wade

WADI *n*

WADIES ▶ wady

WADING ▶ wade

WADINGS ▶ wade

WADIS ▶ wadi

WADMAAL = wadmal

WADMAL *n* coarse thick woollen fabric, formerly woven for outer garments wadmals, wadmel

WADMELS ▶ wadmel

WADMOL = wadmal

WADMOLL = wadmal

WADMOLS ▶ wadmal

WADS ▶ wad

WADSET *vb* pledge or mortgage wadsets, wadsett

WADT = wad

WADTS ▸ wadt

WADY ▸ wadi

WAE old form of ▸ woe

WAEFUL old form of ▸ woeful

WAENESS n sorrow

WAES ▸ wae

WAESOME adj sorrowful

WAESUCK interj alas

WAFER n, vb wafered, wafers, wafery

WAFF n gust or puff of air ▷ vb flutter or cause to flutter waffed

WAFFIE n person regarded as having little worth to society waffies

WAFFING ▸ waff

WAFFLE vb, n waffled, waffler, waffles, waffly

WAFFS ▸ waff

WAFT vb, n waftage, wafted

WAFTER n device that causes a draught wafters

WAFTING ▸ waft

WAFTS ▸ waft

WAFTURE n act of wafting or waving

WAG vb, n

WAGE n, vb waged

WAGER vb, n wagered, wagerer, wagers

WAGES ▸ wage

WAGGA n blanket or bed covering made out of sacks stitched together waggas

WAGGED ▸ wag

WAGGER ▸ wag

WAGGERS ▸ wag

WAGGERY n quality of being humorous

WAGGING ▸ wag

WAGGISH adj jocular or humorous

WAGGLE vb, n waggled

WAGGLER n float only the bottom of which is attached to the fishing line

WAGGLES ▸ waggle

WAGGLY ▸ waggle

WAGGON = wagon

WAGGONS ▸ waggon

WAGING ▸ wage

WAGON n, vb wagoned

WAGONER n person who drives a wagon

WAGONS ▸ wagon

WAGS ▸ wag

WAGSOME another word for ▸ waggish

WAGTAIL n

WAGYU n Japanese breed of beef cattle wagyus

WAHINE n Māori woman, esp a wife wahines

WAHOO n food and game fish of tropical seas wahoos

WAI n in New Zealand, water

WAIATA n Māori song waiatas

WAID ▸ weigh

WAIDE ▸ weigh

WAIF n, vb waifed, waifing, waifish, waifs

WAIFT n piece of lost property found by someone other than the owner waifts

WAIL vb, n wailed, wailer, wailers, wailful, wailing, wails

WAIN vb, n

WAINAGE n carriages, etc, for transportation of goods

WAINED ▸ wain

WAINING ▸ wain

WAINS ▸ wain

WAIR vb spend waired, wairing, wairs

WAIRSH variant spelling of ▸ wersh

WAIRUA n in New Zealand, spirit or soul wairuas

WAIS ▸ wai

WAIST n

WAISTED adj having a waist or waistlike part

WAISTER n sailor performing menial duties

WAISTS ▸ waist

WAIT vb, n waite, waited

WAITER n, vb waiters

WAITES ▸ waite

WAITING ▸ wait

WAITRON n waiter or waitress

WAITS ▸ wait

WAIVE vb waived

WAIVER n act or instance of voluntarily giving up a claim, right, etc waivers

WAIVES ▸ waive
WAIVING ▸ waive
WAIVODE = voivode
WAIWODE = voivode
WAKA n Māori canoe
WAKAME n edible seaweed wakames
WAKANDA n supernatural quality in Native American belief system
WAKAS ▸ waka
WAKE vb, n waked
WAKEFUL adj
WAKEMAN n watchman wakemen
WAKEN vb wakened, wakener, wakens
WAKER ▸ wake
WAKERS ▸ wake
WAKES ▸ wake
WAKF = waqf
WAKFS ▸ wakf
WAKIKI n Melanesian shell currency wakikis
WAKING ▸ wake
WAKINGS ▸ wake
WALD Scots form of ▸ weld
WALDO n gadget for manipulating objects by remote control waldoes, waldos
WALDS ▸ wald
WALE = weal; waled, waler, walers, wales
WALI = vali
WALIER ▸ waly
WALIES ▸ waly
WALIEST ▸ waly
WALING ▸ wale
WALIS ▸ wali
WALISE = valise
WALISES ▸ walise

WALK vb move on foot with at least one foot always on the ground ▸ n short journey on foot, usu for pleasure walked
WALKER n walkers
WALKIES pl n as in go walkies a walk
WALKING adj (of a person) considered to possess the qualities of something inanimate as specified ▸ n act of walking
WALKOUT n
WALKS ▸ walk
WALKUP n building with stairs to upper floors walkups
WALKWAY n
WALL n, vb
WALLA = wallah
WALLABA n type of S American tree
WALLABY n
WALLAH n person involved with or in charge of a specified thing wallahs
WALLAS ▸ walla
WALLED ▸ wall
WALLER ▸ wall
WALLERS ▸ wall
WALLET n wallets
WALLEYE n fish with large staring eyes
WALLIE = wally
WALLIER ▸ wally
WALLIES ▸ wally
WALLING ▸ wall
WALLOP vb, n wallops
WALLOW vb, n wallows
WALLS ▸ wall

WALLY n stupid person ▸ adj fine, pleasing, or splendid
WALNUT n, adj walnuts
WALRUS n
WALTIER ▸ walty
WALTY adj (of a ship) likely to roll over
WALTZ n, vb waltzed
WALTZER n person who waltzes
WALTZES ▸ waltz
WALY = wally
WAMBLE vb move unsteadily ▸ n unsteady movement wambled, wambles, wambly
WAME n belly, abdomen, or womb wamed
WAMEFOU Scots variant of ▸ wameful
WAMEFUL n bellyful
WAMES ▸ wame
WAMMUL n dog wammuls
WAMMUS = wamus
WAMPEE n type of Asian fruit tree wampees
WAMPISH vb wave
WAMPUM n shells woven together, formerly used by Native Americans for money wampums
WAMPUS = wamus
WAMUS n type of cardigan or jacket wamuses
WAN adj, vb
WAND n
WANDER vb, n wanders
WANDLE adj supple

WANDOO n eucalyptus tree of W Australia, having white bark and durable wood **wandoos**

WANDS ▶ wand

WANE vb **waned, wanes, waney**

WANG n cheekbone

WANGAN = wanigan

WANGANS ▶ wangan

WANGLE vb, n **wangled, wangler, wangles**

WANGS ▶ wang

WANGUN = wanigan

WANGUNS ▶ wangun

WANHOPE n delusion

WANIER ▶ wany

WANIEST ▶ wany

WANIGAN n provisions for camp

WANING ▶ wane

WANINGS ▶ wane

WANION n vehemence **wanions**

WANKLE adj unstable

WANLE = wandle

WANLY ▶ wan

WANNA vb spelling of **want to** intended to reflect a dialectal or informal pronunciation

WANNABE adj wanting to be, or be like, a particular person or thing ▷ n person who wants to be, or be like, a particular person or thing

WANNED ▶ wan

WANNEL = wandle

WANNER, wanness,

wannest, wanning ▶ wan

WANNION ▶ wanion

WANNISH adj rather wan

WANS ▶ wan

WANT vb, n

WANTAGE n shortage

WANTED ▶ want

WANTER ▶ want

WANTERS ▶ want

WANTIES ▶ wanty

WANTING adj lacking ▷ prep without

WANTON adj, n, vb **wantons**

WANTS ▶ want

WANTY adj belt

WANY ▶ wane

WANZE vb wane **wanzed, wanzes, wanzing**

WAP vb strike

WAPITI n large N American deer **wapitis**

WAPPED ▶ wap

WAPPEND adj tired

WAPPER vb blink **wappers**

WAPPING ▶ wap

WAPS ▶ wap

WAQF n endowment in Muslim law **waqfs**

An Arabic word meaning the donation of land, property or money for charitable purposes. As one of the Q words without a U, this comes up surprisingly often. It can also be spelt **wakf**.

WAR n, adj, vb

WARAGI n Ugandan alcoholic drink made from bananas **waragis**

WARATAH n

WARB n dirty or insignificant person **warbier**

WARBIRD n vintage military aeroplane

WARBLE vb, n **warbled**

WARBLER n

WARBLES ▶ warble

WARBS ▶ warb

WARBY ▶ warb

WARD n, vb **warded**

WARDEN n, vb **wardens**

WARDER vb, n **warders**

WARDIAN n as in **wardian case** type of glass container for housing delicate plants

WARDING ▶ ward

WARDOG n veteran warrior **wardogs**

WARDROP obsolete form of > **wardrobe**

WARDS ▶ ward

WARE n, vb **wared**

WAREHOU n any of several edible saltwater New Zealand fish

WARES pl n goods for sale

WAREZ pl n illegally copied computer software

WARFARE vb, n

WARHEAD n

WARIER ▶ wary

WARIEST ▶ wary

WARILY ▶ wary

WARING ▶ ware

WARISON n (esp formerly) a bugle note used as an order to a military force to attack

WARK Scots form of ▶ work

WARKED ▶ wark

WARKING ▶ wark

WARKS ▶ wark

WARLESS ▶ war

WARLIKE adj of or relating to war

WARLING n one who is not liked

WARLOCK n

WARLORD n military leader of a nation or part of a nation

WARM adj, vb, n

WARMAN n one experienced in warfare

WARMED ▶ warm

WARMEN ▶ warman

WARMER, warmers, warmest, warming, warmish, warmly, warms ▶ warm

WARMTH n warmths

WARMUP n preparatory exercise routine warmups

WARN vb warned, warner, warners

WARNING n, adj

WARNS ▶ warn

WARP vb, n warpage

WARPATH n

WARPED, warper, warpers, warping, warps ▶ warp

WARRAN = warrant

WARRAND = warrant

WARRANS ▶ warran

WARRANT n, vb

WARRAY vb wage war on warrays

WARRE = war

WARRED ▶ war

WARREN n warrens

WARREY = warray

WARREYS ▶ warrey

WARRING ▶ war

WARRIOR n

WARS ▶ war

WARSAW n type of grouper fish warsaws

WARSHIP n

WARSLE dialect word for ▶ wrestle

WARSLED ▶ warsle

WARSLER ▶ warsle

WARSLES ▶ warsle

WARST obsolete form of ▶ worst

WARSTLE dialect form of ▶ wrestle

WART n warted

WARTHOG n wild African pig with wartlike lumps on the face

WARTIER ▶ wart

WARTIME n, adj

WARTS ▶ wart

WARTY ▶ wart

WARWOLF n Roman engine of war

WARWORK n work contributing to war effort

WARWORN adj worn down by war

WARY adj

WARZONE n area where a war is taking place or there is some other violent conflict

WAS ▶ be

WASABI n Japanese cruciferous plant cultivated for its thick green pungent root wasabis

WASE n pad to relieve pressure of load carried on head wases

WASH vb, n

WASHDAY n day on which clothes and linen are washed, often the same day each week

WASHED ▶ wash

WASHEN ▶ wash

WASHER n, vb washers

WASHERY n plant at a mine where water or other liquid is used to remove dirt from a mineral, esp coal

WASHES ▶ wash

WASHIER ▶ washy

WASHILY ▶ washy

WASHIN n increase in the angle of attack of an aircraft wing towards the wing tip

WASHING n

WASHINS ▶ washin

WASHOUT n

WASHPOT n pot for washing things in

WASHRAG = washcloth

WASHTUB n tub or large container used for washing anything, esp clothes

WASHUP n outcome of a process washups

WASHY adj

WASP n

WASPIE n tight-waisted corset

WASPIER ▶ wasp

WASPIES ▶ waspie

WASPILY ▶ wasp

WASPISH adj

WASPS ▶ wasp

WASPY ▶ wasp

WASSAIL n formerly, festivity when much drinking took place ▷ vb drink health of (a person) at a wassail

WASSUP sentence substitute what is happening?

WAST singular form of the past tense of ▶ be

WASTAGE n

WASTE vb, n, adj wasted

WASTEL n fine bread or cake wastels

WASTER vb waste ▷ n layabout wasters

WASTERY n extravagance

WASTES ▶ waste

WASTING adj

WASTREL n lazy or worthless person

WASTRIE = wastery

WASTRY n wastefulness

WASTS ▶ wast

WAT adj wet; drunken

WATAP n stringy thread made by Native Americans from the roots of conifers watape

WATAPES ▶ watape

WATAPS ▶ watap

WATCH vb, n watched

WATCHER n person who watches

WATCHES ▶ watch

WATCHET n shade of blue

WATE ▶ wit

WATER n, vb watered, waterer, waters

WATERY adj

WATS ▶ wat

WATT n

WATTAGE n

WATTAPE = watap

WATTER ▶ wat

WATTEST ▶ wat

WATTLE n, adj, vb wattled, wattles

WATTS ▶ watt

WAUCHT = waught

WAUCHTS ▶ waucht

WAUFF ▶ waff

WAUFFED ▶ wauff

WAUFFS ▶ wauff

WAUGH vb bark waughed, waughs

WAUGHT vb drink in large amounts waughts

WAUK vb full (cloth) wauked, wauker, waukers, wauking, wauks

WAUL vb cry or wail plaintively like a cat wauled, wauling

WAULK = wauk

WAULKED ▶ waulk

WAULKER ▶ waulk

WAULKS ▶ waulk

WAULS ▶ waul

WAUR obsolete form of ▶ war; waured, wauring, waurs, waurst

WAVE vb, n waved

WAVELET n small wave

WAVEOFF n signal or instruction to an aircraft not to land

WAVER vb, n wavered, waverer, wavers

WAVERY adj lacking firmness

WAVES ▶ wave

WAVESON n goods floating on waves after shipwreck

WAVEY n snow goose or other wild goose waveys

WAVICLE n origin of wave

WAVIER, wavies, waviest, wavily ▶ wavy

WAVING ▶ wave

WAVINGS ▶ wave

WAVY adj, n

WAW another name for ▶ vav

WAWA n speech ▷ vb speak wawaed, wawaing, wawas

WAWE = waw

WAWES ▶ wawe

WAWL = wawl

WAWLED ▶ wawl

WAWLING ▶ wawl

WAWLS ▶ wawl

WAWS ▶ waw

WAX n, vb waxable

WAXBILL n any of various chiefly African finchlike weaverbirds

WAXED ▶ wax

WAXEN adj

WAXER ▶ wax

WAXERS ▶ wax

WAXES ▶ wax

WAXEYE n small New Zealand bird waxeyes

WAXIER ▶ waxy

WAXIEST ▶ waxy

WAXILY ▶ waxy

WAXING ▶ wax

WAXINGS ▶ wax

WAXLIKE ▶ wax

WAXWEED n type of wild flower

WAXWING n type of songbird

WAXWORK n

WAXWORM n waxmoth larva

WAXY adj

WAY n, vb

WAYBILL n document stating the nature, origin, and destination of goods being transported

WAYED ▶ way

WAYFARE vb travel

WAYGONE adj travel-weary

WAYING ▶ way

WAYLAID ▶ waylay

WAYLAY vb waylays

WAYLESS ▶ way

WAYMARK n symbol or signpost marking the route of a footpath ▷ vb mark out with waymarks

WAYMENT vb express grief

WAYPOST n signpost

WAYS ▶ way

WAYSIDE n

WAYWARD adj

WAYWODE n Slavonic governor

WAYWORN adj worn or tired by travel

WAZIR another word for ▶ vizier

WAZIRS ▶ wazir

WAZZOCK n foolish or annoying person

WE pron

WEAK adj

WEAKEN vb weakens

WEAKER ▶ weak

WEAKEST ▶ weak

WEAKISH ▶ weak

WEAKLY adv feebly ▷ adj weak or sickly

WEAKON n subatomic particle weakons

WEAL n

WEALD n open or forested country wealds

WEALS ▶ weal

WEALTH n wealths

WEALTHY adj

WEAMB = wame

WEAMBS ▶ weamb

WEAN vb weaned

WEANEL n recently-weaned child or animal weanels

WEANER n person or thing that weans weaners

WEANING ▶ wean

WEANS ▶ wean

WEAPON vb, n weapons

WEAR vb, n weared, wearer, wearers

WEARIED adj wearied, wearies, wearily ▶ weary

WEARING adj, n

WEARISH adj withered

WEARS ▶ wear

WEARY adj, vb

WEASAND former name for the ▶ trachea

WEASEL n, vb weasels, weasely

WEASON Scots form of ▶ weasand

WEASONS ▶ weason

WEATHER n, vb

WEAVE vb weaved

WEAVER n weavers

WEAVES ▶ weave

WEAVING ▶ weave

WEAZAND = weasand

WEAZEN = wizen

WEAZENS ▶ weazen

WEB n, vb webbed

WEBBIE n person who is well versed in the use of the World Wide Web

WEBBIER ▶ webby

WEBBIES ▶ webbie

WEBBING n

WEBBY adj of, relating to, resembling, or consisting of a web

WEBCAM n camera that transmits images over the internet webcams

WEBCAST n broadcast of an event over the internet ▷ vb make such a broadcast

WEBER n SI unit of magnetic flux webers

WEBFED adj (of printing press) printing from rolls of paper

WEBFEET ▶ webfoot

WEBFOOT n foot having the toes connected by folds of skin

WEBHEAD n person who uses the Internet a lot

WEBIFY vb convert (information) for display on the internet

WEBINAR n interactive seminar conducted over the World Wide Web

WEBLESS ▶ web

WEBLIKE ▶ web

WEBLISH n shorthand form of English that is used in text messaging, chat rooms, etc

WEBLOG n weblogs

WEBMAIL n system of electronic mail accessed via the internet

WEBPAGE n page on website

WEBRING n group of websites organized in a circular structure

WEBS ▶ web

WEBSITE n

WEBSTER archaic word for ▶ weaver

WEBWORK n work done using the World Wide Web

WEBWORM n type of caterpillar

WEBZINE n magazine published on the Internet

WECHT n agricultural tool **wechts**

WED vb wedded

WEDDER dialect form of ▶ weather

WEDDERS ▶ wedder

WEDDING ▶ wed

WEDEL variant of ▶ wedeln

WEDELED ▶ wedel

WEDELN n succession of high-speed turns performed in skiing ▷ vb perform a wedeln **wedelns**

WEDELS ▶ wedel

WEDGE n, vb wedged, wedges

WEDGIE n wedge-heeled shoe

WEDGIER ▶ wedge

WEDGIES ▶ wedgie

WEDGING ▶ wedge

WEDGY ▶ wedge

WEDLOCK n

WEDS ▶ wed

WEE adj, n, vb

WEED n, vb weeded, weeder, weeders

WEEDERY n weed-ridden area

WEEDIER ▶ weedy

WEEDILY ▶ weedy

WEEDING ▶ weed

WEEDS pl n widow's mourning clothes

WEEDY adj (of a person) thin and weak

WEEING ▶ wee

WEEK n, adv

WEEKDAY n

WEEKE = wick

WEEKEND n, vb

WEEKES ▶ weeke

WEEKLY adv, n, adj

WEEKS ▶ week

WEEL Scot word for ▶ well

WEELS ▶ weel

WEEM n underground home **weems**

WEEN vb think or imagine (something) **weened**

WEENIE adj very small ▷ n wiener

WEENIER ▶ weeny

WEENIES ▶ weenie

WEENING ▶ ween

WEENS ▶ ween

WEENSY = weeny

WEENY adj very small

WEEP vb, n

WEEPER n person who weeps, esp a hired mourner **weepers**

WEEPIE, weepier, weepies, weepily ▶ weepy

WEEPING adj

WEEPS ▶ weep

WEEPY adj, n

WEER ▶ wee

WEES ▶ wee

WEEST ▶ wee

WEET dialect form of ▶ wet

WEETE = wit

WEETED ▶ weete

WEETEN = wit

WEETER, weetest, weeting, weets ▶ weet

WEEVER n type of small fish **weevers**

WEEVIL n weevils

WEEVILY another word for ▶ weevilled

WEEWEE vb urinate **weeweed, weewees**

WEFT n, vb

WEFTAGE n texture

WEFTE n forsaken child

WEFTED ▶ weft

WEFTES ▶ wefte

WEFTING ▶ weft

WEFTS ▶ weft

WEID n sudden illness **weids**

WEIGELA n type of shrub

WEIGH vb weighed, weigher, weighs

WEIGHT n, vb weights

WEIGHTY adj

WEIL n whirlpool **weils**

WEINER = wiener

WEINERS ▶ weiner

WEIR vb, n

WEIRD adj, vb weirded, weirder

WEIRDIE = weirdo

WEIRDLY ▶ weird

WEIRDO n weirdos

WEIRDS ▶ weird

WEIRDY n weird person

WEIRED ▶ weir

WEIRING ▶ weir

WEIRS ▶ weir

WEISE = wise

WEISED ▶ weise

WEISES ▶ weise

WEISING ▶ weise

WEIZE = wise

WEIZED ▶ weize

WEIZES ▶ weize

WEIZING ▶ weize

WEKA n flightless New Zealand rail **wekas**

WELAWAY = wellaway

WELCH = welsh

WELCHED ▶ welch

WELCHER ▶ welch

WELCHES ▶ welch

WELCOME vb, n, adj

WELD vb, n welded, welder, welders, welding, weldor

WELDORS ▶ weldor

WELDS ▶ weld

WELFARE n

WELK vb wither; dry up **welke, welked**

WELKES ▶ welke

WELKIN n sky, heavens, or upper air

WELKING ▶ welk

WELKINS ▶ welkin

WELKS ▶ welk

WELKT adj twisted

WELL adv, adj, interj, n, vb welled

WELLIE n wellington boot

WELLIES ▶ welly

WELLING ▶ well

WELLS ▶ well

WELLY n

WELS n type of catfish

WELSH vb welshed, welsher, welshes

WELT n weal

WELTED ▶ welt

WELTER n, vb welters

WELTING ▶ welt

WELTS ▶ welt

WEM = wame

WEMB = wame

WEMBS ▶ wemb

WEMS ▶ wem

WEN n cyst on the scalp

WENA pron South African word for you

WENCH n, vb wenched, wencher, wenches

WEND vb wended

WENDIGO n evil spirit or cannibal

WENDING ▶ wend

WENDS ▶ wend

WENGE n type of tree found in central and West Africa **wenges**

WENNIER, wennish, wenny, wens ▶ wen

WENT n path **wents**

WEPT ▶ weep

WERE vb

WERGELD = wergild

WERGELT = wergild

WERGILD n price set on a man's life, to be paid as compensation by his slayer

WERO n challenge made by an armed Māori warrior to a visitor to a marae **weros**

WERSH adj tasteless **wersher**

WERT singular form of the past tense of ▶ be

WERWOLF = werewolf

WESAND = weasand

WESANDS ▶ wesand

WESKIT informal word for > waistcoat

WESKITS ▶ weskit

WESSAND = weasand

WEST n, adj, adv, vb wested

WESTER vb move or appear to move towards the west ▷ n strong wind or storm from the west

WESTERN adj, n

WESTERS ▶ wester

WESTING n movement, deviation, or distance covered in a westerly direction

WESTLIN *Scots word for* ▸ **western**

WESTS ▸ **west**

WET *adj, n, vb*

WETA *n* type of wingless insect **wetas**

WETHER *n* male sheep, esp a castrated one **wethers**

WETLAND *n* area of marshy land

WETLY ▸ **wet**

WETNESS ▸ **wet**

WETS ▸ **wet**

WETSUIT *n* body suit for diving

WETTED, wetter, wetters, wettest ▸ **wet**

WETTIE *n* wetsuit **wetties**

WETTING ▸ **wet**

WETTISH ▸ **wet**

WETWARE *n* humorous term for the brain

WEX *obsolete form of* ▸ **wax**

> **Wex** is an old word for **wax**, in the sense of grow. It gives a very good score for a three-letter word, and can be extended to **wexe**.

WEXE *obsolete form of* ▸ **wax**

WEXED ▸ **wex**

WEXES ▸ **wex**

WEXING ▸ **wex**

WEY *n* measurement of weight

WEYARD *obsolete form of* ▸ **weird**

WEYS ▸ **wey**

WEYWARD *obsolete form of* ▸ **weird**

WEZAND *obsolete form of* ▸ **weasand**

WEZANDS ▸ **wezand**

WHA *Scot word for* ▸ **who**

WHACK *vb, n,* **whacked, whacker**

WHACKO *n* mad person **whackos**

WHACKS ▸ **whack**

WHACKY *variant spelling of* ▸ **wacky**

WHAE ▸ **wha**

WHAISLE *Scots form of* ▸ **wheeze**

WHAIZLE = **whaisle**

WHALE *n, vb* **whaled**

WHALER *n* ship or person involved in whaling **whalers**

WHALERY *n* whaling

WHALES ▸ **whale**

WHALING *n* whaling

WHALLY *adj* (of eyes) with light-coloured irises

WHAM *interj, n, vb* **whammed**

WHAMMO *n* sound of a sudden collision **whammos**

WHAMMY *n* devastating setback

WHAMO = **whammo**

WHAMPLE *n* strike

WHAMS ▸ **wham**

WHANAU *n* (in Māori societies) a family, esp an extended family **whanaus**

WHANG *vb* strike or be struck so as to cause a resounding noise ▷ *n* resounding noise produced by a heavy blow

WHANGAM *n* imaginary creature

WHANGED ▸ **whang**

WHANGEE *n* tall woody grass grown for its stems, which are used for bamboo canes

WHANGS ▸ **whang**

WHAP = **whop**

WHAPPED ▸ **whap**

WHAPPER = **whopper**

WHAPS ▸ **whap**

WHARE *n* Māori hut or dwelling place **whares**

WHARF *n, vb* **wharfed**

WHARFIE *n* person employed to load and unload ships

WHARFS ▸ **wharf**

WHARVE *n* wooden disc or wheel on a shaft serving as a flywheel or pulley **wharves**

WHAT *pron, interj, adv, n*

WHATA *n* building on stilts or a raised platform for storing provisions **whatas**

WHATEN *adj* what; what kind of **whatna**

WHATNOT *n* similar unspecified thing

WHATS ▸ **what**

WHATSIS *US form of* ▸ **whatsit**

WHATSIT *n* person or thing the name of which is temporarily forgotten

WHATSO n of whatever kind

WHATTEN = **whaten**

WHAUP n curlew **whaups**

WHAUR Scot word for ▸ **where**

WHAURS ▸ **whaur**

WHEAL = **weal**

WHEALS ▸ **wheal**

WHEAR obsolete variant of ▸ **where**

WHEARE obsolete variant of ▸ **where**

WHEAT n

WHEATEN n type of dog ▷ adj made of the grain or flour of wheat

WHEATS ▸ **wheat**

WHEATY adj having a wheat-like taste

WHEE interj exclamation of joy, thrill, etc

WHEECH vb move quickly **wheechs**

WHEEDLE vb

WHEEL n, vb

WHEELED adj having or equipped with a wheel or wheels

WHEELER n horse or other draught animal nearest the wheel

WHEELIE n manoeuvre on a bike in which the front wheel is raised off the ground

WHEELS ▸ **wheel**

WHEELY adj resembling a wheel

WHEEN n few

WHEENGE n Scots form of ▸ **whinge**

WHEENS ▸ **wheen**

WHEEP vb fly quickly and lightly **wheeped**

WHEEPLE vb whistle weakly

WHEEPS ▸ **wheep**

WHEESH vb silence (a person, noise, etc) or be silenced **wheesht**

WHEEZE vb, n **wheezed, wheezer, wheezes**

WHEEZLE vb make hoarse breathing sound

WHEEZY ▸ **wheeze**

WHEFT = **waft**

WHEFTS ▸ **wheft**

WHELK n

WHELKED adj having or covered with whelks

WHELKS ▸ **whelk**

WHELKY ▸ **whelk**

WHELM vb engulf entirely with or as if with water **whelmed, whelms**

WHELP n, vb **whelped, whelps**

WHEMMLE vb overturn

WHEN adv, pron, n

WHENAS conj while; inasmuch as

WHENCE n, adv, pron **whences**

WHENS ▸ **when**

WHENUA n land **whenuas**

WHENWE n White immigrant to South Africa from Zimbabwe **whenwes**

WHERE adv, pron, n

WHEREAS n

WHEREAT adv at or to which place

WHEREBY pron, adv

WHEREIN adv in what place or respect? ▷ pron in which place or thing

WHEREOF adv of what or which person or thing? ▷ pron of which person or thing

WHEREON adv on what thing or place? ▷ pron on which thing, place, etc

WHERES ▸ **where**

WHERESO adv in or to unspecified place

WHERETO adv towards what (place, end, etc)? ▷ pron which place

WHERRET vb strike (someone) a blow ▷ n blow, esp a slap on the face

WHERRIT vb worry or cause to worry

WHERRY n any of certain kinds of half-decked commercial boats ▷ vb travel in a wherry

WHERVE = **wharve**

WHERVES ▸ **wherve**

WHET vb, n

WHETHER conj

WHETS ▸ **whet**

WHETTED ▸ **whet**

WHETTER ▸ **whet**

WHEUGH = **whew**

WHEUGHS ▸ **wheugh**

WHEW interj exclamation expressing relief, delight, etc ▷ vb

express relief
whewed, whewing, whews

WHEY n **wheyey, wheyier, wheyish, wheys**

WHICH pron, adj

WHICKER vb (of a horse) to whinny or neigh

WHID vb move quickly

WHIDAH = whydah

WHIDAHS ▸ whidah

WHIDDED ▸ whid

WHIDDER vb move with force

WHIDS ▸ whid

WHIFF n, vb **whiffed, whiffer**

WHIFFET n insignificant person

WHIFFLE vb think or behave in an erratic or unpredictable way

WHIFFS ▸ whiff

WHIFFY adj smelly

WHIFT n brief emission of air **whifts**

WHIG vb go quickly **whigged, whigs**

WHILE n whiled

WHILERE adv a while ago

WHILES adv at times

WHILING ▸ while

WHILK archaic and dialect word for ▸ **which**

WHILLY vb influence by flattery

WHILOM adv formerly ▸ adj one-time

WHILST = while

WHIM n, vb whimmed

WHIMMY adj having whims

WHIMPER vb, n

WHIMPLE = wimple

WHIMS ▸ whim

WHIMSEY = whimsy

WHIMSY n, adj

WHIN n gorse

WHINE n, vb **whined, whiner, whiners, whines**

WHINEY = whiny

WHINGE vb **whinged, whinger, whinges**

WHINGY adj complaining peevishly, whining

WHINIER ▸ whiny

WHINING ▸ whine

WHINNY vb, n, adj

WHINS ▸ whin

WHINY adj high-pitched and plaintive

WHIO n New Zealand mountain duck with blue plumage **whios**

WHIP n, vb

WHIPCAT n tailor

WHIPPED ▸ whip

WHIPPER ▸ whip

WHIPPET n

WHIPPY adj springy

WHIPRAY n stingray

WHIPS ▸ whip

WHIPSAW n any saw with a flexible blade, such as a bandsaw ▸ vb saw with a whipsaw

WHIPT old past tense of ▸ whip

WHIR n prolonged soft swish or buzz ▸ vb make or cause to make a whir

WHIRL vb, n whirled, whirler, whirls

WHIRLY adj characterized by whirling

WHIRR = whir

WHIRRED ▸ whir

WHIRRET vb strike with sharp blow

WHIRRS ▸ whirr

WHIRRY vb move quickly

WHIRS ▸ whir

WHIRTLE = wortle

WHISH less common word for ▸ swish

WHISHED ▸ whish

WHISHES ▸ whish

WHISHT interj hush! be quiet! ▸ adj silent or still ▸ vb make or become silent **whishts**

WHISK vb, n whisked

WHISKER n

WHISKET = wisket

WHISKEY n Irish or American whisky

WHISKS ▸ whisk

WHISKY n

WHISPER vb, n

WHISS vb hiss whissed, whisses

WHIST = whisht

WHISTED ▸ whist

WHISTLE vb, n

WHISTS ▸ whist

WHIT n

WHITE adj, n

WHITED adj as in whited sepulchre hypocrite

WHITELY adv

WHITEN vb whitens

WHITER ▸ white

WHITES pl n white clothes, as worn for playing cricket

WHITEST ▶ white

WHITHER = wuther

WHITING n

WHITISH ▶ white

WHITLOW n inflamed sore on a finger or toe, esp round a nail

WHITRET n variant of > whittret

WHITS ▶ whit

WHITTAW = whittawer

WHITTER variant spelling of ▶ witter

WHITTLE vb, n

WHIZ ▶ whizz

WHIZZ vb, n whizzed, whizzer, whizzes

WHIZZO ▶ whizzy

WHIZZY adj using sophisticated technology

WHO pron

WHOA interj

WHOEVER pron

WHOLE adj, n wholes

WHOLISM = holism

WHOLIST = holist

WHOLLY adv

WHOM pron

WHOMBLE = whemmle

WHOMMLE = whemmle

WHOMP vb strike; thump whomped, whomps

WHOMSO pron whom; whomever

WHOOBUB = hubbub

WHOOF ▶ woof

WHOOFED ▶ whoof

WHOOFS ▶ whoof

WHOOP n, vb whooped

WHOOPEE n

WHOOPER n type of swan

WHOOPIE = whoopee

WHOOPLA n commotion; fuss

WHOOPS interj exclamation of surprise or of apology

WHOOSH n hissing or rushing sound ▷ vb make or move with a hissing or rushing sound

WHOOSIS n thingamajig

WHOOT obsolete variant of ▶ hoot

WHOOTED ▶ whoot

WHOOTS ▶ whoot

WHOP vb strike, beat, or thrash ▷ n heavy blow or the sound made by such a blow whopped

WHOPPER n

WHOPS ▶ whop

WHORE n, vb whored, whores, whoring, whorish

WHORL n whorled, whorls

WHORT n small shrub bearing blackish edible sweet berries

WHORTLE n whortleberry

WHORTS ▶ whort

WHOSE pron, determiner

WHOSIS n thingamajig

WHOSO archaic word for ▶ whoever

WHOT obsolete variant of ▶ hot

WHOW interj wow

WHUMMLE vb variant of ▶ whemmle

WHUMP vb make a dull thud ▷ n dull thud whumped, whumps

WHUP vb defeat totally whupped, whups

WHY adv, pron, n

WHYDAH n type of black African bird whydahs

WHYEVER adv for whatever reason

WHYS ▶ why

WIBBLE vb wobble wibbled, wibbles

WICCA n cult or practice of witchcraft

WICCAN n member of wicca wiccans

WICCAS ▶ wicca

WICE Scots form of ▶ wise

WICH n variant of wych wiches

WICK n, adj, vb

WICKAPE = wicopy

WICKED adj, n wickeds

WICKEN = quicken

WICKENS ▶ wicken

WICKER adj, n wickers

WICKET n wickets

WICKIES ▶ wicky

WICKING ▶ wick

WICKIUP n crude shelter made of brushwood, mats, or grass and having an oval frame

WICKS ▶ wick

WICKY = quicken

WICKYUP = wickiup

WICOPY n any of various North American trees, shrubs, or herbaceous plants

WIDDER = widow

WIDDERS ▶ widder

WIDDIE = widdy

WIDDIES ▶ widdy

WIDDLE vb urinate ▷ n urine **widdled, widdles**

WIDDY vb rope made of twigs

WIDE adj large from side to side ▷ adv the full extent ▷ n (in cricket) a ball outside a batsman's reach **widely**

WIDEN vb widened, widener, widens

WIDEOUT n footballer who catches passes from the quarterback

WIDER ▶ wide

WIDES ▶ wide

WIDEST ▶ wide

WIDGEON = wigeon

WIDGET n any small device, the name of which is unknown or forgotten **widgets**

WIDGIE n female larrikin or bodgie **widgies**

WIDISH ▶ wide

WIDOW n, vb widowed

WIDOWER n

WIDOWS ▶ widow

WIDTH n widths

WIEL = weel

WIELD vb wielded, wielder, wields

WIELDY adj easily handled, used, or managed

WIELS ▶ wiel

WIENER n kind of smoked beef or pork sausage, similar to a frankfurter **wieners, wienie**

WIENIES ▶ wienie

WIFE n, vb wifed

WIFEDOM n state of being a wife

WIFELY ▶ wife

WIFES ▶ wife

WIFEY n wife **wifeys**

WIFIE n woman **wifies**

WIFING ▶ wife

WIFTIER ▶ wifty

WIFTY adj scatterbrained

WIG n, vb

WIGAN n stiff fabric **wigans**

WIGEON n duck found in marshland **wigeons**

WIGGED ▶ wig

WIGGERY n wigs

WIGGIER ▶ wiggy

WIGGING ▶ wig

WIGGLE vb, n wiggled, wiggler, wiggles, wiggly

WIGGY adj eccentric

WIGHT vb blame ▷ n human being ▷ adj strong and brave **wighted**

WIGHTLY adv swiftly

WIGHTS ▶ wight

WIGLESS ▶ wig

WIGLET n small wig **wiglets**

WIGLIKE ▶ wig

WIGS ▶ wig

WIGWAG vb move (something) back and forth ▷ n system of communication by flag semaphore **wigwags**

WIGWAM n wigwams

WIKI n wikis

WIKIUP = wickiup

WIKIUPS ▶ wikiup

WILCO interj expression indicating that the message just received will be complied with

WILD = wield

WILDCAT n, adj, vb

WILDED ▶ wild

WILDER vb lead or be led astray **wilders**

WILDEST ▶ wild

WILDING n uncultivated plant

WILDISH ▶ wild

WILDLY ▶ wild

WILDS ▶ wild

WILE n trickery, cunning, or craftiness ▷ vb lure, beguile, or entice **wiled**

WILEFUL adj deceitful

WILES ▶ wile

WILFUL adj

WILGA n small drought-resistant tree of Australia **wilgas**

WILI n spirit

WILIER ▶ wily

WILIEST ▶ wily

WILILY ▶ wily

WILING ▶ wile

WILIS ▶ wili

WILJA = wiltja

WILJAS ▶ wilja

WILL vb, n

WILLED adj having a will as specified
WILLER ▸ will
WILLERS ▸ will
WILLEST ▸ will
WILLET n large American shore bird willets
WILLEY = willy
WILLEYS ▸ willey
WILLFUL = wilful
WILLIAM n as in sweet william flowering plant
WILLIE n informal word for a penis
WILLIED ▸ willy
WILLIES ▸ willy
WILLING adj
WILLOW n, vb willows
WILLOWY adj
WILLS ▸ will
WILLY vb clean in willowing-machine
WILT vb, n wilted, wilting
WILTJA n Aboriginal shelter wiltjas
WILTS ▸ wilt
WILY adj
WIMBLE n any of a number of hand tools used for boring holes ▸ vb bore (a hole) with or as if with a wimble wimbled, wimbles
WIMBREL = whimbrel
WIMMIN n common intentional literary misspelling of 'women'
WIMP n, vb as in wimp out; wimped, wimpier, wimping, wimpish

WIMPLE n, vb wimpled, wimples
WIMPS ▸ wimp
WIMPY ▸ wimp
WIN vb, n
WINCE vb, n winced, wincer, wincers, winces
WINCEY n plain- or twill-weave cloth winceys
WINCH n, vb winched, wincher, winches
WINCING ▸ wince
WIND n, vb
WINDAC = windas
WINDACS ▸ windac
WINDAGE n deflection of a projectile as a result of the effect of the wind
WINDAS n windlass
WINDBAG n
WINDED ▸ wind
WINDER n person or device that winds, as an engine for hoisting the cages in a mine shaft winders
WINDGUN n air gun
WINDIER ▸ windy
WINDIGO = wendigo
WINDILY ▸ windy
WINDING ▸ wind
WINDLE vb wind something round continuously windled, windles
WINDOCK = winnock
WINDORE n window
WINDOW n, vb windows, windowy
WINDROW n long low ridge or line of hay or a

similar crop ▸ vb put (hay or a similar crop) into windrows
WINDS ▸ wind
WINDSES pl n ventilation shafts within mines
WINDUP n prank or hoax windups
WINDWAY n part of a wind instrument
WINDY adj
WINE n, adj, vb wined
WINERY n place where wine is made
WINES ▸ wine
WINESAP n variety of apple
WINESOP n old word for an alcoholic
WINEY adj having the taste or qualities of wine
WING n, vb
WINGBOW n distinctive band of colour marking the wing of a bird
WINGE = whinge
WINGED adj furnished with wings
WINGER n wingers
WINGES ▸ winge
WINGIER ▸ wingy
WINGING ▸ wing
WINGLET n small wing
WINGMAN n player in the wing position in Australian Rules wingmen
WINGS ▸ wing
WINGTIP n outermost edge of a wing
WINGY adj having wings

WINIER ▶ winy

WINIEST ▶ winy

WINING ▶ wine

WINISH ▶ wine

WINK vb, n **winked**

WINKER n person or thing that winks **winkers**

WINKING ▶ wink

WINKLE n, vb **winkled**

WINKLER n one who forces person or thing out

WINKLES ▶ winkle

WINKS ▶ wink

WINLESS adj not having won anything

WINN n penny

WINNA vb will not

WINNARD n heron

WINNED ▶ win

WINNER n **winners**

WINNING adj

WINNLE = windle

WINNLES ▶ winnle

WINNOCK n window

WINNOW vb, n **winnows**

WINNS ▶ winn

WINO n **winoes, winos**

WINS ▶ win

WINSEY n **wincey**

WINSEYS ▶ winsey

WINSOME adj

WINTER n, vb **winters**

WINTERY ▶ **wintry**

WINTLE vb reel; stagger **wintled, wintles**

WINTRY adj

WINY ▶ **winey**

WINZE n steeply inclined shaft, as for ventilation between levels **winzes**

WIPE vb, n **wiped**

WIPEOUT n instance of wiping out

WIPER n any piece of cloth, such as a handkerchief, towel, etc, used for wiping **wipers**

WIPES ▶ wipe

WIPING ▶ wipe

WIPINGS ▶ wipe

WIPPEN n part of hammer action in piano **wippens**

WIRABLE adj that can be wired

WIRE n, vb

WIRED adj excited or nervous

WIREMAN n person who installs and maintains electric wiring, cables, etc **wiremen**

WIRER n person who sets or uses wires to snare rabbits and similar animals **wirers**

WIRES ▶ wire

WIRETAP vb obtain information secretly via telegraph or telephone

WIREWAY n tube for electric wires

WIRIER ▶ wiry

WIRIEST ▶ wiry

WIRILDA n SE Australian acacia tree with edible seeds

WIRILY ▶ wiry

WIRING n, adj **wirings**

WIRRA interj exclamation of sorrow or deep concern

WIRRAH n Australian saltwater fish with bright blue spots **wirrahs**

WIRY adj

WIS vb know or suppose (something)

WISARD obsolete spelling of ▶ **wizard**

WISARDS ▶ wisard

WISDOM n **wisdoms**

WISE vb, adj, n

WISEASS n person who thinks he or she is being witty or clever

WISED ▶ wise

WISEGUY n person who wants to seem clever

WISELY ▶ wise

WISENT n European bison **wisents**

WISER ▶ wise

WISES ▶ wise

WISEST ▶ wise

WISH vb, n

WISHA interj expression of surprise

WISHED, wisher, wishers, wishes ▶ **wish**

WISHFUL adj too optimistic

WISHING ▶ wish

WISHT variant of ▶ **whisht**

WISING ▶ wise

WISKET n basket **wiskets**

WISP n, vb **wisped**

WISPIER ▶ wispy

WISPILY ▶ wispy

WISPING ▶ wisp

WISPISH ▶ wisp

WISPS ▶ wisp

WISPY adj thin, fine, or delicate

WISS vb urinate

WISSED ▶ wis

WISSES ▶ wis

WISSING ▶ wis

WIST vb know wisted

WISTFUL adj

WISTING ▶ wist

WISTITI n marmoset

WISTLY adv intently

WISTS ▶ wist

WIT vb, n

WITAN n Anglo-Saxon assembly that met to counsel the king witans

WITCH n, vb, adj

WITCHEN n rowan tree

WITCHES ▶ witch

WITCHY adj like a witch

WITE vb blame wited, wites

WITGAT n type of S African tree witgats

WITH prep, n

WITHAL adv as well

WITHE n strong flexible twig suitable for binding things together ▷ vb bind with withes withed

WITHER vb

WITHERS pl n ridge between a horse's shoulder blades

WITHES ▶ withe

WITHIER ▶ withy

WITHIES ▶ withy

WITHIN adv, prep, n

WITHING ▶ withe

WITHINS ▶ within

WITHOUT prep, adv, n

WITHS ▶ with

WITHY n willow tree, esp an osier ▷ adj (of people) tough and agile

WITING ▶ wite

WITLESS adj

WITLING n person who thinks himself witty

WITLOOF n chicory

WITNESS n, vb

WITNEY n type of blanket; heavy cloth witneys

WITS ▶ wit

WITTED adj having wit

WITTER vb, n witters

WITTIER ▶ witty

WITTILY ▶ witty

WITTING adj deliberate

WITTOL n man who tolerates his wife's unfaithfulness wittols

WITTY adj

WITWALL n golden oriole

WIVE vb marry (a woman) wived

WIVER another word for ▶ wivern

WIVERN = wyvern

WIVERNS ▶ wivern

WIVERS ▶ wiver

WIVES ▶ wife

WIVING ▶ wive

WIZ shortened form of ▶ wizard

> Wiz is a short form of wizard. This is the highest-scoring three-letter word beginning with W, and can be especially useful when there isn't much room to manoeuvre.

WIZARD n, adj wizards

WIZEN vb make or become shrivelled ▷ n archaic word for 'weasand' (the gullet)

WIZENED adj

WIZENS ▶ wizen

WIZES ▶ wiz

WIZIER = vizier

WIZIERS ▶ wizier

WIZZEN = wizen

WIZZENS ▶ wizen

WIZZES ▶ wiz

WO archaic spelling of ▶ woe

WOAD n

WOADED adj coloured blue with woad

WOADS ▶ woad

WOADWAX n small Eurasian leguminous shrub

WOALD = weld

WOALDS ▶ woald

WOBBLE vb, n wobbled, wobbler, wobbles

WOBBLY adj, n

WOCK = wok

WOCKS ▶ wock

WODGE n wodges

WOE n

WOEFUL adj

WOENESS ▶ woe

WOES ▶ woe

WOESOME adj woeful

WOF n fool wofs

WOFUL = woeful

WOFULLY ▶ woful

WOGGLE n ring of leather through which a Scout neckerchief is threaded woggles

WOIWODE = voivode

WOK n

WOKE ▶ wake

WOKEN ▸ wake
WOKKA modifier as in **wokka board** a piece of fibreboard used as a musical instrument
WOKS ▸ wok
WOLD ▸ weld
WOLDS ▸ wold
WOLF n, vb **wolfed**
WOLFER = wolver
WOLFERS ▸ wolfer
WOLFING ▸ wolf
WOLFISH ▸ wolf
WOLFKIN n young wolf
WOLFRAM another name for ▸ **tungsten**
WOLFS ▸ wolf
WOLLIES ▸ wolly
WOLLY n pickled cucumber or olive
WOLVE vb hunt for wolves **wolved**
WOLVER n person who hunts wolves **wolvers**
WOLVES ▸ wolf
WOLVING ▸ wolve
WOLVISH = wolfish
WOMAN n, adj, vb **womaned**
WOMANLY adj
WOMANS ▸ woman
WOMB vb, n
WOMBAT n **wombats**
WOMBED ▸ womb
WOMBIER ▸ womby
WOMBING ▸ womb
WOMBS ▸ womb
WOMBY adj hollow; spacious
WOMEN ▸ woman
WOMERA = woomera
WOMERAS ▸ womera
WOMMERA = woomera

WOMMIT n foolish person **wommits**
WOMYN ▸ woman
WON n standard monetary unit of North Korea ▸ vb live or dwell
WONDER vb, n, adj **wonders**
WONDRED adj splendid
WONGA n money **wongas**
WONGI vb talk informally **wongied, wongis**
WONING ▸ won
WONINGS ▸ won
WONK n person who is obsessively interested in a specified subject
WONKIER ▸ wonky
WONKS ▸ wonk
WONKY adj
WONNED, wonner, wonners, wonning, wons ▸ won
WONT adj, n, vb
WONTED adj accustomed or habituated (to doing something)
WONTING ▸ wont
WONTON n dumpling filled with spiced minced pork **wontons**
WONTS ▸ wont
WOO vb
WOOBUT = woubit
WOOBUTS ▸ woobut
WOOD n, adj, vb
WOODBIN n box for firewood
WOODBOX n box for firewood

WOODCUT n
WOODED adj
WOODEN adj, vb **woodens**
WOODHEN another name for ▸ **weka**
WOODIE n gallows rope
WOODIER ▸ woody
WOODIES ▸ woodie
WOODING ▸ wood
WOODLOT n area restricted to the growing of trees
WOODMAN = woodsman
WOODMEN ▸ woodman
WOODRAT n pack-rat
WOODS pl n closely packed trees forming a forest or wood
WOODSIA n type of small fern with tufted rhizomes and wiry fronds
WOODSY adj of, reminiscent of, or connected with woods
WOODWAX = woodwaxen
WOODY adj
WOOED ▸ woo
WOOER ▸ woo
WOOERS ▸ woo
WOOF vb **woofed**
WOOFER n loudspeaker reproducing low-frequency sounds **woofers**
WOOFIER ▸ woofy
WOOFING ▸ woof
WOOFS ▸ woof
WOOFY adj with close, dense texture

WOOHOO interj

WOOING ▸ woo

WOOINGS ▸ woo

WOOL n

WOOLD vb wind (rope) **woolded**

WOOLDER n stick for winding rope

WOOLDS ▸ woold

WOOLED = woolled

WOOLEN = woollen

WOOLENS ▸ woolen

WOOLER = woolder

WOOLERS ▸ wooler

WOOLFAT = lanolin

WOOLHAT n poor white person in S States

WOOLIE n wool garment

WOOLIER ▸ wooly

WOOLIES ▸ wooly

WOOLLED adj (of animals) having wool

WOOLLEN adj, n

WOOLLY adj, n

WOOLMAN n wool trader **woolmen**

WOOLS ▸ wool

WOOLSEY n cotton and wool blend

WOOLY = woolly

WOOMERA = woomera

WOON = won

WOONED ▸ woon

WOONING ▸ woon

WOONS ▸ woon

WOOPIE n well-off older person **woopies**

WOOPS vb (esp of small child) vomit **woopsed, woopses**

WOORALI less common name for ▸ curare

WOORARA = wourali

WOORARI = wourali

WOOS ▸ woo

WOOSE = wuss

WOOSEL = ouzel

WOOSELL = ouzel

WOOSELS ▸ woosel

WOOSES ▸ woose

WOOSH = whoosh

WOOSHED ▸ woosh

WOOSHES ▸ woosh

WOOT vb wilt thou?

WOOTZ n Middle-Eastern steel **wootzes**

WOOZIER ▸ woozy

WOOZILY ▸ woozy

WOOZY adj

WORD n smallest single meaningful unit of speech or writing ▸ vb express in words

WORDAGE n words considered collectively, esp a quantity of words

WORDED ▸ word

WORDIER ▸ wordy

WORDILY ▸ wordy

WORDING n

WORDISH adj talkative

WORDS ▸ word

WORDY adj

WORE ▸ wear

WORK n, adj, vb

WORKBAG n container for implements, tools, or materials **workbox**

WORKDAY another word for ▸ workaday

WORKED adj made or decorated with evidence of workmanship

WORKER n **workers**

WORKFUL adj hardworking

WORKING n, adj

WORKMAN n **workmen**

WORKOUT n

WORKS ▸ work

WORKSHY adj

WORKTOP n surface used for food preparation

WORKUP n medical examination **workups**

WORLD n, adj

WORLDED adj incorporating worlds

WORLDLY adj, adv

WORLDS ▸ world

WORM n, vb **wormed, wormer, wormers**

WORMERY n piece of apparatus in which worms are kept for study

WORMFLY n type of lure dressed on a double hook

WORMIER ▸ wormy

WORMIL n burrowing larva of type of fly **wormils**

WORMING ▸ worm

WORMISH ▸ worm

WORMS n disease caused by parasitic worms living in the intestines

WORMY adj infested with or eaten by worms

WORN ▸ wear

WORRAL n type of lizard **worrals, worrel**

WORRELS ▸ worrel

WORRIED ▸ worry

WORRIER ▶ worry

WORRIES ▶ worry

WORRIT *vb* tease or worry **worrits**

WORRY *vb, n*

WORSE *vb* worsed

WORSEN *vb* worsens

WORSER *archaic or nonstandard word for* ▶ worse

WORSES ▶ worse

WORSET *n* worsted fabric **worsets**

WORSHIP *vb, n*

WORSING ▶ worse

WORST *n, vb*

WORSTED *n*

WORSTS ▶ worst

WORT *n* any of various plants formerly used to cure diseases

WORTH *prep, n, vb* worthed, worths

WORTHY *adj, vb, n*

WORTLE *n* plate with holes for drawing wire through **wortles**

WORTS ▶ wort

WOS ▶ wo

WOSBIRD *n* illegitimate child

WOST *vb* wit, to know

WOT *vb* wit, to know

WOTCHA ▶ wotcher

WOTCHER *sentence substitute* slang term of greeting

WOTS, wotted, wottest, wotteth, wotting ▶ wot

WOUBIT *n* type of caterpillar **woubits**

WOULD ▶ will

WOULDS = wouldst

WOULDST *singular form of the past tense of* ▶ will

WOUND *vb, n*

WOUNDED *adj* suffering from wounds

WOUNDER ▶ wound

WOUNDS ▶ wound

WOUNDY *adj* extreme

WOURALI *n* plant from which curare is obtained

WOVE ▶ weave

WOVEN *n* article made from woven cloth **wovens**

WOW *interj, n, vb* wowed, wowee

WOWF *adj* mad wowfer, wowfest

This is a Scots word meaning crazy: you are not likely to get the chance to play this very often but if your opponent plays **wow** and you have an F you would be wowf to miss the opportunity of the hook!

WOWING ▶ wow

WOWS ▶ wow

WOWSER *n* puritanical person **wowsers**

WOX ▶ wax

Wox is an old past tense of the verb wax, to grow, and is another of the key words using X.

WOXEN ▶ wax

WRACK *vb* seaweed ▷ *vb* strain or shake

(something) violently **wracked**, **wracks**

WRAITH *n* **wraiths**

WRANG *Scot word for* ▶ wrong

WRANGED ▶ wrang

WRANGLE *vb, n*

WRANGS ▶ wrang

WRAP *vb, n* wrapped

WRAPPER *vb, n*

WRAPS ▶ wrap

WRAPT = rapt

WRASSE *n* colourful sea fish **wrasses**

WRASSLE = wrestle

WRAST = wrest

WRASTED ▶ wrast

WRASTLE = wrestle

WRASTS ▶ wrast

WRATE ▶ write

WRATH *n, adj, vb* wrathed, wraths

WRATHY = wrathful

WRAWL *vb* howl wrawled, wrawls

WRAXLE *vb* wrestle wraxled, wraxles

WREAK *vb* wreaked, wreaker, wreaks

WREATH *n*

WREATHE *vb*

WREATHS ▶ wreath

WREATHY *adj* twisted into wreath

WRECK *vb, n*

WRECKED *adj* in a state of intoxication induced by drugs or alcohol

WRECKER *n* formerly, person who lured ships onto the rocks in order to plunder them

WRECKS ▶ wreck

WREN *n*

WRENCH vb, n

WRENS ▶ wren

WREST vb, n **wrested**, **wrester**

WRESTLE vb, n

WRESTS ▶ wrest

WRETCH n

WRETHE = wreathe

WRETHED ▶ wrethe

WRETHES ▶ wrethe

WRICK variant spelling (chiefly Brit) of ▶ **rick**

WRICKED ▶ wrick

WRICKS ▶ wrick

WRIED, **wrier**, **wries**, **wriest** ▶ wry

WRIGGLE vb, n **wriggly**

WRIGHT n maker **wrights**

WRING vb **wringed**

WRINGER = mangle

WRINGS ▶ wring

WRINKLE n, vb **wrinkly**

WRIST n **wrists**

WRISTY adj characterized by considerable movement of the wrist

WRIT n

WRITE vb

WRITER n **writers**

WRITES ▶ write

WRITHE vb, n **writhed**

WRITHEN adj twisted

WRITHER ▶ writhe

WRITHES ▶ writhe

WRITING ▶ write

WRITS ▶ writ

WRITTEN ▶ write

WRIZLED adj wrinkled

WROATH n unforeseen trouble **wroaths**

WROKE ▶ wreak

WROKEN ▶ wreak

WRONG adj, adv, n, vb **wronged**, **wronger**, **wrongly**, **wrongs**

WROOT obsolete form of ▶ **root**

WROOTED ▶ wroot

WROOTS ▶ wroot

WROTE ▶ write

WROTH adj angry

WROUGHT adj

WRUNG ▶ wring

WRY adj, vb

WRYBILL n New Zealand plover whose bill is bent to one side

WRYER, **wryest**, **wrying**, **wryly** ▶ wry

WRYNECK n woodpecker that has a habit of twisting its neck round

WRYNESS ▶ wry

WRYTHEN adj twisted

WUD Scots form of ▶ **wood**

> W and U are a horrible combination to have on your rack, so this Scots word for wood can be a godsend. And remember that it can also be a verb, meaning to load with wood, so you have **wuds**, **wudding** and **wudded**

WUDDED ▶ wud

WUDDING ▶ wud

WUDJULA n Australian word for a non-Aboriginal person

WUDS ▶ wud

WUDU n practice of ritual washing before daily prayer **wudus**

WULL obsolete form of ▶ **will**

WULLED ▶ will

WULLING ▶ will

WULLS ▶ will

WUNNER = oner

WUNNERS ▶ wunner

WURLEY n Aboriginal hut **wurleys**, **wurlie**

WURLIES ▶ wurlie

WURST n large sausage, esp of a type made in Germany, Austria, etc **wursts**

WURZEL n root **wurzels**

WUS n casual term of address **wuses**

WUSHU n Chinese martial arts **wushus**

WUSS n feeble or effeminate person **wusses**

WUSSIER ▶ wussy

WUSSIES ▶ wussy

WUSSY adj feeble or effeminate ▷ n feeble person

WUTHER vb (of wind) blow and roar **wuthers**

WUXIA n Chinese fiction concerning the adventures of sword-wielding heroes **wuxias**

> This Chinese word for a genre of fiction may get you a decent score from a very difficult-looking rack.

WUZZLE *vb* mix up **wuzzled, wuzzles**

WYCH *n* type of tree having flexible branches **wyches**

WYE *n* y-shaped pipe **wyes**

If you have W and Y on your rack, look for an E on the board

that will allow you to play this name for the letter Y, especially if you can land on a bonus square as a result.

WYLE *vb* entice **wyled, wyles, wyling**

WYN *n* rune equivalent to English 'w'

WYND *n* narrow lane or alley **wynds**

WYNN = wyn

WYNNS ▶ wynn

WYNS ▶ wyn

WYTE *vb* blame **wyted, wytes, wyting**

WYVERN *n* heraldic beast **wyverns**

Xx

Worth 8 points on its own, **X** is one of the best tiles in the game. It doesn't, however, start many two- and three-letter words. There are only two valid two-letter words, **xi** and **xu** (9 points each) beginning with **X**, and only one three-letter word, **xis**. Therefore, if you have an **X** on your rack and need to play short words, you're probably better off thinking of words that end in **X** or have **X** in them rather than those that start with **X**. Particularly good to remember are **zax**, **zex** (19 points each) and **kex** (14 points).

XANTHAM *n* acacia gum **xanthan**

XANTHIC *adj* of, containing, or derived from xanthic acid

XANTHIN *n* any of a group of yellow or orange carotene derivatives

XEBEC *n* small three-masted Mediterranean vessel with both square and lateen sails, formerly used by Algerian pirates and later used for commerce **xebecs**

A kind of small boat, and a good high-scoring word that can easily be missed, as we tend to be slow to consider words beginning with X.

XENIA *n* influence of pollen upon the form of the fruit developing after pollination **xenial, xenias**

XENIC *adj* denoting the presence of bacteria

XENIUM *n* diplomatic gift

XENON *n* **xenons**

XENOPUS *n* African frog

XERAFIN *n* Indian coin

XERARCH *adj* (of a sere) having its origin in a dry habitat

XERASIA *n* dryness of the hair

XERIC *adj* of, relating to, or growing in dry conditions

XEROMA *n* excessive dryness of the cornea **xeromas**

XEROSES ▶ **xerosis**

XEROSIS *n* abnormal dryness of bodily tissues, esp the skin, eyes, or mucous membranes **xerotes, xerotic**

XEROX *n* tradename for a machine employing a xerographic copying process ▷ *vb* produce a copy (of a document, etc) using such a machine **xeroxed, xeroxes**

XERUS *n* ground squirrel **xeruses**

XI *n* 14th letter in the Greek alphabet

XIPHOID *adj* shaped like a sword ▷ *n* part of the sternum

XIS ▸ xi

XOANA ▸ xoanon

XOANON *n* primitive image of a god supposed to have fallen from heaven

> One of the few words starting with X. But be careful: the plural is **xoana** not **xoanons**.

XRAY *n* code word for the letter X **xrays**

XU *n* Vietnamese currency unit

XYLAN *n* yellow polysaccharide consisting of xylose units **xylans**

XYLEM *n* xylems

XYLENE *n* type of hydrocarbon **xylenes**

XYLENOL *n* synthetic resin made from xylene

XYLIC ▸ xylem

XYLIDIN = xylidine

XYLITOL *n* crystalline alcohol used as sweetener

XYLOGEN = xylem

XYLOID *adj* of, relating to, or resembling wood

XYLOL another name (not in technical usage) for ▸ **xylene**

XYLOLS ▸ xylol

XYLOMA *n* hard growth in fungi **xylomas**

XYLONIC *adj* denoting an acid formed from xylose

XYLOSE *n* white crystalline sugar found in wood and straw **xyloses**

XYLYL *n* group of atoms **xylyls**

XYST *n* long portico, esp one used in ancient Greece for athletics

> A kind of court used by ancient Greek athletes for exercises, this is a lovely high-scoring word to play. And if your opponent plays it, you can put an I on it to make **xysti**, as well as an S to make **xysts**.

XYSTER *n* surgical instrument for scraping bone **xysters**

XYSTI ▸ xystus

XYSTOI ▸ xystos

XYSTOS = xyst

XYSTS ▸ xyst

XYSTUS = xyst

Yy

Y can be a useful tile to have on your rack, particularly if you are short of vowels, but it can make it difficult to find bonus words scoring that extra 50 points, and you will normally want to play it off as soon as a good score offers itself. There are only four two-letter words beginning with **Y**, but these are easy to remember as there's one for every vowel except **I: ya, ye, yo** and **yu** (5 points each). There are quite a few useful three-letter words: **yew** (9) and **yob** (8) and remember that **yob** was originally **boy** backwards: if you can't fit in **yob**, you may be able to use **boy** instead. And while his half-brother the **zo** (or **dzo** or **dso** or **zho**) gets all the attention, don't forget that the **yak** (10) earns quite a decent score!

YA *pron* you

YAAR *n* in informal Indian English, a friend **yaars**

YABA *n* informal word for 'yet another bloody acronym' **yabas**

YABBA *n* form of methamphetamine **yabbas**

YABBER *vb* talk or jabber ▷ *n* talk or jabber **yabbers**

YABBIE = yabby

YABBIED ▶ yabby

YABBIES ▶ yabby

YABBY *n, vb*

YACCA *n* Australian plant with a woody stem **yaccas**

YACHT *n, vb* yachted, yachter

YACHTIE *n* yachtsman

YACHTS ▶ yacht

YACK = yak

YACKA = yacca

YACKAS = yacca

YACKED ▶ yack

YACKER = yakka

YACKERS ▶ yacker

YACKING ▶ yack

YACKS ▶ yack

YAD *n* hand-held pointer used for reading the sefer torah **yads**

YAE = ae

YAFF *vb* bark **yaffed, yaffing**

YAFFLE *n* woodpecker with a green back and wings **yaffles**

YAFFS ▶ yaff

YAG *n* artificial crystal

YAGER = jaeger

YAGERS ▶ yager

YAGGER *n* pedlar **yaggers**

YAGI *n* type of highly directional aerial **yagis**

YAGS ▶ yag

YAH *interj* exclamation of derision or disgust ▷ *n* affected upper-class person

YAHOO *n* crude coarse person **yahoos**

YAHS ▶ yah

YAIRD *Scots form of* ▶ yard

YAIRDS ▸ yaird
YAK n, vb
YAKHDAN n box for carrying ice on a pack animal
YAKKA n yakkas
YAKKED ▸ yak
YAKKER = yakka
YAKKERS ▸ yakker
YAKKING ▸ yak
YAKOW n animal bred from a male yak and a domestic cow **yakows**
YAKS ▸ yak
YAKUZA n Japanese criminal organization
YALD adj vigorous
YALE n mythical beast with the body of an antelope (or similar animal) and swivelling horns **yales**
YAM n
YAMALKA = yarmulke
YAMEN n (in imperial China) the office or residence of a public official **yamens**
YAMMER vb whine in a complaining manner ▷ n yammering sound **yammers**
YAMPIES ▸ yampy
YAMPY n foolish person
YAMS ▸ yam
YAMULKA = yarmulke
YAMUN = yamen
YAMUNS ▸ yamun
YANG n (in Chinese philosophy) one of two complementary principles maintaining harmony in the universe **yangs**

YANK vb, n **yanked**
YANKEE n code word for the letter Y **yankees**
YANKER ▸ yank
YANKERS ▸ yank
YANKIE n shrewish woman **yankies**
YANKING ▸ yank
YANKS ▸ yank
YANQUI n slang word for American **yanquis**
YANTRA n diagram used in meditation **yantras**
YAOURT n yoghurt **yaourts**
YAP vb, n, interj
YAPOCK = yapok
YAPOCKS ▸ yapock
YAPOK n type of opossum **yapoks**
YAPON = yaupon
YAPONS ▸ yapon
YAPP n type of book binding
YAPPED ▸ yap
YAPPER ▸ yap
YAPPERS ▸ yap
YAPPIE n young aspiring professional
YAPPIER ▸ yap
YAPPIES ▸ yappie
YAPPING ▸ yap
YAPPS ▸ yapp
YAPPY ▸ yap
YAPS ▸ yap
YAPSTER ▸ yap
YAQONA n Polynesian shrub **yaqonas**
YAR adj nimble
YARD n, vb
YARDAGE n length measured in yards
YARDANG n ridge

formed by wind erosion
YARDARM n outer end of a ship's yard
YARDED ▸ yard
YARDER ▸ yard
YARDERS ▸ yard
YARDING n group of animals displayed for sale
YARDMAN n farm overseer **yardmen**
YARDS ▸ yard
YARE adj ready, brisk, or eager ▷ adv readily or eagerly **yarely, yarer, yarest**
YARFA n peat **yarfas**
YARK vb make ready **yarked, yarking, yarks**
YARN n, vb **yarned, yarner, yarners, yarning, yarns**
YARPHA n peat **yarphas**
YARR n wild white flower
YARRAN n type of small hardy tree of inland Australia **yarrans**
YARROW n wild plant with flat clusters of white flowers **yarrows**
YARRS ▸ yarr
YARTA Shetland word for ▸ heart
YARTAS ▸ yarta
YARTO = yarta
YARTOS ▸ yarto
YASHMAC = yashmak
YASHMAK n yasmak
YASMAKS ▸ yashmak
YATAGAN = yataghan

YATE n type of small eucalyptus tree yielding a very hard timber **yates**

YATTER vb talk at length ▷ n continuous chatter **yatters**

YAUD Scots word for ▶ **mare**

YAUDS ▶ **yaud**

YAULD adj alert, spritely, or nimble

YAUP variant spelling of ▶ **yawp**; **yauped, yauper, yaupers, yauping**

YAUPON n southern US evergreen holly shrub **yaupons**

YAUPS ▶ **yaup**

YAUTIA n Caribbean plant cultivated for its edible leaves and underground stems **yautias**

YAW vb, n ▶ **yawed**

YAWEY ▶ **yaws**

YAWING ▶ **yaw**

YAWL n two-masted sailing boat ▷ vb howl, weep, or scream harshly **yawled, yawling, yawls**

YAWN vb, n **yawned, yawner, yawners, yawnier, yawning, yawns, yawny**

YAWP vb gape or yawn, esp audibly ▷ n shout, bark, yelp, or cry **yawped, yawper, yawpers, yawping, yawps**

YAWS n **yawy**

YAY interj exclamation indicating approval or triumph ▷ n cry of approval **yays**

YBET archaic past participle of ▶ **beat**

YBLENT archaic past participle of ▶ **blend**

YBORE archaic past participle of ▶ **bear**

YBOUND archaic past participle of ▶ **bind**

YBRENT archaic past participle of ▶ **burn**

YCLAD archaic past participle of ▶ **clothe**

YCLED archaic past participle of ▶ **clothe**

YCLEEPE archaic form of ▶ **clepe**

YCLEPED = **yclept**

YCLEPT adj having the name of

YCOND archaic past participle of ▶ **con**

YDRAD archaic past participle of ▶ **dread**

YDRED archaic past participle of ▶ **dread**

YE pron, adj

YEA interj, adv, sentence substitute, n

YEAD vb proceed **yeading, yeads**

YEAH n **yeahs**

YEALDON n fuel

YEALING n person of the same age as oneself

YEALM vb prepare for thatching **yealmed, yealms**

YEAN vb (of a sheep or goat) to give birth to

(offspring) **yeaned yeaning, yeans**

YEAR n

YEARD vb bury **yearded, yeards**

YEAREND n end of year

YEARLY adv (happening) ever or once a year ▷ a occurring, done, appearing once a or every year ▷ n publication, ever that occurs once

YEARN vb **yearne yearner, yearns**

YEARS ▶ **year**

YEAS ▶ **yea**

YEAST n, vb **yeas yeasts**

YEASTY adj of, resembling, or containing yeas

YEBO interj yes ▷ sentence subst expression of affirmation

YECCH = **yech**

YECCHS ▶ **yecc**

YECH expressi disgust

YECHIER ▶ **yec**

YECHS ▶ **yech**

YECHY ▶ **yech**

YEDE = **yead**

YEDES ▶ **yede**

YEDING ▶ **yede**

YEED = **yead**

YEEDING ▶ **yee**

YEEDS ▶ **yeed**

YEELIN n pers same age as **yeelins**

YEGG n burglar or safe-breaker **yeggman**

YEGGMAN ▸ yegg

YEGGS ▸ yegg

YEH = yeah

YELD adj (of an animal) barren or too young to bear young

YELK n yolk of an egg **yelks**

YELL vb, n yelled, yeller, yellers, yelling

YELLOCH vb yell

YELLOW n, adj, vb

YELLOWS n any of various fungal or viral diseases of plants

YELLOWY ▸ yellow

YELLS ▸ yell

YELM ▸ yealm

YELMED ▸ yelm

YELMING ▸ yelm

YELMS ▸ yelm

YELP n, vb yelped, yelper, yelpers, yelping, yelps

YELT n young sow **yelts**

YMMER southwest English form of ▸ ember

YMMERS ▸ yemmer

YEN n, vb yenned, yenning, yens

YENTA n meddlesome woman **yentas, yente**

YENTES ▸ yente

YEOMAN n yeomen

YEP n affirmative statement **yeps**

YERBA n stimulating South American drink made from dried leaves **yerbas**

YERD vb bury **yerded, yerding, yerds**

YERK vb tighten stitches **yerked, yerking, yerks**

YES interj, n, sentence substitute, vb **yeses**

YESHIVA n traditional Jewish school

YESK vb hiccup **yesked, yesking, yesks**

YESSED ▸ yes

YESSES ▸ yes

YESSING ▸ yes

YEST archaic form of ▸ **yeast**

YESTER adj of or relating to yesterday **yestern**

YESTS ▸ yest

YESTY archaic form of ▸ **yeasty**

YET adv

YETI n yetis

YETT n gate or door

YETTIE n young, entrepreneurial, and technology-based (person) **yetties**

YETTS ▸ yett

YEUK vb itch **yeuked**

YEUKIER ▸ yeuky

YEUKING ▸ yeuk

YEUKS ▸ yeuk

YEUKY ▸ yeuk

YEVE vb give **yeven, yeves, yeving**

YEW n

YEWEN adj made of yew

YEWS ▸ yew

YEX vb hiccup **yexed, yexes, yexing**

> This word meaning to hiccup gives you a good score, and the verb forms offer the

chance to expand it if someone else plays it, or if you get the chance later on.

VFERE adv together

YGO archaic past participle of ▸ **go**

YGOE archaic past participle of ▸ **go**

YIBBLES adv perhaps

YICKER vb squeal or squeak **yickers**

YIDAKI n long wooden wind instrument played by the Aboriginal peoples of Arnhem Land **yidakis**

YIELD vb, n **yielded, yielder, yields**

YIKE n argument, squabble, or fight ▸ vb argue, squabble, or fight **yiked**

YIKES interj expression of surprise, fear, or alarm

YIKING ▸ yike

YIKKER vb squeal or squeak **yikkers**

YILL n ale **yills**

YIN Scots word for ▸ **one**

YINCE Scots form of ▸ **once**

YINDIE n person who combines a lucrative career with non-mainstream tastes **yindies**

YINS ▸ yin

YIP n emit a high-pitched bark

YIPE = yipes

YIPES interj expression of surprise, fear, or alarm

YIPPED ▸ yip

YIPPEE interj

YIPPER n golfer who suffers from a failure of nerve **yippers**

YIPPIE n young person sharing hippy ideals **yippies**

YIPPING ▸ yip

YIPPY = yippee

YIPS ▸ yip

YIRD vb bury **yirded, yirding, yirds**

YIRK = yerk

YIRKED ▸ yirk

YIRKING ▸ yirk

YIRKS ▸ yirk

YIRR vb snarl, growl, or yell **yirred, yirring, yirrs**

YIRTH n earth **yirths**

YITE n European bunting with a yellowish head and body and brown streaked wings and tail **yites, yitie**

YITIES ▸ yitie

YITTEN adj frightened

YLEM n original matter from which the basic elements are said to have been formed **ylems**

YLIKE Spenserian form of ▸ alike

YLKE archaic spelling of ▸ ilk

YLKES ▸ ylke

YMOLT Spenserian past participle of ▸ melt

YMOLTEN Spenserian past participle of ▸ melt

YMPE Spenserian form of ▸ imp

YMPES ▸ ympe

YMPING ▸ ympe

YMPT ▸ ympe

YNAMBU n South American bird **ynambus**

YO interj expression used as a greeting ▷ sentence substitute expression used as a greeting

YOB n

YOBBERY n behaviour typical of aggressive surly youths

YOBBISH adj typical of aggressive surly youths

YOBBISM ▸ yob

YOBBO = yob

YOBBOES ▸ yobbo

YOBBOS ▸ yobbo

YOBS ▸ yob

YOCK vb chuckle **yocked, yocking, yocks**

YOD n tenth letter in the Hebrew alphabet

YODE ▸ yead

YODEL vb, n **yodeled, yodeler, yodels**

YODH = yod

YODHS ▸ yodh

YODLE variant spelling of ▸ yodel; **yodled, yodler, yodlers, yodles, yodling**

YODS ▸ yod

YOGA n **yogas**

YOGEE = yogi

YOGEES ▸ yogee

YOGH n character used in Old and Middle English to represent a palatal fricative **yoghs**

YOGHURT = yogurt

YOGI n

YOGIC ▸ yoga

YOGIN = yogi

YOGINI ▸ yogi

YOGINS ▸ yogin

YOGIS ▸ yogi

YOGISM ▸ yogi

YOGISMS ▸ yogi

YOGURT n **yogurts**

YOHIMBE n bark used in herbal medicine

YOICK vb urge on foxhounds **yoicked**

YOICKS interj cry used by huntsmen to urge on the hounds ▷ vb urge on foxhounds

YOJAN n Indian unit of distance **yojana**

YOJANAS ▸ yojana

YOJANS ▸ yojan

YOK vb chuckle

> A useful short word meaning to laugh, with an alternative spelling **yuk**.

YOKE n, vb **yoked**

YOKER vb **yokered**

YOKERS, yokes, yoking, yokings ▸ yoke

YOKKED ▸ yok

YOKKING ▸ yok

YOKS ▸ yok

YOKUL Shetland word for ▸ yes

YOLD archaic past participle of ▸ yield

YOLK n yolked, yolkier, yolks, yolky

YOM n day yomim

YOMP vb walk or trek laboriously yomped, yomping, yomps

YON adj, adv, pron yond

YONDER adv, adj, determiner, n yonders

YONI n female genitalia, regarded as a divine symbol of sexual pleasure

YONIC adj resembling a vulva

YONIS ▶ yoni

YONKER = younker

YONKERS ▶ yonker

YONKS pl n very long time

YONNIE n stone yonnies

YONT ▶ yon

YOOF n non-standard spelling of youth yoofs

YOOP n sob yoops

YORE n, adv yores

YORK vb bowl or try to bowl (a batsman) by pitching the ball under or just beyond the bat yorked

YORKER n ball that pitches just under the bat yorkers

YORKIE n Yorkshire terrier yorkies

YORKING ▶ york

YORKS ▶ york

YORLING n as in yellow yorling yellowhammer

YORP vb shout yorped, yorping, yorps

YOU pron, n

YOUK vb itch youked, youking, youks

YOUNG adj in an early stage of life or growth ▷ n young people in general; offspring younger

YOUNGLY adv youthfully

YOUNGS ▶ young

YOUNGTH n youth

YOUNKER n young man

YOUPON = yaupon

YOUPONS ▶ youpon

YOUR adj

YOURN dialect form of ▶ yours

YOURS pron

YOURT = yurt

YOURTS ▶ yourt

YOUS pron refers to more than one person including the person or persons addressed but not the speaker youse

YOUTH n

YOUTHEN vb render more youthful-seeming

YOUTHLY adv young

YOUTHS ▶ youth

YOUTHY Scots word for ▶ young

YOW vb howl

YOWE Scot word for ▶ ewe

YOWED ▶ yow

YOWES ▶ yowe

YOWIE n legendary Australian apelike creature yowies

YOWING ▶ yow

YOWL n, vb yowled, yowler, yowlers

YOWLEY n yellowhammer (bird) yowleys

YOWLING ▶ yowl

YOWLS ▶ yowl

YOWS ▶ yow

YPERITE n mustard gas

YPIGHT archaic past participle of ▶ pitch

YPLAST archaic past participle of ▶ place

YPLIGHT archaic past participle of ▶ plight

YPSILON = upsilon

YRAPT Spenserian form of ▶ rapt

YRENT archaic past participle of ▶ rend

YRIVD archaic past participle of ▶ rive

YRNEH n unit of reciprocal inductance yrnehs

YSAME Spenserian word for > together

YSHEND Spenserian form of ▶ shend

YSHENDS ▶ yshend

YSHENT ▶ yshend

YSLAKED archaic past participle of ▶ slake

YTOST archaic past participle of ▶ toss

YTTRIA n insoluble solid used mainly in incandescent mantles yttrias

YTTRIC ▶ yttrium

YTTRIUM n silvery metallic element used in various alloys

YU n jade

YUAN n standard monetary unit of the

People's Republic of China **yuans**

YUCA = yucca

YUCAS ▶ yuca

YUCCA n yuccas

YUCCH interj expression of disgust

YUCH interj expression of disgust

YUCK interj exclamation indicating contempt, dislike, or disgust ▷ vb chuckle **yucked, yucker, yuckers**

YUCKIER ▶ yucky

YUCKING ▶ yuck

YUCKO adj disgusting ▷ interj exclamation of disgust

YUCKS ▶ yuck

YUCKY adj disgusting, nasty

YUFT n Russia leather **yufts**

YUG = yuga

YUGA n (in Hindu cosmology) one of the four ages of mankind

YUGARIE variant spelling of ▶ eugarie **yugas**

YUGS ▶ yug

YUK = yuck

YUKATA n light kimono **yukatas**

YUKE vb itch **yuked, yukes**

YUKIER ▶ yuky

YUKIEST ▶ yuky

YUKING ▶ yuke

YUKKED ▶ yuk

YUKKIER ▶ yukky

YUKKING ▶ yuk

YUKKY = yucky

YUKO n score of five points in judo **yukos**

YUKS ▶ yuk

YUKY adj itchy

YULAN n Chinese magnolia with white flowers **yulans**

YULE n Christmas **yules**

YUM interj expression of delight

YUMMIER ▶ yummy

YUMMIES ▶ yummy

YUMMO adj tasty ▷ interj exclamation of delight or approval

YUMMY adj, interj, n

YUMP vb leave the ground when driving over a ridge **yumped**

YUMPIE n young upwardly mobile

person **yumpies**

YUMPING ▶ yump

YUMPS ▶ yump

YUNX n wryneck **yunxes**

YUP n informal affirmative statement

YUPON = yaupon

YUPONS ▶ yupon

YUPPIE n, adj

YUPPIES ▶ yuppy

YUPPIFY vb make yuppie in nature

YUPPY = yuppie

YUPS ▶ yup

YUPSTER ▶ yindie

YURT n circular tent consisting of a framework of poles covered with felt or skins **yurta, yurtas, yurts**

YUS ▶ yu

YUTZ n Yiddish word meaning fool **yutzes**

YUZU n type of citrus fruit **yuzus**

YWIS adv certainly

YWROKE archaic past participle of ▶ wreak

Zz

Scoring the same as **Q** but easier to use, **Z** is normally a good tile to have, but it is not the best when it comes to making bonus words scoring that extra 50 points, so you will normally want to play it off as soon as a good score offers itself. There are only two two-letter words beginning with **Z**, **za** and **zo** (11 points), and remembering this will save you wasting time looking for others. There some very good three-letter words starting with **Z**, however. These include another variant of **zo**, **zho** (15), as well as **zax** and **zex** (19 each), **zap** (14), **zep** (14), **zip** (14) and **zoo** (12).

ZA n pizza

ZABETA n tariff **zabetas**

ZABRA n small sailing vessel **zabras**

ZABTIEH n Turkish police officer

ZACATON n coarse grass

ZACK n Australian five-cent piece **zacks**

ZADDICK adj righteous

ZADDIK n Hasidic Jewish leader **zaddiks**

ZAFFAR = zaffer

ZAFFARS ▶ zaffar

ZAFFER n impure cobalt oxide, used to impart a blue colour to enamels **zaffers, zaffir**

ZAFFIRS ▶ zaffir

ZAFFRE = zaffer

ZAFFRES ▶ zaffre

ZAFTIG adj ripe or curvaceous

ZAG vb change direction sharply **zagged, zagging, zags**

ZAIKAI n Japanese business community **zaikais**

ZAIRE n currency used in the former Zaire **zaires**

ZAITECH n investment in financial markets by a company to supplement its main income

ZAKAT n annual tax on Muslims to aid the poor in the Muslim community **zakats**

ZAKUSKA ▶ zakuski

ZAKUSKI pl n hors d'oeuvres, consisting of tiny open sandwiches

ZAMAN n tropical tree **zamang**

ZAMANGS ▶ zamang

ZAMANS ▶ zaman

ZAMARRA n sheepskin coat **zamarro**

ZAMBUCK n St John ambulance attendant **zambuk**

ZAMBUKS ▶ zambuk

ZAMIA n type of plant of tropical and subtropical America **zamias**

ZAMOUSE n West African buffalo

ZAMPONE n sausage made from pig's trotters **zamponi**

ZANANA = zenana

ZANANAS ▸ zanana

ZANDER n European freshwater pikeperch, valued as a food fish **zanders**

ZANELLA n twill fabric

ZANIED, zanier, zanies, zaniest, zanily ▸ zany

ZANJA n irrigation canal **zanjas**

An irrigation canal in Spanish America, notable for combining the J and Z.

ZANJERO n irrigation supervisor

Someone who supervises the distribution of water in a **zanja** or irrigation canal. This has a fair chance of coming up in actual play, and would make a great bonus.

ZANTE n type of wood **zantes**

ZANY adj, n, vb **zanying, zanyish, zanyism**

ZANZA = zanze

ZANZAS ▸ zanza

ZANZE n African musical instrument **zanzes**

ZAP vb, n, interj

ZAPATA adj (of a moustache) drooping

ZAPATEO n Cuban folk dance

ZAPPED ▸ zap

ZAPPER n remote control for a television etc **zappers**

ZAPPIER ▸ zappy

ZAPPING ▸ zap

ZAPPY adj energetic

ZAPS ▸ zap

ZAPTIAH = zaptieh

ZAPTIEH n Turkish police officer

Watch out for this Turkish policeman, who can also be spelt **zaptieh** or **zaptiah**.

ZARAPE n blanket-like shawl **zarapes**

ZAREBA n stockade or enclosure of thorn bushes around a village or campsite **zarebas, zareeba**

ZARF n (esp in the Middle East) a holder, usually ornamental, for a hot coffee cup **zarfs**

ZARI n thread made from fine gold or silver wire

ZARIBA = zareba

ZARIBAS ▸ zariba

ZARIS ▸ zari

ZARNEC n sulphide of arsenic **zarnecs, zarnich**

ZAS ▸ za

ZATI n type of macaque **zatis**

ZAX variant of ▸ sax

A chopper for trimming slate, and a great word combining X and Z. It has a variant **zex**.

ZAXES ▸ zax

ZAYIN n seventh letter of the Hebrew alphabet **zayins**

ZAZEN n deep meditation undertaken whilst sitting upright with legs crossed **zazens**

ZEA n corn silk

ZEAL n

ZEALANT archaic variant of ▸ zealot

ZEALFUL ▸ zeal

ZEALOT n zealots

ZEALOUS adj extremely eager or enthusiastic

ZEALS ▸ zeal

ZEAS ▸ zea

ZEATIN n cytokinin derived from corn **zeatins**

ZEBEC variant spelling of ▸ xebec

ZEBECK = zebec

ZEBECKS ▸ zebeck

ZEBECS ▸ zebec

ZEBRA n

ZEBRAIC adj like a zebra

ZEBRANO n type of striped wood

ZEBRAS ▸ zebra

ZEBRASS n offspring of a male zebra and a female ass

ZEBRINA n trailing herbaceous plant

ZEBRINE ▸ zebra

ZEBROID ▸ zebra

ZEBRULA n offspring of a male zebra and a female horse **zebrule**

ZEBU n

ZEBUB n large African fly **zebubs**

ZEBUS ▸ zebu

ZECCHIN = zecchino

ZECHIN = zecchino

ZECHINS ▶ zechin

ZED *n* British and New Zealand spoken form of the letter *z*
> A name for the letter Z, and one of the most commonly played Z words.

ZEDOARY *n* dried rhizome of a tropical Asian plant

ZEDS ▶ zed

ZEE *the US word for* ▶ zed
> This word can be very useful because E is the most common tile in Scrabble, so keep it in mind if you draw a Z. Zee scores 12 points.

ZEES ▶ zee

ZEIN *n* protein occurring in maize **zeins**

ZEK *n* Soviet prisoner **zeks**

ZEL *n* Turkish cymbal

ZELANT *alternative form of* ▶ zealant

ZELANTS ▶ zelant

ZELATOR = zelatrix

ZELKOVA = zelatrix

ZELKOVA *n* type of elm tree

ZELOSO *adv* with zeal

ZELS ▶ zel

ZEMSTVA ▶ zemstvo

ZEMSTVO *n* council in Tsarist Russia

ZENAIDA *n* dove

ZENANA *n* part of Muslim or Hindu home reserved for women and girls **zenanas**

ZENDIK *n* unbeliever or heretic **zendiks**

ZENITH *n* **zeniths**

ZEOLITE *n* any of a large group of glassy secondary minerals

ZEP *n* type of long sandwich

ZEPHYR *n* **zephyrs**

ZEPPOLE *n* Italian fritter **zeppoli**

ZEPS ▶ zep

ZERDA *n* fennec **zerdas**

ZEREBA = zareba

ZEREBAS ▶ zereba

ZERIBA = zareba

ZERIBAS ▶ zeriba

ZERK *n* grease fitting **zerks**

ZERO *n, adj, vb, determiner* **zeroed, zeroes, zeroing, zeros**

ZEROTH *adj* denoting a term in a series that precedes the term otherwise regarded as the first term

ZEST *n, vb* **zested**

ZESTER *n* kitchen utensil used to scrape fine shreds of peel from citrus fruits **zesters**

ZESTFUL, zestier, zestily, zesting, zests, zesty ▶ zest

ZETA *n* sixth letter in the Greek alphabet **zetas**

ZETETIC *adj* proceeding by inquiry ▶ *n* investigation

ZEUGMA *n* figure of speech in which a word is used with two

words although appropriate to only one of them **zeugmas**

ZEUXITE *n* ferriferous mineral
> This mineral, a kind of tourmaline, makes an excellent bonus.

ZEX *n* tool for cutting roofing slate **zexes**

ZEZE *n* stringed musical instrument **zezes**

ZHO = zo
> A cross between a yak and a cow; the other forms are **dso, dzo** and **zo**, and it's worth remembering all of them.

ZHOMO *n* female zho **zhomos**

ZHOS ▶ zho

ZIBET *n* large civet of S and SE Asia **zibeth**

ZIBETHS ▶ zibeth

ZIBETS ▶ zibet

ZIFF *n* beard

ZIFFIUS *n* sea monster

ZIFFS ▶ ziff

ZIG = zag

ZIGAN *n* gypsy

ZIGANKA *n* Russian dance

ZIGANS ▶ zigan

ZIGGED ▶ zig

ZIGGING ▶ zig

ZIGS ▶ zig

ZIGZAG *n, vb, adj, adv* **zigzags**

ZIKURAT = ziggurat

ZILA *n* administrative district in India **zilas**

ZILCH *n* nothing **zilches**

ZILL n finger cymbal

ZILLA = zila

ZILLAH = zila

ZILLAHS ▸ zillah

ZILLAS ▸ zilla

ZILLION n extremely large but unspecified number

ZILLS ▸ zill

ZIMB = zebub

ZIMBI n cowrie shell used as money zimbis

ZIMBS ▸ zimb

ZIMOCCA n bath sponge

ZIN short form of > zinfandel

ZINC n, vb

ZINCATE n any of a class of salts derived from the amphoteric hydroxide of zinc

ZINCED ▸ zinc

ZINCIC ▸ zinc

ZINCIER ▸ zinc

ZINCIFY vb coat with zinc

ZINCING ▸ zinc

ZINCITE n red or yellow mineral

ZINCKED ▸ zinc

ZINCKY ▸ zinc

ZINCO n printing plate made from zincography

ZINCODE n positive electrode

ZINCOID ▸ zinc

ZINCOS ▸ zinco

ZINCOUS ▸ zinc

ZINCS ▸ zinc

ZINCY ▸ zinc

ZINE n magazine or fanzine

ZINEB n organic insecticide zinebs

ZINES ▸ zine

ZING n, vb

ZINGANI ▸ zingano

ZINGANO = zingaro

ZINGARA = zingaro

ZINGARE ▸ zingaro

ZINGARI ▸ zingaro

ZINGARO n Italian Gypsy

ZINGED ▸ zing

ZINGEL n small freshwater perch zingels

ZINGER ▸ zing

ZINGERS ▸ zing

ZINGIER ▸ zingy

ZINGING ▸ zing

ZINGS ▸ zing

ZINGY adj vibrant

ZINKE n cornett

ZINKED ▸ zinc

ZINKES ▸ zinke

ZINKIER ▸ zinc

ZINKIFY vb coat with zinc

ZINKING ▸ zinc

ZINKY ▸ zinc

ZINNIA n plant of tropical and subtropical America zinnias

ZINS ▸ zin

ZIP = zipper

ZIPLESS ▸ zip

ZIPLOCK adj fastened with interlocking plastic strips ▸ vb seal (a ziplock storage bag)

ZIPPED ▸ zip

ZIPPER n, vb zippers

ZIPPIER ▸ zippy

ZIPPING ▸ zip

ZIPPO n nothing zippos

ZIPPY adj full of energy

ZIPS ▸ zip

ZIPTOP adj (of a bag) closed with a zip

ZIRAM n industrial fungicide zirams

ZIRCON n zircons

ZIT n spot or pimple

> This little word for a pimple can be very useful for disposing of the Z.

ZITE = ziti

ZITHER n zithern, zithers

ZITI n type of pasta zitis

> Another very useful word for disposing of the Z, ziti is a type of pasta. It has a variant zite. Remember that ziti takes an S to form zitis, but zite does not take an S.

ZITS ▸ zit

ZIZ = zizz

ZIZANIA n aquatic grass

ZIZEL n chipmunk zizels

ZIZIT = zizith

ZIZITH variant spelling of > tsitsith

ZIZZ n short sleep ▸ vb take a short sleep, snooze zizzed, zizzes, zizzing

ZIZZLE vb sizzle zizzled, zizzles

ZLOTE ▸ zloty

ZLOTIES ▸ zloty

ZLOTY n monetary unit of Poland zlotych, zlotys

ZO n Tibetan breed of cattle

ZOA ▶ zoon

ZOAEA = zoea

ZOAEAE ▶ zoaea

ZOAEAS ▶ zoaea

ZOARIA ▶ zoarium

ZOARIAL ▶ zoarium

ZOARIUM n colony of zooids

ZOBO = zo

ZOBOS ▶ zobo

ZOBU = zo

ZOBUS ▶ zobu

ZOCALO n plaza in Mexico zocalos

ZOCCO n plinth zoccolo, zoccos

ZODIAC n zodiacs

ZOEA n free-swimming larva of a crab or related crustacean zoeae, zoeal, zoeas

> One of the most frequently played words in Scrabble, along with its friends zoaea and zooea and the various inflections: remember that these words can take an E in the plural as well as S, giving zoeae, zoaeae and zooeae.

ZOECIA ▶ zoecium

ZOECIUM = zooecium

ZOEFORM ▶ zoecium

ZOETIC adj pertaining to life

ZOFTIG adj ripe or curvaceous

ZOIC adj relating to or having animal life

ZOISITE n grey, brown, or pink mineral

ZOISM n belief in magical animal powers zoisms, zoist, zoists

ZOL n South African slang for a cannabis cigarette zols

ZOMBI = zombie

ZOMBIE n zombies

ZOMBIFY vb turn into a zombie

ZOMBIS ▶ zombi

ZONA n zone or belt zonae

ZONAL adj of, relating to, or of the nature of a zone zonally, zonary

ZONATE adj marked with, divided into, or arranged in zones zonated

ZONDA n South American wind zondas

ZONE n, vb zoned

ZONER n something which divides other things into zones zoners

ZONES ▶ zone

ZONING ▶ zone

ZONINGS ▶ zone

ZONK vb strike resoundingly

ZONKED adj highly intoxicated with drugs or alcohol

ZONKING ▶ zonk

ZONKS ▶ zonk

ZONOID adj resembling a zone

ZONULA n small zone or belt zonulae

ZONULAR ▶ zonule

ZONULAS ▶ zonula

ZONULE n small zone, band, or area zonules

ZONULET n small belt

ZONURE n lizard with ringed tail zonures

ZOO n

ZOOEA = zoea

ZOOEAE ▶ zooea

ZOOEAL ▶ zooea

ZOOEAS ▶ zooea

ZOOECIA > zooecium

ZOOEY ▶ zoo

ZOOGAMY n sexual reproduction in animals

ZOOGENY n doctrine of formation of animals

ZOOGLEA = zoogloea

ZOOGONY = zoogeny

ZOOID n any independent animal body, such as an individual of a coral colony zooidal, zooids

ZOOIER ▶ zoo

ZOOIEST ▶ zoo

ZOOKS short form of > gadzooks

ZOOLITE n fossilized animal

ZOOLITH n fossilized animal

ZOOLOGY n

ZOOM vb, n zoomed, zooming, zooms, zoon

ZOONAL ▶ zoon

ZOONED ▶ zoon

ZOONIC adj concerning animals

ONING ► zoon

ONITE n segment of n articulated animal

ONOMY n science of nimal life

ONS ► zoon

OOPERY n xperimentation on nimals

OOS ► zoo

OOT n as in zoot suit nan's suit consisting f baggy trousers and long jacket

OOTAXY n science of he classification of nimals
The science of classifying animals. An unlikely word to appear on your rack, but you never know, and it would make an impressive bonus!

OOTIER ► zooty

OOTOMY n branch of zoology concerned with the dissection and anatomy of animals

OOTY adj showy

OOTYPE n animal figure used as a symbol

OOZOO n wood pigeon **zoozoos**

OPPA adj syncopated **zoppo**

ORBING n activity of travelling downhill inside a large air-cushioned hollow ball

RORGITE n copper-lead selenide

RORI n Japanese sandal

ZORIL = zorilla

ZORILLA n skunk-like African musteline mammal having a long black-and-white coat **zorille**

ZORILLO = zorille

ZORILS ► zoril

ZORINO n skunk fur **zorinos**

ZORIS ► zori

ZORRO n hoary fox **zorros**

ZOS ► zo

ZOSTER n shingles; herpes zoster **zosters**

ZOUAVE n (formerly) member of a body of French infantry composed of Algerian recruits **zouaves**

ZOUK n style of dance music that combines African and Latin American rhythms **zouks**

ZOUNDS interj mild oath indicating surprise or indignation

ZOWIE interj expression of pleasurable surprise

ZOYSIA n type of grass with short stiffly pointed leaves, often used for lawns **zoysias**

ZUFFOLI ► zuffolo

ZUFFOLO = zufolo

ZUFOLI ► zufolo

ZUFOLO n small flute

ZULU n (in the NATO phonetic alphabet) used to represent z **zulus**

ZUPA n confederation of

Serbian villages

ZUPAN n head of a zupa **zupans**

ZUPAS ► zupa

ZURF = zarf

ZURFS ► zurf

ZUZ n ancient Hebrew silver coin **zuzim, zuzzim**

ZYDECO n type of Black Cajun music **zydecos**

ZYGA ► zygon

ZYGAL ► zygon

ZYGOID = diploid

ZYGOMA n slender arch of bone on each side of the skull of mammals **zygomas**

ZYGON n brain fissure

ZYGOSE ► zygosis

ZYGOSES ► zygosis

ZYGOSIS n direct transfer of DNA between two cells that are temporarily joined

ZYGOTE n fertilized egg cell **zygotes, zygotic**

ZYMASE n mixture of enzymes that is obtained as an extract from yeast and ferments sugars **zymases**

ZYME n ferment **zymes, zymic**

ZYMITE n priest who uses leavened bread during communion **zymites**

ZYMOGEN n any of ~ various inactive precursors of enzymes activated by a kinase

ZYMOID *adj* relating to a ferment

ZYMOME *n* glutinous substance that is insoluble in alcohol **zymomes**

ZYMOSAN *n* insoluble carbohydrate found in yeast

ZYMOSES ▶ zymosis

ZYMOSIS = zymolysis

ZYMOTIC *adj* of, relating to, or causing fermentation ▷ *n* disease

ZYMURGY *n* study of fermentation processes

ZYTHUM *n* Ancient Egyptian beer **zythums**

ZYZZYVA *n* American weevil

ZZZ *n* informal word f sleep **zzzs**